Lecture Notes in Computer Science

# Lecture Notes in Artificial Intelligence  15980
Founding Editor

Jörg Siekmann

Series Editors

Randy Goebel, *University of Alberta, Edmonton, Canada*
Wolfgang Wahlster, *DFKI, Berlin, Germany*
Zhi-Hua Zhou, *Nanjing University, Nanjing, China*

The series Lecture Notes in Artificial Intelligence (LNAI) was established in 1988 as a topical subseries of LNCS devoted to artificial intelligence.

The series publishes state-of-the-art research results at a high level. As with the LNCS mother series, the mission of the series is to serve the international R & D community by providing an invaluable service, mainly focused on the publication of conference and workshop proceedings and postproceedings.

Gian Luca Pozzato · Tarmo Uustalu
Editors

# Automated Reasoning with Analytic Tableaux and Related Methods

34th International Conference, TABLEAUX 2025
Reykjavik, Iceland, September 27–29, 2025
Proceedings

*Editors*
Gian Luca Pozzato  
Università degli Studi di Torino  
Torino, Italy

Tarmo Uustalu  
Reykjavik University  
Reykjavik, Iceland

ISSN 0302-9743   ISSN 1611-3349 (electronic)  
Lecture Notes in Artificial Intelligence  
ISBN 978-3-032-06084-6   ISBN 978-3-032-06085-3 (eBook)  
https://doi.org/10.1007/978-3-032-06085-3

LNCS Sublibrary: SL7 – Artificial Intelligence

© The Editor(s) (if applicable) and The Author(s) 2026. This book is an open access publication.

**Open Access** This book is licensed under the terms of the Creative Commons Attribution 4.0 International License (http://creativecommons.org/licenses/by/4.0/), which permits use, sharing, adaptation, distribution and reproduction in any medium or format, as long as you give appropriate credit to the original author(s) and the source, provide a link to the Creative Commons license and indicate if changes were made.
The images or other third party material in this book are included in the book's Creative Commons license, unless indicated otherwise in a credit line to the material. If material is not included in the book's Creative Commons license and your intended use is not permitted by statutory regulation or exceeds the permitted use, you will need to obtain permission directly from the copyright holder.
This work is subject to copyright. All commercial rights are reserved by the author(s), whether the whole or part of the material is concerned, specifically the rights of translation, reprinting, reuse of illustrations, recitation, broadcasting, reproduction on microfilms or in any other physical way, and transmission or information storage and retrieval, electronic adaptation, computer software, or by similar or dissimilar methodology now known or hereafter developed. Regarding these commercial rights a non-exclusive license has been granted to the publisher.
The use of general descriptive names, registered names, trademarks, service marks, etc. in this publication does not imply, even in the absence of a specific statement, that such names are exempt from the relevant protective laws and regulations and therefore free for general use.
The publisher, the authors and the editors are safe to assume that the advice and information in this book are believed to be true and accurate at the date of publication. Neither the publisher nor the authors or the editors give a warranty, expressed or implied, with respect to the material contained herein or for any errors or omissions that may have been made. The publisher remains neutral with regard to jurisdictional claims in published maps and institutional affiliations.

This Springer imprint is published by the registered company Springer Nature Switzerland AG  
The registered company address is: Gewerbestrasse 11, 6330 Cham, Switzerland

If disposing of this product, please recycle the paper.

# Preface

This volume comprises the proceedings of the 34th International Conference on Automated Reasoning with Analytic Tableaux and Related Methods (TABLEAUX 2025). The conference was held in Reykjavik, Iceland, during September 27–29, 2025, hosted by the ICE-TCS lab of the Department of Computer Science of Reykjavik University. It was colocated with the 15th International Symposium on Frontiers of Combining Systems (FroCoS 2025) and the 16th International Conference on Interactive Theorem Proving (ITP 2025).

TABLEAUX is the main international conference at which research on all aspects—theoretical foundations, implementation techniques, systems development and applications—of tableaux-based reasoning and related methods is presented. The first TABLEAUX conference was held in Lautenbach near Karlsruhe in 1992. Since then it has been organized on an annual basis. Since 2001, TABLEAUX, together with CADE and FroCoS, forms part of IJCAR every two years.

The call for papers of TABLEAUX attracted 47 full submissions (44 regular papers and 3 short papers). Each paper was evaluated by at least 3 programme committee members or additional reviewers in a single-blind review process. A number of papers were discussed extensively. 26 submissions (all of them regular papers) were accepted, one of them was withdrawn after acceptance. The accepted papers cover topics in classical and multi-valued logic, theorem proving, modal and tense logic, dynamic logic, intuitionistic and substructural logic.

Altogether 14 researchers were nominated as invited speaker candidates by members of the programme committee. The following two were invited as a result of a vote in the committee and accepted the invitation:

– Kaustuv Chaudhuri (LIX, Inria and École Polytechnique, France), joint with FroCoS
– Raheleh Jalali (University of Bath, UK)

We are grateful to all who contributed to making TABLEAUX 2025 a success: the authors of the submissions, the invited speakers, the programme committee, the organizing team and the staff of the support units at Reykjavik University. TABLEAUX 2025 was financially supported by the Iceproof project of the Collaboration Fund of the Icelandic Ministry of Culture, Innovation and Higher Education. We are grateful to Springer for sponsoring the conference and publishing these proceedings.

July 2025

Gian Luca Pozzato
Tarmo Uustalu

# Organization

## Programme Committee Chairs

Gian Luca Pozzato — Università degli Studi di Torino, Italy
Tarmo Uustalu — Reykjavik University, Iceland

## Steering Committee

Agata Ciabattoni — Technische Universität Wien, Austria
Anupam Das — University of Birmingham, UK
Hans de Nivelle — Nazarbayev University, Kazakhstan
Didier Galmiche — LORIA, Université de Lorraine, France
Elaine Pimentel — University College London, UK
Revantha Ramanayake — Rijksuniversiteit Groningen, The Netherlands
Renate Schmidt — University of Manchester, UK

## Programme Committee

Matteo Acclavio — University of Sussex, UK
Carlos Areces — Universidad Nacional de Córdoba, Argentina
Davide Bresolin — Università degli Studi di Padova, Italy
Serenella Cerrito — IBISC, Université d'Evry Val-d'Essonne, France
Anupam Das — University of Birmingham, UK
Hans de Nivelle — Nazarbayev University, Kazakhstan
Valeria de Paiva — Topos Institute, USA
José Espírito Santo — Universidade do Minho, Portugal
Christian Fermüller — Technische Universität Wien, Austria
Rajeev Goré — Monash University, Australia
Rosalie Iemhoff — Universiteit Utrecht, The Netherlands
Andrzej Indrzejczak — Uniwersytet Łódzki, Poland
Graham Leigh — Göteborgs Universitet, Sweden
Björn Lellmann — Bundesministerium für Finanzen, Austria
Tim Lyon — Technische Universität Dresden, Germany
Cláudia Nalon — Universidade de Brasília, Brazil
Sara Negri — Università degli Studi di Genova, Italy
Elaine Pimentel — University College London, UK

Francesca Poggiolesi — IHPST, Université Paris 1 Panthéon-Sorbonne, France
Revantha Ramanayake — Rijksuniversiteit Groningen, The Netherlands
Alexis Saurin — IRIF, Université Paris Cité, France
Yaroslav Shramko — Kryvyi Rih State Pedagogical University, Ukraine
Luca Tranchini — Eberhard-Karls-Universität Tübingen, Germany
Josef Urban — České vysoké učení technické v Praze, Czechia

## Local Organizers

Antonis Achilleos — Reykjavik University, Iceland
Matthieu Baty — University of Iceland, Iceland
Bjarki Gunnarsson — University of Iceland, Iceland
Vasiliki Kyriakou — Reykjavik University, Iceland
Yasuaki Morita — Reykjavik University, Iceland
Jacob Neumann — Reykjavik University, Iceland
Tarmo Uustalu — Reykjavik University, Iceland

## Additional Reviewers

Aleksi Anttila
Peter Baumgartner
Kaustuv Chaudhuri
Ivano Ciardelli
Liron Cohen
Jeremy Dawson
Andrea De Domenico
Sebastian Enqvist
Raül Espejo-Boix
Michael Färber
Zhe Hou
Ullrich Hustadt
Raheleh Jalali
Alexander Kocurek
Daniil Kozhemiachenko
Elio La Rosa
Xinghan Liu
Giulia Manara
Ana Oliveira da Costa
Grigory Olkhovikov
Eugenio Orlandelli
Leonardo Pacheco
Fabio Papacchini
Xavier Parent
Paolo Pistone
Paweł Płaczek
Reuben Rowe
Ian Shillito
Will Stafford
Thomas Studer
Henri Thoelke
Jan von Plato
Przemysław Wałęga
Elifnaz Yangin
Michał Zawidzki

# Abstracts of Invited Talks

# Towards a Universal Interactive Theorem Proving Interface

Kaustuv Chaudhuri ⓘ

LIX, Inria and École Polytechnique, France
`kaustuv.chaudhuri@inria.fr`

**Abstract.** Interactive theorem provers are usually designed to use formal languages for expressing proofs and commands. Such languages are rarely portable across different systems, which leads to fragmentation in the community, duplication of effort, and an incumbency bias for existing systems. One way to address this incompatibility is to design an interactive proving interface where proof and command languages have a negligible role. Instead, users build proofs by manipulating the theorem itself using interaction devices such as mice and touch screens, and interaction mechanisms such as clicking, selection, dragging-and-dropping, etc.; in other words, using *direct manipulation*. There have been a number of proposals for such interfaces, most famously the *proof by pointing* approach of the 1990s [1], with several other approaches since then [8, 2, 3, 9].

This talk presents a foundational, proof theoretic, and system independent view of direct manipulation interfaces that generalizes these earlier attempts to *proof by linking* [4], which has been implemented in the interfaces *Profound* [5] and *Actema* [7] for first-order intuitionistic logic. These interfaces are intended to be compatible with arbitrary back-end proof systems, either as plugins or as certifying procedures. For example, *Profound* can be used to produce proofs for Lean 3, Lean 4, Rocq (Coq), Isabelle/HOL, and HOL4 [6]. Linking requires the use of proof calculi of *deep inference*, which are proof systems where logical inferences are allowed in arbitrary formula contexts. This talk presents a particular kind of deep inference called *open deduction*, which was originally developed for classical logic but which is now extended and adapted to intuitionistic logic. In addition to linking, open deduction is suitable for a variety of other front-end features such as hierarchical levels of detail and refactoring by sharing subproofs. We will also discuss current work on extensions of open deduction (and linking) to support dependent type theory and induction.

# References

1. Bertot, Y., Kahn, G., Théry, L.: Proof by pointing. In: Hagiya, M., Mitchell, J.C. (eds.) TACS 1994. LNCS, vol. **789**, pp. 141–160. Springer, Berlin, Heidelberg (1994). https://doi.org/10.1007/3-540-57887-0_94

2. Breitner, J.: Visual theorem proving with the incredible proof machine. In: Blanchette, J.C., Merz, S. (eds.) ITP 2016. LNCS, vol. **9807**, pp. 123–139. Springer, Cham (2016). https://doi.org/10.1007/978-3-319-43144-4_8
3. Callies, E., Laurent, O.: Click and coLLecT: an interactive linear logic prover. In: 5th International Workshop on Trends in Linear Logic and Applications (TLLA 2021). https://hal-lirmm.ccsd.cnrs.fr/lirmm-03271501
4. Chaudhuri, K.: Subformula linking as an interaction method. In: Blazy, S., Paulin-Mohring, C., Pichardie, D. (eds.) ITP 2013. LNCS, vol. **7998**, pp. 386–401. Springer, Berlin, Heidelberg (2013). https://doi.org/10.1007/978-3-642-39634-2_28
5. Chaudhuri, K.: Subformula linking for intuitionistic logic with application to type theory. In: Platzer, A., Sutcliffe, G. (eds.) CADE 2021. LNCS, vol. **12699**, pp. 200–216. Springer, Cham (2021). https://doi.org/10.1007/978-3-030-79876-5_12
6. Chaudhuri, K., Donato, P., Massacci, L., Werner, B.: Certifying proof-by-linking. Tech. rep., INRIA (2022). https://inria.hal.science/hal-04317972
7. Donato, P., Strub, P., Werner, B.: A drag-and-drop proof tactic. In: Popescu, A., Zdancewic, S. (eds.) 11th ACM SIGPLAN Int. Conf. on Certified Programs and Proofs, CPP 2022, pp. 197–209. ACM, New York (2022). https://doi.org/10.1145/3497775.3503692
8. Lerner, S., Foster, S.R., Griswold, W.G.: Polymorphic blocks: formalism-inspired UI for structured connectors. In: 33rd Annual ACM Conf. on Human Factors in Computing Systems, pp. 3063–3072. ACM, New York (2015). https://doi.org/10.1145/2702123.2702302
9. Reis, G., Naeem, Z., Hashim, M.: Sequoia: A playground for logicians (system description). In: Peltier, N., Sofronie-Stokkermans, V. (eds.) IJCAR 2020. LNCS, vol. **12167**, pp. 480–488. Springer, Cham (2020). https://doi.org/10.1007/978-3-030-51054-1_32

# Skolemization Beyond Intuitionistic Logic: The Role of Quantifier Shifts

Raheleh Jalali

Department of Computer Science, University of Bath, UK
rjk53@bath.ac.uk

**Abstract.** Skolemization, the process of simplifying quantified formulas by replacing strong quantifiers (i.e., positive occurrences of the universal quantifier and negative occurrences of the existential quantifier) with fresh function symbols, plays an important role in logic and computer science. While it is sound and complete for classical predicate logic (CQC), Skolemization fails for intuitionistic predicate logic (IQC). In this talk, we provide a full characterization of the intermediate logics which admit Skolemization. We first introduce the so-called quantifier shift principles, commonly used to transform formulas into their equivalent prenex normal form. We call the logic of extending IQC by these principles, QFS. Then, we present our main result, stating that Skolemization is sound and complete for an intermediate logic if and only if it extends QFS. Motivated by the central role QFS plays in this context, we further investigate its logical properties, showing, in particular, that QFS and some of its fragments are Kripke frame-incomplete.

This is joint work with Matthias Baaz, Rosalie Iemhoff and Mariami Gamsakhurdia.

# Contents

## Classical and Multi-valued Logic, Theorem Proving

A Sequent Calculus Perspective on Base-Extension Semantics .............. 3
   *Victor Barroso-Nascimento, Ekaterina Piotrovskaya, and Elaine Pimentel*

A Tableau System for First-Order Logic with Standard Names .............. 22
   *Jens Claßen and Torben Braüner*

Bounded Inquisitive Logics: Sequent Calculi and Schematic Validity ......... 39
   *Tadeusz Litak and Katsuhiko Sano*

Analytic Calculi for Logics of Indicative Conditionals ..................... 59
   *Vitor Greati, Sérgio Marcelino, Miguel Muñoz Pérez,*
   *and Umberto Rivieccio*

Finding Connections via Satisfiability Solving ........................... 82
   *Clemens Eisenhofer, Michael Rawson, and Laura Kovács*

Constraint Learning for Non-confluent Proof Search ....................... 103
   *Michael Rawson, Clemens Eisenhofer, and Laura Kovács*

On Solving String Equations via Powers and Parikh Images ................ 120
   *Clemens Eisenhofer, Theodor Seiser, Nikolaj Bjørner, and Laura Kovács*

## Modal and Tense Logic

A Gödel Modal Logic over Witnessed Crisp Models ....................... 141
   *Mauro Ferrari, Camillo Fiorentini, and Ricardo Oscar Rodriguez*

Refined Tableau Systems for Some Modal Logics of Confluence ............. 161
   *Kiana Samadpour Motalebi, Renate A. Schmidt, and Cláudia Nalon*

The Modal Cube Revisited: Semantics Without Worlds .................... 181
   *Renato Leme, Carlos Olarte, Elaine Pimentel,*
   *and Marcelo Esteban Coniglio*

Non-wellfounded Proof Theory for Interpretability Logic .................. 201
   *Sebastijan Horvat, Borja Sierra Miranda, and Thomas Studer*

Analytic Proofs for Tense Logic ......................................... 220
  Agata Ciabattoni, Timo Lang, and Revantha Ramanayake

Improved Decision Procedures for Multi-modal Tense Logic Using
CEGAR-Tableaux ....................................................... 238
  Rajeev Goré and Cormac Kikkert

Interpolation for Converse PDL ......................................... 258
  Johannes Kloibhofer, Valentina Trucco Dalmas, and Yde Venema

Semi-competitive Differential Game Logic .............................. 278
  Julia Butte and André Platzer

**Intuitionistic and Substructural Logic**

Designing a Safe Forward Chaining Tactic Using Productive Proofs .......... 299
  Kaustuv Chaudhuri, Arunava Gantait, and Dale Miller

Base-Extension Semantics for Intuitionistic Modal Logics (Extended
Abstract) ............................................................. 318
  Yll Buzoku and David J. Pym

Forward Proof Search for Intuitionistic Multimodal K Logics .............. 335
  Niels Voorneveld

A Proof-Theoretic View of Basic Intuitionistic Conditional Logic ........... 354
  Tiziano Dalmonte and Marianna Girlando

Intuitionistic $\mu$-Calculus with the Lewis Arrow ......................... 374
  Bahareh Afshari and Lide Grotenhuis

Justification Logic for Intuitionistic Modal Logic ........................ 393
  Sonia Marin and Paaras Padhiar

Intuitionistic BV ..................................................... 414
  Matteo Acclavio and Lutz Straßburger

An Agda Formalization of Nonassociative Lambek Calculus and its
Metatheory ........................................................... 433
  Niccolò Veltri and Cheng-Syuan Wan

Cyclic System for an Algebraic Theory of Alternating Parity Automata ....... 453
  Anupam Das and Abhishek De

A Sequent Calculus For Trace Formula Implication ......................... 473
  *Niklas Heidler and Reiner Hähnle*

**Author Index** ....................................................... 491

# Classical and Multi-valued Logic,
Theorem Proving

# A Sequent Calculus Perspective on Base-Extension Semantics

Victor Barroso-Nascimento, Ekaterina Piotrovskaya, and Elaine Pimentel

Department of Computer Science, University College London, London, UK
{v.nascimento,kate.piotrovskaya.21,e.pimentel}@ucl.ac.uk

**Abstract.** We define base-extension semantics (BeS) using atomic systems based on sequent calculus rather than natural deduction. While traditional BeS aligns naturally with intuitionistic logic due to its constructive foundations, we show that sequent calculi with multiple conclusions yield a BeS framework more suited to classical semantics. The harmony in classical sequents leads to straightforward semantic clauses derived solely from right introduction rules. This framework enables a Sandqvist-style completeness proof that extracts a sequent calculus proof from any valid semantic consequence. Moreover, we show that the inclusion or omission of atomic cut rules meaningfully affects the semantics, yet completeness holds in both cases.

**Keywords:** Base-extension Semantics · Proof-theoretic Semantics · Sequent Calculus

## 1 Introduction

When proposing a new semantic model for a well-known logic, one must establish its adequacy in at least two ways: first, it should be correct and complete w.r.t. another characterisation of the logic, *e.g.*, a proof system, an axiomatic description, or another semantic model; second, it should exhibit some *novelty* or *advantage* compared to existing formulations.

For example, Kripke semantics is often favoured for counter-model extraction; truth tables are usually easy to compute and understand; and categorical semantics can help bridge logic with other areas since, at an abstract categorical level, different disciplines can end up looking quite similar.

In this work, we will advocate for *proof-theoretic semantics* as an adequate model for reasoning about *classical logics*.

Proof-theoretic semantics (PtS) has recently attracted considerable attention, as it reduces *validity* to *derivability*, making it possible to employ the rich machinery of proof theory to describe the semantics of logical operators [21,24]. Beyond its technical appeal, PtS is grounded in *inferentialism*, offering a compelling philosophical account of the meaning of logical connectives, derived from the inference rules that govern them in a given proof system.

During the genesis of PtS, it was often believed that its close association with natural deduction and apparent reliance on intuitionistic proof-theoretic principles would yield completeness with respect to intuitionistic logic [5,20]. Dummett even made the stronger claim that it would be impossible to obtain proof-theoretic semantics for classical logic without use of classical *canons of reasoning* [8, p. 270], which was later disproven by Sandqvist [22] (see also [11,14]). Such beliefs were also justified by the very fact that the semantic clauses in the first days of PtS were inspired by introduction rules, since the possibility of defining validity through such means was interpreted as a consequence of the harmonic relations between rules that is characteristic of intuitionistic natural deduction [7].

According to traditional readings of the often quoted remark by Gentzen [10], introduction rules can be interpreted as "definitions" of logical connectives [25]. Dummett further argues that this definitional nature has semantic bearing due to making introduction rules self-justifying [8, p. 251]. On the other hand, since classical natural deduction requires intervention of extraneous principles instead of being fully determined by rules for the connectives, it would seem that such definitions are intuitionistic in nature. This is why, absent explicit inclusion of additional canons of reasoning, definitions based on introduction rules were specifically expected to yield intuitionistic semantics.

As remarked by Schroeder-Heister in Section 3.5. of [25], PtS seems to be biased in favour of intuitionistic logic *precisely* due to its reliance on natural deduction. Classical logic is perfectly harmonic if multiple succedent sequent calculus is considered instead [6], arguably even more so than intuitionistic logic. Since validity definitions in PtS rely on proof-theoretic harmony to provide semantics for the logical connectives, one could reasonably expect a sequent-based definition of PtS to yield a semantics for classical logic.

This paper fulfils this expectation by breaking with the PtS tradition of relying on natural deduction and intuitionistic systems and introducing the first Base-extension semantics (BeS) formulated for sequent systems.

BeS is a strand of PtS in which proof-theoretic validity is defined relative to a specified set of inference rules governing basic formulas of the language [23]. These basic formulas are often atomic propositions such as "$a$ is a subset of $b$", "$b$ is a subset of $a$", or "$a$ is equal to $b$". If we represent these as $r$, $s$, and $t$, respectively, a possible inference rule might be:

$$\frac{r \quad s}{t}$$

This resembles the approach of atom definitions [13,15,17,18], where, for instance, set equality can be "defined" in terms of mutual containment[1].

The notion of consequence in BeS is given by an inductively defined semantic judgment, whose base case refers to provability in a given atomic system (or a *base*). That is, for any base $\mathcal{B}$, provability of an atomic formula is defined as:

$$\Vdash_{\mathcal{B}} p \text{ iff } p \text{ is provable in } \mathcal{B}$$

---

[1] We note, however, that this analogy is purely motivational; we are not claiming to define set-theoretic equality within propositional logic.

The remaining semantic clauses are defined inductively. For example, conjunction is handled similarly to Kripke semantics:

$$\Vdash_{\mathcal{B}} A \wedge B \text{ iff } \Vdash_{\mathcal{B}} A \text{ and } \Vdash_{\mathcal{B}} B$$

Beyond this point, the similarity to Kripke semantics fades. For instance, the constant $\bot$ is often defined as *absurdity* in second order logic instantiated to atoms (as in the system **Fat** [9]):

$$\Vdash_{\mathcal{B}} \bot \text{ iff } \Vdash_{\mathcal{B}} p \text{ for all atoms } p$$

The use of semantic clauses making $\bot$ unsatisfiable, as in Kripke semantics, leads to serious issues, as it allows one to prove $\Vdash_{\mathcal{B}} \neg\neg p$ for every atom $p$ [19]. It is still possible, however, to avoid this problem by considering $\bot$ as a basic formula and requiring bases to be consistent (see *e.g.* [1,2]).

Shifting from natural deduction to sequent systems brings a whole new perspective to the meaning of connectives—it also introduces new challenges, as discussed in the next section. Indeed, in classical logic, $\bot$ is introduced from the empty sequent via an invertible rule, and our semantic definition adequately reflects this behaviour:

$$\Vdash_{\mathcal{B}} \bot, \Gamma \text{ iff } \Vdash_{\mathcal{B}} \Gamma$$

This allows the definition of connectives using the invertibility of rules, aligning the semantic clauses closely with the proof rules of classical sequent systems, as well as bringing *proof theory meta-reasoning* to the core of **PtS**.

Moreover, our formulation also supports a constructive proof of completeness for classical logic, mirroring the strategy employed by Sandqvist to prove completeness of traditional **BeS** with respect to intuitionistic logic [23]. In this setting, quantification over atoms, previously used in the semantic clauses for disjunction and $\bot$, is no longer necessary.

Finally, the sequent-style formulation of **BeS** deepens our understanding of general **PtS**. In particular, it makes explicit the semantic role of the cut rule, an aspect often obscured in natural deduction-based approaches.

## 2 Sequent Based Base-Extension Semantics

**BeS** is founded on an inductively defined judgment called *support*, which mirrors the syntactic structure of formulas. The inductive definition begins with a base case: the support of atomic propositions is determined by derivability in a given *base*—a specified collection of inference rules that govern atomic propositions.

In this work, we adapt Sandqvist's terminology [23] to the sequent setting.

### 2.1 Atomic Derivability

The **BeS** begins by defining derivability in a *base*. We use, as does Sandqvist, systems containing rules over basic sentences for the semantical analysis.

The propositional *base language* is assumed to have a set At = $\{p_1, p_2, \ldots\}$ of countably many atomic propositions. The elements of At will be called *basic sentences*, or simply *atoms*.

Let $\Gamma_{At}, \Delta_{At}$ be sets of atoms. An *atomic sequent* is denoted by $\Gamma_{At} \Rightarrow \Delta_{At}$, where $\Rightarrow \Delta_{At}$ denotes $\varnothing \Rightarrow \Delta_{At}$.

**Definition 1 (Base).** *An* atomic sequent system *(or* sequent base*)* $\mathcal{B}$ *is a (possibly empty) set of atomic sequent rules of the form*

$$\frac{\Gamma^1_{At} \Rightarrow \Delta^1_{At} \quad \ldots \quad \Gamma^n_{At} \Rightarrow \Delta^n_{At}}{\Gamma_{At} \Rightarrow \Delta_{At}}$$

*The sequence $\langle \Gamma^1_{At} \Rightarrow \Delta^1_{At}, \ldots, \Gamma^n_{At} \Rightarrow \Delta^n_{At} \rangle$ of premises in a rule can be empty—in this case the rule is called an* atomic axiom.

As in this work we will be referring to sequent systems only, from now on we will drop the word "sequents" from the objects just defined.

**Definition 2 (Extension).** *Let $\mathcal{B}, \mathcal{C}$ be bases. We say that $\mathcal{C}$ is an* extension *of $\mathcal{B}$ (written $\mathcal{C} \supseteq \mathcal{B}$) if $\mathcal{B}$ is a subset of $\mathcal{C}$.*

Before defining atomic derivability, it is important to clarify key distinctions between natural deduction and sequent calculus.

First, sequent calculus derivations always proceed from unconditional tautologies to unconditional tautologies, whereas natural deduction relies on hypothetical assumptions, often treating contexts implicitly. Second, the rules in sequent calculus must explicitly account for contexts—even when arbitrary—while natural deduction may treat contexts implicitly or explicitly.

These differences carry subtle but important consequences. For instance, the identity axiom $A \Rightarrow A$ must be explicitly included in sequent systems, whereas in natural deduction such derivability is implicit in the presence of an assumption $A$. Similarly, consider the contrast between the following rules:

$$\frac{A \vee B \quad \begin{matrix}[A]\\ \vdots \\ C\end{matrix} \quad \begin{matrix}[B]\\ \vdots \\ C\end{matrix}}{C}\vee\text{-elim} \qquad \frac{\Gamma, A \Rightarrow \Delta \quad \Gamma', B \Rightarrow \Delta'}{\Gamma, \Gamma', A \vee B \Rightarrow \Delta, \Delta'} L\vee$$

It is implicitly assumed that $\vee$-elim can be applied regardless of the sets of formulas $\Delta, \Delta'$ and $\Delta''$ used to derive its major premise $A \vee B$ and minor premises $C$, but the rule $L\vee$ represents such contextual sets explicitly (albeit still letting them be arbitrary). It comes as no surprise, then, that natural deduction systems for logics in which context matters (such as linear logic) have to make them explicit again [16].

This distinction becomes critical in atomic systems. In natural deduction, atomic rules can be applied freely, independent of the surrounding context, as illustrated by the rule on the left below—here $p, q, t, r$ are atomic formulas.

$$\frac{\begin{matrix}[p,q]\\ \vdots \\ t\end{matrix}}{r} \qquad \frac{p, q \Rightarrow t}{\Rightarrow r}$$

In contrast, a sequent rule—such as the one on the right above—can only be applied when the exact context $p, q$ is present[2]. This highlights the need to decide how contexts are handled in sequent-style atomic calculi.

If contexts are not treated as arbitrary, three main difficulties arise:

- *Proof rules:* To simulate generality, one rule must be included for every possible atomic context. For example, consider a base that contains a rule of the following form for each set $\Gamma_{At}$ of atomic formulas:

$$\frac{\Gamma_{At}, q \Rightarrow t}{\Gamma_{At} \Rightarrow r}$$

Even if contexts are syntactically fixed, the inclusion of a rule for every conceivable atomic context allows the base to behave as though it included a single rule defined over arbitrary contexts. While this is technically feasible—e.g., through infinitary rule bases—it complicates the system (see [2]).

- *Compositionality:* Fixed contexts restrict derivation composition to cases where sequents match exactly, limiting the expressiveness of the cut rule

$$\frac{\Gamma_{At} \Rightarrow p \quad \Delta_{At}, p \Rightarrow q}{\Gamma_{At}, \Delta_{At} \Rightarrow q} \text{ Cut}$$

To address this, one can close bases w.r.t. atomic cut rules, which allow compositionality through controlled context merging. We will show that adopting this choice will have a direct impact on the semantics principles that can be validated.

- *Context cumulativity:* Consider the following atomic rule

$$\frac{\Gamma_{At} \Rightarrow p \quad \Delta_{At}, q \Rightarrow r}{\Theta_{At} \Rightarrow s}$$

Even though contexts are always carried from premises to conclusion in both natural deduction and sequent calculus, sets of atoms occurring in the premises are not required to be related in any way to the sets occurring in the conclusion if contexts are fixed. This means that in fixed-context settings context accumulation must be enforced at the level of the rules themselves, rather than being built into the notion of deduction. This allows for simpler rule definitions, but undermines general guarantees like context monotonicity across base extensions. Again, atomic cut rules can reintroduce cumulativity, but at the cost of complicating the calculus.

Given these challenges, and motivated by the semantic role of cut in proof-theoretic semantics, we choose to allow arbitrary atomic contexts in our definition of derivability. This ensures generality, supports context cumulativity, and facilitates semantic interpretation. We also adopt an unconditional notion of derivability, in line with sequent calculus traditions, though a hypothetical variant could be used with similar results.

---

[2] This in a premises-to-conclusion reading of the rule, as done in proof-construction. In the bottom-up reading, as done in proof-search, the context should be empty in order to apply this rule.

**Definition 3 (Derivability).** *For every $\mathcal{B}$, the* derivability relation *(written $\vdash_\mathcal{B}$) is defined as follows.*

*(Axiom/Weakening) For any atomic axiom in $\mathcal{B}$ of the form*

$$\Gamma_{At} \Rightarrow \Delta_{At}$$

$\vdash_\mathcal{B} \Theta_{At}, \Gamma_{At} \Rightarrow \Delta_{At}, \Sigma_{At}$ *holds for any sets $\Theta_{At}$ and $\Sigma_{At}$ of atoms;*
*(Mix) If $\vdash_\mathcal{B} \Theta^1_{At}, \Gamma^1_{At} \Rightarrow \Delta^1_{At}, \Sigma^1_{At}, \ldots, \vdash_\mathcal{B} \Theta^n_{At}, \Gamma^n_{At} \Rightarrow \Delta^n_{At}, \Sigma^n_{At}$ hold in $\mathcal{B}$ and the following rule is in $\mathcal{B}$:*

$$\frac{\Gamma^1_{At} \Rightarrow \Delta^1_{At} \quad \cdots \quad \Gamma^n_{At} \Rightarrow \Delta^n_{At}}{\Gamma_{At} \Rightarrow \Delta_{At}}$$

*then $\vdash_\mathcal{B} \Theta^1_{At}, \ldots, \Theta^n_{At}, \Gamma_{At} \Rightarrow \Delta_{At}, \Sigma^1_{At}, \ldots, \Sigma^n_{At}$ holds.*

The following rules play a central role in our framework:

$$\frac{}{\Gamma_{At}, p \Rightarrow p, \Delta_{At}} \text{ Ainit} \qquad \frac{\Gamma^1_{At} \Rightarrow \Delta^1_{At}, p \quad p, \Gamma^2_{At} \Rightarrow \Delta^2_{At}}{\Gamma^1_{At}, \Gamma^2_{At} \Rightarrow \Delta^1_{At}, \Delta^2_{At}} \text{ Acut}$$

Indeed, we will restrict our attention to systems that are closed under the Ainit rule for every atom $p$ and all sets of atoms $\Gamma_{At}, \Delta_{At}$. We observe that, although the contexts $\Gamma_{At}$ and $\Delta_{At}$ in Ainit are not strictly necessary, they simplify certain steps in the completeness proof.

Regarding Acut, we will consider both: systems that are closed under this rule and those that are not.

**Definition 4 (Structural base).** *The structural base $\mathcal{ST}$ is the smallest atomic system closed under atomic axiom and atomic cut.*

**Definition 5 (Cut-free base).** *The cut-free base $\mathcal{HS}$ is the smallest atomic system closed under atomic axiom.*

As will be shown later, even though classical logic is complete with respect to our semantics regardless of the presence or absence of atomic cuts, the cut rule proves to be not only impactful for the semantics of individual bases, but also relevant for determining the shape of the completeness proof—see Sects. 4 and 5.

### 2.2 Semantics

In this subsection we define the proposed semantics and sketch some results that will be key for the soundness and completeness results. Please refer to the technical report [3] for the detailed proofs.

We start with the definition of the support relation, which reduces to derivability in $\mathcal{B}$ in the base case.

**Definition 6 (Support).** *Let $X_{\mathsf{At}} \subseteq \mathsf{At}$ for any set $X_{\mathsf{At}}$. Support in a base $\mathcal{B}$ (written $\Vdash_{\mathcal{B}}$) is defined as follows:*

(At) $\Vdash_{\mathcal{B}} \Gamma_{\mathsf{At}}$ *iff* $\vdash_{\mathcal{B}} \Rightarrow \Gamma_{\mathsf{At}}$;
($\wedge$) $\Vdash_{\mathcal{B}} A \wedge B, \Gamma$ *iff* $\Vdash_{\mathcal{B}} A, \Gamma$ *and* $\Vdash_{\mathcal{B}} B, \Gamma$;
($\vee$) $\Vdash_{\mathcal{B}} A \vee B, \Gamma$ *iff* $\Vdash_{\mathcal{B}} A, B, \Gamma$;
($\to$) $\Vdash_{\mathcal{B}} A \to B, \Gamma$ *iff* $A \Vdash_{\mathcal{B}} B, \Gamma$;
($\bot$) $\Vdash_{\mathcal{B}} \bot, \Gamma$ *iff* $\Vdash_{\mathcal{B}} \Gamma$;
(Inf) $\{A^1, \ldots, A^n\} \Vdash_{\mathcal{B}} \Delta$ *iff for all $C \supseteq \mathcal{B}$ and for all $\{\Theta^i_{\mathsf{At}}\}_{1 \leq i \leq n}$, if $\Vdash_C \Theta^i_{\mathsf{At}}, A^i$ for all $1 \leq i \leq n$ then $\Vdash_C \Theta^1_{\mathsf{At}}, \ldots, \Theta^n_{\mathsf{At}}, \Delta$.*

**Definition 7 (Validity/Cut-free validity).** *We say that an inference from $\Gamma$ to $\Delta$ is valid (cut-free valid), written as $\Gamma \Vdash \Delta$ ($\Gamma \Vdash^{cf} \Delta$), if $\Gamma \Vdash_{\mathcal{B}} \Delta$ for all $\mathcal{B} \supseteq \mathcal{ST}$ ($\mathcal{B} \supseteq \mathcal{HS}$).*

Observe that the BeS approach for the semantic clause for disjunction in intuitionistic logic presented in [23] closely mirrors the disjunction elimination rule in natural deduction:

$$\Vdash_{\mathcal{B}} A \vee B \text{ iff } \forall C \supseteq \mathcal{B}, p \in \mathsf{At}, \text{ if } A \Vdash_C p \text{ and } B \Vdash_C p \text{ then } \Vdash_C p$$

In particular, note the need for the use of quantification over atoms for the definition of semantic clauses.

This is not the case in the sequent presentation of BeS, which is perfectly capable of using only right rules (the sequent calculus equivalent of natural deduction's introduction rules) for the definition of its clauses. In particular, the semantic clause for disjunction reflects the invertible multiplicative right inference rule in sequent calculus (see Fig. 1).

We continue with the standard monotonicity result for bases, which is proven by induction on the complexity of context formulas.

**Lemma 1 (Monotonicity).** *If $\Vdash_{\mathcal{B}} \Delta$ and $C \supseteq \mathcal{B}$, then $\Vdash_C \Delta$.*

This allows to prove the following result about validity:

**Theorem 1 (Validity).** $\Gamma \Vdash \Delta$ *if and only if* $\Gamma \Vdash_{\mathcal{ST}} \Delta$.

*Proof.* ($\Rightarrow$) Immediate by Definition 7—since $\Gamma \Vdash_{\mathcal{B}} \Delta$ holds for all $\mathcal{B} \supseteq \mathcal{ST}$, it holds for $\mathcal{ST}$ in particular.

($\Leftarrow$) Let $\Gamma = \{A^1, \ldots, A^n\}$ and $\Theta^1, \ldots, \Theta^n$ be arbitrary contexts. Assume that $\Vdash_{\mathcal{B}} \Theta^1, A^1, \ldots, \Vdash_{\mathcal{B}} \Theta^n, A^n$ for arbitrary $\mathcal{B} \supseteq \mathcal{ST}$. Then $\Vdash_{\mathcal{B}} \Theta^1, \ldots, \Theta^n, \Delta$ by (Inf). Further, by Lemma 1, $\Vdash_C \Theta^1, \ldots, \Theta^n, \Delta$, as well as $\Vdash_C \Theta^1, A^1, \ldots, \Vdash_C \Theta^n, A^n$, for arbitrary $C \supseteq \mathcal{B}$. Then $\Gamma \Vdash_{\mathcal{B}} \Delta$ by (Inf) again, and since $\mathcal{B}$ is arbitrary, we have that, by Definition 7, $\Gamma \Vdash \Delta$. □

We will next demonstrate that, even though (Inf) is defined via atomic sets, its action can be extended to arbitrary contexts.

**Lemma 2.** $\{A^1, \ldots, A^n\} \Vdash_{\mathcal{B}} \Delta$ *if and only if, for all $C \supseteq \mathcal{B}$ and arbitrary sets of formulas $\Theta^i$, if for $1 \leq i \leq n$, $\Vdash_C \Theta^i, A^i$, then $\Vdash_C \Theta^1, \ldots, \Theta^n, \Delta$.*

*Proof.* ($\Leftarrow$) Immediate by (Inf)—since the statement holds for arbitrary sets of formulas $\Theta^i$, it in particular holds for all atomic sets $\Theta^i_{At}$.

($\Rightarrow$) The result is proven by induction on the degree of $\{\Theta^i\}_{1 \leq i \leq n}$, understood as the sum of the degrees of all formulas occurring in all sets in the collection. $\square$

Finally, we present the admissibility of structural rules.

**Lemma 3 (Right/left weakening).** *If $\Vdash_{\mathcal{B}} \Gamma$ then $\Vdash_{\mathcal{B}} \Gamma, A$. If $\Gamma \Vdash_{\mathcal{B}} \Delta$ then $A, \Gamma \Vdash_{\mathcal{B}} \Delta$.*

*Proof.* Right weakening: We will prove that if $\Vdash_{\mathcal{B}} \Gamma$ then $\Vdash_{\mathcal{B}} \Gamma, A$.

For the base case, consider both $\Gamma$ and $A$ to be atomic, *i.e.* the following clause with $\Gamma = \Gamma_{At}, A = p$ for an arbitrary atom $p$:

$$\text{if } \Vdash_{\mathcal{B}} \Gamma_{At} \text{ then } \Vdash_{\mathcal{B}} \Gamma_{At}, p.$$

By (At), we obtain $\vdash_{\mathcal{B}} \Rightarrow \Gamma_{At}$ from $\Vdash_{\mathcal{B}} \Gamma_{At}$. Since the definition of derivability (Definition 3) allows inclusion of arbitrary contexts on the right, we conclude $\vdash_{\mathcal{B}} \Rightarrow \Gamma_{At}, p$, and, by (At) again, we obtain $\Vdash_{\mathcal{B}} \Gamma_{At}, p$ as desired.

For the inductive case, notice that it does not make a difference whether to consider $\Gamma$ or $A$ to be non-atomic, as in either case, one would end up with *some* non-atomic formula on the right, be it a member of $\Gamma$ or $A$ itself. What truly matters is the ability to break such a formula down into its strict subformulas until, eventually, one ends up solely with atoms on the right.

As an induction hypothesis, thus, take that

$$\text{if } \Vdash_{\mathcal{B}} \Gamma \text{ then } \Vdash_{\mathcal{B}} \Gamma, A$$

holds true with any base in place of $\mathcal{B}$ and any proper subset of $\Gamma$ in place of $\Gamma$. Then proceed with the case analysis, *e.g.*

$\Gamma = \Gamma', B \wedge C$ : we have that $\Vdash_{\mathcal{B}} \Gamma', B \wedge C$. By ($\wedge$), obtain $\Vdash_{\mathcal{B}} \Gamma', B$ and $\Vdash_{\mathcal{B}} \Gamma', C$. By the induction hypothesis, $\Vdash_{\mathcal{B}} \Gamma', B, A$ and $\Vdash_{\mathcal{B}} \Gamma', C, A$, and by ($\wedge$) again, $\Vdash_{\mathcal{B}} \Gamma', B \wedge C, A$.

For the left weakening, we need to prove that if $\Gamma \Vdash_{\mathcal{B}} \Delta$ then $A, \Gamma \Vdash_{\mathcal{B}} \Delta$. Without loss of generality, let $\Gamma = \{A^1, \ldots, A^n\}$ and $\Theta^1_{At}, \ldots, \Theta^n_{At}, \Omega_{At}$ be arbitrary atomic sets. Take an arbitrary $C \supseteq \mathcal{B}$ such that $\Vdash_C \Theta^1_{At}, A^1, \ldots, \Vdash_C \Theta^n_{At}, A^n$ and $\Vdash_C \Omega_{At}, A$. By (Inf), from $\Gamma \Vdash_{\mathcal{B}} \Delta$ and $\Vdash_C \Theta^1_{At}, A^1, \ldots, \Vdash_C \Theta^n_{At}, A^n$ we obtain $\Vdash_C \Theta^1_{At}, \ldots, \Theta^n_{At}, \Delta$. Application of weakening with $\Omega$ on the right yields $\Vdash_C \Theta^1_{At}, \ldots, \Theta^n_{At}, \Delta, \Omega_{At}$. Since also $C \supseteq \mathcal{B}$ such that $\Vdash_C \Theta^1_{At}, A^1, \ldots, \Vdash_C \Theta^n_{At}, A^n$ and $\Vdash_C \Omega_{At}, A$ for arbitrary $\Theta^1_{At}, \ldots, \Theta^n_{At}, \Omega_{At}$, we obtain $A, \Gamma \Vdash_{\mathcal{B}} \Delta$ by (Inf) as required. $\square$

**Lemma 4 (Right/left contraction).** *If $\Vdash_{\mathcal{B}} \Gamma, A, A$ then $\Vdash_{\mathcal{B}} \Gamma, A$. If $\Gamma, A, A \Vdash_{\mathcal{B}} \Delta$ then $\Gamma, A \Vdash_{\mathcal{B}} \Delta$.*

*Proof.* Right contraction: If $\Vdash_S \Gamma, A, A$ then $\Vdash_S \Gamma, A$ follows directly from the fact that $\Gamma, A, A$ and $\Gamma, A$ are the same set of formulas.

$$\frac{A,B,\Gamma \Rightarrow \Delta}{A \wedge B, \Gamma \Rightarrow \Delta} L\wedge \qquad \frac{\Gamma \Rightarrow \Delta, A \quad \Gamma' \Rightarrow \Delta', B}{\Gamma, \Gamma' \Rightarrow \Delta, \Delta', A \wedge B} R\wedge$$

$$\frac{A, \Gamma \Rightarrow \Delta \quad B, \Gamma' \Rightarrow \Delta'}{A \vee B, \Gamma, \Gamma' \Rightarrow \Delta, \Delta'} L\vee \qquad \frac{\Gamma \Rightarrow \Delta, A, B}{\Gamma \Rightarrow \Delta, A \vee B} R\vee$$

$$\frac{\Gamma \Rightarrow \Delta, A \quad B, \Gamma' \Rightarrow \Delta'}{A \to B, \Gamma, \Gamma' \Rightarrow \Delta, \Delta'} L\to \qquad \frac{A, \Gamma \Rightarrow \Delta, B}{\Gamma \Rightarrow \Delta, A \to B} R\to$$

$$\frac{}{\Gamma, A \Rightarrow A, \Delta} \text{init} \qquad \frac{}{\Gamma, \bot \Rightarrow \Delta} L\bot \qquad \frac{\Gamma \Rightarrow \Delta}{\Gamma \Rightarrow \bot, \Delta} R\bot$$

**Fig. 1.** Sequent system CLp.

For the left contraction, we need to prove that if $\Gamma, A, A \Vdash_{\mathcal{B}} \Delta$ then $\Gamma, A \Vdash_{\mathcal{B}} \Delta$. Without loss of generality, let $\Gamma = \{A^1, \ldots, A^n\}$ and $\Theta^1_{\text{At}}, \ldots, \Theta^n_{\text{At}}, \Omega_{\text{At}}$ be arbitrary atomic sets. Choose an arbitrary $C \supseteq \mathcal{B}$ such that $\Vdash_C \Theta^1_{\text{At}}, A^1, \ldots, \Vdash_C \Theta^n_{\text{At}}, A^n$ and $\Vdash_C \Omega_{\text{At}}, A$. From $\Gamma, A, A \Vdash_{\mathcal{B}} \Delta$ and $\Vdash_C \Theta^1_{\text{At}}, A^1, \ldots, \Vdash_C \Theta^n_{\text{At}}, A^n$ and $\Vdash_C \Omega_{\text{At}}, A$ applied twice we obtain $\Vdash_C \Theta^1_{\text{At}}, \ldots, \Theta^n_{\text{At}}, \Omega_{\text{At}}, \Omega_{\text{At}}, \Delta$ by (Inf). Application of contraction on $\Omega_{\text{At}}$ on the right yields $\Vdash_C \Theta^1_{\text{At}}, \ldots, \Theta^n_{\text{At}}, \Omega_{\text{At}}, \Delta$. Since also $C \supseteq \mathcal{B}$ such that $\Vdash_C \Theta^1_{\text{At}}, A^1, \ldots, \Vdash_C \Theta^n_{\text{At}}, A^n$ and $\Vdash_C \Omega_{\text{At}}, A$ for arbitrary $\Theta^1_{\text{At}}, \ldots, \Theta^n_{\text{At}}, \Omega_{\text{At}}$, we obtain $\Gamma, A \Vdash_{\mathcal{B}} \Delta$ by (Inf) as required. □

## 3 Soundness

We shall consider the sequent system CLp for classical propositional logic with rules depicted in Fig. 1. It should be highlighted that, although the presentation is non-standard—using multiplicative inference rules instead of the additive ones—the rules operate over *sets of formulas*.

This section is devoted to proving that CLp is *sound* with respect to our semantics; that is, every provable sequent is semantically valid. This result follows from the fact that the semantic relation $\Vdash$ preserves all inference rules of CLp.

**Theorem 2 (Soundness).** *If there is a proof of $\Gamma \Rightarrow \Delta$ in CLp then $\Gamma \Vdash \Delta$.*

*Proof.* Given that derivations in sequent calculus are defined inductively, it suffices to prove the following:

(Ax)' $\Gamma, A \Vdash A, \Delta$.
($L\wedge$)' If $A, B, \Gamma \Vdash \Delta$ then $A \wedge B, \Gamma \Vdash \Delta$.
($R\wedge$)' If $\Gamma \Vdash \Delta, A$ and $\Gamma' \Vdash \Delta', B$ then $\Gamma, \Gamma' \Vdash \Delta, \Delta', A \wedge B$.
($L\vee$)' If $A, \Gamma \Vdash \Delta$ and $B, \Gamma' \Vdash \Delta'$ then $A \vee B, \Gamma, \Gamma' \Vdash \Delta, \Delta'$.
($R\vee$)' If $\Gamma \Vdash \Delta, A, B$ then $\Gamma \Vdash \Delta, A \vee B$.
($L\to$)' If $\Gamma \Vdash \Delta, A$ and $B, \Gamma' \Vdash \Delta'$ then $A \to B, \Gamma, \Gamma' \Vdash \Delta, \Delta'$.
($R\to$)' If $A, \Gamma \Vdash B, \Delta$ then $\Gamma \Vdash \Delta, A \to B$.
($L\bot$)' $\Gamma, \bot \Vdash \Delta$.
($R\bot$)' If $\Gamma \Vdash \Delta$ then $\Gamma \Vdash \bot, \Delta$.

In what follows, we assume without loss of generality that $\Gamma = A^1, \ldots, A^n$ and $\Gamma' = B^1, \ldots, B^m$. We use $\Theta^1_{At}, \ldots, \Theta^n_{At}, \Sigma^1_{At}, \ldots, \Sigma^m_{At}, \Omega_{At}$ to denote arbitrary atomic contexts.

We include a few illustrative cases below; the full proof is provided in the technical report [3].

Regarding the axiom, the main steps for proving the claim are the following:

**(Ax)'** Recall that by (Inf) $\Gamma, A \Vdash_\mathcal{B} A, \Delta$ iff, for all $C \supseteq \mathcal{B}$ and for all $\{\Theta^i_{At}\}_{1 \le i \le n}$, if $\Vdash_C A^i, \Theta^i_{At}$ for all $1 \le i \le n$ and $\Vdash_C A, \Omega_{At}$, then $\Vdash_C A, \Omega_{At}, \Theta^1_{At}, \ldots, \Theta^n_{At}, \Delta$.

1. Take any $\mathcal{B}$ and any $C \supseteq \mathcal{B}$ such that $\Vdash_C A, \Omega_{At}$ and $\Vdash_C A^i, \Theta^i_{At}$ for all $A^i \in \Gamma$.
2. By applying right weakening (Lemma 3) over $\Vdash_C A, \Omega_{At}$, we have
   $\Vdash_C A, \Omega_{At}, \Theta^1_{At}, \ldots, \Theta^n_{At}, \Delta$.
3. By arbitrariness of $C$ and $\Theta^i_{At}$ we conclude $\Gamma, A \Vdash_\mathcal{B} A, \Delta$.
4. Hence $\Gamma, A \Vdash A, \Delta$ by the arbitrariness of $\mathcal{B}$.

As for the connectives, the following case depict the key ideas of the proof:

**(L →)'** Assume that $\Gamma \Vdash \Delta, A$ and $B, \Gamma' \Vdash \Delta'$, $\Vdash_\mathcal{B} \Theta^1_{At}, A^1, \ldots, \Vdash_\mathcal{B} \Theta^n_{At}, A^n$ and $\Vdash_\mathcal{B} \Sigma^1_{At}, B^1, \ldots, \Vdash_\mathcal{B} \Sigma^m_{At}, B^m$ and $\Vdash_\mathcal{B} \Omega_{At}, A \to B$ for arbitrary $\mathcal{B} \supseteq \mathcal{ST}$.

1. By (→), we have $A \Vdash_\mathcal{B} \Omega_{At}, B$.
2. By (Inf), $\Gamma \Vdash_{\mathcal{ST}} \Delta, A$ and $\Vdash_\mathcal{B} \Theta^1_{At}, A^1, \ldots, \Vdash_\mathcal{B} \Theta^n_{At}, A^n$ yield $\Vdash_\mathcal{B} \Theta^1_{At}, \ldots, \Theta^n_{At}, \Delta, A$.
3. By (Inf), $\Vdash_\mathcal{B} \Theta^1_{At}, \ldots, \Theta^n_{At}, \Delta, A$ and $A \Vdash_\mathcal{B} \Omega_{At}, B$ yield $\Vdash_\mathcal{B} \Theta^1_{At}, \ldots, \Theta^n_{At}, \Omega_{At}, \Delta, B$.
4. $B, \Gamma' \Vdash_{\mathcal{ST}} \Delta'$ and $\Vdash_\mathcal{B} \Sigma^1_{At}, B^1, \ldots, \Vdash_\mathcal{B} \Sigma^m_{At}, B^m$ together with previously obtained $\Vdash_\mathcal{B} \Theta^1_{At}, \ldots, \Theta^n_{At}, \Omega_{At}, \Delta, B$ gives $\Vdash_\mathcal{B} \Theta^1_{At}, \ldots, \Theta^n_{At}, \Sigma^1_{At}, \ldots, \Sigma^m_{At}, \Omega_{At}, \Delta, \Delta'$ by (Inf) again.
5. Hence, for arbitrary $\mathcal{B} \supseteq \mathcal{ST}$, if $\Vdash_\mathcal{B} \Omega_{At}, A \to B$ and $\Vdash_\mathcal{B} \Theta^1_{At}, A^1, \ldots, \Vdash_\mathcal{B} \Theta^n_{At}, A^n$ and $\Vdash_\mathcal{B} \Sigma^1_{At}, B^1, \ldots, \Vdash_\mathcal{B} \Sigma^m_{At}, B^m$ then
   $\Vdash_\mathcal{B} \Theta^1_{At}, \ldots, \Theta^n_{At}, \Sigma^1_{At}, \ldots, \Sigma^m_{At}, \Omega_{At}, \Delta, \Delta'$.
6. By (Inf), we obtain $\Gamma, \Gamma', A \to B \Vdash_{\mathcal{ST}} \Delta, \Delta'$, hence $\Gamma, \Gamma', A \to B \Vdash \Delta, \Delta'$ as required.

In particular, this case highlights the necessity of the multiplicative presentation of the system CLp. While an additive presentation could also be used, it would make the proofs more cumbersome and less readable. □

## 4 Completeness

In this section, we prove that CLp is complete with respect to the semantics; that is, every semantically valid sequent is provable. We begin be returning to Definition 3 and proving a key lemma about composing derivable sequents.

**Lemma 5.** *Let $\mathcal{B}$ be a base. If, for all $C \supseteq \mathcal{B}$, $\vdash_C \Rightarrow \Gamma_{At}$ implies $\vdash_C \Rightarrow \Delta_{At}$, then $\vdash_\mathcal{B} \Gamma_{At} \Rightarrow \Delta_{At}$.*

*Proof.* Assume that for all $C \supseteq \mathcal{B}$, $\vdash_\mathcal{B} \Rightarrow \Gamma_{At}$ implies $\vdash_C \Rightarrow \Delta_{At}$, and let $\mathcal{D}$ be the base obtained by adding to $\mathcal{B}$ an atomic axiom with conclusion $\Rightarrow \Gamma_{At}$. Then we have $\vdash_\mathcal{D} \Rightarrow \Gamma_{At}$, so from our assumption follows $\vdash_\mathcal{D} \Rightarrow \Delta_{At}$. Now consider the deduction $\Pi$ showing $\vdash_\mathcal{D} \Rightarrow \Delta_{At}$. If $\Pi$ does not contain any applications of the new rule it is also a deduction showing $\vdash_\mathcal{B} \Rightarrow \Delta_{At}$, so also $\vdash_\mathcal{B} \Gamma_{At} \Rightarrow \Delta_{At}$ by Definition 3. If $\Pi$ contains applications of the new rule, let $\Pi'$ be the deduction obtained by adding $\Gamma_{At}$ to the left side of the conclusion of any application of the new rule and any rule application below it in the deduction. To exemplify it graphically, the transformation of $\Pi$ into $\Pi'$ is as follows:

$$\begin{array}{c} \overline{\Rightarrow \Gamma_{At}} \\ \Pi \\ \Rightarrow \Delta_{At} \end{array} \quad \text{is transformed into} \quad \begin{array}{c} \overline{\Gamma_{At} \Rightarrow \Gamma_{At}} \\ \Pi' \\ \Gamma_{At} \Rightarrow \Delta_{At} \end{array}$$

It is straightforward to check that, since in $\Pi'$ every instance of the new rule is replaced by an atomic axiom of shape $\Gamma_{At} \Rightarrow \Gamma_{At}$ already contained in $\mathcal{B}$ and the new context is also added to all inferences below each new atomic axiom, $\Pi'$ is the desired deduction showing $\vdash_\mathcal{B} \Gamma_{At} \Rightarrow \Delta_{At}$. □

Completeness in BeS is typically shown by associating a unique atom $p^A$ to each subformula $A$ of $\Gamma \cup \Delta$. Exploiting the validity of $\Gamma \Vdash \Delta$ with respect to every base, we then construct a simulation base $\mathcal{U}$ for $\Gamma \cup \Delta$ in which each $p^A$ mimics the behaviour of $A$ in CLp.

**Definition 8 (Atomic mapping).** *Let $\Sigma$ be a set of formulas. Let $\Sigma_S$ be the set of all subformulas of formulas in $\Sigma$. We say that a function $\alpha : \Sigma_S \to$ At is an atomic mapping for $\Sigma$ if (1) $\alpha$ is injective, (2) $\alpha(p) = p$ for $p \in$ At. If $A \notin$ At, we denote $\alpha(A) =: p^A$.*

**Definition 9 (Simulation base).** *Let $\Sigma$ be a set of formulas, and let $\alpha$ be an atomic mapping on $\Sigma$. A simulation base $\mathcal{U}$ for $\Sigma$ and $\alpha$ is a base that includes exactly the rules in Fig. 2, instantiated for all $A, B \in \Sigma$ and all multisets $\Gamma_{At}, \Delta_{At}, \Gamma'_{At}, \Delta'_{At}$. We write $\mathcal{U}_{ST}$ (resp. $\mathcal{U}_{HS}$) for the closure of $\mathcal{U}$ under $ST$ (resp. $HS$).*

We are now ready to present how the proof simulation works and prove the completeness result.

**Lemma 6.** *Let $\Theta_{At}$ be any (possibly empty) set of atoms, $\Sigma$ any (non-empty) set containing only subformulas of $\Gamma \cup \Delta$ and $\Sigma_{At} = \{p^B | B \in \Sigma\}$. Then, for all $\mathcal{B} \supseteq \mathcal{U}_{ST}$, $\Vdash_\mathcal{B} \Sigma, \Theta_{At}$ if and only if $\vdash_\mathcal{B} \Rightarrow \Sigma_{At}, \Theta_{At}$.*

*Proof.* We prove the result by induction on the complexity of $\Sigma \cup \Theta_{At}$, understood as the number of logical connectives occurring in $\Sigma \cup \Theta_{At}$. We will illustrate with the base case and the inductive case for the implication. All the other cases are in the technical report [3].

For the base case: if the complexity of $\Sigma \cup \Theta_{At}$ is 0, then $\Sigma \cup \Theta_{At}$ is just a set of atoms. Notice that, by virtue of how the mapping is defined, $\alpha(p) = p$ for $p \in$ At, so clearly $\Sigma = \Sigma_{At}$ and the results follow by (At).

$$\frac{p^A, p^B, \Gamma_{\text{At}} \Rightarrow \Delta_{\text{At}}}{p^{A \wedge B}, \Gamma_{\text{At}} \Rightarrow \Delta_{\text{At}}} L\wedge \qquad \frac{\Gamma_{\text{At}} \Rightarrow \Delta_{\text{At}}, p^A \quad \Gamma'_{\text{At}} \Rightarrow \Delta'_{\text{At}}, p^B}{\Gamma_{\text{At}}, \Gamma'_{\text{At}} \Rightarrow \Delta_{\text{At}}, \Delta'_{\text{At}}, p^{A \wedge B}} R\wedge$$

$$\frac{p^A, \Gamma_{\text{At}} \Rightarrow \Delta_{\text{At}} \quad p^B, \Gamma'_{\text{At}} \Rightarrow \Delta'_{\text{At}}}{p^{A \vee B}, \Gamma_{\text{At}}, \Gamma'_{\text{At}} \Rightarrow \Delta_{\text{At}}, \Delta'_{\text{At}}} L\vee \qquad \frac{\Gamma_{\text{At}} \Rightarrow \Delta_{\text{At}}, p^A, p^B}{\Gamma_{\text{At}} \Rightarrow \Delta_{\text{At}}, p^{A \vee B}} R\vee \qquad \frac{\Gamma_{\text{At}} \Rightarrow \Delta_{\text{At}}}{\Gamma_{\text{At}} \Rightarrow \Delta_{\text{At}}, p^\perp} R\perp$$

$$\frac{\Gamma_{\text{At}} \Rightarrow \Delta_{\text{At}}, p^A \quad p^B, \Gamma'_{\text{At}} \Rightarrow \Delta'_{\text{At}}}{p^{A \rightarrow B}, \Gamma_{\text{At}}, \Gamma'_{\text{At}} \Rightarrow \Delta_{\text{At}}, \Delta'_{\text{At}}} L\rightarrow \qquad \frac{p^A, \Gamma_{\text{At}} \Rightarrow \Delta_{\text{At}}, p^B}{\Gamma_{\text{At}} \Rightarrow \Delta_{\text{At}}, p^{A \rightarrow B}} R\rightarrow \qquad \frac{}{\Gamma_{\text{At}}, p^\perp \Rightarrow \Delta_{\text{At}}} L\perp$$

**Fig. 2.** Rules of the simulation base $\mathcal{U}$.

If the complexity of $\Sigma \cup \Theta_{\text{At}}$ is greater than 0, then $\Sigma$ contains at least one formula of shape $A \wedge B$, $A \vee B$ or $A \rightarrow B$. The proof below shows the case when this formula is an implication, with $\Sigma = A \rightarrow B \cup \Omega$.

($\Rightarrow$): Assume $\Vdash_{\mathcal{B}} A \rightarrow B, \Omega, \Theta_{\text{At}}$. Then by ($\rightarrow$) we have $A \Vdash_{\mathcal{B}} B, \Omega, \Theta_{\text{At}}$. Now take any $C \supseteq \mathcal{B}$ with $\vdash_C \Rightarrow p^A$. By the induction hypothesis, we have $\Vdash_C A$. Since $A \Vdash_{\mathcal{B}} B, \Omega, \Theta_{\text{At}}$ and $C \supseteq \mathcal{B}$, it follows that $\Vdash_C B, \Omega, \Theta_{\text{At}}$. Applying the induction hypothesis again, we obtain $\vdash_C \Rightarrow p^B, \Omega_{\text{At}}, \Theta_{\text{At}}$. But then since $C$ is an arbitrary extension of $\mathcal{B}$ with $\vdash_C \Rightarrow p^A$, by Lemma 5 we conclude $\vdash_{\mathcal{B}} p^A \Rightarrow p^B, \Omega_{\text{At}}, \Theta_{\text{At}}$, and we can finally obtain the desired proof of $\vdash_{\mathcal{B}} \Rightarrow p^{A \rightarrow B}, \Omega_{\text{At}}, \Theta_{\text{At}}$ as follows:

$$\frac{\vdots}{\frac{p^A \Rightarrow p^B, \Omega_{\text{At}}, \Theta_{\text{At}}}{\Rightarrow p^{A \rightarrow B}, \Omega_{\text{At}}, \Theta_{\text{At}}}} R\rightarrow$$

($\Leftarrow$): Assume $\vdash_{\mathcal{B}} \Rightarrow p^{A \rightarrow B}, \Omega_{\text{At}}, \Theta_{\text{At}}$, and let $C$ be any $C \supseteq \mathcal{B}$ with $\Vdash_C A, \Pi_{\text{At}}$ for some set of atoms $\Pi_{\text{At}}$. Then by induction hypothesis $\vdash_C \Rightarrow p^A, \Pi_{\text{At}}$ and, since $C$ is an extension of $\mathcal{B}$, we also have $\vdash_C \Rightarrow p^{A \rightarrow B}, \Omega_{\text{At}}, \Theta_{\text{At}}$. Then we can obtain the following deduction in $C$:

$$\frac{\vdots \quad \frac{\vdots}{\Rightarrow p^{A \rightarrow B}, \Omega_{\text{At}}, \Theta_{\text{At}}} \quad \frac{\overline{p^A \Rightarrow p^A} \text{ Axiom} \quad \overline{p^B \Rightarrow p^B} \text{ Axiom}}{p^A, p^{A \rightarrow B} \Rightarrow p^B} L\rightarrow}{\frac{\Rightarrow p^A, \Pi_{\text{At}} \qquad p^A \Rightarrow p^B, \Omega_{\text{At}}, \Theta_{\text{At}}}{\Rightarrow p^B, \Omega_{\text{At}}, \Theta_{\text{At}}, \Pi_{\text{At}}} \text{ Cut}} \text{ Cut}$$

So $\vdash_C \Rightarrow p^B, \Omega_{\text{At}}, \Theta_{\text{At}}, \Pi_{\text{At}}$, and by induction hypothesis $\Vdash_C B, \Omega, \Theta_{\text{At}}, \Pi_{\text{At}}$ (as $\Theta_{\text{At}} \cup \Pi_{\text{At}}$ is still a set of atoms). But $C$ is an arbitrary extension of $\mathcal{B}$ with $\Vdash_C A, \Pi_{\text{At}}$ for an arbitrary set of atoms $\Pi_{\text{At}}$, so we conclude $A \Vdash_{\mathcal{B}} B, \Omega, \Theta_{\text{At}}$ by (Inf), and then $\Vdash_{\mathcal{B}} A \rightarrow B, \Omega, \Theta_{\text{At}}$ by ($\rightarrow$). □

**Theorem 3 (Completeness).** *If* $\Gamma \Vdash \Delta$ *then the sequent* $\Gamma \Rightarrow \Delta$ *is provable in* CLp.

*Proof.* Fix a simulation base $\mathcal{U}_{ST}$ with a mapping $\alpha$ for the set $\Gamma \cup \Delta$. Assume $\Gamma \Vdash \Delta$. Then $\Gamma \Vdash_{\mathcal{U}_{ST}} \Delta$. Now let $\mathcal{B}$ be the system obtained by adding a rule concluding the sequent $\Rightarrow p^B$ from empty premises for all $B \in \Gamma$. So $\vdash_{\mathcal{B}} \Rightarrow p^B$ for all $B \in \Gamma$, hence by Lemma 6 we have $\Vdash_{\mathcal{B}} B$ for all $B \in \Gamma$. From our assumption follows $\Vdash_{\mathcal{B}} \Delta$, and from Lemma 6 we once again have $\vdash_{\mathcal{B}} \Rightarrow \Delta_{At}$, so there must be a proof $\Pi$ in $\mathcal{U}_{ST}$ with conclusion $\Rightarrow \Sigma_{At}$ for some $\Sigma_{At} \subseteq \Delta_{At}$.

If $\Pi$ does not contain applications of the new rules added to $\mathcal{B}$, it is already a deduction in the simulation base $\mathcal{U}_{ST}$, so by adding the context $\Gamma_{At}$ to the left side of all sequents of the deduction we get a deduction $\Pi'$ with conclusion of shape $\Gamma_{At} \Rightarrow \Delta_{At}$. If it does contain applications of the new rules, we define a transformation similar to that of Lemma 5. Let $\Pi'$ be the deduction obtained by adding to each application in $\Pi$ of one of the rules added to $\mathcal{U}_{ST}$ to obtain $\mathcal{B}$ the context $\Gamma_{At}$ on the left side of the sequent, as well as to all rule applications below them. The transformation can be represented graphically as follows:

$$\begin{array}{c} \Rightarrow p^B \\ \Pi \\ \Rightarrow \Delta_{At} \end{array} \quad \text{is transformed into} \quad \begin{array}{c} \Gamma_{At} \Rightarrow p^B \\ \Pi' \\ \Gamma_{At} \Rightarrow \Delta_{At} \end{array}$$

Since $p^B \in \Gamma_{At}$ for every replaced rule due to the definition of $\mathcal{B}$, clearly every instance of one of the new rules becomes an instance of atomic axiom already contained in $\mathcal{U}_{ST}$, so $\Pi'$ is a deduction with conclusion $\vdash_{\mathcal{U}_{ST}} \Gamma_{At} \Rightarrow \Delta_{At}$.

Hence in both cases we have a deduction $\Pi'$ using only the rules in $\mathcal{U}_{ST}$ with conclusion $\Gamma_{At} \Rightarrow \Delta_{At}$. Now let $\Pi''$ be the deduction obtained by replacing every atom $p^B$ in the deduction $\Pi'$ by $B$. Since $\mathcal{U}_{ST}$ contains only instances of atomic axiom, atomic cut, and the rules of a simulation base, $\Pi''$ is a deduction in the classical sequent calculus (with cut) that ends with the sequent $\Gamma \Rightarrow \Delta$. Since the cut rule itself is admissible in CLp we conclude that there is a deduction in the classical sequent calculus that ends with the sequent $\Gamma \Rightarrow \Delta$. □

## 5 Cut-Free Completeness

The proof of completeness just presented makes ostensive use of the cut rule. Since Gentzen's *Hauptsatz* shows that the cut rule is admissible in classical logic, one might be led to think that those uses are only for simplifying the proof, so completeness could also be proved through the same strategy if $\mathcal{U}$ was an extension of $\mathcal{HS}$ instead of $\mathcal{ST}$. However, this is not the case:

**Proposition 1.** *Let $\Theta_{At}$ be any (possibly empty) set of atoms, $\Sigma$ any (non-empty) set containing only subformulas of $\Gamma \cup \Delta$ and $\Sigma_{At} = \{p^B | B \in \Sigma\}$.* **It is not the case** *that, for all $\mathcal{B} \supseteq \mathcal{U}_{HS}$, $\Vdash_{\mathcal{B}} \Sigma, \Theta_{At}$ if and only if $\vdash_{\mathcal{B}} \Rightarrow \Sigma_{At}, \Theta_{At}$.*

*Proof.* As a quick counterexample, consider the consequence $q \wedge r \Vdash q$, which gives $\Gamma \cup \Delta = q \wedge r, q$. Let $\mathcal{B}$ be the extension of $\mathcal{U}_{HS}$ obtained by adding an atomic axiom with conclusion $\Rightarrow p^{q \wedge r}$, where $q$ and $r$ are atomic formulas. By the definition of derivability (Definition 3) we conclude $\vdash_\mathcal{B} \Rightarrow p^{q \wedge r}$. Even though we can still apply the axiom and $L\wedge$ rules to conclude $\vdash_\mathcal{B} p^{q \wedge r} \Rightarrow q$ and $\vdash_\mathcal{B} p^{q \wedge r} \Rightarrow r$, the absence of cut on the base does not allow us to use those deductions in order to obtain the deductions showing $\vdash_\mathcal{B} \Rightarrow q$ and $\vdash_\mathcal{B} \Rightarrow r$ necessary to show $\Vdash_{\mathcal{U}_{HS}} q \wedge r$, so we have to find other deductions. Notice, however, that no rule of the base is capable of producing a deductions with one of the desired conclusions; instances of axiom never have empty antecedents, and the only other rules in $\mathcal{B}$ are the rules in $\mathcal{U}_{HS}$ obtained via the mapping, that is, instances of $L\wedge$ with $p^{q \wedge r}$ on their antecedent and of $R\wedge$ with $p^{q \wedge r}$ in their consequent (given that $\Gamma \cup \Delta = \{q \wedge r, q\}$). Remember that, in virtue of how the mapping is defined, $p^{q \wedge r} \neq p$ and $p^{q \wedge r} \neq p$. Since there are no deductions of $\Rightarrow p$ or $\Rightarrow q$ in $\mathcal{B}$ we conclude $\nVdash_\mathcal{B} p$ and $\nVdash_\mathcal{B} q$, so clearly $\nVdash_\mathcal{B} q \wedge r$. □

The fact that cut is admissible in classical logic *does not entail* that is admissible in all atomic bases. This is essentially due to the fact that cut elimination procedures rely on the structure of rules capable of introducing a formula on the right of the sequent to permute cuts, but such rules can be arbitrary in bases. It is not possible in general to compose a deduction showing $\Rightarrow p$ and a deduction showing $p \Rightarrow q$ to obtain one showing $\Rightarrow q$ if the cut rule is not available, so by taking out such rules we change the semantic content of bases altogether.

This allows us to conclude that atomic cut rules indeed provide substantive semantic content to the bases containing them, but it does not clarify whether this content is essential for the proof of completeness to follow through. Notice that cut is not required in any step of the proof of soundness and, since $\mathcal{ST}$ is an extension of $\mathcal{HS}$, completeness can be shown for $\Vdash^{cf}$ through the strategy employed in Theorem 3 if we require simulation bases $\mathcal{U}_{HS}$ to also contain all instances of atomic cut, whence $\Vdash^{cf}$ is sound and complete w.r.t. classical logic. However, such a completeness proof would still rely on the use of atomic cuts.

As we will now show, completeness can still be proved without relying on bases closed under atomic cut. In the revised proof, all necessary applications of cut are deferred from Lemma 6 to the final step. This is allowed since, at that stage, we are working within a logical calculus rather than with arbitrary bases.

The importance of this proof lies on the fact that it replaces all the semantically meaningful (that is, non-admissible) applications of atomic cut by semantically redundant (admissible) applications of cut on a logical calculus. In other words, even though atomic cut definitely affect bases and the formulas they are capable of supporting, their semantic contents are made redundant at the level of logical connectives if a proof of cut admissibility is provided.

Instead of working with simulation bases, we use the same atomic mappings as before to define quasi-simulation bases $\mathcal{Q}$, which will enable us to prove a result similar to Lemma 6 without relying on applications of cut. Although replacing atoms $p^A$ with formulas $A$ in derivations from $\mathcal{Q}$ does not generally yield valid deductions in the classical sequent calculus, these derivations can be transformed into classical ones via suitable rule replacement procedures. This is possible since the new rules in $\mathcal{Q}$ implicitly incorporate the effect of cut into their structure.

$$\frac{\Gamma_{At} \Rightarrow \Delta_{At}, p^{A\wedge B}}{\Gamma_{At} \Rightarrow \Delta_{At}, p^A} \, Q\wedge_1 \quad \frac{\Gamma_{At} \Rightarrow \Delta_{At}, p^{A\wedge B}}{\Gamma_{At} \Rightarrow \Delta_{At}, p^B} \, Q\wedge_2 \quad \frac{\Gamma_{At} \Rightarrow \Delta_{At}, p^A \quad \Gamma'_{At} \Rightarrow \Delta'_{At}, p^B}{\Gamma_{At}, \Gamma'_{At} \Rightarrow \Delta_{At}, \Delta'_{At}, p^{A\wedge B}} \, R\wedge$$

$$\frac{\Gamma_{At} \Rightarrow \Delta_{At}, p^{A\vee B}}{\Gamma_{At} \Rightarrow \Delta_{At}, p^A, p^B} \, Q\vee \quad \frac{\Gamma_{At} \Rightarrow \Delta_{At}, p^A, p^B}{\Gamma_{At} \Rightarrow \Delta_{At}, p^{A\vee B}} \, R\vee$$

$$\frac{\Gamma_{At} \Rightarrow \Delta_{At}, p^{A\to B} \quad \Gamma'_{At} \Rightarrow \Delta'_{At}, p^A}{\Gamma_{At}, \Gamma'_{At} \Rightarrow \Delta_{At}, \Delta'_{At}, p^B} \, Q\to \quad \frac{p^A, \Gamma_{At} \Rightarrow \Delta_{At}, p^B}{\Gamma_{At} \Rightarrow \Delta_{At}, p^{A\to B}} \, R\to \quad \frac{\Gamma_{At} \Rightarrow \Delta_{At}, p^\bot}{\Gamma_{At} \Rightarrow \Delta_{At}} \, Q\bot$$

**Fig. 3.** Rules of the quasi-simulation base $Q$.

**Definition 10 (Quasi-simulation base).** *Let $\Sigma$ be a set of formulas, and let $\alpha$ be an atomic mapping on $\Sigma$. A quasi-simulation base $Q$ for $\Sigma$ and $\alpha$ is a base closed under $\mathcal{HS}$ that includes exactly the rules in Fig. 3, instantiated for all $A, B \in \Sigma$ and all multisets $\Gamma_{At}, \Delta_{At}, \Gamma'_{At}, \Delta'_{At}$.*

We proceed as follows, with the proof of the next result given in the technical report [3].

**Lemma 7.** *Let $\Theta_{At}$ be any (possibly empty) set of atoms, $\Sigma$ any (non-empty) set containing only subformulas of $\Gamma \cup \Delta$ and $\Sigma_{At} = \{p^B | B \in \Sigma\}$. Then, for all $\mathcal{B} \supseteq Q$, $\Vdash_\mathcal{B} \Sigma, \Theta_{At}$ if and only if $\vdash_\mathcal{B} \Rightarrow \Sigma_{At}, \Theta_{At}$.*

**Theorem 4 (Cut-free completeness).** $\Gamma \Vdash^{cf} \Delta$ *implies that there is a classical proof of the sequent $\Gamma \Rightarrow \Delta$.*

*Proof.* Fix a quasi-simulation base $Q$ with a mapping $\alpha$ for the set $\Gamma \cup \Delta$. Assume that $\Gamma \Vdash^{cf} \Delta$. Then it follows that $\Gamma \Vdash_Q \Delta$. By applying the same procedure used in Theorem 3 we obtain a deduction $\Pi$ showing $\vdash_Q \Gamma_{At} \Rightarrow \Delta_{At}$. Now let $\Pi'$ be the deduction obtained by replacing every atom $p^B$ in the deduction $\Pi$ by $B$. Denote by $Q\wedge_1^*$, $Q\wedge_2^*$, $Q\vee^*$, $Q\to^*$ and $Q\bot^*$ the rules obtained by replacing all atoms $p^B$ by formulas $B$ in the rules $Q\wedge_1$, $Q\wedge_2$, $Q\vee$, $Q\to$ and $Q\bot$, respectively. Now define the following transformation procedures:

$$\frac{\begin{array}{c}\vdots\\ \Theta \Rightarrow A \wedge B, \Sigma\end{array}}{\Theta \Rightarrow A, \Sigma} \, Q\wedge_1^* \quad \mapsto \quad \frac{\begin{array}{c}\vdots\\ \Theta \Rightarrow A \wedge B, \Sigma\end{array} \quad \dfrac{\overline{A, B \Rightarrow A}\,\text{init}}{A \wedge B \Rightarrow A}\,\wedge L}{\Theta \Rightarrow A, \Sigma} \, Cut$$

$$\frac{\begin{array}{c}\vdots\\ \Theta \Rightarrow A \wedge B, \Sigma\end{array}}{\Theta \Rightarrow B, \Sigma} \, Q\wedge_2^* \quad \mapsto \quad \frac{\begin{array}{c}\vdots\\ \Theta \Rightarrow A \wedge B, \Sigma\end{array} \quad \dfrac{\overline{A, B \Rightarrow B}\,\text{init}}{A \wedge B \Rightarrow B}\,\wedge L}{\Theta \Rightarrow B, \Sigma} \, Cut$$

$$
\begin{array}{c}
\vdots \\
\Theta \Rightarrow A \vee B, \Sigma \\
\hline
\Theta \Rightarrow A, B, \Sigma
\end{array} Q\vee^*
\quad \mapsto \quad
\begin{array}{c}
\vdots \\
\Theta \Rightarrow A \vee B, \Sigma \quad
\dfrac{\overline{A \Rightarrow A, \Sigma}\ init \quad \overline{B \Rightarrow B, \Sigma}\ init}{A \vee B \Rightarrow A, B, \Sigma}\vee L \\
\hline
\Theta \Rightarrow A, B, \Sigma
\end{array} Cut
$$

$$
\begin{array}{c}
\vdots \\
\Theta \Rightarrow \bot, \Sigma \\
\hline
\Theta \Rightarrow \Sigma
\end{array} Q\bot^*
\quad \mapsto \quad
\begin{array}{c}
\vdots \\
\Theta \Rightarrow \bot, \Sigma \quad \dfrac{}{\bot \Rightarrow \varnothing}\bot L \\
\hline
\Theta \Rightarrow \Sigma
\end{array} Cut
$$

$$
\begin{array}{c}
\vdots \\
\Theta \Rightarrow A \to B, \Sigma \quad \Theta' \Rightarrow A, \Sigma' \\
\hline
\Theta, \Theta' \Rightarrow B, \Sigma, \Sigma'
\end{array} Q\to^*
$$

$$
\mapsto \quad
\begin{array}{c}
\vdots \\
\Theta \Rightarrow A \to B, \Sigma \quad
\dfrac{\Theta' \Rightarrow A, \Sigma' \quad \dfrac{\overline{A \Rightarrow A}\ init \quad \overline{B \Rightarrow B}\ init}{A \to B, A \Rightarrow B}\to L}{\Theta', A \to B \Rightarrow B, \Sigma'} Cut \\
\hline
\Theta, \Theta' \Rightarrow B, \Sigma, \Sigma'
\end{array} Cut
$$

Let $\Pi''$ be the deduction obtained by applying the procedures depicted above to all instances of $Q\wedge_1^*$, $Q\wedge_2^*$, $Q\vee^*$, $Q\to^*$ and $Q\bot^*$ in $\Pi'$. It is straightforward to check that $\Pi''$ is a deduction with conclusion $\Gamma \Rightarrow \Delta$ in the system obtained by adding the cut rule to our classical sequent calculus, hence since cut is admissible in that system we conclude that there is a deduction of $\Gamma \Rightarrow A$ in the classical sequent calculus. □

## 6 Conclusion

We have presented a novel formulation of base-extension semantics grounded in sequent calculus rather than natural deduction. This shift in perspective brings several benefits. In fact, the use of multiple-conclusion sequents enables a direct and elegant alignment with classical logic, overcoming traditional associations of proof-theoretic semantics with intuitionistic reasoning.

Our approach contrasts sharply with the works in [14,22], not only due to this shift in perspective, but also in how it defines the semantic clauses. In particular, we return to the original inferentialist standpoint, where each connective is assigned meaning in its own right—without relying heavily on De Morgan dualities. Moreover, by exploiting the invertibility and harmony of sequent rules, we obtain semantic clauses that faithfully reflect classical inference patterns without appealing to external reasoning principles.

Also, our new perspective on BeS accommodates both cut-free and cut-inclusive systems, shedding light on the semantic role of the atomic cut rule. We demonstrated that atomic cuts significantly influence the behaviour of specific bases, even though they are not required for completeness at the level of logical connectives. This insight not only refines our understanding of the interplay between structural rules and semantics, but also reveals how semantically meaningful cuts can be modularly absorbed into logical reasoning.

Finally, our sequent-based BeS opens the door to broader applications. The modularity of the framework suggests clear pathways for extending the semantics to substructural and modal logics, as well as to other non-classical systems. For instance, even though the harmony of classical rules allows us to consider only the right side of the sequent when defining atomic support, a stronger clause with added structure could be defined as follows:

$$\Vdash^{\Gamma_{At}}_{\mathcal{B}} \Delta_{At} \text{ iff } \Gamma_{At} \Rightarrow \Delta_{At} \text{ is provable in } \mathcal{B}$$

This use of contexts is somewhat similar to the one observed in [4, 12], but now the contexts $\Gamma_{At}$ are bound by the rules of the base instead of being arbitrary sets of hypotheses. It is also interesting to note that, if a stricter notion of derivability is used, atomic instances of weakening and contraction seem to have a concrete semantic impact on atomic bases, just like the instances of atomic cut rules in the current approach.

By reconstructing PtS in a sequent setting, we hope to contribute to a more general, flexible, and expressive theory of logical meaning—one that is well-positioned to interact with contemporary developments in logic, computation and philosophy.

**Acknowledgments.** Piotrovskaya is supported by the Engineering and Physical Sciences Research Council grants EP/T517793/1 and EP/W524335/1. Barroso-Nascimento and Pimentel are supported by the Leverhulme grant RPG-2024-196. Pimentel has received funding from the European Union's Horizon 2020 research and innovation programme under the Marie Skłodowska-Curie grant agreement Number 101007627. We are grateful for the useful suggestions from the anonymous referees.

## References

1. Barroso-Nascimento, V., Pereira, L.C., Pimentel, E.: An ecumenical view of proof-theoretic semantics. CoRR abs/2306.03656 (2025). https://doi.org/10.48550/arXiv.2306.03656, accepted to Synthese
2. Barroso-Nascimento, V., Piotrovskaya, E., Pimentel, E.: A proof-theoretic approach to the semantics of classical linear logic (2025). https://arxiv.org/abs/2504.08349, to appear in the proceedings of MFPS 2025
3. Barroso-Nascimento, V., Piotrovskaya, E., Pimentel, E.: A sequent calculus perspective on base-extension semantics (technical report) (2025). https://arxiv.org/abs/2505.18589
4. Buzoku, Y.: A proof-theoretic semantics for intuitionistic linear logic. CoRR abs/2402.01982 (2024). https://doi.org/10.48550/arXiv.2402.01982, accepted to Studia Logica
5. de Campos Sanz, W., Oliveira, H.: On dummett's verificationist justification procedure. Synthese **193**(8), 2539–2559 (2015). https://doi.org/10.1007/s11229-015-0865-3
6. Cook, R.: Intuitionism reconsidered. In: The Oxford Handbook of Philosophy of Mathematics and Logic. Oxford University Press (2007). https://doi.org/10.1093/oxfordhb/9780195325928.003.0011
7. Dummett, M.: Frege: Philosophy of Language. Duckworth, London (1973)
8. Dummett, M.: The Logical Basis of Metaphysics. Harvard University Press (1991)
9. Ferreira, F., Ferreira, G.: Atomic polymorphism. J. Symb. Log. **78**(1), 260–274 (2013). https://doi.org/10.2178/jsl.7801180
10. Gentzen, G.: Investigations into logical deduction. In: Szabo, M.E. (ed.) The Collected Papers of Gerhard Gentzen. North-Holland Publishing Company (1969)

11. Gheorghiu, A.V., Buzoku, Y.: Proof-theoretic semantics for classical propositional logic with assertion and denial. CoRR abs/2503.05364 (2025). https://doi.org/10.48550/arXiv.2503.05364
12. Gheorghiu, A.V., Gu, T., Pym, D.J.: Proof-theoretic semantics for intuitionistic multiplicative linear logic. In: Ramanayake, R., Urban, J. (eds.) Automated Reasoning with Analytic Tableaux and Related Methods - 32nd International Conference, TABLEAUX 2023, Prague, Czech Republic, 18–21 September 2023, Proceedings. Lecture Notes in Computer Science, vol. 14278, pp. 367–385. Springer, Cham (2023). https://doi.org/10.1007/978-3-031-43513-3_20
13. Hallnäs, L., Schroeder-Heister, P.: A proof-theoretic approach to logic programming. II. programs as definitions. J. Log. Comput. **1**(5), 635–660 (1991). https://doi.org/10.1093/logcom/1.5.635
14. Makinson, D.: On an inferential semantics for classical logic. Log. J. IGPL **22**(1), 147–154 (2014). https://doi.org/10.1093/jigpal/jzt038
15. Marin, S., Miller, D., Pimentel, E., Volpe, M.: From axioms to synthetic inference rules via focusing. Ann. Pure Appl. Log. **173**(5), 103091 (2022). https://doi.org/10.1016/J.APAL.2022.103091
16. Martins, L.R., Martins, A.T.: Natural deduction and weak normalization for full linear logic. Logic J. IGPL **12**(6), 601–625 (2004). https://doi.org/10.1093/jigpal/12.6.601
17. McDowell, R., Miller, D.: Reasoning with higher-order abstract syntax in a logical framework. ACM Trans. Comput. Log. **3**(1), 80–136 (2002). https://doi.org/10.1145/504077.504080
18. Miller, D., Tiu, A.: A proof theory for generic judgments. ACM Trans. Comput. Log. **6**(4), 749–783 (2005). https://doi.org/10.1145/1094622.1094628
19. Piecha, T., de Campos Sanz, W., Schroeder-Heister, P.: Failure of completeness in proof-theoretic semantics. J. Philos. Log. **44**(3), 321–335 (2014). https://doi.org/10.1007/s10992-014-9322-x
20. Prawitz, D.: Ideas and results in proof theory. In: Fenstad, J. (ed.) Proceedings of the Second Scandinavian Logic Symposium. Studies in Logic and the Foundations of Mathematics, vol. 63, pp. 235–307. Elsevier (1971). https://www.sciencedirect.com/science/article/pii/S0049237X08708498
21. Prawitz, D.: Meaning approached via proofs. Synthese **148**, 507–524 (2006). https://doi.org/10.1007/s11229-004-6295-2
22. Sandqvist, T.: Classical logic without bivalence. Analysis **69**(2), 211–218 (2009). https://doi.org/10.1093/analys/anp003
23. Sandqvist, T.: Base-extension semantics for intuitionistic sentential logic. Logic J. IGPL **23**(5), 719–731 (2015). https://doi.org/10.1093/jigpal/jzv021
24. Schroeder-Heister, P.: Uniform proof-theoretic semantics for logical constants (abstract). J. Symb. Log. **56**, 1142 (1991)
25. Schroeder-Heister, P.: Proof-theoretic semantics. In: Zalta, E.N., Nodelman, U. (eds.) The Stanford Encyclopedia of Philosophy. Metaphysics Research Lab, Stanford University, Winter 2022 edn. (2022). https://plato.stanford.edu/archives/win2022/entries/proof-theoretic-semantics/

**Open Access** This chapter is licensed under the terms of the Creative Commons Attribution 4.0 International License (http://creativecommons.org/licenses/by/4.0/), which permits use, sharing, adaptation, distribution and reproduction in any medium or format, as long as you give appropriate credit to the original author(s) and the source, provide a link to the Creative Commons license and indicate if changes were made.

The images or other third party material in this chapter are included in the chapter's Creative Commons license, unless indicated otherwise in a credit line to the material. If material is not included in the chapter's Creative Commons license and your intended use is not permitted by statutory regulation or exceeds the permitted use, you will need to obtain permission directly from the copyright holder.

# A Tableau System for First-Order Logic with Standard Names

Jens Claßen(✉) and Torben Braüner

Institute for People and Technology, Roskilde University, Roskilde, Denmark
{classen,torben}@ruc.dk

**Abstract.** Levesque and Lakemeyer proposed a logic called $\mathcal{L}$ as a first-order logic for knowledge representation and reasoning in knowledge-based systems. A characteristic feature of this logic is that it uses a countably infinite set of what are called standard names, which are syntactically treated like constants, but which are also isomorphic to a fixed universe of discourse. Quantifiers in $\mathcal{L}$ are then given a substitutional interpretation. This non-standard semantics not only simplifies the proofs for certain meta-theoretic properties, but is also exploited in dedicated reasoning procedures for modal extensions of $\mathcal{L}$ that include notions of belief, actions, time, and more. However, the only sound and complete proof system provided for $\mathcal{L}$ so far is a Hilbert-style axiom system, as well as an iterative reasoning mechanism based on resolution and clause subsumption. In this paper, we present a tableau system for $\mathcal{L}$, and show its soundness and completeness. Completeness is proved first by reduction to the existing axiom system, and involves the cut rule, and then via Hintikka sets, which does not require the cut rule.

**Keywords:** Tableau · First-Order Logic · Standard Names · Substitutional Quantification

## 1 Introduction

The logic $\mathcal{L}$ has been developed and studied by Levesque and Lakemeyer (LL henceforth) as a formalism for knowledge-based systems (their book [21] gives a formal introduction and an overview of recent developments). It is a non-standard first-order logic where so-called *standard names* serve a dual purpose: Syntactically they are treated as a (countable infinite) supply of constants, while semantically they also constitute the fixed universe of discourse, where every name is interpreted by itself. Thus, standard names provide a well-defined notion of the identity of an individual, similar to unique object identifiers in database management. $\mathcal{L}$ forms the basis for a range of modal logics that extend it with notions of belief [21], non-monotonic inference [18], actions [17], programs and temporal specifications [6], and combinations thereof [7], to name but a few. Typically, this involves a type of possible-world semantics where standard names can be viewed as rigid designators in the sense of Kripke [16]. LL argue that this assumption is beneficial not only in terms of simplifying the proofs of certain meta-theoretical properties, but also for defining specific reasoning procedures. For example, the logic

$\mathcal{OL}$ [21] adds modalities for knowledge and "only-knowing". The question of whether only-knowing a knowledge base (KB) $\kappa$ entails knowing a certain query $\alpha$ can then be reduced to logical entailment in the non-modal fragment $\mathcal{L}$, where quantified subformulas are handled by considering all standard names mentioned in $\kappa$ and $\alpha$, plus one extra name to represent all unmentioned names. In a similar way, $\mathcal{L}$ serves as a base logic in an ongoing line of research that is concerned with planning [5], verification [29], and synthesis [11].

Interestingly, to the best of our knowledge, so far there is no implementation of a sound and complete reasoner for $\mathcal{L}$. Moreover, the only sound and complete proof system that has been provided is a Hilbert-style axiom system, which is not suitable for actual reasoning. What comes closest is an implementation of a tractable, yet incomplete reasoner studied in [25], as well as a formal description of a sound and complete reasoning mechanism based on resolution presented in [19]. In principle, the latter could serve as the basis for an implementation, but arguably the method is not analytic. In particular, it involves guessing substitutions for free variables in query clauses, and then testing for subsumption against KB clauses, which is impractical.

In the present paper, we propose an alternative, tableau-based proof system for $\mathcal{L}$ that allows reasoning in a systematic way. To the best of our knowledge, no analytic proof system in the form of tableau-, sequent- or natural deduction systems for $\mathcal{L}$ has been published until now. We show our system to be sound, and give two different completeness results: The first one is via a reduction to LL's axiom system as presented in [21], and requires including the cut rule in the system. It is obviously desirable to avoid the cut rule since it blatantly violates analyticity, and at a more conceptual level, it violates a fundamental idea behind tableau systems, namely that tableau rules break down formulas into smaller formulas. Hence, the result is more of theoretical interest, as it explicates the relation between our new system and LL's existing proof theory. Our second completeness result goes via traditional Hintikka sets, and does not require the cut rule, so lends itself more towards an implementation.

The remainder of this paper is organized as follows. The following section introduces $\mathcal{L}$ formally and presents LL's axiom system for it. In Sect. 3, we then present our tableau system for $\mathcal{L}$ and show its soundness. Afterwards, in Sect. 4, we provide our two completeness results, one wrt. the axiom system and using cuts, and one based on Hintikka sets and not requiring cuts. The paper finishes with a discussion and concluding remarks.

## 2 The Logic $\mathcal{L}$

In this section, we give brief formal description of $\mathcal{L}$ and its proof theory, based on the presentation in [21].

### 2.1 Syntax

In terms of syntax, $\mathcal{L}$ is very similar to the standard first-order predicate calculus with equality and function symbols, but with the addition of standard names that can be used in the same way as constant symbols. Formally:

**Definition 1 (Vocabulary).** *Formulas are built from a set of symbols consisting of:*

1. *a countably infinite supply of* variables, *written as $x, y, z$;*
2. *a countably infinite supply of* standard names *#1, #2, ..., written schematically as $n, m$;*
3. *countably many* predicate symbols *$P, Q, R, \ldots$ with associated arity $k \geq 0$;*
4. *countably many* function symbols *$f, g, h, \ldots$ with associated arity $k \geq 0$;*
5. equality *$=$ and* logical connectives *$\exists, \vee, \neg$.*

**Definition 2 (Terms).** *The* terms *are the smallest set such that*

1. *every variable is a term;*
2. *every standard name is a term;*
3. *if $f$ is a $k$-ary function symbol and $t_1, \ldots, t_k$ are terms, then $f(t_1, \ldots, t_k)$ is a term.*

A *term without variables is a* ground term, *and a ground term with exactly one function symbol is a* primitive term.

**Definition 3 (Formulas).** *The* formulas *are the smallest set such that*

1. *if $P$ is a $k$-ary predicate symbol and $t_1, \ldots, t_k$ are terms, then $P(t_1, \ldots, t_k)$ is an (atomic) formula;*
2. *if $t_1, t_2$ are terms, then $(t_1 = t_2)$ is a formula;*
3. *if $\phi, \psi$ are formulas, then so are $\neg \phi$ and $\phi \vee \psi$;*
4. *if $x$ is a variable and $\phi$ a formula, then $\exists x \phi$ is a formula.*

We treat $\phi \wedge \psi$, $\phi \supset \psi$, $\phi \equiv \psi$, *and* $\forall x \phi$ *as the usual abbreviations. The notions of bound and free variables as well as their scope are defined as usual. By $\phi_t^x$ we denote the result of simultaneously replacing all free occurrences of variable $x$ by term $t$. A* sentence *is a formula without free variables. A* ground atom *is an atomic formula with no variables. A* primitive atom *is ground atom where every $t_i$ is a standard name.*

## 2.2 Semantics

The only non-standard concepts introduced above are those of primitive terms and primitive atoms. They are used in the definition of a model-theoretic semantics as given below. Intuitively, an interpretation (called a *world*) is uniquely defined by means of which primitive atoms $P(n_1, \ldots, n_k)$ are true in it, and to which standard names it maps each primitive term $f(n_1, \ldots, n_k)$. Standard names $n_i$ are always interpreted by themselves, and complex terms and formulas are then evaluated recursively:

**Definition 4 (Semantics).** *A* world *$w$ is a mapping from primitive terms to standard names, and from primitive atoms to truth values $\{0, 1\}$. Let $\mathcal{W}$ be the set of all worlds. The* value *of a ground term $t$ at a world $w$, written as $w(t)$, is defined by*

1. *$w(n) = n$ for every standard name $n$;*
2. *$w(f(t_1, \ldots, t_k)) = w[f(n_1, \ldots, n_k)]$, where $n_i = w(t_i)$.*

The truth *of a sentence $\phi$ in a world $w$, written $w \models \phi$, is then given by*

1. $w \models P(t_1, \ldots, t_k)$ iff $w[P(n_1, \ldots, n_k)] = 1$, where $n_i = w(t_i)$;
2. $w \models (t_1 = t_2)$ iff $w(t_1)$ is the same name as $w(t_2)$;
3. $w \models \neg \phi$ iff it is not the case that $w \models \phi$;
4. $w \models \phi \vee \psi$ iff $w \models \phi$ or $w \models \psi$;
5. $w \models \exists x \phi$ iff for some name $n$, $w \models \phi_n^x$.

*The notions of validity, satisfiability, and logical entailment are defined as usual.*

As mentioned previously, epistemic extensions of $\mathcal{L}$ such as $\mathcal{OL}$ employ possible-world semantics, where an epistemic state is defined as a set of worlds, and a formula is known/believed if it holds in all accessible worlds. While the interpretation of $\mathcal{L}$ formulas does not require such epistemic states, but only single interpretations, we use the term "world" for an interpretation here to keep our terminology consistent with the existing literature.

At least two things here are noteworthy. First, from the second clause for sentences above it can be seen that equality is a built-in predicate of $\mathcal{L}$ with a fixed meaning, namely identity over co-referring standard names. Furthermore, the fifth clause defines quantification to be interpreted substitutionally: A quantified formula such as $\forall x P(x)$ is true in $w$ just in case all of $P(\#1), P(\#2),\ldots$ are true in it. As a consequence, there is no need for valuations or variable maps, but, as we will see, properties about sentences can often be proved by a simple induction over their structure. In such a proof, the case for a quantified sentence $\exists x \phi$ can be reduced to that of its instances $\phi_n^x$, i.e., sentences of smaller size.

## 2.3 Axiom System for $\mathcal{L}$

The Hilbert-style axiom system for $\mathcal{L}$ presented by LL is shown in Fig. 1. Again, the two most unusual aspects relate to standard names: Axiom 6 formalizes equality as identity over standard names. Moreover, the rule for Universal Generalization only requires finitely many instances. Here the intuition is that if we can prove $\alpha_n^x$ for *every* standard name $n$, it is obviously sound to infer $\forall x \alpha$. However, $\alpha$ can only mention finitely many standard names $n_1, \ldots, n_{k-1}$. If we have a proof for every such name, together with one more proof for a single name $n_k$ that is *not* mentioned in $\alpha$, that is enough because the proof for any other unmentioned name $n'$ can be the same as the one for $n_k$, just with all occurrences of $n_k$ replaced by $n'$. The latter works because standard names have no internal structure, except of being distinct from one another. To illustrate these principles, Fig. 2 shows an example axiomatic proof for the substitutivity property for functions. We note:

**Theorem 1** [21]. *The axiom system for $\mathcal{L}$ is sound and complete*

# 3 Sentence Tableaux for $\mathcal{L}$

Drawing inspiration from the axiom system for $\mathcal{L}$, we devised a tableau proof system as depicted in Fig. 3. The first row are standard rules for the Boolean connectives. The second row contains rules for quantification, where the one for existential quantification

---

**Axioms:**

1. $\alpha \supset (\beta \supset \alpha)$
2. $(\alpha \supset (\beta \supset \gamma)) \supset ((\alpha \supset \beta) \supset (\alpha \supset \gamma))$
3. $(\neg\beta \supset \neg\alpha) \supset ((\neg\beta \supset \alpha) \supset \beta)$
4. $\forall x(\alpha \supset \beta) \supset (\alpha \supset \forall x \beta)$, provided that $x$ does not occur freely in $\alpha$
5. $\forall x \alpha \supset \alpha_t^x$
6. $(n = n) \wedge (n \neq m)$ for any distinct $n, m$

**Rules:**

1. From $\alpha$ and $\alpha \supset \beta$, infer $\beta$ (MP).
2. From $\alpha_{n_1}^x, \ldots, \alpha_{n_k}^x$, infer $\forall x \alpha$, provided the $n_i$ range over all names in $\alpha$ and at least one not in $\alpha$ (UG).

---

**Fig. 1.** The axiom system for $\mathcal{L}$ [21].

| | |
|---|---|
| 1. $\#1 = \#1$ | Ax |
| 2. $\forall x(x = x)$ | UG |
| 3. $f(\#1) = f(\#1)$ | MP |
| 4. $\#1 = \#1 \supset f(\#1) = f(\#1)$ | MP |
| 5. $\#1 \neq \#2$ | Ax |
| 6. $\#1 = \#2 \supset f(\#1) = f(\#2)$ | MP |
| 7. $\forall y(\#1 = y \supset f(\#1) = f(y))$ | UG |
| 8. $\forall x \forall y(x = y \supset f(x) = f(y))$ | UG |

**Fig. 2.** Axiomatic proof of the substitutivity property for functions [21].

is non-standard and incorporates the same idea underlying the Universal Generalization inference rule: In addition to considering all standard names that are mentioned on a branch, it suffices to include one additional unmentioned name as representative for all other unmentioned names. The third row lists rules for handling terms that include functions, one for making a case distinction over their possible values (again with the "trick" of using an extra name), and one for substituting a term for its value. The fourth row contains the standard rule for closing a branch with two complementary formulas, the standard rule for closing a branch using inequality, and a non-standard rule for closing a branch based on equality over standard names.

Figure 4 shows an example proof for the substitutivity property for functions to illustrate how existential quantifiers and equality are handled. As for dealing with terms using the (TCut) and (TSub) rules, Fig. 5 depicts a tableau for the set $\{(a = b), P(a, a), \neg P(b, b)\}$, also used in [2] to demonstrate how equality and terms are dealt with in Jeffrey's [12] and Reeves' [23] systems. Intuitively, our system avoids some of the problems that these early systems had in relation to symmetries and unrestricted substitution, as it deconstructs nested terms in a systematic fashion and only uses substitution to remove function symbols. Arguably, our approach aligns more with the ideal of a tableau proof being analytic.

## A Tableau System for First-Order Logic with Standard Names 27

$$\frac{\neg(\phi \vee \psi)}{\neg\phi, \neg\psi} \ (\neg\vee) \qquad \frac{\neg\neg\phi}{\phi} \ (\neg\neg) \qquad \frac{\phi \vee \psi}{\phi \mid \psi} \ (\vee)$$

$$\frac{\exists x \alpha}{\alpha^x_{n_1} \mid \cdots \mid \alpha^x_{n_k}} \ (\exists) \qquad \frac{\neg \exists x \alpha}{\neg \alpha^x_t} \ (\neg\exists)$$

$$\frac{}{(t=n_1) \mid \cdots \mid (t=n_k)} \ (\text{TCut}) \qquad \frac{\phi[t], (t=n)}{\phi[n]} \ (\text{TSub})$$

$$\frac{\phi, \neg\phi}{*} \ (\bot) \qquad \frac{\neg(t=t)}{*} \ (\neq) \qquad \frac{(n=m)}{*} \ (=)$$

**Fig. 3.** Tableau rules for $\mathcal{L}$. In rules ($\exists$) and (TCut), $n_1, \ldots, n_k$ range over all standard names in the branch, plus *one extra*. In rules ($\neg\exists$), (TSub), and ($\neq$), $t$ can be *any* ground term. In rule (TSub), the notation $\phi[t]$ is used to express that $\phi$ mentions ground term $t$, and $\phi[n]$ then means $\phi$ with every occurrence of $t$ simultaneously replaced by $n$. In rule (TCut), $t$ can be any ground term occurring on the branch. In rule (=), $n$ and $m$ are *distinct* names.

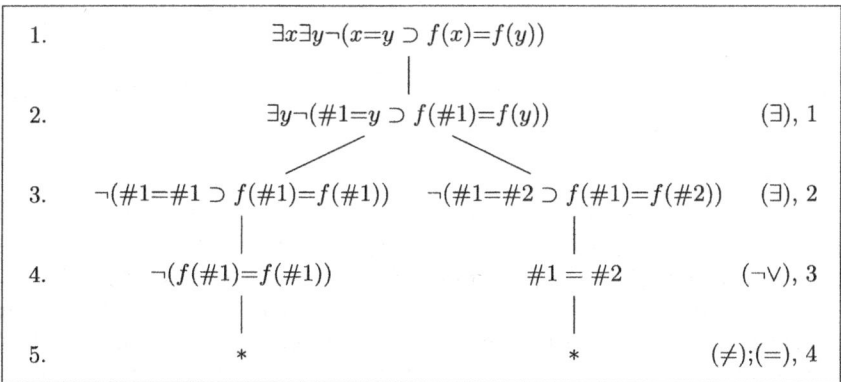

**Fig. 4.** Tableau proof of the substitutivity property for functions.

### 3.1 Soundness

**Theorem 2 (Soundness).** *The system shown in Fig. 3 is sound, i.e., if a sentence $\phi$ is satisfiable, then every tableau for $\phi$ has an open branch.*

*Proof.* As usual, we identify a branch in a tableau with the set of formulas it contains. Clearly, none of the closure rules are applicable in a satisfiable branch. We prove by induction that the expansion rules preserve the property that when being applied to a satisfiable branch, at least one of the resulting branches is satisfiable. Let $B$ be a satisfiable branch. The claim is obvious for rules ($\neg\vee$), ($\neg\neg$), and ($\vee$), and easy to show for rules ($\neg\exists$) and (TSub). The most interesting cases are rules ($\exists$) and (TCut), whose

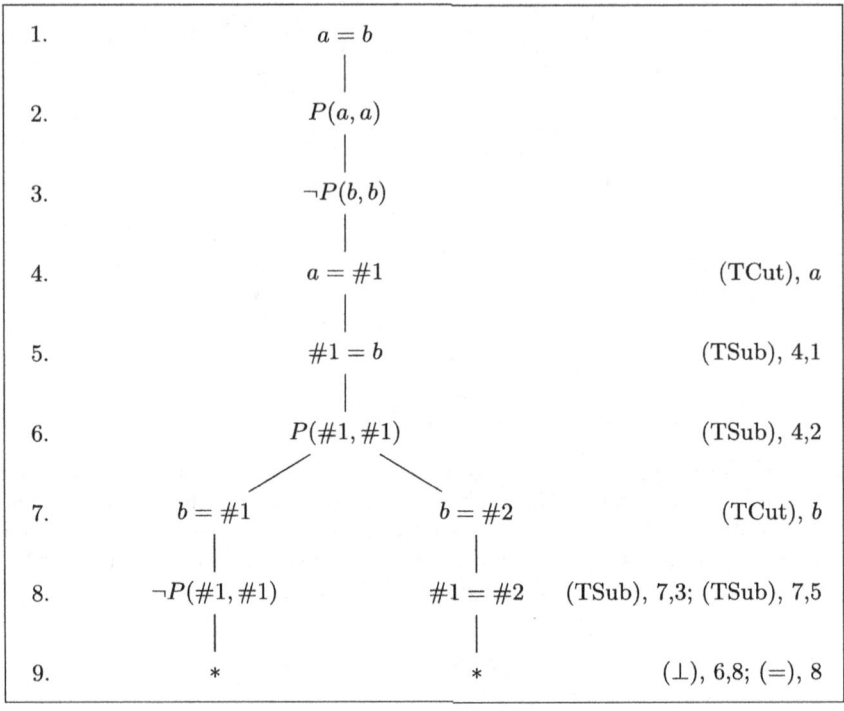

**Fig. 5.** Tableau proof for $\{(a = b), P(a,a), \neg P(b,b)\}$.

proofs work similarly, so we only show the one for (∃) below. Let $w \models \exists x\alpha$. By definition, this means there is a name $n$ such that $w \models \alpha_n^x$. If $n$ is any of the names $n_1, \ldots, n_k$, then by assumption $w \models B \cup \{\alpha_n^x\}$, and we are done. In case that $n$ is a name that is *not* mentioned in $B$ and distinct from the extra name (let's call it $n'$), then let ∗ be a bijection from standard names to standard names that swaps $n$ with $n'$ and leaves all other names unchanged. Similar as in the proof for Theorem 2.8.8 in [21], let $w^*$ be the world such that $w^*[\alpha] = w[\alpha^*]$ for every primitive formula $\alpha$, and $w^*[t] = w[t^*]$ for every primitive term $t$, where $\alpha^*$ and $t^*$ denote the results of simultaneously replacing every name by its mapping under ∗ in $\alpha$ and $t$, respectively. It follows by induction that for any formula $\phi$, $w^* \models \phi$ iff $w \models \phi^*$. Since $B$ does not mention $n'$, $B^* = B$. Hence $w^* \models B \cup \{\alpha_{n'}^x\}$.

The proof above uses a bijection to formalize the following intuition: Because standard names are interchangeable in the sense that their only internal property is being distinct from one another, one "extra" name used in the (∃) and (TCut) rules is enough as it serves as a placeholder (representative) for all other unmentioned names.

## 4 Completeness

As mentioned earlier, we give two different completeness results: The first completeness result is via a reduction to LL's axiom system as presented in [21], and requires including the cut rule in the system. The second completeness result goes via traditional Hintikka sets, and does not require the cut rule. The two are independent from another in the sense that we do not need the first result in the completeness prove for the Cut-free system, but present it merely to explore the relation of our new system to LL's original axiom system.

### 4.1 Completeness via Reduction to an Axiom System (Requiring Cuts)

We take it that most readers of the present paper are familiar with the cut rule, but to make the paper self-contained, we display it anyway:

$$\frac{}{\phi \mid \neg\phi} \text{ (Cut)}$$

So at any stage in the tableau construction, a branch can be split into two branches, where an arbitrary formula $\phi$ is added to one of the branches and the negated formula $\neg\phi$ is added to the other. The cut rule is usually considered undesirable, one reason being that it blatantly violates the idea that tableau rules break down formulas into smaller formulas, but the rule also has its advocates, see for example the paper [8]. See also the discussion of cuts in tableau systems in [9], pages 107–108.

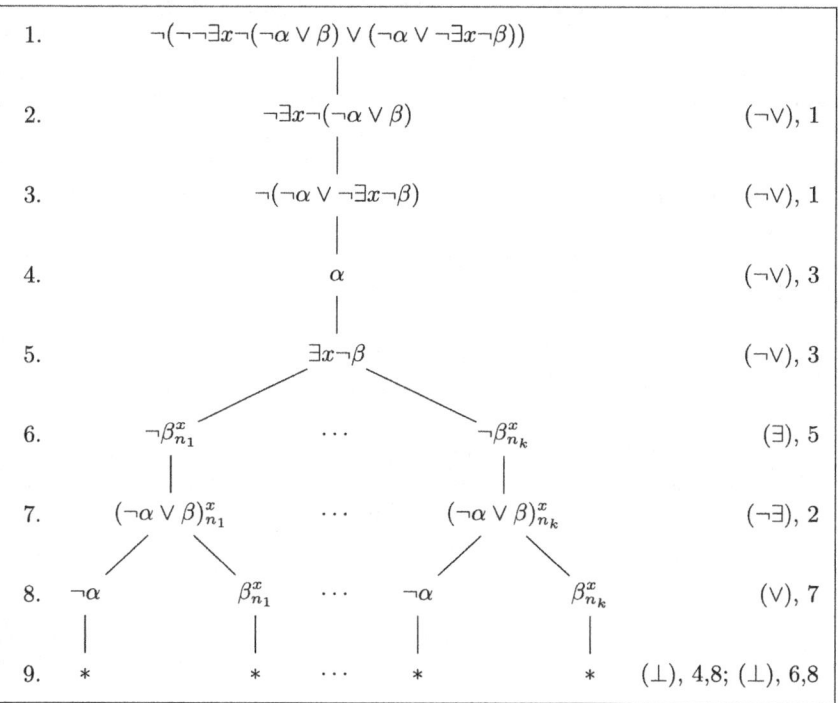

**Fig. 6.** Tableau proof for the negation of Axiom 4. Applications of the ($\neg\neg$) rule are not shown. Step 8 exploits the fact that $\alpha$ does not contain $x$, hence $(\neg\alpha)_n^x = \neg\alpha$.

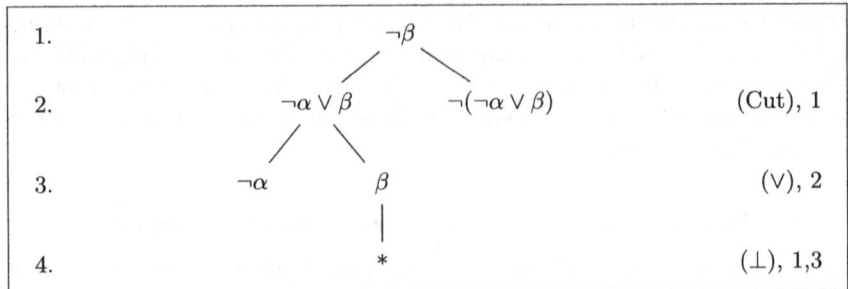

**Fig. 7.** Tableau construction corresponding to the (MP) rule.

**Theorem 3 (Completeness).** *The system comprised of the rules shown in Figs. 3 together with the rule (Cut) is complete, i.e., if a sentence $\phi$ is unsatisfiable, then there is a tableau for $\phi$ all of whose branches are closed.*

*Proof.* The proof is by means of the axiom system shown in Fig. 1. Let $\phi$ be unsatisfiable. Then $\neg\phi$ is valid, and therefore there exists a derivation of $\neg\phi$ using the axioms and rules of Fig. 1, cf. [21]. We show by induction on the structure of the derivation that for every derivable formula $\psi$, there is a corresponding tableau for $\neg\psi$, all of whose branches are closed.

For the base case, we show that this claim is true for the axioms. Axioms 1–3 represent propositional reasoning, and the corresponding tableaux are straightforward, using only the propositional rules $(\neg\vee)$, $(\neg\neg)$, $(\vee)$, and $(\bot)$. Axioms 5 and 6 are similarly easy, requiring an additional application of rules $(\neg\exists)$ as well as $(\neq)$ and $(=)$, respectively. The tableau corresponding to Axiom 4 is shown in Fig. 6.

For the inductive case, we show that the claim is preserved under the application of the (MP) and (UG) rules. In case of (MP), assume that there are closed tableaux for $\neg\alpha$ and $\neg(\neg\alpha \vee \beta)$. Then a closed tableau for $\neg\beta$ can be constructed as shown in Fig. 7, where we can "glue" the given tableaux underneath the $\neg\alpha$ and $\neg(\neg\alpha \vee \beta)$ nodes, respectively. The case of (UG) is similar, requiring only one application each of $(\neg\neg)$ and $(\exists)$.

The overall claim now follows from the observation that if there is a closed tableau for $\neg\neg\phi$, there is also one for $\phi$: Using (Cut), we generate one branch including $\neg\phi$, and one including $\neg\neg\phi$. The former can be closed immediately using $(\bot)$, the latter like in the given closed tableau for $\neg\neg\phi$.

An interesting observation is that the above proof did not make use of the (TCut) and (TSub) rules, so the system is also complete when these rules are not included, as long as the cut rule is present.

### 4.2 Completeness via Hintikka Sets (No Cuts Needed)

The overall structure of our completeness proof follows the one from [20], but we make use of a different tableau construction procedure, based on the lexicographic order given in Definition 7, and used throughout the remaining part of the completeness proof. Moreover, our proof covers a language that includes equality and function symbols.

In the following, when $t$ is a primitive term and $n$ a standard name, we call the formula $(t = n)$ a *primitive assignment*. In the semantics of $\mathcal{L}$, a world $w$ can then be identified by (with) the set of primitive atoms *and* primitive assignments it satisfies. Obviously, for two distinct names $n$ and $m$, it is impossible that both $(t = n)$ and $(t = m)$ are true simultaneously. For the proof, and also for practical reasons, it will be helpful to include the following admissible rule in our system:

$$\frac{(t = n), (t = m)}{*} \; (\stackrel{\circ}{=})$$

**Proposition 1.** *Rule* $(\stackrel{\circ}{=})$ *is admissible wrt the system given in Fig. 3, i.e., for every tableau involving the rule, there is an equivalent one not including it.*

*Proof.* If a branch contains $(t = n)$ and $(t = m)$, then we can add $(n = m)$ by the (TSub) rule, and close it using the (=) rule.

Literals and their complement are defined as usual, and include equalities and inequalities. The subcategory of *flat* literals consists of all primitive atoms, negated primitive atoms, primitive assignments, and equalities and inequalities over standard names.

**Definition 5 (Downward Saturated Set).** *A set $S$ of $\mathcal{L}$ sentences is called* downward saturated *if it satisfies the following conditions:*

1. *If $S$ contains $\neg(\phi \vee \psi)$, then it contains $\neg\phi$ and $\neg\psi$.*
2. *If $S$ contains $\neg\neg\phi$, then it contains $\phi$.*
3. *If $S$ contains $\phi \vee \psi$, then it contains $\phi$ or it contains $\psi$.*
4. *If $S$ contains $\exists x\phi$, then it contains $\phi_n^x$ for some standard name $n$.*
5. *If $S$ contains $\neg\exists x\phi$, then it contains $\neg\phi_n^x$ for all standard names $n$.*
6. *If $S$ contains a non-flat literal $\phi[t]$ in which some primitive term $t$ occurs, then for some standard name $n$, $S$ contains $(t = n)$ and $\phi[n]$.*

**Definition 6 (Hintikka Set).** *A* Hintikka set *is a downward saturated set that does not contain a primitive atom and its negation, does not contain an assignment and its negation, does not contain two assignments $(t = n)$ and $(t = m)$ for the same $t$ and distinct standard names $n, m$, does not contain $\neg(n = n)$ for any standard name, and does not contain $(n = m)$ for any two distinct standard names $n, m$.*

We remark that the definition above corresponds to what is called an *atomic* Hintikka set by Letz [20] and others, since only inconsistencies among or within literals are considered. Obviously, a set $S$ that contains both $\phi$ and $\neg\phi$ for a non-literal formula is also unsatisfiable, which is why the ($\bot$) rule allows to close corresponding branches. However, as we will see, for proving completeness, it suffices to restrict our attention to (flat) literals when closing branches in a tableau. For the sake of brevity, we will still just write "Hintikka set", "closed branch" etc. instead of "atomic Hintikka set", "atomically closed branch" etc.

The reader may have observed that there is a correspondence between most clauses listed in Definition 5 and the tableau expansion rules shown in Fig. 3, except for clause 6, which corresponds to rules (TCut) and (TSub) combined. Indeed, these two rules are often applied directly after one another, and it would be possible to merge them so that branching over standard names and substituting them for $t$ happens in a single step. However, in practice it makes sense to keep them separate since there may be branches that already contain an assignment $(t = n)$ for the primitive term $t$ in question, and there we would only want to apply substitution. In such a case, the merged rule would first branch over all relevant standard names, but then immediately close all but one branches again.

Note that the restriction to primitive terms is sufficient here, as non-primitive ground terms are handled by unnesting them in a recursive fashion. For example, if a set $S$ contains $P(f(a))$ and $f(a) = n$, then $a$ is a primitive term occurring in a non-flat literal, and by clause 6, $S$ has to include $(a = m)$, $P(f(m))$ and $f(m) = n$ for some name $m$. Then $f(m)$ is another primitive term occurring in a non-flat literal, and $S$ subsequently has to include $P(n)$.

**Lemma 1 (Hintikka's Lemma).** *Every Hintikka set is satisfiable.*

*Proof.* Let $S$ be a Hintikka set. The proof is similar to the one presented by Letz in [20], but simpler as it does not need to resort to Herbrand interpretations. In a manner of speaking, Herbrand interpretations are directly "built into" $\mathcal{L}$: A world $w$ is characterized completely by which primitive atoms $P(n_1, \ldots, n_k)$ are true in it, and what names it assigns to primitive terms $f(n_1, \ldots, n_k)$. By assumption, $S$ does not contain any complementary literals over primitive atoms, or over assignments, or two assignments $(t = n)$, $(t = m)$ for distinct names, or unsatisfiable (in-)equalities over standard names. Note that this also excludes the case where $S$ contains $(t \neq n)$ for *every* name $n$, as by clause 6 in Definition 5, $S$ then needs to contain some $(t = n)$ as well. Therefore, there is a world $w$ that satisfies all such literals in $S$.

With these literals as base cases, it then follows by induction on the structure of terms and formulas that $w$ satisfies all sentences in $S$. For example, if $\exists x \phi \in S$, then by Definition 5, $\phi_n^x \in S$ for some standard name $n$. By induction, $w \models \phi_n^x$, and hence $w \models \exists x \phi$ by the substitutional semantics of $\mathcal{L}$. Also, if $\phi[t]$ is a non-flat literal in $S$ with some primitive term $t$, then by Definition 5, $\phi[n] \in S$ for some standard name $n$. Then $w \models \phi[n]$ by induction, and since $w \models (t = n)$, we have $w(t) = w(n)$. Hence by the semantics of $\mathcal{L}$, $w \models \phi[t]$. The other cases are similar.

In what follows, we need total orders over the set of standard names and the set of primitive terms. For standard names, we can use the one where #1 is the first name, #2 the second, and so on. For the primitive terms, we can use any term order. One difference to the standard first-order case, cf. [20], is that we do not consider infinite sets of sentences as input, but only a single sentence (see discussion in the next section).

**Definition 7 (Systematic Tableau Construction).** *We assume that every node in a tableau T is optionally equipped with a natural number label, except for flat literals, which are never assigned a number label. Any such node is assigned a pair $(d, m)$ where $m$ is the number labeling the node in question and $d$ is the depth of this node in the* *tableau tree. We order such pairs with the lexicographic order, that is, $(d,m) < (d',m')$ iff (1) $d < d'$ or (2) $d = d'$ and $m < m'$. Note that the reflexive closure of this order is a total order.*

*Given a tableau $T$ with at least one labeled node, let $(d,m)$ be the lexicographically smallest pair assigned to a labeled node in the tableau tree (such a pair exists because the reflexive closure of the order is total). The leftmost node assigned the pair $(d,m)$ will be called the* usable node *of $T$ (this is well-defined since all nodes assigned $(d,m)$ have the same depth). The systematic tableau sequence $T_0, T_1, \ldots$ for a sentence $\phi$ is then given by:*

- *The tableau $T_0$ is a one-node tableau with root formula $\phi$. If it is not a flat literal, it is assigned number label 1.*
- *Given tableau $T_k$ containing usable node $N$ with number label $m$, $T_{k+1}$ is obtained by expanding each open branch $B$ passing through $N$ in $T_k$ to:*
  1. *$B \oplus \neg \phi \oplus \neg \psi$, if the formula at $N$ is $\neg(\phi \vee \psi)$;*
  2. *$B \oplus \phi$, if the formula at $N$ is $\neg \neg \phi$;*
  3. *$B \oplus \phi \mid \psi$, if the formula at $N$ is $\phi \vee \psi$;*
  4. *$B \oplus \phi_{n_1}^x \mid \cdots \mid \phi_{n_l}^x \mid \phi_{n'}^x$, if the formula at $N$ is $\exists x \phi$, $n_1, \ldots, n_l$ is the ordered sequence of all standard names occurring in $B$, and $n'$ is the least standard name not occurring in $B$;*
  5. *$B \oplus \neg \phi_n^x \oplus \neg \exists x \phi$, if the formula at $N$ is $\neg \exists x \phi$ and $n$ is the $m$-th standard name;*
  6. *If the formula at $N$ is a non-flat literal $\phi$, where $t$ is the least primitive term occurring in $\phi$, we proceed in two steps:*
     
     *(a) First, every open branch $B$ through $N$ that does not contain an assignment for $t$ is expanded to $B \oplus (t = n_1) \mid \cdots \mid (t = n_l) \mid (t = n')$, where $n_1, \ldots, n_l$ is the ordered sequence of all standard names occurring in $B$, and $n'$ is the least standard name not occurring in $B$;*
     
     *(b) Afterwards, every open branch $B$ through $N$ containing an assignment $(t = n)$ is expanded to $B \oplus \phi[n]$.*

  *The number label of the formula at $N$ is removed. If the formula at $N$ is of the form $\neg \exists x \phi$, every new node of the form $\neg \phi_n^x$ is assigned the label 1, if it is not a flat literal, and every new node of the form $\neg \exists x \phi$ is assigned the label $m + 1$. If the formula at $N$ is not of the form $\neg \exists x \phi$, every new node is assigned the number label 1, if it is not a flat literal. Finally, number labels of all nodes at all branches that have become closed (including equalities) by means of the latest expansion are removed.*
- *If $T_k$ has no usable node, it is the last tableau in the sequence.*

The notation $\oplus$ is taken from [20]: Expanding a branch $B$ to $B \oplus \phi$ means extending $B$ and adding the formula $\phi$, and expanding $B$ to $B \oplus \phi \mid \psi$ means splitting $B$ into two branches, where $\phi$ is added to one of the obtained branches and $\psi$ is added to the other.

In clause 5 of the definition above, we add a new copy of a formula $\neg \exists x \phi$ whenever we expand by one of its instances. While this technique may not be standard, it will be helpful in the following proofs, and is also used by Smullyan [26, pp. 58–59] in the classical first-order case. Moreover, some tableaux provers such as leanTAP [3] process universally quantified formulas in a similar fashion.

**Definition 8 (Saturated Systematic Tableau).** *Given a systematic tableau sequence $T_0, T_1, \ldots$ for formula $\phi$, the saturated systematic tableau of $\phi$, denoted $T^*$, is the smallest tree containing all $T_i$ as initial segments. Note that $T^*$ is guaranteed to exist because our tableau system is non-destructive, i.e., if we obtain $T'$ by applying a rule to $T$, $T$ is an initial segment of $T'$. Furthermore, $T^*$ is infinite just in case the sequence is.*

**Lemma 2.** *Consider the saturated systematic tableau $T^*$ for a systematic tableau sequence $T_0, T_1, \ldots$. Let $N$ be a node on an open branch $B$ in $T^*$ containing a formula $\varphi$, which is not a flat literal, and let $T_i$ be the first tableau in the sequence in which $N$ occurs. Then $N$ is the usable node of some tableau $T_j$, where $j \geq i$.*

*Proof.* The proof is based on the following four observations:

- A pair $(d, m)$ is lexicographically smaller than any pair $(d + 1, n)$.
- For any $d$, there are at most finitely many nodes in the tableau $T^*$ with depth less than or equal to $d$.
- The label assigned to a node in a tableau $T_k$ is either unchanged or removed in the embedding of $T_k$ in $T_{k+1}$. Moreover, if the node in question is not selected as usable node in $T_k$, and furthermore the node is on an open branch in $T^*$, then its label will not be removed in the embedding of $T_k$ in $T_{k+1}$.
- If $N$ is not selected as usable node in a tableau $T_k$, then the usable node of $T_k$ is assigned a pair smaller than or equal to the pair assigned to $N$ in $T_k$. Moreover, the usable node of $T_k$ has its number label removed in the embedding of $T_k$ in $T_{k+1}$.

Since $\varphi$ is not a flat literal, it is assigned a number label $m$, and hence some pair $(d, m)$ in the lexicographic order. From the four observations above it follows that for every step succeeding $T_i$, if there is a strictly positive number of nodes assigned the pair $(d, m)$ or a smaller pair, then a smaller number of nodes are assigned the pair $(d, m)$ after the step. Therefore $N$ is selected as the usable node of some tableau $T_j$ with $j \geq i$.

**Proposition 2.** *If $B$ is an open branch of a saturated systematic tableau $T^*$, then the set of formulas it contains is a Hintikka set.*

*Proof.* We first prove that the set of formulas at $B$ is downwards saturated. In the proof we shall frequently make use of the assumption that $B$ is open.

Assume that $\varphi$ is a formula that is not a flat literal on the branch $B$ and let $T_k$ be the first tableau in the tableau sequence where $\varphi$ occurs at the branch. By Lemma 2, the occurrence of $\varphi$ is the usable node of some tableau $T_j$, where $j \geq k$.

If one of the first four clauses in Definition 5 apply, the appropriate nodes are added to the branch.

If the fifth clause in Definition 5 applies, then $\varphi$ is of the form $\neg \exists x \phi$. It follows by inspection of the systematic tableau construction that the occurrence of $\varphi$ in $T_k$, and hence in $T_j$, is labeled with the number 1, and hence in $T_{j+1}$ the formula $\neg \phi^x_{\#1}$ is added to the branch, as well as a new instance of $\neg \exists x \phi$ with label 2. Now, by Lemma 2, the new occurrence of $\neg \exists x \phi$ is in turn the usable node of some tableau $T_i$, where $i \geq j+1$, implying that $\neg \phi^x_{\#2}$ and $\neg \exists x \phi$ (now with label 3) are added to $B$, etc. By induction, it follows that $B$ contains $\neg \phi^x_n$ for every name $n$.

If the sixth clause in Definition 5 applies, we observe that an open branch will never contain more than one assignment for any $t$, and that the number of function symbols occurring in the formula $\phi[n]$ added to the branch is reduced by at least one compared to $\phi$, since $\phi[n]$ is obtained by replacing a primitive term $t$ occurring in $\phi$ by $n$. This concludes the proof that $B$ is downwards saturated.

Finally, note that since $B$ is open, the set of formulas on $B$ cannot contain both a primitive atom and its complement, or both a primitive assignment and its complement, or two different assignments for the same term, or $\neg(n = n)$ for any name $n$, or $(n = m)$ for any distinct names $n, m$. Hence the set of formulas at $B$ is a Hintikka set.

**Theorem 4 (Completeness).** *The system shown in Fig. 3 is complete, i.e., if a sentence $\phi$ is unsatisfiable, then there is a finite tableau for $\phi$ all of whose branches are closed.*

*Proof.* Let $T$ be a saturated systematic tableau for $\phi$. Then $T$ must be closed: Suppose it is not, then there is an open branch $B$, whose formulas by Proposition 2 form a Hintikka set. By Lemma 1, this set would be satisfiable. Since the set includes $\phi$, this would mean that $\phi$ is satisfiable, contradicting the assumption that this formula is unsatisfiable. Furthermore, $T$ being closed implies it being finite: When closing a branch, it will not be extended anymore, so its length remains finite. Because every node has only finitely many successors, the tree $T$ is also finite by König's Lemma.

## 5 Discussion and Concluding Remarks

### 5.1 Compactness

While tableau systems for classical first-order logic can work on infinite sets [20], our system only considers a single sentence as input. In case of the former, compactness of the logic is a corollary of the system's soundness and completeness: It is guaranteed that there exists a finite, closed tableau for any infinite unsatisfiable set. Since that tableau only involves a finite subset of formulas from the input, this subset is also unsatisfiable. So any infinite set is unsatisfiable just in case it has a finite unsatisfiable subset.

The restriction to a finite input is necessary in our case due to the fact that $\mathcal{L}$ is not compact, as observed by LL [21]. To see why, consider the infinite set of sentences $\{\exists x P(x), \neg P(\#1), \neg P(\#2), \neg P(\#3), \ldots\}$. It is clearly unsatisfiable, yet every finite subset is satisfiable, as we can then set $P$ to true for some name that is not mentioned. Intuitively, in order for our system to work on this set, the ($\exists$) rule would need to branch over *all* standard names, since the initial branch enumerates all standard names. That is to say, extending our tableau system to handle infinite sets would require non-finite branching.

In a sense, $\mathcal{L}$ can be viewed as an *infinitary logic* [4] if we interpret $\exists x \alpha$ as the infinite disjunction $\bigvee_n \alpha_n^x$ and $\forall x \alpha$ as the infinite conjunction $\bigwedge_n \alpha_n^x$. Specifically, it bears close resemblance to $\omega$-logic [13], which is defined over a countable sets of constants $n \in \omega$, and admits deriving $\forall x \varphi(x)$ from $\{\varphi(n) \mid n \in \omega\}$. Compactness in the classical sense obviously fails for infinitary logics, but there are adapted notions that involve changing the notion of "finite", including *Barwise Compactness* [1], *Kreisel Compactness* [14], and *Kreisel-Barwise Compactness* [13]. A deeper discussion of how these notions might be applicable to $\mathcal{L}$ is beyond the scope of this paper, and hence left for future work, but in simple terms we conjecture that it would involve identifying the infinite set $\{\neg P(\#1), \neg P(\#2), \ldots\}$ with the equivalent, finite formula $\forall x \neg P(x)$. The set $\{\exists x P(x), \neg P(\#1), \neg P(\#2), \ldots\}$ then coincides with $\{\exists x P(x), \forall x \neg P(x)\}$, and the latter can be proven unsatisfiable using a finite tableau.

### 5.2 Standard Names and Substitutional Quantification

LL [21] say that the original inspiration for standard names stems from "parameters" as described by Smullyan [26]. However, there are significant differences. Smullyan uses standard Tarskian semantics, where the universe can vary between interpretations, and in particular parameters are not identified with the domain of discourse, and are not necessarily distinct from one another. In more modern terminology, parameters are hence merely a countable infinite supply of *constant symbols*. Since Smullyan does not consider function symbols of higher arity, Herbrand bases are then constructed solely from predicates with parameters as arguments.

There has also been a philosophical discussion around substitutional quantification. Kripke [15] rejects earlier criticisms due to Wallace [28] and Tharp [27], among other things the application of criteria of ontological commitment resulting in "an ever-present fear that it will be shown, using substitutional quantification, that nothing exists." Formally, he sees little difference between a substitutional and a referential quantifier in the case that (a) the denotation function for terms is total and (b) all formulae are *transparent*, i.e., their truth value does not change due to substitution by equals. (Both conditions obviously hold for $\mathcal{L}$.) He concludes that there "never was any problem with substitutional quantification".

### 5.3 Implementation

We believe that the presented system lends itself well to an implementation, but clearly, the next step will be to validate this hypothesis through experimentation. Currently, we are working on developing a prototype in Prolog, taking inspiration from similar systems for standard first-order logic [3,10,22]. An interesting observation is that our ($\exists$) rule is very reminiscent of corresponding rules that are used for description logic tableaux [24], where they play a vital role in termination and loop detection, and it will be interesting to study whether similar results can be obtained for decidable fragments of $\mathcal{L}$.

**Acknowledgements.** We thank the anonymous reviewers for their helpful comments, in particular for pointing out an issue in an earlier version of the paper that has now been fixed.

# References

1. Barwise, J.: Infinitary logic and admissible sets. J. Symb. Logic **34**(2), 226–252 (1969). https://doi.org/10.2307/2271099

2. Beckert, B.: Equality and other theories. In: D'Agostino, M., Gabbay, D.M., Hähnle, R., Posegga, J. (eds.) Handbook of Tableau Methods, pp. 197–254. Springer, Dordrecht (1999). https://doi.org/10.1007/978-94-017-1754-0_4
3. Beckert, B., Posegga, J.: LeanTAP: lean tableau-based deduction. J. Autom. Reason. **15**(3), 339–358 (1995)
4. Bell, J.L.: Infinitary Logic. In: Zalta, E.N., Nodelman, U. (eds.) The Stanford Encyclopedia of Philosophy. Metaphysics Research Lab, Stanford University, Fall 2023 edn. (2023)
5. Claßen, J., Eyerich, P., Lakemeyer, G., Nebel, B.: Towards an integration of Golog and planning. In: Veloso, M.M. (ed.) Proceedings of the Twentieth International Joint Conference on Artificial Intelligence (IJCAI 2007), pp. 1846–1851. AAAI Press (2007)
6. Claßen, J., Lakemeyer, G.: A logic for non-terminating Golog programs. In: Brewka, G., Lang, J. (eds.) Proceedings of the Eleventh International Conference on the Principles of Knowledge Representation and Reasoning (KR 2008), pp. 589–599. AAAI Press (2008)
7. Claßen, J., Neuss, M.: Knowledge-based programs with defaults in a modal situation calculus. In: Kaminka, G.A., et al. (eds.) Proceedings of the Twenty-Second European Conference on Artificial Intelligence (ECAI 2016), pp. 1309–1317. IOS Press (2016). https://doi.org/10.3233/978-1-61499-672-9-1309
8. D'Agostino, M., Mondadori, M.: The taming of the cut. Classical refutations with analytical cut. J. Logic Comput. **4**, 285–319 (1994)
9. Fitting, M.: Modal proof theory. In: Blackburn, P., van Benthem, J., Wolter, F. (eds.) Handbook of Modal Logic, pp. 85–138. Elsevier (2007)
10. Fitting, M.: First-Order Logic and Automated Theorem Proving, 2nd edn. Springer, Cham (1996)
11. Hofmann, T., Claßen, J.: LTLf synthesis on first-order agent programs in nondeterministic environments. In: Walsh, T., Shah, J., Kolter, Z. (eds.) Proceedings of the Thirty-Ninth AAAI Conference on Artificial Intelligence (AAAI 2025), pp. 14976–14986. AAAI Press (2025). https://doi.org/10.1609/aaai.v39i14.33642
12. Jeffrey, R.: Formal Logic: Its Scope and Limits. McGraw Hill (1967)
13. Keisler, H.J., Knight, J.F.: Barwise: infinitary logic and admissible sets. Bull. Symb. Logic **10**(1), 4–36 (2004). https://doi.org/10.2178/bsl/1080330272
14. Kreisel, G.: Set theoretic problems suggested by the notion of potential totality. In: Infinitistic Methods (Proc. Sympos. Foundations of Math., Warsaw, 1959), pp. 103–140 (1961)
15. Kripke, S.A.: Is there a problem about substitutional quantification? In: Evans, G., McDowell, J. (eds.) Truth and Meaning: Essays in Semantics, pp. 324–419. Clarendon Press (1976)
16. Kripke, S.A.: Naming and Necessity: Lectures Given to the Princeton University Philosophy Colloquium. Harvard University Press, Cambridge (1980)
17. Lakemeyer, G.: The situation calculus: a case for modal logic. J. Logic Lang. Inform. **19**(4), 431–450 (2010). https://doi.org/10.1007/s10849-009-9117-6
18. Lakemeyer, G., Levesque, H.J.: Only-knowing meets nonmonotonic modal logic. In: Brewka, G., Eiter, T., McIlraith, S.A. (eds.) Proceedings of the Thirteenth International Conference on the Principles of Knowledge Representation and Reasoning (KR 2012). AAAI Press (2012)
19. Lakemeyer, G., Levesque, H.J.: A tractable, expressive, and eventually complete first-order logic of limited belief. In: Kraus, S. (ed.) Proceedings of the Twenty-Eighth International Joint Conference on Artificial Intelligence (IJCAI 2019), pp. 1764–1771. ijcai.org (2019). https://doi.org/10.24963/ijcai.2019/244
20. Letz, R.: First-order tableau methods. In: D'Agostino, M., Gabbay, D.M., Hähnle, R., Posegga, J. (eds.) Handbook of Tableau Methods, pp. 125–196. Springer, Dordrecht (1999). https://doi.org/10.1007/978-94-017-1754-0_3
21. Levesque, H.J., Lakemeyer, G.: The Logic of Knowledge Bases, 2nd edn. College Publications (2022)

22. Posegga, J., Schmitt, P.H.: Implementing semantic tableaux. In: D'Agostino, M., Gabbay, D.M., Hähnle, R., Posegga, J. (eds.) Handbook of Tableau Methods, pp. 581–629. Springer, Dordrecht (1999). https://doi.org/10.1007/978-94-017-1754-0_10
23. Reeves, S.V.: Adding equality to semantic tableaux. J. Autom. Reason. 3(3), 225–246 (1987). https://doi.org/10.1007/BF00243790
24. Schmidt, R.A., Tishkovsky, D.: Using tableau to decide description logics with full role negation and identity. ACM Trans. Comput. Logic 15(1), 7:1–7:31 (2014). https://doi.org/10.1145/2559947
25. Schwering, C.: A reasoning system for a first-order logic of limited belief. In: Bacchus, F., Sierra, C. (eds.) Proceedings of the Twenty-Sixth International Joint Conference on Artificial Intelligence (IJCAI 2017), pp. 5246–5248. AAAI Press (2017)
26. Smullyan, R.M.: First-Order Logic. Springer, New York (1968)
27. Tharp, L.H.: Truth, quantification, and abstract objects. Noûs 5(4), 363–372 (1971)
28. Wallace, J.: Convention T and substitutional quantification. Noûs 5(2), 199–211 (1971)
29. Zarrieß, B., Claßen, J.: Decidable verification of Golog programs over non-local effect actions. In: Schuurmans, D., Wellman, M. (eds.) Proceedings of the Thirtieth AAAI Conference on Artificial Intelligence (AAAI 2016), pp. 1109–1115. AAAI Press (2016)

**Open Access** This chapter is licensed under the terms of the Creative Commons Attribution 4.0 International License (http://creativecommons.org/licenses/by/4.0/), which permits use, sharing, adaptation, distribution and reproduction in any medium or format, as long as you give appropriate credit to the original author(s) and the source, provide a link to the Creative Commons license and indicate if changes were made.

The images or other third party material in this chapter are included in the chapter's Creative Commons license, unless indicated otherwise in a credit line to the material. If material is not included in the chapter's Creative Commons license and your intended use is not permitted by statutory regulation or exceeds the permitted use, you will need to obtain permission directly from the copyright holder.

# Bounded Inquisitive Logics: Sequent Calculi and Schematic Validity

Tadeusz Litak[1](✉) and Katsuhiko Sano[2]

[1] University of Naples Federico II, Naples, Italy
tadeusz.litak@gmail.com
[2] Faculty of Humanities and Human Sciences, Hokkaido University, Sapporo, Japan
v-sano@let.hokudai.ac.jp

**Abstract.** Propositional inquisitive logic is the limit of its $n$-bounded approximations. In the predicate setting, however, this does not hold anymore, as discovered by Ciardelli and Grilletti [11], who also found complete axiomatizations of $n$-bounded inquisitive logics $\mathsf{InqBQ}_n$, for every fixed $n$. We introduce cut-free labelled sequent calculi for these logics. We illustrate the intricacies of *schematic validity* in such systems by showing that the well-known Casari formula is *atomically* valid in (a weak sublogic of) predicate inquisitive logic $\mathsf{InqBQ}$, fails to be schematically valid in it, and yet is schematically valid under the finite boundedness assumption. The derivations in our calculi, however, are guaranteed to be schematically valid whenever a single specific rule is not used.

**Keywords:** inquisitive logic · superintuitionistic predicate logics · labelled sequent calculi · cut elimination · schematic validity · Finite boundedness · constant domains

## 1 Introduction

Inquisitive logic [8,9,12] provides a framework for studying both declarative and interrogative sentences in one setting. On the propositional level, it enriches classical logic with *inquisitive disjunction* $\vee\!\!\vee$, and on the predicate level, it also adds the *inquisitive existential quantifier* $\exists\!\!\exists$. Assuming $S(x,y)$ is the predicate "$x$ sings for $y$", $e$ is the constant denoting Eric Clapton and $g$ denotes Gottlob Frege, we write "Does Eric Clapton sing for Gottlob Frege?" as $?S(e,g) := S(e,g) \vee\!\!\vee \neg S(e,g)$. The question "Who is some person that Eric Clapton sings for?" translates to $\exists\!\!\exists\, x.S(e,x)$, whereas "Which are the people Eric Clapton sings for?" is rendered as $\forall x.?S(e,x)$, and "Is Eric Clapton singing for everybody?" gets expressed as $?\forall x.S(e,x)$.

Semantically, *relational information models* reflect different (combinations of) potential answers to questions as *states*, which are just collections of FO models (structures) over some fixed domain of individuals. A singleton state is maximal under $\supseteq$, settling one way or another all questions. The interpretation of an atomic predicate at a state $s$ is obtained as the intersection of its denotations in members of $s$. Thus, inquisitive logic can be seen not only as an expansion of classical logic with additional operators, but also as a formalism extending (as a set of theorems) the intuitionistic logic of constant domains CD [22]. In other words, $\mathbb{W}$ and $\mathbb{E}$ are just standard intuitionistic connectives, whereas $\vee$ and $\exists$ are simply de Morgan duals of $\wedge$ and $\forall$, respectively. Atomic formulas, however, are evaluated as *regular* upsets satisfying the double negation law. Anyone familiar with, e.g., the Gödel-Gentzen translation [36, Ch. 2.3], [34, Ch. 6–7], [3, Ch. 2] [19,25] can see that formulas involving $\mathbb{W}$ and $\mathbb{E}$ are the only ones that can behave in a non-classical way under this restriction.

The failure of some non-atomic instances of Boolean laws implies that unlike standard superintuitionistic logics, inquisitive logic is not closed under schematic substitutions (see Sect. 3). This naturally leads to the question of *schematic validity* in inquisitive logic: what is its *schematic core/fragment*, i.e., the largest standard superintuitionistic logic contained in it? For the propositional inquisitive logic InqL, Ciardelli [7] established that its schematic fragment is exactly Medvedev's logic ML of finite problems or finite (topless) boolean cubes. Conversely, InqL can be obtained as the negative counterpart of ML, i.e., the collection of formulas whose negatively substituted variants (replacing each atom with its negation) belong to ML. To the best of our knowledge, the corresponding first-order question has not been addressed.

Another set of questions is brought by the idea of restricting the size of the models. Of course, by Trakhtenbrot's theorem, the restriction to (unbounded) finite domains of individuals would block recursive axiomatizability in the presence of at least one binary relation symbol. Moreover, as noted by Ono [30], there are axiom *schemes* in the sense of Sect. 3 that can sense finiteness of the domain of individuals. However, in the inquisitive setting, we can also restrict the cardinality of the *collection of structures*, and consequently of *available states*; note that finite boundedness defined this way is a generalization of the finite model property defined in terms of individuals. In the propositional case, this issue also has been investigated by Ciardelli [7]: not only can all inquisitive non-theorems be refuted with a countable collection of possible worlds/structures, but InqL is in fact the limit of its $n$-bounded approximations. Furthermore, *op.cit.* proves that each such $n$-bounded approximation is obtained as the negative counterpart of ML extended with the axiom limiting the depth of frames to $n$.

The second named author [32] asked whether analogues of boundedness results discussed in the preceding paragraph hold in the predicate case, and provided two complete calculi (Hilbert-style and tree-sequent) for the two-bounded system $\mathsf{InqBQ}_2$. Recently, Ciardelli and Grilletti [11] have provided complete axiomatizations of $\mathsf{InqBQ}_n$ for each $n \in \omega$, and proved that $\mathsf{InqBQ} \subsetneq \bigcap \mathsf{InqBQ}_n$. Disregarding their specific counterexample, one can see this strict inclusion as follows. In the propositional case, *there are no intuitionistic analogues of the Grzegorczyk and Löb formulas, which expresses the presence of infinite ascending chains* [3, p. 175]. On the other hand, there are numerous such formulas are known in the predicate case, both for ascending and descending chains [2,18,26], with the Casari formula [2] being one of the most salient examples (cf. Theorem 2 for its semantic characterization). Such formulas must be schematically valid in $\mathsf{InqBQ}_n$, for any $n \in \omega$. But it does not immediately follow that they fail in InqBQ: the restriction of atoms to regular upsets makes finding relational information countermodels challenging. The negative substitution of the Casari axiom is in fact an intuitionistic theorem (Theorem 1). In the unbounded case there exists a refuting instance of the Casari scheme and a suitable relational information model, but the proof is far from trivial (Theorem 3).

Given the difficulty of providing such semantic proofs, one can wonder if there are convenient proof calculi to work with. Several proof systems have been proposed for propositional inquisitive logic[1]. In the predicate setting, proof calculi have been developed for certain syntactic fragments or for logics tailored to specific classes of models. Grilletti [23] presents a sound and complete natural deduction system for the classical antecedent fragment of first-order inquisitive logic. For $\mathsf{InqBQ}_n$, Ciardelli and Grilletti [11] provide a sound and strongly complete natural deduction calulus, which however does not appear promising in the context of investigating schematic validity in bounded systems, and in several other typical proof-theoretic applications such as proof search (cf. Remark 4 below). We instead leverage the labelled sequent system for $\mathsf{InqBQ}_2$ provided by Sano [32], generalizing it to a semantically complete, cut-free G3-style calculus for $\mathsf{InqBQ}_n$ for any $n \in \omega$. As far as we are aware, this is the first G3-style calculus for such systems. In our sequent calculus, all inference rules are height-preserving invertible, weakening and contraction are height-preserving admissible, and the cut rule is admissible via a syntactic argument (Sano [32] only shows semantic cut elimination for the calculus for $\mathsf{InqBQ}_2$ considered therein). Furthermore, the derivations in our calculi are guaranteed to be schematically valid whenever a single specific rule is not used (Theorem 4).

We proceed as follows: Sect. 2 sets up the syntax of first-order inquisitive logic and its Kripke semantics. Section 3 discusses the issue of validity of the Casari scheme. After introducing our labelled sequent calculus for the finitely bounded first-order inquisitive logics in Sect. 4, Sect. 5 proves the semantic completeness of the calculi, and Sect. 6 establishes the admissibility of cut using a syntactic argument. Tying together the two main threads of the paper, Proposition 6 illustrates how the Casari scheme is derived using structural rules when a specific finite bound is fixed; more such derivations are provided in the accompanying material. Section 7 concludes the paper with further directions of research.

## 2 Preliminaries

Our language L assumes a countably infinite set Var of variables and Pred of predicate symbols (with fixed arities), respectively, and logical connectives $\bot, \wedge, \rightarrow, \forall$ as well as *inquisitive disjunction* $\vee\!\!\!\vee$ and the *inquisitive existential quantifier* $\exists\!\!\!\exists$:

$$\varphi ::= P(x_1,\ldots,x_m) \mid \bot \mid \varphi \rightarrow \varphi \mid \varphi \wedge \varphi \mid \varphi \vee\!\!\!\vee \varphi \mid \forall x.\varphi \mid \exists\!\!\!\exists x.\varphi,$$

where the arity of $P$ is $m$ (when the arity of $P$ is 0, $P$ is regarded as a *propositional variable*). Throughout the paper, $P(\overline{x})$ denotes $P(x_1,\ldots,x_m)$, where $m$ is the arity of $P$. We define $\neg\varphi := \varphi \rightarrow \bot$ and $?\varphi := \varphi \vee\!\!\!\vee \neg\varphi$. By $\varphi[z/x]$, we mean the result of capture-avoiding substitution of free occurrences of $x$ by $z$ in $\varphi$. Note that in order

---

[1] A Hilbert system and a natural deduction system for the propositional inquisitive logic InqB are presented in [13] and [10], respectively. A display calculus for InqB is also provided in [20]. Labelled G3-style sequent calculi for InqB were proposed in [5,27]; see Footnote 2.

to simplify presentation, we assume that our L contains neither identity nor function symbols. An interested reader might compare it with a Rocq formalization by Max Ole Elliger [16, 17], which allows rigid terms.

A *relational information model* is a structure $\mathfrak{M} = (W, D, \mathfrak{I})$ where $W$ is a non-empty set of possible worlds, $D$ is a non-empty set of individuals and $\mathfrak{I} : \mathsf{Pred} \times W \to D^{<\omega}$ is a function sending each $n$-arity predicate symbol $P$ to an element $\mathfrak{I}(P, w)$ of $\mathcal{P}(D^n)$. For a relational information model $\mathfrak{M} = (W, D, \mathfrak{I})$, we say that $s \subseteq W$ is a *state*. Let $\mathfrak{M} = (W, D, \mathfrak{I})$ be a relational information model, $g : \mathsf{Var} \to D$ an assignment and $s \subseteq W$ a state. We define the notion of support $M, s \Vdash_g A$ as follows:

$\mathfrak{M}, s \Vdash_g P(x_1, \ldots, x_m)$ iff $(g(x_1), \ldots, g(x_m)) \in \mathfrak{I}(P, w)$ for all $w \in s$;
$\quad \mathfrak{M}, s \Vdash_g \bot$ iff $s = \emptyset$;
$\quad \mathfrak{M}, s \Vdash_g \varphi \wedge \psi$ iff $\mathfrak{M}, s \Vdash_g \varphi$ and $\mathfrak{M}, s \Vdash_g \psi$;
$\quad \mathfrak{M}, s \Vdash_g \varphi \to \psi$ iff for all $t \subseteq s$: $\mathfrak{M}, t \Vdash_g \varphi$ implies $\mathfrak{M}, t \Vdash_g \psi$;
$\quad \mathfrak{M}, s \Vdash_g \varphi \vee\!\!\!\vee \psi$ iff $\mathfrak{M}, s \Vdash_g \varphi$ or $\mathfrak{M}, s \Vdash_g \psi$;
$\quad \mathfrak{M}, s \Vdash_g \forall x. \varphi$ iff $\mathfrak{M}, s \Vdash_{g[x \mapsto d]} \varphi$ for all $d \in D$;
$\quad \mathfrak{M}, s \Vdash_g \exists x. \varphi$ iff $\mathfrak{M}, s \Vdash_{g[x \mapsto d]} \varphi$ for some $d \in D$.

where $g[x \mapsto d]$ is the same mapping as $g$ except that it sends $x$ to $d$. We say that $\varphi$ is *valid* in a relational information model $\mathfrak{M} = (W, D, \mathfrak{I})$ if $\mathfrak{M}, s \Vdash_g \varphi$ for every assignment $g : \mathsf{Var} \to D$ and every state $s \subseteq W$.

**Proposition 1 (Persistency).** *If $\mathfrak{M}, s \Vdash_g \varphi$ and $s \supseteq t$ then $\mathfrak{M}, t \Vdash_g \varphi$.*

**Definition 1.** *Define $\mathsf{InqBQ}$ to be the set of all the valid formulas in any relational information model M. We also write $\mathsf{InqBQ}_n$ for the collection of formulas forced when cardinality of W is restricted to at most $n$, and $\mathsf{InqBQ}_{<\omega} = \bigcap_{n \in \omega} \mathsf{InqBQ}_n$.*

We note that $\neg\neg P(\overline{x}) \to P(\overline{x}) \in \mathsf{InqBQ}$ for every $P \in \mathsf{Pred}$. Clearly, $\mathsf{InqBQ}_1$ is just the classical logic and for all $n \in \omega$, we have $\mathsf{InqBQ} \subseteq \mathsf{InqBQ}_{<\omega} \subseteq \mathsf{InqBQ}_n$.

## 3 Schematic Validity and The Casari Axiom

The clause for implication and for $\vee\!\!\!\vee$ given above are those of Kripke models for intuitionistic predicate logic, with the accessibility ordering being the reverse inclusion on states. Obviously, neither $\mathsf{InqBQ}$, nor $\mathsf{InqBQ}_{<\omega}$, nor $\mathsf{InqBQ}_n$ for any fixed $n$ is a superintuitionistic predicate logic in the sense of being closed under substitutions of formulas for predicate symbols. In order to formalize such substitutions, Ono [30] employs conventions of Church [6, Ch. III], whereas Gabbay, Shehtman and Skvortsov [21, § 2.2–2.5] follow Bourbaki in using the notion of a *scheme* (which appears to resemble *locally nameless* representation in mechanical reasoning, cf. [4]). The treatment given by Kleene [24, § VII.34, pp. 155–162] appears compact and accessible.

**Definition 2.** *Assume $\overline{a}_1, \ldots, \overline{a}_k$ are $n$-ary lists of variables, $P \in \mathsf{Pred}$ is $n$-ary and $P(\overline{a}_1), \ldots, P(\overline{a}_k)$ are all occurrences of $P$ in $\varphi$. Assume furthermore that $\psi$ is a formula with exactly $n$ free variables. Moreover, for each $i \leq k$, create an $i$-clean instance of $\psi$ by renaming bound variables to ensure no variable in $\overline{a}_i$ becomes captured in $\psi$ after substitution. Then $(\varphi)_P^\psi$ denotes the outcome of syntactic replacement of each $P(\overline{a}_i)$ with the corresponding $i$-clean instance of $\psi(\overline{a}_i)$.*

*Remark 1.* A variant of this definition more faithful to that of Kleene would allow for *at least n* free variables in the formula being substituted instead of *exactly n*. In such a situation, we would need to insist on additional clean-up to ensure that these additional variables do not get captured in $\varphi$ after substituting corresponding occurrences of $P$. The definition would also get require a minor reformulation if our syntax allowed other individual terms than variables.

*Remark 2.* Any intuitionistic Kripke structure forcing some given $\varphi$ also has to force $(\varphi)_P^\psi$ for every suitable choice of $P$ and $\psi$, as one can freely change the interpretation of atomic relations at any node, as long as persistence is respected. However, in a relational information model, the interpretation of atoms at non-singleton states is induced by their singleton substates. Thus, e.g., the atomic validity of double negation elimination does not extend to all its non-atomic instances.

Table 1 present some important examples of schemes to be investigated.

**Table 1.** Formula Schemes

| Name | Scheme |
|---|---|
| Kuroda | $\forall x.\neg\neg\varphi \to \neg\neg\forall x.\varphi$ |
| CD | $\forall x.(\varphi(x) \lor \psi) \to (\forall x.\varphi(x)) \lor \psi$ where $x$ does not appear in $\psi$ |
| CasariAtomic | $(\forall x.((P(x) \to \forall x.P(x)) \to \forall x.P(x))) \to \forall x.P(x)$ |
| CasariDNAtomic | $(\forall x.((\neg\neg P(x) \to \forall x.\neg\neg P(x)) \to \forall x.\neg\neg P(x))) \to \forall x.\neg\neg P(x)$ |
| CasariScheme | $(\forall x.((\varphi(x) \to \forall x.\varphi(x)) \to \forall x.\varphi(x))) \to \forall x.\varphi(x)$ |

**Lemma 1 (Ciardelli & Grilletti).** *Both* Kuroda *and* CD *are in* InqBQ.

In this section, we focus on CasariAtomic and its schematic version CasariScheme from Table 1. The following is not hard to establish, using either a chosen Gentzen-style or Hilbert-style system for intuitionistic predicate logic, or one's preferred proof assistant, or favourite semantics such as Kripke frames.

**Theorem 1.** *Casari scheme instantiated with (doubly) negated atoms is a theorem of intuitionistic logic:* CasariDNAtomic $\in$ IQC. *Consequently,* CasariAtomic $\in$ InqBQ.

**Theorem 2 (Casari [2], Th. 10(2), p. 294).** *A Kripke structure for intuitionistic predicate logic forces* CasariAtomic *(and, consequently,* CasariScheme*) whenever it does not contain infinitely ascending chains.*

As mentioned in the introduction, one is reminded of modal propositional schemes sensitive to the presence of infinite chains. Esakia [18] highlights more such analogies: e.g., between the Kuroda scheme above and the propositional McKinsey scheme.

**Corollary 1.** *All instances of* CasariScheme *are in* InqBQ$_{<\omega}$.

*Proof.* For each $n$, the underlying intuitionistic frames of $\mathsf{InqBQ}_n$ models (with reverse inclusion on states being the partial ordering) do not contain infinitely ascending $\supseteq$-chains, as relational information models induced by finitely many possible worlds contain only finitely many states. □

By contrast, in the light of Remark 2, inquisitively atomic validity and schematic validity may come apart:

**Theorem 3.** CasariScheme *with* $\varphi(x) \equiv \exists\, y.R(x,y)$ *fails in* $\mathsf{InqBQ}$.

*Proof.* Set $W$ and $D$ to be equal to $\omega$. For a fixed $i \in \omega$, we define $\Im(R,i)$ as follows:

$$\forall m \in \omega.\quad ((2m+1),(2m+1)) \in \Im(R,i)$$
$$\forall m, j \in \omega.\quad j \neq i\ \&\ ((j\text{ odd}) \text{ or } (j > 2m)) \implies (2m, j) \in \Im(R, i)$$

As $D = \omega$, for any $n \in \omega$ and any formula $\psi(x)$ whose sole free variable is $x$ we can write "$\mathfrak{M}, s \Vdash \psi(n)$" to denote $\mathfrak{M}, s \Vdash_g \varphi(x)$ for some/any valuation s.t. $g(x) = n$.

*Claim.* $\forall s \subseteq \omega, m \in \omega.\quad \mathfrak{M}, s \Vdash \exists\, y.R(2m+1, y)$.

This is shown by noting that at every possible state, $y = 2m + 1$ does the job.

*Claim.* $\forall s \subseteq \omega, m \in \omega.\quad \mathfrak{M}, s \not\Vdash \exists\, y.R(2m, y)$ iff $s \supseteq \omega - \{0, 2, \ldots, 2m\}$.

(Proof of *Claim.*) To prove the left-to-right implication of this claim, assume that $s \not\supseteq \omega - \{0, 2, \ldots, 2m\}$. This means that there exists $n \notin s$ which is

(∗) either an odd number or an even number strictly greater than $2m$.

This however means that every $i \in s$ is distinct from $n$ and hence $(2m, n) \in \Im(R, i)$ by definition, thus $\mathfrak{M}, s \Vdash \exists\, y.R(2m, y)$. Conversely, assume $s \supseteq \omega - \{0, 2, \ldots, 2m\}$. This means that every $n$ of the form (∗) is a member of $s$. Regardless of $i \in \omega$, every $j \in \omega$ such that $(2m, j) \in \Im(R, i)$ must belong to $s$. But whichever $j$ we would pick to witness $\exists\, y.R(2m, y)$ at $s$, we would get $(2m, j) \notin \Im(R, j)$. (QED of *Claim.*)

These two claims imply that we constructed an ascending-chain-based refutation of the corresponding instance of Casari as needed in Theorem 2. In more detail, setting $\varphi(x)$ to be $\exists\, y.R(x, y)$, by our Claims, entails that the denotation of $\forall\, x.\varphi(x)$ is the collection $E := \{s \subseteq \omega \mid (\exists n \in \omega.(2n+1) \notin s) \vee (\forall m \exists n.2(m+n) \notin s)\}$, i.e., the collection of states that either fail to contain at least one odd number, or whose complement contains infinitely many even numbers. Clearly, $E$ is downward closed, i.e., closed under inclusion. Consequently, we get the following:

- For an odd $m$, the denotation of $\varphi(m) \to \forall\, x.\varphi(x)$ is $E$ and thus the denotation of $(\varphi(m) \to \forall\, x.\varphi(x)) \to \forall\, x.\varphi(x)$ is the whole space of subsets of $\omega$.
- For an even $m$, the denotation of $\varphi(m)$ is the downset of sets not containing at least one element of the form (∗), thus evidence for failure of $\varphi(m) \to \forall\, x.\varphi(x)$ is provided by the set

$$\{s \subseteq \omega \mid (\forall n \in \omega.(2n+1) \in s) \wedge (\exists m' \forall n.2(m'+n) \in s) \wedge (\exists n.2n \notin s \wedge 2n > m)\},$$

i.e., the set of those states that contain all the odd numbers and cofinitely many even ones (thus refuting $\forall x.\varphi(x)$), but fail to contain at least one even number greater than $2m$ (thus satisfying $\varphi(m)$). One easily notes that the superset-closure of this set of states is exactly the complement of $E$, thus the denotation of $\varphi(m) \to \forall x.\varphi(x)$ is exactly $E$, and we finish just like in the odd case.

This shows that the denotation of the antecedent of our instance of CasariScheme is the whole state space. It is not the case for the consequent though (which is $E$), from which the theorem follows. □

*Remark 3.* A reviewer noted that whenever $\varphi(x)$ is *n-coherent* [11] for some finite $n$, the corresponding Casari instance does not fail and asked if this is in fact a necessary and sufficient condition. The same reviewer also suggested a simplified construction proving Theorem 3 with $\Im(R, i)$ defined as $\{(n, k) \mid i < k \text{ or } (k = n \text{ and } n \neq i)\}$. Such questions seem promising experiments for a Rocq mechanization developed by Max Ole Elliger [16, 17]. As in its present form it contains a detailed formalization of our proof of Theorem 3, we leave experiments with the statement and the proof of the theorem to subsequent versions of the paper or follow-up work. Note that the conjecture regarding $n$-coherence being a *necessary* condition for $\varphi(x)$ to yield a non-failing instance appears false, at least without some minimal additional conditions. For example, $\exists x.P(x)$ fails to be coherent even in a transfinite sense [11, Prop 3.3]; merely insisting on $x$ being free does not seem a sufficient refinement. It is generally not obvious whether a refuting instance can be monadic, i.e., involve solely unary predicates, either for the Casari scheme or for other ones that are atomically but not generally valid (we do not have sufficiently many such examples now). It might nevertheless be possible; Rybakov and Shkatov [31] amply illustrate that unary predicates in modal or superintuitionistic predicate logics can often simulate binary ones using the so-called Kripke Trick.

## 4 Labelled Sequent Calculus for The Finite-Bounded Case

From now on we focus on providing the proof calculus promised in the introduction. Its schematic aspects are clarified by Theorem 4 below. We begin by "translating" the satisfaction relation in terms of a labelled formalism, as is common in the literature [15, 28]. Since our target is *finite*-bounded inquisitive logic $\mathsf{InqBQ}_n$ for fixed but arbitrary $n$, we use a non-empty *finite* set $X$ of natural numbers as a label, similar to the labelled tableau calculus for propositional dependence logic [33]. We exclude ∅ from our labels for simplicity. If we impose a constraint $\#X \leq n$, our results in the remainder of the paper instantiate to soundness, completeness and syntactic cut-elimination for $\mathsf{InqBQ}_n$.

**Definition 3.** *A label $X$ is a non-empty finite subset of $\omega$, i.e., $\emptyset \neq X \subseteq_{\text{fin}} \omega$. A labelled formula is an expression of the form $X : \varphi$ where $X$ is a label and $\varphi$ is a formula. The length $|X : \varphi|$ of a labelled formula $X : \varphi$ is the number of all logical connectives in $\varphi$ (including quantifiers), where it is noted that we do not need to count the cardinality $\#X$ of elements in $X$. A sequent, denoted by $\Gamma \Rightarrow \Delta$, is a pair $(\Gamma, \Delta)$ of finite multisets of labelled formulas, where $\Gamma$ is the* antecedent *and $\Delta$ is the* consequent *of the sequent.*

By translating "$\mathfrak{M}, s \Vdash_g \varphi$" to "$X : \varphi$", the satisfaction relation on a relational information model in Sect. 2 naturally provides the axioms and rules in Table 2. Note that the rules ($\Rightarrow$ at) and ($\Rightarrow\rightarrow$) have finitely many premises depending on #$X$ and the number of all non-empty finite subsets of $X$, respectively. Since our labels are finite sets of natural numbers, the propositional fragment of our calculus is simpler than the existing labelled G3-style sequent calculi for inquitive propositional logic **InqB** [5,27] in terms of the number of axioms and rules (see Remark 4). This simplicity also enables us to expand the calculus naturally to the first-order level. If we drop the rule ($\Rightarrow$ at), disregard the labels and remove the repetition of the implication formula from the rule ($\rightarrow\Rightarrow$), the resulting system coincides with **G3c** [35, Definition 3.5.1] [29, p.67], i.e., G3-style sequent calculus for the first-order classical logic.

**Remark 4.** When the syntax is restricted to the propositional fragment, with the standard assumption that the set of propositional variables (predicate symbols of arity 0) is countably infinite, we denote by **G(InqB)** the propositional fragment of **G(FBInqBQ)** where ($\Rightarrow$ at) and (id) are of the following form:

$$\frac{\{\Gamma \Rightarrow \Delta, \{k\} : P \mid k \in X\}}{\Gamma \Rightarrow \Delta, X : P} \ (\Rightarrow \text{at}) \qquad \frac{}{X : P, \Gamma \Rightarrow \Delta, Y : P} \ (\text{id}) \text{ where } X \supseteq Y$$

Since we dispense with atoms such as "$s \subseteq t$" in our calculus, we only have 2 initial sequents and 7 logical rules for the propositional fragment[2]. Note that we have rules with possibly more than or equal to two premises, e.g. ($\Rightarrow$ at), whose number of branches depends on the cardinality of #$X$ of the label $X$ of the formula $X : P(\overline{x})$ in the conclusion of the rule ($\Rightarrow$ at). While this aspect might seem a drawback of the absence of relational atoms, we can conduct the root-first proof search yielding decidability results of our **G(InqB)**. Note that all of our inference rules are height-preserving invertible and the number of possible applications of ($\rightarrow\Rightarrow$) is bounded by $2^{\#X} - 1$ where $X : \varphi \rightarrow \psi$ is the principal formula of ($\rightarrow\Rightarrow$). By contrast, Müller [27, pp.65-6] admits that the algorithm provided in *op.cit.* may generate infinitely many new variables in the course of the proof-search process. We come back to **G(InqB)** also in Remark 7.

**Definition 4.** *We say that a labelled formula not in the context $\Gamma, \Delta$ of the conclusion of a rule is called* principal. *A derivation $\mathcal{D}$ in* **G(FBInqBQ)** *is a finite tree generated from initial sequents* (id) *and* ($\bot \Rightarrow$) *by inference rules of* **G(FBInqBQ)**. *The height of a derivation $\mathcal{D}$ is the length of the longest branch in $\mathcal{D}$. Given a derivation $\mathcal{D}$, $r(\mathcal{D})$ is the last applied rule (including the initial sequents) of $\mathcal{D}$. We say that a sequent $\Gamma \Rightarrow \Delta$ is derivable in* **G(FBInqBQ)** *(written:* **G(FBInqBQ)** $\vdash \Gamma \Rightarrow \Delta$*) if there is a derivation $\mathcal{D}$ whose root is $\Gamma \Rightarrow \Delta$. We write* **G(FBInqBQ)** $\vdash_h \Gamma \Rightarrow \Delta$ *to mean that there is a derivation of $\Gamma \Rightarrow \Delta$ whose height is at most $h$.*

---

[2] Chen's labelled sequent calculus [5] has 3 axioms (initial sequents), 13 logical axioms and 9 rules for relational atoms "$s \subseteq t$", whereas that of Müller [27] has 3 axioms (initial sequents), 10 logical axioms and 11 rules for relational atoms "$s \subseteq t$". The latter reference claims: "Chen and Ma [5] do not provide a modular construction [...] Our system is also much simpler and allows for a more elegant cut-admissibility proof." [27, p.40].

**Table 2.** Sequent Calculus **G(FBInqBQ)**

$$\overline{X : P(\overline{x}), \Gamma \Rightarrow \Delta, Y : P(\overline{x})} \text{ (id) where } X \supseteq Y \qquad \overline{X : \bot, \Gamma \Rightarrow \Delta} \text{ } (\bot \Rightarrow)$$

$$\frac{\{\Gamma \Rightarrow \Delta, \{k\} : P(\overline{x}) \mid k \in X\}}{\Gamma \Rightarrow \Delta, X : P(\overline{x})} \text{ } (\Rightarrow \text{at})$$

$$\frac{\Gamma \Rightarrow \Delta, X : \varphi \quad \Gamma \Rightarrow \Delta, X : \psi}{\Gamma \Rightarrow \Delta, X : \varphi \wedge \psi} \text{ } (\Rightarrow \wedge) \qquad \frac{X : \varphi, X : \psi, \Gamma \Rightarrow \Delta}{X : \varphi \wedge \psi, \Gamma \Rightarrow \Delta} \text{ } (\wedge \Rightarrow)$$

$$\frac{\Gamma \Rightarrow \Delta, X : \varphi, X : \psi}{\Gamma \Rightarrow \Delta, X : \varphi \vee \psi} \text{ } (\Rightarrow \vee) \qquad \frac{X : \varphi, \Gamma \Rightarrow \Delta \quad X : \psi, \Gamma \Rightarrow \Delta}{X : \varphi \vee \psi, \Gamma \Rightarrow \Delta} \text{ } (\vee \Rightarrow)$$

$$\frac{\{Y : \varphi, \Gamma \Rightarrow \Delta, Y : \psi \mid X \supseteq Y\}}{\Gamma \Rightarrow \Delta, X : \varphi \to \psi} \text{ } (\Rightarrow \to)$$

$$\frac{X : \varphi \to \psi, \Gamma \Rightarrow \Delta, Y : \varphi \quad Y : \psi, X : \varphi \to \psi, \Gamma \Rightarrow \Delta}{X : \varphi \to \psi, \Gamma \Rightarrow \Delta} \text{ } (\to \Rightarrow) \text{ where } X \supseteq Y$$

$$\frac{\Gamma \Rightarrow \Delta, X : \varphi[z/x]}{\Gamma \Rightarrow \Delta, X : \forall x.\varphi} \text{ } (\Rightarrow \forall)\dagger \qquad \frac{X : \varphi[y/x], X : \forall x.\varphi, \Gamma \Rightarrow \Delta}{X : \forall x.\varphi, \Gamma \Rightarrow \Delta} \text{ } (\forall \Rightarrow)$$

$$\frac{\Gamma \Rightarrow \Delta, X : \exists x.\varphi, X : \varphi[y/x]}{\Gamma \Rightarrow \Delta, X : \exists x.\varphi} \text{ } (\Rightarrow \exists) \qquad \frac{X : \varphi[z/x], \Gamma \Rightarrow \Delta}{X : \exists x.\varphi, \Gamma \Rightarrow \Delta} \text{ } (\exists \Rightarrow)\dagger$$

where † is the eigenvariable condition: $z$ does not occur in the conclusion.

We define the set of subformulas of $\varphi$ as in Troelstra and Schwichtenberg [35, Definition 1.1.3] by requiring $\mathsf{Sub}(\forall x.\psi) = \{\forall x.\psi\} \cup \{\psi[z/x] \mid z \in \mathsf{Var}\}$ and similarly for $\mathsf{Sub}(\exists x.\psi)$. Given labelled formulas $X : \varphi$ and $Y : \psi$, we say that $Y : \psi$ *is a subexpression of* $X : \varphi$ *if* $\psi$ is a subformula of $\varphi$ and $Y \subseteq X$. Our calculus is trivially proved to be *analytic* in the following sense.

**Proposition 2.** *If $\Gamma \Rightarrow \Delta$ is derivable in* **G(FBInqBQ)** *then $\Gamma \Rightarrow \Delta$ has a derivation in* **G(FBInqBQ)** *such that every labelled subformula in the derivation is a subexpression of a labelled formula in $\Gamma, \Delta$.*

*Example 1.* Let $X \subseteq \omega$ be finite. To derive $\Rightarrow X : \neg\neg P(\overline{x}) \to P(\overline{x})$ by the rule $(\Rightarrow \to)$, it suffices to derive a sequent $Y : \neg\neg P(\overline{x}) \Rightarrow Y : P(\overline{x})$ for all $Y$ such that $X \supseteq Y$. By the rule $(\Rightarrow \text{at})$, it suffices to show the derivability of $Y : \neg\neg P(\overline{x}) \Rightarrow \{k\} : P(\overline{x})$ for each $k \in Y$. Fix any $k \in Y$. Then we proceed as follows:

$$\frac{\dfrac{\overline{\{k\} : P(x), Y : \neg\neg P(x) \Rightarrow \{k\} : P(x), \{k\} : \bot} \text{ (id)}}{Y : \neg\neg P(\overline{x}) \Rightarrow \{k\} : P(\overline{x}), \{k\} : \neg P(\overline{x})} (\Rightarrow \to) \quad \dfrac{\{k\} : \bot, Y : \neg\neg P(\overline{x}) \Rightarrow \{k\} : P(\overline{x})}{} (\bot \Rightarrow)}{Y : \neg\neg P(\overline{x}) \Rightarrow \{k\} : P(\overline{x})} (\to \Rightarrow)$$

where the number of premises of $(\Rightarrow \to)$ above is one. This means that $(\Rightarrow \text{at})$ captures the semantic clause for the atomic formula.

Recall that the persistency in the semantics on a relational information model is formulated as follows: if $s \supseteq t$ and $\mathfrak{M}, s \Vdash_g \varphi$ then $\mathfrak{M}, t \Vdash_g \varphi$ by Proposition 1. This can be expressed in terms of our sequent calculus:

**Proposition 3.** *If $X \supseteq Y$, then $X : \varphi, \Gamma \Rightarrow \Delta, Y : \varphi$ is derivable in* **G(FBInqBQ)** *without applying* $(\Rightarrow \text{at})$.

*Proof.* By induction on $\varphi$, where the rule ($\Rightarrow$ at) is not necessary to conduct an inductive argument. □

*Example 2.* In order to derive the constant domain axiom by the rule ($\Rightarrow\rightarrow$), it suffices to derive all instances of $Y : \forall x.(\varphi \vee \psi) \Rightarrow Y : (\forall x.\varphi) \vee \psi$ (where $x$ does not occur free in $\psi$) for all $Y$ such that $X \supseteq Y$. This is demonstrated as follows.

$$\dfrac{\dfrac{\dfrac{\dfrac{Y : \varphi[z/x], Y : \forall x.(\varphi \vee \psi) \Rightarrow Y : \varphi[z/x], Y : \psi \quad Y : \psi, Y : \forall x.(\varphi \vee \psi) \Rightarrow Y : \varphi[z/x], Y : \psi}{Y : \varphi[z/x] \vee \psi, Y : \forall x.(\varphi \vee \psi) \Rightarrow Y : \varphi[z/x], Y : \psi}\;(\vee \Rightarrow)}{Y : \forall x.(\varphi \vee \psi) \Rightarrow Y : \varphi[z/x], Y : \psi}\;(\forall \Rightarrow)}{Y : \forall x.(\varphi \vee \psi) \Rightarrow Y : (\forall x.\varphi), Y : \psi}\;(\Rightarrow \forall)}{Y : \forall x.(\varphi \vee \psi) \Rightarrow Y : (\forall x.\varphi) \vee \psi}\;(\Rightarrow \vee)$$

where the left and right topsequents are derivable by Proposition 3 and it is noted for the application of the rule ($\forall \Rightarrow$) that $Y : (\varphi \vee \psi)[z/x] \equiv Y : \varphi[z/x] \vee \psi$ since $x$ does not occur free in $\psi$.

Given a relational information model $\mathfrak{M} = (W, D, \mathfrak{J})$, an assignment $g : \mathsf{Var} \to D$ and a mapping $f : \omega \to W$, we define the satisfaction relation $\mathfrak{M}, f \Vdash_g X : \varphi$ for labelled formulas as follows:

$$\mathfrak{M}, f \Vdash_g (X : \varphi) \text{ iff } \mathfrak{M}, f[X] \Vdash_g \varphi.$$

For a sequent $\Gamma \Rightarrow \Delta$, we define $\mathfrak{M}, f \Vdash_g \Gamma \Rightarrow \Delta$ as follows: if $\mathfrak{M}, f \Vdash_g (X : \varphi)$ for all $(X : \varphi) \in \Gamma$, then $\mathfrak{M}, f \Vdash_g (Y : \psi)$ for some $(Y : \psi) \in \Delta$.

**Proposition 4 (Soundness).** *If* $\mathbf{G(FBInqBQ)} \vdash \Gamma \Rightarrow \Delta$ *then* $\mathfrak{M}, f \Vdash_g \Gamma \Rightarrow \Delta$ *holds for every relational information model* $\mathfrak{M} = (W, D, \mathfrak{J})$, *every assignment* $g : \mathsf{Var} \to D$ *and every mapping* $f : \omega \to W$.

*Proof (Sketch).* As an example proof step, we check the validity preservation of ($\Rightarrow$ at). Let $\mathfrak{M} = (W, D, \mathfrak{J})$ be a relational information model, $g : \mathsf{Var} \to D$ an assignment and $f : \omega \to W$ be a mapping. Suppose $\mathfrak{M}, f \Vdash_g \Gamma \Rightarrow \Delta, \{k\} : P(\overline{x})$ for all $k \in X$. We show that $\mathfrak{M}, f \Vdash_g \Gamma \Rightarrow \Delta, X : P(\overline{x})$. Assume that $\mathfrak{M}, f \Vdash_g (Y : \varphi)$ for all $(Y : \varphi) \in \Gamma$ and $\mathfrak{M}, f \nVdash_g (Z : \psi)$ for all $(Z : \psi) \in \Delta$. We show that $\mathfrak{M}, f \Vdash_g X : P(\overline{x})$, i.e., $\mathfrak{M}, f[X] \Vdash_g P(\overline{x})$, which is equivalent to the following: for all $w \in f[X]$, $(g(x_1), \ldots, g(x_n)) \in \mathfrak{J}(P, w)$. So, let us fix $w \in f[X]$. We can find a natural number $k \in X$ such that $f(k) = w$. By assumption, our supposition $\mathfrak{M}, f \Vdash_g \Gamma \Rightarrow \Delta, \{k\} : P(\overline{x})$ gives us that $\mathfrak{M}, f \Vdash_g \{k\} : P(\overline{x})$, which implies our goal.

**Corollary 2.** *If* $\mathbf{G(FBInqBQ)} \vdash \Rightarrow \{1, \ldots, n\} : \varphi$ *then* $\varphi \in \mathsf{InqBQ}_n$.

**Definition 5.** *Let* $(\cdot)^\psi_P$ *be the substitution operation from Definition 2. For a labelled formula* $X : \varphi$, *we define* $(X : \varphi)^\psi_P$ *as* $X : (\varphi)^\psi_P$. *When* $\Gamma = \{X_1 : \varphi_1, \ldots, X_n : \varphi_n\}$, *we define* $\Gamma^\psi_P := \{(X_1 : \varphi_1)^\psi_P, \ldots, (X_n : \varphi_n)^\psi_P\}$.

**Theorem 4.** *If a sequent* $\Gamma \Rightarrow \Delta$ *is derivable in* $\mathbf{G(FBInqBQ)}$ *without applying* ($\Rightarrow$ at), *then* $\Gamma^\psi_P \Rightarrow \Delta^\psi_P$ *is also derivable in* $\mathbf{G(FBInqBQ)}$ *without applying* ($\Rightarrow$ at). *Therefore, if a sequent* $\Rightarrow \{1, \ldots, n\} : \varphi$ *is derivable in* $\mathbf{G(FBInqBQ)}$ *without applying* ($\Rightarrow$ at), *then* $\varphi$ *is schematically valid in* $\mathsf{InqBQ}_n$.

*Proof.* The latter statement follows from the former statement and Proposition 4. So we focus on proving the former by induction on a derivation with no application of ($\Rightarrow$ at) of $\Gamma \Rightarrow \Delta$. For the base case, it is easy to see that the $(\cdot)_P^\psi$-translation of an initial sequent ($\bot \Rightarrow$) is again of the same form ($\bot \Rightarrow$). When $P(\overline{x})$ is not principal of an initial sequent (id), then the $(\cdot)_P^\psi$-translation of the initial sequent is also of the form (id). Otherwise, $X : \psi(\overline{x}), \Gamma_P^\psi \Rightarrow \Delta_P^\psi, Y : \psi(\overline{x})$ is derivable without applying ($\Rightarrow$ at) by Proposition 3. For the inductive step, the argument is straightforward. □

Whether the converse direction of the second statement of Theorem 4 holds is an open question.

## 5 Strong Completeness

This section establishes the converse direction of Corollary 2 in a stronger form, as the semantic strong completeness.

**Definition 6.** *Let $1 \leq n \in \omega$. Given a set $\Psi \cup \{\varphi\}$ of formulas of* L, *we use $\Psi \Vdash_{\mathsf{InqBQ}_n} \varphi$ to mean that, for all relational information models $\mathfrak{M} = (W, D, \mathfrak{I})$ such that $\#W \leq n$, all $g : \mathsf{Var} \to D$ and all $s \subseteq W$, if $\mathfrak{M}, s \Vdash_g \psi$ for every $\psi \in \Psi$ then $\mathfrak{M}, s \Vdash_g \varphi$.*

We note that $\emptyset \Vdash_{\mathsf{InqBQ}_n} \varphi$ iff $\varphi \in \mathsf{InqBQ}_n$. In this subsection, $\Gamma, \Delta$ are possibly infinite in the expression $\Gamma \Rightarrow \Delta$. A (possibly infinite) sequent $\Gamma \Rightarrow \Delta$ is *derivable* in **G(FBInqBQ)** if **G(FBInqBQ)** $\vdash \Gamma' \Rightarrow \Delta'$ for some finite sequent $\Gamma' \Rightarrow \Delta'$ such that $\Gamma' \subseteq \Gamma$ and $\Delta' \subseteq \Delta$.

**Definition 7.** *Let $Z$ be a label, i.e., $\emptyset \neq Z \subseteq_{\mathrm{fin}} \omega$. We say that a possibly infinite sequent $\Gamma \Rightarrow \Delta$ is $Z$-saturated if all the labels in $\Gamma$ or $\Delta$ are subsets of $Z$ and the sequent satisfies the following conditions:*

(unprov) $\Gamma \Rightarrow \Delta$ *is not derivable in* **G(FBInqBQ)**.
(atR) *If $X : P(x_1, \ldots, x_n) \in \Delta$ then $\{k\} : P(x_1, \ldots, x_n) \in \Delta$ for some $k \in X$.*
($\wedge$R) *If $X : \varphi_1 \wedge \varphi_2 \in \Delta$ then $X : \varphi_1 \in \Delta$ or $X : \varphi_2 \in \Delta$.*
($\wedge$L) *If $X : \varphi_1 \wedge \varphi_2 \in \Gamma$ then $X : \varphi_1 \in \Gamma$ and $X : \varphi_2 \in \Gamma$.*
($\vee\!\!\vee$R) *If $X : \varphi_1 \vee\!\!\vee \varphi_2 \in \Delta$ then $X : \varphi_1 \in \Delta$ and $X : \varphi_2 \in \Delta$.*
($\vee\!\!\vee$L) *If $X : \varphi_1 \vee\!\!\vee \varphi_2 \in \Gamma$ then $X : \varphi_1 \in \Gamma$ or $X : \varphi_2 \in \Gamma$.*
($\to$R) *If $X : \varphi_1 \to \varphi_2 \in \Delta$ then $Y : \varphi_1 \in \Gamma$ and $Y : \varphi_1 \in \Delta$ for some $Y \subseteq X$.*
($\to$L) *If $X : \varphi_1 \to \varphi_2 \in \Gamma$ then $Y : \varphi_1 \in \Delta$ or $Y : \varphi_2 \in \Gamma$ for all $Y \subseteq X$.*
($\forall$R) *If $\forall x.\varphi \in \Delta$ then $\varphi[z/x] \in \Delta$ for some variable $z$.*
($\forall$L) *If $\forall x.\varphi \in \Gamma$ then $\varphi[y/x] \in \Gamma$ for all variables $y$.*
($\exists$R) *If $\exists x.\varphi \in \Delta$ then $\varphi[y/x] \in \Delta$ for all variables $y$.*
($\exists$L) *If $\exists x.\varphi \in \Gamma$ then $\varphi[z/x] \in \Gamma$ for some variable $z$.*

**Lemma 2.** *Let $\emptyset \neq Z \subseteq_{\mathrm{fin}} \omega$ and $\Gamma \Rightarrow \Delta$ be a possibly infinite sequent. If $\Gamma \Rightarrow \Delta$ is not derivable in* **G(FBInqBQ)** *and all the labels in $\Gamma, \Delta$ are subsets of $Z$, then there exists a $Z$-saturated sequent $\Gamma^+ \Rightarrow \Delta^+$ such that $\Gamma \subseteq \Gamma^+$ and $\Delta \subseteq \Delta^+$.*

*Proof.* We proceed by a Hintikka-style saturation argument. Suppose that $\mathbf{G(FBInqBQ)} \nvdash \Gamma \Rightarrow \Delta$ and that all the labels are subsets of a fixed label $Z$. We add a countably infinite fresh set of variables to $\mathsf{L}$ to define the expanded syntax $\mathsf{L}^+$. Let $(X_i : \varphi_i)_{i \in \omega}$ be an enumeration of all labelled formulas such that $\varphi_i$ is a formula of $\mathsf{L}^+$ and $X_i \subseteq Z$ is a label and each labelled formula $X_i : \varphi_i$ occurs infinitely many times in the enumeration. Let $(z_i)_{i \in \omega}$ be an enumeration of all the variables in $\mathsf{L}^+$. In what follows, we inductively define an infinite sequence $(\Gamma_i \Rightarrow \Delta_i)_{i \in \omega}$ of labelled sequents such that each sequent $\Gamma_i \Rightarrow \Delta_i$ is not derivable in $\mathbf{G(FBInqBQ)}$, $\Gamma_i \subseteq \Gamma_{i+1}$, and $\Delta_i \subseteq \Delta_{i+1}$ ($i \in \omega$). Then we show that the "limit" $\bigcup_{i \in \omega} \Gamma_i \Rightarrow \bigcup_{i \in \omega} \Delta_i$ of the sequence enjoys all the saturation properties in Definition 7, $\Gamma \subseteq \bigcup_{i \in \omega} \Gamma_i$ and $\Delta \subseteq \bigcup_{i \in \omega} \Delta_i$.

**(Basis)** We put $\Gamma_0 := \Gamma$ and $\Delta_0 := \Delta$. It is clear that the sequent $\Gamma_0 \Rightarrow \Delta_0$ is not derivable in $\mathbf{G(FBInqBQ)}$ by assumption.

**(Inductive Step)** Suppose that we have constructed $(\Gamma_i \Rightarrow \Delta_i)_{i \leq k}$ such that each sequent $\Gamma_i \Rightarrow \Delta_i$ is not derivable in $\mathbf{G(FBInqBQ)}$ ($i \leq k$), $\Gamma_i \subseteq \Gamma_{i+1}$, and $\Delta_i \subseteq \Delta_{i+1}$ ($i < k$). We define a sequent $\Gamma_{k+1} \Rightarrow \Delta_{k+1}$ in terms of the sequent $\Gamma_k \Rightarrow \Delta_k$ and the $k$th element $X_k : \varphi_k$ in the enumeration. The definition is conducted in terms of the following argument by cases.

(at$r$) Let $\varphi_k$ be of the form $P(\overline{x})$ and $X_k : P(\overline{x}) \in \Delta_k$. There is an $m \in X_k$ such that $\mathbf{G(FBInqBQ)} \nvdash \Gamma_k \Rightarrow \Delta_k, \{m\} : P(\overline{x})$. Suppose otherwise. By the rule ($\Rightarrow$ at), we obtain the derivability of $\Gamma_k \Rightarrow \Delta_k$, a contradiction. So let us fix such $m \in X_k$. Then we define $\Gamma_{k+1} := \Gamma_k$ and $\Delta_{k+1} := \Delta_k \cup \{\{m\} : P(\overline{x})\}$.

($\vee r$) Let $\varphi_k$ be of the form $\psi_1 \vee \psi_2$ and $X_k : \psi_1 \vee \psi_2 \in \Delta_k$. Then we define $\Gamma_{k+1} := \Gamma_k$ and $\Delta_{k+1} := \Delta_k \cup \{X_k : \psi_1, X_k : \psi_2\}$. We can prove the underivability of $\Gamma_{k+1} \Rightarrow \Delta_{k+1}$ by the rule ($\Rightarrow \vee$).

Clause ($\wedge l$) is analogous.

($\vee l$) Let $\varphi_k$ be of the form $\psi_1 \vee \psi_2$ and $X_k : \psi_1 \vee \psi_2 \in \Gamma_k$. Either
$$\Gamma_k, X_k : \psi_1 \Rightarrow \Delta_k \text{ or } \Gamma_k, X_k : \psi_2 \Rightarrow \Delta_k$$
is underivable. Suppose otherwise. By the rule ($\vee \Rightarrow$), we obtain the derivability of $\Gamma_k \Rightarrow \Delta_k$, which is a contradiction. Choose one of the underivable sequents as $\Gamma_{k+1} \Rightarrow \Delta_{k+1}$.

Clause ($\wedge r$) is analogous.

($\rightarrow r$) Let $\varphi_k$ be of the form $\psi_1 \rightarrow \psi_2$ and $X_k : \psi_1 \rightarrow \psi_2 \in \Delta_k$. Suppose for contradiction that sequents $Y : \psi_1, \Gamma_k \Rightarrow \Delta_k, Y : \psi_2$ are derivable for all $Y \subseteq X_k$. Then the rule ($\Rightarrow \rightarrow$) gives us the derivability of $\Gamma_k \Rightarrow \Delta_k$, which is a contradiction. Choose one of the underivable sequents as $\Gamma_{k+1} \Rightarrow \Delta_{k+1}$.

($\rightarrow l$) Let $\varphi_k$ be of the form $\psi_1 \rightarrow \psi_2$ and $X_k : \psi_1 \rightarrow \psi_2 \in \Gamma_k$. Let $h := \#(\wp(X_k) \setminus \{\emptyset\})$ and $Z_1, \ldots, Z_h$ be an enumeration of the set. We define an increasing sequence $(\Gamma_k^{(j)} \Rightarrow \Delta_k^{(j)})_{1 \leq j \leq h}$ of sequents inductively as follows. Let $(\Gamma_k^{(1)} \Rightarrow \Delta_k^{(1)})$ be $\Gamma_k \Rightarrow \Delta_k$. Suppose that we have defined an increasing sequence $(\Gamma_k^{(j)} \Rightarrow \Delta_k^{(j)})_{1 \leq j \leq i}$ of sequents such that each sequent is underivable. We define $\Gamma_k^{(i+1)} \Rightarrow \Delta_k^{(i+1)}$ as follows. Suppose for contradiction that both $\Gamma_k^{(i)} \Rightarrow \Delta_k^{(i)}, Z_j : \psi_1$ and $Z_j : \psi_2, \Gamma_k^{(i)} \Rightarrow \Delta_k^{(i)}$ are derivable. By $X_k : \psi_1 \rightarrow \psi_2 \in \Gamma_k$, we obtain the derivability of $\Gamma_k^{(i)} \Rightarrow \Delta_k^{(i)}$ by the rule ($\rightarrow \Rightarrow$). Choose one of the underivable sequents as $\Gamma_k^{(i+1)} \Rightarrow \Delta_k^{(i+1)}$. Define $\Gamma_{k+1} \Rightarrow \Delta_{k+1} := \Gamma_k^{(h)} \Rightarrow \Delta_k^{(h)}$.

($\exists r$) Let $\varphi_k$ be of the form $\exists x.\psi$ and $X_k : \exists x.\psi \in \Delta_k$. We define $\Gamma_{k+1} := \Gamma_k$ and $\Delta_{k+1} := \Delta_k \cup \{X_k : \psi[z_i/x] \mid 0 \leq i \leq k\}$. Suppose for contradiction that $\Gamma_{k+1} \Rightarrow \Delta_{k+1}$ is derivable. By applying ($\Rightarrow \exists$) finitely many times, we obtain the derivability of $\Gamma_k \Rightarrow \Delta_k$, which is a contradiction. Therefore, $\Gamma_{k+1} \Rightarrow \Delta_{k+1}$ is not derivable.
Clause ($\forall l$) is analogous.

($\exists l$) Let $\varphi_k$ be of the form $\exists x.\psi$ and $X_k : \exists x.\psi \in \Gamma_k$. Since $\Gamma_k \Rightarrow \Delta_k$ is finite, we can choose the first fresh variable $z$ in the enumeration $(z_i)_{i \in \omega}$ such that $z$ does not occur free in $\Gamma_k \Rightarrow \Delta_k$. Then we define $\Gamma_{k+1} := \Gamma_k \cup \{X_k : \varphi[z/x]\}$ and $\Delta_{k+1} := \Delta_k$. We can show that $\Gamma_{k+1} \Rightarrow \Delta_{k+1}$ is not derivable by the rule ($\exists \Rightarrow$) since $z$ is a fresh variable not occurring in $\Gamma_k \Rightarrow \Delta_k$.
Clause ($\forall r$) is analogous.

(else) Otherwise. We put $\Gamma_{k+1} := \Gamma_k$ and $\Delta_{k+1} := \Delta_k$.

Finally it is easy to establish that $\bigcup_{i \in \omega} \Gamma_i \Rightarrow \bigcup_{i \in \omega} \Delta_i$ enjoys all the saturation properties (as well as the condition (**unprov**)) in Definition 7, $\Gamma \subseteq \bigcup_{i \in \omega} \Gamma_i$ and $\Delta \subseteq \bigcup_{i \in \omega} \Delta_i$.

**Definition 8.** *Let $\emptyset \neq Z \subseteq_{\text{fin}} \omega$ and $\Gamma \Rightarrow \Delta$ be Z-saturated. We define the derived relational information model $\mathfrak{M}_{(\Gamma,\Delta)} = (Z, \text{Var}, \mathfrak{J}_{(\Gamma,\Delta)})$ from the sequent as follows:*

- $(x_1, \ldots, x_n) \in \mathfrak{J}_{(\Gamma,\Delta)}(P, k)$ iff $\{k\} : P(x_1, \ldots, x_n) \notin \Delta$.

**Lemma 3.** *Let $\emptyset \neq Z \subseteq_{\text{fin}} \omega$ and $\Gamma \Rightarrow \Delta$ be Z-saturated. Then the following hold:*

(i) *if $X : \varphi \in \Gamma$ then $\mathfrak{M}_{(\Gamma,\Delta)}, X \Vdash_{\text{id}} \varphi$;*  (ii) *if $X : \varphi \in \Delta$ then $\mathfrak{M}_{(\Gamma,\Delta)}, X \nVdash_{\text{id}} \varphi$,*

*where* $\text{id} : \text{Var} \to \text{Var}$ *is the identity function.*

*Proof.* We only establish the case where $\varphi \equiv P(\overline{x})$ because the other cases are immediate from the conditions for the Z-saturation of $\Gamma \Rightarrow \Delta$. For (i), suppose that $X : P(\overline{x}) \in \Gamma$. To show that $\mathfrak{M}_{(\Gamma,\Delta)}, X \Vdash P(\overline{x})$, let us fix any $k \in X$. By definition, it suffices to show that $\{k\} : P(\overline{x}) \notin \Delta$. Suppose for contradiction that $\{k\} : P(\overline{x}) \in \Delta$. It follows from $X : P(\overline{x}) \in \Gamma$ that $\Gamma \Rightarrow \Delta$ is an instance of (id), a contradiction with (**unprov**). Next, we move to (ii). We assume that $X : P(\overline{x}) \in \Delta$. To show that $\mathfrak{M}_{(\Gamma,\Delta)}, X \nVdash P(\overline{x})$, it suffices to find some $k \in X$ such that $\{k\} : P(\overline{x}) \in \Delta$. This holds by (atR). □

Write $\{1, \ldots, n\} : \Psi$ for $\{\{1, \ldots, n\} : \psi \mid \psi \in \Psi\}$. Now we can state:

**Theorem 5.** *Fix any $n \in \omega$ and let $\Psi \cup \{\varphi\}$ be a possibly infinite set of formulas. If $\Psi \Vdash_{\text{InqBQ}_n} \varphi$ then $\mathbf{G}(\text{FBInqBQ}) \vdash \{1, \ldots, n\} : \Psi \Rightarrow \{1, \ldots, n\} : \varphi$. In particular, if $\varphi \in \text{InqBQ}_n$ then $\Rightarrow \{1, \ldots, n\} : \varphi$ is derivable in $\mathbf{G}(\text{FBInqBQ})$.*

*Proof.* Let $n \in \omega$ and $Z := \{1, \ldots, n\}$. Suppose that $Z : \Psi \Rightarrow Z : \varphi$ is not derivable in $\mathbf{G}(\text{FBInqBQ})$. By Lemma 2, we can find a Z-saturated sequent $\Gamma \Rightarrow \Delta$ such that $Z : \Psi \subseteq \Gamma$ and $Z : \varphi \in \Delta$. By Lemma 3, we obtain $\mathfrak{M}_{(\Gamma,\Delta)}, Z \Vdash_{\text{id}} \psi$ for all $\psi \in \Psi$ but $\mathfrak{M}_{(\Gamma,\Delta)}, Z \nVdash_{\text{id}} \varphi$ hence $\Psi \nVdash_{\text{InqBQ}_n} \varphi$, as desired. □

*Remark 5.* In the natural deduction system for $\mathsf{InqBQ}_n$ given by Ciardelli and Grilletti [11], a key rôle is played by the $n$-cardinality formula depending on the signature Pred [11, Section 6]. They also established the strong completeness of the natural deduction system for $\mathsf{InqBQ}_n$ in [11, Theorem 8.1]. In our labelled sequent calculus, the cardinality restriction is simply captured by the signature-independent label $\{1,\ldots,n\}$ in Corollary 2 and Theorem 5.

*Remark 6.* The *restricted existential* (*rex*) fragment $\mathsf{L}_{\mathsf{rex}}$ [11] is defined by:

$$\chi ::= P(\overline{x}) \mid \bot \mid \chi \wedge \chi \mid \chi \vee\!\!\vee \chi \mid \varphi \to \chi \mid \forall\, x.\chi,$$

where $\varphi$ is a formula in L. Theorem 9.2 of Ciardelli and Grilletti [11] provides a complete system for the entailments with rex conclusions in terms of a *coherence rule* involving the above-mentioned signature-dependent cardinality formula. However, characterizing entailments with rex conclusions in $\mathbf{G}(\mathsf{FBInqBQ})$ does not require additional inference rules. First, it is a consequence of Theorem 4.3 in *op.cit.* that entailments with rex conclusions are compact. Second, Propositions 3.5 and 5.3 in *op.cit.* imply that, for every $\chi \in \mathsf{L}_{\mathsf{rex}}$, $\chi \in \mathsf{InqBQ}$ iff there exists $n_\chi \in \omega$ such that $\chi \in \mathsf{InqBQ}_{n_\chi}$, where $n_\chi$ is given by Definition 5.2 in *op.cit* and it is recursively computed from $\chi \in \mathsf{L}_{\mathsf{rex}}$. Now, we can show that for every $\Sigma \subseteq \mathsf{L}$ and $\chi \in \mathsf{L}_{\mathsf{rex}}$, the following are equivalent:

(i) $\Sigma \Vdash \chi$;
(ii) $\mathbf{G}(\mathsf{FBInqBQ}) \vdash \Rightarrow \{1,\ldots,n\} : \bigwedge \Sigma' \to \chi$, for some finite subset $\Sigma' \subseteq \Sigma$ and $n \in \omega$.

We can prove the equivalence as follows. By Theorem 4.3 in *op.cit.*, $\Sigma \Vdash \chi$ iff $\Vdash \bigwedge \Sigma' \to \chi$ for some finite subset $\Sigma' \subseteq \Sigma$. Fix such $\Sigma'$. Because $\bigwedge \Sigma' \to \chi$ is still (equivalent to) a rex formula, $\bigwedge \Sigma' \to \chi \in \mathsf{InqBQ}$ iff there exists $n \in \omega$ such that $\bigwedge \Sigma' \to \chi \in \mathsf{InqBQ}_n$ by the observation above. By Corollary 2 and Theorem 5, it is equivalent to $\mathbf{G}(\mathsf{FBInqBQ}) \vdash \Rightarrow \{1,\ldots,n\} : \bigwedge \Sigma' \to \chi$, as desired. The converse direction is immediate.

## 6 Cut Elimination and Derivability of Schematic Validities

First, this section establishes the admissibility of the cut rule on the height-preserving admissibility of weakening rules, inversions of all inference rules of $\mathbf{G}(\mathsf{FBInqBQ})$ and contraction rules. Second, as an application of the admissibility of structural rules and the cut rule, we provide derivations for CasariScheme as well as key axioms underlying the natural deduction system for $\mathsf{InqBQ}_n$ (see Remark 6), except for the signature-specific cardinality formula [11, Section 6].

**Definition 9.** *We say that an inference rule*

$$\frac{\Gamma_1 \Rightarrow \Delta_1 \quad \cdots \quad \Gamma_m \Rightarrow \Delta_m}{\Gamma_0 \Rightarrow \Delta_0}\ (\mathbf{r})$$

*is* height-preserving admissible *in* $\mathbf{G}(\mathsf{FBInqBQ})$ *if whenever* $\mathbf{G}(\mathsf{FBInqBQ}) \vdash_h \Gamma_i \Rightarrow \Delta_i$ *for all* $1 \leq i \leq m$ *we obtain* $\mathbf{G}(\mathsf{FBInqBQ}) \vdash_h \Gamma_0 \Rightarrow \Delta_0$. *When we drop the subscript "h" from all the occurences of "$\vdash_h$", we say that* $(\mathbf{r})$ *is* admissible.

Bounded Inquisitive Logics: Sequent Calculi and Schematic Validity 53

By a standard argument [35, Ch. 3.5] [29], we get the following.

**Proposition 5.** (i) *If* **G(FBInqBQ)** $\vdash_h \Gamma \Rightarrow \Delta$ *then* **G(FBInqBQ)** $\vdash_h \Gamma[z/x] \Rightarrow \Delta[z/x]$, *where* $\Theta[z/x] := \{ X : \varphi[z/x] \mid X : \varphi \in \Theta \}$.
(ii) *The weakening rules are height-preserving admissible in* **G(FBInqBQ)**:

$$\frac{\Gamma \Rightarrow \Delta}{\Gamma \Rightarrow \Delta, X : \varphi} \;(\Rightarrow w) \qquad \frac{\Gamma \Rightarrow \Delta}{X : \varphi, \Gamma \Rightarrow \Delta} \;(w \Rightarrow).$$

(iii) *All the rules of* **G(FBInqBQ)** *are height-preserving invertible, i.e., whenever its conclusion of a rule of* **G(FBInqBQ)** *is derivable, the premises of the same rule are also derivable with no greater derivation height.*
(vi) *The contraction rules are height-preserving admissible in* **G(FBInqBQ)**:

$$\frac{\Gamma \Rightarrow \Delta, X : \varphi, X : \varphi}{\Gamma \Rightarrow \Delta, X : \varphi} \;(\Rightarrow c) \qquad \frac{X : \varphi, X : \varphi, \Gamma \Rightarrow \Delta}{X : \varphi, \Gamma \Rightarrow \Delta} \;(c \Rightarrow).$$

**Theorem 6.** *The rule of cut is admissible in* **G(FBInqBQ)**:

$$\frac{\Gamma \Rightarrow \Delta, X : \varphi \quad X : \varphi, \Pi \Rightarrow \Sigma}{\Gamma, \Pi \Rightarrow \Delta, \Sigma} \;(Cut).$$

*where* $X : \varphi$ *is said to be a* cut formula.

*Proof.* Let $\mathcal{L}$ of $\Gamma \Rightarrow \Delta, X : \varphi$ and $\mathcal{R}$ of $X : \varphi, \Pi \Rightarrow \Sigma$ be derivations in **G(FBInqBQ)**. Our proof is by induction on the lexicographic order of the length c of the cut labelled formula $X : \varphi$ and the cut-height h, i.e., the sum of the height of the derivation $\mathcal{L}$ and the height of the derivation $\mathcal{R}$. We follow the standard argument in G3-style sequent calculus to divide our argument into the following three cases.

1. One of $r(\mathcal{L})$ and $r(\mathcal{R})$ is an initial sequent (id) or ($\bot \Rightarrow$).
2. $r(\mathcal{L})$ or $r(\mathcal{R})$ is a rule where the cut formula is not principal in the rule.
3. $r(\mathcal{L})$ and $r(\mathcal{R})$ are rules where the cut formula is principal in both rules.

We comment on the difference from the standard argument for G3-style sequent calculi [15,28,29]. In particular, we focus on the cases related to the initial sequent (id) and the new rule ($\Rightarrow$ at). First, we comment on Case 1 for the initial sequent (id) of the form $X : P(\overline{x}), \Gamma \Rightarrow \Delta, Y : P(\overline{x})$ where $X \supseteq Y$, where the principal formulas are $X : P(\overline{x})$ and $Y : P(\overline{x})$. Let $r(\mathcal{L})$ or $r(\mathcal{R})$ be (id). When the cut formula is not principal in (id), it is immediate. So we assume that the cut formula is principal in (id). Then we need to consider the following two cases: (i) $(r(\mathcal{L}), r(\mathcal{R})) = ((\text{id}), (\text{id}))$, (ii) $(r(\mathcal{L}), r(\mathcal{R})) = ((\Rightarrow \text{at}), (\text{id}))$. For the case (i), it suffices to consider the following transformation:

$$\frac{\dfrac{}{X : P(\overline{x}), \Gamma \Rightarrow \Delta, Y : P(\overline{x})} \;(\text{id}) \quad \dfrac{}{Y : P(\overline{x}), \Pi \Rightarrow \Sigma, Z : P(\overline{x})} \;(\text{id})}{X : P(\overline{x}), \Gamma, \Pi \Rightarrow \Delta, \Sigma, Z : P(\overline{x})} \;(Cut)$$

$$\rightsquigarrow \frac{}{X : P(\overline{x}), \Gamma, \Pi \Rightarrow \Delta, \Sigma, Z : P(\overline{x})} \;(\text{id})$$

where $X \supseteq Y \supseteq Z$. For case (ii), we have the following derivation:

$$\dfrac{\dfrac{\{\Gamma \Rightarrow \Delta, \{k\} : P(\overline{x}) \mid k \in X\}}{\Gamma \Rightarrow \Delta, X : P(\overline{x})} (\Rightarrow \text{at}) \quad \dfrac{}{X : P(\overline{x}), \Pi \Rightarrow \Sigma, Y : P(\overline{x})} (\text{id})}{\Gamma, \Pi \Rightarrow \Delta, \Sigma, Y : P(\overline{x})} (Cut)$$

where $X \supseteq Y$. By $X \supseteq Y$, we can obtain the following cut-free derivation:

$$\dfrac{\dfrac{\{\Gamma \Rightarrow \Delta, \{k\} : P(\overline{x}) \mid k \in Y\}}{\Gamma \Rightarrow \Delta, Y : P(\overline{x})} (\Rightarrow \text{at})}{\Gamma, \Pi \Rightarrow \Delta, \Sigma, Y : P(\overline{x})} (\Rightarrow w), (w \Rightarrow).$$

Second, we consider Case 2, in particular when $r(\mathcal{L})$ or $r(\mathcal{R})$ is ($\Rightarrow$ at). Here, the cut formula is not principal in ($\Rightarrow$ at). Then we can lift the application of $(Cut)$ for the conclusion of ($\Rightarrow$ at) to an application of $(Cut)$ for the premise. The lifted application of $(Cut)$ can be eliminated since the complexity of the cut formula is the same but the cut height of the rewritten derivation becomes smaller than the original derivation. □

**Corollary 3.** *The following rule is admissible in* **G(FBInqBQ)**: *let* $X \supseteq Y$.

$$\dfrac{Y : \varphi, \Gamma \Rightarrow \Delta}{X : \varphi, \Gamma \Rightarrow \Delta} (\text{Mon}).$$

*Proof.* Let $X \supseteq Y$. Assume that $Y : \varphi, \Gamma \Rightarrow \Delta$ is in **G(FBInqBQ)**. By Proposition 3, $X : \varphi \Rightarrow Y : \varphi$ is derivable in **G(FBInqBQ)**. By the admissibility of the cut rule (Theorem 6), **G(FBInqBQ)** ⊢ $X : \varphi, \Gamma \Rightarrow \Delta$ holds. □

**Proposition 6.** *For every finite subset* $X \subseteq \omega$, *the following sequent*

$$X : \forall x.((\varphi(x) \to \forall x.\varphi(x)) \to \forall x.\varphi(x)) \Rightarrow X : \forall x.\varphi(x)$$

*is derivable in* **G(FBInqBQ)**. *Therefore, a sequent* $\Rightarrow X :$ CasariScheme *is derivable in* **G(FBInqBQ)**, *for every finite subset* $X \subseteq \omega$.

*Proof.* The latter is obtained from the former by applying the rule ($\Rightarrow \to$). Thus we show the former statement by induction on $\#X$. For the base step, we assume $X = \{n\}$. Then we can regard that all the inference rules with the label $\{n\}$ are the same as those for the classical first-order logic, and so the sequent in question is easily derivable in **G(FBInqBQ)**. For the inductive step, let $\#X > 1$.

$$\dfrac{\dfrac{\dfrac{\{\Theta, Y : \varphi(z_1) \Rightarrow Y : \forall x.\varphi(x), X : \varphi(z_1) \mid X \supseteq Y\}}{\Theta \Rightarrow X : \varphi(z_1) \to \forall x.\varphi(x), X : \varphi(z_1)} (\Rightarrow \to) \quad \dfrac{\dfrac{\Theta, X : \varphi(z_1), X : \forall x.\varphi(x) \Rightarrow X : \varphi(z_1)}{\Theta, X : \forall x.\varphi(x) \Rightarrow X : \varphi(z_1)} (\forall \Rightarrow)}{X : \forall x.((\varphi(x) \to \forall x.\varphi(x)) \to \forall x.\varphi(x)), X : (\varphi(z_1) \to \forall x.\varphi(x)) \to \forall x.\varphi(x) \Rightarrow X : \varphi(z_1)} (\to \Rightarrow)}{\dfrac{X : \forall x.((\varphi(x) \to \forall x.\varphi(x)) \to \forall x.\varphi(x)) \Rightarrow X : \varphi(z_1)}{X : \forall x.((\varphi(x) \to \forall x.\varphi(x)) \to \forall x.\varphi(x)) \Rightarrow X : \forall x.\varphi(x)} (\Rightarrow \forall)} (\forall \Rightarrow)$$

where $\Theta := X : \forall x.((\varphi(x) \to \forall x.\varphi(x)) \to \forall x.\varphi(x)), X : (\varphi(z_1) \to \forall x.\varphi(x)) \to \forall x.\varphi(x)$. Since the right topsequent is derivable by Proposition 3, we focus on providing a derivation for a sequent $\Theta, Y : \varphi(z_1) \Rightarrow Y : \forall x.\varphi(x), X : \varphi(z_1)$ for each $Y$ such that

$X \supseteq Y$. Fix any $Y$ such that $X \supseteq Y$. Suppose $Y = X$, then the sequent is derivable by Proposition 3. So, let us assume that $Y \neq X$, which implies $\#Y < \#X$. By induction hypothesis, the sequent $Y : \forall x.((\varphi(x) \to \forall x.\varphi(x)) \to \forall x.\varphi(x)) \Rightarrow Y : \forall x.\varphi(x)$ is derivable. By Corollary 3, $X : \forall x.((\varphi(x) \to \forall x.\varphi(x)) \to \forall x.\varphi(x)) \Rightarrow Y : \forall x.\varphi(x)$ is derivable. By the admissibility of weakening rules (by Proposition 5 (ii)), we obtain our desired derivability of $\Theta, Y : \varphi(z_1) \Rightarrow Y : \forall x.\varphi(x), X : \varphi(z_1)$. □

*Remark 7.* This is a continuation of Remark 4 on the propositional fragment **G(InqB)**. Our syntactic argument for Theorem 6 implies the admissibility of cut rule in **G(InqB)**. We can prove the following soundness and completeness for **InqB**, where we regard **InqB** as the set of valid (propositional) formulas for the propositional reduction of our semantics (we do not need to consider the domain $D$). The following two clauses are equivalent: (i) **G(InqB)** $\vdash \Rightarrow \{1, \ldots, 2^n\} : \varphi$; (ii) $\varphi \in$ **InqB** (note again that propositionally **InqB** coincides with **InqL** [7]), where $n$ is the number of propositional variables in $\varphi$. The direction from (i) to (ii) is already established by Proposition 4. For the direction from (ii) to (i), we proceed as follows. Suppose the negation of (i), i.e., **G(InqB)** $\not\vdash \Rightarrow \{1, \ldots, 2^n\} : \varphi$. We prove $\varphi \notin$ **InqB**. Put $Z = \{1, \ldots, 2^n\}$. By Lemma 2, we can find a (propositionally) $Z$-saturated (finite) labelled sequent $\Gamma \Rightarrow \Delta$ such that $\{1, \ldots, 2^n\} : \varphi \in \Delta$. We define our derived model $\mathfrak{M}_{(\Gamma,\Delta)} = (Z, v)$ as: $k \in v(P)$ iff $\{k\} : P \notin \Delta$ (where $P$ occurs in $\Gamma$ or $\Delta$, otherwise $v(P) := \emptyset$, we use "$v$" instead of $\mathfrak{J}$ here). By Lemma 3, we obtain $\mathfrak{M}_{(\Gamma,\Delta)}, \{1, \ldots, 2^n\} \not\models \varphi$ hence $\varphi \notin$ **InqB**.

# 7 Conclusions

Our results reveal complex interplay between correspondence theory and proof theory of inquisitive logic. We have seen, for example, that the status of the Casari axiom in the base inquisitive logic resembles that of the double negation law: it is valid atomically but not schematically. Its schematic validity is characteristic of **InqBQ**$_{<\omega}$. Remark 3 discusses further challenges and open questions related to these results.

Further intriguing questions regarding notions closely related to boundedness such as *coherence* are raised by Ciardelli and Grilletti [11, § 10]. Several cardinality-related questions posed therein appear related to papers concerning model theory and correspondence theory of extensions of CD [26, 30]. It is not known, for example, if **InqBQ** is complete with respect to relational information models with at most *countable* collection $W$ of possible worlds. It would be also of interest to see if the notion of schematic validity and our labelled sequent apparatus can be useful in resolving Ciardelli and Grilletti's challenge of algorithmically identifying formulas coherent for a fixed cardinality. Remark 6 hints at the relevance of our sequent setup for their question whether the coherence rule is indispensable for entailments with rex conclusions.

Given our proof-theoretic results, it appears natural to consider the Craig interpolation property for logics considered herein. It is also natural to mechanize our calculus in a proof assistant; some spadework in the Rocq proof assistant covering partially our results (but without, e.g., syntactic cut elimination) has been done by Max Ole Elliger [16, 17]. Furthermore, it could be of interest to extend existing computational interpretations of sequent calculi [34, Ch. 7] [14] to our setting. Continuing the topic of CS applications, the discussion of Armstrong relations by Abramsky and Väänänen [1] or

Ciardelli's perspective on *mention-some* questions [8, p. 348 and Ch. 4.7] suggest relationships with database theory that appear rather under-explored by both communities.

**Acknowledgements.** We thank the reviewers of several versions of this paper for their constructive comments. The work of the first named author has been partially funded by the PNRR MUR projects FAIR (No. PE0000013-FAIR). The work of the second named author was partially supported by JSPS KAKENHI Grant-in-Aid for Scientific Research (B) Grant Number JP 22H00597 and (C) Grant Number JP 25K03537. The work of both authors was partially supported by JSPS KAKENHI Grant-in-Aid for Scientific Research (C) Grant Number JP 19K12113. We would also like to acknowledge the feedback of Max Ole Elliger at FAU Erlangen-Nuremberg; his work on formalization was particularly helpful in the context of Sect. 3.

## References

1. Abramsky, S., Väänänen, J.A.: From IF to BI. Synthese **167**, 207–230 (2009)
2. Casari, E.: Intermediate logics. In: Atti degli incontri di logica matematica 1982, Università di Siena, pp. 243–298 (1983)
3. Chagrov, A., Zakharyaschev, M.: Modal Logic, Number 35 in Oxford Logic Guides. Clarendon Press (1997)
4. Charguéraud, A.: The locally nameless representation. J. Autom. Reason. **49**, 363–408 (2012). https://doi.org/10.1007/s10817-011-9225-2
5. Chen, J., Ma, M.: Labelled sequent calculus for inquisitive logic. In: Baltag, A., Seligman, J., Yamada, T. (eds.) LORI 2017. LNCS, vol. 10455, pp. 526–540. Springer, Heidelberg (2017). https://doi.org/10.1007/978-3-662-55665-8_36
6. Church, A.: Introduction to Mathematical Logic, vol. I, 2nd edn. Princeton (1958)
7. Ciardelli, I.: Inquisitive Semantics and Intermediate Logics. Master's thesis, Institute for Logic, Language and Computation, Universiteit van Amsterdam (2009). https://eprints.illc.uva.nl/id/eprint/818
8. Ciardelli, I.: Dependency as question entailment. In: Abramsky, S., Kontinen, J., Väänänen, J., Vollmer, H. (eds.) Dependence Logic, pp. 129–181. Springer, Cham (2016). https://doi.org/10.1007/978-3-319-31803-5_8
9. Ciardelli, I.: Questions as information types. Synthese **195**, 321–365 (2018)
10. Ciardelli, I.: Inquisitive Logic: Consequence and Inference in the Realm of Questions. Springer, Cham (2022)
11. Ciardelli, I., Grilletti, G.: Coherence in inquisitive first-order logic. Ann. Pure Appl. Logic **173**, 103155 (2022)
12. Ciardelli, I., Groenendijk, J., Roelofsen, F.: Inquisitive Semantics. Oxford University Press, Oxford (2017)
13. Ciardelli, I., Roelofsen, F.: Inquisitive logic. J. Philos. Log. **40**, 55–94 (2010)
14. Curien, P.-L., Herbelin, H.: The duality of computation. In: Proceedings of ICFP '00, pp. 233–243 (2000)
15. Dyckhoff, R., Negri, S.: Proof analysis in intermediate logics. Arch. Math. Logic **51**, 71–92 (2011)
16. Elliger, M.O.: Formalization of (bounded) inquisitive first-order logic (2025). https://motrellin.github.io/rocq-docs-inquisitive-logic/
17. Elliger, M.O.: Inquisitive First-Order Logic Bounded and Mechanized. Master's thesis, FAU Erlangen-Nuremberg (2025)

18. Esakia, L.: Quantification in intuitionistic logic with provability smack. Bull. Sect. Logic **27**, 26–28 (1998)
19. Ferreira, G., Oliva, P.: On the relation between various negative translations. In: Berger, U., Schwichtenberg, H. (eds.) Logic, Construction, Computation, Mathematical Logic Series, vol. 3, pp. 227–258. Ontos-Verlag (2012)
20. Frittella, S., Greco, G., Palmigiano, A., Yang, F.: A multi-type calculus for inquisitive logic. In: Väänänen, J., Hirvonen, Å., de Queiroz, R. (eds.) WoLLIC 2016. LNCS, vol. 9803, pp. 215–233. Springer, Heidelberg (2016). https://doi.org/10.1007/978-3-662-52921-8_14
21. Gabbay, D.M., Skvortsov, D., Shehtman, V.: Quantification in Nonclassical Logic, Volume I. In: Studies in Logic and the Foundations of Mathematics, vol. 153. Elsevier (2009)
22. Görnemann, S.: A logic stronger than intuitionism. J. Symb. Logic **36**, 249–261 (1971)
23. Grilletti, G.: Completeness for the classical antecedent fragment of inquisitive first-order logic. J. Logic Lang. Inform. **30**, 725–751 (2021)
24. Kleene, S.: Introduction to metamathematics. North-Holland, Amsterdam-Oxford (1952)
25. Litak, T., Polzer, M., Rabenstein, U.: Negative translations and normal modality. In: Miller, D. (ed.) Proceedings of FSCD 2017, LIPIcs, vol. 84, pp. 27:1–27:18 (2017). http://drops.dagstuhl.de/opus/volltexte/2017/7741
26. Minari, P., Takano, M., Ono, H.: Intermediate predicate logics determined by ordinals. J. Symb. Logic **55**, 1099–1124 (1990)
27. Müller, V.: On the proof theory of inquisitive logic. Master's thesis, Institute for Logic, Language and Computation, Universiteit van Amsterdam (2023). https://eprints.illc.uva.nl/id/eprint/2278
28. Negri, S.: Proof analysis in modal logic. J. Philos. Log. **34**, 507–544 (2005)
29. Negri, S., Von Plato, J.: Structural Proof Theory. Cambridge University Press, Cambridge (2001)
30. Ono, H.: A Study of Intermediate Predicate Logics. Ph.D. thesis, Kyoto University (1973). http://hdl.handle.net/2433/86490
31. Rybakov, M., Shkatov, D.: Variations on the Kripke trick. Stud. Logica. (2024). https://doi.org/10.1007/s11225-023-10093-y
32. Sano, K.: First-order inquisitive pair logic. In: Banerjee, M., Seth, A. (eds.) ICLA 2011. LNCS (LNAI), vol. 6521, pp. 147–161. Springer, Heidelberg (2011). https://doi.org/10.1007/978-3-642-18026-2_13
33. Sano, K., Virtema, J.: Axiomatizing propositional dependence logics. In: Kreutzer, S. (ed.) Proceedings of CSL, LIPIcs, pp. 292–307 (2015)
34. Sørensen, M.H., Urzyczyn, P.: Lectures on the curry-howard isomorphism. Stud. Logic Found. Math. **149** (2006)
35. Troelstra, A.S., Schwichtenberg, H.: Basic Proof Theory, 2nd edn. Cambridge University Press, Cambridge (2000)
36. Troelstra, A.S., van Dalen, D.: Constructivism in mathematics: an introduction. Stud. Logic Found. Math. **121** (1988)

**Open Access** This chapter is licensed under the terms of the Creative Commons Attribution 4.0 International License (http://creativecommons.org/licenses/by/4.0/), which permits use, sharing, adaptation, distribution and reproduction in any medium or format, as long as you give appropriate credit to the original author(s) and the source, provide a link to the Creative Commons license and indicate if changes were made.

The images or other third party material in this chapter are included in the chapter's Creative Commons license, unless indicated otherwise in a credit line to the material. If material is not included in the chapter's Creative Commons license and your intended use is not permitted by statutory regulation or exceeds the permitted use, you will need to obtain permission directly from the copyright holder.

# Analytic Calculi for Logics of Indicative Conditionals

Vitor Greati[1]([✉])[iD], Sérgio Marcelino[2][iD], Miguel Muñoz Pérez[3][iD], and Umberto Rivieccio[3][iD]

[1] Bernoulli Institute, University of Groningen, Groningen, The Netherlands
v.rodrigues.greati@rug.nl
[2] SQIG Instituto de Telecomunicações, Departamento de Matemática – Instituto Superior Técnico, Lisbon, Portugal
smarcel@math.tecnico.ulisboa.pt
[3] Departamento de Lógica, Historia y Filosofía de la Ciencia, UNED, Madrid, Spain
umberto@fsof.uned.es

**Abstract.** We consider a family of non-classical three-valued logics proposed to model *indicative conditionals* in natural language. Among these, systems introduced by B. De Finetti, W.S. Cooper, J. Cantwell and R.J. Farrell, as well as some variants that have not appeared in the literature, but seem nevertheless to be natural objects of interest from a formal point of view. Most of these logics are not easily treatable with the standard techniques of algebraic logic. We therefore resort to non-deterministic structures and multiple-conclusion calculi to provide alternative semantical characterizations and axiomatizations. In the best cases—logics given by a finite monadic matrix—this can be done directly, in a modular way, through a procedure due to Shoesmith and Smiley. In the more involved ones—logics preserving degrees of truth—some ingenuity and more sophisticated techniques are required. We characterize these logics by a partial non-deterministic matrix, and show how to produce analytic (and effective) calculi that are complete with respect to this generalized semantics. In all cases, the calculi thus obtained can be straightforwardly converted, by a uniform procedure, into traditional single-conclusion Hilbert-style axiomatizations.

**Keywords:** Indicative conditionals · Analytic calculi · Axiomatization · Non-deterministic semantics

## 1 Introduction

*Indicative conditionals* are the *if-then* sentences which regard what could be true, whereas counterfactual statements concern eventualities that are no longer possible. For example, 'If Oswald didn't shoot JFK, someone else did' is an indicative conditional, while 'If Oswald hadn't shot JFK, someone else would have' is a counterfactual.

In classical logic, an indicative conditional "if $\varphi$ then $\psi$" is formalized as the material implication $\varphi \to \psi$ (classically equivalent to $\neg\varphi \lor \psi$). From early on, several authors have challenged this classical account. The proposal that conditional statements having a false premise—which are *vacuously true* in classical logic—in fact lack a truth value, can be traced back to Reichenbach (1935), De Finetti (1936), and Quine (1950). The recent survey [11] presents the notion of conditional statements *qua* 'conditional assertions': " the speaker is committed to the truth of the consequent when the antecedent is true, but committed to neither truth nor falsity of the consequent when the antecedent is false" ([11, p. 188]; see also [13] and the references contained therein for more details).

This intuition is formalized by adding a third 'gap' truth value $1/2$ to the Boolean ones, representing conditional sentences with a false antecedent: one would set $0 \to x = 1/2$, whereas in cases such as $1/2 \to x$ intuitions may differ. This leads to a number of alternative truth tables for $\to$, which are shown in Fig. 1. As to the *designated* values (to be preserved in inferences), if one wishes to retain fundamental classical tautologies (e.g. the law of identity, $\varphi \to \varphi$), it is natural to include also $1/2$ (besides $1$). A peculiar consequence of this setup is that there will be valid formulas whose negation is also valid: this makes these logics not just *paraconsistent* but actually *contradictory* in the sense of Wansing [31] (see Example 1 for a derivation of one such formula in the logic $OL_{\land_{OL}}$).

| $\land_{OL}$ | 0 | 1/2 | 1 |     | $\lor_{OL}$ | 0 | 1/2 | 1 |     | $\neg$ |     |     | $\land_K$ | 0 | 1/2 | 1 |     | $\lor_K$ | 0 | 1/2 | 1 |
|---|---|---|---|---|---|---|---|---|---|---|---|---|---|---|---|---|---|---|---|---|---|
| 0   | 0 | 0   | 0 |     | 0   | 0 | 0   | 1 |     | 0   | 1   |     | 0   | 0 | 0   | 0 |     | 0   | 0 | 1/2 | 1 |
| 1/2 | 0 | 1/2 | 1 |     | 1/2 | 0 | 1/2 | 1 |     | 1/2 | 1/2 |     | 1/2 | 0 | 1/2 | 1/2 |   | 1/2 | 1/2 | 1/2 | 1 |
| 1   | 0 | 1   | 1 |     | 1   | 1 | 1   | 1 |     | 1   | 0   |     | 1   | 0 | 1/2 | 1 |     | 1   | 1 | 1   | 1 |

| $\to_{OL}$ | 0 | 1/2 | 1 |     | $\to_{DF}$ | 0 | 1/2 | 1 |     | $\to_F$ | 0 | 1/2 | 1 |
|---|---|---|---|---|---|---|---|---|---|---|---|---|---|
| 0   | 1/2 | 1/2 | 1/2 |   | 0   | 1/2 | 1/2 | 1/2 |   | 0   | 1/2 | 1/2 | 1/2 |
| 1/2 | 0   | 1/2 | 1   |   | 1/2 | 1/2 | 1/2 | 1   |   | 1/2 | 0   | 1/2 | 1/2 |
| 1   | 0   | 1/2 | 1   |   | 1   | 0   | 1/2 | 1   |   | 1   | 0   | 1/2 | 1   |

**Fig. 1.** Connectives of logics of indicative conditionals.

The above constraints determine a family of three-valued propositional *logics of indicative conditionals*, which turn out to be incomparable with classical two-valued logic[1]. For further background and motivation we refer to the papers [11–13], which constitute the main bibliographical source and starting point of the our own research. The more recent papers [20, 27] aimed at obtain-

---

[1] For instance, they may be *connexive* in that they validate the (non-classically valid) formulas known as *Aristotle's* and *Boethius'* theses, respectively: (i) $\neg(\varphi \to \neg\varphi)$ and (ii) $(\varphi \to \psi) \to \neg(\varphi \to \neg\psi)$; $(\varphi \to \neg\psi) \to \neg(\varphi \to \psi)$.

ing a deeper insight—from an algebraic and a proof-theoretic point of view—into Cooper's *logic of ordinary discourse* [10] (formally defined below), with a particular focus on its structural version (dubbed sOL). We established the algebraizability of sOL, studied its algebraic counterpart [27], and provided modular Hilbert-style axiomatizations for the logic in the full language as well as for a number of its fragments [20]. In [28], the focus was expanded to include also the logics introduced by De Finetti, Cantwell and Farrell, classifying each system according to the criteria of algebraic logic.

The present paper continues this work, focusing on the challenges one faces when trying to axiomatize these systems by means of Hilbert-style calculi. In some cases this is relatively straightforward, but the calculi thus obtained are neither standard nor easily readable. We shall therefore resort to a roundabout but systematic route: we will characterize each logic by a (partial non-deterministic) matrix, and show how to produce analytic multiple-conclusion Hilbert-style calculi that are complete with respect to this semantics. We shall then proceed to show that, in all cases, the calculi thus obtained can be straightforwardly converted, by a uniform procedure, into traditional single-conclusion Hilbert-style axiomatizations.

Space limitations oblige us to consider a limited array of logics, but our approach goes beyond the ones to be found in the existing literature: by way of example, we will look at some variations obtained by changing basic parameters (in particular, the designated elements) which appear natural, at least from a formal point of view.

A standard way of introducing a propositional logic is to fix an algebra $\mathbf{A}$ together with a subset $D \subseteq A$ of *designated elements* to be preserved in derivations. Such a pair $\langle \mathbf{A}, D \rangle$ is known as a *(logical) matrix* and (following e.g. [1]) we may unambiguously denote by $\mathrm{Log}\langle \mathbf{A}, D \rangle$ the (single-conclusion) propositional consequence relation determined by the matrix $\langle \mathbf{A}, D \rangle$[2]. For the logics of interest here, the universe of the algebra is always going to be the three-element set $A_3 := \{\mathbf{0}, 1/2, \mathbf{1}\}$, with variations only in the algebraic operations considered, and possibly the set of designated values. Along the paper, we will also work with a multiple-conclusion version of these logics, to be defined in Sect. 2.

**De Finettian Logics.** The logic DF proposed by De Finetti [17] is $\mathrm{Log}\langle\mathbf{DF_3},\{1/2, \mathbf{1}\}\rangle$, where $\mathbf{DF_3} := \langle A_3; \wedge_\mathsf{K}, \vee_\mathsf{K}, \to_\mathsf{DF}, \neg \rangle$. Alternatively, this algebra can be presented in the language $\{\wedge_\mathsf{K}, \vee_\mathsf{K}, \neg, 1/2\}$, replacing the implication $\to_\mathsf{DF}$ by the constant $1/2$. Both presentations are equivalent through the following definitions: $x \to_\mathsf{DF} y = (1/2 \wedge_\mathsf{K} \neg x) \vee_\mathsf{K} (x \wedge_\mathsf{K} y)$, and $1/2 := \neg x \to_\mathsf{DF} (x \to_\mathsf{DF} x)$. The implication-free presentation allows us to view DF as a conservative expansion of Priest's *Logic of Paradox* [26] obtained by just adding the propositional constant $1/2$ to its language. This, in turn, allows one to import key results from Priest's logic (see especially [1]). Likewise, on an algebraic level, the algebraic models of DF may be viewed as a class of *Kleene lattices* [1, Sec. 2.2] enriched with an

---

[2] Likewise, a family of matrices $\{\mathbb{M}_i : i \in I\}$ uniquely determines a logic $\mathrm{Log}\{\mathbb{M}_i : i \in I\}$ given by the intersection of each $\mathrm{Log}\,\mathbb{M}_i$.

extra constant $1/2$ (known as the *center*) required to satisfy $\neg 1/2 = 1/2$: these are known as *centered Kleene lattices* [9].

On an algebraic level, DF inherits the following properties from the Logic of Paradox (see [28] for proofs and further details): (i) DF is non-self-extensional and non-protoalgebraic, hence also non-algebraizable (see [1,18,19,28] for these formal definitions and further background); (ii) DF is, however, truth-equational[3]; (iii) DF may be axiomatized by extending any complete calculus for Priest's LP (see e.g. [1]) with the two rules $\vdash 1/2$ and $\vdash \neg 1/2$; (iv) Further adding the constants $\mathbf{0}, \mathbf{1}$ does not change the above picture.

As DF may be viewed as an expansion of the Logic of Paradox by a single constant, so also a similar strategy may be applied to two other logics defined from Kleene lattices, yielding two natural variations on DF first considered in [28]. *Strong Kleene logic* may be defined as $\mathrm{Log}\langle \mathbf{DF_3}, \{1\}\rangle$ if we view the algebra $\mathbf{DF_3}$ as a pure Kleene lattice (i.e. not including the constant $1/2$ in the language); likewise, *Kleene's logic of order* is given by $\mathrm{Log}\{\langle \mathbf{DF_3}, \{1\}\rangle, \langle \mathbf{DF_3}, \{1/2, 1\}\rangle\}$. Adding suitable rules to their Kleene counterparts, we can obtain an order-preserving *semilattice-based logic*[4] and a $\mathbf{1}$-*assertional*[5] De Finettian logic ($\mathrm{DF}^1$).

$\mathrm{DF}^{\wedge \mathrm{K}}$ is the semilattice-based logic of the variety of centered Kleene lattices, having $\wedge_\mathrm{K}$ as a conjunction, and can be axiomatized by extending any complete calculus for Kleene's logic of order (see e.g. [1, Thm. 3.4]) with the rules $1/2 \vee_\mathrm{K} p \vdash \neg 1/2 \vee_\mathrm{K} p$ and $\neg 1/2 \vee_\mathrm{K} p \vdash 1/2 \vee_\mathrm{K} p$.

$\mathrm{DF}^1 := \mathrm{Log}\langle \mathbf{DF_3}, \{1\}\rangle$—by definition, a strengthening of $\mathrm{DF}^{\wedge \mathrm{K}}$—is the $\mathbf{1}$-assertional logic associated to centered Kleene lattices. As shown in [28], this logic is axiomatized by extending any calculus for $\mathrm{DF}^{\wedge \mathrm{K}}$ with the *disjunctive syllogism* rule: $p \wedge (\neg p \vee q) \vdash q$.

**Logics of Ordinary Discourse.** Cooper's [10] *Logic of Ordinary Discourse* (OL) represents perhaps a more radical departure from classical reasoning than any of the systems mentioned heretofore. Indeed, OL is not Tarskian due to its non-structural character: valuations are forbidden to assign the middle value $1/2$ to propositional letters. Furthermore, OL has not only a connexive implication

---

[3] Algebraizability implies that, on every standard matrix model of a logic L, the designated elements are definable by the witnessing transformer $\tau$. Logics verifying this weaker condition are called *truth-equational*. An important fact that shall often be used in our discussions without further notice is that many logical properties of interest (save for self-extensionality) are preserved by strengthenings: thus, showing that L is not algebraizable (protoalgebraic, etc.) is sufficient to conclude that all logics weaker than L also lack that property.

[4] Order-preserving logics preserve *degrees* of truth rather than "absolute truth". Formally, a logic L is *semilattice-based* (relative to a binary term & and a class $\mathbb{K}$ of semilattices with order $\leq$) when, for every finite set of formulas $\varphi_1, \ldots, \varphi_n, \varphi$, one has $\varphi_1, \ldots, \varphi_n \vdash_\mathrm{L} \varphi$ if and only if $v(\varphi_1) \& \ldots \& v(\varphi_n) \leq v(\varphi)$, for every $\mathbf{A} \in \mathbb{K}$ and every $\mathbf{A}$-valuation $v$.

[5] Semilattice-based logics are contrasted with *($\tau$-)assertional* logics. For a class of algebras $\mathbb{K}$ and a transformer $\tau(x)$, the $\tau$-*assertional logic* of $\mathbb{K}$ is defined by: $\Gamma \vdash \varphi$ if and only if $\tau(\Gamma) \vDash_\mathbb{K} \tau(\varphi)$ for every $\mathbf{A} \in \mathbb{K}$. When $\tau(x)$ is one equation of the form $x \approx \mathbf{1}$ for a constant $\mathbf{1}$, the logic is called $\mathbf{1}$-assertional.

($\to_{OL}$), but also a conjunction ($\wedge_{OL}$) and disjunction ($\vee_{OL}$) that fail to satisfy the distributive law (namely, $(\varphi \wedge_{OL} \psi) \vee_{OL} (\varphi \wedge_{OL} \chi) \nvdash \varphi \wedge_{OL} (\psi \vee_{OL} \chi)$) and disjunction introduction ($\varphi \nvdash \varphi \vee_{OL} \psi$).

The papers [20,27] contain an algebraic and proof-theoretic study of OL, with particular focus on its structural version (sOL), which is obtained in the standard way as $\text{Log}\langle \mathbf{O}_3, \{1/2, 1\}\rangle$. sOL is algebraizable and has as equivalent algebraic semantics the variety $\mathbb{OL}$ of *OL-algebras*. In [27], a finite Hilbert-style axiomatization was introduced for sOL, from which a calculus for OL can be obtained by adding the single *explosion* rule ($p \wedge_{OL} \neg p \vdash q$) restricted to propositional variables.

The primitive language of OL/sOL (consisting of $\wedge_{OL}, \vee_{OL}, \to_{OL}$ and $\neg$) allows us to recover as terms a number of well-known three-valued connectives, notably Kleene's ($\wedge_K$ and $\vee_K$)[6]. The connectives $\wedge_K$, $\wedge_{OL}$ and $\vee_{OL}$ determine semilattice operations that give rise to three independent orderings on $\mathbf{O}_3$ (hence, on every OL-algebra) and to three corresponding logics of order. In addition to the Kleene order ($0 < 1/2 < 1$), we have an order having $\wedge_{OL}$ as meet ($0 < 1 < 1/2$) and one determined by $\vee_{OL}$ as a join-semilattice operation ($1/2 < 0 < 1$); note, in particular, that $\wedge_{OL}$ and $\vee_{OL}$ are not duals of one another. We thus obtain three semilattice-based logics: (i) $\text{OL}_{\wedge_{OL}} := \text{Log}\{\langle \mathbf{O}_3, \{1/2, 1\}\rangle, \langle \mathbf{O}_3, \{1/2\}\rangle\}$, (ii) $\text{OL}_{\wedge_K} := \text{Log}\{\langle \mathbf{O}_3, \{1\}\rangle, \langle \mathbf{O}_3, \{1/2, 1\}\rangle\}$, (iii) $\text{OL}_{\vee_{OL}} := \text{Log}\{\langle \mathbf{O}_3, \{1\}\rangle, \langle \mathbf{O}_3, \{0, 1\}\rangle\}$, as well as two assertional logics (namely, $\text{Log}\langle \mathbf{O}_3, \{1/2\}\rangle$ and $\text{Log}\langle \mathbf{O}_3, \{1\}\rangle$).

As noted in [28], the meet operation dual to $\vee_{OL}$ (denote it by $\vee_{OL}^\delta$) is definable as follows (recall that $\wedge_K$ is itself term-definable): $x \vee_{OL}^\delta y := ((x \vee_K y) \to_{OL} (x \vee_{OL} y)) \to_{OL} (x \wedge_K y)$. Similarly, we have that the join operation dual to $\wedge_{OL}$ (denote it by $\wedge_{OL}^\delta$) is definable as follows: $x \wedge_{OL}^\delta y := (\neg(x \wedge_K y) \to_{OL} \neg(x \wedge_{OL} y)) \to_{OL} (x \vee_K y)$. Thus, we have two lattices $\langle A_3; \vee_{OL}^\delta, \vee_{OL}\rangle$ and $\langle A_3; \wedge_{OL}, \wedge_{OL}^\delta\rangle$ besides the Kleene lattice $\langle A_3; \wedge_K, \vee_K\rangle$.

All the above-mentioned logics of ordinary discourse share the same algebraic counterpart (the variety of OL-algebras), but $\text{Log}\langle \mathbf{O}_3, \{1\}\rangle$ and $\text{Log}\langle \mathbf{O}_3, \{0, 1\}\rangle$ turn out to be non-protoalgebraic, hence also non-algebraizable, due to the lack of valid formulas (*a fortiori*, $\text{OL}_{\wedge_K}$ and $\text{OL}_{\vee_{OL}}$ are also non-algebraizable). However, all the assertional logics based on $\mathbf{O}_3$ become algebraizable if we expand the language with any non-definable constant ($\mathbf{1}$ or $\mathbf{0}$).

The algebraic counterpart of every such algebraizable logic L is the variety of (bounded, if $\mathbf{1}$ is present) OL-algebras. A finite Hilbert-style calculus for each L can then be obtained by translating the algebraic presentation of (bounded) OL-algebras introduced in [27] via the transformers that witness algebraizability. However, the calculi thus obtained may be highly non-standard and not easily readable. Simpler alternative axiomatizations, which are furthermore guaranteed

---

[6] The Kleene connectives may be defined as follows: $x \wedge_K y := (x \to_{OL} x) \vee_{OL} ((x \to_{OL} y) \to_{OL} y)$, $x \vee_K y := \neg(\neg x \wedge_K \neg y)$. The disjunction $\vee_{OL}$ may (and often will) be omitted from the signature, for $x \vee_{OL} y = \neg(\neg x \wedge_{OL} \neg y)$; each of the connectives in $\{\wedge_{OL}, \to_{OL}, \neg\}$ is independent of the other two.

to be analytic, may be obtained via a detour through multiple-conclusion calculi, as we will see.

**Conditional Negation (CN).** This logic—or slight variations thereof—seems to have been (re-)introduced independently by a number of authors at different times. Here, due to space limitations, we shall not deal with CN at any length, but a few observations may help to make the picture of logics of indicative conditionals more complete.

CN may be defined as $\mathrm{Log}\langle \mathbf{CN_3}, \{1/2, 1\}\rangle$, where $\mathbf{CN_3}$ is the three-element algebra in the language $\{\wedge_K, \vee_K, \to_{OL}, \neg\}$[7]. Its motivation and approach (as discussed, e.g., in [8]) are similar to Cooper's. In comparison to sOL, CN represents a less radical departure from classical logic, for while the implication is $\to_{OL}$, the conjunction and disjunction are the more standard (and subclassical) Kleene connectives $\wedge_K$ and $\vee_K$. Hence, CN is by definition a conservative expansion of both Priest's logic and De Finetti's DF.

CN may be viewed as an axiomatic strengthening of Wansing's connexive logic C [30, Sect. 4.5.1], which has been shown to be algebraizable [16]. It follows that CN is also algebraizable with respect to the class of *CN-algebras*, i.e. the variety generated by $\mathbf{CN_3}$ [16, Thm. 50].

As in the previous cases, one may consider variations of CN defined from the same underlying three-element algebra. Regarding assertional logics induced by the matrices $\langle \mathbf{CN_3}, \{1/2\}\rangle$ and $\langle \mathbf{CN_3}, \{1\}\rangle$, one can easily establish the following [28]:

(i) $\mathrm{CN}^{1/2} := \mathrm{Log}\langle \mathbf{CN_3}, \{1/2\}\rangle$ is also algebraizable, and has the class of CN-algebras as its equivalent algebraic counterpart.
(ii) $\mathrm{CN}^{1} := \mathrm{Log}\langle \mathbf{CN_3}, \{1\}\rangle$ is not algebraizable (as before, due to lack of valid formulas ). Algebraizability may be achieved by adding **1** to the language.

The study of CN semilattice-based systems shall be left for further research.

To conclude this brief review, let us mention the logic introduced by R.J. Farrell [14] (see also [15]), defined as $\mathrm{Log}\langle \mathbf{F_3}, \{1/2, 1\}\rangle$, where $\mathbf{F_3}$ is the three-element algebra in the language $\{\wedge_K, \vee_K, \to_F, \neg\}$. Farrell's motivation and discussion are somewhat broader than Cooper's and Cantwell's, for in [14,15] the middle value $1/2$ is read as *inappropriate* (or, "to be ignored"), inappropriate being not only (composite) conditionals with a false antecedent (as in Cooper and Cantwell), but also (atomic) propositions that are ambiguous or expressed in a language that is unfamiliar (to a given audient or reader). Formally, Farrell's logic is identical with CN save for the table of the implication. In fact, both logics are definitionally equivalent, for one can construct $\to_{OL}$ as a term in Farrell's system and, vice-versa, $\to_F$ as a term in CN [28]. The equivalence can be readily verified by direct inspection on Fig. 1. Within Farrell's logic we can define $x \to_{OL} y := \neg((y \to_F x) \to_F \neg y) \to_F ((x \vee_K y) \to_F y)$, and, conversely, in CN

---

[7] Since the Kleene operations are definable in $\mathbf{O_3}$, every OL-algebra has a term-definable CN-algebra structure: thus, CN may be viewed as a sublogic of sOL. One may verify that the OL-algebra operations (e.g. $\wedge_{OL}$) are *not* definable on CN-algebras.

we can let $x \to_F y := x \to_{OL} (x \wedge_K y)$. We may thus regard logics that may be obtained as variations of Farrell—also to be addressed in future research—as essentially notational variations of Conditional Negation.

The above-introduced logics, together with their principal algebraic properties, are summed up in Table 1.

**Table 1.** Logics of indicative conditionals: matrix semantics and algebraic properties. (✓) indicates that the property only holds if the language is expanded with the constant 1. By 'Self' below, we mean 'self-extensional'.

| Log. | Alg. | Desig. | Alg. | Proto. | Truth-Eq. | Self | Algebras |
|---|---|---|---|---|---|---|---|
| DF | $DF_3$ | $\{1/2, 1\}$ | | | | ✓ | CK (centered Kleene lattices) |
| $DF^{\wedge K}$ | $DF_3$ | $\{1\}, \{1/2, 1\}$ | | | | ✓ | CK |
| $DF^1$ | $DF_3$ | $\{1\}$ | | | (✓) | | CK |
| sOL | $OL_3$ | $\{1/2, 1\}$ | ✓ | ✓ | | ✓ | OL (OL-algebras) |
| $OL_{\wedge_{OL}}$ | $OL_3$ | $\{1/2, 1\}, \{1/2\}$ | ? | | | ✓ | OL |
| $OL_{\wedge_K}$ | $OL_3$ | $\{1\}, \{1/2, 1\}$ | | | | ✓ | OL |
| $OL_{\vee_{OL}}$ | $OL_3$ | $\{1\}, \{0, 1\}$ | | | | ✓ | OL |
| $OL^1$ | $OL_3$ | $\{1\}$ | (✓) | (✓) | (✓) | | $OL^1$ (bounded OL-algebras) |
| $OL^{01}$ | $OL_3$ | $\{0, 1\}$ | (✓) | (✓) | (✓) | | $OL^1$ |
| $OL^{1/2}$ | $OL_3$ | $\{1/2\}$ | ✓ | ✓ | ✓ | | OL |
| CN | $CN_3$ | $\{1/2, 1\}$ | ✓ | ✓ | ✓ | | CN (CN-algebras) |
| $CN^{1/2}$ | $CN_3$ | $\{1/2\}$ | ✓ | ✓ | ✓ | | CN |
| $CN^1$ | $CN_3$ | $\{1\}$ | (✓) | (✓) | (✓) | | $CN^1$ (bounded CN-algebras) |
| F | $F_3$ | $\{1/2, 1\}$ | ✓ | ✓ | ✓ | | CN |

## 2 Preliminaries

**Languages and Logics.** A *propositional signature* $\Sigma$ is a collection of *connectives*; to each of them is assigned a natural number called *arity*. We write ⓒ $\in \Sigma_k$ to mean that ⓒ has arity $k \in \mathbb{N}$. Given a countable set $P$ of propositional variables, the *language over $\Sigma$ generated by $P$* is the algebra of terms over $\Sigma$ freely generated by $P$, denoted $\mathbf{L}_\Sigma(P)$. Its carrier is denoted by $L_\Sigma(P)$ and its elements are called *formulas*. Endomorphisms on $\mathbf{L}_\Sigma(P)$ are called *substitutions*. We denote by $\mathsf{subf}(\varphi)$ the collection of all subformulas of a formula $\varphi$.

A *single-conclusion logic (over $\Sigma$)* is a consequence relation $\vdash$ on $L_\Sigma(P)$ and a *multiple-conclusion logic (over $\Sigma$)* is a generalized consequence relation $\rhd$ on $L_\Sigma(P)$—see [23, Secs. 1.12, 1.16] for details. In particular, multiple-conclusion logics satisfy (O)verlap, (D)ilution and (C)ut [29]: (O) if $\Phi \cap \Psi \neq \varnothing$, then $\Phi \rhd \Psi$; (D) if $\Phi \rhd \Psi$, then $\Phi, \Phi' \rhd \Psi, \Psi'$; and (C) if $\Pi, \Phi \rhd \Psi, \overline{\Pi}$ for all $\Pi \subseteq L_\Sigma(P)$, then $\Phi \triangleright \Psi$, which generalize the properties of reflexivity, monotonicity and cut from single-conclusion (Tarskian) logics. The *single-conclusion companion* of a given multiple-conclusion logic $\triangleright$ is the single-conclusion logic $\vdash_\triangleright$ such that $\Phi \vdash_\triangleright \psi$ if, and only if, $\Phi \triangleright \{\psi\}$. We adopt the convention of omitting curly braces when writing sets of formulas in statements involving (generalized) consequence relations. The complement of a given $\triangleright$, i.e., $\mathcal{P}(L_\Sigma(P)) \times \mathcal{P}(L_\Sigma(P)) \setminus \triangleright$, will be denoted by $\blacktriangleright$.

**Hilbert-Style Calculi.** A *multiple-conclusion Hilbert calculus* over $\Sigma$ is traditionally defined as a collection R of *multiple-conclusion rules* r of the form $\frac{\Phi}{\Psi}$, where $\Phi, \Psi \subseteq L_\Sigma(P)$ are called, respectively, the antecedent and the succedent of the rule. Given a substitution $\sigma$, $r^\sigma := \frac{\sigma[\Phi]}{\sigma[\Psi]}$ is called a *rule instance of* r. When writing rules, we usually omit curly braces from the set notation. (See e.g., Fig. 2.) A *proof* of $(\Gamma, \Pi)$ in R is a finite directed rooted tree where each node is labelled either with a set of formulas or with the discontinuation symbol $\star$, such that (i) the root is labelled with a superset of $\Gamma$; (ii) every leaf is labelled either with a set having non-empty intersection with $\Pi$ or with $\star$; (iii) every non-leaf node has children determined by a substitution instance of a rule of inference of R, in the way we now detail. A rule instance $r^\sigma$ applies to a node n when the antecedent of $r^\sigma$ is contained in the label of n. The application results in n having exactly one child node for each formula $\psi$ in the succedent of $r^\sigma$, which is, in turn, labelled with the same formulas as those of (the label of) n plus $\psi$. In case $r^\sigma$ has an empty succedent, then n has a single child node labelled with $\star$. When we display proof trees, it is common to write as labels only the formulas introduced by the rule application, instead of the whole accumulated set of formulas (see Example 1). *Single-conclusion Hilbert calculi* are then just the traditional Hilbert calculi, which can be seen as multiple-conclusion calculi in which only rules of the form $\frac{\Phi}{\psi}$ are allowed, where $\Phi \subseteq L_\Sigma(P)$ and $\psi \in L_\Sigma(P)$. Derivations then can be seen as linear trees, usually displayed simply as sequences of formulas.

We write $\Gamma \triangleright_\mathsf{R} \Psi$ whenever there is a proof of $(\Gamma, \Psi)$ in R. Similarly, we write $\Gamma \vdash_\mathsf{R} \psi$ whenever there is a proof of $(\Gamma, \{\psi\})$ in R. The relation $\triangleright_\mathsf{R}$ is known to be a substitution-invariant multiple-conclusion logic. We say that a Hilbert calculus R *axiomatizes* $\vdash$ in case $\vdash = \vdash_\mathsf{R}$.

A multiple-conclusion Hilbert calculus R is $\Theta$-*analytic*, for $\Theta(p)$ a set of unary formulas, whenever $\Phi \triangleright_\mathsf{R} \Psi$ is witnessed by a derivation using only subformulas of $\Phi \cup \Psi$ or formulas in $\bigcup_{\gamma \in \mathsf{subf}(\Phi \cup \Psi)} \Theta(\gamma)$; in this case, we write $\Phi \triangleright_\mathsf{R}^\Theta \Psi$. Note that $\triangleright_\mathsf{R}^\Theta$ satisfies dilution, cut and overlap. As discussed in [6], $\Theta$-analyticity for finite calculi induces a straightforward exponential-time proof-search procedure. Indeed, to check whether $\Phi \triangleright_\mathsf{R}^\Theta \Psi$, one starts with a node labelled with $\Phi$ and applies the rule instances of R that do not produce formulas outside the allowed ones. Rules that produce a repeated formula do not need to be applied. Then either one reaches a proof of the statement, or extracts a countermodel from the resulting tree. Fully developed examples for both cases may be found in [22]. Thus, if the calculus axiomatizes the logic of a finite matrix, we have an alternative to the truth-table procedure for deciding the induced logic.

**From Multiple- to Single-Conclusion Calculi.** Hilbert-style calculi are a standard way of presenting a logic as a single-conclusion consequence relation, especially in an algebraic logic context. As we are going to see, one can automatically produce *analytic* and *finite* multiple-conclusion calculi from a finite logical matrix. For single-conclusion calculi this is not always the case: indeed, certain finite matrices cannot be finitely axiomatized in single conclusion [25]. It is therefore especially useful to establish sufficient conditions for converting a finite multiple-conclusion calculus into a finite single-conclusion one.

Let ⊢ be a single-conclusion logic over $L_\Sigma(P)$ and ⓒ be a definable connective in $L_\Sigma(P)$. We say that ⓒ is a *disjunction* in ⊢ whenever $\Gamma, \varphi$ ⓒ $\psi \vdash \gamma$ iff $\Gamma, \varphi \vdash \gamma$ and $\Gamma, \psi \vdash \gamma$, for all $\Gamma \cup \{\varphi, \psi, \gamma\} \subseteq L_\Sigma(P)$. Given a multiple-conclusion calculus R, and a disjunction ⊕ in ⊢$_R$, we can convert R into a single-conclusion calculus R$^\oplus$ such that ⊢$_R$ = ⊢$_{R^\oplus}$ [29, Thm. 5.37]. Let us see how the conversion is effected. In what follows, given a set of formulas $\Phi$, let $\Phi \oplus \psi := \{\varphi \oplus \psi : \varphi \in \Phi\}$ and $\bigoplus\{\varphi_1, \ldots, \varphi_m\} := \varphi_1 \oplus (\varphi_2 \oplus \ldots (\ldots \oplus \varphi_n)\ldots)$.

**Definition 1.** *Let R be a multiple-conclusion calculus and ⊕ be a binary connective. We define R$^\oplus$ as the single-conclusion calculus*

$$\left\{\frac{p \oplus p}{p}, \frac{p}{p \oplus q}, \frac{p \oplus q}{q \oplus p}, \frac{p \oplus (q \oplus r)}{(p \oplus q) \oplus r}\right\} \cup \{r^\oplus \mid r \in R\}$$

*where* $r^\oplus$ *is* $\frac{\varnothing}{\bigoplus \Psi}$ *if* $r = \frac{\varnothing}{\Psi}$, $\frac{\Phi \oplus p_0}{(\bigoplus \Psi) \oplus p_0}$ *if* $r = \frac{\Phi}{\Psi}$, *and* $\frac{\Phi \oplus p_0}{p_0}$ *if* $r = \frac{\Phi}{\varnothing}$, *for $p_0$ a propositional variable not occurring in r.*

We thus have a recipe for converting multiple- into single-conclusion calculi, provided a disjunction is available. Note, however, that the conversion does not preserve analyticity. The lack of analyticity in traditional calculi is exactly what is remedied by multiple-conclusion calculi, for these are the calculi that are closest to the logic (differently from tableaux and sequent calculi, no metalanguage is essentially employed) while being still analytic. The following result, though straightforward, is crucial to our approach.

**Proposition 1.** *Every logic considered in the paper has a disjunction in the above-defined sense (see Table 1 for definitions).*

*Proof.* It suffices to observe that, on every algebra based on $A_3$, every set of designated elements is a prime filter of some lattice order. We can thus take as a disjunction the join (which is always term-definable, as we have seen) corresponding to the appropriate lattice order. ∎

**PNmatrices.** A *partial nondeterministic matrix* (PNmatrix) generalizes the notion of logical matrix by having a *multialgebra* instead of an algebra as interpretation structure. Multialgebras are generalizations of algebras that interpret the $k$-ary operation symbols not as functions of type $A^k \to A$ but as *multifunctions* of type $A^k \to \mathcal{P}(A)$. The notion of logic induced by a PNmatrix is defined in the same way as in logical matrices, with the difference that valuations are mappings $v : L_\Sigma(P) \to A$ satisfying

$$v(\copyright(\varphi_1,\ldots,\varphi_k)) \in \copyright_\mathbf{A}(v(\varphi_1),\ldots,v(\varphi_k)). \qquad (1)$$

Let $\mathbb{M} := \langle \mathbf{A}, D \rangle$ be a PNmatrix. The multiple-conclusion logic defined by $\mathbb{M}$, denoted by $\rhd_\mathbb{M}$, is such that $\Phi \rhd_\mathbb{M} \Psi$ iff, for every valuation over $\mathbb{M}$, $v[\Phi] \subseteq D$ implies $v[\Psi] \cap D \neq \varnothing$. Whenever $\Phi \rhd_\mathbb{M} \Psi$ holds we say that the multiple-conclusion rule $\frac{\Phi}{\Psi}$ is *valid* in $\mathbb{M}$. The single-conclusion logic defined by $\mathbb{M}$ is simply $\vdash_{\rhd_\mathbb{M}}$. Any formula $\varphi$ in $k$ variables $p_1,\ldots,p_k$ defines a derived connective that is the multifunction given by $\varphi_\mathbf{A}(a_1,\ldots,a_k) = \{v(\varphi) :$ for a valuation over $\mathbb{M}$ with $v(p_i) = a_i\}$.

For $X \subseteq A$, denote by $\mathbb{M}_X$ the PNmatrix $\langle \mathbf{A}_X, D \cap X \rangle$, where $\mathbf{A}_X := \langle A \cap X, \cdot_{\mathbf{A}_X} \rangle$ is a multialgebra such that $\copyright_{\mathbf{A}_X}(a_1,\ldots,a_k) := \copyright_\mathbf{A}(a_1,\ldots,a_k) \cap X$ for all $a_1,\ldots,a_k \in X$, $k \in \mathbb{N}$ and $\copyright \in \Sigma_k$. This PNmatrix is called *the restriction of $\mathbb{M}$ to $X$*. We say that $X \neq \varnothing$ is a *total component* of $\mathbb{M}$ whenever $\mathbb{M}_X$ is total. A total component $X$ is *maximal* if adding any other value to $X$ leads to a component that is not total. Denote by $\mathbb{T}(\mathbb{M})$ the collection of maximal total components of $\mathbb{M}$. Then we have that $\rhd_\mathbb{M} = \rhd_{\{\mathbb{M}_X : X \in \mathbb{T}(\mathbb{M})\}}$ and $\vdash_\mathbb{M} = \vdash_{\{\mathbb{M}_X : X \in \mathbb{T}(\mathbb{M})\}}$ [7], where by $\rhd_\mathcal{M}$ and $\vdash_\mathcal{M}$, with $\mathcal{M}$ a family of PNmatrices, we mean the intersections of the logics of each matrix in $\mathcal{M}$.

It is known that if $f : S \to A$ is a mapping, where $S \subseteq L_\Sigma(P)$ and $S$ is closed under subformulas, $f$ extends to a homomorphism from the full language $L_\Sigma(P)$ provided $f[S]$ is a subset of values of a total component of $\mathbb{M}$, and Eq. 1 is satisfied for every connective and formulas in $S$ [6]. This result is key for producing countermodels in completeness and analyticity proofs.

**Monadicity and Analyticity.** A PNmatrix $\mathbb{M} := \langle \mathbf{A}, D \rangle$ is *monadic* if there is a unary formula $S(p) \in L_\Sigma(\{p\})$, sometimes called a *separator*, for each pair of truth values $x, y \in A$, such that $S_\mathbf{A}(x) \subseteq D$ and $S_\mathbf{A}(y) \subseteq A \setminus D$ or vice-versa. It is proved in [29] that every finite matrix is finitely axiomatizable by a multiple-conclusion calculus. This result was extended in [6] showing that, when a PNmatrix is monadic, a finite calculus can be effectively generated from the PNmatrix description and is $\Theta$-analytic, where $\Theta$ is the set of separators[8]. The key element is to build a *discriminator for* $\mathbb{M}$, i.e. a family $\{(\Omega_a, \mho_a)\}_{a \in A}$ such that $\Omega_a \cup \mho_a$ completely characterizes every $a \in A$, in the sense that for every valuation $v$ over $\mathbb{M}$ and formula $\varphi$, $v(\varphi) = a$ if and only if $v(\Omega_a(\varphi)) \subseteq D$ and $v(\mho_a(\varphi)) \subseteq \overline{D}$.

---

[8] Similar effective bridges between generalized matrix semantics and proof calculi have been extensively studied in the literature [2–5]. These works, however, resort to metalinguistic objects like sequents, $n$-sequents and semantic labels, while multiple-conclusion calculi keep the metalanguage to a minimum. Indeed, a multiple-conclusion calculus constitutes a logical basis for the logic it axiomatizes, which is particularly useful for the algebraic study of such logics.

## 3  Axiomatizing Single-Matrix Logics

The axiomatization procedure mentioned at the end of the previous section works for any finite monadic PNmatrix. Now, in a three-valued logic, note that if $\neg$ from Fig. 1 is available and $D = \{1\}$, then $\neg p$ separates $1/2$ and $\mathbf{0}$; and if $D = \{1/2, 1\}$, then it separates $1/2$ and $\mathbf{1}$. From this, we get a particular instance of the procedure that applies to many of our (three-valued) logics, namely:

**Theorem 1.** *Let $\Sigma$ be a signature such that $\neg \in \Sigma$ and $\mathbb{M}$ be a three-valued $\Sigma$-matrix that interprets $\neg$ as in Fig. 1 and has $\{1/2, 1\}$ or $\{1\}$ as designated set. Then $\rhd_\mathbb{M}$ is axiomatized by the $\{p, \neg p\}$-analytic calculus*

$$\mathsf{R} := \bigcup_{\copyright \in \Sigma} \mathsf{R}_\copyright,$$

*where each set $\mathsf{R}_\copyright$, $\copyright \in \Sigma$, is generated by the procedure of [6], detailed in [21] for the particular case of logics of three-valued matrices.*

The above procedure is quite modular: if a new connective is added to the semantics, it is readily axiomatized because the discriminator only depends on the presence of $\neg$. As we will see, we will use these calculi as a basis for the calculi for many of the logics considered here. From these base systems, analytic systems for other logics will be obtained by simply adding new rules. For the cases where the designated set is $\{\mathbf{1}, 1/2\}$, we have the base systems displayed in Fig. 2. When it is $\{\mathbf{1}\}$, we have the base systems displayed in Fig. 3. Adequacy and analyticity of these calculi follow from the general proofs in [6]. For what follows, we let $\mathsf{R}_1 := \{\frac{\varnothing}{\top}\}$.

$\mathsf{R}_\neg^{\{1,1/2\}}$

$$\dfrac{p}{\neg\neg p}\,r_1^\neg \qquad \dfrac{\neg\neg p}{p}\,r_2^\neg \qquad \dfrac{}{p,\neg p}\,r_3^\neg$$

$\mathsf{R}_{\wedge_{OL}}^{\{1,1/2\}}$

$$\dfrac{p\wedge q}{p}\,r_1^\wedge \quad \dfrac{p\wedge q}{q}\,r_2^\wedge \quad \dfrac{p,q}{p\wedge q}\,r_3^\wedge \quad \dfrac{p\wedge q, \neg(p\wedge q)}{\neg p}\,r_4^\wedge \quad \dfrac{p\wedge q, \neg(p\wedge q)}{\neg q}\,r_5^\wedge \quad \dfrac{\neg p, \neg q}{\neg(p\wedge q)}\,r_6^\wedge$$

$\mathsf{R}_{\wedge_K}^{\{1,1/2\}}$

$$\dfrac{p\wedge q}{p}\,r_1^\wedge \quad \dfrac{p\wedge q}{q}\,r_2^\wedge \quad \dfrac{p,q}{p\wedge q}\,r_3^\wedge \quad \dfrac{\neg(p\wedge q)}{\neg p,\neg q}\,r_9^\wedge \quad \dfrac{\neg p}{\neg(p\wedge q)}\,r_{10}^\wedge \quad \dfrac{\neg q}{\neg(p\wedge q)}\,r_{11}^\wedge$$

**Fig. 2.** Multiple-conclusion rules for some connectives, when $D = \{\mathbf{1}, 1/2\}$.

**De Finetti's Logic.** By Theorem 1, an analytic calculus for DF is witnessed by $\mathsf{R}_\neg^{\{1,1/2\}} \cup \mathsf{R}_{\wedge_K}^{\{1,1/2\}} \cup \mathsf{R}_{\to_{DF}}^{\{1,1/2\}}$, where $\mathsf{R}_{\to_{DF}}^{\{1,1/2\}}$ consists of the following rules:

$$\dfrac{}{p\to q, p}\,r_1^\to \qquad \dfrac{}{\neg(p\to q), p}\,r_2^\to \qquad \dfrac{}{\neg(p\to q), q}\,r_3^\to \qquad \dfrac{p\to q}{\neg p, q}\,r_4^\to$$

$$\frac{p \to q}{p} r_{10}^{\to} \qquad \frac{p \to q}{q} r_{11}^{\to} \qquad \frac{\neg(p \to q)}{\neg q} r_{12}^{\to} \qquad \frac{\neg(p \to q)}{p} r_{13}^{\to} \qquad \frac{p, \neg q}{\neg(p \to q)} r_{14}^{\to} \qquad \frac{p, q}{p \to q} r_{15}^{\to}$$

$R_{\neg}^{\{1\}}$

$$\frac{p}{\neg\neg p} r_{1}^{\neg} \qquad \frac{\neg\neg p}{p} r_{2}^{\neg} \qquad \frac{p, \neg p}{} r_{4}^{\neg}$$

$R_{\wedge_{OL}}^{\{1\}}$

$$\frac{p, q}{p \wedge q} r_{3}^{\wedge} \qquad \frac{p}{p \wedge q, \neg q} r_{7}^{\wedge} \qquad \frac{q}{p \wedge q, \neg p} r_{8}^{\wedge} \qquad \frac{\neg(p \wedge q)}{\neg p, \neg q} r_{9}^{\wedge} \qquad \frac{\neg p}{\neg(p \wedge q)} r_{10}^{\wedge} \qquad \frac{\neg q}{\neg(p \wedge q)} r_{11}^{\wedge}$$

$$\frac{p \wedge q}{p, q} r_{12}^{\wedge} \qquad \frac{p \wedge q, \neg p}{} r_{13}^{\wedge} \qquad \frac{p \wedge q, \neg q}{} r_{14}^{\wedge} \qquad \frac{p}{p \wedge q, \neg(p \wedge q)} r_{15}^{\wedge} \qquad \frac{q}{p \wedge q, \neg(p \wedge q)} r_{16}^{\wedge}$$

$R_{\wedge_K}^{\{1\}}$

$$\frac{p \wedge q}{p} r_{1}^{\wedge} \qquad \frac{p \wedge q}{q} r_{2}^{\wedge} \qquad \frac{p, q}{p \wedge q} r_{3}^{\wedge}$$

$$\frac{\neg(p \wedge q)}{\neg p, \neg q} r_{9}^{\wedge} \qquad \frac{\neg p}{\neg(p \wedge q)} r_{10}^{\wedge} \qquad \frac{\neg q}{\neg(p \wedge q)} r_{11}^{\wedge} \qquad \frac{\neg(p \wedge q), p}{\neg q} r_{17}^{\wedge} \qquad \frac{\neg(p \wedge q), q}{\neg p} r_{18}^{\wedge}$$

**Fig. 3.** Multiple-conclusion rules for some connectives, when $D = \{1\}$.

$$\frac{\neg(p \to q)}{\neg p, \neg q} r_{5}^{\to} \qquad \frac{\neg p}{p \to q} r_{6}^{\to} \qquad \frac{\neg p}{\neg(p \to q)} r_{7}^{\to} \qquad \frac{\neg q}{\neg(p \to q)} r_{8}^{\to} \qquad \frac{q}{p \to q} r_{9}^{\to}$$

**Variations of** DF. Following Theorem 1, an analytic calculus for $\mathrm{DF}^1$ is given by $R_{\neg}^{\{1\}} \cup R_{\wedge_K}^{\{1\}} \cup R_{\to_{DF}}^{\{1\}}$, where $R_{\to_{DF}}^{\{1\}}$ is defined as including:

$$\frac{p \to q}{p} r_{10}^{\to} \qquad \frac{p \to q}{q} r_{11}^{\to} \qquad \frac{\neg(p \to q)}{\neg q} r_{12}^{\to} \qquad \frac{\neg(p \to q)}{p} r_{13}^{\to} \qquad \frac{p, \neg q}{\neg(p \to q)} r_{14}^{\to} \qquad \frac{p, q}{p \to q} r_{15}^{\to}$$

**Logics of Ordinary Discourse.** By Theorem 1, we can provide analytic calculi for OL and $\mathrm{OL}^1$ as follows. For the former case, take $R_{\neg}^{\{1,1/2\}}$, $R_{\wedge_{OL}}^{\{1,1/2\}}$ and $R_{\to_{OL}}^{\{1,1/2\}}$, where $R_{\to_{OL}}^{\{1,1/2\}}$ is formed by:

$$\frac{}{p \to q, p} r_{1}^{\to} \qquad \frac{}{\neg(p \to q), p} r_{2}^{\to} \qquad \frac{\neg q}{\neg(p \to q)} r_{8}^{\to} \qquad \frac{q}{p \to q} r_{9}^{\to} \qquad \frac{p, p \to q}{q} r_{16}^{\to} \qquad \frac{\neg(p \to q), p}{\neg q} r_{17}^{\to}$$

For $\mathrm{OL}^1$, we can select $R_{\neg}^{\{1\}}, R_{\wedge_{OL}}^{\{1\}}, R_1$ and $R_{\to_{OL}}^{\{1\}}$, where $R_{\to_{OL}}^{\{1\}}$ consists of the rules:

$$\frac{p \to q}{q} r_{11}^{\to} \qquad \frac{\neg(p \to q)}{\neg q} r_{12}^{\to} \qquad \frac{p, \neg q}{\neg(p \to q)} r_{14}^{\to} \qquad \frac{p, q}{p \to q} r_{15}^{\to} \qquad \frac{p \to q, \neg p}{} r_{18}^{\to}$$

$$\frac{\neg(p \to q), \neg p}{} r_{19}^{\to} \qquad \frac{\neg(p \to q), q}{} r_{20}^{\to} \qquad \frac{\neg q}{\neg(p \to q), \neg p} r_{21}^{\to} \qquad \frac{q}{p \to q, \neg p} r_{22}^{\to}$$

**Conditional Negation and Farrell's Logic.** Theorem 1 provides a way of obtaining analytic calculi for $CN, CN^1$ and F. In the first case, pick $R_{\neg}^{\{1,1/2\}}, R_{\wedge_K}^{\{1,1/2\}}$ and $R_{\rightarrow_{OL}}^{\{1,1/2\}}$. In the second case, we can similarly pick $R_{\neg}^{\{1\}}, R_{\wedge_K}^{\{1\}}$, $R_1$ and $R_{\rightarrow_{OL}}^{\{1\}}$. Finally, for F, we can select $R_{\neg}^{\{1,1/2\}}, R_{\wedge_K}^{\{1,1/2\}}$ and $R_{\rightarrow_F}^{\{1,1/2\}}$, where $R_{\rightarrow_F}^{\{1,1/2\}}$ is defined as including the following rules:

$$\frac{}{p \to q, p}r_1^{\to} \qquad \frac{}{\neg(p \to q), p}r_2^{\to} \qquad \frac{\neg(p \to q)}{\neg p, \neg q}r_5^{\to} \qquad \frac{\neg p}{\neg(p \to q)}r_7^{\to}$$

$$\frac{\neg q}{\neg(p \to q)}r_8^{\to} \qquad \frac{q}{p \to q}r_9^{\to} \qquad \frac{p, p \to q}{q}r_{16}^{\to}$$

**Matrices with $D = \{1/2\}$.** When $D = \{1/2\}$, $\neg p$ does not work as separator. For the logics we consider, however, $\to$ can be used, because in any of them we have that $0 \to_{\mathbf{A}} 0 = 1/2 \in D$ and $1 \to_{\mathbf{A}} 1 = 1 \in \overline{D}$, where $\mathbf{A}$ is the underlying algebra for any of them. In other words, $p \to p$ is a separator for the values $0$ and $1$ in these logics. Using $\{p, p \to p\}$ as set of separators yields that $R_{OL}^{1/2} := R_{\neg}^{1/2} \cup R_{\wedge_{OL}}^{1/2} \cup R_{\to}^{1/2}$ axiomatizes $OL^{1/2} = Log\langle \mathbf{OL_3}, \{1/2\}\rangle$, and $R_{CN}^{1/2} := R_{\neg}^{1/2} \cup R_{\wedge_{CN}}^{1/2} \cup R_{\to}^{1/2}$ axiomatizes $CN^{1/2} = Log\langle \mathbf{CN_3}, \{1/2\}\rangle$, where the above-mentioned sets of rules are presented below.

$R_{\neg}^{1/2}$

$$\frac{p}{\neg p}r_5^{\to} \qquad \frac{\neg p}{p}r_6^{\to} \qquad \frac{}{\neg p \to \neg p, p \to p}r_7^{\to} \qquad \frac{\neg p \to \neg p, p \to p}{\neg p}r_8^{\to}$$

$R_{\wedge_{OL}}^{1/2}$

$$\frac{p \wedge q}{p}r_1^{\wedge} \qquad \frac{p \wedge q}{q}r_2^{\wedge} \qquad \frac{p, q}{p \wedge q}r_3^{\wedge}$$

$$\frac{(p \wedge q) \to (p \wedge q)}{p \to p, q \to q}r_{19}^{\wedge} \qquad \frac{(p \wedge q) \to (p \wedge q), p}{q \to q}r_{20}^{\wedge} \qquad \frac{(p \wedge q) \to (p \wedge q), q}{p \to p}r_{21}^{\wedge}$$

$$\frac{p \to p}{(p \wedge q) \to (p \wedge q), p}r_{22}^{\wedge} \qquad \frac{q \to q}{(p \wedge q) \to (p \wedge q), q}r_{23}^{\wedge}$$

$R_{\to}^{1/2}$

$$\frac{q}{p \to q}r_9^{\to} \qquad \frac{p, p \to q}{q}r_{16}^{\to} \qquad \frac{p \to p}{p \to q, p}r_{23}^{\to} \qquad \frac{p \to q}{p \to p, q}r_{24}^{\to}$$

$$\frac{(p \to q) \to (p \to q)}{p \to q, q \to q}r_{25}^{\to} \qquad \frac{q \to q}{(p \to q) \to (p \to q)}r_{26}^{\to}$$

$R_{\wedge_{CN}}^{1/2}$

$$\frac{p, q}{p \wedge q}r_3^{\wedge} \qquad \frac{p \wedge q}{p, q}r_{12}^{\wedge} \qquad \frac{p \to p}{(p \wedge q) \to (p \wedge q)}r_{24}^{\wedge} \qquad \frac{q \to q}{(p \wedge q) \to (p \wedge q)}r_{25}^{\wedge}$$

$$\frac{p \to p, p \wedge q}{p}r_{26}^{\wedge} \qquad \frac{q \to q, p \wedge q}{q}r_{27}^{\wedge} \qquad \frac{p}{(p \wedge q) \to (p \wedge q)}r_{28}^{\wedge} \qquad \frac{q}{(p \wedge q) \to (p \wedge q)}r_{29}^{\wedge}$$

$$\dfrac{p}{q \to q, p \wedge q}\mathsf{r}^{\wedge}_{30} \qquad \dfrac{q}{p \to p, p \wedge q}\mathsf{r}^{\wedge}_{31} \qquad \dfrac{(p \wedge q) \to (p \wedge q)}{p \to p, q \to q}\mathsf{r}^{\wedge}_{32}$$

In the next section, we consider the logics determined by more than one matrix, which correspond to semilattice-based logics.

## 4 Axiomatizing Semilattice-Based Logics

Logics determined by a finite family of finite matrices, arguably the main example being logics of order associated to varieties of algebras as the ones we discussed above, have not been covered in the literature of automatic generation of proof systems for finite-valued logics. Finding good (analytic) proof systems for them, then, might be in principle challenging. In this section, we show the usefulness of partial nondeterministic matrices to deal with these cases. More specifically, we show that the semilattice-based logics we listed above are characterized by single 4-valued PNmatrices. These matrices turn out to be monadic, and therefore amenable to axiomatization by analytic calculi using [6]. Since the latter is a general method and the general proof is not insightful for our concrete logics, we provide here a proof of completeness for one of the presented axiomatizations, whose strategy may be adapted to *all* calculi presented in this paper. In Subsect. 4.3, we justify the above approach by briefly discussing the (im)possibility of characterizing these logics by a single deterministic matrix.

### 4.1 Characterization of Families of Matrices via PNmatrices

We now characterize via PNmatrices the semilattice-based logics listed above, that is, $\mathrm{OL}_{\wedge_{\mathrm{OL}}}$, $\mathrm{OL}_{\vee_{\mathrm{OL}}}$, $\mathrm{OL}_{\wedge_{\mathrm{K}}}$, and $\mathrm{DF}^{\wedge_{\mathrm{K}}}$.

**Definition 2.** *Consider the following PNmatrices, for which the interpretations are given in Fig. 4. We omit the disjunction as it is expressible from the other connectives in these logics.*

1. $\mathbb{M}_{\wedge_{\mathrm{OL}}} := \langle \{0, 1/2, 1^-, 1^+\}, \cdot_{\mathbb{M}_{\wedge_{\mathrm{OL}}}}, \{1/2, 1^+\} \rangle$
2. $\mathbb{M}_{\vee_{\mathrm{OL}}} := \langle \{0^-, 0^+, 1/2, 1\}, \cdot_{\mathbb{M}_{\vee_{\mathrm{OL}}}}, \{1, 0^+\} \rangle$
3. $\mathbb{M}_{\wedge_{\mathrm{K}}} := \langle \{0, 1/2^-, 1/2^+, 1\}, \cdot_{\mathbb{M}_{\wedge_{\mathrm{K}}}}, \{1, 1/2^+\} \rangle$
4. $\mathbb{M}^{\mathrm{DF}}_{\wedge_{\mathrm{K}}} := \langle \{0, 1/2^-, 1/2^+, 1\}, \cdot_{\mathbb{M}^{\mathrm{DF}}_{\wedge_{\mathrm{K}}}}, \{1, 1/2^+\} \rangle$

The intuition behind the design of these matrices is the following. Pick, say, the matrix $\mathbb{M}_{\wedge_{\mathrm{K}}}$. Then erase the value $1/2^-$ from it. Note that the result is a logical matrix isomorphic to $\langle \mathbf{O}_3, \{1/2, 1\} \rangle$. Now do the same, but erasing $1/2^+$. The resulting matrix is isomorphic to $\langle \mathbf{O}_3, \{1\} \rangle$. That is, we have packed the two matrices that determine $\mathrm{OL}_{\wedge_{\mathrm{K}}}$ in a single partial non-deterministic matrix, guaranteeing with empty entries that its maximal total components are exactly the matrices of $\mathrm{OL}_{\wedge_{\mathrm{K}}}$. This is essentially the argument we need for the following.

**Theorem 2.** *(i)* $\mathrm{OL}_{\wedge_{\mathrm{OL}}} = \vdash_{\mathbb{M}_{\wedge_{\mathrm{OL}}}}$ *(ii)* $\mathrm{OL}_{\vee_{\mathrm{OL}}} = \vdash_{\mathbb{M}_{\vee_{\mathrm{OL}}}}$ *(iii)* $\mathrm{OL}_{\wedge_{\mathrm{K}}} = \vdash_{\mathbb{M}_{\wedge_{\mathrm{K}}}}$ *(iv)* $\mathrm{DF}^{\wedge_{\mathrm{K}}} = \vdash_{\mathbb{M}^{\mathrm{DF}}_{\wedge_{\mathrm{K}}}}$.

| $\wedge_{\mathbb{M}_{\wedge_{OL}}}$ | 0 | 1/2 | 1⁻ | 1⁺ |
|---|---|---|---|---|
| 0 | 0 | 0 | 0 | 0 |
| 1/2 | 0 | 1/2 | 1⁻ | 1⁺ |
| 1⁻ | 0 | 1⁻ | 1⁻ | ∅ |
| 1⁺ | 0 | 1⁺ | ∅ | 1⁺ |

| $\rightarrow_{\mathbb{M}_{\wedge_{OL}}}$ | 0 | 1/2 | 1⁻ | 1⁺ |
|---|---|---|---|---|
| 0 | 1/2 | 1/2 | 1/2 | 1/2 |
| 1/2 | 0 | 1/2 | 1⁻ | 1⁺ |
| 1⁻ | 0 | 1/2 | 1⁻ | ∅ |
| 1⁺ | 0 | 1/2 | ∅ | 1⁺ |

| $\neg_{\mathbb{M}_{\wedge_{OL}}}$ | |
|---|---|
| 0 | 1⁻,1⁺ |
| 1/2 | 1/2 |
| 1⁻ | 0 |
| 1⁺ | 0 |

| $\wedge_{\mathbb{M}_{\vee_{OL}}}$ | 0⁻ | 0⁺ | 1/2 | 1 |
|---|---|---|---|---|
| 0⁻ | 0⁻ | ∅ | 0⁻ | 0⁻ |
| 0⁺ | ∅ | 0⁺ | 0⁺ | 0⁺ |
| 1/2 | 0⁻ | 0⁺ | 1/2 | 1 |
| 1 | 0⁻ | 0⁺ | 1 | 1 |

| $\rightarrow_{\mathbb{M}_{\vee_{OL}}}$ | 0⁻ | 0⁺ | 1/2 | 1 |
|---|---|---|---|---|
| 0⁻ | 1/2 | ∅ | 1/2 | 1/2 |
| 0⁺ | ∅ | 1/2 | 1/2 | 1/2 |
| 1/2 | 0⁻ | 0⁺ | 1/2 | 1 |
| 1 | 0⁻ | 0⁺ | 1/2 | 1 |

| $\neg_{\mathbb{M}_{\vee_{OL}}}$ | |
|---|---|
| 0⁻ | 1 |
| 0⁺ | 1 |
| 1/2 | 1/2 |
| 1 | 0⁻,0⁺ |

| $\wedge_{\mathbb{M}_{\wedge_K}}$ | 0 | 1/2⁻ | 1/2⁺ | 1 |
|---|---|---|---|---|
| 0 | 0 | 0 | 0 | 0 |
| 1/2⁻ | 0 | 1/2⁻ | ∅ | 1 |
| 1/2⁺ | 0 | ∅ | 1/2⁺ | 1 |
| 1 | 0 | 1 | 1 | 1 |

| $\rightarrow_{\mathbb{M}_{\wedge_K}}$ | 0 | 1/2⁻ | 1/2⁺ | 1 |
|---|---|---|---|---|
| 0 | 1/2⁻,1/2⁺ | 1/2⁻ | 1/2⁺ | 1/2⁻,1/2⁺ |
| 1/2⁻ | 0 | 1/2⁻ | ∅ | 1 |
| 1/2⁺ | 0 | ∅ | 1/2⁺ | 1 |
| 1 | 0 | 1/2⁻ | 1/2⁺ | 1 |

| $\neg_{\mathbb{M}_{\wedge_K}}$ | |
|---|---|
| 0 | 1 |
| 1/2⁻ | 1/2⁻ |
| 1/2⁺ | 1/2⁺ |
| 1 | 0 |

| $\wedge_{\mathbb{M}^{DF}_{\wedge_K}}$ | 0 | 1/2⁻ | 1/2⁺ | 1 |
|---|---|---|---|---|
| 0 | 0 | 0 | 0 | 0 |
| 1/2⁻ | 0 | 1/2⁻ | ∅ | 1/2⁻ |
| 1/2⁺ | 0 | ∅ | 1/2⁺ | 1/2⁺ |
| 1 | 0 | 1/2⁻ | 1/2⁺ | 1 |

| $\rightarrow_{\mathbb{M}^{DF}_{\wedge_K}}$ | 0 | 1/2⁻ | 1/2⁺ | 1 |
|---|---|---|---|---|
| 0 | 1/2⁻,1/2⁺ | 1/2⁻ | 1/2⁺ | 1/2⁻,1/2⁺ |
| 1/2⁻ | 1/2⁻ | 1/2⁻ | ∅ | 1/2⁻ |
| 1/2⁺ | 1/2⁺ | ∅ | 1/2⁺ | 1/2⁺ |
| 1 | 0 | 1/2⁻ | 1/2⁺ | 1 |

| $\neg_{\mathbb{M}^{DF}_{\wedge_K}}$ | |
|---|---|
| 0 | 1 |
| 1/2⁻ | 1/2⁻ |
| 1/2⁺ | 1/2⁺ |
| 1 | 0 |

**Fig. 4.** Interpretations in $\mathbb{M}_{\wedge_{OL}}$, $\mathbb{M}_{\vee_{OL}}$, $\mathbb{M}_{\wedge_K}$ and $\mathbb{M}^{DF}_{\wedge_K}$.

*Proof.* Let us prove (i); the other items are similar. Item (i) follows directly from the facts that $\vdash_{\mathbb{M}_{\wedge_{OL}}}$ is determined by the family of the maximal total components of $\mathbb{M}_{\wedge_{OL}}$, and that these are, by inspection, the ones induced by the sets $\{0, 1/2, 1^-\}$ and $\{0, 1/2, 1^+\}$, which are isomorphic to the two matrices that define $OL_{\wedge_{OL}}$. ∎

Now that we have PNmatrices for all these logics, we provide analytic calculi for them.

### 4.2 Analytic Axiomatizations

With the characterization via partial non-deterministic matrices, we can now produce analytic calculi for the logics of order. For that, one can run the algorithm from [6] using discriminators described in Figs. 5, and obtain analytic calculi for each of the logics.

| $x$ | $\Omega_x$ | $\mho_x$ |
|---|---|---|
| 0 | $p \to p$ | $p$ |
| $1/2$ | $p, \neg p$ | |
| $1^-$ | | $p, p \to p$ |
| $1^+$ | $p$ | $\neg p$ |

| $x$ | $\Omega_x$ | $\mho_x$ |
|---|---|---|
| 0 | $\neg p$ | $p$ |
| $1/2^-$ | | $p, \neg p$ |
| $1/2^+$ | $p, \neg p$ | |
| 1 | $p$ | $\neg p$ |

| $x$ | $\Omega_x$ | $\mho_x$ |
|---|---|---|
| $0^-$ | $\neg p$ | $p$ |
| $0^+$ | $p$ | $p \to p$ |
| $1/2$ | | $p, \neg p$ |
| 1 | $p, p \to p$ | |

**Fig. 5.** From left-to-right, discriminators for $\mathbb{M}_{\wedge_{\mathsf{OL}}}$, for $\mathbb{M}_{\wedge_{\mathsf{K}}}$ and $\mathbb{M}_{\wedge_{\mathsf{K}}}^{\mathsf{DF}}$, and for $\mathbb{M}_{\vee_{\mathsf{OL}}}$.

**Calculus for** $\mathsf{OL}_{\wedge_{\mathsf{OL}}}$. For $\mathsf{OL}_{\wedge_{\mathsf{OL}}}$ the calculus is $\mathsf{R}_{\mathsf{OL}_{\wedge_{\mathsf{OL}}}} := \mathsf{R}_{\neg_{\wedge_{\mathsf{OL}}}} \cup \mathsf{R}_{\wedge_{\wedge_{\mathsf{OL}}}} \cup \mathsf{R}_{\to_{\wedge_{\mathsf{OL}}}} \cup \{\mathbb{T}_{\wedge_{\mathsf{OL}}}\}$ the latter sets of rules are defined below.

$\mathsf{R}_{\neg_{\wedge_{\mathsf{OL}}}}$

$$\dfrac{p}{\neg\neg p}r_1^{\neg} \qquad \dfrac{\neg\neg p}{p}r_2^{\neg} \qquad \dfrac{\neg p}{p \to p}r_3^{\neg} \qquad \dfrac{}{\neg p \to \neg p, p \to p}r_7^{\neg} \qquad \dfrac{\neg p \to \neg p, p \to p}{\neg p, p}r_9^{\neg}$$

$\mathsf{R}_{\wedge_{\wedge_{\mathsf{OL}}}}$

$$\dfrac{p \wedge q}{p}r_1^{\wedge} \qquad \dfrac{p \wedge q}{q}r_2^{\wedge} \qquad \dfrac{p, q}{p \wedge q}r_3^{\wedge} \qquad \dfrac{p \wedge q, \neg(p \wedge q)}{\neg p}r_4^{\wedge} \qquad \dfrac{p \wedge q, \neg(p \wedge q)}{\neg q}r_5^{\wedge} \qquad \dfrac{\neg p, \neg q}{\neg(p \wedge q)}r_6^{\wedge}$$

$$\dfrac{(p \wedge q) \to (p \wedge q)}{p \to p, q \to q}r_{19}^{\wedge} \qquad \dfrac{(p \wedge q) \to (p \wedge q), p}{q \to q}r_{20}^{\wedge} \qquad \dfrac{(p \wedge q) \to (p \wedge q), q}{p \to p}r_{21}^{\wedge}$$

$$\dfrac{p \to p}{(p \wedge q) \to (p \wedge q), p}r_{22}^{\wedge} \qquad \dfrac{q \to q}{(p \wedge q) \to (p \wedge q), q}r_{23}^{\wedge}$$

$\mathsf{R}_{\to_{\wedge_{\mathsf{OL}}}}$

$$\dfrac{\neg q}{\neg(p \to q)}r_8^{\to} \qquad \dfrac{q}{p \to q}r_9^{\to} \qquad \dfrac{p, p \to q}{q}r_{16}^{\to} \qquad \dfrac{\neg(p \to q), p}{\neg q}r_{17}^{\to} \qquad \dfrac{p \to p}{p \to q, p}r_{23}^{\to}$$

$$\dfrac{p \to q}{p \to p, q}r_{24}^{\to} \qquad \dfrac{(p \to q) \to (p \to q)}{p \to q, q \to q}r_{25}^{\to} \qquad \dfrac{q \to q}{(p \to q) \to (p \to q)}r_{26}^{\to} \qquad \dfrac{p \to q}{\neg(p \to q), p}r_{27}^{\to}$$

$$\dfrac{p}{\neg p, q \to q}\mathbb{T}_{\wedge_{\mathsf{OL}}}$$

The following theorem shows completeness and analyticity for this calculus (soundness follows by the usual checking of preservation of designatedness by the rules of inference). The proof is of course an instantiation of the general proof of [6], but looking at a particular case may help the reader to understand more easily how such proof works.

**Theorem 3.** $\mathsf{R}_{\mathsf{OL}_{\wedge_{\mathsf{OL}}}}$ *is complete for* $\mathsf{OL}_{\wedge_{\mathsf{OL}}}$ *and* $\{p, \neg p, p \to p\}$-*analytic.*

*Proof.* In order to simplify notation, let $\mathsf{R} := \mathsf{R}_{\mathsf{OL}_{\wedge_{\mathsf{OL}}}}$, $\mathbb{M} := \mathbb{M}_{\mathsf{OL}_{\wedge_{\mathsf{OL}}}}$, and $\mathbf{1} := \mathbf{0}$, $\mathbf{2} := 1/2$, $\mathbf{3} := 1^-$ and $\mathbf{4} := 1^+$. By contraposition, assume that $\Gamma \blacktriangleright_{\mathsf{R}}^{\Theta} \Delta$ to prove that $\Gamma \blacktriangleright_{\mathbb{M}} \Delta$. Then, by cut, there is $\Pi \subseteq L_\Sigma(P)$ such that $\Pi \blacktriangleright_{\mathsf{R}}^{\Theta} \overline{\Pi}$,

Analytic Calculi for Logics of Indicative Conditionals    75

with $\Gamma \subseteq \Pi$ and $\Delta \subseteq \overline{\Pi}$. Consider the following mapping on the subformulas of $\Gamma \cup \Delta$:

$$v(\varphi) := \begin{cases} 1 & \text{if } \varphi \to \varphi \in \Pi, \varphi \in \overline{\Pi} \\ 2 & \text{if } \varphi, \neg\varphi \in \Pi \\ 3 & \text{if } \varphi, \varphi \to \varphi \in \overline{\Pi} \\ 4 & \text{if } \varphi \in \Pi, \neg\varphi \in \overline{\Pi} \end{cases}$$

Note that since $(\Pi, \overline{\Pi})$ is a partition of $L_\Sigma(P)$, $v$ is a well-defined function. We now prove that $v$ satisfies $v(\copyright(\varphi_1, \ldots, \varphi_k)) \in \copyright_\mathbb{M}(v(\varphi_1), \ldots, v(\varphi_k))$ for every $\copyright \in \Sigma_k$ and $\varphi_1, \ldots, \varphi_k \in L_\Sigma(P)$.

For $\neg$, we want to prove that $v(\neg\varphi) \in \neg_\mathbb{M}(v(\varphi))$. We have the following cases:

- $v(\varphi) = 1$: We want to show that $v(\neg\varphi) \in \{3, 4\}$. Since $v(\varphi) = 1$, we have $\varphi \to \varphi \in \Pi$ and $\varphi \in \overline{\Pi}$. Suppose by contradiction that $v(\neg\varphi) = 1$. Then we have $\neg\varphi \to \neg\varphi \in \Pi$ and $\neg\varphi \in \overline{\Pi}$. Thus by $r_9^-$ we have $\varphi \to \varphi, \neg\varphi \to \neg\varphi \triangleright_R^\Theta \varphi, \neg\varphi$, contradicting $\Pi \blacktriangleright_R^\Theta \overline{\Pi}$. Now assume that $v(\neg\varphi) = 2$. Then $\neg\varphi, \neg\neg\varphi \in \Pi$. But by $r_2^-$, we have that $\varphi \to \varphi, \neg\varphi, \neg\neg\varphi \triangleright_R^\Theta \varphi$, contradicting that $\Pi \blacktriangleright_R^\Theta \overline{\Pi}$, reaching again a contradiction.
- $v(\varphi) = 2$: derive contradictions by assuming that $v(\neg\varphi) \in \{1, 3, 4\}$, using $r_1^-$ and instances of overlap.
- $v(\varphi) = 3$: by rules $r_7^-$ and $r_3^-$, and instances of overlap.
- $v(\varphi) = 4$: by instances of overlap.

Note that $\{3, 4\} \not\subseteq v[L_\Sigma(P)]$. Indeed, assume the contrary, and pick $\varphi$ and $\psi$ with $v(\varphi) = 3$ and $v(\psi) = 4$. Then $\varphi, \varphi \to \varphi \in \overline{\Pi}$ and $\psi \in \Pi$ and $\neg\psi \in \overline{\Pi}$. By rule the rule $\mathbb{T}_{\wedge_{\text{OL}}}$, i.e., $\frac{p}{\neg p, q \to q}$, and dilution, we have $\psi \triangleright_R^\Theta \neg\psi, \varphi, \varphi \to \varphi$, contradicting $\Pi \blacktriangleright_R^\Theta \overline{\Pi}$. Thus in what follows we do not need to consider the cases $v(\varphi) = 3$ and $v(\psi) = 4$, and vice-versa.

For $\wedge$ and $\to$ we need to show $v(\varphi \wedge \psi) \in v(\varphi) \wedge_\mathbb{M} v(\psi)$ and $v(\varphi \to \psi) \in v(\varphi) \to_\mathbb{M} v(\psi)$. Let $(x, y) := (v(\varphi), v(\psi))$, for lack of space we simply indicate the rules used in each case ($\wedge$ on the left, and $\to$ on the right).

- $x = 1$: $r_1^\wedge, r_{22}^\wedge$
- $y = 1$: $r_2^\wedge, r_{23}^\wedge$
- $x, y = 2, 2$: $r_3^\wedge, r_6^\wedge$
- $x, y = 2, 3$: $r_2^\wedge, r_{20}^\wedge$
- $x, y = 3, 3$: $r_1^\wedge, r_{19}^\wedge$
- $x, y = 3, 2$: $r_1^\wedge, r_{21}^\wedge$
- $x, y = 2, 4$: $r_3^\wedge, r_5^\wedge$
- $x, y = 4, 4$: $r_3^\wedge, r_4^\wedge$
- $x, y = 4, 2$: $r_3^\wedge, r_4^\wedge$

- $x, y = 2, 1$: $\overrightarrow{r_{16}}, \overrightarrow{r_{26}}$
- $x, y = 2, 2$: $\overrightarrow{r_9}, \overrightarrow{r_8}$
- $x, y = 2, 3$: $\overrightarrow{r_{16}}, \overrightarrow{r_{25}}$
- $x, y = 2, 4$: $\overrightarrow{r_9}, \overrightarrow{r_{17}}$
- $x, y = 3, 1$: $\overrightarrow{r_{24}}, \overrightarrow{r_{26}}$
- $x, y = 3, 2$: $\overrightarrow{r_9}, \overrightarrow{r_8}$
- $x, y = 3, 3$: $\overrightarrow{r_{25}}, \overrightarrow{r_{24}}$
- $x, y = 4, 1$: $\overrightarrow{r_{16}}, \overrightarrow{r_{26}}$
- $x, y = 4, 2$: $\overrightarrow{r_9}, \overrightarrow{r_8}$
- $x, y = 4, 4$: $\overrightarrow{r_9}, \overrightarrow{r_{17}}$
- $x = 1$: $\overrightarrow{r_{17}}, \overrightarrow{r_{23}}$

We already saw that $\{3, 4\} \not\subseteq v[\text{subf}(\Gamma \cup \Delta)]$, thus the latter is a subset of values of a total component of $\mathbb{M}$. This means that $v$ extends to a valuation over $L_\Sigma(P)$. Note also that, by definition of $v$, for any $\varphi \in \text{subf}(\Gamma \cup \Delta)$, $v(\varphi) \in \Pi$ iff

$v(\varphi) \in D$, and thus $v(\varphi) \in \overline{\Pi}$ iff $v(\varphi) \in \overline{D}$. Since $\Gamma \subseteq \Pi$ and $\Delta \subseteq \overline{\Pi}$, we have $v[\Gamma] \subseteq D$ and $v[\Delta] \subseteq \overline{D}$, as desired. ∎

We provide below an example of an analytic derivation in $R_{OL_{\wedge_{OL}}}$.

*Example 1.* The $\{p, \neg p, p \to p\}$-analytic derivation in $R_{OL_{\wedge_{OL}}}$ below shows that $\vdash_{OL_{\wedge_{OL}}} \neg p \to (p \to p)$.

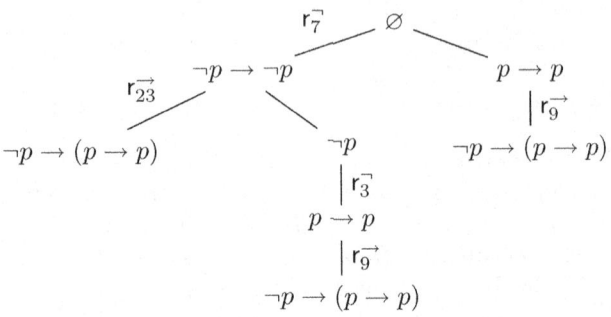

As mentioned earlier, all multiple-conclusion calculi presented here can be converted into single-conclusion ones thanks to the presence of a disjunction connective ⊕. By way of example, we show the single-conclusion rule that translates $\overrightarrow{r_9}$:

$$\frac{(\neg p \to \neg p) \oplus s, (p \to p) \oplus s}{(\neg p \oplus p) \oplus s}$$

Recall that, in this case, $x \oplus y := (\neg(x \wedge_K y) \to_{OL} \neg(x \wedge_{OL} y)) \to_{OL} (x \vee_K y)$.

**Calculus for** $OL_{\wedge_K}$. The calculus is $R_{OL_{\wedge_K}} = R_{\neg_{\wedge_K}} \cup R_{\wedge_{\wedge_K}} \cup R_{\to_{\wedge_K}} \cup \{\mathbb{T}_{\wedge_K}\}$, where the latter sets are defined below.

$R_{\neg_{\wedge_K}}$

$$\frac{p}{\neg\neg p} r_1^{\to} \qquad \frac{\neg\neg p}{p} r_2^{\to}$$

$R_{\wedge_{\wedge_K}}$

$$\frac{p, q}{p \wedge q} r_3^{\wedge} \qquad \frac{\neg p, \neg q}{\neg(p \wedge q)} r_6^{\wedge} \qquad \frac{p}{p \wedge q, \neg q} r_7^{\wedge} \qquad \frac{q}{p \wedge q, \neg p} r_8^{\wedge} \qquad \frac{\neg(p \wedge q)}{\neg p, \neg q} r_9^{\wedge} \qquad \frac{p \wedge q}{p, q} r_{12}^{\wedge}$$

$$\frac{\neg(p \wedge q), p}{\neg q} r_{17}^{\wedge} \qquad \frac{\neg(p \wedge q), q}{\neg p} r_{18}^{\wedge} \qquad \frac{p \wedge q, \neg(p \wedge q)}{p} r_{24}^{\wedge} \qquad \frac{p \wedge q, \neg(p \wedge q)}{q} r_{25}^{\wedge} \qquad \frac{p}{p \wedge q, \neg(p \wedge q)} r_2^{\wedge}$$

$$\frac{q}{p \wedge q, \neg(p \wedge q)} r_{27}^{\wedge} \qquad \frac{p \wedge q, \neg p}{p} r_{28}^{\wedge} \qquad \frac{p \wedge q, \neg p}{q} r_{29}^{\wedge} \qquad \frac{p \wedge q, \neg q}{p} r_{30}^{\wedge} \qquad \frac{p \wedge q, \neg q}{q} r_{31}^{\wedge}$$

$$\frac{\neg p}{\neg(p \wedge q), q} r_{32}^{\wedge} \qquad \frac{\neg q}{\neg(p \wedge q), q} r_{33}^{\wedge}$$

$R_{\to \wedge_K}$

$$\frac{p \to q}{\neg p, q}\vec{r_4} \quad \frac{p, \neg q}{\neg(p \to q)}\vec{r_{14}} \quad \frac{p, q}{p \to q}\vec{r_{15}} \quad \frac{p, p \to q}{q}\vec{r_{16}} \quad \frac{\neg(p \to q), p}{\neg q}\vec{r_{17}} \quad \frac{\neg q}{\neg(p \to q), \neg p}\vec{r_{21}}$$

$$\frac{q}{p \to q, \neg p}\vec{r_{22}} \quad \frac{\neg q, q}{p \to q}\vec{r_{28}} \quad \frac{\neg q, q}{\neg(p \to q)}\vec{r_{29}} \quad \frac{p \to q}{\neg(p \to q), q}\vec{r_{30}} \quad \frac{p \to q}{\neg q, q}\vec{r_{31}} \quad \frac{\neg(p \to q)}{\neg q, q}\vec{r_{32}}$$

$$\frac{p \to q, \neg p}{\neg(p \to q), p}\vec{r_{33}} \quad \frac{\neg(p \to q), \neg p}{p \to q, p}\vec{r_{34}} \quad \frac{\neg(p \to q), q}{p \to q}\vec{r_{35}}$$

$$\frac{p, \neg p}{q, \neg q}\mathbb{T}_{\wedge_K}$$

**Calculus for** $\mathrm{OL}_{\vee_{OL}}$. The calculus is $R_{\mathrm{OL}_{\vee_{OL}}} = R_{\neg_{\vee_{OL}}} \cup R_{\wedge_{\vee_{OL}}} \cup R_{\to_{\vee_{OL}}}$:

$R_{\neg_{\vee_{OL}}}$

$$\frac{p}{\neg\neg p}\vec{r_1} \quad \frac{\neg\neg p}{p}\vec{r_2} \quad \frac{\neg p \to \neg p, p \to p}{}\vec{r_3} \quad \frac{\neg p}{\neg p \to \neg p, p \to p}\vec{r_4}$$

$R_{\wedge_{\vee_{OL}}}$

$$\frac{p, q}{p \wedge q}\hat{r_3} \quad \frac{p}{p \wedge q, \neg q}\hat{r_7} \quad \frac{q}{p \wedge q, \neg p}\hat{r_8} \quad \frac{\neg(p \wedge q)}{\neg p, \neg q}\hat{r_9} \quad \frac{\neg p}{\neg(p \wedge q)}\hat{r_{10}} \quad \frac{\neg q}{\neg(p \wedge q)}\hat{r_{11}} \quad \frac{p \wedge q}{p, q}\hat{r_{12}}$$

$$\frac{p}{p \wedge q, \neg(p \wedge q)}\hat{r_{15}} \quad \frac{q}{p \wedge q, \neg(p \wedge q)}\hat{r_{16}} \quad \frac{p \wedge q, \neg p}{p}\hat{r_{34}} \quad \frac{p \wedge q, \neg q}{q}\hat{r_{35}} \quad \frac{p \to p, q \to q}{(p \wedge q) \to (p \wedge q)}\hat{r_{36}}$$

$$\frac{(p \wedge q) \to (p \wedge q), p}{p \to p}\hat{r_{37}} \quad \frac{(p \wedge q) \to (p \wedge q), q}{q \to q}\hat{r_{38}} \quad \frac{p \to p, p \wedge q}{(p \wedge q) \to (p \wedge q), q}\hat{r_{39}}$$

$$\frac{q \to q, p \wedge q}{(p \wedge q) \to (p \wedge q), p}\hat{r_{40}} \quad \frac{p}{p \to p, p \wedge q}\hat{r_{41}} \quad \frac{q}{q \to q, p \wedge q}\hat{r_{42}}$$

$R_{\to_{\vee_{OL}}}$

$$\frac{p \to q}{q}\vec{r_{11}} \quad \frac{\neg(p \to q)}{\neg q}\vec{r_{12}} \quad \frac{\neg q}{\neg(p \to q), \neg p}\vec{r_{21}} \quad \frac{q}{p \to q, \neg p}\vec{r_{22}} \quad \frac{\neg(p \to q), q}{p \to q}\vec{r_{35}}$$

$$\frac{q}{p \to q, q \to q, p}\vec{r_{36}} \quad \frac{\neg q, p}{p \to p, q}\vec{r_{37}} \quad \frac{\neg q, p}{\neg(p \to q), q}\vec{r_{38}} \quad \frac{p \to q, p}{p \to p}\vec{r_{39}} \quad \frac{p \to p, q}{p \to q}\vec{r_{40}}$$

$$\frac{p \to q, \neg p}{p}\vec{r_{41}} \quad \frac{\neg(p \to q), \neg p}{p \to q}\vec{r_{42}} \quad \frac{(p \to q) \to (p \to q)}{q \to q}\vec{r_{43}} \quad \frac{p \to q, q \to q}{(p \to q) \to (p \to q)}\vec{r_{44}}$$

**Calculus for** $\mathrm{DF}^{\wedge_K}$. The calculus is $R_{\mathrm{DF}^{\wedge_K}} = R_{\neg_{\mathrm{DF}^{\wedge_K}}} \cup R_{\wedge_{\mathrm{DF}^{\wedge_K}}} \cup R_{\to_{\mathrm{DF}^{\wedge_K}}} \cup \{\mathbb{T}_{\wedge_K}\}$:

$R_{\neg_{\mathrm{DF}^{\wedge_K}}}$

$$\frac{p}{\neg\neg p}\vec{r_1} \quad \frac{\neg\neg p}{p}\vec{r_2}$$

$\mathsf{R}_{\wedge_{\mathsf{DF}^\wedge\mathsf{K}}}$

$$\frac{p \wedge q}{p}r_1^\wedge \qquad \frac{p \wedge q}{q}r_2^\wedge \qquad \frac{p,q}{p \wedge q}r_3^\wedge \qquad \frac{\neg(p \wedge q)}{\neg p, \neg q}r_4^\wedge \qquad \frac{\neg p}{\neg(p \wedge q)}r_{10}^\wedge \qquad \frac{\neg q}{\neg(p \wedge q)}r_{11}^\wedge$$

$$\frac{\neg(p \wedge q), p}{q, \neg q}r_{45}^\wedge \qquad \frac{\neg(p \wedge q), q}{p, \neg p}r_{46}^\wedge$$

$\mathsf{R}_{\to_{\mathsf{DF}^\wedge\mathsf{K}}}$

$$\frac{p \to q}{\neg p, q}r_4^\to \qquad \frac{\neg(p \to q)}{\neg p, \neg q}r_5^\to \qquad \frac{p, \neg q}{\neg(p \to q)}r_{14}^\to \qquad \frac{p, q}{p \to q}r_{15}^\to \qquad \frac{p \to q}{\neg(p \to q), p}r_{27}^\to \qquad \frac{\neg q, q}{p \to q}r_{29}^\to$$

$$\frac{p \to q}{\neg(p \to q), q}r_{31}^\to \qquad \frac{p \to q}{\neg q, q}r_{32}^\to \qquad \frac{\neg(p \to q)}{\neg q, q}r_{33}^\to \qquad \frac{p \to q}{\neg p, p}r_{46}^\to \qquad \frac{\neg(p \to q)}{p \to q, p}r_{47}^\to$$

$$\frac{\neg p, p}{p \to q}r_{48}^\to \qquad \frac{\neg p, p}{\neg(p \to q)}r_{49}^\to$$

$$\frac{p, \neg p}{q, \neg q}\mathbb{T}_{\wedge\mathsf{K}}$$

### 4.3 On the Possibility of a Single Matrix Characterization

It is well-known that a multiple-conclusion logic $\triangleright$ is determined by a single (deterministic) matrix if, and only if, it satisfies *multiple-conclusion cancellation* [29, Thm. 15.2]. That is, if $\bigcup_{i \in I} \Gamma_i \triangleright \bigcup_{i \in I} \Delta_i$ and, for every $i \neq j$, the variables of $\Gamma_i \cup \Delta_i$ and $\Gamma_j \cup \Delta_j$ are all distinct, then $\Gamma_i \triangleright \Delta_i$ for some $i \in I$.

Further, a single-conclusion logic $\vdash$ is determined by a single matrix if, and only if, it satisfies *single-conclusion cancellation* [32], that is, $\bigcup_{i \in I} \Gamma_i, \Gamma \vdash \varphi$ and the variables of $\Gamma_i$ are all distinct from the variables in $\Gamma \cup \{\varphi\}$, and none of the $\Gamma_i$ is $\vdash$-explosive, then $\Gamma \vdash \varphi$.

Recall that we have characterized each of the logics of order via PNmatrices, which is an essential step to obtain the axiomatizations. However, could we have done with single deterministic matrices?

It turns out that for none of these cases the multiple-conclusion logic defined by the PNmatrices could be captured by a single matrix. To see this is the case it is enough to consider the incompatible pairs of values (i.e., those that lead to empty entries in the truth tables). Namely, for each $\mathbb{M} \in \{\mathbb{M}_{\wedge_\mathsf{OL}}, \mathbb{M}_{\vee_\mathsf{OL}}, \mathbb{M}_{\wedge_\mathsf{K}}, \mathbb{M}_{\wedge_\mathsf{K}}^{\mathsf{DF}}\}$ and $(a^-, a^+)$, we have $\Omega_{a^-}(p), \Omega_{a^+}(q) \triangleright_\mathbb{M} \mho_{a^-}(p), \mho_{a^+}(q)$ but $\Omega_{a^-}(p) \blacktriangleright_\mathbb{M} \mho_{a^-}(p)$ and $\Omega_{a^+}(q) \blacktriangleright_\mathbb{M} \mho_{a^+}(q)$.

On the other hand, note that $\vdash_{\mathbb{M}_{\wedge_\mathsf{OL}}}$ is characterized by the nine-valued matrix $\mathbb{M}$ that we now describe, and thus satisfies single-conclusion cancellation. Consider $\mathbb{M} := \mathbb{M}_1 \times \mathbb{M}_2$ where $\mathbb{M}_1 := \langle \mathbf{OL_3}, \{1/2\} \rangle$ and $\mathbb{M}_2 := \langle \mathbf{OL_3}, \{1/2, 1\} \rangle$. Soundness follows from the fact that the product operation preserves the single conclusion logic. For completeness, it is enough to observe that $\vdash_\mathbb{M} \subseteq \vdash_{\mathbb{M}'}$

for any submatrix $\mathbb{M}'$ of $\mathbb{M}$, and that $\mathbb{M}_{\{1/2\} \times \{0,1/2,1\}}$ is isomorphic to $\mathbb{M}_2$, and $\mathbb{M}_{\{0,1/2,1\} \times \{1/2\}}$ is isomorphic to $\mathbb{M}_1$, since $1/2$ is designated in both $\mathbb{M}_1$ and $\mathbb{M}_2$ and is closed for the interpretations of the connectives.

It is an open problem whether $\vdash_{\mathbb{M}_{\vee_{OL}}}, \vdash_{\mathbb{M}_{\wedge_K}}$ and $\vdash_{\mathbb{M}_{\wedge_K}^{DF}}$ have single-conclusion cancellation. Still, the path presented in this section, via partial non-determinism, leads to a much simpler semantics, which is clearly monadic and thus finitely axiomatizable as we showed above.

## 5 Future Work

We have demonstrated how to apply the methods developed in [6,24,29] to a wide range of logics of indicative conditionals in order to *uniformly* obtain *analytic* Hilbert-style axiomatizations. As mentioned earlier, in some cases other *ad hoc* methods may also be fruitfully applied (exploiting algebraizability results, connections with other known non-classical logics, etc.). Each of these alternative perspectives provides further insight into semantic and proof-theoretic properties of logics of indicative conditionals, and will be pursued in future research. In particular, the negative results may turn out to be particularly interesting, perhaps revealing unexpected technical difficulties (e.g. establishing the non-algebraizability of the relevant systems, determining which inclusions are strict among the classes of algebras associated to each of them, etc.).

For a different, somewhat broader direction, let us take again into consideration the original motivation behind the logical systems at hand: these aimed at providing a more faithful formalization of indicative conditionals as employed in natural language. We therefore feel that the value of logics in this family—especially those considered here for the first time—should ultimately be assessed through an extensive analysis of natural language reasoning samples, as demonstrated by the exemplary papers [10,14]. This project obviously lies beyond the scope of the present paper; perhaps even beyond our core expertise as mathematical logicians. However, having at hand analytic calculi may greatly simplify the task of analyzing sample arguments, comparing the different systems, establishing which logical principles and inferences each one validates, etc. We therefore hope that our preliminary research will arouse sufficient interest for others in the community to take up the challenge.

**Acknowledgments.** Vitor Greati acknowledges support from the FWF project P33548. Sérgio Marcelino's work is funded by FCT/MECI through national funds and when applicable co-funded EU funds under UID/50008: Instituto de Telecomunicações. Umberto Rivieccio acknowledges support from the I+D+i research project PID2022-142378NB-I00 "PHIDELO", funded by the Ministry of Science and Innovation of Spain.

# References

1. Albuquerque, H., Přenosil, A., Rivieccio, U.: An algebraic view of super-Belnap logics. Stud. Log. **105**(6), 1051–1086 (2017). https://doi.org/10.1007/s11225-017-9739-7
2. Avron, A., Ben-Naim, J., Konikowska, B.: Cut-free ordinary sequent calculi for logics having generalized finite-valued semantics. Log. Univers. **1**(1), 41–70 (2007). https://doi.org/10.1007/s11787-006-0003-6
3. Avron, A., Konikowska, B.: Multi-valued calculi for logics based on non-determinism. Log. J. IGPL **13**(4), 365–387 (2005). https://doi.org/10.1093/jigpal/jzi030
4. Baaz, M., Lahav, O., Zamansky, A.: Finite-valued semantics for canonical labelled calculi. J. Autom. Reason. **51**(4), 401–430 (2013). https://doi.org/10.1007/s10817-013-9273-x
5. Baaz, M., Fermüller, C.G., Salzer, G.: Automated Deduction for Many-Valued Logics, p. 1355–1402. Elsevier Science Publishers B. V., NLD (2001)
6. Caleiro, C., Marcelino, S.: Analytic calculi for monadic PNmatrices. In: Iemhoff, R., Moortgat, M., de Queiroz, R. (eds.) WoLLIC 2019. LNCS, vol. 11541, pp. 84–98. Springer, Heidelberg (2019). https://doi.org/10.1007/978-3-662-59533-6_6
7. Caleiro, C., Marcelino, S.: Modular many-valued semantics for combined logics. J. Symb. Log. 1–54 (2023). https://doi.org/10.1017/jsl.2023.22
8. Cantwell, J.: The logic of conditional negation. Notre Dame J. Formal Log. **49**(3), 245–260 (2008). https://doi.org/10.1215/00294527-2008-010
9. Cignoli, R.: The class of Kleene algebras satisfying an interpolation property and nelson algebras. Algebra Univers. **23**, 262–292 (1986). https://doi.org/10.1007/BF01230621
10. Cooper, W.S.: The propositional logic of ordinary discourse. Inq.: Interdisc. J. Philos. **11**(1-4), 295–320 (1968). https://doi.org/10.1080/00201746808601531
11. Égré, P., Rossi, L., Sprenger, J.: De Finettian logics of indicative conditionals part I: trivalent semantics and validity. J. Philos. Log. **50**(2), 187–213 (2020). https://doi.org/10.1007/s10992-020-09549-6
12. Egré, P., Rossi, L., Spengler, J.: Certain and uncertain inference with indicative conditionals. Preprint available at the arXiv (2023)
13. Égré, P., Rossi, L., Sprenger, J.: De Finettian logics of indicative conditionals part II: proof theory and algebraic semantics. J. Philos. Log. **50**(2), 215–247 (2021). https://doi.org/10.1007/s10992-020-09572-7
14. Farrell, R.J.: Implication and presupposition. Notre Dame J. Formal Log. **27**(1) (1986)
15. Farrell, R.J.: Material implication, confirmation, and counterfactuals. Notre Dame J. Formal Log. **20**(2), 383–394 (1979)
16. Fazio, D., Odintsov, S.P.: An algebraic investigation of the connexive logic C. Stud. Log. (2023). https://doi.org/10.1007/s11225-023-10057-2
17. de Finetti, B.: La logique de la probabilité. In: Actes du Congrés International de Philosophie Scientifique (1936)
18. Font, J.M., Jansana, R.: A General Algebraic Semantics for Sentential Logics. Springer, Cham (2009)
19. Font, J.M.: Abstract Algebraic Logic: An introductory textbook. College Publications (2016)
20. Greati, V., Marcelino, S., Rivieccio, U.: Axiomatizing the logic of ordinary discourse. In: Proceeding of IPMU24 (2024)

21. Greati, V., Greco, G., Marcelino, S., Palmigiano, A., Rivieccio, U.: Generating proof systems for three-valued propositional logics. In: Egré, P., Rossi, L. (eds.) Handbook of Three-Valued Logics. MIT Press (2024). https://arxiv.org/abs/2401.03274
22. Greati, V., Marcelino, S., Marcos, J., Rivieccio, U.: Adding an implication to logics of perfect paradefinite algebras. Math. Struct. Comput. Sci. **34**(10), 1138–1183 (2024). https://doi.org/10.1017/S0960129524000227
23. Humberstone, L.: The Connectives. MIT Press (2011)
24. Marcelino, S., Caleiro, C.: Axiomatizing non-deterministic many-valued generalized consequence relations. Synthese **198**(22), 5373–5390 (2021)
25. Pałasińska, K.: Deductive systems and finite axiomatization properties (1994). https://doi.org/10.31274/rtd-180813-12680
26. Priest, G.: The logic of paradox. J. Philos. Log. **8**(1), 219–241 (1979)
27. Rivieccio, U.: The algebra of ordinary discourse. On the semantics of Cooper's logic. Arch. Math. Log. (2025). https://doi.org/10.1007/s00153-024-00961-2
28. Rivieccio, U., Muñoz-Pérez, M.: Indicative conditionals: some algebraic considerations. In: WoLLIC 2025 (2025, accepted)
29. Shoesmith, D.J., Smiley, T.J.: Multiple-Conclusion Logic. Cambridge University Press, Cambridge (1978). https://doi.org/10.1017/CBO9780511565687
30. Wansing, H.: Connexive modal logic. In: Kracht, M., de Rijke, M., Wansing, H., Zakharyaschev, M. (eds.) Advances in Modal Logic, pp. 367–383. CSLI Publications (2005)
31. Wansing, H.: Constructive logic is connexive and contradictory. Log. Log. Philos. 1–27 (forthcoming). https://doi.org/10.12775/llp.2024.001
32. Wójcicki, R.: Theory of Logical Calculi. Synthese Library, 1 edn. Springer, Dordrecht (1988). https://doi.org/10.1007/978-94-015-6942-2

**Open Access** This chapter is licensed under the terms of the Creative Commons Attribution 4.0 International License (http://creativecommons.org/licenses/by/4.0/), which permits use, sharing, adaptation, distribution and reproduction in any medium or format, as long as you give appropriate credit to the original author(s) and the source, provide a link to the Creative Commons license and indicate if changes were made.

The images or other third party material in this chapter are included in the chapter's Creative Commons license, unless indicated otherwise in a credit line to the material. If material is not included in the chapter's Creative Commons license and your intended use is not permitted by statutory regulation or exceeds the permitted use, you will need to obtain permission directly from the copyright holder.

# Finding Connections via Satisfiability Solving

Clemens Eisenhofer[1](✉)🆔, Michael Rawson[2]🆔, and Laura Kovács[1]🆔

[1] TU Wien, Vienna, Austria
{clemens.eisenhofer,laura.kovacs}@tuwien.ac.at
[2] University of Southampton, Southampton, UK
michael@rawsons.uk

**Abstract.** Commonly used proof strategies by automated reasoners organise proof search either by ordering-based saturation or by reducing goals to subgoals. In this paper, we combine these two approaches and advocate a SAT-based method with symmetry breaking for connection calculi in first-order logic, with the purpose of further pushing the automation in first-order classical logic proofs. In contrast to classical ways of reducing first-order logic to propositional logic, our method encodes the structure of the proof search itself. We present three distinct SAT encodings for connection calculi, analyse their theoretical properties, and discuss the effect of using SAT/SMT solvers on these encodings. We implemented our work in the new solver UPCoP and showcase its practical feasibility.

## 1 Introduction

Search strategies employed by *automated theorem provers for first-order logics* can be divided into two broad classes [16]: *ordering-based* and *subgoal-reduction*. The first class, which contains saturation-based theorem provers including VAMPIRE [35], E [54], and SPASS [60], work by continuously deducing new facts from an existing set of formulas and expanding the search space with these new facts. The second class, containing systems such as SETHEO [38] or leanCoP [45], works by manipulating a partial proof and implementing backtracking if necessary.

The subgoal-reduction class has the disadvantage that redundant, "useless", formulas in the search space may be explored in duplicate manner, unless special care is taken to "remember" where the prover has already been before. Avoiding such redundant cases for the purpose of efficient reasoning is a subject of great interest. Therefore, *global refinement* within the subgoal-reduction approach to theorem proving has been proposed and investigated [11]. In general, such refinements can contain non-trivial propositional structure; for example, the information "if clauses $C$ and $D$ are in the current proof attempt, and the current substitution binds $x \mapsto t$ and $y \mapsto s$, we are in a dead-end and have to backtrack" is a hard formula to reason with.

Backtracking mechanisms are routinely implemented in Boolean satisfiability (SAT) solvers [13], for the purpose of refining the (partial) proof. Modern SAT solvers *learn* relevant information as they go, and even allow users to add constraints during the solver's search for a model, in response to the solver's current (partial) assignment. When a SAT solver cannot find a satisfying assignment, an *explanation* in the form of an unsat core is given. In this paper, we examine these learning and explanation features in the context of first-order theorem proving, which usually makes SAT solvers an ideal vehicle for managing global information and their refinements.

*Here we are interested in the integration of SAT solving and subgoal-reduction,* focusing on Bibel's *connection method* [10]. Connection methods yield powerful calculi for automation of expressive logics, for example, for classical first-order logic [10,38], higher-order logic [2], linear logic [31], and several modal logics [46]. Our work directly encodes the search for connection proofs as a Boolean satisfiability problem, allowing the solver to dictate search decisions and respond by asserting constraints, such that when a satisfying assignment is reached, it represents a complete proof. To this end, we introduce three encodings of connections (Sects. 3–5) and show their complementary nature and power (Sect. 7).

First, we present our method applied to connection *tableaux* (Sect. 3) and highlight some unfortunate properties of this setting. Therefore, we refine our encoding of the connection calculus using a matrix form (Sect. 4). Further, we describe how unsat cores can be used to guide iterative deepening during SAT solving (Sect. 5). The resulting encodings allow many global refinements that are usually not feasible within other methods (Sect. 6).

Our work intends for the SAT solver to return a satisfying assignment of our constraints, where the model encodes a finished proof: matrix or tableau. *In other words, we represent a first-order proof as a propositional model.* This contrasts with most other uses of SAT solvers in theorem proving in which ground unsatisfiability is the aim [59], often witnessing Herbrand-style refutation by instantiation of first-order clauses.

The practical use of our approach is showcased by evaluating our work on the TPTP repository of first-order problems [57]. To this end, we provide a proof-of-concept implementations of our techniques in our new solver UPCoP, where UPCoP uses either the CaDiCaL SAT solver [12] and the Z3 SMT solver [43]. When evaluating UPCoP against the state-of-the-art meanCoP solver [28], our experimental findings demonstrate that our work can solve 179 problems that meanCoP cannot (Sect. 7).

**Summary of Contributions.**

1. We encode the existence of first-order connection calculi proofs as Boolean satisfiability problem, using connection tableaux (Sect. 3), a matrix representation (Sect. 4), and iterative deepening via unsat core refinement (Sect. 5). We show soundness and completeness of our encodings.
2. We explore optimisations to reduce redundancy and symmetry in the encodings (Sect. 6).

3. We discuss our implementation of the encodings in the new prototype solver UPCoP and evaluate it on the TPTP benchmark set (Sect. 7).

## 2 Preliminaries

We use standard syntax and semantics of classical first-order logic [56]. Logical objects such as terms $t$ may be indexed: $t_j^i$. We assume the input problem has been negated and converted to conjunctive normal form (CNF) by a satisfiability-preserving transformation [4]. However, this transformation is optional in theory [10].

### 2.1 Satisfiability Solving

We assume familiarity with Boolean satisfiability (SAT) solving [14] and satisfiability modulo theories (SMT) [58]. In addition to the basic decision procedure for Boolean formulas, many SAT solvers support solving *under assumptions* and *unsatisfiable cores*. Solving under assumptions allows fixing some literals temporarily for the duration of a solving run: afterwards, the solver "forgets" them and their consequences. If the solver detects that the problem is unsatisfiable under assumptions, it may extract a subset of the assumptions used to derive inconsistency: the so-called "unsat core". Cores may not be *minimal*, so inconsistency can be derived with a strict subset of the core. Minimal cores can be generated at additional computational cost [21,40].

Some SAT and SMT solvers, including CADICAL [30] and Z3 [15], allow the user to intervene *during* search by a variety of means, often under the title "user propagation". Such mechanisms allow employing a solver to tackle a broad class of problems efficiently. For our purposes, we assume we can be notified when a SAT variable is assigned true or false, and respond by asserting additional constraints, potentially containing fresh SAT variables. We write $J_1, \ldots, J_n \Vdash F$ to represent that we added (*propagated*) the constraint $J_1 \wedge \ldots \wedge J_n \Rightarrow F$ for some formula $F$ to the solver, given that the solver's current model satisfies all antecedent literals $J_1, \ldots, J_n$. This feature allows us to avoid eagerly generating an extensive set of all possible constraints and add only the currently relevant parts of the encoding. This kind of lazy generation is desirable in our case.

### 2.2 Connection Tableaux

Connection tableaux are essentially clausal tableaux [25] with the additional constraint that each clause added to a branch must have at least one literal *connected* to the current leaf literal [39]. *Two literals are connected if they have the same atom but opposite polarity: they are dual.* Recall that in the first-order case, clauses in the tableau have their variables renamed apart from any other, and a global substitution $\sigma$ is applied to the entire tableau to connect literals (unification). The connection tableau calculus is not *confluent* and requires both backtracking and a fair enumeration of tableaux for completeness.

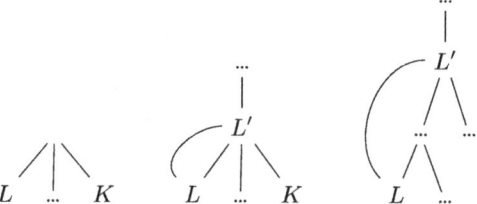

**Fig. 1.** Connection tableau rules, left-to-right: *start*, *extension*, and *reduction*. In *start* and *extension*, $L \vee \ldots \vee K$ is a freshly-renamed copy of a clause from the input problem. In *extension* and *reduction*, $L$ is connected to $L'$ using $\sigma$.

We say that two literals $L, K$ *can* be connected and write $L \bowtie K$ if there exists some substitution $\rho$ such that $\rho(L)$ is connected to $\rho(K)$. A subset of input clauses are considered potential roots of the tableau [39]: we assume these *start* clauses (conjectures) have been chosen in a way that at least one conjecture can be used for finding a proof. Equality is not handled by the basic connection calculus, and it is either axiomatised [44] or preprocessed away by some variation of Brand's modification [18]. We sometimes write $C^k$ to distinguish the $k^{\text{th}}$ copy of the input clause $C$, indexing its variables as $x^k$.

Conventionally, three operations manipulate connection tableaux, shown in Fig. 1. *Start* operations pick a start clause and add it at the root of the tableau. The chosen clause's literals are the initial leaves of the tableau. *Extension* operations add a copy of a clause from the input clause set below a leaf literal of the tableau, connecting at least one of the newly added clause's literals with the leaf. *Reduction* operations connect a leaf literal with another literal on the path from the literal toward the tableau's root. A branch of the tableau is *closed* in case the leaf of that branch is connected to some other literal. The whole tableau is closed, thus representing a proof if all of its branches are closed. In general, all these operations must be backtracked over to achieve completeness.

### 2.3 The Connection Method, Matrices, and Spanning Connections

Connection tableaux are an instance of the connection method [10]. While connection calculi are a rich topic with many facets, we are primarily interested in the following *matrix* representation. We consider matrices in *normal form* and thus define a matrix as a non-empty set of rigid clauses; that means, clauses containing rigid variables. The matrix can contain an arbitrary number of rigid copies of the same input clause, where variables are renamed apart, and a global substitution $\sigma$ is applied. A *path* through a matrix is a set that contains exactly one literal from each copy of the clause in the matrix and is called *closed* if it contains at least one connected pair of literals, otherwise *open*. A *matrix proof*, or a matrix with a *spanning set of connections*, is a matrix for which there are no open paths.

Further, a matrix is *fully connected* with respect to a set of connections if each literal in the matrix is connected to at least one other literal of a different

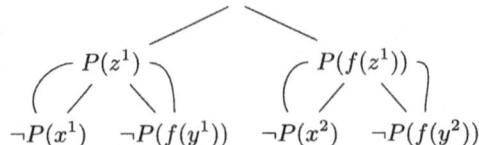

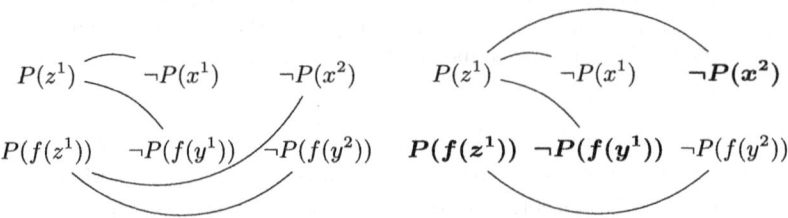

(a) Tableau proof with curved lines indicating connections. $\sigma$ is computed such that, e.g., $\sigma(z^1) = f(y^1)$.

(b) Same proof in matrix form

(c) A matrix that does not represent a proof. An open path is shown in **bold**.

**Fig. 2.** Connection calculus derivations

clause [37]. A matrix proof $M$ is *minimal* if there is no proof using only a strict subset of $M$. Although we can require that there is at least one conjecture in the matrix we could consider as a start clause, there is, in contrast to connection tableau proofs, no inherent tree structure in matrix proofs.

*Example 1.* To illustrate the two representations, consider the unsatisfiable set

$$\{\ \forall x \forall y.\ \neg P(x) \vee \neg P(f(y)),\ \forall z.\ P(z) \vee P(f(z))\ \}$$

and compare matrix and tableau refutations thereof in Fig. 2a and 2b[1]. Figure 2c shows a fully connected matrix that is not a proof as it has an open path.

## 3 Encoding Connection Tableaux

We first encode the search for closed connection tableaux (Sect. 2.2) in a SAT solver. A closed connection tableau is explicitly constructed from a satisfying assignment. We encode that a literal $L$ is a leaf of the tableau at path $U$ using a SAT variable $\langle L; U \rangle$, where $U$ is a set of literals labelling the nodes from $L$ towards the root. $L$ and $U$ are used only to determine the corresponding variable. For example, $\neg P(x^2)$ in Fig. 2a is represented by a variable $\langle \neg P(x^2); \{P(f(z^1))\} \rangle$. The substitution $\sigma$ and unification of connected literals are handled with another family of variables we discuss later.

---

[1] The literals of each clause are written vertically in columns and the order of the clause copies does not matter.

**Connection Tableau Rules as SAT.** We begin by asserting that at least one start clause $S$ must be present in the tableau. Therefore, all literals $L \in S$ must be in the tableau at the root:

$$\bigvee_{S} \bigwedge_{L \in S} \langle L; \emptyset \rangle \tag{1}$$

The SAT solver is free to choose any start clause $S$, but all literals in the chosen $S$ must be present at the root of the tableau. As the solver assigns variables $\langle L; U \rangle$ true we respond by propagating additional requirements. We demand that each literal has either an *extension* $E_{C,K}$ or a *reduction* $R_K$ applied, in order to close the corresponding branch in the final tableau:

$$\langle L; U \rangle \Vdash \bigvee_{C,K} E_{C,K} \vee \bigvee_{K \in U} R_K \tag{2}$$

Each formula $E_{C,K}$ represents applying an extension operation at $L$ using a fresh copy of a clause $C$ containing a literal $K \bowtie L$, which yields

$$E_{C,K} := \left( \langle L \sim K \rangle \wedge \bigwedge_{\substack{K' \in C \\ K' \neq K}} \langle K'; \{L\} \cup U \rangle \right) \tag{3}$$

i.e. that if an extension step $E_{C,K}$ is taken, $L$ and $K$ are connected and other literals $K' \in C$ must be in the tableau with path $\{L\} \cup U$. We write $\langle L \sim K \rangle$ for the SAT variable representing that $L$ and $K$ are connected modulo $\sigma$. Similarly,

$$R_K := \langle L \sim K \rangle \tag{4}$$

where $K \bowtie L$ and $K \in U$. The steps $E_{C,K}$ and $R_K$ are computed based only on the *possible* connection relation $\bowtie$: the current global substitution $\sigma$ maintained by the SAT solver is ignored, otherwise relevant cases may be missed on backtracking. Iterative deepening may be applied as usual [45], for example, by offering no $E_{C,K}$ options if the path length $|U|$ exceeds the depth limit.

*Example 2.* Consider the input clauses from Example 1 and assume the solver assigned literal $\langle \neg P(x^2); \{P(f(z^1))\} \rangle$ true, so the solver considers literal $\neg P(x^2)$ to be within the tableau, below $P(f(z^1))$. The solver propagates

$$\langle \neg P(x^2); \{P(f(z^1))\} \rangle \Vdash$$
$$(\langle P(f(z^2)); \{P(f(z^1)), \neg P(x^2)\} \rangle \wedge \langle \neg P(x^2) \sim P(z^2) \rangle) \vee$$
$$(\langle P(z^2); \{P(f(z^1)), \neg P(x^2)\} \rangle \wedge \langle \neg P(x^2) \sim P(f(z^2)) \rangle) \vee$$
$$\langle \neg P(x^2) \sim P(f(z^1)) \rangle$$

where the first two disjuncts represent applications of the extension rule and the last an application of reduction.

**Unification Constraints.** Variables $\langle L \sim K \rangle$ constrain $\sigma$ such that $\sigma(L)$ is connected to $\sigma(K)$. When the SAT solver assigns such a literal, we check whether this is consistent with the existing set of constraints. This can be done by applying a unification algorithm, perhaps using an efficient data structure such as the *variable trail* [39] to handle backtracking. We note in passing that algebraic datatype solvers [7], which are supported by many SMT solvers, implement a similar decision procedure. If the constraints are not satisfiable, we produce a *conflict clause* containing the reasons as Boolean assignments. For example, if we have $\langle L \sim K \rangle$, $\langle J \sim K \rangle$ and $\langle L \sim J \rangle$, but $\langle L \sim K \rangle \wedge \langle L \sim J \rangle$ is already unsatisfiable, we add the conflict

$$\neg \langle L \sim K \rangle \vee \neg \langle L \sim J \rangle \tag{5}$$

causing the solver to backtrack. This approach also allows a uniform treatment of refinements such as *regularity* based on *disequation constraints* [39].

**SAT Encoding of Closed Connection Tableaux.** We now have all the ingredients for our SAT encoding, which we denote by $\mathcal{E}_T$. By asserting that (i) a start clause must be present (1), (ii) each literal in the tableau must have a reduction or extension rule applied to it (2) and (iii) connections must have a consistent unifier, enforced by unification constraints, our encoding $\mathcal{E}_T$ is finished. Each propositional model of $\mathcal{E}_T$ represents a closed connection tableau.

**Pathological Behaviour.** Our SAT encoding $\mathcal{E}_T$ has drawbacks. Importantly, extension adds a *fresh instance* from the clause set to the tableau, and so the number of different SAT variables $\langle L; U \rangle$ grows rapidly. In turn, this means the resulting SAT problem has only limited propositional structure between variables that the solver can exploit. Search tends to degrade towards the kind of exhaustive enumeration of possible derivations that systems such as leanCoP [45] efficiently implement, but with the added overhead of a SAT solver.

## 4 Encoding Matrix Proofs

To avoid the previously described problems of $\mathcal{E}_T$, we encode matrix proofs (see Sect. 2.3). We denote our matrix-based encoding $\mathcal{E}_M$. Most search routines for spanning sets of connections presented in literature [10,45] restrict connections such that proofs are, or could be, simulated by a connection tableau proof [36]. In our $\mathcal{E}_M$ encoding, we allow arbitrary connections between clauses in the matrix. In this way, a single matrix proof can correspond to numerous tableau proofs [37]. In any event, our new representation $\mathcal{E}_M$ produces a combinatorial problem of finding connections between a set of clauses, which we argue is much more suitable for SAT solvers than $\mathcal{E}_T$.

### 4.1 Encoding Overview

We find a matrix proof with a given *resource limit* and split reasoning in:

1. We encode constraints for a fully-connected matrix (Sect. 4.2).
2. We constrain that the result has a set of spanning connections (Sect. 4.3).

We use the following result to motivate our encoding.

**Theorem 1 (Fully Connected Matrix).** *Suppose M is a minimal matrix proof with a spanning set of connections. Then M is fully connected.*

*Proof.* First, note that this is similar but not identical to Proposition 1 in Letz's work on matings pruning [37]. Suppose, towards contradiction, there is a literal $L \in C \in M$ that is not connected to any other $K$. Now consider the rest of the matrix $M' = M \setminus \{C\}$. Since $M$ is minimal, there is an open path $U$ through $M'$, as otherwise $M'$ would have a spanning set of connections. As $L$ is not connected to any literal, $U \cup \{L\}$ is an open path for $M$, which conflicts with our assumption of $M$ being a proof.

Theorem 1 allows us to restrict our work to fully-connected matrices. This restriction is a good approximation, as few fully-connected matrices do not have a spanning set of connections in practice (see Sect. 7). We use SAT variables of the form $S_C$ to denote that clause $C$ appears in the matrix, sometimes superscripted $S_C^k$ to indicate selecting $C^k$, the $k^{th}$ copy of $C$. We call these $S_C$ *selectors* and call $C$ *selected* if $S_C$ is assigned true. At least one of the start clauses $C$ must be selected, cf. (1):

$$\bigvee S_C^1. \tag{6}$$

In Sect. 3, we apply iterative deepening on the maximum length of a branch. This kind of resource limit cannot be used here, as there is no obvious notion of a *branch*, so we must devise alternatives. We first apply iterative deepening on the matrix's number $d$ of clauses. We immediately see that we need to introduce at most $d$ selectors for each clause. As we always refer to the same copies, the solver can more easily learn sensible conflicts from $\mathcal{E}_M$ than from $\mathcal{E}_T$. We discuss a further enhanced encoding later in Sect. 5.

### 4.2 Fully Connected Matrices

By Theorem 1, we may constrain that each literal in the matrix must connect to at least one other literal. Similarly to (2), we respond to a selection $S_C$ by propagating that each literal must be connected to some other literal in another clause in the matrix by enumerating all possible connections. This other clause could be selected or require selection, but there is no distinction between extension and reduction. Suppose $C$ is selected. For each $L \in C$, we propagate

$$S_C \Vdash \bigvee_D \bigvee_{1 \le k \le d} \bigvee_{K \in D^k} S_D^k \wedge \langle L \sim K \rangle \tag{7}$$

where $K \bowtie L$ is a literal in the input clause $D$ we connect to, and $k$ indicates which copy $D^k$ of that clause is used.

There are several possible options to enforce that at most $d$ clauses are selected for the matrix. We suggest using pseudo-Boolean constraints [20] or a direct encoding [5,14,55] to constrain that "there are no more than $d$ selector variables assigned". We can strengthen this to *exactly* $d$ as we apply iterative deepening, so the less-than-$d$ case was encountered already.

*Example 3.* Assume the situation

$$\{ S^1_{P(z) \vee P(f(z))},\ \neg S^1_{\neg P(x) \vee \neg P(f(y))},\ \langle P(z^1) \sim \neg P(x^1) \rangle,\ \langle P(z^1) \sim \neg P(f(y^1)) \rangle \}$$

which corresponds to the situation in Fig. 2c without the 3$^{\text{rd}}$ clause. Assuming that there are at most two copies of each clause, we would propagate that $P(f(z^1))$ needs to connect somehow. That means,

$$S^1_{P(z) \vee P(f(z))} \Vdash \left( S^1_{\neg P(x) \vee \neg P(f(y))} \wedge \langle P(f(z^1)) \sim \neg P(x^1) \rangle \right) \vee$$
$$\left( S^1_{\neg P(x) \vee \neg P(f(y))} \wedge \langle P(f(z^1)) \sim \neg P(f(y^1)) \rangle \right) \vee$$
$$\left( S^2_{\neg P(x) \vee \neg P(f(y))} \wedge \langle P(f(z^1)) \sim \neg P(x^2) \rangle \right) \vee$$
$$\left( S^2_{\neg P(x) \vee \neg P(f(y))} \wedge \langle P(f(z^1)) \sim \neg P(f(y^2)) \rangle \right)$$

These are all possible options given the available clauses and their copies.

### 4.3 Spanning Sets of Connections

Once we have a fully connected matrix, we check for open paths (see Sect. 2.3). If there are none, we are done and can use the resulting SAT model to output the proof, consisting of the selected clauses, the connections, and the global substitution. Suppose instead there is an open path $U$ – given by the set of literals – through the matrix $M$. At least two literals along $U$ must connect to make $M$ a proof. Let $\bar{S}$ be the set of selectors assigned true. Propagating

$$\bar{S} \Vdash \bigvee_{\{L,K\} \subseteq U} \langle L \sim K \rangle \tag{8}$$

forces the solver to "fix" $M$, likely via backtracking, by requiring that $U$ is not an open path.

*Example 4.* Continuing Example 3, assume the SAT solver further assigns

$$\{ S^2_{\neg P(x) \vee \neg P(f(y))},\ \langle P(f(z^1)) \sim \neg P(f(y^2)) \rangle, \langle P(z^1) \sim \neg P(x^2) \rangle \}$$

true. The result is the fully connected matrix, which is shown in Fig. 2c. We cannot propagate further clauses that are not already satisfied. However, we can find the open path $\{ P(f(z^1)), \neg P(f(y^1)), \neg P(x^2) \}$, which we exclude with

$$S^1_{P(z) \vee P(f(z))}, S^1_{\neg P(x) \vee \neg P(f(y))}, S^2_{\neg P(x) \vee \neg P(f(y))} \Vdash$$
$$\langle P(f(z^1)) \sim \neg P(f(y^1)) \rangle \vee \langle P(f(z^1)) \sim \neg P(x^2) \rangle.$$

As neither $\langle P(f(z^1)) \sim \neg P(f(y^1)) \rangle$ nor $\langle P(f(z^1)) \sim \neg P(x^2) \rangle$ results in a consistent unifier, the SAT solver is required to backtrack.

## 4.4 Correctness and Complexity of Matrix Encodings

Encoding $\mathcal{E}_M$ consists of (6), (7), (8), and constraints for the depth limit. Its models represent fully-connected matrix proofs. We show soundness, completeness, and termination for a given size $d$ in $\mathcal{E}_M$, and describe the respective complexity class of $\mathcal{E}_M$.

**Theorem 2 (Soundness).** *A propositional model of $\mathcal{E}_M$ represents a matrix with a spanning set of connections.*

*Proof.* Whenever the SAT solver finds a propositional model, we first check that it represents a proof, adding constraints if not (Sect. 4.3).

**Theorem 3 (Completeness).** *If a matrix $M$ together with a spanning set of connections exists, there is a propositional model of $\mathcal{E}_M$ at depth $d = |M|$.*

*Proof.* Such a matrix proof $M$ can be represented by setting $S_C^k$ true iff there are at least $k$ copies of $C$ in $M$. The spanning set of connections is represented by setting $L \sim K$ iff $L$ is connected to $K$ in the proof. This model of $\mathcal{E}_M$ and all its submodels are consistent modulo the semantics of $\sim$ and all possible instances of (7). Furthermore, the final model satisfies the depth constraints and contains at least one start clause. Also, we do not block the model with the final check in Sect. 4.3 as the set of connections are spanning.

**Theorem 4 (Complexity Bound).** *Solving our particular encoding $\mathcal{E}_M$ is in the complexity class $\Sigma_2^P$ with respect to the input size and the matrix proof size.*

*Proof.* There are polynomially many SAT variables. To see this, let $c$ be the number of clauses in the input, containing a total of $l$ literals. We have at most $d \cdot c$ selectors $S_C^k$. We also have $O(d^2 l^2)$ possible connection literals $\langle L \sim K \rangle$. Hence, there are only polynomially many instantiations of (7). After adding in the worst case, all of them, the problem is in NP. We can non-deterministically guess an assignment for all polynomially many selectors and unification atoms. Checking the model can be done clearly in deterministic polynomial time. Checking whether a matrix represents a matrix proof is co-NP complete. It can be solved by a separate SAT solver, which checks if the matrix $\sigma(M)$ represented by the SAT model is satisfiable. As we can solve $\mathcal{E}_M$ in NP with a co-NP oracle, the problem of solving our encoding for some fixed limit $d$ is in $\Sigma_2^P$.

As checking the satisfiability of a set of clauses over rigid variables is $\Sigma_2^P$-complete [33], our approach's complexity coincides with its theoretical bound.

**Corollary 1 (Termination).** *A run for solving $\mathcal{E}_M$ at fixed $d$ terminates.*

## 5 Iterative Deepening via Unsat Core Refinement

A downside of our encoding $\mathcal{E}_M$, especially of its constraints from Sect. 4.2, is that we eagerly introduce and use selectors for clause instances that are not required. If there is more than one input clause and the matrix is of size $d$, not all clauses can have $d$ copies in the matrix for arithmetic reasons. Therefore, creating $d$ instances of each clause is overkill. This section addresses this challenge and improves iterative deepening via unsat cores, resulting in a refined encoding $\mathcal{E}_U$.

We use an abstraction-refinement [23] approach to approximate the number of copies required for each clause. This way, we avoid polluting the search space with likely unnecessary clause instances. Instead of a coarse global limit $d$, we estimate how many copies of each clause are required with a *multiplicity* $\mu$ [9]. Initially, we have $\mu(C) = 1$ for start clauses and $\mu(C) = 0$ otherwise. The multiplicity is monotonically increased based on the unsat core of the following encoding. We refine constraint (7) to

$$S_C \Vdash \bigvee_D \bigvee_{1 \leq k \leq \mu(D)+1} \bigvee_{K \in D^k} S_D^k \wedge \langle L \sim K \rangle \qquad (9)$$

as we have $\mu(D)$ copies of $D$. Note that $k$ ranges up to $\mu(D) + 1$. We add temporary assertions[2] $\kappa_D := \neg S_D^{\mu(D)+1}$ so that the solver cannot select $D^{\mu(D)+1}$, but *can* report that finding a proof failed in part due to a lack of copies of $D$. We revise (8), as we can no longer assume that a fully connected matrix has exactly $d$ clauses. A matrix can be fully connected, but the desired matrix proof may in fact be a strict *superset* of the current matrix. As (8) is now too strong, we weaken it to

$$\bar{S} \Vdash \left[ \bigvee_{\{L,K\} \subseteq U} \langle L \sim K \rangle \right] \vee \bigvee_{L \in U} F_L \qquad (10)$$

where $F_L$ is a formula indicating that $L$ could also be connected to another literal in a clause *not yet in the matrix* and $\bar{S}$ a set of selectors as before in (8).

*Example 5.* Assume we have $\mu(P(z) \vee P(f(z))) = \mu(\neg P(x) \vee \neg P(f(y))) := 2$ and let us consider Example 3 again. In this propagation, we would have to additionally list the case that $S^3_{\neg P(x) \vee \neg P(f(y))}$ is true. The case $S^3_{P(z) \vee P(f(z))}$ is not needed, as there is no way to connect it anyway. As we assumed that $S^3_{\neg P(x) \vee \neg P(f(y))}$ is false, the SAT solver will not assign it true, but might report it in its unsat core in case there are feasible ways to proceed, given a higher depth limit. In Example 4, we would have to list the additional cases:

$$S^2_{P(z) \vee P(f(z))} \wedge \langle \neg P(f(y^1)) \sim P(z^2) \rangle, \ S^2_{P(z) \vee P(f(z))} \wedge \langle \neg P(f(y^1)) \sim P(f(z^2)) \rangle,$$

$$S^2_{P(z) \vee P(f(z))} \wedge \langle \neg P(x^2) \sim P(z^2) \rangle, \ S^2_{P(z) \vee P(f(z))} \wedge \langle \neg P(x^2) \sim P(f(z^2)) \rangle,$$

$$S^3_{P(z) \vee P(f(z))}, \ S^3_{\neg P(x) \vee \neg P(f(y))}$$

---

[2] Named $\kappa$ because it indicates that a clause needs more "$\kappa$-city".

As the respective clause selector is assumed false anyway, we do not need to introduce connectedness atoms for clause copies beyond the depth limit. Slight variations and optimisations of the encoding, however, would benefit from encoding those aspects as well. Further, listing both the second and third copies of clause $P(z) \vee P(f(z))$ shows one source of symmetry discussed in Sect. 6.

Whenever the SAT solver reports unsatisfiability, we retrieve the *unsat core* representing a potentially non-minimal subset of $\kappa$ assertions sufficient to yield unsatisfiability. We may increase one or more $\mu(C)$ if the corresponding assertion occurs in the unsat core. However, to retain completeness, we need to ensure that we eventually increment the multiplicity of every clause appearing repeatedly in the unsat core: in other words, we require *fairness*. In case the core is empty, we can conclude that no proof exists. As a result, our SAT encoding $\mathcal{E}_U$ with improved iterative deepening is given by (6), (9), and (10).

*Example 6.* Consider the input problem

$$C := P(a) \qquad D := \forall x.\ \neg P(x) \vee P(f(x)) \qquad E := \forall y.\ \neg P(y)$$

with $C$ as the start clause. $\kappa_D$ will always be contained within the unsat core, no matter its multiplicity. However, a fair enumeration eventually includes $\kappa_E$.

Our improved encoding $\mathcal{E}_U$ remains sound and terminating by similar arguments to Theorems 2 and 4. Completeness requires an adjusted argument.

**Theorem 5 (Completeness).** *If a matrix $M$ together with a spanning set of connections exists, there is a corresponding propositional model of $\mathcal{E}_U$.*

*Proof.* In addition to Theorem 3, we show that if there is a proof using $M$ which our current $\mu$ does not permit, at least one relevant $\kappa_C$ is contained in the unsat core. Fairness then ensures we will eventually find the proof. Consider a maximal subset $M' \subset M$ representable at $\mu$.

1. If $M'$ cannot be fully connected, it contains at least one literal $L$ with no connections. Since $M'$ is maximal and $M$ can be fully connected, $L$ should be connected to some literal in a clause $D$ that is not yet in the matrix. This option is offered in (9), but fails because the respective $\kappa_D$ assumption is forced false. $\kappa_D$ is therefore in the unsat core.
2. If $M'$ can be fully connected, we would have failed to close some open path $U$ and propagated some instance of (10). Some $L \in U$ must connect to at least one literal of a clause not yet in $M'$ by the right disjunct of (10). As $M'$ is maximal, we can add no clauses, so the constraint fails because of the $\kappa$ assumption.

A side effect of encoding $\mathcal{E}_U$ is that it also terminates on some non-theorems.

# 6 Redundancy Elimination

Restricting the SAT solver's search space is beneficial when solving the SAT encodings of Sects. 3–5. In addition to standard techniques, such as tautology elimination [39], we propose some specialised redundancy eliminations.

## 6.1 Multiplicity Symmetry

Our encodings from Sects. 3–5 contain *several symmetries* [1], which we now *avoid*, rather than *break* [51]. The first symmetry is that copies of clauses are interchangeable. Suppose we connect some literal $L$ to literal $K$ in a copy of $C$ not yet in the matrix, and subsequently fail to find a proof in that direction. Nothing prevents the SAT solver from selecting another copy of $C$ and failing for the same reasons. We avoid this by propagating

$$S_C^{i+1} \Vdash S_C^i, \tag{11}$$

enforcing that $C^i$ is selected only if $C^j$ with $j < i$ are selected.

## 6.2 Subsumption and Instance Symmetry

Saturation systems often delete a clause $C$ because it is *subsumed* [47] by some more-general clause $D$. Dynamics in connection systems are somewhat different as new first-order clauses are not deduced, but we can profit by applying some subsumption. If two different clauses $C$ and $D$ are in the current matrix, we can enforce that neither becomes a subset of the other, modulo $\sigma^3$. This restriction preserves completeness, by Bibel's Lemma 6.8 [10].

An obvious extension of this idea is removing clauses from the matrix that are subsumed by other clauses from the input set. This fails, however.

*Example 7.* Consider the four input clauses

$$C := P(a) \quad D := Q(a) \quad E := \forall x.\ \neg P(x) \vee Q(x) \quad F := \forall y.\ \neg Q(y)$$

with $C$ being the only start clause. There is a proof without subsumption via $C$, $E$, and finally $F$; this is the only minimal proof using $C$. However, putting $E$ in the matrix with $\sigma(x) = a$ makes it be subsumed by $D$.

Subsumption in the usual sense of smaller clauses representing any usage of larger clauses fails. This failure occurs because we might lose the *reason to connect* a clause to our current matrix. Keeping larger clauses instead also does not work, as we might not be able to connect all literals of the larger clause. Nonetheless, we can motivate additional symmetry avoidance this way. Define an arbitrary total order $\prec$ on input clauses such that start clauses are the least elements. We assume that the order of each clause in the matrix is the same as the order of the clauses in the input set from which they are a copy.

**Lemma 1 (Instance Symmetry).** *Suppose there is a matrix proof $M$ containing a clause $D$ with $D \succ C$, and that there is a $\rho$ such that $\rho(C) = \sigma(D)$. Then $M$ with $D$ exchanged for $C$ also has a spanning set of connections.*

*Proof.* As all variables in $C$ and $D$ are fresh, we can adapt $\sigma$ according to $\rho$. This way, $C$ may be connected to the same literals as $D$. As $\rho(C)$ has the same literals as $\sigma(D)$, we neither add additional paths that must be closed, nor do we prevent other clauses connecting to $C$ because we dropped the respective literal.

---
[3] We do not apply an additional substitution to either side.

**Corollary 2 (Instance Symmetry Completeness).** *Pruning models containing such clauses D remains complete.*

### 6.3 Substitution Symmetry

Symmetry appears in substitutions applied to different copies of the same clause.

*Example 8.* Consider a literal in two copies of the same clause, $L[x]$ and $L[y]$. Assume that all attempts with $\sigma(x) = a$ and $\sigma(y) = b$ fail. Nothing prevents trying again with all connections "flipped" to the other clause and $\sigma(x) = b$ and $\sigma(y) = a$, introducing an exponential number of branches in the worst case.

We enforce an ordering on the substitutions applied to the *variables in copies of the same clause*. This ordering of terms should be stable under substitution and orient as many terms as possible, but need not have the subterm property and therefore may not be a reduction ordering [3]. We suggest the following order. Assume an arbitrary total ordering $\prec$ over function symbols. Define $f(\bar{t}) \prec g(\bar{s})$ iff (i) $f \prec g$ or (ii) $f = g$ and $\bar{t} \prec \bar{s}$. Sequences of terms $\bar{t} \prec \bar{s}$ are compared lexicographically. Let $\bar{x}$ be the variables occurring left-to-right in clause $C$. Given two instances $C^i$ and $C^j$ of the same clause with $i < j$, we may enforce that $\sigma(\bar{x}_i) \not\succeq \sigma(\bar{x}_j)$ to avoid symmetries over clause substitutions.

**Lemma 2 (Spanning Order).** *Suppose M has a spanning set of connections and contains two copies $C^i$ and $C^j$ of the same clause. Then there is a spanning set of connections that satisfies $\sigma(\bar{x}_i) \not\succeq \sigma(\bar{x}_j)$.*

*Proof.* If this condition does not already hold, we have $\sigma(\bar{x}_i) \succeq \sigma(\bar{x}_j)$. Duplicate clauses are already eliminated, so in fact $\sigma(\bar{x}_i) \succ \sigma(\bar{x}_j)$. Now "swap" $C^i$ and $C^j$ by exchanging their connections to obtain a new spanning set of connections and consistent substitution $\sigma'$. Necessarily, $\sigma'(\bar{x}_i) \prec \sigma'(\bar{x}_j)$.

By iterated application of Lemma 2, it is possible to "reorder" any spanning set of connections into another that respects the order.

**Corollary 3 (Substitution Symmetry Completeness).** *Enforcing an ordering on substitution of variables in copies of the same clause remains complete.*

## 7 Implementation and Experiments

**Implementation.** We implemented the encodings and optimisations of Sects. 3–6 in our new prototype UPCoP[4]. UPCoP uses either the user-propagator of the CADICAL SAT solver [30] or of the Z3 SMT solver [15].

---

[4] At https://github.com/CEisenhofer/UPCoP.

| Solver | UPCoP$_{SAT}$ | UPCoP$_{SMT}$ | UPCoP$_{SAT}$ | UPCoP$_{SMT}$ | UPCoP$_{SAT}$ | UPCoP$_{SMT}$ | meanCoP |
|---|---|---|---|---|---|---|---|
| Enc. | $\mathcal{E}_M$ | | $\mathcal{E}_U$ | | $\mathcal{E}_H$ | | |
| Solved | 928 | 855 | 1,152 | 1,055 | 1,272 | 1,264 | 1,972 |
| Unique | 27 | 20 | 109 | 93 | 105 | 76 | 551 |

**Fig. 3.** Experimental summary. UPCoP$_{SAT}$ and UPCoP$_{SMT}$ denote the UPCoP versions based on CADICAL (SAT) and Z3(SMT). "Unique" lists the number of problems solvable by UPCoP, but not meanCoP, and vice versa.

Due to our encoding via SAT variables, UPCoP can choose an arbitrary atom to be assigned in case of a decision. However, such an arbitrary atom selection conflicts with the notion of goal-directedness. Consider, for example, the initial constraint (6) that at least one selector of a conjecture clause has to be taken. However, this constraint does not require that the solver start by choosing one of those clauses, but only that one start clause is selected in the final model. As a result, the solver might pick an arbitrary selector and derive a submatrix from it that is not connectable to any conjecture. A similar situation may occur when propagating all possible candidates in (7). We therefore force UPCoP always to pick one of the currently relevant options, rather than leaving the choice to the internal heuristics of UPCoP. Further, we make UPCoP to assign currently irrelevant selectors false, rather than true.

We note that UPCoP might spend significant reasoning time upon term equalities and orderings not required by any selected clause in the matrix. To overcome this issue, UPCoP associates every non-ground term uniquely to the clause copy it originates from. This way, we process (in)equalities reported by those non-ground terms only in case the respective selector is assigned true.

**Experimental Setup.** We evaluated UPCoP on the TPTP benchmark set [57] of first-order problems using an AMD EPYC 7502 clocked at roughly 1.8GHz, a limit of 16 GB memory per run, and a 30s timeout. We considered all 6468 provable first-order problems of the TPTP 8.2.0 problem repository by translating them upfront to the SMT-LIB input format [6].

We evaluated UPCoP with three encodings, as follows. First, we used the encodings $\mathcal{E}_M$ and $\mathcal{E}_U$ of Sects. 4–5, respectively. Further, we considered a hybrid approach $\mathcal{E}_H$ which combines $\mathcal{E}_M$ and $\mathcal{E}_U$ in a way such that the capacity of every (non-ground) clause is increased on each failure, but the set of clauses in the matrix is limited by the number of copies available, rather than by a strict upper bound. For each encoding, we separately evaluated UPCoP with user-propagators of CADICAL and Z3. Our experimental results thus report on six different settings of UPCoP, shown in Fig. 3. In addition, we compared UPCoP with the default (complete) mode of meanCoP [28].

**Experimental Analysis.** Our results are summarised in Fig. 3, with all versions of UPCoP solving altogether 1,601 problems. While UPCoP solves less problems than meanCoP, we emphasize that UPCoP solves 179 problems from all different kinds of categories that meanCoP cannot. There are many different reasons for this. There are mainly two reasons apart from the "non-determinism" in the choice of which literals to connect. The first one is that some matrix proofs found by UPCoP are in fact decently smaller than the respective tableau-shaped proof of meanCoP. The second one is that the unsat core-based encodings indeed sometimes deduce that certain clauses are completely irrelevant, and consequently ignore them, resulting in a reasonable speed-up.

Counter-intuitively, UPCoP usually does not get stuck in eliminating non-spanning connections. Most cases in which UPCoP does not terminate are because UPCoP is too slow to find a fully-connected matrix due to the previously discussed points. As soon as a fully-connected matrix is found, it becomes spanning after only a few rejected matrices. Although the spanningness check is co-NP complete, we did not encounter cases where it took a significant time.

We note that $\mathcal{E}_M$ terminates quickly on inputs with small (potentially non-tree-shaped) proofs. $\mathcal{E}_U$ is best suited for large problems with redundant unconnectable clauses, as we will not generate further copies of the redundant clauses. $\mathcal{E}_H$ best pays off on problems whose proofs use most clauses from the input, but each of them only a few times.

**Discussion.** When analysing our experimental results, we note the following aspects for further improvements in UPCoP:

- The SAT/SMT solvers used by UPCoP repeatedly learn additional facts about the underlying proof systems, mostly using new Boolean variables. Hence, the solvers might decide to split on these Boolean variables. This can slow down proof search, as the solver might put a lot of effort into learning facts about partial proofs that cannot be extended to a proper proof. Further, some of these Boolean assignments represent partial proofs that a naive proof enumeration cannot even reach.
- Learning clauses coming from those unfruitful proof spaces also do not necessarily combine: for example, the solver can consider multiple submatrices simultaneously, even though these submatrices can never be combined. The assumption that conflict learning and SAT heuristics will guide the solver towards a more focused search has not been vindicated. Postponing the propagation of possible connections from submatrices not attached to the main matrix helps to reduce the number of Boolean variables and the overhead of propagating potentially unused constraints, but requires additional expensive book-keeping.
- Adjusting the SAT/SMT solvers' decision heuristic to prefer Boolean variables relevant for the current proof state might be beneficial [41]. Yet, such adjustments harm efficient heuristics for variable selection within the solver.
- The encoding $\mathcal{E}_T$ suffers because the conflicts mainly learned depend on the precise paths in the tableau. Similarly, conflicts learned about the Boolean variables in the matrix encodings $\mathcal{E}_M$ and $\mathcal{E}_U$ do not generalise well from one copy to the other in a way such that multiple copies of the same clause are considered in an isomorphic way numerous times.

– Additionally, SAT/SMT solvers incur non-negligible overhead from propagation loops for processing clauses. While simulating a single rule via SAT, a naive proof enumeration solver can process multiple steps within that time.

As shown and discussed before, one way of tackling most of those problems is to implement a custom variant of conflict learning that does not have the discussed behaviours that are mostly inherent to modern SAT solvers. Based on these results, we build a further system hopCoP [49] that implements such a custom conflict learning engine for the tableaux form of connection calculus.

## 8 Related Work

Most first-order theorem provers employ a variety of ground reasoning techniques, predominantly SAT and SMT solvers. Here we must mention the family of instance-based methods [8]: grounding a set of first-order clauses in the hope that they become unsatisfiable, which can be employed with a dedicated calculus [34] or alongside an existing system [50,53]. In the other direction, SMT solvers often integrate quantifier instantiation into satisfiability routines [32,42]. Ground reasoning can also be used for many other combinatorial tasks in first-order theorem provers [52], such as keeping track of clause splitting [59], detecting subsumption [48], or determining if inferences are applicable [24]. MACE-style finite model builders [22] employ SAT solving to determine whether a set of clauses is satisfiable, assuming a fixed-size finite model, using symmetry-breaking [51].

Apart from our other approach [49] using a custom conflict learning engine and restricting ourselves to the direct encoding of proof objects, the ChewTPTP system in both its SAT [26] and SMT [17] incarnations is the closest existing approach to theorem proving via satisfiability solving. ChewTPTP encodes constraints for a closed connection tableau completely ahead of time, then passes the resulting constraints to a SAT or SMT solver. The higher-order systems Satallax [29] and its fork Lash [19] also reduce proof search to the propositional level. However, in contrast to UPCoP, when the Satallax's SAT solver reports unsatisfiability, a proof has been found. We previously published an early version of our ideas in a more general setting [27].

## 9 Conclusion

We encode first-order connection calculi as a propositional problem, improve our SAT encodings for matrix proofs, and guide iterative deepening using unsat cores. We introduce several optimisations to prune symmetries and eliminate unnecessary branches during proof search. Initial experiments with our new UPCoP solver show that our encoding can be used to solve certain problems, other connection solvers fail to solve. Further improvements may come with applying custom garbage-collection and variable selection heuristic strategies in UPCoP due to the discussed problems encountered during solving.

**Acknowledgements.** This research was funded in whole or in part by the ERC Consolidator Grant ARTIST 101002685, the ERC Proof of Concept Grant LEARN 101213411, the TU Wien Doctoral College SecInt, the FWF SpyCoDe Grant 10.55776/F85, the WWTF grant ForSmart 10.47379/ICT22007, and the Amazon Research Award 2023 QuAT.

**Disclosure of Interests.** The authors have no competing interests to declare that are relevant to the content of this article.

# References

1. Aloul, F.A., Sakallah, K.A., Markov, I.L.: Efficient symmetry breaking for Boolean satisfiability. IEEE Trans. Comput. **55**(5), 549–558 (2006). https://doi.org/10.1109/TC.2006.75
2. Andrews, P.B.: On connections and higher-order logic. J. Autom. Reason. **5**(3), 257–291 (1989). https://doi.org/10.1007/BF00248320
3. Baader, F., Nipkow, T.: Term Rewriting and All That. Cambridge University Press, Cambridge (1998)
4. Baaz, M., Egly, U., Leitsch, A.: Normal form transformations. In: Handbook of Automated Reasoning (in 2 volumes), pp. 273–333. Elsevier and MIT Press (2001). https://doi.org/10.1016/B978-044450813-3/50007-2
5. Bailleux, O., Boufkhad, Y.: Efficient CNF encoding of boolean cardinality constraints. In: Rossi, F. (ed.) CP 2003. LNCS, vol. 2833, pp. 108–122. Springer, Heidelberg (2003). https://doi.org/10.1007/978-3-540-45193-8_8
6. Barrett, C., Fontaine, P., Tinelli, C.: The satisfiability modulo theories library (SMT-LIB) (2016). https://www.SMT-LIB.org
7. Barrett, C.W., Shikanian, I., Tinelli, C.: An abstract decision procedure for a theory of inductive data types. J. Satisf. Boolean Model. Comput. **3**(1–2), 21–46 (2007). https://doi.org/10.3233/SAT190028
8. Baumgartner, P., Thorstensen, E.: Instance based methods - a brief overview. Künstliche Intell. **24**(1), 35–42 (2010). https://doi.org/10.1007/S13218-010-0002-X
9. Bibel, W.: Matings in matrices. Commun. ACM **26**(11), 844–852 (1983). https://doi.org/10.1145/182.183
10. Bibel, W.: Automated theorem proving. Artificial intelligence, Vieweg, 2., rev. ed. edn. (1987)
11. Bibel, W.: Comparison of proof methods. In: AReCCa, pp. 119–132 (2023). https://ceur-ws.org/Vol-3613/
12. Biere, A., Fazekas, K., Fleury, M., Heisinger, M.: CaDiCaL, Kissat, Paracooba, Plingeling and Treengeling entering the SAT Competition 2020. In: Proceedings of SAT Competition 2020 – Solver and Benchmark Descriptions, pp. 51–53. Department of Computer Science Report Series B, University of Helsinki (2020)
13. Biere, A., Froleyks, N., Wang, W.: CadiBack: extracting backbones with CaDiCaL. In: SAT. LIPIcs, vol. 271, pp. 3:1–3:12 (2023). https://doi.org/10.4230/LIPICS.SAT.2023.3
14. Biere, A., Heule, M., van Maaren, H., Walsh, T. (eds.): Handbook of Satisfiability - Second Edition, Frontiers in Artificial Intelligence and Applications, vol. 336. IOS Press (2021). https://doi.org/10.3233/FAIA336

15. Bjørner, N.S., Eisenhofer, C., Kovács, L.: Satisfiability modulo custom theories in Z3. In: VMCAI. LNCS, vol. 13881, pp. 91–105 (2023). https://doi.org/10.1007/978-3-031-24950-1_5
16. Bonacina, M.P.: A taxonomy of theorem-proving strategies. In: Wooldridge, M.J., Veloso, M. (eds.) Artificial Intelligence Today. LNCS (LNAI), vol. 1600, pp. 43–84. Springer, Heidelberg (1999). https://doi.org/10.1007/3-540-48317-9_3
17. Bongio, J., Katrak, C., Lin, H., Lynch, C., McGregor, R.E.: Encoding first order proofs in SMT. In: SMT. ENTCS, vol. 198, pp. 71–84 (2007). https://doi.org/10.1016/J.ENTCS.2008.04.081
18. Brand, D.: Proving theorems with the modification method. SIAM J. Comput. **4**(4), 412–430 (1975). https://doi.org/10.1137/0204036
19. Brown, C.E., Kaliszyk, C.: Lash 1.0 (system description). CoRR abs/2205.06640 (2022). https://doi.org/10.48550/ARXIV.2205.06640
20. Chai, D., Kuehlmann, A.: A fast pseudo-Boolean constraint solver. IEEE Trans. Comput. Aided Des. Integr. Circuits Syst. **24**(3), 305–317 (2005). https://doi.org/10.1109/TCAD.2004.842808
21. Cimatti, A., Griggio, A., Sebastiani, R.: Computing small unsatisfiable cores in satisfiability modulo theories. J. Artif. Intell. Res. **40**, 701–728 (2011). https://doi.org/10.1613/JAIR.3196
22. Claessen, K., Sörensson, N.: New techniques that improve MACE-style finite model finding. In: Proceedings of the CADE-19 Workshop: Model Computation-Principles, Algorithms, Applications, pp. 11–27 (2003)
23. Clarke, E.M., Grumberg, O., Jha, S., Lu, Y., Veith, H.: Counterexample-guided abstraction refinement for symbolic model checking. J. ACM **50**(5), 752–794 (2003). https://doi.org/10.1145/876638.876643
24. Coutelier, R., Kovács, L., Rawson, M., Rath, J.: SAT-based subsumption resolution. In: CADE. LNCS, vol. 14132, pp. 190–206 (2023). https://doi.org/10.1007/978-3-031-38499-8_11
25. D'Agostino, M., Gabbay, D.M., Hähnle, R., Posegga, J.: Handbook of Tableau Methods. Springer (2013)
26. Deshane, T., Hu, W., Jablonski, P., Lin, H., Lynch, C., McGregor, R.E.: Encoding first order proofs in SAT. In: Pfenning, F. (ed.) CADE 2007. LNCS (LNAI), vol. 4603, pp. 476–491. Springer, Heidelberg (2007). https://doi.org/10.1007/978-3-540-73595-3_35
27. Eisenhofer, C., Kovács, L., Rawson, M.: Embedding the connection calculus in satisfiability modulo theories. In: AReCCa, pp. 54–63 (2023). https://ceur-ws.org/Vol-3613/
28. Färber, M.: A curiously effective backtracking strategy for connection tableaux. In: AReCCa, pp. 23–40 (2023). https://ceur-ws.org/Vol-3613/
29. Färber, M., Brown, C.: Internal guidance for satallax. In: Olivetti, N., Tiwari, A. (eds.) IJCAR 2016. LNCS (LNAI), vol. 9706, pp. 349–361. Springer, Cham (2016). https://doi.org/10.1007/978-3-319-40229-1_24
30. Fazekas, K., Niemetz, A., Preiner, M., Kirchweger, M., Szeider, S., Biere, A.: IPASIR-UP: user propagators for CDCL. In: SAT. LIPIcs, vol. 271, pp. 8:1–8:13 (2023). https://doi.org/10.4230/LIPICS.SAT.2023.8
31. Galmiche, D.: Connection methods in linear logic and proof nets construction. Theoret. Comput. Sci. **232**(1), 231–272 (2000). https://doi.org/10.1016/S0304-3975(99)00176-0. https://www.sciencedirect.com/science/article/pii/S0304397599001760

32. Ge, Y., Moura, L.: Complete instantiation for quantified formulas in satisfiabiliby modulo theories. In: Bouajjani, A., Maler, O. (eds.) CAV 2009. LNCS, vol. 5643, pp. 306–320. Springer, Heidelberg (2009). https://doi.org/10.1007/978-3-642-02658-4_25
33. Goubault, J.: The complexity of resource-bounded first-order classical logic. In: Enjalbert, P., Mayr, E.W., Wagner, K.W. (eds.) STACS 1994. LNCS, vol. 775, pp. 59–70. Springer, Heidelberg (1994). https://doi.org/10.1007/3-540-57785-8_131
34. Korovin, K.: Inst-gen – a modular approach to instantiation-based automated reasoning. In: Voronkov, A., Weidenbach, C. (eds.) Programming Logics. LNCS, vol. 7797, pp. 239–270. Springer, Heidelberg (2013). https://doi.org/10.1007/978-3-642-37651-1_10
35. Kovács, L., Voronkov, A.: First-order theorem proving and VAMPIRE. In: Sharygina, N., Veith, H. (eds.) CAV 2013. LNCS, vol. 8044, pp. 1–35. Springer, Heidelberg (2013). https://doi.org/10.1007/978-3-642-39799-8_1
36. Kreitz, C., Otten, J., Schmitt, S., Pientka, B.: Matrix-based constructive theorem proving. In: Intellectics and Computational Logic (to Wolfgang Bibel on the occasion of his 60th birthday). Applied Logic Series, vol. 19, pp. 189–205 (2000)
37. Letz, R.: Using matings for pruning connection tableaux. In: CADE. LNCS, vol. 1421, pp. 381–396 (1998). https://doi.org/10.1007/BFB0054273
38. Letz, R., Schumann, J., Bayerl, S., Bibel, W.: SETHEO: a high-performance theorem prover. J. Autom. Reason. 8(2), 183–212 (1992). https://doi.org/10.1007/BF00244282
39. Letz, R., Stenz, G.: Model elimination and connection tableau procedures. In: Handbook of Automated Reasoning (in 2 volumes), pp. 2015–2114. Elsevier and MIT Press (2001). https://doi.org/10.1016/B978-044450813-3/50030-8
40. Lynce, I., Marques-Silva, J.: On computing minimum unsatisfiable cores. In: SAT (2004). http://www.satisfiability.org/SAT04/programme/110.pdf
41. de Moura, L., Bjørner, N.: Relevancy propagation. Technical Report MSR-TR-2007-140, Microsoft Research, Technical report (2007)
42. Moura, L., Bjørner, N.: Efficient E-matching for SMT solvers. In: Pfenning, F. (ed.) CADE 2007. LNCS (LNAI), vol. 4603, pp. 183–198. Springer, Heidelberg (2007). https://doi.org/10.1007/978-3-540-73595-3_13
43. Moura, L., Bjørner, N.: Z3: an efficient SMT solver. In: Ramakrishnan, C.R., Rehof, J. (eds.) TACAS 2008. LNCS, vol. 4963, pp. 337–340. Springer, Heidelberg (2008). https://doi.org/10.1007/978-3-540-78800-3_24
44. Nieuwenhuis, R., Rubio, A.: Paramodulation-based theorem proving. In: Handbook of Automated Reasoning (in 2 volumes), pp. 371–443. Elsevier and MIT Press (2001). https://doi.org/10.1016/B978-044450813-3/50009-6
45. Otten, J.: leanCoP 2.0 and ileanCoP 1.2: high performance lean theorem proving in classical and intuitionistic logic (system descriptions). In: Armando, A., Baumgartner, P., Dowek, G. (eds.) IJCAR 2008. LNCS (LNAI), vol. 5195, pp. 283–291. Springer, Heidelberg (2008). https://doi.org/10.1007/978-3-540-71070-7_23
46. Otten, J.: Implementing connection calculi for first-order modal logics. In: IWIL. EPiC Series in Computing, vol. 22, pp. 18–32. EasyChair (2012). https://doi.org/10.29007/82M9
47. Ramakrishnan, I.V., Sekar, R., Voronkov, A.: Term indexing. In: Handbook of Automated Reasoning (in 2 volumes), pp. 1853–1964. Elsevier and MIT Press (2001). https://doi.org/10.1016/b978-044450813-3/50028-x
48. Rath, J., Biere, A., Kovács, L.: First-order subsumption via SAT solving. In: FMCAD, pp. 160–169 (2022). https://doi.org/10.34727/2022/ISBN.978-3-85448-053-2_22

49. Rawson, M., Eisenhofer, C., Kovács, L.: Constraint learning for non-confluent proof search. In: Pozzatoand, G.L., Uustalu, T. (eds.) TABLEAUX 2025. LNCS (LNAI), vol. 15980, pp.103–119. Springer, Cham (2026). https://doi.org/10.1007/978-3-032-06085-3_6
50. Rawson, M., Reger, G.: Eliminating models during model elimination. In: Das, A., Negri, S. (eds.) TABLEAUX 2021. LNCS (LNAI), vol. 12842, pp. 250–265. Springer, Cham (2021). https://doi.org/10.1007/978-3-030-86059-2_15
51. Reger, G., Riener, M., Suda, M.: Symmetry avoidance in MACE-style finite model finding. In: Herzig, A., Popescu, A. (eds.) FroCoS 2019. LNCS (LNAI), vol. 11715, pp. 3–21. Springer, Cham (2019). https://doi.org/10.1007/978-3-030-29007-8_1
52. Reger, G., Suda, M.: The uses of SAT solvers in VAMPIRE. In: Vampire. EPiC Series in Computing, vol. 38, pp. 63–69 (2015). https://doi.org/10.29007/4W68
53. Schulz, S.: Light-weight integration of SAT solving into first-order reasoners – first experiments. Vampire, pp. 9–19 (2017)
54. Schulz, S., Cruanes, S., Vukmirović, P.: Faster, higher, stronger: E 2.3. In: Fontaine, P. (ed.) CADE 2019. LNCS (LNAI), vol. 11716, pp. 495–507. Springer, Cham (2019). https://doi.org/10.1007/978-3-030-29436-6_29
55. Sinz, C.: Towards an optimal CNF encoding of boolean cardinality constraints. In: van Beek, P. (ed.) CP 2005. LNCS, vol. 3709, pp. 827–831. Springer, Heidelberg (2005). https://doi.org/10.1007/11564751_73
56. Smullyan, R.M.: First-Order Logic. Springer (1968)
57. Sutcliffe, G.: The TPTP problem library and associated infrastructure. from CNF to TH0, TPTP v6.4.0. J. Autom. Reason. **59**(4), 483–502 (2017)
58. Tinelli, C.: A DPLL-based calculus for ground satisfiability modulo theories. In: Flesca, S., Greco, S., Ianni, G., Leone, N. (eds.) JELIA 2002. LNCS (LNAI), vol. 2424, pp. 308–319. Springer, Heidelberg (2002). https://doi.org/10.1007/3-540-45757-7_26
59. Voronkov, A.: AVATAR: the architecture for first-order theorem provers. In: Biere, A., Bloem, R. (eds.) CAV 2014. LNCS, vol. 8559, pp. 696–710. Springer, Cham (2014). https://doi.org/10.1007/978-3-319-08867-9_46
60. Weidenbach, C., Dimova, D., Fietzke, A., Kumar, R., Suda, M., Wischnewski, P.: SPASS version 3.5. In: Schmidt, R.A. (ed.) CADE 2009. LNCS (LNAI), vol. 5663, pp. 140–145. Springer, Heidelberg (2009). https://doi.org/10.1007/978-3-642-02959-2_10

**Open Access** This chapter is licensed under the terms of the Creative Commons Attribution 4.0 International License (http://creativecommons.org/licenses/by/4.0/), which permits use, sharing, adaptation, distribution and reproduction in any medium or format, as long as you give appropriate credit to the original author(s) and the source, provide a link to the Creative Commons license and indicate if changes were made.

The images or other third party material in this chapter are included in the chapter's Creative Commons license, unless indicated otherwise in a credit line to the material. If material is not included in the chapter's Creative Commons license and your intended use is not permitted by statutory regulation or exceeds the permitted use, you will need to obtain permission directly from the copyright holder.

# Constraint Learning for Non-confluent Proof Search

Michael Rawson[1](✉), Clemens Eisenhofer[2], and Laura Kovács[2]

[1] University of Southampton, Southampton, UK
michael@rawsons.uk
[2] TU Wien, Vienna, Austria
{clemens.eisenhofer,laura.kovacs}@tuwien.ac.at

**Abstract.** Proof search in non-confluent tableau calculi, such as the connection tableau calculus, suffers from excess backtracking, but simple restrictions on backtracking are incomplete. We adopt *constraint learning* to reduce backtracking in the classical first-order connection calculus, while retaining completeness. An initial constraint learning language for connection-driven search is iteratively refined to greatly reduce backtracking in practice. The approach may be useful for proof search in other non-confluent tableau calculi.

**Keywords:** Constraint Learning · Connection Tableaux · Backjumping

## 1 Introduction

State-of-the-art methods for automated theorem proving are based on exhaustive search, using a *proof calculus* to explore the space of possible proofs. The search for proofs can be either backtracking or non-backtracking in nature. Backtracking search is required when the underlying calculus allows search to become "stuck" because of choices made previously in the search. These previous choices must be undone, and an alternative choice made, in order for the search to continue, which we call *backtracking*.

Some calculi do not require backtracking, such as confluent tableau calculi. Calculi like superposition and instance generation also fall into this category. Backtrack-free calculi are sometimes preferred and often enjoy theoretical advantages. However, in some cases, a non-confluent calculus is more practically effective, or is preferred for some other reason. We are therefore interested in *improving the behaviour of backtracking proof search*.

Backtracking search is not a problem inherently: state-of-the-art SAT solvers are uniformly based on backtracking procedures. Problems arise when the backtracking behaviour is pathological, backtracking too little, and trying to close the same goals again when the root cause of the dead end has not changed. We note in passing that backtracking *too much* would also cause problems. In SMT solving, for example, adding or removing theory literals to or from their

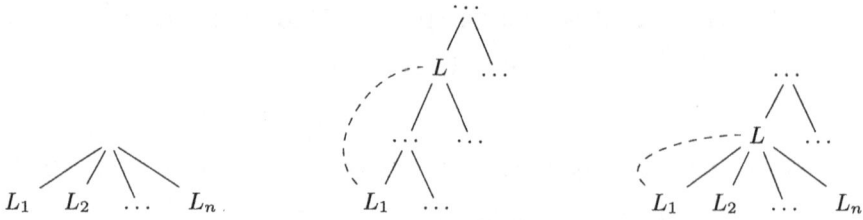

**Fig. 1.** The three inference rules of the clausal connection tableau calculus: *start*, *reduction*, and *extension*. In the *start* and *extension* rules, $C = L_1 \vee L_2 \vee \cdots \vee L_n$ is a clause from the input set, with its variables renamed apart from the tableau. In the *reduction* and *extension* rules we require that $\sigma(\neg L) = \sigma(L_1)$, i.e. $L$ and $L_1$ are *connected* (shown with dashed lines).

respective decision procedures is a relatively expensive operation that should be avoided if possible, which is why smaller backtracking steps are preferred.

We address this here by adapting a technique called *constraint learning*[1] from the constraint satisfaction community. During the search for a closed tableau, we sometimes arrive at a dead end where no further inferences are applicable in the tableau calculus. At this point, we analyse the *reason* that no inference is applicable and *learn* a constraint clause that prevents us from arriving at a similar tableau that is stuck for the same reason. The accumulating constraint database helps to guide the search towards more promising areas, or eventually shows that no closed tableau exists.

> **A potential source of confusion.** Readers familiar with SAT solving, instance generation and/or refutational theorem proving may suspect that we are learning consequences of the input problem, and that if we derive an obviously unsatisfiable constraint like the empty clause or $0 = 1$, the input problem is unsatisfiable. This is *not* the case: we are learning constraints about the search space, and such constraints show that there is no closed tableau to be found (at a particular resource bound).

## 2  Background and Motivation

We assume familiarity with tableau methods [10] and classical first-order logic. The connection method [6], connection tableau calculus [21], model elimination [22], and the method of matings [2] are closely related proof search methods. We will present our work in the language of connection *tableaux*, given the audience. The connection refinement demands that any addition to an open branch is *connected* (contains a literal of opposite polarity) to the leaf literal, which produces a very strong goal-directed effect. This comes at the expense of confluence, even for propositional logic: choosing the wrong extension of the tableau can prevent closing the tableau.

---

[1] Better known as *clause learning* in the context of Boolean satisfiability.

By lifting propositional connection tableau to a free-variable tableau calculus with a global substitution $\sigma$, one obtains a complete calculus for classical first-order logic [21]. We show the three inference rules of the clausal connection tableau calculus in Fig. 1: *start* adds a clause to an empty tableau, *reduction* closes a branch by connecting a leaf literal to a literal on its path, and *extension* adds a clause that is connected to an open branch. With minor modifications, the connection method can be adapted to other logics such as intuitionistic [26] or modal [28] logics, or to non-clausal proof search [29].

The simplicity of the calculus admits very compact theorem provers, often making use of Prolog and related technology [26,31,38]. While tableau methods are no longer the state of the art in classical first-order theorem proving, they are still competitive for proving conjectures in the presence of large numbers of irrelevant axioms (a key application for interactive theorem provers [23]) or in specialised settings [41]. They have also found a new home in experiments applying machine learning to theorem proving [20,36,42], where their simplicity—and to some extent their backtracking—makes them an attractive choice. We assume here that equality has been preprocessed away from the input [8,25,33], although it is possible to extend connection calculi with support for equational reasoning [4,6,32].

### 2.1 Excess Backtracking in Connection-Driven Search

In order to remain complete, propositional connection systems must consider alternative additions to the tableau, but once a branch has been closed, it can remain so. At the first-order level, *alternative ways to close the same branch* must also be considered: this is because closing a branch may bind variables in the global substitution in a way that prevents closing a different branch later.

Otten noticed that this requirement produced an enormous amount of backtracking in some cases [27]. He introduced a Prolog *cut* into leanCoP's search routine, rendering it incomplete but significantly reducing backtracking and increasing performance in many cases. Later, Färber studied the behaviour of these cuts extensively and developed several variants [14]. All of Färber's variants are incomplete, but some are considerably more effective in practice than others. We will use his meanCoP system as a point of comparison in Sect. 6.

### 2.2 Terminology and Convention

We use some terms informally, which we hope will aid understanding rather than cause confusion. As tableau-based first-order theorem provers typically manipulate a tableau and a substitution together, we will refer to both of them simply as "the *tableau*" where it is not confusing. When an inference of the calculus is attempted but cannot be successfully applied, we say it has *failed*. Moreover, if we can detect that a tableau can never be closed, we say it is *stuck*. Both failed inferences and stuck tableaux may be *explained* in terms of a constraint, which we call a *reason*.

We will need to refer explicitly to particular positions in a tableau. We use the obvious scheme where for any position $p$, $p.i$ is the position at the $i^{\text{th}}$ branch below $p$. The empty position stands for the root of the tableau. First-order variables in a tableau are named according to the *position* below which their clause is attached, and are hence *consistent* across backtracking. We simply use $u$, $v$, $w$, $x$, $y$ and $z$ for first-order variables, $c$ and $d$ for constants, $f$ for a function, and $P$, $Q$, $R$, and $S$ for predicates. Finally, we elide parentheses in terms and literals and consider $\neg\neg L$ identical to literal $L$.

### 2.3 Constraint Learning

Constraint learning [11] is a well-known but somewhat vaguely defined approach in constraint satisfaction and artificial intelligence. It is not necessary for our purposes to formally define constraint learning nor explore all of its developments, but the core of the idea is as follows. In a backtracking search for a solution to a set of constraints, we may encounter a dead end, where making a step in any available direction violates some constraint. A subset of the search's previous decisions may be blamed for this situation by a justification extraction process. A constraint enforcing that not all of the elements within the justification may be selected simultaneously is added to the constraint set, which prevents search from running into a similar unfortunate situation again. This *learned* constraint (usually in the form of conflict clauses) can also be used to do *backjumping*: backtracking by more than one level.

Constraint learning was particularly effective for Boolean satisfiability [37] (SAT) solving and is the basis for modern *conflict-driven clause learning* (CDCL) SAT solvers and therefore satisfiability modulo theory (SMT) solvers [5].

### 2.4 Running Example

We use a particular example throughout the paper. Consider the following set of first-order clauses:

$$\forall xyz.\ Px \vee Qy \vee Rxy \vee Pz \tag{1}$$

| | | | |
|---|---|---|---|
| $\forall x.\ \neg Px \vee S$ | (2) | $\neg Pfc$ | (5) |
| $\neg S \vee \neg Pc$ | (3) | $\forall x.\ \neg Rxc$ | (6) |
| $\neg Qd$ | (4) | $\forall x.\ \neg Rdx$ | (7) |

Figure 2 shows a connection tableau built from this set of clauses. It has a single open branch $Rxy$, shown boxed at position 3. The current substitution is $\{\ x \mapsto c,\ y \mapsto d,\ z \mapsto fc,\ w \mapsto x\ \}$. The only available extension steps for $Rxy$ are $\neg Rdv$ or $\neg Rvc$. The tableau is stuck, as neither are possible. At an earlier stage of construction, before $x \mapsto c$ and $y \mapsto d$, both extensions would have been possible. Note that the way in which $Pz$ at position 4 is closed is irrelevant, while the sub-tableaux at 1 and 2 contribute to the dead end.

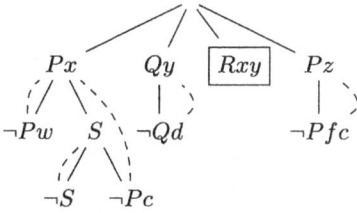

**Fig. 2.** Running example: a connection tableau built from clauses 1–7.

## 3 Learning Constraints

We propose learning and storing constraints during proof search in the connection tableau calculus in order to prevent us from repeatedly reaching dead ends for similar reasons. We will now define a constraint language to explain why no inference step is possible in a given situation, which will allow us to design an improved search procedure in Sect. 4. Suppose that a particular inference step would normally be applicable to an open branch in the tableau. If this step is not applicable, it must be that some rule applications elsewhere in the tableau prevented it. We therefore define our constraint language to be based on the inference rules of the connection tableau calculus. We will refine this language in Sect. 5, but for now, consider the following definition.

**Definition 1 (Simplified Constraint Language).** *Constraints are sets of atoms. Each atom is either:*

1. $\mathcal{S}_C$, *representing starting the tableau with clause $C$;*
2. $\mathcal{R}_p^q$, *representing a reduction from position $p$ to an ancestor $q$ in the tableau;*
3. $\mathcal{E}_{C/i}^p$, *representing extending position $p$ by a connection to the $i^{th}$ literal of clause $C$.*

Note that each atom includes the open goal (or root) to which the step is applied. This language is sufficient to explain why an inference $j$ that would be possible otherwise is currently not possible within the tableau and describes this situation in a way to cover a whole class of similarly affected tableaux. This is done by finding a subset of the inference steps already applied to the tableau that prevent the application of inference $j$.

**Definition 2 (Reasons for failed inferences).** *Take an open branch $B$ in a tableau $T$ constructed by a series of inferences $I$. We construct a sub-tableau $T'$ by applying only those inferences $I' \subseteq I$ which are necessary to produce $B$, i.e. the start clause and a series of extensions along the path to $B$. Suppose that there is an inference $j$ that can be applied to $B$ in $T'$ but not in $T$. A reason for failing to apply $j$ in $T$ is a minimal set $E \subseteq I \setminus I'$ which, if applied additionally to $T'$, prevents applying $j$ at $B$ in the resulting tableau.*

*Example 1 (Reasons for inference failure 1).* Consider the tableau in Fig. 2. To close it, the remaining open branch $Rxy$ must be extended. Suppose that we wish to extend it with clause 7. This would have been initially possible, but by now the global substitution contains $x \mapsto c$ and the extension is impossible.

We can explain this in our language by noticing that the minimal set of previous inferences required to make the extension impossible are those that close the branch at position 1, $Px$. The other two branches at 2 and 3 are irrelevant, even though those branches are also closed and affect the global substitution. If we take the minimal set of previous inferences, we obtain $\{\ S_1, \mathcal{E}^1_{2/1}, \mathcal{E}^{1.2}_{3/1}, \mathcal{R}^1_{1.2.2}\ \}$

*Example 2 (Reasons for inference failure 2).* We return to the tableau in Fig. 2, but now consider extending the open branch with the unit clause 6. Again, we notice that only the branch $Qy$ at position 2 is relevant for explaining why this extension fails, and produce the reason $\{\ S_1, \mathcal{E}^2_{4/1}\ \}$.

Now we turn our attention to explaining why a tableau is stuck. This has two parts: stating that there is an open branch $B$, and showing that no inference can be applied to $B$.

**Definition 3 (Reasons for stuck tableaux).** *Take $T$, $B$, $I$, $T'$ and $I'$ from Definition 2, and take $J$ to be the set of possible inferences from $B$ in $T'$. Suppose that no $j \in J$ can be applied to $B$ in $T$. We compute the set of reasons $R_j$ for each inference $j$ as follows:*

1. *If the calculus prevents $j$ in $T$, we compute an explanation $R_j$ by Definition 2.*
2. *If $j$ is applicable but leads to a tableau that is also stuck, we compute a reason $R'$ for that tableau recursively and set $R_j = R' \setminus \{\ j\ \}$.*

*$I'$ describes $B$ as an open branch, and the union of all inference failure reasons $R_j$ shows that no inference can be applied to $B$. We define*

$$\bigcup_j R_j \cup I'$$

*to be a reason that $T$ is stuck.*

*Example 3 (Reasons for stuck tableaux).* Consider once again the tableau in Fig. 2 and its open branch. If the only possible extensions are with clauses 6 and 7, the tableau is stuck as neither can be applied here. Using the reason set from Examples 1 and 2 and noting that $I'$ is simply $S_1$, we obtain

$$\{\ S_1,\ \mathcal{E}^1_{2/1},\ \mathcal{E}^{1.2}_{3/1},\ \mathcal{R}^1_{1.2.2},\ \mathcal{E}^2_{4/1}\ \}$$

as a reason for $T$ being stuck.

In general, reasons are not unique for any given stuck tableau, both because there could be more than one open branch, and because there could be more than one reason for a failed inference. Choosing one reason suffices, but some are likely to be stronger than others.

**Algorithm 1.** An iterative search routine for finding closed tableaux.

$T \leftarrow$ empty tableau
constraints $\leftarrow \emptyset$
trail $\leftarrow$ nil
**repeat**
  success $\leftarrow$ **false**
  $B \leftarrow$ select_open_branch($T$)
  learn $\leftarrow$ explain($T$, $B$)
  **for all** possible inferences $j$ at $B$ in $T$ **do**
    **if not** apply($T$, $j$) **then**
      learn $\leftarrow$ learn $\cup$ compute_reason($T$, $j$)
    **else if** there is a conflict clause $C \cup \{j\}$ violated by $j$ and the trail **then**
      learn $\leftarrow$ learn $\cup$ $C$
    **else**
      trail $\leftarrow j$ :: trail
      success $\leftarrow$ **true**
      **break**
    **end if**
  **end for**
  **if not** success **then**
    **while** learn is violated **do**
      $i \leftarrow$ pop(trail)
      undo($i$, $T$)
    **end while**
    record_learned_clause(learn)
  **end if**
**until** $T$ is closed or learn is empty

## 4  Search with Learned Constraints

In the previous section, we defined the constraint language so that stuck tableaux can be adequately explained. The search algorithm should now be redesigned to make use of these learned constraints. We implement something similar to that found in CDCL SAT solvers, SMT solvers, or constraint satisfaction systems. Alongside the current tableau, we maintain a *trail* of atoms that are true for the current tableau.

The search algorithm repeatedly applies rules, gets stuck, learns a constraint, and backtracks. It terminates when the tableau is closed or the empty constraint is learned. We maintain the invariant that no learned constraint is *violated* by the current trail: a constraint is violated if all of its atoms are contained in the trail. In case the tableau is empty, a start clause is chosen. Otherwise, at each iteration, an open branch of the tableau is selected for reduction or extension. If any such inference is possible, it is applied to the tableau, and the corresponding atom describing the result of the inference is added to the trail. On the other hand, an inference $j$ may be impossible either:

1. because the calculus does not permit it, or
2. because adding its corresponding atom would violate a learned clause.

In the first case, a reason for the failed inference is computed as in Definition 2. Otherwise, the reason for its failure is the learned constraint it would violate, *minus* the atom corresponding to $j$ (Definition 3) In this way, when all possible inferences at an open branch have failed, a constraint against the stuck tableau is learned such that all the atoms in the constraint are on the trail. To restore the invariant, the system backtracks until at least one violated atom is no longer on the trail.

The overall procedure is shown in Algorithm 1: `compute_reason` computes a reason in the sense of Definition 2, and `explain` computes $I'$ for $B$ as in Definition 3. It is considerably more complex than the usual procedures for finding closed connection tableaux, particularly those embedded in Prolog via the "lean" methodology [26]. However, it is simpler in one aspect: there is no need to remember alternative inferences at backtracking points, which can be quite involved if not implemented in terms of Prolog's existing backtracking mechanism [19].

### 4.1 Resource Bounds

Connection systems typically search by iterative deepening on a particular metric, such as the length of the longest branch. A small limit is set initially, and then a system will begin search, bounded by the current limit. If no tableau exists at one iterative deepening level, the limit is increased and search tried again. We follow this approach here: our search algorithm looks for a tableau bounded by some maximum branch length, and if one does not exist, it will eventually terminate by learning the empty clause.

Constraints learned at one iterative deepening level cannot be reused for the next, as our approach would become incomplete. It is possible to alter the constraint language in order to express constraints that (do not) depend on the depth limit, but this is of limited practical purpose for at least two reasons. Firstly, because the search space at the next iterative deepening level tends to be much larger than the exhausted previous level, reusing constraints independent of the depth limit from the previous level does not help much. Second, in practice, there are few such constraints.

### 4.2 Soundness, Termination and Completeness

We show that Algorithm 1 terminates at any fixed depth limit and use this to show completeness. Soundness is trivial, as the routine searches within an existing sound calculus.

**Lemma 1 (Termination).** *Fix a depth limit. Algorithm 1 terminates.*

*Proof.* First, note that at any depth limit and for any finite set of input clauses, there is a finite number of possible tableaux, all of which are of finite size. Because all tableaux are of finite size, the routine will eventually either close the tableau, terminating immediately, or become stuck. When stuck, the routine learns a constraint which, by construction, is violated by the current trail, and therefore prevents reaching at least this particular tableau again. As constraints are never forgotten within the same depth limit, and there are a finite number of possible tableaux, termination is guaranteed as the solver eventually learns constraints eliminating all possible tableaux. □

**Lemma 2.** *Learned constraints are not violated by any closed tableau reachable in the proof calculus at a given depth limit.*

*Proof.* By induction on the derivation of learned constraints. Suppose a learned constraint $C$ is violated by a closed tableau $T^\star$. By definition, $C$ is a subset of the rules required to construct $T^\star$. Construct the intermediate tableau $T$ generated by $C$. Take the next inference step $j$ from $T$ towards $T^\star$. In Definition 3, $C$ is justified on the basis that all inferences, including $j$, from $T$ are impossible, either because the calculus prevents it (Definition 2), or because another constraint $C'$ is violated. By the induction hypothesis, applying $j$ does not violate any such $C'$, so $j$ must not be legal in the calculus, and we have a contradiction. □

**Theorem 1. (Completeness).** *If a closed tableau exists at a depth limit, it will be found by Algorithm 1.*

*Proof.* By termination and Lemma 2. □

## 5 Refining the Constraint Language

The simple constraint language introduced in Sect. 3 is sufficiently expressive to block classes of similar tableaux, but is quite specific to a particular tableau and fails to block all the similar tableaux we might like. It is also quite clunky to work with and would be difficult to compute inference failure reasons efficiently in practice: see Sect. 6.2.

We therefore decompose each atom into multiple smaller atoms of two kinds: placing literals at positions in a tableau, and binding variables to terms. However, *mutatis mutandis* the search procedure remains the same, pushing one or more such atoms onto the trail for any one inference. As well as being simpler to implement, constraints can be much stronger as they do not block only a particular derivation of a tableau, but any tableau having particular literals and variable bindings.

**Definition 4. (Refined Constraint Language).** *A constraint remains a set of atoms. However, each atom is either*

1. $L@p$, *a literal $L$ being placed at position $p$*
2. $x \mapsto t$, *a variable $x$ is bound to a term $t$ where $t$ itself may be a variable.*

Each inference of the connection tableau calculus can be expressed as some combination of these. Adding clauses in start and extension rules is done by placing their literals at the corresponding positions. Connections of literals in extension and reduction rules are applied by computing the required variable bindings.

*Example 4. (Refined constraint learning).* Take the tableau in Fig. 2. We will explain why it is stuck in terms of the new constraint language. Extending $Rxy$ with $\neg Rvc$ is not possible because $y \mapsto d$, which is on the trail because $Qy$ was connected to $\neg Qd$. Similarly, extending $Rxy$ with $\neg Rdv$ is not possible because $x \mapsto c$. To finish the explanation, we have to say why $Rxy$ needs to be closed in the first place, but this is straightforward: $Rxy@3$. The final explanation is therefore

$$\{ Rxy@3,\ x \mapsto c,\ y \mapsto d \}.$$

## 5.1 No-Connection Atoms

In the proposed language, explaining why an open branch cannot be *reduced* can become overly specific.

*Example 5. (Explaining reduction failure).* Consider an open branch $\neg Pc$ at the depth limit, with path literals $Px$, $Qc$, $Rcd$, $S$ and a substitution containing $x \mapsto d$. Suppose the positions from root to leaf are $p_1 \ldots p_5$. Clearly $\neg Pc$ cannot be reduced. In the case of $Px$, the constraint contains somewhat useful information: if $x$ were not bound to $d$, this branch could be reduced. However, for all other path literals, the only useful information is that they cannot be connected with $\neg Pc$, but this is not in the language, and we must learn

$$\{ \neg Pc@p_5,\ Px@p_1, x \mapsto d,\ Qc@p_2,\ Rcd@p_3,\ S@p_4 \}.$$

This kind of situation occurs often in practice and needlessly specialises the learned constraint to a particular sequence of path literals. To avoid this problem, a new kind of atom $p \not\sim q$ is introduced, representing that no connection can ever be made between the two positions $p$ and $q$, regardless of the substitution. Whenever a literal is added to the tableau at position $q$, its path is checked to see, which literals at positions $p$ it could be reduced with, and where this is impossible, $p \not\sim q$ is added to the trail. In the above example, the learned constraint would be

$$\{ \neg Pc@p_5,\ Px@p_1,\ x \mapsto d,\ p_2 \not\sim p_5,\ p_3 \not\sim p_5,\ p_4 \not\sim p_5 \}.$$

and more general, as it does not specify which literals are at $p_2$, $p_3$, or $p_4$.

## 5.2 Disequations

Classical refinements such as regularity and eliminating tautologies greatly improve the performance of connection systems [21]. These are classically implemented by means of *disequations*. We can support this naturally in the constraint language by adding disequation atoms of the form $s \neq t$. When a disequation is falsified, backtracking can be induced by giving the disequation and the variable bindings required to falsify it as a learned constraint.

## 6 Implementation and Experimental Validation

We implemented a prototype system hopCoP[2] to experiment with constraint learning. So far, the implementation is imperative—although we suspect a lean Prolog implementation may be possible via assert/1 [18]—and owes much to implementation techniques found in the Bare Metal Tableaux Prover [19] and meanCoP [14]. hopCoP implements the clausal connection tableau calculus, without cuts [27] and starting from clauses derived from the conjecture. With the obvious exception of constraint learning, hopCoP's search routine resembles that of meanCoP, if the meanCoP flags --conj --nopaths are set[3]. meanCoP also implements a lemma mechanism [21] that hopCoP so far lacks. In Sects. 6.1 and 6.2 we highlight two aspects of the implementation that may be of interest to implementers of similar systems.

### 6.1 Constraint Management and Detecting Conflicts

A large number of constraints are learned during search, millions with a long enough time limit. However, this seems to be less dramatic than in other settings such as SAT solving, and we did not find any benefit from attempting to garbage-collect old constraints, so hopCoP retains *all* constraints it learns.

It is still necessary to efficiently find conflicts among this large set when adding atoms to the trail. This is done by a 1-watched-literal scheme [24]: there is no need for the 2-watched-literal scheme popular in SAT solving, as all atoms have the same polarity and unit propagation is of little use. More than one conflict may be found when adding an atom to the trail: it is worth trying to choose conflicts that minimise the resulting learned constraint. hopCoP greedily chooses the conflict that adds the fewest atoms to the constraint learned so far.

### 6.2 Computing Explanations

To explain why an inference that connects two literals is not possible, a subset of the current substitution must be computed that prevents their unification. It is no doubt possible to construct a complex variable-tracking scheme to do this quickly, but for our application, the following procedure is acceptably fast.

1. Unify the two literals using a new scratch substitution $\tau$. As the inference was possible with an empty substitution (but not with $\sigma$), this must succeed.
2. Record the current state of $\tau$, say $\tau_0$.
3. For every binding $x \mapsto t$ in $\sigma$ we:
   (a) Try to unify $x$ and $t$ in $\tau$. If this succeeds, continue the loop at step 3.
   (b) Reset $\tau$ to $\tau_0$ and try to unify $x$ and $t$ again. If successful, go to step 2.
   (c) Exit the loop on failure, retaining $x \mapsto t$ in $\tau$.

After this procedure, $\tau$ should contain the necessary subset of $\sigma$. A similar routine can be used to determine why a disequation is falsified.

---
[2] https://github.com/MichaelRawson/hopcop, commit a4a0f66.
[3] Starting with the annotated conjecture clauses (-conj) and preventing input clauses reordering (-nopaths).

## 6.3 Experiments

**Table 1.** The number of extension steps tried in order to determine that there is no closed tableau of a certain depth on PUZ005-1. A proof exists at depth 8.

| depth    | 1 | 2 | 3  | 4   | 5     | 6      | 7         |
|----------|---|---|----|-----|-------|--------|-----------|
| meanCoP  | 1 | 4 | 24 | 108 | 535   | 9,963  | 6,445,008 |
| hopCoP   | 1 | 4 | 89 | 495 | 2,309 | 10,066 | 48,517    |

Having gone to some effort to reduce backtracking in theory, we wish to know whether this also helps in practice. We first manually inspected the behaviour of both meanCoP and hopCoP on problems taken from the PUZ domain of TPTP. meanCoP reports the number of successfully applied extension steps required to exhaust each iterative deepening level, so we instrumented hopCoP to do the same. Table 1 shows the number of steps required for PUZ005-1[4]. At lower iterative deepening levels, the result is mixed due to differences in search decisions and meanCoP's lemma rule, but hopCoP typically extends a clear lead at higher levels. meanCoP maintains a much higher rate of inference: our implementation is not highly optimised, but we suspect that the overhead of maintaining the learned constraints would cause significant inferences-per-second overhead compared to meanCoP even if it were.

hopCoP also ran head-to-head against meanCoP on several popular first-order benchmark sets: FOF and CNF problems from TPTP version 9.0.0 [39], the MPTP challenge problems [1] in *bushy* and *chainy* variants, and the *Miz40* ATP-minimised set [20], of which *M2k* is a subset. Both systems were given a time limit of 10 s per problem and meanCoP was configured with `--conj --nopaths` (to better match hopCoP, see above). We also ran meanCoP with the additional `--cut` argument, which we call !meanCoP: this renders meanCoP incomplete in exchange for significantly reduced backtracking.

We do not wish to claim anything about the relative strength of the systems, only that the data are consistent with the hypothesis that the reduction in backtracking achieved overcomes the overhead in terms of inferences-per-second speed. Table 2 shows the number of solved problems. Readers may also be interested in the very thorough experimental data in Färber's discussion of various backtracking schemes [14].

## 7 Related Work

The most directly related work is the various fixed restrictions on backtracking in connection tableau [14,27]: these are by nature incomplete, but effective. Older techniques such as *failure caching* [3] also achieve a reduction in

---
[4] The first CNF problem of moderate difficulty in the PUZ domain.

**Table 2.** Theorems proved in 10 s by hopCoP, meanCoP, and !meanCoP on various benchmark sets.

|         | M2k   | Miz40  | bushy | chainy | TPTP  |
|---------|-------|--------|-------|--------|-------|
| meanCoP | 795   | 7,592  | 480   | 157    | 3,578 |
| !meanCoP| 878   | 9,748  | 562   | 337    | 3,283 |
| hopCoP  | 1,050 | 13,040 | 589   | 203    | 4,026 |

backtracking and remain complete, but with different mechanisms. The Goéland tableau system exchanges substitution information [9] between concurrent branch explorations: this is likely to reduce backtracking, but again with a different mechanism. Encodings of connection-driven search into SAT or SMT, such as ChewTPTP [12], are complete and will also learn constraints during proof search, but behave very differently and are mostly encoded upfront.

We ourselves have tried various encodings [13] of connection methods into SAT and SMT via *user propagation* [7,15]. We found that SAT/SMT solvers, even with a lazy user-propagator encoding, are not a good match for this kind of proof search, as their internal heuristics have no knowledge of the current state of the tableau. The solver will, for instance, very happily decide or propagate variables that encode some sub-tableau completely disconnected from the current state. Refined encodings such as in Sect. 5 improve the encoding's performance, but allow the solver to partially apply inferences: we are not sure of the performance merits of this, but it is highly confusing.

The first author has also investigated *generating* SAT clauses from instances of clauses found in connection tableau during search [34], as a kind of instance-based method [16]. When the set of SAT clauses becomes unsatisfiable, it shows that the input clause set was also unsatisfiable. While an extension of this instance-generation approach can be used to influence the connection tableau search, it is not the core of the method, unlike the constraint learning approach here. The two are largely orthogonal and could be combined profitably.

Other work that is highly related but may be confusing is the concept of *backjumping* in modal and other tableau [17]: the concept and its origins appears to be similar, but it is used to *avoid* logical conflicts on a branch when looking for a model, rather than to avoid getting stuck when looking for a closed tableau. The MeTTeL$^2$ tableau prover generator [40] has generic support for a similar kind of backjumping, which it calls *conflict-directed backjumping*.

## 8 Outlook

We have integrated a constraint learning approach to guide search and reduce backtracking into a prototype first-order connection theorem prover hopCoP and observe that it reduces the search space significantly, which translates into practical performance. A trade-off is memory use: constraints have to be kept somewhere. This was not excessive in our experience, but may prevent running hopCoP on your iPod® [30].

It is likely that other non-confluent tableau calculi may benefit from such an approach. We would also be interested in the intersection of this kind of learning with the *machine* kind of learning: constraint learning could reduce the options available to a learned heuristic, while a good learned heuristic might rapidly learn useful constraints.

There are some areas for further improvement to the technique. The most irritating are the explicit positions present in the constraint language, which limits the application of learned constraints. Eliminating this would require detecting conflicts modulo structurally equivalent positions, which we suspect may be difficult to do efficiently. A future *lean* implementation may help with this, perhaps based on the recent realisation that *backjumping is exception handling* [35].

**Acknowledgments.** We are grateful to Michael Färber in particular for his meanCoP tool and stimulating discussions on this and related topics. This research was funded in whole or in part by the ERC Consolidator Grant ARTIST 101002685, the ERC Proof of Concept Grant LEARN 101213411, the TU Wien Doctoral College SecInt, the FWF SpyCoDe Grant 10.55776/F85, the WWTF grant ForSmart 10.47379/ICT22007, and the Amazon Research Award 2023 QuAT.

**Disclosure of Interests.** The authors have no competing interests to declare that are relevant to the content of this article.

# References

1. Alama, J., Heskes, T., Kühlwein, D., Tsivtsivadze, E., Urban, J.: Premise selection for mathematics by corpus analysis and kernel methods. J. Autom. Reason. **52**(2), 191–213 (2014). https://doi.org/10.1007/S10817-013-9286-5
2. Andrews, P.B.: Theorem proving via general matings. J. ACM **28**(2), 193–214 (1981). https://doi.org/10.1145/322248.322249
3. Astrachan, O.L., Stickel, M.E.: Caching and lemmaizing in model elimination theorem provers. In: Kapur, D. (ed.) CADE 1992. LNCS, vol. 607, pp. 224–238. Springer, Heidelberg (1992). https://doi.org/10.1007/3-540-55602-8_168
4. Backeman, P., Rümmer, P.: Theorem proving with bounded rigid $E$-unification. In: Felty, A.P., Middeldorp, A. (eds.) CADE 2015. LNCS (LNAI), vol. 9195, pp. 572–587. Springer, Cham (2015). https://doi.org/10.1007/978-3-319-21401-6_39
5. Barrett, C.W., Sebastiani, R., Seshia, S.A., Tinelli, C.: Satisfiability modulo theories. In: Biere, A., Heule, M., van Maaren, H., Walsh, T. (eds.) Handbook of Satisfiability - Second Edition, Frontiers in Artificial Intelligence and Applications, vol. 336, pp. 1267–1329. IOS Press (2021). https://doi.org/10.3233/FAIA201017
6. Bibel, W.: Automated Theorem Proving, 2nd edn. Artificial intelligence, Vieweg (1987). https://www.worldcat.org/oclc/16641802
7. Bjørner, N.S., Eisenhofer, C., Kovács, L.: Satisfiability modulo custom theories in Z3. In: Dragoi, C., Emmi, M., Wang, J. (eds.) VMCAI. LNCS, vol. 13881, pp. 91–105. Springer, Cham (2023). https://doi.org/10.1007/978-3-031-24950-1_5
8. Brand, D.: Proving theorems with the modification method. SIAM J. Comput. **4**(4), 412–430 (1975). https://doi.org/10.1137/0204036

9. Cailler, J., Rosain, J., Delahaye, D., Robillard, S., Bouziane, H.: Goéland: a concurrent tableau-based theorem prover (system description). In: Blanchette, J., Kovács, L., Pattinson, D. (eds.) IJCAR. LNCS, vol. 13385, pp. 359–368. Springer, Cham (2022). https://doi.org/10.1007/978-3-031-10769-6_22
10. D'Agostino, M., Gabbay, D.M., Hähnle, R., Posegga, J., (eds): Handbook of tableau methods. J. Log. Lang. Inf. **10**(4), 518–523 (2001). https://doi.org/10.1023/A:1017520120752
11. Dechter, R.: Learning while searching in constraint-satisfaction-problems. In: Proceedings of the 5th National Conference on Artificial Intelligence, pp. 178–185. Morgan Kaufmann (1986). http://www.aaai.org/Library/AAAI/1986/aaai86-029.php
12. Deshane, T., Hu, W., Jablonski, P., Lin, H., Lynch, C., McGregor, R.E.: Encoding first order proofs in SAT. In: Pfenning, F. (ed.) CADE 2007. LNCS (LNAI), vol. 4603, pp. 476–491. Springer, Heidelberg (2007). https://doi.org/10.1007/978-3-540-73595-3_35
13. Eisenhofer, C., Rawson, M., Kovács, L.: Spanning matrices via satisfiability solving (2025). https://doi.org/to-appear, appears in the same TABLEAUX 2025 inproceeding
14. Färber, M.: A curiously effective backtracking strategy for connection tableaux. In: Otten, J., Bibel, W. (eds.) AReCCa. CEUR Workshop Proceedings, vol. 3613, pp. 23–40. CEUR-WS.org (2023). https://ceur-ws.org/Vol-3613/AReCCa2023_paper2.pdf
15. Fazekas, K., Niemetz, A., Preiner, M., Kirchweger, M., Szeider, S., Biere, A.: IPASIR-UP: user propagators for CDCL. In: Mahajan, M., Slivovsky, F. (eds.) SAT. LIPIcs, vol. 271, pp. 8:1–8:13. Schloss Dagstuhl - Leibniz-Zentrum für Informatik (2023). https://doi.org/10.4230/LIPICS.SAT.2023.8
16. Ganzinger, H., Korovin, K.: New directions in instantiation-based theorem proving. In: LICS, pp. 55–64. IEEE Computer Society (2003). https://doi.org/10.1109/LICS.2003.1210045
17. Hustadt, U., Schmidt, R.A.: Simplification and backjumping in modal tableau. In: de Swart, H. (ed.) TABLEAUX 1998. LNCS (LNAI), vol. 1397, pp. 187–201. Springer, Heidelberg (1998). https://doi.org/10.1007/3-540-69778-0_22
18. ISO/IEC: Information technology—Programming languages—Prolog—Part 1: General Core. Standard, International Organization for Standardization (1995)
19. Kaliszyk, C.: Efficient low-level connection tableaux. In: De Nivelle, H. (ed.) TABLEAUX 2015. LNCS (LNAI), vol. 9323, pp. 102–111. Springer, Cham (2015). https://doi.org/10.1007/978-3-319-24312-2_8
20. Kaliszyk, C., Urban, J., Michalewski, H., Olšák, M.: Reinforcement learning of theorem proving. In: NeurIPS, pp. 8836–8847 (2018). https://proceedings.neurips.cc/paper/2018/hash/55acf8539596d25624059980986aaa78-Abstract.html
21. Letz, R., Stenz, G.: Model elimination and connection tableau procedures. In: Handbook of Automated Reasoning (in 2 volumes), pp. 2015–2114. Elsevier and MIT Press (2001). https://doi.org/10.1016/B978-044450813-3/50030-8
22. Loveland, D.W.: Mechanical theorem-proving by model elimination. J. ACM **15**(2), 236–251 (1968). https://doi.org/10.1145/321450.321456
23. Meng, J., Paulson, L.C.: Translating higher-order clauses to first-order clauses. J. Autom. Reason. **40**(1), 35–60 (2008). https://doi.org/10.1007/S10817-007-9085-Y
24. Moskewicz, M.W., Madigan, C.F., Zhao, Y., Zhang, L., Malik, S.: Chaff: engineering an efficient SAT solver. In: DAC, pp. 530–535. ACM (2001). https://doi.org/10.1145/378239.379017

25. Nieuwenhuis, R., Rubio, A.: Paramodulation-based theorem proving. In: Handbook of Automated Reasoning (in 2 volumes), pp. 371–443 (2001). https://doi.org/10.1016/B978-044450813-3/50009-6
26. Otten, J.: leanCoP 2.0 and ileanCoP 1.2: high performance lean theorem proving in classical and intuitionistic logic (system descriptions). In: Armando, A., Baumgartner, P., Dowek, G. (eds.) IJCAR 2008. LNCS (LNAI), vol. 5195, pp. 283–291. Springer, Heidelberg (2008). https://doi.org/10.1007/978-3-540-71070-7_23
27. Otten, J.: Restricting backtracking in connection calculi. AI Commun. **23**(2–3), 159–182 (2010). https://doi.org/10.3233/AIC-2010-0464
28. Otten, J.: MleanCoP: a connection prover for first-order modal logic. In: Demri, S., Kapur, D., Weidenbach, C. (eds.) IJCAR 2014. LNCS (LNAI), vol. 8562, pp. 269–276. Springer, Cham (2014). https://doi.org/10.1007/978-3-319-08587-6_20
29. Otten, J.: nanoCoP: a non-clausal connection prover. In: Olivetti, N., Tiwari, A. (eds.) IJCAR 2016. LNCS (LNAI), vol. 9706, pp. 302–312. Springer, Cham (2016). https://doi.org/10.1007/978-3-319-40229-1_21
30. Otten, J.: The pocket reasoner – automatic reasoning on small devices. In: NIK. Bibsys Open Journal Systems, Norway (2018). https://ojs.bibsys.no/index.php/NIK/article/view/512
31. Otten, J.: 20 years of leanCoP - an overview of the provers. In: AReCCa. CEUR Workshop Proceedings, vol. 3613, pp. 4–22. CEUR-WS.org (2023). https://ceur-ws.org/Vol-3613/AReCCa2023_paper1.pdf
32. Paskevich, A.: Connection tableaux with lazy paramodulation. J. Autom. Reason. **40**(2–3), 179–194 (2008). https://doi.org/10.1007/S10817-007-9089-7
33. Prusak, G., Kaliszyk, C.: Lazy paramodulation in practice. In: Proceedings of the Workshop on Practical Aspects of Automated Reasoning Co-located with the 11th International Joint Conference on Automated Reasoning (FLoC/IJCAR 2022), Haifa, Israel, 11–12 August 2022. CEUR Workshop Proceedings, vol. 3201. CEUR-WS.org (2022). https://ceur-ws.org/Vol-3201/paper3.pdf
34. Rawson, M., Reger, G.: Eliminating models during model elimination. In: Das, A., Negri, S. (eds.) TABLEAUX 2021. LNCS (LNAI), vol. 12842, pp. 250–265. Springer, Cham (2021). https://doi.org/10.1007/978-3-030-86059-2_15
35. Robbins, E., King, A., Howe, J.M.: Backjumping is exception handling. Theory Pract. Log. Program. **21**(2), 125–144 (2021). https://doi.org/10.1017/S1471068420000435
36. Rømming, F., Otten, J., Holden, S.B.: Connections: Markov decision processes for classical, intuitionistic and modal connection calculi. In: AReCCa. CEUR Workshop Proceedings, vol. 3613, pp. 107–118. CEUR-WS.org (2023). https://ceur-ws.org/Vol-3613/AReCCa2023_paper8.pdf
37. Silva, J.P.M., Sakallah, K.A.: GRASP—a new search algorithm for satisfiability. In: ICCAD, pp. 220–227. IEEE Computer Society/ACM (1996). https://doi.org/10.1109/ICCAD.1996.569607
38. Stickel, M.E.: A Prolog technology theorem prover. In: 9th International Conference on Automated Deduction, Argonne, Illinois, USA, 23–26 May 1988, Proceedings. LNCS, vol. 310, pp. 752–753. Springer, Cham (1988). https://doi.org/10.1007/BFB0012881
39. Sutcliffe, G.: The TPTP problem library and associated infrastructure - from CNF to TH0, TPTP v6.4.0. J. Autom. Reason. **59**(4), 483–502 (2017). https://doi.org/10.1007/S10817-017-9407-7
40. Tishkovsky, D., Schmidt, R.A., Khodadadi, M.: The tableau prover generator MetTeL$^2$. In: del Cerro, L.F., Herzig, A., Mengin, J. (eds.) JELIA 2012. LNCS (LNAI),

vol. 7519, pp. 492–495. Springer, Heidelberg (2012). https://doi.org/10.1007/978-3-642-33353-8_41
41. Wernhard, C., Bibel, W.: Investigations into proof structures. J. Autom. Reason. **68**(4), 24 (2024). https://doi.org/10.1007/S10817-024-09711-8
42. Zombori, Z., Urban, J., Brown, C.E.: Prolog technology reinforcement learning prover. In: Peltier, N., Sofronie-Stokkermans, V. (eds.) IJCAR 2020. LNCS (LNAI), vol. 12167, pp. 489–507. Springer, Cham (2020). https://doi.org/10.1007/978-3-030-51054-1_33

**Open Access** This chapter is licensed under the terms of the Creative Commons Attribution 4.0 International License (http://creativecommons.org/licenses/by/4.0/), which permits use, sharing, adaptation, distribution and reproduction in any medium or format, as long as you give appropriate credit to the original author(s) and the source, provide a link to the Creative Commons license and indicate if changes were made.

The images or other third party material in this chapter are included in the chapter's Creative Commons license, unless indicated otherwise in a credit line to the material. If material is not included in the chapter's Creative Commons license and your intended use is not permitted by statutory regulation or exceeds the permitted use, you will need to obtain permission directly from the copyright holder.

# On Solving String Equations via Powers and Parikh Images

Clemens Eisenhofer[1](✉)[iD], Theodor Seiser[1][iD], Nikolaj Bjørner[2][iD], and Laura Kovács[1][iD]

[1] TU Wien, Vienna, Austria
clemens.eisenhofer@tuwien.ac.at
[2] Microsoft Research, Redmond, USA

**Abstract.** We present a new approach for solving string equations as extensions of Nielsen transformations. Key to our work are the combination of three techniques: a power operator for strings; generalisations of Parikh images; and equality decomposition. Using these methods allows us to solve complex string equations, including less commonly encountered SMT inputs over strings.

**Keywords:** String Equation Solving · SMT · Nielsen Transformation · String Powers · Parikh Image · Equality Decomposition

## 1 Introduction

String solving is used in a wide range of applications, including formal verification [1,9], security analysis [14,15,33,34], and automated reasoning [2,17]. Modern Satisfiability Modulo Theories (SMT) solvers [5], such as Z3 [24], CVC5 [3], or PRINCESS [29], support string constraints via specialised solving techniques for handling length constraints [26], regular expressions [7,30], containment predicates [27], and many others. However, solving string (word) equations that involve long repeated subsequences or contain mutually dependent string variables remains very challenging for state-of-the-art solvers [1,9,10,12,20,23,24,33].

*Example 1 (Motivating Example).* Consider the conjunction of the following two string equations:

$$x_3 x_3 x_4 b x_5 b \simeq x_5 x_5 x_5 x_5 x_4 bb, \quad (E_1)$$
$$x_1 x_1 ac x_2 x_4 x_2 x_5 x_3 ba x_5 x_3 x_4 x_3 \simeq x_2 x_2 abc x_1 x_1 x_3 x_3 x_3 x_4 x_4 a x_4 \quad (E_2)$$

where $\simeq$ denotes (first-order) equality, $x_1, x_2, x_3, x_4, x_5$ are string variables and $a, b, c$ are constant characters. Solving such equations requires reasoning about string variables depending on themselves or mutually on each other needs, which is mostly out of scope of current techniques.

Our work addresses challenges similar to solving equations $(E_1)$–$(E_2)$. Our approach uses *rewriting and generating rules over string equations* (Table 1) as Nielsen transformations (Sect. 3) over Nielsen graphs [17,22,26]. We extend Nielsen transformation rules with:

**Equality decomposition** – to decompose string equations during reasoning into subequations. Using equality decomposition greatly increases the applicability of string power reasoning and Parikh images.

**Explicit power representation** – to solve string equations in which string variables depend on themselves. Furthermore, it allows us to compactly reason on long, but repetitive, strings (Sect. 5).

**Generalized Parikh images** – to detect unsatisfiability when both Nielsen rules and string power reasoning fail (Sect. 6). We adjust generalised forms of Parikh images [25] to string solving.

We implemented our framework as a prototype called ZIPT using the user-propagation framework [8] of the SMT solver Z3 [24]. Our experiments demonstrate the practical potential of our method (Sect. 7) on SMT-LIB2 benchmarks [4] containing equations only.

## 2 Preliminaries

*Strings.* For our purposes, we will use an extended definition of a string term.

**Definition 1 (Token & String Terms).** *We fix a set $\mathcal{K}$ of tokens and denote by $\mathcal{T}$ the set of string terms. A string term $u \in \mathcal{T}$ is a finite sequence of tokens $t \in \mathcal{K}$ and we distinguish between*

– concrete character *tokens, denoted as $a, b, c, d$, whose set is denoted by $\Sigma$;*
– symbolic characters *tokens, written as $o$, whose set is $\mathcal{V}_C$.*
– (string) variable *tokens, denoted as $x, y, z$, whose set is $\mathcal{V}_S$;*
– power *tokens of the form $u^m$, where $u \in \mathcal{T}$ does not contain string variables and $m$ is an arbitrary integer term potentially containing integer variables. We call $u$ the* base *and $m$ the* exponent *of a power token.*

Our token notation might use indices, and we write $@ \in \Sigma \cup \mathcal{V}_C$ to denote (concrete or symbolic) character tokens and $t \in \mathcal{T}$ for a token of any kind. The sets $\Sigma$, $\mathcal{V}_C$, and $\mathcal{V}_S$ are mutually disjoint and $\Sigma$ is additionally finite and non-empty. The set $\mathcal{T}$ of string terms is the set of all finite sequences of tokens. Using regular expression notation, we have $\mathcal{T} := \mathcal{K}^*$ and reserve $\varepsilon$ for the empty sequence of tokens. $\varepsilon$ represents the neutral element of concatenation, and we denote concatenation by juxtaposing tokens. The power token $u^m$ expresses that the token $u$ is repeated $m$ times; that is, $u^0 = \varepsilon$ and $u^m = uu^{m-1}$ if $m > 0$ where $m$ is some integer term. Given how power terms are introduced, negative values for the exponents can be excluded. We denote by $|u|$ the *length* with $u \in \mathcal{T}$; clearly, $|u|$ represents a natural number. We write $u^R$ to denote the reverse string term of $u$. For example, $(ax(ab)^m)^R = (ba)^m x^R a$. Finally, we note that a symbolic character $o$ is equivalent to a string variable $x$ with $|x| = 1$. We nonetheless use symbolic characters to have simpler definitions later on.

*String Equations and Substitutions.* A *string equation* is $u_1 \simeq u_2$ over string terms $u_1, u_2 \in \mathcal{T}$; here, we refer to $u_1$ as the left-hand-side (LHS) of the equation, whereas $u_2$ is the right-hand-side (RHS) of the equation. String equations that only contain string variables and concrete characters are called *plain*; string equations that might also contain symbolic characters and powers are called *extended*. We use $2^u$ to denote the set of *consecutive tokens* within $u$. $||u||$ denotes the number of tokens in $u$, where power tokens in $u$ are considered atomic; we call this the *symbolic length* of $u$: $||\varepsilon|| := 0$ and $||tv|| := 1 + ||v||$. For example, in $u = (abc)^m xb$ we have $2^u = \{\ \varepsilon, a, b, c, (abc)^m, x, ab, bc, (abc)^m x, xb, abc, (abc)^m xb\ \}$ and $||u|| = 3$.

String terms $u \in \mathcal{T}$ containing no string variables are called *ground*. For ground terms $u$ we thus have $2^u \cap \mathcal{V}_S = \emptyset$. Nonetheless, ground terms might contain power and symbolic character tokens.

A *substitution* $\sigma$ maps (i) string variables $x \in \mathcal{V}_S$ to string terms $u \in \mathcal{T}$; and (ii) symbolic characters $o \in \mathcal{V}_C$ to characters $@ \in \Sigma \cup \mathcal{V}_C$. The set of variables $\{x \in \mathcal{V}_S \mid \sigma(x) \neq x\}$ is finite. Similarly, for symbolic characters. We write $(x/u) \in \sigma$ to denote $\sigma(x) = u$. A substitution $\sigma$ is *eliminating* a string variable $x$ if $(x/u) \in \sigma$ and $u$ is ground. The *application of a substitution* $\sigma$ to an expression $C$ is denoted by $C[\sigma]$, where $C$ is a string term or a (set of) string/integer (in)equations.

Substitutions $\sigma$ are assumed to be acyclic and fully extended: For any non-identity $(x/u) \in \sigma$ and $y \in 2^u$ we have $(y/y) \in \sigma$. We write $m_1 \simeq m_2$ and $m_1 \leq m_2$ for integer (in)equations over integer terms $m_1, m_2$.

*Interpretations and Models.* Given a string equation $u \simeq v$, an *interpretation* $\mathcal{M}$ of this equation is a substitution together with an assignment of integer variables to integer values. For every $x \in \mathcal{V}_S \cap (2^u \cup 2^v)$ we have $(x/w) \in \mathcal{M}$, where $w \in \Sigma^*$; further, for every $o \in \mathcal{V}_C \cap (2^u \cup 2^v)$ we have $(o/a) \in \sigma$ with $a \in \Sigma$. An interpretation $\mathcal{M}$ is called a *plain model* of a set $S$ of plain string equations if the application of $\mathcal{M}$ to $S$ results in a simplified set of equations of the form $u \simeq u$ with $u \in \Sigma^*$. If $S$ has a model $\mathcal{M}$, then $S$ is *satisfiable*; otherwise $S$ is *unsatisfiable*. Similarly, an *extended model* of a set of extended string equations and integer (in)equalities simplifies every extended string equation to $u \simeq u$ with $u \in \mathcal{T}^*$ and satisfies all integer constraints. All string variables and symbolic characters in $u$ are implicitly assumed to be universally quantified. Any extended model of a set of plain string equations can be made into a plain model by substituting all symbolic characters with some character of $\Sigma$ and string variables with some element of $\Sigma^*$. Power tokens can be completely unwound by using the integer value of their evaluated power term.

## 3 String Solving – Workflow

Given a non-empty *set $S$ of plain string equations, our task is to decide its satisfiability*. Doing so, we solve extended string equations corresponding to $S$, potentially containing symbolic characters and powers as well as integer (in)equalities.

To this end, we expand Nielsen graphs of string equations (Sects. 3.1) by repeatedly applying an extended set of Nielsen transformation rules (Sects. 3.2). We simplify extended string equations and integer (in)equations, by extending Nielson transformations to arbitrary string terms $u \in \mathcal{T}$ rather than only plain ones. Our approach is summarised in Fig. 1 and detailed in the following.

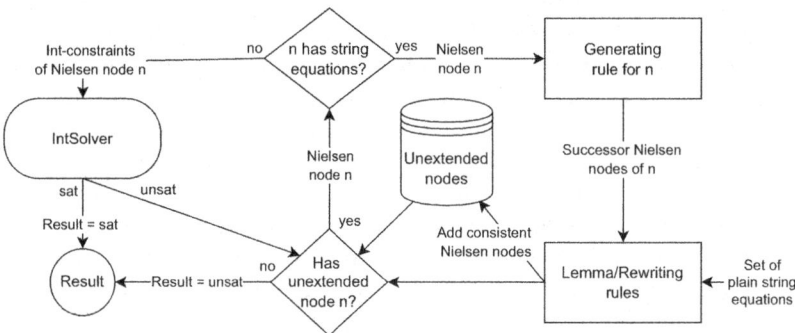

**Fig. 1.** String solving workflow.

### 3.1 Expansion of Nielsen Graphs

We detect the satisfiability of a set of string equations $S$ with the help of Nielsen graphs [26], which we expand and simplify using our Nielsen transformation rules from Sect. 3.2.

*Nielsen Graphs.* Simply put, we consider a *(Nielsen) node* $n$ to be the tuple $\langle \mathcal{E}(n), \mathcal{I}(n) \rangle$, where $\mathcal{E}(n)$ is a finite set of extended string equations and $\mathcal{I}(n)$ is its finite set of integer (in)equalities. In particular, the Nielsen node corresponding to the input set $S$ of plain string equations is $\langle S, \emptyset \rangle$; this node is the *root node* of the Nielsen graph of $S$.

We assume that trivially satisfied constraints in $\mathcal{E}(n)$ and $\mathcal{I}(n)$, such as $\varepsilon \simeq \varepsilon$ or $0 \leq 1$, are implicitly removed from $n$. Given some integer (in)equation $C$, we write $n \models C$ to denote that we can derive $C$ from $\mathcal{I}(n)$.

A Nielsen node $n$ has a finite number of successor nodes and is called *inconsistent* if either (i) $\bot \in \mathcal{E}(n)$, or (ii) $\mathcal{I}(n) \models \bot$, or (iii) all successors nodes of $n$ are inconsistent; where $\bot$ denotes the always false formula. Contrary, $n$ is *satisfied* if (i) $\mathcal{E}(n) = \emptyset$, and (ii) $\mathcal{I}(n) \not\models \bot$. For checking $n \models C$, we assume access to a sound integer reasoner INTSOLVER.

The node $n$ is *extended* if its successor nodes are already added to the Nielsen graph, given that $n$ is neither satisfied nor inconsistent. Dually, a node that is not extended yet is called *unextended*. A Nielsen graph captures dependencies between Nielsen nodes and, as such, witnesses the (un)satisfiability of constraints by a *subgoal reduction*: if the constraints $\mathcal{E}(n) \cup \mathcal{I}(n)$ of node $n$ have a model, then at least one of the successors of $n$ has a model as well. Nielsen graphs can thus be seen as a proof object or a variant of a tableau derivation.

*String Solving via Expansion of Nielsen Graphs.* We use Nielsen graphs to represent and manipulate our (initial) set $S$ of (plain) string equations. Doing so, we apply extended Nielsen transformation rules (Sect. 3.2 and its extension in the succeeding sections) to simplify Nielsen nodes. In the sequel, let simpl($n$) denote the simplified version of Nielsen node $n$.

Satisfiability of the input set $S$ of plain string equations is decided via recursively expanding the Nielsen graph of $S$, as shown in Fig. 1. We start by (i) adding the plain set of equations $S$ to a Nielsen graph in the form of an unextended and simplified Nielsen node simpl($\langle S, \emptyset \rangle$) as the root of the Nielsen graph; here, we use the rewriting and lemma rules of Sect. 3.2. Next, (ii) we choose an arbitrary unextended Nielsen node $n$ of the Nielsen graph and generate its successors $n_1, \ldots, n_k$ via some generating rule from Sect. 3.2. Then, (iii) we consider the simplified versions of the successor nodes simpl($n_i$) of $n$ that are not inconsistent. These simplified successors of $n$ are added as new unexpanded nodes to the Nielsen graph by connecting $n_i$ with $n$ via a respective edge – usually, we loop back to (ii). Once, (iv) a satisfied node $n$, reachable from the root node, is found, we report the initial set of equations $S$ to be satisfiable. Satisfiability of $S$ is implied by the construction of the expanded Nielsen graph: if a node $n$ is satisfied, all its string equations $\mathcal{E}(n)$ have been removed and its remaining integer constraints $\mathcal{I}(n)$ are satisfiable. On the other hand, (v) if there are no unextended Nielsen nodes reachable from the root node anymore and no satisfied node has been found, we conclude the unsatisfiability of the input $S$.

*Remark 1 (Termination of expanding Nielsen graphs).* If a set of plain string equations $S$ is satisfiable, there exists at least one satisfied Nielsen node $n$ that is reachable from the root simpl($\langle S, \emptyset \rangle$). Yet, a fully extended Nielsen graph might be infinitely large and might contain infinitely many satisfied nodes. Termination of unsatisfiable instances is not guaranteed. As our rules (Sect. 3.2) are usually not invertible – $n$ being satisfiable implies only one successors to be satisfiable as well – we require a fair tree traversal methods, such as breadth first or iterative deepening, in practice to make our approach terminate more robustly on satisfiable instances $S$.

## 3.2 Extended Nielsen Transformations Rules

Our string solving expands Nielsen graphs of string equations, by rewriting and generating Nielsen nodes $n$ within the respective Nielsen graphs, as discussed in Sect. 3.1. Namely, we simplify some node $n$ by simpl($n$) via (i) lemma rules, (ii) term rewriting rules, and (iii) equation rewriting rules, in order to obtain the "easier-to-handle" node simpl($n$). We use (iv) generating rules to introduce the successor nodes $n'$ of $n$, where the constraints of $n'$ result from the application of a substitution $\sigma_{n'}$ to the constraints of $n$ and the addition of further constraints $C_{n'}$. That is, $n' = \text{simpl}(\langle \mathcal{E}(n)[\sigma_{n'}], \mathcal{I}(n)[\sigma_{n'}] \cup C_{n'} \rangle)$.

In the sequel, we fix an arbitrary Nielsen node $n$ and introduce the following rules relative to $n$.

**Lemma Rules.** If $\mathcal{E}(n) \cup \mathcal{I}(n)$ contains the power tokens $u^m$, string equations $u \simeq v$, or string variables $x$, we add the respective integer constraints $m \geq 0$, $|u| \simeq |v|$, and $|x| \geq 0$ to $\mathcal{I}(n)$.

**Term Rewriting Rules.** In the sequel, we write $e_1 \rightsquigarrow e_2$ to mean that $e_1$ is replaced by $e_2$ everywhere in the considered Nielsen node. Term rewriting rules are used to simplify length constraints and rewrite power terms, as follows:

$$|uv| \rightsquigarrow |u| + |v| \qquad |u^m| \rightsquigarrow m|u| \qquad \varepsilon^m \rightsquigarrow \varepsilon$$
$$|\varepsilon| \rightsquigarrow 0 \qquad |@| \rightsquigarrow 1 \qquad v^m \rightsquigarrow \varepsilon, \text{ if } n \models m \simeq 0$$
$$(v^{m_1})^{m_2} \rightsquigarrow v^{m_1 m_2} \qquad v^{m_1} v^{m_2} \rightsquigarrow v^{m_1 + m_2} \qquad v^m \rightsquigarrow v, \text{ if } n \models m \simeq 1$$

A term is *fully rewritten* if no more rewriting rule can be applied to it. An (in)equality constraint is *fully rewritten* if all its terms are fully rewritten.

*Example 2 (Computing* $\mathrm{simpl}(n)$ *for Example 1).* Consider the two input equations of Example 1 and let $n$ be their respective node $n$ in the corresponding Nielsen graph. We drop the common $b$ suffix in $(E_1)$ and use lemma rules to add a length constraints for each string equation which can be rewritten into the fully rewritten constraints $2|x_3| \simeq 3|x_5|$ and $2|x_5| \simeq |x_4|$, using respective term rewriting rules. Finally, we add the side constraints $|x_i| \geq 0$ for all $1 \leq i \leq 5$. The resulting set of constraints defines $\mathrm{simpl}(n)$.

**Equation Rewriting and Generating Rules.** Equation rewriting rules remove some prefix of a string equation of $\mathcal{E}(n)$, sometimes under additional side conditions. In case no rewriting rule is applicable over $n$ anymore, a generating rule over $n$ is triggered to add additional information, which usually happens by considering multiple cases in the form of successor nodes.

Equation rewriting/generating rules for an extended string equation $u \simeq v \in \mathcal{E}(n)$ are given based on the first tokens of $u$ and $v$. Our rewriting and generating rules are summarised in Table 1, listed per possible combinations of first tokens, or $\varepsilon$, of the LHS and RHS (columns 1–2 of Table 1). Primed variables $x'$ in the table denote fresh string variables. A rule can be applied if the equation is of the given form and the side condition is satisfied in the current Nielsen node. We note that we can also apply all rules to $v \simeq u$, $u^R \simeq v^R$, and $v^R \simeq u^R$. Finally, any equation rewritten to $\varepsilon \simeq \varepsilon$ is removed from $\mathcal{E}(n)$, and similarly any trivially satisfied integer (in)equation.

Equation rewriting rules replace some equation $u \simeq v$ either by a new equation or detect a conflict $\bot$ (column 4), potentially requiring some side condition to be satisfied (column 3). On the other hand, generating rules apply substitutions (column 5) to $n$ in order to generate successor node(s) $n'$ of $n$ or add additional new (integer) constraints to $n'$ (column 6) to make further equation rewriting rules applicable.

**Table 1.** Equation rewriting rules and generating rules for an extended equation $u \simeq v$.

| LHS | RHS | Rewriting rules | | Generating rules | |
|---|---|---|---|---|---|
| | | Side Cond. | New Equation | Substitution | New Cnstr. |
| $tu$ | $tv$ | – | $u \simeq v$ | – | – |
| $\varepsilon$ | $av$ | – | $\bot$ | – | – |
| $\varepsilon$ | $ov$ | – | $\bot$ | – | – |
| $\varepsilon$ | $xv$ | – | – | $x/\varepsilon$ | – |
| $\varepsilon$ | $w^m v$ | – | – | – | $\{w \simeq \varepsilon\}$ |
| | | | | | $\{m \simeq 0\}$ |
| $au$ | $bv$ | – | $\bot$ | – | – |
| $ou$ | $@v$ | – | – | $o/@$ | – |
| $^{\dagger}@u$ | $xv$ | – | – | $x/\varepsilon$ | – |
| | | | | $x/@x'$ | – |
| $^{\ddagger}@u$ | $w^m v$ | $n \models m \simeq 0$ | $@u \simeq v$ | – | $\{m \simeq 0\}$ |
| | | $n \models m > 0$ | $@u \simeq ww^{m-1}v$ | – | $\{m > 0\}$ |
| $xu$ | $yv$ | – | – | $x/\varepsilon$ | – |
| | | | | $y/\varepsilon$ | $\{|x| > 0\}$ |
| | | | | $y/xy'$ | $\{|x| > 0\}$ |
| | | | | $x/yx'$ | $\{|y| > 0, |x'| > 0\}$ |
| $^{\dagger}xu$ | $w^m v$ | – | – | $x/w^{m'}x'$ | – |
| | | | | $x/w^{m'}p_1$ | $s_1 \cup \{0 \leq m' < m\}$ |
| | | | | ... | ... |
| | | | | $x/w^{m'}p_k$ | $s_k \cup \{0 \leq m' < m\}$ |
| $^{\ddagger}w^{m_1}u$ | $w^{m_2}v$ | $n \models m_1 \geq m_2$ | $w^{m_1-m_2}u \simeq v$ | – | $\{m_1 \geq m_2\}$ |
| | | $n \models m_1 < m_2$ | $u \simeq w^{m_2-m_1}v$ | – | $\{m_1 < m_2\}$ |
| $^{\ddagger}w_1^{m_1}u$ | $w_2^{m_2}v$ | $n \models m_2 \simeq 0$ | $w_1^{m_1}u \simeq v$ | – | $\{m_2 \simeq 0\}$ |
| | | $n \models m_2 > 0$ | $w_1^{m_1}u \simeq w_2 w_2^{m_2-1}v$ | – | $\{m_2 > 0\}$ |

*Example 3 (Generating rules for* simpl($n$) *in Example 1).* Consider the simplified node simpl($n$) computed in Example 2 for Example 1. The set of applicable generating rules is given by the LHS/RHS token combinations of $x_3$ and $x_5$; $x_5^R$ and $b$; $x_1$ and $x_2$; and $x_3^R$ and $x_4^R$.

We stress that expanded Nielsen graphs using the rules of Table 1 correspond to a proof "tree", as illustrated next.

*Example 4 (A fully expanded Nielsen graph for* $xx \simeq yb$). Consider the plain string equation $xx \simeq yb$. We establish its satisfiability by constructing its expanded Nielsen graph, as presented in Sect. 3.1 and using the rules of Table 1. The fully expanded Nielsen graph of $xx \simeq yb$ is shown in Fig. 2. By reusing variable names, a single node could be used rather than multiple isomorphic ones.

Hence, $x' \simeq \varepsilon \wedge |x'| \simeq 0$ and $x'' \simeq \varepsilon \wedge |x''| \simeq 0$ could be contracted to the same node.

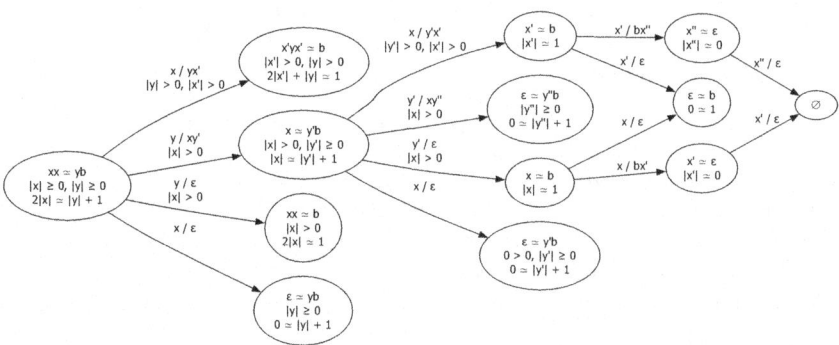

**Fig. 2.** Fully expanded Nielsen graph for the plain string equation $xx \simeq yb$, representing a variant of a tableau derivation.

We conclude this section by noting that the rules of Table 1 annotated by † and ‡ require special care, as discussed in Sect. 5. In particular, the case with $xu$ on the LHS and $w^m v$ on the RHS requires $k+1$ branches given by the finite set $\text{pre}(w) = \{\langle p_1, s_1 \rangle, \ldots, \langle p_k, s_k \rangle\}$ which denotes the set of all syntactic prefixes $p_i$ of $w$ together with potential side conditions $s_i$. The set $\text{pre}(w)$ is detailed in Sect. 5. We optimise the application of those rules by using more extended rules (Sects. 4–6) discussed next.

## 4 Equality Decomposition

This section provides a remedy for some cases when string equations cannot be solved using the Nielsen transformation rules of Sect. 3.2. Intuitively, we decompose string equations into subequations that can be further solved using our transformation rules. Note that the rules of Table 1 can only be applied upon the first (last) tokens of the LHS/RHS of string equations. With equality decomposition, we split equations into smaller ones. As such, the equality decomposition enables us to apply Table 1 on tokens at positions different from the first tokens of LHS/RHS.

In a nutshell, we proceed as follows. Consider an extended string equation $u_1 u_2 \simeq v_1 v_2 \in \mathcal{E}(n)$ and let $d = |u_1| - |v_1|$ be a known integer constant. Equality decomposition is applied by splitting the equation into two equations, potentially padding one side each by $d$ characters. If $d = 0$, the equation $u_1 u_2 \simeq v_1 v_2$ can be decomposed into the set $\{u_1 \simeq v_1, u_2 \simeq v_2\}$ of two smaller equations. If all string terms $u_1, u_2, v_1, v_2$ contain at least one string variable or a power token, we replace $u_1 u_2 \simeq v_1 v_2$ in $\mathcal{E}(n)$ by $\{u_1 \simeq v_1, u_2 \simeq v_2\}$. For example, we decompose $xayw \simeq ybxz$ into $xay \simeq ybx$ and $w \simeq z$, as $|xay| - |ybx| = 0$.

On the other hand, if $d > 0$, then decomposing $u_1u_2 \simeq v_1v_2$ comes with the additional requirement that the last $d$ characters of $u_1$ are the same as the first $d$ characters of $v_2$. To do so, we introduce $|d|$ fresh symbolic character tokens $\bar{o}_d' = o_1', \ldots, o_d'$ to represent these $d$ characters of $u_1$. Note again, this is equivalent to introducing one fresh string variable $x$ with $|x| = d$. Then, $u_1u_2 \simeq v_1v_2$ is decomposed into the equations:

$$\{ u_1 \simeq v_1\bar{o}_d', \; \bar{o}_d'u_2 \simeq v_2 \}.$$

Our equality decomposition approach thus uses length constraints $|u_1| - |v_1|$, which can be facilitated by the integer constraints $\mathcal{I}(n)$ of $n$. Our approach can be seen as a strengthened variant of the usual decomposition rule without padding, primarily used as a preprocessing rule in other solvers: We use $d$ symbolic character tokens for padding string equations in order to enable their decomposition.

*Example 5 (Equality decomposition in Example 1).* Using the lemma and term rewriting rules of Example 2, we derive:

$$2|x_3| \simeq 3|x_5| \wedge 2|x_5| \simeq |x_4|.$$

Consequently, we infer $d = |x_1x_1acx_2x_4x_2x_5| - |x_2x_2abcx_1x_1x_3x_3| = 1$. We decompose $(E_2)$ using a single symbolic character $o$ and replace $(E_2)$ by the resulting two new equations $(E_3)$ and $(E_4)$:

$$x_1x_1acx_2x_4x_2x_5o \quad \simeq \quad x_2x_2abcx_1x_1x_3x_3, \quad (E_3)$$
$$x_3bax_5x_3x_4x_3 \quad \simeq \quad ox_3x_4x_4ax_4 \quad (E_4)$$

In other words, $(E_2)$ is replaced by $(E_3)$ and $(E_4)$ in $\mathcal{E}(n)$, and we further simplify $n$ by lemma and term rewriting rules.

## 5  Ground Power Introduction

We introduce power terms to eliminate lengthy and repetitive substrings in string equations, and compress sequences of rewriting and generating rule applications into power terms. Power terms allow us to eliminate a potentially unbounded number of equation decompositions when applying substitutions of the form $x/@x'$; here, $x'$ is again a fresh string variable. For example, when $xu = axv$ is satisfiable, all its models need $x$ to be $a^m$, for some $m \geq 0$. Finding such models using equality decomposition in combination with the rules of Table 1 requires analysing infinitely many token combinations for some unsatisfiable equations. Even in the case of satisfiable problem instances, the required analysis can become very long. In order to circumvent this, we use rules based on the property that $xu = vx$, with $v \neq \varepsilon$, implies $x = (w_1w_2)^m w_1$, $v = w_1w_2$, and $u = w_2w_1$ for some natural number $m$ and words $w_1$ and $w_2$ [21].

*Power Introduction and Rules* [†] *of Table* 1. The rules of Table 1 that are annotated by [†] are only applied when power introduction is not applicable. In such cases, given a ground string term $w \neq \varepsilon$ and constraint $xu \simeq wxv$, we have:

$$\exists m. \bigvee_{\langle p,s\rangle \in \mathrm{pre}(w)} \left( x \simeq w^m p \wedge \bigwedge s \right) \vee w \simeq \varepsilon \tag{1}$$

where pre($w$) denotes the set of pairs $\langle p, s \rangle$ of possible strict prefixes $p$ of $w$, such that there is only a finite set $s$ of side conditions to constrain $p$. Formally, pre($w$) is defined for a ground string term $w$ as:

- pre($uv$) := pre($u$) $\cup$ $\{\langle up, s\rangle \mid \langle p, s\rangle \in$ pre($v$)$\}$,
- pre($\varepsilon$) := $\emptyset$,
- pre(@) := $\{\langle \varepsilon, \emptyset \rangle\}$,
- pre($u^m$) := $\{\langle u^{m'} p, \{0 \leq m' < m\} \cup s\rangle \mid \langle p, s\rangle \in$ pre($u$)$\}$

where $m'$ is a fresh integer variable.

Let us make the following observation on the interplay between power introductions and prefix pre($w$) analysis. When considering equations $xu \simeq wxv$, an unsoundness problem may arise when $w$ represents $\varepsilon$ in a potential model, as $w$ would have cancelled out. Such cases may happen when $w$ consists of power tokens all becoming $\varepsilon$ because their exponents are zero. Based on the definition of pre($w$), we would introduce a fresh $m'$ integer variable with $0 \leq m' < m$, which yields a conflict when $m = 0$ and thus falsely eliminates a model. As a remedy, we also explicitly split upon $w \simeq \varepsilon$ to cover this case. On the other hand, if $w$ is not $\varepsilon$, power introduction allows us to eliminate string variables $x$ by replacing them with the help of integer constraints, as shown next.

*Example 6 ($xbxa \simeq axbx$).* Without introducing powers, applying the rules of Table 1 would fail to solve the unsatisfiable equation $xbxa \simeq axbx$. Applying the rules from Table 1 leads to an infinite chain of substitutions of the form $x/ax'$, resulting in increasingly longer string terms. By introducing power terms, we eliminate $x$ via the single substitution $x/a^m$: applying this substitution to $xbxa \simeq axbx$ yields $a^m ba^m a \simeq aa^m ba^m$ that can be easily simplified to $\bot$.

*Power Introduction and Rules* ‡ *of Table* 1. We next comment on the use of power introduction together with the Nielsen transformation rules annotated by ‡ in Table 1. When the first token of some side of an equation is a power token, we first check whether the other side of the equation can be rewritten so that it starts with a power token with the same base, so that they can cancel out. For doing so, we apply additional term rewriting rules:

$$ww^m \leadsto w^{m+1} \qquad w_2(w_1 w_2)^m \leadsto (w_2 w_1)^m w_2$$
$$w^m w \leadsto w^{m+1} \qquad (w_1 w_2)^m w_1 \leadsto w_1 (w_2 w_1)^m$$
$$ww \leadsto w^2$$

These additional rules considerably reduce the number of equational decompositions when introducing powers. However, more importantly, they are necessary to handle equations like $a(ba)^m u \simeq (ab)^m v$. In case the solver does not realize that the prefixes can be rewritten into the same power, the rules of Table 1 would suggest an explicit unwinding for each possible value of $m$.

*Strengthening Power Reductions.* We generalize the rule of (1) over $xu \simeq wxv$ to be applicable over sets of equations $EQ \subseteq \mathcal{E}(n)$ given by:

$$EQ := \{\, w_1 x_k u_1 \simeq x_1 v_1,\ w_2 x_1 u_2 \simeq x_2 v_2,\ \ldots,\ w_k x_{k-1} u_k \simeq x_k v_k \,\},$$

with $k \geq 1$, and all terms $w_1, \ldots, w_k$ being ground. Similarly to (1), the set $EQ$ enforces the more general form of power introduction

$$\exists m.\ \bigvee_{1 \leq i \leq k}\ \bigvee_{\langle p,s \rangle \in \mathrm{pre}(\bar{w}_i)} \left( x_i \simeq \bar{w}_i^m p \wedge \bigwedge s \right) \vee \bar{w}_1 \simeq \varepsilon, \tag{2}$$

where $\bar{w}_i := w_i w_{i-1} \ldots w_1 w_k \ldots w_{i+1}$.

*Example 7 (Power introduction in Example 5).* After decomposing $(E_2)$ into $(E_3)$ and $(E_4)$, we introduce a power token that is justified by the prefix of $(E_4)$: the LHS of $(E_4)$ starts with $x_3$ and the RHS with $ox_3$. As the string term consisting only of the symbolic character $o$ is ground and cannot be $\varepsilon$, we apply power introduction and consider only one successor node as $\mathrm{pre}(o) = \{\langle \varepsilon, \emptyset \rangle\}$: the successor is generated by $x_3 / o^{m_1}$ for some fresh constant $m_1$. From a lemma rule, we get $m_1 \geq 0$ and we rewrite the length constraints $|x_3[x_3/o^{m_1}]|$ to $m_1$. The string equations $(E_1)$, $(E_3)$ and $(E_4)$ respectively become:

$$o^{2m_1} x_4 b x_5 \simeq x_5 x_5 x_5 x_5 x_4 b, \tag{$E_1'$}$$

$$x_1 x_1 a c x_2 x_4 x_2 x_5 o \simeq x_2 x_2 a b c x_1 x_1 o^{2m_1}, \tag{$E_3'$}$$

$$o^{m_1} b a x_5 o^{m_1} x_4 o^{m_1} \simeq o o^{m_1} x_4 x_4 a x_4. \tag{$E_4'$}$$

Thanks to the additional rewrite rules introduced previously in this section, token $oo^{m_1}$ on the RHS of $(E_4')$ can be rewritten to $o^{m_1+1}$. As such, common prefixes of $(E_3')$ are removed, and we apply $o/b$. We get the respective equations of $(E_1')$, $(E_3')$ and $(E_4')$ as:

$$b^{2m_1} x_4 b x_5 \simeq x_5 x_5 x_5 x_5 x_4 b, \tag{$E_1''$}$$

$$x_1 x_1 a c x_2 x_4 x_2 x_5 b \simeq x_2 x_2 a b c x_1 x_1 b^{2m_1}, \tag{$E_3''$}$$

$$a x_5 b^{m_1} x_4 b^{m_1} \simeq x_4 x_4 a x_4. \tag{$E_4''$}$$

Further powers can be introduced, either by using $(E_4'')$ because of the suffix $x_4 b^{m_1}$ on the LHS and $x_4$ on the RHS, or via the generalised form of power introduction (2) using equations $(E_1'')$ and $(E_4'')$. In the latter case, we end up with the four successor nodes given by:

$$\{\, x_4/(ab^{2m_1})^{m_2},\ x_4/(ab^{2m_1})^{m_2} ab^{m_3},\ x_5/(b^{2m_1} a)^{m_2} b^{m_3},\ x_5/(b^{2m_1} a)^{m_2} b^{2m_1} \,\}$$

and $m_3 < 2m_1$. In the former case, we have two cases: applying $x_4/b^{m_3}(b^{m_1})^{m_2}$ with $m_3 < m_1$ – which simplifies to $b^{m_1 m_2 + m_3}$ – or adding $b^{m_1} \simeq \varepsilon$. We chose the former case and consider the first successor first: applying $x_4/b^{m_3}(b^{m_1})^{m_2}$.

$$b^{2m_1+m_1m_2+m_3}bx_5 \simeq x_5x_5x_5x_5b^{m_1m_2+m_3}b, \quad (E_1''')$$

$$x_1x_1acx_2b^{m_1m_2+m_3}x_2x_5b \simeq x_2x_2abcx_1x_1b^{2m_1}, \quad (E_3''')$$

$$ax_5b^{2m_1} \simeq b^{2m_1m_2+2m_3}a. \quad (E_4''')$$

As $0 \leq m_3 < m_1$, we derive $m_1 > 0$ and thus we unwind $b^{2m_1}$ to $b^{2m_1-1}b$ in ($E_4'''$) using the respective rule from Table 1, resulting in a conflict. We therefore consider the successor node generated by adding the constraint $b^{m_1} \simeq \varepsilon$. This implies $m_1 = 0$, eliminating all power tokens and allowing us to derive $|x_4| = |x_5| = 0$. After further simplifications, we derive $x_4/\varepsilon$ and $x_5/\varepsilon$. As such, we end up with the Nielsen node containing the single plain string equation:

$$x_1x_1acx_2x_2b \simeq x_2x_2abcx_1x_1.$$

## 6 Parikh Image

Parikh images [25] can be an effective method to prove sets of string constraints to be unsatisfiable by extracting constraints on the number of occurrences of terminal characters [31]. It represents an abstraction of string equations that elides information about character positions, retaining only the number of occurrences. In the following, we establish a method that retains information about the relative positions of characters, resulting in a tighter abstraction. Our method computes a value we call *(error-bounded) multi-sequence Parikh image*.

To formalise the Parikh images, let $\pi_a(u)$ be a function that represents the set of positions on which there is an $a \in \Sigma$ in $u$. The set $\{ (a, \pi_a(u)) \mid a \in \Sigma \}$ is a complete representation of $u$. Let $\alpha_a(u) := |\pi_a(u)|$, then an equation $u \simeq v$ can be over-approximated by $\bigwedge_{a \in \Sigma} \alpha_a(u) \simeq \alpha_a(v)$. For example, $\alpha_a(xay) = \alpha_a(x) + 1 + \alpha_a(y)$ and $\alpha_a(xby) = \alpha_a(x) + \alpha_a(y)$, so the equation $xay \simeq ybx$ can be recognised as unsatisfiable immediately. We note that neither equality decomposition nor ground power introduction combined with the rules of Table 1 can detect this equation as unsatisfiable. Still, Parikh constraints based on single concrete characters fail to capture the infeasibility of equations such as the equation in the only Nielsen node of our running example: $x_1x_1acx_2x_2b \simeq x_2x_2abcx_1x_1$. Our method is going to accomplish this.

### 6.1 Parikh Images for Unbordered Patterns

In the following, we consider Parikh images for strings $w \in \Sigma^+$ of length greater than 1 – we call these $w$ *patterns* – and assume that we have plain string equations. For the scope of this paper, we consider symbolic characters and power tokens as string variables when computing the Parikh image. For example, in the plain equation $xabcy \simeq ybacx$, pattern $bc$ occurs on the LHS of the equation $\alpha_{bc}(xabcy) = \alpha_{bc}(x) + 1 + \alpha_{bc}(y)$ times and $\alpha_{bc}(ybacx) = \alpha_{bc}(y) + \alpha_{bc}(x)$ times on the RHS. The equation is therefore unsatisfiable. Our running example also offers an opportunity to use such a pattern:

*Example 8 (Parikh image in Example 7).* Consider the equation in our running Example 7. We can consider pattern $w = abc$ and thus get $\alpha_w(x_1x_1acx_2x_2b) \simeq \alpha_w(x_2x_2abcx_1x_1)$. This equation can be intuitively rewritten to $\alpha_w(x_1x_1) + \alpha_w(x_2x_2) \simeq \alpha_w(x_2x_2) + 1 + \alpha_w(x_1x_1)$ and further to $0 = 1$ which proves the equation itself, as well as the overall running example unsatisfiable, as all successor Nielsen nodes of the root node are inconsistent. In the following, we will formally define this "intuitive rewriting".

In contrast to usual Parikh images over singleton characters, there is no general notion of $\alpha_w(u)$ that decomposes over string constants and string variables in $u$. For example, we cannot decompose $\alpha_{ab}(ybacx)$ into a sum over the components of $ybacx$ because the value depends on whether $x$ ends with $a$ or not.

We address this limitation by

1. Restricting Parikh images to character sequence patterns $w$ such that no proper suffix of $w$ is a prefix of $w$. Such words are called *unbordered*.
2. Defining over- $\alpha_w^\uparrow(u)$ and under-approximations $\alpha_w^\downarrow(u)$ such that unsatisfiability of a string equation $u \simeq v$ can be established when $\alpha_w^\uparrow(u) - \alpha_w^\downarrow(v)$ or, symmetrically, $\alpha_w^\uparrow(v) - \alpha_w^\downarrow(u)$ rewrite to a negative constant.

Our rewriting rules for $\alpha_w^\uparrow(u)$ and $\alpha_w^\downarrow(u)$ satisfy the following properties:

**Lemma 1 (Correctness of Parikh images for Unbordered Patterns).** *Assume $w$ is an unbordered pattern.*

- *If $u \in \Sigma^*$ then $\alpha_w^\uparrow(u) = \alpha_w^\downarrow(u) =$ number of occurrences of $w$ in $u$.*
- *Assume $\alpha_w^\uparrow(u)$ rewrites to $k + \sum_x c_x \alpha_w(x)$ for natural numbers $c_x$ and $k$. Then for every substitution $\sigma$ from string variables to $\Sigma^*$, $\alpha_w^\uparrow(u[\sigma]) \leq k + \sum_x c_x \alpha_w^\uparrow(x[\sigma])$. A symmetric property holds for $\alpha_w^\downarrow(u)$.*

It remains to define the over- and under-approximations. As the examples suggested, the restriction to unbordered patterns means that there are many cases where the under- and over-approximations coincide.

**Definition 2 ($d$-gaps and $w \bowtie u$).**

*$d$-gaps We call a string term $u$ a $d$-gap (with $d > 1$) iff it is of one of the following forms: $u = xvy$ (with $v \in \Sigma^*$), $u = xv$, or $u = vy$ ($v \in \Sigma^+$ in the latter two cases) and $0 < ||u|| \leq d$.*

*$w \bowtie u$ If $w$ is a pattern and $u$ is a $|w|$-gap, we write $w \bowtie u$ to denote that there can be crossing occurrences of $w$ within a $|w|$-gap $u$. Formally, $w \bowtie u$ is true if $u = xw_2y$ and we can decompose $w = w_1w_2w_3$ ($\{w_1, w_3\} \neq \varepsilon$), otherwise it is false. Similarly, the cases $u = w_1y$ requires $w = w_1w_2$ ($w_2 \neq \varepsilon$) and in cases $u = xw_2$ requires $w = w_1w_2$ ($w_1 \neq \varepsilon$)*

Using the definition of a gap, apply the following term rewriting rules to rewrite stepwise $\alpha_w^\downarrow(u)/\alpha_w^\uparrow(u)$ into the desired grouping for an unbordered pattern $w$:

$$\alpha_w^\uparrow(x) \rightsquigarrow \alpha_w(x)$$
$$\alpha_w^\uparrow(w_2) \rightsquigarrow 0 \qquad \text{if } w_2 \in \Sigma^* \wedge |w_2| < |w|$$
$$\alpha_w^\uparrow(uwv) \rightsquigarrow 1 + \alpha_w^\uparrow(u) + \alpha_w^\uparrow(v)$$
$$\alpha_w^\uparrow(ua_1w_2a_2v) \rightsquigarrow \alpha_w^\uparrow(ua_1w_2) + \alpha_w^\uparrow(w_2a_2v) \quad \text{if } a_1w_2a_2 \in \Sigma^+ \wedge$$
$$|a_1w_2a_2| = |w| \wedge a_1w_2a_2 \neq w$$
$$\alpha_w^\uparrow(uxw_2yv) \rightsquigarrow \alpha_w^\uparrow(uxw_2) + \alpha_w^\uparrow(w_2yv) \quad \text{if } xw_2y \text{ is } |w|\text{-gap and } w \not\trianglelefteq xw_2y$$
$$\alpha_w^\uparrow(aw_2yv) \rightsquigarrow \alpha_w^\uparrow(w_2yv) \qquad \text{if } aw_2y \text{ is } |w|\text{-gap and } w \not\trianglelefteq aw_2y$$
$$\alpha_w^\uparrow(uxw_2a) \rightsquigarrow \alpha_w^\uparrow(uxw_2) \qquad \text{if } xw_2a \text{ is } |w|\text{-gap and } w \not\trianglelefteq xw_2a$$

We now define under- and over-approximations for cases not covered by the previous exact rewrite rules. They are:

$$\alpha_w^\downarrow(x) \rightsquigarrow \alpha_w(x) \qquad \alpha_w^\uparrow(x) \rightsquigarrow \alpha_w(x)$$
$$\alpha_w^\downarrow(w_2u) \rightsquigarrow \alpha_w^\downarrow(u) \qquad \alpha_w^\uparrow(w_2xu) \rightsquigarrow 1 + \alpha_w^\uparrow(xu) \qquad \text{if } w_2 \in \Sigma^+$$
$$\alpha_w^\downarrow(xw_2) \rightsquigarrow \alpha_w(x) \qquad \alpha_w^\uparrow(xw_2) \rightsquigarrow 1 + \alpha_w(x) \qquad \text{if } w_2 \in \Sigma^+$$
$$\alpha_w^\uparrow(xw_2yv) \rightsquigarrow 1 + \alpha_w(x) + \alpha_w^\uparrow(yv) \qquad \text{if } w_2 \in \Sigma^*$$

The correctness of the rewrite rules relies on first applying the non-approximate rules exhaustively before considering the cases presented by the approximations. Informally speaking, we require all $u$ in the remaining $\alpha_w(u)$ to be "concatenations of $|w|$-gaps" that can contain crossing occurrences.

Our procedure for filtering unsatisfiable equations $u \simeq v$ is now as follows:

(i) Enumerate maximal unbordered patterns $w \in \Sigma^*$ occurring in $u$ and $v$. The patterns are maximal only w.r.t. the pattern within the considered side $u$ or $v$.
(ii) For each of these $w$ rewrite $\alpha_w^\uparrow(u) - \alpha_w^\downarrow(v)$ to a sum $k + \sum_x c_x \alpha_w(x)$. If each $c_x$ is 0 and $k < 0$, we can conclude the equation $u \simeq v$ to be unsatisfiable.

*Example 9 (xaxaabbby $\simeq$ xyabababx).* Consider the unbordered pattern $w = ab$, which is maximal within the RHS. Then $\alpha_w^\uparrow(xaxaabbby) \rightsquigarrow 2\alpha_w(x) + 2 + \alpha_w(y)$ and $\alpha_w^\downarrow(xyabababx)$ rewrites to $\alpha_w(y) + 3 + 2\alpha_w(x)$. Thus, $\alpha_w^\uparrow(xaxaabbby) - \alpha_w^\downarrow(xyabababx)$ is $-1$; witnessing that the equation is unsatisifable.

## 7 Implementation and Experiments

*Implementation.* We implemented our approach within a new prototype ZIPT. Our implementation[1] uses the Z3 [24] SMT solver both as the auxiliary integer

---
[1] Available at https://github.com/CEisenhofer/ZIPT.

solver, as well as for the general CDCL($\mathcal{T}$) framework, calling our string solving procedure with the set of plain string equations using user-propagation [8].

Our implementation follows the workflow of Fig. 1, by using the Nielsen transformation rules of Table 1 in combination with equality decomposition 4, power introduction Sect. 5, and Parikh images Sect. 6. If multiple generating rules of Table 1 are applicable, we choose the one predicted to cause faster termination. For example, rules eliminating string variables are prioritised over those that do not.

In addition to the generating rules presented, we use look-ahead heuristics to prefer generating rules in which all but one generated successor node results in a conflict. Examples for such cases are:

- Eliminating some string variable $x$ using $x/\varepsilon$ with $xu_1v_1 \simeq u_2v_2$, where $u_1 \in (\{x\} \cup \mathcal{V}_C \cup \Sigma)^+$ and $u_2 \in (\mathcal{V}_C \cup \Sigma)^+$. Unless a power introduction rule is applicable, we can compute the longest prefix $w$ of $u_2$ such that we can safely apply $x/wx'$. For example, $xxbau \simeq abv$ gives $x/abx'$ without branching, as both $x/\varepsilon$ and $x/a$ would yield a conflict immediately. A similar case applies if $x$ was a power token;
- Unwinding a power token $w_1^m u \simeq w_2 v$ with $w_2 \in (\mathcal{V}_C \cup \Sigma)^+$. Whenever $w_2$ cannot be a prefix or a suffix of any word we can get by unwinding $w_1^m$ at least once, we conclude $m = 0$. For example, $(ab^{m_2}c)^{m_1}u = aav$ enforces $m_1 = 0$ as $aa$ is not a prefix of $ab^{m_2}c$ for any $m_2$ nor is it a suffix;
- Length constraints where we can deduce $n \models |x| > |y|$ in our current Nielsen node $n$. If we consider $xu \simeq yv$, we have to apply $x/yx'$. Similarly, if $n \models |x| = |y|$, we chose $x/y$.

For traversing and expanding the Nielsen graph, we rely on a variant of iterative deepening, in which successors of node $n$ that strictly reduce the constraints of $n$ are expanded in more depth.

*Experimental Setup.* As such, we ran our solver ZIPT on the four QF_S tracks of the woorpje benchmark set [12] of SMT-LIB [4]; this benchmark set consists of 409 benchmark files containing only string equations. We compared our work against the state-of-the-art solvers competing in the most recent SMT-COMP competition[2]. We used a 10 seconds timeout, 8 GB of RAM, and default solver configurations, based on a dedicated core of an Intel i7-13850HX CPU.

*Experimental Analysis.* Our results are summarized in Table 2, showcasing that ZIPT outperforms the state-of-the-art. When solving problems within track 02, our approach benefits from power introduction; this is so because models described by these benchmarks are exponential in the number of string variables. Using (nested) power tokens allows us to solve such examples without taking exponentially many steps, which is a key difference compared to other works.

---

[2] https://smt-comp.github.io/2024/.

**Table 2.** Number of solved problems using string solving benchmarks from the `woorpje` benchmark set of SMT-LIB, organised in four tracks. The number of overall problems in each track is listed in column 8. We compare our solver ZIPT to the related approaches of Z3 [24], CVC5 [3], OSTRICH [9], Z3-NOODLER [10], and Z3STR3 [6].

|          | ZIPT | Z3  | CVC5 | OSTRICH | Z3-NOODLER | Z3STR3 | Total |
|----------|------|-----|------|---------|------------|--------|-------|
| track 01 | 200  | 198 | 191  | 198     | 200        | 200    | 200   |
| track 02 | 9    | 4   | 1    | 4       | 6          | 6      | 9     |
| track 03 | 195  | 176 | 164  | 127     | 190        | 190    | 200   |
| track 04 | 200  | 198 | 200  | 198     | 199        | 200    | 200   |

## 8 Related Work

*Decomposing string equations into subsequences* is typically used mainly as a preprocessing step in string solvers. Even though it is primarily only applied in cases where no padding is required, a different variation of our padding has been described in detail in previous works about string solving [28].

*Recognising self-dependencies in string variables*, especially via explicit powers, is studied in [16,19]. While the languages definable by such equations are generally EDT0L [11], the explicit powers we consider fall within more tractable subclasses. Theoretical results about word equations expressing certain power terms date back even longer [21]. In terms of solver support, the approach of [20] can handle some self-dependencies using regular expressions. In contrast, we identify a broader class of self-dependencies and introduce explicit powers, enabling nesting powers for efficiency (see `track 02` in Sect. 7).

*Parikh images* improve string reasoning via regular expression membership [9, 31]. Most techniques use single-character Parikh images to detect trivial unsatisfiability. We generalize this by considering Parikh information over multiple character sequences simultaneously. Related notions such as Parikh matrices [32] and their role in decidability have been explored in [13]. Our approach of analysing potential crossing occurrences is strongly related to recompression [18], where such occurrences are stepwise eliminated using case distinctions.

## 9 Conclusions

We introduced a string solving approach, based on Nielsen transformation rules extended with equality decomposition, power introduction, and Parikh images. Our initial results show the practical potential of our work. As further work, we plan to improve the analysis via Parikh images by using tighter error approximations and relating the Parikh information from multiple equations rather than considering each equation in isolation. Other steps include heuristically splitting equations using auxiliary variables based on dependency analysis and the introduction of non-ground power terms in order to express dependencies that cannot be represented in our calculus currently. Further, supporting other string-related SMT-LIB functions, including regular expressions, as defined in the SMT-LIB standard [4], is an essential next step.

**Acknowledgements.** This research was funded in whole or in part by the ERC Consolidator Grant ARTIST 101002685, the ERC Proof of Concept Grant LEARN 101213411, the TU Wien Doctoral College SecInt, the FWF SpyCoDe Grant 10.55776/F85, the WWTF grant ForSmart 10.47379/ICT22007, and the Amazon Research Award 2023 QuAT.

**Disclosure of Interests.** The authors have no competing interests to declare that are relevant to the content of this article.

## References

1. Abdulla, P.A., et al.: String constraints for verification. In: Biere, A., Bloem, R. (eds.) CAV 2014. LNCS, vol. 8559, pp. 150–166. Springer, Cham (2014). https://doi.org/10.1007/978-3-319-08867-9_10
2. Amadini, R.: A survey on string constraint solving. ACM Comput. Surv. **55**(2), 16:1–16:38 (2023). https://doi.org/10.1145/3484198
3. Barbosa, H., et al.: cvc5: a versatile and industrial-strength SMT solver. In: TACAS 2022. LNCS, vol. 13243, pp. 415–442. Springer, Cham (2022). https://doi.org/10.1007/978-3-030-99524-9_24
4. Barrett, C., Fontaine, P., Tinelli, C.: The SMT-LIB standard: version 2.7. Technical report, Department of Computer Science, The University of Iowa (2025)
5. Barrett, C.W., Sebastiani, R., Seshia, S.A., Tinelli, C.: Satisfiability modulo theories. In: Handbook of Satisfiability - Second Edition, Frontiers in Artificial Intelligence and Applications, vol. 336, pp. 1267–1329. IOS Press (2021). https://doi.org/10.3233/FAIA201017
6. Berzish, M., Ganesh, V., Zheng, Y.: Z3str3: a string solver with theory-aware heuristics. In: FMCAD, pp. 55–59. IEEE (2017). https://doi.org/10.23919/FMCAD.2017.8102241
7. Berzish, M., et al.: An SMT solver for regular expressions and linear arithmetic over string length. In: Silva, A., Leino, K.R.M. (eds.) CAV 2021. LNCS, vol. 12760, pp. 289–312. Springer, Cham (2021). https://doi.org/10.1007/978-3-030-81688-9_14
8. Bjørner, N.S., Eisenhofer, C., Kovács, L.: Satisfiability modulo custom theories in Z3. In: VMCAI. LNCS, vol. 13881, pp. 91–105. Springer (2023). https://doi.org/10.1007/978-3-031-24950-1_5
9. Chen, T., Hague, M., Lin, A.W., Rümmer, P., Wu, Z.: Decision procedures for path feasibility of string-manipulating programs with complex operations. Proc. ACM Program. Lang. **3**(POPL), 49:1–49:30 (2019). https://doi.org/10.1145/3290362
10. Chen, Y., Chocholatý, D., Havlena, V., Holík, L., Lengál, O., Síc, J.: Z3-noodler: an automata-based string solver. In: TACAS. LNCS, vol. 14570, pp. 24–33. Springer (2024). https://doi.org/10.1007/978-3-031-57246-3_2
11. Ciobanu, L., Diekert, V., Elder, M.: Solution sets for equations over free groups are EDT0L languages. Int. J. Algebra Comput. **26**(5), 843–886 (2016). https://doi.org/10.1142/S0218196716500363

12. Day, J.D., Ehlers, T., Kulczynski, M., Manea, F., Nowotka, D., Poulsen, D.B.: On solving word equations using SAT. In: Filiot, E., Jungers, R., Potapov, I. (eds.) RP 2019. LNCS, vol. 11674, pp. 93–106. Springer, Cham (2019). https://doi.org/10.1007/978-3-030-30806-3_8
13. Day, J.D., Ganesh, V., He, P., Manea, F., Nowotka, D.: The satisfiability of word equations: decidable and undecidable theories. In: Potapov, I., Reynier, P.-A. (eds.) RP 2018. LNCS, vol. 11123, pp. 15–29. Springer, Cham (2018). https://doi.org/10.1007/978-3-030-00250-3_2
14. Emmi, M., Majumdar, R., Sen, K.: Dynamic test input generation for database applications. In: ISSTA, pp. 151–162. ACM (2007). https://doi.org/10.1145/1273463.1273484
15. Eriksson, B., Stjerna, A., Masellis, R.D., Rümmer, P., Sabelfeld, A.: Black ostrich: web application scanning with string solvers. In: SIGSAC, pp. 549–563. ACM (2023). https://doi.org/10.1145/3576915.3616582
16. Ganesh, V., Minnes, M., Solar-Lezama, A., Rinard, M.: Word equations with length constraints: what's decidable? In: Biere, A., Nahir, A., Vos, T. (eds.) HVC 2012. LNCS, vol. 7857, pp. 209–226. Springer, Heidelberg (2013). https://doi.org/10.1007/978-3-642-39611-3_21
17. Hague, M.: Strings at MOSCA. ACM SIGLOG News **6**(4), 4–22 (2019). https://doi.org/10.1145/3373394.3373396
18. Jez, A.: Recompression: a simple and powerful technique for word equations. J. ACM **63**(1), 4:1–4:51 (2016). https://doi.org/10.1145/2743014
19. Karhumäki, J., Mignosi, F., Plandowski, W.: The expressibility of languages and relations by word equations. J. ACM **47**(3), 483–505 (2000)
20. Liang, T., Reynolds, A., Tsiskaridze, N., Tinelli, C., Barrett, C.W., Deters, M.: An efficient SMT solver for string constraints. Formal Methods Syst. Des. **48**(3), 206–234 (2016). https://doi.org/10.1007/S10703-016-0247-6
21. Lyndon, R.C., Schützenberger, M.P., et al.: The equation $a^M = b^N c^P$ in a free group. Michigan Math. J **9**(4), 289–298 (1962)
22. Makanin, G.S.: The problem of solvability of equations in a free semigroup. Matematicheskii Sbornik **145**(2), 147–236 (1977)
23. Mora, F., Berzish, M., Kulczynski, M., Nowotka, D., Ganesh, V.: Z3str4: a multi-armed string solver. In: Huisman, M., Păsăreanu, C., Zhan, N. (eds.) FM 2021. LNCS, vol. 13047, pp. 389–406. Springer, Cham (2021). https://doi.org/10.1007/978-3-030-90870-6_21
24. Moura, L., Bjørner, N.: Z3: an efficient SMT solver. In: Ramakrishnan, C.R., Rehof, J. (eds.) TACAS 2008. LNCS, vol. 4963, pp. 337–340. Springer, Heidelberg (2008). https://doi.org/10.1007/978-3-540-78800-3_24
25. Parikh, R.: On context-free languages. J. ACM **13**(4), 570–581 (1966). https://doi.org/10.1145/321356.321364
26. Przybocki, B., Barrett, C.W.: The termination of Nielsen transformations applied to word equations with length constraints. CoRR (2025). https://doi.org/10.48550/ARXIV.2501.11789
27. Reynolds, A., Nötzli, A., Barrett, C., Tinelli, C.: High-level abstractions for simplifying extended string constraints in SMT. In: Dillig, I., Tasiran, S. (eds.) CAV 2019. LNCS, vol. 11562, pp. 23–42. Springer, Cham (2019). https://doi.org/10.1007/978-3-030-25543-5_2
28. Reynolds, A., Nötzli, A., Barrett, C.W., Tinelli, C.: Reductions for strings and regular expressions revisited. In: FMCAD, pp. 225–235. IEEE (2020). https://doi.org/10.34727/2020/ISBN.978-3-85448-042-6_30

29. Rümmer, P.: A constraint sequent calculus for first-order logic with linear integer arithmetic. In: Cervesato, I., Veith, H., Voronkov, A. (eds.) LPAR 2008. LNCS (LNAI), vol. 5330, pp. 274–289. Springer, Heidelberg (2008). https://doi.org/10.1007/978-3-540-89439-1_20
30. Stanford, C., Veanes, M., Bjørner, N.S.: Symbolic boolean derivatives for efficiently solving extended regular expression constraints. In: PLDI, pp. 620–635. ACM (2021). https://doi.org/10.1145/3453483.3454066
31. Stjerna, A., Rümmer, P.: A constraint solving approach to parikh images of regular languages. Proc. ACM Program. Lang. **8**(OOPSLA1), 1235–1263 (2024). https://doi.org/10.1145/3649855
32. Subramanian, K.G., Huey, A.M., Nagar, A.K.: On parikh matrices. Int. J. Found. Comput. Sci. **20**(2), 211–219 (2009). https://doi.org/10.1142/S0129054109006528
33. Trinh, M., Chu, D., Jaffar, J.: S3: a symbolic string solver for vulnerability detection in web applications. In: SIGSAC, pp. 1232–1243. ACM (2014). https://doi.org/10.1145/2660267.2660372
34. Wassermann, G., Su, Z.: Sound and precise analysis of web applications for injection vulnerabilities. In: SIGPLAN, pp. 32–41. ACM (2007). https://doi.org/10.1145/1250734.1250739

**Open Access** This chapter is licensed under the terms of the Creative Commons Attribution 4.0 International License (http://creativecommons.org/licenses/by/4.0/), which permits use, sharing, adaptation, distribution and reproduction in any medium or format, as long as you give appropriate credit to the original author(s) and the source, provide a link to the Creative Commons license and indicate if changes were made.

The images or other third party material in this chapter are included in the chapter's Creative Commons license, unless indicated otherwise in a credit line to the material. If material is not included in the chapter's Creative Commons license and your intended use is not permitted by statutory regulation or exceeds the permitted use, you will need to obtain permission directly from the copyright holder.

# Modal and Tense Logic

# A Gödel Modal Logic over Witnessed Crisp Models

Mauro Ferrari[1(✉)], Camillo Fiorentini[2], and Ricardo Oscar Rodriguez[3]

[1] Department of Theoretical and Applied Sciences, Università degli Studi dell'Insubria, Varese, Italy
mauro.ferrari@uninsubria.it
[2] Department of Computer Science, Università degli Studi di Milano, Milan, Italy
fiorentini@di.unimi.it
[3] UBA-FCEyN, Departmento de Computación, Buenos Aires, Argentina
ricardo@dc.uba.ar

**Abstract.** This paper considers the bi-modal logic with both $\Box$ and $\Diamond$ arising from Kripke models with crisp accessibility whose propositions are valued over the standard Gödel algebra $[0,1]$. Since this logic lacks the finite model property, we study the logic $\mathbf{GW^c}$ relying on *witnessed* Kripke models where, for each modal formula, there is an assignment where the formula without the modality takes the same value as the modal one. We provide a cut-free sequent calculus and we exploit it to prove that $\mathbf{GW^c}$ is decidable and meets the finite model property. Finally, we explore a connection between the witnessed models and the well-known bi-relational Kripke semantics.

## 1 Introduction

One of the most important challenges in Knowledge Representation and Reasoning is to set up a homogeneous framework to represent and combine the notions of incompleteness, uncertainty and vagueness. In this sense, different many-valued modal logics have become a lingua franca for, among others, the specification and analysis of knowledge and communication in multi-agent and distributed systems. Notably, Gödel Modal Logic $\mathbf{GK}$ has provided an adequate logical foundation for these tasks, so it has been widely studied in the last decade.

In general, $\mathbf{GK}$ semantics rests on Gödel Kripke models (G-*models*), the generalization of the classical Kripke semantics for modal logics, where both propositions at each world and the accessibility relation are valued in the standard Gödel algebra $[0,1]$, namely the algebraic semantics of the well known intermediate Gödel-Dummett Logic. The minimal logics over G-models have been deeply investigated by Caicedo and Rodriguez in [9,10]. A peculiar subclass of this kind of models is obtained by restricting to crisp models ($\mathbf{G}^c$-*models*), where the accessibility relation only takes classical values, i.e., it is valued in $\{0,1\}$. The logic $\mathbf{G^c}$ arising from $\mathbf{G}^c$-models has been characterized in [27]. More general approaches, focusing mainly on finite residuated lattices, have been developed by

Fitting [15,16], Priest [24], and Bou et al. [6], and for other relevant fuzzy logics in [19,30].

In this line of research, we introduce a logic called **GW$^c$**, which is semantically characterized by *witnessed* Gödel crisp Kripke models (GW$^c$-models); in GW$^c$-models, the value of a modal formula $\Box\alpha$ or $\Diamond\alpha$ in a world $w$ coincides with (thus, is witnessed by) the value of $\alpha$ in a world accessible from $w$. A crucial point is that **GW$^c$** has the finite model property (if $\varphi \notin$ **GW$^c$**, than there exists a finite GW$^c$-model falsifying $\varphi$), while such a property fails for the bi-modal logics arising from G-models and from G$^c$-models.

Another important aspect to consider is that the semantical approach to modal many-valued logics considered here differs from the alternative significant framework for modal substructural logics studied, for instance, in [20,23,26]. This latter framework is based on a syntactic definition of the logics, obtained by extending substructural logics with modalities governed by some of the usual axioms and rules for the modalities of classical modal logics. The resulting logics are complete with respect to a bi-relational Kripke semantics, where the evaluation function typical of G-models is replaced by additional relations, similar to the semantics used in intuitionistic modal logics. A prominent contribution of this paper is to establish a simple connection between the semantics of **GW$^c$** and a bi-relational semantics, showing that **GW$^c$** can be naturally embedded within the well-established semantic tradition of intuitionistic modal logics. This connection provides a means to compare a calculus defined under one semantics with that defined under the other.

As for practical reasoning in AI, research has primarily focused on developing efficient calculi for the aforementioned many-valued logics. Metcalfe and Olivetti in [21,22] have provided variants of a hypersequent structure called *sequent of relations calculus* (firstly introduced by Baaz and Fermüller in [2]) for several fragments of **GK**. Galmiche and Salhi use a similar approach in [18] for studying a family of Gödel hybrid logics. Burns in [7] surveys the approaches based on hypersequents; in particular, it is maintained that relational hypersequents provide a unified proof theory for many modal logics with cut-free complete treatments. Here we propose for **GW$^c$** a different approach inspired by the tableau calculus presented in [5], but overcoming some flaws in it.

To sum up, the main result of this paper is the definition of a new calculus $\mathcal{C}_{\mathrm{GW}^c}$ which is sound and complete for the logic **GW$^c$**. We design a terminating decision procedure for $\mathcal{C}_{\mathrm{GW}^c}$ with countermodel generation, consisting in a standard backward proof search strategy for which we provide an implementation, called gwcref (accessible at [13]). Finally we explore a novel and simple connection between the GW$^c$-models and the bi-relational Kripke semantics. For the omitted proofs, we refer the reader to the appendix available online at the URL referenced in [13].

## 2  Basic Definitions

Formulas are built over a countable set of propositional variables $\mathcal{V}$, using the propositional connectives $\wedge$, $\vee$, $\rightarrow$, the constant $\bot$ and the modal connectives

$\Box$, $\Diamond$. We write $\neg\varphi$ as a shorthand for $\varphi \to \bot$. The symbols $\wedge$, $\vee$ and $\to$ are also used to denote algebraic operations.

The *Gödel algebra* is a structure $\langle [0,1], \wedge, \vee, \to \rangle$ where:

$$a \wedge b = \min(a,b) \qquad a \vee b = \max(a,b) \qquad a \to b = \begin{cases} 1 & \text{if } a \leq b \\ b & \text{if } a > b \end{cases}$$

A $\mathbf{G}^c$-*model* (*Gödel crisp model*) $\mathfrak{M}$ is a structure $\langle W, R, e \rangle$ where $W$ is a nonempty set (the set of worlds), $R \subseteq W \times W$ and $e : W \times \mathcal{V} \to [0,1]$.[1] We write $w_1 R w_2$ to mean that $(w_1, w_2) \in R$; in this case, we say that $w_2$ is an $R$-successor of $w_1$. The map $e$ is extended to arbitrary formulas as follows:

- $e(w, \bot) = 0$;
- $e(w, \alpha \star \beta) = e(w, \alpha) \star e(w, \beta)$, for $\star \in \{\wedge, \vee, \to\}$;
- $e(w, \Box\alpha) = \inf(\{e(w', \alpha) \mid wRw'\} \cup \{1\})$;
- $e(w, \Diamond\alpha) = \sup(\{e(w', \alpha) \mid wRw'\} \cup \{0\})$.

Note that:

$$e(w, \neg\alpha) = \begin{cases} 1 & \text{if } e(w,\alpha) = 0 \\ 0 & \text{if } e(w,\alpha) > 0 \end{cases} \qquad e(w, \neg\neg\alpha) = \begin{cases} 1 & \text{if } e(w,\alpha) > 0 \\ 0 & \text{if } e(w,\alpha) = 0 \end{cases}$$

We also recall that $\Box$ and $\Diamond$ are not interdefinable [27]. A formula $\varphi$ is *valid* in $\mathfrak{M} = \langle W, R, e \rangle$ iff $e(w, \varphi) = 1$ for every world $w$ in $W$. If $\varphi$ is not valid in $\mathfrak{M}$, we say that $\mathfrak{M}$ is a *countermodel* for $\varphi$; thus, $\mathfrak{M}$ contains a world $w$ such that $e(w, \varphi) < 1$.

Let $\circ \in \{\Box, \Diamond\}$; a $\mathbf{G}^c$-model $\langle W, R, e \rangle$ is *witnessed* iff every world $w$ having at least one $R$-successor satisfies the following property:

- if $e(w, \circ\varphi) = r$, then there exists $w' \in W$ such that $wRw'$ and $e(w', \varphi) = r$.

Thus, the value $e(w, \circ\varphi)$ is witnessed by the $R$-successor $w'$; hence, in the definitions of $e(w, \Box\alpha)$ and $e(w, \Diamond\alpha)$, the infimum and the superior are just the minimum and the maximum. Note that every finite $\mathbf{G}^c$-model is witnessed. We stress that, if $w$ has no $R$-successors, then $e(w, \Box\varphi) = 1$ and $e(w, \Diamond\varphi) = 0$, even if such values are not witnessed. In the sequel, by $\mathbf{GW}^c$-model, we mean a witnessed $\mathbf{G}^c$-model. Finally, a $\mathbf{GW}^c$-model $\mathfrak{M} = \langle W, R, e \rangle$ is *discrete* if $W$ is finite and the image of $e$ is a finite subset of $[0,1]_{\mathbb{Q}}$, the set of rationals in $[0,1]$.

We introduce the following logics:

- $\mathbf{G}^c$ is the set of formulas valid in every $\mathbf{G}^c$-model (see [27]);
- $\mathbf{GW}^c$ is the set of formulas valid in every $\mathbf{GW}^c$-model.

We recall the axiomatization of $\mathbf{G}^c$ given in [27]. Gödel-Dummett Logic $\mathbf{G}$ can be axiomatized by extending Intuitionistic Propositional Logic **IPL** with the

---

[1] In a general (non-crisp) Gödel model, $R$ is a map $W \times W \to [0,1]$.

linearity axiom $(\alpha \to \beta) \vee (\beta \to \alpha)$. Gödel Modal Logic **GK** is obtained by adding to **G** the following axioms and rules ($\vdash$ refers to provability in **GK**):

$(K_\Box)$ $\Box(\alpha \to \beta) \to (\Box\alpha \to \Box\beta)$  $(K_\Diamond)$ $\Diamond(\alpha \vee \beta) \to (\Diamond\alpha \vee \Diamond\beta)$   $(F_\Diamond)$ $\neg\Diamond\bot$
$(FS_1)$ $\Diamond(\alpha \to \beta) \to (\Box\alpha \to \Diamond\beta)$  $(FS_2)$ $(\Diamond\alpha \to \Box\beta) \to \Box(\alpha \to \beta)$
$(N_\Box)$ $\vdash \alpha$ implies $\vdash \Box\alpha$   $(N_\Diamond)$ $\vdash \alpha \to \beta$ implies $\vdash \Diamond\alpha \to \Diamond\beta$

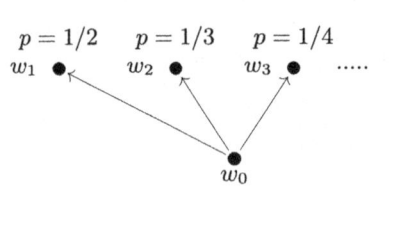

$W = \{w_j \mid j \geq 0\}$
$R = \{(w_0, w_k) \mid k \geq 1\}$
$e(w_k, p) = \frac{1}{k+1}$ $k \geq 1$

$e(w_k, \neg\neg p) = 1$ $k \geq 1$
$e(w_0, \Box\neg\neg p) = 1$
$e(w_0, \Box p) = 0$  $e(w_0, \neg\neg\Box p) = 0$
$e(w_0, \varphi) = 0$

**Fig. 1.** A $\mathbf{G}^c$-model falsifying the formula $\varphi = \Box\neg\neg p \to \neg\neg\Box p$.

The logic $\mathbf{G}^c$ is obtained by adding the axiom $\Box(\alpha \vee \beta) \to (\Box\alpha \vee \Diamond\beta)$ to **GK**. Clearly $\mathbf{G}^c \subseteq \mathbf{GW}^c$; we show that $\varphi = \Box\neg\neg p \to \neg\neg\Box p$ belongs to $\mathbf{GW}^c \setminus \mathbf{G}^c$ (see, e.g., [9]), and this witnesses that the inclusion is strict.

To prove that $\varphi \in \mathbf{GW}^c$, we show that $\varphi$ is valid in all the $\mathbf{GW}^c$-models. Let $\mathfrak{M} = \langle W, R, e \rangle$ be any $\mathbf{GW}^c$-model and $w \in W$. If $e(w, \neg\neg\Box p) = 1$, then $e(w, \varphi) = 1$. Otherwise $e(w, \neg\neg\Box p) = 0$, which implies $e(w, \Box p) = 0$ and, since $w$ has at least one $R$-successor (otherwise, $e(w, \Box p) = 1$) and $\mathfrak{M}$ is witnessed, there is $w' \in W$ such that $wRw'$ and $e(w', p) = 0$. Hence $e(w', \neg\neg p) = 0$, which implies $e(w, \Box\neg\neg p) = 0$; we conclude $e(w, \varphi) = 1$.

Since a finite $\mathbf{G}^c$-model is a $\mathbf{GW}^c$-model, a $\mathbf{G}^c$-countermodel for $\varphi$ must be infinite; accordingly, $\mathbf{G}^c$ does not have the finite model property. A $\mathbf{G}^c$-countermodel $\mathfrak{M} = \langle W, R, e \rangle$ for $\varphi$ is displayed in Fig. 1; note that $\varphi$ is not valid in $\mathfrak{M}$ since $e(w_0, \varphi) = 0$. We stress that $\mathfrak{M}$ is not a $\mathbf{GW}^c$-model: indeed, $e(w_0, \Box p) = 0$, but there is no $R$-successor $w_k$ of $w_0$ such that $e(w_k, p) = 0$.

## 3 The Calculus $\mathcal{C}_{\mathbf{GW}^c}$

We introduce the calculus $\mathcal{C}_{\mathbf{GW}^c}$ for $\mathbf{GW}^c$. We mainly follow [5], where the calculus $\mathcal{T}(\mathbf{KG}_{fb}^2)$ for $\mathbf{KG}_{fb}^2$ is presented. The logic $\mathbf{KG}_{fb}^2$ is an extension of $\mathbf{GW}^c$ over a more expressive language, including an involutive negation and a co-implication. Note that $\mathbf{KG}_{fb}^2$ has the finite model property, hence $\mathbf{KG}_{fb}^2$-models are witnessed.

The constraint language $\mathcal{L}_c$ is defined over a countable set of labels, each representing a world of a $\mathbf{GW}^c$-model, and a countable set of constants, representing elements of $[0, 1]_{\mathbb{Q}}$. Constraints are built using the order relations $<$, $\leq$,

$\triangleleft \in \{<, \leq\}, \quad \triangleright \in \{>, \geq\}$  $\qquad \dfrac{}{\Gamma}$ Ax   if $\text{At}^+(\Gamma)$ is not consistent

$$\dfrac{w : \alpha \triangleright t, \, w : \beta \triangleright t, \, \Gamma}{w : \alpha \wedge \beta \triangleright t, \, \Gamma} \, \wedge\triangleright \qquad \dfrac{w : \alpha \triangleleft t, \, \Gamma \quad w : \beta \triangleleft t, \, \Gamma}{w : \alpha \wedge \beta \triangleleft t, \, \Gamma} \, \wedge\triangleleft$$

$$\dfrac{w : \alpha \triangleleft t, \, w : \beta \triangleleft t, \, \Gamma}{w : \alpha \vee \beta \triangleleft t, \, \Gamma} \, \vee\triangleleft \qquad \dfrac{w : \alpha \triangleright t, \, \Gamma \quad w : \beta \triangleright t, \, \Gamma}{w : \alpha \vee \beta \triangleright t, \, \Gamma} \, \vee\triangleright$$

$$\dfrac{w : \beta \leq b, \, w : \alpha > b, \, b < t, \, \Gamma}{w : \alpha \to \beta < t, \, \Gamma} \, \to < \, (\dagger)$$

$$\dfrac{t \geq 1, \, \Gamma \qquad w : \beta \leq b, \, w : \alpha > b, \, b \leq t, \, \Gamma}{w : \alpha \to \beta \leq t, \, \Gamma} \, \to \leq \, (\dagger)$$

$$\dfrac{w : \alpha \leq a, \, w : \beta \geq a, \, 1 \triangleright t, \, \Gamma \qquad w : \beta \triangleright t, \, \Gamma}{w : \alpha \to \beta \triangleright t, \, \Gamma} \, \to \triangleright \, (\ddagger)$$

$$\dfrac{1 \triangleleft t, \, \Phi^{0,1}(\Gamma) \qquad w_1 : \alpha \triangleleft t, \, \Phi^{\Box,\Diamond}(\Gamma, w, w_1), \, \Gamma}{w : \Box\alpha \triangleleft t, \, \Gamma} \, \Box\triangleleft \quad w_1 \text{ is a new label}$$

$$\dfrac{0 \triangleright t, \, \Phi^{0,1}(\Gamma) \qquad w_1 : \alpha \triangleright t, \, \Phi^{\Box,\Diamond}(\Gamma, w, w_1), \, \Gamma}{w : \Diamond\alpha \triangleright t, \, \Gamma} \, \Diamond\triangleright \quad w_1 \text{ is a new label}$$

$\text{At}^+(\Gamma) = \text{At}(\Gamma) \cup \{1 > t \mid w : \Box\alpha > t \in \Gamma\} \cup \{0 < t \mid w : \Diamond\alpha < t \in \Gamma\}$

$(\dagger) \; b = \begin{cases} w : \beta & \text{if } \beta \in \mathcal{V} \cup \{\bot\} \\ \text{a new constant} & \text{otherwise} \end{cases} \qquad (\ddagger) \; a = \begin{cases} w : \alpha & \text{if } \alpha \in \mathcal{V} \cup \{\bot\} \\ \text{a new constant} & \text{otherwise} \end{cases}$

$\Phi^{\Box,\Diamond}(\Gamma, w, w') = \{w' : \beta \triangleright t \mid w : \Box\beta \triangleright t \in \Gamma\} \cup \{w' : \beta \triangleleft t \mid w : \Diamond\beta \triangleleft t \in \Gamma\}$

$\Phi^{0,1}(\Gamma) = $ replace in $\Gamma$ every constraint of the kind $w' : \Diamond\alpha \blacktriangledown t$ with $0\blacktriangledown t$
and every constraint of the kind $w' : \Box\alpha \blacktriangledown t$ with $1\blacktriangledown t$

**Fig. 2.** The calculus $\mathcal{C}_{\text{GW}^c}$ ($\Gamma$ is a multiset of constraints).

$>, \geq$ over $[0,1]_\mathbb{Q}$. In the following definitions $w$ is a label of $\mathcal{L}_c$, $\varphi$ a formula, $c$ a constant of $\mathcal{L}_c$, $r \in [0,1]_\mathbb{Q}$, $p \in \mathcal{V}$ and $\blacktriangledown \in \{<, \leq, >, \geq\}$.

labelled formula $:= w : \varphi$ \qquad atomic c-term $t := c \mid r \mid w : p \mid w : \bot$

c-term $u := t \mid w : \varphi$ \qquad constraint $\chi := u \blacktriangledown t$

A constraint of the form $t\blacktriangledown t$ is called *atomic*; if $\chi = w : \varphi \blacktriangledown t$ is non-atomic and $\sharp$ is the main connective of $\varphi$, we say that $\chi$ is a $\sharp$-*constraint*. Given a multiset of constraints $\Gamma$, by $\text{At}(\Gamma)$ we denote the set of atomic constraints in $\Gamma$.

Let $\mathfrak{M} = \langle W, R, e \rangle$ be a GW$^c$-model. An $\mathfrak{M}$-interpretation of $\mathcal{L}_c$ is a function $\mathcal{I}$ mapping labels of $\mathcal{L}_c$ to $W$ and constants of $\mathcal{L}_c$ to $[0,1]_\mathbb{Q}$. We extend $\mathcal{I}$ by setting $\mathcal{I}(r) = r$, for every $r \in [0,1]_\mathbb{Q}$, and $\mathcal{I}(w : \varphi) = e(\mathcal{I}(w), \varphi)$. It is easy to check that, for every c-term $u$, $\mathcal{I}(u)$ belongs to $[0,1]_\mathbb{Q}$. We introduce the relations $\models_\mathcal{I}$ and $\models$, where $\mathfrak{M}$ is a GW$^c$-model, $\mathcal{I}$ an $\mathfrak{M}$-interpretation, $\Gamma$ a multiset of constraints.

- $\mathfrak{M} \models_\mathcal{I} u \blacktriangledown t$ iff $\mathcal{I}(u) \blacktriangledown \mathcal{I}(t)$;
- $\mathfrak{M} \models_\mathcal{I} \Gamma$ iff $\mathfrak{M} \models_\mathcal{I} \chi$, for every $\chi \in \Gamma$;
- $\mathfrak{M} \models \Gamma$ iff $\mathfrak{M} \models_\mathcal{I} \Gamma$ for some $\mathfrak{M}$-interpretation $\mathcal{I}$.

A substitution $\sigma$ is a function mapping each atomic c-term of the form $c$ (constant) or $w : p$ to a rational number in $[0,1]_\mathbb{Q}$; $\sigma$ is extended to all the atomic c-terms by setting $\sigma(r) = r$, for $r \in [0,1]_\mathbb{Q}$, and $\sigma(w : \bot) = 0$. Let $\Gamma_{\text{at}}$ be a set of atomic constraints. By $\sigma(\Gamma_{\text{at}})$ we denote the set of constraints obtained by replacing every atomic c-term $t$ occurring in $\Gamma_{\text{at}}$ with $\sigma(t)$; note that $\sigma(\Gamma_{\text{at}})$ is a set of rational constraints of the form $r_1 \blacktriangledown r_2$, with $r_1$ and $r_2$ in $[0,1]_\mathbb{Q}$. Consistency of a set of atomic constraints is defined as follows:

- $\Gamma_{\text{at}}$ is *consistent* iff there exists a substitution $\sigma$ such that all the constraints in $\sigma(\Gamma_{\text{at}})$ hold; we call $\sigma$ a *solution* to $\Gamma_{\text{at}}$.

We remark that consistency of $\Gamma_{\text{at}}$ can be checked by a Constraint Solver over $\mathbb{Q}$: one has to abstract the constants and the c-terms $w : p$ occurring in $\Gamma_{\text{at}}$ by introducing new variables ranging over $[0,1]_\mathbb{Q}$, and then check the consistency of the obtained constraints by exploiting the solver.

Hereafter, $\triangleleft \in \{<, \leq\}$ and $\triangleright \in \{>, \geq\}$. The calculus $\mathcal{C}_{\mathbf{GW}^c}$ is displayed in Fig. 2. It consists of propositional rules, i.e., the axiom rule Ax and rules for the propositional connectives, and of the modal rules $\Box \triangleleft$ and $\Diamond \triangleright$. Differently from $\mathcal{T}(\mathbf{KG}_{\text{fb}}^2)$ [5], some rules of $\mathcal{C}_{\mathbf{GW}^c}$ require the introduction of new constants, since constraints of the form $u \blacktriangledown w : \alpha$ are allowed only in the case $\alpha \in \mathcal{V} \cup \{\bot\}$. E.g., let us compare the rule for $\rightarrow<$ of $\mathcal{T}(\mathbf{KG}_{\text{fb}}^2)$, rewritten in our notation as $\rightarrow<'$, and the rule $\rightarrow<$ of $\mathcal{C}_{\mathbf{GW}^c}$:

$$\frac{w : \alpha > w : \beta,\ w : \beta < t,\ \Gamma}{w : \alpha \rightarrow \beta < t,\ \Gamma} \rightarrow<' \qquad \frac{w : \beta \leq b,\ w : \alpha > b,\ b < t,\ \Gamma}{w : \alpha \rightarrow \beta < t,\ \Gamma} \rightarrow<$$

If $\beta \in \mathcal{V} \cup \{\bot\}$, then $b$ stands for $w : \beta$ and the two rules essentially coincide. If $\beta \notin \mathcal{V} \cup \{\bot\}$, $b$ is a new constant (namely, $b$ does not occur in the conclusion) representing $w : \beta$; to ensure the equivalence between $b$ and $w : \beta$, in the premise we add the constraint $w : \beta \leq b$, the converse constraint $w : \beta \geq b$ can be omitted. The role of the new constants in rules $\rightarrow \leq$ and $\rightarrow \triangleright$ is similar. The modal rules $\Box \triangleleft$ and $\Diamond \triangleright$ introduce a new label $w_1$ in the right premise; we say that $w_1$ *is generated by* $w$. The definitions of $\mathcal{C}_{\mathbf{GW}^c}$-tree and $\mathcal{C}_{\mathbf{GW}^c}$-derivation are the usual ones (see, e.g., [28]). We remark that $\mathcal{C}_{\mathbf{GW}^c}$ has the *subformula property*, namely: if $\mathcal{T}$ is a $\mathcal{C}_{\mathbf{GW}^c}$-tree having $\Gamma_0$ as root, every formula occurring in $\mathcal{T}$ (inside a constraint) is a subformula of a formula in $\Gamma_0$. By $\vdash_{\mathbf{GW}^c} \Gamma$ we mean that there exists a $\mathcal{C}_{\mathbf{GW}^c}$-derivation of $\Gamma$. In the rest of this section we show that $\mathcal{C}_{\mathbf{GW}^c}$ is a sound and complete calculus for $\mathbf{GW}^c$, where soundness and completeness are formalized as follows:

- (Soundness) if $\vdash_{\mathbf{GW}^c} \Gamma$, then $\mathfrak{M} \not\models \Gamma$, for every $\mathfrak{M}$;
- (Completeness) if $\mathfrak{M} \not\models \Gamma$, for every $\mathfrak{M}$, then $\vdash_{\mathbf{GW}^c} \Gamma$.

$$\cfrac{\cfrac{\overline{\varGamma_3}\ \text{Ax}\quad \cfrac{\overline{\varGamma_1}\ \text{Ax}\quad \cfrac{\cfrac{\cfrac{\overline{\varGamma_5}\ \text{Ax}\quad \overline{\varGamma_6}\ \text{Ax}}{w_1:\neg p\le c_2,\,w_1:\bot\ge c_2,\,1>c_0,\,w_1:p\le c_1,\,\varDelta}\to\le\quad \overline{\varGamma_4}\ \text{Ax}}{w_1:p\le c_1,\,w_1:\neg\neg p>c_0,\,\varDelta}\to\rhd}{w:\Box p\le c_1,\,\varDelta}\Box\lhd\quad \overline{\varGamma_2}\ \text{Ax}}{w:\neg\Box p>w:\bot,\,w:\bot\le c_0,\,w:\Box\neg\neg p>c_0,\,c_0<1}\to\rhd}{w:\neg\neg\Box p\le c_0,\,w:\Box\neg\neg p>c_0,\,c_0<1}\to\le}{w:\Box\neg\neg p\to\neg\neg\Box p<1}\to<$$

$\varDelta = w:\bot\ge c_1,\,1>w:\bot,\,w:\bot\le c_0,\,w:\Box\neg\neg p>c_0,\,c_0<1$
$\varGamma_1 = c_0\ge 1,\,w:\Box\neg\neg p>c_0,\,c_0<1$
$\varGamma_2 = w:\bot>w:\bot,\,w:\bot\le c_0,\,w:\Box\neg\neg p>c_0,\,c_0<1$
$\varGamma_3 = 1\le c_1,\,w:\bot\ge c_1,\,1>w:\bot,\,w:\bot\le c_0,\,1>c_0,\,c_0<1$
$\varGamma_4 = w_1:\bot>c_0,\,w_1:p\le c_1,\,\varDelta$
$\varGamma_5 = c_2\ge 1,\,w_1:\bot\ge c_2,\,1>c_0,\,w_1:p\le c_1,\,\varDelta$
$\varGamma_6 = w_1:p>w_1:\bot,\,w_1:\bot\le c_2,\,w_1:\bot\ge c_2,\,1>c_0,\,w_1:p\le c_1,\,\varDelta$

**Fig. 3.** $\mathcal{C}_{\text{GW}^c}$-derivation of $w:\Box\neg\neg p\to\neg\neg\Box p<1$.

Note that in rule Ax it is not enough to check the consistency of $\text{At}(\varGamma)$. Indeed, let $\varGamma = \{w:\Box\alpha > c, c\le 1, c\ge 1\}$; clearly, there are no $\mathfrak{M} = \langle W, R, e\rangle$ and $\mathcal{I}$ such that $\mathfrak{M}\models_{\mathcal{I}}\varGamma$, otherwise we would get $\mathcal{I}(c) = 1$ and $e(\mathcal{I}(w),\Box\alpha) > \mathcal{I}(c)$, a contradiction. We point out that $\text{At}(\varGamma)$ is consistent, but $\varGamma$ is provable in $\mathcal{C}_{\text{GW}^c}$ since rule Ax checks the consistency of $\text{At}^+(\varGamma) = \{1 > c, c\le 1, c\ge 1\}$.

In defining the modal rules $\Box\lhd$ and $\Diamond\rhd$, we have corrected a flaw in [5]. Actually, both rules of $\mathcal{T}(\mathbf{KG}^2_{\text{fb}})$ lack the left premise; the drawback is that such rules are sound only in the case where $R$ is serial (and such a proviso is not assumed in [5]). For instance, let us consider the following application:

$$\cfrac{\overbrace{1\le 1,\,1\ge 1,\,0<1}^{\varGamma_1}\quad \overbrace{w_1:p\le 1,\,w_1:p\ge 1,\,w_1:p<1,\,w:\Box p\ge 1,\,w:\Diamond p<1}^{\varGamma_2}}{\varGamma_0 = w:\Box p\le 1,\,w:\Box p\ge 1,\,w:\Diamond p<1}\Box\lhd$$

The right premise $\varGamma_2$ is an instance of Ax, since the constraints $w_1:p\ge 1$ and $w_1:p<1$ contradict each other; accordingly, if rule $\Box\lhd$ only had the premise $\varGamma_2$ (as in [5]), $\varGamma_0$ would be provable in $\mathcal{C}_{\text{GW}^c}$. This would contradict the soundness of $\mathcal{C}_{\text{GW}^c}$, since taking $\mathfrak{M}$ and $\mathcal{I}$ so that $\mathcal{I}(w)$ has no $R$-successors we would get that $\mathfrak{M}\models_{\mathcal{I}}\varGamma_0$. In $\mathcal{C}_{\text{GW}^c}$, $\varGamma_0$ is not provable since $\varGamma_1$ is not provable.

An example of $\mathcal{C}_{\text{GW}^c}$-derivation is shown in Fig. 3. In representing derivations, we underline the main constraint of a rule application; moreover, we omit redundant constraints (e.g., constraints of the kind $t\le t$ and multiple copies of the same constraint). To prove the soundness of $\mathcal{C}_{\text{GW}^c}$, we need the following:

**Lemma 1.** *Let $\rho$ be an instance of a rule of the calculus $\mathcal{C}_{\text{GW}^c}$, let $\varGamma$ be the conclusion of $\rho$ and let $\mathfrak{M}$ be a $\text{GW}^c$-model. If $\mathfrak{M}\models\varGamma$, then there exists a premise $\varGamma'$ of $\rho$ such that $\mathfrak{M}\models\varGamma'$.*

*Proof.* Let $\rho$ be the rule Ax; since the rule has no premises, we have to show that there is no $\mathfrak{M}$ such that $\mathfrak{M} \models \Gamma$. Let us assume, by contradiction, that there is $\mathfrak{M} = \langle W, R, e \rangle$ and an $\mathfrak{M}$-interpretation $\mathcal{I}$ such that $\mathfrak{M} \models_{\mathcal{I}} \Gamma$. If $w : \Box \alpha > t \in \Gamma$, then $e(\mathcal{I}(w), \Box \alpha) > \mathcal{I}(t)$, hence $1 > \mathcal{I}(t)$, which implies $\mathfrak{M} \models_{\mathcal{I}} 1 > t$. Similarly, if $w : \Diamond \alpha < t \in \Gamma$, then $\mathfrak{M} \models_{\mathcal{I}} 0 < t$. This proves that $\mathfrak{M} \models_{\mathcal{I}} \mathrm{At}^+(\Gamma)$. By exploiting $e$ and $\mathcal{I}$, one can define a solution to $\mathrm{At}^+(\Gamma)$[2]; accordingly, $\mathrm{At}^+(\Gamma)$ is consistent, a contradiction. We conclude that $\mathfrak{M}$ does not exist. The cases concerning the other rules are detailed in the Appendix available at [13]. ∎

**Proposition 2 (Soundness).**

*(i)* If $\vdash_{\mathrm{GW}^c} \Gamma$, then $\mathfrak{M} \not\models \Gamma$, for every $\mathfrak{M}$.
*(ii)* $\vdash_{\mathrm{GW}^c} w : \varphi < 1$ implies $\varphi \in \mathbf{GW}^c$.

*Proof.* Point (i) can be easily proved by induction on the depth of a $\mathcal{C}_{\mathrm{GW}^c}$-derivation of $\Gamma$, by exploiting Lemma 1. To prove (ii), let $\vdash_{\mathrm{GW}^c} w : \varphi < 1$ and assume, by contradiction, $\varphi \notin \mathbf{GW}^c$. Then, there exists a $\mathrm{GW}^c$-model $\mathfrak{M} = \langle W, R, e \rangle$ and a world $w^\star \in W$ such that $e(w^\star, \varphi) < 1$. Let $\mathcal{I}$ be an $\mathfrak{M}$-interpretation mapping $w$ to $w^\star$; then, $\mathfrak{M} \models_{\mathcal{I}} w : \varphi < 1$, in contradiction with (i). We conclude $\varphi \in \mathbf{GW}^c$. ∎

We show that $\mathcal{C}_{\mathrm{GW}^c}$ is *strongly terminating*, namely: there exists a well-founded relation $\prec$ such that, for every application $\rho$ of a rule of $\mathcal{C}_{\mathrm{GW}^c}$, if $\Gamma$ is the conclusion of $\rho$ and $\Gamma'$ any of the premises of $\rho$, then $\Gamma' \prec \Gamma$. Equivalently, given a finite multiset $\Gamma$ and repeatedly applying the rules of $\mathcal{C}_{\mathrm{GW}^c}$ upwards, proof search eventually halts, no matter which strategy is used.

Let $\Theta_1$ and $\Theta_2$ be finite multisets of natural numbers; we set:

$$\Theta_1 \prec_m \Theta_2 \quad \text{iff} \quad \Theta_1 \neq \Theta_2 \wedge (\forall k_1 \in \Theta_1 \setminus \Theta_2. \exists k_2 \in \Theta_2 \setminus \Theta_1. k_1 < k_2).$$

The relation $\prec_m$ is a multiset order, hence $\prec_m$ is well-founded (see [1], Th. 2.5.5 and Lemma 2.5.6). Let $\Gamma$ be a multiset of constraints:

- $|\Gamma|$ is the number of logical connectives occurring in $\Gamma$;
- $\Gamma[w]$ is the multiset of labelled formulas in $\Gamma$ having label $w$;
- $||\Gamma||$ is the multiset of $|\Gamma[w]|$, for every label $w$ occurring in $\Gamma$.

For instance, in the application of rule $\Box \triangleleft$ displayed above, we have $||\Gamma_0|| = \{3\}$, $||\Gamma_1|| = \emptyset$ and $||\Gamma_2|| = \{0, 2\}$ (where $0 = |\Gamma_2[w_1]|$ and $2 = |\Gamma_2[w]|$).

We introduce the following relation $\prec_c$ between finite multisets of constraints:

$$\Gamma_1 \prec_c \Gamma_2 \quad \text{iff} \quad ||\Gamma_1|| \prec_m ||\Gamma_2||.$$

Note that $\Gamma_1 \prec_c \Gamma_0$ and $\Gamma_2 \prec_c \Gamma_0$.

**Proposition 3.** *(i)* The relation $\prec_c$ is well-founded.
*(ii)* The calculus $\mathcal{C}_{\mathrm{GW}^c}$ is strongly terminating.

---

[2] Note that irrational values $e(w, p)$ must be approximated with rationals.

*Proof.* Point (i) follows from the fact that $\prec_m$ is well-founded. Point (ii) holds since $\prec_c$ matches the definition of strong termination for $\mathcal{C}_{\mathrm{GW}^c}$. ∎

By Proposition 3(ii), any backward proof search strategy for $\mathcal{C}_{\mathrm{GW}^c}$ terminates. Following [11,14], we focus on strategies where failure is certified by countermodels, i.e.: if proof search for a multiset of constraints $\Gamma$ fails, a $\mathrm{GW}^c$-model $\mathfrak{M}$ such that $\mathfrak{M} \models \Gamma$ can be built; we call $\mathfrak{M}$ a countermodel for $\Gamma$, since $\mathfrak{M}$ ascertains that $\Gamma$ is not provable in $\mathcal{C}_{\mathrm{GW}^c}$ (by its soundness). Let $\Gamma$ be a multiset of constraints:

- $\Gamma$ is *p-reduced* if no propositional rule of $\mathcal{C}_{\mathrm{GW}^c}$ can be backward applied to $\Gamma$;
- $\Gamma$ is *reduced* if no rule of $\mathcal{C}_{\mathrm{GW}^c}$ can be backward applied to $\Gamma$.

An application of a modal rule $\Box \triangleright$ or $\Diamond \triangleleft$ is *plain* if its conclusion is p-reduced. In such an application, all the constraints in the left premise are atomic; this property is crucial to prove the completeness of $\mathcal{C}_{\mathrm{GW}^c}$ (proof of Lemma 4).

To represent a branch $\mathcal{B}$ of a $\mathcal{C}_{\mathrm{GW}^c}$-tree, we use the notation $\langle \Gamma_0, \ldots, \Gamma_n \rangle$ where, for every $0 \leq i < n$, $\Gamma_i$ is the conclusion of an application $\rho$ of a rule of $\mathcal{C}_{\mathrm{GW}^c}$ and $\Gamma_{i+1}$ is one of the premises of $\rho$; the length of $\mathcal{B}$ is $n+1$. A branch $\mathcal{B} = \langle \Gamma_0, \ldots, \Gamma_n \rangle$ is *saturated* iff the following holds:

- $\Gamma_0$ is finite and $\Gamma_n$ is reduced;
- if $\Gamma_k$ is the conclusion of a modal rule (having $\Gamma_{k+1}$ as one of the premises), then $\Gamma_k$ is p-reduced.

Let $\mathcal{B}$ be a saturated branch, we introduce the following notations:

- $\mathrm{Lab}(\mathcal{B})$ is the set of labels occurring in $\mathcal{B}$;
- $\mathrm{Rel}(\mathcal{B})$ is the set of pairs $(w_1, w_2)$ such that $w_2$ is generated by $w_1$ (thus, $w_2$ is the new label generated by the application of rule $\Box \triangleleft$ or $\Diamond \triangleright$ with main constraint $w_1 : \Box \alpha \triangleleft t$ or $w_1 : \Diamond \alpha \triangleright t$ respectively);
- $\mathrm{Mod}(\mathcal{B})$ is the set of models $\mathfrak{M} = \langle W, R, e \rangle$ such that $W = \mathrm{Lab}(\mathcal{B})$ and $R = \mathrm{Rel}(\mathcal{B})$;
- $\mathrm{I}(\mathcal{B})$ is the set of interpretations $\mathcal{I}$ such that $\mathcal{I}(w) = w$ for every $w \in \mathrm{Lab}(\mathcal{B})$.

Note that every model $\mathfrak{M}$ of $\mathrm{Mod}(\mathcal{B})$ is finite, hence $\mathfrak{M}$ is a $\mathrm{GW}^c$-model. We prove the crucial lemma to state the completeness of $\mathcal{C}_{\mathrm{GW}^c}$.

**Lemma 4.** *Let $\mathcal{B} = \langle \Gamma_0, \ldots, \Gamma_n \rangle$ be a saturated branch. For every $\mathfrak{M} \in \mathrm{Mod}(\mathcal{B})$ and every $\mathcal{I} \in \mathrm{I}(\mathcal{B})$, if $\mathfrak{M} \models_\mathcal{I} \mathrm{At}^+(\Gamma_n)$, then $\mathfrak{M} \models_\mathcal{I} \Gamma_0$.*

*Proof.* Let $\mathfrak{M} = \langle W, R, e \rangle \in \mathrm{Mod}(\mathcal{B})$ and $\mathcal{I} \in \mathrm{I}(\mathcal{B})$ such that $\mathfrak{M} \models_\mathcal{I} \mathrm{At}^+(\Gamma_n)$; we prove $\mathfrak{M} \models_\mathcal{I} \Gamma_0$ by induction on the length of $\mathcal{B}$.

Let $\mathcal{B} = \langle \Gamma_0 \rangle$ and let $\chi \in \Gamma_0$; we prove $\mathfrak{M} \models_\mathcal{I} \chi$. If $\chi$ is atomic, $\mathfrak{M} \models_\mathcal{I} \chi$ follows from $\mathfrak{M} \models_\mathcal{I} \mathrm{At}^+(\Gamma_0)$, since $\chi \in \mathrm{At}^+(\Gamma_0)$. Otherwise, since $\Gamma_0$ is reduced, either $\chi = w : \Box \alpha \triangleright t$ or $\chi = w : \Diamond \alpha \triangleleft t$. Note that $R$ is empty, hence $e(w, \Box \alpha) = 1$ and $e(w, \Diamond \alpha) = 0$. If $\chi = w : \Box \alpha \geq t$ or $\chi = w : \Diamond \alpha \leq t$, we get $\mathfrak{M} \models_\mathcal{I} \chi$. If $\chi = w : \Box \alpha > t$, then $\mathfrak{M} \models_\mathcal{I} \chi$ follows from $1 > t \in \mathrm{At}^+(\Gamma_0)$ and $\mathfrak{M} \models_\mathcal{I} \mathrm{At}^+(\Gamma_0)$. Similarly, if $\chi = w : \Diamond \alpha < t$, then $\mathfrak{M} \models_\mathcal{I} \chi$ follows from $0 < t \in \mathrm{At}^+(\Gamma_0)$.

Let $n > 0$ and let $\mathcal{B}_1 = \langle \Gamma_1, \ldots, \Gamma_n \rangle$; note that $\mathcal{B}_1$ is a saturated branch shorter than $\mathcal{B}$, thus the following induction hypothesis holds:

(IH) for every $\mathfrak{M}' \in \mathrm{Mod}(\mathcal{B}_1)$, if $\mathfrak{M}' \models_\mathcal{I} \mathrm{At}^+(\Gamma_n)$ then $\mathfrak{M}' \models_\mathcal{I} \Gamma_1$.

We proceed by a case analysis on the rule $\rho$ of $\mathcal{C}_{\mathrm{GW^c}}$ applied to get $\Gamma_0$ (thus, $\Gamma_1$ is one of the premises of $\rho$); we only discuss some significant cases.

Let $\rho = \to \leq$; we have two subcases:

(A1) $\Gamma_0 = w : \alpha \to \beta \leq t, \Gamma$ and $\Gamma_1 = t \geq 1, \Gamma$;
(A2) $\Gamma_0 = w : \alpha \to \beta \leq t, \Gamma$ and $\Gamma_1 = w : \beta \leq b, w : \alpha > b, b \leq t, \Gamma$.

Let us consider case (A1). Since $\mathfrak{M} \in \mathrm{Mod}(\mathcal{B}_1)$, by (IH) we get $\mathfrak{M} \models_\mathcal{I} \Gamma$ and $\mathfrak{M} \models_\mathcal{I} t \geq 1$, hence $\mathfrak{M} \models_\mathcal{I} \Gamma_0$. The proof in case (A2) is similar; we point out that, by (IH), $\mathfrak{M} \models_\mathcal{I} w : \beta \leq b$ and $\mathfrak{M} \models_\mathcal{I} w : \alpha > b$ and $\mathfrak{M} \models_\mathcal{I} b \leq t$. It follows that $e(w, \alpha \to \beta) = e(w, \beta)$, hence $\mathfrak{M} \models_\mathcal{I} w : \alpha \to \beta \leq t$.

Let $\rho = \Box \lhd$; we have two subcases:

(B1) $\Gamma_0 = w_0 : \Box \alpha \lhd t, \Gamma$ and $\Gamma_1 = 1 \lhd t, \Phi^{0,1}(\Gamma)$;
(B2) $\Gamma_0 = w_0 : \Box \alpha \lhd t, \Gamma$ and $\Gamma_1 = w_1 : \alpha \lhd t, \Phi^{\Box,\Diamond}(\Gamma, w_0, w_1), \Gamma$, where label $w_1$ is generated by $w_0$.

Since the application of $\Box \lhd$ is plain, $\Gamma_0$ is p-reduced, hence the non-atomic constraints in $\Gamma$ are either $\Box$-constraints or $\Diamond$-constraints. In Case (B1), $\mathcal{B} = \langle \Gamma_0, \Gamma_1 \rangle$ and $R$ is empty, thus $\mathfrak{M} \models_\mathcal{I} \Gamma_0$ can be easily proved. Let us consider case (B2). Let $R_1 = R \setminus \{(w_0, w_1)\}$ and $\mathfrak{M}_1 = \langle W, R_1, e \rangle$; we show that:

(P1) $\mathfrak{M}_1 \models_\mathcal{I} \Gamma_1$.
(P2) Let $\chi = w : \varphi \blacktriangledown t$ be such that $w \neq w_0$. Then, $\mathfrak{M}_1 \models_\mathcal{I} \chi$ iff $\mathfrak{M} \models_\mathcal{I} \chi$.

Property (P1) follows from (IH), since $\mathfrak{M}_1 \in \mathrm{Mod}(\mathcal{B}_1)$ and $\mathfrak{M}_1 \models_\mathcal{I} \mathrm{At}^+(\Gamma_n)$. (P2) can be proved by induction on $\varphi$, observing that $wR_1w'$ iff $wRw'$.

Let $\chi \in \Gamma_0$; we prove $\mathfrak{M} \models_\mathcal{I} \chi$. If $\chi$ is atomic, $\mathfrak{M} \models_\mathcal{I} \chi$ follows from the fact that $\mathfrak{M} \models_\mathcal{I} \mathrm{At}^+(\Gamma_n)$ and $\chi \in \mathrm{At}^+(\Gamma_n)$. Let $\chi$ be non-atomic; since $\Gamma_0$ is p-reduced, $\chi = w : \circ \beta \blacktriangledown t$, with $\circ \in \{\Box, \Diamond\}$. If $w \neq w_0$, then $\chi \in \Gamma$, hence $\mathfrak{M} \models_\mathcal{I} \chi$ follows from (P1) and (P2). The cases $\chi = w_0 : \circ \beta \blacktriangledown t$ require a more refined analysis, since $w_0 R w_1$, but $w_0 R_1 w_1$ does not hold.

Let $\chi = w_0 : \Box \beta \rhd t$, let $w'$ be any $R$-successor of $w_0$ and let $\chi' = w' : \beta \rhd t$; we show that $\mathfrak{M} \models_\mathcal{I} \chi'$. Let $w' \neq w_1$. Since $\chi \in \Gamma$, by (P1) $\mathfrak{M}_1 \models_\mathcal{I} \chi$ and, by the fact that $w_0 R_1 w'$, we get $\mathfrak{M}_1 \models_\mathcal{I} \chi'$; by (P2), we conclude $\mathfrak{M} \models_\mathcal{I} \chi'$. Let $w' = w_1$; then $\chi' \in \Phi^{\Box,\Diamond}(\Gamma, w_0, w_1)$ and $\mathfrak{M} \models_\mathcal{I} \chi'$ follows from (P1) and (P2). We have shown that $\mathfrak{M} \models_\mathcal{I} w' : \beta \rhd t$ for every $w'$ such that $w_0 R w'$, hence $\mathfrak{M} \models_\mathcal{I} w_0 : \Box \beta \rhd t$. The case $\chi = w_0 : \Diamond \beta \lhd t$ is similar.

Let $\chi = w_0 : \Box \alpha \lhd t$. Since $w_1 : \alpha \lhd t \in \Gamma_1$, by (P1) and (P2) we get $\mathfrak{M} \models_\mathcal{I} w_1 : \alpha \lhd t$, hence $\mathfrak{M} \models_\mathcal{I} \chi$. Let $\chi = w_0 : \Box \beta \lhd t$ with $\beta \neq \alpha$; then $\chi \in \Gamma$ and $\mathfrak{M}_1 \models_\mathcal{I} \chi$ by (P1). If $w_0$ has no $R_1$-successors, then $e(w_0, \Box \beta) = 1$ in $\mathfrak{M}_1$; this implies $\chi = w_0 : \Box \beta \leq t$ and $\mathcal{I}(t) = 1$, hence $\mathfrak{M} \models_\mathcal{I} \chi$. Let us assume $w_0 R_1 w^\star$, thus $w_0 R w^\star$. Since $\mathfrak{M}_1 \models_\mathcal{I} \chi$, we get $\mathfrak{M}_1 \models_\mathcal{I} w^\star : \beta \lhd t$. By (P2) $\mathfrak{M} \models_\mathcal{I} w^\star : \beta \lhd t$, hence $\mathfrak{M} \models_\mathcal{I} \chi$. The case $\chi = w_0 : \Diamond \beta \rhd t$ is similar. ∎

Let $\mathcal{B} = \langle \Gamma_0, \ldots, \Gamma_n \rangle$ be a saturated branch; we show how to build a discrete $\mathfrak{M} = \langle W, R, e \rangle \in \mathrm{Mod}(\mathcal{B})$ and $\mathcal{I} \in \mathrm{I}(\mathcal{B})$ such that $\mathfrak{M} \models_\mathcal{I} \Gamma_0$. We set $W = \mathrm{Lab}(\mathcal{B})$, $R = \mathrm{Rel}(\mathcal{B})$ and $\mathcal{I}(w) = w$, for every $w \in W$. It remains to define the valuation $e$ and the values of $\mathcal{I}$ on the constants of $\mathcal{L}_c$. Let $\sigma$ be a solution to $\mathrm{At}^+(\Gamma_n)$ (since $\mathrm{At}^+(\Gamma_n)$ is consistent, at least one $\sigma$ exists); we set:

$$e(w, p) = \begin{cases} \sigma(w : p) & \text{if } w : p \text{ occurs in } \Gamma_n \\ 0 & \text{otherwise} \end{cases} \qquad \mathcal{I}(c) = \begin{cases} \sigma(c) & \text{if } c \text{ occurs in } \Gamma_n \\ 0 & \text{otherwise} \end{cases}$$

We get $\mathfrak{M} \models_\mathcal{I} \mathrm{At}^+(\Gamma_n)$ and, by Lemma 4, we conclude $\mathfrak{M} \models_\mathcal{I} \Gamma_0$. To sum up:

**Proposition 5.** *Let $\mathcal{B} = \langle \Gamma_0, \ldots, \Gamma_n \rangle$ be a saturated branch.*

*(i) There exists a discrete $\mathbf{GW}^c$-model $\mathfrak{M}$ such that $\mathfrak{M} \models \Gamma_0$.*
*(ii) If $\Gamma_0 = \{w : \varphi < 1\}$, then $\varphi \notin \mathbf{GW}^c$.*

$$\mathcal{B} \begin{cases} \dfrac{w_2 : p \leq c_0,\ w_1 : p > c_0,\ w_0 : \Box p > c_0,\ c_0 < 1}{\dfrac{w_1 : \Box p \leq c_0,\ w_1 : p > c_0,\ w_0 : \Box p > c_0,\ c_0 < 1}{\dfrac{w_0 : \Box\Box p \leq c_0,\ w_0 : \Box p > c_0,\ c_0 < 1}{w_0 : \Box p \to \Box\Box p < 1}\ \to<}\ \Box\triangleleft}\ \Box\triangleleft \end{cases}$$

$\mathrm{Lab}(\mathcal{B}) = \{w_0, w_1, w_2\} \qquad \mathrm{Rel}(\mathcal{B}) = \{(w_0, w_1), (w_1, w_2)\}$

$w_2 \bullet\ p \leq \mathcal{I}(c_0)$ 

$w_1 \bullet\ p > \mathcal{I}(c_0)$ 

$w_0 \bullet$

$\boxed{e(w_2, p) \leq \mathcal{I}(c_0) < 1 \qquad e(w_1, p) > \mathcal{I}(c_0)}$

$e(w_0, \Box p) = e(w_1, p) > \mathcal{I}(c_0)$
$e(w_0, \Box\Box p) = e(w_1, \Box p) = e(w_2, p) \leq \mathcal{I}(c_0)$
$e(w_0, \varphi) = e(w_0, \Box\Box p) \leq \mathcal{I}(c_0) < 1$

**Fig. 4.** Countermodel for $\varphi = \Box p \to \Box\Box p$, see Example 6.

*Example 6.* Let $\varphi = \Box p \to \Box\Box p$. At the top of Fig. 4, we show a saturated branch $\mathcal{B} = \langle \Gamma_0, \ldots, \Gamma_3 \rangle$ represented as a path of a tree, where $\Gamma_0 = \{w_0 : \varphi < 1\}$ is the root. We display the rule $\rho$ applied to get $\Gamma_{i+1}$ from $\Gamma_i$ ($0 \leq i < 3$). In the applications of $\Box\triangleleft$ the selected premise is the right one. The new label $w_1$ is generated by $w_0$ and $w_2$ by $w_1$; the application of $\to<$ introduces the new constant $c_0$. Under the branch it is displayed a generic countermodel for $\varphi$ built as discussed above. To get a specific countermodel, namely $\mathfrak{M}$ and $\mathcal{I}$ such that $\mathfrak{M} \models_\mathcal{I} w_0 : \varphi < 1$, we have to fix a value for $e(w_1, p)$, $e(w_2, p)$ and $\mathcal{I}(c_0)$ so that the constraints in the shadowed box are satisfied. ◇

$\Delta_0 = \{w_1 : q \geq c_2, 1 > c_0, w_1 : q \leq c_1, c_1 \leq c_0, c_0 < 1\}$  $\alpha = \neg\neg p \to q$
$\Delta_1 = \Delta_0 \cup \{w_1 : \bot \geq w_1 : p, 1 > w_1 : \bot, w_1 : \bot \leq c_2\}$

$\mathcal{B}$ 
$$\cfrac{\cfrac{\cfrac{\cfrac{\cfrac{\cfrac{\cfrac{\cfrac{\cfrac{\Gamma^\star = c_3 \geq 1, w_2 : q \geq c_3, w_2 : p > c_1, w_0 : \Box\alpha > c_0, \Delta_1}{w_2 : \neg\neg p \leq c_3, w_2 : q \geq c_3, w_2 : p > c_1, w_0 : \Box\alpha > c_0, \Delta_1} \to \leq (l)}{w_2 : p > c_1, w_2 : \alpha > c_0, w_0 : \Box\alpha > c_0, \Delta_1} \to \triangleright(l)}{w_0 : \Diamond p > c_1, w_0 : \Box\alpha > c_0, \Delta_1} \Diamond\triangleright(r)}{\begin{array}{c}\overline{w_1 : \bot \geq w_1 : p, 1 > w_1 : \bot, w_1 : \bot \leq c_2, w_0 : \Diamond p > c_1, w_0 : \Box\alpha > c_0, \Delta_0}\\ w_1 : \neg p > w_1 : \bot, w_1 : \bot \leq c_2, w_0 : \Diamond p > c_1, w_0 : \Box\alpha > c_0, \Delta_0\end{array}} \to \triangleright(l)}{w_1 : \neg\neg p \leq c_2, w_0 : \Diamond p > c_1, w_0 : \Box\alpha > c_0, \Delta_0} \to \leq (r)}{\begin{array}{c}\overline{w_1 : \neg\neg p \leq c_2, w_1 : q \geq c_2, 1 > c_0, w_1 : q \leq c_1,}\\ w_0 : \Diamond p > c_1, c_1 \leq c_0, w_0 : \Box\alpha > c_0, c_0 < 1\end{array}} \to \triangleright(l)}{w_1 : q \leq c_1, w_1 : \alpha > c_0, w_0 : \Diamond p > c_1, c_1 \leq c_0, w_0 : \Box\alpha > c_0, c_0 < 1} \Box\triangleleft(r)}{w_0 : \Box q \leq c_1, w_0 : \Diamond p > c_1, c_1 \leq c_0, w_0 : \Box\alpha > c_0, c_0 < 1} \to \leq (r)}{w_0 : \Diamond p \to \Box q \leq c_0, w_0 : \Box\alpha > c_0, c_0 < 1} \to <}{w_0 : \Box\alpha \to (\Diamond p \to \Box q) < 1}$$

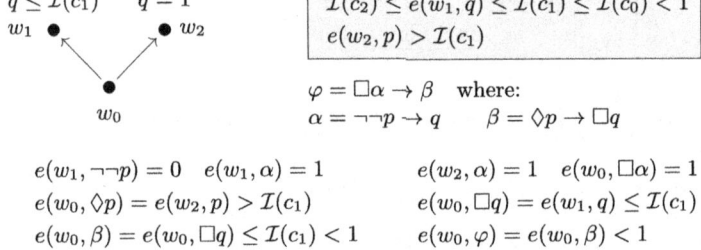

$\varphi = \Box\alpha \to \beta$ where:
$\alpha = \neg\neg p \to q$  $\beta = \Diamond p \to \Box q$

$e(w_1, \neg\neg p) = 0$  $e(w_1, \alpha) = 1$  $e(w_2, \alpha) = 1$  $e(w_0, \Box\alpha) = 1$
$e(w_0, \Diamond p) = e(w_2, p) > \mathcal{I}(c_1)$  $e(w_0, \Box q) = e(w_1, q) \leq \mathcal{I}(c_1)$
$e(w_0, \beta) = e(w_0, \Box q) \leq \mathcal{I}(c_1) < 1$  $e(w_0, \varphi) = e(w_0, \beta) < 1$

**Fig. 5.** Countermodel for $\varphi = \Box(\neg\neg p \to q) \to (\Diamond p \to \Box q)$, see Example 7.

*Example 7.* Let $\varphi = \Box(\neg\neg p \to q) \to (\Diamond p \to \Box q)$. At the top of Fig. 5, we show a saturated branch $\mathcal{B}$ having root $\Gamma_0 = \{w_0 : \varphi < 1\}$; if the applied rule has two premises, the annotation $(l)$ (left) or $(r)$ (right) specifies the selected one. To make reading easier, we introduce some abbreviations, dashed lines mark rewriting steps. Note that both the new labels $w_1$ and $w_2$ are generated by $w_0$. The set $\Gamma_{\mathrm{at}} = \mathrm{At}^+(\Gamma^\star)$ consists of the following constraints:

$c_3 \geq 1$,  $w_2 : q \geq c_3$,  $w_2 : p > c_1$,  $1 > c_0$,  $w_1 : q \geq c_2$,  $w_1 : q \leq c_1$,
$c_1 \leq c_0$,  $c_0 < 1$,  $w_1 : \bot \geq w_1 : p$,  $1 > w_1 : \bot$,  $w_1 : \bot \leq c_2$

Each solution $\sigma$ to $\Gamma_{\mathrm{at}}$ must satisfy $\sigma(c_3) = \sigma(w_2 : q) = 1$ (due to the constraints $c_3 \geq 1$ and $w_2 : q \geq c_3$) and $\sigma(w_1 : p) = 0$ (due to $w_1 : \bot \geq w_1 : p$). A generic countermodel for $\varphi$ is displayed in Fig. 5 (same conventions as in Example 6). ◊

Let Bs be a backward proof search strategy for $\mathcal{C}_{\mathbf{GW}^c}$; we say that Bs is *plain* iff all the modal rule applications performed by Bs are plain; thus, a modal rule is backward applied if and only if no propositional rule is applicable.

**Lemma 8.** *Let Bs be a plain proof search strategy for $\mathcal{C}_{\mathbf{GW}^c}$ and let $\Gamma_0$ be a finite multiset of constraints. If Bs fails to prove $\Gamma_0$, then a discrete countermodel for $\Gamma_0$ can be built.*

*Proof.* Assume that Bs fails. By tracking the computation, we can build an open branch $\mathcal{B}$ having root $\Gamma_0$. Since Bs is plain, the branch $\mathcal{B}$ is saturated, hence from $\mathcal{B}$ a discrete countermodel for $\Gamma_0$ can be extracted (see Proposition 5(i)). ∎

We remark that Bs does not need to implement backtracking.

**Proposition 9 (Completeness).**

*(i) If $\nvdash_{\mathbf{GW}^c} \Gamma$, then there exists a discrete countermodel for $\Gamma$.*
*(ii) If $\nvdash_{\mathbf{GW}^c} w : \varphi < 1$, then $\varphi \notin \mathbf{GW}^c$.*
*(iii) If $\varphi \notin \mathbf{GW}^c$, then then there exists a discrete countermodel for $\varphi$.*

*Proof.* Point (i) follows from Lemma 8. Point (ii) follows from (i), since a countermodel for $w : \varphi < 1$ certifies that $\varphi \notin \mathbf{GW}^c$. Point (iii) follows from (i) since, by soundness of $\mathcal{C}_{\mathbf{GW}^c}$, $\varphi \notin \mathbf{GW}^c$ implies $\nvdash_{\mathbf{GW}^c} w : \varphi < 1$. ∎

By Proposition 9(iii), $\mathbf{GW}^c$ has the finite model property. Let $\varphi \notin \mathbf{GW}^c$ and let $\mathfrak{M}$ be the discrete countermodel extracted from an open branch having root $w_0 : \varphi < 1$. One can easily prove that the depth of $\mathfrak{M}$ is bounded by $|\varphi|$ and that every world of $\mathfrak{M}$ has at most $|\varphi|$ R-successors; this implies that the size of $\mathfrak{M}$ is $O(|\varphi|^{|\varphi|})$ (see Th. 4.1 [5]). Note that it is not possible to build $\mathfrak{M}$ one branch at a time, since the constraints generated during the expansion of a branch have global validity and must be kept throughout the construction. However, by adapting the procedure described in Th. 4.2 [5], one can prove that the decision problem for $\mathbf{GW}^c$ is in PSPACE.

We have implemented both the proof search procedure and the countermodel extraction in the JTabWb framework [12]. The prover, named `gwcref` [13], performs a standard backward depth-first proof search, leveraging the JTabWb engine complemented with the Java implementation of the $\mathcal{C}_{\mathbf{GW}^c}$ rules and of a plain proof-search strategy. The consistency of atomic constraints is checked using the Choco-solver Java library [25]. To our knowledge, the only other prover available for modal fuzzy logic is mNiBLoS [29], an SMT-based solver designed for continuous t-norm-based logics, including Gödel-Dummett Logic. However, mNiBLoS does not support the logic $\mathbf{GW}^c$.

## 4 Bi-relational Kripke Semantics

This section presents an alternative connection between the previously introduced semantics and another well-known bi-relational semantics. This connection has also been considered in [4,17], but our approach is simpler and it does not require knowledge of universal algebras or descriptive set theory. In this sense, our proposal is very easy to understand.

A $GW^c$-*bimodel* is a structure $\mathcal{K} = \langle X, \leq, S, V \rangle$ where $X$ (the set of worlds) is a nonempty finite set, $\leq$ is a partial order relation, $S \subseteq X \times X$, $V$ (the evaluation function) is a map from $X$ to $2^{\mathcal{V}}$ which is persistent ($x \leq y$ implies $V(x) \subseteq V(y)$). We require that $\leq$ satisfies the following connectedness property:

- if $x \leq y$ and $x \leq z$, then $y \leq z$ or $z \leq y$.

The following conditions must be met (see Fig. 6):

(F1) if $x_1 \leq x_2$ and $x_1 S y_1$, there exists $y_2$ such that $x_2 S y_2$ and $y_1 \leq y_2$;
(F2) if $x_1 \leq x_2$ and $x_2 S y_2$, there exists $y_1$ such that $x_1 S y_1$ and $y_1 \leq y_2$;
(F3) if $x_1 S y_1$ and $y_1 \leq y_2$, there exists $x_2$ such that $x_1 \leq x_2$ and $x_2 S y_2$;
(F4) if $x_2 S y_2$ and $y_1 \leq y_2$, there exists $x_1$ such that $x_1 \leq x_2$ and $x_1 S y_1$;
(F5) if $x_1 S y_1$ and $x_1 S y_2$ and $y_1 \leq y_2$, then $y_1 = y_2$;
(F6) if $x_1 S y_1$ and $x_2 S y_1$ and $x_1 \leq x_2$, then $x_1 = x_2$.

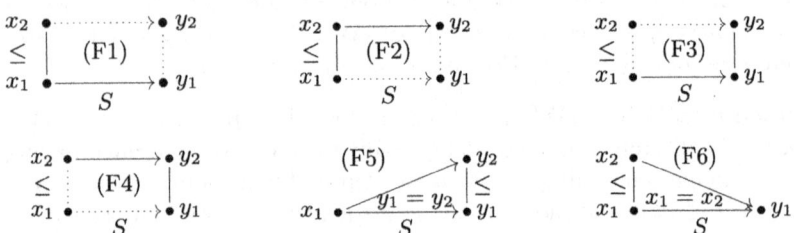

**Fig. 6.** Conditions (F1)–(F6).

The forcing relation $\Vdash$ between worlds of $\mathcal{K}$ and formulas is defined as follows:

- $x \nVdash \bot$;
- $x \Vdash p$ iff $p \in V(x)$, where $p \in \mathcal{V}$;
- $x \Vdash \alpha \wedge \beta$ iff $x \Vdash \alpha$ and $x \Vdash \beta$;
- $x \Vdash \alpha \vee \beta$ iff $x \Vdash \alpha$ or $x \Vdash \beta$;
- $x \Vdash \alpha \to \beta$ iff for every $y \in X$ s.t. $y \geq x$, if $y \Vdash \alpha$ then $y \Vdash \beta$;
- $x \Vdash \Box \alpha$ iff for every $y \in X$, if $xSy$ then $y \Vdash \alpha$;
- $x \Vdash \Diamond \alpha$ iff there exists $y \in X$ s.t. $xSy$ and $y \Vdash \alpha$.

One can easily prove that forcing is persistent, i.e.: if $x \Vdash \varphi$ and $x \leq y$, then $y \Vdash \varphi$; in particular, persistence of $\Diamond$-formulas follows from (F1), persistence of $\Box$-formulas from (F2). In standard bi-relational models, where $\leq$ is any partial order, (F1) and (F2) characterize the Local Intuitionistic Modal Logic **LIK** [3].

A formula $\varphi$ is valid in a $GW^c$-bimodel $\mathcal{K}$ iff $x \Vdash \varphi$, for every world $x$ of $\mathcal{K}$. Let **Lbm** be the set of formulas valid in all the $GW^c$-bimodels; we show that **Lbm** coincides with $\mathbf{GW^c}$. To this aim, we establish a correspondence between the class of discrete $GW^c$-models and the class of $GW^c$-bimodels ensuring that, given any $\mathfrak{M}$, validity in $\mathfrak{M}$ simulates forcing in the corresponding $\mathcal{K}$.

Let $\mathcal{K} = \langle X, \leq, S, V \rangle$ and let $x, y$ be elements of $X$; we set $x \sim y$ iff $x \leq y$ or $y \leq x$. By the connectedness condition on $\leq$, $\sim$ is an equivalence relation; we call *clusters* the $\sim$-equivalence classes. Given two clusters $[x]_\sim$ and $[y]_\sim$, we set:

- $[x]_\sim S[y]_\sim$ iff there is $x' \in [x]_\sim$ and $y' \in [y]_\sim$ such that $x'Sy'$.

Let $[x]_\sim S[y]_\sim$; by properties (F1)–(F4), we get:

(S1) For every $x' \in [x]_\sim$ there is $y' \in [y]_\sim$ such that $x'Sy'$.
(S2) For every $y' \in [y]_\sim$ there is $x' \in [x]_\sim$ such that $x'Sy'$.

A *ranking* over $\mathcal{K} = \langle X, \leq, S, V \rangle$ is a map $\mathrm{Rn} : X \to (0,1]_\mathbb{Q}$ such that:

- if $x$ is $\leq$-minimal, then $\mathrm{Rn}(x) = 1$;
- if $x < y$ then $\mathrm{Rn}(x) > \mathrm{Rn}(y) > 0$;
- if $xSy$, then $\mathrm{Rn}(x) = \mathrm{Rn}(y)$.

A *ranked* $GW^c$-*bimodel* is a pair $(\mathcal{K}, \mathrm{Rn})$, where $\mathcal{K}$ is a $GW^c$-bimodel and $\mathrm{Rn}$ is a ranking over $\mathcal{K}$. Given $(\mathcal{K}, \mathrm{Rn})$, the rank of a formula $\varphi$ in a cluster $[x]_\sim$, denoted by $\mathrm{Rn}(x, \varphi)$ (or else by $\mathrm{Rn}([x]_\sim, \varphi)$), is defined as follows:

$$\mathrm{Rn}(x, \varphi) = \max\left( \{\, \mathrm{Rn}(y) \mid y \in [x]_\sim \text{ and } y \Vdash \varphi \,\} \cup \{0\} \right)$$

Note that $\mathrm{Rn}(x, \varphi) \in \mathrm{Rn}(X) \cup \{0\}$, where $\mathrm{Rn}(X)$ is the image of $\mathrm{Rn}$, moreover:

- $\mathrm{Rn}(x, \varphi) = 0$ iff $y \nVdash \varphi$ for every $y \in [x]_\sim$, iff $y \Vdash \neg \varphi$ for every $y \in [x]_\sim$;
- $\mathrm{Rn}(x, \varphi) = 1$ iff $y \Vdash \varphi$ for every $y \in [x]_\sim$.

*Example 10.* Figure 7 shows the ranked $GW^c$-bimodel $(\mathcal{K}, \mathrm{Rn})$, where the $GW^c$-bimodel $\mathcal{K} = \langle X, \leq, S, V \rangle$ and $\mathrm{Rn}$ are defined as follows. The worlds in $X$ have the form $w_r$, with $w \in \{x, y, z\}$ and $r \in \{0.4, 0.6, 1\}$; we set $\mathrm{Rn}(w_r) = r$. The relation $\leq$ is represented by the straight lines ($x \leq y$ iff $x$ is below or equal to $y$), the relation $S$ is depicted by the arrows. The propositional variables in $V(w_r)$ are displayed to the right of $w_r$. There are three clusters $[x_1]_\sim$, $[y_1]_\sim$ and $[z_1]_\sim$, enclosed in ovals. In the figure, we spell out the ranking of some formulas in the cluster $[x_1]_\sim$. ◊

**Lemma 11.** *Let $\mathcal{K}$ be a $GW^c$-bimodel and $\mathrm{Rn}$ a ranking over $\mathcal{K}$.*

*(i)* $\mathrm{Rn}(x, \alpha \star \beta) = \mathrm{Rn}(x, \alpha) \star \mathrm{Rn}(x, \beta)$, *for* $\star \in \{\wedge, \vee, \to\}$.
*(ii)* $\mathrm{Rn}(x, \Box \alpha) = \min\left( \{\, \mathrm{Rn}(y, \alpha) \mid xSy \,\} \cup \{1\} \right)$.
*(iii)* $\mathrm{Rn}(x, \Diamond \alpha) = \max\left( \{\, \mathrm{Rn}(y, \alpha) \mid xSy \,\} \cup \{0\} \right)$.

A *correspondence* between a discrete $GW^c$-model $\mathfrak{M} = \langle W, R, e \rangle$ and a ranked $GW^c$-bimodel $(\mathcal{K}, \mathrm{Rn})$, where $\mathcal{K} = \langle X, \leq, S, V \rangle$, is a 1–1 map $\Phi$ between the worlds of $\mathfrak{M}$ and the clusters of $\mathcal{K}$ satisfying the following conditions:

- $w_1 R w_2$ iff $\Phi(w_1) \, S \, \Phi(w_1)$, for every $w_1, w_2 \in W$;

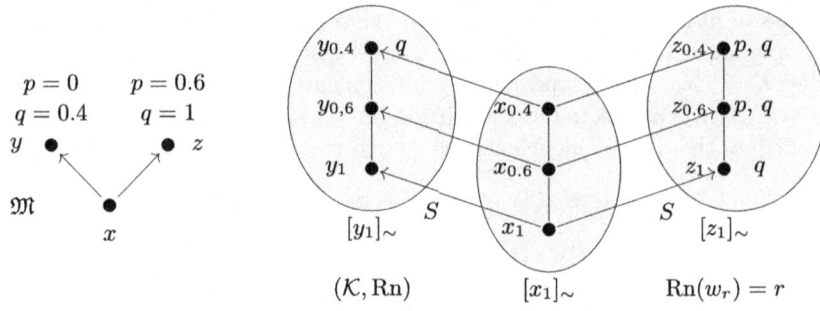

$\alpha = \neg\neg p \to q \quad \beta = \Diamond p \to \Box q \quad \varphi = \Box \alpha \to \beta$

$\mathrm{Rn}(x_1, \Box\alpha) = 1 \quad \mathrm{Rn}(x_1, \Diamond p) = 0.6 \quad \mathrm{Rn}(x_1, \Box q) = 0.4$

$\mathrm{Rn}(x_1, \beta) = 0.4 \quad \mathrm{Rn}(x_1, \varphi) = 0.4$

$\Phi(x) = [x_1]_\sim \quad \Phi(y) = [y_1]_\sim \quad \Phi(z) = [z_1]_\sim$

$e(x, \Box\alpha) = 1 \quad e(x, \Diamond p) = 0.6 \quad e(x, \Box q) = 0.4 \quad e(x, \beta) = 0.4 \quad e(x, \varphi) = 0.4$

**Fig. 7.** Example of correspondence $\Phi$ between $\mathfrak{M}$ and $(\mathcal{K}, \mathrm{Rn})$ (see Example 10 and 12).

- $e(w, p) = \mathrm{Rn}(\Phi(w), p)$, for every $w \in W$ and $p \in \mathcal{V}$.

*Example 12.* In Fig. 7 we show a correspondence $\Phi$ between the discrete $\mathrm{GW}^c$-model $\mathfrak{M} = \langle W, R, e \rangle$ and the ranked $\mathrm{GW}^c$-bimodel $(\mathcal{K}, \mathrm{Rn})$ of Example 10. Note that $\mathfrak{M}$ belongs to the set of models $\mathrm{Mod}(\mathcal{B})$ described in Example 7; $\mathfrak{M}$ is obtained by setting $e(y, p) = 0$, $e(y, q) = 0.4$, $e(z, p) = 0.6$, $e(z, q) = 1$. $\Diamond$

Using Lemma 11, we can prove:

**Proposition 13.** *Let $\Phi$ be a correspondence between $\mathfrak{M}$ and $(\mathcal{K}, \mathrm{Rn})$. For every formula $\varphi$ and every world $w$ of $\mathfrak{M}$, $e(w, \varphi) = \mathrm{Rn}(\Phi(w), \varphi)$.*

To show that **Lbm** and $\mathbf{GW}^c$ coincide, we need the following lemma:

**Lemma 14.**

*(i)* Let $\mathfrak{M}$ be a discrete $\mathrm{GW}^c$-model. Then, there exists a ranked $\mathrm{GW}^c$-bimodel $(\mathcal{K}, \mathrm{Rn})$ and a correspondence $\Phi$ between $\mathfrak{M}$ and $(\mathcal{K}, \mathrm{Rn})$.
*(ii)* Let $(\mathcal{K}, \mathrm{Rn})$ be a ranked $\mathrm{GW}^c$-bimodel. Then, there exists a discrete $\mathrm{GW}^c$-model $\mathfrak{M}$ and a correspondence $\Phi$ between $\mathfrak{M}$ and $(\mathcal{K}, \mathrm{Rn})$.

*Proof.* (i). Let $\mathfrak{M} = \langle W, R, r \rangle$ and let $\mathcal{R} = (e(W) \cup \{1\}) \setminus \{0\}$; since $\mathfrak{M}$ is discrete, $\mathcal{R}$ is a finite subset of $(0, 1]_Q$. The $\mathrm{GW}^c$-bimodel $\mathcal{K} = \langle X, \leq, S, V \rangle$ and the map $\mathrm{Rn}$ are defined as follows:

- $X$ is the set of $w_r$ such that $w \in W$ and $r \in \mathcal{R}$;

- $\text{Rn}(w_r) = r$;
- $(w_1)_{r_1} \leq (w_2)_{r_2}$ iff $w_1 = w_2$ and $r_1 \geq r_2$;
- $(w_1)_{r_1} S (w_2)_{r_2}$ iff $w_1 R w_2$ and $r_1 = r_2$;
- $p \in V(w_r)$ iff $e(w,p) \geq r$.

One can easily check that $\mathcal{K}$ is well-defined. For every $w \in W$, the set of $w_r$ such that $r \in \mathcal{R}$ is a cluster of $\mathcal{K}$; the function $\Phi$ mapping the world $w$ of $\mathfrak{M}$ to the cluster $[w_1]_\sim$ settles a correspondence between $\mathfrak{M}$ and $(\mathcal{K}, \text{Rn})$.

(ii) Let $\mathcal{K} = \langle X, \leq, S, V \rangle$. The $\mathbf{GW^c}$-model $\mathfrak{M} = \langle W, R, e \rangle$ is defined as follows.

- $W$ is the set of $[x]_\sim$ such that $x \in X$;
- $[x_1]_\sim R [x_2]_\sim$ iff $x_1 S x_2$;
- $e([x]_\sim, p) = \text{Rn}([x]_\sim, p)$.

One can easily check that $\mathfrak{M}$ is well-defined. Let $\Phi$ map a world $[x]_\sim$ of $\mathfrak{M}$ to the cluster $[x]_\sim$ of $\mathcal{K}$; then, $\Phi$ is a correspondence between $\mathfrak{M}$ and $(\mathcal{K}, \text{Rn})$. ∎

Now, let $\varphi \notin \mathbf{GW^c}$. By Proposition 9(iii) there exist a discrete $\mathbf{GW^c}$-model $\mathfrak{M} = \langle W, R, e \rangle$ and $w \in W$ such that $e(w, \varphi) < 1$. By Lemma 14(i) there is a ranked $\mathbf{GW^c}$-bimodel $(\mathcal{K}, \text{Rn})$ and a correspondence $\Phi$ between $\mathfrak{M}$ and $(\mathcal{K}, \text{Rn})$. By Proposition 13, $\text{Rn}(\Phi(w), \varphi) = e(w, \varphi)$, hence $\text{Rn}(\Phi(w), \varphi) < 1$. Therefore, there exists $w^\star \in \Phi(w)$ such that $w^\star \nVdash \varphi$; thus $\varphi \notin \mathbf{Lbm}$. This proves that $\mathbf{Lbm} \subseteq \mathbf{GW^c}$. The proof of $\mathbf{GW^c} \subseteq \mathbf{Lbm}$ is similar and relies on Lemma 14(ii). To sum up:

**Proposition 15.** $\mathbf{Lbm} = \mathbf{GW^c}$.

## 5 Conclusions and Future Work

This paper introduces $\mathbf{GW^c}$, a Gödel bi-modal logic characterized by witnessed crisp Kripke models, and presents a sound and complete cut-free sequent calculus for it. While this calculus builds on previous work, notably [5], it corrects critical flaws (e.g., handling empty successor sets) and ensures strong termination through a well founded measure, enabling effective countermodel construction. A PSPACE upper bound for $\mathbf{GW^c}$ can be established following the ideas from [5]. An implementation of the calculus in the JTabWb framework [13] confirms its practical viability, supporting derivation and countermodel generation.

Another contribution of this work lies in connecting $\mathbf{GW^c}$ to intuitionistic modal logics via a bi-relational Kripke semantics. This mapping, while conceptually elegant and technically simple, situates $\mathbf{GW^c}$ within a broader semantic landscape and supports potential future studies on the proof-theoretic dualities. Our construction of a mutual correspondence (Lemma 14 and Proposition 15) clarifies the structure of $\mathbf{GW^c}$ and may facilitate comparisons with other modal systems.

Several research lines remain open. First, while an axiomatization for $\mathbf{G}^c$ exists, an explicit axiomatization for $\mathbf{GW}^c$ is lacking; this would deepen understanding of its proof-theoretic behavior. Second, future work should explore extending $\mathbf{GW}^c$ to first-order logic, which, as noted, remains rare among fuzzy modal logics. Third, although the current results are restricted to crisp models, examining non-crisp variants could elucidate the role of fuzziness in the accessibility relation and broaden applicability. Fourth, although we can reconstruct a proof of the PSPACE upper bound for $\mathbf{GW}^c$ based on [5], we would like to study a more precise complexity characterization using the technique from [8].

Ultimately, this work balances syntactic elegance and semantic insight. While the proposed calculus may not be radically novel, it offers a robust tool for reasoning in a fragment of fuzzy modal logic with the finite model property, a valuable feature in formal verification and AI reasoning tasks where both vagueness and modality are present.

**Acknowledgments.** This project has received funding from the European Union's Horizon 2020 research and innovation programme under the Marie Skłodowska-Curie grant agreement No 101007627. Camillo Fiorentini is member of the Gruppo Nazionale Calcolo Scientifico-Istituto Nazionale di Alta Matematica (GNCS-INdAM).

# References

1. Baader, F., Nipkow, T.: Term Rewriting and All That. Cambridge University Press, Cambridge (1998)
2. Baaz, M., Fermüller, C.G.: Analytic calculi for projective logics. In: Murray, N.V. (eds.) Automated Reasoning with Analytic Tableaux and Related Methods. TABLEAUX 1999. LNCS, vol. 1617, pp. 36–50. Springer, Berlin, Heidelberg (1999). https://doi.org/10.1007/3-540-48754-9_8
3. Balbiani, P., Gao, H., Gencer, Ç., Olivetti, N.: Local intuitionistic modal logics and their calculi. In: Benzmüller, C., Heule, M.J., Schmidt, R.A. (eds.) Automated Reasoning. IJCAR 2024. LNCS, vol. 14740, pp. 78–96. Springer, Cham (2024). https://doi.org/10.1007/978-3-031-63501-4_5
4. Beckmann, A., Preining, N.: Linear Kripke frames and Gödel logics. J. Symb. Log. **72**(1), 26–44 (2007). https://doi.org/10.2178/JSL/1174668382
5. Bílková, M., Frittella, S., Kozhemiachenko, D.: Paraconsistent gödel modal logic. In: Blanchette, J., Kovács, L., Pattinson, D. (eds.) Automated Reasoning. IJCAR 2022. LNCS, vol. 13385, pp. 429–448. Springer, Cham (2022). https://doi.org/10.1007/978-3-031-10769-6_26
6. Bou, F., Esteva, F., Godo, L., Rodríguez, R.O.: On the minimum many-valued modal logic over a finite residuated lattice. J. Log. Comput. **21**(5), 739–790 (2011). https://doi.org/10.1093/LOGCOM/EXP062
7. Burns, S., Zach, R.: Cut-free completeness for modular hypersequent calculi for modal logics K, T, and D. Rev. Symb. Log. **14**(4), 910–929 (2020). https://doi.org/10.1017/s1755020320000180
8. Caicedo, X., Metcalfe, G., Rodríguez, R.O., Rogger, J.: Decidability of order-based modal logics. J. Comput. Syst. Sci. **88**, 53–74 (2017). https://doi.org/10.1016/J.JCSS.2017.03.012

9. Caicedo, X., Rodríguez, R.O.: Standard Gödel modal logics. Stud. Log. **94**(2), 189–214 (2010). https://doi.org/10.1007/S11225-010-9230-1
10. Caicedo, X., Rodríguez, R.O.: Bi-modal Gödel logic over [0,1]-valued Kripke frames. J. Log. Comput. **25**(1), 37–55 (2015). https://doi.org/10.1093/LOGCOM/EXS036
11. Ferrari, M., Fiorentini, C., Fiorino, G.: Contraction-free linear depth sequent calculi for intuitionistic propositional logic with the subformula property and minimal depth counter-models. J. Autom. Reason. **51**(2), 129–149 (2013). https://doi.org/10.1007/s10817-012-9252-7
12. Ferrari, M., Fiorentini, C., Fiorino, G.: JTabWb: a java framework for implementing terminating sequent and tableau calculi. Fund. Inform. **150**(1), 119–142 (2017). https://doi.org/10.3233/FI-2017-1462
13. Ferrari, M., Fiorentini, C., Rodriguez, R.O.: Implementation of a refutation calculus for the Gödel modal logic over witnessed crisp models (GWC). https://github.com/ferram/jtabwb_provers/tree/master/gwc_ref
14. Fiorentini, C., Ferrari, M.: A forward internal calculus for model generation in s4. J. Log. Comput. **31**(3), 771–796 (2021). https://doi.org/10.1093/logcom/exab014
15. Fitting, M.C.: Many-valued modal logics. Fund. Inform. **15**(3–4), 235–254 (1991)
16. Fitting, M.C.: Many-valued modal logics ii. Fund. Inform. **17**(1–2), 55–73 (1992)
17. Flaminio, T., Godo, L., Menchón, P., Rodríguez, R.O.: Algebras and relational frames for Gödel modal logic and some of its extensions. In: Coniglio, M., Kubyshkina, E., Zaitsev, D. (eds.) Many-valued Semantics and Modal Logics: Essays in Honour of Yuriy Vasilievich Ivlev, pp. 179–216. Springer, Cham (2024). https://doi.org/10.1007/978-3-031-56595-3_7
18. Galmiche, D., Salhi, Y.: A family of Gödel hybrid logics. J. Appl. Log. **8**(4), 371–385 (2010). https://doi.org/10.1016/J.JAL.2010.08.008
19. Hansoul, G., Teheux, B.: Extending Łukasiewicz logics with a modality: algebraic approach to relational semantics. Stud. Log. **101**(3), 505–545 (2013). https://doi.org/10.1007/S11225-012-9396-9
20. Kamide, N.: Kripke semantics for modal substructural logics. J. Log. Lang. Inform. **11**(4), 453–470 (2002). https://doi.org/10.1023/A:1019915908844
21. Metcalfe, G., Olivetti, N.: Proof systems for a Gödel modal logic. In: Giese, M., Waaler, A. (eds.) Automated Reasoning with Analytic Tableaux and Related Methods. TABLEAUX 2009. LNCS, vol. 5607, pp. 265–279. Springer, Berlin, Heidelberg (2009). https://doi.org/10.1007/978-3-642-02716-1_20
22. Metcalfe, G., Olivetti, N.: Towards a proof theory of Gödel modal logics. Log. Methods Comput. Sci. **7**(2) (2011). https://doi.org/10.2168/LMCS-7(2:10)2011
23. Ono, H.: Semantics for substructural logics. In: Schroeder-Heister, P., Došen, K. (eds.) Substructural Logics, pp. 259–291. Oxford University Press (1993). https://doi.org/10.1007/978-94-017-3598-8_8
24. Priest, G.: Many-valued modal logics: a simple approach. Rev. Symb. Log. **1**(2), 190–203 (2008). https://doi.org/10.1017/S1755020308080179
25. Prud'homme, C., Godet, A., Fages, J.G.: Choco-solver: an open-source java library for constraint programming. https://github.com/chocoteam/choco-solver
26. Restall, G.: Modalities in substructural logics. Logique et Anal. (N.S.) **36**(141/142), 303–321 (1993)
27. Rodríguez, R.O., Vidal, A.: Axiomatization of crisp Gödel modal logic. Stud. Log. **109**(2), 367–395 (2021). https://doi.org/10.1007/S11225-020-09910-5
28. Troelstra, A., Schwichtenberg, H.: Basic proof theory, 2nd ed. Cambridge Tracts in Theoretical Computer Science, vol. 43. Cambridge University Press, Cambridge (2000). https://doi.org/10.1017/CBO9781139168717

29. Vidal, A.: Mniblos: a SMT-based solver for continuous t-norm based logics and some of their modal expansions. Inf. Sci. **372**, 709–730 (2016). https://doi.org/10.1016/J.INS.2016.08.072
30. Vidal, A., Esteva, F., Godo, L.: On modal extensions of product fuzzy logic. J. Log. Comput. **27**(1), 299–336 (2017). https://doi.org/10.1093/LOGCOM/EXV046

**Open Access** This chapter is licensed under the terms of the Creative Commons Attribution 4.0 International License (http://creativecommons.org/licenses/by/4.0/), which permits use, sharing, adaptation, distribution and reproduction in any medium or format, as long as you give appropriate credit to the original author(s) and the source, provide a link to the Creative Commons license and indicate if changes were made.

The images or other third party material in this chapter are included in the chapter's Creative Commons license, unless indicated otherwise in a credit line to the material. If material is not included in the chapter's Creative Commons license and your intended use is not permitted by statutory regulation or exceeds the permitted use, you will need to obtain permission directly from the copyright holder.

# Refined Tableau Systems for Some Modal Logics of Confluence

Kiana Samadpour Motalebi[1]($^{\boxtimes}$), Renate A. Schmidt[1], and Cláudia Nalon[2]

[1] University of Manchester, Manchester, UK
{kiana.samadpourmotalebi,renate.schmidt}@manchester.ac.uk
[2] University of Brasília, Brasília, Brazil
nalon@unb.br

**Abstract.** We investigate the systematic development of refined tableau systems for a subset of the logics of confluence, which are modal logics comprising of instances of the Scott-Lemmon axioms. In particular, we look at rule refinements aiming to decrease branching, perform fewer inferences and reduce the application of rules which create new labels in the tableau. Propagation rules are common forms of refined rules, that construct smaller pre-models sufficient to determine satisfiability, without needing to construct full concrete models satisfying the correspondence properties which would require a lot more inference steps. These rules have already been developed for the confluence logics that are part of the modal logic cube, but are lacking for some instances outside the cube. Such instances can be awkward, as the nature of their correspondence properties makes the development of propagation rules particularly challenging. These are the logics $K$G0111, $K$G and $K$De for which we propose refined tableau systems. We also present refined tableau systems for the combined logics $K$alt1De, $K$BG0111 and $K$DDe. Soundness and completeness results for all the systems are established.

**Keywords:** Logics of confluence · modal logics · tableau systems · refinement

## 1 Introduction

Modal logics are popular due to their relevance in areas such as agent-based reasoning, artificial intelligence and hardware verification, owing to the expressive capabilities of the dual possibility and necessity operators [3,18]. Other than the basic modal logic $K$, well-known modal logics include $K$T, $K$B, $K$D, $K$4, $K$5, which form part of the standard modal cube. They also belong to the class of logics of confluence, as their defining axioms are specialisations of the axioms of confluence, also known as the Scott-Lemmon or Geach axioms of the form $\Diamond^i \Box^j \phi \to \Box^k \Diamond^l \phi$ [14,19]. They have been the focus of extensive research and several resolution, sequent and tableau systems have been developed for them [5,12,16,24,26].

Tableau systems are a popular method of deduction used in theorem provers. For extensions of modal logic $K$, there are two main types of tableau rules: structural rules and propagation rules. Structural rules create direct reflections of the correspondence properties on the accessibility relation, while propagation rules work by transferring formulae to nodes [5].

Structural rules are easier to develop for axioms whose correspondence property is first-order definable, which is a property that the extra axioms of the logics of confluence fulfil as they are Sahlqvist. However, direct encoding of the first-order formulation of a correspondence property may not lead to an optimal set of inference rules. Propagation rules, first introduced by Fitting in [10], aim to only pass enough information to obtain a proof. Instead of directly enforcing correspondence properties, propagation rules simulate these properties in a syntactic way, which can reduce the number of inferences needed. Tableau systems using propagation rules are considered as refinements and tend to be favoured when implementing tableau provers, because performance is better [15,36].

While refined tableau systems using propagation rules exist for the well-known modal cube logics, there are other extensions of modal logic $K$ in the class of logics of confluence for which it has been noted that constructing such systems poses difficulties [5]. These are the logics $K$G0111, $K$G and $K$De, which feature correspondence properties that require frequent addition of new labels to the tableau for relational edges, which is harder to capture by using propagation rules.

In this paper, we explore the development of refined tableau systems for these special case logics. We explore using the axiomatic translation principle as a starting point. This method is used to partially translate modal logic formulae into first-order logic and has been linked to the propagation rules of the well-studied logics $K$T, $K$B, $K$D, $K$4 and $K$5 [32,36]. We discover that the obtained propagation rules for these 'awkward' logics are not optimal, because they try to emulate the addition of new labels by propagating $\Diamond$ formulae to nodes, which can result in the introduction of several redundant labels. We instead propose almost propagation rules, which refine the structural rules by limiting the creation of new labels.

In this paper, we present refined tableau systems for the logics $K$G0111, $K$G, $K$De, $K$alt1De, $K$BG0111 and $K$DDe. Soundness and completeness proofs are established. Another attractive property of the systems we propose is their modularity, which is beneficial when developing similar systems for other modal logics [24,39]. A basic system is fixed and refined systems are obtained by adding the rules needed for each logic to obtain a complete system. We demonstrate how our completeness proofs are modular by presenting the proofs of all the systems together.

The paper is structured as follows: First, we give some background on modal logic and modal logics of confluence in Sect. 2. Then, in Sect. 3 we describe the tableau method and the concepts related to it. In Sect. 4, related work concerning existing systems for the logics of confluence is explored. In Sect. 5, we present the refined systems, which are the contributions of this paper. Following this, in Sect. 6, we discuss soundness and completeness of the systems using refined rules. The long version of this paper with the omitted proofs is available at the authors' homepages. We conclude with a summary and mention possible future work in the final section.

## 2 Modal Logic

Monomodal logic extends the language of propositional logic with the box ($\Box$) and diamond ($\Diamond$) operators [7]. The syntax for modal formulae is defined by the BNF grammar rule $\phi, \psi := p \mid \neg \phi \mid \Box \phi \mid \Diamond \phi \mid \phi \vee \psi \mid \phi \wedge \psi \mid \bot$, where $p \in P$ which is a denumerable set of *propositional symbols*.

The semantics of modal logics we study is defined as follows. A Kripke frame consists of a non-empty set $W$ of worlds and accessibility relation $R$ over $W$. A Kripke model $\mathcal{M} = (W, R, V)$ consists of a frame and a valuation function $V$ from the set of propositional symbols to subsets of $W$. The meaning of modal formulae at a world $x \in W$ is defined inductively as follows:

$\mathcal{M}, x \models p$      iff    $x \in V(p)$

$\mathcal{M}, x \not\models \bot$

$\mathcal{M}, x \models \neg \phi$      iff    $\mathcal{M}, x \not\models \phi$

$\mathcal{M}, x \models \phi \vee \psi$    iff    $\mathcal{M}, x \models \phi$ or $\mathcal{M}, x \models \psi$

$\mathcal{M}, x \models \Box \phi$      iff    $\mathcal{M}, y \models \phi$ for every $y \in W$ such that $(x, y) \in R$

We regard $\Diamond$ and $\wedge$ as defined operators specified by $\Diamond \phi = \neg \Box \neg \phi$ and $\phi \wedge \psi = \neg(\neg \phi \vee \neg \psi)$.

Axioms are modal formula schemas that are taken to be true at every world of every model. The modal logic $K$ is the smallest set of formulae that satisfy the axioms of propositional logic, the axiom $\mathbf{K} = \Box(\phi \to \psi) \to (\Box \phi \to \Box \psi)$, the necessitation rule $\mathbf{N}$ (if $\phi$ is a theorem, so is $\Box \phi$) and modus ponens $\mathbf{MP}$ (if $\phi$ and $\phi \to \psi$ are theorems, so is $\psi$) [3,16]. Modal logics stronger than $K$ are obtained by adding axioms such as T = $\Box \phi \to \phi$ or B = $\Diamond \Box \phi \to \phi$. The characteristic models for those extensions correspond to particular constraints on the accessibility relation of the frame. For example, the axiom T forces the accessibility relation $R$ in the characteristic models for $K$T to be reflexive. Similarly, the axiom B forces models to be symmetric. Extending modal logic $K$ with a combination of axioms results in more than one restriction placed on the accessibility relation. For example, the modal logic $K$TB has models where the accessibility relation is reflexive and symmetric [30].

Logics of confluence are extensions of modal logic $K$ with axioms of the form $\Diamond^i \Box^j \phi \to \Box^k \Diamond^l \phi$, where $\Diamond^i$ and $\Box^j$ respectively denote a sequence of $i$ diamonds and $j$ boxes with $i \geqslant 0$, $j \geqslant 0$ [26]. For example, when $i = 0$, $j = 1$, $k = 0$, and $l = 0$, we get axiom T. For axiom B, $i = 1$, $j = 1$, $k = 0$ and $l = 0$ [19]. The correspondence property in its generalised form for the general axiom of confluence is: $\forall x, y, z (R^i(x, y) \wedge R^k(x, z) \to \exists u (R^j(y, u) \wedge R^l(z, u)))$, where $R^0(x, y)$ denotes $x \approx y$ and $R^{n+1}(x, y)$ denotes $\exists u (R(x, u) \wedge R^n(u, y))$ for $n > 0$.

**Table 1.** Axioms of confluence and their correspondence properties

| Name | Axiom | Name of corresp. property | Correspondence property |
|---|---|---|---|
| T | $\Box\phi \to \phi$ | Reflexive | $\forall x R(x,x)$ |
| B | $\Diamond\Box\phi \to \phi$ | Symmetric | $\forall x,y(R(x,y) \to R(y,x))$ |
| D | $\Box\phi \to \Diamond\phi$ | Serial | $\forall x \exists y R(x,y)$ |
| 4 | $\Box\phi \to \Box\Box\phi$ | Transitive | $\forall x,y,z((R(x,y) \land R(y,z)) \to R(x,z))$ |
| 5 | $\Diamond\Box\phi \to \Box\phi$ | Euclidean | $\forall x,y,z((R(x,y) \land R(x,z)) \to R(y,z))$ |
| alt1 | $\Diamond\phi \to \Box\phi$ | Functional | $\forall x,y,z((R(x,y) \land R(x,z)) \to y \approx z)$ |
| Ban | $\Diamond\phi \to \phi$ | Modally Banal | $\forall x,y(R(x,y) \to x \approx y)$ |
| G0111 | $\Box\phi \to \Box\Diamond\phi$ | 0,1,1,1-Convergent | $\forall x,y(R(x,y) \to \exists z(R(x,z) \land R(y,z)))$ |
| G | $\Diamond\Box\phi \to \Box\Diamond\phi$ | Confluent | $\forall x,y,z((R(x,y) \land R(x,z)) \to \exists u(R(y,u) \land R(z,u)))$ |
| De | $\Box\Box\phi \to \Box\phi$ | Dense | $\forall x,y(R(x,y) \to \exists z(R(x,z) \land R(z,y)))$ |

This means the correspondence property for T is $\forall x,y,z(R^0(x,y) \land R^0(x,z) \to \exists u(R^1(y,u) \land R^0(z,u))$ which simplifies to $\forall x R(x,x)$, i.e., reflexivity of $R$ [19].

Table 1 lists some of the studied axioms of confluence along with their respective correspondence properties. These are the axioms where $i$, $j$, $k$ and $l$ take the values 0, 1 or 2. The name of axiom $G0111$ comes from [26] and the other axioms are well-known in the literature.

The axioms T, B, D, 4 and 5 form part of the modal cube and are associated with the standard correspondence properties of reflexivity, symmetry, etc. Axioms alt1 and Ban both feature equality in their associated correspondence properties. Their models equate worlds which are related, for Ban, or which have the same predecessor for alt1. Models of logic $K$alt1 are characterised by a partial function, i.e., each world has at most one successor.

The axioms G0111, G and De feature a common aspect. Their associated correspondence properties necessitate the presence of intermediate worlds, which when translated into a tableau system means that, rather than simply propagating modal formulae, the tableau must introduce new labels representing these intermediate worlds. We are interested in developing systems for these logics that are complete, but are also refined to perform only the necessary inferences, despite the complexity of their correspondence properties.

## 3 Tableau

The general idea of semantic tableau is to either construct a model for the given formula or construct a derivation tree in which every branch is closed. We assume that the rules of our tableau systems have the form $X/X_i \mid \ldots \mid X_n$, where $X$ and each $X_i$ are sets of tableau formulae. $X$ is the premise and $X_1, \ldots X_n$ are the conclusions.

The rules are used to construct a tableau derivation, which is a tree. A rule is applicable to a leaf node of the partially constructed tree if it contains formulae that match the formulae in the premise $X$ of the rule. A rule application creates a child node for each conclusion $X_i$ in the rule. These become the new leaf nodes. A branch in a tableau derivation is a sequence $N_0, N_1, N_2, \ldots$ of sets of tableau formulae. $N_0$ is the initial input set of labelled formulae given to the tableau. To determine the satisfiability of a given formula $\phi$, $N_0$ is set to $\{a : \phi\}$. Each subsequent set $N_i$ is obtained by the application of a tableau rule to $N_{i-1}$. Let $N_\infty = \bigcup_{\geq 0} N_i$ denote the formulae on the branch $\mathcal{B}$.

If a contradiction in the form of $\bot$ or a formula and its negation is derived within the same node of a branch, the branch is closed and does not need to be expanded further. If all the branches in a tableau (derivation) are closed, then the tableau is closed and the input set $N_0$ is unsatisfiable. A branch where every applicable rule has been applied and a contradiction has not been derived is called an open branch. A fully expanded tableau derivation with at least one open, fully expanded branch is called an open tableau and means the input set $N_0$ and the given formula $\phi$ are satisfiable [37].

Soundness of a tableau system ensures that an open tableau derivation can be constructed if the input set $N_0$ is satisfiable.[1] It suffices to show that each rule $X/X_i \mid \ldots \mid X_n$ in the system is sound, i.e., if all the formulae in the premise $X$ of a rule are true in a model, then all the formulae in at least one of the conclusions $X_i$ are also true in the model. This means rule application preserves satisfiability [11] and implies that if $N_0$ has a model, then it is possible to construct a fully expanded, open branch.

Completeness of a tableau system, on the other hand, ensures that if a formula is unsatisfiable, a closed tableau can be constructed for it. To prove completeness, it is sufficient to show that given an open, fully expanded branch for $N_0$, we can construct a model from that branch which satisfies all sets (nodes) $N_0, N_1, N_2, \ldots$ on the branch.

The formulae of tableau systems are defined by the BNF grammar rule $F := \bot \mid s : \phi \mid R(s,t) \mid s \approx t$, where $\phi$ denotes a modal logic formula as defined in Sect. 2, $s$ and $t$ denote labels representing worlds with $a$ the designated label representing the initial world of a model that is attempted to be found. $R$ is a binary predicate symbol representing the accessibility relation being constructed. The $\approx$ symbol is interpreted as equality between labels, which is needed in systems featuring equality, such as for the logics $K$Ban and $K$alt1.

A term $f_\psi(s)$ is used to uniquely name the label created from a tableau formula $s : \psi$ where $\psi = \neg \Box \phi$. Technically, $f_\psi$ is a Skolem function taking care of creating successor worlds for diamond formulae. Similarly, other Skolem functions such as $g, h, i$ are used in tableau systems to create witnesses for the

---

[1] Since our tableau systems are proof confluent, in fact any tableau derivation will contain an open, fully expanded branch if $N_0$ is satisfiable. Proof confluence also means that any partial tableau derivation for an unsatisfiable set $N_0$ can be expanded into a closed tableau.

logics $KG0111$, $KG$ and $K$De. Using these Skolem functions enables us to keep track of what formulae were used to create new labels.

The definition of the semantics of tableau formulae uses an interpretation $\mathcal{I} = (U, \cdot^{\mathcal{I}})$, where $U$ is a non-empty set and $\cdot^{\mathcal{I}}$ is an interpretation function mapping labels to elements in $U$, propositional variables to subsets of $U$, $\approx$ to the identity relation over $U$, and $R$ to a relation over $U$.

The meaning of modal formulae in $\mathcal{I}$ is given by a Kripke model $\mathcal{M}$ where $\mathcal{M} = (U, R, v)$ and $v$ is the restriction of $\cdot^{\mathcal{I}}$ to propositional variables. The meaning of modal formulae in $\mathcal{M}$ was defined in the previous section.

Satisfiability in $\mathcal{I}$ of tableau formulae is defined by:

$$\mathcal{I} \models s : \phi \quad \text{iff} \quad \mathcal{M}, s^{\mathcal{I}} \models \phi$$
$$\mathcal{I} \models R(s, t) \quad \text{iff} \quad (s^{\mathcal{I}}, t^{\mathcal{I}}) \in R^{\mathcal{I}}$$
$$\mathcal{I} \models s \approx t \quad \text{iff} \quad s^{\mathcal{I}} = t^{\mathcal{I}}$$

The basic tableau system $Tab_K$, adapted from [35], is given in Table 2. We use the notation $Tab_K^*$ for the basic tableau system without the ($\neg\Box$) rule, which is fixed for all the tableau systems we present. The tableau construction for a formula $\phi$ starts with $N_0 = \{a : \phi\}$. It is sound and complete for modal logic $K$. For example, rule ($\vee$) has as its premise $\{s : \phi \vee \psi\}$, and $\{s : \phi\}$ and $\{s : \psi\}$ as its conclusions. This rule splits the current branch of the tableau derivation into two branches when applied. The $\sim$ operator appearing in the rules ($\neg\Box\phi$) and ($\neg\vee$) is defined as follows: $\sim\phi = \psi$ if $\phi = \neg\psi$ and $\sim\phi = \neg\psi$ if $\phi = \psi$.

Our tableau systems are expanding, i.e., after every application of a rule to a set $N_i$ of a branch, the formulae in the conclusion of the rule are added to the set $N_i$ to obtain $N_{i+1}$ and the formulae in the premise of the rule are not deleted.

Two main types of tableau rules for extensions of modal logic $K$ are known as structural and propagation rules. Structural rules reflect correspondence properties associated with axioms, while propagation rules have flavours of both correspondence properties and axiom schemata [5]. For example, the structural rule for axiom 4 is

$$\frac{R(s,t), R(t,u)}{R(s,u)}$$

reflecting the transitivity property, while the propagation rule for axiom 4 is

$$\frac{R(s,t), s : \Box\phi}{t : \Box\phi}.$$

Structural rules are easier to develop due to their direct relation to correspondence properties of axioms. Development of propagation rules is not as straightforward, but they can be seen as refined rules since they are clever in how much information they add to the tableau to find a proof, instead of adding relational formulae to the tableau every time the rule is applicable.

**Table 2.** The basic tableau system $Tab_K$

| System | Rules | | | | | | | |
|---|---|---|---|---|---|---|---|---|
| $Tab_K$ | ($\Box$) $\dfrac{s : \Box\phi, R(s,t)}{t : \phi}$ | ($\neg\Box$) $\dfrac{s : \neg\Box\phi}{R(s, f_{\neg\Box\phi}(s)), f_{\neg\Box\phi}(s) : \sim\phi}$ | | ($\neg\vee$) $\dfrac{s : \neg(\phi \vee \psi)}{s : \sim\phi, s : \sim\psi}$ |
| | ($\vee$) $\dfrac{s : \phi \vee \psi}{s : \phi \mid s : \psi}$ | ($\bot$) $\dfrac{s : \bot}{\bot}$ | (cl) $\dfrac{s : \phi, s : \neg\phi}{\bot}$ | ($\neg\neg$) $\dfrac{s : \neg\neg\phi}{s : \phi}$ |

## 4 Existing Systems for the Logics of Confluence

Many proof systems exist for instances of the logics of confluence such as resolution, sequent and tableau systems. In the following, we discuss some of the systems that are most relevant to our work.

There are resolution systems for modal logics in general [1,31], and several resolution-based theorem provers have been developed [17,25,40]. The most relevant work is given in [26], where resolution systems for a subset of the logics of confluence, namely the logics $KT$, $KB$, $KD$, $K5$, $KBan$, $Kalt1$, $KG0111$, $KG$ and their combinations are given. The resolution rules are obtained systematically by directly transforming the axioms into a specific clausal normal form. In some sense, they are closely related to propagation rules used in tableau systems.

Many sequent calculi for modal logics of confluence have been developed in the literature. Sequent calculi for basic modal logic $K$ and the logics $KT$, $KB$, $K4$ and $K5$ corresponding to tableau systems using structural rules can be found in [27]. Marin et al. [22] studied intuitionistic modal logics and created a general sequent system for the logics of confluence, which also correspond to structural tableau rules. Their system uses the notion of the generalised form of the correspondence property for the axioms of confluence described in Sect. 2. Natural deduction systems using structural rules have been presented in [39] for the logics $KT$, $KB$, $KD$, $K4$, $K5$, $KG$ and $KDe$.

Sequent systems which correspond to tableau systems using propagational rules also appear in the literature. Nested sequent systems for the logics $KD$, $K4$, $KT$, $KB$ and $K5$ have been developed by Brünnler [4] and Poggiolesi [28]. Fitting [12] studied similar nested sequent systems for the logics $KT$, $KB$, $K4$ and $KD$. Indexed nested sequent systems for axioms of confluence were studied by Marin and Strassburger [23]. They used the general form of the logics of confluence to create indexed sequent systems. Fitting [13] systematically developed cut-free proof systems for the all the logics of confluence in the form of prefixed tableaux and nested sequents by adding extra machinery to rules.

In [21], Lyon presents a method called structural refinement which refines labelled sequent systems for modal and constructive logics. Refinements are made by removing structural rules and adding propagation rules. This method leads to a decrease in the size of proofs. Another work by Lyon [20] uses this methodology to extract nested sequents for intuitionistic modal logics within the family of the logics of confluence. Other relevant works on sequent systems include [38] which develops a nested sequent calculus for grammar logics and [29] which provides syntactic proof of cut-elimination for index nested sequent calculi for the logics of confluence.

Several tableau systems for modal logics have been developed in the literature [2,16,24]. Castillho et al. [5] and del Cerro and Gasquet [9] studied the development of tableau systems based on propagation or structural rules. In their investigations, they identified two groups of systems. One group using propagation rules for the axioms T, 4, B and 5 and one using structural rules for the axioms D, De and G. For the combined systems, they allowed a mixture of propagation and structural rules. In [15], strategies for tableau systems of modal logics in the tableau prover LoTREC [6] are given. Of particular interest is the logic $K$alt1, in which functionality is captured by restricting the ($\Diamond$) rule to only be applied once.

Other work on tableau systems using propagation and structural rules is by Schmidt et al. [36] who developed tableau systems using both types of rules for the logic $K$t(H,R), but the logic considered is different since it is a tense logic with backward and forward looking modalities. An evaluation of the tableau systems showed better performance for systems using propagation rules.

The propagation rules for $K$t(H,R) were created using the axiomatic translation principle [32], which is the same approach we use for developing propagation rules. The axiomatic translation principle creates schema clauses for modal axioms. To translate a modal formula in modal logic $KA$ to first-order logic, the axiomatic translation partially translates the formula to first-order logic and incorporates instances of the schema clause for the axiom $A$ into the translation. The schema clauses for axioms T, B, D, 4, 5 and alt1 are defined in [32].

## 5 Refined Tableau Systems

In this section, we focus on refined tableau systems for the logics $K$G0111, $K$G and $K$De. Structural rules for these logics are easily obtained using the tableau synthesis framework [34], since the restrictions on frames for these logics are first-order definable. However, as noted in the literature, propagation rules usually fare better than structural rules in a tableau derivation [5,21,36]. We start with the axiomatic translation principle as a starting point to derive propagation rules for these logics.

For each logic, first we discuss their tableau system using structural rules. Then, the tableau system obtained using the axiomatic translation principle as a starting point is considered. We note that these systems usually are not complete or can be refined further. Finally, we present the proposed refined tableau system.

### 5.1 Refined Tableau Systems for Single Axiom Extensions

We consider the logic $K$G0111 first. The correspondence property associated with G0111 is
$$\forall x, y(R(x,y) \rightarrow \exists z(R(x,z) \land R(y,z)))$$

and consequently the structural rule for G0111 is

$$\frac{R(s,t)}{R(s,g(s,t)), R(t,g(s,t))}. \tag{1}$$

This rule captures the semantics of the correspondence property associated with G0111, however, the rule will be repeatedly applied after its first application. The conclusion of the rule adds two relational formulae, which means that the rule is applicable again and this can go on indefinitely.

If we follow similar principles as the tableau systems using propagation rules to create a tableau system for $KG0111$, i.e., using the axiomatic translation principle, we can extract two schema clauses from both variants of the G0111 axioms, $\Box\phi \to \Box\Diamond\phi$ and $\Diamond\Box\phi \to \Diamond\phi$. These are $\neg R(x,y) \vee \neg Q_{\Box\phi}(x) \vee Q_{\neg\Box\neg\phi}(y)$ and $\neg R(x,y) \vee \neg Q_{\Box\phi}(y) \vee Q_{\neg\Box\neg\phi}(x)$ and the rules obtained from them are

$$\frac{R(s,t), s : \Box\phi}{t : \neg\Box\neg\phi} \quad \text{and} \quad \frac{R(s,t), t : \Box\phi}{s : \neg\Box\neg\phi}.$$

We need both of the rules, since each rule on its own with the basic calculus does not form a complete system. The tableau system, consisting of the basic calculus and the former rules, also does not form a complete system. Two further rules are needed.

Firstly, the following maxiscoping rule is needed

$$\frac{s : \Box\phi, s : \Box\psi}{s : \Box(\phi \wedge \psi)},$$

which ensures that all the information propagated under $\Box$ formulae ends up in the same world. Secondly, the following rule is needed.

$$\frac{R(s,t), t : \Box\phi}{t : \neg\Box\neg\phi}$$

While the addition of these rules creates a complete tableau system, the propagation rules essentially add $\Diamond$ formulae to the tableau, which in turn create more labels. For the purpose of refinement, more labels could delay closing a tableau.

In our refined tableau system for $KG0111$, we ensure that only the necessary labels are created to find a contradiction or establish satisfiability via an open tableau. The tableau system is given in Table 3. We denote our tableau system by $Tab^{rf}_{G0111}$ and it consists of the basic calculus $Tab_K$ and the refined rules (G0111.1), (G0111.2), (G0111.3) and (G0111.4). These rules were obtained by altering the structural rule (1) for G0111.

To emulate the addition of a new label for every link $R(s,t)$ on the branch similar to the structural rule, we use the label $g(s,t)$ to ensure that no duplicate worlds are created. Unlike the structural rule for G0111, we do not add a new

**Table 3.** The refined tableau systems for single axioms extensions of $K$

| Logic | System | Rules | | | | |
|---|---|---|---|---|---|---|
| $KG0111$ | $Tab^{rf}_{G0111}$ | $Tab_K$, (G0111.1) $\dfrac{R(s,t), t : \Box\phi}{R(s,g(s,t)), g(s,t) : \phi}$ | | | | |
| | | (G0111.2) $\dfrac{R(s,g(s,t)), g(s,t) : \Box\phi}{R(t,g(s,t))}$ | | | | |
| | | (G0111.3) $\dfrac{R(s,t), s : \Box\phi}{R(t,g(s,t)), g(s,t) : \phi}$ | | | | |
| | | (G0111.4) $\dfrac{R(t,g(s,t)), g(s,t) : \Box\phi}{R(s,g(s,t))}$ | | | | |
| $K$De | $Tab^{rf}_{De}$ | $Tab_K$, (De.1) $\dfrac{R(s,t), s : \Box\phi, t : \Box\psi}{i(s,t) : \phi}$, | (De.2) $\dfrac{i(s,t) : \Box\phi}{i(s,t) : \phi, t : \phi}$ | | | |
| $KG$ | $Tab^{rf}_{G}$ | $Tab_K$, (G) $\dfrac{R(s,t), R(s,u)}{R(t,h(s,t,u)), R(u,h(s,t,u))}$ | | | | |

label for every link. Instead, we check for the presence of a $\Box$ formula in the premise of the rule first. This helps create a refined rule that performs just enough steps to derive a contradiction.

The logic $K$De is similar to the logic $KG0111$. The correspondence property associated with De is

$$\forall x, y (R(x,y) \to \exists z (R(x,z) \land R(z,y)))$$

and the structural rule for De is

$$\frac{R(s,t)}{R(s,i(s,t)), R(i(s,t),t)}, \qquad (2)$$

which captures density. This rule adds new links to the branch and is continuously applicable, creating infinitely many labels. This motivates us to explore refinements for $K$De.

The axiomatic translation principle is not a feasible method for deriving propagation rules for $K$De. This is because the axiom De cannot be translated into a single clause, which is necessary for generating a corresponding schema clause from which a rule is derived. We can instead derive two rules directly from the two variants of axiom De:

$$\Box\Box\phi \to \Box\phi \quad \text{and} \quad \Diamond\phi \to \Diamond\Diamond\phi.$$

These are

$$\frac{s : \Box\Box\phi}{s : \Box\phi} \quad \text{and} \quad \frac{s : \neg\Box\phi}{s : \neg\Box\Box\phi},$$

denoted by (De'.1) and (De'.2) respectively.

Neither of the tableau systems created from the union of $Tab_K$ with (De'.1) or (De'.2) or both (De'.1) and (De'.2) are complete. A counterexample for the former system is the formula $\neg\Box\neg p \wedge \Box(\Box\neg p \wedge q)$, which is not satisfied in $K$De. However, using the basic system $Tab_K$ and rule (De'.1), it is not possible to derive a contradiction for it. It is possible to apply box miniscoping for this example, i.e., adding the rule

$$\frac{\Box(p \wedge q)}{\Box p \wedge \Box q}$$

will change the formula $\Box(\Box\neg p \wedge q)$ to the formula $\Box\Box\neg p \wedge \Box q$. The (De'.1) rule can then be applied to eventually derive a contradiction in the tableau. Nevertheless, box miniscoping does not make this system complete either. If we consider the formula $\Box(\Box\neg p \vee \bot)$, then no miniscoping can be done, because $\Box$ does not distribute over disjunction.

A counterexample for the tableau system containing the basic calculus $Tab_K$ and the (De'.2) rule is the following formula: $\neg\Box\neg(p \vee q) \wedge \Box\neg p \wedge \Box\Box\neg q$. Adding rule (De'.1) to the system will derive a contradiction. However, if we replace the subformula $\Box\Box\neg q$ with the formula $\Box(\Box\neg q \vee \bot)$, the rule (De'.1) cannot be applied and no contradiction will be found. Therefore, the system containing $Tab_K$, (De'.1) and (De'.2) is also not complete.

Since these rules do not yield a complete system, we use a similar method to the one used when developing the refined tableau system for the logic $K$G0111. We obtain the tableau system $Tab_{De}^{rf}$ presented in Table 3. These rules do not add new links to the tableau. Instead, a new world is added for every link (if there are $\Box$ formulae), which is reflexive and formulae are propagated by the rules. This ensures that extra labels are not created and the necessary formulae are propagated.

For the logic $K$G, the associated correspondence property is

$$\forall x, y, z (R(x,y) \wedge R(x,z) \to \exists u(R(y,u) \wedge R(z,u)))$$

and the structural rule is

$$\frac{R(s,t), R(s,u)}{R(t, h(s,t,u)), R(u, h(s,t,u))}$$

to capture confluence. This rule does not have the same continuous rule application issue as the structural rules for G0111 and De. The application of the rule does not entail that it is applicable again. However, it might still add unnecessary labels, so we consider whether refinements exist.

The schema clause for G is $\neg R(x,y) \vee \neg R(x,z) \vee \neg Q_{\Box\phi}(y) \vee Q_{\neg\Box\neg\phi}(z)$ and its resulting tableau rule is

$$\frac{R(s,t), R(s,u), t : \Box\phi}{u : \neg\Box\neg\phi}.$$

**Table 4.** Refined tableau systems for combinations of logics

| Logic | System | Rules | | | |
|---|---|---|---|---|---|
| $K$alt1De | $Tab^{rf}_{alt1,De}$ | $Tab^*_K$, (alt1De.1) $\dfrac{a : \neg\Box\phi}{R(a, f(a)), f(a) : \sim\phi}$ | | | |
| | | (alt1De.2) $\dfrac{R(s,t), t : \Box\phi}{t : \phi}$ | | (alt1De.3) $\dfrac{R(s,t), t : \neg\Box\phi}{t : \sim\phi}$ | |
| $K$BG0111 | $Tab^{rf}_{B,G0111}$ | $Tab^{rf}_{G0111}$, (B) $\dfrac{R(s,t), t : \Box\phi}{s : \phi}$ | | | |
| $K$BDe | $Tab^{rf}_{B,De}$ | $Tab^{rf}_{De}$, (B), (BDe) $\dfrac{i(s,t) : \psi, t : \Box\phi}{i(s,t) : \phi}$ | | | |
| $K$DDe | $Tab^{rf}_{D,De}$ | $Tab^{rf}_{De}$, (D) $\dfrac{s : \Box\phi}{s : \neg\Box\sim\phi}$ | | | |

The system consisting of this rule and the rules in $Tab_K$ is not complete. A counterexample for it is the formula $\neg\Box\Box\neg\Box\Box\neg\phi \wedge \neg\Box\Box\neg\Box\Box\phi$.

A system with $Tab_K$, the rules

$$\dfrac{R(s,t), t : \Box\phi}{s : \Box\neg\Box\neg\phi}$$

and maxiscoping is complete. However, this system has the problem of creating redundant labels in the tableau for every occurrence of a formula containing $\Box$. Using a similar method of altering the structural rule results in a better system.

The structural rule for G is universally quantified, so if the formulae $R(s,t)$ and $R(s,u)$ are on the branch, two labels are added, i.e., the labels $h(s,t,u)$ and $h(s,u,t)$. In our tableau system, we add a restriction that rule (G) can only be applied once to the same premise, which results in fewer labels being created.

The rule is also applicable if the premise consists of the same formulae $R(s,t)$ and $R(s,t)$, which results in the creation of the label $h(s,t,t)$. This is necessary to satisfy the property of confluence if a world does not have a successor. However, if it already has a successor, adding another world is superfluous. As a further refinement, our tableau system restricts the application of rule (G) in this case to instances where no successor exists.

### 5.2 Refined Tableau Systems for Combinations

In this section, we present refined tableau systems for combinations of the logics considered in the previous section, namely the logics $K$alt1De, $K$BG0111, $K$BDe and $K$DDe. Developing tableau systems using structural rules for combined logics can be done using a modular approach, but this is not the case for some of the tableau systems using propagation or refined rules. It is not always possible to develop tableau systems by just using the rules we have provided for the individual axioms. This has also been discussed and proven in [8]. Our tableau systems using refined rules for the combinations of logics that we consider are presented in Table 4.

Recall that in a $K$alt1 model, there is at most one successor for every world. Looking at a $K$De model, we know that if two worlds $s$ and $t$ are connected, i.e., $R(s,t)$, then there exists a world $u$ such that $R(s,u)$ and $R(u,t)$. Combining this with $K$alt1, since $R(s,u)$ and $R(s,t)$, we get that $u \approx t$ and since $R(u,t)$, we know that $R(t,t)$ and therefore $t$ is reflexive. The rule (alt1De.1) adds the formula $t : \phi$ to the tableau if the formulae $R(s,t)$ and $t : \Box\phi$ are on the tableau.

Since for every link $R(s,t)$, $t$ is reflexive, any world connected to $t$ is equal to it. This is because if $R(t,t)$ and $R(t,v)$, then $t \approx v$. So a $K$alt1De model can be considered as either just a root world if there are no $\neg\Box$ formulae given, or as a link between the root world and its successor, where the successor world has a reflexive link to it. The rule (alt1De.2) ensures that the information in the successor world is propagated to $t$.

The rule (alt1De.1) replaces the $\neg\Box$ rule in the basic calculus and only adds one successor to $a$, the label representing the root world. All formulae of the form $\neg\phi$ where $a : \neg\Box\phi \in N_\infty$ will be propagated to $f(a)$. Note that we also do not need to include any of the rules from the refined systems of $K$De, because any successor world created for a link $R(s,t)$, i.e. $i(s,t)$ in Rule 2, is equal to $t$.

The logics $K$BG0111 and $K$BDe are equivalent. We can obtain a refined tableau system for this logic modularly using the rules for axioms $B$ and $G$0111. No new rules are needed, because in a $K$BG0111 model, the addition of symmetric links does not require further intermediate witness worlds to be present. If we consider two worlds $s$ and $t$ which are connected, i.e., $R(s,t)$, then by 0,1,1,1-convergence, there exists a world $u$ such that $R(s,u)$ and $R(t,u)$. Due to symmetry, we also have that $R(t,s)$. The 0,1,1,1-convergence property is satisfied for this symmetric link, because there exists a world $u$ where $R(t,u)$ and $R(s,u)$. The density property is also satisfied, since we have $R(t,u)$ and by symmetry, $R(u,s)$.

A more refined tableau system for the logic $K$BG0111 can be obtained by using the rules for axioms B and De. However, only using those rules does not yield a complete system, so this system is not modular. The (BDe) rule is added to obtain a complete system. This rule is needed because our refined system for $K$De adds no links for the new label $i(s,t)$ that is added to the tableau. However, the (B) rule checks if there is a link between two labels $s$ and $t$ and adds information that would emulate the symmetric link between them, i.e., $R(t,s)$. The (BDe) rule ensures that the necessary information is added to the tableau, even though we do not have links between certain worlds.

In $K$D models, all worlds have a successor, i.e., $\forall x \exists y R(x,y)$. The other logics that also require worlds to have successors, namely logics $K$G0111, $K$G and $K$De, satisfy this condition most of the time. Considering the logic $K$DDe, the tableau system for this logic is obtained in a modular way. We can improve the performance of this system by giving the lowest priority to the application of the (D) rule. This is because the (D) rule adds a $\neg\Box\neg\phi$ formula for every $\Box\phi$ formula in the tableau, which emulates adding a successor to worlds in a $K$De model. However, it is not necessary to apply this rule with label $s$ if (De.1) has already been applied to it, because the (De.1) rule creates a successor to $s$.

## 6 Soundness and Completeness Results

In this section, we establish the soundness and completeness of our presented systems. We show how proving completeness can be done in a modular way since all our proofs follow the same structure using the same base lemmas.

Soundness of a tableau system is proved by establishing that every rule in the system is sound. Completeness is proved by showing that the pre-model $\mathcal{I}(\mathcal{B})$ extracted from an open, fully expanded branch can be extended into a concrete model of the respective logic.

**Theorem 1.** $Tab_S^{rf}$ where $S \in \{G0111, De, G, \langle alt1, De\rangle, \langle B, G0111\rangle, \langle B, De\rangle, \langle D, De\rangle\}$ is sound for its corresponding modal logic.

*Proof.* We give a sketch of the soundness proof for the system $Tab_{G0111}^{rf}$. We need to prove that the rules (G0111.1), (G0111.2), (G0111.3) and (G0111.4) are sound. We start with the rules (G0111.1) and (G0111.3), since the other rules' premises depend on their application. Assuming that the premises of the rules (G0111.1) and (G0111.3) are true in $I$, a $KG0111$ model, we know that there exists $u \in U^I$ such that $R^I(s^I, u)$ and $R^I(t^I, u)$. Then, we can create another model $I'$ similar to $I$, where $g(s,t)^I = u$ and then the conclusions of (G0111.1) and (G0111.3) are true in $I$. Using the same model $I'$, since $g(s,t)^I = u$, the conclusions of (G0111.2) and (G0111.4) are also true in $I$.

The proofs for the rest of the systems are delegated to the long version.

**Theorem 2.** *The system $Tab_S^{rf}$ is complete for testing satisfiability of sets of tableau formulae in its respective modal logic where $S \in \{G0111, De, G, \langle alt1, De\rangle, \langle B, G0111\rangle, \langle B, De\rangle, \langle D, De\rangle\}$.*

Suppose that $\mathcal{B} = N_0, N_1, N_2, \ldots$ is an open, fully expanded branch in a $Tab_K$-derivation. Let $N_\infty = \bigcup_{i \geqslant 0} N_i$ denote the formulae on the branch $\mathcal{B}$ and $\mathcal{T}_\mathcal{B}$ denote the set of all labels occurring in the branch $\mathcal{B}$, i.e., $\mathcal{T}_\mathcal{B} = \{s \mid s$ is a label denoting a world occurring in a tableau formula $N_\infty\}$.

The following two lemmas describe the effect of the application of the basic and propagation rules in the considered tableau systems. For Lemma 2, we did not repeat the statements for shared rules between systems.

**Lemma 1 (Basic Rule Application Lemma).**

(i) If $s : \neg\neg\phi \in N_\infty$ then $s : \phi \in N_\infty$.
(ii) If $s : \neg(\phi_1 \vee \ldots \vee \phi_l) \in N_\infty$ then $\{s : \sim\phi_1, \ldots, s : \sim\phi_l\} \subseteq N_\infty$.
(iii) If $s : \phi_1 \vee \ldots \vee \phi_l \in N_\infty$ then $s : \phi_k \in N_\infty$ for some $l$, $1 \leqslant k \leqslant l$.
(iv) If $s : \neg\Box\phi \in N_\infty$ then $\{R(s,z), z : \sim\phi\} \subseteq N_\infty$ for some $z$ such that $f_{\neg\Box\phi}(s) = z$.
(v) If $s : \Box\phi \in N_\infty$ and $R(s,t) \in N_\infty$ then $t : \phi \in N_\infty$.

**Lemma 2 (Rule Application for $Tab_S^{rf}$).**

(i) For $S = G0111$: 1) If $R(s,t)$ and $t : \Box\phi \in N_\infty$ then $R(s, g(s,t)) \in N_\infty$ and $g(s,t) : \phi \in N_\infty$. 2) If $R(s, g(s,t))$ and $g(s,t) : \Box\phi \in N_\infty$ then $R(t, g(s,t)) \in N_\infty$. 3) If $R(s,t)$ and $s : \Box\phi \in N_\infty$ then $R(t, g(s,t)) \in N_\infty$ and $g(s,t) : \phi \in N_\infty$. 4) If $R(t, g(s,t))$ and $g(s,t) : \Box\phi \in N_\infty$ then $R(s, g(s,t)) \in N_\infty$.

(ii) For $S = De$: 1) If $R(s,t) \in N_\infty$, $s : \Box\phi \in N_\infty$ and $t : \Box\psi \in N_\infty$ then $i(s,t) : \phi \in N_\infty$. 2) If $i(s,t) : \Box\phi \in N_\infty$ then $i(s,t) : \phi \in N_\infty$ and $t : \phi \in N_\infty$.

(iii) For $S = G$: If $R(s,t) \in N_\infty$ and $R(s,u) \in N_\infty$ then $R(t, h(s,t,u)) \in N_\infty$ and $R(u, h(s,t,u)) \in N_\infty$.

(iv) For $S = alt1, De$: 1) If $R(s,t) \in N_\infty$ and $t : \Box\phi \in N_\infty$ then $t : \phi \in N_\infty$. 2) If $R(s,t) \in N_\infty$ and $t : \neg\Box\phi \in N_\infty$, then $t : \sim\phi \in N_\infty$. 3) If $a : \neg\Box\phi \in N_\infty$, then $R(a, f(a)) \in N_\infty$ and $f(a) : \sim\phi \in N_\infty$.

(v) For $S = B, G0111$: If $R(s,t) \in N_\infty$ and $t : \Box\phi \in N_\infty$ then $s : \phi \in N_\infty$.

(vi) For $S = B, De$: If $i(s,t) : \psi \in N_\infty$ and $t : \Box\phi$ then $t : \phi \in N_\infty$.

(vii) For $S = D, De$: If $s : \Box\phi \in N_\infty$ then $s : \neg\Box\sim\phi \in N_\infty$.

**Definition 1 (The canonical model).** $\mathcal{I}(\mathcal{B})$ is defined as $(U^{\mathcal{I}(\mathcal{B})}, \cdot^{\mathcal{I}(\mathcal{B})})$ where $U^{\mathcal{I}(\mathcal{B})} = \mathcal{T}_\mathcal{B}$ and $\cdot^{\mathcal{I}(\mathcal{B})}$ is defined on primitive symbols by $s^{\mathcal{I}(\mathcal{B})} = s$ if $s \in \mathcal{T}_\mathcal{B}$, $p^{\mathcal{I}(\mathcal{B})} = \{s \mid s : p \in N_\infty\}$ and $R^{\mathcal{I}(\mathcal{B})} = \{(s,t) \mid R(s,t) \in N_\infty\}$.

Since we start the tableau construction by taking $N_0 = \{a : \phi\}$, there is at least one label in $U^{\mathcal{I}(\mathcal{B})}$. The following properties follow from the definition of the semantics in Sect. 2.

$$s \in (\neg\phi)^{\mathcal{I}(\mathcal{B})} \quad \text{iff} \quad s \in U^{\mathcal{I}(\mathcal{B})} \setminus \phi^{\mathcal{I}(\mathcal{B})}$$
$$s \in (\phi_1 \vee \ldots \vee \phi_k)^{\mathcal{I}(\mathcal{B})} \quad \text{iff} \quad s \in \phi_1^{\mathcal{I}(\mathcal{B})} \cup \ldots \cup \phi_k^{\mathcal{I}(\mathcal{B})}$$
$$s \in (\Box\phi)^{\mathcal{I}(\mathcal{B})} \quad \text{iff} \quad \text{for all } t \in U^{\mathcal{I}(\mathcal{B})}, \text{ if } (s,t) \in R^{\mathcal{I}(\mathcal{B})} \text{ then } t \in \phi^{\mathcal{I}(\mathcal{B})}$$

Since $\mathcal{I}(\mathcal{B})$ is not a $KS$ model, where $KS$ is the logic obtained by extending modal logic $K$ with S, we construct a model $\mathcal{J}(\mathcal{B})$ from $\mathcal{I}(\mathcal{B})$ that is a $KS$ model for each tableau formula on $\mathcal{B}$. In other words, we extend $\mathcal{I}(\mathcal{B})$ by specifying new links to get the appropriate $KS$ model. We define $\mathcal{J}(\mathcal{B}) - (U^{\mathcal{J}(\mathcal{B})}, \cdot^{\mathcal{J}(\mathcal{B})})$ where $U^{\mathcal{J}(\mathcal{B})} = \{s \mid s \in U^{\mathcal{I}(\mathcal{B})}\}$ and $\cdot^{\mathcal{J}(\mathcal{B})}$ is defined on labels by: $s^{\mathcal{J}(\mathcal{B})} = s^{\mathcal{I}(\mathcal{B})} = s$ and on propositional symbols by: $p^{\mathcal{J}(\mathcal{B})} = p^{\mathcal{I}(\mathcal{B})} = \{s \mid s : p \in N_\infty\}$. Further we define:

**For S = G0111:**$R^{\mathcal{J}(\mathcal{B})} = R^{\mathcal{I}(\mathcal{B})} \cup \{(s,s) \mid R(u,s) \in N_\infty \text{ and } s : \Box\phi \notin N_\infty\} \cup$
$\{(t, g(s,t)) \mid R(s, g(s,t)) \in N_\infty, s : \Box\phi \notin N_\infty \text{ and } g(s,t) : \Box\psi \notin N_\infty\} \cup$
$\{(s, g(s,t)) \mid R(t, g(s,t)) \in N_\infty, t : \Box\phi \notin N_\infty \text{ and } g(s,t) : \Box\psi \notin N_\infty\}$

**For S = De:**$R^{\mathcal{J}(\mathcal{B})} = R^{\mathcal{I}(\mathcal{B})} \cup \{(s,s) \mid s : \Box\phi \notin N_\infty \text{ or } s = i(x,y)\} \cup$
$\{(s, i(s,t)) \mid R(s,t) \in N_\infty, s : \Box\phi \in N_\infty, t : \Box\psi \in N_\infty\} \cup$
$\{(i(s,t), t) \mid R(s,t) \in N_\infty, s : \Box\phi \in N_\infty, t : \Box\psi \in N_\infty\}$

**For S = G:**$R^{\mathcal{J}(\mathcal{B})} = R^{\mathcal{I}(\mathcal{B})}$

**For S = alt1,De** $R^{\mathcal{J}(\mathcal{B})} = R^{\mathcal{I}(\mathcal{B})} \cup \{(t,t) \mid R(a,t) \in N_\infty\}$

For **S = B,G0111**: $R^{\mathcal{J}(\mathcal{B})} = R^{\mathcal{I}(\mathcal{B})} \cup \{(t,g(s,t)),(g(s,t),t) \mid$
$R(s,g(s,t)) \in N_\infty, t : \Box\phi \notin N_\infty$ and $g(s,t) : \Box\psi \notin N_\infty\} \cup$
$\{(s,g(s,t)),(g(s,t),s) \mid R(t,g(s,t)) \in N_\infty, s : \Box\phi \notin N_\infty$ and $g(s,t) : \Box\psi \notin$
$N_\infty\} \cup \{(s,s) \mid R(u,s) \in N_\infty$ and $s : \Box\phi \notin N_\infty\} \cup \{(t,s) \mid R(s,t) \in N_\infty\}$

For **S = B,De** $R^{\mathcal{J}(\mathcal{B})} = R^{\mathcal{I}(\mathcal{B})} \cup$
$\{(s,i(s,t)) \mid R(s,t) \in N_\infty, s : \Box\phi \in N_\infty$ and $t : \Box\psi \in N_\infty\} \cup$
$\{(s,s) \mid s : \Box\phi \notin N_\infty$ or $s = i(x,y)\} \cup \{(t,s) \mid R(s,t) \in N_\infty\} \cup$
$\{(i(s,t),t) \mid R(s,t) \in N_\infty, s : \Box\phi \in N_\infty$ and $t : \Box\psi \in N_\infty\} \cup$
$\{(i(s,t),s),(t,i(s,t))) \mid R(s,t) \in N_\infty, s : \Box\phi \in N_\infty, t : \Box\psi \in N_\infty\}$

For **S = D,De:** $R^{\mathcal{J}(\mathcal{B})} = R^{\mathcal{I}(\mathcal{B})} \cup \{(s,s) \mid s : \Box\phi \notin N_\infty$ or $s = i(x,y)\} \cup$
$\{(s,i(s,t)) \mid R(s,t) \in N_\infty, s : \Box\phi \in N_\infty$ and $t : \Box\psi \in N_\infty\} \cup$
$\{(i(s,t),t) \mid R(s,t) \in N_\infty, s : \Box\phi \in N_\infty$ and $t : \Box\psi \in N_\infty\}$

Note that the formulae $\Box\phi$ and $\Box\psi$ are arbitrary. It follows that

$s \in (\neg\phi)^{\mathcal{J}(\mathcal{B})}$ iff $s \in U^{\mathcal{J}(\mathcal{B})} \setminus \phi^{\mathcal{J}(\mathcal{B})}$

$s \in (\phi_1 \vee ... \vee \phi_k)^{\mathcal{J}(\mathcal{B})}$ iff $s \in \phi_1^{\mathcal{J}(\mathcal{B})} \cup ... \cup \phi_k^{\mathcal{J}(\mathcal{B})}$

$s \in (\Box\phi)^{\mathcal{J}(\mathcal{B})}$ iff for all $t \in U^{\mathcal{J}(\mathcal{B})}$, if $(s,t) \in R^{\mathcal{J}(\mathcal{B})}$ then $t \in \phi^{\mathcal{J}(\mathcal{B})}$

**Lemma 3 (Relational Link and Box Lemma for $Tab_S^{rf}$).**

(i) If $R(s,t) \in N_\infty$ then $(s,t) \in R^{\mathcal{J}(\mathcal{B})}$.
(ii) If $(s,t) \in R^{\mathcal{J}(\mathcal{B})}$ and $s : \Box\phi \in N_\infty$ then $t : \phi \in N_\infty$.

*Proof.* i) By definition of $R^{\mathcal{J}(\mathcal{B})}$. There are 7 cases, one for each tableau system.

ii) For $S = G0111$: If $(s,t) \in R^{\mathcal{J}(\mathcal{B})}$ and $s : \Box\phi \in N_\infty$, then $R(s,t) \in N_\infty$ or not. If the former, then by Lemma 1 for the ($\Box$)-rule, $t : \phi \in N_\infty$. If the latter, then if $R(s,t) \notin N_\infty$ and $R(t,s) \notin N_\infty$, then either $t = g(u,s)$ or $t = g(s,u)$. If we assume the former, then $R(u,s) \in N_\infty$ and by Lemma 2, $g(u,s) : \phi \in N_\infty$ and equivalently, $t : \phi \in N_\infty$, so the lemma holds. If we assume the latter, then $R(s,u) \in N_\infty$ and by Lemma 2, $g(s,u) : \phi \in N_\infty$ and equivalently, $t : \phi \in N_\infty$, so the lemma holds.

The proofs for the other cases can be found in the long version of this paper.

**Lemma 4 (Labelled Formula Lemma for $Tab_S^{rf}$).** If $s : \phi \in N_\infty$ then $s \in \phi^{\mathcal{J}(\mathcal{B})}$.

**Lemma 5 (Correspondence Property Lemma for $Tab_S^{rf}$).** *There are 7 cases, one for each value of $S$.*

(i) For $S = G0111$: If $(x,y) \in R^{\mathcal{J}(\mathcal{B})}$ then there exists $u$ such that $(x,u) \in R^{\mathcal{J}(\mathcal{B})}$ and $(y,u) \in R^{\mathcal{J}(\mathcal{B})}$.

(ii) For $S = De$: If $(s,t) \in R^{\mathcal{J}(\mathcal{B})}$, there exists $u$ such that $(s,u) \in R^{\mathcal{J}(\mathcal{B})}$ and $(u,t) \in R^{\mathcal{J}(\mathcal{B})}$.

(iii) For $S = G$: If $(s,t) \in R^{\mathcal{I}(\mathcal{B})}$ and $(s,u) \in R^{\mathcal{I}(\mathcal{B})}$, then there exists $v$ such that $(t,v) \in R^{\mathcal{I}(\mathcal{B})}$ and $(u,v) \in R^{\mathcal{I}(\mathcal{B})}$.

(iv) For $S = alt1, De$: 1) If $(s,t) \in R^{\mathcal{J}(\mathcal{B})}$ and $(s,u) \in R^{\mathcal{J}(\mathcal{B})}$ then $t = u$. 2) If $(s,t) \in R^{\mathcal{J}(\mathcal{B})}$, there exists $u$ such that $(s,u) \in R^{\mathcal{J}(\mathcal{B})}$ and $(u,t) \in R^{\mathcal{J}(\mathcal{B})}$.

(v) For $S = B, G0111$: 1) If $(s,t) \in R^{\mathcal{J}(\mathcal{B})}$ then $(t,s) \in R^{\mathcal{J}(\mathcal{B})}$. 2) If $(x,y) \in R^{\mathcal{J}(\mathcal{B})}$ then there exists $u$ such that $(x,u) \in R^{\mathcal{J}(\mathcal{B})}$ and $(y,u) \in R^{\mathcal{J}(\mathcal{B})}$.

(vi) For $S = B, De$: 1) If $(s,t) \in R^{\mathcal{J}(\mathcal{B})}$ then $(t,s) \in R^{\mathcal{J}(\mathcal{B})}$. 2) If $(s,t) \in R^{\mathcal{J}(\mathcal{B})}$, there exists $u$ such that $(s,u) \in R^{\mathcal{J}(\mathcal{B})}$ and $(u,t) \in R^{\mathcal{J}(\mathcal{B})}$.

(vii) For $S = D, De$: 1) If $s \in U^{\mathcal{J}(\mathcal{B})}$ then there exists $t$ such that $(s,t) \in R^{\mathcal{J}(\mathcal{B})}$. 2) If $(s,t) \in R^{\mathcal{J}(\mathcal{B})}$, there exists $u$ such that $(s,u) \in R^{\mathcal{J}(\mathcal{B})}$ and $(u,t) \in R^{\mathcal{J}(\mathcal{B})}$.

The Relational Link and the Box Lemma 3 [5] check that relational links between two labels on $\mathcal{B}$ also hold in $\mathcal{J}(\mathcal{B})$ and that formulae occurring under the $\Box$ operator in a world $s$ are propagated to all successor worlds as defined in the model $\mathcal{J}(\mathcal{B})$. The Labelled Formula Lemma 4 ensures formula satisfiability by proving that every labelled formula on $\mathcal{B}$ is true in the model $\mathcal{J}(\mathcal{B})$. The Correspondence Property Lemma 5 checks that the restriction(s) imposed on the accessibility relation for the associated logic of each tableau system are satisfied.

**Lemma 6.** $\mathcal{J}(\mathcal{B})$ *is a KS-model and each tableau formula on the branch $\mathcal{B}$ is true in $\mathcal{J}(\mathcal{B})$.*

*Proof.* By Lemmas 3, 4 and 5.

This completes the proof for Theorem 2.

# 7 Conclusion

In this paper, we presented refined systems for the logics $K$G0111, $K$G and $K$De. These logics are characterised by the requirement of creating witness worlds, which is difficult to capture using propagation rules. Our refined rules can be classed as almost propagation rules and they limit the addition of new labels. We also presented refined systems for the combined logics $K$alt1De, $K$BG0111 and $K$DDe. For $K$BG0111, two refined systems were presented. Soundness and completeness proofs were given for the proposed systems.

The logics we consider have the finite model property and terminating systems can be obtained for such logics by incorporating unrestricted blocking [33,36] to provide a basis for decision procedures. The results of [33,36] show that for sound and complete systems using structural rules, simply adding the unrestricted blocking rule ensures decidability. For our systems, formal proofs need to be given to show that adding unrestricted blocking bound on refined rules preserves soundness and completeness.

Further work includes applying the same ideas presented in this paper to develop refined tableau systems for extensions with generalised forms of the axioms we have considered. These include the logics $K$G0111$^\kappa$, $K$G$^\kappa$ and $K$De$^\kappa$ where $\kappa > 0$. More precisely, the axioms G0111$^\kappa$, G$^\kappa$ and De$^\kappa$ are respectively $\Diamond^\kappa \Box \phi \to \Diamond \phi$, $\Diamond^\kappa \Box \phi \to \Box \Diamond^\kappa \phi$ and $\Diamond \Diamond \phi \to \Diamond^\kappa \phi$. The modular nature of our framework can simplify the development and verification of such systems.

# References

1. Areces, C., de Rijke, M., de Nivelle, H.: Resolution in modal, description and hybrid logic. J. Log. Comput. **11**(5), 717–736 (2001). https://doi.org/10.1093/logcom/11.5.717
2. Beckert, B., Goré, R.: Free-variable tableaux for propositional modal logics. Studia Logica **69**(1), 59–96 (2001). http://www.jstor.org/stable/20016338
3. Blackburn, P., de Rijke, M., Venema, Y.: Modal Logic. Cambridge University Press (2001). https://doi.org/10.1017/CBO9781107050884
4. Brünnler, K.: Deep sequent systems for modal logic. In: Governatori, G., Hodkinson, I.M., Venema, Y. (eds.) Advances in Modal Logic 6, p. 107. College Publications (2006). http://www.aiml.net/volumes/volume6/Bruennler.ps
5. Castilho, M.A., del Cerro, L.F., Gasquet, O., Herzig, A.: Modal tableaux with propagation rules and structural rules. Fund. Inform. **32**, 281–297 (1997)
6. Cerro, L.F., Fauthoux, D., Gasquet, O., Herzig, A., Longin, D., Massacci, F.: Lotrec: the generic tableau prover for modal and description logics. In: Goré, R., Leitsch, A., Nipkow, T. (eds.) IJCAR 2001. LNCS, vol. 2083, pp. 453–458. Springer, Heidelberg (2001). https://doi.org/10.1007/3-540-45744-5_38
7. Chellas, B.F.: Modal Logic: An Introduction. Cambridge University Press, Cambridge (1980). https://doi.org/10.1017/CBO9780511621192
8. Ciabattoni, A., Lyon, T., Ramanayake, R., Tiu, A.: Display to labeled proofs and back again for tense logics. ACM Trans. Comput. Log. **22**(3), 1–31 (2021)
9. Cerro, L.F., Gasquet, O.: Tableaux based decision procedures for modal logics of confluence and density. Fund. Inform. **40**(4), 317–333 (1999)
10. Fitting, M.: Tableau methods of proof for modal logics. Notre Dame J. Formal Logic **13**(2), 237–247 (1972). https://doi.org/10.1305/ndjfl/1093894722
11. Fitting, M.: Proof methods for modal and intuitionistic logics. J. Symb. Log. **50**(3), 855–856 (1985). https://doi.org/10.2307/2274341
12. Fitting, M.: Prefixed tableaus and nested sequents. Ann. Pure Appl. Logic **163**(3), 291–313 (2012). https://doi.org/10.1016/j.apal.2011.09.004
13. Fitting, M.: Cut-free proof systems for Geach logics. IfCoLog J. Logics Appl. **2**(2) (2015). https://www.collegepublications.co.uk/downloads/ifcolog00004.pdf#page=27
14. Garson, J.: Modal Logic. In: Zalta, E.N., Nodelman, U. (eds.) The Stanford Encyclopedia of Philosophy. Metaphysics Research Lab, Stanford University (2024)
15. Gasquet, O., Herzig, A., Said, B., Schwarzentruber, F.: Kripke's Worlds: An Introduction to Modal Logics via Tableaux. Studies in Universal Logic, Birkhäuser (2014). https://doi.org/10.1007/978-3-7643-8504-0
16. Goré, R.: Tableau methods for modal and temporal logics. In: D'Agostino, M., Gabbay, D., Hähnle, R., Posegga, J. (eds.) Handbook of Tableau Methods, pp. 297–396. Kluwer (1999)
17. Hustadt, U., Schmidt, R.A.: MSPASS: modal reasoning by translation and first-order resolution. In: Dyckhoff, R. (ed.) TABLEAUX 2000. LNCS (LNAI), vol. 1847, pp. 67–71. Springer, Heidelberg (2000). https://doi.org/10.1007/10722086_7
18. Huth, M., Ryan, M.D.: Logic in Computer Science - Modelling and Reasoning About Systems. Cambridge University Press, Cambridge (2004)
19. Lemmon, E., Scott, D.: The Lemmon Notes: An Introduction to Modal Logic. Basil Blackwell (1977)
20. Lyon, T.S.: Nested sequents for intuitionistic modal logics via structural refinement. In: Das, A., Negri, S. (eds.) TABLEAUX 2021. LNCS (LNAI), vol. 12842, pp. 409–427. Springer, Cham (2021). https://doi.org/10.1007/978-3-030-86059-2_24

21. Lyon, T.S.: Refining labelled systems for modal and constructive logics with applications. Ph.D. thesis, Technische Universität Wien (2021). https://arxiv.org/abs/2107.14487
22. Marin, S., Morales, M., Straßburger, L.: A fully labelled proof system for intuitionistic modal logics. J. Log. Comput. **31**(3), 998–1022 (2021). https://doi.org/10.1093/logcom/exab020
23. Marin, S., Straßburger, L.: Proof theory for indexed nested sequents. In: Schmidt, R.A., Nalon, C. (eds.) TABLEAUX 2017. LNCS (LNAI), vol. 10501, pp. 81–97. Springer, Cham (2017). https://doi.org/10.1007/978-3-319-66902-1_5
24. Massacci, F.: Single step tableaux for modal logics. J. Autom. Reason. **24**, 319–364 (2000). https://doi.org/10.1023/A:1006155811656
25. Nalon, C., Hustadt, U., Dixon, C.: KSP: a resolution-based prover for multimodal K. In: Olivetti, N., Tiwari, A. (eds.) IJCAR 2016. LNCS (LNAI), vol. 9706, pp. 406–415. Springer, Cham (2016). https://doi.org/10.1007/978-3-319-40229-1_28
26. Nalon, C., Marcos, J., Dixon, C.: Clausal resolution for modal logics of confluence. In: Demri, S., Kapur, D., Weidenbach, C. (eds.) IJCAR 2014. LNCS (LNAI), vol. 8562, pp. 322–336. Springer, Cham (2014). https://doi.org/10.1007/978-3-319-08587-6_24
27. Negri, S.: Proof analysis in modal logic. J. Philos. Logic **34**(5/6), 507–544 (2005). http://www.jstor.org/stable/30226848
28. Poggiolesi, F.: The method of tree-hypersequents for modal propositional logic. In: Makinson, D., Malinowski, J., Wansing, H. (eds.) Towards Mathematical Philosophy. TL, vol. 28, pp. 31–51. Springer, Dordrecht (2009). https://doi.org/10.1007/978-1-4020-9084-4_3
29. Ramanayake, R.: Inducing syntactic cut-elimination for indexed nested sequents. Log. Methods Comput. Sci. **14** (2018). https://doi.org/10.23638/lmcs-14(4:18)2018
30. Sahlqvist, H.: Completeness and correspondence in the first and second order semantics for modal logic. In: Studies in Logic and the Foundations of Mathematics, vol. 82, pp. 110–143. Elsevier (1975)
31. Salhi, Y., Sioutis, M.: A resolution method for modal logic S5. In: Gottlob, G., Sutcliffe, G., Voronkov, A. (eds.) GCAI 2015. Global Conference on Artificial Intelligence. EPiC Series in Computing, vol. 36, pp. 252–262. EasyChair (2015). https://doi.org/10.29007/1zgr
32. Schmidt, R.A., Hustadt, U.: The axiomatic translation principle for modal logic. ACM Trans. Comput. Log. **8**(4), 1–55 (2007). https://doi.org/10.1145/1276920.1276921
33. Schmidt, R.A., Tishkovsky, D.: A general tableau method for deciding description logics, modal logics and related first-order fragments. In: Armando, A., Baumgartner, P., Dowek, G. (eds.) IJCAR 2008. LNCS (LNAI), vol. 5195, pp. 194–209. Springer, Heidelberg (2008). https://doi.org/10.1007/978-3-540-71070-7_17
34. Schmidt, R.A., Tishkovsky, D.: Automated synthesis of tableau calculi. In: Giese, M., Waaler, A. (eds.) TABLEAUX 2009. LNCS (LNAI), vol. 5607, pp. 310–324. Springer, Heidelberg (2009). https://doi.org/10.1007/978-3-642-02716-1_23
35. Schmidt, R.A., Waldmann, U.: Modal tableau systems with blocking and congruence closure. In: De Nivelle, H. (ed.) TABLEAUX 2015. LNCS (LNAI), vol. 9323, pp. 38–53. Springer, Cham (2015). https://doi.org/10.1007/978-3-319-24312-2_4
36. Schmidt, R.A., Stell, J.G., Rydeheard, D.E.: Axiomatic and tableau-based reasoning for Kt(H, R). In: Goré, R., Kooi, B.P., Kurucz, A. (eds.) Advances in Modal Logic 10, pp. 478–497. College Publications (2014)

37. Smullyan, R.M.: First-Order Logic. Springer (1968)
38. Tiu, A., Ianovski, E., Goré, R.: Grammar logics in nested sequent calculus: proof theory and decision procedures. In: Bolander, T., Braüner, T., Ghilardi, S., Moss, L.S. (eds.) Advances in Modal Logic 9, pp. 516–537. College Publications (2012). http://www.aiml.net/volumes/volume9/Tiu-Ianovski-Gore.pdf
39. Viganò, L.: Labelled Non-Classical Logics. Kluwer (2000). https://doi.org/10.1007/978-1-4757-3208-5
40. Weidenbach, C., Schmidt, R.A., Hillenbrand, T., Rusev, R., Topic, D.: System description: SPASS version 3.0. In: Pfenning, F. (ed.) CADE 2007. LNCS (LNAI), vol. 4603, pp. 514–520. Springer, Heidelberg (2007). https://doi.org/10.1007/978-3-540-73595-3_38

**Open Access** This chapter is licensed under the terms of the Creative Commons Attribution 4.0 International License (http://creativecommons.org/licenses/by/4.0/), which permits use, sharing, adaptation, distribution and reproduction in any medium or format, as long as you give appropriate credit to the original author(s) and the source, provide a link to the Creative Commons license and indicate if changes were made.

The images or other third party material in this chapter are included in the chapter's Creative Commons license, unless indicated otherwise in a credit line to the material. If material is not included in the chapter's Creative Commons license and your intended use is not permitted by statutory regulation or exceeds the permitted use, you will need to obtain permission directly from the copyright holder.

# The Modal Cube Revisited: Semantics Without Worlds

Renato Leme[1], Carlos Olarte[2], Elaine Pimentel[3(✉)], and Marcelo Esteban Coniglio[1]

[1] Centre for Logic, Epistemology and the History of Science, UNICAMP, Campinas, Brazil
rntreisleme@gmail.com, coniglio@unicamp.br
[2] LIPN, CNRS UMR 7030, Université Sorbonne Paris Nord, Villetaneuse, France
olarte@lipn.univ-paris13.fr
[3] Department of Computer Science, University College London, London, UK
e.pimentel@ucl.ac.uk

**Abstract.** We present a non-deterministic semantic framework for all modal logics in the modal cube, extending prior works by Kearns and others. Our approach introduces modular and uniform multi-valued non-deterministic matrices (Nmatrices) for each logic, where necessitation is captured by the systematic use of level valuations. The semantics is grounded in an eight-valued system and provides a sound and complete decision procedure for each modal logic, extending and refining earlier semantics as particular cases. Additionally, we propose a novel model-theoretic perspective that links our framework to relational (Kripke-style) semantics, addressing longstanding questions regarding the correspondence between modal axioms and semantic conditions in non-deterministic settings. This yields a philosophically robust and technically modular alternative to traditional possible-world semantics.

**Keywords:** Modal logics semantics · Non deterministic matrices

## 1 Introduction

Modal logics are built on top of propositional classical logic (CL) by introducing the modal operators $\Box$ and $\Diamond$, which, under the alethic interpretation, correspond to *necessary* and *possible*, respectively. Thus from a propositional formula $\alpha$, which in CL has value either false (**F**) or true (**T**), one can construct the statements *necessarily* $\alpha$ and *possibly* $\alpha$, denoted by $\Box\alpha$ and $\Diamond\alpha$, respectively.

When interpreting these formulas in Kripke semantics, modalities *qualify* the notion of truth, which now depends on the world in which $\alpha$ is being evaluated. Kripke's concept of *possible worlds* thus provides an elegant framework for capturing the possible values of propositions across different worlds. This natural generalization of the straightforward truth table semantics of CL makes it an ideal foundation for the semantics of modal logics.

A natural question that arises is whether one could define a single finite-valued truth table capable of capturing modal logics. The answer is negative. As early as the 1930s, Gödel [10] proved that intuitionistic logic admits no finite-valued truth-functional semantics and, since it can be faithfully embedded in the modal logic S4, this implies that S4 itself is not finite-valued. In 1940, Dugundji extended this result to the entire modal cube [8] and this largely halted the study of truth tables for modal logics[1].

In an effort to circumvent Dugundji's result–and as a compelling alternative to Kripke semantics–Kearns [13] and Ivlev [12] independently developed frameworks for characterizing certain modal systems[2]. Kearns used four-valued multivalued truth-functions[3], and introduced a constraint on valuations known as *level-valuations* to characterize the modal systems KT, S4, and S5. The idea is that the level-0 corresponds to the standard distribution of truth values (just following the corresponding matrix), while higher levels filter out valuations that violate the necessitation rule, preserving only those that assign the designated truth value to tautologies. Validity is therefore defined as the (infinite) intersection of all level valuations, corresponding to the closure w.r.t. necessitation. This layered structure gives to necessity a *global interpretation*.

Kearns' (and Ivlev's) contributions remained largely overlooked and relatively obscure until they were independently revisited in two separate lines of research. In [4], Coniglio, Fariñas del Cerro, and Peron reconstructed and extended these earlier results, proposing a characterization of the systems KB using four-valued Nmatrices with level-valuations. They also introduced six-valued Nmatrices for a range of modal systems, including KT, S4, S5, KD, KDB, KD4, and KD45. Around the same time, Omori and Skurt, in [24], also began by revisiting Kearns-Ivlev's original framework, and proposed an extension using eight truth values capable of capturing the modal logic K and six truth values for KTB. While there is a considerable conceptual overlap between [4] and [24], the two works were developed independently.

Although conceptually interesting, these works have limited practical applicability, as determining level-valuations requires accounting for the valuations of *all* tautologies across *all* levels. This requires a twofold infinite testing: on formulas *and* levels.

This situation remained unchanged until the work of Grätz [11], whose key contribution was the introduction of a *decision procedure* for Nmatrices that is both sound and complete w.r.t. Kearns' semantics. This breakthrough renewed the attention to an otherwise underexplored area, ultimately leading to the

---

[1] Most recently, in [11] Grätz sealed the fate of this line of inquiry by showing that even non-deterministic finite truth tables are insufficient.

[2] Ivlev proposed semantics for a range of non-normal modal systems lacking the necessitation rule–representing weaker versions of KT and S5 (later extended in, *e.g.*, [5,21,22]). In this work, we will focus on the extension of Kearn's work to the (normal) modal cube. A related approach can be found in [6] and [7].

[3] The notion of multivalued truth-functions was later formalized by Avron and Lev under the term *Nmatrices* [2]. See also [3].

extension of the methods of Kearns and Grätz to a broader class of logics[4]. For instance, [15] presents a semantic characterization of propositional intuitionistic logic (IPL) using a three-valued non-deterministic matrix with a restricted set of valuations, enabling a remarkably simple decision procedure for IPL.

This work follows this path by providing a decision procedure based on multi-valued non-deterministic matrices for *all logics* in the modal cube. In particular, our approach focuses on the following key aspects.

**Modularity.** The results in [4,5,24] share a common limitation: a lack of modularity. These works aim to "explain" or "refine" Kearns' original approach, not addressing the fundamental challenge of uniformly extending it. In fact, different systems use different sets of truth-values, often diverging significantly from standard choices. An alternative axiomatization was proposed by Pawlowski and la Rosa [20], resulting in a modular rule of necessitation to KT, KTB, S4, and S5 (and some non-normal modal logics).

In contrast, our work adopts a fundamentally different approach: we begin (Sect. 3) with a uniform set of eight truth values and systematically develop level-valuations for *all* logics in the modal cube. We demonstrate that, under certain modal axioms, some of these truth values are eliminated, thereby recovering many of the semantics proposed in the *op. cit.* works. Our definitions are guided by a *modal characterization* of the truth values, which enables modular procedures for proving soundness and completeness of the semantics, thus unifying and generalizing existing systems in the literature. Notably, this generalization allowed for new level-semantics for K4, K5, K45, KD4, KD5 and KB5.

**Decision Procedure.** We propose new Nmatrix-based decision procedures for all 15 normal modal logics in the modal cube (Sect. 4). This is achieved uniformly through the modal characterization of truth values. In doing so, we extend Grätz's work on KT and S4 to the entire cube, thereby completing the picture for this family of logics. These results highlight the potential of this alternative semantic framework.

**Modal Semantics without Possible Worlds?** Kearns concludes his paper with the following striking statement [13, p. 86]:

> "The present semantic account [...] is simpler than the standard account in virtue of having dispensed with possible worlds and their relations. I also think that my account is philosophically preferable to the standard account for having done this. For I do not think there are such things as possible worlds, or even that they constitute a useful fiction."

Unfortunately, the price of rejecting possible worlds may seem steep: one must contend with multi-valued truth values, non-deterministic matrices, and–prior to the development of decision procedures–at least two levels of valuations. As a final contribution, we reestablish the connection with Kripke semantics

---

[4] In [14], Lahav and Zohar proved semantic analyticity of Kearns' semantics, thus providing an alternative decidability proof to Grätz's proof for K and KT.

by linking matrix filters to Kripke models, thus providing a more "ecumenical" perspective where the two semantics can coexist. We thus settle a longstanding reflection posed by Omori and Skurt [24, p.27]:

> "One of the virtues of Kripkean semantics is the correspondence between axioms and the accessibility relations of the Kripke frame [...] But a glance at the [Kearnsean] semantics for the systems [...] introduced here reveals that *if there is a correspondence it is not a simple one.*"

## 2 Preliminaries

In what follows, $\mathcal{F}$ is the set of well-formed formulas in a propositional classical language, $\wp(\mathcal{F})$ is the powerset of $\mathcal{F}$, $\alpha, \beta$ (resp. $\Delta, \Gamma, \Lambda$) range over elements of $\mathcal{F}$ (resp. $\wp(\mathcal{F})$), and $\mathcal{L}$ is a Tarskian propositional logic, that is, a pair $(\mathcal{F}, \vdash^{\mathcal{L}})$ where $\vdash^{\mathcal{L}}$ is a consistent Tarskian consequence relation. We say that $\Delta$ is a *consistent set* in $\mathcal{L}$ if there is no formula $\alpha$ such that $\Delta \vdash^{\mathcal{L}} \alpha$ and $\Delta \vdash^{\mathcal{L}} \neg \alpha$. $\Delta$ is *maximally consistent* if it is consistent and $\Delta \cup \{\beta\}$ is inconsistent for all $\beta \in \mathcal{F} \backslash \Delta$. A maximally consistent set $\Delta$ is $\alpha$-*saturated* iff $\Delta \not\vdash^{\mathcal{L}} \alpha$. For any Tarskian logic $\mathcal{L}$, if $\Gamma \not\vdash^{\mathcal{L}} \alpha$, then there is some $\alpha$-saturated set $\Delta$ such that $\Gamma \subseteq \Delta$ (see *e.g.* [25]).

The principle of compositionality states that the truth-value of a formula is fully determined by the truth-values of its subformulas. In the presence of incomplete or uncertain information, this principle is relaxed using non-deterministic matrices (Nmatrices) [2,3], which allows the truth-value of a formula to be selected from a set of possible values (rather than from a single one).

**Definition 1 (Nmatrix).** *An* Nmatrix *for $\mathcal{L}$ is a tuple $\mathcal{M} = \langle \mathcal{V}, \mathcal{D}, \mathcal{O} \rangle$, where:*

- *$\mathcal{V}$ is a non-empty set of truth values.*
- *$\mathcal{D}$ (designated truth values) is a non-empty proper subset of $\mathcal{V}$.*
- *For every n-ary connective $\circledcirc$ in $\mathcal{L}$, $\mathcal{O}$ includes a non-deterministic truth-function $\tilde{\circledcirc} : \mathcal{V}^n \to \wp(\mathcal{V}) \backslash \varnothing$.*

**Definition 2 (Valuation).** *Let $\mathcal{M} = \langle \mathcal{V}, \mathcal{D}, \mathcal{O} \rangle$ be an Nmatrix and $\Lambda \subseteq \mathcal{F}$ closed under subformulas. A partial valuation in $\mathcal{M}$ is a function $v : \Lambda \to \mathcal{V}$ such that, for each n-ary connective $\circledcirc$ in $\mathcal{L}$, the following holds for all $\alpha_0, \ldots, \alpha_n \in \Lambda$: $v(\circledcirc(\alpha_0, \ldots, \alpha_n)) \in \tilde{\circledcirc}(v(\alpha_0), \ldots, v(\alpha_n))$. A partial valuation in $\mathcal{M}$ is a (total) valuation if its domain is $\mathcal{F}$. We denote by $[\mathcal{F} \to \mathcal{V}]_\mathcal{M}$ the set $\{v : \mathcal{F} \to \mathcal{V} \mid v \text{ is a valuation in } \mathcal{M}\}$.*

The syntax of the modal logics considered here is given by the grammar

$$\alpha ::= p \mid \bot \mid \alpha \to \alpha \mid \Box \alpha$$

where $p \in \mathsf{At}$, the set of propositional variable symbols. The other usual connectives for possibility $\Diamond$, conjunction $\wedge$, disjunction $\vee$ and negation $\neg$ are defined as abbreviations, *e.g.* $\neg \alpha$ and $\Diamond \alpha$ abbreviate $\alpha \to \bot$ and $\neg \Box \neg \alpha$, respectively.

The basic modal logic K is obtained by extending the ordinary Hilbert axioms for propositional classical logic with the modal axiom k, along with the rules of necessitation and modus ponens:

$$k : \Box(\alpha \to \beta) \to (\Box\alpha \to \Box\beta) \qquad \frac{\alpha \to \beta \quad \alpha}{\beta} \text{ mp} \qquad \frac{\alpha}{\Box\alpha} \text{ nec}$$

The *modal cube* is formed by extending K with any non-redundant combination of axioms d, t, b, 4 and 5. Such axioms characterize the usual frame conditions in the relational semantics.

$d : \Box\alpha \to \Diamond\alpha$    Seriality
$t : \Box\alpha \to \alpha$    Reflexivity
$b : \alpha \to \Box\Diamond\alpha$    Symmetry
$4 : \Box\alpha \to \Box\Box\alpha$    Transitivity
$5 : \Diamond\alpha \to \Box\Diamond\alpha$    Euclidianness

**Notation 1.** *We use the shorthands below to identify some sets of logics:*

K⋆ = {K, KB, K4, K5, K45}    KD⋆ = {KD, KDB, KD4, KD5, KD45}
KT⋆ = {KT, KTB, KT4, KTB45}    KB45 = {KB45}

*Observe that* KT4 = S4, KTB45 = S5 *and* KB45 = KB5. *In the forthcoming sections,* $\mathcal{L}$ *always ranges over one of these fifteen normal modal logics.*

## 3 Level Valuations for the Modal Cube

As already mentioned in the Introduction, Nmatrices do not capture the behavior of the necessitation rule. Kearns addressed this issue by restricting the set of valuations using *levels*: if a formula $\alpha$ receives a designated value with respect to all possible valuations–that is, if it is a tautology at a certain level–then $\Box\alpha$ will also receive a designated value, being a tautology at the next level. In other words, all valuations $v$ such that $v(\Box\alpha) \notin \mathcal{D}$, and $\alpha$ is a tautology, are eliminated from the set of acceptable valuations.

This section introduces the notion of level-valuation semantics for all the logics in the modal cube in a modular way. We begin by presenting the 8-valued non-deterministic semantics for the logic K which is inspired by, but different from, the version presented in [24] (Sect. 3.1). Truth values are given a *modal characterization*, and we show that some of these values are eliminated in the semantics of certain extensions of K. We then construct Nmatrices for all the logics in the modal cube and prove that the semantics is sound with respect to each logic (Sect. 3.2). Finally, we establish completeness by systematically defining *characteristic functions* directly from the meanings of the values (Sect. 3.3).

## 3.1 About Truth Values and Their Meaning

There are eight ways to "qualify" the truth of a formula $\alpha$: it can be {true, necessary, possible} or not. These combinations are shown in Table 1a, giving rise to the eight truth-values considered in this work: $\mathcal{V} = \{\mathbf{F}, \mathbf{f}, \mathbf{f_1}, \mathbf{f_2}, \mathbf{t_2}, \mathbf{t_1}, \mathbf{t}, \mathbf{T}\}$.

For example, if a formula $\alpha$ has value $\mathbf{F}$, this means that $\alpha$ is impossible: it is neither valid, nor necessary, nor possible. In other words, not only $\alpha$ does not hold ($\neg\alpha$), but its negation is both possible ($\Diamond\neg\alpha$) and necessary ($\Box\neg\alpha$).

This intuitive interpretation will be made precise in Sect. 3.3, but for now, we proceed by developing the concepts guided by this intuition.

**Definition 3 (Value func.).** *Let $\iota \in \mathcal{V}$. The value function $\iota : \mathcal{F} \to \mathcal{F}$ maps each $\alpha \in \mathcal{F}$ to the formula in the second column of Table 1a.*

**Table 1.** Truth-values and distinguished sets

| Truth-value | Intuitive meaning |
|---|---|
| $v(\alpha) = \mathbf{F}$ | $\Diamond\neg\alpha \land \neg\alpha \land \Box\neg\alpha$ |
| $v(\alpha) = \mathbf{f}$ | $\Diamond\neg\alpha \land \neg\alpha \land \Diamond\alpha$ |
| $v(\alpha) = \mathbf{f_1}$ | $\Box\alpha \land \neg\alpha \land \Box\neg\alpha$ |
| $v(\alpha) = \mathbf{f_2}$ | $\Box\alpha \land \neg\alpha \land \Diamond\alpha$ |
| $v(\alpha) = \mathbf{t_2}$ | $\Diamond\neg\alpha \land \alpha \land \Box\neg\alpha$ |
| $v(\alpha) = \mathbf{t_1}$ | $\Box\alpha \land \alpha \land \Box\neg\alpha$ |
| $v(\alpha) = \mathbf{t}$ | $\Diamond\neg\alpha \land \alpha \land \Diamond\alpha$ |
| $v(\alpha) = \mathbf{T}$ | $\Box\alpha \land \alpha \land \Diamond\alpha$ |

(a) Values and *modal characterization*

| Distinguished sets | Main feature |
|---|---|
| $\mathcal{D} = \{\mathbf{T}, \mathbf{t}, \mathbf{t_1}, \mathbf{t_2}\}$ | $\alpha$ is true |
| $\mathcal{D}^\complement = \{\mathbf{F}, \mathbf{f}, \mathbf{f_1}, \mathbf{f_2}\}$ | $\neg\alpha$ is true |
| $\mathcal{N} = \{\mathbf{T}, \mathbf{t_1}, \mathbf{f_2}, \mathbf{f_1}\}$ | $\alpha$ is necessary |
| $\mathcal{I} = \{\mathbf{F}, \mathbf{f_1}, \mathbf{t_2}, \mathbf{t_1}\}$ | $\neg\alpha$ is necessary |
| $\mathcal{P} = \{\mathbf{T}, \mathbf{t}, \mathbf{f_2}, \mathbf{f}\}$ | $\alpha$ is possible |
| $\mathcal{PN} = \{\mathbf{F}, \mathbf{f}, \mathbf{t_2}, \mathbf{t}\}$ | $\neg\alpha$ is possible |

(b) Distinguished sets

Table 1b classifies the truth-values according to the necessity or possibility of $\alpha$ or $\neg\alpha$. For instance, $\mathbf{t}(\alpha) = \Diamond\neg\alpha \land \alpha \land \Diamond\alpha$ and hence this value is in the sets $\mathcal{D}$ (designated), $\mathcal{P}$ ($\alpha$ is possible) and $\mathcal{PN}$ ($\neg\alpha$ is possible). It is worth noticing that the values $\mathbf{t_1}$ and $\mathbf{f_1}$ are, at the same time, necessary ($\mathcal{N}$) and impossible ($\mathcal{I}$). As we will see in Sect. 4.1, these represent, in our relational model, valuations with no successor states, in which both $\Box\alpha$ and $\Box\neg\alpha$ hold trivially.

Next, we show that the intuitive meaning of values is well defined: a consistent set cannot prove both $\iota(\alpha)$ and $\kappa(\alpha)$ for two different truth-values $\iota$ and $\kappa$. Moreover, we show that the truth values $\mathbf{t_1}, \mathbf{f_1}$ are *stable* in the sense that, if they appear in a valuation, then the entire valuation (*i.e.*, the corresponding row in the Nmatrix) is composed solely of these values.

**Lemma 1 (Consistency on Values).** *Let $\mathcal{L}$ be a modal logic, $\iota$ and $\kappa$ be two different truth-values, $\alpha, \beta$ be formulas, and $\Delta$ be a consistent set in $\mathcal{L}$. Then*

1. *if $\Delta \vdash^\mathcal{L} \iota(\alpha)$ then $\Delta \not\vdash^\mathcal{L} \kappa(\alpha)$; and*
2. *if $\iota \in \{\mathbf{t_1}, \mathbf{f_1}\}$, $\Delta \vdash^\mathcal{L} \iota(\alpha)$ and $\Delta \vdash^\mathcal{L} \kappa(\beta)$ then $\kappa \in \{\mathbf{t_1}, \mathbf{f_1}\}$.*

*Proof* (1) follows from the consistency of $\Delta$ and the fact that $\iota(\alpha)$ and $\kappa(\alpha)$ each contain a subformula that contradicts the other. *E.g.* if $\iota = \mathbf{F}$ and $\kappa = \mathbf{f}$, it cannot be the case that both $\Delta \vdash^{\mathcal{L}} \Box\neg\alpha$ and $\Delta \vdash^{\mathcal{L}} \Diamond\alpha$ hold.
For (2), first note that $(\Box\neg\alpha \wedge \Box\alpha) \to \Box\bot$ is an instance of axiom k and that $(\Diamond\alpha \to \Box\beta) \to \Box(\alpha \to \beta)$ is a K-tautology for any $\alpha, \beta$.
Suppose that $\iota \in \{\mathbf{t_1}, \mathbf{f_1}\}$ and $\Delta \vdash^{\mathcal{L}} \iota(\alpha)$. Thus $\Delta \vdash^{\mathcal{L}} \Box\neg\alpha \wedge \Box\alpha$ and hence $\Delta \vdash^{\mathcal{L}} \Box\bot$. Assume now that $\Delta \vdash^{\mathcal{L}} \kappa(\beta)$ with $\kappa \notin \{\mathbf{t_1}, \mathbf{f_1}\}$. Hence, it must be the case that $\Delta \vdash^{\mathcal{L}} \beta'$ where $\beta' \in \{\Diamond\beta, \Diamond\neg\beta\}$. Suppose $\beta' = \Diamond\beta \equiv \neg\Box\neg\beta$. Since $\Delta \vdash^{\mathcal{L}} (\Diamond\beta \to \Box\bot) \to \Box(\beta \to \bot)$, by mp we have $\Delta \vdash^{\mathcal{L}} \Box\neg\beta$, which is a contradiction. The case where $\beta' = \Diamond\neg\beta$ is similar. □

### 3.2 Matrices and Level Semantics

Before introducing the Nmatrices for all the logics in the modal cube, it is important to note that not all eight truth values are required for every logic. The set of values used depends on the specific axioms that characterize each system. For example, consider the axiom $\mathsf{T} = \Box\alpha \to \alpha$. This axiom rules out certain combinations of truth values: specifically, any valuation that assigns to formulas

**Table 2.** Multifunctions for all the logics in the modal cube.

| $\alpha \tilde{\to} \beta$ | F | f | $f_1$ | $f_2$ | $t_2$ | $t_1$ | t | T |
|---|---|---|---|---|---|---|---|---|
| F | {T} | {T} | {T} | {T} | {T} | {T} | {T} | {T} |
| f | {t} | {T,t} | {$t_1$} | {T} | {t} | {T} | {T,t} | {T} |
| $f_1$ | {$t_2$} | {t} | {$t_1$} | {T} | {$t_2$} | {$t_1$} | {t} | {T} |
| $f_2$ | {$t_2$} | {t} | {$t_1$} | {T} | {$t_2$} | {$t_1$} | {t} | {T} |
| $t_2$ | {$f_2$} | {$f_2$} | {$f_2$} | {$f_2$} | {T} | {T} | {T} | {T} |
| $t_1$ | {F} | {f} | {$f_1$} | {$f_2$} | {$t_2$} | {$t_1$} | {$t_2$} | {T} |
| t | {f} | {f,$f_2$} | {$f_2$} | {$f_2$} | {t} | {T} | {T,t} | {T} |
| T | {F} | {f} | {$f_1$} | {$f_2$} | {$t_2$} | {$t_1$} | {t} | {T} |

$\tilde{\bot}\{\mathbf{F}, \mathbf{f_1}\}$

(a) $\tilde{\bot}$ and $\tilde{\to}$ for all the families, where $\alpha/\beta$-values are the rows/columns.

| $\alpha$ | $\tilde{\Box}^{\mathsf{K}}\alpha$ | $\tilde{\Box}^{\mathsf{KB}}\alpha$ | $\tilde{\Box}^{\mathsf{K4}}\alpha$ | $\tilde{\Box}^{\mathsf{K5}}\alpha$ | $\tilde{\Box}^{\mathsf{K45}}\alpha$ |
|---|---|---|---|---|---|
| F | {F,f,$f_2$} | {F} | {F,f,$f_2$} | {F} | {F} |
| f | {F,f,$f_2$} | {F} | {F,f,$f_2$} | {F} | {F} |
| $f_1$ | {$t_1$} | {$t_1$} | {$t_1$} | {$t_1$} | {$t_1$} |
| $f_2$ | {T,t,$t_2$} | {$t_2$} | {T} | {T,$t_2$} | {T} |
| $t_2$ | {F,f,$f_2$} | {F,f,$f_2$} | {F,f,$f_2$} | {F} | {F} |
| $t_1$ | {$t_1$} | {$t_1$} | {$t_1$} | {$t_1$} | {$t_1$} |
| t | {F,f,$f_2$} | {F,f,$f_2$} | {F,f,$f_2$} | {F} | {F} |
| T | {T,t,$t_2$} | {T,t,$t_2$} | {T} | {T,$t_2$} | {T} |

(b) $\tilde{\Box}$ for family K⋆

| $\alpha$ | $\tilde{\Box}^{\mathsf{KB45}}\alpha$ |
|---|---|
| F | {F} |
| f | {F} |
| $f_1$ | {$t_1$} |
| $t_1$ | {$t_1$} |
| t | {F} |
| T | {T} |

(c) $\tilde{\Box}$ for family KB45

| $\alpha$ | $\tilde{\Box}^{\mathsf{KD}}\alpha$ | $\tilde{\Box}^{\mathsf{KDB}}\alpha$ | $\tilde{\Box}^{\mathsf{KD4}}\alpha$ | $\tilde{\Box}^{\mathsf{KD5}}\alpha$ | $\tilde{\Box}^{\mathsf{KD45}}\alpha$ |
|---|---|---|---|---|---|
| F | {F,f,$f_2$} | {F} | {F} | {F} | {F} |
| f | {F,f,$f_2$} | {F} | {F,f,$f_2$} | {F} | {F} |
| $f_2$ | {T,t,$t_2$} | {$t_2$} | {T} | {T,$t_2$} | {T} |
| $t_2$ | {F,f,$f_2$} | {F,f,$f_2$} | {F} | {F} | {F} |
| t | {F,f,$f_2$} | {F,f,$f_2$} | {F,f,$f_2$} | {F} | {F} |
| T | {T,t,$t_2$} | {T,t,$t_2$} | {T} | {T,$t_2$} | {T} |

(d) $\tilde{\Box}$ for family KD⋆

| $\alpha$ | $\tilde{\Box}^{\mathsf{KT}}\alpha$ | $\tilde{\Box}^{\mathsf{KTB}}\alpha$ | $\tilde{\Box}^{\mathsf{KT4}}\alpha$ | $\tilde{\Box}^{\mathsf{KTB45}}\alpha$ |
|---|---|---|---|---|
| F | {F} | {F} | {F} | {F} |
| f | {F,f} | {F} | {F,f} | {F} |
| t | {F,f} | {F,f} | {F,f} | {F} |
| T | {T,t} | {T,t} | {T} | {T} |

(e) $\tilde{\Box}$ for family KT⋆

the values $\mathbf{f_1}$, $\mathbf{f_2}$, $\mathbf{t_1}$ or $\mathbf{t_2}$ would violate the axiom by allowing both $\Box\alpha$ and $\neg\alpha$ to hold simultaneously. Thus, such valuations render the axiom unsound. As a result, these four values cannot appear in any model of the logic KT or its extensions, and the semantics effectively collapses to the four-valued framework proposed by Kearns in [13]. Similarly, the axiom $\mathsf{D} = \Box\alpha \to \Diamond\alpha$ excludes the values $\mathbf{f_1}$ and $\mathbf{t_1}$ from the logic KD, since $\Box\alpha$ and $\Box\neg\alpha$ cannot both hold. This restriction gives rise to the six-valued semantics presented in [4].

Accordingly, each family of logics introduced in Notation 1 corresponds to a distinct subset of truth values, as detailed next.

**Definition 4 (Nmatrices for the modal cube).** *The set of admissible truth-values for each family of logics is as follows:*

$$\mathcal{V}(\mathsf{K}\star) = \{\mathbf{F},\mathbf{f},\mathbf{f_1},\mathbf{f_2},\mathbf{t_2},\mathbf{t_1},\mathbf{t},\mathbf{T}\} \quad \mathcal{V}(\mathsf{KB45}) = \{\mathbf{F},\mathbf{f},\mathbf{f_1},\mathbf{t_1},\mathbf{t},\mathbf{T}\}$$
$$\mathcal{V}(\mathsf{KD}\star) = \{\mathbf{F},\mathbf{f},\mathbf{f_2},\mathbf{t_2},\mathbf{t},\mathbf{T}\} \quad \mathcal{V}(\mathsf{KT}\star) = \{\mathbf{F},\mathbf{f},\mathbf{t},\mathbf{T}\}$$

*The set of values for a logic $\mathcal{L}$ in the family* L, *denoted $\mathcal{V}(\mathcal{L})$, is $\mathcal{V}(\mathsf{L})$; the set of designated values of $\mathcal{L}$, denoted $\mathcal{D}(\mathcal{L})$, is $\mathcal{D}(\mathcal{L}) = \mathcal{V}(\mathsf{L}) \cap \mathcal{D}$; and the corresponding set of non-designated values, denoted $\mathcal{D}^\complement(\mathcal{L})$, is $\mathcal{D}^\complement(\mathcal{L}) = \mathcal{V}(\mathsf{L}) \cap \mathcal{D}^\complement$. The Nmatrix $\mathcal{M}$ associated to $\mathcal{L}$ is determined by its set of values $\mathcal{V}(\mathcal{L})$, its designated values $\mathcal{D}(\mathcal{L})$, the non-deterministic functions for $\to$ (restricted to the domain $\mathcal{V}(\mathcal{L})$) and $\bot$ in Table 2a, and the appropriate non-deterministic function for $\Box$ in Table 2.*

Matrices for the derived connectives can be defined in the usual way. For example, the matrix for $\Diamond$ is fully dual to that of $\Box$, obtained via negation. Note that the matrix for $\neg\alpha$ is already included in Table 2a, as it corresponds to the special case $\alpha \to \bot$. Finally, we note that our Nmatrices are refinements of those presented in [24], in the sense that certain valuations–those that would be excluded by level-valuations–have already been omitted.

While Kearns addressed the issue of necessitation in Nmatrices through level-valuations, our approach introduces an additional layer of complexity: it requires a uniform and general definition that applies coherently across all the logics in the modal cube. Hence, at level-0, besides considering only valuations that follow the corresponding Nmatrix, we also incorporate the condition imposed by the presence of *stable values* (see Lemma 1). Moreover, a valuation is not removed iff it assigns a designated $\mathcal{N}$-value to tautologies in the previous level.

**Definition 5 (Level-valuation in $\mathcal{M}$).** *The $n$-level-valuation for an Nmatrix $\mathcal{M}$ is a set of total valuations defined inductively as follows:*

- $\mathscr{L}_0(\mathcal{M}) = \{v \in [\mathcal{F} \to \mathcal{V}]_\mathcal{M} \mid (\exists \alpha, v(\alpha) \in \{\mathbf{f_1},\mathbf{t_1}\}) \Rightarrow \forall \beta, v(\beta) \in \{\mathbf{f_1},\mathbf{t_1}\}\}$;
- $\mathscr{L}_{n+1}(\mathcal{M}) = \{v \in \mathscr{L}_n(\mathcal{M}) \mid \forall \alpha, \vDash_n^\mathcal{M} \alpha \Rightarrow v(\alpha) \in \{\mathbf{T},\mathbf{t_1}\}\}$

*where $\vDash_n^\mathcal{M} \alpha$ denotes $\forall w \in \mathscr{L}_n(\mathcal{M}), w(\alpha) \in \mathcal{D}$. The set of level-valuations in $\mathcal{M}$ is given by $\mathscr{L}(\mathcal{M}) = \bigcap_{n=0}^\infty \mathscr{L}_n(\mathcal{M})$. The level-semantic consequence relation $\vDash^\mathcal{M}$ is defined as: $\Gamma \vDash^\mathcal{M} \alpha$ iff $\forall v \in \mathscr{L}(\mathcal{M}) : (\forall \beta \in \Gamma : v(\beta) \in \mathcal{D}) \Rightarrow v(\alpha) \in \mathcal{D}$. A formula $\alpha$ is valid in $\mathcal{M}$ if $\vDash^\mathcal{M} \alpha$.*

As already noted by Kearns, $\mathscr{L}_n(\mathcal{M})$ is not closed under necessitation as illustrated below for the family KT$_\star$ (left) and family KD$_\star$ (right).

| | $p$ | $p \to p$ | $\Box(p \to p)$ | $\Box\Box(p \to p)$ | ... |
|---|---|---|---|---|---|
| 1 | **F** | **T** | **T** | {**T**, t} | |
| 2 | **F** | **T** | t | {**F**, f} | |
| 3 | f | t | {**F**, f} | {**F**, f} | |
| ⋮ | | | | | |

| | $p$ | $p \to p$ | $\Box(p \to p)$ | $\Box\Box(p \to p)$ | ... |
|---|---|---|---|---|---|
| 1 | **F** | **T** | **T** | {**T**, t, $t_2$} | |
| 2 | **F** | **T** | t | {**F**, f, $f_2$} | |
| 3 | **F** | **T** | $t_2$ | {**F**, f, $f_2$} | |
| ⋮ | | | | | |

Each line in these tables actually represents multiple valuations. For instance, line 1 on the left table corresponds to two valuations: one where $\Box\Box(p \to p)$ takes the value **T** and another where it takes the value t. As we move through the levels, some of these valuations are discarded. For example, in the left table, line 3 is eliminated at level 1 because $p \to p$ is a tautology at level 0, and so $\Box(p \to p)$ must hold at level 1. Similarly, line 2 is discarded at level 2. The right table illustrates that, in the family KD$_\star$, the $\Box$ non-deterministic function can map designated values to non-designated ones.

Unlike earlier definitions of level-valuations, our definition of $\mathscr{L}_0$ includes an extra constraint on the values $\mathbf{t_1}$ and $\mathbf{f_1}$. Such a constraint is a natural consequence of the statement (2) in Lemma 1. Furthermore, in logics that include the axioms t or d, the values $\mathbf{t_1}$ and $\mathbf{f_1}$ are excluded altogether, and the definition reduces to the standard one in the literature. Finally, the definition of $\mathscr{L}_n$ for $n \geq 1$ refines and unifies previous approaches as it considers the only truth values "persist" under necessitation: for every non-deterministic function $\tilde{\Box}$ in Definition 4, if $\iota \in \{\mathbf{T}, \mathbf{t_1}\}$ then $\tilde{\Box}(\iota) \in \mathcal{D}$ (which is not the case for t and $\mathbf{t_2}$).

We are now ready to state and prove soundness.

**Theorem 1 (Soundness).** *For $\mathcal{L}$, $\Gamma \vdash^{\mathcal{L}} \alpha$ implies $\Gamma \vDash^{\mathcal{M}} \alpha$.*

*Proof.* We first show (**Part I**), by induction on $n$, that if $\vdash^{\mathcal{L}} \alpha$ with length $n+1$ then $\vDash_n^{\mathcal{M}} \alpha$. In the base case ($n = 0$), $\alpha$ is an axiom and it is straightforward to verify that all axioms are tautologies, *i.e.*, $\vDash_0^{\mathcal{M}} \alpha$. In the inductive step, assume the statement holds for all proofs of length less than $n + 1, n \geq 0$.

- Suppose $\alpha$ is obtained by mp to $\gamma \to \alpha$ and $\gamma$. By induction, $\vDash_n^{\mathcal{M}} \gamma \to \alpha$ and $\vDash_n^{\mathcal{M}} \gamma$. Hence $v(\gamma), v(\gamma \to \alpha) \in \{\mathbf{T}, \mathbf{t_1}\}$ for any $v \in \mathscr{L}_{n+1}$. A direct inspection of the truth table for implication (see Table 2a) shows that in this case, $v(\alpha) \in \mathcal{D}$.
- Suppose $\alpha = \Box\gamma$ is derived by nec. Again, by the inductive hypothesis, $\vDash_n^{\mathcal{M}} \gamma$ and then $v(\gamma) \in \{\mathbf{T}, \mathbf{t_1}\}$. But this implies that $v(\Box\gamma) \in \mathcal{D}$.

We now generalize the result above. Assume that $\Gamma \vdash^{\mathcal{L}} \alpha$ with length $n + 1$. We will prove that $\Gamma \vDash_n^{\mathcal{M}} \alpha$. There are two cases to consider.

- $\alpha$ is a tautology. Hence $\vdash^{\mathcal{L}} \alpha$ and this case follows directly from (**Part I**).
- There are $\gamma_1, \ldots, \gamma_k \in \Gamma$ such that $\vdash^{\mathcal{L}} \bigwedge_{i=1}^{k} \gamma_i \to \alpha$. From (**Part I**), $\vDash_n^{\mathcal{M}} \bigwedge_{i=1}^{k} \gamma_i \to \alpha$ and hence $\Gamma \vDash_n^{\mathcal{M}} \alpha$.

Since every valuation is, in particular, an $n$-level valuation for some $n$, it follows that if $\Gamma \vdash^{\mathcal{L}} \alpha$ then $\Gamma \vDash^{\mathcal{M}} \alpha$. □

## 3.3 Completeness of the Level Semantics

In this section, we prove the completeness of the level semantics. The proof of this theorem relies on the well-known Lindenbaum-Łoś construction method, showing that every consistent set can be extended to a maximally consistent set. In the level semantics, a key step in this construction is to define a *characteristic function*, which we later show to be a valid level valuation. Interestingly enough, we can define such a function directly from the interpretation of the semantic values presented in Table 1a (see the notation $\iota(\alpha)$ in Definition 3).

**Definition 6. (Characteristic function for Nmatrices).** *Let $\mathcal{L}$ be a modal logic and $\Delta$ be a maximally consistent set in $\mathcal{L}$. The characteristic function $v_\Delta^\mathcal{L} : \mathcal{F} \to \mathcal{V}(\mathcal{L})$ is defined as $v_\Delta^\mathcal{L}(\alpha) = \iota$ iff $\Delta \vdash^\mathcal{L} \iota(\alpha)$.*

We observe that, by part (1) of Lemma 1, $v_\Delta^\mathcal{L}(\cdot)$ is indeed a well-defined function. Moreover, the characteristic function is unique for all logics in a family. For example, the characteristic function for any logic $\mathcal{L}$ in the family KT⋆ is:

$$v_\Delta^\mathcal{L}(\alpha) = \begin{cases} \mathbf{F} & \text{iff } \Delta \vdash^\mathcal{L} \Box\neg\alpha \\ \mathbf{f} & \text{iff } \Delta \vdash^\mathcal{L} \neg\alpha \text{ and } \Delta \vdash^\mathcal{L} \Diamond\alpha \\ \mathbf{t} & \text{iff } \Delta \vdash^\mathcal{L} \alpha \text{ and } \Delta \vdash^\mathcal{L} \Diamond\neg\alpha \\ \mathbf{T} & \text{iff } \Delta \vdash^\mathcal{L} \Box\alpha \end{cases}$$

Note that we use a simplified version of the definition. Rather than writing "$\mathbf{T}$ iff $\Delta \vdash^\mathcal{L} \Box\alpha \wedge \alpha \wedge \Diamond\alpha$", we simply write "$\mathbf{T}$ iff $\Delta \vdash^\mathcal{L} \Box\alpha$". This simplification is justified since, in this family of systems, the axiom T guarantees that from $\Delta \vdash^\mathcal{L} \Box\alpha$ we can derive both $\Delta \vdash^\mathcal{L} \alpha$ and $\Delta \vdash^\mathcal{L} \Diamond\alpha$.

The following results show that, for any modal logic $\mathcal{L}$, the corresponding characteristic function is a level-valuation. We start by considering level 0.

**Lemma 2 (Adequacy of $v_\Delta^\mathcal{L}$).** *For any modal logic $\mathcal{L}$ with Nmatrix $\mathcal{M}$, and maximally consistent set $\Delta$ in $\mathcal{L}$, $v_\Delta^\mathcal{L} \in [\mathcal{F} \to \mathcal{V}]_\mathcal{M}$.*

*Proof.* Let $\alpha = \odot(\alpha_0, \ldots \alpha_n)$ be a formula with main connective $\odot$. We proceed by case analysis on $\odot$ to show that $v_\Delta^\mathcal{L}(\alpha) \in \tilde{\odot}(v_\Delta^\mathcal{L}(\alpha_0), \ldots, v_\Delta^\mathcal{L}(\alpha_n))$. Consider the case $\odot = \Box$ and assume that $v_\Delta^\mathcal{L}(\alpha_0)$ is some value $\iota$. By definition,

$$\Delta \vdash^\mathcal{L} \iota(\alpha_0) \tag{1}$$

Assume that $\tilde{\Box}(\iota)$ is a set $V$. Our goal is to show that: $v_\Delta^\mathcal{L}(\Box\alpha_0) \in V$ which, by definition, is equivalent to proving:

$$\Delta \vdash^\mathcal{L} \bigvee_{\kappa \in V} \kappa(\Box\alpha_0) \tag{2}$$

Using any deductive system for $\mathcal{L}$, it suffices to show that (1) implies (2). All resulting proof obligations are detailed in the technical report [16]. □

**Lemma 3.** *For every level $n$ and maximally consistent set $\Delta$, $v_\Delta^\mathcal{L} \in \mathscr{L}_n(\mathcal{M})$.*

*Proof.* We proceed by induction on $n$. The base case was proved in Lemma 2. Assume that $\vDash_n^{\mathcal{M}} \alpha$ for some formula $\alpha$ and suppose that $\alpha$ is not a theorem in $\mathcal{L}$, that is, $\nvdash^{\mathcal{L}} \alpha$. Thus there is a maximally consistent set $\Theta$ such that $\Theta \nvdash^{\mathcal{L}} \alpha$, which means that $\Theta \vdash^{\mathcal{L}} \neg \alpha$. Hence, $v_\Theta^{\mathcal{L}}(\alpha) \notin \mathcal{D}$. However, by IH, $v_\Theta^{\mathcal{L}} \in \mathcal{L}_n(\mathcal{M})$ and, by hypothesis, $\vDash_n^{\mathcal{M}} \alpha$, implying $v_\Theta^{\mathcal{L}}(\alpha) \in \mathcal{D}$, a contradiction. Therefore, $\vdash^{\mathcal{L}} \alpha$ and, by (nec), $\vdash^{\mathcal{L}} \Box \alpha$. Hence, for every maximally consistent set $\Delta$, $\Delta \vdash^{\mathcal{L}} \alpha$ and $\Delta \vdash^{\mathcal{L}} \Box \alpha$. By definition, $v_\Delta^{\mathcal{L}}(\alpha) \in \mathcal{D}$ and $v_\Delta^{\mathcal{L}}(\Box \alpha) \in \mathcal{D}$ and hence, $v_\Delta^{\mathcal{L}}(\alpha) \in \mathcal{N} \cap \mathcal{D}$ (see the set $\mathcal{N}$ in Table 1) and $v_\Delta^{\mathcal{L}} \in \mathcal{L}_{n+1}$ as needed. □

**Theorem 2 (Completeness).** *For every modal logic $\mathcal{L}$ and associated Nmatrix $\mathcal{M}$, if $\Gamma \vDash^{\mathcal{M}} \alpha$ then $\Gamma \vdash^{\mathcal{L}} \alpha$.*

*Proof* If $\Gamma \nvdash^{\mathcal{L}} \alpha$ then there is some $\alpha$-saturated set $\Delta$ such that $\Gamma \subseteq \Delta$. By Lemma 3, $v_\Delta^{\mathcal{L}}$ is a level valuation and $\Delta \nvdash^{\mathcal{L}} \alpha$; hence $v_\Delta^{\mathcal{L}}(\alpha) \notin \mathcal{D}(\mathcal{L})$ and, given that $\Delta \vdash^{\mathcal{L}} \beta$, for every $\beta \in \Delta$, then $v_\Delta^{\mathcal{L}}(\beta) \in \mathcal{D}(\mathcal{L})$. Therefore, $\Gamma \nvDash^{\mathcal{M}} \alpha$. □

## 4 Decision Procedures for the Modal Cube

The previous section introduced level semantics for all the logics in the modal cube, providing new results for K4, K5, K45, KD4, KD5, and KB5. However, in practice, checking level semantics is challenging, as each step involves verifying whether a given formula is a tautology (see Definition 5). To address this, the current section introduces a *partial valuation* semantics (see Definition 2), which offers a sound and complete finitary method for validating formulas across all the logics in the modal cube.

We show that such partial valuations can be *extended* to total valuations, and that these total valuations are also valid level-valuations. This property, known as *analyticity*, is a key step for establishing the soundness of this semantics. We then prove *co-analyticity*, showing that restricting a level-valuation to a closed set of formulas yields a valid partial valuation. Using co-analyticity and Theorem 2, we prove completeness of the partial valuation semantics.

Our decision procedures not only generalize those proposed by Grätz in [11] by covering the entire modal cube, but also show how such procedures can be *systematically* and *modularly* derived from the functions that define truth values (Definition 3). Additionally, we bridge the Kearns interpretation and traditional Kripke semantics by identifying, based on the interpretation of truth values, the dependencies and relational conditions (in the Kripke sense) that partial valuations must satisfy. These conditions determine how partial valuations are extended and provide a modular approach to proving the results in this section.

Our method thus brings valuations and possible-world semantics into closer alignment by demonstrating that the derived relational conditions correspond to the standard frame conditions of the respective modal logics.

### 4.1 From Truth Values to Dependencies and Relational Conditions

*Relational Models on Valuations.* The algorithm introduced in [11] for building (finite) truth tables (*i.e.*, partial valuations) consists of two steps. First, compute the full truth table for a set of formulas closed under subformulas following the Nmatrix. Since the resulting table is not necessarily sound (it may assign non-designated values to tautologies), the algorithm systematically removes "non valid" partial valuations (*i.e.*, rows in the table). A key contribution of our work is to propose uniform criteria for all the considered logic by identifying "non valid" partial valuations as those whose *dependencies* are not properly satisfied, as explained below.

Consider a partial valuation $v$ and a formula $\alpha$ such that $v(\alpha) = \mathbf{t}$. This truth value indicates that $\alpha$ is *contingently true*: $\alpha$ is true but *possibly false* (recall that $\mathbf{t}(\alpha) = \Diamond\neg\alpha \wedge \alpha \wedge \Diamond\alpha$). Therefore, there must exist a valuation $w$ in which $\alpha$ is false (*i.e.*, $\Diamond\neg\alpha$ holds). This means that the column corresponding to $\alpha$ must contain at least one non-designated value. If no such a valuation/row exists, then $\alpha$ is not contingently true but *necessarily true*—contradicting the assumption that $v(\alpha) = \mathbf{t}$. In that case, $v$ is not a valid valuation and must be discarded. We thus say that assigning $v(\alpha) = \mathbf{t}$ imposes a *dependency* on $v$: it requires the existence of another valuation $w$ to satisfy the semantics. The same reasoning applies to all truth values $\iota$ in the sets $\mathcal{P}$ and $\mathcal{PN}$, due to the presence of the formulas $\Diamond\alpha$ and $\Diamond\neg\alpha$ in its modal characterization.

However, the mere existence of the above valuation $w$ is not sufficient: it must properly *support* the values assigned by $v$. Suppose, for instance, that for some formula $\beta$, we have $v(\beta) \in \mathcal{N}$, that is, $\beta$ is necessarily true at $v$. Then, by nec, $w(\beta)$ must be a designated value. Moreover, the modal axioms of the logic in question may impose stricter requirements. For example, in any extension of K4, if $v(\beta) \in \mathcal{N}$, then $w(\beta)$ must not only be designated but must itself also belong to $\mathcal{N}$. We refer to these additional constraints as *relational conditions* (see Table 3): they determine the criteria that a valuation $w$ must satisfy in order to support a given valuation $v$.

Below, we formalize the above intuitions.

**Definition 7 (Model).** *Let $\mathcal{M} = \langle \mathcal{V}, \mathcal{D}, \mathcal{O} \rangle$ be an Nmatrix for a logic $\mathcal{L}$ and $\Lambda \subseteq \mathcal{F}$ closed under subformulas. A* pre-model *in $\mathcal{L}$ is a pair $\langle \Pi, R \rangle$, where $\Pi \subseteq [\Lambda \to \mathcal{V}]_\mathcal{M}$ is a set of partial valuations, and $R \subseteq \Pi \times \Pi$ relates valuations s.t for all $v \in \Pi$ and $\alpha \in \Lambda$:*

*(1) If $v(\alpha) \in \mathcal{P}$, then $\exists w \in \Pi$ such that $vRw$ and $w(\alpha) \in \mathcal{D}$;*
*(2) If $v(\alpha) \in \mathcal{PN}$, then $\exists w \in \Pi$ such that $vRw$ and $w(\alpha) \notin \mathcal{D}$.*

*A* K-model *is a pre-model $\langle \Pi, R \rangle$ s.t. $R$ additionally satisfies the condition* nec *in Table 3. For a logic $\mathcal{L}$, extending* K*, an $\mathcal{L}$-model is a* K-model *where for all (frame) properties in Table 3 that holds in $\mathcal{L}$, $R$ and all $v \in \Pi$ additionally satisfy the respective relational conditions in Table 3. We say that $v$ is a partial* level-valuation *if there exists a $\mathcal{L}$-model $\langle \Pi, R \rangle$ s.t. $v \in \Pi$.* □

**Table 3.** Relational conditions on models.

| Property | | Condition | Implies |
|---|---|---|---|
| nec | any | $w(\alpha) \in \mathcal{N}$ and $wRw'$ | $w'(\alpha) \in \mathcal{D}$ |
| | | $w(\alpha) \in \mathcal{I}$ and $wRw'$ | $w'(\alpha) \notin \mathcal{D}$ |
| t | $\Box\alpha \to \alpha$ | $w(\alpha) \in \mathcal{N}$ | $w(\alpha) \in \mathcal{D}$ |
| | | $w(\alpha) \in \mathcal{I}$ | $w(\alpha) \notin \mathcal{D}$ |
| d | $\Box\alpha \to \Diamond\alpha$ | $w(\alpha) \in \mathcal{N}$ | $w(\alpha) \in \mathcal{P}$ |
| | | $w(\alpha) \in \mathcal{I}$ | $w(\alpha) \in \mathcal{PN}$ |
| b | $\alpha \to \Box\Diamond\alpha$ | $w(\alpha) \in \mathcal{D}$ and $wRw'$ | $w'(\alpha) \in \mathcal{P}$ |
| | | $w(\alpha) \notin \mathcal{D}$ and $wRw'$ | $w'(\alpha) \in \mathcal{PN}$ |
| 4 | $\Box\alpha \to \Box\Box\alpha$ | $w(\alpha) \in \mathcal{N}$ and $wRw'$ | $w'(\alpha) \in \mathcal{N}$ |
| | | $w(\alpha) \in \mathcal{I}$ and $wRw'$ | $w'(\alpha) \in \mathcal{I}$ |
| 5 | $\Diamond\alpha \to \Box\Diamond\alpha$ | $w(\alpha) \in \mathcal{P}$ and $wRw'$ | $w'(\alpha) \in \mathcal{P}$ |
| | | $w(\alpha) \in \mathcal{PN}$ and $wRw'$ | $w'(\alpha) \in \mathcal{PN}$ |
| | $\Box\Box\alpha \to \Box\Box\Box\alpha$ | $w(\alpha), w'(\alpha) \in \mathcal{N}$, $wRw'$ and ($wRw''$ or $w'Rw''$) | $w''(\alpha) \in \mathcal{N}$ |
| | | $w(\alpha), w'(\alpha) \in \mathcal{I}$, $wRw'$ and ($wRw''$ or $w'Rw''$) | $w''(\alpha) \in \mathcal{I}$ |

The above definition provides a *procedure* to check whether a set of partial valuations is legal, *i.e.*, it forms a *model*. It suffices to check that whenever $v(\alpha) = \iota$ is a $(\mathcal{P} \cup \mathcal{PN})$-value, $v$ must be supported by another valuation $w$ (*i.e.*, $vRw$) and $v$ and $w$ must satisfy the *relational conditions* imposed by the logic at hand. For concreteness, we show the resulting model conditions in Fig. 1 where the following notation is used.

**Notation 2.** *Let $\iota \in \mathcal{V}, V \subseteq \mathcal{V}$. We will adopt the following notation:*

- $\iota \Rightarrow^R V$: *"$\forall \alpha \in \mathcal{F}$, if $v(\alpha) = \iota$ and $vRw$, then $w(\alpha) \in V$".*
- $\iota \rightarrowtail V$: *"$\forall \alpha \in \mathcal{F}$, if $v(\alpha) = \iota$, there must exist $w$ s.t. $vRw$ and $w(\alpha) \in V$".*

*Any value $\iota$ in $\mathcal{P}, \mathcal{PN}$ must be supported in the sense of Definition 7; that is, $\iota \rightarrowtail V$ for some $V$. This means that if $\iota \Rightarrow^R V'$ then $V$ in $\iota \rightarrowtail V$ must satisfy:*

- *to be a support for a value $\iota \in \mathcal{P}$, $V = V' \cap \mathcal{D}(\mathcal{L})$;*
- *to be a support for a value $\iota \in \mathcal{PN}$, $V = V' \cap \mathcal{D}^{\complement}(\mathcal{L})$.*

Note that **t** and **f** belong to both $\mathcal{P}$ and $\mathcal{PN}$. Therefore, each must be supported by both a designated and a non-designated value. This implies that, in every logic, we have $\mathbf{t} \rightarrowtail V_1$ and $\mathbf{t} \rightarrowtail V_2$ for some $V_1 \neq V_2$, and similarly for **f**.

*Seriality.* In logics where d holds–such as extensions of KD and KT–the d-condition requires that $\mathcal{N}$-values (respectively, $\mathcal{I}$-values) must also be $\mathcal{P}$-values (respectively, $\mathcal{PN}$-values). This excludes from these logics the values $\mathbf{t}_1$ and $\mathbf{f}_1$, which, as noted, characterize valuations without successors. For the other logics, note that these values are not in $\mathcal{P}$ or $\mathcal{PN}$, and therefore cannot appear on the left of $\rightarrowtail$. Moreover, since both are in $\mathcal{N}$ and $\mathcal{I}$, the nec-condition implies that if $v(\alpha) = \mathbf{t_1}$ and $vRw$, then $w(\alpha) \in \mathcal{D}$ and $w(\alpha) \notin \mathcal{D}$–a contradiction. This justifies the notation $\mathbf{t_1} \Rightarrow^R \bullet$ and $\mathbf{f_1} \Rightarrow^R \bullet$ in Fig. 1, as a valuation containing these values cannot be related to any other (see Lemma 1).

*Reflexivity.* In logics where t holds (and hence d), the t-condition further excludes the values $\mathbf{t_2}$ and $\mathbf{f_2}$ since, *e.g.*, the latter is in $\mathcal{N}$ but it is not designated. Moreover, checking the supports ($\rightarrowtail$) becomes simpler as shown in Fig. 1. For instance, in KT, we do not have to check whether $\mathbf{t} \rightarrowtail \mathbf{T}, \mathbf{t}$ since this condition trivially holds by reflexivity. Furthermore, observe that, for every $\iota \Rightarrow^R V$ in logics extending KT, $\iota \in V$ (which of course is not the case for values $\mathbf{t_2}, \mathbf{f_2}, \mathbf{f_1}, \mathbf{t_1}$ in other logics).

*Symmetry and Transitivity.* Regarding the b-condition, note that instead of $\mathbf{T} \Rightarrow^R \mathbf{T}, \mathbf{t}, \mathbf{t_1}, \mathbf{t_2}$ as in K, we have $\mathbf{T} \Rightarrow^R \mathbf{T}, \mathbf{t}$ in KB since $\mathbf{t_1}$ and $\mathbf{t_2}$ are not in $\mathcal{P}$. In logics where the axiom 4 holds, the relation is further restricted to $\mathbf{T} \Rightarrow^R \mathbf{T}$ (since $\mathbf{t}$ is not in $\mathcal{N}$).

*Euclidianity.* In any logic extending K5, $\mathbf{T} \Rightarrow^R \mathbf{T}, \mathbf{t}$, but $\mathbf{t} \not\Rightarrow^R \mathbf{T}$. For this reason, besides the condition for axiom 5, we add a further condition derived from the formula $\Box\Box\alpha \to \Box\Box\Box\alpha$ (a theorem in any system extending K5). Its twofold purpose is to ensure that, for every 5-model: (1) if $wRv$ and $wRv'$, then if $w(\alpha) \in \mathcal{N}$ (or $\mathcal{I}$) and $v(\alpha) = \mathbf{T}$ (or $\mathbf{F}$), then $v'(\alpha) = \mathbf{T}$ (or $\mathbf{F}$); (2) if $wRv$ and $vRv''$, then if $w(\alpha) \in \mathcal{N}$ (or $\mathcal{I}$) and $v(\alpha) = \mathbf{T}$ (or $\mathbf{F}$), then $v''(\alpha) = \mathbf{T}$ (or $\mathbf{F}$). This guarantees that $wRv \wedge wRv'$ implies $vRv'$.

A fundamental property of our model is that the relation $\Rightarrow^R$ induced by any logic $\mathcal{L}$ satisfies the standard frame conditions associated with $\mathcal{L}$. This marks a significant step toward reconciling Kripke semantics with Kearns' semantics–a completely new feature not present in previous works.

**Theorem 3 (Frame Properties).** *(1) If axiom* t/b/4/5 *is valid in the logic $\mathcal{L}$, then the induced $\Rightarrow^R$ is reflexive/symmetric/transitive/Euclidian, respectively; (2) If axiom* d *is valid in $\mathcal{L}$, for all $\iota \in \mathcal{V}(\mathcal{L})$, $\iota \rightarrowtail V$ for some $V$; and (3) If axiom* d/t/b/4/5 *is valid in $\mathcal{L}$, and $\langle \Pi, R \rangle$ is an $\mathcal{L}$-model, then there exists a $\mathcal{L}$-model $\langle \Pi, R' \rangle$ s.t. $R' \supseteq R$ and $R'$ is serial/reflexive/symmetric/transitive/Euclidian.*

*Proof.* Statement (1) follows by inspecting the induced $\Rightarrow^R$ for each $\mathcal{L}$. For symmetry in KB, we can check that $\iota \Rightarrow^R V_\iota$ implies that for all $\kappa \in V_\iota$, $\kappa \Rightarrow^R V_\kappa$ and $\iota \in V_\kappa$. For euclidianness in (extensions of) K5, the interesting case is when $\kappa \in \mathcal{N} \cup \mathcal{I}$, and it is solved as explained above due to the condition imposed by $\Box\Box\alpha \to \Box\Box\Box\alpha$. For (2), note that in all extensions of KD (including logics where t holds), all the values of the logic appear on the left of $\rightarrowtail$. For (3), note that $R$ in $\langle \Pi, R \rangle$ does not necessarily satisfy the usual frame conditions. However, due to (1), $R$ can always by extended to a $R' \supseteq R$ that satisfies such conditions. □

|  (a) K | (b) KB | (c) K4 | (d) K5 | (e) K45 | (f) KB45 | (g) KD |
|---|---|---|---|---|---|---|
| $T \Rightarrow^R T, t$ | $T \Rightarrow^R T, t$ | | $T \Rightarrow^R T, t$ | $T \Rightarrow^R T$ | | |
| $t \Rightarrow^R T, t, f, f_2$ | | | $t \Rightarrow^R t, f$ | $t \Rightarrow^R t, f$ | | |
| $T \Rightarrow^R T, t, t_1, t_2$ | $t_1 \Rightarrow^R \bullet$ | $T \Rightarrow^R T, t_1$ | $t_1 \Rightarrow^R \bullet$ | $t_1 \Rightarrow^R \bullet$ | $T \Rightarrow^R T$ | |
| $t_1 \Rightarrow^R \bullet$ | $t_2 \Rightarrow^R f, f_2$ | $t_1 \Rightarrow^R \bullet$ | $t_2 \Rightarrow^R F, f$ | $t_2 \Rightarrow^R F$ | $t \Rightarrow^R t, f$ | |
| $t_2 \Rightarrow^R F, f, f_1, f_2$ | $f_2 \Rightarrow^R t, t_2$ | $t_2 \Rightarrow^R F, f_1$ | $f_2 \Rightarrow^R T, t$ | $f_2 \Rightarrow^R T$ | $t_1 \Rightarrow^R \bullet$ | $T \Rightarrow^R T, t, t_2$ |
| $f_2 \Rightarrow^R T, t, t_1, t_2$ | $f_1 \Rightarrow^R \bullet$ | $f_2 \Rightarrow^R T, t_1$ | $f_1 \Rightarrow^R \bullet$ | $f_1 \Rightarrow^R \bullet$ | $f_1 \Rightarrow^R \bullet$ | $t_2 \Rightarrow^R F, f, f_2$ |
| $f_1 \Rightarrow^R \bullet$ | $f \Rightarrow^R F, f, t_2$ | $f_1 \Rightarrow^R \bullet$ | $f \Rightarrow^R t, f$ | $f \Rightarrow^R t, f$ | $f \Rightarrow^R t, f$ | $f_2 \Rightarrow^R T, t, t_2$ |
| $F \Rightarrow^R F, f, f_1, f_2$ | $F \Rightarrow^R F, f$ | $F \Rightarrow^R F, f_1$ | $F \Rightarrow^R F, f$ | $F \Rightarrow^R F$ | $F \Rightarrow^R F$ | $F \Rightarrow^R F, f, f_2$ |

|  (h) KDB | (i) KD4 | (j) KD5 | (k) KD45 | (l) KT | (m) KTB | (n) KT4 | (o) KTB45 |
|---|---|---|---|---|---|---|---|
| $T \Rightarrow^R T, t$ | | $T \Rightarrow^R T, t$ | $T \Rightarrow^R T$ | | | | |
| $t \Rightarrow^R T, t, f, f_2$ | | $t \Rightarrow^R t, f$ | $t \Rightarrow^R t, f$ | $t \mapsto F, f$ | | $t \mapsto F, f$ | $t \mapsto f$ |
| $t_2 \Rightarrow^R f, f_2$ | $T \Rightarrow^R T$ | $t_2 \Rightarrow^R F, f$ | $t_2 \Rightarrow^R F$ | $f \mapsto T, t$ | $T \Rightarrow^R T, t$ | $f \mapsto T, t$ | $T \Rightarrow^R T$ |
| $f_2 \Rightarrow^R t, t_2$ | $t_2 \Rightarrow^R F$ | $f_2 \Rightarrow^R T, t$ | $f_2 \Rightarrow^R T$ | | $t \Rightarrow^R T, t, f$ | | $t \Rightarrow^R t, f$ |
| $f \Rightarrow^R F, f, t_2 f_2 \Rightarrow^R T$ | $f \Rightarrow^R t, f$ | $f \Rightarrow^R t, f$ | $T \Rightarrow^R T, t$ | $f \Rightarrow^R F, t, f$ | $T \Rightarrow^R T$ | $f \Rightarrow^R t, f$ |
| $F \Rightarrow^R F, f$ | $F \Rightarrow^R F$ | $F \Rightarrow^R F, f$ | $F \Rightarrow^R F$ | $F \Rightarrow^R F, f$ | $F \Rightarrow^R F, f$ | $F \Rightarrow^R F$ | $F \Rightarrow^R F$ |

**Fig. 1.** Relational Model. The absence of an entry $\iota \Rightarrow^R V$ is interpreted as $\iota \Rightarrow^R \mathcal{V}(\mathcal{L})$ (any value supports $\iota$). For an $\mathcal{L}$ not extending KT where $\iota \Rightarrow^R V$, we further have: for any $\iota \in \mathcal{P}$ (and $\iota \in \mathcal{PN}$), $\iota \mapsto V \cap \mathcal{D}(\mathcal{L})$ (and $\iota \mapsto V \cap \mathcal{D}^{\complement}(\mathcal{L})$).

*Analyticity.* Recall that Grätz's original algorithm constructs the entire truth table *before* eliminating any rows. This naturally raises the question: is there a way to generate only valid partial valuations from the start, thereby avoiding the need for post hoc filtering?

In the truth table method, we start by assigning all possible values to the atomic propositions. A new column for a formula $\alpha$ is introduced only once all its subformulas have been added to the table. When working with the partial valuations defined here, one might worry that adding such columns–and checking the associated constraints–could lead to the elimination of some valuations (*i.e.*, rows in the table), potentially resulting in an empty model. This would be problematic, as it would undermine the entire model construction process.

The following lemmas show, however, that all valid partial valuations in a model can be extended. To ensure this, we propose an algorithm that, in nondeterministic cases, selects one admissible value in a way that guarantees that all rows are preserved and correctly extended. As a by-product, if the algorithm always selects *every* admissible value (instead of only one), it will build a set containing all and only the valid partial valuations, which corresponds to the filtered truth table of Grätz's original algorithm.

**Notation 3 (Extensions).** *Assume that $\Lambda \subseteq \mathcal{F}$ and $\Lambda \cup \{\beta\}$ are both closed under subformulas, and let $v : \Lambda \to \mathcal{V}$ and $v' : \Lambda \cup \{\beta\} \to \mathcal{V}$ be two partial valuations. We say that $v'$ extends $v$, notation $v \sqsubseteq v'$, if $v(\alpha) = v'(\alpha)$ for all $\alpha \in \Lambda$. Let $M = \langle \Pi, R \rangle$ and $M' = \langle \Pi', R' \rangle$ be $\mathcal{L}$-models defined, respectively on $\Lambda$ and $\Lambda \cup \{\beta\}$. We say that $M'$ extends $M$, notation $M \sqsubseteq M'$, if either $\Pi = \emptyset$ or there is a bijection $f : \Pi \to \Pi'$ such that $v \sqsubseteq f(v)$ and $vRw$ iff $f(v)R'f(w)$.*

**Lemma 4 (Extension Lemma).** *Let $\Lambda \subseteq \mathcal{F}$ and $\Lambda \cup \{\alpha\}$ be closed under subformulas, and $\langle \Pi, R \rangle$ be a $\mathcal{L}$-model where $\Pi \subseteq [\Lambda \to \mathcal{V}]_{\mathcal{M}}$. Then, there exists $\langle \Pi', R' \rangle$ s.t. $\Pi' \subseteq [\Lambda \cup \{\alpha\} \to \mathcal{V}]_{\mathcal{M}}$ and $\langle \Pi, R \rangle \sqsubseteq \langle \Pi', R' \rangle$.*

*Proof.* If $\alpha \in \mathsf{At}$, we consider two cases: If $\Pi = \emptyset$, then the needed model is the set of valuations with domain $\alpha$ ($\Pi = [\{\alpha\} \to \mathcal{V}]_{\mathcal{M}}$) and $R = \{(v_1, v_2) \mid v_1(\alpha) \rightarrowtail v_2(\alpha)\}$; otherwise, we choose any $\beta \in \Lambda$ and extend all $v$ with $v(\alpha) = v(\beta)$. It is easy to show that "copying" a column is a valid extension.

Consider the case of $\Box \alpha$ with $\alpha \in \mathrm{dom}(\Pi)$. Since the interpretation $\tilde{\Box}$ is not necessarily deterministic, we must ensure that all partial valuations in the model are extended in a *deterministic* manner. The extension procedure depends on the logic in question. For example, in the case of KT, the situation is as follows:

$$\begin{array}{cc} \alpha\ldots\ \Box\alpha\ldots & \alpha\ldots\Box\alpha\ldots \\ v:\ldots\mathbf{f},\mathbf{t}\ldots\mathbf{F}?\mathbf{f}?\ldots & v:\ldots\mathbf{T}\ldots\mathbf{T}?\mathbf{t}?\ldots \end{array}$$

meaning that if $v(\alpha) \in \{\mathbf{f}, \mathbf{t}\}$, the non-deterministic function dictates that the resulting value is either $\mathbf{F}$ or $\mathbf{f}$ (similarly for the figure on the right). The criterion to extend $v$ is the following: If there are $v', v''$ s.t. $vRv'$, $vRv''$, $v'(\alpha) = \mathbf{T}$ and $v''(\alpha) \neq \mathbf{T}$, then extend with the lowercase values; otherwise with the uppercase values. The rationale is that, if there is no $v'$, $vRv'$, such that $v'(\alpha) = \mathbf{T}$ or $v'(\alpha) \neq \mathbf{T}$ then, in the first case, $\Box \alpha$ is always false (hence, impossible), while, in the second case (which corresponds to choose $\mathbf{T}$ in the figure on the right), $\Box \alpha$ is always true (hence, necessary). Similarly, if there are both $v'(\alpha) = \mathbf{T}$ and $v'(\alpha) \neq \mathbf{T}$, then we can safely infer that $\Box \alpha$ is contingently false or true (lowercase values). The other cases assume similar criteria, and they can be found in the technical report [16].

Consider the case $\alpha \to \beta$ for KD (similarly for all logics since they share $\overset{\sim}{\to}$):

$$\begin{array}{ccc} \alpha\ldots\quad \beta\ldots\alpha\to\beta & \alpha\ldots\quad \beta\ldots\alpha\to\beta & \alpha\ldots\beta\ldots\alpha\to\beta \\ v:\ldots\mathbf{f},\mathbf{f_2}\ldots\mathbf{f}\ldots\mathbf{T}?\mathbf{t}?\ldots & v:\ldots\mathbf{t},\mathbf{f}\ldots\mathbf{t}\ldots\mathbf{T}?\mathbf{t}?\ldots & v:\ldots\mathbf{t}\ldots\mathbf{f}\ldots\mathbf{f}?\mathbf{f_2}?\ldots \end{array}$$

The criterion is: if there is $v'$ such that $vRv'$, $v'(\alpha) \in \mathcal{D}$ and $v'(\beta) \notin \mathcal{D}$, then extend with $\mathbf{t}$ and $\mathbf{f}$; otherwise, extend with $\mathbf{T}$ and $\mathbf{f_2}$. Since the implication is classical, $\alpha \to \beta$ is falsified only when $\alpha$ is designated but $\beta$ is not. In the first case, the implication $\alpha \to \beta$ is contingently true ($\mathbf{t}$) and $v$ can be extended with $\mathbf{t}$ and $\mathbf{f}$. In the second case, the implication is not falsified and we can infer that $\alpha \to \beta$ is necessarily true ($\mathbf{T}$). Observe that, although $\mathbf{f_2}$ is a non-designated value, it is a $\mathcal{N}$-value, and then, if $\alpha \to \beta$ is always true "onward", then $\alpha \to \beta$ is false "now" but necessarily true ($\mathbf{f_2}$).

**Theorem 4 (Analyticity).** *Every partial level-valuation can be extended to a level-valuation.*

**Definition 8 (Partial Valuation Semantics).** *Given $\Gamma \subseteq \mathcal{F}$, we write $\lceil \Gamma \rceil$ to denote the smallest set containing $\Gamma$ that is closed under subformulas. We say that $\alpha$ is a* partial-semantic consequence *of $\Gamma$ in logic $\mathcal{L}$, notation $\Gamma \vDash^{\mathcal{L}} \alpha$, iff*
$$\forall v \in [\lceil \Gamma \cup \{\alpha\} \rceil] \to \mathcal{V}]_{\mathcal{M}} : (\forall \beta \in \Gamma : v(\beta) \in \mathcal{D}) \Rightarrow v(\alpha) \in \mathcal{D}.$$

**Theorem 5 (Soundness).** *For every $\mathcal{L}$, $\Gamma \vdash^{\mathcal{L}} \alpha \Rightarrow \Gamma \vDash^{\mathcal{L}} \alpha$.*

*Proof* We proceed by induction on the derivation of $\Gamma \vdash^{\mathcal{L}} \alpha$. The case for mp relies on Lemma 4, which ensures that any valuation $v$ with domain $\lceil \Gamma \cup \{\alpha\} \rceil$ can be extended to the domain $\lceil \Gamma \cup \{\alpha \to \beta\} \rceil$.

*Co-analyticity.* The completeness proof for the partial valuation semantics relies on Theorem 2. Accordingly, we must show that level (*i.e.*, full) valuations, when restricted to a set $\Lambda$ closed under subformulas, yield valid partial valuations. We denote the restriction of a valuation $v$ to the domain $\Lambda$ by $v \downarrow_\Lambda$.

**Theorem 6 (Co-analyticity).** *For every level-valuation $v \in \mathscr{L}(\mathcal{M})$ and every set closed under subformulas $\Lambda$, $v \downarrow_\Lambda$ is a partial level-valuation.*

*Proof.* Following Grätz, we consider *partial'* valuations [11], where partial valuations are supported by level-valuation. By systematically reducing level to partial valuation, the two definitions of partial valuations are shown to be equivalent. Now we prove that level valuations are indeed partial' valuations. Given a formula $\alpha$, let $\alpha[\iota]$ denote the values that result when evaluating the corresponding multifunctions in the connectives of $\alpha$ with $\iota$ as in $(\alpha \wedge \Box \alpha)[\mathbf{f}] = \bigcup_\iota \tilde{\wedge}(\mathbf{f}, \iota)$ where $\iota \in \tilde{\Box}(\mathbf{f})$. Let $v$ be a level-valuation and assume that $v_p = v \downarrow_\Lambda$ is not partial', *i.e.*, there exists $\alpha \in \Lambda$ s.t. $v(\alpha) = \iota$ is not supported. Assume that $\iota \rightarrowtail V_\iota$, $\kappa \Rightarrow^R V_\kappa$ in $\mathcal{L}$ and the following situation

$$v_p \quad \frac{\beta_0 \quad \beta_1 \quad \alpha \quad \beta_2 \quad \psi_\iota(\alpha) \quad \beta_3 \cdots}{\kappa \quad \kappa \quad \iota \quad \kappa \qquad \qquad \kappa}$$

To show that there is no $w$ s.t. $vRw$, we choose $\kappa$, $\Delta = \{\beta_0 \cdots\}$, and $\psi_\iota(\alpha)$ s.t. $\psi_\iota(\alpha)[\iota] \in \{\mathbf{t}, \mathbf{t_2}\}$, $\beta_i[\kappa] = \{\mathbf{T}\}$, and $w(\alpha) \in V_\iota$ iff $w(\psi_\iota(\alpha)) \notin \mathcal{D}$ (if $\Delta = \emptyset$ the proof below is the same.) The choices are guided by the modal characterization of the truth values (e.g., in KT $\psi_\mathbf{f}(\alpha) = \mathbf{F}(\alpha) \vee \mathbf{f}(\alpha)$, the other cases are in the technical report [16]). The idea is to show that, if $w$ respects the $\Rightarrow^R$-conditions, then it cannot assign the expected supporting value in $w(\alpha)$, i.e., $w(\psi_\iota(\alpha)) \notin \mathcal{D}$ iff there is some $i \geq 0$ such that $w(\beta_i) \notin \mathcal{D}$. Hence, $\Delta \vDash^{\mathcal{L}} \psi_\iota(\alpha)$. By completeness (of level-semantics) $\Delta \vdash^{\mathcal{L}} \psi_\iota(\alpha)$, and by compactness of $\mathcal{L}$, $\Delta' \vdash^{\mathcal{L}} \psi_\iota(\alpha)$ for a finite $\Delta \supseteq \Delta' = \{\gamma_0, \cdots, \gamma_n\}$. By nec and the deduction theorem, $\vdash^{\mathcal{L}} \Box(\gamma_0 \to \cdots \to \gamma_n \to \psi_\iota(\alpha))$. By soundness (of level-semantics), $\vDash^{\mathcal{L}} \Box(\gamma_0 \to \cdots \to \gamma_n \to \psi_\iota(\alpha))$. We then find a contradiction since, using the Nmatrices, we can check that $v(\Box(\gamma_0 \to \cdots \to \gamma_n \to \psi_\iota(\alpha))) \notin \mathcal{D}$.

**Theorem 7 (Completeness).** *For every $\mathcal{L}$, $\Gamma \vDash^{\mathcal{L}} \alpha \Rightarrow \Gamma \vdash^{\mathcal{L}} \alpha$.*

## 5 Concluding Remarks

This paper generalizes previous non-deterministic semantic approaches to the entire modal cube of normal modal logics. First, Kearns' semantics based on Nmatrices with level valuations was extended to the full modal cube, starting from an 8-valued Nmatrix for the basic logic K. Second, the decision procedure for KT and S4 using partial valuations over a 3-valued Nmatrix proposed by Grätz, was extended to all systems of the modal cube, again starting from the 8-valued Nmatrix for K. A distinctive feature of our framework is that it bridges Nmatrix semantics with Kripke semantics by ensuring that the resulting models satisfy the standard frame conditions associated with each modal system.

Our results are supported by prototypical tools [1]. An OCaml implementation generates truth tables and visualizes models, making the Kripke correspondence explicit (and helping us to prove, *e.g.*, that modal axioms are indeed tautologies). We have a very preliminary and partial formalization of our results in Rocq, initially focusing on S5. Given the central role of analyticity in our approach, we developed a Maude specification [9,19] to explore all possible extensions (Lemma 4) and automatically verify their validity.

Future work includes extending our framework to intuitionistic and ecumenical [17,18,23] modal logics by combining it with the approach from [15]. Another line of investigation involves the relationship between Kripke and Nmatrix countermodels. For instance, the minimal Kripke countermodel for $\Diamond \alpha \to \Box \alpha$ in KT involves two worlds, which is mirrored in the matrix semantics by a two-row model assigning $\mathbf{t}, \mathbf{F}$ to $\alpha$. Understanding this correspondence may yield insights into the complexity-theoretic aspects of the frameworks. Finally, we intend to describe the Nmatrices and the level valuation restrictions analytically using swap structures, as done e.g., in [7]. This representation should enable the generalization of the decision procedures proposed here to a broader class of modal systems.

**Acknowledgments.** This study was financed, in part, by the São Paulo Research Foundation (FAPESP), Brasil. Process Number n. 2023/16021-9 and n. 2021/01025-3. The work of Olarte was partially funded by the NATO Science for Peace and Security Programme through grant number G6133 (project SymSafe) and the SGR project PROMUEVA (BPIN 2021000100160) under the supervision of Minciencias Colombia. Pimentel is supported by the Leverhulme grant RPG-2024-196 and has received funding from the European Union's Horizon 2020 research and innovation programme under the Marie Skłodowska-Curie grant agreement Number 101007627. Coniglio acknowledges support by an individual research grant from the National Council for Scientific and Technological Development (CNPq, Brazil), grant 309830/2023-0. He was also supported by the São Paulo Research Foundation (FAPESP, Brazil), thematic project *Rationality, logic and probability – RatioLog*, grant 2020/16353-3. We are grateful for the useful suggestions from Carlos Caleiro and Sergio Marcelino, as well as the anonymous referees. The collaboration of Coniglio and Olarte was possible thanks to the project CAPES/COFECUB 88881.878969/2023-01.

# References

1. Nmatrices for the Modal Cube. https://github.com/nmatrices
2. Avron, A., Lev, I.: Non-deterministic multiple-valued structures. J. Log. Comput. **15**(3), 241–261 (2005). https://doi.org/10.1093/logcom/exi001
3. Avron, A., Zamansky, A.: Non-deterministic semantics for logical systems, pp. 227–304. Springer, Dordrecht (2011). https://doi.org/10.1007/978-94-007-0479-4_4
4. Coniglio, M.E., del Cerro, L.F., Peron, N.M.: Finite non-deterministic semantics for some modal systems. J. Appl. Non Class. Logics **25**(1), 20–45 (2015). https://doi.org/10.1080/11663081.2015.1011543
5. Coniglio, M.E., del Cerro, L.F., Peron, N.M.: Modal logic with non-deterministic semantics: part I - propositional case. Log. J. IGPL **28**(3), 281–315 (2020). https://doi.org/10.1093/jigpal/jzz027
6. Coniglio, M.E., Pawlowski, P., Skurt, D.: Modal logics - RNmatrices vs. Nmatrices. In: Indrzejczak, A., Zawidzki, M. (eds.) Proceedings Eleventh International Conference on Non-Classical Logics. Theory and Applications, NCL 2024, Łódź, Poland, 5–8 September 2024. EPTCS, vol. 415, pp. 138–149 (2024). https://doi.org/10.4204/EPTCS.415.14
7. Coniglio, M.E., Pawlowski, P., Skurt, D.: RNmatrices for Modal Logics. Rev. Symb. Logic (2025, to appear). https://doi.org/10.1017/S1755020325100737
8. Dugundji, J.: Note on a property of matrices for lewis and langford's calculi of propositions. J. Symb. Log. **5**(4), 150–151 (1940). https://doi.org/10.2307/2268175
9. Durán, F., et al.: Programming and symbolic computation in Maude. J. Log. Algebraic Methods Program. **110** (2020). https://doi.org/10.1016/j.jlamp.2019.100497
10. Feferman, S., Dawson, J.W., Kleene, S.C., Moore, G.H., Solovay, R.M., van Heijenoort, J.: Kurt Gödel: Collected Works. Vol. 1: Publications 1929-1936. Oxford University Press (1986)
11. Grätz, L.: Truth tables for modal logics T and S4, by using three-valued non-deterministic level semantics. J. Log. Comput. **32**(1), 129–157 (2022). https://doi.org/10.1093/logcom/exab068
12. Ivlev, J.: A semantics for modal calculi. Bull. Sect. Logic **17**(3–4), 114–121 (1988)
13. Kearns, J.T.: Modal semantics without possible worlds. J. Symb. Log. **46**(1), 77–86 (1981). https://doi.org/10.2307/2273259
14. Lahav, O., Zohar, Y.: Effective semantics for the modal logics K and KT via non-deterministic matrices. In: Blanchette, J., Kovács, L., Pattinson, D. (eds.) Automated Reasoning - 11th International Joint Conference, IJCAR 2022, Haifa, Israel, August 8-10, 2022, Proceedings. Lecture Notes in Computer Science, vol. 13385, pp. 468–485. Springer (2022). https://doi.org/10.1007/978-3-031-10769-6_28
15. Leme, R., Coniglio, M.E., Lopes, B.: A new decision method for intuitionistic logic by 3-valued non-deterministic truth-tables (2025, submitted)
16. Leme, R., Olarte, C., Pimentel, E., Coniglio, M.E.: The modal cube revisited: semantics without worlds (technical report) (2025). https://arxiv.org/abs/2505.12824
17. Marin, S., Pereira, L.C., Pimentel, E., Sales, E.: Ecumenical modal logic. In: Martins, M.A., Sedlár, I. (eds.) Dynamic Logic. New Trends and Applications - Third International Workshop, DaLí 2020, Prague, Czech Republic, 9–10 October 2020, Revised Selected Papers. Lecture Notes in Computer Science, vol. 12569, pp. 187–204. Springer (2020). https://doi.org/10.1007/978-3-030-65840-3_12
18. Marin, S., Pereira, L.C., Pimentel, E., Sales, E.: A pure view of ecumenical modalities. In: Silva, A., Wassermann, R., de Queiroz, R.J.G.B. (eds.) Logic, Language,

Information, and Computation - 27th International Workshop, WoLLIC 2021, Virtual Event, 5–8 October 2021, Proceedings. Lecture Notes in Computer Science, vol. 13038, pp. 388–407. Springer (2021). https://doi.org/10.1007/978-3-030-88853-4_24
19. Olarte, C., Pimentel, E., Rocha, C.: A rewriting logic approach to specification, proof-search, and meta-proofs in sequent systems. J. Log. Algebraic Methods Program. **130**, 100827 (2023). https://doi.org/10.1016/J.JLAMP.2022.100827
20. Pawlowski, P., Rosa, E.L.: Modular non-deterministic semantics for T, TB, S4, S5 and more. J. Log. Comput. **32**(1), 158–171 (2022). https://doi.org/10.1093/logcom/exab079
21. Pawlowski, P., Skurt, D.: 8 valued non-deterministic semantics for modal logics. J. Philos. Log. **53**(2), 351–371 (2024). https://doi.org/10.1007/s10992-023-09733-4
22. Pawlowski, P., Skurt, D.: ◊ and □ in eight-valued non-deterministic semantics for modal logics. J. Log. Comput. **35**(2) (2025). https://doi.org/10.1093/logcom/exae010
23. Pimentel, E., Pereira, L.C.: A tour on ecumenical systems (invited talk). In: Baldan, P., de Paiva, V. (eds.) 10th Conference on Algebra and Coalgebra in Computer Science, CALCO 2023, 19–21 June 2023, Indiana University Bloomington, IN, USA. LIPIcs, vol. 270, pp. 3:1–3:15. Schloss Dagstuhl - Leibniz-Zentrum für Informatik (2023). https://doi.org/10.4230/LIPICS.CALCO.2023.3
24. Skurt, D., Omori, H.: More modal semantics without possible worlds. FLAP **3**(5), 815–846 (2016)
25. Wójcicki, R.: Lectures on Propositional Calculi. Pub. House of the Polish Academy of Sciences, Ossolineum [Poland] (1984)

**Open Access** This chapter is licensed under the terms of the Creative Commons Attribution 4.0 International License (http://creativecommons.org/licenses/by/4.0/), which permits use, sharing, adaptation, distribution and reproduction in any medium or format, as long as you give appropriate credit to the original author(s) and the source, provide a link to the Creative Commons license and indicate if changes were made.

The images or other third party material in this chapter are included in the chapter's Creative Commons license, unless indicated otherwise in a credit line to the material. If material is not included in the chapter's Creative Commons license and your intended use is not permitted by statutory regulation or exceeds the permitted use, you will need to obtain permission directly from the copyright holder.

# Non-wellfounded Proof Theory for Interpretability Logic

Sebastijan Horvat[1], Borja Sierra Miranda[2](✉) , and Thomas Studer[2]

[1] Department of Mathematics, Faculty of Science, University of Zagreb, Zagreb, Croatia
sebastijan.horvat@math.hr
[2] University of Bern, Bern, Switzerland
{borja.sierra,thomas.studer}@unibe.ch

**Abstract.** We provide a simple cut elimination proof for the interpretability logic of IL. To achieve this, we introduce a traditional Gentzen-style sequent calculus for IL and a non-wellfounded version of it. The non-wellfounded calculus makes it possible to avoid diagonal formulas. Hence, we can give a simple argument based on a general proof-theoretic method for calculi of this kind. Our results provide a useful basis for further research; in particular, they will allow us to establish uniform interpolation for IL.

**Keywords:** Proof theory · Interpretability logic · Cut elimination

## 1 Introduction

This paper is concerned with the proof theory of interpretability logic IL (see [15]), i.e., the extension of provability logic with a binary modality formalizing interpretability. We introduce two new calculi for IL: a wellfounded Gentzen calculus GIL and a non-wellfounded local progress calculus $G^\infty$IL. We show proof-theoretically the equivalence of these two calculi and also their equivalence to the usual Hilbert-style calculus for IL. Our procedure is displayed in Fig. 1.

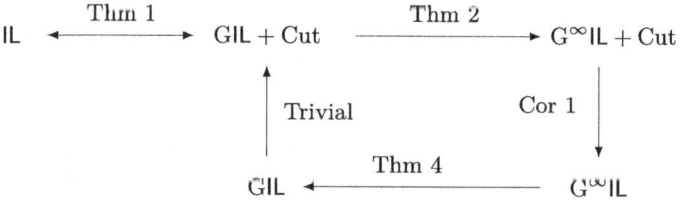

**Fig. 1.** The plan

Thus, the contributions of this paper are threefold:

---

Research supported by the Swiss National Science Foundation project 200021_214820.

1. We refine our previous work on developing a general proof theory of non-wellfounded local progress calculi. In particular, we introduce the notions of admissible, locally admissible, eliminable, and locally eliminable rules and study their relationship.
2. We present a simple syntactic cut elimination method for interpretability logic. In particular, the cut reductions will mimic the cut reductions of IK4, i.e., IL without Löb's axiom. To do so, we introduce a traditional Gentzen-style sequent calculus for IL and a non-wellfounded version of it.
3. Our non-wellfounded proofs exhibit a regular structure (i.e., they lead to cyclic proofs), which makes them a useful base for studying uniform interpolation for IL. Due to constraints of space, this part of the work has been moved to a future publication.

**Related Work.** There are two directions of closely related work. The first one is non-wellfounded and cyclic proof theory. The structure and methodology of this paper has been inspired by the seminal paper [12]. We follow the trend started in that paper of defining a non-wellfounded Gentzen calculi from a finite one where cut elimination becomes easier to show. There are many proposed methods for cut elimination in non-wellfounded and cyclic proofs. The interested reader may consult [1–3,5,7,11–14], among others.

We use our own method of cut elimination, described in detail in [14], as it simplifies the non-wellfounded cut elimination to the point of making it completely analogue to the finitary case.

The second one is the proof theoretical study of interpretability logics. Sasaki's work [8–10] has been a fundamental reference for this paper. Part of our motivation was to simplify his approach with the use of modern tools (e.g. non-wellfounded proof theory) and build from them. More recently, [6] has also studied the proof theory of subsystems of IL.

**Summary of Sections.** In the next section we will introduce the basic concepts of interpretability logic and non-wellfounded proof theory needed for the rest of the paper. Section 3 will introduce the Gentzen calculi $G^\infty IL$ and GIL. Section 4 is devoted to showing the equivalence of IL and GIL + Cut. Section 5 shows the central square of Fig. 1, thus providing a simple cut elimination procedure for GIL.

## 2 Preliminaries

In this section we will introduce the basic concepts needed for future sections.

### 2.1 Interpretability Logic

In this subsection we will define the interpretability logic that we will be working with. We will also prove that certain formulas, which will be useful to us in the next sections, are theorems of this logic.

The syntax of interpretability logic is given by

$$\phi ::= p \mid \bot \mid \phi \to \phi \mid \phi \triangleright \phi,$$

where $p$ ranges over a fixed infinite countable set of propositional variables. We call formulas of this language IL-formulas. If it will be clear from the context that we are talking about IL-formula, we will just write formula instead of IL-formula. Other Boolean connectives can be defined as abbreviations as usual. $\Box \phi$ can be defined as an abbreviation, namely $\Box \phi = \neg \phi \triangleright \bot$ and we set $\Diamond \phi = \neg \Box \neg \phi$. We will also use the abbreviations $\blacksquare \phi = (\phi \triangleright \bot) \wedge \phi$ and $\boxdot \phi = \phi \wedge \Box \phi$. A formula of the form $\phi \triangleright \psi$ will be called a $\triangleright$-formula.

We use lower case Latin letters $p$, $q$, ..., possibly with subscripts, for propositional variables and lower case Greek letters $\phi$, $\psi$, ..., possibly with subscripts, for IL-formulas. To avoid too many parentheses in longer formulas, we treat $\triangleright$ as having higher priority than $\to$, but lower than other Boolean connectives. Unary operators $\Box$, $\Diamond$ and $\neg$ have the highest priority.

The idea of interpretability logics originates by extending the usual interpretation of modal logic inside arithmatic $T$ by adding a binary modality $\triangleright$. Then $\phi \triangleright \psi$ is understood as $T+\psi$ is relative interpretable in $T+\phi$. Some interpretability logics are sound and complete with respect to this semantics, e.g., ILM when we choose $T$ to be Peano Arithmetic. IL, the logic we are going to study, is sound with respect to many arithmetical theories, but incomplete. However, it contains a good portion of the rest of interpretability logics and it is an appealing logic from the modal point of view. For details the reader is encouraged to read [15].

In some proofs we will use the following auxiliary definition of a size of an IL-formula.

**Definition 1.** *The* size $|\phi|$ *of an* IL-*formula $\phi$ is defined recursively as follows:*

$$|\bot| = 0, \qquad |p| = 1, \qquad |\phi \to \psi| = |\phi \triangleright \psi| = |\phi| + |\psi| + 1.$$

Note that, contrary to the usual definition, the size of $\bot$ is smaller than the size of any other formula.

We define the interpretability logic we will consider in this paper.

**Definition 2.** *Interpretability logic* IL *is the smallest set of* IL-*formulas that contains all the classical propositional tautologies and axioms*

(K) $\Box(\phi \to \psi) \to (\Box \phi \to \Box \psi)$,    (4) $\Box \phi \to \Box \Box \phi$,
(L) $\Box(\Box \phi \to \phi) \to \Box \phi$,    (J1) $\Box(\phi \to \psi) \to (\phi \triangleright \psi)$,
(J2) $(\phi \triangleright \chi) \wedge (\chi \triangleright \psi) \to (\phi \triangleright \psi)$,    (J3) $(\phi \triangleright \psi) \wedge (\chi \triangleright \psi) \to (\phi \vee \chi) \triangleright \psi$,
(J4) $\phi \triangleright \psi \to (\Diamond \phi \to \Diamond \psi)$.    (J5) $\Diamond \phi \triangleright \phi$

*and is closed under modus ponens and necessitation:*

$$\dfrac{\phi \to \psi \quad \phi}{\psi}, \qquad \dfrac{\phi}{\Box \phi}.$$

*Sometimes we will be referring to axiom (L) as* **Löb** *axiom.*

In the following lemma we will put together some basic properties of IL. These results will be used in some proofs in the remainder of this paper.

**Lemma 1.** *Let $\phi, \psi$ be formulas and $\Sigma$ be a non-empty finite multiset of formulas. Then*

1. $\mathsf{IL} \vdash \phi \to \psi$ *implies* $\mathsf{IL} \vdash \phi \rhd \psi$.
2. *(Löb's rule in* $\mathsf{IL}$*)* $\mathsf{IL} \vdash \psi \land \bigwedge(\Sigma \rhd \bot) \to \bigvee \Sigma$ *implies* $\mathsf{IL} \vdash \psi \rhd \bigvee \Sigma$.
3. $\mathsf{IL} \vdash \phi \rhd \blacksquare \phi$.

*Proof.* The proof of 1. is trivial using necessitation and (J1). Let us prove 2. and 3. in detail.

Assume $\mathsf{IL} \vdash \psi \land \bigwedge(\Sigma \rhd \bot) \to \bigvee \Sigma$. From classical propositional reasoning we obtain $\mathsf{IL} \vdash \psi \to \bigvee \Sigma \lor \bigvee(\Diamond \Sigma)$, so by using 1. we obtain

$$\mathsf{IL} \vdash \psi \rhd \left(\bigvee \Sigma \lor \bigvee \Diamond \Sigma\right) \qquad (i)$$

Let $\Sigma = \{\phi_0, \ldots, \phi_m\}$ and notice that $\mathsf{IL} \vdash \Diamond \phi_j \rhd \phi_j$ for each $j \leq m$ thanks to (J5). For each $j \leq m$ we also have by 1. that $\mathsf{IL} \vdash \phi_j \rhd \phi_j$, so we get by (J3) that $\mathsf{IL} \vdash (\phi_j \lor \Diamond \phi_j) \rhd \phi_j$. Also from $\mathsf{IL} \vdash \phi_j \to \bigvee_{i \leq m} \phi_i$ by 1. we get $\mathsf{IL} \vdash \phi_j \rhd \bigvee_{i \leq m} \phi_i$. Then, using (J2) we obtain $\mathsf{IL} \vdash (\phi_j \lor \Diamond \phi_j) \rhd \bigvee_{i \leq m} \phi_i$ for each $j \leq m$ and, by (J3),

$$\mathsf{IL} \vdash \left(\bigvee_{i \leq m}(\phi_i \lor \Diamond \phi_i)\right) \rhd \bigvee_{i \leq m} \phi_i. \qquad (ii)$$

Since the formulas $\left(\bigvee_{i \leq m} \phi_i\right) \lor \left(\bigvee_{i \leq m} \Diamond \phi_i\right)$ and $\bigvee_{i \leq m}(\phi_i \lor \Diamond \phi_i)$ are equivalent in classical propositional logic by 1. we obtain

$$\mathsf{IL} \vdash \left(\bigvee \Sigma \lor \bigvee \Diamond \Sigma\right) \rhd \left(\bigvee_{i \leq m}(\phi_i \lor \Diamond \phi_i)\right) \qquad (iii)$$

where we used that $\left(\bigvee_{i \leq m} \phi_i\right) \lor \left(\bigvee_{i \leq m} \Diamond \phi_i\right)$ is just the same formula as $\bigvee \Sigma \lor \bigvee \Diamond \Sigma$. So using (i), (ii), (iii) and the (J2) axiom gives us

$$\mathsf{IL} \vdash \psi \rhd \bigvee_{i \leq m} \phi_i,$$

as desired.

Proof of 3. By Löb's axiom we obtain that $\mathsf{IL} \vdash \Box(\Box \neg \phi \to \neg \phi) \to \Box \neg \phi$. Unfolding some definitions of $\Box$ we get $\mathsf{IL} \vdash \neg(\Box \neg \phi \to \neg \phi) \rhd \bot \to \neg \neg \phi \rhd \bot$. Since $\mathsf{IL} \vdash \neg \neg \phi \leftrightarrow \phi$ and $\mathsf{IL} \vdash \neg(\Box \neg \phi \to \neg \phi) \leftrightarrow (\Box \neg \phi \land \phi)$, using 1. and (J2) we get $\mathsf{IL} \vdash (\Box \neg \phi \land \phi) \rhd \bot \to \phi \rhd \bot$, or in other words $\mathsf{IL} \vdash ((\neg \neg \phi \rhd \bot) \land \phi) \rhd \bot \to \phi \rhd \bot$. Using again that $\mathsf{IL} \vdash \neg \neg \phi \leftrightarrow \phi$ with 1. and (J2) (multiple times) we obtain $\mathsf{IL} \vdash ((\phi \rhd \bot) \land \phi) \rhd \bot \to \phi \rhd \bot$, i.e., $\mathsf{IL} \vdash \blacksquare \phi \rhd \bot \to \phi \rhd \bot$. Adding $\phi$ on both sides we have $\mathsf{IL} \vdash \phi \land (\blacksquare \phi \rhd \bot) \to \phi \land \phi \rhd \bot$, or analogously, $\mathsf{IL} \vdash \phi \land (\blacksquare \phi \rhd \bot) \to \blacksquare \phi$. Using 2. we conclude the desired $\mathsf{IL} \vdash \phi \rhd \blacksquare \phi$.

## 2.2 Non-wellfounded Proof Theory

We introduce the basic concepts of (non-wellfounded) proof theory that we are going to use. The details can be found in [14]. We start with the definition of non-wellfounded finitely branching trees, from now own simply called *trees*.

**Definition 3.** *A tree with labels in $A$ is a function $T$ such that*

1. $\mathrm{Dom}(T) \subseteq \mathbb{N}^{<\omega}$ *is closed under prefixes and* $\mathrm{Im}(T) \subseteq A$.
2. *For each $w \in \mathrm{Dom}(T)$ there is an unique $k$, called the* arity *of $w$, such that $wi \in \mathrm{Dom}(T)$ if and only if $i < k$.*

*The elements of* $\mathrm{Dom}(T)$ *are called* nodes *of $T$.*

*Given a tree $T$ an* (infinite) branch *is an infinite sequence $b \in \mathbb{N}^\omega$ such that for each $i \in \mathbb{N}$, $b\!\restriction\! i \in \mathrm{Dom}(T)$, where $b\!\restriction\! i = b_0 \cdots b_{i-1}$.*

**Basics of Local Progress Calculi.** We use upper case Greek letters $\Gamma$, $\Delta$, $\Sigma$, $\Gamma'$, $\Delta'$, ..., possibly with subscripts, for finite multisets of formulas. The expression $\Gamma \triangleright \bot$ denotes the multiset $\{\phi \triangleright \bot \mid \phi \in \Gamma\}$. By a sequent, we mean an ordered pair $\langle \Gamma, \Delta \rangle$ usually denoted as $\Gamma \Rightarrow \Delta$. We use upper case Latin letters $S$, $S'$, ..., possibly with subscripts, for sequents. We will write $\Gamma, \Delta$ to mean $\Gamma \cup \Delta$ and $\phi, \Gamma$ or $\Gamma, \phi$ to mean $\{\phi\} \cup \Gamma$, as usual.[1] Also, we will write expressions like $(\Gamma, \phi, \Delta) \triangleright \bot$ to mean $(\Gamma \triangleright \bot) \cup \{\phi \triangleright \bot\} \cup (\Delta \triangleright \bot)$. Sequences of sequents like $S_n, \ldots, S_0$ will be denoted as $[S_i]_{n\ldots i \ldots 0}$.

**Definition 4.** *An $n$-ary* rule *is a set of $n+1$-tuples $\langle S_0, \ldots, S_n \rangle$ where each $S_i$ is a sequent. The elements of a rule are called its* instances.

*A* local progress sequent calculus *is a pair $G = \langle \mathcal{R}, L \rangle$ where*

1. $\mathcal{R}$ *is a set of rules.*
2. $L$ *is a function such that given a $n$-ary rule $R$ and a rule instance $\langle S_0, \ldots, S_n \rangle$ of $R$ returns a subset of $\{0, \ldots, n-1\}$, called* progressing premises. $L$ *is called the* progressing function.

**Definition 5.** *Let $G$ be a local progress sequent calculus. A* preproof $\pi$ *in $G$ is a non wellfounded tree, whose nodes are annotated by a sequent and a rule of $G$, that is generated by the rules of $G$. In other words, for any $n$-ary node $w$ of $\pi$ we have that $\langle S_0, \ldots, S_{n-1}, S \rangle \in R$, where $R$ is the rule at $w$, $S$ is the sequent at $w$ and $S_i$ is the sequent at $wi$ (the $i$-th successor of $w$).*

*Given a preproof $\pi$ in $G$ and an infinite branch $b$ in $\pi$ we will say that $b$* progresses at $i$ *iff $b_{i+1} \in L_R(S_0, \ldots, S_{n-1}, S)$ where the node $b\!\restriction\! i$ is $n$-ary, $R$ is the rule at node $b\!\restriction\! i$, $S$ is the sequent at node $b\!\restriction\! i$ and $S_j$ is the sequent at node $(b\!\restriction\! i)j$ for $j < n$. A preproof $\pi$ in $G$ is said to be a* proof *in $G$ iff for any infinite branch $b$ of $\pi$ the set $\{i \in \mathbb{N} \mid b \text{ progresses at } i\}$ is infinite. We will write $G \vdash S$*

---

[1] Note that in particular $\Gamma_0, \ldots, \Gamma_n$ could be either $\Gamma_0 \cup \cdots \cup \Gamma_n$ or a sequence of multisets of formulas with first element $\Gamma_0$ and last element $\Gamma_n$. The meaning of this expression should be clear by context.

to mean that there is a proof in $G$ whose conclusion is $S$ and $\pi \vdash_G S$ to mean that $\pi$ is a proof in $G$ with conclusion $S$ (we will omit $G$ when it is clear from the context).

A local progress calculus is said to be *wellfounded iff* its local progress function is the constant function always returning ∅. Given a local progress calculus $G$ and a rule $R$ not in $\mathcal{R}$ we will define the local progress calculus $G + R$ by adding the rule $R$ to the calculus and extending the local progress function such that no premise of an instance of $R$ is a progressing premise.

**The Method of Translations.** In [14] we developed a method to prove translations between local progress calculi, i.e., to provide functions transforming proofs of one calculus into proofs (not necessarily of the same sequent) in another calculus. Here, we will introduce informally the concepts and methods, the interested reader should consult [14] for more details.

The idea goes as follows. Given a proof $\pi$ in a local progress calculus $G$ we can define a partition of its nodes, the elements of the partition will be called *local fragments*. Two nodes will belong to the same local fragment if the smallest path between them does not go through progress. Here, with passing through progress we mean going from the premise to the conclusion of a rule instance, or from conclusion to premise, such that the premise is progressing in the rule instance. Thanks to the condition that any infinite branch progresses infinitely often, it is easy to see that each local fragment will be a finite tree, in other words, this slices the non-wellfounded tree into (possibly infinitely many) finite trees. Figure 2 shows how the slicing can look in this setting, where each triangle represents a local fragment.

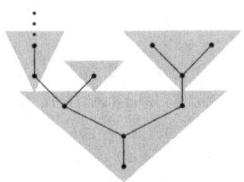

**Fig. 2.** Structure of proofs in local progress calculi

The bottom-most local fragment, i.e., the one to which the root belongs to, is called the *main local fragment*. We define the *local height* of a proof $\pi$, denoted as $\text{lhg}(\pi)$, as the height of its main local fragment (which is a finite tree, so indeed it has a height).

Finally, the translation method goes as follows. To define a function from local progress Gentzen calculus $G$ to local progress Gentzen calculus $G'$, it suffices to provide another function (called *corecursive step*) that, given a proof $\pi$ in $G$, returns:

1. a local fragment in $G'$, i.e., a finite tree generated by the rules of $G'$ where every leaf is either axiomatic or a progressing premise and every progressing premise is a leaf;
2. for each non-axiomatic leaf (of the local fragment) with sequent $S$, a proof of $S$ in $G$.

Then, the desired translation function is obtained by extending this corecursive step via corecursion. The procedure is displayed in Fig. 3.

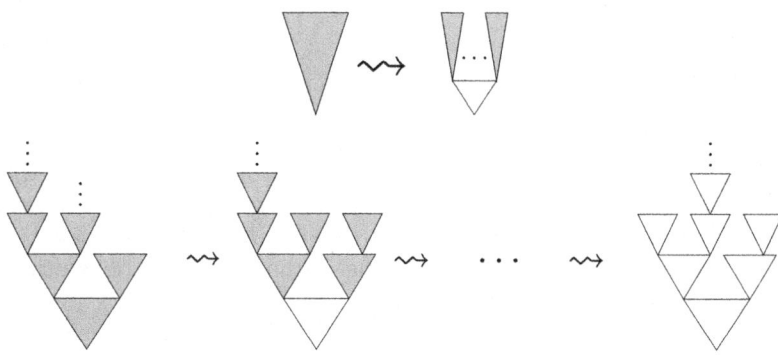

**Fig. 3.** Corecursive step function (top) and its extension from proofs to proofs (bottom). Tall gray (white) triangles represent proofs in $G$ ($G'$) and short gray (white) triangles represent local fragments in $G$ ($G'$).

**Properties of Rules.** Finally we introduce some properties of rules and proofs that will be fundamental to show cut elimination.

**Definition 6.** *Let $R$ be an $n$-ary rule, $G$ be a local progress Gentzen calculus and $\pi$ a proof in $G + R$. We say that*

1. *$R$ is admissible in $G$ iff for any instance $\langle S_0, \ldots, S_{n-1}, S \rangle$ of the rule $R$, $G \vdash S_0, \ldots, G \vdash S_{n-1}$ implies that $G \vdash S$.*
2. *$R$ is invertible iff for each $i < n$, the rule*

$$R_i^{-1} = \{\langle S_n, S_i \rangle \mid \text{Exists } S_0, \ldots, S_{i-1}, S_{i+1}, \ldots S_{n-1}. \langle S_0, \ldots, S_n \rangle \in R\}$$

*is admissible. In words, if each of the rules which says that from the conclusion you can infer the premises is admissible.*
3. *$R$ is eliminable in $G$ iff for any sequent $S$ if $G + R \vdash S$ then $G \vdash S$.*
4. *$\pi$ is locally $R$-free iff it contains no instances of $R$ in its main local fragment.*
5. *$R$ is locally admissible in $G$ iff for any instance $\langle S_0, \ldots, S_{n-1}, S \rangle$ of the rule if $G \vdash S_0, \ldots, G \vdash S_{n-1}$ with locally $R$-free proofs, then there is a locally $R$-free proof of $G \vdash S$.*
6. *$R$ is locally eliminable iff for any $S$, if $G + R \vdash S$ then there is a locally $R$-free proof in $G + R$ of $S$.*

*All the previous properties can be understood as asserting the existence of a proof $\pi$ from the assumption that some proofs $\tau_0, \ldots, \tau_{n-1}$ exist. Let P be a property of proofs, we say that any of the properties above holds* preserving P *if, adding the extra assumption that $\tau_0, \ldots, \tau_{n-1}$ fulfill P, $\pi$ also fulfills P.*

Note that the usual proof of admissibility implying eliminability does not hold for non-wellfounded proofs, as it requires an induction on the height of a non-wellfounded proof (which does not exist). For that reason we introduce the new notions of local admissibility and local eliminability. The main application of the method of translations is the following lemma, which relates these new notions to eliminability.

**Lemma 2.** *For any local progress sequent calculi, the following holds*

$$R \text{ eliminable iff } R \text{ locally eliminable iff } R \text{ locally admissible.}$$

*Proof.* That $R$ is eliminable trivially implies that $R$ is locally admissible. To show that $R$ locally admissible implies $R$ locally eliminable it suffices to do an induction in the local height. Finally, to show that $R$ locally eliminable implies that $R$ is eliminable it suffices to apply the method of translations using local eliminability to define a corecursive step.

## 3 Sequent Calculi for IL

In this section we introduce two sequent calculi for IL. Let us introduce a useful convention for describing the rules of these calculi. In case $X \subseteq \mathbb{N}$ we will define the sets

$$\Phi_X := \{\phi_i \mid i \in X\} \quad \text{and} \quad \Psi_X := \{\psi_i \mid i \in X\}.$$

In particular $X$ will always be an interval like $(i,j)$, $[i,j]$ or $[i,j)$.

$$\frac{}{p, \Gamma \Rightarrow p, \Delta} \text{ ax} \qquad \frac{}{\bot, \Gamma \Rightarrow \Delta} \bot\text{L} \qquad \frac{\Gamma \Rightarrow \Delta, \chi \quad \chi, \Gamma \Rightarrow \Delta}{\Gamma \Rightarrow \Delta} \text{ Cut}$$

$$\frac{\Gamma \Rightarrow \Delta, \phi \quad \psi, \Gamma \Rightarrow \Delta}{\phi \rightarrow \psi, \Gamma \Rightarrow \Delta} \rightarrow\text{L} \qquad \frac{[\psi_i, (\psi_i, \Phi_{[0,i)}, \phi) \triangleright \bot \Rightarrow \Phi_{[0,i)}, \phi]_{m\ldots i \ldots 0}}{\{\phi_i \triangleright \psi_i\}_{i<m}, \Gamma \Rightarrow \psi_m \triangleright \phi, \Delta} \triangleright_\text{IL}$$

$$\frac{\phi, \Gamma \Rightarrow \Delta, \psi}{\Gamma \Rightarrow \Delta, \phi \rightarrow \psi} \rightarrow\text{R} \qquad \frac{[\psi_i, (\Phi_{[0,i)}, \phi) \triangleright \bot \Rightarrow \Phi_{[0,i)}, \phi]_{m\ldots i \ldots 0}}{\{\phi_i \triangleright \psi_i\}_{i<m}, \Gamma \Rightarrow \psi_m \triangleright \phi, \Delta} \triangleright_\text{IK4}$$

**Fig. 4.** Sequent rules

**Definition 7.** *We define the sequent calculus* GIL *as the wellfounded calculus given by the rules of Fig. 4 without rules $\triangleright_{\text{IK4}}$ and* Cut.

*We define the sequent calculus* $G^\infty$IL *as the local progress sequent calculus given by the rules of Fig. 4 without rules $\triangleright_{\text{IL}}$ and* Cut. *Progress only occurs at the premises of $\triangleright_{\text{IK4}}$.*

In the rules ax, $\bot L$, $\to L$ and $\to R$ of Fig. 4 the explicitly displayed formula in the conclusion is called the *principal formula*. In $\rhd_{\mathsf{IL}}$ and $\rhd_{\mathsf{IK4}}$ the formula $\psi_m \rhd \phi$ is called *principal*, and multisets of formulas $\Gamma$ and $\Delta$ are called the *weakening part* of these rules. In $\rhd_{\mathsf{IL}}$ the formula $\psi_m \rhd \bot$ appearing at the left hand side of the first premise is called *diagonal formula*. The absence of diagonal formula at $\rhd_{\mathsf{IK4}}$ is what simplifies the treatment of Cut elimination. The explicitly displayed formula in the Cut rule is called the cut formula.

The calculus GIL is inspired from the calculus for IK4 in [9]. It provides a simplification of the calculus defined there, as we are capable of give a much more concrete shape to the modal rule. However, we notice a peculiar property of our calculus: the premises depend on an ordering of the $\rhd$-formulas of the conclusion. This implies that the same conclusion could have been obtained in multiple ways, depending on the ordering chosen. The necessity of an order comes from the axiom (J2) of IL.

The following lemma will be used in many proofs in the rest of this paper, as usual it is proven by induction on the size of $\phi$. When we use this lemma in a proof we will simply write Ax just as we write ax for the rule in Fig. 4.

**Lemma 3.** *Let $\phi$ be a formula. Then in $\mathsf{GIL}$ and in $\mathsf{G}^\infty\mathsf{IL}$ we have that*

$$\vdash \phi, \Gamma \Rightarrow \phi, \Delta.$$

*Proof.* This is a simple proof by induction on $|\phi|$. Cases where $\phi$ is $\bot$ or an atomic variable are trivial, and the case where $\phi$ is an implication is as usual. Assume $\phi = \phi_0 \rhd \phi_1$. Then we provide the following proof for GIL

$$\dfrac{\dfrac{}{\phi_0 \rhd \bot, \phi_0, \phi_0 \rhd \bot, \phi_1 \rhd \bot \Rightarrow \phi_0, \phi_1} \text{I.H.} \quad \dfrac{}{\phi_1 \rhd \bot, \phi_1, \phi_1 \rhd \bot \Rightarrow \phi_1} \text{I.H.}}{\Gamma, \phi_0 \rhd \phi_1 \Rightarrow \phi_0 \rhd \phi_1, \Delta} \rhd_{\mathsf{IL}}$$

and this other proof for $\mathsf{G}^\infty\mathsf{IL}$

$$\dfrac{\dfrac{}{\phi_0, \phi_0 \rhd \bot, \phi_1 \rhd \bot \Rightarrow \phi_0, \phi_1} \text{I.H.} \quad \dfrac{}{\phi_1, \phi_1 \rhd \bot \Rightarrow \phi_1} \text{I.H.}}{\Gamma, \phi_0 \rhd \phi_1 \Rightarrow \phi_0 \rhd \phi_1, \Delta} \rhd_{\mathsf{IK4}}$$

where, in both cases, we applied the rule $\rhd_{\mathsf{IL}}$ with ordering $\phi_0 \rhd \phi_1$ and principal formula $\phi_0 \rhd \phi_1$.

We state the eliminability of some rules that will be useful, they are proved by showing admissibility or local admissibility (depending on the calculus) which is shown by induction on the height or local height, respectively.

**Lemma 4.** *The rules*

$$\dfrac{\Gamma \Rightarrow \Delta}{\Gamma, \Gamma' \Rightarrow \Delta, \Delta'} \text{Wk} \qquad \dfrac{\Gamma \Rightarrow \Delta, \bot}{\Gamma \Rightarrow \Delta} \bot\text{R}$$

*are eliminable in $\mathsf{GIL}(+\mathrm{Cut})$ and in $\mathsf{G}^\infty\mathsf{IL}(+\mathrm{Cut})$. In addition*

1. *In $\mathsf{GIL}(+\mathrm{Cut})$ they are eliminable preserving height.*

2. In $\mathsf{G}^\infty\mathsf{IL}(+\mathrm{Cut})$ *they are eliminable preserving local height and local* Cut-*freeness.*

**Lemma 5.** *The rules* $\to L$ *and* $\to R$ *are invertible in* $\mathsf{GIL}(+\mathrm{Cut})$, *preserving height; and in* $\mathsf{G}^\infty\mathsf{IL}(+\mathrm{Cut})$, *preserving local height and local* Cut-*freeness.*

Notice that in $\mathsf{G}^\infty\mathsf{IL}(+\mathrm{Cut})$ we added a preservation of local height and local Cut-freeness. It is not hard to see, that if we show local admissibility preserves these properties while extending local admissibility to eliminability this preservation remains. For preservation of height in $\mathsf{GIL}(+\mathrm{Cut})$ a similar argument applies.

**Lemma 6.** *The rule*
$$\dfrac{\phi, \Sigma \triangleright \bot \Rightarrow \Sigma}{\Sigma \triangleright \bot, \Gamma \Rightarrow \phi \triangleright \bot, \Delta}\ \mathrm{Nec}$$
*is admissible in* $\mathsf{GIL}(+\mathrm{Cut})$ *and in* $\mathsf{G}^\infty\mathsf{IL}(+\mathrm{Cut})$.

*Proof.* We show it for $\mathsf{GIL}(+\mathrm{Cut})$, the other proof being similar. Assume $\pi \vdash \phi, \Sigma \triangleright \bot \Rightarrow \Sigma$ in $\mathsf{GIL}(+\mathrm{Cut})$ and let us enumerate $\Sigma$ as $\{\phi_0, \ldots, \phi_{m-1}\}$ (note that then $\Sigma = \Phi_{[0,m)}$). Then, the desired proof for $\mathsf{GIL}$ is

$$\dfrac{\dfrac{\overset{\pi}{\phi, \Phi_{[0,m)} \triangleright \bot \Rightarrow \Phi_{[0,m)}}}{\phi, (\phi, \Phi_{[0,m)}, \bot) \triangleright \bot \Rightarrow \Phi_{[0,m)}, \bot}\ \mathrm{Wk} \quad \dfrac{}{\bot, \ldots \Rightarrow \ldots}\ \bot\mathrm{L} \quad \ldots}{\Sigma \triangleright \bot, \Gamma \Rightarrow \phi \triangleright \bot, \Delta}\ \triangleright_{\mathsf{IL}}$$

where in the right-most dots we are omitting some proofs by $\bot\mathrm{L}$.

Finally, we note some nice properties of the Cut-free calculi.

**Proposition 1.** *Any preproof of* $\mathsf{G}^\infty\mathsf{IL}$ *is a proof of* $\mathsf{G}^\infty\mathsf{IL}$.

*Proof.* The rules $\to \mathrm{L}$ and $\to \mathrm{R}$ reduce the size of the sequent (which is just the sum of the sizes of each formula ocurrence in it). So any infinite branch in a preproof must have infinitely many instances of $\triangleright_{\mathsf{IK4}}$.

Due to the shape of the rules we need to slightly change the usual definition of subformula set. This definition allows to establish the subformula property for $\mathsf{GIL}$ and $\mathsf{G}^\infty\mathsf{IL}$.

**Definition 8.** *Let $\phi$ be a formula. We define the set* $\mathrm{Sub}_\triangleright(\phi)$ *as follows:*

$$\mathrm{Sub}_\triangleright(p) = \{p\}, \quad \mathrm{Sub}_\triangleright(\bot) = \{\bot\},$$
$$\mathrm{Sub}_\triangleright(\phi \to \psi) = \{\phi \to \psi\} \cup \mathrm{Sub}_\triangleright(\phi) \cup \mathrm{Sub}_\triangleright(\psi),$$
$$\mathrm{Sub}_\triangleright(\phi \triangleright \psi) = \{\phi \triangleright \psi, \phi \triangleright \bot, \psi \triangleright \bot, \bot\} \cup \mathrm{Sub}_\triangleright(\phi) \cup \mathrm{Sub}_\triangleright(\psi).$$

*If $\Gamma$ is a multiset,* $\mathrm{Sub}_\triangleright(\Gamma) = \bigcup\{\mathrm{Sub}_\triangleright(\phi) \mid \phi \in \Gamma\}$; *and if* $S = (\Gamma \Rightarrow \Delta)$ *is a sequent, then* $\mathrm{Sub}_\triangleright(S) = \mathrm{Sub}_\triangleright(\Gamma \cup \Delta)$.

**Proposition 2 (Subformula property).** *Let* $\pi \vdash S$ *in* $\mathsf{G}^\infty\mathsf{IL}$ *or* $\mathsf{GIL}$ *and $\phi$ be a formula occurring in $\pi$. Then* $\phi \in \mathrm{Sub}_\triangleright(S)$.

## 4 Equivalence of IL and GIL + Cut

We show the equivalence of Hilbert style proofs in IL and sequent proofs in the calculus GIL+Cut. First we remember the interpretation of sequents as formulas.

**Definition 9.** *Given a sequent $S = (\Gamma \Rightarrow \Delta)$, we define $S^\sharp = (\bigwedge \Gamma \to \bigvee \Delta)$.*

**Lemma 7.** *Let $\mathsf{IL} \vdash \phi$, then $\mathsf{GIL} + \mathsf{Cut} \vdash \Rightarrow \phi$.*

*Proof.* By induction on the length of the Hilbert-style proof of $\phi$. The case of classical propositional tautologies is trivial, the proofs in GIL of the modal axioms are easy to construct. For modus ponens case it suffices to use Lemma 5 and Cut. For necessitation case it suffices to use Lemma 6.

The converse of the previous lemma is a simple consequence of the following.

**Theorem 1.** *For any sequent $S$, $\mathsf{IL} \vdash S^\sharp$ if and only if $\mathsf{GIL} + \mathsf{Cut} \vdash S$.*

*Proof.* Let $S = (\Gamma \Rightarrow \Delta)$. Using Lemma 7, we have that $\mathsf{IL} \vdash S^\sharp$ implies $\mathsf{GIL} + \mathsf{Cut} \vdash \Rightarrow \bigwedge \Gamma \to \bigvee \Delta$. Then, using invertibility of $\to L, \to R$ and admissibility of $\bot R$, we obtain $\mathsf{GIL} + \mathsf{Cut} \vdash \Gamma \Rightarrow \Delta$.

For the other direction, let $\pi \vdash S$ in $\mathsf{GIL} + \mathsf{Cut}$. We proceed by induction on the height of $\pi$ and cases in the last rule of $\pi$. The cases where the last rule of $\pi$ is either $ax, \bot L, \to L, \to R, \mathsf{Cut}$ follow from simple propositional tautologies. So we focus on the $\rhd_{\mathsf{IL}}$ case. Then $\pi$ is of shape

$$\cfrac{\left[\cfrac{\pi_i}{\psi_i, (\psi_i, \Phi_{[0,i)}, \phi) \rhd \bot \Rightarrow \Phi_{[0,i)}, \phi}\right]_{m...i...0}}{\{\phi_i \rhd \psi_i\}_{i<m}, \Gamma \Rightarrow \psi_m \rhd \phi, \Delta} \rhd_{\mathsf{IL}}.$$

By the induction hypothesis we get

$$\mathsf{IL} \vdash (\psi_i \rhd \bot) \land \psi_i \land \bigwedge (\Phi_{[0,i)} \rhd \bot) \land (\phi \rhd \bot) \to \bigvee \Phi_{[0,i)} \lor \phi, \quad \text{for } i \leq m,$$

so by Löb's rule we have $\mathsf{IL} \vdash ((\psi_i \rhd \bot) \land \psi_i) \rhd (\bigvee \Phi_{[0,i)} \lor \phi)$, or equivalently $\mathsf{IL} \vdash \blacksquare \psi_i \rhd (\bigvee \Phi_{[0,i)} \lor \phi)$ for $i \leq m$. Using Lemma 1 with (J2) we have $\mathsf{IL} \vdash \psi_i \rhd (\bigvee \Phi_{[0,i)} \lor \phi)$, for $i \leq m$. By induction on $i \leq m$ we show that $\mathsf{IL} \vdash (\bigwedge_{k<m} \phi_k \rhd \psi_k) \to \psi_i \rhd \phi$, so assume $\mathsf{IL} \vdash (\bigwedge_{k<m} \phi_k \rhd \psi_k) \to \psi_j \rhd \phi$, for $j < i$. Using (J3) we get $\mathsf{IL} \vdash (\bigwedge_{k<m} \phi_k \rhd \psi_k) \to (\bigvee_{j<i} \psi_j) \rhd \phi$ and by (J2) $\mathsf{IL} \vdash (\bigwedge_{k<m} \phi_k \rhd \psi_k) \to (\bigvee \Phi_{[0,i)}) \rhd \phi$. Also $\mathsf{IL} \vdash \phi \rhd \phi$, so we get $\mathsf{IL} \vdash (\bigwedge_{k<m} \phi_k \rhd \psi_k) \to (\bigvee \Phi_{[0,i)} \lor \phi) \rhd \phi$. But $\mathsf{IL} \vdash \psi_i \rhd (\bigvee \Phi_{[0,i)} \lor \phi)$ so by the use of (J2) we conclude the desired $\mathsf{IL} \vdash (\bigwedge_{k<m} \phi_k \rhd \psi_k) \to \psi_i \rhd \phi$.

## 5 Equivalence of GIL(+Cut) and G$^\infty$IL(+Cut)

In this section we will provide a Cut elimination method for GIL by translating to G$^\infty$IL and back. Thanks to G$^\infty$IL being a local progress calculus, we can show Cut eliminability by just proving local admissibility. Finally, the translation to and back from the local progress calculus will be defined by recursion.

### 5.1 From GIL + Cut to G$^\infty$IL + Cut

First, we will prove that anything provable in GIL + Cut is also provable in G$^\infty$IL + Cut.

**Lemma 8.** *We have that* G$^\infty$IL $\vdash \phi \triangleright \psi, \psi \triangleright \chi \Rightarrow \phi \triangleright \chi$ *and* G$^\infty$IL $\vdash \Rightarrow \phi \triangleright \blacksquare \phi$.

*Proof.* Proof of G$^\infty$IL $\vdash \phi \triangleright \psi, \psi \triangleright \chi \Rightarrow \phi \triangleright \chi$. We have the proof

$$\cfrac{\cfrac{}{\phi, \phi \triangleright \bot, \ldots \Rightarrow \phi, \ldots}\text{Ax} \quad \cfrac{}{\psi, \psi \triangleright \bot, \ldots \Rightarrow \psi, \ldots}\text{Ax} \quad \cfrac{}{\chi, \chi \triangleright \bot \Rightarrow \chi}\text{Ax}}{\phi \triangleright \psi, \psi \triangleright \chi \Rightarrow \phi \triangleright \chi}\triangleright_{\text{IK4}}.$$

Proof of G$^\infty$IL $\vdash \Rightarrow \phi \triangleright \blacksquare \phi$. Define the proof $\pi$ as

$$\cfrac{\cfrac{\cfrac{\boxed{\phi, (\blacksquare\phi, \bot) \triangleright \bot \Rightarrow \blacksquare\phi, \bot} \quad \cfrac{\bot, \bot \triangleright \bot \Rightarrow \bot}{}\bot\text{L}}{\phi, (\blacksquare\phi, \bot) \triangleright \bot \Rightarrow \phi \triangleright \bot, \bot}\triangleright_{\text{IK4}} \quad \cfrac{}{\phi, (\blacksquare\phi, \bot) \triangleright \bot \Rightarrow \phi, \bot}\text{Ax}}{\cfrac{\phi, (\blacksquare\phi, \bot) \triangleright \bot \Rightarrow (\phi \triangleright \bot) \wedge \phi, \bot}{\boxed{\phi, (\blacksquare\phi, \bot) \triangleright \bot \Rightarrow \blacksquare\phi, \bot}}}\wedge\text{R}$$

where the gray box at the top indicates the start of a non-wellfounded branch obtained by copying the proof from the gray box at the bottom infinitely often. Note that we applied $\triangleright_{\text{IK4}}$ with ordering $\blacksquare\phi \triangleright \bot$ and principal formula $\phi \triangleright \bot$. The desired proof is

$$\cfrac{\cfrac{\cfrac{\pi}{\phi, (\blacksquare\phi, \bot) \triangleright \bot \Rightarrow \blacksquare\phi, \bot} \quad \cfrac{\bot, \ldots \Rightarrow \ldots}{}\bot\text{L}}{\phi, \blacksquare\phi \triangleright \bot \Rightarrow \phi \triangleright \bot}\triangleright_{\text{IK4}} \quad \cfrac{}{\phi, \blacksquare\phi \triangleright \bot \Rightarrow \phi}\text{Ax}}{\cfrac{\phi, \blacksquare\phi \triangleright \bot \Rightarrow (\phi \triangleright \bot) \wedge \phi}{\cfrac{\phi, \blacksquare\phi \triangleright \bot \Rightarrow \blacksquare\phi}{\Rightarrow \phi \triangleright \blacksquare\phi}\triangleright_{\text{IK4}}}}\wedge\text{R}$$

**Theorem 2.** *Let S be a sequent. If* GIL + Cut $\vdash S$, *then* G$^\infty$IL + Cut $\vdash S$.

*Proof.* Let $\pi \vdash S$ in GIL + Cut. We proceed by induction on the height of the proof $\pi$ and case analysis in the last rule applied. The only interesting case is when the last rule is $\triangleright_{\text{IL}}$, so $\pi$ is of shape

$$\cfrac{\left[\cfrac{\pi_i}{\psi_i, (\psi_i, \Phi_{[0,i)}, \phi) \triangleright \bot \Rightarrow \Phi_{[0,i)}, \phi}\right]_{m \ldots i \ldots 0}}{\{\phi_i \triangleright \psi_i\}_{i<m}, \Gamma \Rightarrow \Delta, \psi_m \triangleright \phi}\triangleright_{\text{IL}}.$$

So by induction hypothesis we get a proof $\pi_i'$ in G$^\infty$IL + Cut proving the same sequent as $\pi_i$, for $i \leq m$. First, define a proof $\tau_i$ in G$^\infty$IL + Cut for $i \leq m$ as

$$\cfrac{\cfrac{\pi_i'}{\psi_i, (\psi_i, \Phi_{[0,i)}, \phi) \triangleright \bot \Rightarrow \Phi_{[0,i)}, \phi}}{\blacksquare\psi_i, (\Phi_{[0,i)}, \phi) \triangleright \bot \Rightarrow \Phi_{[0,i)}, \phi}\wedge\text{L}.$$

Then define the proof $\rho$ in $G^\infty IL + Cut$ as

$$\dfrac{\left[\dfrac{\tau_i}{\blacksquare\psi_i,(\Phi_{[0,i)},\phi)\rhd\bot\Rightarrow\Phi_{[0,i)},\phi}\right]_{m...i...0}}{\{\phi_i\rhd\blacksquare\psi_i\}_{i<m},\Gamma\Rightarrow\Delta,\blacksquare\psi_m\rhd\phi}\rhd_{IK4}.$$

We have the following proofs $\rho_i$ in $G^\infty IL + Cut$ for $i < m$

$$\dfrac{\dfrac{\overline{\Rightarrow\psi_i\rhd\blacksquare\psi_i}\ \text{Lm 8}}{\phi_i\rhd\psi_i\Rightarrow\phi_i\rhd\blacksquare\psi_i,\psi_i\rhd\blacksquare\psi_i}\ \text{Wk}\quad \dfrac{}{\psi_i\rhd\blacksquare\psi_i,\psi_i\rhd\blacksquare\psi_i\Rightarrow\phi_i\rhd\blacksquare\psi_i}\ \text{Lm 8}}{\phi_i\rhd\psi_i\Rightarrow\phi_i\rhd\blacksquare\psi_i}\ \text{Cut}$$

and the following proof $\rho_m$ in $G^\infty IL + Cut$

$$\dfrac{\dfrac{\overline{\Rightarrow\psi_m\rhd\blacksquare\psi_m}\ \text{Lm 8}}{\blacksquare\psi_m\rhd\phi\Rightarrow\psi_m\rhd\phi,\psi_m\rhd\blacksquare\psi_m}\ \text{Wk}\quad \dfrac{}{\psi_m\rhd\blacksquare\psi_m,\blacksquare\psi_m\rhd\phi\Rightarrow\psi_m\rhd\phi}\ \text{Lm 8}}{\blacksquare\psi_m\rhd\phi\Rightarrow\psi_m\rhd\phi.}\ \text{Cut.}$$

The desired proof is obtained cutting the proofs $\rho$ and $\rho_i$ for $i \leq m$.

## 5.2 From $G^\infty IL + Cut$ to $G^\infty IL$

We turn to the proof of Cut elimination for $G^\infty IL$. To make the proof simpler, we will show eliminability of contraction.

**Lemma 9.** *Define the rule* Ctr *as having instances*

$$\dfrac{\phi,\phi,\Gamma\Rightarrow\Delta}{\phi,\Gamma\Rightarrow\Delta}\ \text{Ctr}\qquad \dfrac{\Gamma\Rightarrow\phi,\phi,\Delta}{\Gamma\Rightarrow\phi,\Delta}\ \text{Ctr}$$

*Then* Ctr *is eliminable in* $G^\infty IL(+Cut)$ *preserving local* Cut*-freeness.*

*Proof.* We are going to show that Ctr is locally admissible without introducing any new cuts, obtaining the preservativity condition. We proceed by induction on the local height of the proof and cases in the last rule applied. The only interesting case[2] is when $\pi$ is of shape

$$\dfrac{\left[\dfrac{\pi_i}{\psi_i,(\Phi_{[0,i)},\phi)\rhd\bot\Rightarrow\Phi_{[0,i)},\phi}\right]_{m...i...0}}{\{\phi_i\rhd\psi_i\}_{i<m},\Gamma\Rightarrow\Delta,\psi_m\rhd\phi}\rhd_{IK4}$$

and both formulas we desire to contract occur in the conclusion at $\{\phi_i\rhd\psi_i\}_{i<m}$. So there are $j<k<m$ such that $\phi_j\rhd\psi_j=\phi_k\rhd\psi_k$ and we want to show that

---

[2] The rest of the cases are manages as usual, applying inversion if necessary.

the sequent $\{\phi_i \triangleright \psi_i\}_{i<m, i\neq k}, \Gamma \Rightarrow \Delta, \psi_m \triangleright \phi$ is provable. For each $i > k$ define the proof $\rho_i$ in $G^\infty IL(+Cut) + Ctr$ as [3]

$$\cfrac{\cfrac{\cfrac{\cfrac{\pi_i}{\psi_i, (\Phi_{[0,i)}, \phi) \triangleright \bot \Rightarrow \Phi_{[0,i)}, \phi}}{\psi_i, (\Phi_{[k+1,i)}, \phi_k, \Phi_{[0,k)}, \phi) \triangleright \bot \Rightarrow \Phi_{[k+1,i)}, \phi_k, \Phi_{[0,k)}, \phi}}{\psi_i, (\Phi_{[k+1,i)}, \Phi_{[0,k)}, \phi) \triangleright \bot \Rightarrow \Phi_{[k+1,i)}, \phi_k, \Phi_{[0,k)}, \phi} \, \text{Ctr}}{\psi_i, (\Phi_{[k+1,i)}, \Phi_{[0,k)}, \phi) \triangleright \bot \Rightarrow \Phi_{[k+1,i)}, \Phi_{[0,k)}, \phi} \, \text{Ctr}$$

where in order to apply Ctr we used that $\phi_k = \phi_j \in \Phi_{[0,k)}$. Then, the desired proof (which is trivially locally Ctr-free), is

$$\cfrac{\rho_m \quad \cdots \quad \rho_{k+1} \quad \pi_{k-1} \quad \cdots \quad \pi_0}{\{\phi_i \triangleright \psi_i\}_{i<m, i\neq k}, \Gamma \Rightarrow \psi_m \triangleright \phi, \Delta} \, \triangleright_{\text{IK4}}$$

where $\triangleright_{\text{IK4}}$ has been applied with ordering $\phi_0 \triangleright \psi_0, \ldots, \phi_{k-1} \triangleright \psi_{k-1}, \phi_{k+1} \triangleright \psi_{k+1}, \ldots, \phi_{m-1} \triangleright \psi_{m-1}$ and principal formula $\psi_m \triangleright \phi$.

**Theorem 3 (Local Cut-admissibility).** *Assume we have proofs $\pi \vdash \Gamma \Rightarrow \Delta, \chi$ and $\tau \vdash \chi, \Gamma \Rightarrow \Delta$ in $G^\infty IL + Cut$ which are locally Cut-free. Then there is $\rho \vdash \Gamma \Rightarrow \Delta$ in $G^\infty IL + Cut$ which is locally Cut-free.*

*Proof.* By induction on the lexicographic order of the pairs $\langle |\chi|, \text{lhg}(\pi) + \text{lhg}(\tau) \rangle$, i.e., the size of the formula and the sum of the local heights of $\pi$ and $\tau$.

The only interesting case is when both proofs end in an application of $\triangleright_{\text{IK4}}$, the cut formula is principal in $\pi$ and occurs in the ordering used in $\tau$. Then $\pi$ and $\tau$ are of the following shape:

$$\cfrac{\left[\cfrac{\pi_i}{\psi_i, (\Phi_{[0,i)}, \phi) \triangleright \bot \Rightarrow \Phi_{[0,i)}, \phi}\right]_{m\ldots i\ldots 0}}{\{\phi_i \triangleright \psi_i\}_{i<m}, \Gamma_0 \Rightarrow \Delta_0, \psi_m \triangleright \phi} \, \triangleright_{\text{IK4}}$$

$$\cfrac{\left[\cfrac{\tau_i}{\psi'_j, (\Phi'_{[0,j)}, \phi') \triangleright \bot \Rightarrow \Phi'_{[0,j)}, \phi'}\right]_{n\ldots j\ldots 0}}{\{\phi'_j \triangleright \psi'_j\}_{j<n}, \Gamma_1 \Rightarrow \Delta_1, \psi'_n \triangleright \phi'} \, \triangleright_{\text{IK4}},$$

where $\chi = \chi_0 \triangleright \chi_1 = \psi_m \triangleright \phi = \phi'_k \triangleright \psi'_k$ for some $k < n$ and

$$(\{\phi_i \triangleright \psi_i\}_{i<m}, \Gamma_0 \Rightarrow \Delta_0) = (\{\phi'_j \triangleright \psi'_j\}_{j<n, j\neq k}, \Gamma_1 \Rightarrow \Delta_1, \psi'_n \triangleright \phi'). \tag{i}$$

Subcase 1: $\chi_0 = \bot$. We are going to define proofs $(\rho_j)_{k<j\leq n}$ such that

$$\rho_j \vdash \psi'_j, (\Phi'_{(k,j)}, \Phi'_{[0,k)}, \phi') \triangleright \bot \Rightarrow \Phi'_{(k,j)}, \Phi'_{[0,k)}, \phi'.$$

---

[3] We will use dashed lines to reexpress sequents. This is just a notation and does not affect the structure of the proof.

Then, the desired proof will be (which is trivially locally Cut-free).[4]

$$\dfrac{\rho_n \quad \cdots \quad \rho_{k+1} \quad \tau_{k-1} \quad \cdots \quad \tau_0}{\{\phi'_j \rhd \psi'_j\}_{j<n, j\neq k}, \Gamma_1 \Rightarrow \Delta_1, \psi'_n \rhd \phi'}\rhd_{\text{IK4}}$$

We notice that $\chi_0 = \bot$ implies that $\phi'_k = \bot$, so we define $\tau'_j$ for $j > k$ by applying $\bot$R from Lemma 4 to $\tau_j$ (thus deleting $\phi'_k = \bot$ from the right hand side of the conclusion). We define $\rho_j$ as

$$\dfrac{\dfrac{\bot, \bot \rhd \bot \Rightarrow \bot}{\cdots \Rightarrow \cdots, \bot \rhd \bot}\bot L \rhd_{\text{IK4}} \qquad \dfrac{\dfrac{\tau'_j}{\psi'_j, (\Phi'_{[0,j)}, \phi') \rhd \bot \Rightarrow \Phi'_{[0,k)}, \Phi'_{(k,j)}, \phi'}}{\psi'_j, (\Phi'_{(k,j)}, \bot, \bar{\Phi}'_{[0,k)}, \phi') \rhd \bot \Rightarrow \Phi'_{(k,j)}, \bar{\Phi}'_{[0,k)}, \phi'}}{\psi'_j, (\Phi'_{(k,j)}, \Phi'_{[0,k)}, \phi') \rhd \bot \Rightarrow \Phi'_{(k,j)}, \Phi'_{[0,k)}, \phi'} \text{Cut}$$

**Subcase 2:** $\chi_0 \neq \bot$. Let us write $\Sigma = \{\phi_i \rhd \psi_i\}_{i<m}$ and $\Sigma' = \{\phi'_j \rhd \psi'_j\}_{j<n, j\neq k}$. Define $\Gamma_2 := \Gamma_0 \setminus (\Sigma' \setminus \Sigma) = \Gamma_1 \setminus (\Sigma \setminus \Sigma')$, where the equality holds thanks to (i). Then

$$\Gamma_2, \Sigma \cap \Sigma', \Sigma \setminus \Sigma', \Sigma' \setminus \Sigma = \{\phi_i \rhd \psi_i\}_{i<m}, \Gamma_0 = \{\phi'_j \rhd \psi'_j\}_{j<n, j\neq k}, \Gamma_1.$$

We also notice that contracting $\Gamma_2, \Sigma, \Sigma'$ we can obtain the desired sequent. Let us define proofs $(\rho_i)_{i<m}, (\rho'_j)_{j\leq n, j\neq k}$ such that

$$\rho'_j \vdash \psi'_j, (\Phi'_{(k,j)}, \Phi'_{[0,m)}, \Phi'_{[0,k)}, \phi') \rhd \bot \Rightarrow \Phi'_{(k,j)}, \Phi'_{[0,m)}, \Phi'_{[0,k)}, \phi', \text{ for } k < j \leq n,$$

$$\rho_i \vdash \psi_i, (\Phi_{[0,i)}, \Phi'_{[0,k)}, \phi') \rhd \bot \Rightarrow \Phi_{[0,i)}, \Phi'_{[0,k)}, \phi', \text{ for } i < m,$$

$$\rho'_j \vdash \psi'_j, (\Phi'_{[0,j)}, \phi') \rhd \bot \Rightarrow \Phi'_{[0,j)}, \phi', \text{ for } j < k.$$

Then we get the following (locally Cut-free) proof $\rho$

$$\dfrac{\rho'_n \quad \cdots \quad \rho'_{k+1} \quad \rho_{m-1} \quad \cdots \quad \rho_0 \quad \rho'_{k-1} \quad \cdots \quad \rho'_0}{\{\phi_i \rhd \psi_i\}_{i<m}, \{\phi'_j \rhd \psi'_j\}_{j<n, j\neq k}, \Gamma_2 \Rightarrow \Delta', \psi'_n \rhd \phi'} \rhd_{\text{IK4}}$$

where $\rhd_{\text{IK4}}$ is applied with ordering

$$\phi'_0 \rhd \psi'_0, \ldots, \phi'_{k-1} \rhd \psi'_{k-1}, \phi_0 \rhd \psi_0, \ldots, \phi_{m-1} \rhd \psi_{m-1}, \phi'_{k+1} \rhd \psi'_{k+1}, \ldots, \phi'_{n-1} \rhd \psi'_{n-1}$$

and main formula $\psi'_n \rhd \phi'$. The desired proof will be obtained by applying contraction, i.e., Lemma 9 to $\rho$ as contraction preserves local Cut-freeness.

We define $\rho'_j$ for $j < k$ as $\tau_j$, so we only need to define $\rho'_j$ for $k < j \leq n$ and $\rho_i$ for $i < m$. To define $\rho'_j$ for $k < j \leq n$ we notice we have the following proofs:

$$\tau_j \vdash \psi'_j, (\Phi'_{(k,j)}, \chi_0, \Phi'_{[0,k)}, \phi') \rhd \bot \Rightarrow \Phi'_{(k,j)}, \chi_0, \Phi'_{[0,k)}, \phi',$$

---

[4] When defining the $\rho_i$'s we can freely use Cut, since all these instances of Cut will not appear in the local fragment of the desired proof.

$\pi_m \vdash \chi_0, (\Phi_{[0,m)}, \chi_1) \triangleright \bot \Rightarrow \Phi_{[0,m)}, \chi_1, \qquad \tau_k \vdash \chi_1, (\Phi_{[0,k)}, \phi') \triangleright \bot \Rightarrow \Phi'_{[0,k)}, \phi'.$

Applying Lemma 6 to $\pi_m$ and to $\tau_k$ we obtain proofs $\pi'_m$ and $\tau'_k$ such that $\pi'_m \vdash (\Phi_{[0,m)}, \chi_1) \triangleright \bot \Rightarrow \chi_0 \triangleright \bot$, $\tau'_k \vdash (\Phi'_{[0,k)}, \phi') \triangleright \bot \Rightarrow \chi_1 \triangleright \bot$. Then the desired proof $\rho'_j$ is (where wk indicates an application of admissibility of weakening)

$$\chi_1 \triangleright \bot \quad \cfrac{\text{wk}(\tau'_k) \quad \chi_0 \triangleright \bot \quad \cfrac{\text{wk}(\pi'_m) \quad \text{wk}(\tau_j)}{\psi'_j, (\Phi, \chi_1) \triangleright \bot \Rightarrow \Phi, \chi_0, \chi_1} \text{Cut} \quad \text{wk}(\pi_m)}{\cfrac{\cfrac{\psi'_j, (\Phi, \chi_1) \triangleright \bot \Rightarrow \Phi, \chi_1}{\chi_1 \cfrac{\psi'_j, \Phi \triangleright \bot \Rightarrow \Phi, \chi_1}{\psi'_j, \Phi \triangleright \bot \Rightarrow \Phi} \text{Cut} \quad \text{wk}(\tau_k)}{\psi'_j, \Phi \triangleright \bot \Rightarrow \Phi} \text{Cut}} \text{Cut}} \text{Cut}$$

where we denoted $\Phi'_{(k,j)}, \Phi_{[0,m)}, \Phi'_{[0,k)}, \phi'$ as $\Phi$ and annotated the cut formula at the left of the rule application.

All that is left is to define proofs $\rho_i$ for $i < m$. We remember that we have the following proofs:

$\pi_i \vdash \psi_i, (\Phi_{[0,i)}, \chi_1) \triangleright \bot \Rightarrow \Phi_{[0,i)}, \chi_1 \qquad \tau_k \vdash \chi_1, (\Phi'_{[0,k)}, \phi') \triangleright \bot \Rightarrow \Phi'_{[0,k)}, \phi'.$

Applying Lemma 6 we obtain $\tau'_k \vdash (\Phi'_{[0,k)}, \phi') \triangleright \bot \Rightarrow \chi_1 \triangleright \bot$. Then the desired proof $\rho_i$ is defined as

$$\chi_1 \triangleright \bot \quad \cfrac{\text{wk}(\tau'_k) \quad \cfrac{\text{wk}(\tau'_k) \quad \text{wk}(\pi_i)}{\psi_i, \Phi \triangleright \bot \Rightarrow \Phi, \chi_1} \text{Cut} \quad \text{wk}(\tau_k)}{\chi_1 \cfrac{}{\psi_i, \Phi \triangleright \bot \Rightarrow \Phi} \text{Cut}}$$

where we denoted $\phi_{[0,i)}, \phi'_{[0,k)}, \phi'$ as $\Phi$ and annoted the cut formula at the left of the rule application.

**Corollary 1** (G$^\infty$IL **Cut elim.**). *If* G$^\infty$IL $+$ Cut $\vdash S$, *then* G$^\infty$IL $\vdash S$.

### 5.3  From G$^\infty$IL to GIL

Finally we show how to return from G$^\infty$IL to GIL. For this step the absence of the Cut rule is fundamental.

**Theorem 4.** *For any $\Lambda$ finite set of formulas, we have that* G$^\infty$IL $\vdash \Gamma \Rightarrow \Delta$ *implies* GIL $\vdash \Lambda \triangleright \bot, \Gamma \Rightarrow \Delta$.

*Proof.* Let $\pi \vdash \Gamma \Rightarrow \Delta$ in G$^\infty$IL. By induction on the lexicographical order $\langle |\text{Sub}_\triangleright(\Gamma \Rightarrow \Delta) \setminus \Lambda|, \text{lhg}(\pi) \rangle$ and the case analysis in the last rule of $\pi$.[5] The only interesting case is when the last rule of $\pi$ is $\triangleright_{\text{IK4}}$. So $\pi$ is of shape

$$\cfrac{\left[ \cfrac{\pi_i}{\psi_i, (\Phi_{[0,i)}, \phi) \triangleright \bot \Rightarrow \Phi_{[0,i)}, \phi} \right]_{m \ldots i \ldots 0}}{\{\phi_i \triangleright \psi_i\}_{i<m}, \Gamma \Rightarrow \psi_m \triangleright \phi, \Delta} \triangleright_{\text{IK4}}$$

---

[5] Note that in the presence of Cut this measure would not work.

and let us denote the conclusion of $\pi_i$ as $S_i$ and the conclusion of $\pi$ as $S$. We want to show that $\mathsf{GIL} \vdash \Lambda \rhd \bot, \{\phi_i \rhd \psi_i\}_{i<m}, \Gamma \Rightarrow \psi_m \rhd \phi, \Delta$. For $i \leq m$ we define proofs $\tau_i \vdash \psi_i, (\psi_i, \Phi_{[0,i)}, \Lambda, \phi) \rhd \bot \Rightarrow \Phi_{[0,i)}, \Lambda, \phi$ so the desired proof is

$$\frac{\tau_m \quad \cdots \quad \tau_0 \quad \rho_{n-1} \quad \cdots \quad \rho_0}{\Lambda \rhd \bot, \{\phi_i \rhd \psi_i\}_{i<m}, \Gamma \Rightarrow \psi_m \rhd \phi, \Delta} \rhd_{\mathrm{IL}}$$

where the last rule was applied with the ordering $\chi_0 \rhd \bot, \ldots, \chi_{n-1} \rhd \bot, \phi_0 \rhd \psi_0, \ldots, \phi_{m-1} \rhd \psi_{m-1}$ and principal formula $\psi_m \rhd \phi$. We define the $\tau_i$'s by cases.

Case 1. If $\psi_i \in \Lambda$ then we define $\tau_i$ as

$$\frac{}{\psi_i, (\psi_i, \Phi_{[0,i)}, \Lambda, \phi) \rhd \bot \Rightarrow \Phi_{[0,i)}, \Lambda, \phi} \mathrm{Ax}$$

since the formula $\psi_i$ appears on both sides of this sequent.

Case 2. If $\psi_i \notin \Lambda$ then, since $\psi_i \in \mathrm{Sub}_\rhd(S_i)$ and $\mathrm{Sub}_\rhd(S_i) \subseteq \mathrm{Sub}_\rhd(S)$, we have $|\mathrm{Sub}_\rhd(S_i) \setminus (\Lambda \cup \{\psi_i\})| < |\mathrm{Sub}_\rhd(S_i) \setminus \Lambda| \leq |\mathrm{Sub}_\rhd(S) \setminus \Lambda|$. So by induction hypothesis applied to $\pi_i$ with set $\Lambda \cup \{\psi_i\}$ we obtain a proof $\pi'_i$ in GIL such that $\pi'_i \vdash \psi_i, (\psi_i, \Phi_{[0,i)}, \Lambda, \phi) \rhd \bot \Rightarrow \Phi_{[0,i)}, \phi$. We define $\tau_i$ applying Wk to $\pi'_i$ so $\tau_i \vdash \psi_i, (\psi_i, \Phi_{[0,i)}, \Lambda, \phi) \rhd \bot \Rightarrow \Phi_{[0,i)}, \Lambda, \phi$ in GIL. Let $\Lambda = \{\chi_0, \ldots, \chi_{n-1}\}$. We define $\rho_j$ for $j < n$ as the following proof in GIL

$$\frac{}{\bot, (\bot, \Lambda_{[0,j)}, \phi) \rhd \bot \Rightarrow \Lambda_{[0,j)}, \phi} \bot \mathrm{L}.$$

By Theorem 2, Corollary 1 and Theorem 4 we obtain:

**Corollary 2** (GIL cut elim.). *If* GIL $+$ Cut $\vdash S$, *then* GIL $\vdash S$.

# 6 Conclusion

We have defined two new sequent calculi for IL, a wellfounded and a local progress (non-wellfounded) one. Both have a nice subformula property appering first in [9] for IK4 (IL without Löb's axiom). However, we have used a much more concrete modal rules simplifying their treatment.

Local progress proof theory, with our addition of local admissibility, allows to show cut elimination for IL without the complications that usually appear in (wellfounded) calculi for GL-like logics or the complications of eliminating cuts in non-wellfounded proofs. For this reason, we believe that local progress proof theory provides the correct set of tools to study many provability logics proof theoretically.

Finally, the present work forms the foundation for establishing uniform interpolation for IL. For reasons of space, this result will appear in a separate future publication.

We leave it as future work to study extensions of IL (see [15] for definitions), in particular ILP should be easy to handle following the same ideas as [10]. However, the logics ILW and ILM should provide bigger challenges as they are known to lack Craig interpolation (see [4]). This hints at the inexistence of a nice sequent calculus for them.

# References

1. Acclavio, M., Curzi, G., Guerrieri, G.: Infinitary cutelimination via finite approximations (extended version) (2024). arXiv:2308.07789 [cs.LO]
2. Afshari, B., Kloibhofer, J.: Cut elimination for cyclic proofs: a case study in temporal logic. In: Proceedings Twelfth International Workshop on Fixed Points in Computer Science. Electronic Proceedings in Theoretical Computer Science (to appear)
3. Afshari, B., Leigh, G.E., Turata, G.M.: Demystifying $\mu$ (2025). arXiv:2401.01096 [math.LO]
4. Areces, C., Hoogland, E., de Jongh, D.: Interpolation, definability and fixed points in interpretability logics. In: Kracht , M., et al. (eds.) Advances in Modal Logic, pp. 53–76. CSLI Publications (1998)
5. Das, A., Pous, D.: Non-wellfounded proof theory for (kleene+ action) (algebras+lattices). In: Ghica, D.R., Jung, A. (eds.) 27th EACSL Annual Conference on Computer Science Logic (CSL 2018). Leibniz International Proceedings in Informatics (LIPIcs), vol. 119, pp. 19:1–19:18. Schloss Dagstuhl – Leibniz-Zentrum für Informatik, Dagstuhl (2018). https://doi.org/10.4230/LIPIcs.CSL.2018.19. ISBN 978-3-95977-088-0
6. Iwata, S., Kurahashi, T., Okawa, Y.: The persistence principle over weak interpretability logic. Math. Log. Q. **70**(1), 37–63 (2024)
7. Miranda, B.S., Studer, T.: Cut elimination for a nonwellfounded system for the master modality (2025). arXiv:2505.02700 [math.LO]
8. Sasaki, K.: A cut-free sequent system for the smallest interpretabili ty logic. Stud. Log. **70**, 353–372 (2002). https://doi.org/10.1023/A:1015150314504
9. Sasaki, K.: A sequent system for a sublogic of the smallest interpretability logic. Acad. Math. Sci. Inf. Eng.: J. Nanzan Acad. Soc. **3**, 1–17 (2003). https://doi.org/10.15119/00000018
10. Sasaki, K.: A sequent system for the interpretability logic with the persistence axiom. Acad. Math. sci. inf. eng.: j. Nanzan Acad. Soc. **2**, 25–34 (2002). https://doi.org/10.15119/00000117
11. Saurin, A.: A linear perspective on cut-elimination for non-wellfounded sequent calculi with least and greatest fixed-points. In: Ramanayake, R., Urban, J. (eds.) TABLEAUX 2023. LNCS, vol. 14278, pp. 203–222. Springer, Cham (2023). https://doi.org/10.1007/978-3-031-43513-3_12. ISBN 978-3-031-43513-3
12. Savateev, Y., Shamkanov, D.: Non-well-founded proofs for the Grzegorczyk modal logic. Rev. Symb. Log. **14** (2018). https://doi.org/10.1017/S1755020319000510.
13. Shamkanov, D.: On structural proof theory of the modal logic K+ extended with infinitary derivations (2023). arXiv:2310.10309 [math.LO]
14. Miranda, B.S., Studer, T., Zenger, L.: Coalgebraic proof translations of non-wellfounded proofs. In: Ciabattoni, A., Gabelaia, D., Sedlar, I. (eds.) Advances in Modal Logic, vol. 15, pp. 527–548. College Publications (2024)
15. Visser, A.: Interpretability logic. In: Petkov, P.P. (ed.) Mathematical Logic, pp. 175–209. Springer, Boston (1990). https://doi.org/10.1007/978-1-4613-0609-2_13. ISBN 978-1-4613-0609-2

**Open Access** This chapter is licensed under the terms of the Creative Commons Attribution 4.0 International License (http://creativecommons.org/licenses/by/4.0/), which permits use, sharing, adaptation, distribution and reproduction in any medium or format, as long as you give appropriate credit to the original author(s) and the source, provide a link to the Creative Commons license and indicate if changes were made.

The images or other third party material in this chapter are included in the chapter's Creative Commons license, unless indicated otherwise in a credit line to the material. If material is not included in the chapter's Creative Commons license and your intended use is not permitted by statutory regulation or exceeds the permitted use, you will need to obtain permission directly from the copyright holder.

# Analytic Proofs for Tense Logic

Agata Ciabattoni[1], Timo Lang[2,3], and Revantha Ramanayake[4(✉)]

[1] Technische Universität Wien (TU Wien), Vienna, Austria
agata@logic.at
[2] Huawei Ireland Research Centre, Dublin, Ireland
[3] University College London (UCL), London, UK
timo.lang@ucl.ac.uk
[4] University of Groningen, Groningen, The Netherlands
d.r.s.ramanayake@rug.nl

**Abstract.** The first algorithm to transform a proof in Nishimura's sequent calculus **GKt** for tense logic **Kt** into an analytic proof of the same sequent is presented. In an analytic proof, every rule instance is analytic i.e., each formula in every premise is a subformula of some formula in its conclusion. We call this algorithm *analytic restriction* to convey that it extends analytic cut-restriction where just the cut-rule instances are made analytic. This distinction is essential in tense logic since cut and modal rules can both cause non-analyticity. Analytic cut-restriction is itself an extension of cut-elimination so our work contributes to a broader program of transforming arbitrary sequent proofs into ones constructed from a designated set of formulas—not necessarily subformulas. As with cut-elimination, the aim is to limit the proof search space and support proof-theoretic and meta-logical investigations.

**Keywords:** tense logic · analytic proofs · sequent calculus · analytic restriction · cut-elimination

## 1 Introduction

Following Gentzen's [12] seminal work on cut-elimination for the sequent calculus in the 1930s, the primary goal of structural proof theory has been to obtain this result for the numerous non-classical logics of interest. Cut-elimination is an algorithm to remove instances of the cut-rule by transforming the given proof. In many cases it implies the subformula property (every formula in the proof is a subformula of the formula to be proved), and the latter in turn implies a significant constraint on the proof search space, aiding the establishment of metalogical results like decidability, complexity and interpolation. Of course, cut-elimination is important in its own right e.g., for the analysis of mathematical proofs [13] and as computation via the Curry-Howard (proofs-as-programs) correspondence [25].

Unfortunately, the cut-elimination result does not hold in the framework of the sequent calculus for most logics of interest. While the traditional response in structural proof theory has been the use of elaborate extensions of the sequent calculus such as hypersequent calculi [1], labeled sequent calculi [11, 19, 28], display calculi [3], this has the drawback of introducing a syntax-heavy framework that complicates or even impedes further investigation.

Ciabattoni et al. [5] propose an alternative to cut-elimination called *cut-restriction* that stays with the sequent calculus: this is a proof transformation algorithm that takes an arbitrary sequent calculus proof as input and outputs a proof where cuts are restricted to a specified and restricted set of formulas. In the case that cut is the only rule in the sequent calculus that can violate analyticity, the cut-restriction result often retains the benefits of cut-elimination, namely a significant constraint on proof search leading to applications, see e.g., [5, 17, 23]. However, a significant drawback of the argument in [5] is its reliance on cut-elimination in the richer hypersequent calculus as an intermediate step. In particular, as the hypersequent cut-elimination cannot be simulated in the sequent calculus, this approach can be said to substantially distort the original sequent proof in the process of deriving the cut-restricted version. Additionally, due to this reliance, the argument applies only to logics having a cut-free hypersequent calculus. In hindsight, Takano's [22] proof for the modal logic **S5** appears to be the first example of a cut-restriction result. Unfortunately, Takano's argument is technically intricate and not widely understood.

A general and direct—i.e., one that stays within the sequent calculus—algorithm that transforms a sequent proof into a cut-restricted sequent proof still remains beyond reach. This has motivated attempts to investigate specific cases, the idea being that techniques applicable in such cases will reveal what a general argument must incorporate. *Analytic*[1] *cut-restriction* [21], where the cut-formulas are restricted to subformulas of their conclusion, is a special case. Recently, [6] identified abstract sufficient conditions for analytic cut-restriction with transformations that stay within the sequent calculus.

In this paper, we consider Nishimura's sequent calculus **GKt** [20] for the normal basic tense logic **Kt**. As already observed in [20], cut-elimination fails in **GKt**, and hence cuts cannot be avoided. Our main result here is an algorithm for transforming any proof in **GKt** into an analytic proof. This work extends the results in [5] in a crucial way: the algorithm here is direct in the sense that the transformations stay *within* the sequent calculus (indeed, there is no cut-free hypersequent calculus for **Kt**). Moreover, the form of restriction that we obtain is a strong form, namely analytic. Note that the analytic cut-restriction algorithm in [6] only applied to a limited class of sequent calculi, those whose rules (i) introduce only one formula at a time (on either the left or right side of the sequent), and (ii) satisfy the subformula property, with the exception of the cut-rule. **GKt** satisfies neither condition, so our algorithm needs to go beyond the one given in [6]. In particular, the cut-rule *and* the modal rules in **GKt** can both cause non-analyticity, so our proof transformation shows how to restrict the rule instances of *all* these rules. To convey that this result constitutes an extension of analytic cut-restriction, we call it *analytic restriction*. To encourage

---

[1] The term 'analytic' follows the tradition, dating back to Leibniz, of referring to proofs which only employs notions that are contained in the statement being proved.

adaptation to other logics, we present our transformation so as to make the algorithm—rather than just the proof of its correctness—explicit.

**Related Literature.** In Takano's paper establishing analytic cut-restriction for **S5**, it is observed [22, Digression 1.2] that every provable sequent in **GKt** and **GKt**4 has an analytic proof. Note that this is based on semantic considerations, as opposed to the proof transformation algorithm given here. Nishimura [20] presents an alternative proof calculus for **Kt** that witnesses completeness of its analytic proofs but it is not a sequent calculus. Indeed, cut-free calculi for **Kt** have been presented in several complex proof frameworks such as the display calculus [14,18,29] and labeled sequent systems [19,28]; for the axiomatic extension **Kt4.3**, a cut-free hypersequent calculus has been provided in [16] but it does not contain **GKt** as subcalculus.

More generally, there is a body of work demonstrating the existence of cut-restricted proofs using semantic methods, without providing an explicit proof transformation algorithm, e.g., [2,8,10,17]. We observe that this situation contrasts with that of cut-elimination, where it is the syntactic arguments that are standard, and semantic approaches (see e.g., [9,24]) are relatively rare.

## 2 Preliminaries

The tense logic **Kt** extends the normal basic modal logic **K** (which has a single modal operator $\Box$) by a second modal operator $\blacksquare$ and a necessitation rule for it, and the following axiom schemes [4]. The latter two are called *converse axioms*.

$$\blacksquare(A \to B) \to (\blacksquare A \to \blacksquare B) \qquad A \to \Box\neg\blacksquare\neg A \qquad A \to \blacksquare\neg\Box\neg A$$

**Kt** aims to provide a minimal[2] setup for temporal reasoning, where $\Box A$ is read as '$A$ holds at every point in the future' and $\blacksquare A$ is read as '$A$ holds at every point in the past'. The corresponding diamond operators can be defined from the box operators using negation.

A *sequent* is a pair of formula multisets, written as $\Gamma \Rightarrow \Delta$. Nishimura's sequent calculus **GKt** [20] for **Kt** appears in Fig. 1. The reader may observe that what is labeled here as the cut-rule is in fact Gentzen's mix (i.e., multicut) rule. This is a standard generalization of cut that is convenient for simplifying the cut-elimination argument in the presence of the contraction rule. To simplify terminology, we use cut as a shorthand for multicut throughout.

The reader may find the modal rules of **GKt** (below) somewhat unfamiliar.

$$\frac{\Gamma \Rightarrow A, \blacksquare\Delta}{\Box\Gamma \Rightarrow \Box A, \Delta} \ (\Box) \qquad \frac{\Gamma \Rightarrow A, \Box\Delta}{\blacksquare\Gamma \Rightarrow \blacksquare A, \Delta} \ (\blacksquare)$$

The above rules can be conveniently remembered as the usual **K** rule which adds a modality going from premise to conclusion, plus an additional succedent context $\Delta$ which adds the other modality but this time from conclusion to premise.

---

[2] Properties like transitivity/antisymmetry are not imposed on the temporal relation.

$$\overline{p \Rightarrow p} \ (init) \qquad \frac{\Gamma \Rightarrow \Delta}{\Sigma, \Gamma \Rightarrow \Delta, \Pi} \ (w) \qquad \frac{\Sigma, \Gamma, \Gamma \Rightarrow \Delta, \Delta, \Pi}{\Sigma, \Gamma \Rightarrow \Delta, \Pi} \ (c)$$

$$\frac{\Gamma \Rightarrow A, \Delta}{\Gamma, \neg A \Rightarrow \Delta} \ (\neg_L) \qquad \frac{\Gamma, A \Rightarrow \Delta}{\Gamma \Rightarrow \neg A, \Delta} \ (\neg_R)$$

$$\frac{\Gamma, A, B \Rightarrow \Delta}{\Gamma, A \wedge B \Rightarrow \Delta} \ (\wedge_L) \qquad \frac{\Gamma \Rightarrow A, \Delta \quad \Gamma \Rightarrow B, \Delta}{\Gamma \Rightarrow A \wedge B, \Delta} \ (\wedge_R)$$

$$\frac{\Gamma \Rightarrow A, \blacksquare\Delta}{\Box\Gamma \Rightarrow \Box A, \Delta} \ (\Box) \qquad \frac{\Gamma \Rightarrow A, \Box\Delta}{\blacksquare\Gamma \Rightarrow \blacksquare A, \Delta} \ (\blacksquare)$$

$$\frac{\Gamma \Rightarrow A^k, \Delta \quad \Sigma, A^l \Rightarrow \Pi}{\Sigma, \Gamma \Rightarrow \Delta, \Pi} \ (cut) \ k, l > 0$$

**Fig. 1.** Nishimura's sequent calculus **GKt** for **Kt**.

In the familiar Kripke semantics for **Kt**, the rule ($\Box$) asserts that if the premise $\Gamma \Rightarrow A, \blacksquare\Delta$ is valid so is the conclusion $\Box\Gamma \Rightarrow \Box A, \Delta$. This can be easily verified by reasoning contrapositively: suppose that that the conclusion is not true at some world $w$. That means that $\Gamma$ holds at any single future step from $w$, $A$ fails at some single future step (call that world $w'$), and every formula in $\Delta$ fails at $w$. From the perspective of $w'$, we have that $\Gamma$ holds and $A$ fails and every formula in $\Delta$ fails at some single past step (this is witnessed by $w$). Hence the premise is not true at $w'$. The ($\blacksquare$) rule can be interpreted in the semantics in a similar way.

**Definition 1.** *A* rule instance *is* analytic *if every formula in every premise is a subformula of some formula in the conclusion, otherwise it is* non-analytic.

If a rule instance is non-analytic, any formula in the premise that is not a subformula of any formula in the conclusion is said to be *non-analytic* for that instance.

An *analytic proof* has the property that every rule instance in it is analytic. By inspection, a non-analytic proof in **GKt** must contain either an

(i) instance of ($\Box$) (resp. ($\blacksquare$)) where some context formula $\blacksquare B \in \blacksquare\Delta$ (resp. $\Box B \in \Box\Delta$) is not a subformula of the conclusion, or an
(ii) instance of (*cut*) where the cut-formula is not a subformula of the conclusion

The reason is that none of the other rules has non-analytic rule instances.

Nishimura already observed that cut-elimination fails for **GKt**, since the axiom instance $p \to \Box\neg\blacksquare\neg p$ is provable in **Kt**, but unprovable without cut. Indeed, here is a proof using cut.

$$\frac{\dfrac{\dfrac{\dfrac{\dfrac{\dfrac{p \Rightarrow p}{\neg p \Rightarrow \neg p}}{\blacksquare\neg p \Rightarrow \blacksquare\neg p}}{\Rightarrow \neg\blacksquare\neg p, \blacksquare\neg p}}{\Rightarrow \Box\neg\blacksquare\neg p, \neg p} \quad \dfrac{p \Rightarrow p}{\neg p, p \Rightarrow}}{p \Rightarrow \Box\neg\blacksquare\neg p} \ (cut)$$

This sequent cannot be proved without cut since the only rule instance with conclusion $p \Rightarrow \Box\neg\blacksquare\neg p$ is weakening (and that would certainly not lead to a proof). Observe, however, that the above proof is analytic. In particular, the cut-formula $\neg p$ is a subformula of the formula $\Box\neg\blacksquare\neg p$ in the conclusion of cut.

## 3 A High-Level Overview of the Transformation

Gentzen's cut-elimination argument for **LK** and **LJ** can be summarized at a high-level as follows:

> Given a proof where only the last rule instance is cut: permute the cut upwards in each premise until it is principal in both premises of cut. Now, making use of the form of the rules which—viewed upwards—decompose the principal formula into formulas that are strictly smaller in the sense of being strictly smaller in grade (i.e., formula size), or the same grade but occurring closer to the leaves of the proof. Hence, we can transform the original proof to a proof that has strictly smaller cuts. Cut-elimination follows through an induction on the underlying measure.

In this section, in the spirit of the latter text, we give a high-level overview of the algorithm for **GKt** that transforms a proof into an analytic one. This is illustrated with a running example. Another example of a transformed proof appears at the end of Sect. 4. The formal argument is given in the next section.

For a start, consider a proof where only the last rule instance is non-analytic. The latter must be an instance of (i) one of the modal rules, or (ii) the cut-rule.

**Case (i):** Suppose that the last rule instance is modal and non-analytic. The formal version of the sketch here appears in Proposition 1. If it is ($\Box$)—the case of ($\blacksquare$) is analogous—then the formulas that witness the non-analyticity constitute some $\Delta$ in the conclusion that becomes $\blacksquare\Delta$ in the premise.

---

Let us consider the following non-analytic proof as a running example.

$$\dfrac{\dfrac{\dfrac{\dfrac{\dfrac{\dfrac{p, p \Rightarrow p}{p \wedge p \Rightarrow p}}{\neg p, p \wedge p \Rightarrow}}{\neg p \Rightarrow \neg(p \wedge p)}}{\blacksquare\neg p \Rightarrow \blacksquare\neg(p \wedge p)} \ (\blacksquare) \text{ critical rule instance}}{\Rightarrow \neg\blacksquare\neg p, \blacksquare\neg(p \wedge p)} \ (\neg_R)}{\Rightarrow \Box\neg\blacksquare\neg p, \neg(p \wedge p)} \ (\Box)$$

Only the ($\Box$) rule instance is non-analytic. The witness is the $\blacksquare\neg(p \wedge p)$ in its premise; it is not a subformula of any formula in its conclusion.

---

The idea is to trace—using the familiar parametric ancestor relation from structural proof theory, see e.g., [3]—the formulas in $\Delta$ upwards until a modal rule instance that decomposes them is reached (this is called a *critical instance*). A formula in the *premise context of a critical instance* that is not a parametric ancestor (of some formula in $\Delta$) is called a *critical formula*. Starting from the desired endsequent we apply cut-rules upwards using every critical formula.

---

In our example, there is one rule instance that is critical (i.e., a rule instance that, viewed upwards, decomposes the $\blacksquare\neg(p \wedge p)$ into $\neg(p \wedge p)$). The premise of that rule instance is $\neg p \Rightarrow \neg(p \wedge p)$. Of the two formulas in this sequent, $\neg(p \wedge p)$ is a parametric ancestor of the $\blacksquare\neg(p \wedge p)$, but $\neg p$ is not. Hence there is one critical formula: $\neg p$. Here is the cut introducing $\neg p$.

$$\frac{\Rightarrow \Box\neg\blacksquare\neg p, \neg(p \wedge p), \neg p \qquad \neg p \Rightarrow \Box\neg\blacksquare\neg p, \neg(p \wedge p)}{\Rightarrow \Box\neg\blacksquare\neg p, \neg(p \wedge p)} \text{ (cut)}$$

---

To prove the premises of the cuts on critical formulas that we introduced, we use portions of the original proof, either by weakening, or by adapting a subproof of the original proof. Specifically, the adaptation is to replace the ancestors of the formulas witnessing non-analyticity with critical formulas.

---

We utilize the original proof to obtain analytic proofs of $\Rightarrow \Box\neg\blacksquare\neg p, \neg(p \wedge p), \neg p$ and $\neg p \Rightarrow \Box\neg\blacksquare\neg p, \neg(p \wedge p)$. The latter sequent is obtained by applying weakening on $\Box\neg\blacksquare\neg p$ to a subproof of the original proof, as shown below.

$$\frac{\dfrac{\dfrac{\dfrac{\dfrac{p, p \Rightarrow p}{p \wedge p \Rightarrow p}}{\neg p, p \wedge p \Rightarrow}}{\neg p \Rightarrow \neg(p \wedge p)}}{\neg p \Rightarrow \Box\neg\blacksquare\neg p, \neg(p \wedge p)} \text{ (w)}}$$

To obtain $\Rightarrow \Box\neg\blacksquare\neg p, \neg(p \wedge p), \neg p$, the idea is to reason backwards, first by removing the undesirable formula $\neg(p \wedge p)$ that witnessed the non-analyticity using (w) upwards, and then following the original proof upwards—use the introduced critical formula $\neg p$ in place of $\neg(p \wedge p)$—until the conclusion of the critical instance is reached:

$$\frac{\dfrac{\dfrac{\dfrac{\blacksquare\neg p \Rightarrow \blacksquare\neg p}{\Rightarrow \neg\blacksquare\neg p, \blacksquare\neg p} (\neg R)}{\Rightarrow \Box\neg\blacksquare\neg p, \neg p} (\Box)}{\Rightarrow \Box\neg\blacksquare\neg p, \neg(p \wedge p), \neg p} \text{ (w)}}$$

The uppermost sequent in the above is a quasi-initial sequent i.e., a sequent of the form $\Gamma, A \Rightarrow \Delta, A$, easily seen to be provable (in this paper, an initial sequent is taken to have the form $p \Rightarrow p$). As we shall see, this is not a coincidence.

**Case (ii):** Suppose that the last rule instance is the cut-rule and non-analytic. Permute the cut upwards in the usual way by decomposing propositional connectives. The interesting case is when the cut-rule is non-analytic and principal in both premises by a modal rule. Non-analyticity implies that the cut-formula is not a subformula of the conclusion, from which we can deduce that the cut-formula must be principal in the left premise of the cut (Claim 7). Apply a standard $K$-style cut-reduction step to identify a cut on a formula of strictly smaller grade (yielding an analytic proof by IH), followed by an application of the modal rule. By inspection, the latter must have strictly smaller grade so the result follows from Case (i).

In general, the transformation we described might not immediately yield an analytic proof, as it may introduce new rule instances that are non-analytic although with strictly smaller grade. To account for these, we consider the multiset of grades of all the non-analytic rule instances in the proof and note that the transformation applied to topmost non-analytic rule instances leads to a strictly smaller multiset under the Dershowitz-Manna multiset ordering. Termination—and hence an analytic proof—follows.

## 4 Analytic Restriction for Tense Logic

In this section we establish the main theorem. See Sect. 3 for the definitions of analytic rule, analytic proof, and non-analytic formula in a non-analytic rule instance. The grade of a formula defined as the number of symbols in it.

**Definition 2.** *The* grade *of a non-analytic rule instance is the maximal grade of a non-analytic formula in it.*

For technical reasons, it is convenient to allow only *atomic* initial sequents $p \Rightarrow p$ in **GKt**. Let us call *quasi-initial* every sequent of the form $\Gamma, A \Rightarrow A, \Delta$. The following can be proved by a simple induction:

**Lemma 1 (Axiom expansion).** *Every quasi-initial sequent has an analytic* **GKt**-*proof.*

The *ancestor relation* between formula occurrences in **GKt**-proofs is defined in the usual way: every occurrence in the context of the conclusion of a rule instance is related to corresponding occurrences in the context of the premise(s), and an occurrence of a principal formula is related to the occurrences of its auxiliary formulas in the premise(s).

An ancestor of a formula is either a subformula or, due to the rules (□) and (■), a subformula prefixed by a string of modalities. Due to contraction a formula can have multiple ancestors in the same sequent. Moreover, as we allow the cut-rule, not every formula in a proof is necessarily an ancestor of some formula in the endsequent.

The high-level intuition of Case (i) in Sect. 3 is formalized in the following.

**Proposition 1.** *Let $\alpha$ be a **GKt**-proof that is analytic apart from its last rule, which is a modal rule instance of grade $k > 0$. Then there is a **GKt**-proof $\alpha^*$ of the same endsequent all of whose non-analytic rule instances are of grade $< k$.*

*Proof.* We first construct $\alpha^*$ and then prove the desired reduction in grade.

**1. Construction of $\alpha^*$.**

The construction consists of three steps: (I) Preprocessing, (II) Tracing non-analytic ancestors, and (III) Restructuring the proof.

**(I) Preprocessing (remove trivial cuts).** Every cut in $\alpha$ where the cut formula appears in the lower sequent is trivially eliminable. Such a cut must have the following form with $s + u > 0$ or $t + v > 0$.

$$\frac{A^s, \Gamma \Rightarrow A^k, \Delta, A^t \quad A^u, \Sigma, A^l \Rightarrow \Pi, A^v}{A^{s+u}, \Gamma, \Sigma \Rightarrow \Delta, \Pi, A^{t+v}} \text{ (cut)}$$

If $s + u > 0$ and $t + v > 0$ then either premise can be used to obtain the conclusion via (w) and (c). Else, suppose that $s + u = 0$ (the case of $t + v = 0$ is analogous). Then, noting that $t + v > 0$, proceed as

$$\frac{\Gamma \Rightarrow A^k, \Delta, A^t}{\Gamma, \Sigma \Rightarrow \Delta, \Pi, A^{t+v}} \text{ (w), (c)}$$

Henceforth, without loss of generality we will assume that $\alpha$ is preprocessed.

**(II) Tracing Non-analytic Ancestors.** The purpose of this step is to identify the rule instances and formulas that will be crucial in the next step. In particular, this step does not modify the proof.

Suppose that the last rule is ($\Box$) (the case ($\blacksquare$) is analogous). Then write $\alpha$ as follows, where $\blacksquare\Delta$ is the multiset of non-analytic formulas in the rule instance. This means that every formula in $\blacksquare\Pi$ is analytic i.e., a subformula of $\Box\Gamma \Rightarrow \Box A, \Delta, \Pi$.

$$\frac{\boxed{\alpha_0}}{\dfrac{\Gamma \Rightarrow A, \blacksquare\Delta, \blacksquare\Pi}{\Box\Gamma \Rightarrow \Box A, \Delta, \Pi}} \text{ ($\Box$)}$$

Of course, every formula in $\Gamma \Rightarrow A$ is analytic as well. By hypothesis, only the last rule in $\alpha$ is non-analytic, so the subproof $\alpha_0$ is analytic.

Since the initial sequents are on propositional variables, tracing the ancestors of any element from non-empty $\blacksquare\Delta$ upwards must lead to a weakening or a modal rule instance. More specifically, we have the following:

**Claim 1.** *Every lowermost modal rule instance in $\alpha_0$ either*

1. *contains no ancestor of $\blacksquare\Delta$, or*

2. contains exactly one ancestor of $\blacksquare\Delta$, which is principal in the rule instance.

Rule instances of type 2. will be called *critical instances*.
*Proof of Claim* 1. Assume towards a contradiction that an ancestor of $\blacksquare\Delta$ is a context formula in the conclusion of a lowermost modal rule instance. Due to the modal rule instance being lowermost, this ancestor is unchanged from the original formula i.e., it is some $\blacksquare B \in \blacksquare\Delta$. Due to the form of the rule instances ($\square$) and ($\blacksquare$), the premise of this lowermost modal rule instance contains a formula $\heartsuit\blacksquare B$, where $\heartsuit \in \{\square, \blacksquare\}$. By analyticity of $\alpha_0$, it follows that $\heartsuit\blacksquare B$ is a subformula of $\Gamma \Rightarrow A, \blacksquare\Delta, \blacksquare\Pi$ and so in particular $\blacksquare B$ is a subformula of $\square\Gamma \Rightarrow \square A, \Delta, \Pi$. However, $\blacksquare\Delta$ was chosen such that every formula in it is non-analytic, so we have reached a contradiction. ◁

In light of Claim 1, we write $\alpha$ as follows where $i \in I$ enumerates the critical instances and $\blacksquare B^i$ is the unique ancestor of $\blacksquare\Delta$ in the $i$-th critical instance.

$$\boxed{\beta_i}$$

$$\dfrac{\Sigma^i \Rightarrow B^i, \square\Psi^i}{\blacksquare\Sigma^i \Rightarrow \blacksquare B^i, \Psi^i}\,(\blacksquare)^i \quad i \in I$$

$$\boxed{core(\alpha_0)}$$

$$\dfrac{\Gamma \Rightarrow A, \blacksquare\Delta, \blacksquare\Pi}{\square\Gamma \Rightarrow \square A, \Delta, \Pi}\,(\square)$$

Following the usual terminology, a derivation of $s_0$ from the sequents $\{s_1, \ldots, s_n\}$ is a proof-like structure except that every leaf is either initial sequents of **GKt** or an element from $\{s_1, \ldots, s_n\}$. Then $core(\alpha_0)$ is the subderivation (of $\alpha$) of $\Gamma \Rightarrow A, \blacksquare\Delta, \blacksquare\Pi$ from the sequents $\blacksquare\Sigma^i \Rightarrow \blacksquare B^i, \Psi^i$ for $i \in I$, that is, from the conclusions of the critical instances. Note that $core(\alpha_0)$ also contains all lowermost modal rule instances that are non-critical together with their subderivations but these are not shown in the picture above.

A *critical formula* is a formula that appears in some $\Sigma^i$'s or $\square\Psi^i$. i.e., some premise context of a critical instance. Let $\Xi$ be the set of all critical formulas.

**(III) Restructuring the Proof.** Let $\Xi = \{C_1, C_2, \ldots\}$. Starting from the desired endsequent $\square\Gamma \Rightarrow \square A, \Delta, \Pi$ (this is the endsequent of $\alpha$), introduce cuts bottom-up on all critical formulas, as follows:

$$\dfrac{\dfrac{\vdots}{\square\Gamma \Rightarrow \square A, \Delta, \Pi, C_1, C_2} \quad \dfrac{\vdots}{C_2, \square\Gamma \Rightarrow \square A, \Delta, \Pi, C_1}}{\square\Gamma \Rightarrow \square A, \Delta, \Pi, C_1}\,(cut) \quad \dfrac{\dfrac{\vdots}{C_1, \square\Gamma \Rightarrow \square A, \Delta, \Pi, C_2} \quad \dfrac{\vdots}{C_1, C_2, \square\Gamma \Rightarrow \square A, \Delta, \Pi}}{C_1, \square\Gamma \Rightarrow \square A, \Delta, \Pi}\,(cut)$$
$$\square\Gamma \Rightarrow \square A, \Delta, \Pi$$

First observe that every introduced cut is analytic.

**Claim 2.** *Every critical formula is a subformula of the endsequent $\square\Gamma \Rightarrow \square A, \Delta, \Pi$ of $\alpha$.*

$$
\begin{array}{c}
\boxed{\beta_i} \\
\dfrac{\Sigma^i \Rightarrow B^i, \Box\Psi^i}{\blacksquare\Sigma^i \Rightarrow \blacksquare B^i, \Psi^i}\ (\blacksquare)^i \\
\boxed{core(\alpha_0)} \\
\dfrac{\Gamma \Rightarrow A, \blacksquare\Delta, \blacksquare\Pi}{\Box\Gamma \Rightarrow \Box A, \Delta, \Pi}\ (\Box)
\end{array}
\quad\rightsquigarrow\quad
\begin{array}{c}
\boxed{\beta_i} \\
\dfrac{\Sigma^i \Rightarrow B^i, \Box\Psi^i}{\Xi_1, \Box\Gamma \Rightarrow \Box A, \Delta, \Pi, \Xi_2}\ (\text{w}), (\text{c}) \\
(\Xi_1; \Xi_2)\ \text{aligned}
\end{array}
\qquad
\begin{array}{c}
\boxed{\text{axiom expansion}} \\
\Xi_1^{-\Box}, \blacksquare\Sigma^i \Rightarrow \Psi^i, \blacksquare\Xi_2^* \\
\boxed{core(\alpha_0)^{\Xi_1^{-\Box}, \blacksquare\Xi_2^*}} \\
\dfrac{\Xi_1^{-\Box}, \Gamma \Rightarrow A, \blacksquare\Pi, \blacksquare\Xi_2^*}{\dfrac{\Xi_1, \Box\Gamma \Rightarrow \Box A, \Pi, \Xi_2^*}{\Xi_1, \Box\Gamma \Rightarrow \Box A, \Delta, \Pi, \Xi_2}\ (\text{w})}\ (\Box) \\
(\Xi_1; \Xi_2)\ \text{unaligned}
\end{array}
$$

$$
\boxed{\text{cuts on critical formulas}}
$$
$$
\Box\Gamma \Rightarrow \Box A, \Delta, \Pi
$$

**Fig. 2.** From $\alpha$ to $\alpha^*$.

*Proof.* Let $C$ be a critical formula. As $\alpha_0$ is analytic, $C$ is a subformula of its endsequent $\Gamma \Rightarrow A, \blacksquare\Delta, \blacksquare\Pi$. Moreover, only the formulas in $\blacksquare\Delta$ are non-analytic in the last rule instance. So it suffices to show that $C \notin \blacksquare\Delta$. Towards a contradiction, suppose that $C \in \blacksquare\Delta$. As $C$ is a critical formula we have $C \in \Sigma^i$ for some $i$ (the case that $C \in \Box\Psi^i$ is impossible because $C \in \blacksquare\Delta$ begins with $\blacksquare$). As $\blacksquare\Sigma^i$ is in the conclusion of the $i$-th critical instance, we see that $\blacksquare C$ appears in $\alpha_0$ and hence, by analyticity of $\alpha_0$, it is a subformula of $\Gamma \Rightarrow A, \blacksquare\Delta, \blacksquare\Pi$. It follows that $C$ is a subformula of $\Box\Gamma \Rightarrow \Box A, \Delta, \Pi$, which, together with the assumption $C \in \blacksquare\Delta$, contradicts the non-analyticity of $\blacksquare\Delta$.   ◁

Next, observe that the above derivation is a binary tree with $2^{|\Xi|}$-many leaves, each of which is of the following form for some partition $\Xi_1 \cup \Xi_2 = \Xi$:

$$\Xi_1, \Box\Gamma \Rightarrow \Box A, \Delta, \Pi, \Xi_2$$

See Fig. 2 for a pictorial representation of the transformation $\alpha \mapsto \alpha^*$.

Call a partition and its associated sequent *aligned* if there is some $i \in I$ such that $\Xi_1$ contains all formulas in $\Sigma^i$ and $\Xi_2$ contains all formulas in $\Box\Psi^i$, and *unaligned* otherwise. Informally, $(\Xi_1; \Xi_2)$ aligned means that there exists $i \in I$ such that $\Xi_1$ contains $\Sigma^i$, and $\Xi_2$ contains $\Box\Psi^i$.

(a) **Proof of a sequent with an aligned partition** $(\Xi_1; \Xi_2)$

Suppose that $i \in I$ witnesses that $(\Xi_1; \Xi_2)$ is aligned. Then, noting that $B^i \in \Delta$, we can obtain a proof of the aligned sequent from the conclusion of $\beta_i$—this is the proof of the premise of the $i$ th critical instance, see Fig. 2—using weakening and contraction.

$$
\boxed{\beta_i}
$$
$$
\dfrac{\Sigma^i \Rightarrow B^i, \Box\Psi^i}{\Xi_1, \Box\Gamma \Rightarrow \Box A, \Delta, \Pi, \Xi_2}\ (\text{w}), (\text{c})
$$

Contraction is required because $(\Sigma_i, \Box\Psi^i)$ is a pair of multisets, and $(\Xi_1; \Xi_2)$ a pair of sets that we read inside a sequent as multisets in the obvious way (an element is in the set iff the element has multiplicity 1 in the multiset).

(b) **Proof of a sequent with an unaligned partition $(\Xi_1; \Xi_2)$**

Working bottom-up from a unaligned sequent, consider the following derivation, where $\Xi_1^{-\Box} := \{C \mid \Box C \in \Xi_1^*\}$ and $\Xi_2^* := \Xi_2 \cap (\bigcup_i \Sigma^i)$.

$$\Xi_1^{-\Box}, \blacksquare\Sigma^i \Rightarrow \Psi^i, \blacksquare\Xi_2^*$$

$$\boxed{core(\alpha_0)^{\Xi_1^{-\Box}, \blacksquare\Xi_2^*}}$$

$$\frac{\dfrac{\Xi_1^{-\Box}, \Gamma \Rightarrow A, \blacksquare\Pi, \blacksquare\Xi_2^*}{\Xi_1, \Box\Gamma \Rightarrow \Box A, \Pi, \Xi_2^*} (\Box)}{\Xi_1, \Box\Gamma \Rightarrow \Box A, \Delta, \Pi, \Xi_2} (w)$$

Here $core(\alpha_0)^{\Xi_1^{-\Box}, \blacksquare\Xi_2^*}$ is obtained from $core(\alpha_0)$ by the following operation: In every sequent containing an ancestor of $\blacksquare\Delta$, remove all such ancestors and add $\Xi_1^{-\Box}$ in the antecedent and $\blacksquare\Xi_2^*$ in the succedent. Leave sequents without ancestors of $\blacksquare\Delta$ unchanged.

The following shows that it is well-defined.

**Claim 3.** $core(\alpha_0)^{\Xi_1^{-\Box}, \blacksquare\Xi_2^*}$ *is a derivation of* $\Xi_1^{-\Box}, \Gamma \Rightarrow A, \blacksquare\Pi, \Xi_2^*$ *from the premises* $\Xi_1^{-\Box}, \blacksquare\Sigma^i \Rightarrow \Psi^i, \blacksquare\Xi_2^*$, *for all* $i \in I$.

*Proof.* By Claim 1 and the definition of critical instance, the part of $core(\alpha_0)$ below the critical instances contains only propositional rule instances. Since propositional rule instances do not have side conditions, $core(\alpha_0)^{\Xi_1^{-\Box}, \blacksquare\Xi_2^*}$ is indeed a derivation. ◁

Hence we have a derivation of the unaligned sequent $\Xi_1, \Box\Gamma \Rightarrow \Box A, \Delta, \Pi, \Xi_2$ from $\{\Xi_1^{-\Box}, \blacksquare\Sigma^i \Rightarrow \Psi^i, \blacksquare\Xi_2^*\}_{i \in I}$. The following shows that every leaf of $core(\alpha_0)^{\Xi_1^{-\Box}, \blacksquare\Xi_2^*}$ is a quasi-initial sequent (and hence has an analytic proof, by Lemma 1). Hence we obtain a proof of the unaligned sequent.

**Claim 4.** *If $(\Xi_1; \Xi_2)$ is unaligned, then some formula appears both in the antecedent and the succedent of $\Xi_1^{-\Box}, \blacksquare\Sigma^i \Rightarrow \Psi^i, \blacksquare\Xi_2^*$.*

*Proof of Claim 4.* As $(\Xi_1; \Xi_2)$ is unaligned, either $\Xi_1$ does not contain some formula in $\Sigma^i$ or $\Xi_2$ does not contain some formula in $\Box\Psi^i$. Since multiset union $\Xi_1 \sqcup \Xi_2 = \Xi$, in the first case that there exists $C \in \Sigma^i \cap \Xi_2$, and hence $\blacksquare C \in \blacksquare\Sigma^i \cap \blacksquare\Xi_2^*$. In the second case, there exists $C \in \Box\Psi^i \cap \Xi_1$, which means that $C$ is necessarily of the form $\Box D$ owing to membership in $\Box\Psi^i$, and therefore $D \in \Psi^i \cap \Xi_1^{-\Box}$. ◁

This concludes the description of the construction of $\alpha^*$.

## 2. Proof of Grade Reduction.

The sole non-analytic rule instance of $\alpha$ of grade $k$ has been eliminated in $\alpha^*$. Since non-analyticity in **GKt** may occur in any modal or cut-rule instance, and since an analytic instance may become non-analytic when formulas in it are replaced, we show that every new and modified rule instance in $\alpha^*$ is either analytic, or non-analytic of grade $< k$. This is shown in the following two claims.

**Claim 5.** *The grade of the following rule instance that appears in the proof of an unaligned sequent—see 1. Construction of $\alpha^*$/step (III)/case b—is $< k$.*

$$\frac{\Xi_1^{-\Box}, \Gamma \Rightarrow A, \blacksquare\Pi, \blacksquare\Xi_2^*}{\Xi_1, \Box\Gamma \Rightarrow \Box A, \Pi, \Xi_2^*} \; (\Box)$$

*Proof of Claim 5.* Let $(\Box)^*$ denote the instance of $(\Box)$ in the statement.

By inspection, if a formula $D$ in the premise $\Xi_1^{-\Box}, \Gamma \Rightarrow A, \blacksquare\Pi, \blacksquare\Xi_2^*$ of $(\Box)^*$ is not a subformula of some formula in $\Xi_1, \Box\Gamma \Rightarrow \Box A, \Pi, \Xi_2^*$—i.e., $(\Box)^*$ is non-analytic—then $D$ must occur in either $\blacksquare\Pi$ or $\blacksquare\Xi_2^*$.

Suppose $D \in \blacksquare\Pi$. We know that $D$ is a subformula of some formula in the conclusion $\Box\Gamma \Rightarrow \Box A, \Delta, \Pi$ of the last rule instance in $\alpha$—see Fig. 2—since the non-analytic formulas in that instance are exclusively in $\blacksquare\Delta$. It follows that $D$ is either a subformula of a formula in $\Box\Gamma \Rightarrow \Box A, \Pi$ and hence analytic in $(\Box)^*$, or a subformula of a formula in $\Delta$, and hence of grade $< k$ (else $\blacksquare\Delta$ would contain a formula with grade $\geq k+1$ which would contradict the hypothesis).

Finally, suppose $D \in \blacksquare\Xi_2^* = \blacksquare(\Xi_2 \cap (\bigcup_i \Sigma^i))$. Hence $D \in \blacksquare\Sigma^i$ for some $i \in I$. Let $D_0$ be an occurrence of $D$ in the conclusion of the $i$-th critical instance. Starting from $D_0$ in the conclusion of the $i$-th critical instance, we now identify a sequence $D_0, D_1, \ldots, D_{end}$ of occurrences—one in each successive sequent below it in $core(\alpha_0)$—until we reach a formula $D_{end}$ in $\Gamma \Rightarrow A, \blacksquare\Delta, \blacksquare\Pi$ (this is the root of $core(\alpha_0)$, and the premise of the last rule instance in $\alpha$; see Fig. 2).

1. If $D_l$ is the ancestor of some formula $D'$ in the sequent below it, $D_{l+1} := D'$.
2. If $D_l$ is not the ancestor of any formula in the sequent below it, then $D_l$ must be the cut-formula of an analytic cut. Due to analyticity, $D_l$ must be a subformula of some formula $D'$ in the sequent below it. Set $D_{l+1} := D'$.

The rule instances along the sequents from which the sequence $D_0, D_1, \ldots, D_{end}$ are constructed were analytic, so $D$ is a subformula of $D_{end}$. If $D_{end}$ appears in $\Gamma \Rightarrow A$ then $D$ is analytic in $(\Box)^*$. Else, if $D_{end}$ appears in $\blacksquare\Pi$, then $D$ must appear in $\Pi$ or $\Delta$ (by consideration of the last rule instance in $\alpha$), and hence it is analytic in $(\Box)^*$ or of grade $< k$. Else, it must be the case that $D_{end}$ appears in $\blacksquare\Delta$. Since $D_0$ was not an ancestor of $\blacksquare\Delta$ in $\alpha_0$—indeed, $D$ is a critical formula so it appears in the context of the critical instance, and by Claim 1, if the conclusion of the critical instance contains an ancestor, it is unique and principal—at some index $l+1$ in the construction of $D_0, D_1, \ldots, D_{end}$, condition 2 in the construction must have been applied to obtain $D_{l+1}$ from $D_l$. This implies that $D_{l+1} \neq D_l$, since otherwise the cut would be trivial, and trivial cuts were removed in the preprocessing. Thus $D_0$ is a *proper* subformula of $D_{end} \in \blacksquare\Delta$. It follows that the grade of $D$ in $(\Box)^*$ is $< k$. ◁

**Claim 6.** *The grade of every non-analytic rule instance in $core(\alpha_0)^{\Xi_1^{-\Box}, \blacksquare \Xi_2^*}$ (the derivation that appears in the proof of an unaligned sequent) is $< k$.*

*Proof.* Recall that $core(\alpha_0)$ is analytic, and $core(\alpha_0)^{\Xi_1^{-\Box}, \blacksquare \Xi_2^*}$ arises from $core(\alpha_0)$ by considering every sequent containing an ancestor of the $\blacksquare \Delta$ in the endsequent, removing every such ancestor from the sequent and adding $\Xi_1^{-\Box}$ in the antecedent and $\blacksquare \Xi_2^*$ in the succedent. Every rule instance in $core(\alpha_0)$ is analytic. Suppose that $core(\alpha_0)^{\Xi_1^{-\Box}, \blacksquare \Xi_2^*}$ contains some non-analytic instance $r'$ that was an analytic instance $r$ in $core(\alpha_0)$. As $r$ contains ancestors of $\blacksquare \Delta$ it is not a modal non-critical instance (Claim 1), and it cannot be a critical instance since $core(\alpha_0)$ does not contain those. It must therefore be a cut, since all the other rules of the calculus are analytic. A cut-rule instance is non-analytic only if the cut-formula $C$ is not a subformula of any formula in the conclusion. Comparing the conclusion sequents of $r$ and $r'$, the only formulas that are in the former and not the latter are the formulas of $\blacksquare \Delta$ (since we removed these). Since $r$ is analytic and $r'$ is not, $C$ must be a subformula of some $\blacksquare D \in \blacksquare \Delta$. Now $C$ cannot be $\blacksquare D$ since $r$ would then be a trivial cut instance since $C$ appears in its conclusion, and trivial cut instances were removed in the preprocessing step on $\alpha$. So, $C$ must be a proper subformula of $\blacksquare D$. Hence $r'$ has grade $< k$.   ◁

This concludes the proof of Proposition 1.   **QED**

We are ready to prove the main theorem.

**Theorem 1.** *Every provable sequent in* **GKt** *has an analytic proof.*

*Proof.* We show that a proof where only the last rule instance is non-analytic can be transformed into an analytic proof of the same sequent. The desired result follows from this: if $\pi_0$ is a proof of sequent $s$ in **GKt**, replacing a subproof in $\pi_0$ whose only non-analytic rule instance is the last rule with the analytic proof obtained through the latter, we obtain a proof $\pi_1$ of $s$ that contains one less non-analytic rule; iterating this step, we ultimately reach an analytic proof of $s$.

Suppose that $\alpha$ is a proof of $s$ where only the last rule instance $r$ is non-analytic. We proceed by primary induction on the grade of $r$, and secondary induction on the sum of the heights of the premises of $r$.

First suppose that $r$ is a modal rule. Applying Proposition 1, we obtain a proof $\alpha^*$ of $s$ in which all non-analytic rule instances have strictly lower grade. At each subsequent step, we use the induction hypothesis to replace the subproof ending in a topmost non-analytic rule instances with analytic proofs with strictly lower grade. This process terminates by well-foundedness of the Dershowitz–Manna multiset ordering—i.e., replacing an element in the multiset by strictly smaller ones yields a strictly smaller multiset—as each application of Proposition 1 strictly decreases the multiset of grades of non-analytic rule instances. At termination we obtain an analytic proof of $s$.

The remaining case is that $r$ is a non-analytic cut with analytic premises.

$$\dfrac{\overset{\alpha_1}{\Gamma \Rightarrow A^k, \Delta} \quad \overset{\alpha_2}{\Sigma, A^l \Rightarrow \Pi}}{\Gamma, \Sigma \Rightarrow \Delta, \Pi} \ (cut)$$

Suppose that the last rule in $\alpha_1$ or $\alpha_2$ is an analytic cut $r_1$. Permuting $r$ above $r_1$ turns it into a non-analytic cut $r'$ with smaller sum of premise heights, and hence an analytic proof is obtained by IH. The analytic cut $r_1$ (with cut formula $A_1$, say) that was permuted downwards (call it $r'_1$) may have now become a non-analytic. Since $r_1$ was analytic and $r'_1$ is not, it must be that $A_1$ is a subformula of $A$. If $A_1 = A$ then $r_1$ would have been a trivial cut (since $A$ occurs in the premises of $r$), but these were removed in preprocessing. So $A_1$ is a proper subformula of $A$, hence we obtain an analytic proof by IH. If the last rule is a structural rule of weakening or contraction, the standard reductions apply. It remains to consider when the last rule in $\alpha_1$ and $\alpha_2$ is a logical rule.

If the main connective in $A$ is not modal, then neither the last rule instance in $\alpha_1$ nor $\alpha_2$ is modal. Apply the usual propositional cut reduction steps leading to new cuts of smaller grade, or the same grade and smaller sum of premise height. The subproof concluding the new cuts can be made analytic by the IH, and any subsequent propositional rules that follow will, of course, preserve analyticity.

Finally, suppose that the main connective in $A$ is modal. The last rule in $\alpha_1$ ($\alpha_2$) may be a propositional rule instance making some formula in $\Gamma, \Delta$ (resp. $\Sigma, \Pi$) principal. Apply the usual steps to reduce a propositional cut. We are left with the case when the last rule instance in $\alpha_1$ and $\alpha_2$ are modal rules.

**Claim 7.** *If the last rule instance in $\alpha_1$ is a modal rule, then $A$ is its principal formula and $k = 1$.*

*Proof.* Otherwise, one occurrence of $A$ would be non-principal in the modal rule instance and therefore—due to the form of the modal rules—appear as $\Box A$ or $\blacksquare A$ in the premise of $\alpha_1$'s last rule instance. As $\alpha_1$ is analytic by assumption this implies that $\Box A$ or $\blacksquare A$ is a subformula of $\Gamma \Rightarrow A^k, \Delta$ and hence of $\Gamma \Rightarrow \Delta$, implying that the multicut on $A$ is analytic, contrary to the assumption.  ◁

We have reached the following situation (an analogous argument applies when it is an instance of ($\blacksquare$)). Recall that only the last rule instance is non-analytic.

$$\dfrac{\dfrac{\Gamma \Rightarrow A, \blacksquare\Delta}{\Box\Gamma \Rightarrow \Box A, \Delta}\,(\Box) \quad \dfrac{\Sigma, A^l \Rightarrow B, \blacksquare\Pi}{\Box\Sigma, \Box A^l \Rightarrow \Box B, \Pi}\,(\Box)}{\Box\Gamma, \Box\Sigma \Rightarrow \Box B, \Delta, \Pi}\,(\text{cut})$$

Applying a multicut to $\Gamma \Rightarrow A, \blacksquare\Delta$ and $\Sigma, A^l \Rightarrow B, \blacksquare\Pi$ we get a proof of $\Gamma, \Sigma \Rightarrow B, \blacksquare\Delta, \blacksquare\Pi$. By IH, we have an analytic proof of this sequent. Now we apply ($\Box$) to get the desired endsequent:

$$\dfrac{\Gamma, \Sigma \Rightarrow B, \blacksquare\Delta, \blacksquare\Pi}{\Box\Gamma, \Box\Sigma \Rightarrow \Box B, \Delta, \Pi}\,(\Box)$$

If the last rule instance is non-analytic, then there is a formula $\blacksquare D \in \blacksquare\Delta \cup \blacksquare\Pi$ that is not a subformula of any formula in the conclusion. Since the two rule instances of ($\Box$) before the reduction were analytic, this can only be the case if $\blacksquare D$ is a subformula of $\Box A$. But clearly $\blacksquare D \neq \Box A$, so in fact $\blacksquare D$ is a proper subformula of $\Box A$. Hence the grade of this instance is strictly less than the grade of the original cut formula $\Box A$. By IH we obtain the desired sequent.
**QED**

*Example 1.* Consider the proof

$$\dfrac{\dfrac{\dfrac{\dfrac{p \Rightarrow p}{p \Rightarrow p \vee q}}{\blacksquare p \Rightarrow \blacksquare(p \vee q)}\ (\blacksquare)}{\Rightarrow \blacksquare(p \vee q), \neg \blacksquare p}}{\Rightarrow p \vee q, \Box \neg \blacksquare p}\ (\Box)$$

The rule instance of ($\Box$) is non-analytic as $\blacksquare(p \vee q)$ is not a subformula of the endsequent. The corresponding critical instance is ($\blacksquare$) above, with a single critical formula $p$. The transformed proof thus starts with a cut on $p$:

$$\dfrac{\dfrac{\dfrac{\dfrac{p \Rightarrow p}{\blacksquare p \Rightarrow \blacksquare p}\ (\blacksquare)}{\Rightarrow \blacksquare p, \neg \blacksquare p}}{\Rightarrow p, \Box \neg \blacksquare p}\ (\Box) \qquad \dfrac{p \Rightarrow p}{p \Rightarrow p \vee q}}{\Rightarrow p \vee q, \Box \neg \blacksquare p}\ (cut)$$

Let us use this example to illustrate the semantic intuition behind the proof transformation. As in other proof systems for modal logic, derivations in **GKt** can be understood as structured searches for countermodels. The process begins with a partially constructed countermodel for the endsequent, where *formulas in the antecedent are treated as true, and those in the succedent as false.* As the proof unfolds upward, this model is incrementally extended with additional information until a contradiction is reached, which means that no countermodel is possible, and hence, the endsequent must be valid. In this dynamic view, an instance of ($\Box$) (resp. ($\blacksquare$)) corresponds to transitioning from one world in the countermodel to a future (resp. past) world.

Looking through this lens at the proof before the transformation (we are reading upwards from the endsequent), we observe a step into the future via ($\Box$) followed two rules later by a step back into the present via ($\blacksquare$), with one true formula $\blacksquare p$ that was 'learned' in the future pulled back to the present as $p$. This additional formula is then used to derive contradiction, witnessed by $p \Rightarrow p$.

Consider now the transformed proof. Rather than moving into the future, we remain in the present and perform a case distinction (a cut) on $p$. In right branch, where the learned formula $p$ is assumed true, we derive a contradiction as before. Only in the case where the learned formula is assumed false we take it into the future, where it becomes $\blacksquare p$ fails. But we already know that in the future we can learn that $\blacksquare p$ is in fact true, and this gives the desired contradiction.

## 5 Conclusions and Future Work

Although our analytic restriction proof is carried out within **GKt**, the core idea is adaptable to related logics, by slightly modifiying the methodology. The situation is analogous to a cut-elimination strategy which, though originally developed for a specific calculus, is then extended to other calculi with similar structural characteristics—we recall Valentini's cut-elimination for provability logic [15,26], which was subsequently adapted to various structurally similar systems [7,27]. The proof presented in this paper can also be adapted to the logic **KB**, obtained by adding the following to the classical calculus.

$$\frac{\Gamma \Rightarrow A, \Box \Delta}{\Box \Gamma \Rightarrow \Box A, \Delta} \ (B)$$

We expect these methods to apply to some further extensions of the classical sequent calculus with non-analytic modal rules that meet the following conditions:

1. If the cut-formula is principal in both premises by the modal rule, it can be transformed to cuts on proper subformulas (reduction of principal cuts)
2. The rules are non-analytic with respect to a single type of modality, which may prefix formulas in the premise that are unmodalized in the conclusion.
3. Formulas prefixed by a modality in the conclusion (premise) are unmodalized (modalized with the same operator) in the premises (conclusion), and formulas. All formulas remain on the same side of the sequent as they appear in the conclusion, and no additional formula is introduced in the premises.

As future work, we intend to formalize these intuitive conditions and develop a general cut restriction proof applicable to a broad class of logics, and consider the algorithmic complexity and potential computational interpretations.

**Acknowledgements.** Agata Ciabattoni is supported by Work supported by the FWF project I 6372-N [doi: 10.55776/I6372]. Timo Lang is supported by UK EPSRC through Research Grants EP/S013008/1 and EP/R006865/1. Revantha Ramanayake is supported by the Austrian Science Fund (FWF) project P33548, and the Dutch Research Council (NWO) project OCENW.M.22.258.

# References

1. Avron, A.: The method of hypersequents in the proof theory of propositional non-classical logics. In: Logic: From Foundations to Applications (Staffordshire, 1993), pp. 1–32. Oxford Univ. Press, New York (1996)
2. Avron, A., Lahav, O.: A unified semantic framework for fully structural propositional sequent systems. ACM Trans. Comput. Log. **14**(4) (2013)
3. Belnap, N.D.: Display logic. J. Philos. Log. **11**(4), 375–417 (1982)
4. Blackburn, P., de Rijke, M., Venema, I.: Modal Logic. Cambridge Tracts in Theoretical Computer Science, vol. 53. Cambridge University Press, Cambridge (2001)
5. Ciabattoni, A., Lang, T., Ramanayake, R.: Bounded-analytic sequent calculi and embeddings for hypersequent logics. J. Symb. Log. **86**(2), 635–668 (2021)
6. Ciabattoni, A., Lang, T., Ramanayake, R.: Cut-restriction: From cuts to analytic cuts. In: 38th Annual ACM/IEEE Symposium on Logic in Computer Science, LICS 2023, Boston, MA, USA, 26–29 June 2023, pp. 1–13. IEEE (2023). https://doi.org/10.1109/LICS56636.2023.10175785

7. Ciabattoni, A., Olivetti, N., Parent, X., Ramanayake, R., Rozplokhas, D.: Analytic proof theory for åqvist's system F. In: Maranhão, J., Peterson, C., Straßer, C., van der Torre, L. (eds.) Deontic Logic and Normative Systems - 16th International Conference, DEON 2023, Trois-Rivières, QC, Canada, 5–7 July 2023, pp. 79–98. College Publications (2023)
8. D'Agostino, M., Mondadori, M.: The taming of the cut. Classical refutations with analytic cut. J. Log. Comput. **4**, 285–319 (1994)
9. Belardinelli, F., Jipsen, P., Ono, H.: Algebraic aspects of cut elimination. Stud. Log. **68**, 1–32 (2001)
10. Fitting, M.: Subformula results in some propositional modal logics. Stud. Log. **37**(4), 387–391 (1978)
11. Gabbay, D.: Labelled Deductive Systems, vol. 1—Foundations. Oxford University Press, Oxford (1996)
12. Gentzen, G.: Untersuchungen über das logische Schließen **39**, 176–210, 405–431 (1934/35). english translation in: American Philosophical Quarterly 1 (1964), 288–306 and American Philosophical Quarterly 2 (1965), 204–218, as well as in: *The Collected Papers of Gerhard Gentzen*, (ed. M.E. Szabo), pp. 68–131. Amsterdam, North Holland (1969)
13. Girard, J.Y.: Proof Theory and Logical Complexity, Studies in Proof Theory. Monographs, vol. 1. Bibliopolis, Naples (1987)
14. Goré, R., Postniece, L., Tiu, A.: On the correspondence between display postulates and deep inference in nested sequent calculi for tense logics. Log. Methods Comput. Sci. **7**(2), 2:8, 38 (2011)
15. Goré, R., Ramanayake, R.: Valentini's cut-elimination for provability logic resolved. Rev. Symb. Log. **5**(2), 212–238 (2012)
16. Indrzejczak, A.: Cut elimination in hypersequent calculus for some logics of linear time. Rev. Symb. Log. **12**(4), 806–822 (2019)
17. Kowalski, T., Ono, H.: Analytic cut and interpolation for bi-intuitionistic logic. Rev. Symb. Log. **10**(2), 259–283 (2017)
18. Kracht, M.: Power and weakness of the modal display calculus. In: Proof Theory of Modal Logic (Hamburg, 1993), Appl. Log. Ser., vol. 2, pp. 93–121. Kluwer Acad. Publ., Dordrecht (1996)
19. Negri, S.: Proof analysis in modal logic. J. Philos. Log. **34**(5–6), 507–544 (2005)
20. Nishimura, H.: A study of some tense logics by gentzen's sequential method. Publ. Res. Inst. Math. Sci. **16**(2), 343–353 (1980)
21. Smullyan, R.M.: Analytic cut. J. Symb. Log. **33**, 560–564 (1968)
22. Takano, M.: Subformula property as a substitute for cut-elimination in modal propositional logics. Math. Japon. **37**, 1129–1145 (1992)
23. Takano, M.: A modified subformula property for the modal logics K5 and K5D. Bull. Sect. Log. **30** (2001). https://doi.org/10.18778/0138-0680.48.1.02
24. Terui, K.: Which structural rules admit cut elimination? An algebraic criterion. J. Symb. Log. **72**(3), 738–754 (2007)
25. Troelstra, A.S., Schwichtenberg, H.: Basic Proof Theory, Cambridge Tracts in Theoretical Computer Science, vol. 43, second edn. Cambridge University Press, Cambridge (2000)
26. Valentini, S.: The modal logic of provability: cut-elimination. J. Philos. Log. **12**(4), 471–476 (1983)
27. Valentini, S.: A syntactic proof of cut-elimination for $gl_{lin}$. Z. Math. Logik Grundlag. Math. **32**(2), 137–144 (1986)

28. Viganò, L.: Labelled Non-Classical Logics. Kluwer Academic Publishers, Dordrecht (2000). with a foreword by Dov M. Gabbay
29. Wansing, H.: Displaying Modal Logic, Trends in Logic. Springer, Cham (1998). https://doi.org/10.1007/978-94-017-1280-4

**Open Access** This chapter is licensed under the terms of the Creative Commons Attribution 4.0 International License (http://creativecommons.org/licenses/by/4.0/), which permits use, sharing, adaptation, distribution and reproduction in any medium or format, as long as you give appropriate credit to the original author(s) and the source, provide a link to the Creative Commons license and indicate if changes were made.

The images or other third party material in this chapter are included in the chapter's Creative Commons license, unless indicated otherwise in a credit line to the material. If material is not included in the chapter's Creative Commons license and your intended use is not permitted by statutory regulation or exceeds the permitted use, you will need to obtain permission directly from the copyright holder.

# Improved Decision Procedures for Multi-modal Tense Logic Using CEGAR-Tableaux

Rajeev Goré[1]($\boxtimes$) and Cormac Kikkert[2]

[1] Faculty of Information Technology, Monash University, Melbourne, Australia
rajeev.gore@monash.edu
[2] Cormac Kikkert Research, Canberra, Australia

**Abstract.** We extend the mono-modal CEGAR-tableaux of Goré and Kikkert to normal multi-modal logic $K_n$ with global assumptions. We then extend these CEGAR-tableaux to multi-modal tense logic $Kt_n$ without global assumptions by "compiling in" the residuation conditions between "future" and "past" modalities. Our new implementation CEGARBox++ uses $C^{++}$ and includes multiple optimisations which speed up proof-search. CEGARBox++ is the best satisfiability-checker for mono-modal tense logic $Kt_1$ but is not competitive for global assumptions.

## 1 Introduction

Propositional modal, temporal and description logics are of fundamental importance in logic-based artificial intelligence, hardware and software verification and knowledge representation and reasoning (KRR) [1,21]. Thus efficient decision procedures for modal satisfiability are an important area of research.

Such automated reasoning has not matched the advances in SAT-solving, until recently, when various authors independently used a SAT-solver for modal satisfiablity [7,9,14,18] using a technique originally due to Claessens and Rosén [4] for propositional intuitionistic logic, which was, itself, "inspired" by the work of Goré et al. [11] on "modal clause learning" using binary decision diagrams.

We previously [9] presented a new type of tableaux calculus which uses a SAT-solver and the standard counter-example guided abstraction refinement (CEGAR) methodology [5] to search for a rooted Kripke model for a given formula in modal clausal normal form (mcnf). We showed how to modify the initial mcnf to "compile in" the axioms T and 4 via a preprocessing stage, adding a standard loop-check for termination when required. Our Haskell implementation CEGARBox was, overall, the best over the standard benchmarks for the modal logics K, KT and S4, sometimes by orders of magnitude.

We have extended CEGAR-tableaux as follows: (1) to handle the multi-modal (description) logic $K_n$ (aka $\mathcal{ALC}$); (2) to handle $K_n$ with global assumptions (aka TBoxes); (3) to handle multi-modal tense (description) logic $Kt_n$ ($\mathcal{ALCI}$); (4) re-implemented satisfiability checkers for these logics in CEGARBox++ using C++; (5)

$M, w \Vdash \langle \alpha \rangle \varphi$ iff $\exists v. R_\alpha(w,v)$ & $M, v \Vdash \varphi$
$M, w \Vdash [\alpha] \varphi$ iff $\forall v. R_\alpha(w,v) \Rightarrow M, v \Vdash \varphi$
$M, w \Vdash \langle \bar{\alpha} \rangle \varphi$ iff $\exists v. R_\alpha(v,w)$ & $M, v \Vdash \varphi$
$M, w \Vdash [\bar{\alpha}] \varphi$ iff $\forall v. R_\alpha(v,w) \Rightarrow M, v \Vdash \varphi$

**Fig. 1.** Kripke semantics for multi-modal logic $Kt_n$ (aka $\mathcal{ALCI}$)

tested these solvers on existing mono-modal tense benchmarks, and on our own new multi-modal benchmarks with and without global assumptions.

We thank Robert McArthur for contributions to C++ and Ullrich Hustadt and Claudia Nalon for helpful discussions.

## 2 Syntax, Semantics and Local/Global Logical Consequence

Let $Ag$ be a non-empty finite set of agent names, let $\overline{Ag} = \{\bar{\alpha} \mid \alpha \in Ag\}$ be a finite set of converse (inverse) agent names and let $Agt := Ag \cup \overline{Ag}$. Let $Atm$ be a set of atomic formulae with $Atm \cap Agt = \emptyset$. Consider the language of formulae defined from atoms $p \in Atm$ and $\alpha \in Ag$ by the BNF grammar:

$$\varphi ::= \bot \mid \top \mid p \mid \neg \varphi \mid \varphi \wedge \varphi \mid \varphi \vee \varphi \mid [\alpha]\varphi \mid \langle \alpha \rangle \varphi \mid [\bar{\alpha}]\varphi \mid \langle \bar{\alpha} \rangle \varphi$$

Define $(\varphi_1 \to \varphi_2) := (\neg \varphi_1 \vee \varphi_2)$ and $\varphi_1 \leftrightarrow \varphi_2 := ((\varphi_1 \to \varphi_2) \wedge (\varphi_2 \to \varphi_1))$. Let $[\alpha]^0 \varphi := \varphi$ and $[\alpha]^{n+1} \varphi := [\alpha][\alpha]^n \varphi$. The modal-degree of a formula is the maximum number of nested modalities in it. For a finite set $\Gamma = \{\varphi_1, \cdots, \varphi_k\}$ let $\widehat{\Gamma} = (\varphi_1 \wedge \cdots \wedge \varphi_k)$ and let $[\alpha]\Gamma := \{[\alpha]\varphi_1, \cdots, [\alpha]\varphi_k\}$.

Putting $Ag$ as the singleton · (say), and ignoring $\overline{Ag}$ gives the syntax of basic mono-modal logic K where $[\cdot]\varphi/\langle \cdot \rangle \varphi$ mean "necessarily/possibly $\varphi$". Putting $Ag$ as the singleton $\alpha$ (say), and including $\bar{\alpha} \in \overline{Ag}$ gives the syntax of basic mono-modal tense logic Kt where $[\alpha]/\langle \alpha \rangle \varphi$ means "always/sometime in the future $\varphi$" and $[\bar{\alpha}]/\langle \bar{\alpha} \rangle \varphi$ means "always/sometime in the past $\varphi$". Putting $Ag = \{\alpha_1, \cdots, \alpha_n\}$, and $\overline{Ag} = \{\bar{\alpha}_1, \cdots, \bar{\alpha}_n\}$ for $n > 1$ gives the syntax of multi-modal tense logic $Kt_n$ [19], also known as the description logic $\mathcal{ALCI}$ [1] from KRR.

The semantics for these multi-modal (description) logics extend the truth-tables of classical propositional logic (cpl) using Kripke models which are tuples $M := \langle W, \{R_\alpha\}_{\alpha \in Ag}, \vartheta \rangle$ over a non-empty set $W$ (of possible worlds), and binary relations $R_\alpha$ over $W$ for every agent $\alpha \in Ag$, and a valuation $\vartheta(w,p) \subseteq W \times Atm$ telling us the truth value of each atomic formula $p$ at each world $w \in W$. Atomic valuations extend to a "forcing" relation $M, w \Vdash \varphi$ on the structure of $\varphi$. The semantics in Fig. 1 allow us to use only $vR_\alpha w$ as the "converse" of $wR_\alpha v$.

For a finite set $\Gamma$ of formulae and a Kripke model $M$, let $M \Vdash \Gamma$ mean $\forall \varphi \in \Gamma. \forall w \in M. M, w \Vdash \varphi$. Let $GA$ be a finite set of (TBox) formulae called the global assumptions. Let $LA$ be a finite set of (ABox) formulae called the local assumptions. Let $\mathcal{L}$ be any logic mentioned above with a corresponding class of $\mathcal{L}$-models. A formula $\varphi$ is $\mathcal{L}$-satisfiable if there is an $\mathcal{L}$-model $M$ containing a world $w$ such that $M, w \Vdash \varphi$. A formula $\varphi$ is $\mathcal{L}$-valid if $\neg\varphi$ is not $\mathcal{L}$-satisfiable. Formulae $\varphi$ and $\psi$ are logically equivalent if $\varphi \leftrightarrow \psi$ is $\mathcal{L}$-valid. Formulae $\varphi$ and $\psi$ are equi-satisfiable if $\varphi$ is $\mathcal{L}$-satisfiable iff $\psi$ is $\mathcal{L}$-satisfiable. A formula $\varphi$ is a global logical consequence of $GA$ in $\mathcal{L}$ iff $\forall M$. $M \Vdash GA$ implies $M \Vdash \varphi$. A formula $\varphi$ is a local logical consequence of $LA$ in $\mathcal{L}$ iff $\forall M. \forall w. M, w \Vdash (\widehat{LA} \to \varphi)$ A formula $\varphi$ is $\mathcal{L}$-satisfiable with global assumptions $\Gamma$ if there exists a Kripke $\mathcal{L}$-model $M$ containing a world $w$ such that $M, w \Vdash \varphi$ and $M \Vdash \Gamma$.

## 3 Two Different Modal Clausal Normal Forms for $Kt_n$

We give the modal clausal normal forms for $Kt_n$ only.

A *positive literal* is an atomic formula $p$. A *negative literal* is a negated atomic formula $\neg p$. A *literal* is a positive literal $p$ or else a negative literal $\neg p$. We use $a$ to $f$ and $l$ and $r$ for literals. We use $A$, $B$, $C$ and $D$ for a set of literals. Let $\overline{l} := \neg p$ if $l = p$ and $\overline{l} := p$ if $l = \neg p$ so that $\overline{\overline{l}} = l$. A formula is in *negation normal form* (NNF) if it is implication-free and negations appear only in front of atomic formulae. An NNF can be created with a linear descent of the formula.

**Proposition 1.** *A formula $\varphi_0$ of modal depth $\kappa$ can be converted into a logically equivalent formula $nnf(\varphi_0)$ in NNF which is at most polynomially longer.*

A modal clause is any formula of one of the following forms [10, 15, 20]:

cpl-clause: a formula $l_1 \wedge \cdots \wedge l_i \to r_1 \vee \cdots \vee r_j$ of literals;
box-clause: a formula $a \to [\alpha]b$ with literals $a$ and $b$ and agent name $\alpha \in Agt$;
dia-clause: a formula $c \to \langle\alpha\rangle d$ with literals $c$ and $d$ and agent name $\alpha \in Agt$.

For any set $\mathcal{C}$ of (multi-) modal clauses, let $\mathcal{C}^{cpl}$ be the cpl-clauses in $\mathcal{C}$, let $\mathcal{C}^{box} := \bigcup_{\alpha \in Agt}\{a \to [\alpha]b \mid (a \to [\alpha]b) \in \mathcal{C}\}$ and let $\mathcal{C}^{dia} := \bigcup_{\alpha \in Agt}\{c \to \langle\alpha\rangle d \mid (c \to \langle\alpha\rangle d) \in \mathcal{C}\}$. Using ";" for set-union, the set $\mathcal{C} = (\mathcal{C}^{cpl} ; \mathcal{C}^{box} ; \mathcal{C}^{dia})$ can be partitioned into its cpl-clauses and box-clauses and dia-clauses. We often write $\mathcal{C}$ rather than $\widehat{\mathcal{C}}$ as $\mathcal{C}$ is thought of as the conjunction of its members.

One of our modal clausal normal forms requires notation to succinctly express finite sequences of modalities such as $[\alpha_1][\alpha_2]\cdots[\alpha_k]$ which naturally correspond to all finite paths $w_1 R_{\alpha_1} w_2 R_{\alpha_2} \cdots R_{\alpha_k} w_k$ in a Kripke model. We therefore abuse notation to extend the language of formulae using constructs from regular expressions even though they are not part of the official syntax.

Specifically, we use the composition operator ";" from regular expressions to write $[\alpha_1; \alpha_2; \cdots ; \alpha_k]$ instead of $[\alpha_1][\alpha_2]\cdots[\alpha_k]$, use $\epsilon$ for the empty regular expression and write $w_1 R_{\alpha_1;\cdots;\alpha_k} w_k$ for $w_1 R_{\alpha_1} w_2 R_{\alpha_2} \cdots R_{\alpha_k} w_k$. Let $Ag^*/Agt^*$ be the set of all finite regular expressions over $Ag/Agt$ that use only ";", and let $Ag^k/Agt^k$ be the set of all finite regular expressions of length $k$ over $Ag/Agt$ that use only ";". For any such regular expression $\sigma$, let $\sigma^0 = \epsilon$, let $\sigma^{n>0} = (\sigma; \sigma^n)$, and let $(\sigma; \epsilon) = (\epsilon; \sigma) = \sigma$. Then, using | for parallel composition and .* for finite iteration, we define the universal modality $u$ as $(\alpha_1 \mid \overline{\alpha}_1 \mid \cdots \mid \alpha_n \mid \overline{\alpha}_n)^*$, encoding "everywhere $\varphi$" and "somewhere $\varphi$" as:

everywhere $\varphi$: $M, w \Vdash [u]\varphi$ iff for all $\sigma \in Agt^*$ if $wR_\sigma v$ then $M, v \Vdash \varphi$ and
somewhere $\varphi$: $M, w \Vdash \langle u \rangle \varphi$ iff there is some $\sigma \in Agt^*$ and $wR_\sigma v$ and $M, v \Vdash \varphi$.

**Proposition 2.** *A formula $\varphi_0$ of modal depth $\kappa$ can be put into two equi-satisfiable modal clausal normal forms $r \wedge \widehat{mcnf(\varphi_0)}$ and $r \wedge [u]\widehat{mcnfg(\varphi_0)}$ by naming subformulae using new atomic propositions, using $r$ as the name for $\varphi_0$, and where each $\mathcal{C}$ below is a finite set of modal clauses (essentially the $SNF_{ml}$ and SNF of Nalon et al. [16] who prove this proposition in detail):*

$$mcnf(\varphi_0) := \mathcal{C}_\epsilon\ ;\ \bigcup_{\sigma \in Agt^1} [\sigma]\mathcal{C}_\sigma\ ;\ \cdots\ ;\ \bigcup_{\sigma \in Agt^\kappa} [\sigma]\mathcal{C}_\sigma$$
$$mcnfg(\varphi_0) := \mathcal{C}_\epsilon\ ;\ \bigcup_{\sigma \in Agt^1} \mathcal{C}_\sigma\ ;\ \cdots\ ;\ \bigcup_{\sigma \in Agt^\kappa} \mathcal{C}_\sigma$$

*Example 1.* Consider the negation $\varphi_0 := \neg([\alpha](p \to q) \to ([\alpha]p \to [\alpha]q))$ of the K axiom with modal depth $\kappa = 1$. Its NNF is $[\alpha](\neg p \vee q) \wedge [\alpha]p \wedge \langle \alpha \rangle \neg q$. Putting $r$ as the name for $\varphi_0$ gives us: $\mathcal{C}_\epsilon := r \to [\alpha]b\ ;\ r \to [\alpha]p\ ;\ r \to \langle \alpha \rangle \neg q$ and $\mathcal{C}_\alpha := b \to \neg p \vee q$ with $mcnf(\varphi_0) = (\mathcal{C}_\epsilon\ ;\ [\alpha]\mathcal{C}_\alpha)$ and $mcnfg(\varphi_0) = (\mathcal{C}_\epsilon\ ;\ \mathcal{C}_\alpha)$.

These definitions clumsily try to capture the following intuitions. The set $\mathcal{C}_\epsilon$ excludes $r$ so we must add it explicitly to form $(r\ ;\ mcnf(\varphi_0))$ and $(r\ ;\ mcnfg(\varphi_0))$. Moreover, the modal clauses $\mathcal{C}_\sigma$ "live" at the top level in $mcnfg(\varphi_0)$ while they must be "pushed" to the appropriate modal level as $[\sigma]\mathcal{C}_\sigma$ in $mcnf(\varphi_0)$.

## 4 SAT-Solvers as CPL-Oracles

The original CEGAR-tableaux from Goré and Kikkert [9] assume we have access to a SAT-solver s, to which we can add a cpl-clause $\varphi$ via addClause(s, $\varphi$), and which accepts a set of literals $\mathcal{A}$ called unit assumptions, such as MiniSAT [6]. The intuition is that we want all literals in $\mathcal{A}$ to be assigned to true.

When pre-loaded with a set $\mathcal{C}^{cpl}$ of cpl-clauses and called with solve(s, $\mathcal{A}$), such a SAT-solver returns one of two results:

$(sat, \vartheta)$: if $(\mathcal{A}\ ;\ \mathcal{C}^{cpl})$ is true under the cpl-valuation $\vartheta \supseteq \mathcal{A}$ or-else
$(unsat, UC)$: if $UC \subseteq \mathcal{A}$ is a, not necessarily unique, minimal "unsatisfiable core" of $\mathcal{A}$ such that $(UC\ ;\ \mathcal{C}^{cpl})$ is cpl-unsatisfiable

$UC$ itself may be cpl-satisfiable but the term "unsatisfiable core" is standard.
Strictly speaking, since SAT-solvers handle classical propositional logic, they should return a cpl-valuation $\vartheta \subseteq Atm$ as the cpl-part of a modal valuation $\vartheta(w, p) \subseteq W \times Atm$. That is, strictly speaking, a cpl-valuation $\vartheta$ is just a set of atomic formulae. But in concrete applications, from KRR say, it may be more useful for a user to assert "I know that atomic formula $c$ is false", which can be achieved with $\neg c \in \mathcal{A}$. To ensure the returned valuation obeys $\vartheta \supseteq \mathcal{A}$, the SAT-solver returns a "complete" valuation that contains a truth value for every atomic formula that appears in the mcnf. So if the mcnf contains $n$ atomic formulae, each cpl-valuation $\vartheta$ returned is actually a finite set of $n$ literals.

*Example 2.* From our previous example, $\varphi_0$ is equi-satisfiable with $(r \ ; \ \mathcal{C}_\epsilon \ ; \ [\alpha]\mathcal{C}_\alpha)$. Create a SAT-solver s0 for modal depth 0, pre-load s0 with $\mathcal{C}_\epsilon^{cpl} = \emptyset$, the cpl-part of $\mathcal{C}_\epsilon$, put $\mathcal{A}_\epsilon = \{r\}$ because $r$ must be true at modal depth 0, and call solve(s0, $\mathcal{A}_\epsilon$): it must return $(sat, \vartheta_\epsilon)$ where $\vartheta_\epsilon = \{r, \cdots\} \supseteq \mathcal{A}_\epsilon$ since $(\mathcal{A}_\epsilon ; \mathcal{C}_\epsilon^{cpl}) = (r \ ; \ \emptyset) = \{r\}$ is true under $\vartheta_\epsilon = \{r, \cdots\}$.

Create a SAT-solver s1 for modal depth 1, pre-load s1 with $\mathcal{C}_\alpha^{cpl} = \{b \to \neg p \vee q\}$, the cpl-part of $\mathcal{C}_\alpha$, put $\mathcal{A}_\alpha = \{b, p, \neg q\}$, and call solve(s1, $\mathcal{A}_\alpha$): it must return $(unsat, UC_\alpha)$ where $UC_\alpha = \{b, p, \neg q\} \subseteq \mathcal{A}_\alpha$ since $(UC_\alpha \ ; \ \mathcal{C}_\sigma^{cpl}) = \{b, p, \neg q, b \to \neg p \vee q\}$ is cpl-unsatisfiable but every proper subset is cpl-satisfiable.

Finally, add $\neg r$ to s0 via addClause(s0, $\neg r$), and restart it via solve(s0, $\mathcal{A}_\epsilon$): it must return $(unsat, UC_\epsilon)$ where $UC_\epsilon = \{r\} \subseteq \mathcal{A}_\epsilon$ because $(UC_\epsilon \ ; \ (\mathcal{C}_\epsilon^{cpl} \ ; \ \neg r)) = (r \ ; \ \neg r)$ is cpl-unsatisfiable but no proper subset is so.

---

**Algorithm 1** CEGARTab($A$, Trie[$\sigma$])

1: {Inputs: $A$ is a set of unit assumptions,
    Trie[$\sigma$] is a node in our Trie containing modal clauses and a SAT-solver.}
2: Let $t_\sigma :=$ solve(Trie[$\sigma$].sat, $A$) {*is $\mathcal{C}_\sigma^{cpl}$ cpl-satisfiable*}
3: **if** $t_\sigma =$ (unsat, $UC_\sigma$) **then**
4:     **return** Unsatisfiable($UC_\sigma$) {*because $\mathcal{C}_\sigma$ is $K_n$-unsatisfiable*}
5: **else if** $t_\sigma =$ (sat, $\vartheta_\sigma$) **then**
6:     {*Check box and diamond clauses that fire under classical valuation $\vartheta_\sigma$*}
7:     **for** $(c \to \langle\alpha\rangle d) \in$ Trie[$\sigma$].DiaCl with $c \in \vartheta_\sigma$ **do**
8:         Let $B = \{b \mid (a \to [\alpha]b) \in$ Trie[$\sigma$].BoxCl and $a \in \vartheta_\sigma\}$
9:         {*evaluate the next $\alpha$-successor using the jump rule*}
10:        **if** CEGARTab$((d; B)$, Trie[$\sigma$].child$(\alpha)) =$ Unsatisfiable$(UC_{\sigma;\alpha})$ **then**
11:            $CS := \{c\} \cup \{a \mid (a \to [\alpha]b) \in$ Trie[$\sigma$].BoxCl and $a \in \vartheta_\sigma$ and $b \in UC_{\sigma;\alpha}\}$
12:            Let $\varphi := \bigvee_{l \in CS} \neg l$
13:            addClause(Trie[$\sigma$].sat, $\varphi$) { *Learn new clause* $\varphi := \neg \bigwedge CS$}
14:            **return** CEGARTab($A$, Trie[$\sigma$]) { *apply (restart)* }
15:        **end if**
16:    **end for**
17:    **return** Satisfiable {*because every fired diamond is fulfilled*}
18: **end if**

**Fig. 2.** Algorithm of CEGARTab for multi-modal (description) logic $K_n$ ($\mathcal{ALC}$)

## 5  CEGAR-Tableaux for Multi-modal Logic $K_n$ (aka $\mathcal{ALC}$)

We now describe the CEGAR-tableaux procedure from Goré and Kikkert [9] extended to multi-modal logic $K_n$ (aka $\mathcal{ALC}$) directly.

Conceptually, the extension from mono-modal logic K to multi-modal logic $K_n$ is easy because there are no interactions between the different modalities, so we essentially have $n$ "copies" of K, one for each modality $[\alpha]$ for every agent $\alpha \in Ag$. In particular, there are no "converse" modalities $[\bar{\alpha}]/\langle\bar{\alpha}\rangle$ in the given formula $\varphi_0$, nor global assumptions, nor local assumptions.

We give the extension of the main CEGARTab algorithm from Goré and Kikkert [9] as Algorithm 1 in Fig. 2, and make the connection to the general form of mcnf($\varphi_0$) but with $Ag$ instead of $Agt$ as there is no converse:

$$\text{mcnf}(\varphi_0) := \mathcal{C}_\epsilon \; ; \; \bigcup_{\sigma \in Ag^1}[\sigma]\mathcal{C}_\sigma \; ; \; \cdots \; ; \; \bigcup_{\sigma \in Ag^\kappa}[\sigma]\mathcal{C}_\sigma$$

Because CEGARBox handled only mono-modal logics, the mcnf of a given formula $\varphi_0$ of modal depth $\kappa$ was as below for a singleton $Ag = \{\alpha\}$ (say):

$$\text{mcnf}(\varphi_0) := \mathcal{C}_\epsilon \; ; \; [\alpha]\mathcal{C}_\alpha \; ; \; [\alpha^2]\mathcal{C}_{\alpha^2} \; ; \; \cdots \; ; \; [\alpha^\kappa]\mathcal{C}_{\alpha^\kappa}$$

Conceptually, these "modal contexts" were stored in a (linear) Trie data structure with Node[0] initialised to contain $\mathcal{C}_\epsilon$ and node Node[i], for $i > 0$, initialised to contain $\mathcal{C}_{\alpha^i}$, eliding the box-prefix $[\alpha^i]$ without loss of generality.

In the multi-modal case, we use a multi-dimensional trie and all trie-edges are labelled by an agent name and the trie-root is labelled with $\epsilon$. For a regular expression $\sigma$, we write Trie[$\sigma$] for the corresponding TrieNode. For example, from the trie-root node Trie[$\epsilon$] $= \mathcal{C}_\epsilon$ there is a trie-path labelled by an $\alpha$-edge followed by a $\beta$-edge to the trie-node Trie[$\alpha;\beta$] $= \mathcal{C}_{\alpha;\beta}$.

In Algorithm 1 in Fig. 2, and in the implementation, each $\mathcal{C}_\sigma$ is stored at trie-position Trie[$\sigma$] in four fields by partitioning it into its three disjoint components $\mathcal{C}_\sigma = (\mathcal{C}_\sigma^{cpl} \; ; \; \mathcal{C}_\sigma^{dia} \; ; \; \mathcal{C}_\sigma^{box})$ and adding "next" pointers as follows:

1. Trie[$\sigma$].sat is a dedicated SAT-solver for this trie-node pre-loaded with $\mathcal{C}_\sigma^{cpl}$
2. Trie[$\sigma$].DiaCl contains $\mathcal{C}_\sigma^{dia} := \bigcup_{\alpha \in Ag}\{c \rightarrow \langle\alpha\rangle d \mid (c \rightarrow \langle\alpha\rangle d) \in \mathcal{C}_\sigma\}$
3. Trie[$\sigma$].BoxCl contains $\mathcal{C}_\sigma^{box} := \bigcup_{\alpha \in Ag}\{a \rightarrow [\alpha]b \mid (a \rightarrow [\alpha]b) \in \mathcal{C}_\sigma\}$
4. Trie[$\sigma$].Child($\alpha$) is (a pointer to) the node Trie[$\sigma;\alpha$], for each $\alpha \in Ag$.

The second and third fields are structured further so that we can select the dia-clauses and box-clauses for a particula agent $\alpha \in Ag$ via Trie[$\sigma$].DiaCl($\alpha$) and Trie[$\sigma$].BoxCl($\alpha$), respectively. We often write "formula in a TrieNode" or even "$\varphi \in$ Trie[$\sigma$]" to refer to formulae that are stored in one of these fields.

Recall that $r$ names the initial formula but it is not in the root Trie[$\epsilon$]. Now we simply start by calling CEGARTab($\{r\}$, Trie[$\epsilon$]) as shown in Fig. 2.

*Example 3.* Let us continue with our example. We know that $\varphi_0$ is equi-satisfiable with $r \; ; \; \mathcal{C}_\epsilon \; ; \; [\alpha]\mathcal{C}_\alpha$, where $\mathcal{C}_\epsilon^{cpl} = \emptyset$ and $\mathcal{C}_\epsilon^{dia} = (r \rightarrow \langle\alpha\rangle\neg q)$ and $\mathcal{C}_\epsilon^{box} = (r \rightarrow [\alpha]b \; ; \; r \rightarrow [\alpha]p)$, meaning Trie[$\epsilon$].sat is s0. We also have $\mathcal{C}_\alpha^{cpl} = (b \rightarrow \neg p \vee q)$ and $\mathcal{C}_\alpha^{dia} = \emptyset$ and $\mathcal{C}_\alpha^{box} = \emptyset$, meaning Trie[$\alpha$].sat is s1.

*Recursion 0.* The initial call to CEGARTab($\{r\}$, Trie[$\epsilon$]) sets $\sigma := \epsilon$ and $A := \{r\} = \mathcal{A}_\epsilon$ so line 2 is solve(s0, $\mathcal{A}_\epsilon$): it returns $(sat, \vartheta_\epsilon)$ where $\vartheta_\epsilon = \{r, \cdots\}$ so we enter the "then" part of line 5. At line 7, there is only one "fired" dia-clause $(r \to \langle\alpha\rangle\neg q) \in$ Trie[$\epsilon$].DiaCl $= \mathcal{C}_\epsilon^{dia}$ with $r \in \vartheta_\epsilon$, so $c := r$ and $d := (\neg q)$ and we know that $\langle\alpha\rangle\neg q$ must be (modally) true at modal depth 0. Under $\vartheta_\epsilon = \{r, \cdots\}$, every box-clause in $\mathcal{C}_\epsilon^{box}$ "fires", thus the set $\{[\alpha]b, [\alpha]p\}$ is (modally) true at modal depth 0, and hence the set $B = \{b, p\}$ formed at line 8 must be classically true at some $R_\alpha$-successor for $\neg q$ at modal depth 1. To evaluate this $R_\alpha$-successor, we compute $(d; B) = \{b, p, \neg q\}$ at line 10 and recurse via CEGARTab($\{b, p, \neg q\}$, Trie[$\alpha$].Child($\alpha$)).

*Recursion 1.* So $\sigma := \alpha$ and $A := \{b, p, \neg q\} = \mathcal{A}_\alpha$ and the relevant SAT-solver is the "next" one so Trie[$\alpha$].sat $=$ s1. Line 2 calls this SAT-solver, so this is the call solve(s1, $\mathcal{A}_\alpha$): it must return $(unsat, UC_\alpha)$ where $UC_\alpha = \{b, p, \neg q\}$ so we return Unsatisfiable($\{b, p, \neg q\}$) at line 4 and pop the recursion stack.

*Recursion 0.* We return to line 11 where $\sigma := \epsilon$ and so $(\sigma; \alpha) = \alpha$, so $UC_{\sigma;\alpha} = UC_\alpha = \{b, p, \neg q\}$. We know the chosen $\vartheta_\epsilon$ at modal depth 0 caused a clash at modal depth 1 involving $\{b, p, \neg q\}$, and hence that $\{[\alpha]b, [\alpha]p, \langle\alpha\rangle\neg q\}$ cannot be jointly true at modal depth 0. At line 11 we trace the relevant box- and dia-clauses to find the conflict set $CS = \{r\}$ at modal depth 0. To avoid this "mistake", we compute the "refinement" $\varphi = \neg r$ at line 12 of level 0. Line 13 is then just addClause(s0, $\neg r$) so $\mathcal{C}_\epsilon^{cpl} = \{\neg r\}$. The refined mcnf($\varphi_0$) demands $r$ is false at the root. At line 14, we recurse again via CEGARTab($\{r\}$, Trie[$\epsilon$]) but we stay at the current SAT-solver at modal depth 0.

*Recursion 1.* Line 2 calls solve(s0, $\mathcal{A}_\epsilon$): it returns $(unsat, UC_\epsilon)$ where $UC_\epsilon = r$ which returns Unsatisfiable($\{r\}$) to line 14 of Recursion 0: our final answer.

**Theorem 1.** *If* Trie *contains mcnf($\varphi_0$) and $r$ names $\varphi_0$ then* CEGARTab($\{r\}$, Trie[$\epsilon$]) *terminates, and returns satisfiable iff $\varphi_0$ is* $K_n$-*satisfiable.*

*Proof.* A simple modification of the proofs for mono-modal K from Goré and Kikkert [9] which proceeds by induction on the number of restarts.

## 6 Multi-modal $K_n$ with Global Assumptions

The following proposition shows that global logical consequence requires the global assumption $GA$ to be true "everywhere" from where $r$ is true.

**Proposition 3.** $\varphi_0$ *is a global logical consequence of $GA$, in multi-modal logic* $K_n$, *if and only if* $r \wedge \widehat{mcnf(\neg\varphi_0)} \wedge [u]\widehat{mcnfg}(GA)$ *is* $K_n$-*unsatisfiable.*

This justifies the following transformation where we intuitively just "broadcast" the single set of modal clauses mcnfg($GA$) to every trie-node in the Trie.

**Proposition 4.** *If $mcnf(\neg\varphi_0)$ is stored in a trie* `Trie`, *then adding $mcnfg(GA)$ to every trienode* `Trie[σ]` *is sound.*

But that is not sufficient because mcnfg $(GA)$ may contain a dia-clause $c \to \langle\gamma\rangle d$ (say). We need to ensure that if this dia-clause is triggered at any trie-node in the `Trie`, then the $\gamma$-successor created by it will also contain mcnfg $(GA)$, and so on. The solution is simple: for every dia-clause $c \to \langle\gamma\rangle d \in \text{mcnf}(GA)$ we extend every trie-node in `Trie` with a new $\langle\gamma\rangle$-child that contains mcnfg $(GA)$ only, and which is $\delta$-reflexive for every dia-clause $x \to \langle\delta\rangle y \in \text{mcnf}(GA)$.

Consider augmenting an initial `Trie` for $\langle\alpha\rangle\langle\alpha\rangle\langle\alpha\rangle p$ with global assumptions $GA = \{\langle\beta\rangle\langle\beta\rangle q\}$ as in Fig. 3. Every original node in the `Trie` for $\langle\alpha\rangle\langle\alpha\rangle\langle\alpha\rangle p$ begets mcnfg $(GA) = (\top \to \langle\beta\rangle y_1 \; ; \; y_1 \to \langle\beta\rangle q)$. We need to extend the `Trie` with a *new* $\beta$.child for every node, and put its contents to be the clauses mcnfg $(GA)$ only, and then make this new child $\beta$-reflexive. Intuitively, all $\beta$-children of the new leaves will force mcnfg $(GA)$, as required. But only these introduced nodes are $\beta$-reflexive because they have no clauses from $\varphi_0$. If the initial trie in Fig. 3 contained a $\beta$-child for some node, the $\beta$-reflexive node would instead be the new $\beta$-child of that $\beta$-child.

To stop `CEGARTab` looping forever on such reflexive nodes, we use loop-check.

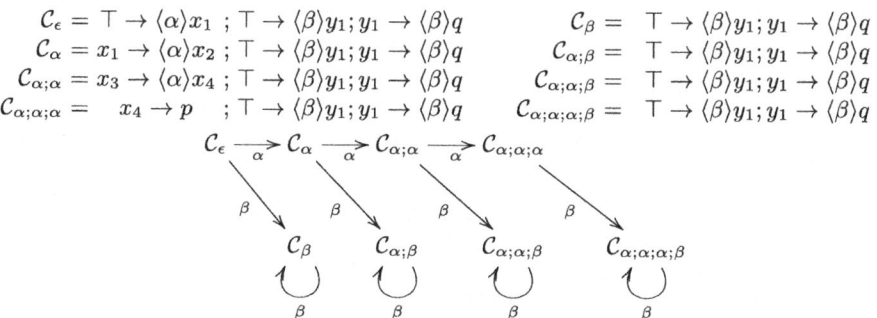

**Fig. 3.** A Trie for $\langle\alpha\rangle\langle\alpha\rangle\langle\alpha\rangle p$ augmented with global assumptions $\langle\beta\rangle\langle\beta\rangle q$. For illustrative purposes we rename $p$ as $x_4$, though our implementation would not.

### 6.1 Loop-Check for Multi-modal Logic $K_n$ with Global Assumptions

We assume familiarity with the standard notion of rooted tree models.

CEGAR-tableaux mimic traditional tableaux in trying to create a rooted tree model by "saturating and jumping", except that CEGAR-tableaux outsource the "saturation" part to a SAT-solver. In this setting, it is well-known that global assumptions require loop-check (blocking) for termination. For example, naive proof search on a root node containing only $GA = \{\langle\alpha\rangle p\}$ will create an infinite sequence of worlds, each making $(p; \langle\alpha\rangle p)$ true.

For many logics, including $K_n$, it suffices to stop when a jump creates a node which appears already on the unique path back to the root, giving a finite rooted

Kripke model, with ancestor loops: see Wu and Goré [22] for a formally verified construction. For the construction to be successful when global assumptions are involved, we just have to ensure that every node "contains" $GA$.

We extend CEGARTab with a third argument - a history $\mathcal{H}$ of classical valuations of ancestor worlds on the unique path back to the root, and add an ancestor loop-check as shown in Algorithm 2 in Fig. 6. Before calling the SAT-solver with unit assumptions $A$, we immediately return Satisfiable if $A \in \mathcal{H}$.

**Theorem 2.** *If the* Trie *for* mcnf($\varphi_0$) *is augmented with* mcnfg $(\widehat{GA})$ *as described above then* CEGARTab($\{r\}$, Trie[$\epsilon$], $\emptyset$) *returns Satisfiable if and only if $\varphi_0$ is $K_n$-satisfiable with global assumptions $GA$.*

*Proof.* Loop-check ensures termination.

Left to right: Suppose CEGARTab returns Satisfiable. Thus the final run had no restarts, every jump succeeded and each node $w_\sigma$ on the path $\sigma$ from the root node contains Trie[$\sigma$] $\supseteq$ mcnfg $(\widehat{GA})$. The root node contains $r$, thus there is a rooted tree model with ancestor loops which forces $r$ at the root and which makes mcnfg $(\widehat{GA})$ true "everywhere" (from the root). Now use Proposition 2 to obtain a rooted tree model with ancestor loops which forces $\varphi_0$ at the root and which makes $\widehat{GA}$ true "everywhere", as required.

Right to left: Suppose CEGARTab returns Unsatisfiable on the set $X$ of modal clauses. Proceed by induction on the number of restarts. The base case is when there are no restarts, so the first call to the SAT-solver Trie[$\epsilon$].sat returned unsat. That is, the cpl-part of $X$ is cpl-unsatisfiable. But then it must be $K_n$-unsatisfiable as well, meaning that no $K_n$-model forces $GA$ everywhere and forces $\varphi_0$ somewhere.

Assume the lemma holds for all runs of the algorithm with $m$ restarts and consider the first restart when there are $m + 1$ restarts.

The algorithm called some SAT-solver s, found a cpl-valuation that made $C$ true and jumped on the triggered diamonds, but one of the jumps returned Unsatisfiable, so it added the cpl-clause $\varphi = \neg C$ to s and restarted s. That is, the valuation which put $C$ to true led to Unsatisfiable as did the valuation that put $C$ to false. The SAT-solver in the jump-child that returned Unsatisfiable falls under the induction hypothesis as it was restarted at most $m$ times. It returned Unsatisfiable so the formulae in the jump-child are really $K_n$-unsatisfiable, thus $X; C$ is $K_n$-unsatisfiable. The restarted SAT-solver $X; \neg C$ also falls under the induction hypothesis as it is restarted at most $m$ times, and it returned Unsatisfiable, so $X; \neg C$ is $K_n$-unsatisfiable. This is just a semantic cut on $C$ and so the current node $X$ is $K_n$-unsatisfiable.

## 7 From Multi-modal $K_n$ to Multi-modal Tense Logic $Kt_n$

By adding the interaction axioms $\langle \bar{\alpha} \rangle [\alpha] p \to p$ and $\langle \alpha \rangle [\bar{\alpha}] p \to p$ to the Hilbert calculi for $K_n$, we ensure that $(\langle \bar{\alpha} \rangle, [\alpha])$ and $(\langle \alpha \rangle, [\bar{\alpha}])$ form an adjoint (or residuated) pair which is often the basis of nested sequent calculi [13] and display calculi [12]. The resulting normal modal logic is usually known as multi-modal tense logic $Kt_n$ or the description logic $\mathcal{ALCI}$ [1]. A reduction from $\mathcal{ALCI}$ to $\mathcal{ALC}$ [3,8] is known, but a direct $Kt_n$-model is more accessible to users.

**Lemma 1 (Residuation).** $a \to [\bar{\alpha}] b$ is $Kt_n$-valid iff $\langle \alpha \rangle a \to b$ is $Kt_n$-valid.

*Proof.* Left to right, assume $a \to [\bar{\alpha}] b$ is $Kt_n$-valid but $\langle \alpha \rangle a \to b$ is not. Hence some $w$ in some $Kt_n$-model $M$ obeys $M, w \Vdash \langle \alpha \rangle a; \neg b$. So $w$ has an $R_\alpha$-successor $w R_\alpha v$ with $M, v \Vdash a$. But $a \to [\bar{\alpha}] b$ is $Kt_n$-valid, so $M, v \Vdash a \to [\bar{\alpha}] b$, giving $M, v \Vdash [\bar{\alpha}] b$, whence $M, w \Vdash b$: contradiction. The other direction is similar.

But look: $\langle \alpha \rangle a \to b$ is just $\bar{b} \to [\alpha] \bar{a}$ in disguise! This justifies the following modifications to the `Trie`.

Residuation: For every context $\sigma$ and every $\alpha \in Agt$, if $(a \to [\bar{\alpha}] b) \in \texttt{Trie}[\sigma; \alpha]$ then put $(\bar{b} \to [\alpha] \bar{a}) \in \texttt{Trie}[\sigma]$ (this does not cause a cycle of additions);
$Kt_n$-modification: For every agent $\alpha$, and regular expressions $\sigma$ and $\tau$, if $\varphi \in \texttt{Trie}[\sigma; \alpha; \bar{\alpha}; \tau]$ then create $\texttt{Trie}[\sigma; \tau]$ if it does not already exist, and put $\varphi \in \texttt{Trie}[\sigma; \tau]$ as $\varphi$ contains the "definitions" for $b$ under residuation.

Under the $Kt_n$-modification, the number of modal contexts can grow exponentially. For example consider $\varphi \in \texttt{Trie}[(\alpha; \bar{\alpha}; \beta)^m]$. Each of the $m$ occurrences of $\alpha; \bar{\alpha}$ can either be left alone or collapsed, which results in $\varphi$ being placed in $2^m$ different modal contexts! This is clearly inefficient, and implementing this in CEGARTab, will lead to memory outs. We instead aim to maintain a linear number of modal contexts by grouping them together arbitrarily, as follows.

### 7.1 Representing $mcnf(\varphi_0)$ in a Grid Using the Sum-Heuristic

Suppose the number of agents in $Ag$ is exactly $n$ for some fixed $n \geq 1$.

**Lemma 2.** *If the `Trie` is for $mcnf(\varphi_0)$ then for all (arbitrary) agent regular expressions $\sigma$ and $\tau$ such that $Trie[\sigma]$ and $Trie[\tau]$ exist, for any modal clause $\psi \in Trie[\sigma]$, we can add $\psi$ to $Trie[\tau]$, with CEGARTab preserving equi-satisfiabilty.*

*Proof.* Left to right: if the original $\varphi_0$ is $Kt_n$-satisfiable, Proposition 2 implies that so are $(r; mcnf(\varphi_0))$ and $(r; [u] mcnfg(\varphi_0))$. But $\psi \in Trie[\sigma]$ implies $\psi \in \mathcal{C}_\sigma$ implies $[u] \psi \in [u] mcnfg(\varphi_0)$. So the transformation preserves $Kt_n$-satisfiability. Right to left: if CEGARTab, invoked appropriately on the modified $Trie[\tau]$ returns Satisfiable, it must do the same on $Trie[\sigma] \subseteq Trie[\tau]$ (seen as sets of formulae).

**Corollary 1.** *Merging clauses in `TrieNodes` arbitrarily is sound and complete.*

Corollary 1 allows us to avoid the exponential blowup of modal contexts. We define an equivalence class on modal contexts, balancing the need to have a linear number of SAT-solvers, with the desire to have each SAT-solver focus on a unique part of the input problem. We aim to ensure that if two modal contexts can "map" onto the same world (e.g. $\epsilon$ and $\alpha; \overline{\alpha}$), they share an equivalence class. To do so, our `Trie` becomes a `Grid`, as described next.

Define a binary function $\Sigma(\alpha, \sigma)$ that counts the number of occurrences of $\alpha$ in the regular expression $\sigma$ and subtracts the number of occurrences of $\overline{\alpha}$ in $\sigma$ as below, where $\alpha$ and $\beta$ are from $Agt$:

$$\Sigma(\alpha, \epsilon) = 0 \qquad \Sigma(\alpha, \alpha) = 1 \qquad \Sigma(\alpha, \beta \neq \alpha) = 0$$
$$\Sigma(\alpha, \alpha; \sigma) = \Sigma(\alpha, \sigma) + 1 \qquad \Sigma(\alpha, \overline{\alpha}; \sigma) = \Sigma(\alpha, \sigma) - 1$$
$$\Sigma(\alpha, \beta; \sigma) = \Sigma(\alpha, \sigma) \text{ if } \alpha \neq \beta \neq \overline{\alpha}$$

Define the grid position `GridPos`($\mathcal{C}_\sigma$) and the contents of `GridCls`($i_1, \cdots, i_n$):

$$\texttt{GridPos}(\mathcal{C}_\sigma) = (\Sigma(\alpha_1, \sigma), \cdots, \Sigma(\alpha_n, \sigma))$$
$$\texttt{GridCls}(i_1, i_2, \cdots, i_n) = \bigcup \{\mathcal{C}_\tau \mid \Sigma(\alpha_1, \tau) = i_1 \ \& \ \cdots \ \& \ \Sigma(\alpha_n, \tau) = i_n\}$$

Intuitively, a modal context $\mathcal{C}_\sigma$ gives an $n$-tuple where the $i$-th element counts the number of $\alpha_i$ modalities in $\sigma$ minus the number of $\overline{\alpha_i}$ modalities in $\sigma$.

*Example 4.* For example, if $Ag := \{\alpha; \beta\}$ with $\alpha \neq \beta$ and the maximum modal degree of $\varphi_0$ is 2, then mcnf($\varphi_0$) gives rise to the `Grid` below:

| Modal Context $\sigma$ | | | | | GridPos($\sigma$) |
|---|---|---|---|---|---|
| $\epsilon$ | $\alpha; \overline{\alpha}$ | $\beta; \overline{\beta}$ | $\overline{\alpha}; \alpha$ | $\overline{\beta}; \beta$ | $(0,0)$ |
| | | $\alpha$ | | | $(1,0)$ |
| | | $\beta$ | | | $(0,1)$ |
| | $\alpha; \beta$ | | $\beta; \alpha$ | | $(1,1)$ |
| | $\overline{\alpha}; \beta$ | | $\beta; \overline{\alpha}$ | | $(-1,1)$ |

| Modal Context $\sigma$ | | GridPos($\sigma$) |
|---|---|---|
| $\alpha; \overline{\beta}$ | $\overline{\beta}; \alpha$ | $(1,-1)$ |
| $\overline{\alpha}; \overline{\beta}$ | $\overline{\beta}; \overline{\alpha}$ | $(-1,-1)$ |
| $\alpha; \alpha$ | | $(2,0)$ |
| $\beta; \beta$ | | $(0,2)$ |
| $\overline{\alpha}; \overline{\alpha}$ | | $(-2,0)$ |
| $\overline{\beta}; \overline{\beta}$ | | $(0,-2)$ |

We modify our trie datastructure to create equivalence-classes in a corresponding grid datastructure as explained next.

## 7.2 Implementation of CEGARTab($Kt_n$) without global assumptions

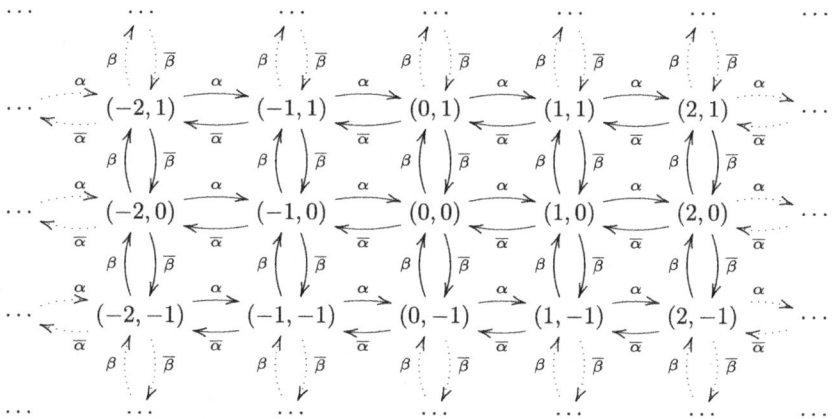

**Fig. 4.** A complete grid for $Ag = \{\alpha, \beta \neq \alpha\}$

Let $\text{Trie}[\sigma_1] \sim \text{Trie}[\sigma_2]$ if $\text{GridPos}(\mathcal{C}_{\sigma_1}) = \text{GridPos}(\mathcal{C}_{\sigma_2})$, defining an equivalence class $[\text{Trie}[\sigma_1]]$. We merge all TrieNodes sharing an equivalence class into a single GridNode, by replacing $\text{Trie}[\sigma]$ with $\text{Grid}[\sigma] := [\text{Trie}[\sigma]]$. Each $\text{Grid}[\sigma]$ contains a SAT-solver, cpl-clauses, dia-clauses, and box-clauses. For every $\text{Trie}[\sigma_1].child(\alpha_i) = \text{Trie}[\sigma_2]$, we put $\text{Grid}[\sigma_1].child(\alpha_i) = \text{Grid}[\sigma_2]$, because $\sigma_1$ and $\sigma_2$ are necessarily adjacent on the grid as $\text{GridPos}(\sigma_2)$ differs from $\text{GridPos}(\sigma_1)$ by one at the $i$-th element only. A complete grid for the case where $Ag = \{\alpha, \beta \neq \alpha\}$ is shown in Fig. 4: we may not generate all edges.

The new underlying data structure allows us to use the same algorithm in Fig. 2 for $Kt_n$, with TrieNode just being replaced with GridNode, as shown in Fig. 6. The only caveat is that we must also enable loop check (blocking).

### 7.3 Loop-Check for Multi-modal Tense Logic $Kt_n$

One downside of using a SAT-solver inside CEGARTab is that its non-deterministic choices may "activate" unnecessary subformulae. If a diamond clause $c \rightarrow \langle \alpha \rangle d$ is activated, because the SAT-solver just happens to put $c$ true, this leads to an unnecessary jump. We [9] mitigated this by taking every modal clause, for example $c \rightarrow \langle \alpha \rangle d$ or $a \rightarrow [\alpha]b$, and biasing all SAT-solvers to put both $a$ and $c$ to be false. This is not perfect, however, and superfluous jumps still happen, but they are not an issue for termination in K because every jump moves us down one level in a Trie of finite length. Thus eventually we reach a leaf node in the Trie, containing no dia-clauses, and terminate. However, now that we use a grid, the jump rule can happen indefinitely, as there is no "end" to the grid.

Consider $\text{Grid}[\epsilon] : (a \rightarrow \langle \alpha \rangle \top)$ and $\text{Grid}[\alpha] : (b \rightarrow \langle \bar{\alpha} \rangle \top)$, where we write $\text{Grid}[\sigma] : \varphi$ to mean $\varphi \in \text{Grid}[\sigma]$. At modal context $\epsilon$, the SAT-solver may superfluously put $a$ to true, triggering an $\alpha$-successor. We then jump, the SAT-solver with modal context $[\alpha]$ may superfluously put $b$ to true, in which case we jump again to $\alpha;\overline{\alpha}$, and as $[\texttt{Grid}[\epsilon]] \equiv [\texttt{Grid}[\alpha;\overline{\alpha}]]$ we jump back to the root, where the SAT-solver may again put $a$ to true, and so on, giving an infinite loop.

Thus we enable loop-check in the same manner as presented in Sect. 6.1.

### 7.4 Tense Logic Example

$$\begin{array}{lll}
\mathcal{C}_\epsilon := & r \to \langle\overline{\alpha}\rangle x_1 \ ; \ r \to \langle\alpha\rangle y_1 & \mathcal{C}_{\overline{\alpha}} := \quad x_1 \to [\alpha]x_2 \\
\mathcal{C}_{\overline{\alpha};\alpha} := & x_2 \to p \ ; \ x_2 \to q & \mathcal{C}_\alpha := \quad y_1 \to [\overline{\alpha}]y_2 \\
\mathcal{C}_{\alpha;\overline{\alpha}} := & y_2 \to \neg p \vee \neg q &
\end{array}$$

$$\text{Residuation plus Sum Heuristic}$$

$$\begin{array}{lll}
\Sigma(\alpha,\sigma)=-1 & \Sigma(\alpha,\sigma)=0 & \Sigma(\alpha,\sigma)=1 \\
\hline
x_1 \to [\alpha]x_2 & r \to \langle\overline{\alpha}\rangle x_1 \ ; \ r \to \langle\alpha\rangle y_1 & y_1 \to [\overline{\alpha}]y_2 \\
 & x_2 \to p \ ; \ x_2 \to q \ ; \ y_2 \to \neg p \vee \neg q & \\
 & \overline{x_2} \to [\overline{\alpha}]\overline{x_1} \ ; \ \overline{y_2} \to [\alpha]\overline{y_1} &
\end{array}$$

**Fig. 5.** Tense logic example where $\sigma \in \{\epsilon, \alpha, \overline{\alpha}, (\alpha \ ; \ \overline{\alpha}), (\overline{\alpha} \ ; \ \alpha)\}$

*Example 5.* Consider axioms $\langle\overline{\alpha}\rangle[\alpha]\varphi \to \varphi$ and $\varphi \to [\alpha]\langle\overline{\alpha}\rangle\varphi$, where $\varphi := p \wedge q$. They imply that $\langle\overline{\alpha}\rangle[\alpha]\varphi \to [\alpha]\langle\overline{\alpha}\rangle\varphi$. We explain how to prove this in CEGARtab.

The negation of $\langle\overline{\alpha}\rangle[\alpha](p \wedge q) \to [\alpha]\langle\overline{\alpha}\rangle(p \wedge q)$ in NNF is $\langle\overline{\alpha}\rangle[\alpha](p \wedge q) \ ; \ \langle\alpha\rangle[\overline{\alpha}](\neg p \vee \neg q)$ and its mcnf is in the top half of Fig. 5. Residuation on $x_1 \to [a]x_2 \in \mathcal{C}_{\overline{\alpha}}$ adds $\overline{x_2} \to [\overline{\alpha}]\overline{x_1}$ to $\mathcal{C}_\epsilon$ and residuation on $y_1 \to [\overline{a}]y_2 \in \mathcal{C}_\alpha$ adds $\overline{y_2} \to [\alpha]\overline{y_1}$ giving $\mathcal{C}_\epsilon = r \to \langle\overline{\alpha}\rangle x_1 \ ; \ r \to \langle\alpha\rangle y_1 \ ; \ \overline{x_2} \to [\overline{\alpha}]\overline{x_1} \ ; \ \overline{y_2} \to [\alpha]\overline{y_1}$. Computing sums and grouping modal contexts into equivalence classes gives a 1-dimensional grid (a line) with an origin at $\Sigma(\alpha,\sigma) = 0$: see Fig. 5.

Putting $r$ to true at the origin will trigger $r \to \langle\overline{\alpha}\rangle x_1$ and $r \to \langle\alpha\rangle y_1$, giving a $\langle\overline{\alpha}\rangle$-successor and a $\langle\alpha\rangle$-successor. If the SAT-solver at the origin puts $x_2 = \bot$ this triggers $\overline{x_2} \to [\overline{\alpha}]\overline{x_1}$ giving a clash at the $\langle\overline{\alpha}\rangle$-successor containing $(x_1 \ ; \ \overline{x_1})$. Similarly, putting $y_2 = \bot$ triggers $\overline{y_2} \to [\alpha]\overline{y_1}$ and gives a clash at the $\langle\alpha\rangle$-successor containing $(y_1 \ ; \ \overline{y_1})$. Thus, after some clause learning, this SAT-solver puts $x_2 = y_2 = \top$, which gives a clash as the origin contains $x_2 \to p \ ; \ x_2 \to q \ ; \ y_2 \to \neg p \vee \neg q$, so this SAT-solver returns $(unsat, \{r\})$ giving Unsatisfiable.

### 7.5 Termination, Soundness and Completeness for Kt$_n$

CEGARtab($\{r\}$, Grid$[\epsilon]$, $\emptyset$) tries to create a rooted tree-K$_n$-model $M$ with ancestor loops for the mcnf in the Grid. We need to show that $M$ is in fact a Kt$_n$-model.

**Definition 1 (compatibility).** *Two worlds $(w,v)$ created by our procedure are an $\alpha$-pair if $v$ is the (jump) child of $w$ from some dia-clause $c \to \langle\alpha\rangle d$ that fires* from $w$. If our procedure creates a rooted $K_n$-treemodel $M$, such a parent-child $\alpha$-pair $(w,v)$ is $Kt_n$-compatible if (1) $M, w \Vdash \{a_1, a_1 \to [\,\alpha\,]b_1\}$ implies $M, v \Vdash b_1$ and (2) $M, v \Vdash \{a_2, a_2 \to [\,\bar{\alpha}\,]b_2\}$ implies $M, w \Vdash b_2$.

**Lemma 3.** *If the initial* `Trie` *is modified using the residuation and the $Kt_n$-modification to obtain a* `Grid` *then every parent-child $\alpha$-pair $(w,v)$ in the rooted tree $K_n$-model $M$ created by our algorithm is $Kt_n$-compatible.*

*Proof.* To show (1), suppose $M, w \Vdash \{a_1, a_1 \to [\,\alpha\,]b_1\}$: we have to show that $M, v \Vdash b_1$. But this is guaranteed by the definition of the $\alpha$-child at line 16 in Algorithm 2 since $b_1 \in B$. To show (2), suppose $v$ is an $\alpha$-child of $w$ and suppose $M, v \Vdash \{a_2, a_2 \to [\,\bar{\alpha}\,]b_2\}$: we have to show that $M, w \Vdash b_2$. For a contradiction, suppose $M, w \nVdash b_2$ meaning that $M, w \Vdash \bar{b_2}$. Residuation implies $M, w \Vdash \{\bar{b_2}, \bar{b_2} \to [\,\alpha\,]\bar{a_2}\}$ which by (1) implies that $M, v \Vdash \bar{a_2}$: contradiction.

**Theorem 3.** CEGARTab$(Kt_n)$ *is a sound, complete and terminating decision procedure for multi-modal tense logic $Kt_n$ without global assumptions.*

*Proof.* Termination is via loop-check as explained above. The original `Trie` is just a sound representation of mcnf($\varphi_0$), preserving equi-satisfiability with $\varphi_0$. For soundness, all modifications to this `Trie` are sound as they are based upon residuation, which is a valid principle for $Kt_n$. Applying the sum-heuristic to the modified `Trie` preserves equi-satisfiability via Corollary 1 giving us a `Grid` as outlined above. So CEGARTab($\{r\}$, `Grid`$[\epsilon], \emptyset$) returning Unsatisfiable implies that the original formula $\varphi_0$ is $Kt_n$-unsatisfiable. For completeness, suppose that CEGARTab($\{r\}$, `Grid`$[\epsilon], \emptyset$) returns Satisfiable, possibly with some ancestor loops. All jumps implement the traditional tableaux rule for each $K_\alpha$ from premise $\langle \alpha \rangle d; [\,\alpha\,]B$ to conclusion $d; B$ since the algorithm has stabilised with no restarts. Consider any loop node $x_s$ (for source) whose valuation $A$ appears in the history and suppose $A$ causes some $l \to \langle \alpha \rangle d$ to fire at $x_s$, with $l$ possibly being a negative literal $\neg c$ (say). Currently, $x_s$ has no explicit $\alpha$-successor containing $d$ because its creation was blocked by a subset loop-check $A \subseteq \vartheta \in \mathcal{H}$. But the valuations returned by our SAT-solvers are "complete" sets of literals, not just atomic formulae, so the loop-target $x_t$ will have fired $l \to \langle \alpha \rangle d$ and created an $\alpha$-successor $y$ containing $d$ and possibly many more formulae than required. Directing every such loop-node $x_s$ to $y$ gives a $K_n$ parent-child pair $(x_s, y)$. But our `Grid` already contains all residuation modifications and preserves equi-satisfiability, so Lemma 3 guarantees that every parent-child in this $K_n$-model is $Kt_n$-compatible. Thus our $K_n$-model is actually a $Kt_n$-model.

## 8 Moving from Haskell to C++ and Various Optimisations

Our new implementation CEGARBox++ uses C++ for several reasons: (i) is to allow comparability with other modal satisfiability solvers which are also written in C/C++, such as bddtab, FaCT++, and $K_SP$, and perhaps benefit from the speed of C++; (ii) is to integrate with other SAT solvers, as we provide an abstract class that can be easily replaced with any other SAT solver implemented in C++, as well as an IPASIR API (the standard interface for incremental satisfiability solving), which allows us to easily plug in more modern SAT solvers - though by default we still use Minisat [6]; (iii) is that C++ gives finer control over memory and performance, which is particularly important for large problems, where our Haskell solver CEGARBox may have run out of memory.

## 8.1 Various Optimisations

We keep our previous optimisation which biases all SAT-solvers to put literals (e.g. $c$) to false, hoping to avoid needless modal jumps via a dia-clause $c \to \langle\rangle d$.

We again implement caching of $Kt_n$-satisfiable valuations, to avoid repeatedly determining the satisfiability of the same unit assumptions $A$. We do not cache unsatisfiability results as clause learning handles this. However, adding loop check for $Kt_n$ makes caching more difficult. We previously [9] outlined how worlds should only be cached, once all worlds in a loop are deemed satisfiable, and gave two-phase caching as a solution, which we have also implemented in CEGARBox++.

While inspecting Grid$[\sigma]$.Cache or the history $\mathcal{H}$ for loop-check, we replaced an exact "hit" on the unit assumptions $A$ with a subset "hit" $A \subseteq \vartheta$ by instead storing the full valuation $\vartheta_\sigma$ in Grid$[\sigma]$.Cache/$\mathcal{H}$ at line 23/16 in Algorithm 2. This gives more "cache hits" as every exact "hit" implies a subset "hit" but not vice versa. However, "exact hits" can be implemented in sub-linear time with respect to the size of the cache/history, while "subset hits" is slower as we must check whether $A \subseteq \vartheta$ for every $\vartheta$ in the cache/history. We used bitsets to implement subset-hits efficiently but the risk of exponential memory usage remains. We changed the restart procedure at line 20 to goto line 8 in Algorithm 2, instead of recursing, thus avoiding unnecessarily checking the cache when we implement caching and loop-check. We checked that CEGARBox++ outperforms CEGARBox on the standard benchmarks used by Goré and Kikkert [9].

## 9 New Benchmarks

There are few dedicated solvers and no comprehensive set of multi-modal benchmarks. As far as we know, the only benchmarks for $Kt_n$ are the MQBF $\mathcal{ALCI}$ benchmarks which used to be available at http://users.cecs.anu.edu.au/~rpg/software.html but which now exist only on the way back machine: https://web.archive.org/ However, these benchmarks are for mono-modal $Kt_1$ and do not use global assumptions (TBoxes). We have therefore extended the Logics Workbench (LWB) benchmarks [2] to create a new set of multi-modal benchmarks, with and without global assumptions in the manner of Nalon et al. [17]: https://github.com/cormackikkert/LWB-benchmark-generator.

**Algorithm 2** CEGARTab($A$, Grid[$\sigma$], $\mathcal{H}$)

1: {Inputs: $A$ is a set of unit assumptions, Grid[$\sigma$] is a node in our Grid containing modal clauses and a SAT-solver, $\mathcal{H}$ is a list of ancestor world valuations}
2: **if** $A \subseteq \vartheta$ for some $\vartheta \in \mathcal{H}$ **then**
3:     **return** Satisfiable {*subset loop check succeeds*}
4: **end if**
5: **if** $A \subseteq \vartheta$ for some $\vartheta \in$ Grid[$\sigma$].Cache **then**
6:     **return** Satisfiable {*subset cache check succeeds*}
7: **end if**
8: Let $t_\sigma :=$ solve(Grid[$\sigma$].sat, $A$) {*is $\mathcal{C}_\sigma^{cpl}$ cpl-satisfiable*}
9: **if** $t_\sigma = $ (unsat, $UC_\sigma$) **then**
10:     **return** Unsatisfiable($UC_\sigma$)
11: **else if** $t_\sigma = $ (sat, $\vartheta_\sigma$) **then**
12:     {*Check box and diamond clauses that fire under classical valuation $\vartheta_\sigma$*}
13:     **for** $(c \to \langle \alpha \rangle d) \in$ Grid[$\sigma$].DiaCl with $c \in \vartheta_\sigma$ **do**
14:         Let $B = \{b \mid (a \to [\alpha]b) \in$ Grid[$\sigma$].BoxCl and $a \in \vartheta_\sigma\}$
15:         {*evaluate the next $\alpha$-child where :: is list-concatenation*}
16:         **if** CEGARTab(($d; B$), Grid[$\sigma$].child($\alpha$), $\vartheta_\sigma :: \mathcal{H}$) = Unsatisfiable(UC) **then**
17:             $C := \{c\} \cup \{a \mid (a \to [\alpha]b) \in$ Grid[$\sigma$].BoxCl and $a \in \vartheta_\sigma$ and $b \in UC\}$
18:             Let $\varphi := \bigvee_{l \in C} \neg l$
19:             addClause(Grid[$\sigma$].sat, $\varphi$) { *Learn new clause $\varphi := \neg \bigwedge C$ by adding it to $\mathcal{C}_\sigma^{cpl}$*}
20:             **goto** line 8 { *apply (restart)* }
21:         **end if**
22:     **end for**
23:     Grid[$\sigma$].Cache := Grid[$\sigma$].Cache $\cup\, \vartheta_\sigma$ {*add current valuation to the cache*}
24:     **return** Satisfiable {*because every fired diamond is fulfilled*}
25: **end if**

**Fig. 6.** Multi-modal tense logic CEGARTab with loop-check and caching

Following Nalon et al. we build our $K_n$-unsatisfiable benchmarks from the following originally unsatisfiable classes k_branch_p, k_path_p, k_ph_p, k_poly_p, k_t4p_p, 20 from each giving 100 new $K_n$-unsatisfiable formulae. Our $K_n$-satisfiable benchmarks are based on the five originally satisfiable classes k_poly_n, s4_md_n, s4_ph_n, s4_path_n, s4_s5_n, again 20 from each class giving 100 new $K_n$-satisfiable formula. For originally unsatisfiable benchmarks we replace all propositional literals $p$ with $p \vee \phi_p$, where $\phi_p$ is the $K_n$-unsatisfiable formula $\phi_p := [\alpha_i]p \wedge \langle \alpha_i \rangle \neg p$ for a random modality $\alpha_i$. For originally satisfiable benchmarks we replace each $p$ with $p \wedge \psi_p$, where $\psi_p$ is the $K_n$-satisfiable formula $\psi_p := \langle \alpha_i \rangle p \wedge [\alpha_j] \neg p$, where $\alpha_i$ and $\alpha_j$ are random modalities that do not interfere. Note that $\psi_p$ is K(1)-unsatisfiable if a solver only reasons in one modality.

Global assumptions encode particular scenarios: for example, they might describe the obstacles in a room through which a robot has to navigate. Thus it makes no sense to have a set of global assumptions that are unsatisfiable. Alas, ksp [16] supports local assumptions or global assumptions, but not both, so we had to construct $K_n$-unsatisfiable global assumptions, as explained next.

For global assumptions we put $LA = \{\top\}$. For each new $K_n$-satisfiable benchmark $\varphi$ we simply put $GA = \{\varphi\}$ as this is sound for global reasoning. For the new $K_n$-unsatisfiable benchmarks we modify the benchmarks slightly so that they require the use of global assumptions to prove unsatisfiability. We take the new $K_n$-unsatisfiable benchmark (say $\varphi$) of modal depth $\kappa$ and replace it with $(\varphi \vee \langle \alpha \rangle \top) \wedge [\alpha]^{2\kappa} \bot$, ensuring that the resulting formula is $K_n$-unsatisfiable with global reasoning, but $K_n$-satisfiable with local reasoning.

## 10 Experimental Results

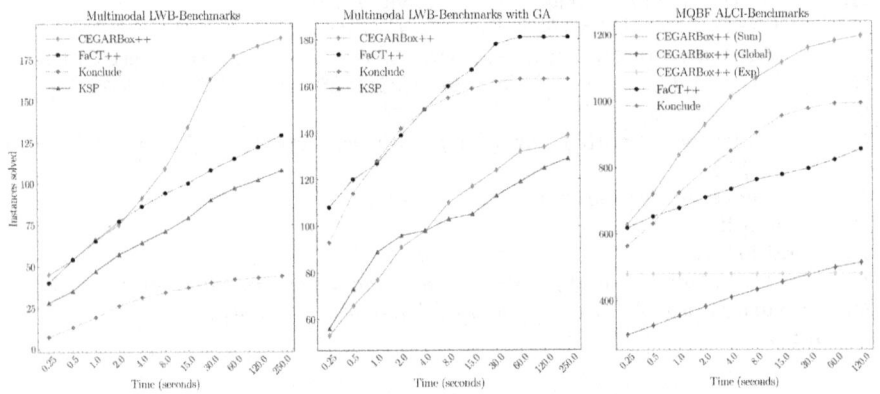

**Fig. 7.** Results for $K_n$, $K_n$ with global assumptions, and $Kt_1$

We used an Intel Xeon E5-2640@2.40 GHz CPU with 8 GB of RAM for our $Kt_1$ benchmarks and used an Intel i7-11700F@2.50 GHz CPU with 16 GB of RAM for the rest. Our code is here: https://github.com/cormackikkert/CEGARBoxCPP

We tested against FaCT++1.6.5 and Konclude0.7.0 as these are two of the best current reasoners for description logics extending $\mathcal{ALCI}$. Our comparison does not do full justice to these reasoners as they handle much more expressive logics, but we have no choice as reasoners for just $Kt_n$ are rare. We allocate a fixed number of seconds for every problem instance and plot the number of problem instances that can be solved in that time. The time includes conversion to normal form. We omit solvers such as bddtab and inKreSat that do not handle tense logic directly. We also checked that all solvers gave the same answers.

We compare against three variants of CEGARBox++. CEGARBox++ (Sum) which implements the sum heuristic presented in Sect. 7 and requires loop-check. CEGARBox++ (Exp), does not group modal contexts, requires no loop check, but instead creates an exponential number of TrieNodes. Finally CEGARBox++

(Global) uses one modal context that stores all clauses. CEGARBox++ (Sum) can be thought of as a middle ground between these two approaches.

The leftmost graph in Fig. 7 shows that CEGARBox++ is clearly superior for our new benchmarks for $K_n$-satisfiability ($\mathcal{ALC}$) without global assumptions, solving 125/200 problems under 15 s while the next-best solver, FaCT++, requires 250 s: an improvement of one order of magnitude.

The middle graph in Fig. 7 shows that CEGARBox++ is clearly inferior to the description logic (DL) reasoners for our extended $K_n$ ($\mathcal{ALC}$) benchmarks with global assumptions (TBoxes). This is not surprising as they handle global assumptions in a more sophisticated way while we use naive loop-check.

The rightmost graph in Fig. 7 shows that CEGARBox++(Sum) is clearly superior on the MQBF $Kt_n$ ($\mathcal{ALCI}$) benchmarks but with the caveat that these only contain formulae for $n = 1$. CEGARBox++ (Exp) does not solve any more problems after the 0.25 s mark because it memory-outs for large problems. CEGARBox++ (Global) also performs poorly, though worse than one might expect. This is likely because the slowdown isn't just coming from the SAT-solver becoming congested, and thus taking a longer time for each call, but also because having more subformulae in the SAT-solver leads to more superfluous jumps.

## 11 Further Work and Conclusions

Our experiments show that CEGARBox++ is state-of-the-art for $K_n$. This is not surprising, as CEGARBox++ is state-of-the-art for K, and our extension to multi-modal logic is simple and introduces no overhead. However, our new global assumption benchmarks highlights a big weakness in CEGARBox++ that was previously unnoticed - the loop-check procedure. The main reason is that global assumptions cannot be separated into clause-sets that "live" at the appropriate modal level, meaning that CEGAR-tableaux can no longer separate clauses into multiple modal contexts. Interestingly, our procedure for $Kt_n$ uses loop check but still outperforms other solvers. Indeed, CEGARBox++(Global) is essentially our global assumptions solver, which highlights the performance gains of the sum heuristic. Grouping modal contexts into equivalence classes is a general technique that can be refined further to avoid exponential blowup.

## References

1. Baader, F., Horrocks, I., Sattler, U.: Description logics. In: van Harmelen, F., Lifschitz, V., Porter, B.W. (eds.) Handbook of Knowledge Representation. Foundations of Artificial Intelligence, vol. 3, pp. 135–179. Elsevier (2008)
2. Balsiger, P., Heuerding, A., Schwendimann, S.: A benchmark method for the propositional modal logics K, KT, S4. J. Autom. Reason. **24**(3), 297–317 (2000)
3. Calvanese, D., De Giacomo, G., Rosati, R.: A note on encoding inverse roles and functional restrictions in ALC knowledge bases. In: Franconi, E., De Giacomo, G., MacGregor, R.M., Nutt, W., Welty, C.A. (eds.) Proceedings of the 1998 International Workshop on Description Logics (DL 1998), IRST, Povo - Trento, Italy, 6–8 June 1998. CEUR Workshop Proceedings, vol. 11. CEUR-WS.org (1998)

4. Claessen, K., Rosén, D.: SAT modulo intuitionistic implications. In: Davis, M., Fehnker, A., McIver, A., Voronkov, A. (eds.) LPAR 2015. LNCS, vol. 9450, pp. 622–637. Springer, Heidelberg (2015). https://doi.org/10.1007/978-3-662-48899-7_43
5. Clarke, E.M., Grumberg, O., Jha, S., Yuan, L., Veith, H.: Counterexample-guided abstraction refinement for symbolic model checking. J. ACM **50**(5), 752–794 (2003)
6. Een, N., Sörensson, N.: http://minisat.se/Papers.html. Accessed 10 Feb 2020
7. Geatti, L., Gigante, N., Montanari, A.: BLACK: a fast, flexible and reliable LTL satisfiability checker. In: Monica, D.D., Pozzato, G.L., Scala, E. (eds.) Proceedings of the 3rd Workshop on Artificial Intelligence and Formal Verification, Logic, Automata, and Synthesis hosted by the Twelfth International Symposium on Games, Automata, Logics, and Formal Verification (GandALF 2021), Padua, Italy, 22 September 2021. CEUR Workshop Proceedings, vol. 2987, pp. 7–12. CEUR-WS.org (2021)
8. Giacomo, G.: Eliminating "converse" from converse PDL. J. Logic Lang. Inform. **5**(2), 193–208 (1996)
9. Goré, R., Kikkert, C.: CEGAR-tableaux: improved modal satisfiability via modal clause-learning and SAT. In: Das, A., Negri, S. (eds.) TABLEAUX 2021. LNCS (LNAI), vol. 12842, pp. 74–91. Springer, Cham (2021). https://doi.org/10.1007/978-3-030-86059-2_5
10. Goré, R., Nguyen, L.A.: Clausal tableaux for multimodal logics of belief. Fundam. Inform. **94**(1), 21–40 (2009)
11. Goré, R., Thomson, J.: An improved BDD method for intuitionistic propositional logic: BDDIntKt system description. In: Bonacina, M.P. (ed.) CADE 2013. LNCS (LNAI), vol. 7898, pp. 275–281. Springer, Heidelberg (2013). https://doi.org/10.1007/978-3-642-38574-2_19
12. Belnap Jr, N.D.: Display logic. J. Philos. Log. **11**(4), 375–417 (1982)
13. Kashima, R.: Cut-free sequent calculi for some tense logics. Stud. Log. **53**(1), 119–136 (1994)
14. Li, J., Zhu, S., Pu, G., Vardi, M.Y.: SAT-based explicit LTL reasoning. In: Piterman, N. (ed.) HVC 2015. LNCS, vol. 9434, pp. 209–224. Springer, Cham (2015). https://doi.org/10.1007/978-3-319-26287-1_13
15. Mints, G. (1990). Gentzen-type systems and resolution rules part I propositional logic. In: Martin-Löf, P., Mints, G. (eds.) COLOG-88. LNCS, vol. 417, pp. 198–231. Springer, Heidelberg (1988). https://doi.org/10.1007/3-540-52335-9_55
16. Nalon, C., Hustadt, U., Dixon, C.: KSP: a resolution-based prover for multimodal K, abridged report. In: Sierra, C. (ed.) Proceedings of the Twenty-Sixth International Joint Conference on Artificial Intelligence, IJCAI 2017, Melbourne, Australia, 19–25 August 2017, pp. 4919–4923. ijcai.org (2017)
17. Nalon, C., Hustadt, U., Papacchini, F., Dixon, C.: Local reductions for the modal cube. In: Blanchette, J., Kovács, L., Pattinson, D. (eds.) IJCAR 2022. LNCS, vol. 13385, pp. 486–505. Springer, Cham (2022). https://doi.org/10.1007/978-3-031-10769-6_29
18. Pagram, T.: Using decision diagrams for modal and intuitionistic theorem proving. Honours thesis, Research School of Computer Science, The Australian National University (2015). https://github.com/tpagram
19. Prior, A.N.: Time and Modality. Oxford University Press (1957)
20. Tseytin, G.S.: On the complexity of derivation in propositional calculus. In: Slisenko, A.O. (ed.) Studies in Constructive Mathematics and Mathematical Logic, Part II. Seminars in Mathematics, pp. 115–125. Steklov Mathematical Institute (1970)

21. Vardi, M.Y.: From philosophical to industrial logics. In: Ramanujam, R., Sarukkai, S. (eds.) ICLA 2009. LNCS (LNAI), vol. 5378, pp. 89–115. Springer, Heidelberg (2008). https://doi.org/10.1007/978-3-540-92701-3_7
22. Wu, M., Goré, R.: Verified decision procedures for modal logics. In: Harrison, J., O'Leary, J., Tolmach, A. (eds.) 10th International Conference on Interactive Theorem Proving, ITP 2019, 9–12 September 2019, Portland, OR, USA. LIPIcs, vol. 141, pp. 31:1–31:19. Schloss Dagstuhl - Leibniz-Zentrum für Informatik (2019)

**Open Access** This chapter is licensed under the terms of the Creative Commons Attribution 4.0 International License (http://creativecommons.org/licenses/by/4.0/), which permits use, sharing, adaptation, distribution and reproduction in any medium or format, as long as you give appropriate credit to the original author(s) and the source, provide a link to the Creative Commons license and indicate if changes were made.

The images or other third party material in this chapter are included in the chapter's Creative Commons license, unless indicated otherwise in a credit line to the material. If material is not included in the chapter's Creative Commons license and your intended use is not permitted by statutory regulation or exceeds the permitted use, you will need to obtain permission directly from the copyright holder.

# Interpolation for Converse PDL

Johannes Kloibhofer[1], Valentina Trucco Dalmas[2(✉)], and Yde Venema[1]

[1] ILLC, University of Amsterdam, Amsterdam, The Netherlands
{j.kloibhofer,y.venema}@uva.nl
[2] University of Groningen, Groningen, The Netherlands
f.c.trucco.dalmas@rug.nl

**Abstract.** Converse PDL is the extension of propositional dynamic logic with a converse operation on programs. Our main result states that Converse PDL enjoys the (local) Craig Interpolation Property, with respect to both atomic programs and propositional variables. As a corollary we establish the Beth Definability Property for the logic.

Our interpolation proof is based on an adaptation of Maehara's proof-theoretic method. For this purpose we introduce a sound and complete cyclic sequent system for this logic. This calculus features an analytic cut rule and uses a focus mechanism for recognising successful cycles.

**Keywords:** propositional dynamic logic · converse modalities · cyclic proof system · interpolation

## 1 Introduction

Propositional Dynamic Logic (abbreviated: PDL) was introduced by Fischer & Ladner [8] in 1979 as a propositional formalism to reason about the behaviour of programs. The language of PDL features an infinite collection of modalities, the intended interpretation of $\langle \alpha \rangle \varphi$ being that 'after some execution of the program $\alpha$, the formula $\varphi$ holds'. The inductive structure of programs is reflected by the syntax of PDL, where complex programs are constructed from atomic ones and formula tests, by means of program constructors for sequential composition, nondeterministic choice and iteration.

Converse PDL or CPDL, also defined in [8], extends PDL with a converse operator on programs, which facilitates backwards reasoning about programs. PDL and CPDL also have applications in for instance knowledge representation [2], where the program expressions represent *roles* between objects, and the program constructions correspond to natural operations on such roles; in particular, the converse operator corresponds to *inverse roles*.

PDL and CPDL both have the small-model property and an EXPTIME-complete satisfiability problem, as established by Fischer & Ladner [8] and Pratt [17]). A natural axiomatisation was given by Segerberg [19] and proved to

---

Johannes Kloibhofer: The research of this author has been made possible by a grant from the Dutch Research Council NWO, project nr. 617.001.857.

be complete by Parikh [16] and others. Generally, PDL and related formalisms have been recognized as important modal logics for quite some time now, see for instance Troquard & Balbiani [21] for a recent survey.

Here we study interpolation properties for CPDL. A logic has the *Craig Interpolation Property* (CIP) if any pair $\varphi, \psi$ of formulas such that $\varphi \models \psi$ has an *interpolant*, that is, a formula $\theta$ in the common vocabulary of $\varphi$ and $\psi$ such that $\varphi \models \theta$ and $\theta \models \psi$. (Here $\models$ denotes the local consequence relation, that is: we have $\varphi \models \psi$ iff the implication $\varphi \to \psi$ is valid.) A related property is the Beth Definability Property, which informally states that any concept which can implicitly be defined in the logic, in fact also has an explicit definition. Interpolation and definability are generally considered to be attractive properties of a formalism; applications in computer science include the modularisation and optimisation of reasoning [6,10,14,18]. Both properties have been studied extensively in the literature on modal logic, see Gabbay & Maksimova [9] for a survey.

Our main result states that CPDL has the Craig Interpolation Property indeed, with respect to both atomic programs and propositional variables. As a direct corollary we obtain the Beth Definability Property for CPDL.

We prove Craig interpolation following Maehara's proof-theoretic method, adapted to our logic. That is, we first introduce a sound and complete cyclic proof system for this logic. This calculus features an analytic cut rule and uses a focus mechanism for recognising successful cycles. To prove interpolation we consider a version of the proof system that operates on *split sequents*, that is, pairs of finite sets of formulas. Given a pair $\varphi, \psi$ of formulas such that $\varphi \models \psi$, we fix a derivation $\pi$ of the split sequent $\overline{\psi} \mid \varphi$. This derivation induces a system of equations, whose solution would immediately yield an interpolant of $\varphi$ and $\psi$. As in the case for standard PDL, a straightforward approach would result in a system of equations that cannot be solved *inside* CPDL itself. To solve this problem we employ an idea from Borzechowski [4]: based on an *auxiliary structure* rather than on $\pi$ itself, we set up an alternative system of equations, which *does* have a solution in CPDL, thus providing us with the desired interpolant.

*Related Work.* Maehara's method has been extended to cyclic proof systems by Shamkanov [20], Afshari & Leigh [1] and Marti & Venema [13], in order to prove interpolation properties for, respectively, Godel-Lob logic, the modal $\mu$-calculus $\mathcal{L}_\mu$ and its alternation-free fragment. Closely related to our work is the paper by Borzechowski et al. [5], who use ideas from Borzechowski [4] to establish interpolation for PDL. Our work extends [5] to include converse modalities: notable differences are that our proof system features a cut rule and a more involved modal rule, while on the other hand our rules for the program constructors are simpler than those in [5]. Kloibhofer & Venema establish Craig interpolation for the two-way $\mu$-calculus [11]. Our cyclic proof system is much simpler, since it avoids the use of trace atoms and can restrict to a simple focus annotation system; the construction of our interpolants is rather more intricate, however.

## 2 Converse PDL

### 2.1 Syntax

**Definition 1.** *Let* Prop *be an infinite set of atomic propositions and* Act *an infinite set of atomic programs. We assume an involution operation* $\breve{\phantom{a}}$ : Act $\to$ Act *such that for every* $a \in$ Act *it holds that* $a \neq \breve{a}$ *and* $a = \breve{\breve{a}}$. *The sets of formulas and programs of* CPDL *are given by the following mutual induction:*

$$\varphi ::= \top \mid \bot \mid p \mid \overline{p} \mid \varphi \wedge \varphi \mid \varphi \vee \varphi \mid \langle \alpha \rangle \varphi \mid [\alpha]\varphi$$
$$\alpha ::= a \mid \breve{a} \mid \alpha; \alpha \mid \alpha \cup \alpha \mid \alpha^* \mid \varphi?$$

*where* $p \in$ Prop *and* $a \in$ Act[1] .

The *vocabulary of* $\varphi$, written $\mathsf{Voc}(\varphi)$, is the set of propositions and actions occurring in $\varphi$, with the proviso that we include both $a$ and $\breve{a}$ in the vocabulary of any expression in which $a$ or $\breve{a}$ occurs. We refer to formulas of the form $\langle \alpha \rangle \varphi$ and $[\alpha]\varphi$ as, respectively, *diamond* and *box formulas*. Formulas of the form $\langle \alpha^* \rangle \varphi$ or $[\alpha^*]\varphi$ are called *fixpoint formulas*.

We think of the formula $\overline{p}$ as the negation of $p$, and inductively extend the map $p \mapsto \overline{p}$ to a full-blown negation operation as follows:

$$\overline{\top} := \bot \qquad \overline{\varphi \wedge \psi} := \overline{\varphi} \vee \overline{\psi} \qquad \overline{[\alpha]\varphi} := \langle \alpha \rangle \overline{\varphi}$$
$$\overline{\bot} := \top \qquad \overline{\overline{p}} := p \qquad \overline{\varphi \vee \psi} := \overline{\varphi} \wedge \overline{\psi} \qquad \overline{\langle \alpha \rangle \varphi} := [\alpha]\overline{\varphi}$$

For a set of formulas $\Gamma$ we define $\overline{\Gamma} = \{\overline{\varphi} \mid \varphi \in \Gamma\}$. Note that $\overline{\overline{\varphi}} = \varphi$ for every formula $\varphi$.

Similarly, we extend the converse operator to arbitrary programs by putting $(\alpha; \beta)^{\smile} := \breve{\beta}; \breve{\alpha}$, $(\alpha \cup \beta)^{\smile} := \breve{\alpha} \cup \breve{\beta}$, $(\alpha^*)^{\smile} := \breve{\alpha}^*$ and $(\tau?)^{\smile} := \tau?$. Thus we may think indeed of CPDL as extending PDL with a converse operation on programs.

We let $\varphi[\psi/p]$ denote the result of substituting all occurrences of $p$ in the formula $\varphi$ with the formula $\psi$ (and all occurrences of $\overline{p}$ with $\overline{\psi}$).

**Definition 2.** *Let* $\varphi$ *and* $\psi$ *be formulas. We write* $\varphi \to_C \psi$ *if*

1. $\varphi = \chi_0 \wedge \chi_1$ *and* $\psi \in \{\chi_0, \chi_1\}$ *or* $\varphi = \chi_0 \vee \chi_1$ *and* $\psi \in \{\chi_0, \chi_1\}$;
2. $\varphi = \langle a \rangle \chi$ *and* $\psi = \chi$, *or* $\varphi = [a]\chi$ *and* $\psi = \chi$;
3. $\varphi = \langle \alpha; \beta \rangle \chi$ *and* $\psi = \langle \alpha \rangle \langle \beta \rangle \chi$, *or* $\varphi = [\alpha; \beta]\chi$ *and* $\psi = [\alpha][\beta]\chi$;
4. $\varphi = \langle \alpha \cup \beta \rangle \chi$ *and* $\psi \in \{\langle \alpha \rangle \chi, \langle \beta \rangle \chi\}$, *or* $\varphi = [\alpha \cup \beta]\chi$ *and* $\psi \in \{[\alpha]\chi, [\beta]\chi\}$;
5. $\varphi = \langle \tau? \rangle \chi$ *and* $\psi \in \{\tau, \chi\}$, *or* $\varphi = [\tau?]\chi$ *and* $\psi \in \{\overline{\tau}, \chi\}$;
6. $\varphi = \langle \alpha^* \rangle \chi$ *and* $\psi \in \{\langle \alpha \rangle \langle \alpha^* \rangle \chi, \chi\}$, *or* $\varphi = [\alpha^*]\chi$ *and* $\psi \in \{[\alpha][\alpha^*]\chi, \chi\}$.

A *trace* is a sequence $(\varphi_n)_{0 \leq n < \kappa}$ (with $\kappa \leq \omega$) such that $\varphi_n \to_C \varphi_{n+1}$ for all $i < \kappa$. We define the *trace relation* $\twoheadrightarrow_C$ on formulas as the reflexive-transitive closure of $\to_C$. We write $\varphi \equiv_C \psi$ if both $\varphi \twoheadrightarrow_C \psi$ and $\psi \twoheadrightarrow_C \varphi$. We define the *Fischer-Ladner closure* of a sequent $\Gamma$ as the set $\mathsf{FL}(\Gamma) := \{\psi \mid \varphi \twoheadrightarrow_C \psi \text{ for some } \varphi \in \Gamma\}$ and put $\mathsf{FL}^{\neg}(\Gamma) := \mathsf{FL}(\Gamma) \cup \mathsf{FL}(\overline{\Gamma})$.

---

[1] In our set-up the atomic actions come in pairs $a, \breve{a}$. This has some technical advantages over the approach where the converse operation $\smile$ is an explicit syntactic symbol.

**Proposition 3.** *Let $t = (\varphi_n)_{n<\omega}$ be an infinite trace. Then infinitely many $\varphi_n$ are fixpoint formulas, and either cofinitely many $\varphi_n$ are diamond formulas, or cofinitely many $\varphi_n$ are box formulas.*

## 2.2 Semantics

CPDL-formulas are interpreted in (poly-modal) Kripke models. It will be convenient for us to present the semantics in terms of an evaluation game. This game-theoretic semantics is equivalent to the standard one, but for lack of space we cannot prove this equivalence here.

**Definition 4.** *A Kripke model $\mathbb{S} = (S, R, V)$ consists of a set $S$ of states; a family of binary relations $R = \{R_a \subseteq S^2 \mid a \in \mathsf{Act}\}$ on $S$ such that $(s, s') \in R_a$ iff $(s', s) \in R_{\check{a}}$; and a valuation $V : \mathsf{Prop} \to \mathcal{P}(S)$. A pointed model is a pair $(\mathbb{S}, s)$ where $\mathbb{S}$ is a Kripke model and $s \in S$.*

Let $\mathbb{S} = (S, R, V)$ be a Kripke model. The *evaluation game* $\mathcal{E}(\mathbb{S})$ is the following infinite two-player game. Its positions are pairs of the form $(\varphi, s)$, where $\varphi$ is a formula and $s \in S$, and its ownership function and admissible moves are given in the following table.

| Position | Owner | Admissible moves | Position | Owner | Admissible moves |
|---|---|---|---|---|---|
| $(\varphi \vee \psi, s)$ | $\exists$ | $\{(\varphi, s), (\psi, s)\}$ | $(\varphi \wedge \psi, s)$ | $\forall$ | $\{(\varphi, s), (\psi, s)\}$ |
| $(\langle a \rangle \varphi, s)$ | $\exists$ | $\{(\varphi, t) \mid (s, t) \in R_a\}$ | $([a]\varphi, s)$ | $\forall$ | $\{(\varphi, t) \mid (s, t) \in R_a\}$ |
| $(\langle \alpha; \beta \rangle \varphi, s)$ | - | $\{(\langle \alpha \rangle \langle \beta \rangle \varphi, s)\}$ | $([\alpha; \beta]\varphi, s)$ | - | $\{([\alpha][\beta]\varphi, s)\}$ |
| $(\langle \alpha \cup \beta \rangle \varphi, s)$ | $\exists$ | $\{(\langle \alpha \rangle \varphi, s), (\langle \beta \rangle \varphi, s)\}$ | $([\alpha \cup \beta]\varphi, s)$ | $\forall$ | $\{([\alpha]\varphi, s), ([\beta]\varphi, s)\}$ |
| $(\langle \alpha^* \rangle \varphi, s)$ | $\exists$ | $\{(\langle \alpha \rangle \langle \alpha^* \rangle \varphi, s), (\varphi, s)\}$ | $([\alpha^*]\varphi, s)$ | $\forall$ | $\{([\alpha][\alpha^*]\varphi, s), (\varphi, s)\}$ |
| $(\langle \psi? \rangle \varphi, s)$ | $\forall$ | $\{(\psi, s), (\varphi, s)\}$ | $([\psi?]\varphi, s)$ | $\exists$ | $\{(\overline{\psi}, s), (\varphi, s)\}$ |

Whenever a position $(\varphi, s)$ is reached with $\varphi = \bot, \top, p, \overline{p}$, the game ends and is won by $\exists$ if $\varphi = \top$; $\varphi = p$ and $s \in V(p)$; or $\overline{p}$ and $s \notin V(p)$, and is won by $\forall$ else. Note that the left projection $(\varphi_n)_{n<\kappa}$ of any (partial) match $(\varphi_n, s_n)_{n<\kappa}$ is a trace. An infinite match is won by $\forall$ if its left projection features infinitely many diamond fixpoint formulas (or, equivalently, cofinitely many diamond formulas) and by $\exists$ else. (This corresponds to the standard definition of winning conditions for evaluation games for fixpoint formulas, cf. Proposition 3.) It is clear that this game can be presented as a parity game, and as such it is positionally determined.

**Definition 5.** *Let $\mathbb{S}, s$ be a pointed model, let $f$ be a strategy for $\exists$ in $\mathcal{E}(\mathbb{S})$ and let $\varphi$ be a formula. We write $\mathbb{S}, s \Vdash_f \varphi$ if $f$ is winning for $\exists$ at $(\varphi, s)$, and $\mathbb{S}, s \Vdash \varphi$ if $\mathbb{S}, s \Vdash_f \varphi$ for some strategy $f$ for $\exists$. We say that a formula $\varphi$ is satisfiable if there exists $\mathbb{S}, s$ such that $\mathbb{S}, s \Vdash \varphi$ and unsatisfiable otherwise.*

## 3 Proof System

An *annotated formula* is a pair $(\varphi, o)$, usually denoted as $\varphi^o$, where $o$ is either $u$ (*unfocused*) or $f$ (*in focus*). An *annotated sequent* $\Gamma$ is a set of annotated formulas, such that at most one formula in $\Gamma$ is in focus. Given a set of formulas $\Delta$, we define the annotated sequent $\Delta^u := \{\varphi^u \mid \varphi \in \Delta\}$. For an annotated sequent $\Gamma$ we define $\Gamma^- := \{\varphi \mid \varphi^o \in \Gamma\}$ and $\Gamma^u := \{\varphi^u \mid \varphi^o \in \Gamma\}$. We read annotated sequents *conjunctively* and say that $\Gamma$ is *satisfiable* if $\bigwedge \Gamma^-$ is satisfiable and call $\Gamma$ *unsatisfiable* else. If no confusion is likely, we will call annotated sequents just sequents.

The rules of the proof system $\mathsf{CPDL}_f$ are given in Fig. 1. Note that the calculus aims to derive sequents that are *unsatisfiable*. Apart from the annotations the rules are as expected. In the rules $\langle a \rangle$, $\wedge$, $\vee$, $\langle ; \rangle$, $[;]$, $\langle \cup \rangle$, $[\cup]$, $\langle ? \rangle$, $[?]$, $\langle * \rangle$, $[*]$ and weak we call the single explicitly written formula in its conclusion the *principal formula* of the rule. We only allow applications of rules R with a principal formula different from $\langle \alpha \rangle \varphi$ if the principal formula is unfocused. (Hence, to apply such a rule to a formula in focus, first a u rule has to be applied.) The modal rule $\langle a \rangle$ is only allowed if its principal formula $\langle a \rangle \varphi$ is in focus.

In applications of acut we demand that $\varphi \in \mathsf{FL}^-(\Gamma)$. For a modal rule $\langle a \rangle$ with conclusion $\Theta = \langle a \rangle \varphi^f, [a]\Sigma, \Gamma$ the sequent $\langle \breve{a} \rangle \Gamma$ is defined as $\langle \breve{a} \rangle \Gamma := \{\langle \breve{a} \rangle \chi^u \mid \chi^u \in \Gamma \text{ and } \langle \breve{a} \rangle \chi \in \mathsf{FL}^-(\Theta)\}$. This ensures that all rules are analytic.

| | | | | | | | |
|---|---|---|---|---|---|---|---|
| Ax1: $\dfrac{}{\varphi^{o_1}, \overline{\varphi}^{o_2}, \Gamma}$ | | Ax2: $\dfrac{}{\perp^u, \Gamma}$ | | $\wedge$: $\dfrac{\varphi^u, \psi^u, \Gamma}{\varphi \wedge \psi^u, \Gamma}$ | | $\vee$: $\dfrac{\varphi^u, \Gamma \quad \psi^u, \Gamma}{\varphi \vee \psi^u, \Gamma}$ | |
| $\langle ; \rangle$: $\dfrac{\langle \alpha \rangle \langle \beta \rangle \varphi^o, \Gamma}{\langle \alpha; \beta \rangle \varphi^o, \Gamma}$ | | $[;]$: $\dfrac{[\alpha][\beta]\varphi^u, \Gamma}{[\alpha; \beta]\varphi^u, \Gamma}$ | | $\langle \cup \rangle$: $\dfrac{\langle \alpha \rangle \varphi^o, \Gamma \quad \langle \beta \rangle \varphi^o, \Gamma}{\langle \alpha \cup \beta \rangle \varphi^o, \Gamma}$ | | | |
| $\langle * \rangle$: $\dfrac{\langle \alpha \rangle \langle \alpha^* \rangle \varphi^o, \Gamma \quad \varphi^o, \Gamma}{\langle \alpha^* \rangle \varphi^o, \Gamma}$ | | $[*]$: $\dfrac{[\alpha][\alpha^*]\varphi^u, \varphi^u, \Gamma}{[\alpha^*]\varphi^u, \Gamma}$ | | $[\cup]$: $\dfrac{[\alpha]\varphi^u, [\beta]\varphi^u, \Gamma}{[\alpha \cup \beta]\varphi^u, \Gamma}$ | | | |
| $\langle ? \rangle$: $\dfrac{\psi^u, \varphi^o, \Gamma}{\langle \psi ? \rangle \varphi^o, \Gamma}$ | | $[?]$: $\dfrac{\overline{\psi}^u, \Gamma \quad \varphi^u, \Gamma}{[\psi ?]\varphi^u, \Gamma}$ | | $\langle a \rangle$: $\dfrac{\varphi^f, \Sigma, \langle \breve{a} \rangle \Gamma}{\langle a \rangle \varphi^f, [a]\Sigma, \Gamma}$ | | | |
| acut: $\dfrac{\Gamma, \varphi^u \quad \overline{\varphi}^u, \Gamma}{\Gamma}$ | | weak: $\dfrac{\Gamma}{\varphi^u, \Gamma}$ | | f: $\dfrac{\varphi^f, \Gamma}{\varphi^u, \Gamma}$ | | u: $\dfrac{\varphi^u, \Gamma}{\varphi^f, \Gamma}$ | |

**Fig. 1.** Rules of $\mathsf{CPDL}_f$

**Definition 6 (Derivation).** *A* $\mathsf{CPDL}_f$ *derivation* $\pi = (T, \lessdot, \Lambda, \mathsf{R})$ *is a proof tree defined from the rules in Fig. 1 such that* $(T, \lessdot)$ *is a, possibly infinite, tree with nodes* $T$ *and parent relation*[2] $\lessdot$; $\Lambda$ *maps each node* $u \in T$ *to an annotated*

---
[2] We write $s \lessdot t$ if $s$ is the parent of $t$.

sequent $\Lambda_u$; and R is a function that maps every node $u \in T$ to either (i) the name of a rule in Fig. 1 or (ii) an extra value e, such that every node labelled with e is a leaf. Leaves labelled by e are called assumptions. We require the maps $\Lambda$ and R to be in accordance with the formulation of the rules, as usual.

An assumption $l$ is called a repeat leaf *if it has a proper ancestor $v$ of $l$ that such that $\Lambda_l = \Lambda_v$. In this case the nearest such ancestor of $l$ is called its* companion *and we denote it by $c(l)$.*

Given a CPDL$_f$ derivation $\pi = (T, \lessdot, \Lambda, \mathsf{R})$ we define the usual *proof tree* $\mathcal{T}_\pi = (T, \lessdot)$ and the *proof tree with back edges* $\mathcal{T}_\pi^C = (T, \triangleleft)$, where $\triangleleft\, =\, \lessdot \cup\, \{(l, c(l)) \mid l$ is a repeat leaf$\}$. Note that we think of trees as growing *upwards*. We call $\pi$ *regular* if it has finitely many distinct subderivations. We define $<$ and $\leq$ to be the transitive and reflexive-transitive closures of $\lessdot$, respectively, and $\triangleleft^+$ and $\triangleleft^*$ to be the transitive and reflexive-transitive closures of $\triangleleft$, respectively.

**Definition 7.** *A finite path $\tau$ in a CPDL$_f$ derivation is* successful *if*

1. *every sequent on $\tau$ has a formula in focus, and*
2. *there is a node on $\tau$ where the formula in focus is principal.*

Let $l$ be a repeat leaf in a CPDL$_f$ derivation $\pi$ with companion $c(l)$, and let $\tau_l$ denote the repeat path of $l$ in $\mathcal{T}_\pi$ from $c(l)$ to $l$. We say that $l$ is a discharged assumption *if the path $\tau_l$ is successful. A leaf is called* closed *if it is either a discharged assumption or labelled by an axiom, and is called* open *otherwise.*

**Definition 8 (Cyclic proof).** *Let $\mathcal{A}$ be a set of sequents. A CPDL$_f$ proof with assumptions $\mathcal{A}$ is a finite CPDL$_f$ derivation $\pi$, where every leaf of $\pi$ is either closed or labeled by a sequent in $\mathcal{A}$. If the root of such a proof $\pi$ is labeled with a sequent $\Gamma$, we write $\pi : \mathcal{A} \vdash \Gamma$. We say that CPDL$_f$ proves a sequent $\Gamma$ with assumptions $\mathcal{A}$ and write $\mathcal{A} \vdash \Gamma$, if we have $\pi : \mathcal{A} \vdash \Gamma$ for some $\pi$. If $\mathcal{A}$ is empty, we write $\vdash \Gamma$. For a set of unannotated formulas $\Delta$ we define $\vdash \Delta$ as $\vdash \Delta^u$.*

The following theorem states the soundness and completeness of this system. This result follows as a special case of the soundness and completeness of the split proof system that we introduce in the next section.

**Theorem 9 (Soundness & Completeness).** *A sequent $\Gamma$ is unsatisfiable iff $\vdash \Gamma$.*

## 4 Split Proof System

One of the core ideas underlying Maehara's proof-theoretic approach towards Craig interpolation is to work with a version of the derivation system that operates on so-called *split sequents*. Here a *split sequent* $(\Gamma, \Delta)$, usually written as $\Gamma \mid \Delta$, is a pair of annotated sequents, of which at most one can be focused. Note that we do not require $\Gamma$ and $\Delta$ to be disjoint. Given a split sequent $\Sigma = \Gamma \mid \Delta$, we will write $\Sigma^l$ for its *left component* $\Gamma$ and $\Sigma^r$ for its *right component* $\Delta$. We will use $d$ as a variable ranging over the set $\{l, r\}$. If $\Gamma$ (respectively $\Delta$) contains a formula in focus, we call $\Gamma$ (respectively $\Delta$) the *focused component* of $\Gamma \mid \Delta$.

The rules of the split proof system $\mathsf{SCPDL}_f$ are obtained from the rules of $\mathsf{CPDL}_f$ by applying the rules to one of the components. Formally, let $\mathsf{R} \; \dfrac{\Gamma_1, \Delta_1 \quad \cdots \quad \Gamma_n, \Delta_n}{\Gamma, \Delta}$ be a rule of Fig. 1. Then $\mathsf{R}^l \; \dfrac{\Gamma_1 \mid \Delta_1 \quad \cdots \quad \Gamma_n \mid \Delta_n}{\Gamma \mid \Delta}$
is a *left rule*, if the following conditions are satisfied:

1. if R is not an axiom and $\mathsf{R} \neq \langle a \rangle$, then $\Delta_i = \Delta$ for $1 \leq i \leq n$,
2. if $\mathsf{R} = \mathsf{acut}$, then $\varphi \in \mathsf{FL}^\neg(\Gamma)$,
3. if $\mathsf{R} = \langle a \rangle$, then $\langle a \rangle^l$ is of the form $\langle a \rangle^l : \dfrac{\varphi^f, \Sigma, \langle \breve{a} \rangle \Lambda \mid \Pi, \langle \breve{a} \rangle \Theta}{\langle a \rangle \varphi^f, [a] \Sigma, \Lambda \mid [a] \Pi, \Theta}$ where
$\langle \breve{a} \rangle \Lambda := \{ \langle \breve{a} \rangle \chi^u \mid \chi^u \in \Lambda \text{ and } \langle \breve{a} \rangle \chi \in \mathsf{FL}^\neg(\Gamma) \}$ and $\langle \breve{a} \rangle \Theta := \{ \langle \breve{a} \rangle \chi^u \mid \chi^u \in \Theta \text{ and } \langle \breve{a} \rangle \chi \in \mathsf{FL}^\neg(\Delta) \}$.[3]

*Right rules* are defined analogously. *Split rules* are either left or right rules. Note that the only split rules with interactions between the components are axioms and modal rules. Notions defined in Sect. 3 translate straightforwardly to $\mathsf{SCPDL}_f$ derivations.

**Definition 10.** *An $\mathsf{SCPDL}_f$ derivation is defined analogously to a $\mathsf{CPDL}_f$ derivation, where each node is now labelled by a split sequent and a split rule. A finite path $\tau$ in an $\mathsf{SCPDL}_f$ derivation is* successful *if every node on $\tau$ features a formula in focus and there is a node on $\tau$ where the formula in focus is principal. An $\mathsf{SCPDL}_f$ proof with assumptions $\mathcal{A}$ is a finite $\mathsf{SCPDL}_f$ derivation, where every leaf is either closed or labelled by a sequent in $\mathcal{A}$. The relation $\vdash$ is defined as for $\mathsf{CPDL}_f$ proofs.*

## 5 Soundness and Completeness of Split Proofs

We prove the soundness and completeness of $\mathsf{SCPDL}_f$ by *game-theoretic* means. Given a split sequent $\Sigma$, we define a proof-search game $\mathcal{G}(\Sigma)$ in which one player (Prover) aims to find a proof of $\Sigma$, while the other player (Builder) aims to construct a model where $\Sigma$ is satisfied. Winning strategies for Prover and Builders then correspond to, respectively, proofs and models for $\Sigma$. To tighten the correspondence between winning strategies for Prover and proofs we will work with infinite $\mathsf{SCPDL}_f^\infty$ proofs. These are $\mathsf{SCPDL}_f$ derivations, where instead of cycles we allow infinite branches satisfying a corresponding success condition.

### 5.1 Infinite $\mathsf{SCPDL}_f^\infty$ Proofs

**Definition 11.** *An infinite path $\tau$ in an $\mathsf{SCPDL}_f$ derivation is* successful *if*

1. *on cofinitely many sequents on $\tau$ there is a formula in focus, and*
2. *there are infinitely many nodes on $\tau$ where the formula in focus is principal.*

---
[3] Note that here $\Gamma = \langle a \rangle \varphi^f, [a] \Sigma, \Lambda$ and $\Delta = [a] \Pi, \Theta$.

**Definition 12 (Infinitary proof).** *An* SCPDL$_f^\infty$ *proof is an* SCPDL$_f$ *derivation, where every leaf is labelled by an axiom and every infinite path is successful.*

The correspondence between regular SCPDL$_f^\infty$ proofs and SCPDL$_f$ proofs is standard in cyclic proof theory.

**Lemma 13.** *There is a regular* SCPDL$_f^\infty$ *proof of* $\Gamma \mid \Delta$ *iff* SCPDL$_f \vdash \Gamma \mid \Delta$.

## 5.2 Proof Search Game

A *rule instance* is a triple $(\Sigma, \mathsf{R}, \langle \Sigma_1, ..., \Sigma_n \rangle)$ such that $\mathsf{R}\ \dfrac{\Sigma_1 \ \cdots \ \Sigma_n}{\Sigma}$ is a valid rule application in SCPDL$_f$. We let conc be the function mapping rule instances to their conclusions. A rule instance is *cumulative* if all premises are componentwise supersets of the conclusion and *productive* if each premise is distinct from the conclusion. We call a rule instance of u *conceding*, if its principal formula is of the form $\langle \alpha \rangle \varphi$ and *unblocking* otherwise.

Let $\Phi$ be a split sequent. We define the proof search game $\mathcal{G}(\Phi)$, with players Prover and Builder. Its positions are given by $\mathsf{Seq}_\Phi \cup \mathsf{Inst}_\Phi$, where $\mathsf{Seq}_\Phi$ is the set of split sequents and $\mathsf{Inst}_\Phi$ the set of rule instances containing formulas in $\mathsf{FL}^-(\Phi)$. The ownership function and admissible moves are given in the table below. An infinite match is won by Prover iff the resulting infinite path is successful.

| Position | Owner | Admissible moves |
| --- | --- | --- |
| $\Sigma$ | Prover | $\{i \in \mathsf{Inst}_\Phi \mid \mathsf{conc}(i) = \Sigma\}$ |
| $(\Sigma, \mathsf{R}, \langle \Sigma_1, \cdots, \Sigma_n \rangle)$ | Builder | $\{\Sigma_i \mid i = 1, \cdots, n\}$ |

Interestingly, we may assume that winning strategies in $\mathcal{G}(\Phi)@\Phi$ are positional, that is, only depend on the current position of the game, and not on the history of the play leading up to this position. The key observations here is that $\mathcal{G}(\Phi)$ can be formulated as a parity game, since parity games are well known to enjoy positional determinacy [7,15]. To see that $\mathcal{G}(\Phi)$ is a parity game, we may assign the following priorities to its positions. $\Omega(\Sigma) := 0$ for any sequent position, and for the other positions we put

$$\Omega(\Sigma, \mathsf{R}, \langle \Sigma_1, \cdots, \Sigma_n \rangle) := \begin{cases} 3 & \text{if } \Sigma \text{ has no formula in focus} \\ 2 & \text{if } \Sigma \text{ has a formula in focus and } \mathsf{R} = \langle a \rangle \\ 1 & \text{if } \Sigma \text{ has a formula in focus and } \mathsf{R} \neq \langle a \rangle. \end{cases}$$

An SCPDL$_f^\infty$ proof of a split sequent $\Phi$ may be identified with a winning strategy of Prover in $\mathcal{G}(\Phi)@\Phi$, and thus, as a consequence of positional determinacy we may assume that CPDL$_f^\infty$ proofs are regular.

## 5.3 Soundness

Given a $\mathsf{CPDL}_f^\infty$ proof of a split sequent $\Sigma = \Gamma \,|\, \Delta$ we want to show that $\Gamma \cup \Delta$ is unsatisfiable. Equivalently, given a pointed model $\mathbb{S}, s$ that satisfies $\Gamma \cup \Delta$ we provide a winning strategy for Builder in $\mathcal{G}(\Sigma)@(\Sigma)$. To prove this is standard.

**Theorem 14 (Soundness).** *If* $\mathsf{SCPDL}_f \vdash \Gamma \,|\, \Delta$, *then* $\Gamma, \Delta$ *is unsatisfiable.*

## 5.4 Completeness

For any unsatisfiable sequent $\Gamma, \Delta$ we have to find a $\mathsf{SCPDL}_f^\infty$ proof of $\Sigma = \Gamma \,|\, \Delta$, in other words a winning strategy of Prover in $\mathcal{G}(\Sigma)@\Sigma$. We will show an even stronger statement: By restricting the strategy of Prover we show that for every unsatisfiable split sequent we obtain an $\mathsf{SCPDL}_f^\infty$ proof in a certain normal form. These *uniform* proofs will be instrumental in our interpolation proof.

**Definition 15 (Uniform Split Derivation).** *A set of formulas $\Gamma$ is called* saturated, *if no axiom or cumulative and productive $\mathsf{CPDL}_f$ rule may be applied to $\Gamma^u$. This definition is equivalent to $\Gamma^u$ being a saturated set in the usual sense. A split derivation $\pi$ is* uniform *if it satisfies the following conditions:*

U0. *If possible an axiom is applied.*
U1. *Else if possible a cumulative and productive rule is applied to a formula in an unfocused component.*
U2. *Let $t_1$ and $t_2$ be nodes labelled with split sequents $\Gamma_1 \,|\, \Delta$ and $\Gamma_2 \,|\, \Delta$ in $\pi$, respectively. Assume that their common component $\Delta$ is focused, while their unfocused components $\Gamma_1$ and $\Gamma_2$ are both saturated. Then at both $t_1$ and $t_2$ the same rule with the same principal formula in $\Delta$ is applied. If possible, this rule is cumulative and productive with an unfocused principal formula, and else it is productive with its principal formula in focus.*
U3. *The analogous condition to (U2) for split sequents $\Gamma \,|\, \Delta_1$ and $\Gamma \,|\, \Delta_2$.*

We thus aim to show the following completeness theorem. Due to lack of space we only present a proof sketch.

**Theorem 16 (Completeness).** *If $\Gamma, \Delta$ is unsatisfiable then there is a uniform* $\mathsf{SCPDL}_f$ *proof of* $\Gamma \,|\, \Delta$.

*Proof (Sketch).* Let $\Sigma = \Gamma \,|\, \Delta$. By contraposition, given a winning strategy for Builder in $\mathcal{G}(\Sigma)@\Sigma$ we have to show that $\Gamma, \Delta$ is satisfiable. Let $f$ be a *positional* winning strategy for Builder in $\mathcal{G}(\Sigma)@\Sigma$, we construct a pointed model $\mathbb{S}^f, s$ and a strategy $\underline{f}$ for $\exists$ in $\mathcal{E}(\mathbb{S}^f)$ such that $\mathbb{S}^f, s \Vdash_{\underline{f}} \Sigma$.

Let $\mathcal{T}$ be the subtree of the game-tree of $\mathcal{G}(\Sigma)@\Sigma$, where Builder plays the strategy $f$ and Prover picks rule instances such that the uniformity conditions are satisfied. We want to define a model $\mathbb{S}^f$ from $\mathcal{T}$. A maximal path $\rho$ in $\mathcal{T}$ not containing rule instances of $\langle a \rangle$, f and conceding instances of u is called a *local path*. It follows that every local path is finite: Only finitely many cumulative and productive rule instances may be applied, and in the only non-cumulative rule instances that we apply the principal formula is in focus, hence there can also only be finitely many as $f$ is a winning strategy for Builder.

For local paths $\rho, \tau$ we define $\rho \xrightarrow{a} \tau$ if $\tau$ is above $\rho$ in $\mathcal{T}$ only separated by an instance of $\langle a \rangle$ and (possibly) instances of f and conceding instances of u. We let $\Lambda(\rho) := \bigcup \{\Sigma^l \cup \Sigma^r \mid \Sigma \text{ occurs in } \rho\}$.

We now define the model $\mathbb{S}^f = (S^f, R^f, V^f)$. We let $S^f$ be the set of local paths in $\mathcal{T}$, define $V^f(p) := \{\rho \in S^f \mid p \in \Lambda(\rho)^-\}$ and $R^f = \{R_a^f\}_{a \in \mathsf{Act}}$, where

$$\rho R_a \tau \quad :\Leftrightarrow \quad \rho \xrightarrow{a} \tau \text{ or } \tau \xrightarrow{\breve{a}} \rho$$

For the definition of the strategy $\underline{f}$ for $\exists$ in $\mathcal{E}(\mathbb{S}^f)$ we use the fact that $\Lambda(\rho)$ is a saturated set for every local path $\rho$. For instance, at position $(\varphi \vee \psi, \rho)$ the formula $\varphi$ or $\psi$ is in $\Lambda(\rho)^-$ and $\underline{f}$ picks one that is. At position $(\langle a \rangle \varphi, \rho)$ the strategy $\underline{f}$ picks some $\tau$ such that $\rho \xrightarrow{a} \tau$.

Now let $\psi_0 \in \Sigma$ and let $\rho_0$ be a local path containing $\Sigma$. Let $\mathcal{M}$ be an $\underline{f}$-guided $\mathcal{E}(\mathbb{S}^f)$-match starting at $(\psi_0, \rho_0)$. Then we can prove that for every position $(\psi, \rho)$ in $\mathcal{M}$ it holds that $\psi \in \Lambda(\rho)$ and consequently that $\exists$ wins $\mathcal{M}$. This shows that $\mathbb{S}^f, \rho_0 \Vdash_f \Sigma$.

## 6 Interpolation

As mentioned in the introduction, the following theorem is the main contribution of this paper.

**Theorem 17 (Craig Interpolation).** *Let $\varphi$ and $\psi$ be CPDL-formulas such that $\varphi \models \psi$. Then there is a CPDL-formula $\theta$ such that $\mathsf{Voc}(\theta) \subseteq \mathsf{Voc}(\varphi) \cap \mathsf{Voc}(\psi)$ and $\varphi \models \theta$ and $\theta \models \psi$.*

As an immediate consequence of this we obtain Beth definability. Where $\varphi(p)$ is a CPDL-formula, we use $\varphi(p_i)$ as an abbreviation of $\varphi[p_i/p]$.

**Corollary 18 (Beth Definability).** *Let $\varphi(p)$ be a CPDL-formula, and let $p_0, p_1$ be fresh variables. If $\varphi(p_0), \varphi(p_1) \models p_0 \leftrightarrow p_1$, then there is a CPDL-formula $\chi$ with $\mathsf{Voc}(\chi) \subseteq \mathsf{Voc}(\varphi) \setminus \{p\}$ and $\varphi(p) \models p \leftrightarrow \chi$.*

*Proof.* Apply Craig interpolation to $\varphi(p_0), p_0 \models \varphi(p_1) \rightarrow p_1$.

The remainder of the paper is devoted to the proof of Theorem 17. In this section we will use the split sequent system to find Craig interpolants for CPDL. We first transfer the concept of interpolation from formulas to split sequents, calling a formula $\theta$ an *interpolant* for an unsatisfiable split sequent $\Gamma \mid \Xi$ if $\mathsf{Voc}(\theta) \subseteq \mathsf{Voc}(\Gamma) \cap \mathsf{Voc}(\Xi)$, and both sequents $\Gamma \mid \theta$ and $\overline{\theta} \mid \Xi$ are unsatisfiable. Since we have $\varphi \models \psi$ iff $\overline{\psi} \mid \varphi$ is unsatisfiable, it is easy to see that a formula $\theta$ is an interpolant for the formulas $\varphi$ and $\psi$ iff it is an interpolant for the split sequent $\overline{\psi} \mid \varphi$. By the completeness of the split sequent system it therefore suffices to prove the following result.

**Theorem 19.** *If* $\vdash \Gamma \mid \varXi$ *then the split sequent* $\Gamma \mid \varXi$ *has an interpolant.*

The proof of Theorem 19 easily follows from the Lemmas 20 and 21 below. The key notion in the proof is that of a *cluster*; to introduce clusters, let $s, t$ be nodes in a uniform $\mathsf{SCPDL}_f$ proof $\pi$. We define the relation $\equiv_c$ by putting:

$$s \equiv_c t \text{ iff } s \vartriangleleft^* t \text{ and } t \vartriangleleft^* s.$$

It is easily verified that the relation $\equiv_c$ is an equivalence relation, whose equivalence classes, called *clusters*, are the maximal strongly connected components of $\vartriangleleft$. Non-singleton clusters are called *proper*. Note that for any pair $s, t$ of nodes of a proper cluster there are $\vartriangleleft$-paths from $s$ to $t$ and vice versa. Every proper cluster of $\pi$ is in fact a *subtree* of the underlying tree of $\pi$, in the sense that the structure $(C, \lessdot\!\upharpoonright_C)$ is a tree itself (here $\lessdot\!\upharpoonright_C$ denotes the parent-child relation of $\pi$, restricted to $C$). In particular, every proper cluster has a root. We refer to the children of $C$-nodes which lie outside of $C$ as the *exit nodes* of $C$—in the case of a singleton cluster these are just the children of the cluster's unique member.

We prove Theorem 19 by induction on the size of the derivation of $\Gamma \mid \varXi$. Lemma 20 takes care of leaves and of the induction step in the case where the root of the derivation forms a singleton cluster. We omit its proof, which is a straightforward adaptation of Maehara's method for well-founded proofs.

**Lemma 20.** *Let* $\pi$ *be an* $\mathsf{SCPDL}_f$ *proof of* $\Gamma \mid \varXi$. *Assume that the root* $r$ *of* $\pi$ *forms a singleton cluster, and that for every child* $t$ *of* $r$ *we have an interpolant* $\theta_t$ *for the split sequent* $\Lambda_t^l \mid \Lambda_t^r$. *Then* $\Gamma \mid \varXi$ *has an interpolant.*

The key task is to obtain interpolants for the roots of proper clusters.

**Lemma 21.** *Let* $\pi$ *be a uniform* $\mathsf{SCPDL}_f$ *proof of* $\Gamma \mid \varXi$, *assume that the root* $r$ *of* $\pi$ *belongs to a proper cluster* $C$, *and that for every exit node* $t$ *of* $C$ *we have an interpolant* $\theta_t$ *for the split sequent* $\Lambda_t^l \mid \Lambda_t^r$. *Then* $\Gamma \mid \varXi$ *has an interpolant.*

Fix $\pi, C, r, \Gamma, \varXi$ for the remainder of the paper.

For reasons of symmetry we may confine our attention to the case where $\varXi$ is focused. Furthermore, we will assume that $\Gamma$ is non-empty, since if $\Gamma = \emptyset$ we may simply define the interpolant to be the formula $\bot$.

**Proper Clusters.** We first discuss proper clusters in some more detail. Let

$$C^+ := C \cup \{s \in \pi \mid t \lessdot s, \text{ for some } t \in C\}$$

be the set of nodes that either belong to $C$ or are the child of a node in $C$. Then $C^+ \backslash C$ is the set of exit nodes of $C$. The following lemma will be used implicitly.

**Lemma 22.** *For all* $t \in C$, *the following hold: (1)* $\Lambda_t^r$ *and* $\Lambda_t^l$ *are both non-empty; (2)* $\Lambda_t^r$ *is focused; (3) all children of* $t$ *are in* $C^+$, *and at least one is in* $C$; *(4) if a right rule is applied at* $t$ *then* $\Lambda_t^r \neq \Lambda_u^r$, *for every child* $u$ *of* $t$.

**Definition 23.** *We let $\mathcal{F}_C$ denote the sets of sequents occurring as a right component in $C$, namely $\mathcal{F}_C := \{\Lambda_t^r \mid t \in C\}$, and likewise for $\mathcal{F}_{C^+}$. Given a sequent $\Delta \in \mathcal{F}_{C^+}$, we define $C_\Delta := \{t \in C \mid \Lambda_t^r = \Delta\}$, $C_\Delta^+ := \{t \in C^+ \mid \Lambda_t^r = \Delta\}$ and we let $C_\Delta^l$ ($C_\Delta^r$, respectively), denote the set of nodes in $C_\Delta$ where a left rule (a right rule, respectively) is applied.*

**Lemma 24.** *For all sequents $\Delta$, the following hold:*

1. *$C_\Delta = C_\Delta^l \uplus C_\Delta^r$.*
2. *If $t \in C_\Delta^l$ then the rule applied at $t$ is not the modal rule.*
3. *If $t \in C_\Delta^l$ then all of its children belong to $C_\Delta^+$, and at least one to $C_\Delta$.*
4. *If $C_\Delta$ is not empty then $C_\Delta^r$ is not empty.*

By uniformity of $\pi$, for each $\Delta \in \mathcal{F}_C$ there is a unique right rule $R_\Delta$ which is applied at each $t \in C_\Delta^r$ (provided $C_\Delta^r \neq \emptyset$). If $R_\Delta$ is the modal rule we call $\Delta$ a modal sequent. If $\Delta \in \mathcal{F}_{C^+} \setminus \mathcal{F}_C$, we call $\Delta$ an exit sequent.

**Lemma 25.** *If $\Delta$ is neither a modal nor an exit sequent then there are sequents $\Pi_1, \ldots, \Pi_n$ such that $\bigwedge \Delta \equiv \bigvee_i \bigwedge \Pi_i$, and, for all $t \in C_\Delta^r$, the children of $t$ can be listed as $u_1, \ldots, u_n$ such that $\Lambda_{u_i}^l = \Lambda_t^l \mid \Pi_i$, for all $i = 1, \ldots, n$.*

**Quasi-proofs.** We can now introduce the pivotal structure in our interpolation proof: the *quasi-proof* $\mathsf{Q} = (Q, <_\mathsf{Q}, k, \Psi)$ associated with the cluster $C$. Roughly, $\mathsf{Q}$ is a finite labeled tree that represents the focused part of $C$. In particular, its labeling is a map $\Psi : Q \to \mathcal{F}_{C^+}$ that respects the labeling of $C$ as suggested by Lemma 25; also, any node labeled with an exit sequent is a leaf of $\mathsf{Q}$. To ensure that $\mathsf{Q}$ is based on a *finite* tree, we make sure that every repeat node is a leaf.

To explain the role of the typing map $k$ in $\mathsf{Q}$, note that the purpose of $\mathsf{Q}$ is to help find an interpolant for the root $r$ of $C$. We will do this by inductively associating with each node in $\mathsf{Q}$ an auxiliary formula that we will call a *pre-interpolant*. To facilitate this definition we construct $\mathsf{Q}$ in such a way that its internal nodes come in *triples*. The subsequent nodes of such a triple are all labeled with the same sequent in $\mathcal{F}_{C^+}$, but they have a different *type* (respectively, 1, 2 and 3). This typing will play a role in the actual definition of the pre-interpolants.

**Definition 26.** *Given the cluster $C$ we construct a structure $\mathsf{Q} = (Q, <_\mathsf{Q}, k, \Psi)$, called a* quasi-proof, *step by step. Here $(Q, <_\mathsf{Q})$ will be a finite tree, $k : Q \to \{1, 2, 3\}$ types the nodes of $\mathsf{Q}$ and $\Psi : Q \to \mathcal{F}_{C^+}$ is a labeling.*

*To start the construction, we put a root node $r_\mathsf{Q}$ in $\mathsf{Q}$ and let $r_\mathsf{Q}$ have type 1 and label $\Xi$. Inductively, given a node $x \in Q$, define the children of $x$ as follows:*

**Case** $k(x) = 1$. *If $x$ is a repeat in $\mathsf{Q}$ (i.e., there exists $y \in Q$ such that $y$ is an ancestor of $x$ and $\Psi_x = \Psi_y$) or an exit (i.e., $\Psi_x$ is an exit sequent), then $x$ is a leaf. Otherwise, $x$ has a unique child with type 2 and label $\Psi_x$.*
**Case** $k(x) = 2$. *Then $x$ has a unique child with type 3 and label $\Psi_x$.*
**Case** $k(x) = 3$. *In this case[4] $C_{\Psi_x}^r \neq \emptyset$. If $\Psi_x$ is modal, say, it is of the form $\langle a \rangle \varphi^f, [a]\Sigma, \Pi$ then $x$ has a unique child $y$ with type 1 and label $\varphi^f, \Sigma, \langle \breve{a} \rangle \Pi$.*

---

[4] Every type-3 node is the grandchild of a type-1 node with the same label, but any type-1 node $z$ such that $C_{\Psi_z}^r = \emptyset$ is a leaf.

If $\Psi_x$ is not modal then by Lemma 25 there exist $\Pi_1, \ldots, \Pi_n$ such that $\bigwedge \Psi_x \equiv \bigvee_i \bigwedge \Pi_i$ and for all $t \in C^r_{\Psi_x}$, the children of $t$ can be listed as $u_1, \ldots, u_n$ with $\Lambda_{u_i} = \Lambda^l_t \mid \Pi_i$, for all $i$. We define the children of $x$ in $Q$ as $y_1, \ldots, y_n$, where each $y_i$ has type 1 and label $\Pi_i$.

Given the repeat condition it is fairly easy to check that $Q$ is a finite tree.

**Definition 27.** We let $<_Q$ and $\leq_Q$ denote, respectively, the transitive and the reflexive-transitive closure of $\lessdot_Q$. For a repeat leaf $z \in Q$, we let $c(z)$ be the *companion* of $z$, defined as the unique node $x$ such that $x <_Q z$, $k(x) = k(z) = 1$ and $\Psi_x = \Psi_z$. We let $\mathsf{L}_Q$ and $\mathsf{K}_Q$ denote, respectively, the sets of repeats and companions of $Q$, in particular $\mathsf{K}_Q := \{c(z) \mid z \in \mathsf{L}_Q\}$. Given $x \in Q$ we set

$$\mathsf{L}_{<x} := \{z \in \mathsf{L}_Q \mid c(z) <_Q x \leq_Q z\} \quad \text{and} \quad \mathsf{K}_{<x} := \{c(z) \mid z \in \mathsf{L}_{<x}\}.$$

A *repeat path* in $Q$ is a sequence of the form $(x_k)_{0 \leq k \leq n}$ such that for some leaf $z$ we have $x_0 = c(z)$, $x_n = z$ and $x_i \lessdot_Q x_{i+1}$ for all $i < n$.

**Lemma 28.** *Let $Q$ be a quasi-proof and let $x \in Q$. Then the following hold:*

1. *$\Psi_x$ is focused.*
2. *If $x$ is a leaf or a companion node in $Q$, then $k(x) = 1$.*
3. *$\mathsf{L}_{<r_Q} = \mathsf{K}_{<r_Q} = \emptyset$.*
4. *$x \notin \mathsf{K}_{<x}$.*
5. *If $x$ is not a companion then $\mathsf{L}_{<x} = \bigcup_{x \lessdot_Q y} \mathsf{L}_{<y}$ and $\mathsf{K}_{<x} = \bigcup_{x \lessdot_Q y} \mathsf{K}_{<y}$.*
6. *If $x$ only has one child, say, $y$, then $\mathsf{L}_{<x} \subseteq \mathsf{L}_{<y}$ and $\mathsf{K}_{<x} \subseteq \mathsf{K}_{<y}$.*
7. *Every repeat path features nodes with distinct formulas in focus.*

As mentioned before, each node $x$ in $Q$ represents a certain (not necessarily connected) subset $R_x$ of $C^+$, which we call its *region*:

$$R_x := \begin{cases} C^+_{\Psi_x} & \text{if } k(x) = 1, 2 \\ C^r_{\Psi_x} & \text{if } k(x) = 3. \end{cases}$$

**Lemma 29.** *Let $x \in Q$ with $k(x) = 3$. If we list the children of $x \in Q$ as $z_1, \ldots, z_n$ then for all $t \in R_x$, the children of $t$ may be listed as $s_1, \ldots, s_n$ so that $s_i \in R_{z_i}$ for all $1 \leq i \leq n$.*

**Pre-interpolants and the Interpolant.** We are now ready to define the interpolant $\theta_r$ for the root $r$ of $C$. The key idea underlying this definition is to first associate with each node $x$ in the quasi-proof $Q$ a so-called *pre-interpolant* $\iota_x$. These pre-interpolants are auxiliary formulas that will be defined by a leaf-to-root induction on the tree $(Q, <_Q)$; once we have arrived at the root $r_Q$ of $Q$ we simply define the interpolant $\theta_r$ as $\theta_r := \iota_{r_Q}$. For the definition of these pre-interpolants we extend the language with a set $\{q_x \mid x \in K_Q\}$ of internal variables, and with every set $\Delta \in \mathcal{F}_{C^+}$ we associate an 'exit interpolant':

$$\theta_\Delta := \bigwedge \{\theta_t \mid t \in C^+_\Delta \setminus C_\Delta\}.$$

**Definition 30.** *By a leaf-to-root induction, we define for all nodes $x, y \in Q$ a formula $\psi_x$ and a family of programs $\{\alpha_{x,y} \mid y \in \mathsf{K}_{<x}\}$. In all applicable cases, $z$ denotes the unique successor of $x$, and in the case where $x$ is a modal node of type 3, $a$ denotes the leading atomic program of the formula in focus in $\Psi_x$. Note that for exit nodes $x$, we have $\mathsf{K}_{<x} = \emptyset$, so no definition of $\alpha_{x,y}$ is required.*

| Case | $\psi_x$ | $\alpha_{x,y}$ |
|---|---|---|
| $x$ is a repeat | $\bot$ | $\top?$ |
| $x$ is an exit | $\theta_{\Psi_x}$ | – |
| $x$ is a companion | $\langle \alpha^*_{z,x} \rangle \psi_z$ | $\alpha^*_{z,x}; \alpha_{z,y}$ |
| $x$ is otherwise of type 1 | $\psi_z$ | $\alpha_{z,y}$ |
| $x$ is of type 2 | $\langle \theta_{\Psi_x}? \rangle \psi_z$ | $\theta_{\Psi_x}?; \alpha_{z,y}$ |
| $x$ is of type 3, not modal | $\bigvee \{\psi_z \mid x <_\mathsf{Q} z\}$ | $\bigcup \{\alpha_{z,y} \mid x <_\mathsf{Q} z, y \in \mathsf{K}_{<z}\}$ |
| $x$ is of type 3, modal | $\langle a \rangle \psi_z$ | $a; \alpha_{z,y}$ |

*Based on these expressions the* pre-interpolant $\iota_x$ *of a node $x \in Q$ is defined as:*

$$\iota_x := \psi_x \vee \bigvee_{y \in \mathsf{K}_{<x}} \langle \alpha_{x,y} \rangle q_y.$$

Note that the programs $\alpha_{x,y}$ and formulas $\psi_x$ do not contain internal variables.

**Definition 31.** *We define the interpolant $\theta_r$ of the root $r$ of the cluster $C$ as*

$$\theta_r := \iota_{r_\mathsf{Q}}.$$

## 7 Correctness of the Interpolant

To prove Lemma 21 and thereby establish the Craig interpolation property for CPDL, we verify that the formula $\theta_r$ from Definition 31 satisfies the requirements of an interpolant for $\Gamma \mid \Xi$. The vocabulary condition is straightforward and omitted. The remaining conditions are proved in Lemmas 35 and 38, respectively. We need an auxiliary lemma that follows from the assumptions of Lemma 21.

**Lemma 32.** *For any exit sequent $\Delta$ we have that $\vdash \overline{\theta_\Delta} \mid \Delta$ and $\vdash \Lambda^l_t \mid \theta_\Delta$, for all $t \in C^+_\Delta \setminus C_\Delta$.*

In the proof of $\vdash \Gamma \mid \theta_r$ we also need the following definition and lemma.

**Definition 33.** *Let $\pi$ be some split proof, possibly with assumptions. We call $\pi$ right-focused if the path from the root of $\pi$ to any of its assumptions is right-focused (that is, the right component of each node on such a path is focused).*

**Lemma 34.** *Let $\mathcal{S}$ and $\mathcal{A}$ be finite sets of respectively (unfocused) sequents and split sequents, let $\alpha$ be some program, $q$ a proposition not occurring in either $\mathcal{S}, \mathcal{A}$ or $\alpha$, and $\chi$ some formula. Assume that for every $\Sigma \in \mathcal{S}$ there are right-focused proofs $\pi_\Sigma : \{\Pi \mid q^f : \Pi \in \mathcal{S}\} \vdash \Sigma \mid \langle\alpha\rangle q^f$ and $\rho_\Sigma : \mathcal{A} \vdash \Sigma \mid \chi^\circ$. Then we may construct a right-focused proof witnessing that $\mathcal{A} \vdash \Sigma \mid \langle\alpha^*\rangle\chi^\circ$.*

Note that assumption-free proofs are automatically right-focused, and that $\rho_\Sigma : \mathcal{A} \vdash \Sigma \mid \chi^u$ can only be right-focused if $\mathcal{A} = \emptyset$.

**Lemma 35.** $\vdash \Gamma \mid \theta_r$.

*Proof.* The intuition underlying the proof is to show, by means of a leaf-to-root induction, that for each node $x$ of $\mathsf{Q}$ and for each $t \in R_x$ we can find a right-focused proof $\pi : \mathcal{C}_x \vdash \Lambda_t^l \mid \iota_x^f$, where $\mathcal{C}_x$ is some suitable set of assumptions. In the case where $x$ is a companion, the idea is to *discharge* some of the assumptions, so that, when we arrive at the root $r_\mathsf{Q}$ of $\mathsf{Q}$ we obtain an assumption-free proof of the split sequent $\Lambda_t^l \mid \iota_{r_\mathsf{Q}}^f = \Gamma \mid \theta_r^f$. For a proper proof-theoretic execution of this elimination procedure we need to prove a somewhat stronger claim, which involves separate statements on the constituting parts of the pre-interpolants.

*Claim.* For all $x \in Q$, for all $y \in \mathsf{K}_{<x}$ and all $t \in R_x$ we have that (1) $\vdash \Lambda_t^l \mid \psi_x^u$ and (2) there is a right-focused proof of $\Lambda_t^l \mid \langle\alpha_{x,y}\rangle q_y^f$ with assumptions $\mathcal{A}_y := \{(\Lambda_s^l \mid q_y^f) \mid s \in R_y\}$.

*Proof (of Claim).* We prove the Claim by a leaf-to-root induction on $x$. For the base case we treat only the case where $x$ is an exit. Then $\mathsf{K}_{<x} = \emptyset$, so it suffices to show $\vdash \Lambda_t^l \mid \psi_x^u$. But since, by definition, $\psi_x = \theta_{\Psi_x}$, this follows from Lemma 35.

For the induction step we treat only the case where $x$ is a companion and prove item (2). Then $x$ has a unique child $z$ and $\mathsf{K}_{<z} = \mathsf{K}_{<x} \cup \{x\}$ and $\alpha_{x,y} = \alpha_{z,x}^*; \alpha_{z,y}$. Let $y$ and $t$ be as in the claim, and note that $y \neq x$ since $x \notin \mathsf{K}_{<x}$ (Lemma 28). By the induction hypothesis on $z$ we have right-focused proofs witnessing $\{\Lambda_s^l \mid q_x^f : s \in R_x\} \vdash \Lambda_t^l \mid \langle\alpha_{z,x}\rangle q_x^f$ and $\mathcal{A}_y \vdash \Lambda^l \mid \langle\alpha_{z,y}\rangle q_y^f$. Then we may apply Lemma 34, with $\mathcal{A} = \mathcal{A}_y$, $\mathcal{S} = \{\Lambda_s^l : s \in R_x\}$, $\alpha = \alpha_{z,x}$, $q = q_x$ and $\chi = \langle\alpha_{z,y}\rangle q_y$. This yields a right-focused proof witnessing $\mathcal{A}_y \vdash \Lambda^l \mid \langle\alpha_{z,x}^*\rangle\langle\alpha_{z,y}\rangle q_y^f$, so that with one right application of $\langle;\rangle$ we find that $\mathcal{A}_y \vdash \Lambda^l \mid \langle\alpha_{z,x}^*; \alpha_{z,y}\rangle q_y^f$. This suffices, since we have $\alpha_{x,y} = \alpha_{z,x}^*; \alpha_{z,y}$. This finishes the proof of the Claim.

Now consider the root $r_\mathsf{Q}$ of $\mathsf{Q}$. Since we have $\mathsf{K}_{<r_\mathsf{Q}} = \emptyset$ the Claim yields that $\vdash \Lambda_t^l \mid \psi_{r_\mathsf{Q}}^u$ for all $t \in R_{r_\mathsf{Q}}$. In particular, the root $r$ of the cluster $C$ belongs to $R_{r_\mathsf{Q}}$ and, since $\Lambda_r^l = \Gamma$, we find that $\vdash \Gamma \mid \psi_{r_\mathsf{Q}}^u$. Finally, unravelling the definitions we find that $\theta_r = \iota_{r_\mathsf{Q}}$, and, again since $\mathsf{K}_{<r_\mathsf{Q}} = \emptyset$, that $\iota_{r_\mathsf{Q}} = \psi_{r_\mathsf{Q}} \vee \bot$. But then from $\vdash \Gamma \mid \psi_{r_\mathsf{Q}}^u$ we easily obtain $\vdash \Gamma \mid \theta_r$, as required.

The second interpolation condition states that the split sequent $\overline{\theta_r} \mid \Xi$ is unsatisfiable. We will show this by providing an actual derivation as well, but here we use the unrestricted cut rule. We let $\vdash^c$ denote derivability in the version of $\mathsf{SCPDL}_f$ where we allow the unrestricted cut rules $\mathsf{cut}^l$ and $\mathsf{cut}^r$.

Before providing the proof that $\vdash^c \overline{\theta_r} \mid \Xi$, we first state the following definition and lemma, with the purpose of simplifying the proofs.

**Definition 36.** *Let $x$ be a node in $Q$, and let $\rho : \mathcal{A} \vdash^c \Sigma^l \mid \Sigma^r$ be a proof with assumptions. We say that $\rho$ is $(Q,x)$-shaped if $\mathcal{A} = \{(\overline{q_y}^u \mid \Psi_y) \mid y \in \mathsf{K}_{<x}\}$, $\Sigma^r = \Psi_x$ and for every open leaf $\ell$ of $\rho$ labeled with an assumption $\overline{q_y}^u \mid \Psi_y$ there is a repeat $z$ in $Q$ with $c(z) = y$, and such that the list of formulas in focus on the $Q$-path from $x$ to $z$ is, up to repetitions, equal to the list of formulas in focus on the path in $\rho$ from the root to $\ell$.*

**Lemma 37.** *Let $\varphi$ and $\psi$ be equivalent CPDL formulas. Then we can transform any $(Q,x)$-shaped proof $\rho : \mathcal{A} \vdash^c \varphi^u \mid \Delta$ into a $(Q,x)$-shaped proof $\rho' : \mathcal{A} \vdash^c \psi^u \mid \Delta$.*

*Proof.* By completeness, there is a proof $\sigma$ of the split sequent $\overline{\varphi}^u, \psi^u \mid \Delta$. Using this, we construct the desired proof as follows:

$$\rho': \quad \mathsf{cut}^l \frac{\begin{array}{c} \mathcal{A} \\ \vdots \rho \\ \varphi^u \mid \Delta \end{array} \quad \begin{array}{c} \vdots \sigma \\ \overline{\varphi}^u, \psi^u \mid \Delta \end{array}}{\psi^u \mid \Delta}$$

It is easy to verify that $\rho'$ is $(Q,x)$-shaped if $\rho$ is so. This concludes the proof.

**Lemma 38.** $\vdash^c \overline{\theta_r} \mid \Xi$.

*Proof.* By a leaf-to-root induction on $Q$ we will prove the following claim, where we write $\mathcal{B}_x := \{(\overline{q_y}^u \mid \Psi_y) \mid y \in \mathsf{K}_{<x}\}$.

*Claim.* For every $x \in Q$ there is a $(Q,x)$-shaped proof $\pi_x : \mathcal{B}_x \vdash^c \overline{\iota_x}^u \mid \Psi_x$.

*Proof (of Claim).*

**Case $x$ is a repeat.** Here we have $\mathsf{K}_{<x} = \emptyset$ and thus $\mathcal{B}_x = \{(\overline{q_{c(x)}}^u \mid \Psi_x)\}$. By definition, $\iota_x = \psi_x \vee \langle \alpha_{x,c(x)} \rangle q_{c(x)}$, where $\alpha_{x,c(x)} = \top?$ and $\psi_x = \bot$. It is then straightforward to find a (cut-free) $(Q,x)$-shaped proof $\pi_x : \mathcal{B}_x \vdash \overline{\iota_x}^u \mid \Psi_x$.

**Case $x$ is an exit.** By definition we have $\iota_x = \theta_{\Psi_x}$ and by Lemma 32 that $\vdash \overline{\theta_{\Psi_x}}^u \mid \Psi_x$.

**Case $x$ is a companion.** Here $x$ has a unique child $z$, for which we have $\Psi_x = \Psi_z$; we will write $\Psi := \Psi_x$. Furthermore recall that by the definition of pre-interpolants we have $\iota_x \equiv \iota_z[\iota_x/q_x]$. By completeness this means that there is some proof $\rho : \vdash \overline{\iota_x}^u, \iota_z[\iota_x/q_x]^u \mid \Psi$.

By the inductive hypothesis we have a $(Q,z)$-shaped proof $\pi_z : \mathcal{B}_x \cup \{\overline{q_x}^u \mid \Psi\} \vdash^c \overline{\iota_z}^u \mid \Psi$. Substituting $q_x$ with $\iota_x$ everywhere in $\pi_z$ we obtain a proof $\pi_z[\iota_x]$ which we may cut with $\rho$ to obtain the following proof $\pi_x$ with assumptions:

$$\pi_x \quad \mathsf{cut}^l \frac{\begin{array}{c} \mathcal{B}_x \cup \{\overline{\iota_x}^u \mid \Psi\} \\ \vdots \pi_z[\iota_x] \\ \overline{\iota_z[\iota_x/q_x]}^u \mid \Psi \end{array} \quad \begin{array}{c} \vdots \rho \\ \iota_z[\iota_x/q_x]^u, \overline{\iota_x}^u \mid \Psi \end{array}}{\overline{\iota_x}^u \mid \Psi}$$

Note that all paths from the root of $\pi_x$ to assumptions of the form $\overline{\iota_x}^u \mid \Psi$ are successful, because $\pi_z$ is $(Q,x)$-shaped and Lemma 28(7). Therefore all assumptions $\overline{\iota_x}^u \mid \Psi$ in $\pi_x$ are discharged. This implies that the proof $\pi_x$ : $\mathcal{B}_x \vdash^c \overline{\iota_x}^u \mid \Psi$ is $(Q,x)$-shaped.

**Case $k(x) = 1$, $x$ is neither a leaf nor a companion.** In this case $x$ has a unique child $z$, for which we have $\alpha_{x,y} = \alpha_{z,y}$, $\psi_x = \psi_z$ and thus $\iota_x = \iota_z$. Furthermore we have $\Psi_z = \Psi_x$ and $\mathcal{B}_z = \mathcal{B}_x$. Since $R_x = R_z$, the inductive hypothesis directly applies to $z$, providing us with a $(Q,z)$-shaped proof $\pi_z : \mathcal{B}_z \vdash^c \overline{\iota_z}^u \mid \Psi_z$. We may now simply take $\pi_x := \pi_z$.

**Case $k(x) = 2$.** In this case $x$ has a unique child $z$, for which we have $\Psi_x = \Psi_z$ and $\mathcal{B}_x = \mathcal{B}_z$. Write $\mathcal{B} := \mathcal{B}_x$ and $\Psi := \Psi_x$. By the inductive hypothesis we have a $(Q,z)$-shaped proof $\pi_z : \mathcal{B} \vdash^c \overline{\iota_z}^u \mid \Psi$, and by Lemma 32 we have $\vdash \overline{\theta_\Psi}^u \mid \Psi$.

Applying the $[?]^l$ rule we obtain a $(Q,z)$-shaped proof witnessing that $\mathcal{B} \vdash^c [\theta_\Psi ?]\overline{\iota_z}^u \mid \Delta$. It is straightforward to verify that $[\theta_\Psi ?]\overline{\iota_z} \equiv \overline{\iota_x}$. But then by Lemma 37 we obtain the desired proof $\pi_x : \mathcal{B} \vdash^c \overline{\iota_x}^u \mid \Psi$.

**Case $k(x) = 3$, $\Psi_x$ is not modal.** In this case $x$ has $n > 0$ children $z_1, \ldots, z_n$ in Q. Recall that by the uniformity of $\pi$, the same right rule R is applied at each $t \in C^r_{\Psi_x} = R_x$.

By the inductive hypothesis, for each $z_i$, we have a $(Q,z_i)$-shaped proof of $\mathcal{B}_{z_i} \vdash^c \overline{\iota_{z_i}}^u \mid \Psi_{z_i}$. By repeated applications of the rules weak$^l$ and $\wedge^l$, we obtain, for each $z_i$, a $(Q,z_i)$-shaped proof of $\pi_{z_i} : \mathcal{B}_{z_i} \vdash^c \bigwedge_{1 \leq i \leq n} \overline{\iota_{z_i}}^u \mid \Psi_{z_i}$. By an application of the rule R we obtain a $(Q,x)$-shaped proof

$$\pi_x : \bigcup_{1 \leq i \leq n} \mathcal{B}_{z_i} \vdash^c \bigwedge_{1 \leq i \leq n} \overline{\iota_{z_i}}^u \mid \Psi_x$$

By Lemma 28, it follows that $\bigcup_{1 \leq i \leq n} \mathcal{B}_{z_i} = \mathcal{B}_x$ and thus, that $\pi_x : \mathcal{B}_x \vdash^c \bigwedge_{1 \leq i \leq n} \overline{\iota_{z_i}}^u \mid \Psi_x$.

It is easy to see that $\bigwedge_{1 \leq i \leq n} \overline{\iota_{z_i}} \equiv \overline{\iota_x}$, and therefore Lemma 37, concludes the case.

**Case $k(x) = 3$, $\Psi_x$ is modal.** In this case $x$ has a unique child $z$, for which we have $\iota_x \equiv \langle a \rangle \iota_z$ and $\mathcal{B}_x = \mathcal{B}_z$. Write $\mathcal{B} = \mathcal{B}_x$. By the inductive hypothesis there exists a $(Q,z)$-shaped proof of $\mathcal{B} \vdash^c \overline{\iota_z}^u \mid \Psi_z$. By an application of the rule $\langle a \rangle^r$ to the formula in focus in $\Psi_z$ we obtain a $(Q,x)$-shaped proof $\mathcal{B} \vdash^c [a]\overline{\iota_z}^u \mid \Psi_x$. But since we have $[a]\overline{\iota_z} \equiv \overline{\iota_x}$, we may use Lemma 37 to transform this proof into a $(Q,x)$-shaped proof of $\mathcal{B} \vdash^c \overline{\iota_x}^u \mid \Psi_x$, as required.

This finishes the proof of the Claim.

To finish the proof of Lemma 38, for the root $r_Q$ of Q the Claim yields that $\mathcal{B}_{r_Q} \vdash^c \overline{\iota_{r_Q}}^u \mid \Psi_{r_Q}$. But since $K_{<r_Q} = \emptyset$, we find $\mathcal{B}_{r_Q} = \emptyset$, and as $\Psi_{r_Q} = \Xi$ and $\theta_r = \iota_{r_Q}$, we may conclude that $\vdash^c \overline{\theta_r} \mid \Xi$, as required.

## 8 Conclusions

We presented a sound and complete cyclic proof system for CPDL and used it to show that the logic enjoys the Craig Interpolation Property. As a corollary we established that CPDL also has the Beth Definability Property.

With some minor modifications we can make our approach work to prove interpolation for PDL itself as well. First, we simplify the rule $\langle a \rangle$ to the standard rule for (one-way) modal logic:

$$\frac{\varphi^f, \Sigma}{\langle a \rangle \varphi^f, [a]\Sigma, \Gamma}$$

We then verify that, with minor adaptations (that are in fact simplifications), the completeness proof still holds. Finally, we observe that the current definition of the interpolant will not involve the use of the converse modality, and check that the correctness proofs for the interpolant can be adapted to the system with the new modal rule. We hope to supply the details of this approach in an expanded version of this paper.

Finally, it would be interesting to see whether one can find a proof system for CPDL, such that the proof of correctness of the interpolant can be proven inside the system without the need of adding unrestricted cut. Achieving this seems to require adding admissible rules to $CPDL_f$. Another open question is whether our method can be extended to other variants of PDL such as PDL with intersection [12] or deterministic PDL [3].

## References

1. Afshari, B., Leigh, G.E.: Lyndon interpolation for modal $\mu$-calculus. In: Özgün, A., Zinova, Y. (eds.) TbiLLC 2019. LNCS, vol. 13206, pp. 197–213. Springer, Cham (2022). https://doi.org/10.1007/978-3-030-98479-3_10
2. Baader, F., Lutz, C.: Description logics. In: Blackburn, P., van Benthem, J., Wolter, F. (eds.) Handbook of Modal Logic, Studies in logic and practical reasoning, vol. 3, pp. 757–820. North-Holland (2007). https://doi.org/10.1016/S1570-2464(07)80015-2
3. Ben-Ari, M., Halpern, J.Y., Pnueli, A.: Deterministic propositional dynamic logic: finite models, complexity, and completeness. J. Comput. Syst. Sci. **25**(3), 402–417 (1982). https://doi.org/10.1016/0022-0000(82)90018-6
4. Borzechowski, M.: Tableau-Kalkül für PDL und Interpolation. Master's thesis, Department of Mathematics, Freie Universität Berlin (1988)
5. Borzechowski, M., Gattinger, M., Hansen, H.H., Ramanayake, R., Dalmas, V.T., Venema, Y.: Propositional dynamic logic has Craig interpolation: a tableau-based proof (2025). https://arxiv.org/abs/2503.13526
6. Cate, B., Franconi, E., Seylan, I.: Beth definability in expressive description logics. J. Artif. Intell. Res. **48**, 347–414 (2013). https://doi.org/10.1613/JAIR.4057
7. Emerson, E., Jutla, C.: The complexity of tree automata and logics of programs. SIAM J. Comput. **29**(1), 132–158 (1999)

8. Fischer, M.J., Ladner, R.E.: Propositional dynamic logic of regular programs. J. Comput. Syst. Sci. **18**(2), 194–211 (1979). https://doi.org/10.1016/0022-0000(79)90046-1
9. Gabbay, D.M., Maksimova, L.: Interpolation and Definability: Modal and Intuitionistic Logics. Oxford University Press (2005)
10. Jung, J.C., Lutz, C., Pulcini, H., Wolter, F.: Separating data examples by description logic concepts with restricted signatures. In: Proceedings of the 18th International Conference on Principles of Knowledge Representation and Reasoning, KR (2021). https://doi.org/10.24963/KR.2021/37
11. Kloibhofer, J., Venema, Y.: Interpolation for the two-way modal $\mu$-calculus. In: 40th Annual ACM/IEEE Symposium on Logic in Computer Science (LICS 2025) (2025). to appear
12. Lutz, C.: PDL with intersection and converse is decidable. In: Ong, L. (ed.) CSL 2005. LNCS, vol. 3634, pp. 413–427. Springer, Heidelberg (2005). https://doi.org/10.1007/11538363_29
13. Marti, J., Venema, Y.: Focus-style proof systems and interpolation for the alternation-free $\mu$-calculus. CoRR **abs/2103.01671** (2021). https://arxiv.org/abs/2103.01671
14. McMillan, K.L.: Applications of craig interpolants in model checking. In: Halbwachs, N., Zuck, L.D. (eds.) TACAS 2005. LNCS, vol. 3440, pp. 1–12. Springer, Heidelberg (2005). https://doi.org/10.1007/978-3-540-31980-1_1
15. Mostowski, A.: Games with forbidden positions (1991), technical Report 78, Instytut Matematyki, Uniwersytet Gdański, Poland
16. Parikh, R.: The completeness of propositional dynamic logic. In: Winkowski, J. (ed.) MFCS 1978. LNCS, vol. 64, pp. 403–415. Springer, Heidelberg (1978). https://doi.org/10.1007/3-540-08921-7_88
17. Pratt, V.: A near-optimal method for reasoning about action. J. Comput. Syst. Sci. **20**, 231–254 (1980). https://doi.org/10.1016/0022-0000(80)90061-6
18. Renardel de Lavalette, G.R.: Interpolation in computing science: the semantics of modularization. Synthese **164**(3), 437–450 (2008). https://doi.org/10.1007/S11229-008-9358-Y
19. Segerberg, K.: A completeness theorem in the modal logic of programs. Not. Am. Math. Soc. **24**, 522 (1977). http://eudml.org/doc/209235
20. Shamkanov, D.S.: Circular proofs for the Gödel-Löb provability logic. Math. Notes **96**(3–4), 575–585 (2014). https://doi.org/10.1134/s0001434614090326
21. Troquard, N., Balbiani, P.: Propositional dynamic logic. In: Zalta, E.N., Nodelman, U. (eds.) The Stanford Encyclopedia of Philosophy. Metaphysics Research Lab, Stanford University, Fall 2023 edn. (2023). https://plato.stanford.edu/archives/fall2023/entries/logic-dynamic/

**Open Access** This chapter is licensed under the terms of the Creative Commons Attribution 4.0 International License (http://creativecommons.org/licenses/by/4.0/), which permits use, sharing, adaptation, distribution and reproduction in any medium or format, as long as you give appropriate credit to the original author(s) and the source, provide a link to the Creative Commons license and indicate if changes were made.

The images or other third party material in this chapter are included in the chapter's Creative Commons license, unless indicated otherwise in a credit line to the material. If material is not included in the chapter's Creative Commons license and your intended use is not permitted by statutory regulation or exceeds the permitted use, you will need to obtain permission directly from the copyright holder.

# Semi-competitive Differential Game Logic

### Julia Butte[✉][id] and André Platzer[id]

Karlsruhe Institute of Technology, Karlsruhe, Germany
{julia.butte,platzer}@kit.edu

**Abstract.** This paper introduces *semi-competitive differential game logic* $\mathsf{dG\mathcal{L}}_{sc}$, which enables verification of safety-critical applications that involve interactions between two agents. In $\mathsf{dG\mathcal{L}}_{sc}$, these interactions are specified as games on hybrid systems with two players that *may* collaborate with each other when helpful and *may* compete when necessary. The players in the hybrid games of $\mathsf{dG\mathcal{L}}_{sc}$ have individual goals that may overlap, leading to nonzero-sum games. This makes $\mathsf{dG\mathcal{L}}_{sc}$ especially well-suited for verifying situations where players, e.g., share safety objectives but otherwise pursue different goals, so that zero-sum assumptions lead to overly conservative results. Additionally, $\mathsf{dG\mathcal{L}}_{sc}$ solves the subtlety that even though each player may benefit from knowledge of the other player's goals, e.g., concerning shared safety objectives, unsafe situations might still occur if every player were to mutually assume the other player would act to avoid unsafety. The syntax and semantics, as well as a sound and relatively complete proof calculus are presented for $\mathsf{dG\mathcal{L}}_{sc}$. The relationship between $\mathsf{dG\mathcal{L}}_{sc}$ and zero-sum differential game logic $\mathsf{dG\mathcal{L}}$ is discussed and the purpose of $\mathsf{dG\mathcal{L}}_{sc}$ illustrated in a canonical example.

**Keywords:** Differential game logic · Hybrid systems · Hybrid games · Nonzero-sum games · Cooperative games · Competitive games

## 1 Introduction

The safety of cyber-physical systems (CPS) is of significant interest to avoid damage to persons and goods due to faulty programs [9,13,24]. Cyber-physical systems include trains, planes, robots and autonomous cars [8,13]. Particularly challenging are situations involving two CPSs, due to their possible interactions which frequently occur in aerial collision avoidance or steering of autonomous cars. To verify, for example, two planes on a collision course, different approaches can be used: The situation could be regarded as one hybrid system, and its safety verified using differential dynamic logic ($\mathsf{d\mathcal{L}}$) [12,20,21,23–25]. This corresponds to all planes being centrally controlled, which is infeasible for larger numbers of planes. Or the situation can be modeled with games, regarding each plane as a player which represents the fact that planes are normally steered independently. Collision avoidance could then be verified assuming adversarial players using differential game logic ($\mathsf{dG\mathcal{L}}$) [9,22]. This assumption results in a zero-sum game, i.e. exactly one player wins. But if one pilot is trying to avoid a collision, the intruder pilot does *not* in fact have the opposite goal of causing a collision! Flying under a zero-sum assumption gives safe but unnecessarily conservative results.

Instead, many games are non-zero-sum, where players have individual goals which often overlap. The planes, for example, both do not want to crash, but they still want to fly into different directions. Such partially shared goals open up the possibility of cooperating, which leads to new winning strategies. Alas, the possibility and will to cooperate is no guarantee that everything goes smoothly. Misunderstandings might still happen, leading for example, to unintentional crashes.

To verify the safety of these two-player non-zero sum games, this paper introduces the *semi-competitive differential game logic* ($dG\mathcal{L}_{sc}$) which offers a natural way of expressing and reasoning about non-zero sum hybrid games. $dG\mathcal{L}_{sc}$ supports players that behave *semi-competitively*, i.e., both players have individual goals and are open for cooperation but will compete if necessary. They both try to reach their goal while being aware of the other player's goal and can collaborate to jointly meet their respective goals. This strategy provides a solution to the challenging question of when players should cooperate. The possibility of cooperation adds more winning strategies thus enabling safety proofs for situations that are unsafe under conservative zero-sum game assumptions.

To underline the semantics' suitability, the paper derives an alternative representation of semi-competitive games in $dG\mathcal{L}$. Theoretically, this is possible, since all mixed (co)inductive concepts are definable in $dG\mathcal{L}$ [22]. But as $dG\mathcal{L}$ is fundamentally designed for zero-sum, this requires manual coding, causes redundancies, and duplicates verification effort.

The structure of this paper is as follows: First, Sect. 2 relates and compares relevant logics to $dG\mathcal{L}_{sc}$. After that, the logic $dG\mathcal{L}$ whose correspondence to $dG\mathcal{L}_{sc}$ will be proved later on, is reviewed in Sect. 3. Then, Sect. 4 introduces the notion of semi-competitiveness and defines the syntax and semantics of $dG\mathcal{L}_{sc}$. Section 5 establishes important properties of $dG\mathcal{L}_{sc}$ and its relation to $dG\mathcal{L}$. Afterward, a proof calculus for $dG\mathcal{L}_{sc}$ is introduced in Sect. 6 and its soundness and relative completeness proven.

## 2 Related Work

Non-zero sum games is a wide field of study that has been addressed by various communities. Game theory provides fundamental definitions of non-zero sum games and studies of their equilibria [15–17] which lay the basis for our work. In terms of game theory, the games played in $dG\mathcal{L}_{sc}$ are non-zero sum sequential games with perfect information and binary payoffs. Whether a player can reach their goal can be considered by backward induction in $dG\mathcal{L}_{sc}$, similar to the determination of a subgame perfect equilibrium [5]. But $dG\mathcal{L}_{sc}$ has the advantage that the backward induction is done without game trees, which might have uncountable, infinite breadth and unbounded depth due to continuous dynamics and consequently would be hard to handle.

In the field of synthesis, multi-player non-zero sum games played on a graph have been investigated by Fisman et al. who developed rational synthesis [10].

Although the assumptions about the players' behavior are very similar to dG$\mathcal{L}_{sc}$, their work pursues a different aim: Rational synthesis can be used to construct correct systems, while dG$\mathcal{L}_{sc}$ instead can be used to verify already existing systems.

In purely discrete settings, non-zero sum games have already been addressed by Chaterjee et al. who introduced strategy logic [7]. This is a logic that allows modelling two-player non-zero sum games played on a graph. As explicit quantifications over strategies are possible, the logic is more powerful than e.g. alternating-time temporal logic (ATL) [3] or propositional game logic [18] but also more complex. Therefore, it is better suited for theoretical investigations than for practical use, which dG$\mathcal{L}_{sc}$ supports. Additionally, continuous dynamics cannot be expressed in strategy logic.

For a hybrid setting, there exist rectangular hybrid games [11] or STORMED games [26] which both model players with hybrid automata. While STORMED games are able to express more varieties of continuous dynamics than rectangular hybrid games, it is possible for both of them to perform model checking and controller synthesis. But unlike dG$\mathcal{L}_{sc}$, both of these hybrid games assume the players to act adversarially. Another work on hybrid games which also assumes adversarial players, by Mitchell et al. [14], computes backwards reachable sets for hybrid games which resemble winning regions in dG$\mathcal{L}_{sc}$. Unlike dG$\mathcal{L}_{sc}$, they do not use a comparatively simple state-based semantics, but instead compute these sets by numerically solving Hamilton-Jacobi-Isaac partial differential equations.

Other logics dealing with multi-player settings are e.g., coalition logic [19], ATL [3] or stochastic game logic [4]. These logics are able to verify that a coalition of arbitrarily many players is able to reach a certain goal. The game that is played is defined in the semantics. That has the disadvantage that validity demands a formula to be true for all games, which is only the case for very general statements. Our logic includes the game's definition in the formula, so that safety guarantees can be made for a specific game. Furthermore, the referenced works [3,4,19] only consider reachability of outcomes, whereas our work includes goals for all players.

Agotnes et al. [2] include a preference relation in their logic but keep reachability of outcomes and their preferability separate which leaves information unused. Moreover, games are not composable whereas our logic allows modularizing games so that proofs can be reused. Additionally, the players in our work take each other's goals into account to improve their strategies.

Closest to our work are the propositional game logic developed by Parikh [18] which addresses zero-sum two-player games, and differential game logic dG$\mathcal{L}$ by Platzer [22] which extends game logic to include continuous dynamics. Relations to the $\mu$-calculus are discussed in prior work [1]. Our work takes these logics a step further by allowing non-zero sum games instead.

## 3 Preliminaries

For better understanding of the content of the paper, the logic dG$\mathcal{L}$ [22] will be recalled briefly in this section. In dG$\mathcal{L}$, there are two players called *Angel* and

*Demon*. These players play a *hybrid game* which is specified as part of a logical formula. In the following, syntax, semantics and a proof calculus for dG$\mathcal{L}$ will briefly be explained, based on the book [24].

The syntax of dG$\mathcal{L}$ is based on first-order logic. Additionally, there are two modalities $\langle\alpha\rangle P$ and $[\alpha]P$. The first one states that Angel can win the game $\alpha$ by achieving her goal $P$. The second modality means that Demon can win game $\alpha$ by reaching his goal $P$. Formally, the syntax is defined as follows:

**Table 1.** Hybrid games

| Game | Name | Meaning |
| --- | --- | --- |
| $x := e$ | Assignment game | assigns $e$ to $x$ |
| $x' = f(x) \& Q$ | Continuous game | Angel evolves ordinary differential equation (ODE) to change value of $x$ while evolution domain constraint $Q$ has to hold |
| $?Q$ | Test game | tests if Angel fulfills $Q$, if not, she loses and Demon wins automatically |
| $\alpha \cup \beta$ | Choice game | Angel chooses to play either $\alpha$ or $\beta$ |
| $\alpha; \beta$ | Sequential game | $\alpha$ and $\beta$ are played sequentially |
| $\alpha^d$ | Dual game | controls in $\alpha$ are swapped between Angel and Demon |
| $\alpha^*$ | Repetition game | $\alpha$ is played repeatedly until Angel wants to stop after finite rounds |

**Definition 1 (dG$\mathcal{L}$ Syntax).** *Formulas of* dG$\mathcal{L}$ *are defined by the grammar*

$$P, Q ::= e \geq \tilde{e} \mid \neg P \mid P \wedge Q \mid \forall x P \mid \exists x P \mid \langle\alpha\rangle P \mid [\alpha]P$$

*where $x$ is a variable, $e, \tilde{e}$ terms, $P, Q$ formulas and $\alpha$ a hybrid game (Table 1).*

The formulas are interpreted over states. Each state is a function $\omega : \mathcal{V} \to \mathbb{R}$ which assigns a real value to each variable. The variable values in state $\omega_x^r$ are the same as in $\omega$, except for $x$ whose value is $r$. The semantics is defined as a function $[\![\cdot]\!] : Fml \to \mathcal{P}(\mathcal{S})$ which returns the states where a formula is true. The semantics for the first-order formulas is as usual. The semantics for the two modalities is defined using two functions that retrace from which states a player must have started to reach their goal at the end of the game.

**Definition 2.** (Semantics) *The* dG$\mathcal{L}$ *semantics is:*

- $[\![\langle\alpha\rangle P]\!] = \varsigma_\alpha([\![P]\!])$
- $[\![[\alpha]Q]\!] = \delta_\alpha([\![Q]\!])$

*Angel's function for her winning region $\varsigma_\alpha(\cdot)$ is defined as follows:*

- $\varsigma_{x:=e}(X) = \{\omega \in \mathcal{S} \mid \omega_x^{\omega[\![e]\!]} \in X\}$

- $\varsigma_{x'=f(x)\&Q}(X) = \{\varphi(0) \in \mathcal{S} \mid \varphi(r) \in X \text{ for some } r \geq 0 \text{ and (differentiable)}$
  $\varphi : [0,r] \rightarrow \mathcal{S} \text{ such that } \varphi(s) \in [\![Q]\!] \text{ and } \frac{d\varphi(t)(x)}{dt}(s) = \varphi(s)[\![f(x)]\!] \text{ for all }$
  $0 \leq s \leq r\} \stackrel{def}{=} \{\varphi(0) \in \mathcal{S} \mid \varphi(r) \in X \text{ for some } r \geq 0 \text{ with } \varphi \models x' = f(x) \land Q\}$
- $\varsigma_{?Q}(X) = [\![Q]\!] \cap X$
- $\varsigma_{\alpha \cup \beta}(X) = \varsigma_\alpha(X) \cup \varsigma_\beta(X)$
- $\varsigma_{\alpha;\beta}(X) = \varsigma_\alpha(\varsigma_\beta(X))$
- $\varsigma_{\alpha^d}(X) = \varsigma_\alpha(X^\mathbf{C})^\mathbf{C}$
- $\varsigma_{\alpha^*}(X) = \bigcap\{Z \subseteq \mathcal{S} \mid X \cup \varsigma_\alpha(Z) \subseteq Z\}$

Demon's winning region is defined by $\delta_\alpha(X) = \varsigma_\alpha(X^\mathbf{C})^\mathbf{C}$ ([22, Th. 3.1]), i.e., Demon wins whenever Angel fails to reach the opposite of his goal, because he wins whenever Angel loses.

The proof calculus for dG$\mathcal{L}$ shown in Table 2, consists of all proof rules for first-order logic and one axiom for each game in Angel's modality. Additionally, there is also a determinacy axiom that links Angel's modality to Demon's. All axioms for Demon's modality can be derived using this axiom. Furthermore, the calculus contains a monotonicity rule and a fixpoint rule that handles repetition games.

**Table 2.** dG$\mathcal{L}$ proof calculus

| | | | |
|---|---|---|---|
| [·] | $[\alpha]P \leftrightarrow \neg\langle\alpha\rangle\neg P$ | $\langle\cup\rangle$ | $\langle\alpha \cup \beta\rangle P \leftrightarrow \langle\alpha\rangle P \vee \langle\beta\rangle P$ |
| $\langle :=\rangle$ | $\langle x := e\rangle p(x) \leftrightarrow p(e)$ | $\langle ;\rangle$ | $\langle\alpha;\beta\rangle P \leftrightarrow \langle\alpha\rangle\langle\beta\rangle P$ |
| $\langle '\rangle$ | $\langle x' = f(x)\rangle P \leftrightarrow \exists t \geq 0 \, \langle x := y(t)\rangle P \quad (y' = f(y))$ | $\langle d\rangle$ | $\langle\alpha^d\rangle P \leftrightarrow \neg\langle\alpha\rangle\neg P$ |
| $\langle ?\rangle$ | $\langle ?Q\rangle P \leftrightarrow Q \wedge P$ | $\langle *\rangle$ | $\langle\alpha^*\rangle P \leftrightarrow P \vee \langle\alpha\rangle\langle\alpha^*\rangle P$ |
| M | $\dfrac{P \to Q}{\langle\alpha\rangle P \to \langle\alpha\rangle Q}$ | FP | $\dfrac{P \vee \langle\alpha\rangle Q \to Q}{\langle\alpha^*\rangle P \to Q}$ |

## 4 Semi-competitive Differential Game Logic

The logic dG$\mathcal{L}_{sc}$ supports two players called *Angel* and *Demon*. They semi-competitively play a game defined in the dG$\mathcal{L}_{sc}$ formula.

After the game has ended, *both* want to have achieved their goal. Each player has a separate goal which is independent of the other player's goal. The game is *non-zero sum*, both players can win or lose at the same time.

### 4.1 Semi-competitiveness

To describe the player's behavior in the logic, the notion of "semi-competitiveness" is introduced in this paper. *Semi-competitiveness means that players cooperate where it is helpful for them, and compete where it is necessary.* More precisely, a player will only choose options that help them reach their goal. They will never lose on purpose. If there are multiple options that all make the player win, the player will *always* choose an option that also helps the other player win. If no option makes the player win, they will not altruistically help the other player instead. In terms of game theory, the players play a cooperative game, if collaboration is possible, and a non-cooperative game otherwise.

This gameplay is chosen to ensure the greatest cooperation among players, especially in games with multiple steps. Here, uncooperative behavior in a previous step might have negative consequences later. For example, if Angel and Demon pick candy for each other and Angel gives Demon a lemon candy, although he wanted a strawberry candy, he might in turn give Angel a candy she does not want because he already lost the game and will not help Angel anymore. If, on the other hand, Angel indeed gives him a strawberry candy, Demon will give her the candy she wants because now all options make him win, so he will help Angel.

Additionally, this gameplay ensures monotonicity of the logic, i.e., a greater goal means more possibilities to win. Monotonicity ensures that the logic behaves intuitively. Furthermore, it guarantees the existence of fixpoints which are needed later on to define parts of the semantics. Helping other players is a necessary assumption to obtain monotonicity: If the players' behavior does not also help the other player win and players choose randomly between all options they are indifferent to, then monotonicity is lost.

### 4.2 Syntax

The syntax of $\mathsf{dG\mathcal{L}}_{sc}$ consists of first-order logic and two modalities. The modality $\langle\alpha\rangle(P,Q)$ expresses that Angel has a winning strategy to win the game $\alpha$ by achieving her goal $P$ while knowing that Demon's goal is $Q$. $[\alpha](P,Q)$ means that Demon has a winning strategy to achieve $Q$ by playing $\alpha$ while knowing that Angel's goal is $P$.

**Definition 3. ($\mathsf{dG\mathcal{L}}_{sc}$ Syntax).** *The following grammar defines the $\mathsf{dG\mathcal{L}}_{sc}$ formulas:*

- $\alpha, \beta ::= x := e \mid x' = f(x) \& Q \mid ?Q \mid \alpha \cup \beta \mid \alpha; \beta \mid \alpha^d \mid \alpha^*$
- $P, Q ::= e \geq \tilde{e} \mid \neg P \mid P \wedge Q \mid \forall x P \mid \exists x P \mid \langle\alpha\rangle(P,Q) \mid [\alpha](P,Q)$

*where $\alpha, \beta$ are hybrid games, $P, Q$ are $\mathsf{dG\mathcal{L}}_{sc}$ formulas, $x$ is a variable, $f$ is a function and $e, \tilde{e}$ are terms.*

The hybrid games in Definition 3 have the same effects as the ones for $\mathsf{dG\mathcal{L}}$ described in Table 1. So in the game $((x := x + 1 \cup x := x - 1); \{x' = -1\}^d)^*$, for example, the outermost game is a repetition game. Here, Angel chooses after each round, if she wants to play again. She might also choose to play 0 rounds. If she does play a round, Angel first chooses whether to increase or to decrease $x$ by one. After that follows a continuous game. As it is marked with $^d$, this game is under Demon's control, so he chooses how long to evolve the ODE to decrease $x$. That means, time passes and $x$ changes according to the ODE until Demon stops time. In this example, the new value of $x$ would be $x - t$ after time $t$. Then, Angel chooses again whether she wants to play another round or not.

The main difference now to dG𝓛 is not in the effects of games but rather in the behavior of the players: If we have $\langle (x := 1 \cup x := 0)^d \rangle x = 1$ in dG𝓛, Demon will choose an option that hinders Angel at achieving her goal due to his adversarial behavior, i.e., $x := 0$ here. In dG𝓛$_{sc}$ the formula could be $\langle (x := 1 \cup x := 0)^d \rangle (x = 1, \top)$, including the information that Demon's goal is *true*. As Demon can win in any case, Demon helps Angel by choosing $x := 1$ due to his semi-competitive behavior.

*Example 1.* As the verification of an aerial collision avoidance system is a fully-fledged case study, the two planes in this example are still standing on the ground. Angel and Demon are replenishing the stocks for their respective plane, but Angel is missing 3l of orange juice while Demon needs 5l of tomato juice (more would not fit in the tank, less and some passengers will stay thirsty). Fortunately, Angel has plenty of tomato juice and Demon's stock is full of orange juice (enough, so that they do not have to worry about running out). In dG𝓛$_{sc}$, filling up each other's stock can be modeled using two continuous games:

$$o = 0 \wedge t = 0 \to \langle \{t' = 1\}; \{o' = 1\}^d \rangle (o = 3, t = 5)$$

First, Angel, at a constant rate, fills tomato juice into Demon's tank. Then, Demon fills orange juice into her tank. Note how the goals of both players are visible at the end of the formula. Although these goals are not directly overlapping, the players' semi-competitive behavior ensures their cooperation which leads to them both winning the game. This would not have been possible if they played adversarially because they have no control over the variable that matters for their goal. Even with indifference towards Demon's goal, Angel could not have won the game. If she would not care about the amount of tomato juice she gave to Demon, Demon would probably have refused to cooperate with her, making her lose as well.

### 4.3 Semantics

The semantics of the formulas is defined in the following section. This is done via a function $[\![\cdot]\!] : Fml \to \mathcal{P}(\mathcal{S})$ that maps a formula to the set of states where the formula is true. $\mathcal{S}$ is the set of all states. A state is a mapping $\omega : \mathcal{V} \to \mathbb{R}$ that maps all variables to a real number. The state $\omega_x^r$ denotes a state that coincides with the state $\omega$ in all variable values, except for $x$ whose value is replaced by $r$.

The semantics of first-order operators is as expected. To define the semantics of Angel's and Demon's modality, the functions $\varsigma_\alpha(\cdot, \cdot)$ and $\delta_\alpha(\cdot, \cdot)$ resp., are used which describe the winning region of a game. These functions take two inputs each: The first one is Angel's goal and the second is Demon's goal. Since Angel and Demon know each other's goal, this knowledge is needed for determining the winning regions. Unlike in dG𝓛, Demon's semantics cannot be defined as a function of Angel's winning region $\varsigma_\alpha(\cdot, \cdot)$ anymore, because their winning regions are no longer complementary. Instead, their winning regions partially overlap and there are also states that belong to neither winning region.

Still, the semantics of the assignment, test, and sequential game is similar to dGL as the effects of the game are the same, and the players' decisions cannot differ from those they would make in dGL because these games do not involve choices. A little tweak for the semantics of the sequential game is needed nonetheless, as the winning regions in dGL$_{sc}$ take two arguments instead of one. To win the sequential game $\alpha;\beta$, the player has to reach their winning region for $\beta$ after $\alpha$, so they can reach their goal after $\beta$. The same applies for the other player except their respective winning region operator is needed, instead, so the semantics of the sequential game is:

$$\varsigma_{\alpha;\beta}(X,Y) = \varsigma_\alpha(\varsigma_\beta(X,Y), \delta_\beta(X,Y)) \text{ and } \delta_{\alpha;\beta}(X,Y) = \delta_\alpha(\varsigma_\beta(X,Y), \delta_\beta(X,Y))$$

For Angel, the semantics of the continuous game and the choice game also correspond to the semantics in dGL. The winning region only returns states in which Angel *has* an option so that she can win but which one she will *actually* choose is invisible. Locally, only her goal matters to her because she has control which is also why she cannot expect help from Demon in this step. Globally, semi-competitiveness comes into play through nested games, e.g., the games Angel chooses from in the choice game. Especially important here is the dual game because in this game Demon's goals matter for Angel which then inductively matter for Angel through the whole game.

Demon's semantics of the continuous game and choice game does differ from the one in dGL though. His winning regions are extended by states where Angel, who is in control, will help him. As they act semi-competitively, Angel will help him in states where both of their goals can be reached simultaneously. Therefore, Demon's semantics for the continuous game $\delta_{x'=f(x)\&Q}(X,Y)$ is:

$$\{\varphi(0) \in \mathcal{S} \mid \varphi(r) \in Y \text{ for all } r \text{ with } \varphi \models x' = f(x) \wedge Q\}$$
$$\cup \ \{\varphi(0) \in \mathcal{S} \mid \varphi(r) \in X \cap Y \text{ for some } r \text{ with } \varphi \models x' = f(x) \wedge Q\}$$

The definition of the semantics uses a function from time to states $\varphi$. Over the course of this function, $x$ changes such that $x' = f(x)$ and the evolution domain constraint $Q$ holds in every state in $\varphi$. If Demon stays in his goal $Y$ for all states in $\varphi$, he can definitely win the game (left-hand side of the union). If Angel can reach a state by evolving the ODE (i.e. there is a state in $\varphi$) where both of their goals are fulfilled, she will stop there because she behaves semi-competitively, making both of them win (right-hand side of the union). The definition for the semantics of the choice game follows a corresponding idea:

$$\delta_{\alpha \cup \beta}(X,Y) = (\delta_\alpha(X,Y) \cap \delta_\beta(X,Y)) \cup (\delta_\alpha(X,Y) \cap \varsigma_\alpha(X,Y))$$
$$\cup \ (\delta_\beta(X,Y) \cap \varsigma_\beta(X,Y))$$

If Demon can win both $\alpha$ and $\beta$, i.e. he is in the winning region of $\alpha$ and $\beta$, he can definitely win the game. If he and Angel can both win $\alpha$, i.e. the current state is part of both Angel's and Demon's winning region for $\alpha$, Demon can also win the game because Angel will choose $\alpha$ due to her semi-competitive behavior. A similar argument applies, if both of them can win $\beta$.

In the dual game, the controls between Angel and Demon are swapped. This is simulated in the semantics by letting Angel keep control but making her play for Demon, i.e. trying to achieve his goal. In exchange, Demon plays with Angel's goal. As Angel now wins, if Demon's goal is achieved, her winning region actually denotes the states where Demon wins, as well as vice versa. Consequently, Angel and Demon swap goals and winning regions in the definitions of the dual game:

$$\varsigma_{\alpha^d}(X,Y) = \delta_\alpha(Y,X) \text{ and } \delta_{\alpha^d}(X,Y) = \varsigma_\alpha(Y,X)$$

The main idea to define the semantics of the repetition game is that allowing one more round of $\alpha$ should not change the winning region. Consequently, the winning region for Angel should be some kind of fixpoint of the form $X \cup \varsigma_\alpha(\varsigma_{\alpha^*}(X,Y), \delta_{\alpha^*}(X,Y)) = \varsigma_{\alpha^*}(X,Y)$ as Angel either is already in her goal, or she can reach it after one more round of $\alpha$. The problem is that by the same idea, Demon's winning region should also be a fixpoint, so using a definition like this would result in complex nested fixpoints. Additionally, this fixpoint is not unique yet. To solve the first problem, a case distinction is made between competitive and cooperative behavior, resulting in two fixpoints. If they compete, the other's goal is the complement of the fixpoint because they have complementary goals, while in the cooperative case, the other's goal is the same fixpoint, as they share the same goal. Consequently, a candidate $Z$ for Angel's first fixpoint should fulfill $X \cup \varsigma_\alpha(Z, Z^C) = Z$ and for the second it should fulfill $(X \cap Y) \cup (\varsigma_\alpha(Z,Z) \cap \delta_\alpha(Z,Z)) = Z$. The intersection of their winning regions rules out that one player wins and fulfills both goals (otherwise they would not cooperate), but the other one loses, e.g., by failing a test. To make the fixpoints unique, either the greatest or the least fixpoint can be chosen. $\mathcal{S}$ as the greatest possible set fulfills the equation, but this does not contain much information, so the least fixpoint is used. It can be computed as the intersection of all pre-fixpoints (sets that fulfill the equation only with set inclusion). Taken together, the semantics for Angel is:

$$\varsigma_{\alpha^*}(X,Y) = \bigcap \{Z \subseteq \mathcal{S} \mid X \cup \varsigma_\alpha(Z, Z^C) \subseteq Z\}$$
$$\cup \bigcap \{Z \subseteq \mathcal{S} \mid (X \cap Y) \cup (\varsigma_\alpha(Z,Z) \cap \delta_\alpha(Z,Z))\}$$

The definition of Demon's winning region follows the same idea. The second fixpoint is identical because here, both of them win. If Demon competes with Angel, he can only win for sure if he always stays in his goal, no matter how many rounds Angel plays. Consequently, Demon needs to be in his goal now, and he should be in his winning region, even if one more round of $\alpha$ is allowed: $Z = Y \cap \delta_\alpha(Z^C, Z)$. Because the least fixpoint in this case is the empty set, which does not contain much information, the greatest fixpoint is used. It can be computed by union of all pre-fixpoints. Thus, the semantics for Demon are:

$$\delta_\alpha(X,Y) = \bigcup \{Z \subseteq \mathcal{S} \mid Z \subseteq Y \cap \delta_\alpha(Z^C, Z)\}$$
$$\cup \bigcap \{Z \subseteq \mathcal{S} \mid (X \cap Y) \cup (\varsigma_\alpha(Z,Z) \cap \delta_\alpha(Z,Z))\}$$

The full definition of the semantics can be found in the long version [6].

*Remark 1.* As in dG$\mathcal{L}$, goals can still be converted to tests at the end, i.e. there is an equivalent formulation for each modality where the goals are replaced by *true* and the original goals appear as tests at the end of the program. As Angel's and Demon's winning regions are not complementary anymore, this conversion is much more subtle than in dG$\mathcal{L}$ because Angel does not always win if Demon loses. Additionally, Demon's ability to win influences his choices and thus Angel's ability to win and vice versa. Therefore, tests for both goals must be incorporated, and Angel and Demon, resp., need to pass them in any order (either test Angel first, or test Demon first) to ensure that they do not only win because the other one loses. This also demonstrates that the opponent's goals matter to both players. For the full statement, reference the long version [6, L. 8].

## 5 dG$\mathcal{L}_{sc}$ Properties and Relation to Zero-Sum dG$\mathcal{L}$

In this section, some important results for dG$\mathcal{L}_{sc}$ are proven. The first result proves monotonicity which ensures that the logic behaves in an intuitive way: A larger goal can be reached from a larger winning region. The first lemma states that the logic is monotone if both goals are increased. In this case, both Angel's and Demon's winning region will increase. The proof for this lemma is a straightforward structural induction over $\alpha$.

**Lemma 1. (Monotonicity).** *The logic* dG$\mathcal{L}_{sc}$ *is monotone, i.e.*

$$X \subseteq A, Y \subseteq B \text{ implies } \varsigma_\alpha(X,Y) \subseteq \varsigma_\alpha(A,B) \text{ and } \delta_\alpha(X,Y) \subseteq \delta_\alpha(A,B)$$

See proof in the long version [6].

The second lemma states that if Angel's and Demon's goals are disjoint, Angel's winning region expands by increasing her goal while Demon's goal may change arbitrarily. Intuitively, all parts in the semantics covering cooperation are empty since the goals are disjoint. Then, proving that the remaining sets grow by increasing the goal is fairly easy. After that, the parts where Angel and Demon cooperate, can be added. Thus, the winning region can only increase. The proof for Demon's statement is conducted similarly.

The following lemma is especially helpful if Angel and Demon have opposing goals, before and after the increase of one goal. In this case, enlarging one goal means that the other shrinks. Therefore, the first monotonicity Lemma 1 is not applicable but Lemma 2 can be used.

**Lemma 2. (Disjoint Monotonicity).** *If the goals of Angel and Demon are initially disjoint, then* dG$\mathcal{L}_{sc}$ *is monotone in each argument:*

$$X \subseteq A, X \cap Y = \emptyset \text{ implies } \varsigma_\alpha(X,Y) \subseteq \varsigma_\alpha(A,B) \text{ and}$$
$$Y \subseteq B, X \cap Y = \emptyset \text{ implies } \delta_\alpha(X,Y) \subseteq \delta_\alpha(A,B)$$

*Sets A and B may overlap. For each case the other goal can be chosen arbitrarily.*

See proof in the long version [6].

Another important property is that the logic behaves as intended. But how can this be checked? If the players have complementary goals, they have to compete and will behave adversarially. The same setting can also be expressed in dGL (which is assumed to be defined suitably). Consequently, both formulas should also have the same truth values. This holds indeed, as Lemma 3 shows:

**Lemma 3. (Complementary dGL Equivalence).** *If Angel and Demon have complementary goals, the logic dGL$_{sc}$ reduces to dGL, i.e. it holds that*

$$\varsigma_\alpha(X, X^C) = \varsigma_\alpha X \quad \text{and} \quad \delta_\alpha(X^C, X) = \delta_\alpha X$$

See proof in the long version [6].

In the proof it is shown via structural induction that all parts in the semantics that differ between dGL$_{sc}$ and dGL cancel out, if the goals oppose.

*Remark 2.* If there were a super-logic that contained both dGL$_{sc}$ and dGL, the previous lemma could be rendered as the syntactic equivalences

$$\langle \alpha \rangle (P, \neg P) \leftrightarrow \langle \alpha \rangle P \quad \text{and} \quad [\alpha](\neg P, P) \leftrightarrow [\alpha]P$$

**Notation 1.** *In the following, $\langle \alpha \rangle (P, \neg P)$ will be abbreviated with $\langle \alpha \rangle P$ and $[\alpha](\neg Q, Q)$ with $[\alpha]Q$, as well as $\varsigma_\alpha(X, X^C)$ with $\varsigma_\alpha X$ and $\delta_\alpha(Y^C, Y)$ with $\delta_\alpha Y$. These two formulas express the same and have the same winning regions in dGL$_{sc}$ and dGL respectively(Lemma 3). The abbreviations allow for staying in the logic dGL$_{sc}$ without having to write $P, Q, X, Y$ twice.*

Consequently, determinacy holds even though it only does for complementary goals, which will be useful for the proof calculus later on.

**Corollary 1 (Complementary Determinacy).** *Determinacy holds if Angel and Demon have complementary goals, i.e. the following equivalence is valid:*

$$\neg \langle \alpha \rangle (P, \neg P) \leftrightarrow [\alpha](P, \neg P)$$

See proof in the long version [6].

To show that dGL$_{sc}$'s definition is reasonable for the general case, first observe the following: If Angel and Demon compete in a later game, they will not cooperate in an earlier game because they will not reach both goals at the same time anyway. Similarly, if Angel and Demon cooperate in a later game, they can already do so for earlier games because they can win together. Inductively, this means that Angel and Demon can already decide at the start whether to cooperate or to compete! As competing players try to achieve mutually exclusive goals, each of them might as well play against an adversarial player because the other one might hinder them at achieving their goal in order to reach their own. Two cooperating players can also be modeled as an adversarial game: The coalition is regarded as one player and tries to reach both goals, playing against an adversarial player with no control. Since one of the two cases always applies, every semi-competitive game can be split into two adversarial games. Using this alternative description, the definition of dG$\mathcal{L}_{sc}$ can be checked against dG$\mathcal{L}$ again. The equivalence holds indeed, as Lemma 4 shows. The $^{-d}$ indicates the removal of all dual operators to transfer all controls to the coalition player. Although the conversion is possible, there are *two* winning regions in dG$\mathcal{L}$ instead of one in dG$\mathcal{L}_{sc}$ which doubles the work for proving formulas. On top, the formulas are linked by disjunction which makes it impossible to get rid of one part if each formula only holds for certain cases. Additionally, dG$\mathcal{L}_{sc}$ offers a much more intuitive way of expressing games where both players have an individual goal.

**Lemma 4 (General dG$\mathcal{L}$ Equivalence).** *Winning regions in* dG$\mathcal{L}_{sc}$ *correspond to those in* dG$\mathcal{L}$ *as follows:*

$$\varsigma_\alpha(X,Y) = \varsigma_{\alpha^{-d}}(X \cap Y) \cup \varsigma_\alpha(X) \quad and \quad \delta_\alpha(X,Y) = \varsigma_{\alpha^{-d}}(X \cap Y) \cup \delta_\alpha(Y)$$

*where $\alpha$ is a hybrid game, $X, Y$ are sets of states and $\alpha^{-d}$ is defined in Table 3.*

See proof in the long version [6].

As a corollary for Lemma 4, it can be stated that players will cooperate, iff both can win the game.

**Corollary 2 (Joint Cooperation).** *It holds that*

$$\varsigma_\alpha(X,Y) \cap \delta_\alpha(X,Y) = \varsigma_{\alpha^{-d}}(X \cap Y)$$

See proof in the long version [6].

## 6 Proof Calculus

For making practical use of dG$\mathcal{L}_{sc}$, a proof calculus is provided in this section. The proof calculus includes two axioms for each hybrid game, one for Angel and one for Demon. They correspond to the game's semantic definitions and decompose formulas into smaller parts.

**Table 3.** Hybrid system $\alpha^{-d}$ is the *systematization* of hybrid game $\alpha$

$(x := e)^{-d} \equiv x := e$  $\qquad (\alpha; \beta)^{-d} \equiv \alpha^{-d}; \beta^{-d}$

$(x' = f(x)\&Q)^{-d} \equiv x' = f(x)\&Q$  $\qquad (\alpha^d)^{-d} \equiv \alpha^{-d}$

$(?Q)^{-d} = ?Q$  $\qquad (\alpha^*)^{\ d} \equiv (\alpha^{\ d})^*$

$(\alpha \cup \beta)^{-d} \equiv \alpha^{-d} \cup \beta^{-d}$

$\langle := \rangle$  $\langle x := e \rangle (p(x), q(x)) \leftrightarrow p(e)$
$\langle ' \rangle$  $\langle x' = f(x) \rangle (P, Q) \leftrightarrow \exists t{\geq}0 \, \langle x := y(t) \rangle (P, Q)$  $\hfill (y' = f(y))$
$\langle ? \rangle$  $\langle ?R \rangle (P, Q) \leftrightarrow R \wedge P$
$\langle \cup \rangle$  $\langle \alpha \cup \beta \rangle (P, Q) \leftrightarrow \langle \alpha \rangle (P, Q) \vee \langle \beta \rangle (P, Q)$
$\langle ; \rangle$  $\langle \alpha ; \beta \rangle (P, Q) \leftrightarrow \langle \alpha \rangle (\langle \beta \rangle (P, Q), [\beta](P, Q))$
$\langle ^d \rangle$  $\langle \alpha^d \rangle (P, Q) \leftrightarrow [\alpha](Q, P)$
$\langle ^* \rangle$  $\langle \alpha^* \rangle (P, Q) \leftrightarrow P \vee \langle \alpha ; \alpha^* \rangle (P, Q)$

$$\text{FP} \quad \frac{P \vee \langle \alpha \rangle R_1 \to R_1 \quad (P \wedge Q) \vee (\langle \alpha \rangle (R_2, R_2) \wedge [\alpha](R_2, R_2)) \to R_2}{\langle \alpha^* \rangle (P, Q) \to R_1 \vee R_2}$$

$[:=]$  $[x := e](p(x), q(x)) \leftrightarrow q(e)$
$[']$  $[x' = f(x)](P, Q) \leftrightarrow \forall t{\geq}0 \, [x{:=}x(t)](P, Q) \vee \exists t{\geq}0 \, \langle x{:=}x(t) \rangle (P \wedge Q, Q)$  $(x' = f(x))$
$[?]$  $[?R](P, Q) \leftrightarrow \neg R \vee Q$
$[\cup]$  $[\alpha \cup \beta](P, Q) \leftrightarrow ([\alpha](P, Q) \wedge [\beta](P, Q)) \vee ([\alpha](P, Q) \wedge \langle \alpha \rangle (P, Q)) \vee ([\beta](P, Q) \wedge \langle \beta \rangle (P, Q))$
$[;]$  $[\alpha ; \beta](P, Q) \leftrightarrow [\alpha](\langle \beta \rangle (P, Q), [\beta](P, Q))$
$[^*]$  $[\alpha^*](P, Q) \leftrightarrow (P \wedge Q) \vee (\langle \alpha ; \alpha^* \rangle (P, Q) \wedge [\alpha ; \alpha^*](P, Q)) \vee (Q \wedge [\alpha ; \alpha^*]Q)$

$$\text{M}\langle\rangle \quad \frac{P_1 \to P_2 \quad Q_1 \to Q_2}{\langle \alpha \rangle (P_1, Q_1) \to \langle \alpha \rangle (P_2, Q_2)}$$

$$\text{M}_2\langle\rangle \quad \frac{P_1 \to P_2 \quad P_1 \wedge Q_1 \to \bot}{\langle \alpha \rangle (P_1, Q_1) \to \langle \alpha \rangle (P_2, Q_2)}$$

det  $\neg \langle \alpha \rangle P \leftrightarrow [\alpha] \neg P$

**Fig. 1.** Proof calculus for $\mathsf{dGL}_{sc}$

Additionally, there is the determinacy axiom det, which corresponds to Corollary 1 and links Angel and Demon's modality, if they have opposing goals. The fixpoint rule FP is, like the other rules, written with the premises at the top and the conclusion at the bottom. The rule characterizes $\langle \alpha^* \rangle (P, Q)$ as the union of two least fixpoints. If $R_1$ is a pre-fixpoint for the first fixpoint and $R_2$ is a pre-fixpoint for the second, then $R_1 \vee R_2$ holds whenever $\langle \alpha^* \rangle (P, Q)$ holds. As a subtle detail, $R_1$ and $R_2$ do not need to be the same because Angel can rarely achieve the same by competing and by cooperating with Demon. Unlike axiom $\langle ^* \rangle$, the rule does not feature more instances of repetition games in the premises. Demon's induction rule is not included because it can be derived from FP. The other two proof rules M$\langle\rangle$ and M$_2\langle\rangle$ correspond to the two monotonicity lemmas. Unlike the axioms, the monotonicity rules for Demon can be derived by using $\langle ^d \rangle$. For the monotonicity rules, it is irrelevant that this changes the game. But for Demon's axioms, the dual game introduced by $\langle ^d \rangle$ prevents the use of any other axiom to derive them.

Additionally, the proof calculus includes all rules for first-order logic. The proof calculus' rules are listed in Fig. 1, except for the first-order rules which are left out for reasons of space limitations and readability.

*Example 2.* With these proof rules on hand, it can now be proved that Angel is actually able to win the game seen in Example 1 and gets enough orange juice to supply all her passengers but not so much that it spills everywhere. In the proof, the hybrid game is straightforwardly broken down using the continuous, dual and assignment axioms:

$$
\begin{array}{c}
\vee\text{R, wR, }\langle:=\rangle\text{, }\exists\text{R} \;\dfrac{\mathbb{R}\;\dfrac{*}{o=0, t=0 \;\vdash\; y+5=5 \wedge o+3=3}}{o=0, t=0 \;\vdash\; \forall s\geq 0[o:=o+s](t+5=5, o=3)} \\[2ex]
\exists\text{R, }\langle:=\rangle \;\dfrac{[']\;\dfrac{\vee\exists s\geq 0\langle o=o+s\rangle(t+5=5 \wedge o=3, o=3)}{o=0, t=0 \;\vdash\; [x'=1](t+5=5, o=3)}}{o=0, t=0 \;\vdash\; \exists s\geq 0\langle t:=t+s\rangle([x'=1](t=5, o=3),} \\[2ex]
\langle'\rangle \;\dfrac{\langle x'=1\rangle(t=5, o=3))}{o=0; t=0 \;\vdash\; \langle y'=1\rangle([x'=1](t=5, o=3),} \\[2ex]
\langle;\rangle, \langle^d\rangle, [^d] \;\dfrac{\langle x'=1\rangle(t=5, o=3))}{o\doteq 0, t=0 \;\vdash\; \langle\{t'=1\}; \{o'=1\}^d\rangle(o=3, t=5)}
\end{array}
$$

Notably, the point where the proof splits into two cases (cooperation or competition), only occurs in the penultimate step of the proof. In this case it is already conceivable which option is provable, and the other branch can be eliminated, but usually this is hard to see. Therefore, this saves considerable effort compared to using dG$\mathcal{L}$ where both cases had to be considered from the start.

To be of any use, soundness of the proof calculus is crucial. Soundness means that all formulas that can be proven in the proof calculus are actually valid. If a false formula could be proven, anything could be, rendering it useless. Therefore, the soundness of the proof calculus is proven in the following theorem:

**Theorem 1 (Soundness).** *The* dG$\mathcal{L}_{sc}$ *proof calculus is sound.*

See proof in the long version [6].

Another important property of a proof calculus is completeness. Completeness means that any valid formula can be proven in the proof calculus. But how can this property be shown for dG$\mathcal{L}_{sc}$? For dG$\mathcal{L}$ it is already known that it is relatively complete [22]. This means that any valid formula can be proved if all tautologies may be assumed in the antecedent, i.e. the notion is less strict than completeness. For dG$\mathcal{L}_{sc}$ only relative completeness can be proven, as this logic builds on top of dG$\mathcal{L}$. Adapting the definitions from [22], relative completeness is defined as:

**Definition 4 (Expressiveness** *[22]***).** *A logic L is* expressive *(for* dG$\mathcal{L}_{sc}$*), if for every formula $\phi$, there exists an equivalent formula $\phi^\flat$ of L, i.e. $\models \phi \leftrightarrow \phi^\flat$. The logic L is called* differentially expressive, *if it is expressive and all equivalences of the form $\langle x' = \theta\rangle(P, Q) \leftrightarrow (\langle x' = \theta\rangle(P, Q))^\flat$ and $[x' = \theta](P, Q) \leftrightarrow ([x' = \theta](P, Q))^\flat$ are provable in the proof calculus. It is assumed that the logic L is closed under first-order logic.*

**Definition 5 (Relative completeness** *[22]***).** *A logic is* complete relative to *an expressive logic L, if every valid formula can be proved in the calculus from L tautologies.*

If now, the dG$\mathcal{L}_{sc}$ proof calculus could be converted to the dG$\mathcal{L}$ proof calculus, relative completeness could be proven almost for free. In the semantics this conversion is possible by Lemma 4. The proof calculus though, does not contain any axioms that syntactically rephrase this lemma. The inclusion of a corresponding axiom would also run counter to the intended compositionality principles of dG$\mathcal{L}_{sc}$. Fortunately, this is also unnecessary, as Theorem 2 shows a core insight: The two complementarization axioms (C.A. 1, 2) that split one modality with two individual player goals into two modalities with complementary goals, are *admissible!* Consequently, the set of provable formulas is unaffected by adding them. Hence, similar to Gentzen's cut elimination theorem, the compositional axioms of dG$\mathcal{L}_{sc}$ prove every dG$\mathcal{L}_{sc}$ formula that the complementarization axioms would reduce to dG$\mathcal{L}$, thereby guaranteeing relative completeness for free.

**Theorem 2 (Complementarization Elimination).** *The complementarization axioms are admissible in the proof calculus:*

- *Complementarization axiom 1:* $\langle \alpha \rangle(P, Q) \leftrightarrow \langle \alpha^{-d} \rangle(P \wedge Q) \vee \langle \alpha \rangle P$
- *Complementarization axiom 2:* $[\alpha](P, Q) \leftrightarrow \langle \alpha^{-d} \rangle(P \wedge Q) \vee [\alpha]Q$

See proof in the long version [6].

Using Theorem 3, the relative completeness of dG$\mathcal{L}_{sc}$ can easily be proven:

**Theorem 3 (Completeness).** *The dG$\mathcal{L}_{sc}$ proof calculus is complete relative to any differentially expressive logic L.*

*Proof* (Sketch) With complementarization, every formula of dG$\mathcal{L}_{sc}$ can be transformed to a formula where all modalities feature opposing goals. The complementarization axioms are admissible by Theorem 2, so the rewrite can be mimicked using only the rules available in the dG$\mathcal{L}_{sc}$ proof calculus. For opposing goals, the rules in the proof calculus correspond to the rules of the proof calculus for dG$\mathcal{L}$ which is complete relative to any differentially expressive logic $L$ [22]. Consequently, the proof calculus for dG$\mathcal{L}_{sc}$ is also relatively complete.

See full proof in the long version [6].

# 7 Conclusion

This paper introduces the logic dG$\mathcal{L}_{sc}$ for reasoning about hybrid games with two players that have individual goals. dG$\mathcal{L}_{sc}$ helps determine if a player is able to achieve their goal after playing a given game while taking into account the goal of the other player to *compete or collaborate if needed*. Additionally, the paper introduces the notion of "semi-competitiveness" to characterize the players' behavior.

Syntax, semantics and a proof calculus for dG$\mathcal{L}_{sc}$ are given in this paper. Monotonicity is shown to hold for dG$\mathcal{L}_{sc}$ and the winning regions of dG$\mathcal{L}_{sc}$ coincide with those of zero-sum dG$\mathcal{L}$ for complementary goals. Furthermore, complementarization has been proven admissible, illustrating the semi-competitive behavior of the players and justifying that the semantics is defined suitably.

In the future, several extensions of dG$\mathcal{L}_{sc}$ would be interesting. First, players might behave suboptimally by not always cooperating when necessary. In this case, players would need to actively agree on cooperating. As zero-sum three player games can be reduced to non-zero sum two-player games [17], dG$\mathcal{L}_{sc}$ could also be extended to a three-player logic. This logic could then be used for safety proofs of more complex scenarios with more players like overtaking maneuvers.

**Acknowledgements.** This work was funded by an Alexander von Humboldt Professorship and by KiKIT, the Pilot Program for Core-Informatics at the KIT of the Helmholtz Association.

# References

1. Abou El Wafa, N., Platzer, A.: Complete game logic with sabotage. In: Sobocinski, P., Lago, U.D., Esparza, J. (eds.) LICS, pp. 1:1–1:15. ACM, New York (2024). https://doi.org/10.1145/3661814.3662121
2. Ågotnes, T., van der Hoek, W., Wooldridge, M.J.: On the logic of coalitional games. In: Nakashima, H., Wellman, M.P., Weiss, G., Stone, P. (eds.) 5th International Joint Conference on Autonomous Agents and Multiagent Systems (AAMAS 2006), Hakodate, Japan, May 8–12, 2006, pp. 153–160. ACM (2006). https://doi.org/10.1145/1160633.1160659
3. Alur, R., Henzinger, T.A., Kupferman, O.: Alternating-time temporal logic. J. ACM **49**(5), 672–713 (2002). https://doi.org/10.1145/585265.585270
4. Baier, C., Brázdil, T., Größer, M., Kucera, A.: Stochastic game logic. In: Fourth International Conference on the Quantitative Evaluation of Systems (QEST 2007), 17–19 September 2007, Edinburgh, Scotland, UK, pp. 227–236. IEEE Computer Society (2007). https://doi.org/10.1109/QEST.2007.38
5. Bielefeld, R.S.: Reexamination of the perfectness concept for equilibrium points in extensive games. In: Models of Strategic Rationality, pp. 1–31. Springer Netherlands, Dordrecht (1988). https://doi.org/10.1007/978-94-015-7774-8-1
6. Butte, J., Platzer, A.: Semi-competitive differential game logic. CoRR abs/2505.14688 (2025). https://doi.org/10.48550/ARXIV.2505.14688
7. Chatterjee, K., Henzinger, T.A., Piterman, N.: Strategy logic. In: Caires, L., Vasconcelos, V.T. (eds.) CONCUR 2007, Lisbon, Portugal, September 3–8, 2007, Proceedings. LNCS, vol. 4703, pp. 59–73. Springer (2007). https://doi.org/10.1007/978-3-540-74407-8-5
8. Chattopadhyay, A., Lam, K.: Security of autonomous vehicle as a cyber-physical system. In: 7th International Symposium on Embedded Computing and System Design, ISED 2017, Durgapur, India, December 18–20, 2017, pp. 1–6. IEEE (2017). https://doi.org/10.1109/ISED.2017.8303906
9. Cleaveland, R., Mitsch, S., Platzer, A.: Formally verified next-generation airborne collision avoidance games in ACAS x. ACM Trans. Embed. Comput. Syst. **22**(1), 1–30 (2023). https://doi.org/10.1145/3544970
10. Fisman, D., Kupferman, O., Lustig, Y.: Rational synthesis. In: Esparza, J., Majumdar, R. (eds.) TACAS 2010, Paphos, Cyprus, March 20–28, 2010. Proceedings. LNCS, vol. 6015, pp. 190–204. Springer (2010). https://doi.org/10.1007/978-3-642-12002-2-16

11. Henzinger, T.A., Horowitz, B., Majumdar, R.: Rectangular hybrid games. In: Baeten, J.C.M., Mauw, S. (eds.) CONCUR 1999, Eindhoven, The Netherlands, August 24–27, 1999, Proceedings. LNCS, vol. 1664, pp. 320–335. Springer (1999). https://doi.org/10.1007/3-540-48320-9-23
12. Jeannin, J., et al.: A formally verified hybrid system for the next-generation airborne collision avoidance system. In: Baier, C., Tinelli, C. (eds.) TACAS. LNCS, vol. 9035, pp. 21–36. Springer (2015). https://doi.org/10.1007/978-3-662-46681-0-2
13. Kabra, A., Mitsch, S., Platzer, A.: Verified train controllers for the Federal Railroad Administration train kinematics model: balancing competing brake and track forces. IEEE Trans. Comput. Aided Des. Integr. Circuits Syst. **41**(11), 4409–4420 (2022). https://doi.org/10.1109/TCAD.2022.3197690
14. Mitchell, I., Bayen, A., Tomlin, C.: A time-dependent hamilton-jacobi formulation of reachable sets for continuous dynamic games. IEEE Trans. Autom. Control **50**(7), 947–957 (2005). https://doi.org/10.1109/TAC.2005.851439
15. Nash, J.F.: Equilibrium points in n-person games. Proc. Natl. Acad. Sci. **36**(1), 48–49 (1950). https://doi.org/10.1073/pnas.36.1.48
16. Nash, J.F.: Non-cooperative games. In: The Foundations of Price Theory Vol 4, pp. 329–340. Routledge (2024). https://doi.org/10.2307/1969529
17. von Neumann, J., Morgenstern, O.: Theory of Games and Economic Behavior. Princeton University Press, Princeton (2004). https://doi.org/10.1515/9781400829460
18. Parikh, R.: The logic of games and its applications. In: Karplnski, M., van Leeuwen, J. (eds.) Topics in the Theory of Computation, North-Holland Mathematics Studies, vol. 102, pp. 111–139. North-Holland (1985). https://doi.org/10.1016/S0304-0208(08)73078-0
19. Pauly, M.: A modal logic for coalitional power in games. J. Log. Comput. **12**(1), 149–166 (2002). https://doi.org/10.1093/LOGCOM/12.1.149
20. Platzer, A.: Differential dynamic logic for hybrid systems. J. Autom. Reas. **41**(2), 143–189 (2008). https://doi.org/10.1007/s10817-008-9103-8
21. Platzer, A.: Logical Analysis of Hybrid Systems: Proving Theorems for Complex Dynamics. Springer, Heidelberg (2010). https://doi.org/10.1007/978-3-642-14509-4
22. Platzer, A.: Differential game logic. ACM Trans. Comput. Log. **17**(1), 1:1–1:51 (2015). https://doi.org/10.1145/2817824
23. Platzer, A.: A complete uniform substitution calculus for differential dynamic logic. J. Autom. Reason. **59**(2), 219–265 (2016). https://doi.org/10.1007/s10817-016-9385-1
24. Platzer, A.: Logical Foundations of Cyber-Physical Systems. Springer, Cham (2018). https://doi.org/10.1007/978-3-319-63588-0
25. Platzer, A., Tan, Y.K.: Differential equation invariance axiomatization. J. ACM **67**(1), 6:1–6:66 (2020). https://doi.org/10.1145/3380825
26. Vladimerou, V., Prabhakar, P., Viswanathan, M., Dullerud, G.E.: Specifications for decidable hybrid games. Theor. Comput. Sci. **412**(48), 6770–6785 (2011). https://doi.org/10.1016/J.TCS.2011.08.036

**Open Access** This chapter is licensed under the terms of the Creative Commons Attribution 4.0 International License (http://creativecommons.org/licenses/by/4.0/), which permits use, sharing, adaptation, distribution and reproduction in any medium or format, as long as you give appropriate credit to the original author(s) and the source, provide a link to the Creative Commons license and indicate if changes were made.

The images or other third party material in this chapter are included in the chapter's Creative Commons license, unless indicated otherwise in a credit line to the material. If material is not included in the chapter's Creative Commons license and your intended use is not permitted by statutory regulation or exceeds the permitted use, you will need to obtain permission directly from the copyright holder.

# Intuitionistic and Substructural Logic

# Designing a Safe Forward Chaining Tactic Using Productive Proofs

Kaustuv Chaudhuri[✉], Arunava Gantait, and Dale Miller

Inria Saclay & LIX, Institut Polytechnique Paris, Palaiseau, France
kaustuv.chaudhuri@inria.fr

**Abstract.** We present a proof-theoretic treatment of forward chaining and saturation within a multisorted, first-order intuitionistic logic with equality. The notions of *polarity* and *focused proofs* are central to our approach since they provide a characterization of geometric implications as *bipolar formulas* as well as a natural setting to describe forward chaining and the concept of *productive proofs*. We identify conditions under which forward chaining with a given set of formulas is guaranteed to saturate in a finite number of steps. The motivation for this research stems, in part, from exploring avenues to automate the Abella theorem prover, which relies on relational specifications, and where theorems in typical proof developments are essentially bipolar formulas. We illustrate the potential benefits of automating forward chaining and saturation for Abella by presenting examples that compute congruence closure and assist in other equational and relational reasoning tasks.

## 1 Introduction

When attempting to prove a theorem in an interactive theorem prover, the user is typically presented with a collection of *proof states* or *subgoals* where each such state consists of two key elements:

1. A *context* that consists of a collection $\Sigma$ of (eigen-)variables, the collection $\mathcal{L}$ of previously loaded axioms and verified theorems, and a set $\Gamma$ of local assumptions relevant to the position of the subgoal in the entire proof.[1]
2. A *goal* (which we write $E$) that needs to be established within the combined context of $\Sigma$, $\mathcal{L}$, and $\Gamma$.

We can write this proof state as the *sequent* $\Sigma :: \mathcal{L}, \Gamma \vdash E$. To reduce notational clutter, we will usually omit $\mathcal{L}$ and instead assume that all previously proved theorems are included in $\Gamma$; we will also often omit the $\Sigma ::$ if those variables are not relevant.

---

[1] In formalisms based on dependent type theory, the two categories of variables and assumptions are merged; however, in logic and in proof theory they correspond to two separate and distinct connectives – universal quantification $\forall$ and implication $\supset$.

In interactive provers, there are broadly two kinds of logical actions that can be performed on any proof state that correspond to the two *sides* of the sequent. The first kind analyzes the goal formula $E$ and decomposes the proof state into possibly several proof states with simpler goals. The other kind of action looks at one or more facts in $\Gamma$ and then uses rules such as case-analysis, inversion, etc. to decompose the facts into simpler facts. In both kinds of actions, the formulas in $\Gamma$) can also participate, and the user generally intends such formulas to serve as recipes for the creation of high level inference rules. For example, suppose the user defines the binary relation $\leq$ (on natural numbers, say) and establishes its transitivity by proving $\forall x \forall y \forall z. (x \leq y \wedge y \leq z \supset x \leq z)$. The user expects that this lemma will yield the following two inference rules:

- *Backward chaining*: In order to prove $t \leq s$, prove instead $t \leq u$ and $u \leq s$ for some interpolant term $u$, using the inference rule[2]

$$\frac{\Gamma \vdash t \leq u \quad \Gamma \vdash u \leq s}{\Gamma \vdash t \leq s}.$$

This rule is an action of the first kind as it modifies the goal but not the proof context. Organizing proof search using backward chaining is well understood and has been used to justify the design of logic programming languages [19].
- *Forward chaining*: If the proof context contains $t \leq u$ and $u \leq s$ then produce the additional assumption $t \leq s$, which corresponds to the following rule, which only modifies the proof context but not the goal:

$$\frac{\Gamma, t \leq u, u \leq s, t \leq s \vdash E}{\Gamma, t \leq u, u \leq s \vdash E}.$$

Observe that in either formulation of these derived inference rules, only the relational atoms are present; indeed, none of the compound subformulas of the transitivity lemma are present.

In this paper we will use Gentzen's *sequent calculus* to analyze and transform proof states, i.e., sequents. The ordinary sequent calculus provides a foundational framework that is able to represent actions on both the proof context and the goal formula as left and right introduction rules, respectively; moreover, both of the above kinds of chaining correspond to applications of $\forall$-left, $\supset$-left, and initial rules. However, the rules of the sequent calculus operate on individual connectives at a time, so the space of sequent proofs also contains many other unprincipled proofs that do not follow the forward or backward chaining protocol, and leave partially instantiated and applied versions of lemmas in the proof contexts. The general topic of converting lemmas into more *synthetic* inference rules has been explored since at least the work of Negri [23,24], and appears more recently in a more systematic fashion in the work on *focused proof systems*, which is the setting we will use in this paper. Focused proof systems were

---

[2] We shall read all inference rules in this paper from the conclusion to the premises.

initially designed as a particular kind of protocol for (linear) logic programming by Andreoli [3], but in a more modern presentation they define a normal form for sequent proofs that respects a *polarity* distinction. This perspective allows focused proofs to be defined for classical and intuitionistic logics as well where the polarities of connectives are not predetermined but assignable [15]. Both the forward chaining and the backward chaining interpretations of lemmas described above arise in focused proofs simply as a consequence of assigning the right polarities to the logical connectives and atomic formulas [10,17].

In this paper we are principally concerned with the forward chaining interpretation of lemmas, which arises out of assigning a positive polarity to the conjunction and all atomic formulas. This interpretation has the obvious problem that the premise sequents can be *more* complex than the conclusions, since they may contain additional assumptions that were generated from the existing assumptions. Thus, automated proof search using this interpretation will be immediately non-terminating without further controls. Similar issues of non-termination with forward chaining have been considered in the context of bottom-up logic programming (see e.g. [22]), and termination sometimes needs to be explicitly engineered in such approaches with the use of global program transformations [5].

In this paper we will identify a class of lemmas for which termination can be achieved by direct analysis of focused proofs. In particular, we identify a notion of *productive proof rule* as a synthetic inference rule that tries to create a fact that was not already provable in a single focused phase. We can then run the forward chaining interpretation as long as the inferences stay productive. We show that this search strategy terminates on a fairly natural class of lemmas that consist of *bipolar formulas* that have an additional *safety* condition.

We also implement this strategy as a new forward chaining tactic in the Abella theorem prover, and show experimentally that it reduces much of the tedium of lemma applications. In fact, we show how to implement certain other well known operations such as transitive closure (on finite graphs) and congruence closure. We use Abella because of its proof-theoretic basis and its use of (an extension of) intuitionistic first-order logic; however, the approach of this paper can be used to define similar tactics using forward chaining in other proof assistants.

## 2 Focused Proofs for Intuitionistic Logic with Equality

### 2.1 Polarities and Formulas

In a two-sided sequent presentation of linear logic, every logical connective has the property that either its right-introduction rules are invertible or its left-introduction rules are invertible (never both). This allows us to classify every connective into two *polarities*, with those with right-introduction rules being invertible called *negative* and those with left-introduction rules being invertible called *positive*. For intuitionistic and classical (non-linear) logics, this definition of polarity is not directly applicable, since there are connectives such as conjunction $\wedge$ that can be given invertible rules on both sides of the sequent arrow, as is the case with the popular *G3* and *G3i* proof systems [25]. Particular choices of rules may give particular *polarizations* of these connectives with ambiguous polarities; for example, Gentzen's *LJ* and *LK* calculi [14] treats conjunction as uniquely negative. (Atomic formulas in every one of these logics also have ambiguous polarities, but this is only relevant in the presence of the *focusing* restriction described in the next subsection.)

One common technique in logics such as intuitionistic logic is to include both *polarizations* of connectives that can have ambiguous polarities. In our setting, the conjunction $\wedge$ and its unit t will both have two polarized forms, namely, $\wedge^-$, $\wedge^+$, and $t^-$, $t^+$. To be precise, we should maintain a distinction between *formulas* and *polarized formulas*. The latter class of formulas will not contain t or $\wedge$, but may include $t^-$, $t^+$, $\wedge^-$, and $\wedge^+$. Given a polarized formula $B$, we define its unpolarized form $\tilde{B}$ as that formula obtained by replacing every occurrence of $\wedge^-$ and $\wedge^+$ in $B$ with $\wedge$, and every instance of $t^-$ and $t^+$ in $B$ with t. When this distinction is clear from the context, we may sometimes refer to polarized formulas simply as formulas.

The multisorted first-order intuitionistic logic we consider in this paper contains the following connectives.

- Equality = is a logical connective and is polarized positively.
- The quantifiers $\forall_\tau$ and $\exists_\tau$ are first-order: i.e., the types $\tau$ range over primitive types. Of these, $\forall_\tau$ has negative polarity and $\exists_\tau$ has positive polarity.
- The propositional connectives are divided into *positive connectives* ($\wedge^+$, $t^+$, $\vee$, f) and the *negative connectives* ($\wedge^-$, $t^-$, $\supset$).

A non-atomic formula is *negative* if its top-level connective is negative, and is *positive* if its top-level connective is positive. In this paper, atomic formulas are always polarized positively.

## 2.2 The Multifocused Proof System $LJF^=$

Figure 1 contains the $LJF^=$ proof system in which all formulas in all sequents are polarized. There are three kinds of sequents in this proof system:

$$\Sigma :: \Gamma \Uparrow \Theta \vdash \Delta \Uparrow \Upsilon \quad \text{(unfocused sequent)}$$
$$\Sigma :: \Gamma \vdash P \Downarrow \quad \text{(right-focused sequent)}$$
$$\Sigma :: \Gamma \Downarrow \Theta \vdash P \quad \text{(left-focused sequent)}$$

Here, $\Gamma$ is a *set* of negatively polarized formulas or atoms, and $\Theta$, $\Delta$, and $\Upsilon$ are multisets of polarized formulas with $\Upsilon$ restricted to positive formulas. Given that we are working with intuitionistic logic, we insist that the multiset union of $\Delta$ and $\Upsilon$ is a singleton multiset in unfocused sequents, i.e., one of $\Delta$ or $\Upsilon$ is a singleton and the other is empty. The introduction rules introduce connectives only within the $\Theta$ and $\Delta$ zones. Whenever $\Theta$ or $\Delta$ is empty, we indicate it with an empty space; furthermore, in the case of unfocused sequents, we also elide the corresponding $\Uparrow$. Sequents of the form $\Gamma \vdash P$ (i.e., $\Gamma \Uparrow \vdash \Uparrow P$) will be called *border sequents*.

STRUCTURAL RULES

$$\dfrac{\Sigma :: \Gamma \vdash P \Downarrow}{\Sigma :: \Gamma \vdash P} \, D_r \qquad \dfrac{\Sigma :: \Gamma \Uparrow \Theta \vdash \, \Uparrow P}{\Sigma :: \Gamma \Uparrow \Theta \vdash P \Uparrow} \, S_r \qquad \dfrac{\Sigma :: \Gamma \vdash N \Uparrow}{\Sigma :: \Gamma \vdash N \Downarrow} \, R_r$$

$$\dfrac{\Sigma :: \Gamma \Downarrow \mathcal{N} \vdash P}{\Sigma :: \Gamma \vdash P} \, D_l \qquad \dfrac{\Sigma :: C, \Gamma \Uparrow \Theta \vdash \Delta \Uparrow \Upsilon}{\Sigma :: \Gamma \Uparrow C, \Theta \vdash \Delta \Uparrow \Upsilon} \, S_l \qquad \dfrac{\Sigma :: \Gamma \Uparrow \mathcal{P} \vdash P}{\Sigma :: \Gamma \Downarrow \mathcal{P} \vdash P} \, R_l$$

Here, $\mathcal{P}$ is a multiset of positive formulas and $\mathcal{N}$ is a non-empty multiset of negative formulas such that every formula in $\mathcal{N}$ is in the set $\Gamma$.

INITIAL RULE $\qquad \dfrac{}{\Sigma :: \Gamma, P \vdash P \Downarrow} \, I_r$, $P$ atomic

INVERTIBLE INTRODUCTION RULES

$$\dfrac{\Sigma :: \Gamma \Uparrow \Theta \vdash B_1 \Uparrow \quad \Sigma :: \Gamma \Uparrow \Theta \vdash B_2 \Uparrow}{\Sigma :: \Gamma \Uparrow \Theta \vdash B_1 \wedge^- B_2 \Uparrow} \qquad \dfrac{}{\Sigma :: \Gamma \Uparrow \Theta \vdash \mathsf{t}^- \Uparrow}$$

$$\dfrac{x{:}\tau, \Sigma :: \Gamma \Uparrow \Theta \vdash B \Uparrow}{\Sigma :: \Gamma \Uparrow \Theta \vdash \forall x_\tau.B \Uparrow} \qquad \dfrac{\Sigma :: \Gamma \Uparrow \Theta, B_1 \vdash B_2 \Uparrow}{\Sigma :: \Gamma \Uparrow \Theta \vdash B_1 \supset B_2 \Uparrow}$$

$$\dfrac{\Sigma :: \Gamma \Uparrow \Theta \vdash \Delta \Uparrow \Upsilon}{\Sigma :: \Gamma \Uparrow \mathsf{t}^+, \Theta \vdash \Delta \Uparrow \Upsilon} \qquad \dfrac{\Sigma :: \Gamma \Uparrow B_1, B_2, \Theta \vdash \Delta \Uparrow \Upsilon}{\Sigma :: \Gamma \Uparrow B_1 \wedge^+ B_2, \Theta \vdash \Delta \Uparrow \Upsilon}$$

$$\dfrac{}{\Sigma :: \Gamma \Uparrow \mathsf{f}, \Theta \vdash \Delta \Uparrow \Upsilon} \qquad \dfrac{\Sigma :: \Gamma \Uparrow B_1, \Theta \vdash \Delta \Uparrow \Upsilon \quad \Sigma :: \Gamma \Uparrow B_2, \Theta \vdash \Delta \Uparrow \Upsilon}{\Sigma :: \Gamma \Uparrow B_1 \vee B_2, \Theta \vdash \Delta \Uparrow \Upsilon}$$

$$\dfrac{x{:}\tau, \Sigma :: \Gamma \Uparrow B, \Theta \vdash \Delta \Uparrow \Upsilon}{\Sigma :: \Gamma \Uparrow \exists x_\tau.B, \Theta \vdash \Delta \Uparrow \Upsilon}$$

$$\dfrac{(\theta = \mathrm{mgu}(t,s)) \quad \Sigma\theta :: \Gamma\theta \Uparrow \Theta\theta \vdash \Delta\theta \Uparrow \Upsilon\theta}{\Sigma :: \Gamma \Uparrow s = t, \Theta \vdash \Delta \Uparrow \Upsilon} \qquad \dfrac{(t \text{ and } s \text{ not unifiable})}{\Sigma :: \Gamma \Uparrow s = t, \Theta \vdash \Delta \Uparrow \Upsilon}$$

NON-INVERTIBLE INTRODUCTION RULES

$$\dfrac{}{\Sigma :: \Gamma \vdash t = t \Downarrow} \qquad \dfrac{}{\Sigma :: \Gamma \vdash \mathsf{t}^+ \Downarrow} \qquad \dfrac{\Sigma :: \Gamma \vdash B_i \Downarrow}{\Sigma :: \Gamma \vdash B_1 \vee B_2 \Downarrow} \, i \in \{1, 2\}$$

$$\dfrac{\Sigma :: \Gamma \vdash B_1 \Downarrow \quad \Sigma :: \Gamma \vdash B_2 \Downarrow}{\Sigma :: \Gamma \vdash B_1 \wedge^+ B_2 \Downarrow} \qquad \dfrac{(\Sigma \vdash t : \tau) \quad \Sigma :: \Gamma \vdash [t/x]B \Downarrow}{\Sigma :: \Gamma \vdash \exists x_\tau.B \Downarrow}$$

$$\dfrac{\Sigma :: \Gamma \vdash B_1 \Downarrow \quad \Sigma :: \Gamma \Downarrow B_2, \Theta \vdash P}{\Sigma :: \Gamma \Downarrow B_1 \supset B_2, \Theta \vdash P} \qquad \dfrac{\Sigma :: \Gamma \Downarrow B_i, \Theta \vdash P}{\Sigma :: \Gamma \Downarrow B_1 \wedge^- B_2, \Theta \vdash P}$$

$$\dfrac{(\Sigma \vdash t : \tau) \quad \Sigma :: \Gamma \Downarrow [t/x]B, \Theta \vdash P}{\Sigma :: \Gamma \Downarrow \forall x_\tau.B, \Theta \vdash P}$$

$\Gamma$ ranges over a set of negatively polarized formulas or atoms; $\Delta, \Theta$ range over multisets of polarized formulas; $\Upsilon$ ranges over multisets of positive formulas; $P$ denotes a positive formula; $N$ denotes a negative formula; $C$ denotes either a negative formula or a (positive) atom; and $B$ denotes any polarized formula. The multiset union of $\Delta$ and $\Upsilon$ must be a singleton. Parenthesized premises are to be interpreted as side conditions.

**Fig. 1.** The $LJF^=$ proof system: multifocused version

The $LJF^=$ proof system is *multifocused* in the sense that in the left-focused sequent $\Gamma \Downarrow \Theta \vdash C$ the zone of foci $\Theta$ can have multiple formulas. Multifocusing is a generalization of ordinary focusing that permits the parallel application of synthetic inference rules [7,9]. It is important to note that the focus zone is treated in a *linear* fashion in the sense that contraction and weakening are not available for formulas in that zone. We will exploit multifocusing in Sect. 4.1 when we deal with forward chaining and saturation.

Focused proofs are constructed in two phases. The *invertible phase* (a.k.a. *negative* or *asynchronous* phase) involves unfocused sequents and uses invertible rules on principal formulas drawn from $\Theta$ or $\Delta$. The *non-invertible* phase (a.k.a. *positive* and *synchronous* phase) involves focused sequents. Transitions between these two phases happen with a collection of structural rules, where the *release* rules ($R_l$ and $R_r$) transition from a focused conclusion to an unfocused premise, while the *decide* rules ($D_l$ and $D_r$) transition from an unfocused conclusion to a focused premise. Note that the conclusions of both decide rules are border sequents. In the invertible phase, the two *store* rules ($S_l$ and $S_r$) are used to transfer a formula from $\Theta$ and $\Delta$ to $\Gamma$ and $\Upsilon$, respectively, when no further invertible rules can be applied to that formula; these store rules are internal to the invertible phase. The initial rule $I_r$ is part of the non-invertible phase and requires a right focus on a (positive) atom.

The $LJ^=$ proof system is defined as the unfocused version of $LJF^=$; that is, $LJ^=$ results from taking all the inference rules of $LJF^=$ and replacing $\Uparrow$ and $\Downarrow$ with commas and replacing all polarized formulas with their unpolarized forms. The result of doing this replacement on the store rules ($S_l$ and $S_r$) and the release rules ($R_l$ and $R_r$) would equate their conclusions and premises, so we drop these rules from $LJ^=$. Wherever an $LJF^=$ rule is restricted to formulas of a certain polarity, the corresponding $LJ^=$ rule drops the restriction. Thus, the $D_l$ rule becomes the contraction rule in $LJ^=$.

**Theorem 1 (Soundness and Completeness of $LJF^=$ wrt $LJ^=$).** *Let $B$ be a polarized formula defined over the variables in $\Sigma$. Then the sequent $\Sigma :: \cdot \Uparrow \vdash B \Uparrow$ is provable in $LJF^=$ if and only if the sequent $\Sigma :: \cdot \vdash \tilde{B}$ is provable in $LJ^=$.*

*Proof (Sketch).* The forward direction (soundness) is immediate. The converse (completeness) is more involved but follows by modifying the proof for the completeness of the singly focused version of $LJF$ in [15] to also account for equality (following the treatment of equality in, say, [18]). This use of $LJF$ assumes that all atomic formulas are polarized positively. When completeness holds for the singly focused proof system, it immediately holds for the multifocused system which includes the singly focused system. □

## 3 Bipolar Formulas and Productive Proofs

### 3.1 Purely Positive and Bipolar Formulas

A polarized formula is *purely positive* if the only logical connectives in it are positive. Let $\mathbb{P}$ be the set of all purely positive formulas. The following theorem shows that $LJF^=$ proofs of purely positive formulas are particularly simple.

**Theorem 2.** *For any $P \in \mathbb{P}$:*

1. *If the sequent $\Sigma :: \Gamma \vdash P \Downarrow$ has an $LJF^=$ proof, it has a proof that is exactly one non-invertible phase composed only of right-introduction rules.*
2. *It is decidable whether or not $\Sigma :: \Gamma \vdash P \Downarrow$ is provable.*

*Proof.* By immediate inspection of the inference rules in Fig. 1. □

The dual set $\mathbb{N}$ of purely negative formulas consists of formulas $N$ with the grammar $N ::= \mathsf{t}^- \mid N_1 \wedge^- N_2 \mid P \supset N \mid \forall_\tau x.N$ (where $P \in \mathbb{P}$). It is easy to show that a formula in $\mathbb{N}$ is provably equivalent in $LJF^=$ to $\mathsf{t}^-$. As a result, we shall generally be able to ignore these formulas. Note that purely negative formulas can have positive subformulas, but only as antecedents of implications.

A more interesting class of formulas are the *bipolar* formulas which are negative formulas with the grammar $B ::= \mathsf{t}^- \mid B_1 \wedge^- B_2 \mid P_1 \supset P_2 \mid \forall_\tau x.B$ (where $P_1$ and $P_2$ are in $\mathbb{P}$). It is not difficult to show that every bipolar formula is logically equivalent to the conjunction ($\wedge^-$) of formulas of the form

$$\forall \bar{x}.(A_1 \wedge^+ \cdots \wedge^+ A_n \supset P), \quad (n \geq 0)$$

where $P \in \mathbb{P}$, the $A_i$s are atoms, and the empty $\wedge^+$ is written as $\mathsf{t}^+$. Following [23], we shall call formulas of this shape *geometric implications*, and we say that the *head* of this implication is $P$. If $B$ is a bipolar formula, we write $[\![B]\!]$ to denote the multiset of all such geometric implications in this conjunction. We extend this function to sets of bipolar formulas, i.e., $[\![B_1, \ldots, B_m]\!] = [\![B_1]\!] \cup \cdots \cup [\![B_m]\!]$. A derivation that starts (reading conclusion-upwards) with $D_l$ on such a formula would have the following non-invertible phase in $LJF^=$:

$$\cfrac{\cfrac{\cfrac{\cfrac{\overline{\Gamma, A_1\theta, \ldots, A_n\theta \vdash A_1\theta \wedge^+ \cdots \wedge^+ A_n\theta \Downarrow}\ \dagger \quad \cfrac{\Gamma, A_1\theta, \ldots, A_n\theta \Uparrow P\theta \vdash C}{\Gamma, A_1\theta, \ldots, A_n\theta \Downarrow P\theta \vdash C}}{\Gamma, A_1\theta, \ldots, A_n\theta \Downarrow A_1\theta \wedge^+ \cdots \wedge^+ A_n\theta \supset P\theta \vdash C}}{\Gamma, A_1\theta, \ldots, A_n\theta \Downarrow \forall \bar{x}.(A_1 \wedge^+ \cdots \wedge^+ A_n \supset P) \vdash C}\ \ddagger}{\Gamma, A_1\theta, \ldots, A_n\theta \vdash C}\ D_l,$$

where the derivation marked † consists of $n - 1$ applications of $\wedge^+$-right and $I_r$, and that marked ‡ consists of repeated applications of $\forall$-left. We say that forward chaining on $\forall \bar{x}.(A_1 \wedge^+ \cdots \wedge^+ A_n \supset P)$ succeeds if some instance of $A_1, \ldots, A_n$ is present in the proof context of the root sequent and the information present in the same instance of the head $P$ is added to the proof context.

In the rest of this paper we will present a complete proof search strategy for formulas of the form $(B_1 \wedge^+ \cdots \wedge^+ B_n) \supset B_0$ where $B_0, \ldots, B_n$ ($n \geq 0$) are bipolar formulas. The border sequents within an $LJF^=$ proof of such a formula are of the form $B_1, \ldots, B_n, \mathcal{A} \vdash P$, where $P$ is in $\mathbb{P}$ and $\mathcal{A}$ is a set of atomic formulas: we shall call such sequents *reduced* sequents. The $LJF^=$ system restricted to these border sequents can be simplified by requiring the goal formulas to be purely positive, and removing the now redundant $R_r$ and $S_r$ rules.

If we abstract the structure of $LJF^=$ proofs of reduced sequents as a tree of occurrences of decide rules, then every occurrence of a $D_r$ rule is a terminal node and every occurrence of a $D_l$ rule is an internal node. Additionally, a formula occurrence under left focus in the conclusion of a left-introduction rule corresponds uniquely to a formula occurrence under left focus in exactly one of the premises of that rule. As a consequence, if an instance of $D_l$ selects $m \geq 1$ formulas for its focus, then the $R_l$ rule at the top of that non-invertible phase also has $m$ formulas as the left foci.

### 3.2 Productive Proofs

An application of the $R_l$ rule (where $\mathcal{P}$ is a multiset of purely positive formulas)

$$\frac{\Sigma :: \Gamma \Uparrow \mathcal{P} \vdash Q}{\Sigma :: \Gamma \Downarrow \mathcal{P} \vdash Q} \; R_l$$

is *unproductive* if there is a $P \in \mathcal{P}$ such that $\Sigma :: \Gamma \vdash P \Downarrow$ is provable. An instance of $R_l$ is *productive* in case it is not unproductive. A proof is productive if all occurrences of $R_l$ are productive. The intuition here is that if $\Sigma :: \Gamma \vdash P \Downarrow$ is provable then the information content of $P$ is already in $\Gamma$: using $R_l$ on $\Sigma :: \Gamma \Downarrow P \vdash Q$ would then add the content of $P$ to $\Gamma$, which is redundant.

In order to prove the completeness of productive proofs, we first consider the following cut-style rule where $P$ and $Q$ are restricted to be purely positive:

$$\frac{\Sigma :: \Gamma \vdash P \Downarrow \quad \Sigma :: \Gamma \Uparrow P, \Theta \vdash Q}{\Sigma :: \Gamma \Uparrow \Theta \vdash Q} \; cut \Updownarrow$$

**Theorem 3 (Elimination of $cut \Updownarrow$).** *If a reduced border sequent has a proof in $LJF^=$ plus $cut \Updownarrow$ then it has a proof in $LJF^=$ (without $cut \Updownarrow$).*

*Proof.* Say that an instance of $cut \Updownarrow$ has size $n$ if there are $n$ occurrences of logical connectives in the cut formula $P$. The size of a proof with possible occurrences of $cut \Updownarrow$ is the sum of the size of all occurrences of $cut \Updownarrow$ rules it contains.

If the size of a proof is 0 then any occurrence of $cut \Updownarrow$ in it involves an atomic cut formula. Without loss of generality, we can assume that all such occurrences $cut \Updownarrow$ have their right premise proved by storing $A$ using $S_l$ (otherwise that last inference rule can be permuted below the cut rule):

$$\dfrac{\Sigma :: \Gamma \vdash A \Downarrow \quad I_r \quad \dfrac{\Xi}{\Sigma :: \Gamma, A \Uparrow \Theta \vdash Q}\ S_l}{\Sigma :: \Gamma \Uparrow \Theta \vdash Q}\ cut \Updownarrow.$$

Since $A$ is a member of $\Gamma$ (and since multiplicity in the set $\Gamma$ does not matter), the endsequent of $\Xi$ is the same as $\Sigma :: \Gamma \Uparrow \Theta \vdash E$: hence, we can replace this derivation with $\Xi$. This reduces the number of atomic instances of $cut \Updownarrow$ by one.

Assume that the size of the proof is $n > 0$. We can prove by induction on the structure of cut formulas that we can lower this measure by pushing the $cut \Updownarrow$ upwards in the usual way. Note that since there are no occurrences of $R_l$ in the left premise of a proof that ends with $cut \Updownarrow$, no new instances of $R_l$ occur in the process of removing $cut \Updownarrow$. □

**Theorem 4 (Completeness of productive proofs).** *If a reduced sequent has an $LJF^=$ proof, it has a productive $LJF^=$ proof.*

*Proof.* Every occurrence of an unproductive $R_l$ can be replaced with possibly several instances of $cut \Updownarrow$. In particular, consider the following unproductive $R_l$ rule along with the $D_l$ rule that occurs below it in the same phase.

$$\dfrac{\dfrac{\Xi}{\Sigma :: \Gamma \Uparrow P_1, \ldots, P_n, \mathcal{P} \vdash Q}}{\Sigma :: \Gamma \Downarrow P_1, \ldots, P_n, \mathcal{P} \vdash Q}\ R_l$$

$$\vdots$$

$$\dfrac{\Sigma :: \Gamma \Downarrow N_1, \ldots, N_n, \mathcal{N} \vdash Q}{\Sigma :: \Gamma \vdash Q}\ D_l$$

Also assume that we have for $1 \le i \le n$, $\Xi_i$ is a proof of $\Gamma \vdash P_i \Downarrow$ ($n \ge 1$) and that $N_i$ is the antecedent of $P_i$. We can now reorganize this proof as follows.

$$\dfrac{\Xi_n}{\Gamma \vdash P_n \Downarrow} \quad \dfrac{\dfrac{\Xi_1}{\Gamma \vdash P_1 \Downarrow} \quad \dfrac{\Xi}{\Gamma \Uparrow P_1, \ldots, P_n, \mathcal{P} \vdash Q}}{\Gamma \Uparrow P_2, \ldots, P_n, \mathcal{P} \vdash Q}\ cut \Updownarrow$$

$$\vdots$$

$$\dfrac{\Gamma \Uparrow P_n, \mathcal{P} \vdash Q}{\Gamma \Uparrow \mathcal{P} \vdash Q}\ cut \Updownarrow$$

$$\vdots$$

$$\dfrac{\Gamma \Downarrow \mathcal{N} \vdash Q}{\Gamma \vdash Q}\ D_l$$

Theorem 3 guarantees a cut-free proof that does not contain new occurrences of $R_l$. Thus, the resulting proof is productive. □

An immediate consequence of this completeness theorem is that we only need to search for productive proofs when attempting to prove a reduced sequent.

## 4 Forward Chaining and Saturation

### 4.1 Eliminating the Non-determinism of $D_l$

The search for a proof of a reduced sequent in $LJF^=$ begins by choosing between $D_l$ or $D_r$. If $D_r$ is chosen, then the proof will terminate within the non-invertible phase above the $D_r$ rule, ending with one of $I_r$, $t_r^+$, or $=_r$ (see Theorem 2). Otherwise, when choosing $D_l$ we must also choose a subset of the bipolar formulas in $\Gamma$ as well as choose their multiplicity in the multiset that is the left-focus zone. In this case, the entire non-invertible left-focused phase can fail if any of the selected foci cannot be successfully used in the forward direction (e.g., if the body of a geometric implication does not hold in the current context). While there can be clever reasons for selecting certain formulas as foci—say, because the user indicates them as part of a proof script—the general problem of what formulas to pick is not simplified by the ability to pick multiple foci. Indeed, from an implementation standpoint it is better to select the left foci one at a time, which is a non-deterministic choice with finitely many possibilities, rather than to backtrack over the infinite possibilities of selecting a multiset from a set.

We now motivate a variant of the $D_l$ rule that becomes deterministic by having it select *all* bipolar formulas in $\Gamma$ with a rule similar to the following:

$$\frac{\Sigma :: \Gamma \Downarrow \mathcal{N} \vdash P}{\Sigma :: \Gamma \vdash P} D_l,$$

where $\mathcal{N}$ is the multiset of the negative formulas in $\Gamma$ (all given multiplicity 1). As written, this rule has four significant problems.

First, the multiple foci in a left-focused sequent are intended to be *independent*. If there are rigid dependencies between the foci, then the non-invertible phase would immediately fail. For example, consider the sequent $r, r \supset s, s \supset q \Uparrow \vdash \Uparrow q$, for propositional constants $r, s, q$. Clearly, the $D_l$ rule should not place both $r \supset s$ and $s \supset q$ in the focus that initiates the non-invertible phase since only one of these has a premise currently holding in the proof context.

Second, if $B_1 \wedge^- B_2$ is among the left foci, then the $\wedge_l^-$ rules would replace that conjunction with either $B_1$ or $B_2$. However, it may be that *both* $B_1$ and $B_2$ can be foci simultaneously: in that case, it would be better to initially chose *two* copies of $B_1 \wedge^- B_2$ in the original focus so that both conjuncts could be explored.

The third problem, similar to the second problem, concerns geometric formulas. It might be possible to find multiple instances of the antecedent of such an implication but only one of these can contribute a successful forward-chaining step. For example, the sequent $p\ a, p\ b, \forall x. p\ x \supset q\ x \Uparrow \vdash \Uparrow q\ a \wedge^+ q\ b$ has an $LJF^=$ proof with exactly one left-focused non-invertible phase that starts by using $D_l$ with two copies of $\forall x. p\ x \supset q\ x$ in focus. Once again, the benefit of multifocusing is lost if we can pick only one copy of each formula in the $D_l$ rule.

Finally, the $D_l$ rule might lead to a non-productive $R_l$ rule (in the sense of Sect. 3.2).

## 4.2 Refined Processing of Geometric Implications

While the problems outlined above cannot be solved for the full logic, they can be addressed successfully when we restrict our attention to reduced border sequents. All four of these problems are addressed by changing the interpretation of left-focused sequents $\Gamma \Downarrow \Theta \vdash P$. In $LJF^=$, following the tradition of focusing calculi, the context of left foci $\Theta$ is treated as linear, without allowing for any weakening or contraction, since such foci are explicitly added with $D_l$ and removed with $R_l$. The problems above seem to indicate that this restriction is too strong, since we may need to back off from a decision to focus on a formula if we discover it has an antecedent that is not satisfied by the proof context, or to duplicate a focus if we find multiple possible uses for it during the non-invertible phase. One way to achieve this could be to add structural contraction and weakening rules to the foci $\Theta$ in such sequents:

$$\frac{\Sigma :: \Gamma \Downarrow \Theta \vdash P}{\Sigma :: \Gamma \Downarrow N, \Theta \vdash P} \qquad \frac{\Sigma :: \Gamma \Downarrow N, N, \Theta \vdash P}{\Sigma :: \Gamma \Downarrow N, \Theta \vdash P}$$

We do not take this option since adding these rules introduces non-deterministic choice points in the proof with contraction, in particular, restoring the infinite choices problem we were attempting to avoid with our naive $D_l$ rule.

To improve our treatment of the above problems with the naive $D_l$, we will eventually build a new proof system called $\mathbb{FC}$ that resembles $LJF^=$ except that it is more sophisticated in its manipulations of the left multifocus zone. We justify the design of this new proof system by addressing the problems listed above in the order of easiest to hardest.

*Handling Non-productivity:* In Sect. 3.2 we classified the $R_l$ rule as productive if and only if the focus being released is on a formula that is not immediately provable in a single phase. This can be implemented as part of the $R_l$ rule where we simply filter out all the provable formulas with the following rule:

$$\frac{\Sigma :: \Gamma \Uparrow Q_1, \ldots, Q_n \vdash R \quad (\Sigma :: \Gamma \vdash P_i \Downarrow)_{i=1}^{m} \quad (\Sigma :: \Gamma \nvdash Q_j \Downarrow)_{j=1}^{n}}{\Sigma :: \Gamma \Downarrow P_1, \ldots, P_m, Q_1, \ldots, Q_n \vdash R} R_l^d.$$

Here, the notation $\nvdash$ stands for the corresponding right-focused sequent not being provable. Note that by Theorem 2, provability of sequents of the form $\Gamma \vdash P \Downarrow$ is decidable. The items in parentheses above the horizontal line are side conditions: in particular, the proof tree that is constructed using the $R_l^d$ rule has only one premise.

*Enabling the Restriction to Geometric Implications:* The second problem identified above is already solved by the restriction of $\Theta$ to geometric implication formulas, which have no occurrences of $\wedge^-$. However, this requires a further change to $D_l$ because the formulas in $\Gamma$ are bipolar, not necessarily geometric implications. However, as we have already seen, each bipolar formula $B$ is related to a multiset of geometric formulas $[\![B]\!] = \{N_1, \ldots, N_n\}$ such that $B$ is logically equivalent to $N_1 \wedge^- \cdots \wedge^- N_n$ (or $\mathbf{t}^-$ if $n = 0$). Therefore, we can change the $D_l$ rule to the rule

$$\frac{\Sigma :: \Gamma \Downarrow [\![\mathcal{N}]\!] \vdash P}{\Sigma :: \Gamma \vdash P} \; [\![D_l]\!],$$

where $\mathcal{N}$ is the multiset of the negative formulas in $\Gamma$ (all given multiplicity 1).

*Handling Multiple Proofs of Antecedents:* The first and third problems both deal with the logical rules in the non-invertible phase. In our case, since our left-foci are guaranteed to be geometric implications after a $[\![D_l]\!]$, we can replace the three left-introduction rule in the non-invertible phase $LJF^=$ (Fig. 1) with the following rule of *forward chaining*:

$$\frac{(\Sigma :: \Gamma \vdash P\theta_i \Downarrow)_{i=1}^n \quad \Sigma :: \Gamma \Downarrow Q\theta_1, \ldots, Q\theta_n, \Theta \vdash R}{\Sigma :: \Gamma \Downarrow \forall \bar{x}.(P \supset Q), \Theta \vdash R} \; fc$$

where there are exactly $n \geq 0$ *ground* substitutions $\theta_1, \ldots, \theta_n$ for the variables $\bar{x}$ such that each of the $\theta_i$, the sequent $\Sigma :: \Gamma \vdash P\theta_i \Downarrow$ is provable. Note that if the antecedent $P$ is not provable with any substitution, then $n = 0$ and the effect of this rule is the removal of the geometric implication from the focus. Likewise, for each instance of the antecedent $P$ that is proved, the corresponding instance of the head $Q$ is added to the foci, which handles the third problem outlined above.

Without any additional restriction, it is not always the case that there is a finite number of ground substitutions such that $\Sigma :: \Gamma \vdash P\theta \Downarrow$ is provable (which is a necessary requirement for the $fc$ rule). We make one additional restriction on the structure of bipolar formulas: we require that every geometric implication $\forall \bar{x}.(A_1 \wedge^+ \cdots \wedge^+ A_n \supset P)$ in $[\![B]\!]$ is such that the free variables of its head $P$ are also free in at least one of $A_1, \ldots, A_n$. This restriction is commonly used in logic and relational programming: in [16] such formulas are called *allowed clauses*. This restriction formally eliminates some bipolar formulas: for example, $\forall x.(\mathbf{t}^+ \supset x \leq x)$. (Note that the empty $\wedge^+$ is $\mathbf{t}^+$.) However, the formula $\forall x.(nat\, x \supset x \leq x)$ does satisfy this restriction, where $nat$ is an atomic predicate. Following this example, we can convert every bipolar formula into one that satisfies the allowed clause restriction by making typed quantification more explicit as predicates. That is, for every primitive type $\tau$, we allow $\tau$ to be used also as a predicate of one argument and then replace quantifiers as follows: $\forall_\tau x.P\,x$ with $\forall x.(\tau x \supset P\,x)$ and $\exists_\tau x.P\,x$ with $\exists x.(\tau x \wedge^+ P\,x)$.

Figure 2 shows the $\mathbb{FC}$ proof system that results from modifying the proof system in Fig. 1 as follows: replace $\wedge_l^-$ and $D_l$ with $[\![D_l]\!]$, replace $\forall_l$ and $\supset_l$ with $fc$, and replace $R_l$ with $R_l^d$. Also, since $\mathbb{FC}$ will only be used to prove reduced sequents, the invertible right-introduction rules can be removed as well. It is easy to show that if a reduced sequent has an $\mathbb{FC}$ proof then it has an $LJF^=$ proof. The main advantage of using the $\mathbb{FC}$ proof system is that we need no cleverness in choosing the formulas to use with the $D_l$ rule: instead we can select

NEW RULES

$$\frac{\Sigma :: \Gamma \Downarrow [\![\mathcal{N}]\!] \vdash P}{\Sigma :: \Gamma \vdash P} \; [\![D_l]\!], \text{ where } \mathcal{N} \text{ contains the negative formulas in } \Gamma$$

$$\frac{(\Sigma :: \Gamma \vdash P\theta_i \Downarrow)_{i=1}^n \quad \Sigma :: \Gamma \Downarrow Q\theta_1, \ldots, Q\theta_n, \Theta \vdash R}{\Sigma :: \Gamma \Downarrow \forall \bar{x}.(P \supset Q), \Theta \vdash R} \; fc$$

$$\frac{\Sigma :: \Gamma \Uparrow Q_1, \ldots, Q_n \vdash R \quad (\Sigma :: \Gamma \vdash P_i \Downarrow)_{i=1}^m \quad (\Sigma :: \Gamma \nvdash Q_j \Downarrow)_{j=1}^n}{\Sigma :: \Gamma \Downarrow P_1, \ldots, P_m, Q_1, \ldots, Q_n \vdash R} \; R_l^d.$$

STRUCTURAL RULES

$$\frac{\Sigma :: \Gamma \vdash P \Downarrow}{\Sigma :: \Gamma \vdash P} \; D_r \quad \frac{\Sigma :: \Gamma \Uparrow \Theta \vdash \Uparrow P}{\Sigma :: \Gamma \Uparrow \Theta \vdash P \Uparrow} \; S_r \quad \frac{\Sigma :: \Gamma \vdash N \Uparrow}{\Sigma :: \Gamma \vdash N \Downarrow} \; R_r \quad \frac{\Sigma :: C, \Gamma \Uparrow \Theta \vdash \Delta \Uparrow \Upsilon}{\Sigma :: \Gamma \Uparrow C, \Theta \vdash \Delta \Uparrow \Upsilon} \; S_l$$

INITIAL RULE

$$\overline{\Sigma :: \Gamma, P \vdash P \Downarrow} \; I_r, \; P \text{ atomic}$$

INVERTIBLE INTRODUCTION RULES

$$\frac{\Sigma :: \Gamma \Uparrow \Theta \vdash \Delta \Uparrow \Upsilon}{\Sigma :: \Gamma \Uparrow t^+, \Theta \vdash \Delta \Uparrow \Upsilon} \qquad \frac{\Sigma :: \Gamma \Uparrow B_1, B_2, \Theta \vdash \Delta \Uparrow \Upsilon}{\Sigma :: \Gamma \Uparrow B_1 \wedge^+ B_2, \Theta \vdash \Delta \Uparrow \Upsilon}$$

$$\overline{\Sigma :: \Gamma \Uparrow f, \Theta \vdash \Delta \Uparrow \Upsilon} \qquad \frac{\Sigma :: \Gamma \Uparrow B_1, \Theta \vdash \Delta \Uparrow \Upsilon \quad \Sigma :: \Gamma \Uparrow B_2, \Theta \vdash \Delta \Uparrow \Upsilon}{\Sigma :: \Gamma \Uparrow B_1 \vee B_2, \Theta \vdash \Delta \Uparrow \Upsilon}$$

$$\frac{x{:}\tau, \Sigma :: \Gamma \Uparrow B, \Theta \vdash \Delta \Uparrow \Upsilon}{\Sigma :: \Gamma \Uparrow \exists x_\tau.B, \Theta \vdash \Delta \Uparrow \Upsilon}$$

$$\frac{(\theta = \mathrm{mgu}(t,s)) \quad \Sigma\theta :: \Gamma\theta \Uparrow \Theta\theta \vdash \Delta\theta \Uparrow \Upsilon\theta}{\Sigma :: \Gamma \Uparrow s = t, \Theta \vdash \Delta \Uparrow \Upsilon} \qquad \frac{(t \text{ and } s \text{ not unifiable})}{\Sigma :: \Gamma \Uparrow s = t, \Theta \vdash \Delta \Uparrow \Upsilon}$$

NON-INVERTIBLE INTRODUCTION RULES

$$\overline{\Sigma :: \Gamma \vdash t = t \Downarrow} \qquad \overline{\Sigma :: \Gamma \vdash t^+ \Downarrow} \qquad \frac{\Sigma :: \Gamma \vdash B_i \Downarrow}{\Sigma :: \Gamma \vdash B_1 \vee B_2 \Downarrow} \; i \in \{1,2\}$$

$$\frac{\Sigma :: \Gamma \vdash B_1 \Downarrow \quad \Sigma :: \Gamma \vdash B_2 \Downarrow}{\Sigma :: \Gamma \vdash B_1 \wedge^+ B_2 \Downarrow} \qquad \frac{(\Sigma \vdash t : \tau) \quad \Sigma :: \Gamma \vdash [t/x]B \Downarrow}{\Sigma :: \Gamma \vdash \exists x_\tau.B \Downarrow}$$

The conventions and restrictions on schema variables here are the same as in Figure 1.

**Fig. 2.** The FC proof system for reduced sequents.

all available bipolar formulas for that rule, and then dynamically adjust the foci when searching for a productive proof.

A *forward-chaining phase* is a partial proof that has $[\![D_l]\!]$ as its last rule, has $R_l^d$ as its uppermost rules, and only *fc* for its internal rules. A forward chaining phase is a *useless phase* if every occurrence of $R_l^d$ has border sequents as premises because the $R_l^d$ rules discards all the foci: for example,

$$\cfrac{\cfrac{\Xi_1 \atop \Sigma :: \Gamma \Uparrow \vdash Q}{\Sigma :: \Gamma \Downarrow \mathcal{P}_1 \vdash Q}\, R_l^d \quad \cdots \quad \cfrac{\Xi_n \atop \Sigma :: \Gamma \Uparrow \vdash Q}{\Sigma :: \Gamma \Downarrow \mathcal{P}_n \vdash Q}\, R_l^d}{\cfrac{\Sigma :: \Gamma \Downarrow [\mathcal{N}] \vdash Q}{\Sigma :: \Gamma \vdash Q}\, [\![D_l]\!]}\, fc *.$$

The endsequents of any of the proofs $\Xi_i$ match that of the useless phase itself. The proof context $\langle \Sigma, \Gamma \rangle$ of a border sequent $\Sigma :: \Gamma \vdash Q$ is said to be *saturated* if the $\mathbb{FC}$ proof of this sequent must end in either a useless phase or $D_r$. Any attempt to use $D_l$ for this sequent would be unproductive.

*Example 1.* Assume that $i$ is a primitive type, $f$ is a unary constructor for $i$, $p$ is unary predicate for type $i$, and $t$ is a $\Sigma$-term of type $i$.

- If $\Gamma$ contains $p\,t$ and $\forall_i x.(p\,x \supset p(f\,x))$, then $\langle \Sigma, \Gamma \rangle$ is not saturated.
- If $\Gamma$ is the two element set containing $p\,t$ and $\forall_i x.(p\,x \supset \exists y.p\,y)$, then $\langle \Sigma, \Gamma \rangle$ is saturated.
- If $\leq$ is a binary predicate on type $i$ and $\Gamma$ contains $p\,t$ and $\forall_i x.(p\,x \supset \exists_i y.(p\,y \wedge^+ x \leq y))$, then $\langle \Sigma, \Gamma \rangle$ is not saturated.

### 4.3 Safe for Saturation

One of the reasons to identify saturated sequents is that they provide a simple decision procedure for proving $\mathbb{P}$ formulas. In particular, if $\langle \Sigma, \Gamma \rangle$ is saturated then determining if it entails a purely positive formula is immediate in $\mathbb{FC}$ (and hence in $LJF^=$). Every forward chaining phase that concludes with $\Sigma :: \Gamma \vdash Q$ will be useless by definition, so it will be provable if and only if $\Sigma :: \Gamma \vdash Q \Downarrow$ is provable, which is decidable by Theorem 2.

We say that a border sequent is *safe for saturation in n steps* (for a natural number $n$) if it has an $\mathbb{FC}$ phase that ends with a non-useless forward chaining phase, and each of the border sequents in the premises of that phase has a saturated context or is safe for saturation in $n-1$ steps. We say that the sequent is *safe for saturation* if there is an $n$ such that it is safe for saturation in $n$ steps. Any border sequent that is safe for saturation has decidable provability because one can simply compute repeatedly forward-chaining phases (of which there will be finitely many), and if any border sequent premise is saturated then its provability is decidable as argued below. Furthermore, there are no infinitely deep branches for that border sequent along non-useless forward chaining phases because the length of that branch (counting the instances of $D_l$) is bounded above by some finite number $n$.

The next theorem identifies a natural class of sequents that are safe for saturation.

**Theorem 5.** Let $\langle \Sigma, \Gamma \rangle$ be a proof context and let $\mathcal{N}$ be the multiset of bipolar formulas in $\Gamma$. This context is safe for saturation if for every geometric implication in $[\![\mathcal{N}]\!]$ of the form $\forall \bar{x}.(P \supset Q)$ it is the case that $Q$ is composed of only f, $\vee$, $\mathsf{t}^+$, $\wedge^+$, equality, and atomic formulas without constructors of non-zero arity.

*Proof.* Let the proof context $\langle \Sigma, \Gamma \rangle$ be divided into the negative (bipolar) formulas $\mathcal{N}$ and the positive (atomic) formulas $\mathcal{P}$. Define the *cover* of this proof context $\langle \Sigma, \mathcal{N}, \mathcal{P} \rangle^\circ$ as the set of atomic formulas of the form $p\ t_1 \cdots t_n$ where $p$ is any $n$-ary predicate occurring in formulas in either $\mathcal{N}$ or $\mathcal{P}$ and the terms $t_1, \ldots, t_n$ are either subterms of terms appearing in the atoms of $\mathcal{P}$ or constructors of arity 0 (i.e., constants). Note that $\langle \Sigma, \mathcal{N}, \mathcal{P} \rangle^\circ$ is a finite set. Now consider the following productive forward-chaining phase:

$$\cfrac{\cfrac{\cfrac{\cdots \quad \Sigma\theta :: \mathcal{N}\theta, \mathcal{P}\theta, \mathcal{P}' \vdash Q\theta \quad \cdots}{\Sigma :: \mathcal{N}, \mathcal{P} \Uparrow \mathcal{P}'' \vdash Q} \text{ invertible phase}}{\Sigma :: \mathcal{N}, \mathcal{P} \Downarrow [\![\mathcal{N}]\!] \vdash Q}\, fc^*, R_l^d}{\Sigma :: \mathcal{N}, \mathcal{P} \vdash Q}\, [\![D_l]\!]$$

Here $\theta$ is a substitution (possibly the identity) resulting from possible occurrences of the $=_l$ rule in the invertible phase, and $\mathcal{P}'$ is a multiset of atomic formulas that are not present in $\mathcal{P}\theta$. Since this is a productive proof, either $\mathcal{P}'$ is not empty or the phase is useless (and can be collapsed). We make the following observations about the forward-chaining phase above.

1. $\langle \Sigma\theta, \mathcal{N}\theta, \mathcal{P}\theta \cup \mathcal{P}' \rangle^\circ \subseteq \langle \Sigma, \mathcal{N}, \mathcal{P} \rangle^\circ$. This follows simply from the fact that since ($i$) there are no existential quantifiers in the head of bipolar formulas, no new eigenvariables are introduced into the proof context and ($ii$) since the head of geometric clauses do not contain constructors of non-zero arity, any substitution instance of such head will be composed of subterms on the $\mathcal{P}$ component of the context.
2. Both $\mathcal{P} \subseteq \langle \Sigma, \mathcal{N}, \mathcal{P} \rangle^\circ$ and $\mathcal{P}\theta \cup \mathcal{P}' \subseteq \langle \Sigma, \mathcal{N}, \mathcal{P} \rangle^\circ$.
3. If the forward chaining phase is not useless, then $\mathcal{P}'$ is non-empty and the number of elements in $\mathcal{P}\theta \cup \mathcal{P}'$ is strictly greater than the number of elements in $\mathcal{P}$ (ignoring multiplicity).

As a result of these observations, the number of not useless forward-chaining phases must be limited by the size of the set $\langle \Sigma, \mathcal{N}, \mathcal{P} \rangle^\circ$. $\square$

Theorem 5 provides a useful criterion for determining when one can expect the saturation process to terminate. Undoubtedly, many other criteria can also be developed.

### 4.4 Implementing a Forward Chaining Tactic (in Abella)

Abella [4] is an interactive theorem prover based on the $\mathcal{G}$ logic [13], which is $LJ^=$ extended with inductive and co-inductive fixed points, quantification over simply typed $\lambda$-terms (instead of just multisorted first-order terms), and the $\nabla$

quantifier [20] and associated nominal constants. Given that $LJ^=$ is contained withing $\mathcal{G}$, it has been straightforward to design and prototype a forward chaining tactic based on $\mathbb{FC}$ in the Abella.[3]

The implementation of the $[\![D_l]\!]$ rule of $\mathbb{FC}$ has to be adapted for the implementation because Abella is intended as a general purpose system where we cannot *a priori* limit the shape of the elements of $\Gamma$: users are allowed to write any theorems they want, even those that are not bipolar formulas. We implement a variant of the system where the user picks the specific multiset of lemmas to decide on, and the geometric implication set $[\![B]\!]$ of every lemma $B$ is computed on the fly. The implementation also does not currently detect whether the lemmas the user indicates for saturation are safe for saturation. Instead, the saturation mechanism is run with an implicit finite *phase height* bound, which bounds the number of instances of $D_l$ needed on any branch of the derivation.

Another key difference with $\mathbb{FC}$ is that the implementation does not keep the context $\Gamma$ as a set. This is mainly for performance reasons, since transforming a multiset into a set is a worst-case quadratic operation that should therefore not be done too often.

## 5 Related and Future Work

Focused proof systems offer a framework to account for various synthetic inference rules found in the literature [17]. For instance, the work of Negri [23,24] can be explained by polarizing atomic formulas positively, while the synthetic inference rules developed by Viganò [26] can be explained by polarizing atoms negatively. Furthermore, the phases of goal-reduction and backchaining, commonly found in logic programming, can be interpreted as the two phases of focused proofs when atomic formulas are polarized negatively [19].

Although this paper primarily focuses on bipolar formulas and geometric implications, such formulas appear in a wide range of contexts. For example, Horn clauses are inherently bipolar formulas, as are many axioms describing algebraic structures. A formal process known as *geometrisation* can also be employed to reduce arbitrary first-order logical theories exclusively to geometric theories [11]. Examining published proofs, for instance, in Abella, reveals that a large majority of theorems proved in these settings are bipolar. As an illustration, every theorem in the development of a library for multisets [8][4] is a geometric implication. Even in meta-theoretic papers, such as [1,2], the collection of theorems is either entirely or almost exclusively composed of bipolar formulas.

A number of examples in the extended version of this paper [6] explicitly represent terms using the *administrative normal form* (ANF) [12], a representation that allows for explicitly sharing term structures. As shown in [21], ANF can be seen as representing terms as focused proofs of their types when primitive

---

[3] See https://abella-prover.org/fc for a page dedicated to this implementation, with installation instruction and browsable examples.

[4] See: https://github.com/meta-logic/abella-reasoning/tree/master/lib.

types are given positive polarity. We plan to explore the synergy around positive polarization in both term structure and forward chaining. Also, since the proof theory of the $\nabla$-quantifier can be layered on $LJ^=$, we hope to generalize forward chaining to also work with term structures that contain bindings. As a result, the approach to the congruence closure described in [6, Appendix B] might be lifted in a natural way to account for congruences on such terms.

## 6 Conclusion

This paper introduces a proof-theoretic framework for defining forward chaining and saturation within a multisorted, first-order intuitionistic logic with equality. Key to this framework are the notions of polarity and focused proofs, which provide a principled interpretation of forward chaining and *productive proofs*. We also define the notion of *safe for saturation* under which forward chaining is guaranteed to terminate and exhibit a natural class of formulas that are shown to be safe in this sense. This theoretical analysis motivates and supports the implementation of a novel forward chaining tactic within the Abella theorem prover, which has been shown to reduce manual proof effort by automating lemma applications and facilitating tasks like congruence closure and various equational and relational reasoning.

## References

1. Accattoli, B.: Proof pearl: abella formalization of lambda calculus cube property. In: Hawblitzel, C., Miller, D. (eds.) Second International Conference on Certified Programs and Proofs. LNCS, vol. 7679, pp. 173–187. Springer, Cham (2012)
2. Accattoli, B., Blanc, H., Coen, C.S.: Formalizing functions as processes. In: Naumowicz, A., Thiemann, R. (eds.) 14th International Conference on Interactive Theorem Proving (ITP 2023). Leibniz International Proceedings in Informatics (LIPIcs), vol. 268, pp. 5:1–5:21. Schloss Dagstuhl – Leibniz-Zentrum für Informatik, Dagstuhl, Germany (2023). https://doi.org/10.4230/LIPIcs.ITP.2023.5, https://drops.dagstuhl.de/opus/volltexte/2023/18380
3. Andreoli, J.M.: Logic programming with focusing proofs in linear logic. J. Logic Comput. **2**(3), 297–347 (1992). https://doi.org/10.1093/logcom/2.3.297
4. Baelde, D., et al.: Abella: a system for reasoning about relational specifications. J. Formalized Reasoning **7**(2), 1–89 (2014). https://doi.org/10.6092/issn.1972-5787/4650
5. Bancilhon, F., Maier, D., Sagiv, Y., Ullman, J.D.: Magic sets and other strange ways to implement logic programs. In: Silberschatz, A. (ed.) Proceedings of the Fifth ACM SIGACT-SIGMOD Symposium on Principles of Database Systems, pp. 1–15. ACM (1986). https://doi.org/10.1145/6012.15399
6. Chaudhuri, K., Gantait, A., Miller, D.: Designing a safe forward chaining tactic using productive proofs. Tech. rep., Inria (2025). https://hal.archives-ouvertes.fr/hal-05157939
7. Chaudhuri, K., Hetzl, S., Miller, D.: A multi-focused proof system isomorphic to expansion proofs. J. Logic Comput. **26**(2), 577–603 (2016). https://doi.org/10.1093/logcom/exu030

8. Chaudhuri, K., Lima, L., Reis, G.: Formalized meta-theory of sequent calculi for linear logics. Theor. Comput. Sci. **781**, 24–38 (2019). https://doi.org/10.1016/j.tcs.2019.02.023. logical and Semantic Frameworks with Applications
9. Chaudhuri, K., Miller, D., Saurin, A.: Canonical sequent proofs via multi-focusing. In: Ausiello, G., Karhumäki, J., Mauri, G., Ong, L. (eds.) TCS 2008. IIFIP, vol. 273, pp. 383–396. Springer, Boston, MA (2008). https://doi.org/10.1007/978-0-387-09680-3_26
10. Chaudhuri, K., Pfenning, F., Price, G.: A logical characterization of forward and backward chaining in the inverse method. J. Autom. Reasoning **40**(2-3), 133–177 (2008). https://doi.org/10.1007/s10817-007-9091-0
11. Dyckhoff, R., Negri, S.: Geometrisation of first-order logic. Bull. Symb. Log. **21**(02), 123–163 (2015)
12. Flanagan, C., Sabry, A., Duba, B.F., Felleisen, M.: The essence of compiling with continuations. ACM SIGPLAN Notices **28**(6), 237–247 (1993). https://doi.org/10.1145/155090.155113
13. Gacek, A., Miller, D., Nadathur, G.: Nominal abstraction. Inf. Comput. **209**(1), 48–73 (2011). https://doi.org/10.1016/j.ic.2010.09.004
14. Gentzen, G.: Investigations into logical deduction. In: Szabo, M.E. (ed.) The Collected Papers of Gerhard Gentzen, pp. 68–131. North-Holland, Amsterdam (1935). https://doi.org/10.1007/BF01201353. translation of articles that appeared in 1934-35. Collected papers appeared in 1969
15. Liang, C., Miller, D.: Focusing and polarization in linear, intuitionistic, and classical logics. Theoret. Comput. Sci. **410**(46), 4747–4768 (2009). https://doi.org/10.1016/j.tcs.2009.07.041. Abstract Interpretation and Logic Programming: A Special Issue in Honor of Professor Giorgio Levi
16. Lloyd, J., Topor, R.: A basis for deductive database systems II. J. Log. Program. **3**(1), 55–67 (1986). https://doi.org/10.1016/0743-1066(86)90004-X
17. Marin, S., Miller, D., Pimentel, E., Volpe, M.: From axioms to synthetic inference rules via focusing. Ann. Pure Appl. Logic **173**(5), 1–32 (2022). https://doi.org/10.1016/j.apal.2022.103091
18. McDowell, R., Miller, D.: Cut-elimination for a logic with definitions and induction. Theoret. Comput. Sci. **232**, 91–119 (2000). https://doi.org/10.1016/S0304-3975(99)00171-1
19. Miller, D.: A survey of the proof-theoretic foundations of logic programming. Theory Pract. Logic Program. **22**(6), 859–904 (2022). https://doi.org/10.1017/S1471068421000533. published online November 2021
20. Miller, D., Tiu, A.: A proof theory for generic judgments. ACM Trans. Comput. Logic **6**(4), 749–783 (2005). https://doi.org/10.1145/1094622.1094628
21. Miller, D., Wu, J.H.: A positive perspective on term representations. In: Klin, B., Pimentel, E. (eds.) 31st EACSL Annual Conference on Computer Science Logic (CSL 2023). Leibniz International Proceedings in Informatics (LIPIcs), vol. 252, pp. 3:1–3:21. Schloss Dagstuhl–Leibniz-Zentrum fuer Informatik, Dagstuhl, Germany (2023). https://doi.org/10.4230/LIPIcs.CSL.2023.3
22. Naughton, J.F., Ramakrishnan, R.: Bottom-up evaluation of logic programs. In: Lassez, J., Plotkin, G.D. (eds.) Computational Logic - Essays in Honor of Alan Robinson, pp. 640–700. The MIT Press (1991)
23. Negri, S.: Contraction-free sequent calculi for geometric theories with an application to Barr's theorem. Arch. Math. Logic **42**, 389–401 (2003). https://doi.org/10.1007/s001530100124
24. Negri, S., Plato, J.: Cut elimination in the presence of axioms. Bull. Symbolic Logic **4**(4), 418–435 (1998). https://doi.org/10.2307/420956

25. Troelstra, A.S., Schwichtenberg, H.: Basic Proof Theory, 2nd edn. Cambridge University Press, Cambridge (2000)
26. Viganò, L.: Labelled Non-Classical Logics. Kluwer Academic Publishers, Dordrecht (2000)

**Open Access** This chapter is licensed under the terms of the Creative Commons Attribution 4.0 International License (http://creativecommons.org/licenses/by/4.0/), which permits use, sharing, adaptation, distribution and reproduction in any medium or format, as long as you give appropriate credit to the original author(s) and the source, provide a link to the Creative Commons license and indicate if changes were made.

The images or other third party material in this chapter are included in the chapter's Creative Commons license, unless indicated otherwise in a credit line to the material. If material is not included in the chapter's Creative Commons license and your intended use is not permitted by statutory regulation or exceeds the permitted use, you will need to obtain permission directly from the copyright holder.

# Base-Extension Semantics for Intuitionistic Modal Logics (Extended Abstract)

Yll Buzoku[1]( ) and David J. Pym[1,2]

[1] University College London, London WC1E 6BT, UK
{y.buzoku,d.pym}@ucl.ac.uk
[2] Institute of Philosophy, University of London, London WC1H 0AR, UK

**Abstract.** The proof theory and semantics of intuitionistic modal logics have been studied by Simpson in terms of Prawitz-style labelled natural deduction systems and Kripke models. An alternative to model-theoretic semantics is provided by proof-theoretic semantics, which is a logical realization of inferentialism, in which the meaning of constructs is understood through their use. The key idea in proof-theoretic semantics is that of a base of atomic rules, all of which refer only to propositional atoms and involve no logical connectives. A specific form of proof-theoretic semantics, known as base-extension semantics (B-eS), is concerned with the validity of formulae and provides a direct counterpart to Kripke models that is grounded in the provability of atomic formulae in a base. We establish, systematically, B-eS for Simpson's intuitionistic modal logics and, also systematically, obtain soundness and completeness theorems with respect to Simpson's natural deduction systems.

**Keywords:** inferentialism · proof-theoretic semantics · base-extension semantics · intuitionistic modal logics · labelled natural deduction

## 1 Introduction

Simpson [25] introduces a family of natural deduction systems for a range of intuitionistic modal logics (iMLs). These natural deduction systems are shown to be both sound and complete with respect to meta-logical derivations in the intuitionistic first-order meta-theory that is assumed. This result is shown by defining a bidirectional translation of modal formulae to intuitionistic first-order formulae and showing that theorems of the natural deduction systems, under the translation, correspond to a particular type of (intuitionistic) first-order derivation. Simpson also defines a Kripke semantics for his intuitionistic modal logics based on the interpretation of first-order expressions in the Kripke semantics of first-order intuitionistic logic. The resulting modal models are then used to establish the soundness and completeness of his natural deduction systems.

Proof-theoretic semantics is an alternative conception of a semantic theory that is grounded in the philosophical position known as inferentialism, in which the meanings of language constructs are considered to be determined by their use. In proof-theoretic semantics, which may be seen as a logical realization of the inferentialist position, meaning is given to a logical language through proof, rather than truth. This idea has deep roots in the works of Wittgenstein, with his principle that the meaning of a word should be reflected in its use [26], but also more recently in works such as those of Dummett [6] and Brandom [1,2,15].

Proof-theoretic semantics can usefully be seen as having two main branches. One, proof-theoretic validity (P-tV) is concerned—in a sense articulated by Prawitz [20], Dummett [6], and Schroeder-Heister [17,18,23,24]—with what constitutes a valid proof. The other, base-extension semantics (B-eS) is concerned with what constitutes a valid formula and is the focus of this paper: we provide a uniform B-eS for the iMLs studied by Simpson [25].

Sandqvist [22] obtains a sound and complete B-eS for intuitionistic propositional logic (IPL). This is achieved by defining the concept of an atomic rule as an inference figure such as $\mathcal{R}$ in Fig. 1 (which we may write linearly as $((P_1 \Rightarrow q_1), \ldots, (P_n \Rightarrow q_n)) \Rightarrow r)$), and then defining a relation of atomic derivability $\vdash_{\mathscr{B}}$ over sets of atomic rules $\mathscr{B}$, between sets of atoms and atoms. Crucially, the rules make mention only of atoms and the relation of atomic derivability, as the name suggests, is thus capable only of observing judgements between sets of atoms and individual atoms. One can imagine the $\mathscr{B}$ as being a natural deduction like construct whose elements are not schemas, but, in fact, instances of rules. Thus, in the same way that NJ can be viewed as generating the consequence relation $\vdash_{\mathrm{NJ}}$, the relation $\vdash_{\mathscr{B}}$ can be understood as the consequence relation generated by $\mathscr{B}$. Sandqvist then conservatively extends this relation to a relation of support $\Vdash_{\mathscr{B}}$ over a base $\mathscr{B}$ which relates sets of IPL formulae to an IPL formula.

$$\frac{[P_1] \quad [P_n]}{q_1 \;\cdots\; q_n} \mathcal{R}$$
$$r$$

(Ref) $P, p \vdash_{\mathscr{B}} p$

(App$_{\mathcal{R}}$) if $((P_1 \Rightarrow q_1), \ldots, (P_n \Rightarrow q_n)) \Rightarrow r)$ and, for all $i \in [1, n]$, $P, P_i \vdash_{\mathscr{B}} q_i$, then $P \vdash_{\mathscr{B}} r$

(At) for atomic $p$, $\Vdash_{\mathscr{B}} p$ iff $\vdash_{\mathscr{B}} p$

(∨) $\Vdash_{\mathscr{B}} \phi \vee \psi$ iff, for every atomic $p$ and every $\mathscr{C} \supseteq \mathscr{B}$, if $\phi \Vdash_{\mathscr{C}} p$ and $\psi \Vdash_{\mathscr{C}} p$, then $\Vdash_{\mathscr{C}} p$

(⊃) $\Vdash_{\mathscr{B}} \phi \supset \psi$ iff $\phi \Vdash_{\mathscr{B}} \psi$

(⊥) $\Vdash_{\mathscr{B}} \bot$ iff, for all atomic $p$, $\Vdash_{\mathscr{B}} p$

(∧) $\Vdash_{\mathscr{B}} \phi \wedge \psi$ iff $\Vdash_{\mathscr{B}} \phi$ and $\Vdash_{\mathscr{B}} \psi$

(Inf) for $\Theta \neq \emptyset$, $\Theta \Vdash_{\mathscr{B}} \phi$ iff, for every $\mathscr{C} \supseteq \mathscr{B}$, if $\Vdash_{\mathscr{C}} \theta$, for every $\theta \in \Theta$, then $\Vdash_{\mathscr{C}} \phi$

**Fig. 1.** Sandqvist's B-eS for Intuitionistic Propositional Logic

The need to consider base extensions, of the form $\mathscr{C} \supseteq \mathscr{B}$, in entailments defined by $\Vdash_{\mathscr{B}}$ is analogous to the need to consider accessible worlds in Kripke models of intuitionistic implication. As Prawitz [20] explains, we wish the semantics to yield a construction of an implication $\phi \supset \psi$, say, as a construction of $\psi$ from $\phi$ that, together with a construction of $\phi$, yields a construction of $\psi$. For a fixed base $\mathscr{B}$, the condition as formulated above would be vacuously satisfied in the absence of a construction of $\phi$ relative to $\mathscr{B}$. This would be a rather weak condition and, unsurprisingly, the semantics requires that all base-extensions $\mathscr{C} \supseteq \mathscr{B}$ be used. See also [10] to explore further some related issues.

It is a support relation of this form that provides our main semantic tool in giving a uniform B-eS for iMLs.

The semantics as defined in Fig. 1 is sound and complete for IPL. In this framework, an IPL sequent $(\Gamma : \phi)$ is deemed valid iff for all bases $\mathscr{B}$, we have that $\Gamma \Vdash_{\mathscr{B}} \phi$ (where $\Gamma$ is a set of IPL formulae and $\phi$ is an IPL formula). This is somewhat analogous to what one might expect in a Kripke-like semantics, where one would say something like $\phi$ is valid iff for all models $\mathcal{M}$ we have that $\mathcal{M} \vDash \phi$. It is crucial, though, that bases are *not* the same as models and that this difference is easily observed in the fact that the meanings of the connectives—that is, the semantic clauses—are very different in some cases from the familiar Kripke semantics for IPL. For example, the form of the clause for disjunction in Fig. 1 can be understood either as following the second-order definition of $\vee$ or, perhaps more proof-theoretically, as following the form of the $\vee$-elimination rule in NJ (see, e.g., [10,19,21])—cf. also Beth's semantics; for example, [16] provides an illuminating discussion. That said, the treatment of $\bot$ follows, for example, Dummett [6]. Sandqvist proves, in [22], soundness and completeness of the B-eS relative to NJ [19]. We sketch the arguments below.

**Theorem 1 (IPL Soundness).** *If $\Gamma \vdash_{NJ} \phi$, then $\Gamma \Vdash \phi$.* □

In this case, by the inductive definition of $\vdash_{NJ}$, it is sufficient to consider simply every rule of NJ as a series of meta-logical expressions with us assuming the hypothesis of every rule is valid and showing that the conclusion of every rule is also valid. For example, for $\supset_I$, we show that if $\Gamma, \phi \Vdash_{\emptyset} \psi$, then $\Gamma \Vdash_{\emptyset} \phi \supset \psi$ (note, using the base $\emptyset$ is equivalent to the validity condition mentioned above).

**Theorem 2 (IPL Completeness).** *If $\Gamma \Vdash \phi$, then $\Gamma \vdash_{NJ} \phi$.* □

The proof of completeness is more involved, but amounts to showing that, for any valid sequent, we can always construct a base $\mathcal{N}$ whose rules simulate NJ. Since $\mathcal{N}$ does not contain schemas, every NJ rule must be simulated for every subformula of the valid sequent. Since the valid sequent is indeed valid, we can therefore construct an NJ proof of the sequent using the rules of $\mathcal{N}$, and then translate it faithfully to give us an NJ proof of the valid sequent.

For B-eS for iMLs, we take Simpson [25] and Sandqvist [22] as starting points and combine them to give B-eS for iMLs with natural deduction systems defined by Simpson in [25]. We do this in a very similar fashion to that described for IPL [22]. Crucially, however, more organizational structure within the formulation of bases is necessary.

As mentioned above, Simpson [25] shows that there is a translation, the standard translation, between intuitionistic first-order formulae and the modal formulae that he considers for his proof systems. The modal formulae would better be described as being 'labelled' modal formulae, whose intuitive reading is as being the 'world' at which that formula holds. Similarly, Simpson allows additionally for a special type of *non-logical* object to be present in the hypothesis of any rules in his natural deduction systems; that of relations between the worlds.

These objects are, in the inferentialist spirit of bases, inherently non-logical— they simply describe which labels are related to one other and do not involve logical constants. Accordingly, we consider these objects alongside atomic propositions (to which we now also attach a label) to be 'first-class citizens' in bases. Consequently, our notion of atomic rule can contain both world relations and labelled atoms. However, in keeping with the spirit of the natural deduction systems of Simpson, we do not generally allow for a rule to conclude such relations. That is to say, whereas it might be desirable to be able to directly express rules of the form $\mathcal{R}$, we can, and do, express them in form $\mathcal{R}'$

$$\frac{xRy \quad yRz}{xRz}\,\mathcal{R} \qquad \frac{xRy \quad yRz \quad \genfrac{}{}{0pt}{}{[xRz]}{p^v}}{p^v}\,\mathcal{R}'$$

where $p^v$ is an atom. Doing so allows us to build bases whose proof structures mimic those of the natural deduction systems of Simpson. Thus, soundness and, especially, completeness are proven exactly as in [22]; however, extra care is taken with respect to the modal connectives.

Building on all this, we give a brief summary of the organization of this paper. Section 2 introduces natural deduction systems for intuitionistic modal logics in the sense of Simpson [25]. Section 3 introduces the notion of derivability in a base, extending the work of Sandqvist [22] to include labelled atoms and relations on labels. This notion of derivability is extended to incorporate labelled formulae and to give a conception of a semantic theory through relational, or 'frame', properties. From this grounding, a B-eS in the sense of Sandqvist [22] is given for the family of modal logics described by the relational properties. Sections 4 and 5 then establish that this semantics is sound and complete with respect to the natural deduction systems given by Simpson for their respective logics— some of the details of the proofs are deferred to [4]. We conclude, in Sect. 6, with a summary of our contribution and a brief discussion of directions for further research.

In recent work by Gheorghiu, Gu, and Pym [12] on inferentialist semantics for substructural logics—and also work by Eckhardt and Pym [7,8] on classical modal logics—it has been shown that B-eS has significant potential as a modelling tool. As well as being a fundamental contribution in logic, demonstrating the scope of proof-theoretic semantics, the work presented herein adds to the collection of logics that are available to support that line of enquiry.

## 2 Intuitionistic Modal Logics

We begin by fixing some definitions that are required throughout the paper. Discussions of these definitions can be found in Simpson's comprehensive 'The Proof Theory and Semantics of Intuitionistic Modal Logics' [25].

Fix a countable set of variables $\mathbb{W}$ which we call labels, and propositional atoms $\mathbb{A}$.

**Definition 1 (Modal formulae).** *Propositional modal formulae are defined by the grammar:* $\phi, \psi ::= p \in \mathbb{A} \mid \phi \wedge \psi \mid \phi \vee \psi \mid \phi \supset \psi \mid \Box \phi \mid \Diamond \phi \mid \bot \mid \top$ □

We enrich formulae to labelled formulae. The intuitive reading of such objects is that they express the 'locale' at which the formula holds true.

**Definition 2 (Labelled formula).** *A labelled formula is an ordered pair $\langle x, \phi \rangle$, which we write as $\phi^x$, where $x \in \mathbb{W}$ and $\phi$ is a propositional modal formula.* □

**Definition 3 (Sequent).** *An intuitionistic modal sequent is an ordered pair $\langle \Gamma, \phi^x \rangle$ which we write as $(\Gamma : \phi^x)$, where $\Gamma$ is a (finite) set of labelled formulae and $\phi^x$ is a labelled formula.* □

We introduce relational assumptions, treated similarly to propositional atoms.

**Definition 4 (Relational assumption).** *A relational assumption is an ordered pair $\langle x, y \rangle$ where $x, y \in \mathbb{W}$, though we will write this as $xRy$.* □

Relational assumptions act like edges of a directed graph. This intuition will be useful for understanding the proof theory of the intuitionistic modal logics. To make this precise, recall the definition of a graph.

**Definition 5 (Graph).** *A graph is a pair $\mathcal{G} = (X, \mathfrak{R})$ where $X \subseteq \mathbb{W}$ is a non-empty set of labels and $\mathfrak{R}$ is a binary relation on $X$. We write $x \mathfrak{R} y$ to mean that $xRy \in \mathfrak{R}$.* □

Given a graph $\mathcal{G} = (X, \mathfrak{R})$, we can require that the relations be subject to different global properties (i.e., properties on all $x \in X$) such as those in Fig. 2. The properties in Fig. 2 are conventionally called *frame conditions* in the context of modal logic and we adopt this terminology herein. We denote a (possibly empty) subset of these frame conditions and represent this by a letter $\gamma$, which should be understood as $\gamma \subseteq \{\gamma_D, \gamma_T, \gamma_B, \gamma_4, \gamma_5, \gamma_2\}$. By fixing such a $\gamma$, we fix a particular intuitionistic modal logic, with the empty subset $\gamma = \emptyset$ denoting the modal logic iK.

**Definition 6 (Intuitionistic modal derivability).** *Given a set of frame conditions $\gamma$, a sequent $(\Gamma : \phi^x)$, and a graph $\mathcal{G} = (X, \mathfrak{R})$ whose vertex set $X$ contains at least every label of the elements of $\Gamma$ and $x$, whose edge-set $\mathfrak{R}$ satisfies the conditions $\gamma$, then the relation of derivability for the specific intuitionistic modal logic satisfying the modal axioms corresponding to the frame conditions $\gamma$ is defined by the schemas of Fig. 3 and the schemas corresponding to the frame conditions of Fig. 4. The resulting consequence relation is written $\Gamma \vdash_{\mathcal{G}}^{\gamma} \phi^x$.* □

The schemas of Fig. 3 form the base natural deduction system $N_{\Box \Diamond}$, which corresponds to a natural deduction system for the logic iK. We extend this natural deduction system to other intuitionistic modal logics by adding to $N_{\Box \Diamond}$

| Axiom Schema | Label | Name | Relational property |
|---|---|---|---|
| $\Diamond \top$ | $\gamma_D$ | Seriality | $\forall x.\, \exists y.\, xRy$ |
| $\Box \phi \supset \phi$ | $\gamma_T$ | Reflexivity | $\forall x.\, xRx$ |
| $\phi \supset \Box \Diamond \phi$ | $\gamma_B$ | Symmetry | $\forall x.\, \forall y.\, xRy \Rightarrow yRx$ |
| $\Box \phi \supset \Box \Box \phi$ | $\gamma_4$ | Transitivity | $\forall x.\, \forall y.\, \forall z.\, xRy \,\&\, yRz \Rightarrow xRz$ |
| $\Diamond \phi \supset \Box \Diamond \phi$ | $\gamma_5$ | Euclidean | $\forall x.\, \forall y.\, \forall z.\, xRy \,\&\, xRz \Rightarrow yRz$ |
| $\Diamond \Box \phi \supset \Box \Diamond \phi$ | $\gamma_2$ | Directed | $\forall x.\, \forall y.\, \forall z.\, xRy \,\&\, yRz \Rightarrow \exists w.\, yRw \,\&\, zRw$ |

**Fig. 2.** Frame conditions

additional inference figures from Fig. 4, which represent the necessary relational properties of those logics. That this is justified is shown by Simpson in [25]. We write $N_{\Box\Diamond}(\gamma)$ to denote the natural deduction system $N_{\Box\Diamond}$ extended by the rules that correspond to the frame conditions $\gamma$. Thus, the consequence relation $\Gamma \vdash^\gamma_{\mathcal{G}} \phi^x$ should be read as saying that there is a derivation in $N_{\Box\Diamond}(\gamma)$ of $\phi^x$ from open assumptions $\Gamma$ and $\mathfrak{R}$, where $\mathcal{G} = (X, \mathfrak{R})$, recalling that $X = \{x \mid \psi^x \in \Gamma \cup \{\phi^x\}\}$. Of interest is the trivial graph: $\tau = (x, \emptyset)$.

The soundness and completeness of the natural deduction systems $N_{\Box\Diamond}(\gamma)$ with respect to their intuitionistic modal logics is proven in [25].

**Definition 7 (Theorem of $N_{\Box\Diamond}(\gamma)$).** *A labelled formula $\phi^x$ is called a theorem of $N_{\Box\Diamond}(\gamma)$ if $\vdash^\gamma_\tau \phi^x$ holds. We write this as $\vdash^\gamma \phi^x$.* □

## 3 Derivability in a Base and Base-Extension Semantics

Following the approach of Sandqvist [22], we start by defining a notion of atomic derivability, which is the basis of the B-eS.

**Definition 8 (Basic sentence).** *A basic sentence is either a labelled atom or a relational assumption. $\mathbb{B}$ denotes the set of basic sentences.* □

We adopt the convention that lower case Latins refer to basic sentences, except for the variable letters $v, w, x, y, z, a, b$. Lower case Greeks, except for $\gamma$, will refer to intuitionistic modal formulae and uppercase Latins and Greeks, except for the relation symbol $R$, refer to finite sets thereof. A basic sentence written without a superscript is taken to be *either* a labelled atom *or* a relational assumption. We henceforth use the word atom to mean *labelled atom*.

**Definition 9 (Basic sequent).** *A basic sequent is an ordered pair $\langle P, p \rangle$ where $P$ is a (finite) set of basic sentences and $p$ is a labelled atom if $P \neq \emptyset$. Else $p$ is a basic sentence. We write this pair as $P \Rightarrow p$ and omit the $P$ if it is empty.* □

**Definition 10 (Basic rule).** *A basic rule is an ordered pair $\langle \mathbf{Q}, r \rangle$ where $\mathbf{Q}$ is a (finite) set of basic sequents and $r$ is a labelled atom if $\mathbf{Q} \neq \emptyset$. Else, $r$ is a basic sentence. We write this as $(P_1 \Rightarrow p_1, \ldots, P_n \Rightarrow p_n) \Rightarrow r$ where each $P_i \Rightarrow p_i \in \mathbf{Q}$ and omit the $(P_1 \Rightarrow p_1, \ldots, P_n \Rightarrow p_n)$ if $\mathbf{Q}$ is empty.* □

$$\frac{}{\top^x} \top_I \qquad\qquad \frac{\bot^x}{\phi^y} \bot_E$$

$$\frac{\begin{array}{c}[\phi^x]\\ \psi^x\end{array}}{(\phi \supset \psi)^x} \supset_I \qquad\qquad \frac{(\phi \supset \psi)^x \quad \phi^x}{\psi^x} \supset_E$$

$$\frac{\phi^x \quad \psi^x}{(\phi \wedge \psi)^x} \wedge_I \qquad\qquad \frac{(\phi \wedge \psi)^x}{\phi^x} \wedge_{1E} \quad \frac{(\phi \wedge \psi)^x}{\psi^x} \wedge_{2E}$$

$$\frac{\phi^x}{(\phi \vee \psi)^x} \vee_{1I} \quad \frac{\psi^x}{(\phi \vee \psi)^x} \vee_{2I} \qquad \frac{(\phi \vee \psi)^x \quad \begin{array}{c}[\phi^x]\\ \chi^y\end{array} \quad \begin{array}{c}[\psi^x]\\ \chi^y\end{array}}{\chi^y} \vee_E$$

$$\frac{\begin{array}{c}[xRy]\\ \phi^y\end{array}}{(\Box \phi)^x} \Box_I^* \qquad\qquad \frac{(\Box \phi)^x \quad xRy}{\phi^y} \Box_E$$

$$\frac{\phi^y \quad xRy}{(\Diamond \phi)^x} \Diamond_I \qquad\qquad \frac{(\Diamond \phi)^x \quad \begin{array}{c}[\phi^y]\,[xRy]\\ \psi^z\end{array}}{\psi^z} \Diamond_E^{**}$$

$*$ The label $y$ is different to $x$ and the labels of any open assumptions.

$**$ The label $y$ is different to $x$ and $z$ and the labels of any open assumptions.

**Fig. 3.** The natural deduction system $N_{\Box\Diamond}$ for intuitionistic modal logic iK

**Definition 11 (Base).** *A base is a set of basic rules.* □

**Definition 12 (Basic derivability relation).** *Given a set of frame conditions $\gamma$ and a base $\mathcal{B}$, we inductively define derivability on basic sequents:*

(Ref)  $S, p \vdash_{\mathcal{B}}^{\gamma} p$  (App)  *If* $((P_1 \Rightarrow p_1, \ldots, P_n \Rightarrow p_n) \Rightarrow r) \in \mathcal{B}$ *and* $S, P_i \vdash_{\mathcal{B}}^{\gamma} p_i$ *for each $i$, then* $S \vdash_{\mathcal{B}}^{\gamma} r$

(D)  *If $\gamma_D \in \gamma$ and there exists a $y$ such that $S, xRy \vdash_{\mathcal{B}}^{\gamma} p^z$, then $S \vdash_{\mathcal{B}}^{\gamma} p^z$*

(T)  *If $\gamma_T \in \gamma$ and $S, xRx \vdash_{\mathcal{B}}^{\gamma} p^y$, then $S \vdash_{\mathcal{B}}^{\gamma} p^y$*

(B)  *If $\gamma_B \in \gamma$, $S \vdash_{\mathcal{B}}^{\gamma} xRy$ and $S, yRx \vdash_{\mathcal{B}}^{\gamma} p^z$, then $S \vdash_{\mathcal{B}}^{\gamma} p^z$*

(4)  *If $\gamma_4 \in \gamma$, $S \vdash_{\mathcal{B}}^{\gamma} xRy$, $S \vdash_{\mathcal{B}}^{\gamma} yRz$, and $S, xRz \vdash_{\mathcal{B}}^{\gamma} p^w$, then $S \vdash_{\mathcal{B}}^{\gamma} p^w$*

(5)  *If $\gamma_5 \in \gamma$, $S \vdash_{\mathcal{B}}^{\gamma} xRy$, $S \vdash_{\mathcal{B}}^{\gamma} xRz$, and $S, yRz \vdash_{\mathcal{B}}^{\gamma} p^w$, then $S \vdash_{\mathcal{B}}^{\gamma} p^w$*

(2)  *If $\gamma_2 \in \gamma$, $S \vdash_{\mathcal{B}}^{\gamma} xRy$, $S \vdash_{\mathcal{B}}^{\gamma} xRz$, and there exists a $w$ such that $S, yRw, zRw \vdash_{\mathcal{B}}^{\gamma} p^v$, then $S \vdash_{\mathcal{B}}^{\gamma} p^v$.*

*The last six cases we call the* modal cases *of the derivability relation. In the case of (D), the label $y$ cannot appear as the label of any $s \in S$ or be equal to $x$ or $z$. In the case of (2), the label $w$ cannot appear as the label of any $s \in S$ or be equal to $x, y, z, v$.* □

$$\frac{[xRy]}{\phi^z}\ (R_D)^*\qquad\qquad \frac{[xRx]}{\phi^y}\ (R_T)$$

$$\frac{xRy\quad \overset{[yRx]}{\phi^z}}{\phi^z}\ (R_B)\qquad\qquad \frac{xRy\quad yRz\quad \overset{[xRz]}{\phi^w}}{\phi^w}\ (R_4)$$

$$\frac{xRy\quad xRz\quad \overset{[yRz]}{\phi^w}}{\phi^w}\ (R_5)\qquad\qquad \frac{xRy\quad xRz\quad \overset{[yRw]\,[zRw]}{\phi^v}}{\phi^v}\ (R_2)^{**}$$

\* The label $y$ is different to $x$ and the labels of any open assumptions.

\*\* The label $w$ is different to $v, x, y, z$ and the labels of any open assumptions.

**Fig. 4.** Rules which extend $N_{\Box\Diamond}$ that express the properties of the relational assumptions

The proofs of Lemmas 1, 2, and 3 are provided in [4]. They are minor variants of similar proofs given in [22].

**Lemma 1.** *If* $U \Vdash^\gamma_\mathscr{B} u$, *then* $T, U \Vdash^\gamma_\mathscr{B} u$. □

**Lemma 2.** $T \Vdash^\gamma_\mathscr{B} u$ *if and only if, for all* $\mathscr{C} \supseteq \mathscr{B}$ *such that if, for all* $t \in T$, *we have* $\Vdash^\gamma_\mathscr{C} t$, *then* $\Vdash^\gamma_\mathscr{C} u$. □

**Lemma 3 (Monotonicity).** *If* $S \Vdash^\gamma_\mathscr{B} p$, *then, for all* $\mathscr{C} \supseteq \mathscr{B}$, $S \Vdash^\gamma_\mathscr{C} p$. □

**Definition 13 (Extended sequent).** *An extended sequent is a pair* $(\Gamma, \phi)$ *that we write* $(\Gamma : \phi)$ *where* $\Gamma$ *is a set of intuitionistic modal formulae and relational assumptions and* $\phi$ *is an intuitionistic modal formula or, if* $\Gamma$ *is empty, also possibly a relational assumption.* □

**Definition 14 (Support).** *Given a set of frame conditions* $\gamma$ *and a base* $\mathscr{B}$, *we can inductively define a relation of support on extended sequents as follows:*

(At)  $\Vdash^\gamma_\mathscr{B} p^x$ iff $\vdash^\gamma_\mathscr{B} p^x$
(Rel) $\Vdash^\gamma_\mathscr{B} xRy$ iff $\vdash^\gamma_\mathscr{B} xRy$
($\wedge$) $\Vdash^\gamma_\mathscr{B} (\phi \wedge \psi)^x$ iff $\Vdash^\gamma_\mathscr{B} \phi^x$ and $\Vdash^\gamma_\mathscr{B} \psi^x$
($\vee$) $\Vdash^\gamma_\mathscr{B} (\phi \vee \psi)^x$ iff for all $\mathscr{C} \supseteq \mathscr{B}$ and $p^z$,
  if $\phi^x \Vdash^\gamma_\mathscr{C} p^z$ and $\psi^x \Vdash^\gamma_\mathscr{C} p^z$, then $\Vdash^\gamma_\mathscr{C} p^z$
($\supset$) $\Vdash^\gamma_\mathscr{B} (\phi \supset \psi)^x$ iff $\phi^x \Vdash^\gamma_\mathscr{B} \psi^x$
($\Box$) $\Vdash^\gamma_\mathscr{B} (\Box\phi)^x$ iff $xRy \Vdash^\gamma_\mathscr{B} \phi^y$, for all labels $y$
($\Diamond$) $\Vdash^\gamma_\mathscr{B} (\Diamond\phi)^x$ iff for all $\mathscr{C} \supseteq \mathscr{B}$ and $p^z$,
  if $xRy, \phi^y \Vdash^\gamma_\mathscr{C} p^z$ for all labels $y$, then $\Vdash^\gamma_\mathscr{C} p^z$
($\bot$) $\Vdash^\gamma_\mathscr{B} \bot^x$ iff $\Vdash^\gamma_\mathscr{B} p^z$, for all $p^z$
($\top$) $\Vdash^\gamma_\mathscr{B} \top^x$ always
(Inf) $\Gamma \Vdash^\gamma_\mathscr{B} \phi$ iff for all $\mathscr{C} \supseteq \mathscr{B}$ such that $\Vdash^\gamma_\mathscr{C} \psi$, for each $\psi \in \Gamma$,
  implies $\Vdash^\gamma_\mathscr{C} \phi$ □

**Definition 15 (Validity).** *The sequent* $(\Gamma : \phi^x)$ *is said to be valid if and only if for all bases* $\mathscr{B}$, *it is the case that* $\Gamma \Vdash^\gamma_\mathscr{B} \phi^x$ *holds.* □

**Lemma 4.** *The sequent* $(\Gamma : \phi^x)$ *is valid if and only if* $\Gamma \Vdash^\gamma_\emptyset \phi^x$

*Proof.* Going left to right, we have that for all bases $\mathscr{B}$, it is the case that $\Gamma \Vdash^\gamma_\mathscr{B} \phi^x$. Thus, we can pick $\mathscr{B} = \emptyset$. Going right to left, we obtain the result by monotonicity as the empty base is the smallest subset of every base. □

So, we are justified in writing a valid sequent as $\Gamma \Vdash^\gamma \phi^x$. Before moving on, a brief discussion of the clause for $\Diamond$ is in order. One would perhaps wish to see a clause for $\Diamond$ that says something along the lines of $\Vdash^\gamma_\mathscr{B} (\Diamond\phi)^x$ iff $\exists y(\Vdash^\gamma_\mathscr{B} xRy$ and $\Vdash^\gamma_\mathscr{B} \phi^y)$. Doing so, however, quickly presents problems in proving both soundness and completeness. If we understand the presence of the existential as an infinite, meta-level disjunction, then we can understand this problem as being of the same kind faced by Sandqvist [22] in trying to define disjunction. In fact, the clause for $\Diamond$ amounts to an infinitary version of Sandqvist's clause for disjunction.

More specifically, suppose one gives a naïve Kripke-like definition for intuitionistic disjunction; that is, $\Vdash_\mathscr{B} \phi \vee \psi$ iff $\Vdash_\mathscr{B} \phi$ or $\Vdash_\mathscr{B} \psi$. One could instead write this definition as $\exists \chi \in \Delta$ s.t. $\Vdash_\mathscr{B} \chi$, where $\Delta = \{\phi, \psi\}$. This definition, as shown by de Campos Sanz and Piecha in [5], doesn't work.

Instead, the clause $\forall \mathscr{C} \supseteq \mathscr{B}, \forall p, \forall \chi \in \Delta, \chi \Vdash_\mathscr{C} p$ implies $\Vdash_\mathscr{C} p$—corresponding to the second-order definition of $\vee$ or to the elimination rule in NJ—does (again, see [10] for more discussion). Something similar follows for $\Diamond$. If one attempts to give $\Diamond$ a Kripke-like definition, that is, $\Vdash^\gamma_\mathscr{B} (\Diamond\phi)^x$ iff $\exists y$ s.t. ($\Vdash^\gamma_\mathscr{B} xRy$ and $\Vdash^\gamma_\mathscr{B} \phi^y$), then, similarly to before, this definition fails to be sound and complete. Instead, as demonstrated below, the clause $\forall \mathscr{C} \supseteq \mathscr{B}, \forall p^z, \forall y \in \mathbb{W}(\phi^y, xRy \Vdash_\mathscr{C} p^z)$ implies $\Vdash_\mathscr{C} p^z$, again based on the elimination rule, is sound and complete. Note that, in both cases, we have taken definitions that are meta-level disjunctive in the Kripke semantics, and turned them around into meta-level conjunctive in their proof-theoretic semantics.

## 4 Soundness

The soundness of the B-eS we have given with respect to natural deduction system $N_{\Box\Diamond}(\gamma)$ is stated as follows: if $\Gamma \vdash^\gamma \phi^x$, then $\Gamma \Vdash^\gamma \phi^x$.

By the inductive definition of derivability in $N_{\Box\Diamond}(\gamma)$, it suffices to show the following:

(R) $\Gamma, \phi^x \Vdash \phi^x$
($\wedge$I) If $\Gamma \Vdash \phi^x$ and $\Gamma \Vdash \psi^x$, then $\Gamma \Vdash (\phi \wedge \psi)^x$
($\wedge$E) If $\Gamma \Vdash (\phi \wedge \psi)^x$, then $\Gamma \Vdash \phi^x$ and $\Gamma \Vdash \psi^x$
($\vee$I) If $\Gamma \Vdash \phi^x$ or $\Gamma \Vdash \psi^x$, then $\Gamma \Vdash (\phi \vee \psi)^x$
($\vee$E) If $\Gamma \Vdash (\phi \vee \psi)^x$ and $\Gamma, \phi^x \Vdash \chi^y$ and $\Gamma, \psi^x \Vdash \chi^y$, then $\Gamma \Vdash \chi^y$
($\supset$I) If $\Gamma, \phi^x \Vdash \psi^x$, then $\Gamma \Vdash (\phi \supset \psi)^x$
($\supset$E) If $\Gamma \Vdash (\phi \supset \psi)^x$ and $\Gamma \Vdash \phi^x$, then $\Gamma \Vdash \psi^x$
($\bot$E) If $\Gamma \Vdash \bot^x$, then $\Gamma \Vdash \chi^y$

($\Box$I) If $\Gamma, xRy \Vdash^\gamma \phi^y$ for $y$ different to $x$ and not a label of any element of $\Gamma$, then $\Gamma \Vdash^\gamma (\Box\phi)^x$

($\Box$E) If $\Gamma \Vdash^\gamma (\Box\phi)^x$ and $\Gamma \Vdash^\gamma xRy$, then $\Gamma \Vdash^\gamma \phi^y$

($\Diamond$I) If $\Gamma \Vdash^\gamma \phi^v$ and $\Gamma \Vdash^\gamma xRv$, then $\Gamma \Vdash^\gamma (\Diamond\phi)^x$

($\Diamond$E) If $\Gamma \Vdash^\gamma (\Diamond\phi)^x$ and $\Gamma, \phi^a, xRa \Vdash^\gamma \psi^z$ for $a$ different to $x$ and $z$ and not a label of any element of $\Gamma$, then $\Gamma \Vdash^\gamma \psi^z$.

Additionally, if $\gamma \neq \emptyset$ we must show the following:

($R_D$) If $\gamma_D \in \gamma$ and $\Gamma, xRa \Vdash^\gamma \phi^z$, for $a$ different to $x$ and $z$ and not a label of any element of $\Gamma$, then $\Gamma \Vdash^\gamma \phi^z$

($R_T$) If $\gamma_T \in \gamma$ and $\Gamma, xRx \Vdash^\gamma \phi^y$ then $\Gamma \Vdash^\gamma \phi^y$

($R_B$) If $\gamma_B \in \gamma$ and $\Gamma \Vdash^\gamma xRy$ and $\Gamma, yRx \Vdash^\gamma \phi^z$ then $\Gamma \Vdash^\gamma \phi^z$

($R_4$) If $\gamma_4 \in \gamma$ and $\Gamma \Vdash^\gamma xRy$ and $\Gamma \Vdash^\gamma yRz$ and $\Gamma, xRz \Vdash^\gamma \phi^w$ then $\Gamma \Vdash^\gamma \phi^w$

($R_5$) If $\gamma_5 \in \gamma$ and $\Gamma \Vdash^\gamma xRy$ and $\Gamma \Vdash^\gamma xRz$ and $\Gamma, yRz \Vdash^\gamma \phi^w$ then $\Gamma \Vdash^\gamma \phi^w$

($R_2$) If $\gamma_2 \in \gamma$ and $\Gamma \Vdash^\gamma xRy$ and $\Gamma \Vdash^\gamma xRz$ and $\Gamma, yRw, zRw \Vdash^\gamma \phi^v$, for $w$ different to $x, y, z, v$ and not a label of any element of $\Gamma$, then $\Gamma \Vdash^\gamma \phi^v$.

Soundness, Theorem 3, is proved in detail in [4]. Here we provide some of the more important cases, emphasising modality, frame axioms, and, in order to stress the connection with the underlying issues in IPL, disjunction.

**Theorem 3 (Soundness).** *If $\Gamma \vdash^\gamma \phi^x$, then $\Gamma \Vdash^\gamma \phi^x$.*

*Proof.* We proceed by proving a selection of the cases listed above, under the additional hypothesis that we are in an arbitrary base $\mathscr{B}$ s.t., for all $\theta \in \Gamma$, $\Vdash^\gamma_\mathscr{B} \theta$.

(R) $\phi^x \Vdash^\gamma_\mathscr{B} \phi^x$. This case is immediate by (Inf).

($\vee$E) If $\Vdash^\gamma_\mathscr{B} (\phi \vee \psi)^x$ and $\phi^x \Vdash^\gamma_\mathscr{B} \chi^y$ and $\psi^x \Vdash^\gamma_\mathscr{B} \chi^y$, then $\Vdash^\gamma_\mathscr{B} \chi^y$. We proceed by an inductive argument over the structure of the labelled formula $\chi^y$. We give just a few key cases.

- $\chi = \Box\alpha$. Our goal will be to show that, $yRa \Vdash^\gamma_\mathscr{B} \alpha^a$ holds, for all labels $a$. With this in mind, we fix an arbitrary label $a$ and consider all bases $\mathscr{C} \supseteq \mathscr{B}$, where $\Vdash^\gamma_\mathscr{C} yRa$ holds. We are left with showing $\Vdash^\gamma_\mathscr{C} \alpha^a$. To this end, consider the hypothesis $\phi^x \Vdash^\gamma_\mathscr{B} (\Box\alpha)^y$. We immediately have that $\phi^x \Vdash^\gamma_\mathscr{C} (\Box\alpha)^y$ by monotonicity. This is equivalent to considering all bases $\mathscr{D} \supseteq \mathscr{C}$ for which $\Vdash^\gamma_\mathscr{D} \phi^x$ implies $\Vdash^\gamma_\mathscr{D} (\Box\alpha)^y$. The consequent of the previous implication is equivalent to considering all labels $b$ such that $yRb \Vdash^\gamma_\mathscr{D} \alpha^b$ which implies that in particular $yRa \Vdash^\gamma_\mathscr{D} \alpha^a$. Since, by hypothesis, we have that $\Vdash^\gamma_\mathscr{C} yRa$ and $\mathscr{D} \supseteq \mathscr{C}$, then it is the case that $\Vdash^\gamma_\mathscr{D} \alpha^a$. It thus follows that $\phi^x \Vdash^\gamma_\mathscr{C} \alpha^a$. The same argument gives that $\psi^x \Vdash^\gamma_\mathscr{C} \alpha^a$, so, by the inductive hypothesis, we can therefore obtain $\Vdash^\gamma_\mathscr{C} \alpha^a$, as required.

- $\chi = \Diamond\alpha$. We start by fixing a base $\mathscr{C} \supseteq \mathscr{B}$ and an atom $p^w$, where $yRz, \alpha^z \Vdash^\gamma_\mathscr{C} p^w$, for all $z$. We must show that $\Vdash^\gamma_\mathscr{C} p^w$. The second hypothesis, by monotonicity, gives $\phi^x \Vdash^\gamma_\mathscr{C} (\Diamond\alpha)^y$. This equivalently gives us that, for all bases $\mathscr{D} \supseteq \mathscr{C}$, $\Vdash^\gamma_\mathscr{D} \phi^x$ implies that, for all bases $\mathscr{E} \supseteq \mathscr{D}$ and atoms $p^a$, if $yRz, \alpha^z \Vdash^\gamma_\mathscr{E} p^a$, for all $z$, then $\Vdash^\gamma_\mathscr{E} p^a$. Thus, we can conclude that $\Vdash^\gamma_\mathscr{D} p^w$ and therefore $\phi^x \Vdash^\gamma_\mathscr{C} p^w$. Similarly, we obtain $\psi^x \Vdash^\gamma_\mathscr{C} p^w$, and so, by the first hypothesis, we conclude $\Vdash^\gamma_\mathscr{C} p^w$, as required.

($\lozenge$E) If $\Vdash^\gamma_{\mathscr{B}} (\lozenge\phi)^x$ and $\phi^a, xRa \Vdash^\gamma_{\mathscr{B}} \psi^z$ for $a$ different to $x$ and $z$, then $\Vdash^\gamma_{\mathscr{B}} \psi^z$. We break the proof into a case analysis over the structure of $\psi^z$.

- $\psi = \alpha \vee \beta$. In this case, further fix a base $\mathscr{C} \supseteq \mathscr{B}$ and an atom $p^w$ such that $\alpha^z \Vdash^\gamma_{\mathscr{C}} p^w$ and $\beta^z \Vdash^\gamma_{\mathscr{C}} p^w$. We want to show that $\Vdash^\gamma_{\mathscr{C}} p^w$. By monotonicity, taking the second hypothesis is equivalent to considering all $\mathscr{D} \supseteq \mathscr{C}$ such that $\Vdash^\gamma_{\mathscr{D}} \phi^a$ and $\Vdash^\gamma_{\mathscr{D}} xRa$ implies $\Vdash^\gamma_{\mathscr{D}} (\alpha \vee \beta)^z$. By definition, this is equivalent to considering all bases $\mathscr{E} \supseteq \mathscr{D}$ and atoms $p^w$ such that $\alpha^z \Vdash^\gamma_{\mathscr{E}} p^w$ and $\beta^z \Vdash^\gamma_{\mathscr{E}} p^w$ implies $\Vdash^\gamma_{\mathscr{E}} p^w$. Since we have that $\alpha^z \Vdash^\gamma_{\mathscr{C}} p^w$ and $\beta^z \Vdash^\gamma_{\mathscr{C}} p^w$, then we can conclude that we have $\Vdash^\gamma_{\mathscr{D}} p^w$. Thus we have that $xRa, \phi^a \Vdash^\gamma_{\mathscr{C}} p^w$, which implies that $xRy, \phi^y \Vdash^\gamma_{\mathscr{C}} p^w$, for all $y$. Hence, by the first hypothesis, we get $\Vdash^\gamma_{\mathscr{C}} p^w$, as required.

- $\psi = \Box\alpha$. In this case, further fix a label $v$ and a base $\mathscr{C} \supseteq \mathscr{B}$, such that $\Vdash^\gamma_{\mathscr{C}} zRv$. We are left to show that $\Vdash^\gamma_{\mathscr{C}} \alpha^v$. By monotonicity, the second hypothesis gives, for all $\mathscr{D} \supseteq \mathscr{C}$, that $\Vdash^\gamma_{\mathscr{D}} xRa$ and $\Vdash^\gamma_{\mathscr{D}} \phi^a$ implies that, for all $y$, we have $zRy \Vdash^\gamma_{\mathscr{D}} \alpha^y$. Therefore, in particular, we have that $zRv \Vdash^\gamma_{\mathscr{D}} \alpha^v$. Since $\Vdash^\gamma_{\mathscr{C}} zRv$, we therefore conclude that $xRa, \phi^a \Vdash^\gamma_{\mathscr{C}} \alpha^v$. By the arbitrariness of $a$, we therefore have that $xRa, \phi^a \Vdash^\gamma_{\mathscr{C}} \alpha^v$, for all $y$. Since, by monotonicity, we have that $\Vdash^\gamma_{\mathscr{C}} (\lozenge\phi)^x$, by applying the inductive hypothesis, we therefore obtain $\Vdash^\gamma_{\mathscr{C}} \alpha^v$, as required.

- $\psi = \lozenge\alpha$. In this case, further fix a base $\mathscr{C} \supseteq \mathscr{B}$ and an atom $p^w$ for which $zRv, \phi^v \Vdash^\gamma_{\mathscr{C}} p^w$ holds for all $v$. We want to show that $\Vdash^\gamma_{\mathscr{C}} p^w$. By monotonicity, the second hypothesis gives that, for all $\mathscr{D} \supseteq \mathscr{C}$, $\Vdash^\gamma_{\mathscr{D}} \phi^a$ and $\Vdash^\gamma_{\mathscr{D}} xRa$ implies $\Vdash^\gamma_{\mathscr{D}} (\lozenge\alpha)^z$. The conclusion of the previous implication is equivalent to considering all bases $\mathscr{E} \supseteq \mathscr{D}$ and atoms $p^b$ such that if $zRv, \phi^v \Vdash^\gamma_{\mathscr{E}} p^b$ for all $v$, then $\Vdash^\gamma_{\mathscr{E}} p^b$. Thus we conclude that $\Vdash^\gamma_{\mathscr{C}} p^w$ and so that $xRa, \phi^a \Vdash^\gamma_{\mathscr{C}} p^w$. Therefore, we have that $xRy, \phi^y \Vdash^\gamma_{\mathscr{C}} p^w$ for all $y$ from which, by the first hypothesis, we conclude that $\Vdash^\gamma_{\mathscr{C}} p^w$, as required.

Now we consider the cases where $\gamma \neq \emptyset$. In each case, we assume that $\gamma$ contains that particular condition. We give just the cases of $(R_D)$ for disjunction and modality. The others are similar.

$(R_D)$ If $xRa \Vdash^\gamma_{\mathscr{B}} \phi^z$, for $a$ different to $x$, then $\Vdash^\gamma_{\mathscr{B}} \phi^z$. We proceed by induction on the structure of $\phi^z$.

- If $\phi = \alpha \vee \beta$, then we have that $xRa \Vdash^\gamma_{\mathscr{B}} (\alpha \vee \beta)^z$. Given a base $\mathscr{C} \supseteq \mathscr{B}$ and an atom $p^w$ such that $\phi^z \Vdash^\gamma_{\mathscr{C}} p^w$ and $\psi^z \Vdash^\gamma_{\mathscr{C}} p^w$, we want to show that $\Vdash^\gamma_{\mathscr{C}} p^w$. We start by considering that, by monotonicity, we have $xRa \Vdash^\gamma_{\mathscr{C}} (\alpha \vee \beta)^z$, which is equivalent to considering all bases $\mathscr{D} \supseteq \mathscr{C}$ for which $\Vdash^\gamma_{\mathscr{D}} xRa$ implies $\Vdash^\gamma_{\mathscr{D}} (\alpha \vee \beta)^z$. The conclusion of the previous implication is equivalent to considering all bases $\mathscr{E} \supseteq \mathscr{D}$ and atoms $q^v$, where $\phi^z \Vdash^\gamma_{\mathscr{E}} q^v$ and $\psi^z \Vdash^\gamma_{\mathscr{E}} q^v$ implies $\Vdash^\gamma_{\mathscr{E}} q^v$. Since we have by hypothesis that $\phi^z \Vdash^\gamma_{\mathscr{C}} p^w$, $\psi^z \Vdash^\gamma_{\mathscr{C}} p^w$, and $\mathscr{E} \supseteq \mathscr{C}$, we therefore conclude that $xRa \Vdash^\gamma_{\mathscr{C}} p^v$, and thus that there exists a $y$ such that $xRa \Vdash^\gamma_{\mathscr{C}} p^v$. By the definition of $\Vdash^\gamma_{\mathscr{C}}$, we obtain $\Vdash^\gamma_{\mathscr{C}} p^v$, as desired.

- If $\phi = \Box\alpha$, then we have that $xRa \Vdash^\gamma_{\mathscr{B}} (\Box\alpha)^z$ and we must show, given a base $\mathscr{C} \supseteq \mathscr{B}$ such that $\Vdash^\gamma_{\mathscr{C}} zRw$ for an arbitrary $w$, that $\Vdash^\gamma_{\mathscr{C}} \alpha^w$. By monotonicity, we have $xRy \Vdash^\gamma_{\mathscr{C}} (\Box\alpha)^z$, which is equivalent to considering all bases $\mathscr{D} \supseteq \mathscr{C}$ for which $\Vdash^\gamma_\mathscr{D} xRy$ implies $\Vdash^\gamma_\mathscr{D} (\Box\alpha)^z$. The conclusion of the previous implication is equivalent to considering all labels $v$ such that $zRv \Vdash^\gamma_\mathscr{D} \alpha^v$. Since we have $\Vdash^\gamma_\mathscr{C} zRw$, then we have, in particular, that $\Vdash^\gamma_\mathscr{D} \alpha^v$ and thus $xRa \Vdash^\gamma_\mathscr{C} \alpha^w$. We therefore have that there exists a $y$ such that $xRa \Vdash^\gamma_\mathscr{C} \alpha^w$. By the inductive hypothesis, we obtain $\Vdash^\gamma_\mathscr{C} \alpha^w$, as required.

- If $\phi = \Diamond\alpha$, then we have that $xRa \Vdash^\gamma_\mathscr{B} (\Diamond\alpha)^z$. To show this, we begin by fixing a base $\mathscr{C} \supseteq \mathscr{B}$ and an atom $p^w$ such that $zRa, \alpha^a \Vdash^\gamma_\mathscr{C} p^w$ for all $a$, with the goal of showing that $\Vdash^\gamma_\mathscr{C} p^w$. By monotonicity, we have that $xRa \Vdash^\gamma_\mathscr{C} (\Diamond\alpha)^z$, which gives that, for all $\mathscr{D} \supseteq \mathscr{C}$, we have that $\Vdash^\gamma_\mathscr{D} xRy$ implies, for all $\mathscr{E} \supseteq \mathscr{D}$ and all atoms $q^v$, if $zRb, \alpha^b \Vdash^\gamma_\mathscr{E} q^v$ for all $b$, then $\Vdash^\gamma_\mathscr{E} q^v$. Since we have $zRa, \alpha^a \Vdash^\gamma_\mathscr{C} p^w$, we therefore can obtain by monotonicity that $\Vdash^\gamma_\mathscr{D} p^w$ and therefore $xRa \Vdash^\gamma_\mathscr{C} p^w$, and thus that there exists a $y$ such that $xRy \Vdash^\gamma_\mathscr{C} p^w$. Thus, by the definition of $\Vdash^\gamma_\mathscr{C}$, we conclude $\Vdash^\gamma_\mathscr{C} p^w$, as desired.

This concludes the proof of soundness. □

## 5 Completeness

We show that, given an arbitrary valid sequent $(\Gamma : \phi^x)$, there exists an $N_{\Box\Diamond}(\gamma)$ proof of it. We construct a special base, called $\mathscr{N}$, whose rules will mimic the natural deduction rules of $N_{\Box\Diamond}(\gamma)$, with basic sentences playing the role of (or simulating) the subformulae of the arbitrary sequent. Since the base rules can only be in terms of basic sentences and not formulae, we must be careful, as described below, about how we choose the assignment of basic sentences.

We then show that derivations in $\mathscr{N}$ directly correspond to natural deduction derivations of the formulae being simulated. Thus, in effect, we show that the sequent $(\Gamma : \phi^x)$ is provable in $N_{\Box\Diamond}(\gamma)$ by constructing the proof.

To this end, we fix an arbitrary valid sequent $\mathfrak{S} = (\Gamma : \phi^x)$ and let $\Xi$ be the set of generalized subformulae of the sequent. We define the generalized subformulae of a formula $\phi$ as follows:

- if $\phi^x$ is an atom $p^x$, then the only generalized subformula of $p^x$ is $p^x$ itself
- if $\phi^x$ is either $\top^x$ or $\bot^x$, then the only generalized subformula of $\phi^x$ is $\top^x$ or $\bot^x$, respectively
- if $\phi^x$ is $(\alpha \circ \beta)^x$ for $\circ \in \{\wedge, \vee, \supset\}$, then the generalized subformulae of $\phi^x$ are $\phi^x, \alpha^x$, and $\beta^x$
- if $\phi^x$ is $(\circ\alpha)^x$ for $\circ \in \{\Box, \Diamond\}$, then the generalized subformulae of $\phi^x$ are $\phi^x$, $\alpha^z$, and $xRz$, for all $z \in \mathbb{W}$.

Define the set $\mathrm{Lab}(\Xi) = \{a \mid \xi^a \in \Xi\} \cup \{a, b \mid aRb \in \Xi\}$ as the set of labels of each element of $\Xi$. We define an injection $(\cdot)^\flat : \Xi \to \mathbb{W} \times \mathbb{A}$, called the flattening map, such that: it is the identity map on atoms and on $\top^x$ and $\bot^x$; for non-atomic formulae, $\alpha^x$, and relational assumption $vRw$, it picks an $p^x$, where $p^x \notin \Xi$, and, for all $\alpha^x, \beta^y \in \Xi$, if $\alpha^x \neq \beta^y$, then $(\alpha^x)^\flat \neq (\beta^y)^\flat$. $(\cdot)^\flat$ has a left inverse $(\cdot)^\natural$,

$$\frac{}{(\top^x)^\flat} \top_I^\flat \qquad\qquad \frac{(\bot^x)^\flat}{p^z} \bot_E^\flat$$

$$\frac{\begin{array}{c}[(\phi^x)^\flat]\\ (\psi^x)^\flat\end{array}}{((\phi \supset \psi)^x)^\flat} \supset_I^\flat \qquad\qquad \frac{((\phi \supset \psi)^x)^\flat \quad (\phi^x)^\flat}{(\psi^x)^\flat} \supset_E^\flat$$

$$\frac{(\phi^x)^\flat \quad (\psi^x)^\flat}{((\phi \wedge \psi)^x)^\flat} \wedge_I^\flat \qquad\qquad \frac{((\phi \wedge \psi)^x)^\flat}{(\phi^x)^\flat} \wedge_{1E}^\flat \qquad \frac{((\phi \wedge \psi)^x)^\flat}{(\psi^x)^\flat} \wedge_{2E}^\flat$$

$$\frac{(\phi^x)^\flat}{((\phi \vee \psi)^x)^\flat} \vee_{1I}^\flat \qquad \frac{(\psi^x)^\flat}{((\phi \vee \psi)^x)^\flat} \vee_{2I}^\flat \qquad \frac{((\phi \vee \psi)^x)^\flat \quad \begin{array}{c}[(\phi^x)^\flat]\\ p^z\end{array} \quad \begin{array}{c}[(\psi^x)^\flat]\\ p^z\end{array}}{p^z} \vee_E^\flat$$

$$\frac{\begin{array}{c}[(xRy)^\flat]\\ (\phi^y)^\flat\end{array}}{((\Box\phi)^x)^\flat} \Box_I^\flat \qquad\qquad \frac{((\Box\phi)^x)^\flat \quad (xRz)^\flat}{(\phi^z)^\flat} \Box_E^\flat$$

$$\frac{(\phi^z)^\flat \quad (xRz)^\flat}{((\Diamond\phi)^x)^\flat} \Diamond_I^\flat \qquad\qquad \frac{((\Diamond\phi)^x)^\flat \quad \begin{array}{c}[(\phi^y)^\flat][(xRy)^\flat]\\ p^z\end{array}}{p^z} \Diamond_E^\flat$$

**Fig. 5.** Simulation base $\mathscr{N}$

defined by: the identity map on basic sentences and on $\top^x$ and $\bot^x$; the original labelled formula, otherwise. These functions are defined to be distributing over sets; that is, given a set of labelled formulae $\Gamma$, we define $\Gamma^\flat = \{(\gamma^x)^\flat \mid \gamma^x \in \Gamma\}$ and $\Gamma^\natural = \{(\gamma^x)^\natural \mid \gamma^x \in \Gamma\}$.

We can now define the simulation base $\mathscr{N}$ relative to $\Xi$ and $(\cdot)^\flat$, according to the rules of Fig. 5, where $p^z$ ranges over all atoms, $\phi^x$, $\phi^z$, and $\psi^x$ range over elements of $\Xi$ and

- the formula $\phi^y$ in the rule ($\Box_I^\flat$) ranges over all elements of $\Xi$ such that $y \neq x$ for each $((\Box\phi)^x)^\flat$,
- the formula $\phi^y$ in the rule ($\Diamond_E^\flat$) ranges over all elements of $\Xi$ such that $y \neq x$ and $y \neq z$, for each $((\Diamond\phi)^x)^\flat$ and $p^z$.

If $\gamma \neq \emptyset$, we must also add rules to $\mathscr{N}$ to express the frame conditions. We do this by adding the rules $(R_i)^\flat$ from Fig. 6 to $\mathscr{N}$, for each axiom $\gamma_i \in \gamma$, as follows: if the rule does not contain a relation with the letter $y$, then we add to $\mathscr{N}$ the rule concluding each $p^a$, where all labels range over $\text{Lab}(\Xi)$; if the rule contains a relation with the letter $y$, then we add to $\mathscr{N}$ the rule concluding each $p^a$, where the label $y$ ranges over all $\mathbb{W}$ and all other labels range over $\text{Lab}(\Xi)$, with the condition that $y$ is never equal to any of the other labels in that rule; that is, $y \neq x, a$, in the case of $(R_D)^\flat$, and $y \neq x, z, v, w, a$, in the case of $(R_2)^\flat$.

$$\frac{[(xRy)^\flat]}{p^a}\ (R_D)^\flat \qquad\qquad \frac{[(xRx)^\flat]}{p^a}\ (R_T)^\flat$$

$$\frac{(xRz)^\flat \quad \overset{[(zRx)^\flat]}{p^a}}{p^a}\ (R_B)^\flat \qquad\qquad \frac{(xRw)^\flat \quad (wRz)^\flat \quad \overset{[(xRz)^\flat]}{p^a}}{p^a}\ (R_4)^\flat$$

$$\frac{(xRw)^\flat \quad (xRz)^\flat \quad \overset{[(wRz)^\flat]}{p^a}}{p^a}\ (R_5)^\flat \qquad\qquad \frac{(xRw)^\flat \quad (xRz)^\flat \quad \overset{[(wRy)^\flat][(zRy)^\flat]}{p^a}}{p^a}\ (R_2)^\flat$$

**Fig. 6.** Rules which extend $\mathcal{N}$ to express the properties of the relational assumptions

**Theorem 4 (Completeness).** *If $\Gamma \Vdash^\gamma \phi^x$, then $\Gamma \vdash^\gamma \phi^x$.*

*Proof.* Let $(\cdot)^\flat$ be a flattening map with $(\cdot)^\natural$ being its corresponding left inverse and $\mathcal{N}$ be a simulation base the sequent $(\Gamma : \phi^x)$. We start by considering $\Gamma \Vdash^\gamma \phi^x$, which, since it is valid, implies in particular that $\Gamma \Vdash^\gamma_\mathcal{N} \phi^x$ holds. By Lemma 5, this is equivalent to $\Gamma^\flat \Vdash^\gamma_\mathcal{N} (\phi^x)^\flat$. By the (At) clause of the definition of $\Vdash^\gamma_\mathcal{N}$ and Lemma 2, we have that this is equivalent to $(\Gamma)^\flat \vdash^\gamma_\mathcal{N} (\phi^x)^\flat$. Finally, by Lemma 6, this implies that $(\Gamma^\flat)^\natural \vdash^\gamma ((\phi^x)^\flat)^\natural$, which is $\Gamma \vdash^\gamma \phi^x$, as desired. □

**Proposition 1.** *The following hold for all $\mathcal{B} \supseteq \mathcal{N}$:*

- $\vdash^\gamma_\mathcal{B} ((\phi \wedge \psi)^x)^\flat$ *iff* $\vdash^\gamma_\mathcal{B} (\phi^x)^\flat$ *and* $\vdash^\gamma_\mathcal{B} (\psi^x)^\flat$
- $\vdash^\gamma_\mathcal{B} ((\phi \vee \psi)^x)^\flat$ *iff for all $\mathcal{C} \supseteq \mathcal{B}$ and atoms $p^z$ if $\phi^x \Vdash^\gamma_\mathcal{C} p^z$ and $\psi^x \Vdash^\gamma_\mathcal{C} p^z$, then $\Vdash^\gamma_\mathcal{C} p^z$.*
- $\vdash^\gamma_\mathcal{B} (\bot^x)^\flat$ *iff* $\vdash^\gamma_\mathcal{B} p^z$, *for all atoms $p^z$.*
- $\vdash^\gamma_\mathcal{B} ((\Box \phi)^x)^\flat$ *iff for all labels $y$, we have $(xRy)^\flat \vdash^\gamma_\mathcal{B} (\phi^y)^\flat$.*
- $\vdash^\gamma_\mathcal{B} ((\Diamond \phi)^x)^\flat$ *iff for all $\mathcal{C} \supseteq \mathcal{B}$ and atoms $p^z$, if $(xRy)^\flat, (\phi^y)^\flat \vdash^\gamma_\mathcal{C} p^z$ for all $y$, then $\vdash^\gamma_\mathcal{C} p^z$.*

*Proof.* We defer the proof of all cases to [4] and give just the case of $\Diamond$ as an interesting example. Going left to right, we start by fixing an arbitrary base $\mathcal{C} \supseteq \mathcal{B}$ and atom $p^z$ such that $(xRy)^\flat, (\phi^y)^\flat \vdash^\gamma_\mathcal{B} p^z$ for all $y$. Our goal will be to show that $\vdash^\gamma_\mathcal{N} p^z$. To this end, we note that, as we have $(xRy)^\flat, (\phi^y)^\flat \vdash^\gamma_\mathcal{B} p^z$ for all $y$, we can pick some $y = a$ where $a \neq x, z$ to obtain $(xRa)^\flat, (\phi^a)^\flat \vdash^\gamma_\mathcal{B} p^z$. Furthermore, by monotonicity, we also have that $\vdash^\gamma_\mathcal{C} ((\Diamond \phi)^x)^\flat$. Therefore, by (App) applied to the appropriate $(\Diamond^\flat_E)$ rule which concludes $p^z$ (since there is one for each $y$ not equal to $x$ or $z$), we obtain $\vdash^\gamma_\mathcal{C} p^z$, as required.

Going right to left, the hypothesis gives that for all $\mathcal{C} \supseteq \mathcal{B}$ and atoms $p^z$, if $(xRy)^\flat, (\phi^y)^\flat \vdash^\gamma_\mathcal{C} p^z$ for all $y$, then $\vdash^\gamma_\mathcal{C} p^z$. We start by considering $\mathcal{C} = \mathcal{B}$ and $p^z = ((\Diamond \phi)^x)^\flat$. Given an arbitrary variable $a$, we know that $(xRa)^\flat, (\phi^a)^\flat \vdash^\gamma_\mathcal{B} (\phi^a)^\flat$ and $(xRa)^\flat, (\phi^a)^\flat \vdash^\gamma_\mathcal{B} (xRa)^\flat$ both hold by (Ref). Therefore, by (App) applied to the appropriate $(\Diamond^\flat_I)$ rule, we have $(xRa)^\flat, (\phi^a)^\flat \vdash^\gamma_\mathcal{B} ((\Diamond \phi)^x)^\flat$ for arbitrary $a$. Thus, $(xRy)^\flat, (\phi^y)^\flat \vdash^\gamma_\mathcal{B} ((\Diamond \phi)^x)^\flat$ holds for all $y$, from which we conclude, by the assumed implication, that $\vdash^\gamma_\mathcal{B} ((\Diamond \phi)^x)^\flat$. □

The proofs of Lemmas 5 and 6 are given in [4]. They are very similar to those of corresponding results in [22].

**Lemma 5.** $\Vdash_{\mathscr{B}}^{\supset} \phi^x$ *if and only if* $\Vdash_{\mathscr{B}}^{\supset} (\phi^x)^\flat$. □

**Lemma 6.** *If* $L \Vdash_{\mathscr{N}}^{\supset} p^x$ *then* $L^\natural \Vdash^{\supset} (p^x)^\natural$, *for any* $L \subseteq \mathbb{A}$ *and* $p \in \mathbb{A}$. □

A question to ask is whether in the cases of $\Box_I$ and $\Diamond_E$, the side-conditions are actually being adhered to? This is indeed the case because of the way in which $\mathscr{N}$ is defined. Recall that the schemas $\Box_I$ and $\Diamond_E$ are simulated by ensuring that the base $\mathscr{N}$ contains an instance of the rule for every possible allowed combination of labels. That this always guarantees the existence of the rule with the right kind of label is because of the way we add rules to the base. Recall that if a sequent contains a modal formula, say $(\Box p)^x$, then the set of generalized subformulae $\Xi$ will contain not only $(\Box p)^x$, but also $p^y$ and $xRy$, for all $y \in \mathbb{W}$. Thus, the only rules in $\mathscr{N}$ that allow introduction of $((\Box p)^x)^\flat$ are those that satisfy the side-conditions. Similar reasoning holds for $\Diamond_E$. Therefore, when translating our proofs in $\mathscr{N}$ under $(\cdot)^\natural$, we always obtain a valid $N_{\Box\Diamond}(\gamma)$ proof.

# 6 Conclusion

We have provided an inferentialist interpretation of a core family of intuitionistic modal logics, as defined by Simpson [25], through a B-eS that uniformly and conservatively extends Sandqvist's B-eS for IPL. Soundness and completeness properties have been established. This work makes essential use of the idea of labelling in proof systems that is familiar in work on tableaux systems and sequent calculi. The set-up presented here readily generalizes to Simpson's generalized soundness and completeness results.

The approach here stands in contrast to the work of Eckhardt and Pym on proof-theoretic semantics for classical modal logics [7,8] in which 'modal relations' are imposed on bases. Further work to understand the relationships between the two approaches would be valuable.

B-eS has also been developed for substructural logics, including intuitionistic multiplicative linear logic [11,13], linear logic with additives and exponentials [3], and the bunched logic BI [14].

These logics typically come along with a 'resource interpretation' or 'resource semantics'. For example, in linear logic, propositions occurring in proofs can be interpreted as resources that can be consumed in the construction described by proof. Alternatively, in the logic of bunched implications (BI) [9,12], a resource semantics resides in its Kripke-style models, with the intuitionistic connectives characterizing the sharing of resources and the multiplicative connectives characterizing the separation of resources. BI's resource semantics gives rise to Separation Logic, which is significant in program analysis and verification.

Gheorghiu, Gu, and Pym [12] have shown that BI's B-eS provides a unifying framework for the resource readings described above. Furthermore, they show how B-eS can be deployed as a system-modelling technology. Such a technology would be very much enriched by the inclusion of modal operators of the kind treated here and in [7,8]. The use of B-eS in system modelling appears to be a promising line of enquiry. This suggests that it would be worthwhile to explore automated reasoning tools for B-eS for modal and substructural logics. Such a programme is beyond the scope of this paper.

# References

1. Brandom, R.B.: Making it Explicit. Harvard University Press (1994)
2. Brandom, R.B.: Articulating Reasons: An Introduction to Inferentialism. Harvard University Press (2000). https://doi.org/10.2307/j.ctvjghvz0
3. Buzoku, Y.: A proof-theoretic semantics for intuitionistic linear logic (2025). https://arxiv.org/abs/2402.01982
4. Buzoku, Y., Pym, D.J.: Base-extension semantics for intuitionistic modal logics (2025). https://arxiv.org/abs/2507.06834
5. Campos Sanz, W., Piecha, T.: A critical remark on the BHK interpretation of implication. Philos. Sci. **3**(18–3), 13–22 (2014). https://doi.org/10.4000/philosophiascientiae.965
6. Dummett, M.: The Logical Basis of Metaphysics. The William James Lectures Delivered at Harvard University. Harvard University Press (1991). https://books.google.co.uk/books?id=lvsVFxK3BPcC
7. Eckhardt, T., Pym, D.: Base-extension semantics for modal logic. Log. J. IGPL **3**(2) (2024). https://doi.org/10.1093/jigpal/jzae004
8. Eckhardt, T., Pym, D.: Base-extension semantics for S5 modal logic. Log. J. IGPL (2025). https://doi.org/10.1093/jigpal/jzae131
9. Gheorghiu, A., Pym, D.: Semantical analysis of the logic of bunched implications. Stud. Log. **111** (01 2023). https://doi.org/10.1007/s11225-022-10028-z
10. Gheorghiu, A., Pym, D.: From proof-theoretic validity to base-extension semantics for intuitionistic propositional logic. Stud. Log. (2025). https://doi.org/10.1007/s11225-024-10163-9
11. Gheorghiu, A.V., Gu, T., Pym, D.J.: Proof-theoretic semantics for intuitionistic multiplicative linear logic. In: Ramanayake, R., Urban, J. (eds.) TABLEAUX 2023. LNCS, vol. 14278, pp. 367–385. Springer, Cham (2023). https://doi.org/10.1007/978-3-031-43513-3_20
12. Gheorghiu, A.V., Gu, T., Pym, D.J.: Inferentialist resource semantics. Electron. Notes Theor. Inform. Comput. Sci. **4**, 9 (2024). https://doi.org/10.46298/entics.14727, https://entics.episciences.org/14727
13. Gheorghiu, A.V., Gu, T., Pym, D.J.: Proof-theoretic semantics for intuitionistic multiplicative linear logic. Stud. Log. (2024). https://doi.org/10.1007/s11225-024-10158-6
14. Gu, T., Gheorghiu, A.V., Pym, D.J.: Proof-theoretic semantics for the logic of bunched implications (2023). https://arxiv.org/abs/2311.16719
15. Hlobil, U., Brandom, R.: Reasons for Logic, Logic for Reasons: Pragmatics, Semantics, and Conceptual Roles. Routledge (2024)
16. Lambek, J., Scott, P.: Introduction to Higher-Order Categorical Logic. Cambridge University Press (1986)
17. Piecha, T.: Completeness in proof-theoretic semantics. In: Piecha, T., Schroeder-Heister, P. (eds.) Advances in Proof-Theoretic Semantics. TL, vol. 43, pp. 231–251. Springer, Cham (2016). https://doi.org/10.1007/978-3-319-22686-6_15

18. Piecha, T., Campos Sanz, W., Schroeder-Heister, P.: Failure of completeness in proof-theoretic semantics. J. Philos. Log. **44**(3), 321–335 (2015)
19. Prawitz, D.: Natural Deduction: A Proof-Theoretical Study. Dover Books on Mathematics, Dover Publications (2006). https://books.google.co.uk/books?id=sJj3DQAAQBAJ
20. Prawitz, D.: Ideas and results in proof theory. In: Fenstad, J. (ed.) Studies in Logic and the Foundations of Mathematics, vol. 63, pp. 235–307. Elsevier (1971). https://doi.org/10.1016/S0049-237X(08)70849-8
21. Pym, D., Ritter, E., Robinson, E.: Categorical proof-theoretic semantics. Stud. Log. **113**, 125–162 (2025)
22. Sandqvist, T.: Base-extension semantics for intuitionistic sentential logic. Log. J. IGPL **23**, 719–731 (2015). https://api.semanticscholar.org/CorpusID:7310523
23. Schroeder-Heister, P.: Uniform proof-theoretic semantics for logical constants. J. Symb. Log. **56**, 1142 (1991)
24. Schroeder-Heister, P.: Proof-theoretic versus model-theoretic consequence. In: Pelis, M. (ed.) The Logica Yearbook 2007. Filosofia (2008)
25. Simpson, A.K.: The proof theory and semantics of intuitionistic modal logic. Ph.D. thesis, University of Edinburgh (1994)
26. Wittgenstein, L.: Philosophical Investigations. Wiley-Blackwell, New York (1953)

**Open Access** This chapter is licensed under the terms of the Creative Commons Attribution 4.0 International License (http://creativecommons.org/licenses/by/4.0/), which permits use, sharing, adaptation, distribution and reproduction in any medium or format, as long as you give appropriate credit to the original author(s) and the source, provide a link to the Creative Commons license and indicate if changes were made.

The images or other third party material in this chapter are included in the chapter's Creative Commons license, unless indicated otherwise in a credit line to the material. If material is not included in the chapter's Creative Commons license and your intended use is not permitted by statutory regulation or exceeds the permitted use, you will need to obtain permission directly from the copyright holder.

# Forward Proof Search for Intuitionistic Multimodal K Logics

Niels Voorneveld

Cybernetica AS, Tallinn, Estonia
niels.voorneveld@cyber.ee

**Abstract.** We consider intuitionistic multimodal logics with modalities satisfying axiom K and the axiom of Necessity, as well as collections of axioms for transforming, removing and splitting modalities, specified by a relation between modalities and sequences of modalities. These axioms can be used for systems of knowledge and belief, describing multiple environments of truth and their awareness of each other. We extend Gentzen's decidable cut-free calculus to accommodate such multimodal systems, using a modal shift operation on contexts to extend the cut elimination proof in a novel way. We then adapt the inverse method to formulate a correct and complete forward proof search for these logics, which can be interpreted in a Fitch-style manner. Proof derivation is streamlined by implementing most derivations using the cut rule. The resulting proof search allows for making multiple queries, building a database of assumptions and their consequences which can be fine-tuned and updated to fit an application.

**Keywords:** Epistemic logic · Sequent calculi · Cut elimination · Inverse method

## 1 Introduction

Intuitionistic logics may be used to build guarantees from sets of assumptions (see e.g. [12]). Unlike classical logics, intuitionistic predicates cannot simply be decomposed into Boolean statements to be fed to a SAT solver. Yet an intuitionistic proof has many benefits, as they are inherently constructive [24] and adaptable to computer formalisation following the proofs as types paradigm [9].

Modalities can be used to give more context to pieces of knowledge. They may explain when and where a statement is given, who said or hears or believes the statement, and how a statement is communicated. We can consider each modality as framing some domain in which logical properties can be considered: a domain of knowledge. Modalities satisfying axiom K and Necessity are particularly useful for this purpose. That is, those modalities $\mathcal{M}$ where, if $B$ can be derived from a (possibly empty) sequence of assumptions $A_1, \ldots, A_n$, then $\mathcal{M}B$ can be derived

---

This research has been supported by Estonian Research Council, grant No. PRG1780.
© The Author(s) 2026
G. L. Pozzato and T. Uustalu (Eds.): TABLEAUX 2025, LNAI 15980, pp. 335–353, 2026.
https://doi.org/10.1007/978-3-032-06085-3_18

from $\mathcal{M}A_1, \ldots, \mathcal{M}A_n$. This proof principle allows us to combine statements from the same domain, and reason from the perspective of this domain. The modality of *necessity* $\Box$ is a foundational example, studied intuitionistically in [23,26].

Further modal axioms can be used to specify the relation between knowledge domains. Particularly interesting is the specification of how domains can *reflect* on each other. The famous axiom 4, $\Box A \Rightarrow \Box\Box A$, asserts that $\Box$ can reflect and refer to their own statements. In case of multiple modalities, $\mathcal{M}A \Rightarrow \mathcal{N}\mathcal{M}A$ states that $\mathcal{N}$ is aware of and can reflect on statements made in domain $\mathcal{M}$. By extension, an axiom $\mathcal{M}A \Rightarrow \mathcal{N}\mathcal{R}A$ expresses a similar kind of awareness, except for the fact that $\mathcal{N}$ sees domain $\mathcal{M}$ differently, appearing to it as domain $\mathcal{R}$.

Having specified a collection of domains and their relations, the important next step is to establish what is true in each domain. That is, establishing a decidable proof search [13,14,21] for such systems with certain selections of awareness axioms. See for instance [7,10] for related approaches. What is difficult in this endeavour is that axioms $\mathcal{M}A \Rightarrow \mathcal{N}\mathcal{R}A$ have the potential to increase the size of the formulas, potentially leading to non-terminating proof searches.

In this paper, we explore a method for establishing decidability for such logics in a way which is compatible with Gentzen's original decidability proof [8] and Pfenning's cut elimination proof [22], adapting the decidable cut-free sequent calculus for intuitionistic logic. See [20, Ch. 4] for an overview on sequent calculi for intuitionistic logics. At the core of the method of this paper is the *modal shift operation* on contexts. That is, for each modality $\mathcal{M}$ we formulate an operation $\mathcal{M}^{-1}$ which, when applied to a context $\Gamma$, extracts all statements which are *readily* true within domain $\mathcal{M}$ given formulas from $\Gamma$. So if $\mathcal{M}A$ exists in $\Gamma$, then $A$ will exist in $\mathcal{M}^{-1}\Gamma$, but $B \wedge \mathcal{M}A$ does not yield a formula in $\mathcal{M}^{-1}\Gamma$ as it is not immediately evident that $\mathcal{M}A$ holds without inspecting the formula.

The main proof rule associated to modalities then becomes: If $A$ can be concluded from assumptions $\mathcal{M}^{-1}\Gamma$, then $\mathcal{M}A$ can be concluded from $\Gamma$. This operation is similar yet not exactly the same as the adjoint operator used in Fitch-style approaches [4], as it could discard important formulas. The key to establishing decidability here is that $\mathcal{M}^{-1}\Gamma$ only contains subformulas of $\Gamma$, and hence can be seen as a reduced context compared to $\Gamma$.

To increase efficiency of proof search, we adapt the *inverse method* [5,16,17] to implement a forward proof search for our logic. Here we generate from the sequent we want to prove a collection of trivially true sequents and derivation rules, and explore all possible ways to build more sequents from these. Differently from the usual application of the inverse method, we shall unify most derivation rules into a single cut-rule, structuring the sequents to be accommodating to disjunctions and modalities, allowing for the optimization of the derivation process. For instance, conjunctions $A \wedge B$ are proven by applying the cut rule to the sequent $A, B \vdash A \wedge B$. This is similar in spirit to for instance the Mints-style resolution technique [19] which uses a singular resolution rule.

Forward proof search does lead to another risk: when abandoning the bottom-up goal oriented proof derivation, you leave the door open to deriving a lot of sequents which were not needed to prove the result. This need not just be seen as an unnecessary byproduct however. In many practical application it may be useful to derive all relevant consequences of a set of assumptions. Take for instance the situation in which a company makes several claims, which we could mark by some modality $\mathcal{M}$. It is useful for the company to derive any relevant consequences of such claims, so they can check what facts they are implying.

The problem statement is as follows: Given a finite set of possible assumptions !A and a finite set of possible questions or goals ?Q, derive for any context $\Gamma \subseteq$ !A and consequent $A \in$ ?Q whether $\Gamma \vdash A$ is provable. The idea is to systematically generate all such provable sequents $\Gamma \vdash A$ where $\Gamma$ is minimal w.r.t. the provability of this statement, and store them in some database. Then, to check whether a sequent $\Gamma' \vdash A$ is true, we need only query the database whether there is a derived sequent $\Gamma \vdash A$ with $\Gamma \subseteq \Gamma'$. Searching the database for a matching sequent can be done optimally if the database is appropriately structured.

This method allows one to query the same database multiple times for different sequents. Not only that, supposing we wanted to add more assumptions or questions to !A and ?Q, we can reuse the already generated database, and derive further sequents relevant to the new assumptions and questions. This creates a dynamic proof search system which allows one to optimize for assumptions and questions relevant to a certain scenario.

Decidability of K4 intuitionistic modal logics and variations have been established in for instance [7,10], and there is a manuscript describing a forward proof search with the inverse method in [18], and moreover a bidirectional search in [11]. In this paper, we give an alternative proof of decidability of K4 in a more traditional style, as well as extending them to more general multimodal systems, avoiding the need for considering Kripke worlds. Moreover, our forward proof search unifies all multi-premise derivations into a single cut rule, which can be efficiently implemented.

The paper is divided into three parts. First, we consider multimodal axiomatic systems to which the method of this paper can be applied in Sect. 2. Then in Sect. 3 we lay out the proof of decidability using a traditional style decidable cut-free sequent calculus. An accompanying forward proof search of cuts is then laid out in Sect. 4. Finally, in Sect. 5 we briefly consider two extensions, involving consistency and unitality axioms.

## 2 Domains of Knowledge

Before going into the full definition of the multimodal intuitionistic logic, let us first consider the axiomatic systems of modalities. We suppose given some set of formulas $\mathbb{F}$ closed under a set of unary operations called modalities $\mathbb{M}$, which need not be finite. We are interested in the truth of sequents $A_1, \ldots, A_n \vdash B$ given by a sequence of assumptions $A_1, \ldots, A_n$ and a conclusion $B$. Modal axioms dictate some ways of proving sequents.

We assume first that all modalities satisfy axiom K and necessity N. This means that for any modality $\mathcal{M} \in \mathbb{M}$, if sequent $A_1, \ldots, A_n \vdash B$ is provable then $\mathcal{M}A_1, \ldots, \mathcal{M}A_n \vdash \mathcal{M}B$ is provable. This effectively means each $\mathcal{M}$ forms an endofunctor on the multi-category of formulas and proofs.

On top of K and N we specify an axiom scheme defined using a relation $\Rightarrow$ between $\mathbb{M}$ and $\mathbb{M}^*$ (lists over $\mathbb{M}$), which tells us how to *elaborate* on some modality. The statement $\mathcal{M} \Rightarrow \mathcal{N}_1 \ldots \mathcal{N}_n$ asserts the axiom $\forall A \in \mathbb{F}.\mathcal{M}A \vdash \mathcal{N}_1 \ldots \mathcal{N}_n A$. Here we associate modal application to the right, so $\mathcal{N}\mathcal{R}A = \mathcal{N}(\mathcal{R}A)$.

We require the following properties on $\Rightarrow$, adapting endorelational properties:

- $\Rightarrow$ is *reflexive* if for any $\mathcal{M}$, $\mathcal{M} \Rightarrow \mathcal{M}$.
- $\Rightarrow$ is *transitive* if $\mathcal{M} \Rightarrow \alpha \mathcal{N} \beta$ and $\mathcal{N} \Rightarrow \gamma$ implies $\mathcal{M} \Rightarrow \alpha \gamma \beta$.

Neither conditions puts restrictions on the logics we can formulate:

**Lemma 1.** *Any sequent calculus which admits cuts and has proofs $A \vdash A$ for each $A$, has the same collection of provable sequents given $(\mathbb{M}, \Rightarrow)$ as it does given $(\mathbb{M}, \Rightarrow^*)$, where $\Rightarrow^*$ is the reflexive transitive closure of $\Rightarrow$.*

The next property does put some restrictions on possible axiom schemes, and is used to deal with $\mathcal{M} \Rightarrow \mathcal{N}\mathcal{R}$ axioms. They are used to ensure decidability:

- $\Rightarrow$ is *decomposable* if for any $\mathcal{M}, \mathcal{N} \in \mathbb{M}$ there is a finite set $(\mathcal{M} \ominus \mathcal{N}) \subseteq \mathbb{M}$ s.t.:
  - For any $\mathcal{R} \in (\mathcal{M} \ominus \mathcal{N})$, $\mathcal{M} \Rightarrow \mathcal{N}\mathcal{R}$.
  - For any non-empty $\alpha \in \mathbb{M}^*$ such that $\mathcal{M} \Rightarrow \mathcal{N}\alpha$ there is an $\mathcal{R} \in \mathcal{M} \ominus \mathcal{N}$ such that $\mathcal{R} \Rightarrow \alpha$.[1]
- Decomposition is *terminating* if there is a preorder on modalities $\preceq$ s.t.:
  - For any $\mathcal{M}$ the set $\{\mathcal{N} \mid \mathcal{N} \preceq \mathcal{M}\}$ is finite.
  - For any $\mathcal{M}$ and $\mathcal{N}$, and $\mathcal{R} \in (\mathcal{M} \ominus \mathcal{N})$, then $\mathcal{R} \preceq \mathcal{M}$.
  - For any $\mathcal{M}$ and $\mathcal{N}$, then for at most one $\mathcal{R} \in (\mathcal{M} \ominus \mathcal{N})$, $\mathcal{M} \preceq \mathcal{R}$.

The first property in particular is included for the succinct formulation of proof rules for modal formulas, in such a way that we have cut-elimination. The second property is then needed to show that the resulting calculus has a kind of *subformula property*, as well as to ensure that cut elimination is terminating.

*Example 1.* One of the core examples is the $\square$ modality, which satisfies $\square A \vdash A$ and $\square A \vdash \square \square A$. This can be encapsulated in the axiom scheme where $\square \Rightarrow \square^n$ for any $n \in \mathbb{N}$, hence $\Rightarrow$ is the total relation between $\{\square\}$ and $\{\square\}^*$. We define $(\square \ominus \square) = \{\square\}$. The $\square$ modality can also enhance other multimodal systems by signifying globally known statements. Given modalities $\mathbb{M} \cup \{\square\}$ we assume on top of the $\square$ axioms that $\square A \vdash \mathcal{M}\square A$ for any $\mathcal{M} \in \mathbb{M}$. From this it is provable that $\square A \vdash \mathcal{M}A$. We can fold this into a scheme where $\square \Rightarrow \alpha$ for any sequence of modalities $\alpha$, and $\mathcal{M} \Rightarrow \mathcal{M}$ for any $\mathcal{M} \in \mathbb{M}$. We can define $(\square \ominus \mathcal{M}) = \{\square\}$, and $(\mathcal{M} \ominus \mathcal{N}) = \emptyset$ for any $\mathcal{M}, \mathcal{N} \in \mathbb{M}$, unless one assumes more axioms.

*Example 2.* Suppose we have a set of modalities $\mathbb{M}$ equipped with a reflexive and transitive relation $\triangleleft$ expressing *awareness*. The statement $\mathcal{M} \triangleleft \mathcal{N}$ means $\mathcal{M}$ is aware of all knowledge in $\mathcal{N}$, which is asserted with the axiom $\mathcal{N}A \vdash \mathcal{M}\mathcal{N}A$. So we assert $\mathcal{N} \Rightarrow \alpha\mathcal{N}$ when $\alpha\mathcal{N}$ is a sequence of modalities where for each subsequent pair $\mathcal{R}$ and $\mathcal{T}$ in $\alpha$, $\mathcal{R} \triangleleft \mathcal{T}$. Note that this is reflexive and transitive. Moreover, we define $(\mathcal{M} \ominus \mathcal{N}) = \{\mathcal{M}\}$ if $\mathcal{N} \triangleleft \mathcal{M}$, and otherwise $(\mathcal{M} \ominus \mathcal{N}) = \emptyset$.

---

[1] Note that if $\mathcal{M} \ominus \mathcal{N}$ is empty, there cannot be any $\mathcal{R}$ such that $\mathcal{M} \Rightarrow \mathcal{N}\mathcal{R}$.

*Example 3.* We can define lattices of modalities as well. Suppose we have a set of agents $\mathbb{A}$, and for each non-empty subset $S$ a modality $[S]$. The modality $[\{a\}]$ expresses claims made by agent $a$, whereas $[S]$ expresses truth by combining all claims from all agents $a \in S$. We simply assert $[S] \Rightarrow [Z]$ if $S \subseteq Z$. Note there is a useful distinction between $[\{a,b\}](B)$ and $[\{a\}](B) \vee [\{b\}](B)$, since the former can be derived from $[\{a\}](A)$ and $[\{b\}](A) \vdash [\{b\}](B)$ whereas the latter cannot.

Note that we can combine all examples into a single framework, as long as we take care of the required properties. For instance, we can add $\Box$ to the other two examples, or add awareness to our lattice by e.g. taking $Z \triangleleft S$ if $S \subseteq Z$.

## 2.1 Modal Shifts

We suppose contexts $\Gamma, \Delta, \Phi$ are given by sets of formulas. We define an order on contexts, for specifying a stronger weakening property on sequents. First, for two formulas $A$ and $B$ we write $A \sqsubseteq B$ if either $A = B$ or $A = \mathcal{M}C$ and $B = \mathcal{N}C$ for some triple $\mathcal{M}, \mathcal{N}, C$ such that $\mathcal{N} \Rightarrow \mathcal{M}$. For two contexts $\Gamma$ and $\Delta$, we write $\Gamma \sqsubseteq \Delta$ if for any formula $A \in \Gamma$ there is a formula $B \in \Delta$ such that $A \sqsubseteq B$. Note that if $\Gamma \subseteq \Delta$ then $\Gamma \sqsubseteq \Delta$, and that $\sqsubseteq$ is a reflexive and transitive relation. When $\Gamma \sqsubseteq \Delta$, then we say that the assumptions of $\Delta$ *cover* or directly imply the assumptions of $\Gamma$.

Fundamental to the formulation of the sequent calculus is the *modal shift* operation. For any modality $\mathcal{M}$ and context $\Gamma$, we define a context $\mathcal{M}^{-1}(\Gamma)$:

$$\mathcal{M}^{-1}(\Gamma) = \{A \mid \mathcal{N}A \in \Gamma, \mathcal{N} \Rightarrow \mathcal{M}\} \cup \{\mathcal{R}A \mid \mathcal{N}A \in \Gamma, \mathcal{R} \in (\mathcal{N} \ominus \mathcal{M})\}$$

This modal shift has two main principles underpinning it. First is that if $\Gamma$ has some $\mathcal{N}A$ for which $\mathcal{N} \Rightarrow \mathcal{M}\alpha$, and hence $\mathcal{M}\alpha(A)$ can be derived and $\alpha(A)$ is known within $\mathcal{M}$, then $\mathcal{M}^{-1}\Gamma$ has some $B$ directly implying $\alpha(A)$ (either $B = A$ and $\alpha = \cdot$, or $B = \mathcal{T}A$ and $\mathcal{T} \Rightarrow \alpha$). Secondly, any formula $A$ in $\Gamma$ only contributes at most one formula of the same $\preceq$ size to $\mathcal{M}^{-1}\Gamma$, with all other formulas of a lower $\preceq$ size. This is vital in order to formulate a cut-elimination algorithm which terminates.

In short, the modal shift operator tells you, given a collection of concrete assumptions $\Gamma$, a sufficiently complete set of assumption to use within domain $\mathcal{M}$, given the modal axioms. Both $\mathcal{M}^{-1}$ and $\sqsubseteq$ look at formulas in a shallow manner, only considering the top level modalities. So $\mathcal{M}^{-1}(A \wedge \mathcal{M}B)$ is empty, and $\mathcal{M}A \not\sqsubseteq \mathcal{M}B$ if $A \neq B$.

*Example 4.* Following 1, suppose we have the context $\Gamma = A \Rightarrow \Box B, \Box C, \Box\Box D$, then $\Box^{-1}(\Gamma) = C, \Box C, \Box D, \Box\Box D$. Following example 2, suppose $\mathcal{N} \triangleleft \mathcal{M}$ but not $\mathcal{N} \triangleleft \mathcal{R}$, and let $\Gamma = \mathcal{M}A, \mathcal{R}B, \mathcal{N}C$, then $\mathcal{N}^{-1}(\gamma) = \mathcal{M}A, C, \mathcal{N}C$.

We have three main lemmas:

**Lemma 2.** *If $\Gamma \sqsubseteq \Delta$, then $\mathcal{M}^{-1}\Gamma \sqsubseteq \mathcal{M}^{-1}\Delta$.*
**Lemma 3.** *If $\mathcal{M} \Rightarrow \mathcal{N}$ then $\mathcal{M}^{-1}\Gamma \sqsubseteq \mathcal{N}^{-1}\Gamma$.*
**Lemma 4.** *Suppose $\mathcal{T} \in \mathcal{M} \ominus \mathcal{N}$, then $\mathcal{M}^{-1}\Gamma \sqsubseteq \mathcal{T}^{-1}(\mathcal{N}^{-1}\Gamma)$.*

## 3  Decidable Cut-Free Calculus

Formulas of the logic are inductively generated according to the following rules:

$$A, B := a \mid A \wedge B \mid A \vee B \mid A \Rightarrow B \mid \mathcal{M}A \mid \top \mid \bot$$

Where $a$ ranges over some set of basic formulas. Contexts $\Gamma, \Delta$ are given by sets of formulas, and can be expressed using concatenation. We define the subformula relation $\preceq$ on formulas as the reflexive transitive closure of the following rules:

- $A \preceq A \wedge B$, $B \preceq A \wedge B$, $A \preceq A \vee B$, $B \preceq A \vee B$, $A \preceq A \Rightarrow B$, $B \preceq A \Rightarrow B$,
- $A \preceq \mathcal{M}A$, and lastly $\mathcal{N}A \preceq \mathcal{M}A$ if $\mathcal{N} \preceq \mathcal{M}$.

Importantly, for any formula $A$ the set $\{B \mid B \preceq A\}$ is finite.

The rules for the sequent calculus are outlined in Fig. 1. Since contexts are sets, the order and multiplicity of formulas in the context does not matter. This also means some rules, like ($\wedge$L) may not make any progress if the extracted formulas $A$ and $B$ were already in $\Gamma$. Alternatively, one could have started with lists of formulas for contexts instead, and established contraction and commutativity as lemmas. But we take a more structural approach.

$$\frac{}{\Gamma, a \vdash a}(\text{Var}) \quad \frac{}{\Gamma \vdash \top}(\top\text{R}) \quad \frac{}{\Gamma, \bot \vdash A}(\bot\text{L})$$

$$\frac{\Gamma \vdash A \quad \Gamma \vdash B}{\Gamma \vdash A \wedge B}(\wedge\text{R}) \quad \frac{\Gamma, A \wedge B, A, B \vdash C}{\Gamma, A \wedge B \vdash C}(\wedge\text{L})$$

$$\frac{\Gamma \vdash A}{\Gamma \vdash A \vee B}(\vee\text{R1}) \quad \frac{\Gamma \vdash B}{\Gamma \vdash A \vee B}(\vee\text{R2}) \quad \frac{\Gamma, A \vee B, A \vdash C \quad \Gamma, A \vee B, B \vdash C}{\Gamma, A \vee B \vdash C}(\vee\text{L})$$

$$\frac{\Gamma, A \vdash B}{\Gamma \vdash A \Rightarrow B}(\Rightarrow\text{R}) \quad \frac{\Gamma, A \Rightarrow B \vdash A \quad \Gamma, A \Rightarrow B, B \vdash C}{\Gamma, A \Rightarrow B \vdash C}(\Rightarrow\text{L})$$

$$\frac{\Gamma, \mathcal{M}A, A \vdash B \quad \mathcal{M} \Rightarrow \cdot}{\Gamma, \mathcal{M}A \vdash B}(\text{ModL}) \quad \frac{\mathcal{M}^{-1}\Gamma \vdash A}{\Gamma \vdash \mathcal{M}A}(\text{Mod})$$

**Fig. 1.** The Sequent Calculus

*Example 5.* Let $\mathcal{M}, \mathcal{N}, \mathcal{R}$ and $\mathcal{T}$ be distinct modalities such that $\mathcal{M} \Rightarrow \mathcal{NR}$ and $\mathcal{M} \ominus \mathcal{N} = \{\mathcal{T}\}$, so $\mathcal{T} \Rightarrow \mathcal{R}$. Then $\mathcal{N}A \Rightarrow A, \mathcal{N}(\mathcal{R}A \Rightarrow A) \vdash \mathcal{M}A \Rightarrow A$. Here the (Id) rule is the forthcoming Identity Lemma 6.

$$\cfrac{\cfrac{\cfrac{\cfrac{A \vdash A}{\mathcal{R}A \Rightarrow A, \mathcal{T}A \vdash \mathcal{R}A}(\text{Id})\ (\text{Mod}) \quad \cfrac{}{\mathcal{R}A \Rightarrow A, A \vdash A}(\text{Id})}{\mathcal{R}A \Rightarrow A, \mathcal{T}A \vdash A}(\Rightarrow\text{L})}{\cfrac{\mathcal{N}A \Rightarrow A, \mathcal{N}(\mathcal{R}A \Rightarrow A), \mathcal{M}A \vdash \mathcal{N}A}(\text{Mod}) \quad \cfrac{}{\mathcal{N}A \Rightarrow A, \mathcal{N}(\mathcal{R}A \Rightarrow A), \mathcal{M}A, A \vdash A}(\text{Id})}{\mathcal{N}A \Rightarrow A, \mathcal{N}(\mathcal{R}A \Rightarrow A), \mathcal{M}A \vdash A}(\Rightarrow\text{L})}}{\mathcal{N}A \Rightarrow A, \mathcal{N}(\mathcal{R}A \Rightarrow A) \vdash \mathcal{M}A \Rightarrow A}(\Rightarrow\text{R})$$

## 3.1 Sequent Calculus Properties

Let us look at some properties of the calculus. Note first that it has the *subformula property*; given a proof of a sequent $\Gamma \vdash A$, then for any formula $B$ mentioned anywhere in the proof, there is a formula $C \in \Gamma, A$ such that $B \preceq C$.

**Lemma 5 (Generalized weakening).** *If $\Gamma \vdash A$ is provable by some proof tree P and $\Gamma \sqsubseteq \Delta$, then $\Delta \vdash A$ is provable by a tree of the same shape as P (same sequence of proof rules, only the sequents have changed).*

*Proof.* We prove this by induction on the sizes of the proof tree P, doing case analysis on the last proof step. We only consider the two modal cases as the rest of the cases are standard (note that if a formula $B$ does not start with a modality, and $B \in \Gamma \sqsubseteq \Delta$, then $B \in \Delta$).

**ModL** We have a proof P of $\Gamma, \mathcal{M}A, A \vdash B$, with $\mathcal{M} \Rrightarrow \cdot$. Since $\Gamma, \mathcal{M}A \sqsubseteq \Delta$ we have $\Gamma, \mathcal{M}A \sqsubseteq \Delta, A$, and hence by the induction hypothesis we have a proof P' of $\Delta, A \vdash B$. Given $\mathcal{M}A \sqsubseteq \Delta$, then $\Delta$ must have some $\mathcal{N}A$ such that $\mathcal{N} \Rrightarrow \mathcal{M}$ (special case being $\mathcal{M} = \mathcal{N}$). By transitivity of $\Rrightarrow$, it holds that $\mathcal{N} \Rrightarrow \cdot$, and hence we can apply (ModL) to P' to get a proof of $\Delta \vdash B$.
**Mod** We have proof P of $\mathcal{M}^{-1}\Gamma \vdash A$. By Lemma 2, $\mathcal{M}^{-1}\Gamma \sqsubseteq \mathcal{M}^{-1}\Delta$, and hence by the induction hypothesis we have a proof P' of $\mathcal{M}^{-1}\Delta \vdash A$. Applying the (Mod) rule, we get a proof of $\Delta \vdash \mathcal{M}A$.

We get the usual consequence of the subformula property.

**Corollary 1.** *It is decidable whether any sequent $\Gamma \vdash A$ has a proof following the sequent calculus of Fig. 1.*

**Lemma 6 (Identity Lemma).** *For any context $\Gamma$ and formula $A$, the sequent $\Gamma, A \vdash A$ is provable. So in particular, $A \vdash A$ is provable.*

*Proof.* We show this by induction on $A$. We only consider the modal case:

- If $A = \mathcal{M}B$, then since $\mathcal{M} \Rrightarrow \mathcal{M}$ we have that $B \in \mathcal{M}^{-1}(\Gamma, A)$, so by the induction hypothesis we have a proof of $\mathcal{M}^{-1}(\Gamma, A) \vdash B$. Hence by applying the (Mod) rule, we have a proof of $\Gamma, \mathcal{M}B \vdash \mathcal{M}B$.

With the next result, we can conclude that the calculus of Fig. 1 coincides with natural deduction on intuitionistic modal logic with axiom scheme $\Rrightarrow$.

**Proposition 1.** *The calculus admits a cut rule.*

*Proof.* We follow Gentzen's and later Pfenning's cut elimination proof [8,22], and add to this the new modal proof rules. Concretely, suppose we have a proof $\mathsf{D} = \frac{\mathsf{D}_1 \ldots \mathsf{D}_n}{\Gamma \vdash A}$ and a proof $\mathsf{E} = \frac{\mathsf{E}_1 \ldots \mathsf{E}_m}{\Gamma, A \vdash B}$, then we can construct a proof $\mathsf{F} = \frac{\mathsf{F}_1 \ldots \mathsf{F}_k}{\Gamma \vdash B}$. This is done by mutual induction on $A$, $\mathsf{D}$ and $\mathsf{E}$, in that order. That is, induction hypothesis may be called when:

- $A$ is reduced. We call this (IH-A).
- Size of $A$ remains the same, but D is reduced. We call this (IH-D)
- Size of $A$ and D is the same, but E is reduced. We call this (IH-E).

Here it should be noted that the size of a proof is determined by its shape, and weakening sequents following Lemma 5 gives a proof of the same size. Moreover, the size of formulas is determined by the $\preceq$ order, where $B$ is the same size as $A$ if $B \preceq A$ and $A \preceq B$, and $B$ is smaller than $A$ if $B \preceq A$ and $A \not\preceq B$ (cut elimination terminates since we cannot have an infinite chain $A_1 \succeq A_2 \succeq A_2 \ldots$).

We consider a formula $A$ in a proof of $\Gamma, A \vdash B$ *principal* if the proof ended with a rule targeting $A$, that is: either a left rule which targets $A$ specifically, or a (Mod) rule which targets all formulas. Cases covered in the literature are:

- When D is the (Var) rule or a Left rule.
- When $A$ is not principal in E,
- When $A$ is a non-modal formula and principal in both D and E.

We have three new cases:

1. D ends with a right rule, E with a (Mod) rule, and $A$ is non-modal.

$$E = \dfrac{\dfrac{E_1}{\mathcal{M}^{-1}(\Gamma, A) \vdash B} \text{(e1)}}{\Gamma, A \vdash \mathcal{M} B} \text{(Mod)}$$

In this case, $\mathcal{M}^{-1}(\Gamma, A) = \mathcal{M}^{-1}\Gamma$, and hence E also proves $\Gamma \vdash \mathcal{M} B$.

2. D ends with a (Mod) rule proving $\mathcal{M} A$, and E with (ModL) targeting $\mathcal{M} A$.

$$D = \dfrac{\dfrac{D_1}{\mathcal{M}^{-1}\Gamma \vdash A} \text{(d1)}}{\Gamma \vdash \mathcal{M} A} \text{(Mod)} \qquad E = \dfrac{\dfrac{E_1}{\Gamma, \mathcal{M} A, A \vdash B} \text{(e1)}}{\Gamma, \mathcal{M} A \vdash B} \text{(ModL)}$$

In this case, $\mathcal{M} \Rightarrow \cdot$. We construct a proof of $\Gamma \vdash A$, and use this to cut the formula with (IH-A).

Starting with $\Gamma \vdash A$ at the bottom, apply (ModL) as many times as possible, leading to $\Phi \vdash A$ for some context $\Phi$ such that: $\Gamma \subseteq \Phi$ and for any $\mathcal{N} C \in \Gamma$ where $\mathcal{N} \Rightarrow \cdot$, $C \in \Phi$. We see that $\mathcal{M}^{-1}\Gamma \sqsubseteq \Phi$ since:

- For $C \in \mathcal{M}^{-1}\Gamma$ from $\mathcal{N} C \in \Gamma$ and $\mathcal{N} \Rightarrow \mathcal{M}$. Then $\mathcal{N} \Rightarrow \cdot$, hence $C \in \Phi$.
- For $\mathcal{R} C \in \mathcal{M}^{-1}\Gamma$ from $\mathcal{N} C \in \Gamma$ and $\mathcal{R} \in (\mathcal{N} \ominus \mathcal{M})$. Then $\mathcal{N} \Rightarrow \mathcal{M R} \Rightarrow \mathcal{R}$, and hence $\mathcal{R} C \sqsubseteq \mathcal{N} C \subseteq \Phi$.

We conclude that $\mathcal{M}^{-1}\Gamma \sqsubseteq \Phi$, and hence by Lemma 5, $D_1$ proves $\Phi \vdash A$. Applying the aforementioned (ModL) gives a proof G of $\Gamma \vdash A$.
We construct F by performing two consecutive cuts:

$$F = \dfrac{\dfrac{G}{\Gamma \vdash A} \qquad \dfrac{\dfrac{\dfrac{D_1}{\mathcal{M}^{-1}(\Gamma, A) \vdash A} \text{(d1)}}{\Gamma, A \vdash \mathcal{M} A} \text{(Mod)} \qquad \dfrac{E_1}{\Gamma, \mathcal{M} A, A \vdash B} \text{(e1)}}{\Gamma, A \vdash B} \text{(IH-E)}}{\Gamma \vdash B} \text{(IH-A)}$$

Here $D_1$ was weakened to perform the initial cut of $\mathcal{M}A$ as well.
3. Both D and E end with a (Mod) rule.

$$D = \dfrac{\dfrac{D_1}{\mathcal{M}^{-1}\Gamma \vdash A}\,(d1)}{\Gamma \vdash \mathcal{M}A}\,(\text{Mod}) \qquad E\,\dfrac{\dfrac{E_1}{\mathcal{N}^{-1}(\Gamma, \mathcal{M}A) \vdash B}\,(e1)}{\Gamma, \mathcal{M}A \vdash \mathcal{N}B}\,(\text{Mod})$$

By assumption, $\mathcal{M} \ominus \mathcal{N} = \{\mathcal{R}_1, \ldots, \mathcal{R}_n\}$ for some sequence of modalities, such that $\mathcal{R}_i \preceq \mathcal{M}$ for all $i$, and $\mathcal{R}_1$ is the only modality with $\mathcal{M} \preceq \mathcal{R}_1$. We have that $\mathcal{N}^{-1}(\Gamma, \mathcal{M}A) = \mathcal{N}^{-1}\Gamma, \mathcal{R}_1 A, \ldots, \mathcal{R}_n A$ or $\mathcal{N}^{-1}(\Gamma, \mathcal{M}A) = \mathcal{N}^{-1}\Gamma, \mathcal{R}_1 A, \ldots, \mathcal{R}_n A, A$, where the $A$ is included when $\mathcal{M} \Rrightarrow \mathcal{N}$.
We want to cut each formula $B \in \mathcal{R}_1 A, \ldots, \mathcal{R}_n A, A$ with a proof of $\mathcal{N}^{-1}\Gamma \vdash B$. For all but $\mathcal{R}_1 A$, we have a reduced formula, and hence we can use (IH-A). So we want to cut $\mathcal{R}_1 A$ first, using (IH-E), and then cut all other formulas using (IH-A). We only need the proofs for cutting the formulas.

 - Cutting $\mathcal{R}_i A$. By Lemma 4, $\mathcal{M}^{-1}\Gamma \sqsubseteq \mathcal{R}_i^{-1}\mathcal{N}^{-1}\Gamma$, so we can weaken $D_1$ to a proof of $\mathcal{R}_i^{-1}(\mathcal{N}^{-1}\Gamma) \vdash A$ using Lemma 5. Applying the (Mod) rule, we get a proof of $\mathcal{N}^{-1}\Gamma \vdash \mathcal{R}_i A$, and this proof is the same size as D.
 - Cutting $A$, which is only necessary when $\mathcal{M} \Rrightarrow \mathcal{N}$. By Lemma 3 we have $\mathcal{M}^{-1}\Gamma \sqsubseteq \mathcal{N}^{-1}\Gamma$, so we can also weaken $D_1$ to prove $\mathcal{N}^{-1}\Gamma \vdash A$.

The number of formulas to cut varies. To illustrate the construction of F, suppose for example $\mathcal{M} \Rrightarrow \mathcal{N}$ and $\mathcal{M} \ominus \mathcal{N} = \{\mathcal{R}\}$, then we take F =

$$\dfrac{\dfrac{D_1''}{\mathcal{N}^{-1}\Gamma \vdash A}\,(d1) \qquad \dfrac{\dfrac{\dfrac{D_1'}{\mathcal{R}^{-1}(\mathcal{N}^{-1}\Gamma) \vdash A}\,(d1)}{\mathcal{N}^{-1}\Gamma \vdash \mathcal{R}A}\,(\text{Mod}) \qquad \dfrac{E_1}{\mathcal{N}^{-1}\Gamma, \mathcal{R}A, A \vdash B}\,(e1)}{\dfrac{\mathcal{N}^{-1}\Gamma, A \vdash B}{\mathcal{N}^{-1}\Gamma \vdash B}\,(\text{IH-A})}\,(\text{IH-E})}$$

To establish completeness with respect to intuitionistic multimodal logic with $\mathcal{M} \Rrightarrow \alpha$ axioms, we can use the completeness of the original decidable sequent calculus for intuitionistic logic, and note that the two Mod rules extend this naturally. Concretely, we can show the following:

**Lemma 7.** *If $\mathcal{M} \Rrightarrow \alpha$, then $\mathcal{M}A \vdash \alpha A$ is provable for any $A$.*

*Proof.* If $\mathcal{M} \Rrightarrow \cdot$, then $\mathcal{M}A \vdash A$ via (ModL) and the identity lemma (Lemma 6). By induction on the length of $\alpha$, we can show that if $\mathcal{M} \Rrightarrow \mathcal{N}\alpha$, then $\mathcal{M}A \vdash \mathcal{N}\alpha A$. If $\alpha$ empty, then $\mathcal{M} \Rrightarrow \mathcal{N}$, and hence $\mathcal{M}A \vdash \mathcal{N}A$ can be derived from (Mod) since $A \in \mathcal{N}^{-1}(\mathcal{M}A)$. If $\alpha$ is non-empty, then there is an $\mathcal{R} \in (\mathcal{M} \ominus \mathcal{N})$ such that $\mathcal{R} \Rrightarrow \alpha$. So by induction hypothesis, $\mathcal{R}A \vdash \alpha A$ and hence by (Mod), $\mathcal{N}\mathcal{R}A \vdash \mathcal{N}\alpha A$. Moreover, $\mathcal{M}A \vdash \mathcal{N}\mathcal{R}A$ can be derived using (Mod) and the identity lemma. Applying the cut rule, we get $\mathcal{M}A \vdash \mathcal{N}\alpha A$.

*Remark 1.* For the purposes of constructing counter models, which are not the focus of this paper, we can follow the usual approach for implementing *Kripke semantics* [15] for intuitionistic modal logics [23] with modalities satisfying axiom K and Necessity. A Kripke model for the intuitionistic logic with $(\mathbb{M}, \Rightarrow)$ involves a set of worlds $W$, a preorder $\leq$ to accommodate intuitionistic implication, and a relation $\mathcal{R}_\mathcal{M}$ on $W$ for any $\mathcal{M} \in \mathbb{M}$. Necessity and axiom K can be implemented in the usual sense, Our axioms can be implemented as follows: If $\mathcal{M} \Rightarrow \mathcal{N}_1 \ldots \mathcal{N}_n$ then the composition of relations $\mathcal{R}_{\mathcal{N}_1} \ldots \mathcal{R}_{\mathcal{N}_n}$ should be included in $\mathcal{R}_\mathcal{M}$. In particular, if $\mathcal{M} \Rightarrow \cdot$, then $\mathcal{R}_\mathcal{M}$ is reflexive.

## 4 Forward Proof Search

Rules ($\vee$L), ($\Rightarrow$R), and the new rule (Mod) of Fig. 1 are especially cumbersome to deal with in any practical proof search, since the order of application matters greatly, exponentially increasing the execution time of the proof search. Accompanying the decidable calculus, we formulate a terminating forward proof search scheme for our logic in an attempt to bypass these issues, adapting the inverse method [5]. We use an alternative here to avoid having to consider too many multi-premise derivation rules, which require more computation power to exhaustively check for in practice. Instead, we include only one rule with more than one sequent in its premise; the analytic cut. In order to facilitate this method we need to assume some further finiteness properties, defined in the next subsection, which will be automatically satisfied if $\mathbb{M}$ is finite.

The general scheme is as follows. Instead of asking ourselves whether a particular sequent $\Gamma \vdash A$ is true, we consider the following two sets of formulas:

- A set of *questions* or *goals* ?Q. These are properties we are interested in proving. We may write ?$A$ for $A \in$ ?Q.
- A set of *answers* or *assumptions* !A. These are properties we may use to prove our questions. We may write !$A$ for $A \in$ !A.

We are then interested in establishing the provability of any sequent $\Gamma \vdash A$ such that $\Gamma \subseteq$ !A (also denoted as !$\Gamma$) and $A \in$ ?Q. In terms of the inverse method, our questions are the *right formulas*, and our assumptions are the *left formulas*.

When you want to know the truth of a particular sequent $\Gamma \vdash A$, you would take !A $= \Gamma$ and ?Q $= \{A\}$, run the proof search and check the result. Our proof search algorithm gathers the minimal set of provable sequents for a given set of questions and answers. These are stored in a database optimized for searchability. This database can then be queried in order to check whether a certain sequent is provable. If necessary, you can also remove questions and answers from the database you no longer need for later queries.

In order to streamline the derivation process in forward search, we combine all derivation steps with multiple premises into a single rule: the cut rule. To facilitate this, we add specific sequents to represent proof rules, like $A, B \vdash A \wedge B$ and $A \wedge B \vdash A$ when ?$A \wedge B$ and !$A \wedge B$ respectively. With this more streamlined approach, we need only check any pair of sequents once to see if any relevant consequences can be derived. Note that regardless of approach, we are already forced to consider cuts anyway, given the ($\vee$L) rule in the sequent calculus.

### 4.1 Derivations

In order to facilitate both disjunctions and modalities, and enable all necessary derivations using the analytic cut rule, we extend standard sequents in two ways: we allow for multiple consequents as is usual in sequent calculi, and we consider two contexts separated by a modality. This second extension is in line with the Fitch-style approach to modal calculi [4,6]. Given sets of formulas $\Phi$, $\Gamma$ and $\Delta$, and given $\mathcal{M} \in \mathbb{M} \cup \{id\}$ such that (1) $\Delta$ is non-empty, and (2) If $\mathcal{M} = id$ then $\Phi$ is empty. We write the sequent:

$$\Phi \mid_{\mathcal{M}} \Gamma \Vdash \Delta, \qquad \text{we may write} \quad \Gamma \Vdash \Delta \quad \text{if } \mathcal{M} = id$$

This is interpreted as the statement: Given all of $\Phi$, then within domain $\mathcal{M}$ the multi consequent sequent $\Gamma \Vdash \Delta$ is true. The $\Delta$ is interpreted disjunctively as usual, so the sequent means that given all of $\Gamma$ then one of $\Delta$ holds. As a single formula, $\Phi \mid_{\mathcal{M}} \Gamma \Vdash \Delta$ is interpreted as (where $\mathcal{M}(A) = A$ if $\mathcal{M} = id$):

$$\bigwedge \Phi \Rightarrow \mathcal{M}\left(\bigwedge \Gamma \Rightarrow \bigvee \Delta\right)$$

We define an order on sequents: $\Phi \mid_{\mathcal{M}} \Gamma \Vdash \Delta \subseteq \Phi' \mid_{\mathcal{N}} \Gamma' \Vdash \Delta'$ if $\Phi \subseteq \Phi'$, $\Gamma \subseteq \Gamma'$, $\Delta \subseteq \Delta'$ and either $\mathcal{M} \Rightarrow \mathcal{N}$ or $\mathcal{M} = id$. The order expresses when the first sequent covers the second. Note that if $\mathcal{M} = id$ then $\Phi = \emptyset$, so the implication holds by necessity. We call a sequent $\Phi \mid_{\mathcal{M}} \Gamma \Vdash \Delta$ *trivial* if $\Gamma \cap \Delta \neq \emptyset$.

When building a database of true sequents during our forward proof search, we shall only include non-trivial and minimal sequents. That is, we do not add a sequent $\alpha$ if the database already has a sequent $\beta$ such that $\beta \subseteq \alpha$. Moreover, when a new sequent $\alpha$ is added, all sequents $\beta$ in the database such that $\alpha \subseteq \beta$ are removed. As such, when making a derivation you use only minimal sequents from the database as premises, and only add the result if it was not yet covered by the database. We say that the database is *saturated* by a rule if the rule does not yield any uncovered sequents.

To deal with modalities, we assume the existence of operations $s : \mathbb{M} \to \mathcal{P}(\mathbb{M} \times \mathbb{M})$ and $\triangledown : \mathbb{M} \times \mathbb{M} \to \mathcal{P}(\mathbb{M})$ producing finite sets such that:

- $s\mathcal{M}$ is finite and forms a basis for all splitting axioms, that is:
  - For any $(\mathcal{N}, \mathcal{R}) \in s\mathcal{M}$, $\mathcal{R} \in (\mathcal{M} \ominus \mathcal{N})$.
  - For any $\mathcal{R} \in \mathcal{M} \ominus \mathcal{N}$, there is a $(\mathcal{T}, \mathcal{R}) \in s\mathcal{M}$ such that $\mathcal{T} \Rightarrow \mathcal{N}$.
- $\mathcal{M} \triangledown \mathcal{N}$ is finite and forms a basis for all modalities above $\mathcal{M}$ and $\mathcal{N}$, that is:
  - For any $\mathcal{R} \in (\mathcal{M} \triangledown \mathcal{N})$, $\mathcal{M} \Rightarrow \mathcal{R}$ and $\mathcal{N} \Rightarrow \mathcal{R}$.
  - If $\mathcal{M} \Rightarrow \mathcal{R}$ and $\mathcal{N} \Rightarrow \mathcal{R}$, then there is a $\mathcal{T} \in (\mathcal{M} \triangledown \mathcal{N})$ such that $\mathcal{T} \Rightarrow \mathcal{R}$.
- For any finite set of modalities $S$, the smallest set including $S$ and closed under $\triangledown$ is finite[2].

---

[2] A counter example is $\mathbb{M} = \{\mathcal{M}_i, \mathcal{N}_i \mid i \in \mathbb{N}\}$ where $\mathcal{M}_i \Rightarrow \mathcal{N}_j$ and $\mathcal{N}_i \Rightarrow \mathcal{M}_j$ if $i < j$. Though $\mathcal{M}_i \triangledown \mathcal{N}_i$ can be chosen to be $\{\mathcal{M}_{i+1}, \mathcal{N}_{i+1}\}$, closure of $S = \{\mathcal{M}_0, \mathcal{N}_0\}$ is $\mathbb{M}$.

The last condition puts some limitation on axiom schemes we can accommodate, but will automatically hold if we only have a finite number of modalities.

We extend $\nabla$ to $\mathbb{M} \cup \{id\}$ by taking $id \nabla \mathcal{M} = \{\mathcal{M}\} = \mathcal{M} \nabla id$. Our main tool for deriving new sequents is the cut rule, given as follows:

$$\frac{\Phi \mid_{\mathcal{M}} \Gamma, A \Vdash \Delta \qquad \Phi' \mid_{\mathcal{N}} \Gamma' \Vdash \Delta', A \qquad \mathcal{R} \in \mathcal{M} \nabla \mathcal{N}}{\Phi, \Phi' \mid_{\mathcal{R}} \Gamma \cup \Gamma' \Vdash \Delta \cup \Delta'}$$

Note that the number of sequents derivable from two sequents by cutting is at most the number of elements of $\mathcal{M} \nabla \mathcal{N}$, since if there are multiple cuttable formulas, both results will yield a trivial formula.

Not all derivations can be implemented by cuts. We formulate a collection of unary derivation rules for sequents, which we call *catch-rules* since we catch and apply them to formulas derived by the cut rule. We consider two catch-rules:

$$\frac{\Phi \mid_{\mathcal{M}} \Gamma, A \Vdash A \Rightarrow B}{\Phi \mid_{\mathcal{M}} \Gamma \Vdash A \Rightarrow B} \qquad \frac{\Phi \mid_{\mathcal{N}} \cdot \Vdash A \qquad ?\mathcal{M}A \qquad \mathcal{N} \Rightarrow \mathcal{M} \text{ or } \mathcal{N} = id}{\Phi \Vdash \mathcal{M}A}$$

Note that if the first rule is applicable, it will yield a sequent which is stronger than the input sequent, so they can immediately replace the premise. In fact, we could add it as a structural rule on sequents instead, and get a *cut-only* derivation scheme for intuitionistic logic. The second rule refers to $?\mathcal{M}A$, which is a needed condition lest we accidentally generate infinite sequences of modalities.

## 4.2 Forward Proof Search Rules

Suppose that a set of questions ?Q, answers !A, and a collection of sequents K are given. We call such collections of sequents a *knowledge database*. Initially, K will be empty, unless one reuses a database generated by earlier queries. We separate the proof search rules into two phases: Firstly, the *initiation rules* are given in Fig. 2, which investigate answers and questions, spinning up new questions and answers together with simple sequents needed to use and prove them. Secondly, the *accumulation rules* in Fig. 3 generate logical consequences of our sequents and does not yield any new question and answers.

Our treatment of implications is slightly different than usual, attempting to avoid the practically cumbersome ($\Rightarrow$-L) rule to instead use the cut rule more. Instead of deriving $\Gamma \Vdash A \Rightarrow B$ directly from $\Gamma, A \Vdash B$, we instead note that $B \Vdash A \Rightarrow B$, perform a cut with $\Gamma, A \Vdash B$ to get $\Gamma, A \Vdash A \Rightarrow B$. We then can apply the second rule of Fig. 3 to remove $A$. Importantly, the second rule of 3 only applies when there is but one formula in the consequent. We can for instance prove $\Vdash A \Rightarrow (B \Rightarrow A)$ by cutting $A \Vdash B \Rightarrow A$ and $B \Rightarrow A \Vdash A \Rightarrow (B \Rightarrow A)$, and removing the $A$.

There are three rules which require multiple premises. The cut rule lies at the core of all derivations and covers, in tandem with the simple sequents generated in the initiation phase, most necessary proof derivations rules. New sequents generated by the cut rule are then checked and potentially *caught* and processed by the two catch-rules. We allow for multiple consequents in a sequent in order

$$\frac{}{\Vdash \top} ?\top \qquad \frac{!\bot}{\bot \Vdash A} ?A$$

$$\frac{!(A \wedge B)}{A \wedge B \Vdash A \quad A \wedge B \Vdash B \quad !A \quad !B} \qquad \frac{?(A \wedge B)}{A, B \Vdash A \wedge B \quad ?A \quad ?B}$$

$$\frac{!(A \vee B)}{A \vee B \Vdash A, B \quad !A \quad !B} \quad \frac{}{A \Vdash A \vee B} \qquad \frac{?(A \vee B)}{B \Vdash A \vee B \quad ?A \quad ?B}$$

$$\frac{!(A \Rightarrow B)}{A, A \Rightarrow B \Vdash B \quad ?A \quad !B} \qquad \frac{?(A \Rightarrow B)}{B \Vdash A \Rightarrow B \quad !A \quad ?B}$$

$$\frac{!\mathcal{M}A}{!A \quad \mathcal{M}A \mid_{\mathcal{M}} \cdot \Vdash A \quad \cdot \mid \mathcal{M}A \Vdash A \text{ if } \mathcal{M} \Rightarrow \cdot} \qquad \frac{?\mathcal{M}A}{?A}$$
$$\forall (\mathcal{N},\mathcal{R}) \in s\mathcal{M}. \ \mathcal{M}A \mid_{\mathcal{N}} \cdot \Vdash \mathcal{R}A \qquad \forall (\mathcal{N},\mathcal{R}) \in s\mathcal{M}. \ !\mathcal{R}A$$

**Fig. 2.** Forward search initiation phase rules.

$$\frac{\Phi \mid_{\mathcal{M}} \Gamma, A \Vdash \Delta \quad \Phi' \mid_{\mathcal{N}} \Gamma' \Vdash \Delta', A \quad \mathcal{R} \in \mathcal{M} \triangledown \mathcal{N}}{\Phi \cup \Phi' \mid_{\mathcal{R}} \Gamma \cup \Gamma' \Vdash \Delta \cup \Delta'}$$

$$\frac{\Phi \mid_{\mathcal{M}} \Gamma, A \Vdash A \Rightarrow B}{\Phi \mid_{\mathcal{M}} \Gamma \Vdash A \Rightarrow B} \qquad \frac{\Phi \mid_{\mathcal{N}} \cdot \Vdash A \quad ?\mathcal{M}A \quad \mathcal{N} \Rightarrow \mathcal{M} \text{ or } \mathcal{N} = id}{\Phi \Vdash \mathcal{M}A}$$

**Fig. 3.** Forward search accumulation phase rules.

to enable the cut rule to admit the (∨-L) rule from Fig. 1, which is a particularly cumbersome rule to work with in practice when performing a proof search. Setting the forward proof search up in this way focuses all computation efforts into the cut rule.

There are two other multi-premise rules besides the cut rule, but neither have more than one sequent in the premise, and hence can be more easily dealt with. In fact, the !⊥ rule can be omitted if we simply assert that !⊥ holds from the get-go, and add the sequents ⊥ ⊩ A directly to the respective cases of ?A. Note that we do not allow for sequents without any consequents. This is to allow us to apply cuts on ⊥ in order to make further derivations.

Last but not least is the multi-premise catch-rule for ?$\mathcal{M}A$, which is there to avoid deriving infinite sequences of modalities. We could actually omit ?$\mathcal{M}A$ from the premises in the absence of any modality splitting axiom $\mathcal{M} \Rightarrow \mathcal{N}\mathcal{R}$ and a finite number of modalities, but this is a strong restriction.

**Definition 1.** *We call a triple* (?Q, !A, K) *saturated if it is closed under both the initiation and the derivation rules.*

We say a sequent $\Phi \mid_{\mathcal{M}} \Gamma \Vdash \Delta$ is *valid* if the sequent $\Phi \vdash \mathcal{M}(\bigwedge \Gamma \Rightarrow \bigvee \Delta)$ is provable in the sequent calculus of Fig. 1. A knowledge base is *valid* if each included sequent $\Phi \mid_{\mathcal{M}} \Gamma \Vdash \Delta$ is valid. The following lemma holds as all derivable sequents are provable.

**Lemma 8.** *Suppose given a triple* (!A, ?Q, K) *where* K *is valid, and take the saturated closure of the triples. Then the resulting knowledge base is valid.*

**Proposition 2.** *Given any triple* (!A, ?Q, K), *the process of closing under the initiation and derivation rules is terminating.*

*Proof.* Note first that each further question and answer generated by the initiation rules is a subformula of an already existing question and answer. This includes in particular $!\mathcal{R}A$ generated from $!\mathcal{M}A$ when $(\mathcal{N}, \mathcal{R}) \in s\mathcal{M}$, in which case $\mathcal{R} \in (\mathcal{M} \ominus \mathcal{N})$ and hence $\mathcal{R} \preceq \mathcal{M}$. As such, the initiation process generates only finitely many questions and answers, during which it only generates a finite number of sequents (consider for instance that $s\mathcal{M}$ is finite).

Moreover, we only have a finite number of *separating modalities*, those used separate the two contexts. Given that the closure of any finite set under $\triangledown$ must again be finite by assumption, and that the only new separating modalities which can be generated by the derivation process are created by the cut-rule with $\triangledown$, we know that we only have a finite number of separating modalities.

Now, for any sequent $\Phi \mid_\mathcal{M} \Gamma \Vdash \Delta$ added by the initiation rules, $(\Phi, \Gamma, \Delta) \subseteq$ (!A∪?Q), meaning that all formulas mentioned are drawn from some finite pool. In addition, all three derivation rules only produces sequents whose formulas where already contained in the sequents and questions of their respective assumptions. As such, we can conclude that any derived sequent must only have formulas existing within the finite set of questions and answers generated at initiation.

Hence, there are only finitely many sequents $\Phi \mid_\mathcal{M} \Gamma \Vdash \Delta$ which can be derived, which means the process of accumulation is terminating.

We moreover have that the accumulation process is *confluent*, in the sense that whatever order we made derivations, the final set of questions, answers and sequents $\Gamma \Vdash \Delta$ is the same. Last but not least, we have *completeness* of the forward proof search. For conciseness, we write $\Gamma \Vvdash A$ to say either $A \in \Gamma$ or $\Gamma' \Vdash A$ is derivable for some $\Gamma' \subseteq \Gamma$.

**Proposition 3.** *Suppose given a saturated triple* (?Q, !A, K). *Then for any* $\Gamma \subseteq$ !A *and* $A \in$ ?Q, *if* $\Gamma \vdash A$ *is provable in the sequent calculus, then* $\Gamma \Vvdash A$.

*Proof.* Note first that $\Vvdash$ is closed under cuts since $\Vdash$ is closed under cuts, that is: if $\Gamma \Vvdash A$ and $\Gamma, A \Vvdash B$, then $\Gamma \Vvdash B$.

Suppose given a proof P of $\Gamma \vdash A$ such that !$\Gamma$ and ?$A$. We show that $\Gamma \Vvdash A$ by induction on P. Note that if $A \in \Gamma$, then the statement is trivially true. Supposing $A \notin \Gamma$, we do a case analysis on the last proof step of the proof tree:

**Var** This is a vacuous case, since $a \in \Gamma, a$.

⊤ **R** If ?⊤, then $\Vdash A$ is added in the initiation phase, which fulfills the requirement since $\emptyset \subseteq \Gamma$.

⊥ **L** This gives a proof of $\Gamma, \bot \vdash A$. By assumption, !⊥ and ?$A$, and hence $\bot \Vdash A$ is added in the initiation phase and $\bot \subseteq (\Gamma, \bot)$.

∧**R** We have two trees $P_1$ and $P_2$ proving $\Gamma \vdash A$ and $\Gamma \vdash B$ respectively. We have $\Gamma \subseteq$ !A, and since $A \wedge B \in$ ?Q we have $A \in$ ?Q, $B \in$ ?Q and $A, B \Vdash A \wedge B$. By the induction hypothesis, $\Gamma \Vvdash A$, and $\Gamma \Vvdash B$. By cutting $A, B \Vvdash A \wedge B$ with both $\Gamma \Vvdash A$ and $\Gamma \Vvdash B$ we get $\Gamma, B \Vvdash A \wedge B$ and $\Gamma \Vvdash A \wedge B$.

∧**L** We have a tree P proving $\Gamma, A \wedge B, A, B \vdash C$. By assumption, $C \in \text{?Q}$, and $\Gamma, A \wedge B \subseteq \text{!A}$. Since $A \wedge B \in \text{!A}$, then $A \in \text{!A}$, $B \in \text{!A}$, $A \wedge B \Vdash A$ and $A \wedge B \Vdash B$ were added in the initiation phase. By the induction hypothesis, $\Gamma, A \wedge B, A, B \Vvdash C$, and by consecutive cutting, $\Gamma, A \wedge B, B \Vvdash C$ and $\Gamma, A \wedge B \Vvdash C$, as required.

∨**R1** We have a tree P proving $\Gamma \vdash A$, and $\Gamma \subseteq \text{!A}$, and $A \vee B \in \text{?Q}$. The latter implies that $A \in \text{?Q}$, and $A \Vdash A \vee B$. By the induction hypothesis, $\Gamma \Vvdash A$, and cutting this with $A \Vvdash A \vee B$ we get $\Gamma \Vvdash A \vee B$.

∨**R2** Similar to the previous case.

∨**L** We have trees $\mathsf{P}_1$ and $\mathsf{P}_2$ proving $\Gamma, A \vee B, A \vdash C$ and $\Gamma, A \vee B, B \vdash C$ respectively, $\Gamma, A \vee B \subseteq \text{!A}$ and $C \in \text{?Q}$. From $A \vee B \subseteq \text{!A}$, we derive that $A, B \in \text{!A}$ and $A \vee B \Vdash A, B$. Hence $\Gamma, A \vee B, A \subseteq \text{!A}$ and $\Gamma, A \vee B, B \subseteq \text{!A}$, and by the induction hypothesis, $\Gamma, A \vee B, A \Vvdash C$ and $\Gamma, A \vee B, B \Vvdash C$. By consecutive cutting, $\Gamma, A \vee B \Vvdash C, B$ and $\Gamma, A \vee B \Vvdash C$.

⇒**R** We have a tree P proving $\Gamma, A \vdash B$, and $\Gamma \subseteq \text{!A}$ and $A \Rightarrow B \in \text{?Q}$. The latter implies $A \in \text{!A}$, $B \in \text{?Q}$ and $B \Vdash A \Rightarrow B$. By the induction hypothesis on P we derive that $\Gamma, A \Vvdash B$. Cutting this with $B \Vvdash A \Rightarrow B$ we get $\Gamma, A \Vvdash A \Rightarrow B$. Hence $\Gamma' \Vdash A \Rightarrow B$ for some $\Gamma' \subseteq \Gamma, A$, so either $\Gamma' \subseteq \Gamma$, or $\Gamma' = \Gamma'', A$ and $\Gamma'' \subseteq \Gamma$, in which case we can apply the catch rule to get $\Gamma'' \Vdash A \Rightarrow B$. Either way, we have $\Gamma \Vvdash A \Rightarrow B$.

⇒**L** We have proofs $\mathsf{P}_1$ and $\mathsf{P}_2$ of $\Gamma, A \Rightarrow B \vdash A$ and $\Gamma, A \Rightarrow B, C \vdash C$ respectively, and $\Gamma, A \Rightarrow B \subseteq \text{!A}$ and $C \in \text{?Q}$. By $A \Rightarrow B \in \text{!A}$, $A \in \text{?Q}$, $B \in \text{!A}$ and $A, A \Rightarrow B \Vdash B$. By the induction hypothesis on $\mathsf{P}_2$, we get $\Gamma, A \Rightarrow B, B \Vvdash C$, which cutting this with $A, A \Rightarrow B \Vdash B$ we get $\Gamma, A, A \Rightarrow B \Vvdash C$. By the induction hypothesis on $\mathsf{P}_1$ we get $\Gamma, A \Rightarrow B \Vvdash A$, and cutting this with $\Gamma, A, A \Rightarrow B \Vvdash C$ we get $\Gamma, A \Rightarrow B \Vvdash C$.

**ModL** We have a proof P of $\Gamma, \mathcal{M}A, A \vdash B$ with $\mathcal{M} \Rightarrow \cdot$, proving $\Gamma, \mathcal{M}A \vdash B$ via ModL. Moreover, we have $\Gamma, \mathcal{M}A \subseteq \text{!A}$ and $B \in \text{?Q}$ by assumption. Since !$\mathcal{M}A$ we have !$A$ and $\mathcal{M}A \Vdash A$, and hence $\Gamma, \mathcal{M}A, A \subseteq \text{!A}$. By the induction hypothesis on P, $\Gamma, \mathcal{M}A, A \Vvdash B$ and by cutting this with $\mathcal{M}A \Vdash A$ we get $\Gamma, \mathcal{M}A \Vvdash B$ as required.

**Mod** We have a proof P of $\mathcal{M}^{-1}\Gamma \vdash A$, and $\Gamma \subseteq \text{!A}$ and $\mathcal{M}A \in \text{?Q}$. From the latter we can derive $A \in \text{?Q}$. Given that $\Gamma \subseteq \text{!A}$, we prove the following two properties at the same time: $\mathcal{M}^{-1}\Gamma \subseteq \text{!A}$, and for each $B \in \mathcal{M}^{-1}\Gamma$ there is a $C \in \Gamma$ such that we have $C \mid_\mathcal{N} \cdot \Vdash B$ for some $\mathcal{N} \Rightarrow \mathcal{M}$.

- Suppose $B \in \mathcal{M}^{-1}\Gamma$ from $\mathcal{N}B \in \Gamma$ and $\mathcal{N} \Rightarrow \mathcal{M}$. Then $\mathcal{N}B \in \text{!A}$ implies $B \in \text{!A}$ as required. Moreover, we have $\mathcal{N}B \mid_\mathcal{N} \cdot \Vdash B$ where $\mathcal{N} \Rightarrow \mathcal{M}$.
- Suppose $\mathcal{R}B \in \mathcal{M}^{-1}\Gamma$ from $\mathcal{N}B \in \Gamma$ and $\mathcal{R} \in \mathcal{N} \ominus \mathcal{M}$. Then there is a $(\mathcal{T}, \mathcal{R}) \in s\mathcal{N}$ such that $\mathcal{T} \Rightarrow \mathcal{M}$. We know that $\mathcal{R}B \in \text{!A}$ since $\mathcal{N}B \in \text{!A}$. Moreover, from $\mathcal{N}B \in \text{!A}$ we also have $\mathcal{N}B \mid_\mathcal{T} \cdot \Vdash \mathcal{R}B$ where $\mathcal{T} \Rightarrow \mathcal{M}$.

We can apply the induction hypothesis on P to derive $\mathcal{M}^{-1}\Gamma \Vvdash A$. If $\mathcal{M}^{-1}\Gamma$ is non-empty, then by repeatedly cutting, using for each $B \in \mathcal{M}^{-1}\Gamma$ the derived $C \mid_\mathcal{N} \cdot \Vdash B$ where $C \in \Gamma$ and $\mathcal{N} \Rightarrow \mathcal{M}$, we get $\Gamma \mid_\mathcal{R} \cdot \Vdash B$ for some $\mathcal{R} \Rightarrow \mathcal{M}$ (this $\mathcal{R}$ will be some $\triangledown$ combination of all used $\mathcal{N}$). If $\mathcal{M}^{-1}\Gamma$ is empty, simply note that $\cdot \mid_{id} \cdot \Vdash A$. Since $\mathcal{M}A \in \text{?Q}$ we can use the catch-rule to derive $\Gamma \Vvdash \mathcal{M}A$ as required.

*Example 6.* One of the motivating examples is the necessity modality $\Box$ from Example 1. We consider the example $\Box A, \Box(\Box A \Rightarrow B) \vdash \Box\Box B$.

$$\cfrac{\cfrac{\overline{\Box A, A, \Box(\Box A \Rightarrow B), \Box A \Rightarrow B \vdash \Box A}\,(\text{Id}) \quad \overline{\Box A, A, \Box(\Box A \Rightarrow B), \Box A \Rightarrow B, B \vdash B}\,(\text{Id})}{\cfrac{\Box A, A, \Box(\Box A \Rightarrow B), \Box A \Rightarrow B \vdash B}{\cfrac{\Box A, A, \Box(\Box A \Rightarrow B), \Box A \Rightarrow B \vdash \Box B}{\Box A, \Box(\Box A \Rightarrow B) \vdash \Box\Box B}\,(\text{Mod})}\,(\text{Mod})}\,(\Rightarrow\text{L})}{}$$

In the forward search we have $!\Box A$, $!\Box(\Box A \Rightarrow B)$, and $?\Box\Box B$.

- From $!\Box A$, we have $\Box A \mid_\Box \cdot \Vdash A$, and $\Box A \mid_\Box \cdot \Vdash \Box A$.
- From $!\Box(\Box A \Rightarrow B)$, we have $\Box(\Box A \Rightarrow B) \mid_\Box \cdot \Vdash \Box A \Rightarrow B$, and $\Box(\Box A \Rightarrow B) \mid_\Box \cdot \Vdash \Box(\Box A \Rightarrow B)$, as well as $!\Box A \Rightarrow B$.
- From $!\Box A \Rightarrow B$ we have $\Box A, \Box A \Rightarrow B \Vdash B$.
- From $?\Box\Box B$ we get $?\Box B$.
- We cut $\Box A, \Box A \Rightarrow B \Vdash B$ with $\Box A \mid_\Box \cdot \Vdash \Box A$ and $\Box(\Box A \Rightarrow B) \mid_\Box \cdot \Vdash \Box A \Rightarrow B$ to get $\Box A, \Box(\Box A \Rightarrow B) \mid_\Box \cdot \Vdash B$.
- Since $?\Box B$ and $\Box A, \Box(\Box A \Rightarrow B) \mid_\Box \cdot \Vdash B$, derive $\Box A, \Box(\Box A \Rightarrow B) \Vdash \Box B$.
- We can again cut this with $\Box A \mid_\Box \cdot \Vdash \Box A$ and $\Box(\Box A \Rightarrow B) \mid_\Box \cdot \Vdash \Box(\Box A \Rightarrow B)$ to get $\Box A, \Box(\Box A \Rightarrow B) \mid_\Box \cdot \Vdash \Box B$.
- Since $?\Box\Box B$, we can again catch to get $\Box A, \Box(\Box A \Rightarrow B) \Vdash \Box\Box B$.
- Note that we can still derive $\Box A, \Box(\Box A \Rightarrow B) \mid_\Box \cdot \Vdash \Box\Box B$, but this is where the process stops, since we do not have $?\Box\Box\Box B$.

### 4.3 Optimizations

The completeness result of Proposition 3 is established as a completeness of saturated triples $(?\mathsf{Q}, !\mathsf{A}, \mathsf{K})$. This can be strengthened by stating that $(?\mathsf{Q}, !\mathsf{A}, \mathsf{K})$ need only be saturated with respect to minimal sequents of $\mathsf{K}$, allowing us to remove from $\mathsf{K}$ any $\Gamma \Vdash A$ covered by $\Gamma' \Vdash A$ where $\Gamma' \subsetneq \Gamma$ during the forward proof search process.

We can moreover fine-tune data structures to be optimized for applying cuts on non-trivial sequents. Particularly, with a sorting order on formulas, we may design a sequent as a sorted list of formulas together with a Boolean value denoting whether the formula is an assumption or a consequent. Collections of sequents can be stored in a *tree data structure*, whose nodes are labeled by formulas, each with three branches for collecting all sequents which assume, conclude or not consider the formula in question. Proofs and refutations are then stored at the leaves. Checking, merging and applying cuts with such tree data structures can be done more efficiently then on sorted lists of sequents.

Finally, further optimizations are possible when we limit the situations in which we apply cuts. Checking the proof of Proposition 3, we see that we can maintain completeness even if we limit cuts to:

- those producing sequents $\Vdash \Gamma \vdash \Delta$ or $\Phi \mid_\mathcal{M} \Gamma \Vdash A$.
- those such that at most one premise of the cut has multiple consequents.
- $\Phi \mid_\mathcal{M} \Gamma \Vdash A$ produced by a cut is only included when $?\mathcal{N}A$ for some $\mathcal{M} \Rightarrow \mathcal{N}$.

## 5 Conclusions

We have proven decidability of intuitionistic logic with multiple modalities satisfying axiom K, N and selections of axioms of the form $\mathcal{M}X \Rightarrow X$, $\mathcal{M}X \Rightarrow \mathcal{N}X$ and $\mathcal{M}X \Rightarrow \mathcal{N}\mathcal{R}X$. This makes use of the modal shift operation $\mathcal{M}^{-1}$ on contexts which is used for a modal proof rule in a cut-free decidable calculus. The approach necessitates the existence of the shifted modalities $\mathcal{M} \ominus \mathcal{N}$, that is: If $\mathcal{M}X \Rightarrow \mathcal{N}\mathcal{R}_1 \ldots \mathcal{R}_n X$ where $n \geq 1$, then $\mathcal{M} \ominus \mathcal{N}$ includes some $\mathcal{T}$ such that $\mathcal{M}X \Rightarrow \mathcal{N}\mathcal{T}X$, and $\mathcal{T}X \Rightarrow \mathcal{R}_1 \ldots \mathcal{R}_n X$. Let us consider two possible extensions.

One extension is to include *consistency axioms* $\mathcal{M}\bot \Rightarrow \bot$. To facilitate these in the cut-free sequent calculus, we can include the rule: $\frac{\mathcal{M}^{-1}\Gamma \vdash \bot}{\Gamma \vdash A}$, that is, we have a new way of proving each $A$. Allowing this for each $A$ (as opposed to just $\bot$) gives way to a cut elimination proof. To extend the forward proof search accordingly, you need to assert $?\mathcal{M}\bot$, $?\bot$, and $\mathcal{M}\bot \Vdash \bot$ to ensure completeness.

Another extension is to include *unitality axioms* of the form $X \Rightarrow \mathcal{M}X$, which are stronger than the axiom of necessity (which states $\vdash X$ implies $\vdash \mathcal{M}X$). In order to facilitate these, we can add $\Gamma$ to $\mathcal{M}^{-1}\Gamma$ whenever $X \Rightarrow \mathcal{M}X$ is assumed. In order to keep a terminating cut elimination proof, the set $\mathcal{N} \ominus \mathcal{M}$ set can now *only* contain smaller modalities, since $\mathcal{N}X \Rightarrow \mathcal{M}\mathcal{N}X$ always holds.

The forward proof search does not cleanly produce countermodels of false statements, as in [7,25]. However, in case the search does not prove a statement, the generated database itself could collectively be considered a kind of countermodel. The idea is to take each context which does not prove $\bot$ as a possible Kripke world [15], and use the $\sqsubseteq$ ordering of contexts as order on worlds. We then record which atomic statements hold in which contexts. This is subject to future research. Other more direct approaches to generating countermodels using the inverse method exist as well [2,3], and could be adapted.

Proofs generated by the forward proof search can be imported into a Fitch-style modal calculus, as employed in *modal dependent type* theory [1]. These include contexts with multiple separations by modalities, allowing for a completely *substitutive* calculus. The proof search employed in this paper may be applied to find proofs in a fragment of modal type theory, but this must be further investigated.

## References

1. Birkedal, L., Clouston, R., Mannaa, B., Møgelberg, R.E., Pitts, A.M., Spitters, B.: Modal dependent type theory and dependent right adjoints. Math. Struct. Comput. Sci. **30**, 118–138 (2018). https://doi.org/10.1017/S0960129519000197
2. Chaudhuri, K., Pfenning, F.: A focusing inverse method theorem prover for first-order linear logic. In: Nieuwenhuis, R. (ed.) CADE 2005. LNCS (LNAI), vol. 3632, pp. 69–83. Springer, Heidelberg (2005). https://doi.org/10.1007/11532231_6
3. Chaudhuri, K., Pfenning, F., Price, G.: A logical characterization of forward and backward chaining in the inverse method. In: Furbach, U., Shankar, N. (eds.) IJCAR 2006. LNCS (LNAI), vol. 4130, pp. 97–111. Springer, Heidelberg (2006). https://doi.org/10.1007/11814771_9

4. Clouston, R.: Fitch-style modal lambda calculi. In: Baier, C., Dal Lago, U. (eds.) FoSSaCS 2018. LNCS, vol. 10803, pp. 258–275. Springer, Cham (2018). https://doi.org/10.1007/978-3-319-89366-2_14
5. Degtyarev, A., Robinson, J., Voronkov, A.: The inverse method. In: Robinson, A., Voronkov, A. (eds.) Handbook of Automated Reasoning, vol. 1, pp. 179–272. North-Holland, Amsterdam (2001). https://doi.org/10.1016/b978-044450813-3/50006-0
6. Fitch, F.B.: Symbolic Logic: An Introduction. Roland Press Co., New York (1952)
7. Garg, D., Genovese, V., Negri, S.: Countermodels from sequent calculi in multi-modal logics. In: Proceedings of 27th Annual IEEE Symposium on Logic in Computer Science (LICS '12), pp. 315–324. IEEE, Los Alamitos, CA (2012). https://doi.org/10.1109/lics.2012.42
8. Gentzen, G.: Untersuchungen über das logische SchlieSSen. I. Math. Z. **39**(1), 176–210 (1935). https://doi.org/10.1007/bf01201353
9. Girard, J.Y., Taylor, P., Lafont, Y.: Proofs and Types, Cambridge Tracts in Theoretical Computer Science, vol. 7. Cambridge University Press, Cambridge (1989)
10. Girlando, M., Kuznets, R., Marin, S., Morales, M., StraSSburger, L.: Intuitionistic S4 is decidable. In: Proceedings of 38th Annual ACM/IEEE Symposium on Logic in Computer Science (LICS '23), pp. 1–13. IEEE, Los Alamitos, CA (2023). https://doi.org/10.1109/lics56636.2023.10175684
11. Heilala, S., Pientka, B.: Bidirectional decision procedures for the intuitionistic propositional modal logic **IS4**. In: Pfenning, F. (ed.) CADE 2007. LNCS (LNAI), vol. 4603, pp. 116–131. Springer, Heidelberg (2007). https://doi.org/10.1007/978-3-540-73595-3_9
12. Heyting, A.: Intuitionism: An Introduction, Studies in Logic and the Foundations of Mathematics, vol. 17. North-Holland, Amsterdam (1956). https://www.sciencedirect.com/bookseries/studies-in-logic-and-the-foundations-of-mathematics/vol/17
13. Ketonen, O.: Untersuchungen zum Prädikatenkalkul. J. Symb. Logic **10**(4), 127–130 (1945). https://doi.org/10.2307/2269018
14. Kleene, S.C.: Introduction to Metamathematics. P. Noordhoff N.V, Groningen (1952)
15. Kripke, S.A.: Semantical analysis of intuitionistic logic I. In: Crossley, J., Dummett, M. (eds.) Formal Systems and Recursive Functions, Studies in Logic and the Foundations of Mathematics, vol. 40, pp. 92–130. Elsevier (1965). https://doi.org/10.1016/s0049-237x(08)71685-9
16. Maslov, S.Y.: Invertible sequential variant of constructive predicate calculus. In: Slisenko, A.O. (ed.) Studies in Constructive Mathematics and Mathematical Logic: Part I, Seminars in Mathematics: V. A. Steklov Mathematical Institute, Leningrad, vol. 4, pp. 36–42. Consultants Bureau, New York (1969). https://doi.org/10.1007/978-1-4684-8968-2_10
17. McLaughlin, S., Pfenning, F.: Efficient intuitionistic theorem proving with the polarized inverse method. In: Schmidt, R.A. (ed.) CADE 2009. LNCS (LNAI), vol. 5663, pp. 230–244. Springer, Heidelberg (2009). https://doi.org/10.1007/978-3-642-02959-2_19
18. McLaughlin, S., Pfenning, F.: The focused constraint inverse method for intuitionistic modal logics (2010). https://www.cs.cmu.edu/~fp/papers/inviml10.pdf, manuscript
19. Mints, G.: Gentzen-type systems and resolution rules part I propositional logic. In: Martin-Löf, P., Mints, G. (eds.) COLOG 1988. LNCS, vol. 417, pp. 198–231. Springer, Heidelberg (1990). https://doi.org/10.1007/3-540-52335-9_55

20. Negri, S., von Plato, J.: Structural Proof Theory. Cambridge University Press, Cambridge (2001). https://doi.org/10.1017/cbo9780511527340
21. Ono, K.: Logische Untersuchungen über die Grundlagen der Mathematik. J. Fac. Sci. Imperial Univ. Tokyo, Section I **3**(7), 329–389 (1939)
22. Pfenning, F.: Structural cut elimination: I. intuitionistic and classical logic. Inf. Comput. **157**(1), 84–141 (2000). https://doi.org/10.1006/inco.1999.2832
23. Simpson, A.K.: The Proof Theory and Semantics of Intuitionistic Modal Logic. Ph.D. thesis, University of Edinburgh (1994). https://hdl.handle.net/1842/407
24. Troelstra, A.S., Dalen, D.: Constructivism in Mathematics: An Introduction, Studies in Logic and the Foundations of Mathematics, vol. 121. North-Holland, Amsterdam (1988). https://www.sciencedirect.com/bookseries/studies-in-logic-and-the-foundations-of-mathematics/vol/121/
25. Troelstra, A.S., Schwichtenberg, H.: Basic Proof Theory, Cambridge Tracts in Theoretical Computer Science, vol. 43. Cambridge University Press, 2nd edn. (2000). https://doi.org/10.1017/cbo9781139168717
26. Wolter, F., Zakharyaschev, M.: Intuitionistic modal logic. In: Cantini, A., Casari, E., Minari, P. (eds.) Logic and Foundations of Mathematics, Synthese Library, vol. 280, pp. 227–238. Kluwer, Dordrecht (1999). https://doi.org/10.1007/978-94-017-2109-7_17

**Open Access** This chapter is licensed under the terms of the Creative Commons Attribution 4.0 International License (http://creativecommons.org/licenses/by/4.0/), which permits use, sharing, adaptation, distribution and reproduction in any medium or format, as long as you give appropriate credit to the original author(s) and the source, provide a link to the Creative Commons license and indicate if changes were made.

The images or other third party material in this chapter are included in the chapter's Creative Commons license, unless indicated otherwise in a credit line to the material. If material is not included in the chapter's Creative Commons license and your intended use is not permitted by statutory regulation or exceeds the permitted use, you will need to obtain permission directly from the copyright holder.

# A Proof-Theoretic View of Basic Intuitionistic Conditional Logic

Tiziano Dalmonte[1](✉) and Marianna Girlando[2]

[1] Free University of Bozen-Bolzano, Bolzano, Italy
[2] University of Amsterdam, Amsterdam, The Netherlands

**Abstract.** Intuitionistic conditional logic, studied by Weiss, Ciardelli and Liu, and Olkhovikov, aims at providing a constructive analysis of conditional reasoning. In this framework, the *would* and the *might* conditional operators are no longer interdefinable. The intuitionistic conditional logics considered in the literature are defined by setting Chellas' conditional logic CK, whose semantics is defined using selection functions, within the constructive and intuitionistic framework introduced for intuitionistic modal logics. This operation gives rise to a constructive variant of might-free-CK, which we call ConstCK$^{\Box\!\rightarrow}$, and an intuitionistic variant of CK, called IntCK. Building on the proof systems defined for CK and for intuitionistic modal logics, in this paper we introduce a nested calculus for IntCK and a sequent calculus for ConstCK$^{\Box\!\rightarrow}$. Based on the sequent calculus, we define ConstCK, a conservative extension of Weiss' logic ConstCK$^{\Box\!\rightarrow}$ with the might operator. We introduce a class of models and an axiomatisation for ConstCK, and extend these result to some extensions of ConstCK.

**Keywords:** Conditional logic · Intuitionistic modal logic · Sequent calculus · Nested sequents

## 1 Introduction

Intuitionistic conditional logic aims at providing a constructive analysis of conditional reasoning by combining the intuitionistic implication ($\rightarrow$) with the *would* $\Box\!\rightarrow$ and the *might* $\Diamond\!\rightarrow$ conditional operators. These modalities have been extensively studied from the 1970s, and several possible-world semantics have been proposed for them, including *selection function* [7], *sphere models* [16] and *preferential semantics* [6]. Conditional operators have mostly been studied in a classical setting; the goal is now to interpret them constructively, providing a formal and modular framework for their analysis. This line of research shares several insights with the definition of *intuitionistic modal logics*, where the intuitionistic implication is combined with the modalities $\Box$ and $\Diamond$. In this direction, *constructive* variants of modal logic K have been defined, inspired by a computational interpretation [1,27], while *intuitionistic* versions of K rely on the correspondence with first-order intuitionistic logic [12,22].

The study of intuitionistic variants of conditional logics is a relatively new field of research. This analysis started with the study of intuitionistic variants of

Chellas' 'basic' conditional logic CK [7]. This logic, one of the simplest normal conditional logics, constitutes the 'core' of several other systems, including preferential conditionals [6] and Lewis' counterfactuals [16]. The first intuitionistic counterpart of CK was the system ICK (which we call ConstCK$^{\Box\rightarrow}$) proposed by Weiss in [25] and extended by Ciardelli and Liu in [8] with additional conditional axioms. Axiomatic extensions of $ConstCKbox$ were also recently studied in [11][1]. These logics are defined in a language with $\Box\rightarrow$ as the only conditional modality. While in classical conditional logics the might operator $\Diamond\rightarrow$ is definable via the relation $(\varphi \Diamond\rightarrow \psi) \leftrightarrow \neg(\varphi \Box\rightarrow \neg\psi)$ [16], the same is generally assumed not to hold intuitionistically. Weiss, Ciardelli and Liu leave open the question of how to extend ConstCK$^{\Box\rightarrow}$ with the might operator $\Diamond\rightarrow$.

An answer was given by Olkhovikov in [18], with the definition of logic IntCK, inspired by the Fisher Servi-style *bi-relational semantics* for intuitionistic modal logic. While IntCK supports a meaningful interpretation of $\Diamond\rightarrow$, it validates $\Box\rightarrow$-principles that are not valid in ConstCK$^{\Box\rightarrow}$, so that IntCK is *not* a conservative extensions of Weiss' system. This is analogous to what happens for intuitionistic modal logics where, as pointed out in [10], logic iK, the $\Box$-fragment of constructive K [4,28] differs from IK, the intuitionistic variant of modal logic comprising both $\Box$ and $\Diamond$ [12,22]. And indeed, as observed by Weiss [25] and Olkhovikov [18], by defining $\Box$ and $\Diamond$ in terms of conditionals (through $\top \Box\rightarrow \varphi$ and $\top \Diamond\rightarrow \varphi$, respectively) one can reconstruct iK and IK within ConstCK$^{\Box\rightarrow}$ and IntCK, respectively.

Very few proof-theoretical accounts of intuitionistic conditionals exist in the literature. A labelled calculus for a constructive conditional logic representing access control policies is introduced in [13], while a natural deduction system supporting a BHK interpretation of counterfactual inferences is defined in [26].

In this paper we explore the proof theory of intuitionistic conditional logic, and we propose an alternative answer to the question posed by Weiss, Ciardelli and Liu. We first present a nested sequent calculus N.IntCK for IntCK. This calculus is defined by suitably combining Straßburger's nested calculus for IK [23] and Alenda, Olivetti and Pozzato's nested calculus for CK [2,3]. In particular, N.IntCK inherits from [23] the treatment of the intuitionistic base, and from [2,3] the indexing of nested components to treat antecedents of conditional sentences.

We then introduce S.ConstCK$^{\Box\rightarrow}$, a sequent calculus for ConstCK$^{\Box\rightarrow}$ based on Pattinson and Schröder's calculus for classical CK [19]. While this calculus does not require to enrich the structure of Gentzen-style sequents, the number of premises of the conditional rules is bounded by the number of conditional operators appearing in the conclusion. S.ConstCK$^{\Box\rightarrow}$ is defined by restricting Pattinson and Schröder's calculus to single-succedent sequents.

The choice of the formalism employed (nested sequents or sequent calculus) depends on the logic under scope. In particular, no Gentzen-style sequent calculus is known for intuitionistic modal logic IK (but other kinds of proof systems have been introduced for the logic, e.g., labelled calculi [17]). On the other hand, sequent calculi are available both for CK [19] and for constructive modal logics

---

[1] In the literature, CK also denotes the constructive version of K. We here use CK for Chellas' logic, and use the prefix Const for the 'constructive' version of a logic.

[27]. To define proof systems for both IntCK and ConstCK$^{\square\!\rightarrow}$, we thus select the 'simplest' kind of proof system known for the logic.

Proof-theory serves as a guide to integrate the might operator into ConstCK$^{\square\!\rightarrow}$. We first define the classical rules for $\diamond\!\!\rightarrow$ as duals of the rules for $\square\!\rightarrow$ in Pattinson and Schröder's calculus. By adding the single-succedent restriction, we obtain a proof-theoretic characterization of a new system, which we call ConstCK, comprising both $\square\!\rightarrow$ and $\diamond\!\!\rightarrow$. We propose an axiomatisation and a class of models for ConstCK. Since the $\diamond\!\!\rightarrow$-free fragment of ConstCK corresponds to ConstCK$^{\square\!\rightarrow}$, this logic represents a natural answer to the question of how to integrate the $\diamond\!\!\rightarrow$ modality in ConstCK$^{\square\!\rightarrow}$. We conclude by discussing extensions of ConstCK with *identity, conditional modus ponens* and *conditional excluded middle*.

The paper is structured as follows. In Sect. 2 we introduce axiomatisations and semantics for intuitionistic conditional logics. Then, in Sect. 3 we present the nested calculus N.IntCK for IntCK. In Sect. 4 we introduce the sequent calculus S.ConstCK$^{\square\!\rightarrow}$ for ConstCK$^{\square\!\rightarrow}$, and the new logic ConstCK. Finally, in Sect. 5 we discuss extensions of ConstCK, and we conclude with directions for future works in Sect. 6. Full proofs of our results can be found in a technical report [9].

## 2 Preliminaries

Fixed a countable set of propositional atoms $Atm$, the formulas of $\mathcal{L}$ are generated as follows, for $p \in Atm$: $\varphi ::= p \mid \bot \mid \varphi \wedge \varphi \mid \varphi \vee \varphi \mid \varphi \rightarrow \varphi \mid \varphi \square\!\!\rightarrow \varphi \mid \varphi \diamond\!\!\rightarrow \varphi$. We assume the convention that $\wedge, \vee$ bind stronger than $\rightarrow, \square\!\!\rightarrow, \diamond\!\!\rightarrow$. We define $\neg \varphi := \varphi \rightarrow \bot$, $\top := \neg \bot$ and $\varphi \leftrightarrow \psi := (\varphi \rightarrow \psi) \wedge (\psi \rightarrow \varphi)$. The formulas of $\mathcal{L}^{\square\!\rightarrow}$ are defined as those of $\mathcal{L}$, but by removing the operator $\diamond\!\!\rightarrow$. For $\circ\!\!\rightarrow \in \{\square\!\!\rightarrow, \diamond\!\!\rightarrow\}$, we call $\circ\!\!\rightarrow$-formula (or *conditional* formula) any formula whose main connective is $\circ\!\!\rightarrow$. We use capital Latin letters $A, B, C, ...$ to denote *sets* of formulas, and capital Greek letters $\Gamma, \Delta, \Sigma, ...$ to denote *multisets* of formulas.

The classical (resp. intuitionistic) conditional logics we consider are defined extending any axiomatisation of classical (resp. intuitionistic) propositional logic CPL (resp. IPL) including the *modus ponens* rule, with suitable axioms and rules, as summarised in Fig. 1.

As usual, we say that a rule $A/\varphi$ is *derivable* in a logic L if there is a finite sequence of formulas $\psi_1, ..., \psi_n$ such that $\psi_n = \varphi$ and for all $1 \leq i \leq n$, $\psi_i \in A$, or it is an (instance of an) axiom of L, or it is obtained from previous formulas by the application of a rule of L. Moreover, a formula $\varphi$ is *derivable* in L (written $\vdash_L \varphi$), if $\emptyset/\varphi$ is derivable. Finally, we say that $\psi$ is derivable in L from a set of formulas $A$ (written $A \vdash_L \varphi$) if there are $\psi_1, ..., \psi_n \in A$ such that $\vdash_L \psi_1 \wedge ... \wedge \psi_n \rightarrow \varphi$.

Logic ConstCK$^{\square\!\rightarrow}$ was introduced in [8,25] (under the name ICK), while IntCK is from [18]. In [18], Olkhovikov shows that if $\varphi$ is derivable in ConstCK$^{\square\!\rightarrow}$, then it is derivable in IntCK. However, similarly to what happens in the intuitionistic modal case, IntCK is a non-conservative extension of ConstCK$^{\square\!\rightarrow}$: formula $\neg\neg(\top\square\!\!\rightarrow\bot)\rightarrow(\top\square\!\!\rightarrow\bot)$ is derivable in IntCK, but it is *not* derivable in ConstCK$^{\square\!\rightarrow}$ [18]. Finally, CK$_\diamond$ is derivable in *IntCK*, we added it to Fig. 1 as it will be used in Sec. 4 to define the logic *CCK*.

A Proof-Theoretic View of Basic Intuitionistic Conditional Logic     357

$$\text{CM}_\Box \quad (\varphi \Box\!\!\to \psi \wedge \chi) \to (\varphi \Box\!\!\to \psi) \wedge (\varphi \Box\!\!\to \chi)$$
$$\text{CC}_\Box \quad (\varphi \Box\!\!\to \psi) \wedge (\varphi \Box\!\!\to \chi) \to (\varphi \Box\!\!\to \psi \wedge \chi)$$
$$\text{CN}_\Box \quad \varphi \Box\!\!\to \top$$
$$\text{CM}_\Diamond \quad (\varphi \Diamond\!\!\to \psi) \vee (\varphi \Diamond\!\!\to \chi) \to (\varphi \Diamond\!\!\to \psi \vee \chi)$$
$$\text{CC}_\Diamond \quad (\varphi \Diamond\!\!\to \psi \vee \chi) \to (\varphi \Diamond\!\!\to \psi) \vee (\varphi \Diamond\!\!\to \chi)$$
$$\text{CN}_\Diamond \quad \neg(\varphi \Diamond\!\!\to \bot)$$
$$\text{CW} \quad (\varphi \Diamond\!\!\to \psi) \wedge (\varphi \Box\!\!\to \chi) \to (\varphi \Diamond\!\!\to \psi \wedge \chi)$$
$$\text{CFS} \quad ((\varphi \Diamond\!\!\to \psi) \to (\varphi \Box\!\!\to \chi)) \to (\varphi \Box\!\!\to (\psi \to \chi))$$
$$\text{CK}_\Diamond \quad (\varphi \Box\!\!\to (\psi \to \chi)) \to ((\varphi \Diamond\!\!\to \psi) \to (\varphi \Diamond\!\!\to \chi))$$
$$\text{def}_\Diamond \quad (\varphi \Diamond\!\!\to \psi) \leftrightarrow \neg(\varphi \Box\!\!\to \neg\psi)$$

$$\text{RA}_\Box \ \dfrac{\varphi \leftrightarrow \rho}{(\varphi \Box\!\!\to \psi) \leftrightarrow (\rho \Box\!\!\to \psi)}$$

$$\text{RC}_\Box \ \dfrac{\psi \leftrightarrow \chi}{(\varphi \Box\!\!\to \psi) \leftrightarrow (\varphi \Box\!\!\to \chi)}$$

$$\text{RA}_\Diamond \ \dfrac{\varphi \leftrightarrow \rho}{(\varphi \Diamond\!\!\to \psi) \leftrightarrow (\rho \Diamond\!\!\to \psi)}$$

$$\text{RC}_\Diamond \ \dfrac{\psi \leftrightarrow \chi}{(\varphi \Diamond\!\!\to \psi) \leftrightarrow (\varphi \Diamond\!\!\to \chi)}$$

| System name | Language | Prop. base | Conditional axioms and rules |
|---|---|---|---|
| $\text{CK}^{\Box\!\!\to}$ | $\mathcal{L}^{\Box\!\!\to}$ | CPL | $\text{RA}_\Box$, $\text{RC}_\Box$, $\text{CM}_\Box$, $\text{CC}_\Box$, $\text{CN}_\Box$. |
| CK | $\mathcal{L}$ | CPL | $\text{RA}_\Box$, $\text{RC}_\Box$, $\text{CM}_\Box$, $\text{CC}_\Box$, $\text{CN}_\Box$, $\text{def}_\Diamond$. |
| ConstCK$^{\Box\!\!\to}$ | $\mathcal{L}^{\Box\!\!\to}$ | IPL | $\text{RA}_\Box$, $\text{RC}_\Box$, $\text{CM}_\Box$, $\text{CC}_\Box$, $\text{CN}_\Box$. |
| IntCK | $\mathcal{L}$ | IPL | $\text{RA}_\Box$, $\text{RC}_\Box$, $\text{RA}_\Diamond$, $\text{RC}_\Diamond$, $\text{CM}_\Box$, $\text{CM}_\Diamond$, $\text{CC}_\Box$, $\text{CC}_\Diamond$, $\text{CN}_\Box$, $\text{CN}_\Diamond$, CW, CFS. |

**Fig. 1.** Conditional axioms and rules, and axiomatic systems.

We introduce the bi-relational Kripke models for ConstCK$^{\Box\!\!\to}$ and IntCK from [25] and [18] respectively. We first present some general definitions.

**Definition 2.1.** *A basic birelational Chellas model (basic model for short) is a tuple $M = \langle W, \leq, R, V \rangle$ consisting of $W$, a non-empty set of elements called worlds, a binary relation $\leq$ over $W$ which is reflexive and transitive, and a monotone valuation function $V : W \longrightarrow 2^{Atm}$, that is, for $w, w' \in W$, if $w \leq w'$ then $V(w) \subseteq V(w')$. Finally, $R \subseteq W \times \mathcal{P}(W) \times W$ is a relation associating to every $X \subseteq W$ a binary relation $R_X$ on $W$.*

**Definition 2.2.** *For $M$ basic model, $X \subseteq W$, we consider the properties (Fig. 2):*

Left commutativity:   $\forall w, w', v(w \leq w' R_X v \Rightarrow \exists v'(w R_X v' \leq v))$.
Right commutativity:  $\forall w, w', v(w R_X v \leq v' \Rightarrow \exists w'(w \leq w' \ \& \ w' R_X v'))$.
Church-Rosser:        $\forall w, w', v(w \leq w' \ \& \ w R_X v \Rightarrow \exists v'(w' R_X v' \ \& \ v \leq v'))$.

**Definition 2.3.** *For $M$ basic model, $w$ world of $M$ and $\varphi$ formula, the satisfaction relation $M, w \Vdash \varphi$ is defined inductively as follows. For $[\![\psi]\!] = \{w \in W \mid M, w \Vdash \psi\}$, conditionals have a local (L) or global (G) interpretation:*

- $M, w \Vdash p$ iff $p \in V(w)$;
- $M, w \not\Vdash \bot$;
- $M, w \Vdash \varphi \wedge \psi$ iff $M, w \Vdash \varphi$ and $M, w \Vdash \psi$;
- $M, w \Vdash \varphi \vee \psi$ iff $M, w \Vdash \varphi$ or $M, w \Vdash \psi$;
- $M, w \Vdash \varphi \to \psi$ iff *for all* $w' \in W$ s.t. $w \leq w'$, if $M, w' \Vdash \varphi$ then $M, w' \Vdash \psi$;
- (L$\Box\!\!\to$) $M, w \Vdash \varphi \Box\!\!\to \psi$ iff *for all* $v \in W$ s.t. $w R_{[\![\varphi]\!]} v$, $M, v \Vdash \psi$;

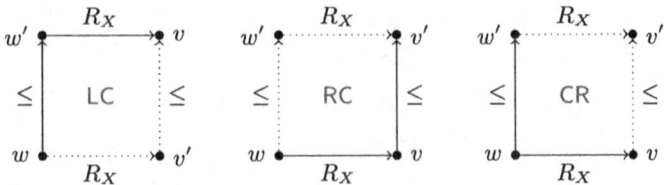

**Fig. 2.** Left commutativity, right commutativity and Church-Rosser

- $(G\Box\!\!\rightarrow)$ $M, w \Vdash \varphi \Box\!\!\rightarrow \psi$ iff *for all* $w', v \in W$ *s.t.* $w \leq w' R_{[\![\varphi]\!]} v$, $M, v \Vdash \psi$;
- $(L\diamond\!\!\rightarrow)$ $M, w \Vdash \varphi \diamond\!\!\rightarrow \psi$ iff *there is* $v \in W$ *s.t.* $w R_{[\![\varphi]\!]} v$ *and* $M, v \Vdash \psi$;
- $(G\diamond\!\!\rightarrow)$ $M, w \Vdash \varphi \diamond\!\!\rightarrow \psi$ iff *for all* $w' \in W$ *s.t.* $w \leq w'$ *there is* $v \in W$ *s.t.* $w' R_{[\![\varphi]\!]} v$ *and* $M, v \Vdash \psi$.

Global and local interpretation clauses for the conditional operators reflect different ways of satisfying the *hereditary property (hp)*, namely that for all models $M$ and all worlds $w$, $v$ of $M$, if $M, w \Vdash \varphi$ and $w \leq v$, then $M, v \Vdash \varphi$. Satisfaction of hp is a crucial condition in order for the axioms of IPL to be valid over the whole conditional language. While global clauses automatically ensure hp (see e.g. Definition 4.7 below), local clauses typically need to be combined with frame properties among those of Definition 2.2. This situation is witnessed by the models for ConstCK$^{\Box\!\!\rightarrow}$ and IntCK, respectively defined in [18,25] as follows.

**Definition 2.4.** *A* Weiss model *is a basic model satisfying* left commutativity. *For* $\varphi \in \mathcal{L}^{\Box\!\!\rightarrow}$, *the satisfaction relation* $M, w \Vdash \varphi$ *is inductively defined by the propositional clauses in Definition 2.3 and* $(L\Box\!\!\rightarrow)$.

**Definition 2.5.** *An* Olkhovikov model, *or* intuitionistic Chellas model, *is a basic model satisfying* right commutativity *and* Church-Rosser. *For* $\varphi \in \mathcal{L}$, *the satisfaction relation* $M, w \Vdash \varphi$ *is inductively defined by the propositional clauses in Definition 2.3,* $(G\Box\!\!\rightarrow)$ *and* $(L\diamond\!\!\rightarrow)$.

Weiss' and Olkhovikov's models adapt to the conditional language some preexisting semantics for their corresponding constructive vs. intuitionistic unary modal systems (cf. [22] for a discussion of alternative constructive and intuitionistic modal semantics). Note in particular the semantics of IntCK, that mimics the global interpretation of $\forall$ and the local interpretation of $\exists$ in intuitionistic first-order semantics. For $M$ any kind of model above, a formula $\varphi$ is *valid in* $M$ if it is satisfied by all its worlds. For $\varphi \in \mathcal{L}^{\Box\!\!\rightarrow}$, $\varphi$ is derivable in ConstCK$^{\Box\!\!\rightarrow}$ iff it is valid in all Weiss models [25], and for $\psi \in \mathcal{L}$, $\psi$ is derivable in IntCK iff it is valid in all Olkhovikov models [18].

## 3 Nested Sequent Calculus for IntCK

In this section we present a nested sequent calculus N.IntCK for logic IntCK. The proof system 'combines' the nested proof system for classical conditional logic

CK from Alenda et al. in [2,3] with the nested sequent calculus for intuitionitstic modal logic IK introduced by Straßburger in [23]. In particular, the treatment of the intuitionistic base is from [23], while the idea of indexing nested components with formulas to evaluate conditional operators is from [2,3].

For convenience, we employ *polarised* formulas, as in [23]. We associate to formulas $\varphi$ of $\mathcal{L}$ a *input polarity*, $-^{\bullet}$, or a *output polarity*, $-^{\circ}$. Polarities indicate the position of the formulas within two-sided sequents: input formulas $\varphi^{\bullet}$ can be thought as occurring in the antecedent of a sequent, while output formulas $\varphi^{\circ}$ as formulas occurring in the consequent. Our nested sequents are 'single-succedent', meaning that we allow *exactly one* output formula in a nested sequent. As it is usual for nested sequents, we enrich the structure of Gentzen-style sequent with an additional structural connective [ ], which is now indexed with a non-polarised formula acting as index, or placeholder. A colon separates the index formulas from the rest of the nested sequent. The formal definition is given below.

**Definition 3.1.** Intuitionistic conditional nested sequents $\Gamma$ (nested sequents for short) are generated as follows, for $\varphi, \psi$ (polarized) formulas of the language:

$$\Lambda ::= \emptyset \mid \Lambda, \varphi^{\bullet} \mid \Lambda, [\psi : \Lambda] \qquad \Gamma ::= \Lambda, \varphi^{\circ} \mid \Lambda, [\psi : \Gamma]$$

Objects $\Lambda$ containing only input/$\bullet$-formulas are input sequents, while objects $\Gamma$ containing exactly one output/$\circ$-formula are nested sequents. The formula interpretation of both objects is defined as:

$$i(\emptyset) := \top \qquad\qquad i(\Lambda, \varphi^{\circ}) := i(\Lambda) \to \varphi$$
$$i(\Lambda, \varphi^{\bullet}) := i(\Lambda) \wedge \varphi \qquad i(\Lambda, [\psi : \Gamma]) := i(\Lambda) \to \big(\psi \,\Box\!\!\to i(\Gamma)\big)$$
$$i(\Lambda, [\psi : \Lambda']) := i(\Lambda) \wedge \big(\psi \,\Diamond\!\!\to i(\Lambda')\big)$$

Observe that, according to our definition, nested sequents cannot be empty. A *context* is a input or nested sequent containing a *hole*, $\{,\}$, to be filled with a input or nested sequent. This notion is needed to apply rules 'deep' within nested sequents.

**Definition 3.2.** We inductively define the notion of context, denoted $\Gamma\{\,\}$, and depth of a context, denoted $depth(\Gamma\{\,\})$, for $\Delta$ input or nested sequent and $\varphi$ formula:

- $\{\,\}$ is a context with $depth(\{\,\}) = 0$;
- $\Delta, \Gamma\{\,\}$ is a context with $depth(\Delta, \Gamma\{\,\}) = depth(\Gamma\{\,\})$;
- $[\varphi : \Gamma\{\,\}]$ is a context with $depth([\varphi : \Gamma\{\,\}]) = depth(\Gamma\{\,\}) + 1$.

A context containing only $\bullet$-formulas is a $\bullet$-*context*, and a context containing exactly one $\circ$-formula is a $\circ$-*context*. A $\bullet$-*context* filled with an input sequent is an input sequent, while a $\bullet$-context filled with a nested sequent is a nested sequent. A $\circ$-context can only be filled with an input sequent.

$$\text{init} \frac{}{\Gamma\{p^\bullet, p^\circ\}} \quad \bot^\bullet \frac{}{\Gamma\{\bot^\bullet\}} \quad \wedge^\bullet \frac{\Gamma\{\varphi^\bullet, \psi^\bullet\}}{\Gamma\{\varphi \wedge \psi^\bullet\}} \quad \wedge^\circ \frac{\Gamma\{\varphi^\circ\} \quad \Gamma\{\psi^\circ\}}{\Gamma\{\varphi \wedge \psi^\circ\}}$$

$$\vee^\bullet \frac{\Gamma\{\varphi^\bullet\} \quad \Gamma\{\psi^\bullet\}}{\Gamma\{\varphi \vee \psi^\bullet\}} \quad \vee^\circ \frac{\Gamma\{\varphi^\circ\}}{\Gamma\{\varphi \vee \psi^\circ\}} \quad \vee^\circ \frac{\Gamma\{\psi^\circ\}}{\Gamma\{\varphi \vee \psi^\circ\}} \quad \to^\bullet \frac{\Gamma^{\downarrow}\{\varphi \to \psi^\bullet, \varphi^\circ\} \quad \Gamma\{\psi^\bullet\}}{\Gamma\{\varphi \to \psi^\bullet\}}$$

$$\to^\circ \frac{\Gamma\{\varphi^\bullet, \psi^\circ\}}{\Gamma\{\varphi \to \psi^\circ\}} \quad \Box{\mapsto}^\bullet \frac{\varphi^\bullet, \eta^\circ \quad \eta^\bullet, \varphi^\circ \quad \Gamma\{\varphi \Box{\mapsto} \psi^\bullet, [\eta : \psi^\bullet, \Delta]\}}{\Gamma\{\varphi \Box{\mapsto} \psi^\bullet, [\eta : \Delta]\}} \quad \Box{\mapsto}^\circ \frac{\Gamma\{[\varphi : \psi^\circ]\}}{\Gamma\{\varphi \Box{\mapsto} \psi^\circ\}}$$

$$\Diamond{\mapsto}^\bullet \frac{\Gamma\{[\varphi : \psi^\bullet]\}}{\Gamma\{\varphi \Diamond{\mapsto} \psi^\bullet\}} \quad \Diamond{\mapsto}^\circ \frac{\varphi^\bullet, \eta^\circ \quad \eta^\bullet, \varphi^\circ \quad \Gamma\{[\eta : \psi^\circ, \Delta]\}}{\Gamma\{\varphi \Diamond{\mapsto} \psi^\circ, [\eta : \Delta]\}}$$

**Fig. 3.** The rules of N.IntCK.

*Example 3.3.* $\Lambda\{\} = \varphi^\bullet, \psi^\bullet, [\eta : \zeta^\bullet, \{\}]$ is a •-context, $\chi^\bullet$ is an input sequent, and $\Delta = \chi^\bullet, [\gamma : \xi^\circ]$ is a nested sequent. $\Lambda\{\chi^\bullet\} = \varphi^\bullet, \psi^\bullet, [\eta : \zeta^\bullet, \chi^\bullet]$ is an input sequent, and $\Lambda\{\Delta\} = \varphi^\bullet, \psi^\bullet, [\eta : \zeta^\bullet, \chi^\bullet, [\gamma : \xi^\circ]]$ is a nested sequent. $\Gamma\{\} = \varphi^\bullet, \psi^\bullet, [\eta : \zeta^\circ, \{\}]$ is a ○-context; $\Gamma\{\chi^\bullet\}$ is a nested sequent, while $\Gamma\{\Delta\}$ is *not* a nested sequent, as it contains two output formulas.

The rules of N.IntCK are defined in Fig. 3. Every object $GCSigma$ appearing in the rules is a nested sequent. Propositional rules are standard (refer, e.g., to [24]). For $\Gamma\{\}$ context, $\Gamma^{\downarrow}\{\}$ denotes the result of removing the ○-formula from $\Gamma\{\}$. The conditional rules, inspired from [3], 'exemplify' the semantic conditions for $\Box{\mapsto}$ and $\Diamond{\mapsto}$. The rule $\Box{\mapsto}^\circ$, read bottom-up, creates a new nested component indexed with $\varphi$, representing the set of worlds accessible through $R_{[\![\varphi]\!]}$. The rule $\Box{\mapsto}^\bullet$ 'moves' formula $\psi^\bullet$ to a nested component indexed with $\eta$, under the condition that $\eta$ and $\varphi$ are equivalent, i.e., that derivations of both $\varphi^\bullet, \eta^\circ$ and $\eta^\bullet, \varphi^\circ$ can be constructed. A *proof*, or *derivation*, of a nested sequent $\Gamma$ in N.IntCK is a tree whose root is labeled with $\Gamma$, whose leaves are occupied by instances of init or $\bot^\bullet$, and such that the nested sequents occurring at intermediate nodes are obtained through application of N.IntCK-rules. If there is a proof of $\Gamma$ in N.IntCK, then $\Gamma$ is *derivable* in N.IntCK.

The proof of soundness of N.IntCK follows the structure of the soundness proof for intuitionistic nested sequents in [23]. Refer to [9] for details.

**Theorem 3.4.** *If a nested sequent $\Gamma$ is derivable in* N.IntCK, *then* $\vdash_{\text{IntCK}} i(\Gamma)$.

Next, we shall give a *syntactic* proof of completeness of N.IntCK, inspired from [2,3]. We wish to prove that cut is eliminable (Fig. 4); however, to do so, we need to prove eliminability of the *index-replacement* rule rep. So, after proving admissibility the structural rules (Lemma 3.6), we show how to 'simulate' instances of cut and of rep, in Lemma 3.7 and 3.8 . In Theorem 3.9, we show how to transform derivations in N.IntCK ∪ {cut} into derivations in N.IntCK.

For $\varphi$ formula of $\mathcal{L}$, the *weight* of $\varphi$ is defined as the number of binary connectives occurring in $\varphi$. The *height* of a N.IntCK derivation $\mathcal{D}$, denoted by $h(\mathcal{D})$, is the length of its longest branch, minus 1. In the cut rule as displayed

$$\mathsf{w}\,\frac{\Gamma\{\emptyset\}}{\Gamma\{\Lambda\}} \qquad [\mathsf{nec}]\,\frac{\Gamma}{[\eta:\Gamma]} \qquad [\mathsf{m}]\,\frac{\Gamma\{[\eta:\Delta_1]\} \quad \Gamma\{[\eta:\Delta_2]\}}{\Gamma\{[\eta:\Delta_1,\Delta_2]\}} \qquad \mathsf{c}\,\frac{\Gamma\{\varphi^\bullet,\varphi^\bullet\}}{\Gamma\{\varphi^\bullet\}}$$

$$\mathsf{cut}\,\frac{\Gamma^\downarrow\{\xi^\circ\} \quad \Gamma\{\xi^\bullet\}}{\Gamma\{\emptyset\}} \qquad \mathsf{rep}\,\frac{\varphi^\bullet,\eta^\circ \quad \eta^\bullet,\varphi^\circ \quad \Gamma\{[\varphi:\Delta]\}}{\Gamma\{[\eta:\Delta]\}}$$

**Fig. 4.** The structural rules of *weakening, necessitation, box-medial, contraction* and *cut*, and the *index-replacement* rule. In the w rule, $\Lambda$ needs to be an input sequent.

in Fig. 4, we call $\xi$ the *cut formula*. The *rank* of an application of the cut rule is set to be the weight of the cut formula, plus 1. The *rank* of a derivation $\mathcal{D}$ in N.IntCK $\cup$ {cut}, denoted by $r(\mathcal{D})$, is the maximum of all the ranks of rules cut occurring in $\mathcal{D}$. In the rep rule as displayed in Fig. 4, we call $\varphi$ the *rep-formula*.

Given a rule $\mathsf{R} = \psi_1,..,\psi_n/\chi$ and a proof system $\mathcal{P}$, R is *admissible* in $\mathcal{P}$ if, whenever there are $\mathcal{P}$-proofs $\mathcal{D}_1,..,\mathcal{D}_n$ of $\psi_1,..,\psi_n$, then there is a $\mathcal{P}$-proof $\mathcal{D}$ of $\chi$. R is *height-preserving (hp-) admissible* in $\mathcal{P}$ if $h(\mathcal{D}) \leq \max(h(\mathcal{D}_1),..,h(\mathcal{D}_n))$, and it is *rank-preserving (rk-) admissible* in $\mathcal{P}$ if $r(\mathcal{D}) \leq \max(r(\mathcal{D}_1),..,r(\mathcal{D}_n))$. Moreover, R is *invertible* in $\mathcal{P}$ if, whenever there is a $\mathcal{P}$-proof $\mathcal{D}$ of $\chi$, then there are $\mathcal{P}$-proofs $\mathcal{D}_1,..,\mathcal{D}_n$ of $\psi_1,..,\psi_n$. If, for every $i \leq n$, $h(\mathcal{D}_i) \leq h(\mathcal{D})$, the rule is *hp-invertible*, and if $r(\mathcal{D}_i) \leq r(\mathcal{D})$ the rule is *rp-invertible*.

The following result can easily be proved by induction on $w(\varphi)$. We then report the structural result needed to prove the Cut-elimination Theorem (3.9).

**Proposition 3.5.** *Every sequent of the form $\Gamma\{\varphi^\bullet,\varphi^\circ\}$ is derivable in N.IntCK.*

**Lemma 3.6.** *The following hold in N.IntCK $\cup$ {cut, rep}:*

*a) The rules of w, [nec], [m] and c are hp- and rp-admissible;*
*b) Rules $\wedge^\bullet$, $\wedge^\circ$, $\vee^\bullet$, $\to^\circ$, $\Box\!\!\to^\bullet$, $\Box\!\!\to^\circ$ and $\Diamond\!\!\to^\bullet$ are hp- and rp-invertible.*

*Proof (Sketch).* All the statements follow by routine induction on the height of the available derivation. The constructions are similar to the proofs in [5,23] (for the modal rules) and to the proofs in [3] (for the conditional rules). Some cases are detailed in [9]. □

**Lemma 3.7.** *If $\mathcal{D}^1, \mathcal{D}^2, \mathcal{D}^3$ are N.IntCK$\cup$ {cut} derivations of $\varphi^\bullet,\eta^\circ$ and $\eta^\bullet,\varphi^\circ$ and $\Gamma\{[\varphi:\Delta]\}$ respectively, then there is a N.IntCK $\cup$ {cut} derivation $\mathcal{D}$ of $\Gamma\{[\eta:\Delta]\}$, such that $r(\mathcal{D}) = \max(r(\mathcal{D}^1),r(\mathcal{D}^2),r(\mathcal{D}^3),w(\varphi) + 1)$.*

*Proof.* By induction on the height $n$ of the derivation $\mathcal{D}$ of $\Gamma\{[\varphi:\Delta]\}$. We consider only the case in which the last rule applied in $\mathcal{D}$ is $\Box\!\!\to^\bullet$. The derivations of the premises of rep are the following, where $\mathcal{D}^3$ is the rightmost derivation:

$$\begin{array}{ccc} \overset{\mathcal{D}^1}{\triangledown} & \overset{\mathcal{D}^2}{\triangledown} & \Box\!\!\to^\bullet\,\dfrac{\overset{\mathcal{D}^3_1}{\triangledown}\quad \overset{\mathcal{D}^3_2}{\triangledown}\quad \overset{\mathcal{D}^3_3}{\triangledown}}{\Gamma\{\chi\Box\!\!\to\vartheta^\bullet,[\varphi:\Delta]\}} \\ \varphi^\bullet,\eta^\circ & \eta^\bullet,\varphi^\circ & \chi^\bullet,\varphi^\circ \quad \varphi^\bullet,\chi^\circ \quad \Gamma\{\chi\Box\!\!\to\vartheta^\bullet,[\varphi:\vartheta^\bullet,\Delta]\} \end{array}$$

We construct $\mathcal{D}$ as follows, where the double line denotes (possibly multiple) applications of the admissible rules, and the dotted line signifies an application of the inductive hypothesis $(ih)$. Since the cut rules have $\varphi$ as cut-formula, $r(\mathcal{D}) = \max(r(\mathcal{D}_1), r(\mathcal{D}_2), r(\mathcal{D}_3), w(\varphi)+1)$.

$$\mathrm{cut}\,\frac{\mathcal{D}_1^3\;\;\;\;\;\mathcal{D}^1\\ \chi^\circ,\varphi^\circ\;\;\;\; \mathrm{w}\overline{\overline{\chi^\bullet,\varphi^\bullet,\eta^\circ}}\;\;\;\;\varphi^\bullet,\eta^\circ}{\chi^\bullet,\eta^\circ} \boxminus \;\;\; \mathrm{cut}\,\frac{\mathcal{D}_2\;\;\;\;\;\;\mathcal{D}_2^3\\ \eta^\bullet,\varphi^\circ\;\;\; \mathrm{w}\overline{\overline{\eta^\bullet,\varphi^\bullet,\chi^\circ}}\;\;\;\varphi^\bullet,\chi^\circ}{\eta^\bullet,\chi^\circ}$$

$$\frac{\Gamma\{\chi \boxminus \vartheta^\bullet, [\eta:\Delta]\}}{}$$

$$ih\,\frac{\Gamma\{\chi \boxminus \vartheta^\bullet, [\varphi:\vartheta^\bullet,\Delta]\}\;\;\;\mathcal{D}_3^3}{\Gamma\{\chi \boxminus \vartheta^\bullet, [\eta:\vartheta^\bullet,\Delta]\}}$$

$\square$

**Lemma 3.8.** *If $\mathcal{D}^1$, $\mathcal{D}^2$ are N.IntCK $\cup$ {cut} derivations of $\Gamma^{\downarrow}\{\xi^\circ\}$ and $\Gamma\{\xi^\bullet\}$ such that $r(\mathcal{D}^1) = r(\mathcal{D}^2) = w(\xi)$, then there is a N.IntCK $\cup$ {cut, rep} derivation $\mathcal{D}$ of $\Gamma\{\emptyset\}$ s.t. $r(\mathcal{D}) = w(\xi)$. Every rep-formula $\zeta$ in $\mathcal{D}$ is s.t. $w(\zeta) < w(\xi)$.*

*Proof.* By induction on $m+n$, the sum of heights of $\mathcal{D}^1$ and $\mathcal{D}^2$. We here report one case. Suppose that the cut formula is $\varphi \boxminus \psi$ is principal in the last rule applied in both $\mathcal{D}^1, \mathcal{D}^2$. Then, for $\Delta$ and $[\eta:\Delta]$ input sequents, we have:

$$\boxminus^\circ\,\frac{\mathcal{D}_1^1\\\Gamma^{\downarrow}\{[\varphi:\psi^\circ],[\eta:\Delta]\}}{\Gamma^{\downarrow}\{\varphi\boxminus\psi^\circ,[\eta:\Delta]\}} \;\;\;\;\; \boxminus^\bullet\,\frac{\mathcal{D}_1^2\;\;\;\mathcal{D}_2^2\;\;\;\mathcal{D}_3^2\\ \varphi^\bullet,\eta^\circ\;\;\;\eta^\bullet,\varphi^\circ\;\;\;\Gamma\{\varphi\boxminus\psi^\bullet,[\eta:\psi^\bullet,\Delta]\}}{\Gamma\{\varphi\boxminus\psi^\bullet,[\eta:\Delta]\}}$$

We construct the following derivation $\mathcal{D}$, where $\mathcal{Q} = \Gamma\{\varphi\boxminus\psi^\bullet, [\eta:\psi^\bullet,\Delta]\}$:

$$\mathrm{cut}\,\frac{\mathrm{rep}\,\frac{\mathcal{D}_1^2\;\;\;\;\mathcal{D}_2^2\;\;\;\;\mathcal{D}_1^1\\\varphi^\bullet,\eta^\circ\;\;\;\;\eta^\bullet,\varphi^\circ\;\;\;\;\Gamma^{\downarrow}\{[\varphi:\psi^\circ],[\eta:\Delta]\}}{\Gamma^{\downarrow}\{[\eta:\psi^\circ],[\eta:\Delta]\}}}{\mathrm{w}\,\overline{\overline{\Gamma^{\downarrow}\{[\eta:\psi^\circ,\Delta],[\eta:\Delta]\}}}} \;\;\;\; ih\,\frac{\boxminus^\circ\,\frac{\mathcal{D}_1^1\\\Gamma^{\downarrow}\{[\varphi:\psi^\circ],[\eta:\Delta]\}}{\mathrm{w}\,\frac{\Gamma^{\downarrow}\{\varphi\boxminus\psi^\circ,[\eta:\Delta]\}}{\Gamma^{\downarrow}\{\varphi\boxminus\psi^\circ,[\eta:\psi^\bullet,\Delta]\}}}\;\;\;\mathcal{Q}}{\mathrm{w}\,\frac{\Gamma\{[\eta:\psi^\bullet,\Delta]\}}{\Gamma\{[\eta:\psi^\bullet,\Delta],[\eta:\Delta]\}}}$$

$$\mathrm{c,[m]}\,\frac{\Gamma\{[\eta:\Delta],[\eta:\Delta]\}}{\Gamma\{[\eta:\Delta]\}}$$

The application of the inductive hypothesis is justified, since the sum of heights of the two subderivations above $ih$ is smaller than $m+n$. Next, we need to check that $r(\mathcal{D}) \leq w(\varphi\boxminus\psi)$. From Lemma 3.7, we have that $r(\Gamma^{\downarrow}\{[\eta:\psi^\circ],[\eta:\Delta]\}) = \max(r(\mathcal{D}_1^2), r(\mathcal{D}_2^2), r(\mathcal{D}_1^1), w(\varphi)+1)$. By $ih$, $r(\Gamma\{[\eta:\psi^\bullet,\Delta]\}) \leq w(\varphi\boxminus\psi)$. Then, $r(\mathcal{D}) = \max(r(\mathcal{D}_1^2), r(\mathcal{D}_2^2), r(\mathcal{D}_1^1), w(\varphi)+1, w(\varphi\boxminus\psi), w(\psi)+1)$. By assumption, $r(\mathcal{D}_j^i) \leq w(\varphi\boxminus\psi)$, for $i \in \{1,2\}$ and $j \in \{1,2,3\}$. Moreover, $w(\varphi)+1 \leq$

$w(\varphi \mathbin{\square\!\!\rightarrow} \psi)$, and $w(\psi) + 1 \leq w(\varphi \mathbin{\square\!\!\rightarrow} \psi)$. Thus, $r(\mathcal{D}) \leq w(\varphi \mathbin{\square\!\!\rightarrow} \psi)$. Finally, the rep-formula $\varphi$ of the new application of rep in the derivation is such that $w(\varphi) < w(\varphi \mathbin{\square\!\!\rightarrow} \psi)$. □

**Theorem 3.9 (Cut-elimination).** *If $\Gamma$ is derivable in* N.IntCK $\cup$ {cut}, *then $\Gamma$ is derivable in* N.IntCK.

*Proof.* Suppose that $\mathcal{D}$ is a derivation of $\Gamma$ in N.IntCK $\cup$ {cut}; we show how to construct a derivation $\mathcal{D}^*$ of $\Gamma$ in N.IntCK, reasoning by induction on $r(\mathcal{D})$. If $r(\mathcal{D}) = 0$, set $\mathcal{D}^* = \mathcal{D}$. If $r(\mathcal{D}) = n+1$, select a topmost applications of cut in $\mathcal{D}$ having rank $n+1$ and conclusion $\Gamma$. Thus, the cut formula $\xi$ of this occurrence of cut has weight $w(\xi) = n$, and the two subderivations of the premises of cut have rank $n$. By Lemma 3.8 we obtain a derivation $\mathcal{D}'$ of $\Gamma$ such that $r(\mathcal{D}') = n$. The derivation $\mathcal{D}'$ might contain occurrences of rep, whose rep-formulas $\zeta$ are such that $w(\zeta) < w(\xi)$. Next, take the topmost occurrence of rep in $\mathcal{D}'$, and apply Lemma 3.7 to its premises. Iterate this procedure until all applications of rep have been 'removed' from $\mathcal{D}'$. The resulting derivation $\mathcal{D}^\dagger$ is such that $r(\mathcal{D}^\dagger) \leq n$. Consider the 'full' derivation $\mathcal{D}$, modified by replacing its subderivation $\mathcal{D}'$ with $\mathcal{D}^\dagger$. Select a topmost cut of highest rank, and repeat the procedure. □

Thanks to the cut elimination result, we can now prove completeness of N.IntCK. For $A$ set of formulas, let $A^\bullet = \{\gamma^\bullet \mid \gamma \in A\}$.

**Theorem 3.10.** *For $A \cup \{\varphi\}$ finite set of formulas in $\mathcal{L}$, if $A \vdash_{\mathsf{IntCK}} \varphi$ then the nested sequent $A^\bullet, \varphi^\circ$ is derivable in* N.IntCK.

*Proof.* By showing that the axioms and rules of IntCK are derivable and admissible in N.IntCK $\cup$ {cut}, and then using Theorem 3.9 to remove occurrences of cut. Derivations of some axioms and rules can be found in [9]. □

## 4 Basic Constructive Conditional Logic

We now move to the analysis of constructive conditional logics. We first present a Gentzen-style sequent calculus for ConstCK$^{\square\!\!\rightarrow}$ obtained as the single-succedent restriction of (a two-sided formulation of) the sequent calculus for CK$^{\square\!\!\rightarrow}$ defined in [19]. We then consider sequent rules explicitly dealing with $\diamond\!\!\rightarrow$, and define on their basis logic ConstCK, which is an extension of ConstCK$^{\square\!\!\rightarrow}$ in the full language $\mathcal{L}$. Other than the sequent calculus, we shall introduce both an Hilbert-style axiom system and a class of models for ConstCK.

Since we now deal with Gentzen-style sequents, we drop the polarities of formulas and use the standard two-sided notation. A *sequent* is a pair $\Gamma \Rightarrow \Delta$ of finite, possibly empty multisets of formulas. A sequent is called *single-succedent* if $|\Delta| \leq 1$, that is, if it contains *at most one* formula in the consequent. A sequent $\Gamma \Rightarrow \Delta$ is interpreted via the *formula interpretation* $\iota$ as $\bigwedge \Gamma \rightarrow \bigvee \Delta$ if $\Gamma \neq \emptyset$, and as $\bigvee \Delta$ if $\Gamma = \emptyset$, where $\bigvee \emptyset$ is interpreted as $\bot$. We use $\Gamma \Leftrightarrow \Delta$ as an abbreviation for the two sequents $\Gamma \Rightarrow \Delta$ and $\Delta \Rightarrow \Gamma$. The rules of calculus S.ConstCK$^{\square\!\!\rightarrow}$ for ConstCK$^{\square\!\!\rightarrow}$ can be found on top of Fig. 5.

$$\text{init} \frac{}{\Gamma, p \Rightarrow p} \qquad \bot_\text{L} \frac{}{\Gamma, \bot \Rightarrow \Delta} \qquad \wedge_\text{L} \frac{\Gamma, \varphi, \psi \Rightarrow \Delta}{\Gamma, \varphi \wedge \psi \Rightarrow \Delta} \qquad \wedge_\text{R} \frac{\Gamma \Rightarrow \varphi \quad \Gamma \Rightarrow \psi}{\Gamma \Rightarrow \varphi \wedge \psi}$$

$$\vee_\text{L} \frac{\Gamma, \varphi \Rightarrow \Delta \quad \Gamma, \psi \Rightarrow \Delta}{\Gamma, \varphi \vee \psi \Rightarrow \Delta} \qquad \vee_\text{R}^1 \frac{\Gamma \Rightarrow \varphi}{\Gamma \Rightarrow \varphi \vee \psi} \qquad \vee_\text{R}^2 \frac{\Gamma \Rightarrow \psi}{\Gamma \Rightarrow \varphi \vee \psi} \qquad \to_\text{R} \frac{\Gamma, \varphi \Rightarrow \psi}{\Gamma \Rightarrow \varphi \to \psi}$$

$$\to_\text{L} \frac{\Gamma, \varphi \to \psi \Rightarrow \varphi \quad \Gamma, \psi \Rightarrow \Delta}{\Gamma, \varphi \to \psi \Rightarrow \Delta} \qquad \Box\mapsto \frac{\{\varphi \Leftrightarrow \rho_i\}_{i \leq n} \quad \sigma_1, ..., \sigma_n \Rightarrow \psi}{\Gamma, \rho_1 \Box\mapsto \sigma_1, ..., \rho_n \Box\mapsto \sigma_n \Rightarrow \varphi \Box\mapsto \psi}$$

$$\Diamond\mapsto \frac{\{\varphi \Leftrightarrow \rho_i\}_{i \leq n} \quad \varphi \Leftrightarrow \eta \quad \sigma_1, ..., \sigma_n, \psi \Rightarrow \vartheta}{\Gamma, \rho_1 \Box\mapsto \sigma_1, ..., \rho_n \Box\mapsto \sigma_n, \varphi \Diamond\mapsto \psi \Rightarrow \eta \Diamond\mapsto \vartheta}$$

$$\Diamond\mapsto_\bot \frac{\{\varphi \Leftrightarrow \rho_i\}_{i \leq n} \quad \sigma_1, ..., \sigma_n, \psi \Rightarrow}{\Gamma, \rho_1 \Box\mapsto \sigma_1, ..., \rho_n \Box\mapsto \sigma_n, \varphi \Diamond\mapsto \psi \Rightarrow \Delta}$$

**Fig. 5.** **Top**: Rules of S.ConstCK$^{\Box\mapsto}$, for $0 \leq |\Delta| \leq 1$ and $n \geq 0$. **Bottom**: Additional rules of S.ConstCK.

We shall prove soundness and completeness of S.ConstCK$^{\Box\mapsto}$ as a consequence of soundness and completeness of an extension of S.ConstCK$^{\Box\mapsto}$ with rules for the might operator $\Diamond\mapsto$. To define such an extension, we start from a calculus S.CK for classical CK with explicit rules for both $\Box\mapsto$ and $\Diamond\mapsto$. Such a calculus can be obtained by extending the standard G3-style rules for CPL from [24] with the following rules obtained by integrating $\Diamond\mapsto$ into the rules of [19] (cf. e.g. [14] for analogous rules for unary modal logics):

$$\frac{\{\varphi \Leftrightarrow \rho_i\}_{i \leq n} \quad \{\varphi \Leftrightarrow \eta_j\}_{j \leq k} \quad \sigma_1, ..., \sigma_n \Rightarrow \psi, \chi_1, ..., \chi_k}{\Gamma, \rho_1 \Box\mapsto \sigma_1, ..., \rho_n \Box\mapsto \sigma_n \Rightarrow \varphi \Box\mapsto \psi, \eta_1 \Diamond\mapsto \chi_1, ..., \eta_k \Diamond\mapsto \chi_k, \Delta} \quad (n, k \geq 0)$$

$$\frac{\{\varphi \Leftrightarrow \rho_i\}_{i \leq n} \quad \{\varphi \Leftrightarrow \eta_j\}_{j \leq k} \quad \sigma_1, ..., \sigma_n, \psi \Rightarrow \chi_1, ..., \chi_k}{\Gamma, \rho_1 \Box\mapsto \sigma_1, ..., \rho_n \Box\mapsto \sigma_n, \varphi \Diamond\mapsto \psi \Rightarrow \eta_1 \Diamond\mapsto \chi_1, ..., \eta_k \Diamond\mapsto \chi_k, \Delta} \quad (n, k \geq 0)$$

By restricting S.CK to single-succedent sequents, we obtain the calculus S.ConstCK defined by adding to the rules of S.ConstCK$^{\Box\mapsto}$ the $\Diamond\mapsto$ rules at the bottom of Fig. 5. We now turn to investigating the structural properties of S.ConstCK$^{\Box\mapsto}$ and S.ConstCK.

**Theorem 4.1 (Structural Properties).** *The rules* $\wedge_\text{L}$, $\wedge_\text{R}$, $\vee_\text{L}$, $\vee_\text{R}^1$, $\vee_\text{R}^2$, $\to_\text{R}$ *are height-preserving invertible, and the rule* $\to_\text{L}$ *is height-preserving invertible with respect to the right premiss. Moreover, the following weakening and contraction rules are height-preserving admissible in S.ConstCK, and the following rule* cut *is admissible in S.ConstCK.*

$$\text{w}_\text{L} \frac{\Gamma \Rightarrow \Delta}{\Gamma, \varphi \Rightarrow \Delta} \qquad \text{w}_\text{R} \frac{\Gamma \Rightarrow}{\Gamma \Rightarrow \varphi} \qquad \text{c} \frac{\Gamma, \varphi, \varphi \Rightarrow \Delta}{\Gamma, \varphi \Rightarrow \Delta} \qquad \text{cut} \frac{\Gamma \Rightarrow \varphi \quad \Gamma', \varphi \Rightarrow \Delta}{\Gamma, \Gamma' \Rightarrow \Delta}$$

*Proof.* The proof of hp-admissibility of $\text{w}_\text{L}$, $\text{w}_\text{R}$ and c and of the hp-invertibility of the propositional rules is essentially the standard one for G3ip (cf. e.g. [24]) without major modification induced by the addition of the conditional rules.

A Proof-Theoretic View of Basic Intuitionistic Conditional Logic 365

Admissibility of cut is proved by induction on lexicographically ordered pairs $(c, h)$, where $c$ is the weight of the cut formula $\varphi$, and $h$ is the sum of the heights of the derivations of the two premises of cut. As an example, consider the following:

$$\diamondsuit\!\!\!\rightarrow \frac{\begin{array}{ccccc} \mathcal{D}_1 & \mathcal{D}_2 & \mathcal{D}_3 & \mathcal{D}_4 & \mathcal{D}_5 \\ \varphi \Rightarrow \rho & \rho \Rightarrow \varphi & \varphi \Rightarrow \eta & \eta \Rightarrow \varphi & \sigma, \psi \Rightarrow \vartheta \end{array}}{\Gamma, \rho \,\square\!\!\!\rightarrow \sigma, \varphi \diamondsuit\!\!\!\rightarrow \psi \Rightarrow \eta \diamondsuit\!\!\!\rightarrow \vartheta} \qquad \diamondsuit\!\!\!\rightarrow_\bot \frac{\begin{array}{ccc} \mathcal{D}_6 & \mathcal{D}_7 & \mathcal{D}_8 \\ \eta \Rightarrow \xi & \xi \Rightarrow \eta & \chi, \vartheta \Rightarrow \end{array}}{\Gamma', \xi \,\square\!\!\!\rightarrow \chi, \eta \diamondsuit\!\!\!\rightarrow \vartheta \Rightarrow}$$

with the conclusion $\Gamma, \Gamma', \rho \,\square\!\!\!\rightarrow \sigma, \xi \,\square\!\!\!\rightarrow \chi, \varphi \diamondsuit\!\!\!\rightarrow \psi \Rightarrow$ of cut derivable as follows, where dotted lines represent applications of the induction hypothesis:

$$\diamondsuit\!\!\!\rightarrow_\bot \frac{\begin{array}{cc} \mathcal{D}_1 & \mathcal{D}_2 \\ \varphi \Rightarrow \rho & \rho \Rightarrow \varphi \end{array} \quad \frac{\begin{array}{cc} \mathcal{D}_3 & \mathcal{D}_6 \\ \varphi \Rightarrow \eta & \eta \Rightarrow \xi \end{array}}{\varphi \Rightarrow \xi} \quad \frac{\begin{array}{cc} \mathcal{D}_7 & \mathcal{D}_4 \\ \xi \Rightarrow \eta & \eta \Rightarrow \varphi \end{array}}{\xi \Rightarrow \varphi} \quad \frac{\begin{array}{cc} \mathcal{D}_5 & \mathcal{D}_8 \\ \sigma, \psi \Rightarrow \vartheta & \chi, \vartheta \Rightarrow \end{array}}{\sigma, \chi, \psi \Rightarrow}}{\Gamma, \Gamma', \rho \,\square\!\!\!\rightarrow \sigma, \xi \,\square\!\!\!\rightarrow \chi, \varphi \diamondsuit\!\!\!\rightarrow \psi \Rightarrow} \qquad \square$$

Next, we define an axiomatic system ConstCK equivalent to S.ConstCK, and prove that ConstCK is a conservative extension of ConstCK$^{\square\!\!\!\rightarrow}$.

**Definition 4.2 (ConstCK).** *The logic* ConstCK *is defined in the language* $\mathcal{L}$ *extending any axiomatisation of* IPL *(formulated in the language* $\mathcal{L}$*), containing modus ponens, with the axioms* $CM_\square$, $CC_\square$, $CN_\square$, $CN_\diamondsuit$, $CK_\diamondsuit$ *and the rules* $RA_\square$, $RC_\square$, $RA_\diamondsuit$, $RC_\diamondsuit$ *from Fig. 1.*

**Theorem 4.3 (Syntactic Equivalence).** $\Gamma \Rightarrow \Delta$ *is derivable in* S.ConstCK *if and only if* $\iota(\Gamma \Rightarrow \Delta)$ *is derivable in* ConstCK.

*Proof.* Both directions of this claim are proved by induction on the height of the derivations in the respective proof system. From left to right, we observe that for every rule $\mathcal{S}_1, ..., \mathcal{S}_k/\mathcal{S}$ of S.ConstCK, the corresponding rule $\iota(\mathcal{S}_1), ..., \iota(\mathcal{S}_k)/\iota(\mathcal{S})$ is derivable in ConstCK. For instance, for $n = 2, \Gamma = \emptyset$, the rule corresponding to $\diamondsuit\!\!\!\rightarrow$ has the following form: $\varphi \leftrightarrow \rho_1, \varphi \leftrightarrow \rho_2, \varphi \leftrightarrow \eta, \sigma_1 \wedge \sigma_2 \wedge \psi \rightarrow \vartheta/(\rho_1 \,\square\!\!\!\rightarrow \sigma_1) \wedge (\rho_2 \,\square\!\!\!\rightarrow \sigma_2) \wedge (\varphi \diamondsuit\!\!\!\rightarrow \psi)) \rightarrow (\eta \diamondsuit\!\!\!\rightarrow \vartheta)$. To derive these rules, we can make use of the rules $RM_\square$, $RM_\diamondsuit$ and the axiom CW, which are easily derivable in ConstCK. In the other direction, we can show that all axioms and rules of ConstCK are derivable, respectively admissible, in S.ConstCK, with modus ponens simulated as usual by cut. $\square$

The following result is a consequence of the analysis of S.ConstCK, by removing the cases dealing with $\diamondsuit\!\!\!\rightarrow$, $\diamondsuit\!\!\!\rightarrow_\bot$ from all proofs.

**Theorem 4.4.** $\Gamma \Rightarrow \Delta$ *is derivable in* S.ConstCK$^{\square\!\!\!\rightarrow}$ *if and only if* $\iota(\Gamma \Rightarrow \Delta)$ *is derivable in* ConstCK$^{\square\!\!\!\rightarrow}$.

We are now ready to prove that the $\diamondsuit\!\!\!\rightarrow$-free fragment of ConstCK amounts to ConstCK$^{\square\!\!\!\rightarrow}$, as desired.

**Theorem 4.5.** *If $\varphi \in \mathcal{L}^{\Box\rightarrowtail}$, then $\varphi$ is derivable in ConstCK if and only if it is derivable in ConstCK$^{\Box\rightarrowtail}$.*

*Proof.* Suppose that $\varphi \in \mathcal{L}^{\Box\rightarrowtail}$ is derivable in ConstCK. Then, $\Rightarrow \varphi$ is derivable in S.ConstCK. Since S.ConstCK is analytic, the derivation $\mathcal{D}$ of $\Rightarrow \varphi$ does not contain any formula with occurrences of $\Diamond\rightarrowtail$, meaning that $\mathcal{D}$ does not employ the rules $\Diamond\rightarrowtail$ and $\Diamond\rightarrowtail_\bot$. Since all other rules of S.ConstCK also belong to S.ConstCK$^{\Box\rightarrowtail}$, $\mathcal{D}$ is a derivation of $\Rightarrow \varphi$ in S.ConstCK$^{\Box\rightarrowtail}$, thus $\varphi$ is derivable in ConstCK$^{\Box\rightarrowtail}$. □

As already mentioned, ConstCK$^{\Box\rightarrowtail}$ and IntCK naturally correspond to known intuitionistic unary modal logics. Similarly, we can show that the modal correspondent of ConstCK is the propositional fragment of Wijesekera's logic CCDL, often denoted WK [10]. This fragment is defined in a language $\mathcal{L}_m$, containing $\Box, \Diamond$, by extending IPL with the rule $\varphi/\Box\varphi$ and the axioms $\Box(\varphi \rightarrow \psi) \rightarrow (\Box\varphi \rightarrow \Box\psi)$, $\Box(\varphi \rightarrow \psi) \rightarrow (\Diamond\varphi \rightarrow \Diamond\psi)$, $\neg\Diamond\bot$. Let $(\cdot)^\tau$ be a translation $\mathcal{L}_m \longrightarrow \mathcal{L}$ such that $p^\tau = p$, $\bot^\tau = \bot$, $(\rho \circ \psi)^\tau = \rho^\tau \circ \psi^\tau$ for $\circ \in \{\land, \lor, \rightarrow\}$, and $(\circ\psi)^\tau = \top \circ\!\!\rightarrowtail \psi^\tau$ for $\circ \in \{\Box, \Diamond\}$.

**Theorem 4.6.** *For all $\varphi \in \mathcal{L}_m$, $\vdash_{\mathsf{WK}} \varphi$ if and only if $\vdash_{\mathsf{ConstCK}} \varphi^\tau$.*

*Proof.* Considering S.WK, the propositional fragment of the sequent calculus for WK in [27], and transforming every derivation in S.ConstCK into a derivation in S.WK by replacing every application of $\Box\rightarrowtail$, $\Diamond\rightarrowtail$, $\Diamond\rightarrowtail_\bot$ with an application of the corresponding modal rule, and vice versa. □

### 4.1 Semantics

We now present a semantics for ConstCK defined in terms of basic Chellas models.

**Definition 4.7 (Constructive Chellas Model).** *We call constructive Chellas model (ccm for short) any basic model (Definition 2.1) where the satisfaction relation $M, w \Vdash \varphi$ is inductively defined by the propositional clauses in Definition 2.3 and the global interpretations $(G\Box\rightarrowtail)$ and $(G\Diamond\rightarrowtail)$ for $\Box\rightarrowtail$ and $\Diamond\rightarrowtail$.*

By an easy induction on the construction of the formulas, one can prove that ccms satisfy the hereditary property. Moreover, one can prove that ConstCK is sound with respect to ccms, by showing that all axioms and rules of ConstCK are valid, respectively validity-preserving, in every ccm.

We now prove that ConstCK is complete with respect to ccms. The proof is based on a canonical model construction inspired from [27]. In the following, $\vdash$ only refers to $\vdash_{\mathsf{ConstCK}}$. A set $A$ of formulas of $\mathcal{L}$ is *prime* if it is consistent ($A \nvdash \bot$), deductively closed (if $A \vdash \varphi$, then $\varphi \in A$), and satisfies the disjunction property (if $\varphi \lor \psi \in A$, then $\varphi \in A$ or $\psi \in A$). We denote by $[\varphi]$ the set of all prime sets $A$ such that $\varphi \in A$. The following lemma can be proved via a routine extension of the proof of [21] for IPL to the conditional language $\mathcal{L}$.

# A Proof-Theoretic View of Basic Intuitionistic Conditional Logic 367

**Lemma 4.8.** *If $A \not\vdash \varphi$, then there is a prime set $B$ such that $A \subseteq B$ and $\varphi \notin B$.*

**Definition 4.9 (Canonical Element).** *A canonical element (ce) is a pair $(A, \mathscr{R})$, where $A$ is a prime set, and $\mathscr{R}$ is a set of pairs $(\alpha, \beta)$ such that*

- $\alpha = [\varphi]$ for some $\varphi \in \mathcal{L}$;
- $\beta$ is a set of prime sets such that, for all $\psi \in \mathcal{L}$:
  - if $\varphi \square\!\!\rightarrow \psi \in A$, then for all $B \in \beta$, $\psi \in B$,
  - if $\varphi \diamond\!\!\rightarrow \psi \in A$, then there is $B \in \beta$ such that $\psi \in B$;
- for all $(\alpha, \beta), (\alpha', \beta') \in \mathscr{R}$, $\alpha = \alpha'$ implies $\beta = \beta'$;
- if $\varphi \diamond\!\!\rightarrow \psi \in A$, then there is $\beta$ such that $([\varphi], \beta) \in \mathscr{R}$.

We denote by $\langle \varphi \rangle$ the set of all ces $(A, \mathscr{R})$ such that $\varphi \in A$. For every set $A \subseteq \mathcal{L}$, we denote by $\varphi \square\!\!\rightarrow^{-}(A)$ the set $\{\psi \mid \varphi \square\!\!\rightarrow \psi \in A\}$.

**Lemma 4.10.** *For every prime set $A$:*

1. *There is a ce $(A, \mathscr{R})$;*
2. *If $\varphi \square\!\!\rightarrow \psi \notin A$, then there is a ce $(A, \mathscr{R})$ and a pair $([\varphi], \beta) \in \mathscr{R}$ such that $\psi \notin B$ for some $B \in \beta$;*
3. *If $\varphi \diamond\!\!\rightarrow \psi \notin A$, then there is a ce $(A, \mathscr{R})$ and a pair $([\varphi], \beta) \in \mathscr{R}$ such that $\psi \notin B$ for all $B \in \beta$.*

**Definition 4.11 (Canonical Model).** *The canonical model for ConstCK is the tuple $M = \langle W, \leq, R, V \rangle$, where:*

- *$W$ is the set of all canonical elements;*
- *$(A, \mathscr{R}) \leq (A', \mathscr{R}')$ iff $A \subseteq A'$;*
- *$(A, \mathscr{R}) R_X (B, \mathscr{U})$ iff there are $\varphi, \beta$ s.t. $X = \langle \varphi \rangle$, $([\varphi], \beta) \in \mathscr{R}$ and $B \in \beta$;*
- *$p \in V((A, \mathscr{R}))$ iff $p \in A$.*

It is easy to verify that the canonical model for ConstCK is a ccm.

**Lemma 4.12.** *For all $\varphi \in \mathcal{L}$ and all prime sets $A$, $\varphi \in A$ iff $(A, \mathscr{R}) \Vdash \varphi$ for all ces $(A, \mathscr{R})$.*

*Proof.* Note that the claim is equivalent to $\llbracket \varphi \rrbracket = \langle \varphi \rangle$. The proof is by induction on the construction of $\varphi$. We only show the case $\varphi = \rho \square\!\!\rightarrow \psi$. Assume $\rho \square\!\!\rightarrow \psi \in A$ and $(A, \mathscr{R}) \leq (A', \mathscr{R}') R_{\llbracket \rho \rrbracket}(B, \mathscr{U})$. Then $A \subseteq A'$, which implies $\rho \square\!\!\rightarrow \psi \in A'$, and by i.h., $(A', \mathscr{R}') R_{\langle \rho \rangle}(B, \mathscr{U})$. By definition of $R_X$, there is $\beta$ such that $([\rho], \beta) \in \mathscr{R}'$ and $B \in \beta$, then by definition of ce, $\psi \in B$. Thus by i.h., $(B, \mathscr{U}) \Vdash \psi$, hence $(A, \mathscr{R}) \Vdash \rho \square\!\!\rightarrow \psi$. Now assume $\rho \square\!\!\rightarrow \psi \notin A$. By Lemma 4.10, there are $(A, \mathscr{R})$, $\beta$, $B$ such that $([\rho], \beta) \in \mathscr{R}$, $B \in \beta$ and $\psi \notin B$. Moreover, there exists a ce $(B, \mathscr{U})$. Then $(A, \mathscr{R}) R_{\langle \rho \rangle}(B, \mathscr{U})$, and by i.h., $(A, \mathscr{R}) R_{\llbracket \rho \rrbracket}(B, \mathscr{U})$ and $(B, \mathscr{U}) \not\Vdash \psi$. Therefore $(A, \mathscr{R}) \not\Vdash \rho \square\!\!\rightarrow \psi$. □

**Theorem 4.13 (Completeness).** *If $\varphi$ is valid in all ccms if and only if it is derivable in ConstCK.*

| | | System name | Axiomatisation |
|---|---|---|---|
| ID$_\Box$ | $\varphi \Box\!\!\rightarrow \varphi$ | ConstCKID | ConstCK + ID$_\Box$ |
| MP$_\Box$ | $(\varphi \Box\!\!\rightarrow \psi) \to (\varphi \to \psi)$ | ConstCKMP | ConstCK + MP$_\Box$, MP$_\Diamond$ |
| MP$_\Diamond$ | $\varphi \wedge \psi \to (\varphi \Diamond\!\!\!\rightarrow \psi)$ | ConstCKMPID | ConstCK + MP$_\Box$, MP$_\Diamond$, ID$_\Box$ |
| CEM$_\Box$ | $(\varphi \Box\!\!\rightarrow \psi) \vee (\varphi \Box\!\!\rightarrow \neg\psi)$ | ConstCKCEM | ConstCK + CEM$_\Diamond$ |
| CEM$_\Diamond$ | $(\varphi \Diamond\!\!\!\rightarrow \psi) \wedge (\varphi \Diamond\!\!\!\rightarrow \chi) \to (\varphi \Diamond\!\!\!\rightarrow \psi \wedge \chi)$ | | |

**Fig. 6.** Conditional axioms and extensions of ConstCK.

*Proof.* If $\not\vdash \varphi$, then by Lemma 4.8 there is $A$ prime such that $\varphi \notin A$, then by Lemma 4.10 there is a $ce$ $(A, \mathscr{R})$ that by Definition 4.11 belongs to the canonical model for ConstCK, hence by Lemma 4.12, $(A, \mathscr{R}) \not\Vdash \varphi$, thus $\varphi$ is not valid in all ccms. □

We conclude this section by analysing the relation between ccms and Weiss models. From Theorems 4.5 and 4.13, it follows that ccms and Weiss models are equivalent with respect to $\mathcal{L}^{\Box\!\!\rightarrow}$. The same equivalence can be proved directly by means of model transformations. In one direction, note that every Weiss model $M$ is also a ccm, where however $\Box\!\!\rightarrow$ is interpreted globally rather than locally. By an easy induction on the construction of formulas, one can prove that the two models are pointwise equivalent with respect to formulas of $\mathcal{L}^{\Box\!\!\rightarrow}$. In the other direction, every ccm model $M = \langle W, \leq, R, V \rangle$ can be transformed into a Weiss model $M^* = \langle W, \leq, R^*, V \rangle$ by defining, for each $X \subseteq W$, $wR^*_X v$ iff there is $w'$ such that $w \leq w' R_X v$. As before, the two models can be shown pointwise equivalent by induction on the construction of formulas. At present, we do not know whether a direct extension of Weiss models can provide a semantics for ConstCK over the full language $\mathcal{L}$.

## 5 Beyond Basic Constructive Conditional Logic

Similarly to what happens in classical CK, axioms and frame conditions can be added to ConstCK$^{\Box\!\!\rightarrow}$, ConstCK and IntCK. Several extensions of ConstCK$^{\Box\!\!\rightarrow}$ are studied in [8] while, to the best of our knowledge, extensions of IntCK or ConstCK have not been investigated. In this section, we define sequent calculi, axiom systems and classes of models for ConstCK extended with *identity* and *conditional modus ponens*. While we focus on ConstCK for this section, by removing the $\Diamond\!\!\!\rightarrow$-rules from our proof systems, we obtain sequent calculi for the corresponding extensions of ConstCK$^{\Box\!\!\rightarrow}$, defined in [8]. We also provide a sequent calculus and an axiom system for ConstCK extended with the *conditional excluded middle*, but a semantic characterisation of the logic is left to future work.

To define proof systems for extensions of ConstCK, we consider the sequent calculi of [19] for the extensions of CK$^{\Box\!\!\rightarrow}$ with the axioms ID$_\Box$, MP$_\Box$ and CEM$_\Box$ (Fig. 6). We integrate the rules of these calculi with $\Diamond\!\!\!\rightarrow$, and reduce them to single-succedent sequents, obtaining the constructive conditional rules and calculi in Fig. 7. We first consider extensions of ConstCK with ID$_\Box$ and MP$_\Box$. Take S.ConstCK* ∈ {S.ConstCKID, S.ConstCKMP, S.ConstCKMPID}.

A Proof-Theoretic View of Basic Intuitionistic Conditional Logic    369

$$\square\!\!\rightarrow^{id} \frac{\{\varphi \Leftrightarrow \rho_i\}_{i \leq n} \quad \sigma_1, ..., \sigma_n, \varphi \Rightarrow \psi}{\Gamma, \rho_1 \square\!\!\rightarrow \sigma_1, ..., \rho_n \square\!\!\rightarrow \sigma_n \Rightarrow \varphi \square\!\!\rightarrow \psi}$$

$$\diamondsuit\!\!\rightarrow^{id}_{\bot} \frac{\{\varphi \Leftrightarrow \rho_i\}_{i \leq n} \quad \sigma_1, ..., \sigma_n, \varphi, \psi \Rightarrow}{\Gamma, \rho_1 \square\!\!\rightarrow \sigma_1, ..., \rho_n \square\!\!\rightarrow \sigma_n, \varphi \diamondsuit\!\!\rightarrow \psi \Rightarrow \Delta}$$

$$\diamondsuit\!\!\rightarrow^{id} \frac{\{\varphi \Leftrightarrow \rho_i\}_{i \leq n} \quad \varphi \Leftrightarrow \eta \quad \sigma_1, ..., \sigma_n, \varphi, \psi \Rightarrow \vartheta}{\Gamma, \rho_1 \square\!\!\rightarrow \sigma_1, ..., \rho_n \square\!\!\rightarrow \sigma_n, \varphi \diamondsuit\!\!\rightarrow \psi \Rightarrow \eta \diamondsuit\!\!\rightarrow \vartheta}$$

$$\mathsf{mp}_\square \; \frac{\Gamma, \varphi \square\!\!\rightarrow \psi \Rightarrow \varphi \quad \Gamma, \varphi \square\!\!\rightarrow \psi, \psi \Rightarrow \Delta}{\Gamma, \varphi \square\!\!\rightarrow \psi \Rightarrow \Delta} \qquad \mathsf{mp}_\diamondsuit \; \frac{\Gamma \Rightarrow \varphi \quad \Gamma \Rightarrow \psi}{\Gamma \Rightarrow \varphi \diamondsuit\!\!\rightarrow \psi}$$

$$\diamondsuit\!\!\rightarrow^{cem} \frac{\{\varphi \Leftrightarrow \rho_i\}_{i \leq n} \quad \{\varphi \Leftrightarrow \xi_j\}_{j \leq k} \quad \varphi \Leftrightarrow \eta \quad \sigma_1, ..., \sigma_n, \chi_1, ..., \chi_k, \psi \Rightarrow \vartheta}{\Gamma, \rho_1 \square\!\!\rightarrow \sigma_1, ..., \rho_n \square\!\!\rightarrow \sigma_n, \xi_1 \diamondsuit\!\!\rightarrow \chi_1, ..., \xi_k \diamondsuit\!\!\rightarrow \chi_k, \varphi \diamondsuit\!\!\rightarrow \psi \Rightarrow \eta \diamondsuit\!\!\rightarrow \vartheta}$$

$$\diamondsuit\!\!\rightarrow^{cem}_{\bot} \frac{\{\varphi \Leftrightarrow \rho_i\}_{i \leq n} \quad \{\varphi \Leftrightarrow \xi_j\}_{j \leq k} \quad \sigma_1, ..., \sigma_n, \chi_1, ..., \chi_k, \psi \Rightarrow}{\Gamma, \rho_1 \square\!\!\rightarrow \sigma_1, ..., \rho_n \square\!\!\rightarrow \sigma_n, \xi_1 \diamondsuit\!\!\rightarrow \chi_1, ..., \xi_k \diamondsuit\!\!\rightarrow \chi_k, \varphi \diamondsuit\!\!\rightarrow \psi \Rightarrow \Delta}$$

| Calculus | Conditional rules | Calculus | Conditional rules |
|---|---|---|---|
| S.ConstCKID | $\square\!\!\rightarrow^{id}$, $\diamondsuit\!\!\rightarrow^{id}$, $\diamondsuit\!\!\rightarrow^{id}_\bot$ | S.ConstCKMPID | $\square\!\!\rightarrow^{id}$, $\diamondsuit\!\!\rightarrow^{id}$, $\diamondsuit\!\!\rightarrow^{id}_\bot$, $\mathsf{mp}_\square$, $\mathsf{mp}_\diamondsuit$ |
| S.ConstCKMP | $\square\!\!\rightarrow$, $\diamondsuit\!\!\rightarrow$, $\diamondsuit\!\!\rightarrow_\bot$, $\mathsf{mp}_\square$, $\mathsf{mp}_\diamondsuit$ | S.ConstCKCEM | $\square\!\!\rightarrow$, $\diamondsuit\!\!\rightarrow^{cem}$, $\diamondsuit\!\!\rightarrow^{cem}_\bot$ |

**Fig. 7.** Conditional rules and calculi for extensions, where $0 \leq |\Delta| \leq 1$ and $n, k \geq 0$.

The proof of the following theorem extends or slightly modifies the proofs of Theorem 4.1 with the new conditional rules.

**Theorem 5.1.** *The rules* $\mathsf{w_L}$, $\mathsf{w_R}$, $\mathsf{c}$ *are height-preserving admissible, and the rule* $\mathsf{cut}$ *is admissible in* S.ConstCK*.

For every calculus S.ConstCK* we define a corresponding axiomatic system ConstCK*, see Fig. 6, and prove their equivalence with the sequent calculus characterisation.

**Theorem 5.2.** $\Gamma \Rightarrow \Delta$ *is derivable in* S.ConstCK* *if and only if* $\iota(\Gamma \Rightarrow \Delta)$ *is derivable in* ConstCK*.

By extending the completeness proof for ConstCK, we can show that these logics are characterised by exactly those classes of ccms that satisfy the frame properties of Chellas models for their classical counterparts (c.f. [7]).

**Theorem 5.3.** *Formula $\varphi$ is derivable in* ConstCKID, *resp.* ConstCKMP, *resp.* ConstCKMPID *if and only if it is valid in all ccms satisfying the property (id), resp. the property (mp), resp. both properties (id) and (mp) below:*

(id) *if* $wR_Xv$, *then* $v \in X$;   (mp) *if* $w \in X$, *then* $wR_Xw$.

*Proof.* Soundness is easy. For completeness, in the case of ConstCKID we need to show that the canonical model satisfies (id): Suppose $(A, \mathscr{R})R_X(B, \mathscr{U})$. By definition, $X = \langle \varphi \rangle$ for some $\varphi \in \mathcal{L}$, and there is $\beta$ such that $([\varphi], \beta) \in \mathscr{R}$

and $B \in \beta$. Since $\varphi \Box\!\!\rightarrow \varphi \in A$, by Def. 4.9, $\varphi \in B$ for all $B \in \beta$, that is $B \subseteq [\varphi]$, therefore $(B, \mathcal{U}) \in \langle\varphi\rangle$. For ConstCKMP, we need to slightly modify the construction of $ces$ in the proof of Lemma 4.10. First, call $MP$-$ce$ any $ce$ $(A, \mathcal{R})$ such that if $(\alpha, \beta) \in \mathcal{R}$, $\alpha = [\varphi]$ and $\varphi \in A$, then $A \in \beta$. Moreover, in item (i) of the proof, let $\beta$ be defined as before as a set containing a witness for every $\varphi \Diamond\!\!\rightarrow \vartheta \in A$. We now define $\beta^* = \beta$ if $\varphi \notin A$, and $\beta^* = \beta \cup \{A\}$ if $\varphi \in A$, and define $\mathcal{R}$ as a set of pairs $([\varphi], \beta^*)$. Then $([\varphi], \beta^*)$ is still a $ce$, in particular if $\varphi \Box\!\!\rightarrow \psi, \varphi \in A$, then by $MP_\Box$, $\psi \in A$. We define $W$ in the canonical model for ConstCKMP as the set of all MP-ces. It is easy to verify that the model satisfies (mp). For ConstCKMPID, we consider the same canonical model construction and show that it satisfies (id). □

Let us consider $CEM_\Box$. This case is particularly interesting, as there is no agreement in the literature about how a constructive variant of it should, or could, be defined. According to Weiss [25], intuitionistic analogues of these logics are not possible, since $\varphi \vee \neg\varphi$ becomes derivable in presence of $MP_\Box$ and $CEM_\Box$. Against this claim, Ciardelli and Liu [8] observe that by replacing $CEM_\Box$ with $(\varphi \Box\!\!\rightarrow \psi \vee \chi) \to (\varphi \Box\!\!\rightarrow \psi) \vee (\varphi \Box\!\!\rightarrow \chi)$, which is classically but not intuitionistically equivalent to $CEM_\Box$, one can define intuitionistic conditional systems that do not collapse into classical logic. Our proof-theoretical approach suggests at least one alternative constructive variant of the logics with $CEM_\Box$. The classical sequent rule of [19] for $CK^{\Box\!\!\rightarrow} + CEM_\Box$ has the following shape:

$$\frac{\{\varphi_1 \Leftrightarrow \rho_i\}_{i \leq n} \quad \sigma_1, ..., \sigma_n \Rightarrow \psi_1, ..., \psi_m}{\Gamma, \rho_1 \Box\!\!\rightarrow \sigma_1, ..., \rho_n \Box\!\!\rightarrow \sigma_n \Rightarrow \varphi_1 \Box\!\!\rightarrow \psi_1, ..., \varphi_m \Box\!\!\rightarrow \psi_m, \Delta} \ (n \geq 0, m \geq 1)$$

The single-succedent restriction of this rule simply collapses into $\Box\!\!\rightarrow$. However, by integrating $\Diamond\!\!\rightarrow$ into the classical calculus we add $k \geq 1$ principal $\Diamond\!\!\rightarrow$-formulas in the premiss of conditional rules, which are preserved by their single-succedent restriction. The resulting rules are displayed in Fig. 7. Using these rules, one can derive axiom $CEM_\Diamond$ (Fig. 6), which is the characterising axiom of ConstCKCEM:

$$\frac{\dfrac{\dfrac{\varphi \Leftrightarrow \varphi \quad \varphi \Leftrightarrow \varphi \quad \psi, \chi \Rightarrow \psi \wedge \chi}{\varphi \Diamond\!\!\rightarrow \psi, \varphi \Diamond\!\!\rightarrow \chi \Rightarrow \varphi \Diamond\!\!\rightarrow \psi \wedge \chi}\Diamond\!\!\rightarrow\text{cem}}{(\varphi \Diamond\!\!\rightarrow \psi) \wedge (\varphi \Diamond\!\!\rightarrow \chi) \Rightarrow \varphi \Diamond\!\!\rightarrow \psi \wedge \chi}\wedge_L}{\Rightarrow (\varphi \Diamond\!\!\rightarrow \psi) \wedge (\varphi \Diamond\!\!\rightarrow \chi) \to (\varphi \Diamond\!\!\rightarrow \psi \wedge \chi)}\to_R$$

**Theorem 5.4.** *Weakening and contraction are height-preserving admissible, and* cut *is admissible in* S.ConstCKCEM. *If* $\Gamma \Rightarrow \Delta$ *is derivable in* S.ConstCKCEM *if and only if* $\iota(\Gamma \Rightarrow \Delta)$ *is derivable in* ConstCKCEM.

## 6 Conclusions

We have investigated the proof theory of intuitionistic conditional logics, by defining a nested sequent calculus for IntCK and a sequent calculus for

ConstCK$^{\Box\to}$. The calculi are obtained by imposing a single-succedent restriction to a nested and a sequent calculus for classical CK respectively. Then, inspired by the sequent calculus rules, we have defined logic ConstCK, a natural extension of ConstCK$^{\Box\to}$ with the $\Diamond\to$ modality. We have introduced a class of models for the logic, and showed its soundness and completeness with respect to its axiomatisation. Finally, we have defined extensions of ConstCK with *identity, conditional modus ponens* and *conditional excluded middle*, and investigated their proof theory and semantics. Similarly to ConstCK, the definition of its extensions was proof-theoretically driven, as the logics resulted from the restriction of sequent calculi for their classical counterparts.

In future work, we would like to employ our proof systems to determine decision procedures for intuitionistic conditional logics, thus giving the first complexity bounds for these logics. Moreover, we are interested in exploring extensions of ConstCK and IntCK with further axioms and frame conditions coming from classical conditional logics. As a first candidate, we plan to cover ConstCK with *cautious monotonicity*, taking inspiration from the classical rules proposed in [20]. Regarding IntCK, we conjecture that the nested sequent calculi defined in [2,3] for extensions of classical CK can be adapted to our nested sequent framework. The rule for *conditional excluded middle* poses a problem though, as it does not seem to expand the set of derivable sequents in the single-succedent setting of N.IntCK. Switching to a multi-succedent nested calculus as the one in [15] might provide further insight on the definition of intuitionistic logics with conditional excluded middle. Finally, we are interested in investigating the semantics and the proof theory of stronger conditional logics, such as preferential logics and Lewis' counterfactuals, in a constructive setting.

**Acknowledgements.** Tiziano Dalmonte acknowledges financial support from the 'Abstractron' project funded by the Autonome Provinz Bozen - Südtirol (Autonomous Province of Bolzano/Bozen) through the Research Südtirol/Alto Adige 2022 Call.

# References

1. Alechina, N., Mendler, M., de Paiva, V., Ritter, E.: Categorical and kripke semantics for constructive s4 modal logic. In: Fribourg, L. (ed.) CSL 2001. LNCS, vol. 2142, pp. 292–307. Springer, Heidelberg (2001). https://doi.org/10.1007/3-540-44802-0_21
2. Alenda, R., Olivetti, N., Pozzato, G.L.: Nested sequent calculi for conditional logics. In: del Cerro, L.F., Herzig, A., Mengin, J. (eds.) JELIA 2012. LNCS (LNAI), vol. 7519, pp. 14–27. Springer, Heidelberg (2012). https://doi.org/10.1007/978-3-642-33353-8_2
3. Alenda, R., Olivetti, N., Pozzato, G.L.: Nested sequent calculi for normal conditional logics. J. Log. Comput. **26**(1), 7–50 (2016)
4. Božić, M., Došen, K.: Models for normal intuitionistic modal logics. Stud. Logica **43**, 217–245 (1984)
5. Brünnler, K.: Deep sequent systems for modal logic. Arch. Math. Logic **48**(6), 551–577 (2009). https://doi.org/10.1007/s00153-009-0137-3

6. Burgess, J.P.: Quick completeness proofs for some logics of conditionals. Notre Dame J. Formal Logic **22**(1), 76–84 (1981)
7. Chellas, B.F.: Basic conditional logic. J. Philosophic. Logic 133–153 (1975)
8. Ciardelli, I., Liu, X.: Intuitionistic conditional logics. J. Philos. Log. **49**(4), 807–832 (2020). https://doi.org/10.1007/S10992-019-09538-4
9. Dalmonte, T., Girlando, M.: A proof-theoretic view of basic intuitionistic conditional logic (extended version) (2025). https://arxiv.org/abs/2507.02767
10. Das, A., Marin, S.: On intuitionistic diamonds (and lack thereof). In: Ramanayake, R., Urban, J. (eds.) Automated Reasoning with Analytic Tableaux and Related Methods - 32nd International Conference, TABLEAUX 2023, Prague, Czech Republic, 18–21 September 2023, Proceedings. Lecture Notes in Computer Science, vol. 14278, pp. 283–301. Springer (2023). https://doi.org/10.1007/978-3-031-43513-3_16
11. Dufty, B., de Groot, J.: Filling in the semantics for intuitionistic conditional logic. arXiv:2508.11972 (2025)
12. Fischer Servi, G.: Axiomatizations for some intuitionistic modal logics. Rendiconti del Seminario Matematico - PoliTO **42**(3), 179–194 (1984). https://doi.org/10.1093/logcom/exs040
13. Genovese, V., Giordano, L., Gliozzi, V., Pozzato, G.L.: Logics in access control: a conditional approach. J. Log. Comput. **24**(4), 705–762 (2014). https://doi.org/10.1093/LOGCOM/EXS040
14. Indrzejczak, A.: Sequents and Trees. Birkhäuser Cham (2021)
15. Kuznets, R., Straßburger, L.: Maehara-style modal nested calculi. Arch. Math. Logic **58**(3), 359–385 (2019)
16. Lewis, D.: Counterfactuals. Blackwell (1973)
17. Marin, S., Morales, M., Straßburger, L.: A fully labelled proof system for intuitionistic modal logics. J. Log. Comput. **31**(3), 998–1022 (2021)
18. Olkhovikov, G.K.: An intuitionistically complete system of basic intuitionistic conditional logic. J. Philos. Log. **53**(5), 1199–1240 (2024). https://doi.org/10.1007/S10992-024-09763-6
19. Pattinson, D., Schröder, L.: Generic modal cut elimination applied to conditional logics. Log. Methods Comput. Sci. **7**(1) (2011). https://doi.org/10.2168/LMCS-7(1:4)2011
20. Schröder, L., Pattinson, D., Hausmann, D.: Optimal tableaux for conditional logics with cautious monotonicity. In: Coelho, H., Studer, R., Wooldridge, M.J. (eds.) ECAI 2010 - 19th European Conference on Artificial Intelligence, Lisbon, Portugal, 16–20 August 2010, Proceedings. Frontiers in Artificial Intelligence and Applications, vol. 215, pp. 707–712. IOS Press (2010). https://doi.org/10.3233/978-1-60750-606-5-707
21. Segerberg, K.: Propositional logics related to heyting's and johansson's. Theoria **34**(1), 26–61 (1968)
22. Simpson, A.K.: The proof theory and semantics of intuitionistic modal logic (1994)
23. Straßburger, L.: Cut elimination in nested sequents for intuitionistic modal logics. In: Pfenning, F. (ed.) FoSSaCS 2013. LNCS, vol. 7794, pp. 209–224. Springer, Heidelberg (2013). https://doi.org/10.1007/978-3-642-37075-5_14
24. Troelstra, A.S., Schwichtenberg, H.: Basic Proof Theory. Cambridge University Press (2000)
25. Weiss, Y.: Basic intuitionistic conditional logic. J. Philos. Log. **48**(3), 447–469 (2019). https://doi.org/10.1007/S10992-018-9471-4
26. Więckowski, B.: On the proof-theoretic structure of counterfactual inference. Bull. Symb. Logic 1–51 (2025)

27. Wijesekera, D.: Constructive modal logics i. Ann. Pure Appl. Logic **50**(3), 271–301 (1990)
28. Wolter, F., Zakharyaschev, M.: Intuitionistic modal logic. In: Logic and Foundations of Mathematics: Selected Contributed Papers of the Tenth International Congress of Logic, Methodology and Philosophy of Science, Florence, pp. 227–238. Springer (1995)

**Open Access** This chapter is licensed under the terms of the Creative Commons Attribution 4.0 International License (http://creativecommons.org/licenses/by/4.0/), which permits use, sharing, adaptation, distribution and reproduction in any medium or format, as long as you give appropriate credit to the original author(s) and the source, provide a link to the Creative Commons license and indicate if changes were made.

The images or other third party material in this chapter are included in the chapter's Creative Commons license, unless indicated otherwise in a credit line to the material. If material is not included in the chapter's Creative Commons license and your intended use is not permitted by statutory regulation or exceeds the permitted use, you will need to obtain permission directly from the copyright holder.

# Intuitionistic $\mu$-Calculus with the Lewis Arrow

Bahareh Afshari[1] and Lide Grotenhuis[2(✉)]

[1] Department of Philosophy, Linguistics and Theory of Science, University of Gothenburg, Gothenburg, Sweden
bahareh.afshari@gu.se
[2] Institute of Logic, Language and Computation, University of Amsterdam, Amsterdam, The Netherlands
l.m.grotenhuis@uva.nl

**Abstract.** We present an intuitionistic counterpart of the modal $\mu$-calculus formulated with the binary Lewis arrow, a generalisation of the $\Box$-operator. Using Ruitenburg's theorem, we prove that every formula is equivalent to a guarded one. We then provide a sound and complete non-wellfounded proof system for the logic that is cut-free, and obtain as a corollary that the logic is decidable and admits a cyclic proof system. A game semantics for the logic is developed which acts as a mediator between the formal proof system and the relational semantics.

**Keywords:** Intuitionistic Modal Logic · Fixpoint Logic · Sequent Calculus · Non-wellfounded Proof Theory · Game Semantics

## 1 Introduction

The modal $\mu$-calculus, well-known for its succinctness in specification and verification of computer systems, is obtained by adding explicit fixpoint operators to the modal language, thereby allowing one to express complex fairness properties, including path-based quantification. The result is a highly expressive logic which, at the same time, enjoys many desirable meta-logical properties [9]: it is decidable, satisfies uniform interpolation, has a small model property and a finitary axiomatisation. Syntactically, the logic is characterised particularly well by non-wellfounded and cyclic proof systems, which capture (co)inductive reasoning implicitly through cycles or infinitely long branches in the proof-tree dispensing the explicit inference rules for (co)induction. Consequently, such systems are better suited for proof search, and they have proven useful in lifting the barrier of applying proof-theoretic machinery to fixpoint languages, examples of which include interpolation and cut-elimination results such as [1,5,16,30].

The modal $\mu$-calculus is a classical logic. Recently, there has been increasing interest in fixpoint modal logics over intuitionistic propositional logic (IPL). Examples include intuitionistic linear-time temporal logic [3,6–8,15], intuitionistic common knowledge logic (ICK) [20], intuitionistic Gödel-Löb logic (IGL)

[12,18,31] and the constructive modal $\mu$-calculus [28]. The motivations behind these logics are diverse. Fernández-Duque [15] aims at developing a formalisation of the theory of dynamical topological systems; another motivation for intuitionistic or constructive temporal logic lies in *metaprogramming*, where temporal modalities are used to model processes such as binding-time analysis and staged computation (see e.g. [13,22,23]). Jäger and Marti [20] introduce ICK as a system for reasoning about common knowledge from the perspective of the intuitionist, thus providing a philosophical justification. Das, van der Giessen and Marin [12] study IGL as it provides a computational interpretation of the classical provability logic GL via a Gödel-Gentzen negative translation.

The current work is part of a larger programme to establish a general framework and proof-theoretic techniques for studying intuitionistic fixpoint modal logics. In particular, we aim at transferring the techniques from non-wellfounded and cyclic proof theory from the classical to the intuitionistic realm building on recently developed non-wellfounded proof systems for two versions of intuitionistic linear-time temporal logic [3] and a cyclic system for intuitionistic modal logic with the master modality [4]. In this paper, we present a non-wellfounded calculus for an intuitionistic version of the modal $\mu$-calculus. To keep the framework as general as possible, we have chosen to add fixpoint operators to an intuitionistic modal logic with the binary *Lewis arrow* (denoted by $\mathrel{-3}$), which generalises the more commonly used unary $\Box$-operator.

The Lewis arrow is the historical ancestor of the $\Box$-operator [25]. In classical modal logic, the Lewis arrow is interdefinable with $\Box$; one can define $\varphi \mathrel{-3} \psi$ as $\Box(\varphi \to \psi)$ and $\Box\varphi$ as $\top \mathrel{-3} \varphi$. Intuitionistically, however, the situation is more subtle. Given a bi-relational Kripke model $(W, \leq, R, V)$, where $\leq$ provides the intuitionistic ordering and $R$ the modal accessibility relation, a natural way to define the relational semantics of the Lewis arrow is

$$w \models \varphi \mathrel{-3} \psi \quad \text{iff} \quad \text{for all } v \text{ such that } wRv, \text{ if } v \models \varphi \text{ then } v \models \psi.$$

In this setting, one can still define $\Box\varphi$ as $\top \mathrel{-3} \varphi$, but cannot define $\mathrel{-3}$ in terms of $\Box$. This was first observed in the study of *preservativity logics*, led by Visser and Iemhoff (see e.g. [17,19,33]).

Following Litak and Visser's notation in [26], we consider the Lewisian logic iA. The language of iA consists of the language of IPL extended with the $\mathrel{-3}$-operator. Syntactically, iA can be characterised by a Hilbert system containing[1]

(Tr) $\varphi \mathrel{-3} \psi \to (\psi \mathrel{-3} \chi \to \varphi \mathrel{-3} \chi)$,
(K$_a$) $\varphi \mathrel{-3} \psi \to (\varphi \mathrel{-3} \chi \to \varphi \mathrel{-3} (\psi \wedge \chi))$,
(Di) $\varphi \mathrel{-3} \chi \to (\psi \mathrel{-3} \chi \to (\varphi \vee \psi) \mathrel{-3} \chi)$,

and axioms for IPL, together with the inference rules *modus ponens* and the Lewisian version of necessitation: if $\vdash \varphi \to \psi$ then $\vdash \varphi \mathrel{-3} \psi$. Semantically, iA is the logic of all (finite) bi-relational models $(W, \leq, R, V)$ that satisfy triangle

---

[1] We follow the convention that $\mathrel{-3}$ binds tighter than $\to$.

confluence: if $s \leq tRu$ then $sRu$. Triangle confluence is the minimal frame condition necessary to obtain the *monotonicity lemma*: for all formulas $\varphi$, if $s \leq t$ and $s \models \varphi$ then $t \models \varphi$. The $\square$-fragment of iA, defined as the theorems containing only occurrences of $\prec$ of the form $\top \prec \varphi$, is equal to the 'minimal' intuitionistic modal logic iK, obtained by adding the K-axiom $\square(A \to B) \to (\square A \to \square B)$ and the necessitation rule to a Hilbert system for IPL.

**Contribution.** We extend the language of iA with explicit fixpoint operators and interpret formulas over triangle confluent bi-relational Kripke models; the resulting logic is called $\text{iL}_\mu$ (Sect. 2). We provide game semantics for $\text{iL}_\mu$ (Sect. 3) and use *Ruitenburg's theorem* [29] to show that a standard yet important result for the classical $\mu$-calculus, namely that every formula is equivalent to one that is *guarded* (see e.g. [14, §8.3.5]), still holds in our intuitionistic setting (Sect. 4). Lastly, we introduce a cut-free, non-wellfounded proof system for $\text{iL}_\mu$ (Sect. 5). We prove soundness and guarded completeness with respect to the game semantics. For the latter, we set up a *validity game* between two players, Prover and Refuter, in the spirit of [27]. The crux of the completeness proof lies in constructing a countermodel from a winning strategy for Refuter; compared to the classical setting, the intuitionistic case involves the extra hurdle of satisfying the frame conditions ensuring monotonicity. For triangle confluent frames, however, this is relatively simple, as one need not adjust the intuitionistic relation but only extend the modal accessibility relation to obtain a triangle confluent model. As the validity game is $\omega$-regular, we obtain as a corollary that $\text{iL}_\mu$ is decidable and has a finitary proof system (Sect. 6). The adequacy proof of the games and the completeness proof of the calculus are inspired by their classical counterparts as presented in [32].

## 2 Syntax and Relational Semantics

Fix a countable set of atomic variables Var. We define *formulas* of $\text{iL}_\mu$ by

$$\varphi, \psi ::= \bot \mid \top \mid X \mid \varphi \wedge \psi \mid \varphi \vee \psi \mid \varphi \to \psi \mid \varphi \prec \psi \mid \mu X.\varphi \mid \nu X.\varphi$$

with $X \in \text{Var}$. For the formation of bound formulas $\eta X.\varphi$ with $\eta \in \{\mu, \nu\}$, we require that $X$ is *positive* in $\varphi$, i.e. when breaking $\varphi$ down to an occurrence of $X$ one meets an even number of '$\to$'s and '$\prec$'s. We let $X, Y, \ldots$ range over bound variables and $P, Q, \ldots$ over unbounded variables (also called *propositions*). We call formulas of the form $\varphi \prec \psi$ *modal formulas* and formulas of the form $\eta.X\varphi$ *fixpoint formulas*. Moreover, we define $\square \varphi := \top \prec \varphi$, and we call a formula $\psi$ a $\square$-*formula* if every occurrence of $\prec$ in $\psi$ is of the form $\top \prec \varphi$.

It will be useful to extend the notion of polarity from variables to formulas and to make this polarity explicit whenever we talk about subformulas. A *polarised formula*, denoted by $\varphi^p$, is a pair consisting of a formula $\varphi$ and a *polarity* $p \in \mathbb{F}_2 = \{+, -\}$. If $p = +$ (resp. $-$) then we call $\varphi^p$ a *positive* or *right* (resp. *negative* or *left*) formula. We use $A, B, \ldots$ to range over polarised formulas

We can then state the winning condition of $\mathcal{E}(\psi, M)$ as follows: an infinite play $\pi$ of $\mathcal{E}(\psi, M)$ is won by $\exists$ if $\tau_\pi$ is a right $\nu$-trace or a left $\mu$-trace.

Note that $\mathcal{E}(\psi, M)$ is a *parity game*: we can define a priority mapping $\Omega$ by assigning even numbers to positive $\nu$- and negative $\mu$-variables and odd numbers to negative $\nu$- and positive $\mu$-variables in such a way that higher ranking variables obtain a higher priority. Thus $\mathcal{E}(\psi, M)$ is positionally determined.

The following lemma follows directly from the symmetry between the admissible moves of $\exists$ and $\forall$.

**Lemma 5.** *For any position $q$ in the game $\mathcal{E}(\psi, M)$, we have that $q$ is winning for $\exists$ iff $-q$ is winning for $\forall$.*

Adequacy of the game semantics can be proven in a purely game-theoretic way as done in [32] for the classical $\mu$-calculus, appealing to *unfolding games* as a semantics for fixpoints. Given a set $W$, a monotone function $f : \mathcal{P}(W) \to \mathcal{P}(W)$ and a binder $\eta \in \{\mu, \nu\}$, the unfolding game $\mathcal{U}^\eta(f)$ is defined as follows.

| Position | Player | Admissible moves |
|---|---|---|
| $s \in W$ | $\exists$ | $\{V \subseteq W : s \in f(V)\}$ |
| $V \subseteq W$ | $\forall$ | $V$ |

An infinite play of $\mathcal{U}^\eta(f)$ is won by $\exists$ if $\eta = \nu$ and won by $\forall$ if $\eta = \mu$. It is known that the set of winning positions for $\exists$ in $\mathcal{U}^\eta(f)$ is equal to the least fixed point of $f$ if $\eta = \mu$ and equal to the greatest fixed point of $f$ if $\eta = \nu$.[5] Moreover, $\mathcal{U}^\eta(f)$ is clearly a parity game and therefore positionally determined.

**Theorem 1.** *Let $\psi$ be a clean formula. For any pointed model $(M, s)$, we have $M, s \models \psi$ if and only if $(\psi^+, s)$ is winning for $\exists$ in $\mathcal{E}(\psi, M)$.*

*Proof (sketch).* We proceed by induction on $\psi$, and at the inductive step for a fixpoint formula $\eta X.\varphi$ we use the unfolding game to 'paste together' plays of the evaluation game for $\varphi$. The key insight here is the shift from standard to polarised formulas, which enables a smooth adaptation from the classical proof.

## 4 Guarded Formulas

In the classical modal $\mu$-calculus, formulas are called *guarded* if every fixpoint variable occurs in the scope of a modality. Guarded fixpoint formulas are easier to work with than general fixpoint formulas, as tracing such a formula $\eta X.\varphi$ to its fixpoint variable $X$ always involves 'progress' in the form of a modal step. In our context, the notion of guardedness can be defined as follows.

---

[5] See e.g. Prop. 1.5.1. in [2] or Thm. 3.14 in [32].

**Definition 3.** *Given a formula $\varphi$ and a variable $X$, we call $X$ guarded in $\varphi$ if every occurrence of $X$ in $\varphi$ is in the scope of some $\rightarrow$ operator.[6] A formula $\varphi$ is guarded if for every subformula $\eta X.\psi$ of $\varphi$, $X$ is guarded in $\psi$.*

It is well-known that every classical modal $\mu$-formula is equivalent to one that is guarded. Intuitively, this is due to the fact that adding fixpoint operators to classical propositional logic does not increase its expressive power; this fact is easily shown by appealing to normal forms, which fail to exist in intuitionistic propositional logic (IPL). Nevertheless, Ruitenburg [29] showed, with a rather involved syntactic proof, that this result also holds for IPL.

**Theorem 2 (Ruitenburg).** *Let $\varphi$ be a formula of IPL and $X$ a propositional letter such that $X$ is positive in $\varphi$. Define $\varphi_X^0 := X$ and $\varphi_X^{n+1} := \varphi[\varphi_X^n/X]$. Then there exists an $N$ such that $\varphi_X^N \equiv \varphi_X^{N+1}$.*

To derive guardedness of $iL_\mu$, we use Ruitenburg's theorem and the 'golden lemma' of the $\mu$-calculus. As for the classical case, this lemma follows easily from the game semantics.

**Lemma 6 (Golden Lemma).** *Let $X$ and $Y$ be positive in $\varphi$ and $\eta \in \{\mu, \nu\}$. Then we have $\eta X.\eta Y.\varphi \equiv \eta X.\varphi[X/Y] \equiv \eta Y.\eta X.\varphi$.*

**Theorem 3.** *Every formula of $iL_\mu$ is equivalent to a guarded one.*

*Proof.* We prove the statement by induction on $\varphi$ and only treat the case that $\varphi$ is of the form $\mu X.\psi$ with $\psi$ guarded. Suppose that $X$ occurs unguarded in $\psi$. If $X$ occurs unguarded inside a subformula $\eta Y.\chi$ of $\psi$, then we can replace $\eta Y.\chi$ with its unfolding $\chi[\eta Y.\chi/Y]$. As $Y$ is guarded in $\chi$, doing so only adds guarded occurrences of $X$. So we may assume that the unguarded occurrences of $X$ in $\psi$ are all outside the scope of fixpoint operators. Let $\zeta$ be obtained from $\psi$ by replacing every unguarded occurrence of $X$ by $X_0$ and every guarded occurrence of $X$ by $X_1$. Then we have $\mu X.\psi \equiv \mu X_0.\mu X_1.\zeta \equiv \mu X_1.\mu X_0.\zeta$ by Lemma 6. Let $\hat{\zeta}$ be obtained from $\zeta$ by replacing each maximal fixpoint or modal subformula $\chi$ of $\psi$ by a fresh propositional letter $P_\chi$; 'maximal' here means in terms of the subformula-relation. Note that, by construction, no such $\chi$ contains the variable $X_0$ and $\hat{\zeta}$ does not contain $X_1$. As $\hat{\zeta}$ is an IPL formula, by Theorem 2 there exists an $N$ such that $\hat{\zeta}_{X_0}^N \equiv \hat{\zeta}_{X_0}^{N+1}$. As none of the $\chi$ contains $X_0$, note that $\zeta_{X_0}^N$ is identical to the formula obtained from $\hat{\zeta}_{X_0}^N$ by substituting for each $P_\chi$ its corresponding subformula $\chi$ back in. Since $\hat{\zeta}_{X_0}^N \equiv \hat{\zeta}_{X_0}^{N+1}$, it follows that $\zeta_{X_0}^N \equiv \zeta_{X_0}^{N+1}$, which implies $\mu X_0.\zeta \equiv \zeta_{X_0}^N[\bot/X_0]$. Now $\zeta_{X_0}^N[\bot/X_0]$ only contains guarded occurrences of $X_1$ and we have $\mu X_1.\zeta_{X_0}^N[\bot/X_0] \equiv \mu X_1.\mu X_0.\zeta \equiv \mu X.\psi$.

## 5  A Non-wellfounded Proof System

In this section, we introduce a non-wellfounded sequent calculus for $iL_\mu$ and show its completeness with respect to guarded formulas.

---

[6] Note that the scope of a $\rightarrow$-operator consists of both the antecedent and the consequent, thus $X$ may occur on either side of a $\rightarrow$-operator.

## 5.1 The Calculus NWiL

We define a *sequent* as a finite set of polarised formulas. We use $\Gamma, \Delta, \ldots$ to range over sets of plain formulas and write $\Gamma \Rightarrow \Delta$ to refer to the sequent $\{\varphi^- : \varphi \in \Gamma\} \cup \{\varphi^+ : \varphi \in \Delta\}$. The *interpretation* of $\Gamma \Rightarrow \Delta$ is $\bigwedge \Gamma \to \bigvee \Delta$.

In the rest of this section, we assume we are working within the context of some clean formula, i.e. we have fixed sets of free and bound variables and a function $X \mapsto (\eta_X, \varphi_X)$ mapping bound variables to their binder and bound formula.

**Definition 4.** *The sequent calculus* NWiL *is given by the rules in Fig. 2. Here $P$ is a free variable, $X$ a bound variable and $\eta \in \{\mu, \nu\}$. In the $\prec_n$-rule, we have $n \geq 0$ and the sets $\Gamma_j \subseteq \{\gamma_1, \ldots, \gamma_n\}$ and $\Delta_j \subseteq \{\delta_1, \ldots, \delta_n\}$ range over all $2^n$ pairs of subsets such that for all $i \leq n$ we have $\gamma_i \in \Gamma_j$ if and only if $\delta_i \notin \Delta_j$.*

$$\frac{}{\Gamma, P \Rightarrow P, \Delta} \text{ id} \qquad \frac{}{\Gamma, \bot \Rightarrow \Delta} \bot \qquad \frac{}{\Gamma \Rightarrow \top} \top$$

$$\frac{\Gamma, \varphi_X \Rightarrow \Delta}{\Gamma, X \Rightarrow \Delta} \text{ XL} \qquad \frac{\Gamma, \varphi \Rightarrow \Delta \quad \Gamma, \psi \Rightarrow \Delta}{\Gamma, \varphi \vee \psi \Rightarrow \Delta} \text{ VL} \qquad \frac{\Gamma, \varphi, \psi \Rightarrow \Delta}{\Gamma, \varphi \wedge \psi \Rightarrow \Delta} \wedge\text{L}$$

$$\frac{\Gamma \Rightarrow \varphi_X, \Delta}{\Gamma \Rightarrow X, \Delta} \text{ XR} \qquad \frac{\Gamma \Rightarrow \varphi, \psi, \Delta}{\Gamma \Rightarrow \varphi \vee \psi, \Delta} \text{ VR} \qquad \frac{\Gamma \Rightarrow \varphi, \Delta \quad \Gamma \Rightarrow \psi, \Delta}{\Gamma \Rightarrow \varphi \wedge \psi, \Delta} \wedge\text{R}$$

$$\frac{\Gamma, \varphi \Rightarrow \Delta}{\Gamma, \eta X.\varphi \Rightarrow \Delta} \eta\text{L} \qquad \frac{\Gamma, \varphi \to \psi \Rightarrow \varphi, \Delta \quad \Gamma, \psi \Rightarrow \Delta}{\Gamma, \varphi \to \psi \Rightarrow \Delta} \to\text{L}$$

$$\frac{\Gamma \Rightarrow \varphi, \Delta}{\Gamma \Rightarrow \eta X.\varphi, \Delta} \eta\text{R} \qquad \frac{\Gamma, \varphi \Rightarrow \psi}{\Gamma \Rightarrow \varphi \to \psi, \Delta} \to\text{R}$$

$$\frac{\{\Gamma_j, \varphi \Rightarrow \psi, \Delta_j\}_{j \leq 2^n}}{\Pi, \{\delta_i \prec \gamma_i\}_{i \leq n} \Rightarrow \varphi \prec \psi, \Sigma} \prec_n$$

**Fig. 2.** The rules of the calculus NWiL.

For example, the $\prec_0$ and $\prec_1$ rule are given by

$$\frac{\varphi \Rightarrow \psi}{\Pi \Rightarrow \varphi \prec \psi, \Sigma} \prec_0 \qquad \frac{\varphi \Rightarrow \psi, \delta \quad \gamma, \varphi \Rightarrow \psi}{\Pi, \delta \prec \gamma \Rightarrow \varphi \prec \psi, \Sigma} \prec_1$$

Observe that the calculus NWiL does not contain a cut-rule. Moreover, we have two pairs of 'fixpoint rules': one for the bound variables and one for the fixpoint formulas.[7] Also note that all rules except →R and $\prec_n$ are invertible

---
[7] The presented fixpoint rules are possible since we are working with clean formulas and thereby with proofs that are defined in the context of a bound variable mapping $X \mapsto (\eta_X, \phi_X)$.

in the sense that the conclusion is valid if and only if all premises are. We therefore refer to $\dashv_n$ and $\to$R as the *non-invertible* rules and to the other rules as *invertible*. The rules id, $\bot$ and $\top$ are called *axioms*. We call an application of $\dashv_n$ to a sequent $\sigma$ *full* if $n$ equals the number of left $\dashv$-formulas in $\sigma$. For each rule except $\dashv_n$, the distinguished formula in the conclusion is called *principal* and the distinguished formula(s) in the premises are called its *residual(s)*. For example, for $\to$L the principal formula is $(\varphi \to \psi)^-$ and its residuals are $(\varphi \to \psi)^-, \varphi^+$ and $\psi^-$. For the rule $\dashv_n$, all formulas in the conclusion are called principal and each distinguished modal formula in the conclusion has its antecedent and consequent as residual in the premises where they occur (formulas in $\Pi$ and $\Sigma$ have no residuals); for example, in the above application of $\dashv_1$, the formula $(\delta \dashv \gamma)^-$ has $\delta^+$ as residual in the left premise and $\gamma^-$ as residual in the right premise. In every rule application, any formula that is neither principal nor residual is called a *side formula*. Although residual formulas are often structurally smaller than their corresponding principal formula, the $\to$L-rule is an exception to this; we call the residual formula $(\varphi \to \psi)^-$ in an application of $\to$L *non-progressing*, and we call the other two residual formulas *progressing*. For other rules, every residual formula is considered to be progressing.

As we are working with set sequents, formulas can simultaneously function as principal and as side formulas. We call a rule application *succinct* if every principal formula does not occur as a side formula. For example, the application of $\wedge$L as depicted above is succinct if $A \wedge B \notin \Gamma$. Note that applications of the non-invertible rules $\dashv_n$ and $\to$R are always succinct.

A *derivation* in NWiL of a sequent $\sigma$ is a finite or infinite tree whose nodes are labelled by sequents according to the rules of NWiL and whose root is labelled by $\sigma$. We read derivations 'upwards', so the premise of a rule is considered to be a successor of the conclusion. A *path* through a derivation $\Pi$ is a sequence of nodes $(\rho_i)_i$ in $\Pi$ where for each $i$ the node $\rho_{i+1}$ (if it exists) is a direct successor of $\rho_i$. A path is *maximal* if it ends in a leaf or is infinite. A *branch* is a maximal path that starts at the root. We will often tacitly identify a node in a derivation with the sequent labelling it and thereby paths with sequences of sequents.

**Definition 5.** *Let $\rho$ be a path through a derivation $\Pi$. A trace on $\rho$ is a sequence of polarised formulas $\tau = (A_i)_{i<\alpha}$ with $\alpha = |\rho|$ such that for all $i < \alpha$ we have:*

*(1) $A_i$ occurs in the sequent labelling $\rho_i$;*
*(2) if $i+1 < \alpha$ and $A_i$ is principal, then $A_{i+1}$ is one of its residuals;*
*(3) if $i+1 < \alpha$ and $A_i$ is a side formula, then $A_{i+1} = A_i$.*

We call an infinite trace $\tau$ on $\rho$ *progressing* if for every $i$ there exists a $j > i$ such that $A_j$ is a progressing residual formula in $\Pi$.

A trace $\tau$ on a path in a derivation of $\Gamma \Rightarrow \Delta$ can be 'condensed' into a trace $\hat\tau$ in the formula $\bigwedge \Gamma \to \bigvee \Delta$ by deleting all possible repetitions due to side formulas and non-progressing residuals of $\to$L.

**Definition 6.** *Let $\tau$ be a progressing trace on a path through a derivation. Its condensation $\hat\tau$ is the subsequence $(\tau_{l(i)})_i$ of $\tau$ with $l(0) = 0$ and for $i > 0$, $l(i)$ is the least index such that $\tau_{l(i)}$ is a progressing residual formula of $\tau_{l(i-1)}$.*

By Lemma 1 and 2, the condensation of a progressing trace $\tau$ has a well-defined type and polarity. We call $\tau$ *good* if it is progressing and its condensation is either a right $\nu$-trace or a left $\mu$-trace.

**Definition 7.** *A derivation $\Pi$ of a sequent $\sigma$ is a* proof *of $\sigma$ if every leaf in $\Pi$ is labelled by an axiom and every infinite branch of $\Pi$ has a good trace.*

**Theorem 4.** *Every clean formula provable in* NWiL *is valid over $\rightarrow$-models.*

*Proof (sketch).* By Theorem 1, it suffices to prove soundness with respect to the game semantics. Let $\Pi$ be a proof of $\Rightarrow \varphi$ and suppose, for contradiction, that there is a pointed $\rightarrow$-model $(M,s)$ such that $(\varphi^+, s)$ is winning for $\forall$ in $\mathcal{E}(\varphi, M)$. Let $f$ be $\forall$'s positional winning strategy. We construct an infinite branch $\beta$ of $\Pi$ and an infinite sequence $s$ in $W$ such that any trace $\tau$ on $\beta$ induces an $f$-guided play $\pi_\tau$ of the form $(\tau_{l(i)}, s_{l(i)}, b_i)_i$ in $\mathcal{E}(\varphi, M)@(\varphi^+, s)$, for some monotone map $l$ and sequence of bits $b$. As $\Pi$ is a proof, $\beta$ must have a good trace $\tau_*$. But then the play $\pi_{\tau_*}$ induced by $\tau_*$ must be won by $\exists$, contradicting that it is $f$-guided.

We construct $\beta$ and $s$ by induction such that for every $i$: ($*$) for every polarised formula $A$ in $\beta_i$, the position $(A, s_i)$ is winning for $\forall$. Let $\beta_0$ be the root of $\Pi$ and let $s_0 = s$. Given $\beta_i$ and $s_i$, we define the next step by a case distinction on the rule applied at $\beta_i$. We treat the $\rightarrow_n$-case as an example. Let $\delta_j \rightarrow \gamma_j^-$, with $j \le n$, and $\varphi_1 \rightarrow \varphi_2^+$ be the principal formulas. Note that it is $\forall$'s turn at position $(\varphi_1 \rightarrow \varphi_2^+, s_i)$, so we can let $s_{i+1}$ be the modal successor of $s_i$ picked out by $f$. Then by ($*$) and definition of $f$, $(\varphi_1^-, s_{i+1})$ and $(\varphi_2^+, s_{i+1})$ are still winning for $\forall$. Define $\Gamma := \{\gamma_j : s_{i+1} \models \gamma_j\}$ and $\Delta := \{\delta_j : s_{i+1} \not\models \gamma_j\}$, and let $\beta_{i+1}$ be the premise of $\beta_i$ labelled by $\Gamma, \varphi_1 \Rightarrow \varphi_2, \Delta$. By ($*$) (and adequacy of the game semantics), we must have $s_i \models \bigwedge_{j \le n} \delta_j \rightarrow \gamma_j$. Thus, since $s_i R s_{i+1}$, this implies that $s_{i+1} \not\models \delta_j$ for each $\delta_j \in \Delta$, ensuring that ($*$) is satisfied for $i+1$.

## 5.2 Completeness

In this section, we prove completeness of NWiL with respect to guarded formulas. For the rest of this section, we therefore assume that formulas are guarded.

Given a clean formula $\psi$, we define a *validity game* $\mathcal{V}(\psi)$ between Prover and Refuter. Intuitively, Prover tries to show that $\psi$ is provable in NWiL, while Refuter tries to show that $\psi$ is invalid. Determinacy of this game will then provide the desired completeness result. Positions in $\mathcal{V}(\psi)$ are sequents $\sigma$ or tuples $(\sigma, A)$ with $\sigma \subseteq Sub(\psi^+)$ and $A \in \sigma$. Given a sequent position $\sigma$, Prover chooses which formula $A \in \sigma$ will become principal in the next rule application. Subsequently, Refuter picks which premise of this rule application he wishes to refute. The game continues either infinitely or until an axiomatic sequent is reached.

Due to the intuitionistic $\rightarrow$L-rule, left implications are preserved in the left premise even for succinct rule applications. To remedy this, we temporarily extend our syntax with the binary connective $\dot\rightarrow$ and replace the $\rightarrow$L-rule by

$$\frac{\Gamma, A \dot\rightarrow B \Rightarrow A, \Delta \quad \Gamma, B \Rightarrow \Delta}{\Gamma, A \rightarrow B \Rightarrow \Delta} \dot\rightarrow L$$

The point is that we may only apply $\to$L to $\to$-formulas and not to $\dashrightarrow$-formulas. We call the latter *marked* implications. Given a sequent $\sigma$, we let $\overline{\sigma}$ denote the sequent obtained from $\sigma$ by removing all markings of left implications.

Let $Prem(\sigma, A)$ denote the set of sequents that can occur as a premise in a **succinct** and **full** rule application to $\sigma$ in which $A$ is principal. Then we can define the validity game $\mathcal{V}(\psi)$ by the following table:

| Position | Player | Admissible moves |
|---|---|---|
| $\sigma$ axiom | Refuter | $\emptyset$ |
| $\sigma$ non-axiom | Prover | $\{(\sigma, A) : A \in \sigma\}$ |
| $(\sigma, A)$ with $A \in At(\psi)$, $A = \varphi_1 \dashv \varphi_2^-$ or $\varphi_1 \dashrightarrow \varphi_2^-$ | Prover | $\emptyset$ |
| $(\sigma, A)$ with $A = \varphi_1 \to \varphi_2^+$ or $A = \varphi_1 \dashv \varphi_2^+$ | Refuter | $Prem(\overline{\sigma}, A)$ |
| $(\sigma, A)$ with $\sigma$ and $A$ not as above | Refuter | $Prem(\sigma, A)$ |

Here $At(\psi)$ contains the *atoms of* $\psi$, that is subformulas $\varphi^p$ of $\psi^+$ with $\varphi \in FV(\psi) \cup \{\bot, \top\}$. By construction, an infinite play $\pi$ of the game $\mathcal{V}(\psi)@\{\psi^+\}$ corresponds to a branch $\beta_\pi$ in a derivation of $\psi$: given a sequent position $\sigma$ in $\pi$, the subsequent position $(\sigma, A)$ indicates which rule is to be applied at $\sigma$. Thus, for $\pi$ given by

$$\sigma_0, (\sigma_0, A_0), \sigma_1, (\sigma_1, A_1), \ldots,$$

the branch $\beta_\pi$ is simply equal to $(\sigma_i)_{i<\omega}$. An infinite play $\pi$ is won by Prover if $\beta_\pi$ has a good trace, and won by Refuter otherwise.

The validity game $\mathcal{V}(\psi)@\{\psi^+\}$ is not necessarily a parity game, but it is an $\omega$-regular game. Note that the set $\Sigma$ of all possible positions in $\mathcal{V}(\psi)@\{\psi^+\}$ is finite, as $\psi^+$ only has finitely many polarised subformulas. Taking $\Sigma$ as our alphabet, we can then define a non-deterministic parity automaton $\mathcal{A}$ with set of states $Sub(\psi^+)$ and initial state $\psi^+$ such that, when given an infinite play $\pi \in \Sigma^*$, $\mathcal{A}$ non-deterministically picks out a formula trace in $\beta_\pi$. If we define the priority mapping so that positive $\nu$- and negative $\mu$-variables are assigned an even number and negative $\nu$- and positive $\mu$-variables are assigned an odd number in a way that respects the subsumption order, then $\mathcal{A}$ accepts $\pi$ exactly when $\pi$ is won by Prover. It therefore follows that $\mathcal{V}(\psi)$ is determined, so either Prover or Refuter has a winning strategy in $\mathcal{V}(\psi)@\{\psi^+\}$.

A winning strategy for Prover induces an NWiL-proof of $\psi$. In fact, due to $\omega$-regularity, we may assume that the resulting non-wellfounded proof is *regular*, i.e. only has finitely many distinct subproofs.

**Theorem 5.** *If Prover has a winning strategy in $\mathcal{V}(\psi)@\{\psi^+\}$, then $\psi$ has a regular proof in* NWiL.

*Proof (sketch).* Starting with the sequent $\Rightarrow \psi$, Prover's strategy tells us which rule should be applied to a particular sequent, and the resulting derivation $\Pi$

will be a proof due the winning conditions for Prover. Moreover, by $\omega$-regularity, we may assume that the winning strategy of Prover has *finite memory*[8] and therefore that this strategy can only assign different subproofs to finitely many different sequents.

For the completeness result, we are thus left to show that a winning strategy $f_R$ for Refuter in $\mathcal{V}(\psi)@\{\psi^+\}$ induces a countermodel for $\psi$. In order to define this countermodel, we need to consider $f_R$-guided plays in which Prover adheres to a *saturating* playing strategy.

**Definition 8.** *A subformula of $\psi$ is* saturated *if it is an atom of $\psi$, a modal formula, a left $\dashrightarrow$-formula, or a right implication. A sequent $\sigma$ is* saturated *if it only contains saturated formulas.*

**Definition 9.** *A strategy for Prover in $\mathcal{V}(\psi)$ is* saturating *if the following hold: (1) at positions $\sigma$, Prover only picks formulas of the form $\varphi \dashv \chi^+$ or $\varphi \to \chi^+$ if $\sigma$ is saturated; and (2) Prover only picks formulas in $At(\psi)$ or formulas of the form $\varphi \dashv \chi^-$ or $\varphi \dashrightarrow \chi^-$ if she has no other option.*

Note that saturating strategies for Prover always exist: as long as $\sigma$ is not saturated, she can keep picking unsaturated formulas, and if $\sigma$ is saturated she prioritises right modal formulas and implications.

A partial play $\pi$ in $\mathcal{V}(\psi)$ is called *local* if Prover never picks a right implication or modal formula in $\pi$. Intuitively, local plays in $\mathcal{V}(\psi)$ describe plays in the evaluation game that take place at the same world. A local play $\pi$ is called *saturated* if Prover adheres to a saturating strategy in $\pi$ and $\pi$ is maximal, i.e. $\pi$ is a full play or ends in a saturated sequent. By guardedness, the marking of left implications and the succinctness of invertible rules, we obtain the following.

**Lemma 7.** *Every local play is finite.*

**Definition 10.** *A finite partial play $\pi$ is* locally partitionable *if there exist saturated local plays $\lambda_0, \ldots, \lambda_n$ and positions $(\sigma_0, A_0), \ldots, (\sigma_{n-1}, A_{n-1})$ such that*

$$\pi = \lambda_0 \cdot (\sigma_0, A_0) \cdots \lambda_{n-1} \cdot (\sigma_{n-1}, A_{n-1}) \cdot \lambda_n.$$

Given a winning strategy $f_R$ for Refuter in $\mathcal{V}(\psi)$, we define the model $M_R := (W, \leq, R, V)$ as follows.

(1) Let $W$ be the set of all locally partitionable $f_R$-guided plays in $\mathcal{V}(\psi)$.
(2) Given two plays $w, v \in W$, we define $w <_0 v$ iff there exists a right implication $A$ such that $v = w \cdot (\sigma, A) \cdot \lambda$ for some saturated local play $\lambda$. Let $\leq$ be the reflexive transitive closure of $<_0$.

---

[8] See e.g. Corollary 15.1.29 in [14]. Formally, having finite memory means that there exists an equivalence relation $\sim$ of finite index $k$ on the finite partial plays of $\mathcal{V}(\psi)@\{\psi^+\}$ such that $f((\pi_i)_{i \leq n}) = f((\pi'_i)_{i \leq n'})$ whenever $(\pi_i)_{i < n} \sim (\pi'_i)_{i < n'}$ and $\pi_n = \pi'_{n'}$.

(3) Given two plays $w, v \in W$, we define $wR_0 v$ iff there exists a right modal formula $A$ such that $v = w \cdot (\sigma, A) \cdot \lambda$ for some saturated local play $\lambda$. Let $R$ be the composition $\leq; R_0$.
(4) Given $w \in W$, $V(w) := \{P \in \mathit{Prop}(w) : P^-$ occurs in the last position of $w\}$.

Note that $M_R$ is indeed a ⫟-model: given $v \leq wRu$, we have $w \leq sR_0 u$ for some $s$ by definition of $R$, and so we have $v \leq sR_0 u$ (by transitivity of $\leq$) and thus $vRu$. We now show that $M_R$ is also a countermodel for $\psi$.

**Proposition 1.** *Let $w_0 \in W$ be a saturated local play with starting position $\{\psi^+\}$. Then $M_R, w_0 \not\models \psi$.*

*Proof (sketch).* We define a winning strategy $f_\forall$ for $\forall$ in $\mathcal{E} := \mathcal{E}(\psi, M_R)@(\psi^+, w_0)$. The idea is that an infinite $f_\forall$-guided play $\pi$ in $\mathcal{E}$ will correspond to a trace $\tau$ on an infinite, $f_R$-guided extension of the play $w_0$ in $\mathcal{V} := \mathcal{V}(\psi)@\{\psi^+\}$. As $f_R$ is winning for Refuter, such a trace cannot be good, which implies that $\forall$ wins the play $\pi$.

We construct the $\mathcal{E}$-play $\pi$ and the trace $\tau$ by simultaneous induction, while we extend the $\mathcal{V}$-play $w_0$ by tracing through the model $M_R$ and let Refuter's choices in the extension of $w_0$ guide the choices for $\forall$. The formal construction is a bit tricky, as the development of the $\mathcal{E}$-play $\pi$ and the form of the model $M_R$ need not align perfectly. Note that game positions in $\mathcal{E}$ consist of both a polarised formula and a location in $M_R$, say $w$. This location $w$ will be some locally partitionable play in $\mathcal{V}$. By moving to an intuitionistic successor, the location of the $\mathcal{E}$-play may 'jump' over some local $\mathcal{V}$-plays to an extension of $w$, while the rules applied along these local plays are still relevant for the evolution of the formula of the $\mathcal{E}$-play. The location of $\pi$ may therefore be a few steps ahead of the construction of the trace $\tau$, as $\tau$ is keeping track of which formula the play $\pi$ is at. In order to be able to extend the $\mathcal{V}$-play at non-invertible rule applications, we ensure that the trace $\tau$ has caught up with $\pi$ whenever a positive implication or positive modal formula is reached.

**Corollary 1.** *Every guarded validity of* $\mathsf{iL}_\mu$ *is provable in* $\mathsf{NWiL}$.

## 6  Discussion

The intuitionistic $\mu$-calculus with the Lewis arrow $\mathsf{iL}_\mu$ proposed in this paper can be viewed as a natural starting point for the study of intuitionistic modal fixpoint logic: it is *basic* in the sense that it only includes a universal modal operator and involves minimal frame conditions for monotoniticy[9], yet *general* in the sense that we have explicit fixpoint operators for all (weakly) positive formulas and a modal operator ⫟ that is more expressive than $\Box$. Lemma 4 shows that the logic of $\Box$-validities $\mathsf{iL}_\mu^\Box$ is simply a fragment of $\mathsf{iL}_\mu$. The intuitionistic

---

[9] In particular, we have no existential $\Diamond$-operator; see Das & Marin [11] for a clear overview of intuitionistic versions of the modal logic K with and without $\Diamond$.

logic with the master modality considered in [4] can also be viewed as a fragment of i$L_\mu$. Let us note that i$L_\mu$ is neither an extension nor a fragment of Pacheco's 'constructive $\mu$-calculus' studied in [28], which is obtained by adding fixpoints to CK; the latter contains both $\Box$ and $\Diamond$ and involves minimal frame conditions for monotonicity.[10]

The results in this paper show that i$L_\mu$ is in many ways just as well-behaved as its classical counterpart, the modal $\mu$-calculus. First of all, we have seen that the semantics of i$L_\mu$ can be elegantly presented in terms of evaluation games over polarised formulas. Secondly, we have proven that every formula is equivalent to a guarded one, which shows that when working with i$L_\mu$, we may restrict ourselves to the well-behaved guarded fragment. Thirdly, we have provided a complete non-wellfounded calculus NWiL that is cut-free and therefore analytic.

The presented calculus NWiL is a multi-conclusion calculus. Multi-conclusion calculi are particularly well-suited for proof search, and therefore streamline game-theoretic completeness proofs like the one presented here. However, as we are working with intuitionistic logic, one might expect that a single-conclusion calculus should attainable as well. Indeed, the logic i$L_\mu$ satisfies the disjunction property, and so the single-conclusion $\lor$R-rule is admissible. However, it is not clear to us what the single-conclusion version of the $\prec$-rule should be.[11]

Note that we have presented the completeness of NWiL for guarded formulas only. By Theorem 3, we still get a 'full' completeness result in the sense that for every valid i$L_\mu$-formula we can find an equivalent formula that is NWiL-provable. However, we expect that determinacy of the validity game can also be used to show completeness of NWiL for unguarded formulas. The problem with unguarded formulas is that local plays need not be finite anymore. In the classical case, one can solve this problem by considering finite 'representations' of these infinite local plays [32], and we expect this strategy to work here as well.

The completeness of NWiL has nice meta-logical consequences for i$L_\mu$. Since the validity game $V(\psi)$ based on NWiL is $\omega$-regular, the validity problem is decidable. Moreover, $\omega$-regularity implies that every NWiL-provable formula $\psi$

---

[10] Pacheco introduces game semantics to obtain a constructive version of the classical result that the $\mu$-calculus over S5-frames collapses to the logic S5. The game semantics for i$L_\mu$ presented here were developed independently but are very similar in spirit; the main difference is that we make the two roles of $\forall$ and $\exists$ explicit by using polarised formulas, whereas Pacheco leaves these roles implicit. Moreover, our adequacy proof of the game semantics is purely game-theoretic, whereas Pacheco's proof appeals to decreasing signatures.

[11] A natural candidate would be the rule

$$\frac{\varphi \Rightarrow \delta_1 \quad \gamma_1, \varphi \Rightarrow \delta_2 \quad \ldots \quad \gamma_1, \ldots, \gamma_n, \varphi \Rightarrow \psi}{\Gamma, \{\delta_i \prec \gamma_i\}_{i \leq n} \Rightarrow \varphi \prec \psi} \prec_n$$

This rule is sound, but does not provide a complete system: it is easy to check that one cannot prove the axiom Di with this rule.

has a regular NWiL-proof (Theorem 5), so NWiL can be used to construct a cyclic proof system with a local soundness condition.[12]

Let us close with an open problem. Recall the Hilbert system for iA given in the introduction. A natural way to extend this to $iL_\mu$ is by adding the axioms $\varphi(\mu X.\varphi(X)) \to \mu X.\varphi(X)$ and $\nu X.\varphi(X) \to \varphi(\nu X.\varphi(X))$ and the rules

$$\frac{\varphi(\psi) \to \psi}{\mu X.\varphi(X) \to \psi} \qquad \frac{\psi \to \varphi(\psi)}{\psi \to \nu X.\varphi(X)}$$

Is this extended Hilbert system complete for $iL_\mu$? Extrapolating from the classical case, one might hope for a positive answer. However, Walukiewicz's completeness proof [34] of Kozen's Hilbert system for the classical modal $\mu$-calculus is infamously involved, and seems to crucially depend on the existence of certain normal forms in classical modal logic. It is therefore unclear to us whether this proof strategy is adaptable to the intuitionistic case.

**Acknowledgments.** Funded by the Dutch Research Council [OCENW.M20.048] and the Knut and Alice Wallenberg Foundation [2020.0199]. We are grateful to Yde Venema for advice on the set-up of the game semantics and insights to simplify the proof of Theorem 3. We also thank the anonymous referees for their valuable feedback.

# References

1. Acclavio, M., Curzi, G., Guerrieri, G.: Infinitary cut-elimination via finite approximations. In: Murano, A., Silva, A. (eds.) 32nd EACSL Annual Conference on Computer Science Logic (CSL 2024). Leibniz International Proceedings in Informatics (LIPIcs), vol. 288, pp. 8:1–8:19. Schloss Dagstuhl – Leibniz-Zentrum für Informatik, Dagstuhl (2024). https://doi.org/10.4230/LIPIcs.CSL.2024.8
2. Aczel, P.: An introduction to inductive definitions. In: Handbook of Mathematical Logic, Studies in Logic and the Foundations of Mathematics, vol. 90, pp. 739–782. Elsevier (1977)
3. Afshari, B., Grotenhuis, L., Leigh, G.E., Zenger, L.: Ill-founded proof systems for intuitionistic linear-time temporal logic. In: Ramanayake, R., Urban, J. (eds.) TABLEAUX 2023. LNCS, vol. 14278, pp. 223–241. Springer, Cham (2023). https://doi.org/10.1007/978-3-031-43513-3_13
4. Afshari, B., Grotenhuis, L., Leigh, G.E., Zenger, L.: Intuitionistic master modality. In: Ciabattoni, A., Gabelaia, D., Sedlár, I. (eds.) Advances in Modal Logic, AiML 2024, Prague, Czech Republic, 19–23 August 2024, pp. 19–40. College Publications (2024)
5. Afshari, B., Leigh, G.E., Menéndez Turata, G.: Uniform interpolation from cyclic proofs: the case of modal mu-calculus. In: Das, A., Negri, S. (eds.) TABLEAUX 2021. LNCS (LNAI), vol. 12842, pp. 335–353. Springer, Cham (2021). https://doi.org/10.1007/978-3-030-86059-2_20

---

[12] This follows for example from Theorem 4.6 in [35] and the main result in [24]. However, the key idea in the construction, stems from [21].

6. Balbiani, P., Boudou, J., Diéguez, M., Fernández-Duque, D.: Intuitionistic linear temporal logics. ACM Trans. Comput. Logic **21**(2) (2019). https://doi.org/10.1145/3365833
7. Boudou, J., Diéguez, M., Fernández-Duque, D.: A decidable intuitionistic temporal logic. In: Goranko, V., Dam, M. (eds.) 26th EACSL Annual Conference on Computer Science Logic (CSL 2017). Leibniz International Proceedings in Informatics (LIPIcs), vol. 82, pp. 14:1–14:17. Schloss Dagstuhl–Leibniz-Zentrum fuer Informatik, Dagstuhl (2017). https://doi.org/10.4230/LIPIcs.CSL.2017.14
8. Boudou, J., Diéguez, M., Fernández-Duque, D.: Complete intuitionistic temporal logics for topological dynamics. J. Symb. Log. **87**(3), 995–1022 (2022)
9. Bradfield, J., Walukiewicz, I.: The mu-calculus and Model Checking. In: Clarke, E.M., Henzinger, T.A., Veith, H., Bloem, R. (eds.) Handbook of Model Checking, pp. 871–919. Springer, Cham (2018). https://doi.org/10.1007/978-3-319-10575-8_26
10. Curzi, G., Das, A.: Computational expressivity of (circular) proofs with fixed points. In: 2023 38th Annual ACM/IEEE Symposium on Logic in Computer Science (LICS), pp. 1–13. IEEE (2023)
11. Das, A., Marin, S.: On intuitionistic diamonds (and lack thereof). In: Ramanayake, R., Urban, J. (eds.) TABLEAUX 2023. LNCS, vol. 14278, pp. 283–301. Springer, Cham (2023). https://doi.org/10.1007/978-3-031-43513-3_16
12. Das, A., van der Giessen, I., Marin, S.: Intuitionistic Gödel-Löb logic, à la Simpson: labelled systems and birelational semantics. In: Murano, A., Silva, A. (eds.) 32nd EACSL Annual Conference on Computer Science Logic (CSL 2024), pp. 22:1–22:18. Leibniz International Proceedings in Informatics, LIPIcs, Schloss Dagstuhl (2024). https://doi.org/10.4230/LIPIcs.CSL.2024.22
13. Davies, R., Pfenning, F.: A modal analysis of staged computation. J. ACM **48**(3), 555–604 (2001). https://doi.org/10.1145/382780.382785
14. Demri, S., Goranko, V., Lange, M.: Temporal Logics in Computer Science: Finite-State Systems. Cambridge Tracts in Theoretical Computer Science. Cambridge University Press (2016). https://doi.org/10.1017/CBO9781139236119
15. Fernández-Duque, D.: The intuitionistic temporal logic of dynamical systems. Log. Methods Comput. Sci. **14** (2018)
16. Fortier, J., Santocanale, L.: Cuts for circular proofs: semantics and cut-elimination. In: Rocca, S.R.D. (ed.) Computer Science Logic 2013 (CSL 2013), CSL 2013, 2–5 September 2013, Torino, Italy. LIPIcs, vol. 23, pp. 248–262. Schloss Dagstuhl - Leibniz-Zentrum für Informatik (2013). https://doi.org/10.4230/LIPICS.CSL.2013.248
17. Iemhoff, R.: Preservativity logic: an analogue of interpretability logic for constructive theories. Math. Log. Q.: Math. Log. Q. **49**(3), 230–249 (2003)
18. Iemhoff, R.: Reasoning in circles. In: van Eijck, J., Iemhoff, R., Joosten, J.J. (eds.) Liber Amicorum Alberti: A Tribute to Albert Visser. College Publications (2016)
19. Iemhoff, R., Jongh, D., Zhou, C.: Properties of intuitionistic provability and preservativity logics. Log. J. IGPL **13**(6), 615–636 (2005)
20. Jäger, G., Marti, M.: Intuitionistic common knowledge or belief. J. Appl. Log. **18**, 150–163 (2016)
21. Jungteerapanich, N.: Tableau systems for the modal $\mu$-calculus. Ph.D. thesis, The University of Edinburgh (2010)
22. Kavvos, G.A.: The many worlds of modal $\lambda$-calculi: I. Curry–howard for necessity, possibility and time. arXiv preprint arXiv:1605.08106 (2016)
23. Kojima, K., Igarashi, A.: Constructive linear-time temporal logic: proof systems and kripke semantics. Inf. Comput. **209**(12), 1491–1503 (2011)

24. Leigh, G.E., Wehr, D.: From GTC to: generating reset proof systems from cyclic proof systems. Ann. Pure Appl. Logic 103485 (2024)
25. Lewis, C.I., Langford, C.H.: Symbolic Logic. Dover (1932)
26. Litak, T., Visser, A.: Lewis meets Brouwer: constructive strict implication. Indagationes Math. **29**(1), 36–90 (2018). https://doi.org/10.1016/j.indag.2017.10.003, https://www.sciencedirect.com/science/article/pii/S0019357717301167
27. Niwinski, D., Walukiewicz, I.: Games for the mu-calculus. Theoret. Comput. Sci. **163**(1&2), 99–116 (1996)
28. Pacheco, L.: Game semantics for the constructive $\mu$-calculus. arXiv preprint arXiv:2308.16697 (2024)
29. Ruitenburg, W.: On the period of sequences (an(p)) in intuitionistic propositional calculus. J. Symb. Log. **49**(3), 892–899 (1984)
30. Saurin, A.: A linear perspective on cut-elimination for non-wellfounded sequent calculi with least and greatest fixed-points. In: Ramanayake, R., Urban, J. (eds.) TABLEAUX 2023. LNCS, vol. 14278, pp. 203–222. Springer, Cham (2023). https://doi.org/10.1007/978-3-031-43513-3_12
31. Sierra-Miranda, B.: Cyclic proofs for iGL via corecursion. In: Fixed Points in Computer Science 2024 (2024). https://www.irif.fr/_media/users/saurin/fics2024/pre-proceedings/fics-2024-sierra-miranda.pdf
32. Venema, Y.: Lectures on the modal $\mu$-calculus (2024). https://staff.fnwi.uva.nl/y.venema/teaching/ml/notes/20241212-mu-coursenotes.pdf
33. Visser, A.: Propositional combinations of $\sigma$-sentences in Heyting's arithmetic. Utrecht Univ. Log. Group Preprint Ser. **117** (1994)
34. Walukiewicz, I.: Completeness of Kozen's axiomatisation of the propositional $\mu$-calculus. Inf. Comput. **157**(1–2), 142–182 (2000)
35. Wehr, D.: An abstract framework for the analysis of cyclic derivations. Master's thesis, University of Amsterdam (2021)

**Open Access** This chapter is licensed under the terms of the Creative Commons Attribution 4.0 International License (http://creativecommons.org/licenses/by/4.0/), which permits use, sharing, adaptation, distribution and reproduction in any medium or format, as long as you give appropriate credit to the original author(s) and the source, provide a link to the Creative Commons license and indicate if changes were made.

The images or other third party material in this chapter are included in the chapter's Creative Commons license, unless indicated otherwise in a credit line to the material. If material is not included in the chapter's Creative Commons license and your intended use is not permitted by statutory regulation or exceeds the permitted use, you will need to obtain permission directly from the copyright holder.

# Justification Logic for Intuitionistic Modal Logic

Sonia Marin[✉] and Paaras Padhiar[✉]

School of Computer Science, University of Birmingham, Birmingham, UK
s.marin@bham.ac.uk, pxp367@student.bham.ac.uk

**Abstract.** Justification logic is an explication of modal logic: boxes are replaced with proof terms formally through realisation theorems. This can be achieved syntactically using a cut-free proof system for a modal logic, e.g., using sequent, hypersequent, or nested sequent calculi. In constructive modal logic, boxes and diamonds are decoupled and not De Morgan dual. Previous work provides a justification counterpart to constructive modal logic CK (and some extensions) by making diamonds explicit and introducing new terms called satisfiers. We continue this line of work and provide a justification counterpart to intuitionistic modal logic IK and its extensions with the t and 4 axioms. We extend the syntax of proof terms to accommodate the additional axioms of intuitionistic modal logic and provide an axiomatisation of these justification logics with a syntactic realisation procedure using a cut-free nested sequent system for intuitionistic modal logic.

**Keywords:** Justification logic · Intuitionistic modal logic · Realisation theorem · Nested sequents

## 1 Introduction

Justification logics are a family of logics which refine modal logics by replacing modal operators with explicit *proof terms*. In a similar way to how a modal formula $\Box A$ can be read as *A is provable* in provability logics, it can be given an explicit justification counterpart $t{:}A$ for some proof term $t$, to be read as *there exists a proof $t$ of $A$*.

The first such justification logic is the Logic of Proofs, LP, introduced by Artemov [2,3] which is an explicitation of the modal logic S4. Artemov showed that this logic, which can be seen as provability semantics to intuitionistic logic (IPL) via the Gödel translation of IPL into S4, enjoys an arithmetic interpretation into Peano Arithmetic (PA). The formal connection between LP and S4 is made through a *realisation theorem*, which translates each theorem of S4 into a corresponding theorem of LP by *realising* every modalities with proof terms. The first realisation theorem was proved syntactically by Artemov using a cut-free sequent calculus for S4 and Fitting later provided an alternative semantic method [22].

LP was also further generalised, and realisation theorems were obtained for instance for the modal S5 cube and the family of Geach logics (see [7] for a survey) as Artemov's method for realisation can be adapted to modal logics if they have a cut-free sequent calculus (see [29]). Moreover, this syntactic method was expanded to more exotic cut-free proof systems: based on the formalism of hypersequents [9] and of nested sequents [12,15,25].

Since the early days of justification logic, there has been an interest in their intuitionistic variants, originally as a way to unify the treatment of terms between LP and the $\lambda$-calculus [4]. Another line of research that has brought justification logic into the realm of intuitionistic modal logics, is the investigation of the provability logic of Heyting Arithmetic (HA). Some propositions for an intuitionistic version of LP have been put forward in [8,18], as a building block towards a justification logic corresponding to HA in the way that LP corresponds to PA. Other intuitionistic variants of justification logics have been considered as a basis for type systems for computations that have access to some of their execution [44]. The semantics and the proof theory of some of these logics have also been partially studied [27,36,37]; however none of these work provide counterparts to an intuitionistic modal logic which contains both the box and the diamond modalities.

The first justification logic for an intuitionistic modal logic which makes the diamond explicit was postulated in [30] as a justification counterpart to *constructive modal logic* CK [10,11,42] via a syntactic realisation procedure. As $\Box$ is replaced by a proof term $t$; so is the diamond operator $\Diamond$ replaced with a *satisfier* term $\mu$.

We expand this line of work to provide a justification counterpart to the intuitionistic variant of modal logic IK, as defined originally by [19–21,39]. Interestingly, intuitionistic modal logic IK is remarkably more expressive than constructive modal logic CK as it not only provides more validities about the $\Diamond$ operator (in particular, that it is normal), but it also permits the derivation of more $\Diamond$-free theorems [17]. One such theorem is the Gödel-Gentzen (double-negation) translation, which makes for example the relationship of IK with classical K more akin to the relationship of HA with PA than could be obtained with CK, and is also more amenable to functional interpretations.

We present an axiomatisation of our justification counterpart to IK and extensions with the t and 4 axioms and establish a formal connection through a syntactic realisation procedure using a cut-free system for IK and extensions [45] using nested sequents [13,14,16,28,40,41].

## 2 Modal and Justification Logics

### 2.1 Intuitionistic Modal Logic

*Formulas* of intuitionistic modal logic, $\mathcal{L}_\Box$, are given by the grammar:

$$A ::= \bot \mid p \mid (A \wedge A) \mid (A \vee A) \mid (A \to A) \mid \Box A \mid \Diamond A$$

where $p$ ranges over a countable set of propositional atoms Prop. We will drop the outermost brackets when it is not required. We will assume $\wedge$ and $\vee$ are associative, $\wedge$ is commutative, and $\to$ is right associative.

| | | | | | | |
|---|---|---|---|---|---|---|
| $k_1$ | : | $\Box(A \to B) \to (\Box A \to \Box B)$ | $t_\Box$ | : | $\Box A \to A$ | |
| $k_2$ | : | $\Box(A \to B) \to (\Diamond A \to \Diamond B)$ | $t_\Diamond$ | : | $A \to \Diamond A$ | nec $\dfrac{\vdash A}{\vdash \Box A}$ |
| $k_3$ | : | $\Diamond(A \vee B) \to (\Diamond A \vee \Diamond B)$ | $4_\Box$ | : | $\Box A \to \Box \Box A$ | |
| $k_4$ | : | $(\Diamond A \to \Box B) \to \Box(A \to B)$ | $4_\Diamond$ | : | $\Diamond \Diamond A \to \Diamond A$ | |
| $k_5$ | : | $\Diamond \bot \to \bot$ | | | | |

**Fig. 1.** Intuitionistic modal axioms

| | |
|---|---|
| $\mathsf{jk}_1 : s{:}(A \to B) \to (t{:}A \to s \cdot t{:}B)$ | |
| $\mathsf{jk}_2 : s{:}(A \to B) \to (\mu{:}A \to s \star \mu{:}B)$ | $\mathsf{j}{+} : s{:}A \to (s+t){:}A$ $\quad \mathsf{jt}_\Box : t{:}A \to A$ |
| $\mathsf{jk}_3 : \mu{:}(A \vee B) \to (\mu{:}A \vee \mu{:}B)$ | $\mathsf{j}{+} : t{:}A \to (s+t){:}A$ $\quad \mathsf{jt}_\Diamond : A \to \mu{:}A$ |
| $\mathsf{jk}_4 : (\mu{:}A \to t{:}B) \to \mu \triangleright t{:}(A \to B)$ | $\mathsf{j}\sqcup : \mu{:}A \to (\mu \sqcup \nu){:}A$ $\quad \mathsf{j}4_\Box : t{:}A \to !t{:}t{:}A$ |
| $\mathsf{jk}_5 : \mu{:}\bot \to \bot$ | $\mathsf{j}\sqcup : \nu{:}A \to (\mu \sqcup \nu){:}A$ $\quad \mathsf{j}4_\Diamond : \mu{:}\nu{:}A \to \nu{:}A$ |

**Fig. 2.** Intuitionistic justification axioms.

On Fig. 1 we list the modal axioms that we consider in this work. *Constructive* modal logic CK [10] is an extension of intuitionistic propositional logic IPL with axioms $k_1$ and $k_2$ and the necessitation inference. *Intuitionistic* modal logic IK [19–21,39] is an extension of CK with axioms $k_3$, $k_4$ and $k_5$. We will also study extensions of IK: with axioms $t_\Box$ and $t_\Diamond$ to logic IT, with axioms $4_\Box$ and $4_\Diamond$ to logic IK4, and finally to logic IS4 with all four axioms.

### 2.2 Justification Logic

*Formulas* of intuitionistic justification logic, $\mathcal{L}_J$, are given by the grammar:

$$A ::= \bot \mid p \mid (A \wedge A) \mid (A \vee A) \mid (A \to A) \mid t{:}A \mid \mu{:}A$$

where $p$ ranges over a countable set propositional atoms Prop, $t$ ranges over *proof terms* PrfTm and $\mu$ ranges over *satisfiers* SatTm.

*Proof terms* $t, s, \ldots$ and *satisfiers* $\mu, \nu, \ldots$ are generated as follows:

$$t ::= x, y \mid c \mid (t+t) \mid (t \cdot t) \mid (\mu \triangleright t) \mid \, !t$$
$$\mu ::= \alpha, \beta \mid (\mu \sqcup \mu) \mid (t \star \mu)$$

where $x, y$ range over proof variables PrfVar, $\alpha, \beta$ over satisfier variables SatVar, and $c$ over proof constants PrfConst. A term is called *ground* if it contains neither proof nor satisfier variables. For a formula $A$, we write var($A$) for the set $\{x \in \mathsf{PrfVar} \mid x \text{ occurs in } A\} \cup \{\alpha \in \mathsf{SatVar} \mid svar \text{ occurs in } A\}$.

We define the *justification counterpart of modal logic* IK, which we call JIK, as the extension of IPL with axioms $\mathsf{jk}_1 - \mathsf{jk}_5$, $\mathsf{j}{+}$ and $\mathsf{j}\sqcup$ on Fig. 2, together with the *constant axiom necessitation rule*:

$$\text{can} \, \dfrac{}{c_n{:}\ldots{:}c_1{:}A}$$

where $c_1, \ldots, c_n \in \mathsf{PrfConst}$ and $A$ is any axiom instance in Fig. 2.

We furthermore define justification counterparts to the extensions of IK introduced previously using the additional axioms on Fig. 2:

$$\mathsf{JIT} = \mathsf{JIK} + \mathsf{jt}_\Box + \mathsf{jt}_\Diamond \quad \mathsf{JIK4} = \mathsf{JIK} + \mathsf{j4}_\Box + \mathsf{j4}_\Diamond \quad \mathsf{JIS4} = \mathsf{JIK} + \mathsf{jt}_\Box + \mathsf{jt}_\Diamond + \mathsf{j4}_\Box + \mathsf{j4}_\Diamond$$

The operations *proof sum* $+$, *application* $\cdot$ and *proof checker* $!$ are the standard justification operations relating to proof manipulations. To build intuition for the application operator, recall the $\mathsf{jk}_1$ axiom $s{:}(A \to B) \to (t{:}A \to s \cdot t{:}B)$. It internalises *modus ponens*, namely that a proof $t$ of $A$ and a proof $s$ of $A \to B$ can be composed to obtain a proof $s \cdot t$ of $B$.

The proof terms embed an abstract notion of *global reasoning* in the way that they assert the *validity* of statements wrt. any model. Satisfiers give us a seemingly dual notion of *local reasoning*, where $\mu{:}A$ could be read as $\mu$ is a *model* where $A$ is satisfied, or that $\mu$ asserts the *consistency* of $A$.

The operations on satisfiers of *propagation* $\star$ and *disjoint union* $\sqcup$ were introduced in [30]. The operation $\star$, which builds a satisfier from a proof term and a satisfier, can be seen as a combination of local and global reasoning, e.g., suppose that we have $\mu{:}A$, we can use the proof $t$ of $A \to (A \vee B)$ to locally establish $t \star \mu{:}(A \vee B)$ using axiom $\mathsf{jk}_2$. While $A \vee B$ is true whenever $A$ is, the justification used is different in that the former involves a valid transition from $A$ to $A \vee B$ justified by $t$. Hence, instead of using the same satisfier $\mu$, we record our reasoning in the new satisfier $t \star \mu$.

The operation $\sqcup$ is akin to that of a disjoint union of models. For sets, disjoint union is often defined $X \sqcup Y := (X \times \{0\}) \cup (Y \times \{1\})$ to create separate copies of $X$ and $Y$ to avoid intersection. We adopt the same notion to our disjoint model union. Any overlaps of $\mu$ and $\nu$ are resolved before the models are combined and no connection between the $\mu$ and $\nu$ parts of the satisfier $\mu \sqcup \nu$ exists.

In this work, we introduce the new operation of *local update* $\triangleright$ which carries the intuition that if local reasoning implies global reasoning, one can update this global reasoning with the local. Restating the $\mathsf{jk}_4$ axiom here, $(\mu{:}A \to t{:}B) \to \mu \triangleright t{:}(A \to B)$, the satisfier $\mu$ locally reasons about $A$ and implies the proof term $t$ globally reasoning about $B$, so this notion is *updated* into global reasoning about $A \to B$ being kept track by the proof term $\mu \triangleright t$.

### 2.3 From JL to L – and back

From now, we will write L for any logic in $\{\mathsf{IK}, \mathsf{IT}, \mathsf{IK4}, \mathsf{IS4}\}$ and JL for the corresponding logic in $\{\mathsf{JIK}, \mathsf{JIT}, \mathsf{JIK4}, \mathsf{JIS4}\}$. The main point of this work is to establish a syntactic correspondence between the logics introduced in previous sections.

**Definition 1 (Forgetful projection).** *The forgetful projection is a map*

$$(\cdot)^{\mathsf{f}} : \mathcal{L}_\mathsf{J} \to \mathcal{L}_\Box$$

*inductively defined as follows:*

$$\bot^{\mathsf{f}} := \bot \qquad\qquad (t{:}A)^{\mathsf{f}} := \Box A^{\mathsf{f}}$$
$$p^{\mathsf{f}} := p \qquad\qquad (\mu{:}A)^{\mathsf{f}} := \Diamond A^{\mathsf{f}}$$
$$(A * B)^{\mathsf{f}} := (A^{\mathsf{f}} * B^{\mathsf{f}}) \text{ where } * \in \{\wedge, \vee, \rightarrow\}$$

**Theorem 2.** *Let $A \in \mathcal{L}_\mathsf{J}$. If $\mathsf{JL} \vdash A$ then $\mathsf{L} \vdash A^{\mathsf{f}}$.*

*Proof.* This follows from the fact that the forgetful projection on axioms of JL and conclusions of the can rule are theorems of L.

**Definition 3 (Realisation).** *A realisation is a map $(\cdot)^r : \mathcal{L}_\Box \to \mathcal{L}_\mathsf{J}$ such that $(A^r)^{\mathsf{f}} = A$ for each $A \in \mathcal{L}_\Box$.*

**Theorem 4.** *Let $A \in \mathcal{L}_\Box$. If $\mathsf{L} \vdash A$, then there exists a realisation $r$ such that $\mathsf{JL} \vdash A^r$.*

The goal of this paper is to prove this theorem. We first need to introduce the main technical ingredients of the proof.

### 2.4 Realisation over Annotations

A subformula of A is *positive* if its position in the formula tree of A is reached from the root by following the left branch of an $\rightarrow$ an even number of times; otherwise it is called *negative*.

A realisation is *normal* if when $t : B$ (resp. $\mu : B$) is a negative subformula of $A^r$, then $t \in \mathsf{PrfVar}$ (resp. $\mu \in \mathsf{SatVar}$) and occurs in $A$ exactly once.

We follow and expand the methodology introduced in [25] using nested sequents to prove a realisation theorem. Due to the complexity of the sequent structure, some extra machinery is required to ensure a careful bookkeeping during the proof manipulations.

**Definition 5 (Annotated formula).** *Annotated formulas are built as in $\mathcal{L}_\Box$ but using annotated boxes $\Box_n$ and diamonds $\Diamond_n$ for $n \in \mathbb{N}$.
For an annotated formula A, define $\mathsf{ann}(A) := \{n \in \mathbb{N} \mid \Box_n \text{ or } \Diamond_n \text{ occurs in } A\}$.*

**Definition 6 (Properly annotated).** *A formula A is properly annotated if:*

- *modalities are annotated by pairwise distinct indexes;*
- *a $\Box$ (resp. $\Diamond$) is indexed by n iff $n = 0, 1 \mod 4$ (resp. $n = 2, 3 \mod 4$);*
- *a modality indexed by n occurs in a positive (resp. negative) position iff n is even (resp. odd).*

*The set of properly annotated formulas is denoted $\mathcal{L}_\Box^{\mathsf{ann}}$.*

For $\mathsf{L} \in \{\mathsf{IK}, \mathsf{IT}, \mathsf{IK4}, \mathsf{IS4}\}$, we will write $\mathsf{L} \vdash A$ for $A \in \mathcal{L}_\Box^{\mathsf{ann}}$, when the unannotated version of $A$ is a theorem of L.

We assume that we have fixed an enumeration of proof variables $\mathsf{PrfVar} = \{x_1, x_2, \ldots, y_1, y_2, \ldots\}$ and of satisfier variables $\mathsf{SatVar} = \{\alpha_1, \alpha_2, \ldots, \beta_1, \beta_2, \ldots\}$.

**Definition 7 (Realisation on annotations).** A realisation on annotations *is a partial function*
$$r : \mathbb{N} \to \mathsf{PrfTm} \cup \mathsf{SatTm}$$
where $r(4n) \in \mathsf{PrfTm}$, $r(4n+1) = x_n$, $r(4n+2) \in \mathsf{SatTm}$, $r(4n+3) = \alpha_n$ when defined. Denote the domain of $r$ as $\mathrm{dom}(r) := \{n \in \mathbb{N} \mid r(n) \text{ is defined}\}$.

Given $\mathrm{ann}(A) \subseteq \mathrm{dom}(r)$, denote $r|_A$ the restriction of the partial function $r$ onto the domain $\mathrm{ann}(A)$.

A realisation on annotations $r$ can be applied to an annotated formula $A$ such that $\mathrm{dom}(r) \subseteq \mathrm{ann}(A)$ inductively:

- $\bot^r := \bot$
- $p^r := p$
- $(A * B)^r := (A^r * B^r)$ where $* \in \{\wedge, \vee, \to\}$
- $(\square_n A)^r := r(n){:}A^r$
- $(\lozenge_n A)^r := r(n){:}A^r$ with the *satisfier self-referentiality restriction* that: if $n = 4k+3$, $\alpha_k$ does not occur in $A^r$. $(*)$

By first annotating properly all modalities occurring in it and then replacing each of them by the term $r(n)$ given by the realisation on annotations, we henceforth obtain a realisation $A^r$ for a formula $A \in \mathcal{L}_\square$, which is in particular *normal* and *restricted* (in the sense of the $(*)$ condition above).

Indeed, when a properly annotated formula $A \in \mathcal{L}_\square^{\mathrm{ann}}$ is realised through this algorithm, it fixes automatically some of the variables that occur in $A^r$. Namely, $\{x_n \in \mathsf{PrfVar} \mid \square_{4n+1} \text{ occurs in } A\} \cup \{\alpha_n \in \mathsf{SatVar} \mid \lozenge_{4n+3} \text{ occurs in } A\}$ designates a set of fixed variables, which we will call $\mathrm{negvar}(A)$.

The satisfier self-referentiality restriction is required when handling realisations over annotated formula. It will become apparent in the proof of Lemma 29.

## 3 Nested Sequent Calculus

A (full nested) sequent $\Gamma$ is comprised of two distinct parts: an LHS sequent $\Lambda$ and an RHS sequent $\Pi$. Formally, these sequents are unordered multisets generated from the following grammar:

$$\Lambda ::= \varnothing \mid A^\bullet \mid \langle \Lambda \rangle \mid \Lambda, \Lambda \qquad \Pi ::= A^\circ \mid [\Gamma] \qquad \Gamma ::= \Lambda, \Pi$$

where $A$ ranges over $\mathcal{L}_\square$. The dots can be seen as marking the polarity of a formula in a sequent: $\bullet$ represents the antecedent; $\circ$ represents the succedent – hence, the restriction of only one $\circ$-formula in a sequent $\Pi$ is a rendering of Gentzen's intuitionistic restriction [45].

The formula interpretation of nested sequents is defined as follows:

$\mathrm{form}(\varnothing) := \top$
$\mathrm{form}(A^\bullet) := A$
$\mathrm{form}(\langle \Lambda \rangle) := \lozenge \mathrm{form}(\Lambda)$
$\mathrm{form}(\Lambda_1, \Lambda_2) := \mathrm{form}(\Lambda_1) \wedge \mathrm{form}(\Lambda_2)$

$\mathrm{form}(A^\circ) := A$
$\mathrm{form}([\Gamma]) := \square \mathrm{form}(\Gamma)$
$\mathrm{form}(\Lambda, \Pi) := \mathrm{form}(\Lambda) \to \mathrm{form}(\Pi)$

**Definition 8 (Contexts).** *A context $\Delta\{\}$ is like a sequent but contains a hole wherever a formula may otherwise occur. We formally distinguish between* output *context $\Lambda\{\}$ and* input *context $\Gamma\{\}$:*

$$\Lambda\{\} ::= \{\} \mid \Lambda, \Lambda\{\} \mid \langle\Lambda\{\}\rangle \qquad \Gamma\{\} ::= \Lambda\{\}, \Pi \mid \Lambda, \Gamma\{\} \mid [\Gamma\{\}]$$

*Remark 9.* An *input context* $\Gamma\{\}$ contains an ∘-formula, so the hole only needs to be filled with a LHS sequent to give a sequent.
For example, if $\Gamma\{\} = \Lambda_1, [\langle\Lambda_2\rangle, \{\}, A^\circ]$, then $\Gamma\{\Lambda_3\} = \Lambda_1, [\langle\Lambda_2\rangle, \Lambda_3, A^\circ]$.
An *output context* $\Lambda\{\}$ on the other hand does not contain an ∘-formula, so if the hole is filled with a LHS sequent one simply gets a LHS sequent.
For example, if $\Lambda\{\} = \Lambda_1, \langle\langle\Lambda_2\rangle, \{\}\rangle$, then $\Lambda\{\Lambda_3\} = \Lambda_1, \langle\langle\Lambda_2\rangle, \Lambda_3\rangle$.
To obtain a sequent, the hole in $\Lambda\{\}$ needs to be filled with a sequent too. Furthermore, when doing so, note the need to flip some brackets from $\langle\cdot\rangle$ to $[\cdot]$ (along the path from the root to the hole).
For example, if $\Lambda\{\} = \Lambda_1, \langle\langle\Lambda_2\rangle, \{\}\rangle$, then $\Lambda\{\Lambda_3, A^\circ\} = \Lambda_1, [\langle\Lambda_2\rangle, \Lambda_3, A^\circ]$.

**Definition 10 (Depth).** *The depth of a context is defined inductively:*

$$\begin{aligned} \text{depth}(\{\}) &:= 0 & \text{depth}(\Lambda\{\}, \Pi) &:= \text{depth}(\Lambda\{\}) \\ \text{depth}(\Lambda_1, \Lambda_2\{\}) &:= \text{depth}(\Lambda_2\{\}) & \text{depth}(\Lambda, \Gamma\{\}) &:= \text{depth}(\Gamma\{\}) \\ \text{depth}(\langle\Lambda\{\}\rangle) &:= \text{depth}(\Lambda\{\}) + 1 & \text{depth}([\Gamma\{\}]) &:= \text{depth}(\Gamma\{\}) + 1 \end{aligned}$$

**Definition 11.** *For every input context $\Gamma\{\}$, its* output pruning $\Gamma^\downarrow\{\}$ *is an output context with the hole in the same position as $\Gamma\{\}$ but with the output formula in $\Gamma\{\}$ removed and brackets changed from $[\cdot]$ to $\langle\cdot\rangle$ as necessary. Formally,*

$$(\Lambda\{\}, \Pi)^\downarrow := \Lambda\{\}, \Pi^\downarrow \qquad (\Lambda, \Gamma\{\})^\downarrow := \Lambda, \Gamma^\downarrow\{\} \qquad ([\Gamma\{\}])^\downarrow := \langle\Gamma^\downarrow\{\}\rangle$$

*where $\Pi^\downarrow$ is given inductively by $(A^\circ)^\downarrow := \varnothing$ and $([\Lambda, \Pi])^\downarrow := \langle\Lambda, \Pi^\downarrow\rangle$.*

For example, if $\Gamma\{\} = \Lambda_1, [\langle\Lambda_2\rangle, \{\}, A^\circ]$, then $\Gamma^\downarrow\{\} = \Lambda_1, \langle\langle\Lambda_2\rangle, \{\}\rangle$.

The proof system nIK consists of the rules given in Fig. 3. The addition of the rules in Fig. 4 yields the proof systems $\mathsf{nL} \in \{\mathsf{nIK}, \mathsf{nIT}, \mathsf{nIK4}, \mathsf{nIS4}\}$ by picking and mixing rules corresponding to axioms t and 4.

A proof of a nested sequent $\Gamma$ in nL is constructed as trees from these rules with root $\Gamma$ and leaves closed by axiomatic rules; we then write $\mathsf{nL} \vdash \Gamma$.

**Theorem 12 (Straßburger [45]).** *Let $\mathsf{L} \in \{\mathsf{IK}, \mathsf{IT}, \mathsf{IK4}, \mathsf{IS4}\}$. For $A \in \mathcal{L}_\square$:*

$$\mathsf{L} \vdash A \iff \mathsf{nL} \vdash A^\circ$$

The completeness is proved via a cut-elimination argument where the cut rule is of the shape

$$\text{cut} \frac{\Gamma^\downarrow\{A^\circ\} \quad \Gamma\{A^\bullet\}}{\Gamma\{\varnothing\}}$$

$$\bot^\bullet \frac{}{\Gamma\{\bot^\bullet\}} \qquad \text{id} \frac{}{\Lambda\{p^\bullet, p^\circ\}}$$

$$c^\bullet \frac{\Gamma\{\Lambda, \Lambda\}}{\Gamma\{\Lambda\}} \qquad \wedge^\bullet \frac{\Gamma\{A^\bullet, B^\bullet\}}{\Gamma\{A \wedge B^\bullet\}} \qquad \wedge^\circ \frac{\Lambda\{A^\circ\} \quad \Gamma\{B^\circ\}}{\Lambda\{A \wedge B^\circ\}}$$

$$\vee^\bullet \frac{\Gamma\{A^\bullet\} \quad \Gamma\{B^\bullet\}}{\Gamma\{A \vee B^\bullet\}} \qquad \vee^\circ_1 \frac{\Lambda\{A^\circ\}}{\Lambda\{A \vee B^\circ\}} \qquad \vee^\circ_2 \frac{\Lambda\{B^\circ\}}{\Lambda\{A \vee B^\circ\}}$$

$$\rightarrow^\bullet \frac{\Gamma^+\{A^\circ\} \quad \Gamma\{B^\bullet\}}{\Gamma\{A \rightarrow B^\bullet\}} \qquad \rightarrow^\circ \frac{\Lambda\{A^\bullet, B^\circ\}}{\Lambda\{A \rightarrow B^\circ\}}$$

$$\Box^\bullet_{[\cdot]} \frac{\Lambda\{[A^\bullet, \Gamma]\}}{\Lambda\{\Box A^\bullet, [\Gamma]\}} \qquad \Box^\bullet_{\langle\cdot\rangle} \frac{\Gamma\{\langle A^\bullet, \Lambda\rangle\}}{\Gamma\{\Box A^\bullet, \langle\Lambda\rangle\}} \qquad \Box^\circ \frac{\Lambda\{[A^\circ]\}}{\Lambda\{\Box A^\circ\}}$$

$$\Diamond^\bullet \frac{\Gamma\{\langle A^\bullet\rangle\}}{\Gamma\{\Diamond A^\bullet\}} \qquad \Diamond^\circ \frac{\Lambda_1\{[A^\circ, \Lambda_2]\}}{\Lambda_1\{\Diamond A^\circ, \langle\Lambda_2\rangle\}}$$

**Fig. 3.** System nIK.

$$t^\bullet \frac{\Gamma\{A^\bullet\}}{\Gamma\{\Box A^\bullet\}} \qquad t^\circ \frac{\Lambda\{A^\circ\}}{\Lambda\{\Diamond A^\circ\}}$$

$$4^\bullet_{[\cdot]} \frac{\Lambda\{[\Box A^\bullet, \Gamma]\}}{\Lambda\{\Box A^\bullet, [\Gamma]\}} \qquad 4^\bullet_{\langle\cdot\rangle} \frac{\Gamma\{\langle\Box A^\bullet, \Lambda\rangle\}}{\Gamma\{\Box A^\bullet, \langle\Lambda\rangle\}} \qquad 4^\circ \frac{\Lambda_1\{[\Diamond A^\circ, \Lambda_2]\}}{\Lambda_1\{\Diamond A^\circ, \langle\Lambda_2\rangle\}}$$

**Fig. 4.** Modal rules for t and 4.

Cut-freeness is in fact a critical property to use a proof system for a syntactic realisation result, see [6, Chapter 8.8] for details.

Another key detail concerns the use of an explicit contraction rule, which the system in [45] does not use, as it is admissible due to the shape of the rules. For the purposes of our work, we require to decouple contraction from the rules similarly to the system in [35].

*Example 13.* This is an example of a proof in nIK:

$$\rightarrow^\circ \frac{\Box^\bullet \frac{\bot^\bullet \frac{}{\bot^\circ, \langle\bot^\bullet\rangle}}{\Box\bot^\bullet, \bot^\circ, \langle\varnothing\rangle}}{\rightarrow^\bullet \frac{\Box\bot \rightarrow \bot^\circ, \langle\varnothing\rangle \quad \bot^\bullet \frac{}{\bot^\bullet, [\bot^\circ]}}{\Box^\circ \frac{(\Box\bot \rightarrow \bot) \rightarrow \bot^\bullet, [\bot^\circ]}{\rightarrow^\circ \frac{((\Box\bot \rightarrow \bot) \rightarrow \bot)^\bullet, \Box\bot^\circ}{((\Box\bot \rightarrow \bot) \rightarrow \bot) \rightarrow \Box\bot^\circ}}}}$$

Note that this is a theorem of IK but not of CK [17]. We will expand this example later to illustrate how our system allows us to provide a realisation of it.

## 3.1 Annotated Sequents

**Definition 14 (Annotated sequents).** *An annotated sequent/context is a sequent/context in which only annotated formulas occur, and brackets $[\cdot]$ and $\langle \cdot \rangle$ are indexed by some $n \in \mathbb{N}$, written $[\cdot]_n$ and $\langle \cdot \rangle_n$.*

$$\mathrm{form}(\langle \Lambda \rangle_n) := \Diamond_n \mathrm{form}(\Lambda) \qquad \mathrm{form}([\Gamma]_n) := \Box_n \mathrm{form}(\Gamma)$$

Most definitions for annotated formulas and for nested sequents transfer directly to annotated sequents. However, the concept of output pruning requires some careful handling as not only the brackets need to be possibly flipped, but their annotations need to be accordingly and appropriately changed as well.

For example, if $\Gamma\{\} = \langle \Lambda_1, \{\} \rangle_{4k+3}, [\Lambda_2, C^\circ]_{4n}$, then for some $m \in \mathbb{N}$ and a re-annotated version of $\Lambda_2$ given as $\Lambda'_2$, we define $\Gamma^\downarrow\{\} = \langle \Lambda_1, \{\} \rangle_{4k+3}, \langle \Lambda'_2 \rangle_{4m+3}$. Finally, $\Gamma^\downarrow\{A^\circ\} = [\Lambda_1, A^\circ]_{4l}, \langle \Lambda'_2 \rangle_{4m+3}$ for some $l \in \mathbb{N}$. This is necessary to ensure square brackets are annotated by even numbers and angle brackets by odd numbers.

The annotated rules are also mainly the same as the ones without annotations. The contraction rule, however, applies in principle to the same sequent, but needs to distinguish annotations, that is, it should be written:

$$\mathsf{c} \bullet \frac{\Gamma\{\Lambda_1, \Lambda_2\}}{\Gamma\{\Lambda_3\}}$$

where $\Lambda_1$, $\Lambda_2$ and $\Lambda_3$ represent the same unannotated sequent but do not share annotation indices.

The subtlety of the annotated output pruning is key to the $\to^\bullet$-rule.

*Example 15.* This is illustrated on the following instance of $\to^\bullet$:

$$\to^\bullet \frac{[\Lambda_1, A^\circ]_{4l}, \langle \Lambda'_2 \rangle_{4m+3} \qquad \langle \Lambda_1, B^\bullet \rangle_{4k+3}, [\Lambda''_2, C^\circ]_{4n}}{\langle \Lambda_1, A \to B^\bullet \rangle_{4k+3}, [\Lambda_2, C^\circ]_{4n}}$$

where $\Lambda_2, \Lambda'_2, \Lambda''_2$ represent the same unannotated sequent but do not share annotations.

From now on, a nested sequent system nL will casually refer to the annotated version. We note that Theorem 12 also holds for the annotated case – for any unannotated derivation in the nested sequent system, properly annotate the endsequent and propagate the annotations upwards.

*Example 16.* Proof from Example 13 in an annotated version:

$$\to^\circ \cfrac{\to^\circ \cfrac{\Box^\circ \cfrac{\to^\bullet \cfrac{\Box^\bullet_{\langle \cdot \rangle} \cfrac{\bot^\bullet \cfrac{}{\bot^\circ, \langle \bot^\bullet \rangle_3}}{\Box_1 \bot^\bullet, \bot^\circ, \langle \varnothing \rangle_3}}{\Box_1 \bot \to \bot^\circ, \langle \varnothing \rangle_3} \qquad \bot^\bullet \cfrac{}{\bot^\bullet, [\bot^\circ]_0}}{(\Box_1 \bot \to \bot) \to \bot^\bullet, [\bot^\circ]_0}}{((\Box_1 \bot \to \bot) \to \bot)^\bullet, \Box_0 \bot^\circ}}{((\Box_1 \bot \to \bot) \to \bot) \to \Box_0 \bot^\circ}$$

We observe moreover that the soundness of the $\to^\bullet$ rule combines modal reasoning for the $k_4$ axiom and propositional reasoning for implication. It is helpful in the realisation proof to decouple these two aspects and replace each occurrence of $\to^\bullet$ in a proof with a macro rule composed of $\to^\bullet_s$, $\triangleright$ and $c^\bullet$ rules:

$$\to^\bullet_s \frac{\Lambda_1\{\Lambda_2\{A^\circ\}, \Lambda\} \quad \Lambda_1\{\Lambda_2\{B^\bullet\}, \Pi\}}{\Lambda_1\{\Lambda_2\{A \to B^\bullet\}, \Lambda, \Pi\}} \qquad \triangleright \frac{\Gamma\{\langle\Lambda_1\rangle_{4k+3}, [\Lambda_2, \Pi]_{4n}\}}{\Gamma\{[\Lambda_1, \Lambda_2, \Pi]_{4n}\}}$$

where $\Lambda_1$ and $\Lambda_2$ are annotated LHS sequents and $\Pi$ is an annotated RHS sequent. The soundness of the $\to^\bullet_s$ rule only makes use of basic modal reasoning and propositional reasoning for implication and the soundness of the $\triangleright$ rule makes use of the $k_4$ axiom. For a detailed proof of how an occurrence of the $\to^\bullet$ rule is replaced, the reader is referred to [34].

*Example 17.* We rewrite the annotated rule instance of Example 15 with these macro rules:

$$\to^\bullet_s \frac{[\Lambda_1, A^\circ]_{4l}, \langle\Lambda'_2\rangle_{4m+3} \quad \langle\Lambda_1, B^\bullet\rangle_{4k+3}, [\Lambda''_2, C^\circ]_{4n}}{\triangleright \frac{\langle\Lambda_1, A \to B^\bullet\rangle_{4k+3}, \langle\Lambda'_2\rangle_{4m+3}, [\Lambda''_2, C^\circ]_{4n}}{c^\bullet \frac{\langle\Lambda_1, A \to B^\bullet\rangle_{4k+3}, [\Lambda'_2, \Lambda''_2, C^\circ]_{4n}}{\langle\Lambda_1, A \to B^\bullet\rangle_{4k+3}, [\Lambda_2, C^\circ]_{4n}}}}$$

where the contraction rule $c^\bullet$ applies to the LHS sequents $\Lambda'_2, \Lambda''_2$ to obtain a differently annotated sequent $\Lambda_2$ but all representing the same sequent. Reading the derivation bottom-up, we note that the annotations of brackets on the left premiss of the $\to^\bullet_s$ are changed to accommodate the change of bracket type.

## 4 Realisation Theorem

A realisation can be extended to an annotated sequent $\Sigma$ as $\Sigma^r := \text{form}(\Sigma)^r$.

The goal of this section is to prove the following theorem.

**Theorem 18 (Realisation Theorem).** *Let* $L \in \{IK, IT, IK4, IS4\}$. *Let* $\Gamma$ *be an annotated sequent. If*

$$nL \vdash \Gamma$$

*then there exists a realisation function $r$ on $\Gamma$ such that*

$$JL \vdash \Gamma^r$$

The high-level idea is to systematically scan through the proof of $\Gamma$ top down. In the leaves, a basic realisation is given to any axiomatic sequent $\Sigma$ defined as:

$$\text{for any } n \text{ an annotation in } \Sigma, \ r(n) := \begin{cases} y_m & \text{if } n = 4m \\ x_m & \text{if } n = 4m+1 \\ \beta_m & \text{if } n = 4m+2 \\ \alpha_m & \text{if } n = 4m+3 \end{cases}$$

*Example 19.* On the annotated proof from Example 16, at each stage of the proof, the realisation procedure will yields a justification formula for each sequent in the derivation tree. These formulas can be linked by derivations in the Hilbert system of the justification logics. The variables $y_i$ and $\beta_j$ are step-by-step substituted top-down by larger and larger terms according to the JL axioms.

$$\cfrac{\cfrac{\cfrac{\cfrac{\cfrac{\cfrac{\bot^\bullet}{\alpha_0{:}\bot \to \bot}}{(\alpha_0{:}\top \land x_0{:}\bot) \to \bot} \Box^\bullet}{\alpha_0{:}\top \to (x_0{:}\bot \to \bot)} \to^\circ \quad \cfrac{\bot^\bullet}{\bot \to y_0{:}\bot}}{((x_0{:}\bot \to \bot) \to \bot) \to t(\alpha_0 \triangleright y_0){:}\bot} \to^\bullet}{((x_0{:}\bot \to \bot) \to \bot) \to t(\alpha_0 \triangleright y_0){:}\bot} \Box^\circ}{((x_0{:}\bot \to \bot) \to \bot) \to t(\alpha_0 \triangleright y_0){:}\bot} \to^\circ$$

The proof term $t(\alpha_k \triangleright y_m)$ will be constructed from the steps given in Lemma 26. Using the $\mathsf{jk}_4$ axiom

$$\mathsf{JL} \vdash (\alpha_k{:}\top \to y_m{:}\bot) \to \alpha_k \triangleright y_m{:}(\top \to \bot)$$

and using the Lifting Lemma 21 on the propositional theorem

$$\mathsf{JL} \vdash (\top \to \bot) \to \bot$$

there exists a proof term $t(\alpha_k \triangleright y_m)$ such that

$$\mathsf{JL} \vdash \alpha_k \triangleright y_m{:}(\top \to \bot) \to t(\alpha_k \triangleright y_m){:}\bot$$

In the following subsections we will provide some of the key lemmas that allow us to eventually complete the realisation proof. They all apply for any $\mathsf{JL} \in \{\mathsf{JIK}, \mathsf{JIT}, \mathsf{JIK4}, \mathsf{JIS4}\}$.

### 4.1 Lifting

**Lemma 20 (Internalised neccessitation).** *Let $A \in \mathcal{L}_\mathsf{J}$. If $\mathsf{JL} \vdash A$, then there exists a ground term $t$ such that $\mathsf{JL} \vdash t{:}A$.*

*Proof.* The proof is the same as the classical case. Example proofs can be found in [6,33]. □

**Lemma 21 (Lifting Lemma).** *Let $B_1, \ldots, B_n, C, A \in \mathcal{L}_\mathsf{J}$ for some $n \in \mathbb{N}$.*

1. *If $\mathsf{JL} \vdash B_1 \to B_2 \to \ldots \to B_n \to A$, then for proof terms $s_1, \ldots, s_n$, there exists a proof term $t(s_1, \ldots, s_n)$ such that*

$$\mathsf{JL} \vdash s_1{:}B_1 \to \ldots \to s_n{:}B_n \to t(s_1, \ldots, s_n){:}A$$

2. *If $\mathsf{JL} \vdash B_1 \to B_2 \to \ldots \to B_n \to C \to A$, then for proof terms $s_1, \ldots, s_n$ and satisfier $\nu$, there exists a satisfier $\mu(s_1, \ldots, s_n, \nu)$ such that*

$$\mathsf{JL} \vdash s_1{:}B_1 \to \ldots \to s_n{:}B_n \to \nu{:}C \to \mu(s_1, \ldots, s_n, \nu){:}A$$

*Proof.* A proof of 1. can be found in [6,33]. A proof of 2. can be found in [30]. The proof is not sensitive to the additional axioms and operators used here. □

## 4.2 Merging

**Definition 22 (Substitution).** *A substitution is a map* $\sigma$ : PrfVar $\to$ PrfTm *and* $\sigma$ : SatVar $\to$ SatTm. *Substitutions can then be inductively extended to* PrfTm, SatTm *and* $\mathcal{L}_J$ *as standard. We will write* $\chi\sigma$ *for* $\sigma(\chi)$ *for some* $\chi \in$ PrfTm $\cup$ SatTm $\cup \mathcal{L}_J$.

*The domain of* $\sigma$ *is the set* $dom(\sigma) := \{\chi \in$ PrfVar $\cup$ SatVar $\mid \chi\sigma \neq \chi\}$.

**Lemma 23 (Substitution Lemma).** *Let* $A \in \mathcal{L}_J$. *Let* $\sigma$ *be a substitution. If* JL $\vdash A$, *then* JL $\vdash A\sigma$.

*Proof.* This is a routine proof which follows precisely from the fact that given any axiom instance $A$, $A\sigma$ is an axiom instance, and hence, for a conclusion of the can rule $c_n{:}\ldots{:}c_1{:}A$, the result of applying a substitution on it: $(c_n{:}\ldots{:}c_1{:}A)\sigma = c_n{:}\ldots{:}c_1{:}(A\sigma)$ is a conclusion of the can rule. □

**Theorem 24 (Realisation merging).** *Let* $A \in \mathcal{L}_\square^{\mathsf{ann}}$. *Let* $r_1$ *and* $r_2$ *be realisations on* $A$. *Then there exists a realisation function* $r$ *on* $A$ *and a substitution* $\sigma$ *such that:*

1. *For every positive subformula* $X$ *of* $A$, JL $\vdash X^{r_1}\sigma \to X^{r_2}\sigma \to X^r$
2. *For every negative subformula* $X$ *of* $A$, JL $\vdash X^r \to X^{r_i}\sigma$ *where* $i \in \{1,2\}$.

*where* $dom(\sigma) \subseteq negvar(A)$ *and* $x\sigma$ *contains no new variables for each* $x$.

*Proof.* This is an adaptation of Fitting [23,24]. The original proof is in the setting of classical Logic of Proofs but does not make use of classical reasoning or the $\mathsf{jt}_\square$ and $\mathsf{j4}_\square$ axioms. The proof can be adapted to deal with satisfiers and has a similar treatment to proof terms, with $\sqcup$ playing for satisfiers the role played by $+$ for proof terms. □

These notions are similarly extended to annotated sequents.

**Corollary 25.** *Let* $\Gamma$ *be an annotated sequent and* $\Lambda$ *an annotated LHS sequent. Let* $r_1$ *and* $r_2$ *be realisation functions. Then there exists a realisation function* $r$ *and a substitution* $\sigma$ *such that:*

1. JL $\vdash \Gamma^{r_1}\sigma \to \Gamma^{r_2}\sigma \to \Gamma^r$ *where* $dom(\sigma) \subseteq negvar(\Gamma)$ *and* $x\sigma$ *contains no new variables*
2. JL $\vdash \Lambda^r \to \Lambda^{r_i}\sigma$ *where* $i \in \{1,2\}$, $dom(\sigma) \subseteq negvar(\Gamma)$ *and* $x\sigma$ *contains no new variables.*

## 4.3 Proving Realisation

Given an instance of a rule $\in \{\text{id}, \wedge^\circ, \vee^\circ, \rightarrow^\circ, \Box^\circ, \Diamond^\circ, \Box^\bullet_{[\cdot]}, \text{t}^\circ, 4^\circ, 4^\bullet_{[\cdot]}, \triangleright\}$, for some $k \leq 2$, it will be of the shape:

$$\text{rule} \; \frac{\Lambda\{\Gamma_1\} \quad \cdots \quad \Lambda\{\Gamma_k\}}{\Lambda\{\Gamma_0\}}$$

As these rules behave similarly to classical rules, following [25] we can show:

**Lemma 26.** *For any realisations $r_i$ on $\Lambda\{\Gamma_i\}$ for $i \leq k$, there exist a realisation $r$ on $\Lambda\{\Gamma_0\}$ and substitutions $\sigma_i$ for $i \leq k$, such that*

$$\mathsf{JL} \vdash (\Lambda\{\Gamma_1\}^{r_1}\sigma_1 \wedge \ldots \wedge \Lambda\{\Gamma_k\}^{r_k}\sigma_k) \rightarrow \Lambda\{\Gamma_0\}^r$$

*Proof (Sketch).* We proceed by induction on $\Lambda\{\}$. See [34] for the full details.

The base case, $\Lambda = \varnothing$, relies on a bespoke proof for each specific rule. These are similar to the classical case for id, $\vee^\circ, \wedge^\circ$ and $\rightarrow^\circ$. Note the particular case of id where the empty conjunction reduces and the particular case of $\wedge^\circ$ whose branching requires the merging property (Theorem 24). However, rules that involve a $\Diamond$-formula (or $\langle \cdot \rangle$-brackets) require a novel treatment as they should introduce satisfier terms, rather than the classical treatment through duality with $\Box$ which would only introduce proof terms.

The inductive cases, $\Lambda = \Lambda^\bullet, \Lambda'$ and $\Lambda = \langle \Lambda' \rangle$, follow the shallow-to-deep approach first devised in [25] but using intuitionistic reasoning and applying lifting (Lemma 21) for both proof and satisfier terms. □

Given an instance of a rule $\in \{\bot^\bullet, \vee^\bullet, \wedge^\bullet, \Box^\bullet, \Diamond^\bullet, \rightarrow^\bullet_s, \mathsf{c}^\bullet, \mathsf{t}^\bullet, 4^\bullet\}$, for some $k \leq 2$, it will be of the shape:

$$\text{rule} \; \frac{\Gamma\{\Lambda_1\} \quad \cdots \quad \Gamma\{\Lambda_k\}}{\Gamma\{\Lambda_0\}}$$

This can be further refined depending of the precise position of the $\Lambda_i$ within context $\Gamma\{\}$. If the principal formula is among the LHS part of $\Gamma\{\}$, the rule can be rewritten:

$$\text{rule} \; \frac{\Lambda\{\Lambda_1\}, \Pi \quad \cdots \quad \Lambda\{\Lambda_k\}, \Pi}{\Lambda\{\Lambda_0\}, \Pi}$$

In this case, we get the following upside-down reading of the previous lemma:

**Lemma 27.** *For any realisations $r_i$ on $\Lambda\{\Lambda_i\}$ for $i \leq k$, there exist a realisation $r$ on $\Lambda\{\Lambda_0\}$ and substitutions $\sigma_i$ for $i \leq k$, such that*

$$\mathsf{JL} \vdash \Lambda\{\Lambda_0\}^r \rightarrow (\Lambda\{\Lambda_1\}^{r_1}\sigma_1 \vee \ldots \vee \Lambda\{\Lambda_k\}^{r_k}\sigma_k)$$

*Proof (Sketch).* As before, this proceeds by induction on $\Lambda\{\}$. See [34] for details. Again, in the case of the axiomatic $\bot^\bullet$, the empty disjunction reduces to $\bot$, and in the case of the branching $\vee^\bullet$, merging (Theorem 24) is required to reconcile the realisations of the branches. The details for $\vee^\bullet$ are given as Lemma 29 in Appendix; it also illustrate the need for the *diamond self-referential restriction*. □

On the other hand, if the principal formula is among the RHS of $\Gamma\{\}$, rule presents itself as

$$\text{rule} \frac{\Lambda, \Pi\{\Lambda_1\} \quad \cdots \quad \Lambda, \Pi\{\Lambda_k\}}{\Lambda, \Pi\{\Lambda_0\}}$$

which lets us prove a similar lemma to the classical case and Lemma 26:

**Lemma 28.** *For any realisations $r_i$ on $\Lambda\{\Gamma_i\}$ for $i \leq k$, there exist a realisation $r$ on $\Lambda\{\Gamma_0\}$ and substitutions $\sigma_i$ for $i \leq k$, such that*

$$\mathsf{JL} \vdash (\Pi\{\Lambda_1\}^{r_1}\sigma_1 \wedge \ldots \wedge \Pi\{\Lambda_k\}^{r_k}\sigma_k) \to \Pi\{\Lambda_0\}^r$$

*Proof (Sketch).* The proof proceeds by induction on $\Pi\{\}$. See all details in [34]. The base case, when $\Pi\{\} = A^\circ, \{\}$ for some $A \in \mathcal{L}_\square^{\mathsf{ann}}$, depends on the logical content of each rule. The inductive case, when $\Pi = [\Gamma\{\}]$, is where the complexity resides. Indeed, it presents the same dichotomy as described above, where the principal formula can occur in the LHS or the RHS of $\Gamma\{\}$. In the latter, the inductive hypothesis applies readily, while in the former, we need Lemma 27 to conclude. The details for $\vee^\bullet$ are given as Lemma 30 in Appendix. □

Finally, putting all the ingredients together,

*Proof (Proof of Theorem 18).* We proceed by induction on the structure of the proof $\pi$ of $\Gamma$ in nL. For the base case, $\Gamma$ is a conclusion of the id or $\perp^\bullet$ rule. For the inductive case, $\Gamma$ is the conclusion of the following rule rule

$$\text{rule} \frac{\overset{\pi_1}{\nabla} \quad \overset{\pi_i}{\nabla}}{\Gamma_1 \quad \cdots \quad \Gamma_i}$$

for smaller proofs $\pi_1, \ldots, \pi_k$ and premisses $\Gamma_1, \ldots, \Gamma_k$ where $i \in \{1, \ldots, k\}$. By the inductive hypothesis, we have realisations $r_i$ on $\Gamma_i$ such that

$$\mathsf{JL} \vdash \Gamma_i^{r_i}$$

Applying Lemma 26 or 27 corresponding to the rule rule, there exists a realisation $r$ on $\Gamma$ and substitutions $\sigma_1, \ldots, \sigma_i$ (which can be Id if not mentioned in the Lemmas) such that

$$\mathsf{JL} \vdash (\Gamma_1^{r_1}\sigma_1 \wedge \ldots \wedge \Gamma_i^{r_i}\sigma_i) \to \Gamma^r$$

or equivalently

$$\mathsf{JL} \vdash \Gamma_1^{r_1}\sigma_1 \to \ldots \to \Gamma_i^{r_i}\sigma_i \to \Gamma^r$$

By the Substitution Lemma 23

$$\mathsf{JL} \vdash \Gamma_j^{r_j}\sigma_j$$

for each $j \in \{1, \ldots, i\}$. Using modus ponens, we achieve

$$\mathsf{JL} \vdash \Gamma^r$$

□

We thus obtain the realisation theorem as a corollary:

*Proof (Proof of Theorem 4).* By Theorem 12, there is a nested sequent derivation of $A^\circ$ and we apply Theorem 18 to construct a realisation. □

## 5 Conclusion and Future Work

We have presented a justification counterpart for intuitionistic modal logic, with a modified merging theorem for realisations and a method for a realisation theorem using intuitionistic nested sequents. This method should be adaptable to other cut-free nested sequent systems, e.g., for the IS5 cube [35,45], and to some logics of the CS5 cube [1] – the challenge here being finding suitable justification counterparts for other modal axioms of the cube.

The restriction of only one output formula in the nested sequent system can be removed to recover a proof system for the modal logics over a classical base [31]. The method of realisation presented in this work can also be adapted to this system. It would provide an alternative realisation result for classical modal logics, this time with both □ and ◇ being made explicit. Given that IK and its extensions satisfy Simpson's requirements [43], namely the addition of the law of excluded middle recovers the corresponding classical modal logic, this could provide an axiomatic direction to understanding a classical version of satisfiers.

Justification logic for classical modal logic can be understood semantically over various classes of models [5,22,32,38]. Some of these have been adapted to a basic constructive setting, with no ◇-modalities, in [36] using birelational models, which are standardly used for intuitionistic/constructive modal logics [43]. These could therefore provide a starting point to understand justification logics for CK [30] and for IK (this work) semantically. There could furthermore be a way to understand the $jk_3, jk_4, jk_5$ axioms modularly similar to the case in intuitionistic modal logic [26].

Logic of Proofs LP, i.e., the justification logic for classical modal logic S4, is in particular complete with respect to an arithmetic interpretation into PA [2]. Previous investigations towards justification logics interpretable into HA were performed without the ◇-modality and required heavy machinery to recover the full power of HA. We know however that by adding ◇-modalities we at least regain access to the Gödel-Gentzen (double-negation) translation. It would be interesting to compare the strength of the justification logic we obtained here for IS4 wrt. arithmetical completeness, and whether we can make progress towards an intuitionitic logic of proofs ILP.

## A  Appendix

We illustrate the technicalities required in the proof of the realisation theorem on the case of the $\vee^\bullet$ rule.

**Lemma 29 (Lemma 27 for $\vee^\bullet$).** *Given realisation functions $r_1$ on $\Lambda\{A^\bullet\}$ and $r_2$ on $\Lambda\{B^\bullet\}$, there exist a substitution $\sigma$ with $\text{dom}(\sigma) \subseteq \text{negvar}(\Lambda\{A \vee B^\bullet\})$ and a realisation function $r$ on $\Lambda\{A \vee B^\bullet\}$ such that*

$$\mathsf{JL} \vdash \Lambda\{A \vee B^\bullet\}^r \to (\Lambda\{A^\bullet\}^{r_1}\sigma \vee \Lambda\{B^\bullet\}^{r_2}\sigma)$$

*Proof.* We proceed by induction on the depth of $\Lambda\{\}$.

For the base case, $\Lambda\{\} = \Lambda_0, \{\}$ for some annotated LHS sequent $\Lambda_0$. Using Theorem 24 and Corollary 25 there exist a realisation $r$ and substitution $\sigma$ such that $\Lambda_0^r \to \Lambda_0^{r_i}\sigma$, $A^r \to A^{r_1}\sigma$ and $B^r \to B^{r_2}\sigma$ are theorems of JL. It follows by propositional reasoning that

$$\mathsf{JL} \vdash (\Lambda_0, A \vee B^\bullet)^r \to ((\Lambda_0, A^\bullet)^{r_1}\sigma \vee (\Lambda_0, B^\bullet)^{r_2}\sigma)$$

since $(\Lambda_0, A \vee B^\bullet)^r = (\Lambda_0^r \wedge (A^r \vee B^r))$ and $(\Lambda_0, A^\bullet)^{r_i}\sigma = (\Lambda_0^{r_i}\sigma \wedge A^{r_i}\sigma)$ for each $i \in \{1, 2\}$.

For the inductive case, $\Lambda\{\ \} = \Lambda_0, \langle \Lambda_1\{\ \} \rangle_{4i+3}$ for some annotated LHS sequent $\Lambda_0$. By the inductive hypothesis, there exist a realisation $r'$ on $\Lambda_1\{A \vee B^\bullet\}$ and substitution $\sigma'$ with $\text{dom}(\sigma') \subseteq \text{negvar}(\Lambda_1\{A \vee B^\bullet\})$ such that

$$\mathsf{JL} \vdash \Lambda_1\{A \vee B^\bullet\}^{r'} \to (\Lambda'\{A^\bullet\}^{r_1}\sigma_1 \vee \Lambda'\{B^\bullet\}^{r_2}\sigma_1)$$

Note that $(\sigma' \circ r_i)|_{\Lambda_0}$ is a realisation on $\Lambda_0$ for each $i \in \{1, 2\}$. By Corollary 25, there exist a realisation $r''$ on $\Lambda_0$ and substitution $\sigma''$ with $\text{dom}(\sigma'') \subseteq \text{negvar}(\Lambda_0)$ such that

$$\mathsf{JL} \vdash \Lambda_0^{r''} \to \Lambda_0^{\sigma' \circ r_i}\sigma'' = \Lambda_0^{\sigma'' \circ \sigma' \circ r_i}$$

for each $i \in \{1, 2\}$. By the Substitution Lemma 23

$$\mathsf{JL} \vdash \Lambda_1\{A \vee B^\bullet\}^{\sigma'' \circ r'} \to (\Lambda_1\{A^\bullet\}^{r_1}(\sigma'' \circ \sigma') \vee \Lambda_1\{B^\bullet\}^{r_2}(\sigma \circ \sigma'))$$

as $\Lambda_1\{A \vee B^\bullet\}^{\sigma'' \circ r'} = \Lambda_1\{A \vee B^\bullet\}^{r'}\sigma''$. By the Lifting Lemma 21, there exists a satisfier term $\mu(\alpha_k)$ such that

$$\mathsf{JL} \vdash \alpha_k{:}\Lambda_1\{A \vee B^\bullet\}^{\sigma'' \circ r'} \to \mu(\alpha_k){:}(\Lambda_1\{A^\bullet\}^{r_1}(\sigma'' \circ \sigma') \vee \Lambda_1\{B^\bullet\}^{r_2}(\sigma \circ \sigma'))$$

Using the $\mathsf{jk}_3$ axiom and transitivity

$$\mathsf{JL} \vdash \alpha_k{:}\Lambda_1\{A \vee B^\bullet\}^{\sigma'' \circ r'} \to (\mu(\alpha_k){:}\Lambda_1'\{A^\bullet\}^{r_1}(\sigma'' \circ \sigma') \vee \mu(\alpha_k){:}\Lambda_1'\{A^\bullet\}^{r_2}(\sigma'' \circ \sigma'))$$

Set $\sigma'''$ as the substitution with $\alpha_k \mapsto \mu(\alpha_k)$. With the satisfier self-referential restriction,

$$\langle \Lambda_1\{A^\bullet\} \rangle_{4k+3}{}^{r_1}(\sigma''' \circ \sigma'' \circ \sigma') = \mu(\alpha_k){:}\Lambda_1\{A^\bullet\}^{r_1}(\sigma'' \circ \sigma')$$
$$\langle \Lambda_1\{B^\bullet\} \rangle_{4k+3}{}^{r_2}(\sigma''' \circ \sigma'' \circ \sigma') = \mu(\alpha_k){:}\Lambda_1\{B^\bullet\}^{r_2}(\sigma'' \circ \sigma')$$

The Substitution Lemma 23 gives

$$\mathsf{JL} \vdash \Lambda_0^{\sigma''' \circ r''} = \Lambda_0^{r''}\sigma''' \to \Lambda_0^{\sigma'' \circ \sigma' \circ r_i}\sigma''' = \Lambda_0^{\sigma''' \circ \sigma'' \circ \sigma' \circ r_i}$$

Set $\sigma = \sigma''' \circ \sigma'' \circ \sigma'$. By propositional reasoning

$$\mathsf{JL} \vdash (\Lambda_0^{\sigma''' \circ r''} \wedge \alpha_k{:}\Lambda_1\{A \vee B^\bullet\}^{\sigma'' \circ r'})$$
$$\to ((\Lambda_0, \langle \Lambda_1\{A^\bullet\}\rangle_{4k+3})^{r_1}\sigma \vee (\Lambda_0, \langle \Lambda_1\{B^\bullet\}\rangle_{4k+3})^{r_2}\sigma)$$

since $((\Lambda_0^{r_i}(\sigma'' \circ \sigma') \wedge \mu(\alpha_k){:}\Lambda_1\{A^\bullet\}^{r_i}(\sigma'' \circ \sigma')) = (\Lambda_0, \langle \Lambda_1\{A^\bullet\}\rangle_{4k+3})^{r_i}\sigma$ for each $i \in \{1, 2\}$.

Finally set $r := (\sigma''' \circ r'')|_{\Lambda_0} \cup (\sigma'' \circ r')|_{\Lambda_1\{A \vee B^\bullet\}} \cup \{(4k+3, \alpha_k)\}$ which is a realisation function on $\Lambda\{A \vee B^\bullet\}$. □

**Lemma 30 (Lemma 28 for $\vee^\bullet$).** *Given realisation functions $r_1$ and $r_2$ on $\Gamma\{A^\bullet\}$ and $\Gamma\{B^\bullet\}$ respectively, there exist a realisation function $r$ and a substitution $\sigma$ such that*

$$\mathsf{JL} \vdash \Gamma\{A^\bullet\}^{r_1}\sigma \to \Gamma\{B^\bullet\}^{r_2}\sigma \to \Gamma\{A \vee B^\bullet\}^r$$

*Proof.* We rewrite $\Gamma\{\}$ as $\Gamma\{\Lambda\{\}, \Pi\}$ and proceed by induction on depth$(\Gamma\{\ \})$.

For the base case, $\Gamma\{\Lambda\{\}, \Pi\} = \Lambda\{\}, \Pi$. By Corollary 25, there exist a realisation $r'$ on $\Pi$ and a substitution $\sigma'$ with dom$(\sigma') \subseteq$ negvar$(\Pi)$ such that

$$\mathsf{JL} \vdash \Pi^{r_1}\sigma' \to \Pi^{r_2}\sigma' \to \Pi^{r'}$$

Note that $(\sigma' \circ r_1)|_{\Lambda\{A^\bullet\}}$ and $(\sigma' \circ r_2)|_{\Lambda\{B^\bullet\}}$ are realisation functions. By Lemma 29, there exist a realisation $r''$ on $\Lambda\{A \vee B^\bullet\}$ and a substitution $\sigma''$ with dom$(\sigma'') \subseteq$ negvar$(\Lambda\{A \vee B^\bullet\})$ such that

$$\mathsf{JL} \vdash \Lambda\{A \vee B^\bullet\}^{r''} \to (\Lambda\{A^\bullet\}^{\sigma' \circ r_1}\sigma'' \vee \Lambda\{B^\bullet\}^{\sigma' \circ r_2}\sigma'')$$

By the Substitution Lemma 23,

$$\mathsf{JL} \vdash \Pi^{r_1}(\sigma'' \circ \sigma') \to \Pi^{r_2}(\sigma'' \circ \sigma') \to \Pi^{r'}\sigma''$$

Equivalently

$$\mathsf{JL} \vdash \Pi^{r_1}(\sigma'' \circ \sigma') \to \Pi^{r_2}(\sigma'' \circ \sigma') \to \Pi^{\sigma'' \circ r'}$$

and by propositional reasoning

$$\mathsf{JL} \vdash (\Lambda\{A^\bullet\}^{r_2}(\sigma'' \circ \sigma') \to \Pi^{r_1}(\sigma'' \circ \sigma'))$$
$$\to (\Lambda\{B^\bullet\}^{r_2}(\sigma'' \circ \sigma') \to \Pi^{r_2}(\sigma'' \circ \sigma'))$$
$$\to (\Lambda\{A \vee B^\bullet\}^{r''} \to \Pi^{\sigma'' \circ r'})$$

Set $r := r' \cup (\sigma'' \circ r')$ and $\sigma := \sigma'' \circ \sigma'$.

For the inductive case, $\Gamma\{\ \} = \Lambda, [\Gamma'\{\ \}]_{4n}$ for some annotated LHS sequent $\Lambda$ and context $\Gamma'\{\ \}$. Using the inductive hypothesis, there exists a realisation $r'$ on $\Gamma'\{A \vee B^\bullet\}$ and substitution $\sigma'$ with $\mathrm{dom}(\sigma) \subseteq \mathrm{negvar}(\Gamma'\{A \vee B^\bullet\})$ such that

$$\mathsf{J} \vdash \Gamma'\{A^\bullet\}^{r_1}\sigma' \to \Gamma'\{B^\bullet\}^{r_2}\sigma' \to \Gamma'\{A \vee B^\bullet\}^{r'}$$

Similarly, $(\sigma' \circ r_i)|_\Lambda$ is a realisation on $\Lambda$ for each $i \in \{1, 2\}$. By Corollary 25, there exist a realisation $r''$ on $\Lambda$ and substitution $\sigma''$ with $\mathrm{dom}(\sigma'') \subseteq \mathrm{negvar}(\Lambda)$ such that $\mathsf{J} \vdash \Lambda^{r''} \to \Lambda^{\sigma' \circ r_i}\sigma''$ for $i \in \{1, 2\}$. By the Substitution Lemma 23

$$\mathsf{J} \vdash \Gamma'\{A^\bullet\}^{r_1}(\sigma'' \circ \sigma') \to \Gamma'\{B^\bullet\}^{r_2}(\sigma'' \circ \sigma') \to \Gamma'\{A \vee B^\bullet\}^{r'}\sigma''$$

Set $\sigma = \sigma'' \circ \sigma$. By the Lifting Lemma 21, there exists a proof term $t \equiv t((\sigma \circ r_1)(4n), (\sigma \circ r_2)(4n))$ such that

$$\mathsf{J} \vdash (\sigma \circ r_1)(4n){:}\Gamma'\{A^\bullet\}^{r_1}\sigma \to (\sigma \circ r_2)(4n){:}\Gamma'\{B^\bullet\}^{r_1}\sigma \to t{:}\Gamma'\{A \vee B^\bullet\}^{\sigma'' \circ r'}$$

Set $r := (\sigma'' \circ r') \cup r'' \cup \{(4n, t)\}$ which is a realisation function on the sequent $(\Lambda, [\Gamma'\{A \wedge B^\circ\}]_{4n})$ and by propositional reasoning

$$\mathsf{J} \vdash (\Lambda, [\Gamma'\{A^\circ\}]_{4n})^{r_1}\sigma \to (\Lambda, [\Gamma'\{B^\circ\}]_{4n})^{r_2}\sigma \to (\Lambda, [\Gamma'\{A \wedge B^\circ\}]_{4n})^{r}$$

□

## References

1. Arisaka, R., Das, A., Straßburger, L.: On nested sequents for constructive modal logics. Log. Methods Comput. Sci. **11**(3), 1–33 (2015). https://doi.org/10.2168/LMCS-11(3:7)2015
2. Artemov, S.N.: Operational modal logic. Technical report MSI 95-29, Cornell University (1995). https://sartemov.ws.gc.cuny.edu/files/2014/01/download-3.pdf
3. Artemov, S.N.: Explicit provability and constructive semantics. Bull. Symb. Log. **7**(1), 1–36 (2001). https://doi.org/10.2307/2687821
4. Artemov, S.N.: Unified semantics for modality and λ-terms via proof polynomials. In: Vermeulen, K., Copestake, A. (eds.) Algebras, Diagrams and Decisions in Language, Logic and Computation - Lecture Notes, pp. 89–119. Centre for the Study of Language & Information, Stanford University (2002)
5. Artemov, S.N.: The ontology of justifications in the logical setting. Stud. Logica **100**(1–2), 17–30 (2012). https://doi.org/10.1007/s11225-012-9387-x
6. Artemov, S.N., Fitting, M.: Justification Logic: Reasoning with Reasons. Cambridge Tracts in Mathematics, vol. 216. Cambridge University Press (2019). https://doi.org/10.1017/9781108348034
7. Artemov, S.N., Fitting, M., Studer, T.: Justification logic. In: Zalta, E.N. (ed.) The Stanford Encyclopedia of Philosophy. Metaphysics Research Lab, Stanford University, fall edn. (2024). https://plato.stanford.edu/archives/fall2024/entries/logic-justification
8. Artemov, S.N., Iemhoff, R.: The basic intuitionistic logic of proofs. J. Symb. Log. **72**(2), 439–451 (2007). https://doi.org/10.2178/jsl/1185803617

9. Artemov, S.N., Kazakhov, E., Shapiro, D.: On logic of knowledge with justifications. Technical report CFIS 99-12, Cornell University (1999)
10. Bellin, G., de Paiva, V., Ritter, E.: Extended Curry-Howard correspondence for a basic constructive modal logic. In: Proceedings for Methods for Modalities 2. Amsterdam, Netherlands (2001)
11. Bierman, G., Paiva, V.: On an intuitionistic modal logic. Stud. Logica **65**(3), 383–416 (2000). https://doi.org/10.1023/A:1005291931660
12. Borg, A., Kuznets, R.: Realization theorems for justification logics: full modularity. In: De Nivelle, H. (ed.) TABLEAUX 2015. LNCS (LNAI), vol. 9323, pp. 221–236. Springer, Cham (2015). https://doi.org/10.1007/978-3-319-24312-2_16
13. Brünnler, K.: Deep sequent systems for modal logic. In: Governatori, G., Hodkinson, I., Venema, Y. (eds.) Advances in Modal Logic, vol. 6, pp. 107–119. College Publications, Noosa (2006). https://www.aiml.net/volumes/volume6/Bruennler.ps
14. Brünnler, K.: Deep sequent systems for modal logic. Arch. Math. Logic **48**(6), 551–577 (2009). https://doi.org/10.1007/s00153-009-0137-3
15. Brünnler, K., Goetschi, R., Kuznets, R.: A Syntactic Realization Theorem for Justification Logics. In: Beklemishev, L., Goranko, V., Shehtman, V. (eds.) Advances in Modal Logic, vol. 8, pp. 39–58. College Publications, Moscow (2010). https://www.aiml.net/volumes/volume8/Bruennler-Goetschi-Kuznets.pdf
16. Bull, R.A.: Cut elimination for propositional dynamic logic without ∗. Math. Log. Q. **38**(1), 85–100 (1992). https://doi.org/10.1002/malq.19920380107
17. Das, A., Marin, S.: On intuitionistic diamonds (and lack thereof). In: Ramanayake, R., Urban, J. (eds.) TABLEAUX 2023. LNCS, vol. 14278, pp. 283–301. Springer, Cham (2023). https://doi.org/10.1007/978-3-031-43513-3_16
18. Dashkov, E.: Arithmetical completeness of the intuitionistic logic of proofs. J. Log. Comput. **21**(4), 665–682 (2011). https://doi.org/10.1093/logcom/exp041
19. Fischer Servi, G.: On modal logic with an intuitionistic base. Stud. Logica **36**(3), 141–149 (1977)
20. Fischer Servi, G.: Semantics for a class of intuitionistic modal calculi. In: Dalla Chiara, M.L. (ed.) Italian Studies in the Philosophy of Science. Boston Studies in the Philosophy and History of Science, vol. 47, pp. 59–72. Springer, Dordrecht (1980). https://doi.org/10.1007/978-94-009-8937-5_5
21. Fischer Servi, G.: Axiomatizations for some intuitionistic modal logics. Rendiconti Seminario Matematico Università e Politecnico di Torino **42**(3), 179–194 (1984)
22. Fitting, M.: The logic of proofs, semantically. Ann. Pure Appl. Log. **132**(1), 1–25 (2005). https://doi.org/10.1016/j.apal.2004.04.009
23. Fitting, M.: Realizations and LP. In: Artemov, S.N., Nerode, A. (eds.) LFCS 2007. LNCS, vol. 4514, pp. 212–223. Springer, Heidelberg (2007). https://doi.org/10.1007/978-3-540-72734-7_15
24. Fitting, M.: Realizations and LP. Ann. Pure Appl. Logic **161**(3), 368–387 (2009). https://doi.org/10.1016/j.apal.2009.07.010
25. Goetschi, R., Kuznets, R.: Realization for justification logics via nested sequents: modularity through embedding. Ann. Pure Appl. Logic **163**(9), 1271–1298 (2012). https://doi.org/10.1016/j.apal.2012.02.002
26. de Groot, J., Shillito, I., Clouston, R.: Semantical analysis of intuitionistic modal logics between CK and IK. In: 2025 40th Annual ACM/IEEE Symposium on Logic in Computer Science (LICS). IEEE, Singapore (2025). https://doi.org/10.48550/arXiv.2408.00262

27. Hill, B., Poggiolesi, F.: An analytic calculus for the intuitionistic logic of proofs. Notre Dame J. Formal Log. **60**(3) (2019). https://doi.org/10.1215/00294527-2019-0008
28. Kashima, R.: Cut-free sequent calculi for some tense logics. Stud. Logica **53**(1), 119–135 (1994). https://doi.org/10.1007/BF01053026
29. Kuznets, R.: Complexity issues in justification logic. Ph.D. thesis, City University of New York (2008). https://academicworks.cuny.edu/gc_etds/1439
30. Kuznets, R., Marin, S., Straßburger, L.: Justification logic for constructive modal logic. J. Appl. Log.—IfCoLog J. Log. their Appl. **8**(8), 2313–2332 (2021)
31. Kuznets, R., Straßburger, L.: Maehara-style modal nested calculi. Arch. Math. Log. **58**(3-4), 359–385 (2019). https://doi.org/10.1007/s00153-018-0636-1
32. Kuznets, R., Studer, T.: Justifications, ontology, and conservativity. In: Bolander, T., Braüner, T., Ghilardi, S., Moss, L. (eds.) Advances in Modal Logic, vol. 9, pp. 437–458. College Publications, Copenhagen (2012). http://www.aiml.net/volumes/volume9/Kuznets-Studer.pdf
33. Kuznets, R., Studer, T.: Logics of Proofs and Justifications, Studies in Logic, vol. 80. College Publications (2019)
34. Marin, S., Padhiar, P.: Justification logic for intuitionistic modal logic (extended technical report) (2025). https://doi.org/10.48550/arxiv.2507.09427
35. Marin, S., Straßburger, L.: Label-free modular systems for classical and intuitionistic modal logics. In: Goré, R., Kooi, B., Kurucz, A. (eds.) Advances in Modal Logic, vol. 10, pp. 387–406. College Publications, Groningen (2014). http://www.aiml.net/volumes/volume10/Marin-Strassburger.pdf
36. Marti, M., Studer, T.: Intuitionistic modal logic made explicit. IFCoLog J. Log. Appl. **3**(5), 877–901 (2016)
37. Marti, M., Studer, T.: The internalized disjunction property for intuitionistic justification logic. In: Bezhanishvili, G., D'Agostino, G., Metcalfe, G., Studer, T. (eds.) Advances in Modal Logic, vol. 12, pp. 511–529. College Publications, Bern (2018). https://www.aiml.net/volumes/volume12/Marti-Studer.pdf
38. Mkrtychev, A.: Models for the logic of proofs. In: Adian, S., Nerode, A. (eds.) LFCS 1997. LNCS, vol. 1234, pp. 266–275. Springer, Heidelberg (1997). https://doi.org/10.1007/3-540-63045-7_27
39. Plotkin, G., Stirling, C.: A framework for intuitionistic modal logics: extended abstract. In: Halpern, J.Y. (ed.) Proceedings of the 1986 Conference on Theoretical Aspects of Reasoning about Knowledge, TARK 1986, pp. 399–406. Morgan Kaufmann Publishers Inc., Monterey (1986)
40. Poggiolesi, F.: The method of tree-hypersequents for modal propositional logic. In: Makinson, D., Malinowski, J., Wansing, H. (eds.) Towards Mathematical Philosophy. TL, vol. 28, pp. 31–51. Springer, Dordrecht (2009). https://doi.org/10.1007/978-1-4020-9084-4_3
41. Poggiolesi, F.: Gentzen Calculi for Modal Propositional Logic. Trends in Logic, vol. 32. Springer, Dordrecht (2011). https://doi.org/10.1007/978-90-481-9670-8
42. Prawitz, D.: Natural deduction: a proof-theoretical study. Ph.D. thesis, Stockholm University (1965)
43. Simpson, A.K.: The proof theory and semantics of intuitionistic modal logic. Ph.D. thesis, University of Edinburgh (1994). http://hdl.handle.net/1842/407
44. Steren, G., Bonelli, E.: Intuitionistic hypothetical logic of proofs. In: de Paiva, V., Benevides, M., Nigam, V., Pimentel, E. (eds.) Proceedings of the 6th Workshop on Intuitionistic Modal Logic and Applications (IMLA 2013). Electronic Notes in Theoretical Computer Science, vol. 300, pp. 89–103. Elsevier, Rio de Janeiro (2014). https://doi.org/10.1016/j.entcs.2013.12.013

45. Straßburger, L.: Cut elimination in nested sequents for intuitionistic modal logics. In: Pfenning, F. (ed.) FoSSaCS 2013. LNCS, vol. 7794, pp. 209–224. Springer, Heidelberg (2013). https://doi.org/10.1007/978-3-642-37075-5_14

**Open Access** This chapter is licensed under the terms of the Creative Commons Attribution 4.0 International License (http://creativecommons.org/licenses/by/4.0/), which permits use, sharing, adaptation, distribution and reproduction in any medium or format, as long as you give appropriate credit to the original author(s) and the source, provide a link to the Creative Commons license and indicate if changes were made.

The images or other third party material in this chapter are included in the chapter's Creative Commons license, unless indicated otherwise in a credit line to the material. If material is not included in the chapter's Creative Commons license and your intended use is not permitted by statutory regulation or exceeds the permitted use, you will need to obtain permission directly from the copyright holder.

# Intuitionistic BV

Matteo Acclavio[1](✉)[iD] and Lutz Straßburger[2][iD]

[1] Sussex University, Brighton, UK
[2] INRIA Saclay, Palaiseau, France
https://matteoacclavio.com/

**Abstract.** We present the logic IBV, which is an intuitionistic version of BV, in the sense that its restriction to the MLL connectives is exactly IMLL, the intuitionistic version of MLL. For this logic we give a deep inference proof system and show cut elimination. We also show that the logic obtained from IBV by dropping the associativity of the new non-commutative seq-connective is an intuitionistic variant of the recently introduced logic NML. For this logic, called INML, we give a cut-free sequent calculus.

## 1 Introduction

The logic BV is a conservative extension of multiplicative linear logic with mix ($\text{MLL}_\text{mix}$) with a self-dual non-commutative connective (◂) called *seq*. It was introduced by Guglielmi in [11,13] in the attempt of providing cut-free deduction system for Retoré's pomset logic [20,22].[1] To this end, Guglielmi developed the deep inference formalism of the calculus of structures to deal with the limitations of the traditional proof systems based on Gentzen's work (sequent calculi and natural deduction). In fact, as shown by Tui in [26], the presence of the non-commutative connective ◂ makes it impossible to define a cut-free sequent calculus for BV. Nonetheless, the logic BV has found applications in the formalisation of process algebras (e.g., [7] and [15,16]), in typing linear lambda calculus with explicit substitutions [23], and in describing quantum computations through *BV-categories* [5,24].

Our motivation for this work is to develop a proof-theoretic framework that could serve as a basis for the definition of type systems that treat *sequentiality* as a first-class citizen of the language. In this context, the logic BV appears to be a natural candidate, as it provides a non-commutative connective capable of expressing sequentiality.[2] However, BV is not intuitionistic, and thus cannot serve as a basis for type systems aligned with tradition of type theory developed for functional programming languages.

This leads us to the central question of this work: *Is it possible to define an intuitionistic version of* BV*?* More precisely, we are interested in a system

---

[1] The inclusion of BV in pomset has been known since the introduction of BV [25]. However, that this inclusion is strict has only been proven recently [18,19].
[2] Indeed, the deep inference formalism was developed by Guglielmi after various attempt in defining sequent calculi including a logic operator modeling sequentiality [9,10].

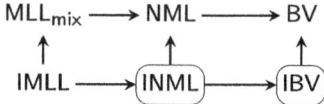

**Fig. 1.** Proof systems discussed in this paper. The ones in the boxes are new.

that conservatively extends intuitionistic multiplicative linear logic (IMLL) and introduces a connective that internalizes sequentiality within the logic itself.

The biggest obstacle towards the definition of an intuitionistic variant of BV is the fact that in BV the unit $\mathbb{I}$ is *self-dual* and is shared not only by the connectives $\otimes$ and $\mathbin{\text{⅋}}$, but also the new *self-dual* connective ◁. It is well-known that intuitionistic multiplicative linear logic (IMLL) can be obtained by polarizing formulas in multiplicative linear logic (MLL). But the self-duality of the unit $\mathbb{I}$ and the seq-connective ◁ makes it difficult to extend this polarization to BV. Our solution to this problem is to make the unit $\mathbb{I}$ only 'half a unit'. That means that we no longer have $A \triangleleft \mathbb{I} \equiv A \equiv \mathbb{I} \triangleleft A$; but only $A \multimap A \triangleleft \mathbb{I}$ and $A \multimap \mathbb{I} \triangleleft A$.

In classical BV the triple $\langle \otimes, \mathbin{\text{⅋}}, \mathbb{I} \rangle$ forms an *isomix category* [8], and the connective ◁ is a *degenerate linear functor* (in the sense of [5]), that is, it validates the following implication.[3]

$$((A \triangleleft B) \otimes (C \triangleleft D)) \multimap ((A \otimes C) \triangleleft (B \otimes D)) \tag{1}$$

We define *intuitionistic* BV (IBV) by extending intuitionistic multiplicative linear logic (IMLL), where the triple $\langle \otimes, \multimap, \mathbb{I} \rangle$ forms a symmetric monoidal closed structure, with a non-commutative connective ◁ validating Eq. (1) and the unit laws $A \multimap (\mathbb{I} \triangleleft A)$ and $A \multimap (A \triangleleft \mathbb{I})$.[4]

*Contributions.* We give a deep inference proof system for IBV (Sects. 2 and 3), and we prove cut elimination via a *splitting lemma* (in Sect. 4). We argue that IBV is indeed the intuitionistic version of BV, by showing that (i) IBV is a conservative extension of IMLL (Sect. 5), and that (ii) the unit-free version of BV is a conservative extension of the unit-free version of IBV (Sect. 6).[5]

Finally, in Sect. 7, we present a weaker logic, called INML, in which the connective ◁ is not associative. We give a cut-free sequent calculus for INML, which is obtained by considering a single-conclusion two-sided version of the sequent calculus for the *non-commutative multiplicative logic* (NML) from [2,3]. We prove that INML is another conservative extension of IMLL, which can be conservatively extended to NML and to IBV (see Fig. 1).

Details of the proofs can be found in the extended version [4] of this paper.

---

[3] The fact that the unit $\mathbb{I}$ of the $\otimes$ and $\mathbin{\text{⅋}}$ is also the (left and right) unit for ◁ is a consequence of the definition of degenerate linear functor [5].

[4] If $(\mathbb{I} \triangleleft A) \multimap A$ and $(A \triangleleft \mathbb{I}) \multimap A$ were valid in IBV, then the connectives $\otimes$ and ◁ would collapse. See Proposition 18 for details.

[5] Note that BV is not conservative over MLL, because it is conservative over MLL$_{\text{mix}}$, and MLL$_{\text{mix}}$ is not conservative over MLL.

$$\text{ai}^\circ_\downarrow \frac{\mathbb{I}}{a \multimap a}\,{}_\circ \qquad \text{u}^\triangleleft_\downarrow \frac{A}{\mathbb{I} \triangleleft A}\,{}_\circ \qquad \text{u}^\triangleright_\downarrow \frac{A}{A \triangleleft \mathbb{I}}\,{}_\circ \qquad \text{ref}^\circ \frac{A \otimes B}{A \triangleleft B}\,{}_\circ \qquad \text{ref}^\bullet \frac{A \triangleleft B}{A \otimes B}\,{}_\bullet$$

$$\text{s}^\circ_\text{L} \frac{A \otimes (B \multimap C)}{(A \multimap B) \multimap C}\,{}_\circ \qquad \text{s}^\circ_\text{R} \frac{(A \multimap B) \otimes C}{A \multimap (B \otimes C)}\,{}_\circ \qquad \text{s}^\bullet_\text{L} \frac{(A \multimap B) \multimap C}{A \otimes (B \multimap C)}\,{}_\bullet \qquad \text{s}^\bullet_\text{R} \frac{A \multimap (B \otimes C)}{(A \multimap B) \otimes C}\,{}_\bullet$$

$$\text{sq}^\circ_\text{L} \frac{(A \multimap B) \triangleleft C}{A \multimap (B \triangleleft C)}\,{}_\circ \qquad \text{sq}^\circ_\text{R} \frac{B \triangleleft (A \multimap C)}{A \multimap (B \triangleleft C)}\,{}_\circ \qquad \text{sq}^\bullet_\text{L} \frac{(A \otimes B) \triangleleft C}{A \otimes (B \triangleleft C)}\,{}_\bullet \qquad \text{sq}^\bullet_\text{R} \frac{B \triangleleft (A \otimes C)}{A \otimes (B \triangleleft C)}\,{}_\bullet$$

$$\text{q}^\circ_\downarrow \frac{(A \multimap B) \triangleleft (C \multimap D)}{(A \triangleleft C) \multimap (B \triangleleft D)}\,{}_\circ \qquad \text{q}^\bullet_\downarrow \frac{(A \otimes B) \triangleleft (C \otimes D)}{(A \triangleleft C) \otimes (B \triangleleft D)}\,{}_\bullet$$

---

$$\text{com}^\otimes \frac{A \otimes B}{B \otimes A} \qquad \text{asso}^\otimes \frac{(A \otimes B) \otimes C}{A \otimes (B \otimes C)} \qquad \text{asso}^\triangleleft_\text{L} \frac{(A \triangleleft B) \triangleleft C}{A \triangleleft (B \triangleleft C)} \qquad \text{asso}^\triangleleft_\text{R} \frac{A \triangleleft (B \triangleleft C)}{(A \triangleleft B) \triangleleft C}$$

$$\text{u}^\otimes_\downarrow \frac{A}{\mathbb{I} \otimes A} \qquad \text{u}^{\multimap}_\downarrow \frac{A}{\mathbb{I} \multimap A} \qquad \text{cur} \frac{(A \otimes B) \multimap C}{A \multimap (B \multimap C)} \qquad \text{ruc} \frac{A \multimap (B \multimap C)}{(A \otimes B) \multimap C}$$

**Fig. 2.** Inference rules for system IBV

$$\text{ai}^\bullet_\uparrow \frac{a \multimap a}{\mathbb{I}}\,{}_\bullet \qquad \text{u}^\triangleleft_\uparrow \frac{\mathbb{I} \triangleleft A}{A}\,{}_\bullet \qquad \text{u}^\triangleright_\uparrow \frac{A \triangleleft \mathbb{I}}{A}\,{}_\bullet \qquad \text{u}^\otimes_\uparrow \frac{\mathbb{I} \otimes A}{A} \qquad \text{u}^{\multimap}_\uparrow \frac{\mathbb{I} \multimap A}{A}$$

$$\text{q}^\circ_\uparrow \frac{(A \triangleleft C) \otimes (B \triangleleft D)}{(A \otimes B) \triangleleft (C \otimes D)}\,{}_\circ \qquad \text{q}^\bullet_\uparrow \frac{(A \triangleleft C) \multimap (B \triangleleft D)}{(A \multimap B) \triangleleft (C \multimap D)}\,{}_\bullet$$

**Fig. 3.** Additional rules for SIBV.

## 2 Formulas and Inference Rules

We consider **formulas** generated from a countable set $\mathcal{A} = \{a, b, c, \ldots\}$ of atoms, a unit $\mathbb{I}$, and the binary connectives implication $\multimap$, tensor $\otimes$, and seq $\triangleleft$:

$$A, B := a \mid \mathbb{I} \mid A \otimes B \mid A \multimap B \mid A \triangleleft B \qquad a \in \mathcal{A} \qquad (2)$$

A formula is **unit-free** if it contains no occurrences of $\mathbb{I}$. In order to define the deep inference rules for our systems, we need to define **contexts**, which are formulas where one atom occurrence is replaced by a hole $[\cdot]$. In the intuitionistic setting we have to distinguish between **positive contexts**, denoted by $P[\cdot]$, and **negative contexts**, denoted by $N[\cdot]$, depending on the position of the 'hole':

$$\begin{aligned} P[\cdot] &:= [\cdot] \mid P[\cdot] \otimes A \mid A \otimes P[\cdot] \mid A \multimap P[\cdot] \mid N[\cdot] \multimap A \mid P[\cdot] \triangleleft A \mid A \triangleleft P[\cdot] \\ N[\cdot] &:= \phantom{[\cdot] \mid} N[\cdot] \otimes A \mid A \otimes N[\cdot] \mid A \multimap N[\cdot] \mid P[\cdot] \multimap A \mid N[\cdot] \triangleleft A \mid A \triangleleft N[\cdot] \end{aligned} \qquad (3)$$

The inference rules for the **system IBV** are shown in Fig. 2. The reader familiar with classical BV might be surprised at the large number of inference rules. But note that (i) because we are in the intuitionistic setting, we need two versions of each rule: one for positive contexts and one for negative contexts,[6] (ii) because the $\multimap$ is not commutative, we need a left and a right version of each s-rule (called ***switch***), and (iii) because the $\mathbb{I}$ is not a proper unit of the $\triangleleft$, we need the different versions of the ref- and sq-rules, which would just be instances of the q↓-rule in classical BV.[7]

We use the ○ and • decoration on the inference rules to indicate whether it applies in a positive or negative context, respectively. Finally, the rules below the dashed line have no such decoration, which indicates that they can be applied in positive and negative contexts. Furthermore, we use dotted lines for the rules to indicate that they correspond to what is usually given as equational theory in classical BV. They comprise associativity, commutativity, unit-equations, and currying.

From the inference rules, we can now define derivations. We are going to use the *open deduction* style [12], and again, because of the intuitionistic setting, we have ***positive*** and ***negative derivations***, which are defined inductively as follows:

$$\text{Positive:} \quad \mathcal{P}, \mathcal{Q} ::= A \ \Big|\ \mathcal{P} \otimes \mathcal{Q} \ \Big|\ \mathcal{P} \triangleleft \mathcal{Q} \ \Big|\ \mathcal{N} \multimap \mathcal{P} \ \Big|\ \mathsf{r}\frac{\mathcal{P}}{\mathcal{Q}}\!\circ \ \Big|\ \mathsf{r}\frac{\mathcal{P}}{\mathcal{Q}}$$

$$\text{Negative:} \quad \mathcal{N}, \mathcal{M} ::= A \ \Big|\ \mathcal{N} \otimes \mathcal{M} \ \Big|\ \mathcal{N} \triangleleft \mathcal{M} \ \Big|\ \mathcal{P} \multimap \mathcal{N} \ \Big|\ \mathsf{r}\frac{\mathcal{N}}{\mathcal{M}}\!\bullet \ \Big|\ \mathsf{r}\frac{\mathcal{N}}{\mathcal{M}}$$

(4)

where $A$ is the identity derivation with premise $A$ and conclusion $A$. The composition by r is only allowed if the premise of r is the conclusion of the derivation $\mathcal{P}$ (resp. $\mathcal{N}$), and the conclusion of r is the premise of the derivation $\mathcal{Q}$ (resp. $\mathcal{M}$). Then the premise of the resulting derivation is the premise of $\mathcal{P}$ (resp. $\mathcal{N}$) and its conclusion is the conclusion of $\mathcal{Q}$ (resp. $\mathcal{M}$).

Let X be a set of inference rules. We write $\mathcal{P}\|_{\mathsf{X}}\genfrac{}{}{0pt}{}{A}{B}$ (resp. $\mathcal{N}\|_{\mathsf{X}}\genfrac{}{}{0pt}{}{A}{B}$) for a positive derivation $\mathcal{P}$ (resp. negative derivation $\mathcal{N}$) whose inference rules are all from X, whose premise is $A$ and whose conclusion is $B$. A *proof* of $A$ is a positive derivation $\mathcal{P}$ with premise $\mathbb{I}$ and conclusion $A$, which may be denoted $\genfrac{}{}{0pt}{}{\mathcal{P}\|\mathsf{X}}{A}$, and we write $\vdash_{\mathsf{X}} A$ if there is a proof of $A$ in X. In the following, we will omit X in derivations if X = IBV.

Consider now the inference rules in Fig. 3. They are the up-versions of the down-rules (i.e., the ones with a down-arrow in the name) of IBV. The rules of IBV without an arrow in the name are part of both, the up- and the down-fragment. We call *system* **SIBV** the union of the rules in Figs. 2 and 3. The

---

[6] This would correspond to rules on the left and rules on the right of the turnstile in the sequent calculus.

[7] See [17,18,21] for unit-free versions of BV, also having these rules.

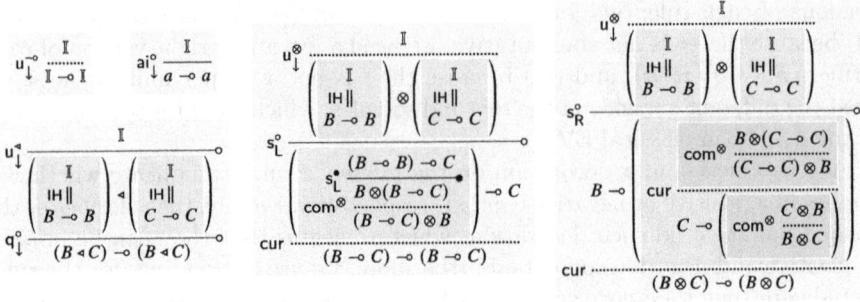

**Fig. 4.** Derivability of $\mathsf{i}^\circ_\downarrow$ in IBV.

'S' in SIBV stands for *symmetric*, and we follow here the naming scheme that is common in deep inference [6,13,23].

Of course, in the next sections, we will show that the two systems SIBV and IBV are equivalent, i.e., prove the same formulas: $\vdash_{\mathsf{SIBV}} A$ iff $\vdash_{\mathsf{IBV}} A$.

*Remark 1.* It is common in deep inference, and in particular for BV, to consider formulas modulo an equivalence relation, covering associativity, commutativity, and units for the connectives. In our system, this would correspond to the rules marked with a dotted line in Figs. 2 and 3. We chose not to do this in this paper because (i) the unit $\mathbb{I}$ is only half a unit for the $\triangleleft$ connective, and the rules $\mathsf{u}^\triangleleft_\downarrow$, $\mathsf{u}^\triangleright_\downarrow$, $\mathsf{u}^\triangleleft_\uparrow$, $\mathsf{u}^\triangleright_\uparrow$ would be needed anyway, (ii) it might be confusing to the reader to have implicit currying, and (iii) making everything explicit makes derivations easier to read.

## 3 Properties of the Systems

In this section we show some basic properties of IBV and SIBV. For this, consider the two rules

$$\mathsf{i}^\circ_\downarrow \frac{\mathbb{I}}{A \multimap A}^\circ \quad \text{and} \quad \mathsf{i}^\bullet_\uparrow \frac{A \multimap A}{\mathbb{I}}^\bullet \tag{5}$$

called *identity* and *cut*. Their atomic versions $\mathsf{ai}\!\downarrow$ and $\mathsf{ai}\!\uparrow$ have already been shown in Figs. 2 and 3.

**Lemma 2.** *We have the following results:*

1. $\mathsf{i}^\circ_\downarrow$ *is derivable in* IBV;
2. $\mathsf{i}^\bullet_\uparrow$ *is derivable in* SIBV;
3. $\mathsf{ai}^\bullet_\uparrow$, $\mathsf{q}^\circ_\uparrow$, *and* $\mathsf{q}^\bullet_\uparrow$ *are derivable in* IBV $\cup \{\mathsf{i}^\bullet_\uparrow, \mathsf{u}^\otimes_\uparrow, \mathsf{u}^{\multimap}_\uparrow\}$.

*Proof.* The first point is proven by induction on $A$ as shown in Fig. 4. The second point is proven dually. For the third point, $\mathsf{ai}^\bullet_\uparrow$ is a special case of $\mathsf{i}^\bullet_\uparrow$, and derivability of $\mathsf{q}^\circ_\uparrow$ and $\mathsf{q}^\bullet_\uparrow$ follows via the derivations shown in Fig. 5, where $P$ and $Q$ (resp. $R$ and $S$) are the premise and conclusion of $\mathsf{q}^\circ_\uparrow$ (resp. $\mathsf{q}^\bullet_\uparrow$). □

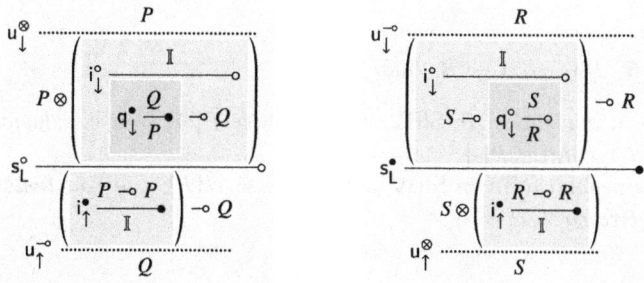

**Fig. 5.** Using $\mathsf{i}^\bullet_\uparrow$ to derive $\mathsf{q}^\circ_\uparrow$ and $\mathsf{q}^\bullet_\uparrow$

**Lemma 3.** *The following are equivalent:*
1. $\vdash_{\mathsf{IBV}} A \multimap B$;
2. $\vdash_{\mathsf{IBV}} P[A] \multimap P[B]$ *for any positive context* $P[\cdot]$;
3. $\vdash_{\mathsf{IBV}} N[B] \multimap N[A]$ *for any negative context* $N[\cdot]$;

*Proof.* Note that 1 is a special case of 2. We prove $1 \Rightarrow 2$ and $1 \Rightarrow 3$ and $2 \Leftrightarrow 3$ simultaneously by induction on the context, see (3). We show only two cases:

$$\mathsf{cur}\frac{\mathsf{s}^\circ_\mathsf{L}\frac{\mathsf{u}^\otimes_\downarrow\frac{I}{\left(\frac{I}{N[B]\,\mathsf{IH}\,N[A]}\right)\otimes\left(\mathsf{i}^\circ_\downarrow\frac{I}{C\multimap C}\right)}}{\mathsf{com}^\otimes\frac{\mathsf{s}^\bullet_\mathsf{L}\frac{(N[B]\multimap N[A])\multimap C}{N[B]\otimes(N[A]\multimap C)}}{(N[A]\multimap C)\otimes N[B]}\multimap C}}{(N[A]\multimap C)\multimap(N[B]\multimap C)}$$

$$\mathsf{cur}\frac{\mathsf{com}^\otimes\frac{\mathsf{s}^\bullet_\mathsf{L}\frac{\left(\mathsf{i}^\circ_\downarrow\frac{I}{C\multimap C}\right)\multimap P[A]\;\;\;\frac{I}{P[A]\,\mathsf{IH}\,P[B]}}{C\otimes(C\multimap P[A])}\multimap P[B]}{(C\multimap P[A])\otimes C}}{(C\multimap P[A])\multimap(C\multimap P[B])}$$

where we have to switch between 2 and 3 because in the cases $N[\cdot] = P[\cdot] \multimap C$ and $P[\cdot] = N[\cdot] \multimap C$ the left-hand side of the $\multimap$ has opposite polarity. □

**Theorem 4 (Deduction Theorem).** *Let $A$ and $B$ be formulas. Then*

$$\vdash_{\mathsf{SIBV}} A \multimap B \iff \text{there is a derivation } \begin{array}{c} A \\ \mathcal{P} \,\|\, \mathsf{SIBV} \\ B \end{array}.$$

*Proof.* Via the following two derivations:

$$\mathsf{s}^\circ_\mathsf{R}\frac{\mathsf{u}^\otimes_\downarrow\frac{A}{A\otimes\left(\frac{I}{\|\,\mathsf{SIBV}\,A\multimap B}\right)}}{\mathsf{u}^{\multimap}_\uparrow\frac{\left(\mathsf{i}^\bullet_\uparrow\frac{A\multimap A}{I}\right)\multimap B}{B}} \qquad \mathsf{i}^\circ_\downarrow\frac{I}{A\multimap\left(\frac{A}{\|\,\mathsf{SIBV}}\right)}$$ □

**Corollary 5.** *If* $\vdash_{\mathsf{SIBV}} A \multimap B$, *then*

- *there is a derivation in* SIBV *with premise* $P[A]$ *and conclusion* $P[B]$ *for any positive context* $P[\cdot]$;
- *there is a derivation in* SIBV *with premise* $N[B]$ *and conclusion* $N[A]$ *for any negative context* $N[\cdot]$;

*Proof.* Consequence of the Deduction Theorem and Lemma 3. □

We conclude this section by proving that the *Modus Ponens* is a valid logical inference in SIBV.

**Corollary 6 (Modus Ponens).** *Let $A$ and $B$ be formulas. If $\vdash_{\mathsf{SIBV}} A \multimap B$ and $\vdash_{\mathsf{SIBV}} A$, then $\vdash_{\mathsf{SIBV}} B$.*

*Proof.* By hypothesis, we have a proof $\mathcal{P}_A$ with conclusion $A$, and the Deduction Theorem ensures the existence of a derivation $\mathcal{P}_{A \multimap B}$ with premise $A$ and conclusion $B$. We conclude by composing 'vertically' the two derivations. □

## 4 Cut Elimination

In this section we show that the cut rule $\mathsf{i}^\bullet_\uparrow$, given in (5), is admissible for IBV. To prove this, we will first show that the two systems SIBV and IBV are equivalent, that is, any formula provable in SIBV is also provable in IBV. In other words, we will show that all up-rules shown in Fig. 3 are admissible for IBV. Then the admissibility of cut will follow from Lemma 2.

**Theorem 7.** *The rules* $\mathsf{u}^\triangleleft_\uparrow$, $\mathsf{u}^\triangleright_\uparrow$, $\mathsf{u}^\otimes_\uparrow$, $\mathsf{u}^{\multimap}_\uparrow$, $\mathsf{ai}^\bullet_\uparrow$, $\mathsf{q}^\circ_\uparrow$, *and* $\mathsf{q}^\bullet_\uparrow$ *are admissible for* IBV.

**Corollary 8.** *The systems* SIBV *and* IBV *are equivalent.*

**Corollary 9.** *The rule* $\mathsf{i}^\bullet_\uparrow$ *is admissible for* IBV.

It therefore remains to prove Theorem 7. For this, we will use a *splitting lemma* as common for deep inference systems [1,11,14,25]. But to our knowledge, this is the first version of a splitting lemma for an intuitionistic system, and there are certain subtleties, for example, the number of cases doubles, for the same reason as the number of inference rules doubles. Here is the statement of the general splitting lemma for IBV:

**Lemma 10 (Splitting).** *Let $A$, $B$ and $K$ be formulas.*

- *If* $\vdash_{\mathsf{IBV}} K \multimap (A \otimes B)$, *then there are formulas $K_A$ and $K_B$ such that*

$$\frac{K_A \otimes K_B}{K} \quad \text{and} \quad \frac{\|}{K_A \multimap A} \quad \text{and} \quad \frac{\|}{K_B \multimap B} \;.$$

- If $\vdash_{\mathsf{IBV}} (A \multimap B) \multimap K$, then there are formulas $K_A$ and $K_B$ such that
$$\begin{array}{c} K_A \multimap K_B \\ \| \\ K \end{array} \quad \text{and} \quad \begin{array}{c} \mathbb{I} \\ K_A \multimap A \end{array} \quad \text{and} \quad \begin{array}{c} \mathbb{I} \\ B \multimap K_B \end{array}.$$

- If $\vdash_{\mathsf{IBV}} K \multimap (A \triangleleft B)$, then there are formulas $K_A$ and $K_B$ such that
$$\begin{array}{c} K_A \triangleleft K_B \\ \| \\ K \end{array} \quad \text{and} \quad \begin{array}{c} \mathbb{I} \\ K_A \multimap A \end{array} \quad \text{and} \quad \begin{array}{c} \mathbb{I} \\ K_B \multimap B \end{array}.$$

- If $\vdash_{\mathsf{IBV}} (A \triangleleft B) \multimap K$, then there are formulas $K_A$ and $K_B$ such that
$$\begin{array}{c} K_A \triangleleft K_B \\ \| \\ K \end{array} \quad \text{and} \quad \begin{array}{c} \mathbb{I} \\ A \multimap K_A \end{array} \quad \text{and} \quad \begin{array}{c} \mathbb{I} \\ B \multimap K_B \end{array}.$$

*Proof.* The proof is by induction on the derivation, considering the bottom-most (non-dotted) rule instance in the derivation. In Fig. 6 we show the most general forms of the non-trivial cases to take into account. In that figure, we abuse the dotted line notation to indicate that there might be more than one application of a 'dotted line' inference rule from Fig. 2. More details are provided in [4]. □

We also need a version of splitting for the atoms.

**Lemma 11 (Atomic Splitting).** *Let $a$ be an atom and $K$ a formula. Then:*

1. *if $\vdash_{\mathsf{IBV}} K \multimap a$, then there is a negative derivation* $\begin{array}{c} a \\ \| \\ K \end{array}$ ;

2. *if $\vdash_{\mathsf{IBV}} a \multimap K$, then there is a positive derivation* $\begin{array}{c} a \\ \| \\ K \end{array}$ .

*Proof.* Again, by induction on the derivation and a case analysis on the bottom-most rule instance. We have the following non-trivial cases:
$$\mathsf{s}_L^\circ \frac{K_1 \otimes (K_2 \multimap a)}{(K_1 \multimap K_2) \multimap a} \quad \mathsf{s}_R^\circ \frac{(a \multimap K_1) \otimes K_2}{a \multimap (K_1 \otimes K_2)} \quad \mathsf{sq}_L^\circ \frac{(a \multimap K_1) \triangleleft K_2}{a \multimap (K_1 \triangleleft K_2)} \quad \mathsf{sq}_R^\circ \frac{K_1 \multimap (a \multimap K_2)}{a \multimap (K_1 \triangleleft K_2)}$$

We conclude by applying the inductive hypothesis on the premise of the rule after remarking that, because of splitting, if $\vdash_{\mathsf{IBV}} A \otimes B$ or $\vdash_{\mathsf{IBV}} A \triangleleft B$, then $\vdash_{\mathsf{IBV}} A$ and $\vdash_{\mathsf{IBV}} B$ must hold. The derivations to prove the statement are recursively defined as follows:

| Point 1. | Point 2. |
|---|---|

$$\mathsf{u}_\downarrow^{\multimap} \frac{a}{\left(\begin{array}{c} \mathbb{I} \\ \| \\ K_1 \end{array}\right) \multimap \left(\begin{array}{c} a \\ \mathsf{IH} \| \\ K_2 \end{array}\right)} \qquad \mathsf{u}_\downarrow^{\otimes} \frac{a}{\left(\begin{array}{c} a \\ \mathsf{IH} \| \\ K_1 \end{array}\right) \otimes \left(\begin{array}{c} \mathbb{I} \\ \| \\ K_2 \end{array}\right)} \qquad \mathsf{u}_\downarrow^{\triangleleft} \frac{a}{\left(\begin{array}{c} \mathbb{I} \\ \| \\ K_1 \end{array}\right) \triangleleft \left(\begin{array}{c} a \\ \mathsf{IH} \| \\ K_2 \end{array}\right)} \qquad \mathsf{u}_\downarrow^{\triangleright} \frac{a}{\left(\begin{array}{c} a \\ \mathsf{IH} \| \\ K_1 \end{array}\right) \triangleleft \left(\begin{array}{c} \mathbb{I} \\ \| \\ K_2 \end{array}\right)}$$

□

$$K_1 \multimap \left( \mathsf{s}_\mathsf{R}^\circ \frac{(K_2 \multimap (A_2 \otimes B_2)) \otimes (A_1 \otimes B_1)}{K_2 \multimap ((A_2 \otimes B_2) \otimes (A_1 \otimes B_1))}^\circ \right)$$
$$\overline{(K_1 \otimes K_2) \multimap ((A_1 \otimes A_2) \otimes (B_1 \otimes B_2))}$$
Case 1

$$K_1 \multimap \left( \mathsf{s}_\mathsf{L}^\circ \frac{(A_1 \otimes B_1) \otimes ((A_2 \otimes B_2) \multimap K_2)}{((A_1 \otimes B_1) \multimap (A_2 \otimes B_2)) \multimap K_2}^\circ \right)$$
$$\overline{((A_1 \otimes A_2) \multimap (B_1 \otimes B_2)) \multimap (K_1 \otimes K_2)}$$
Case 2

$$\left( \mathsf{s}_\mathsf{L}^\bullet \frac{((K_1 \multimap (A_1 \otimes B_1)) \multimap (A_2 \multimap B_2))}{(K_1 \otimes ((A_1 \otimes B_1) \multimap (A_2 \multimap B_2)))}^\bullet \right) \multimap K_2$$
$$\overline{(A_1 \otimes A_2) \multimap (B_1 \multimap B_2) \multimap (K_1 \multimap K_2)}$$
Case 3

$$\left( \mathsf{s}_\mathsf{R}^\bullet \frac{(A_1 \otimes B_1) \multimap ((A_2 \multimap B_2) \otimes K_2)}{((A_1 \otimes B_1) \multimap (A_2 \multimap B_2)) \otimes K_2}^\bullet \right) \multimap K_1$$
$$\overline{((A_1 \otimes A_2) \multimap (B_1 \multimap B_2)) \multimap (K_2 \multimap K_1)}$$
Case 4

$$K_1 \multimap \left( \mathsf{q}_\downarrow^\circ \frac{(K_2 \multimap A_1) \triangleleft (K_3 \multimap (A_3 \triangleleft B))}{(K_2 \triangleleft K_3) \multimap (A_1 \triangleleft (A_2 \triangleleft B))}^\circ \right)$$
$$\overline{(K_1 \otimes (K_2 \triangleleft K_3)) \multimap ((A_1 \triangleleft A_2) \triangleleft B)}$$
Case 5 (left associativity)

$$K_1 \multimap \left( \mathsf{q}_\downarrow^\circ \frac{(K_2 \multimap (A \triangleleft B_1)) \triangleleft (K_3 \multimap B_2)}{(K_2 \triangleleft K_3) \multimap ((A \triangleleft B_1) \triangleleft B_2)}^\circ \right)$$
$$\overline{(K_1 \otimes (K_2 \triangleleft K_3)) \multimap (A \triangleleft (B_1 \triangleleft B_2))}$$
Case 5 (right associativity)

$$\left( \mathsf{q}_\downarrow^\bullet \frac{(A_1 \otimes K_1) \triangleleft ((A_2 \triangleleft B) \otimes K_2)}{(A_1 \triangleleft (A_2 \triangleleft B)) \multimap (K_1 \triangleleft K_2)}^\bullet \right) \multimap K_3$$
$$\overline{((A_1 \triangleleft A_2) \triangleleft B) \multimap ((K_1 \triangleleft K_2) \multimap K_3)}$$
Case 6 (left associativity)

$$\left( \mathsf{q}_\downarrow^\bullet \frac{((A \triangleleft B_1) \otimes K_1) \triangleleft (B_2 \otimes K_2)}{(A \triangleleft (B_1 \triangleleft B_2)) \multimap (K_1 \triangleleft K_2)}^\bullet \right) \multimap K_3$$
$$\overline{(A \triangleleft (B_1 \triangleleft B_2)) \multimap ((K_1 \triangleleft K_2) \multimap K_3)}$$
Case 6 (right associativity)

$$K_1 \multimap \left( \mathsf{q}_\downarrow^\circ \frac{(A_1 \multimap K_2) \triangleleft ((A_2 \triangleleft B) \multimap K_3)}{((A_1 \triangleleft A_2) \triangleleft B) \multimap (K_2 \triangleleft K_3)}^\circ \right)$$
$$\overline{((A_1 \triangleleft A_2) \triangleleft B) \multimap (K_1 \multimap (K_2 \triangleleft K_3))}$$
Case 7 (left associativity)

$$K_1 \multimap \left( \mathsf{q}_\downarrow^\circ \frac{((A \triangleleft B_1) \multimap K_2) \triangleleft (B_2 \multimap K_3)}{(A \triangleleft (B_1 \triangleleft B_2)) \multimap (K_2 \triangleleft K_3)}^\circ \right)$$
$$\overline{(A \triangleleft (B_1 \triangleleft B_2)) \multimap (K_1 \multimap (K_2 \triangleleft K_3))}$$
Case 7 (right associativity)

**Fig. 6.** Cases for the splitting lemma.

In order to use the splitting lemmas for proving Theorem 7, we need to be able to employ them in arbitrary contexts. For this, we use the context reduction lemma.

**Lemma 12 (Context Reduction).** *Let $A$ be a formula, $P[\cdot]$ a positive context, and $N[\cdot]$ a negative context.*

1. *If $\vdash_\mathsf{IBV} P[A]$, then there is a formula $K$ and derivations*

$$\begin{array}{c} K \multimap X \\ \mathcal{P}_X \| \\ P[X] \end{array} \quad \text{and} \quad \begin{array}{c} \mathcal{P}_A \| \\ K \multimap A \end{array} \quad \text{for any formula } X.$$

2. *If $\vdash_\mathsf{IBV} N[A]$, then there is a formula $K$ and derivations*

$$\begin{array}{c} X \multimap K \\ \mathcal{P}_X \| \\ N[X] \end{array} \quad \text{and} \quad \begin{array}{c} \mathcal{P}_A \| \\ A \multimap K \end{array} \quad \text{for any formula } X.$$

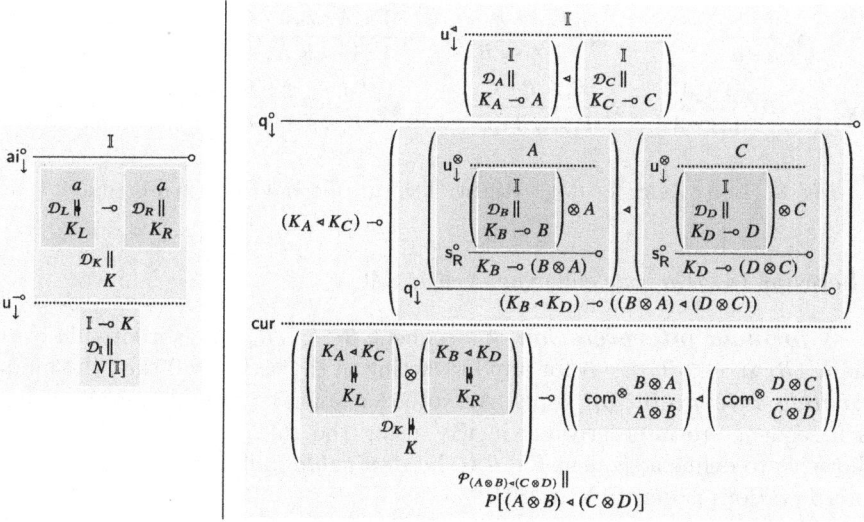

**Fig. 7.** Derivations for admissibility of $\mathsf{ai}_\uparrow^\bullet$ and $\mathsf{q}_\uparrow^\circ$. The case for $\mathsf{q}_\uparrow^\bullet$ is similar. All subderivations exist by splitting and context reduction lemmas.

*Proof.* By induction on the structure of (positive and negative) contexts, see (3). Except for the trivial cases $P[\cdot] = H \multimap [\cdot]$ and $N[\cdot] = [\cdot] \multimap H$, the discussion of each case requires to apply the splitting lemma once to get derivations to be used, together with the inductive case, to construct the derivations $\mathcal{P}_X$ and $\mathcal{N}_X$. More details are provided in [4]. □

*Proof (for Theorem 7).* We can remove all instances of the up-rules in a derivation, starting with a topmost one. Given such an instance $\mathsf{r}\uparrow$, we apply context reduction and splitting to the premise or $\mathsf{r}\uparrow$ (once for $\mathsf{u}_\uparrow^\triangleleft$, $\mathsf{u}_\uparrow^\triangleright$, $\mathsf{u}_\uparrow^\otimes$, $\mathsf{u}_\uparrow^{-\circ}$, and twice for $\mathsf{ai}_\uparrow^\bullet$, $\mathsf{q}_\uparrow^\bullet$, $\mathsf{q}_\uparrow^\circ$). The derivations we obtained are then assembled to construct a derivation of the conclusion of $\mathsf{r}\uparrow$. For $\mathsf{ai}_\uparrow^\bullet$ and $\mathsf{q}_\uparrow^\circ$, these derivations are shown in Fig. 7. More details are given in [4]. □

## 5 From IMLL to IBV

In this section we show that IBV is a conservative extension of intuitionistic multiplicative linear logic (IMLL): every IMLL-formula that is provable in IBV is also provable in IMLL.

We assume the reader to be familiar with sequent calculi and cut-elimination. A ***sequent*** is a pair $\Gamma \vdash A$, where $\Gamma$ is a (possibly empty) set of occurrences of formulas, and $A$ is a formula. Figure 8 shows the inference rules of the sequent calculus for IMLL, and it's well known that it admits cut elimination.

**Theorem 13.** *The rule* AX *is derivable in* IMLL.

$$\text{ax}\,\frac{}{a \vdash a} \qquad \multimap_R \frac{\Gamma, A \vdash B}{\Gamma \vdash A \multimap B} \qquad \multimap_L \frac{\Gamma \vdash A \quad B, \Delta \vdash C}{\Gamma, A \multimap B, \Delta \vdash C} \qquad \text{cut}\,\frac{\Gamma \vdash A \quad A, \Delta \vdash C}{\Gamma, \Delta \vdash C}$$

$$\mathbb{I}_R\,\frac{}{\vdash \mathbb{I}} \qquad \mathbb{I}_L\,\frac{\Gamma \vdash A}{\Gamma, \mathbb{I} \vdash A} \qquad \otimes_L\,\frac{\Gamma, A, B \vdash C}{\Gamma, A \otimes B \vdash C} \qquad \otimes_R\,\frac{\Gamma \vdash A \quad \Delta \vdash B}{\Gamma, \Delta \vdash A \otimes B} \qquad \text{AX}\,\frac{}{A \vdash A}$$

**Fig. 8. Left:** Rules for IMLL **Right:** The cut rule and the generalized axiom

**Theorem 14.** *The rule* cut *is admissible* IMLL.

A ***formula interpretation*** of a sequent $B_1, \ldots, B_n \vdash A$ is a formula of the shape $(B_1 \otimes \cdots \otimes B_n) \multimap A$ for any bracketing of the $\otimes$. If $n = 0$ then the unique ***formula interpretation*** is just $A$. Note that any two formula interpretations of a sequent are interderivable in IBV using the rules com$^\otimes$ and asso$^\otimes$. This allows us to define a sequent $\Gamma \vdash B$ to be ***derivable*** in IBV if any of its formula interpretations is derivable in IBV.

**Lemma 15.** *Let* r *be an inference rule of* IMLL. *If every premise of and instance of* r *is derivable in* IBV, *then so is its conclusion.*

*Proof.* For the rules $\mathbb{I}$ and $\otimes_L$ this is trivial. For ax it follows by a single instance of ai$\downarrow$. For $\multimap_R$, observe that a formula interpretation of its conclusion can be obtained via the cur-rule from a formula interpretation of its premise. Finally, for the rules $\multimap_L$ and $\otimes_R$, formula interpretations of their conclusions are derived via the following derivations:

$$\text{cur}\,\frac{\mathsf{s}_L^\circ\,\dfrac{(\Gamma \multimap A) \otimes \left(\text{cur}\,\dfrac{\mathcal{D}' \| \atop (\Delta \otimes B) \multimap C}{B \multimap (\Delta \multimap C)}\right)}{\mathsf{s}_R^\bullet\,\dfrac{(\Gamma \multimap A) \multimap (B \otimes \Delta)}{\left(\mathsf{s}_L^\bullet\,\dfrac{(\Gamma \multimap A) \multimap B}{\Gamma \otimes (A \multimap B)}\right) \otimes \Delta}\multimap C}}{(\Gamma \otimes \Delta \otimes (A \multimap B)) \multimap C} \quad \text{and} \quad \mathsf{s}_R^\circ\,\dfrac{\mathcal{D}' \| \atop (\Gamma \multimap A) \otimes (\Delta \multimap B)}{\Gamma \multimap \left(\text{com}^\otimes\,\dfrac{A \otimes (\Delta \multimap B)}{\mathsf{s}_R^\circ\,\dfrac{(\Delta \multimap B) \otimes A}{\Delta \multimap (A \otimes B)}}\right)}$$
$$\text{ruc}\,\frac{}{(\Gamma \otimes \Delta) \multimap (A \otimes B)}$$

where $\mathcal{D}'$ are derivations of formula interpretations of their premises. □

**Lemma 16.** *(i) Let* r $\in$ IBV, *and let* $A$ *and* $B$ *be formulas not containing any occurrence of* $\triangleleft$. *If* r $\dfrac{A}{B}\circ$ *then* $A \vdash B$ *is derivable in* IMLL, *and if* r $\dfrac{A}{B}\bullet$ *then* $B \vdash A$ *is derivable in* IMLL. *(ii) Let* $P[\cdot]$ *and* $N[\cdot]$ *be a positive and a negative $\triangleleft$-free context, respectively. If* $A \vdash B$ *is derivable in* IMLL, *then so are* $P[A] \vdash P[B]$ *and* $N[B] \vdash N[A]$.

Intuitionistic BV    425

*Proof.* (i) Cases for the rule $\mathsf{u}_\downarrow^\otimes$, $\mathsf{u}_\downarrow^{-\circ}$, $\mathsf{com}^\otimes$, and $\mathsf{asso}^\otimes$ are the standard derivations to prove that associativity and commutativity of $\otimes$, and the fact that $\mathbb{I}$ is the unit for $\otimes$ and the left-unit of $-\circ$. Cases for rules $\mathsf{ai}_\downarrow^\circ$ and $\mathsf{cur}$ are the following:

$$\mathsf{I}_L \frac{\mathsf{ax} \overline{a \vdash a}}{\mathbb{I}, a \vdash a} \qquad 2 \times {-\circ}_L \frac{\mathsf{ax}\,\overline{A \vdash A} \quad \mathsf{ax}\,\overline{B \vdash B} \quad \mathsf{ax}\,\overline{C \vdash C}}{A \multimap (B \multimap C), A, B \vdash C} \qquad {-\circ}_L + {\otimes}_R \frac{\mathsf{ax}\,\overline{A \vdash A} \quad \mathsf{ax}\,\overline{B \vdash B} \quad \mathsf{ax}\,\overline{C \vdash C}}{(A \otimes B) \multimap C, A, B \vdash C}$$
$${-\circ}_L \frac{}{\mathbb{I} \vdash a \multimap a} \qquad {-\circ}_R + {\otimes}_L \frac{}{A \multimap (B \multimap C) \vdash (A \otimes B) \multimap C} \qquad 2 \times {-\circ}_R \frac{}{(A \otimes B) \multimap C \vdash A \multimap (B \multimap C)}$$

If $r \in \{\mathsf{s}_L^\circ, \mathsf{s}_R^\circ, \mathsf{s}_R^\bullet, \mathsf{s}_L^\bullet\}$, then we have either the following derivations

$${-\circ}_L + {\otimes}_R \frac{\mathsf{ax}\,\overline{A \vdash A} \quad \mathsf{ax}\,\overline{B \vdash B} \quad \mathsf{ax}\,\overline{C \vdash C}}{(A \multimap B), C, A \vdash B \otimes C} \qquad 2 \times {-\circ}_L \frac{\mathsf{ax}\,\overline{A \vdash A} \quad \mathsf{ax}\,\overline{B \vdash B} \quad \mathsf{ax}\,\overline{C \vdash C}}{A, B \multimap C, A \multimap B \vdash C}$$
$${-\circ}_R + {\otimes}_L \frac{}{(A \multimap B) \otimes C \vdash A \multimap (B \otimes C)} \qquad {-\circ}_R + {\otimes}_L \frac{}{A \otimes (B \multimap C) \vdash (A \multimap B) \multimap C}$$
(6)

(ii) is shown by induction on the context, where both statements are proved simultaneously. □

**Theorem 17.** *IBV is a conservative extension of IMLL.*

*Proof.* Given a proof $\pi$ in IMLL, we can construct by induction a proof in IBV of the formula interpretation of its conclusion using Lemma 15.

Conversely, assume we have proof $\mathcal{P}_A$ in IBV of a formula $A$ in IBV. We construct a proof $\pi_A$ in IMLL with the same conclusion by induction on the number of rules in $\mathcal{P}_A$. We consider as base case $\mathsf{ai}\downarrow$, whose conclusion derivable in IMLL using $\mathsf{ax}$ and ${-\circ}_R$. For the inductive case, consider a bottommost rule instance $r$ in $\mathcal{P}_A$, as shown on the left below. The desired cut-free derivation in IMLL is obtained by applying cut-elimination (Theorem 14) to the derivation in the middle below:

$$\mathcal{P}_A = C\left[ r \frac{B'}{B} \right]^{\mathsf{IBV}} \rightsquigarrow \mathsf{cut} \frac{\overset{\pi_1}{\nabla}_{C[B']} \quad \overset{\pi_2}{\nabla}_{C[B'] \vdash C[B]}}{\vdash C[B]} \xRightarrow{\text{cut-elim.}} \overset{\pi_A}{\nabla}_{\vdash C[B]} \qquad (7)$$

where $C[\cdot]$ is positive if $r$ is a $\circ$-rule and negative if $r$ is a $\bullet$-rule. Then $\pi_1$ exists by induction hypothesis and the existence of $\pi_2$ is guaranteed by Lemma 16. □

We conclude this section by making precise the statement in Footnote 4. The two connectives $\triangleleft$ and $\otimes$ would collapse if the two implications $(\mathbb{I} \triangleleft A) \multimap A$ and $(A \triangleleft \mathbb{I}) \multimap A$ were added to IBV. By this, we mean that the two connectives would be logically equivalent, i.e., the formulas $(A \triangleleft B) \multimap (A \otimes B)$ and $(A \otimes B) \multimap (A \triangleleft B)$ and would both be provable in IBV.

**Proposition 18.** *If $(\mathbb{I} \triangleleft A) \multimap A$ and $(A \triangleleft \mathbb{I}) \multimap A$ are added to IBV, then $\triangleleft$ and $\otimes$ collapse (i.e., the formulas $A \triangleleft B$ and $A \otimes B$ become logically equivalent).*

$$\mathsf{ai}{\downarrow}^{\circ}\frac{\phantom{B}}{a \multimap a}\circ \quad \mathsf{ai}{\downarrow}^{\circ}\frac{B}{(a \multimap a) \otimes B}\circ \quad \mathsf{ai}{\downarrow}^{\bullet}\frac{B}{(a \multimap a) \multimap B}\bullet \quad \mathsf{ai}{\downarrow}^{\circ}\frac{B}{(a \multimap a) \triangleleft B}\circ \quad \mathsf{ai}{\downarrow}^{\circ}\frac{B}{B \triangleleft (a \multimap a)}\circ$$

**Fig. 9.** ai↓-rules for IBV⁻.

*Proof.* The implication $(A \otimes B) \multimap (A \triangleleft B)$ already holds in BV and IBV (it suffices to apply a ref• and a $\mathsf{i}{\downarrow}^{\circ}$). For the other implication $(A \triangleleft B) \multimap (A \otimes B)$, assume we have $(\mathbb{I} \triangleleft A) \multimap A$ and $(A \triangleleft \mathbb{I}) \multimap A$ for every $A$. By Lemma 3, there should be negative derivations $\mathcal{D}_{\mathbb{I} \triangleleft}$ and $\mathcal{D}_{\triangleleft \mathbb{I}}$ in SIBV with premise $A$ and conclusion $\mathbb{I} \triangleleft A$ and $A \triangleleft \mathbb{I}$ respectively, for any formula $A$. Then, we could construct a proof of $(A \triangleleft B) \multimap (A \otimes B)$ in IBV by applying up-rules elimination (Theorem 7) to the following derivation in SIBV:

$$\mathsf{i}{\downarrow}\frac{\mathbb{I}}{\mathsf{q}{\downarrow}^{\bullet}\frac{\left(\mathcal{D}_{\triangleleft\mathbb{I}}\Vert\begin{array}{c}A\\A\triangleleft\mathbb{I}\end{array}\right)\otimes\left(\mathcal{D}_{\mathbb{I}\triangleleft}\Vert\begin{array}{c}B\\\mathbb{I}\triangleleft B\end{array}\right)}{\left(\mathsf{u}{\uparrow}^{\otimes}\frac{A\otimes\mathbb{I}}{A}\right)\triangleleft\left(\mathsf{u}{\uparrow}^{\otimes}\frac{\mathbb{I}\otimes B}{B}\right)}} \multimap (A \otimes B)$$

□

## 6  From IBV to BV

One might expect that also BV is a conservative extension of IBV, in the same sense as MLL is a conservative extension of IMLL. Unfortunately, this is not true because of the collapse of the units in BV. However, if we look at the unit-free versions of the two systems, we can get our expected result. The unit-free version of IBV, denoted by **IBV⁻**, is obtained from IBV (see Fig. 2) by removing all versions of u↓ and by replacing the ai↓ by the rules shown in Fig. 9.

Similarly, the **BV⁻-*formulas*** are the BV formulas without the unit, i.e., they are generated from the countable set $\mathcal{A}$ of atoms and the binary connectives par ($\bindnasrepma$), tensor ($\otimes$), and seq ($\triangleleft$), using the following grammar:

$$A, B := a \mid a^\perp \mid A \otimes B \mid A \bindnasrepma B \mid A \triangleleft B \qquad a \in \mathcal{A} \qquad (8)$$

We can define the negation $(\cdot)^\perp$ for all BV⁻-formulas via DeMorgan duality:

$$a^{\perp\perp} = a \quad (A \otimes B)^\perp = A^\perp \bindnasrepma B^\perp \quad (A \bindnasrepma B)^\perp = A^\perp \otimes B^\perp \quad (A \triangleleft B)^\perp = A^\perp \triangleleft B^\perp$$

The inference rules for ***system* BV⁻** are shown in Fig. 10. It is the unit-free version of BV described in [17–19]. The rule ≡ is defined by the equations for associativity of the connectives $\otimes$, $\triangleleft$, and $\bindnasrepma$, and commutativity of $\otimes$ and $\bindnasrepma$.

$$\equiv \frac{A}{B} \quad \operatorname{ai}^{\otimes}\!\downarrow \frac{}{a \mathbin{\gamma} a^{\perp}} \quad \operatorname{ai}^{\triangleleft}\!\downarrow \frac{B}{(a \mathbin{\gamma} a^{\perp}) \triangleleft B} \quad \operatorname{ai}^{\triangleright}\!\downarrow \frac{B}{B \triangleleft (a \mathbin{\gamma} a^{\perp})} \quad \operatorname{ai}^{\otimes}\!\downarrow \frac{B}{(a \mathbin{\gamma} a^{\perp}) \otimes B} \quad \operatorname{mix} \frac{A \otimes B}{A \mathbin{\gamma} B}$$

$$\operatorname{s} \frac{A \otimes (B \mathbin{\gamma} C)}{(A \otimes B) \mathbin{\gamma} C} \quad \operatorname{sq_R} \frac{(A \mathbin{\gamma} B) \triangleleft C}{A \mathbin{\gamma} (B \triangleleft C)} \quad \operatorname{sq_L} \frac{A \triangleleft (B \mathbin{\gamma} C)}{(A \triangleleft C) \mathbin{\gamma} B} \quad \operatorname{q}\!\downarrow \frac{(A \mathbin{\gamma} B) \triangleleft (C \mathbin{\gamma} D)}{(A \triangleleft C) \mathbin{\gamma} (B \triangleleft D)} \quad \operatorname{ref} \frac{A \triangleleft B}{A \mathbin{\gamma} B}$$

- - - - - - - - - - - - - - - - - - - - - - - - - - - - - - - - - - - - - - - - - -

$$A \otimes (B \otimes C) \equiv (A \otimes B) \otimes C \qquad A \otimes B \equiv B \otimes A$$
$$A \mathbin{\gamma} (B \mathbin{\gamma} C) \equiv (A \mathbin{\gamma} B) \mathbin{\gamma} C \qquad A \mathbin{\gamma} B \equiv B \mathbin{\gamma} A \qquad A \triangleleft (B \triangleleft C) \equiv (A \triangleleft B) \triangleleft C$$

**Fig. 10.** Rules for the system BV⁻. The side condition for the ≡-rule is that $A$ and $B$ are equivalent modulo the equivalence relation generated by the relation ≡, defined below the dashed line.

We define an embedding $(\cdot)^{\flat}$ from unit-free formulas (see Sect. 2) into BV⁻-formulas as follows:

$$a^{\flat} = a \quad (A \otimes B)^{\flat} = A^{\flat} \otimes B^{\flat} \quad (A \multimap B)^{\flat} = (A^{\flat})^{\perp} \mathbin{\gamma} B^{\flat} \quad (A \triangleleft B)^{\flat} = A^{\flat} \triangleleft B^{\flat} \quad (9)$$

This allows us to state the main theorem of this section.

**Theorem 19.** *Let $A$ be a unit-free formula. We have $\vdash_{\mathsf{IBV^-}} A$ iff $\vdash_{\mathsf{BV^-}} A^{\flat}$.*

For proving it, we define two subsets of BV⁻-formulas, called **positive formulas** and **negative formulas**:

$$\begin{aligned} \text{positive:} \quad & A^{\circ}, B^{\circ} := a \mid A^{\circ} \otimes B^{\circ} \mid A^{\bullet} \mathbin{\gamma} B^{\circ} \mid A^{\circ} \triangleleft B^{\circ} \\ \text{negative:} \quad & A^{\bullet}, B^{\bullet} := a^{\perp} \mid A^{\circ} \otimes B^{\bullet} \mid A^{\bullet} \mathbin{\gamma} B^{\bullet} \mid A^{\bullet} \triangleleft B^{\bullet} \end{aligned} \quad (10)$$

with $a \in \mathcal{A}$. Clearly, a BV⁻-formula can either be positive (e.g., $a \otimes a$) or negative (e.g., $a^{\perp} \mathbin{\gamma} a^{\perp}$) or neither (e.g., $a^{\perp} \otimes a^{\perp}$), but never both. We call a BV⁻-formula that is neither positive nor negative **unpolarisable**.

**Lemma 20.** *A BV⁻-formula $A$ is positive iff it is in the image of $(\cdot)^{\flat}$.*

*Proof.* By induction on $A$, proving at the same time that $A$ is negative iff $A^{\perp}$ is in the image of $(\cdot)^{\flat}$. □

*Proof (for Theorem 19).* Let us first assume we have a derivation of $A$ in IBV⁻. We can apply the mapping $(\cdot)^{\flat}$ to every formula in that derivation and obtain a valid BV⁻ derivation. For the converse, it suffices to observe that all rules of BV⁻ either preserve the positive polarity of the whole formula (every proof starts with a positive atomic interaction), or break it. And no inference rule of BV⁻ can transform an unpolarisable formula back into one with positive polarity. Furthermore, enumerating all possible polarity-preserving assignments to the rules in Fig. 10 yields the rules of IBV⁻.[8] Now the result follows from Lemma 20. (See [4] for an alternative proof). □

---

[8] This is, in fact, the method by which we found the inference rules for IBV.

$$\text{ax} \frac{}{\vdash a, a^\perp} \qquad \mathbin{\text{⅋}} \frac{\vdash \Gamma, A, B}{\vdash \Gamma, A \mathbin{⅋} B} \qquad \otimes \frac{\vdash \Gamma, A \quad \vdash \Delta, B}{\vdash \Gamma, \Delta, A \otimes B} \qquad \triangleleft \frac{\vdash \Gamma, A_1, \ldots, A_n \quad \vdash \Delta, B_1, \ldots, B_n}{\vdash \Gamma, \Delta, A_1 \triangleleft B_1, \ldots, A_n \triangleleft B_n} n \geq 0$$

**Fig. 11.** Sequent calculus for unit-free NML⁻.

## 7 Associative or Not Associative, that is the Question

The argument of Tiu [26] that there is no shallow proof system for BV makes crucial use of the associativity of $\triangleleft$. This inspired [2] to design the logic NML, which is a conservative extension of MLL with a non-commutative and *non-associative* self-dual connective, and which has a cut-free sequent calculus.

In this section, we investigate the intuitionistic version of that logic, that we call **INML**, and which is obtained from the sequent calculus of IMLL (shown in Fig. 8) extended by the rule $\triangleleft$ shown below:

$$\triangleleft \frac{\Gamma, A_1, \ldots, A_n \vdash A \quad \Delta, B_1, \ldots, B_n \vdash B}{\Gamma, \Delta, A_1 \triangleleft B_1, \ldots, A_n \triangleleft B_n \vdash A \triangleleft B} n \geq 0 \qquad (11)$$

**Theorem 21.** *The rule* AX *is derivable in* INML.

**Theorem 22.** *The rule* cut *is admissible in* INML.

*Proof.* The proof is the same as for IMLL, with one cut-elimination step added for the $\triangleleft$-rule:

$$\text{cut} \frac{\triangleleft \frac{\Gamma_1 \vdash A \quad \Gamma_2 \vdash B}{\Gamma \vdash A \triangleleft B} n \quad \triangleleft \frac{A, \Delta_1 \vdash C \quad B, \Delta_2 \vdash D}{A \triangleleft B, \Delta \vdash C \triangleleft D} m+1}{\Gamma, \Delta \vdash C \triangleleft D} \leadsto \triangleleft \frac{\text{cut} \frac{\Gamma_1 \vdash A \quad A, \Delta_1 \vdash C}{\Gamma_1, \Delta_1 \vdash C} \quad \text{cut} \frac{\Gamma_2 \vdash B \quad B, \Delta_2 \vdash D}{\Gamma_2, \Delta_2 \vdash D}}{\Gamma, \Delta \vdash C \triangleleft D} n+m$$

where $\Gamma$ (resp. $\Delta$) can contain formulas of the shape $E \triangleleft F$, which are decomposed in $\Gamma_1$ and $\Gamma_2$ (resp. $\Delta_1$ and $\Delta_2$). □

The logic INML is indeed the same logic as we would obtain by removing associativity of $\triangleleft$ from IBV.

**Theorem 23.** *Let $A$ be a formula. Then* $\vdash_{\text{INML}} A$ *iff* $\vdash_{\text{IBV}\setminus\{\text{asso}_R^\triangleleft, \text{asso}_L^\triangleleft\}} A$.

*Proof.* Most of the work has already been done in Lemmas 15 and 16. It remains to show that (i) Lemma 15 also applies to the rule $\triangleleft$ in (11), and that $\text{asso}_R^\triangleleft$, $\text{asso}_L^\triangleleft$ are not needed for this, and (ii) that Lemma 16 also applies to the q↓-, sq-, and ref-rules, when we use INML instead of IMLL. □

Unsurprisingly, we have for INML the same conservativity results as we proved for IBV in the previous two sections.

$$w \frac{\Gamma \vdash B}{\Gamma, A \vdash C} \qquad c \frac{\Gamma, A, A \vdash C}{\Gamma, A \vdash C}$$

$$w \downarrow \frac{I}{A} \qquad c \downarrow \frac{A \otimes A}{A}$$

$$\mathsf{LJ} \longrightarrow \boxed{\mathsf{NLJ}} \longrightarrow \boxed{\mathsf{BLJ}}$$
$$\uparrow \qquad \uparrow \qquad \uparrow$$
$$\mathsf{IMLL} \longrightarrow \mathsf{INML} \longrightarrow \mathsf{IBV}$$

**Fig. 12. Left:** Rules for weakenning and contraction in the sequent calculus and in deep inference. **Right:** Possible extensions of LJ with a non-commutative connective.

**Theorem 24.** INML *is a conservative extension of* IMLL.

*Proof.* It suffices to remark that all rules in INML have the subformula property, so any proof of a ◁-free formula in INML can only use rules in IMLL. □

We now would like to show that NML is conservative over INML, but we encounter the same problems with the units as in BV. We therefore consider only unit-free formulas, and the unit-free version of NML, that we call **NML⁻**, and which is shown in Fig. 11.

**Theorem 25.** *Let $A$ be a unit-free formula. We have* $\vdash_{\mathsf{INML}} A$ *iff* $\vdash_{\mathsf{NML}^-} A^\flat$.

*Proof.* This follows in the same way as (unit-free) $\mathsf{MLL}_{\mathsf{mix}}$ is conservative over unit-free IMLL. See [4] for more details. □

We conclude this section by observing that the cut restricted to associativity of ◁ is enough to obtain from INML a sequent calculus for IBV. To this end, we introduce the following ***associative-cut*** rules:

$$\text{a-cut}_L \frac{\Gamma \vdash (A \triangleleft B) \triangleleft C \quad A \triangleleft (B \triangleleft C), \Delta \vdash D}{\Gamma, \Delta \vdash D} \qquad \text{a-cut}_R \frac{\Gamma \vdash A \triangleleft (B \triangleleft C) \quad (A \triangleleft B) \triangleleft C, \Delta \vdash D}{\Gamma, \Delta \vdash D} \quad (12)$$

**Theorem 26.** *Let $A$ be a formula. Then* $\vdash_{\mathsf{IBV}} A$ *iff* $\vdash_{\mathsf{INML} \cup \{\text{a-cut}_L, \text{a-cut}_R\}} A$.

*Proof.* As before, it suffices to extend Lemmas 15 and 16. Note that for simulating a-cut$_L$ and a-cut$_R$ in IBV, we use $i^\bullet_\uparrow$ and then apply Corollary 9. □

*Remark 27.* A sequent calculus for BV could be obtained by adding to the cut-free sequent system NML with the unit from [2] the one-side version of the rule a-cut$_R$.

## 8 Conclusion and Future Work

In this paper, we have defined two logics, IBV and INML, which are the intuitionistic counterparts of the non-commutative logics BV and NML, respectively. In order to show that both systems are conservative extensions of the multiplicative intuitionistic linear logic IMLL, for IBV we have implemented the first splitting proof for an intuitionistic system, and for INML we have shown that cut-elimination holds for the sequent system INML.

In future work, we will study extensions of our systems with contraction and weakening, in order to obtain conservative extensions of intuitionistic logic with a non-commutative connective. In particular, since one could see intuitionsitic logic as an extension of IMLL with the contraction and weakening rules, one could define a system NLJ = INML ∪ {w, c}, as well as extending IBV with the deep inference rules $w_\downarrow^\bullet$ and $c_\downarrow^\bullet$ corresponding to weakening and contraction (see Fig. 12). Note that the deep inference versions of weakening and contraction can only be applied in a negative context, as the weakening and contraction can only be applied on the left-hand side of a sequent in sequent calculus.

These systems could be used as a framework for defining typing disciplines for imperative programming languages in which the sequentiality of the order of instructions is modeled with the new non-commutative connective.

## References

1. Acclavio, M., Horne, R., Mauw, S., Straßburger, L.: A graphical proof theory of logical time. In: Felty, A.P. (ed.) 7th International Conference on Formal Structures for Computation and Deduction (FSCD 2022). Leibniz International Proceedings in Informatics (LIPIcs), vol. 228, pp. 22:1–22:25. Dagstuhl Publishing, Saarbrücken/Wadern (2022). https://doi.org/10.4230/lipics.fscd.2022.22
2. Acclavio, M., Manara, G.: Proofs as execution trees for the π-calculus. arXiv eprint 2411.08847 [cs.LO] (2024). https://doi.org/10.48550/arXiv.2411.08847
3. Acclavio, M., Manara, G., Montesi, F.: Formulas as processes, deadlock-freedom as choreographies. In: Vafeiadis, V. (ed.) ESOP 2025. LNCS, vol. 15694, pp. 23–55. Springer, Cham (2025). https://doi.org/10.1007/978-3-031-91118-7_2
4. Acclavio, M., Straßburger, L.: Intuitionistic BV (extended version). arXiv eprint 2505.13284 [cs.LO] (2025). https://doi.org/10.48550/arXiv.2505.13284
5. Blute, R., Panangaden, P., Slavnov, S.: Deep inference and probabilistic coherence spaces. Appl. Categ. Struct. **20**(3), 209–228 (2012). https://doi.org/10.1007/s10485-010-9241-0
6. Brünnler, K., Tiu, A.F.: A local system for classical logic. In: Nieuwenhuis, R., Voronkov, A. (eds.) LPAR 2001. LNCS (LNAI), vol. 2250, pp. 347–361. Springer, Heidelberg (2001). https://doi.org/10.1007/3-540-45653-8_24
7. Bruscoli, P.: A purely logical account of sequentiality in proof search. In: Stuckey, P.J. (ed.) ICLP 2002. LNCS, vol. 2401, pp. 302–316. Springer, Heidelberg (2002). https://doi.org/10.1007/3-540-45619-8_21
8. Cockett, J.R.B., Seely, R.A.G.: Proof theory for full intuitionistic linear logic, bilinear logic, and mix categories. Theory Appl. Categ. **3**(5), 85–131 (1997). http://www.tac.mta.ca/tac/volumes/1997/n5/3-05abs.html

9. Guglielmi, A.: Concurrency and plan generation in a logic programming language with a sequential operator. In: van Hentenryck, P. (ed.) Logic Programming: 11th International Conference, pp. 240–254. MIT Press, Cambridge (1994). https://doi.org/10.7551/mitpress/4316.003.0030
10. Guglielmi, A.: Sequentiality by linear implication and universal quantification. In: Desel, J. (ed.) Structures in Concurrency Theory. Workshops in Computing, pp. 160–174. Springer, London (1995). https://doi.org/10.1007/978-1-4471-3078-9_11
11. Guglielmi, A.: A system of interaction and structure. ACM Trans. Comput. Log. **8**(1) (2007). https://doi.org/10.1145/1182613.1182614
12. Guglielmi, A., Gundersen, T., Parigot, M.: A proof calculus which reduces syntactic bureaucracy. In: Lynch, C. (ed.) 21st International Conference on Rewriting Techniques and Applications (RTA 2010). Leibniz International Proceedings in Informatics (LIPIcs), vol. 6, pp. 135–150. Dagstuhl Publishing, Saarbrücken/Wadern (2010). https://doi.org/10.4230/lipics.rta.2010.135
13. Guglielmi, A., Straßburger, L.: Non-commutativity and MELL in the calculus of structures. In: Fribourg, L. (ed.) CSL 2001. LNCS, vol. 2142, pp. 54–68. Springer, Heidelberg (2001). https://doi.org/10.1007/3-540-44802-0_5
14. Guglielmi, A., Straßburger, L.: A system of interaction and structure V: the exponentials and splitting. Math. Struct. Comput. Sci. **21**(3), 563–584 (2011). https://doi.org/10.1017/s096012951100003x
15. Horne, R., Tiu, A., Aman, B., Ciobanu, G.: Private names in non-commutative logic. In: Desharnais, J., Jagadeesan, R. (eds.) 27th International Conference on Concurrency Theory (CONCUR 2016). Leibniz International Proceedings in Informatics (LIPIcs), vol. 59, pp. 31:1–31:16. Dagstuhl Publishing, Saarbrücken/Wadern (2016). https://doi.org/10.4230/lipics.concur.2016.31
16. Horne, R., Tiu, A., Aman, B., Ciobanu, G.: De Morgan dual nominal quantifiers modelling private names in non-commutative logic. ACM Trans. Comput. Logic **20**(4), 22:1–22:44 (2019). https://doi.org/10.1145/3325821
17. Kahramanoğulları, O.: System BV without the Equalities for Unit. In: Aykanat, C., Dayar, T., Körpeoğlu, İ (eds.) ISCIS 2004. LNCS, vol. 3280, pp. 986–995. Springer, Heidelberg (2004). https://doi.org/10.1007/978-3-540-30182-0_99
18. Nguyên, L.T.D., Straßburger, L.: A system of interaction and structure III: the complexity of BV and pomset logic. Log. Methods Comput. Sci. **19**(4), 25:1–25:60 (2023). https://doi.org/10.46298/lmcs-19(4:25)2023
19. Nguyên, L.T.D., Straßburger, L.: BV and pomset logic are not the same. In: Manea, F., Simpson, A. (eds.) 30th EACSL Annual Conference on Computer Science Logic (CSL 2022). Leibniz International Proceedings in Informatics (LIPIcs), vol. 216, pp. 3:1–3:17. Dagstuhl Publishing, Saarbrücken/Wadern (2022). https://doi.org/10.4230/lipics.csl.2022.3
20. Retoré, C.: Réseaux et séquents ordonnés. Ph.D. thesis, Université Paris VII (1993)
21. Retoré, C.: Pomset logic as a calculus of directed cographs. In: Abrusci, V.M., Casadio, C. (eds.) Dynamic Perspectives in Logic and Linguistics, pp. 221–247. Bulzoni Editore, Roma (1999). Also available as INRIA Rapport de Recherche RR-3714
22. Retoré, C.: Pomset logic: the other approach to noncommutativity in logic. In: Casadio, C., Scott, P.J. (eds.) Joachim Lambek: The Interplay of Mathematics, Logic, and Linguistics. Outstanding Contributions to Logic, vol. 20, pp. 299–345. Springer, Cham (2021). https://doi.org/10.1007/978-3-030-66545-6_9
23. Roversi, L.: Linear lambda calculus and deep inference. In: Ong, L. (ed.) TLCA 2011. LNCS, vol. 6690, pp. 184–197. Springer, Heidelberg (2011). https://doi.org/10.1007/978-3-642-21691-6_16

24. Simmons, W., Kissinger, A.: Higher-order causal theories are models of BV-logic. In: Szeider, S., Ganian, R., Silva, A. (eds.) 47th International Symposium on Mathematical Foundations of Computer Science (MFCS 2022). Leibniz International Proceedings in Informatics (LIPIcs), vol. 241, pp. 80:1–80:14. Dagstuhl Publishing, Saarbrücken/Wadern (2022). https://doi.org/10.4230/lipics.mfcs.2022.80
25. Straßburger, L.: Linear logic and noncommutativity in the calculus of structures. Ph.D. thesis, Technische Universität Dresden (2003)
26. Tiu, A.: A system of interaction and structure II: the need for deep inference. Log. Methods Comput. Sci. **2**(2), 4:1–4:24 (2006). https://doi.org/10.2168/lmcs-2(2:4)2006

**Open Access** This chapter is licensed under the terms of the Creative Commons Attribution 4.0 International License (http://creativecommons.org/licenses/by/4.0/), which permits use, sharing, adaptation, distribution and reproduction in any medium or format, as long as you give appropriate credit to the original author(s) and the source, provide a link to the Creative Commons license and indicate if changes were made.

The images or other third party material in this chapter are included in the chapter's Creative Commons license, unless indicated otherwise in a credit line to the material. If material is not included in the chapter's Creative Commons license and your intended use is not permitted by statutory regulation or exceeds the permitted use, you will need to obtain permission directly from the copyright holder.

# An Agda Formalization of Nonassociative Lambek Calculus and its Metatheory

Niccolò Veltri[id] and Cheng-Syuan Wan[✉][id]

Tallinn University of Technology, Tallinn, Estonia
{niccolo,cswan}@cs.ioc.ee

**Abstract.** This paper presents a formalization of the nonassociative Lambek calculus in the Agda proof assistant. The sequent calculus for this logic has sequents with binary trees as antecedents, in which formulae are stored as leaves. The shape of the antecedents creates subtleties when proving logical properties, since in many cases one needs to analyze equalities involving sequentially-composed trees. We formally characterize these equalities and show how to employ the resulting technical lemma to prove cut admissibility and the Maehara interpolation properly, which implies Craig interpolation. We show that both the cut rule and the interpolation procedure are well-defined wrt. a certain notion of equivalence of derivations. We additionally prove a proof-relevant version of Maehara interpolation, exhibiting the interpolation procedure as a right inverse of the admissible cut rule.

**Keywords:** nonassociative Lambek calculus · Agda · cut admissibility · Maehara interpolation · proof-relevant interpolation

## 1 Introduction

From the perspective of sequent calculus, substructural logics are characterized by the absence of at least one structural rule. A notable instance is Lambek's syntactic calculus [15], which forbids the structural rules of weakening, contraction and exchange. Its non-associative variant, also introduced by Lambek [16], further disallows associativity. The Lambek calculus (both its associative and nonassociative variants) has been extensively studied in the literature, especially for its linguistic applications [20].

In its sequent calculus presentation, sequents in the associative Lambek calculus (L) are of the form $\Gamma \vdash C$, where $\Gamma$ is a *list* of formulae and $C$ is a single formula, while sequents in the nonassociative Lambek calculus (NL) are of the form $T \mid C$ where $T$ is a *binary tree* in which formulae are stored in the leaves. This structural difference makes the proofs of logical properties for NL trickier than for the associative variant. For example, when proving cut admissibility, in certain cases, one must determine whether the cut formula coincides with the principal formula of the conclusion. For L, the flat antecedents make the situation clear: there are three possibilities–either the cut formula is to the left of the principal formula, to the right, or it is the principal formula itself.

For NL, the situation is more involved, as there are more cases to examine. For example, consider the proof of cut admissibility, in which we wish to compose the derivations of sequents $U \vdash D$ and $\mathcal{C}[D] \vdash C$. Here $\mathcal{C}$ is a context, i.e. a tree with a hole, and $\mathcal{C}[D]$ is the tree resulting from plugging the formula $D$ in the hole. If the derivation of the second sequent ends with an application of the left $\Rightarrow$L-introduction rule, then its antecedent is of the form $\mathcal{C}'[U', A \Rightarrow B]$ for some context $\mathcal{C}'$, tree $U'$ and formulae $A, B$ (where $\mathcal{C}'[U', A \Rightarrow B]$ is the tree arising from substituting the tree $(U', A \Rightarrow B)$ in context $\mathcal{C}'$). This means that we are given an equality of trees $\mathcal{C}[D] = \mathcal{C}'[U', A \Rightarrow B]$ and we need to precisely characterize the structural relationship between the cut formula $D$ and the tree $(U, A \Rightarrow B)$ within the contexts $\mathcal{C}$ and $\mathcal{C}'$. This relationship is not as simple as in the associative Lambek calculus, it involves a more complex splitting of the contexts from which more cases arise.

We can intuitively understand what occurs in the proof of cut admissibility, since it is not too difficult to compute all possible cases. However, what about more complex properties? For example, consider proving that the admissible cut rule is associative, i.e. the two ways of cutting three sequents of the form $U \vdash D$, $\mathcal{C}[D] \vdash E$ and $\mathcal{C}'[E] \vdash C$ produce equal derivations. Because of the large number of cases arising from the induction on the shape of derivations and, mostly, from the analysis of equalities of trees discussed in the previous paragraph, establishing the associativity of cut becomes very challenging to perform with pen and paper, as it is hard to keep track of all the possible cases to consider. On the other hand, interactive theorem provers are very good tools for dealing with large inductive proofs and keeping track of all existing proof obligations.

In this work, we present the formalization of the sequent calculus for NL and its metatheory in the Agda proof assistant. We start by formally describing all possible cases arising from equalities of sequentially-composed trees of the form $\mathcal{C}[U] = \mathcal{C}'[U']$, which is the main technical lemma that we employ in the proof of logical properties. In particular, cut admissibility and properties of the admissible cut rule: associativity, commutativity and unitality wrt. the axiom rule.

We then present the formal proof of the Maehara interpolation property, originating from Maehara's proof of Craig interpolation [7] for classical logic [18]. Maehara's method has been applied and adapted to several logics, especially to substructural logics that admit a cut-free sequent calculus [21]. The Maheara interpolation property states that, given a sequent $\mathcal{C}[U] \vdash C$, there exist a formula $D$ and derivations of sequents $U \vdash D$ and $\mathcal{C}[D] \vdash C$, such that all the atomic formulae appearing in $D$ appear also in $U$, as well as in $\mathcal{C}, C$. More precisely, we formalize a proof-relevant (in the sense of Čubrić [8,9] and Saurin [24]) variant of Maehara interpolation: we aim to capture not only the existence of interpolants but also their relationship to the admissible cut rule. In order to achieve this, we first introduce an equivalence relation $\overset{\circ}{=}$ on derivations, capturing all the possible permutative conversions. We then show that both the cut rule and the interpolation procedure are well-defined wrt. to the relation $\overset{\circ}{=}$. Then we show that the interpolation procedure is a right inverse of the admissible cut rule, in the sense that running the interpolation algorithm on a derivation $f$ of a sequent $\mathcal{C}[U] \vdash C$ and successively cutting the resulting two derivations along the interpolant formula results in a derivation that is $\stackrel{\circ}{=}$-related to $f$.

Summarizing, this work makes the following contributions: (*i*) we formalize a technical lemma for dealing with equalities of the form $\mathcal{C}[U] = \mathcal{C}'[U']$; (*ii*) we employ the lemma to formally define effective procedures for cut admissibility and Maehara (and consequently Craig) interpolation; (*iii*) we prove proof-relevant versions of the latter, by introducing an equivalence of derivations $\stackrel{\circ}{=}$ and formally establishing many properties of the defined procedures: cut is associative, commutative and unital; cut and interpolation are well-defined wrt. $\stackrel{\circ}{=}$; interpolation is a right inverse of cut. We notice that contribution (*iii*) is completely novel in the study of the metatheory of NL, not only its mechanization in a proof assistant.

*Related Work.* There is some previous work on the formalization of NL in proof assistants. Chapter 4 of Anoun et al.'s tutorial [2] presents a Coq formalization of the nonassociative Lambek calculus, covering axiomatic calculus, natural deduction and sequent calculus. Tian [25] ported the above Coq formalization to HOL4. Kokke [14] formalized the nonassociative Lambek-Grishin calculus in Agda. These earlier formalizations primarily focus on implementing the calculi and proving cut admissibility with potential linguistic applications in mind.

The Craig interpolation property for intuitionistic logic has been formalized in Isabelle/HOL by Ridge [22] and in Nominal Isabelle by Chapman et al. [6]. For classical logic, there is a formalization in Isabelle/HOL by Michealis and Nipkow [19]. Recently, Férée and van Gool [11] have formalized uniform interpolation for intuitionistic logic in Coq, which was extended to a class of modal logics by Férée et al. [10]. As far as we know, there are no formalized proofs of Craig/Maehara interpolation for substructural logics in the literature.

We would like to add that the (pen-and-paper, non-formalized) proof of Maehara interpolation for NL is uncommon in the literature, as we were unable to find a reference for it. For NL (and its extensions with modalities, additive connectives, etc.) researchers have traditionally been interested in other interpolation properties, involving a different condition on atomic formulae, which are useful for establishing the finite model property and the relationship between Lambek grammars and context-free grammars [3–5,12,13,17].

*Formalization.* All our constructions have been formalized in Agda. The code is freely available online at https://github.com/cswphilo/nonassociative-Lambek/tree/main/code. Throughout the paper each result is accompanied by a clickable link, in the form of the Agda logo ( ♡ ), directing to the corresponding line in the Agda code.

## 2 Basics on Trees

In this section, we introduce the core elements of our Agda formalization: trees, paths within trees and substitutions. We mainly aim at proving a technical lemma characterizing equalities of the form $\mathcal{C}[U] = \mathcal{C}'[U']$. Intuitively, this lemma states that either (i) $U = U'$, (ii) $U$ is a subtree of $U'$, (iii) $U'$ is a subtree of $U$, or (iv) $U$ and $U'$ are disjoint subtrees. Formally, one needs also to characterize the shape of contexts $\mathcal{C}$ and $\mathcal{C}'$ in all these cases. The technical lemma is fundamental to our subsequent formalization of cut admissibility and Maehara interpolation for NL, as well as for establishing properties of these procedures.

### 2.1 Formulae, Trees, Substitutions

Formulae of NL are inductively generated by the grammar

$$A, B ::= X \mid A \Leftarrow B \mid B \Rightarrow A \mid A \otimes B$$

where $X$ is drawn from a set At of atomic formulae, $\otimes$ is multiplicative conjunction and $\Leftarrow, \Rightarrow$ are left and right implications (also called residuals). In our formalization, we postulate the existence of a type At of atomic formulae. We consistently use letters $X, Y, Z$ to denote atomic formulae. The type Fma ( 𝒰 ) of formulae is defined as the following inductive type:

> data Fma : Set where
> at : At → Fma
> \_⇐\_ : Fma → Fma → Fma
> \_⇒\_ : Fma → Fma → Fma
> \_⊗\_ : Fma → Fma → Fma

Underscores indicate infix operators, e.g. $A \otimes B$ is a formula for any $A, B$ : Fma.

In the literature on NL [20], trees (also called structures) are defined inductively by the grammar $T, U ::= A \mid (T, U)$ where $A$ is a single formula. Contexts are trees with a hole, inductively specified by the grammar $\mathcal{C} ::= [\bullet] \mid (\mathcal{C}, T) \mid (T, \mathcal{C})$. In our formalization, we conflate the two notions and define a type Tree ( 𝒰 ) of trees possibly containing more than one hole. This representation becomes convenient in the specification of the technical lemma. We will see in Sect. 3 that allowing the presence of holes in trees is unproblematic, as antecedents of valid sequents are necessarily free of holes.

> data Tree : Set where
> • : Tree
> η : Fma → Tree
> \_⊛\_ : Tree → Tree → Tree

The base constructor • corresponds to a hole, the constructor $\eta$ corresponds to a leaf containing a formula, while ⊛ is the node constructor.

We introduce a type Path $T$ ( 𝒰 ) whose terms are paths in the tree $T$. These are sequences of left (◄) or right (►) moves from the root node of $T$ to a hole •. The type family Path is the following inductive type family:

```
data Path : Tree → Set where
  • : Path •
  _◀_ : ∀ {T} (p : Path T) U → Path (T ⊛ U)
  _▶_ : ∀ T {U} (p : Path U) → Path (T ⊛ U)
```

Curly brackets are used in Agda to denote implicit arguments. The constructor name • is overloaded: we have that • : Tree is a tree consisting of a single hole and • : Path • is the unique path to the hole in that tree.

In the literature on NL [20], the substitution $\mathcal{C}[U]$ of a tree $U$ into a hole of a context $\mathcal{C}$ is defined by structural recursion on $\mathcal{C}$:

$$[\bullet][U] = U$$
$$(\mathcal{C}, V)[U] = (\mathcal{C}[U], V)$$
$$(V, \mathcal{C})[U] = (V, \mathcal{C}[U])$$

In Agda, the substitution function replaces a hole in $T$, specified by a given path, by another tree $U$. This is defined by pattern-matching on the path ( ⟳ ).

```
sub : ∀{T} → Path T → Tree → Tree
sub • U        = U
sub (p ◀ V) U = sub p U ⊛ V
sub (V ▶ p) U = V ⊛ sub p U
```

Two paths $p$ : Path $T$ and $q$ : Path $U$ can be concatenated, resulting in a path $p \mathbin{+\!\!+} q$ : Path (sub $p\ U$) in the tree obtained by substituting $U$ in the hole specified by path $p$. Concatenation is defined by pattern-matching on $p$ ( ⟳ ).

*Example 1.* Consider the tree $T = (\eta X \circledast \bullet) \circledast \eta Y$, which contains a single hole. The path to the hole is $p = (\eta X \blacktriangleright \bullet) \blacktriangleleft \eta Y$, which indicates that, starting from the root node, we take one step to the left followed by one step to the right, after which we reach the hole. Given another tree $U = \eta Z \circledast \bullet$ and a path $q = \eta Z \blacktriangleright \bullet$ in $U$, the concatenation of paths $p$ and $q$ is $p \mathbin{+\!\!+} q = (\eta X \blacktriangleright (\eta Z \blacktriangleright \bullet)) \blacktriangleleft \eta Y$, which is a path in the tree sub $p\ U = (\eta X \circledast (\eta Z \circledast \bullet)) \circledast \eta Y$.

Given paths $p$ : Path $T$ and $q$ : Path $U$, substituting a tree $V$ in the concatenation $p \mathbin{+\!\!+} q$ is the same as first substituting $V$ in $q$ and then substituting the result in $p$, i.e. sub $(p \mathbin{+\!\!+} q)\ V \equiv$ sub $p$ (sub $q\ V$) ( ⟳ ), where $\equiv$ is Agda's propositional equality type. Agda allows the extension of its evaluation relation with new computation rules using the flag --rewriting. This enabled us to turn the latter propositional equality into a judgemental one. This is only used to *simplify* the proofs of cut admissibility and Maehara interpolation (and their properties). All our formalized results remain valid when the equality is propositional instead of judgemental.

Path concatenation is also associative, i.e. $(p \mathbin{+\!\!+} q) \mathbin{+\!\!+} r \equiv p \mathbin{+\!\!+} (q \mathbin{+\!\!+} r)$ for $p$ : Path $T$, $q$ : Path $U$ and $r$ : Path $V$ ( ⟳ ). Notice that the latter is a well-formed equality type, since the term $(p \mathbin{+\!\!+} q) \mathbin{+\!\!+} r$ has type Path (sub $(p \mathbin{+\!\!+} q)\ V$) while

$p \mathbin{+\!\!+} (q \mathbin{+\!\!+} r)$ has type Path (sub $p$ (sub $q$ $V$)), but these types are judgementally equal (due to the discussion in the previous paragraph).

## 2.2 Equality of Substituted Trees

When proving cut admissibility and Maehara interpolation for NL, a common step is determining all possible cases arising from equalities of the form $\mathcal{C}_1[U_1] = \mathcal{C}_2[U_2]$. In our Agda formalization, these will be propositional equalities of the form sub $p_1$ $U_1$ ≡ sub $p_2$ $U_2$, where $p_1$ and $p_2$ are paths in some trees $T_1$ and $T_2$ respectively. This subsection is dedicated to providing a concrete characterization of the equality type sub $p_1$ $U_1$ ≡ sub $p_2$ $U_2$, i.e. we are after a type SubEq $p_1$ $p_2$ $U_1$ $U_2$ that is equivalent to sub $p_1$ $U_1$ ≡ sub $p_2$ $U_2$. We only need to employ one direction of this equivalence ( ♡ ):

$$\begin{aligned}\text{subeq} : &\forall \{T_1\ T_2\}\ U_1\ U_2\ (p_1 : \text{Path } T_1)\ (p_2 : \text{Path } T_2)\\ &\to (eq : \text{sub } p_1\ U_1 \equiv \text{sub } p_2\ U_2) \to \text{SubEq } p_1\ p_2\ U_1\ U_2\end{aligned} \quad (1)$$

The type SubEq $p_1$ $p_2$ $U_1$ $U_2$ ( ♡ ) is the disjoint union of all the cases that can occur, of which there are 7:

```
data SubEq (p₁ : Path T₁) (p₂ : Path T₂) (U₁ U₂ : Tree) : Set where
  case₁ : Same p₁ p₂ U₁ U₂     → SubEq p₂ p₁ U₁ U₂
  case₂ : ∈Left p₁ p₂ U₁ U₂    → SubEq p₂ p₁ U₁ U₂
  case₃ : ∈Right p₁ p₂ U₁ U₂   → SubEq p₂ p₁ U₁ U₂
  case₄ : ∈Left p₂ p₁ U₂ U₁    → SubEq p₂ p₁ U₁ U₂
  case₅ : ∈Right p₂ p₁ U₂ U₁   → SubEq p₂ p₁ U₁ U₂
  case₆ : Disj p₁ p₂ U₁ U₂     → SubEq p₂ p₁ U₁ U₂
  case₇ : Disj p₂ p₁ U₂ U₁     → SubEq p₂ p₁ U₁ U₂
```

Let us go through them one by one.

*Case 1 ($U_1$ is equal to $U_2$).* In this case, $T_1$ must be equal to $T_2$ and $p_1$ equal to $p_2$. We collect this information in the record type Same $p_1$ $p_2$ $U_1$ $U_2$ ( ♡ ).

```
record Same (p₁ : Path T₁) (p₂ : Path T₂) (U₁ U₂ : Tree) : Set where
  field
    eqT : T₁ ≡ T₂
    eqU : U₁ ≡ U₂
    eqp : subst Path eqT p₁ ≡ p₂
```

Terms of this type are triples consisting of three equalities about the outer trees, the inner trees used for substitution into holes, and paths, respectively. Notice that paths $p_1$ and $p_2$ have different types, so to be able to equate them one needs to first substitute $T_2$ for the equal tree $T_1$ in the type of $p_1$. This is what the application of subst in the type of $eqp$ is used for.

*Case 2 ($U_1$ contains $U_2$ in its left subtree)*. In this case, there exist trees $W_1$ and $W_2$ and a path $q$ in $W_1$ such that $U_1$ is equal to the tree sub $q$ $U_2 \circledast W_2$. Moreover, $p_2$ is equal to the concatenation of $p_1$ with $q \blacktriangleleft W_2$. Visually, an example of a tree sub $p_2$ $U_2$ (equal to sub $p_1$ $U_1$) for this case is

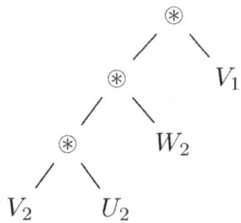

We can break apart this tree and identify all the relevant component trees and paths (the latter marked in red):

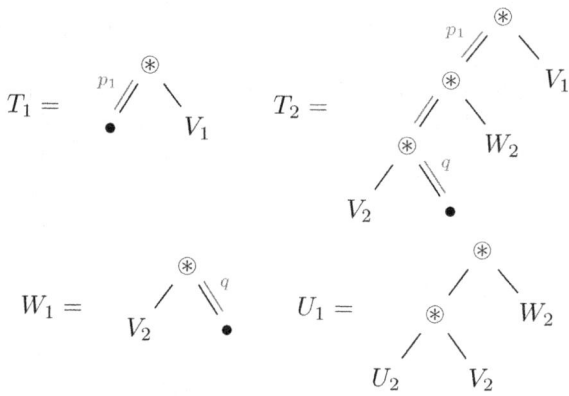

This information is collected in the record type ∈Left $p_1$ $p_2$ $U_1$ $U_2$ ( 👁 ):

    record ∈Left ($p_1$ : Path $T_1$) ($p_2$ : Path $T_2$) ($U_1$ $U_2$ : Tree) : Set where
      field
        {$W_1$ $W_2$} : Tree
        $q$        : Path $W_1$
        eqT      : $T_2 \equiv$ sub $p_1$ ($W_1 \circledast W_2$)
        eqU      : $U_1 \equiv$ sub ($q \blacktriangleleft W_2$) $U_2$
        eqp      : subst Path eqT $p_2 \equiv p_1$ ++ ($q \blacktriangleleft W_2$)

Terms of this type are tuples consisting of trees $W_1$ and $W_2$ (which are implicit), as well as a path $q$ : Path $W_1$, which indicates how to extend $p_1$. Additionally, there are three equalities characterizing $T_2$, $U_1$, and $p_2$.

*Case 3 ($U_1$ contains $U_2$ in its right subtree)*. This case is similar to the previous one, with the difference that now $q$ is a path in $W_2$ and $U_1$ is equal to $W_1 \circledast$

sub $q$ $U_2$. Moreover, $p_2$ is equal to the concatenation of $p_1$ with $W_1 \blacktriangleright q$. This information is collected in the record type ∈Right $p_1$ $p_2$ $U_1$ $U_2$ ( e℧ ):

> record ∈Right ($p_1$ : Path $T_1$) ($p_2$ : Path $T_2$) ($U_1$ $U_2$ : Tree) : Set where
> field
> $\{W_1\ W_2\}$ : Tree
> $q$        : Path $W_2$
> $eqT$    : $T_2 \equiv$ sub $p_1$ $(W_1 \circledast W_2)$
> $eqU$    : $U_1 \equiv$ sub $(W_1 \blacktriangleright q)$ $U_2$
> $eqp$     : subst Path $eqT$ $p_2 \equiv p_1$ ++ $(W_1 \blacktriangleright q)$

*Case 4 ($U_2$ contains $U_1$ in its left subtree).* This case corresponds to an element of type ∈Left $p_2$ $p_1$ $U_2$ $U_1$.

*Case 5 ($U_2$ contains $U_1$ in its right subtree).* This case corresponds to an element of type ∈Right $p_2$ $p_1$ $U_2$ $U_1$.

*Case 6 ($U_1$ and $U_2$ are disjoint and $U_1$ is on the left of $U_2$).* In this case, $p_1$ and $p_2$ share a common initial path $q$, but then split at a node where they take different directions: $p_1$ continues on the left branch while $p_2$ continues on the right branch. This means that there exist two trees $W_1$ and $W_2$, as well as two paths $p_1$ : Path $W_1$ and $p_2$ : Path $W_2$, such that $p_1$ is equal to the concatenation of $q$ with $q_1 \blacktriangleleft W_2$, while $p_2$ is equal to the concatenation of $q$ with $W_1 \blacktriangleright q_2$. Visually, an example of a tree sub $p_2$ $U_2$ (equal to sub $p_1$ $U_1$) for this case is

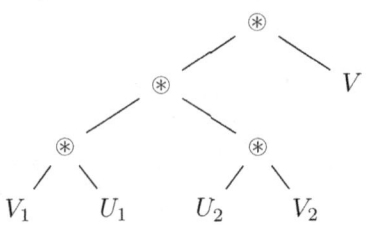

We can break apart this tree and identify all the relevant component trees and paths (the latter marked in red):

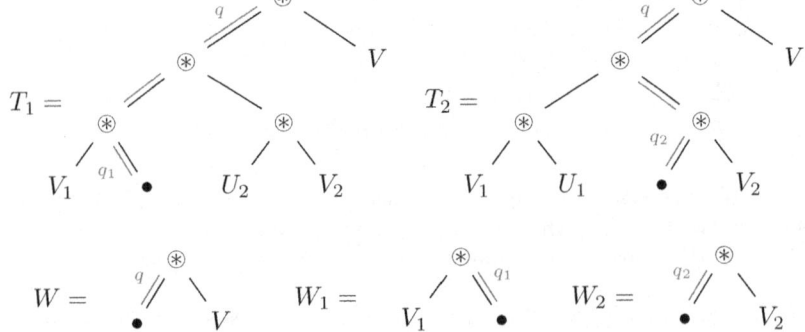

This information is collected in the record type Disj $p_1$ $p_2$ $U_1$ $U_2$ ( ♡ ):

record Disj ($p_1$ : Path $T_1$) ($p_2$ : Path $T_2$) ($U_1$ $U_2$ : Tree) : Set where
  field
  $\{W\ W_1\ W_2\}$ : Tree
  $q$           : Path $W$
  $q_1$         : Path $W_1$
  $q_2$         : Path $W_2$
  $eqT_1$       : $T_1 \equiv$ sub $q$ ($W_1$ ⊛ sub $q_2$ $U_2$)
  $eqT_2$       : $T_2 \equiv$ sub $q$ (sub $q_1$ $U_1$ ⊛ $W_2$)
  $eqp_1$       : subst Path $eqT_1$ $p_1 \equiv q$ ++ ($q_1$ ◀ $W_2$)
  $eqp_2$       : subst Path $eqT_2$ $p_2 \equiv q$ ++ ($W_1$ ▶ $q_2$)

Terms of this type are tuples consisting of three (implicit) trees $W$, $W_1$, and $W_2$. The tree $W$ contains the common path $q$ and it is the largest common prefix tree of both $T_1$ and $T_2$. The tree $W_1$ is the subtree where $U_1$ will be substituted, while $W_2$ the one where $U_2$ will be substituted. The remaining equalities characterize $T_1$, $T_2$, $p_1$ and $p_2$.

*Case 7 ($U_1$ and $U_2$ are disjoint and $U_2$ is on the left of $U_1$).* This case is similar to the previous one, all information is recorded in the type Disj $p_2$ $p_1$ $U_2$ $U_1$.

One can check that the 7 previous cases are mutually disjoint and exhaustive, and that the type SubEq $p_1$ $p_2$ $U_1$ $U_2$ is indeed equivalent to sub $p_1$ $U_1 \equiv$ sub $p_2$ $U_2$. The right-to-left direction of this equivalence corresponds to the construction of the function subeq in (1), which is defined by pattern-matching on the given paths $p_1$ and $p_2$. Conversely, the left-to-right direction of the equivalence is established by the function subeq$^{-1}$ ( ♡ ), which is defined by pattern-matching on the argument $s$ of type SubEq $p_1$ $p_2$ $U_1$ $U_2$:

$$\text{subeq}^{-1} : \forall \{T_1\ T_2\}\ U_1\ U_2\ (p_1 : \text{Path}\ T_1)\ (p_2 : \text{Path}\ T_2)$$
$$\to (s : \text{SubEq}\ p_1\ p_2\ U_1\ U_2) \to \text{sub}\ p_1\ U_1 \equiv \text{sub}\ p_2\ U_2$$

## 3 The Nonassociative Lambek Calculus

We now present the sequent calculus for NL and its cut admissibility property. A sequent in NL takes the form $T \vdash C$, where $T$ is a tree and $C$ is a single formula. The inference rules of the calculus are given below:

$$\frac{}{X \vdash X}\,\text{ax} \quad \frac{A, T \vdash B}{T \vdash A \Rightarrow B}\,\Rightarrow\text{R} \quad \frac{T, A \vdash B}{T \vdash B \Leftarrow A}\,\Leftarrow\text{R} \quad \frac{T \vdash A \quad U \vdash B}{T, U \vdash A \otimes B}\,\otimes\text{R}$$
$$\frac{U \vdash A \quad \mathcal{C}[B] \vdash C}{\mathcal{C}[U, A \Rightarrow B] \vdash C}\,\Rightarrow\text{L} \quad \frac{U \vdash A \quad \mathcal{C}[B] \vdash C}{\mathcal{C}[B \Leftarrow A, U] \vdash C}\,\Leftarrow\text{L} \quad \frac{\mathcal{C}[A, B] \vdash C}{\mathcal{C}[A \otimes B] \vdash C}\,\otimes\text{L} \qquad (2)$$

Notice that the axiom rule ax operates only on atomic formulae $X$. A general axiom rule, with $X$ replaced by an arbitrary formula $A$, is admissible.

In our Agda formalization, the entailment relation $\vdash$ ( 🌑 ) is implemented as an inductive type family indexed over the types Tree and Fma, i.e. $T \vdash C$ is a type for each $T$ : Tree and $C$ : Fma. There is one constructor for each rule in (2). The types of the constructors mimic closely the inference rules, but they use paths to describe the exact position of each hole and they employ the function sub for the implementation of substitution in a hole. Here we only show the constructors associated to two rules ax and $\Rightarrow$L:

```
data _⊢_ : Tree → Fma → Set where
  ax  : ∀{X} → η (at X) ⊢ at X
  ⇒L : ∀{T U A B C} (p : Path T) (f : U ⊢ A) (g : sub p (η B) ⊢ C)
       → sub p (U ⊛ η (A ⇒ B)) ⊢ C
```

It is possible to show that, if the type $T \vdash C$ is inhabited, i.e. the sequent admits a derivation, then the tree $T$ does not contain any holes.

### 3.1 Cut Admissibility

The cut rule in NL takes the form

$$\frac{U \vdash D \quad C[D] \vdash C}{C[U] \vdash C} \text{ cut}$$

which in Agda becomes the function cut ( 🌑 ):

```
cut : {p : Path T} (f : U ⊢ D) (g : W ⊢ C) (eq : W ≡ sub p (η D))
      → sub p U ⊢ C
```

Notice that some implicit arguments ($T, U, W, D$ and $C$) have been omitted to shorten the specification of cut and improve readability. We will similarly omit implicit arguments later in the paper. The function cut takes an extra equality proof $eq$, which allows us to pattern-match on $g$. Without $eq$, i.e. if we assumed an argument $g$ : sub $p$ ($\eta$ $D$) $\vdash C$ instead, Agda would not allow pattern-matching on $g$, as it is unable to unify the antecedent sub $p$ ($\eta$ $D$) with the ones appearing in the conclusion of inference rules.

Concretely, we are constructing a function cut that takes two derivations $f : U \vdash D$ and $g : W \vdash C$ (and an equality proof $eq : W \equiv$ sub $p$ ($\eta$ $D$)) and produces a new derivation cut $f$ $g$ $eq$ : sub $p$ $U \vdash C$. Since there is no primitive cut rule in our calculus (2), all derivations $f$, $g$ and cut $f$ $g$ $eq$ are cut-free. This construction should therefore be understood as a proof of *cut admissibility*, not as a procedure for cut elimination. An alternative approach would have been introducing a second sequent calculus that includes a primitive cut rule and constructing a cut elimination procedure that translates derivations in the calculus with primitive cut rule in the calculus (2).

The construction of the function cut proceeds by pattern-matching on $g$. Similarly to the pen-and-paper proof, when $g$ ends with an application of a left-introduction rule, we need to determine the relative positions of the cut formula and the principal formula. For instance, when $g = \otimes$L $g'$, we have the following situation:

$$\cfrac{U \vdash D \quad \cfrac{\cfrac{g'}{\mathcal{C}'[A, B] \vdash C}}{\mathcal{C}'[A \otimes B] \vdash C} \otimes\text{L}}{\mathcal{C}[U] \vdash C} \text{cut}$$

with $\mathcal{C}'[A \otimes B] = \mathcal{C}[D]$.

In the Agda formalization, the latter (propositional) equality appears as the type sub $p'$ $(\eta\ (A \otimes B)) \equiv$ sub $p$ $(\eta\ D)$ of the argument $eq$, where $p'$ is a path in another tree $T'$. At this point we apply the technical lemma subeq of (1) to the equality proof $eq$ in order to identify the different possible cases. Here there are only three non-vacuous cases: case$_1$ (where $D$ is exactly the principal formula $A \otimes B$), case$_6$ (where $D$ and $A \otimes B$ are in different subtrees with $A \otimes B$ on the left and $D$ on the right), and case$_7$ (the dual case). For the latter two cases, we permute the $\otimes$L rule downward and continue recursively. For the first case, we introduce an auxiliary function cut$\otimes$L ( ♡ ), defined by mutual recursion with cut:

cut$\otimes$L : $\{p : \text{Path } T\}$ $(f : U \vdash A \otimes B)$ $(g : \text{sub } p\ (\eta\ A \circledast \eta\ B) \vdash C)$
$\to$ sub $p\ U \vdash C$

The construction of cut$\otimes$L proceeds by pattern-matching on $f$, mirroring the pen-and-paper proof where one further inducts on the derivation of the first premise when the cut formula coincides with the principal formula. In the definition of cut, the cases when the derivation $g$ ends with an application of rules $\Rightarrow$L and $\Leftarrow$L also require special care, similar to the case of $\otimes$L described above, i.e. an application of the technical lemma subeq and the definition of two auxiliary functions cut$\Rightarrow$L and cut$\Leftarrow$L for the cases when the cut formula $D$ coincides with the principal formula. The functions cut$\Rightarrow$L ( ♡ ) and cut$\Leftarrow$L ( ♡ ) are defined by mutual recursion with cut and cut$\otimes$L.

cut$\Rightarrow$L : $\{p : \text{Path } T\}$ $(f : U \vdash A \Rightarrow B)$ $(g : V \vdash A)$ $(g' : \text{sub } p\ (\eta\ B) \vdash C)$
$\to$ sub $p\ (V \circledast U) \vdash C$
cut$\Leftarrow$L : $\{p : \text{Path } T\}$ $(f : U \vdash B \Leftarrow A)$ $(g : V \vdash A)$ $(g' : \text{sub } p\ (\eta\ B) \vdash C)$
$\to$ sub $p\ (U \circledast V) \vdash C$

$$\dfrac{\overline{X \vdash X}\ \mathsf{ax} \quad \mathcal{C}[X] \vdash C\ {}^{g}}{\mathcal{C}[X] \vdash C}\ \mathsf{cut} \;=\; \mathcal{C}[X] \vdash C\ {}^{g}$$

$$\dfrac{\dfrac{V \vdash D\ {}^{f}\quad \mathcal{C}'[D] \vdash E\ {}^{g}}{\mathcal{C}'[V] \vdash E}\ \mathsf{cut} \quad \mathcal{C}[E] \vdash C\ {}^{h}}{\mathcal{C}[\mathcal{C}'[V]] \vdash C}\ \mathsf{cut} \;=\; \dfrac{V \vdash D\ {}^{f}\quad \dfrac{\mathcal{C}'[D] \vdash E\ {}^{g}\quad \mathcal{C}[E] \vdash C\ {}^{h}}{\mathcal{C}[\mathcal{C}'[D]] \vdash C}\ \mathsf{cut}}{\mathcal{C}[\mathcal{C}'[V]] \vdash C}\ \mathsf{cut}$$

$$\dfrac{T \vdash D\ {}^{f}\quad \dfrac{U \vdash E\ {}^{g}\quad \mathcal{C}[\mathcal{C}_1[D],\mathcal{C}_2[E]] \vdash C\ {}^{h}}{\mathcal{C}[\mathcal{C}_1[D],\mathcal{C}_2[U]] \vdash C}\ \mathsf{cut}}{\mathcal{C}[\mathcal{C}_1[T],\mathcal{C}_2[U]] \vdash C}\ \mathsf{cut} \;=\; \dfrac{U \vdash E\ {}^{g}\quad \dfrac{T \vdash D\ {}^{f}\quad \mathcal{C}[\mathcal{C}_1[D],\mathcal{C}_2[E]] \vdash C\ {}^{h}}{\mathcal{C}[\mathcal{C}_1[T],\mathcal{C}_2[E]] \vdash C}\ \mathsf{cut}}{\mathcal{C}[\mathcal{C}_1[T],\mathcal{C}_2[U]] \vdash C}\ \mathsf{cut}$$

**Fig. 1.** Unitality, associativity, and commutativity of cut.

*Remark 1.* Alternatively, cut can be defined by pattern-matching on the first argument $f$ instead of $g$ and then distinguishing cases where $f$ ends with an application of a right-introduction rule. The latter approach results in an equivalent but longer definition of cut, since it requires a larger number of applications of the function subeq. This in turn has a negative impact on the type-checking time of the whole development, especially of proofs of properties of cut.

The admissible cut rule satisfies the set of equations in Fig. 1, which shows that cut is unital wrt. the rule ax ( ♡ ), sequential composition of cut is associative ( ♡ ), and parallel composition of cut is commutative ( ♡ ). The proofs of these results are quite technical and we highly benefited from the employment of Agda for keeping track of all proof obligations. The technical lemma subeq was also indispensable for this task.

## 4  Equivalence of Derivations

In logic, one often distinguishes between the proposition $T \vdash C$ ("$T$ proves $C$") and the collection of its proofs. In Agda, the two perspectives are unified: the sequent $T \vdash C$ is a type and a term $f : T \vdash C$ is a specific derivation of the sequent. Different terms $f, g : T \vdash C$ correspond to different witnesses of the validity of the sequent.

Nevertheless, some derivations are "morally" the same, they only differ by some "inessential" permutation of rules in their proof tree. In the literature on substructural logic, one would say that these derivations are different sequentialization of the same proof net. We introduce a congruence relation $\stackrel{\circ}{=}$ ( ♡ ) relating precisely these derivations in NL. The congruence $\stackrel{\circ}{=}$ is generated by twenty-seven permutative conversions, of which we present three in Fig. 2. These are representative examples of three classes of permutative conversions: ($i$) left rules permute with right rules (⊗L permutes with ⇒R in the figure); ($ii$) sequential application of left rules can be permuted ($\otimes$L permutes with $\Rightarrow$L in the figure); (iii) parallel application of left rules can be permuted ($\Rightarrow$L permutes with $\Rightarrow$L in the figure).

$$\cfrac{\cfrac{\overset{f}{A',C[A,B]\vdash B'}}{C[A,B]\vdash A'\Rightarrow B'}\Rightarrow\mathsf{R}}{C[A\otimes B]\vdash A'\Rightarrow B'}\otimes\mathsf{L} \;\overset{\circ}{=}\; \cfrac{\cfrac{\overset{f}{A',C[A,B]\vdash B'}}{A',C[A\otimes B]\vdash B'}\otimes\mathsf{L}}{C[A\otimes B]\vdash A'\Rightarrow B'}\Rightarrow\mathsf{R}$$

$$\cfrac{\cfrac{\overset{f}{C[A',B']\vdash A}\quad \overset{g}{C'[B]\vdash C}}{C'[C[A',B']],A\Rightarrow B]\vdash C}\Rightarrow\mathsf{L}}{C'[C[A'\otimes B'],A\Rightarrow B]\vdash C}\otimes\mathsf{L} \;\overset{\circ}{=}\; \cfrac{\cfrac{\overset{f}{C[A',B']\vdash A}}{C[A'\otimes B']\vdash A}\otimes\mathsf{L} \quad \overset{g}{C'[B]\vdash C}}{C'[C[A'\otimes B'],A\Rightarrow B]\vdash C}\Rightarrow\mathsf{L}$$

$$\cfrac{\overset{f}{U\vdash A}\quad \cfrac{\overset{f'}{V\vdash A'}\quad \overset{g}{C[\mathcal{C}_1[B],\mathcal{C}_2[B']]\vdash C}}{C[\mathcal{C}_1[B],\mathcal{C}_2[V,A'\Rightarrow B']]\vdash C}\Rightarrow\mathsf{L}}{C[\mathcal{C}_1[U,A\Rightarrow B],\mathcal{C}_2[V,A'\Rightarrow B']]\vdash C}\Rightarrow\mathsf{L} \;\overset{\circ}{=}\; \cfrac{\overset{f'}{V\vdash A'}\quad \cfrac{\overset{f}{U\vdash A}\quad \overset{g}{C[\mathcal{C}_1[B],\mathcal{C}_2[B']]\vdash C}}{C[\mathcal{C}_1[U,A\Rightarrow B],\mathcal{C}_2[B']]\vdash C}\Rightarrow\mathsf{L}}{C[\mathcal{C}_1[U,A\Rightarrow B],\mathcal{C}_2[V,A'\Rightarrow B']]\vdash C}\Rightarrow\mathsf{L}$$

**Fig. 2.** Examples of permutative conversions.

In Agda, the relation $\overset{\circ}{=}$ is implemented as an inductive type family indexed over pairs of derivations. This means that $f \overset{\circ}{=} g$ is a type for each $f, g : T \vdash C$, whose terms are proofs of $f$ being $\overset{\circ}{=}$-equivalent to $g$. The Agda definition of $\overset{\circ}{=}$ includes: (i) a constructor for each permutative conversion, (ii) constructors for reflexivity, symmetry and transitivity of $\overset{\circ}{=}$, and (iii) constructors evidencing the compatibility of $\overset{\circ}{=}$ with the inference rules of NL, i.e. that $\overset{\circ}{=}$ is a congruence relation. Here we present three indicative examples, one for each class of equational generators: (i) the constructor $\otimes$L$\Rightarrow$R associated to the first example of permutative conversion in Fig. 2; (ii) the constructor sym$\overset{\circ}{=}$ witnessing that $\overset{\circ}{=}$ is a symmetric relation; (iii) the constructor cong$\Rightarrow$L witnessing the compatibility of $\overset{\circ}{=}$ wrt. $\Rightarrow$L.

$$\otimes\mathsf{L}{\Rightarrow}\mathsf{R} \;:\; (p : \mathsf{Path}\ T)\ (f : \eta A' \circledast \mathsf{sub}\ p\ (\eta A \circledast \eta B) \vdash B')$$
$$\to\; \otimes\mathsf{L}\ p\ (\Rightarrow\mathsf{R}\ f) \overset{\circ}{=} \Rightarrow\mathsf{R}\ (\otimes\mathsf{L}\ (\bullet \blacktriangleright p)\ f)$$
$$\mathsf{sym}\overset{\circ}{=} \;:\; (f\ g : T \vdash C)\ (eq : f \overset{\circ}{=} g) \to g \overset{\circ}{=} f$$
$$\mathsf{cong}{\Rightarrow}\mathsf{L} \;:\; (p : \mathsf{Path}\ T)\ (f\ f' : U \vdash A)\ (g\ g' : \mathsf{sub}\ p\ \eta B \vdash C)$$
$$\to\; (eq : f \overset{\circ}{=} f')\ (eq' : g \overset{\circ}{=} g') \to\; \Rightarrow\mathsf{L}\ p\ f\ g \overset{\circ}{=} \Rightarrow\mathsf{L}\ p\ f'\ g'$$

The admissible cut rule satisfies the set of equivalences in Fig. 3, which shows that cut and left rules in the first premise are permutable up to $\overset{\circ}{=}$ ( ↻ ). These equations arise from our implementation of cut admissibility, which proceeds by structural recursion on the second premise. If cut were defined by pattern-matching on the first premise instead, as discussed in Remark 1, then we would have equivalences showing that cut and right rules in the second premise are permutable up to $\overset{\circ}{=}$. In Agda, the proofs of the equivalences in Fig. 3 also proceeds by induction on the second premise.

$$\dfrac{\dfrac{\overset{f}{V \vdash A} \quad \overset{h}{C'[B] \vdash D}}{C'[V, A \Rightarrow B] \vdash D} \Rightarrow\text{L} \quad \overset{g}{C[D] \vdash C}}{C[C'[V, A \Rightarrow B]] \vdash C} \text{cut} \quad \overset{\circ}{=} \quad \dfrac{\overset{f}{V \vdash A} \quad \dfrac{\overset{h}{C'[B] \vdash D} \quad \overset{g}{C[D] \vdash C}}{C[C'[B]] \vdash C} \text{cut}}{C[C'[V, A \Rightarrow B]] \vdash C} \Rightarrow\text{L}$$

$$\dfrac{\dfrac{\overset{f}{V \vdash A} \quad \overset{h}{C'[B] \vdash D}}{C'[B \Leftarrow A, V] \vdash D} \Leftarrow\text{L} \quad \overset{g}{C[D] \vdash C}}{C[C'[B \Leftarrow A, V]] \vdash C} \text{cut} \quad \overset{\circ}{=} \quad \dfrac{\overset{f}{V \vdash A} \quad \dfrac{\overset{h}{C'[B] \vdash D} \quad \overset{g}{C[D] \vdash C}}{C[C'[B]] \vdash C} \text{cut}}{C[C'[B \Leftarrow A, V]] \vdash C} \Leftarrow\text{L}$$

$$\dfrac{\dfrac{\overset{h}{C'[A, B] \vdash D}}{C'[A \otimes B] \vdash D} \otimes\text{L} \quad \overset{g}{C[D] \vdash C}}{C[C'[A \otimes B]] \vdash C} \text{cut} \quad \overset{\circ}{=} \quad \dfrac{\dfrac{\overset{h}{C'[A, B] \vdash D} \quad \overset{g}{C[D] \vdash C}}{C[C'[A, B]] \vdash D} \text{cut}}{C[C'[A \otimes B]] \vdash C} \otimes\text{L}$$

**Fig. 3.** Permutation of cut and left rules.

Since we consider $\overset{\circ}{=}$-related derivations as being equal, all admissible rules (e.g. cut) and constructions on derivations (e.g. Maehara interpolation in the next section) must be well-defined wrt. to $\overset{\circ}{=}$. This means that the cut procedure must produce $\overset{\circ}{=}$-related outputs when applied to $\overset{\circ}{=}$-related inputs. In Agda, this statement can be split in the following two terms, which are defined by mutual induction, witnessing that cut respects $\overset{\circ}{=}$ in each of its arguments ( ○ ):

$\text{cut}\overset{\circ}{=}_1 : \{f\ f' : U \vdash D\}\ \{g : W \vdash C\}\ (eq_1 : W \equiv \text{sub}\ p\ \eta\ D)\ (eq_2 : f \overset{\circ}{=} f')$
$\quad \to \text{cut}\ f\ g\ eq_1 \overset{\circ}{=} \text{cut}\ f'\ g\ eq_1$
$\text{cut}\overset{\circ}{=}_2 : \{f : U \vdash D\}\{g\ g' : W \vdash C\}\ (eq_1 : W \equiv \text{sub}\ p\ \eta\ D)\ (eq_2 : g \overset{\circ}{=} g')$
$\quad \to \text{cut}\ f\ g\ eq_1 \overset{\circ}{=} \text{cut}\ f\ g'\ eq_1$

We define $\text{cut}\overset{\circ}{=}_2$ by pattern-matching on $eq_2$, i.e. the proof of equivalence of derivations. The main challenge is handling the thirty-six cases that arise from the pattern-match, with further numerous subcases arising from the applications of subeq, which are necessary for the cut function to compute. The use of Agda was invaluable here, helping us examine all possible cases systematically and verifying the correctness of the completed proof.

## 5  Proof-Relevant Maehara Interpolation

The Maehara interpolation property is a property of a cut-free sequent calculus. It originates from Maehara's proof of Craig interpolation for the sequent calculus for classical logic LK [18]. The method has been subsequently used to prove Craig interpolation for various logics. For the associative Lambek calculus, the Maehara interpolation property is formulated as follows [21]: given a derivation $f : \Gamma_0, \Gamma_1, \Gamma_2 \vdash C$, there exist a formula $D$ and two derivations $g : \Gamma_1 \vdash D$ and $h : \Gamma_0, D, \Gamma_2 \vdash C$ such that $\text{var}(D) \subseteq \text{var}(\Gamma_1) \cap \text{var}(\Gamma_0, \Gamma_2, C)$. Here $\text{var}(A)$ denotes the set of atomic formulae appearing in $A$, which can be extended naturally to lists of formulae.

Maehara interpolation for NL has the following form: given a derivation $f : \mathcal{C}[U] \vdash C$, there exist a formula $D$ and two derivations $g : \mathcal{C}[D] \vdash C$ and $h : U \vdash D$ such that $\text{var}(D) \subseteq \text{var}(U) \cap \text{var}(\mathcal{C}, C)$. This property, not including the variable condition (discussed later), is implemented in Agda as the record type MIP ( ♡ ):

> record MIP $(p : \text{Path } T)$ $(U : \text{Tree})$ $(C : \text{Fma})$ : Set where
>   field
>     $D$ : Fma
>     $g$ : sub $p$ $(\eta\ D) \vdash C$
>     $h : U \vdash D$

Elements of type MIP $p\ U\ C$ are triples consisting of a formula $D$ and two derivations $g$ and $h$. Proving the Maehara interpolation property translates to constructing the function mip ( ♡ ):

> mip : $(f : V \vdash C)$ $(eq : V \equiv \text{sub } p\ U) \to$ MIP $p\ U\ C$

The construction of the mip function proceeds by pattern-matching on the derivation $f$. Similar to our implementation of cut admissibility, there are cases when we need to determine whether the tree $U$ and the principal formula of the conclusion of an inference rule coincide. This analysis is again handled by the subeq function, which helps us systematically identifying and processing all possible cases that may arise during the construction.

The variable condition of Maehara interpolation is implemented in Agda as follows. We first introduce a type $X \in A$ ( ♡ ) whose terms correspond to occurrences of the atomic formula $X$ in the formula $A$. This can be lifted to a type $X \in^{\mathsf{T}} T$ ( ♡ ), whose terms are occurrences of $X$ in any formula appearing as a leaf of $T$. The variable condition can then be expressed as a record type VarCond ( ♡ ):

> record VarCond $(p : \text{Path } T)$ $(U : \text{Tree})$ $(C\ D : \text{Fma})$ : Set where
>   field
>     $varg : \forall\{X\} \to X \in D \to X \in^{\mathsf{T}} T \uplus X \in C$
>     $varh : \forall\{X\} \to X \in D \to X \in^{\mathsf{T}} U$

Here $\uplus$ is the disjoint union of types in Agda. Terms of the above type are pairs of functions: varg sends each occurrence of atomic formula $X$ in $D$ to an occurrence of $X$ in $T, C$, while varh sends occurrences of X in $D$ to occurrence of

$X$ in $U$. In Agda we verify that the interpolant formula $D$ produced by the mip procedure satisfies this variable condition by constructing the function varcond (🗘):

$$\begin{aligned}\text{varcond} : (f : V \vdash C)\ (eq : V \equiv \text{sub}\ p\ U) \\ \rightarrow \text{VarCond}\ p\ U\ C\ (\text{MIP}.D\ (\text{mip}\ f\ eq))\end{aligned}$$

The definition of varcond follows the structure of mip, ensuring that the variable condition is preserved through all cases of the interpolation algorithm. In the type above, MIP.$D$ (mip $f$ $eq$) is the interpolant formula $D$ produced by mip $f$ $eq$.

Similarly to the cut rule, the procedure mip must also be well-defined wrt. the relation $\stackrel{\circ}{=}$. To this end, we need to pick an appropriate notion of equivalence of terms of type MIP $p$ $U$ $C$. For NL, we say that two interpolant triples $(D, g, h)$ and $(D', g', h')$ of type MIP $p$ $U$ $C$ are equivalent when $D \equiv D'$, $g$ is $\stackrel{\circ}{=}$-related to $g'$ and $h$ is $\stackrel{\circ}{=}$-related to $h'$. This is a quite strong notion of equivalence, as interpolant formulae $D$ and $D'$ are required to be syntactically equal. In Agda, equivalences of interpolant triples are terms of the record type MIP$\stackrel{\circ}{=}$ (🗘):

$$\begin{aligned}&\text{record MIP}\stackrel{\circ}{=}\ (m_1\ m_2 : \text{MIP}\ p\ U\ C) : \text{Set where} \\ &\quad \text{field} \\ &\quad\quad eqD : D \equiv D' \\ &\quad\quad eqg : \text{subst}\ (\lambda x.\ \text{sub}\ p\ (\eta\ x) \vdash C)\ eqD\ g \stackrel{\circ}{=} g' \\ &\quad\quad eqh : \text{subst}\ (\lambda x.\ U \vdash x)\ eqD\ h \stackrel{\circ}{=} h'\end{aligned}$$

The well-definedness of Maehara interpolation wrt. $\stackrel{\circ}{=}$ in Agda corresponds to the construction of the function mip$\stackrel{\circ}{=}$ (🗘), which proceeds by pattern-matching on $eq_2$:

$$\begin{aligned}\text{mip}\stackrel{\circ}{=} : \{f\ f' : V \vdash C\}\ (eq_1 : V \equiv \text{sub}\ p\ U)\ (eq_2 : f \stackrel{\circ}{=} f') \\ \rightarrow \text{MIP}\stackrel{\circ}{=}\ (\text{mip}\ f\ eq_1)\ (\text{mip}\ f'\ eq_1)\end{aligned}$$

We have established a procedure mip for effectively splitting a derivation $f : \mathcal{C}[U] \vdash C$ into two derivations $g : U \vdash D$ and $h : \mathcal{C}[D] \vdash C$, with $D$ being "minimal" in the sense of satisfying an appropriate variable condition. A natural question arises: what happens when we compose derivations $g$ and $h$ using the admissible cut rule? Intuition suggests that we should recover the original derivation $f$, at least modulo $\stackrel{\circ}{=}$. Similar questions have been considered by Čubrić [8,9] for intuitionistic propositional logic and by Saurin [24] for (extensions) of classical linear logic. They call *proof-relevant interpolation* the study of interpolation procedures in relationship to the cut rule and equivalence of proofs, like our $\stackrel{\circ}{=}$. In particular, Čubrić and Saurin show that interpolation procedures are in a way "right inverses" of the cut rule. Here we show the same for NL: if $g : \mathcal{C}[D] \vdash C$ and $h : U \vdash D$ are derivations obtained by applying the mip procedure on a derivation $f : \mathcal{C}[U] \vdash C$, then $\text{cut}(h, g)$ is $\stackrel{\circ}{=}$-related to $f$.

In Agda, proving proof-relevant interpolation translates to the construction of the function cut-intrp ( 💱 ) :

cut-intrp : $(f : V \vdash C)$ $(eq : V \equiv \text{sub } p \ U)$
$\to$ cut (MIP.$h$ (mip $f$ $eq$)) (MIP.$g$ (mip $f$ $eq$)) refl $\stackrel{\circ}{=}$ subst $(\lambda x.\ x \vdash C)$ $eq$ $f$

The term $f$ has type $V \vdash C$, while the derivation on the left-hand-side of $\stackrel{\circ}{=}$ has type sub $p$ $U \vdash C$, so we fix this mismatch with an application of subst. The definition of cut-intrp proceeds by pattern-matching on the argument $f$, again crucially employing the technical lemma subeq.

## 6 Conclusions

We have presented an Agda formalization of NL, showcasing the proofs of two major logical properties: cut admissibility and proof-relevant Maehara interpolation. The key technical contribution is the formal characterization of equality of substituted trees, which serves as a fundamental lemma for the formalization of the aforementioned properties (and for proving other properties in the future, such as uniform interpolation [1] for an extension of NL with additives). While cut admissibility and the standard Maehara interpolation property for NL have been established in previous research, our formalization also offers some new theoretical results: a proof-relevant version of Maehara interpolation and the well-definedness of cut and mip with respect to permutative conversions.

For many substructural logics, the variable condition in the Maehara interpolation property can be strengthened to include the multiplicity [20] and the polarity [23] of occurrences of atomic formulae. This is true for NL and we plan to formalize these upgrades of the variable condition VarCond in future work.

The well-definedness of mip wrt. $\stackrel{\circ}{=}$ is attainable in NL, but it cannot be proved for more structured logics (such as the associative Lambek calculus, or even a semi-associative fragment [26]) without relaxing the equivalence of interpolation triples. In particular, one cannot expect the interpolant formulae to be syntactically equal, as in our type MIP$\stackrel{\circ}{=}$ $m_1$ $m_2$. A possible relaxation would be replacing equality by logical equivalence.

We would also like to employ our Agda formalization, especially the formalized interpolation procedure and its properties, as a stepping stone towards the formalization of the relationship between context-free languages and nonassociative Lambek calculus [3,13].

From a practical perspective, it is worth mentioning that this Agda formalization is computationally intensive. The type-checking time for some files is quite substantial: the well-definedness proof mip$\stackrel{\circ}{=}$ takes $\sim$10 min to type-check, while the associativity of cut and the well-definedness proofs cut$\stackrel{\circ}{=}_1$ and cut$\stackrel{\circ}{=}_2$ require >2 h on a MacBook Pro 2020 with 2 GHz Intel Core i5. In future work, we plan to work on the code in order to reduce the compilation time.

**Acknowledgments.** This work was supported by the Estonian Research Council grant PSG749.

# References

1. Alizadeh, M., Derakhshan, F., Ono, H.: Uniform interpolation in substructural logics. Rev. Symb. Log. **7**(3), 455–483 (2014). https://doi.org/10.1017/s175502031400015x
2. Anoun, H., Castéran, P., Moot, R.: Proof automation for type-logical grammars. Lecture notes for ESSLLI 2004 (2004). https://www.labri.fr/perso/moot/esslli_reader.pdf, https://github.com/rocq-archive/lambek
3. Buszkowski, W.: Generative capacity of nonassociative Lambek calculus. Bull. Pol. Acad. Sci. Math. **34**(7–8), 507–516 (1986)
4. Buszkowski, W.: Interpolation and FEP for logics of residuated algebras. Log. J. IGPL **19**(3), 437–454 (2010). https://doi.org/10.1093/jigpal/jzp094
5. Buszkowski, W., Farulewski, M.: Nonassociative Lambek calculus with additives and context-free languages. In: Grumberg, O., Kaminski, M., Katz, S., Wintner, S. (eds.) Languages: From Formal to Natural. LNCS, vol. 5533, pp. 45–58. Springer, Heidelberg (2009). https://doi.org/10.1007/978-3-642-01748-3_4
6. Chapman, P., McKinna, J., Urban, C.: Mechanising a proof of Craig's interpolation theorem for intuitionistic logic in nominal isabelle. In: Autexier, S., Campbell, J., Rubio, J., Sorge, V., Suzuki, M., Wiedijk, F. (eds.) CICM 2008. LNCS (LNAI), vol. 5144, pp. 38–52. Springer, Heidelberg (2008). https://doi.org/10.1007/978-3-540-85110-3_5
7. Craig, W.: Three uses of the Herbrand-Gentzen theorem in relating model theory and proof theory. J. Symb. Log. **22**(3), 269–285 (1957). https://doi.org/10.2307/2963594
8. Čubrić, D.: Results in categorical proof theory. Ph.D. thesis, McGill University (1993). https://escholarship.mcgill.ca/concern/theses/pv63g1818
9. Čubrić, D.: Interpolation property for bicartesian closed categories. Arch. Math. Log. **33**(4), 291–319 (1994). https://doi.org/10.1007/bf01270628
10. Férée, H., van der Giessen, I., van Gool, S., Shillito, I.: Mechanised uniform interpolation for modal logics K, GL, and iSL. In: Benzmüller, C., Heule, M.J.H., Schmidt, R.A. (eds.) IJCAR 2024. LNCS, vol. 14740, pp. 43–60. Springer, Cham (2024). https://doi.org/10.1007/978-3-031-63501-4_3
11. Férée, H., van Gool, S.: Formalizing and computing propositional quantifiers. In: Krebbers, R., Traytel, D., Pientka, B., Zdancewic, S. (eds.) Proceedings of 12th ACM SIGPLAN International Conference on Certified Programs and Proofs, CPP 2023, pp. 148–158. ACM (2023). https://doi.org/10.1145/3573105.3575668
12. Jäger, G.: Residuation, structural rules and context freeness. J. Log. Lang. Inf. **13**(1), 47–59 (2004). https://doi.org/10.1023/a:1026175817625
13. Kandulski, M.: The equivalence of nonassociative Lambek categorial grammars and context-free grammars. Z. Math. Log. Grundl. Math. **34**(1) (1988). https://doi.org/10.1002/malq.19880340106
14. Kokke, P.: Formalising type-logical grammars in Agda. In: Extended abstracts of the ESSLLI 2015 workshop TYTLES: Types Theory and Lexical Semantics, pp. 83–90 (2015). https://www.lirmm.fr/tytles/Articles/Kokke.pdf, https://github.com/wenkokke/msla2014/blob/b880cf25ed8e81b9a965ea9aad18377008d68a9f/src/LambekGrishinCalculus.agda
15. Lambek, J.: The mathematics of sentence structure. Amer. Math. Monthly **65**(3), 154–170 (1958). https://doi.org/10.2307/2310058
16. Lambek, J.: On the calculus of syntactic types. In: Jakobson, R. (ed.) Structure of Language and Its Mathematical Aspects, Proceedings of Symposium in Applied

Mathematics, vol. 12, pp. 166–178. American Mathematical Society, Providence (1961). https://doi.org/10.1090/psapm/012
17. Lin, Z.: Non-associative Lambek calculus with modalities: interpolation, complexity and FEP. Log. J. IGPL **22**(3), 494–512 (2014). https://doi.org/10.1093/jigpal/jzt042
18. Maehara, S.: Craig's interpolation theorem. Sûgaku **12**(4), 235–237 (1961). https://doi.org/10.11429/sugaku1947.12.235
19. Michaelis, J., Nipkow, T.: Formalized proof systems for propositional logic. In: Abel, A., Forsberg, F.N., Kaposi, A. (eds.) Proceedings of 23rd International Conference on Types for Proofs and Programs (TYPES 2017). Leibniz International Proceedings in Informatics, vol. 104, pp. 5:1–5:16. Dagstuhl Publishing, Saarbrücken/Wadern (2019). https://doi.org/10.4230/lipics.types.2017.5
20. Moot, R., Retore, C.: The Logic of Categorial Grammars: A Deductive Account of Natural Language Syntax and Semantics. LNCS, vol. 6850. Springer, Heidelberg (2012). https://doi.org/10.1007/978-3-642-31555-8
21. Ono, H.: Proof-theoretic methods in nonclassical logic: an introduction. In: Dezani-Ciancaglini, M., Okada, M., Takahashi, M. (eds.) Theories of Types and Proofs. Mathematical Society Memoirs, vol. 2, pp. 207–254. Mathematical Society of Japan (1998). https://doi.org/10.2969/msjmemoirs/00201c060
22. Ridge, T.: Craig's interpolation theorem formalised and mechanised in Isabelle/HOL. arXiv eprint arXiv:cs/0607058 [cs.LO] (2006). https://doi.org/10.48550/arxiv.cs/0607058
23. Roorda, D.: Resource logics: proof-theoretical investigations. Ph.D. thesis, Universiteit van Amsterdam (1991). https://pure.knaw.nl/ws/portalfiles/portal/1821261/Roorda_1991_Resource_Logics_Proof_theoretical_Investigations.pdf
24. Saurin, A.: Interpolation as cut-introduction: on the computational content of Craig-Lyndon interpolation. In: Fernández, M. (ed.) Proceedings of 10th International Conference on Formal Structures for Computation and Deduction (FSCD 2025). Leibniz International Proceedings in Informatics, vol. 337, pp. 32:1–32:21. Dagstuhl Publishing, Saarbrücken/Wadern (2025). https://doi.org/10.4230/lipics.fscd.2025.32
25. Tian, C.: Formalized Lambek calculus in higher order logic HOL4. arXiv eprint arXiv:1705.07318 [cs.CL] (2017). https://doi.org/10.48550/arXiv.1705.07318, https://github.com/binghe/informatica-public/tree/master/lambek
26. Veltri, N., Wan, C.-S.: Craig interpolation for a semi-substructural logic. Stud. Log. (to appear). https://doi.org/10.1007/s11225-025-10189-7

**Open Access** This chapter is licensed under the terms of the Creative Commons Attribution 4.0 International License (http://creativecommons.org/licenses/by/4.0/), which permits use, sharing, adaptation, distribution and reproduction in any medium or format, as long as you give appropriate credit to the original author(s) and the source, provide a link to the Creative Commons license and indicate if changes were made.

The images or other third party material in this chapter are included in the chapter's Creative Commons license, unless indicated otherwise in a credit line to the material. If material is not included in the chapter's Creative Commons license and your intended use is not permitted by statutory regulation or exceeds the permitted use, you will need to obtain permission directly from the copyright holder.

# Cyclic System for an Algebraic Theory of Alternating Parity Automata

Anupam Das and Abhishek De

University of Birmingham, Birmingham, UK
{a.das,a.de}@bham.ac.uk

**Abstract.** $\omega$-regular languages are a natural extension of the regular languages to the setting of infinite words. Likewise, they are recognised by a host of automata models, one of the most important being Alternating Parity Automata (APAs), a generalisation of Büchi automata that symmetrises both the transitions (with universal as well as existential branching) and the acceptance condition (by a parity condition).

In this work, we develop a cyclic proof system manipulating APAs, represented by an algebraic notation of Right Linear Lattice expressions. This syntax dualises that of previously introduced Right Linear Algebras, which comprised a notation for non-deterministic finite automata. Our main result is the soundness and completeness of our system for $\omega$-language inclusion, heavily exploiting game-theoretic techniques from the theory of $\omega$-regular languages.

**Keywords:** Cyclic Proofs · $\omega$-regular Languages · Alternating Parity Automata · Parity Games · Determinacy · Proof Search · Fixed Points

## 1 Introduction

The theory of $\omega$-regular languages is among the most important in all of computer science. *Büchi automata*, the classical characterisation of $\omega$-regularity, are a variation of usual finite state automata that run on infinite words rather than finite ones. Büchi's famous complementation theorem for these automata is the engine underlying his proof of the decidability of monadic second-order logic (MSOL) over infinite words [34]. Its extension to infinite trees, *Rabin's Tree Theorem* [33], is often referred to as the 'mother of all decidability results'.

Büchi automata can be generalised in two ways: (i) by considering more expressive acceptance conditions, such as Muller or parity; and (ii) by symmetrising the transition relation, allowing both existential and *universal* branching. Combining these gives *alternating parity automata* (APAs), a symmetric model that leads to beautiful accounts of $\omega$-language theory via the theory of positional and finite memory games (see, e.g., [4,20,31]). Indeed, their features more closely mimic those of logical settings where such symmetries abound, e.g. the linear-time $\mu$-calculus ($\mu$LTL) and MSOL over infinite words.

**Contribution.** In this work we design a system for reasoning *natively* about APAs, in the form of *right-linear lattice* (RLL) expressions. This syntax is a dualisation of previously studied *right-linear algebra* (RLA) expressions [9,10], which comprise a notation for non-deterministic finite word automata (NFAs). While RLA expressions model existential nondeterminism by a join-semilattice structure $(0, +)$, and resolve cycles of an automaton by *least* fixed points $\mu$, RLL expressions can further model universal nondeterminism by a lattice structure $(0, +, \top, \cap)$ and resolve infinite paths of an automaton by a combination of least and *greatest* fixed points $\nu$, modelling the parity condition.

Our system, $\mathsf{CRLL}_\mathcal{L}$, is a two-sided sequent calculus admitting *cyclic proofs*: proof trees may be non-wellfounded but regular. Our main result is the soundness and completeness of $\mathsf{CRLL}_\mathcal{L}$ with respect to the usual model of $\omega$-languages. The techniques we employ in this work draw heavily from the literature on cyclic proofs, in particular the *game theoretic* approach dating back to Niwiński and Walukiewicz [30]. Soundness of $\mathsf{CRLL}_\mathcal{L}$ is established via an infinite descent argument that is typical of cyclic proof theory, here formulated as a reduction to the adequacy of certain *evaluation games*. Completeness of $\mathsf{CRLL}_\mathcal{L}$ further exploits the finite-memory determinacy of the associated *proof search game*, implied by the well-known Büchi-Landweber theorem for $\omega$-regular games [6].

**Related Work.** Using fixed points to model parity conditions is an old idea, going back to work of Streett and Emerson [36] in the setting of the modal $\mu$-calculus. The latter's linear-time restriction $\mu$LTL offers an alternative syntax for APAs, but one that differs somewhat from the RLL expressions of this work. $\mu$LTL formulas, built over classical logic, are equipped with native complementation, while RLL expressions are not. Furthermore, while $\mu$LTL formulas are interpreted as subsets of $\mathbb{N}$, over a *fixed* $\omega$-word, RLL expressions are interpreted directly as sets of $\omega$-words. These differences have effects on the resulting proof theory of these logics. Previously studied systems for $\mu$LTL include a complete axiomatisation due to Kaivola [23] (see also [17]) and, most related to this work, a cyclic system due to Dax, Hofmann and Lange [15].

Our algebraic syntax is rather inspired by the tradition of *regular algebras* (see, e.g., [2,3,24,26,35]), structures interpreting regular expressions, in particular their extensions by lattice structure (see, e.g., [1,25,32]). $\omega$-*regular expressions* are a modification of regular expressions for notating $\omega$-regular languages. They have enjoyed both axiomatic treatments (see, e.g., [7,8,29,38]) and more recently a cyclic system [21], building on the cyclic system of [14] for Kleene Algebra.

**Full Version.** Detailed proofs and further examples can be found in [12].

## 2 Right-Linear Lattice Expressions

Let us fix a finite set $\mathcal{A}$ (the **alphabet**) of **letters**, written $a, b$, etc., and a countable set $\mathcal{V}$ of **variables**, written $X, Y$, etc.

## 2.1 Syntax and Semantics of Right-Linear Lattice Expressions

In this subsection, we introduce the basic syntax and semantics we shall work with, before relating them to automaton models later.

**Definition 1.** *Right-linear lattice expressions, or simply (**RLL** expressions, written $e, f$, etc. are generated as follows,*

$$e, f, \ldots ::= X \quad | \quad ae \quad | \quad 0 \quad | \quad e + f \quad | \quad \mu X e$$
$$| \quad \top \quad | \quad e \cap f \quad | \quad \nu X e$$

*where $X \in \mathcal{V}$ and $a \in \mathcal{A}$. The **free variables** of an expression are defined as expected, understanding $\mu$ and $\nu$ as variable binders. A **closed** expression is one with no free variables. A (closed) expression $e$ is **guarded** if each of its variable occurrences $X$ occurs free in a subexpression of form $af$.*

We may sometimes refer to expressions as 'formulas' when it is more natural (e.g. 'subformula', or 'principal formula'). The intended semantics of expressions is given by languages of infinite words:

**Definition 2 (Language semantics).** *Let us temporarily expand the syntax of expressions to include each language $A \subseteq \mathcal{A}^\omega$ as a constant symbol. We interpret each closed expression (of this expanded syntax) as a subset of $\mathcal{A}^\omega$ inductively:*

$$\begin{aligned}
\mathcal{L}(A) &:= A & \mathcal{L}(ae) &:= \{aw \mid w \in \mathcal{L}(e)\} \\
\mathcal{L}(0) &:= \varnothing & \mathcal{L}(\top) &:= \mathcal{A}^\omega \\
\mathcal{L}(e + f) &:= \mathcal{L}(e) \cup \mathcal{L}(f) & \mathcal{L}(e \cap f) &:= \mathcal{L}(e) \cap \mathcal{L}(f) \\
\mathcal{L}(\mu X e(X)) &:= \bigcap \{A \mid A \supseteq \mathcal{L}(e(A))\} & \mathcal{L}(\nu X e(X)) &:= \bigcup \{A \mid A \subseteq \mathcal{L}(e(A))\}
\end{aligned}$$

The interpretation of $a\cdot, 0, \top, +, \cap$ should be familiar from formal language theory. For the binders, the idea is that $\mathcal{L}$ interprets $\mu X e(X)$ and $\nu X e(X)$ as the least and greatest fixed points, respectively, of the operation $A \mapsto \mathcal{L}(e(A))$. Note that each such operation is *monotone*, i.e. $A \subseteq B \implies \mathcal{L}(e(A)) \subseteq \mathcal{L}(e(B))$, by a straightforward induction on the structure of $e$. Thus by the *Knaster-Tarski Theorem* $A \mapsto \mathcal{L}(e(A))$ indeed has a least and greatest fixed point in $\mathcal{L}$, given by the definitions of $\mathcal{L}(\mu X e(X))$ and $\mathcal{L}(\nu X e(X))$.

*Example 3.* We have $\mathcal{L}(\mu X X) = \varnothing$ and $\mathcal{L}(\nu X X) = \mathcal{A}^\omega$. Thus we can say that the structure $\mathcal{L}$ satisfies $0 = \mu X X$ and $\top = \nu X X$. We also have $\mathcal{L}(\nu X(aX)) = a^\omega$ and $\mathcal{L}(\nu X(aX + bX)) = \{a, b\}^\omega$.

In previous work [9,10] we studied expressions without $\top, \cap$ and $\nu$, called *right-linear algebra (RLA) expressions*, which semantically denote languages of finite words rather than $\omega$-words.[1] The terminology 'right-linear' is drawn from the formal grammar literature, as both RLA expressions and RLL expressions

---

[1] More precisely, one must include a constant symbol 1, with $\mathcal{L}(1) := \{\varepsilon\}$, so that expressions do not trivially always denote the empty language.

allow products $ef$ only when $e$ is a letter $a \in \mathcal{A}$. RLA expressions can be construed as a notation for non-deterministic finite automata (equivalently, right-linear grammars) over *finite* words, and duly denote just the regular languages. As RLL expressions denote languages of infinite words, we are interested in the corresponding notion of regularity.

**Definition 4 ($\omega$-regular languages).** *A language $L \subseteq \mathcal{A}^\omega$ is $\omega$-**regular** if we have $L = \bigcup_{i<n} B_i C_i^\omega$ for some $B_i, C_i$ regular and $\varepsilon \notin C_i$.*

There are now several equivalent presentations of $\omega$-regular languages. The one above is often called the *Kleene closure* of regular languages. The most common presentations are via $\omega$-automata, such as Büchi automata and parity automata, and we shall (briefly) see *alternating* parity automata later.

It turns out that RLL expressions denote just the $\omega$-regular languages. One direction, that RLL expressions *exhaust* the $\omega$-regular languages, was already observed in previous work:

**Proposition 5 [9].** *For every $\omega$-regular language $L \subseteq \mathcal{A}^\omega$ there is a guarded expression $e$ with $L = \mathcal{L}(e)$.*

[9,10] further studied the extension of RLA expressions by $\nu$ (but without $\top, \cap$), so-called $\nu$RLA expressions; indeed the above result holds already for $e$ free of $\top, \cap$. The proof theory of $\nu$RLA expressions developed in [9,10] is much simpler (but less symmetric) than that of RLL expressions presented in this work. Indeed the presence of $\top$ and $\cap$ renders our syntax fully symmetric: $\top$ is dual to 0, + is dual to $\cap$, and $\mu$ is dual to $\nu$. While $\nu$RLA expressions correspond to *non-deterministic* parity automata, RLL expressions correspond to *alternating* parity automata.

*Example 6 ((In)finitely many).* Let us fix the alphabet $\mathcal{A} = \{a, b\}$. We have:

- $f_a := \mu X(aX + bX + \nu Y(bY))$ denotes (in $\mathcal{L}$) the set of words with only finitely many $a$s.
- $i_a := \nu X \mu Y(aX + bY)$ denotes the set of words with infinitely many $a$s.
- $\mathcal{L}(i_a \cap f_b)$ is the set of words with infinitely many $a$s but finitely many $b$s.
- $f_a \cap f_b$ and $i_a \cap f_a$ both denote the empty language.

*Remark 7 (Comparison to $\mu$LTL, syntax and semantics).* For the reader familiar with linear-temporal logic (LTL), our syntax may look familiar to its extension by least and greatest fixed points, $\mu$LTL (see, e.g., [28]). Indeed there are many high-level similarities, in particular with both syntaxes enjoying a form of symmetry and, as we shall soon see, serving as notations for alternating parity automata. Let us point out two subtle differences:

- RLL expressions do not have a native complementation operation, unlike $\mu$LTL formulas. They are based in the language of lattice theory rather than that of Boolean algebras.

- RLL expressions are interpreted as *sets* of $\omega$-words, while $\mu$LTL formulas are interpreted as subsets of $\mathbb{N}$, within a structure given by a *single* $\omega$-word.

At the level of automata and language theory these differences are quite minor, but they will ultimately have a more significant effect on the resulting proof theory for RLL expressions we present in Sect. 3 later.

### 2.2 Expressions as Automata

In this subsection, we shall introduce a textbook automaton model for computing $\omega$-languages, essentially following the exposition in [4].

An **alternating parity automaton** (APA) is a tuple $\mathbf{A} = (Q, \Delta, X_0, c)$:

- $Q$ is a finite set of **states**, partitioned into **existential** states $E$ and **universal** states $A$.
- $\Delta$ is a set of **transitions** or **productions** of form $X \xrightarrow{\varepsilon} Y$ or $X \xrightarrow{a} Y$, for $X, Y \in Q$ and $a \in \mathcal{A}$.
- $X_0 \in Q$ is the **initial** state.
- $c : Q \to \{0, \ldots, n\}$ is called the **colouring**.

A **run-tree** of a word $w \in \mathcal{A}^\omega$ is a tree of nodes of form $(v, X)$ where $v$ is a (infinite) suffix of $w$ and $X$ is a state, generated by:

- The root is $(w, X_0)$.
- A node $(v, X)$, where $X \in E$, must have exactly one child, either $(v, X)$ with $X \xrightarrow{\varepsilon} Y$ in $\Delta$, or $(v', X)$ with $X \xrightarrow{a} Y$ in $\Delta$ and $v = av'$.
- A node $(v, X)$, where $X \in A$, must have children $(v, Y)$ for all transitions $X \xrightarrow{\varepsilon} Y$ in $\Delta$ and children $(v', Y)$ for all transitions $X \xrightarrow{a} Y$ if $v = av'$.

An infinite path $\pi$ of a run-tree from $w$ is **accepting** $w$ if the least colour among its infinitely occurring states is even (otherwise $\pi$ is **rejecting**). An APA $\mathbf{A}$ **accepts** $w$ if there is a run-tree from $w$ in which every infinite path is accepting (otherwise $\mathbf{A}$ **rejects** $w$). We write $\mathcal{L}(\mathbf{A})$ for the set of $\omega$-words accepted by $\mathbf{A}$.

Notably, it is well known that APAs give yet another characterisation of the $\omega$-regular languages:

**Fact 8 (See, e.g., [4]).** $L \subseteq \mathcal{A}^\omega$ *is $\omega$-regular* $\iff$ *there is an APA* $\mathbf{A}$ *s.t.* $\mathcal{L}(\mathbf{A}) = L$.

Note that we have allowed '$\varepsilon$-transitions' of the form $X \xrightarrow{\varepsilon} Y$, to mimic the syntax of RLL-expressions as closely as possible. We shall draw APAs in a similar fashion to usual finite word automata:

*Example 9 (Expressions vs automata).* The following APAs compute the languages from Example 6:

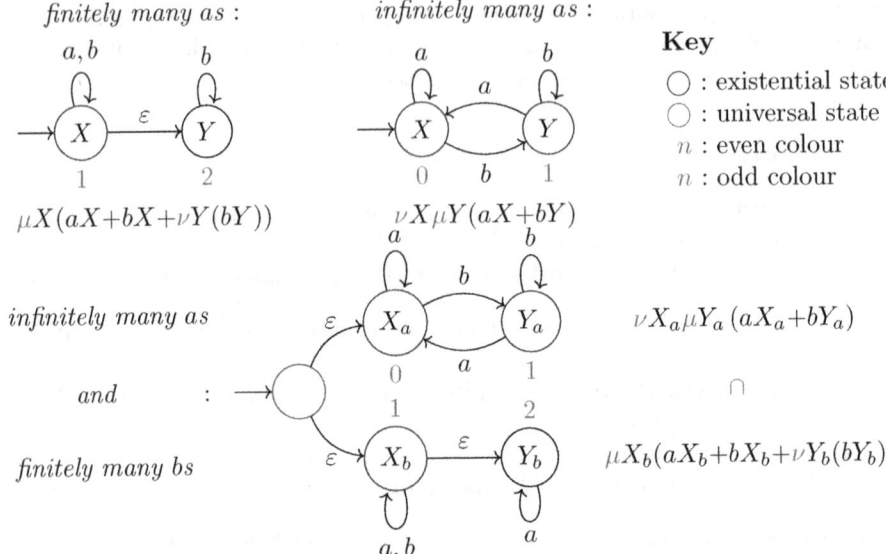

We have repeated the expressions from Example 6 for the corresponding languages above too, now with colouring suggestive of how APAs and RLL expressions correspond to each other (more on this later). For states that are black/uncoloured, it does not matter whether they are universal or existential, as there is a unique transition from them.

The preceding example suggested an association between expressions and APAs. We can make this formal:

**Theorem 10.** *For every closed RLL-expression $e$, there is an APA $\mathbf{A}_e$ such that $\mathcal{L}(e) = \mathcal{L}(\mathbf{A}_e)$.*

Together with Fact 8 we thus obtain:

**Corollary 11.** *For any closed RLL expression $e$, $\mathcal{L}(e)$ is $\omega$-regular.*

In fact, Proposition 5 can itself be refined: RLL expressions can be construed as a *notation* for APAs, but a full development is beyond the scope of this work.

## 3  A Cyclic System for RLL Expressions

In this section, we shall present a sequent-style system for RLL expressions and associated notions of 'non-wellfounded' and 'cyclic' proof.

Let us take a moment to remark upon some principles valid in the intended interpretation $\mathcal{L}$ of RLL expressions, in order to motivate the proof systems we are about to introduce. As usual we write $e \leq f$ for $e + f = f$, equivalently $e = e \cap f$ (so in $\mathcal{L}$, $\leq$ just means $\subseteq$).

1. $(0, \top, +, \cap)$ forms a bounded distributive lattice.
2. Each $a \in \mathcal{A}$ is a (lower) semibounded lattice homomorphism:
   - $a0 = 0$
   - $a(e + f) = ae + af$
   - $a(e \cap f) = ae \cap af$
3. The ranges of $a \in \mathcal{A}$ partition $\mathcal{P}(\mathcal{A}^\omega)$:
   - $ae \cap bf = 0$ if $a \neq b$
   - $\top = \sum_{a \in \mathcal{A}} a\top$

**$\mathcal{A}$ rules:**

$$\text{p-}l\, \frac{}{ae, bf \to}\, a \neq b \qquad \text{h}_a\, \frac{\Gamma \to \Delta}{a\Gamma \to a\Delta}\, \Gamma \neq \emptyset \qquad \text{p-}r\, \frac{\{\to \Gamma_a\}_{a \in \mathcal{A}}}{\to \{a\Gamma_a\}_{a \in \mathcal{A}}}$$

**Structural rules:**

$$\text{w-}l\, \frac{\Gamma \to \Delta}{\Gamma, e \to \Delta} \qquad \text{w-}r\, \frac{\Gamma \to \Delta}{\Gamma \to \Delta, e}$$

**Left logical rules:**

$$\text{0-}l\, \frac{}{\Gamma, 0 \to \Delta} \qquad \text{+-}l\, \frac{\Gamma, e \to \Delta \quad f \to \Delta}{\Gamma, e+f \to \Delta} \qquad \mu\text{-}l\, \frac{\Gamma, e(\mu X e(X)) \to \Delta}{\Gamma, \mu X e(X) \to \Delta}$$

$$\top\text{-}l\, \frac{\Gamma \to \Delta}{\Gamma, \top \to \Delta} \qquad \cap\text{-}l\, \frac{\Gamma, e, f \to \Delta}{\Gamma, e \cap f \to \Delta} \qquad \nu\text{-}l\, \frac{\Gamma, e(\nu X e(X)) \to \Delta}{\Gamma, \nu X e(X) \to \Delta}$$

**Right logical rules:**

$$\text{0-}r\, \frac{\Gamma \to \Delta}{\Gamma \to \Delta, 0} \qquad \text{+-}r\, \frac{\Gamma \to \Delta, e, f}{\Gamma \to \Delta, e+f} \qquad \mu\text{-}r\, \frac{\Gamma \to \Delta, e(\mu X e(X))}{\Gamma \to \Delta, \mu X e(X)}$$

$$\top\text{-}r\, \frac{}{\Gamma \to \Delta, \top} \qquad \cap\text{-}r\, \frac{\Gamma \to \Delta, e \quad \Gamma \to \Delta, f}{\Gamma \to \Delta, e \cap f} \qquad \nu\text{-}r\, \frac{\Gamma \to \Delta, e(\nu X e(X))}{\Gamma \to \Delta, \nu X e(X)}$$

**Fig. 1.** Rules of the system $\widehat{\text{LRLL}}_\mathcal{L}$.

### 3.1 A Sequent System

A **sequent** is an expression $\Gamma \to \Delta$, where $\Gamma$ and $\Delta$ are sets of expressions (called **cedents**). The intended reading of a sequent $\Gamma \to \Delta$ is the inequality $\bigcap \Gamma \leq \sum \Delta$.

**Definition 12.** *The system $\widehat{\text{LRLL}}_\mathcal{L}$ is given by the rules of Fig. 1, where we write $a\Gamma := \{ae \mid e \in \Gamma\}$.*

By the properties we identified for the language model earlier, Items 1 to 3:

**Proposition 13 (Local soundness).** *Each rule of* $\widehat{\mathsf{LRLL}}_{\mathcal{L}}$ *is sound for* $\mathcal{L}$. *I.e. for each inference step* $\mathsf{r} \dfrac{\Gamma_1 \to \Delta_1 \quad \cdots \quad \Gamma_n \to \Delta_n}{\Gamma \to \Delta}$ *of* $\widehat{\mathsf{LRLL}}_{\mathcal{L}}$, *if for* $i = 1, \ldots, n$ *we have* $\mathcal{L}(\bigcap \Gamma_i) \subseteq \mathcal{L}(\sum \Delta_i)$, *then also* $\mathcal{L}(\bigcap \Gamma) \subseteq \mathcal{L}(\sum \Delta)$.

*Remark 14 (*p-r*).* Let us explain further the p-r rule. Recall that LHSs of sequents are interpreted as intersections, so an empty LHS corresponds to a nullary intersection i.e., the top element, which in our case is $\mathcal{A}^\omega$. Therefore, p-r rule states that if, for each $a \in \mathcal{A}$, we have $\mathcal{A}^\omega = \Gamma_a$, then $\mathcal{A}^\omega = \sum_{a \in \mathcal{A}} a\Gamma_a$. This is justified by Item 3 at the beginning of the section, and explains why we have a premiss for each letter $a \in \mathcal{A}$.

However, notice that we have not included any (co)induction rules in $\widehat{\mathsf{LRLL}}_{\mathcal{L}}$: in fact this system does not distinguish $\mu X e$ and $\nu X e$ at the level of rules. Rather, their distinction is controlled by a notion of infinite proof that we shall soon see.

*Remark 15 (Sequents vs hypersequents).* Systems for regular and $\omega$-regular expressions, e.g. [14,21], worked with a form of hypersequent, $\Gamma \to S$, where $\Gamma$ is a list of formulas and $S$ is a set of lists. Our sequents for RLL expressions avoid such extra structure on the RHS, due to the absence of multiplication, while recovering symmetry on the LHS, due to native lattice operations $\top, \cap$.

### 3.2 Non-wellfounded and Cyclic Proofs

We introduce a form of *non-wellfounded* proof to recover (co)inductive reasoning:

**Definition 16 (Preproofs).** *A **preproof** (of* $\widehat{\mathsf{LRLL}}_{\mathcal{L}}$*) is generated coinductively from the rules of* $\widehat{\mathsf{LRLL}}_{\mathcal{L}}$. *In other words, it is a possibly infinite tree of sequents generated by the rules of* $\widehat{\mathsf{LRLL}}_{\mathcal{L}}$. *A preproof is **cyclic** or **regular** if it has only finitely many distinct sub-preproofs.*

While usual inductively generated proofs can be represented as finite trees or DAGs of sequents, cyclic preproofs are rather represented as *graphs* of sequents, possibly with cycles (we shall see examples shortly). Of course, non-wellfounded reasoning can be fallacious, so genuine 'proofs' must satisfy further conditions. This is given by a 'global trace condition', as per usual in cyclic proof theory.

As usual for structural and logical steps, the **principal** formula is the distinguished formula on the LHS or RHS, respectively, of the lower sequent, as typeset in Fig. 1. Any distinguished formulas on the LHS or RHS, respectively, of the upper sequent are called **auxiliary**. For an inference step r, a formula $e'$ in the LHS/RHS of a premiss is an **immediate ancestor** of a formula $e$ in the LHS/RHS, respectively, of the conclusion if:

- r is structural or logical, $e$ is principal and $e'$ is auxiliary; or,

- r is a $h_a$ step and $e = ae'$; or,
- r is a p-$r$ step, $e'$ occurs in the $a$-premiss and $e = ae'$; or,
- $e = e'$.

**Definition 17 (Traces).** *For an infinite branch B (of some preproof), a (B-)trace is a maximal path along the graph of immediate ancestry, restricted to B. An LHS or RHS trace is one that remains in the LHS or RHS respectively. We say that an infinitely often principal trace $\tau$ is **progressing** if:*

- *$\tau$ is LHS with smallest infinitely often principal formula a $\mu$-formula; or,*
- *$\tau$ is RHS with smallest infinitely often principal formula a $\nu$-formula.*

We shall examine some more low-level properties of traces in the next section, in particular addressing the existence of 'smallest infinitely often principal formulas'. We shall also see some examples of traces (and preproofs) soon, in the next subsection. However, for now, let us finally give our definition of cyclic proof:

**Definition 18 (CRLL$_\mathcal{L}$ system).** *A $\widehat{\mathsf{LRLL}}_\mathcal{L}$ preproof is **progressing** if every infinite branch has a progressing trace. Write CRLL$_\mathcal{L}$ for the class of regular progressing $\widehat{\mathsf{LRLL}}_\mathcal{L}$-preproofs, which we may simply call CRLL$_\mathcal{L}$-**proofs** henceforth. We may write, say, CRLL$_\mathcal{L} \vdash \Gamma \to \Delta$ if there is a CRLL$_\mathcal{L}$-proof of $\Gamma \to \Delta$.*

*Remark 19 (Proof checking).* While the progressing condition for proofhood may look complex, let us emphasise that it is indeed decidable for regular preproofs. The set of progressing branches of a regular preproof $P$ forms an $\omega$-regular language over the alphabet of (the finitely many) sequents in $P$, and so progressiveness can be decided in **PSPACE** by reduction to universality of Büchi automata (see, e.g., [16,30], for similar developments for the modal $\mu$-calculus).

We are now in a position to state the main result of this work:

**Theorem 20 (Soundness and completeness).** CRLL$_\mathcal{L} \vdash \Gamma \to \Delta \iff \bigcap_{e \in \Gamma} \mathcal{L}(e) \subseteq \bigcup_{f \in \Lambda} \mathcal{L}(f)$, *for $\Gamma, \Delta$ containing only guarded expressions.*

The proof is involved, requiring a detour through the theory of $\omega$-regular games. We shall develop this formally over the course of Sects. 4 and 5. Note that the restriction to guarded sequents above is harmless in the sense that each expression is equivalent to a guarded one, over $\mathcal{L}$, cf. Proposition 5 (see also, e.g., [5] for the related setting of the modal $\mu$-calculus). One useful consequence of this restriction is:

**Observation 21.** *If $\Gamma, \Delta$ consists of only guarded formulas and $P$ is a $\widehat{\mathsf{LRLL}}_\mathcal{L}$ preproof of $\Gamma \to \Delta$, then no infinite trace in $P$ is eventually stable.*

*Remark 22 (Comparison to μLTL, system).* Recalling Remark 7, let us point out that cyclic systems for μLTL have appeared in the literature too, in particular in [15]. Here the differences of syntax and semantics between RLL expressions and μLTL formulas become more telling.

As μLTL formulas are based in classical logic with full negation/duality, sequents are (without loss of generality) one-sided with just one initial rule for identity, $\dfrac{}{\to p, \bar p}$.[2] On the other hand RLL sequents are necessarily two-sided, as there is no native complementation operation. Instead the homomorphism rules in the top line of Fig. 1 are carefully designed in order to admit an appropriate proof search strategy, for completeness, as we shall see in Definition 34 later.

Finally, while the logical rules of $\widehat{\mathsf{LRLL}}_\mathcal{L}$ behave like the analogous rules of μLTL in [15], let us point out that this is for semantically slightly different reasons: as mentioned in Remark 7, while μLTL-formulas are interpreted within the complete lattice of subsets of $\mathbb{N}$, RLL expressions are interpreted in the complete lattice of ω-languages.

### 3.3 Some Examples

We conclude this section with some examples of cyclic proofs pertinent to ω-language theory. Recall the expressions $f_a := \mu X(aX + bX + \nu Y(bY))$ and $i_a := \nu X \mu Y(aX + bY)$ from Example 6, denoting the languages of finitely many $a$s and infinitely many $a$s respectively, when $\mathcal{A} = \{a, b\}$. Let us point out that both $f_a$ and $i_a$ are guarded. In what follows, we write $i'_a := \mu Y(ai_a + bY)$.

Recall $\mathcal{L}(\nu X(aX)) = a^\omega$ from Example 3. The following $\mathsf{CRLL}_\mathcal{L}$-proofs shows that $a^\omega$ has infinitely many $a$s.

$$\cfrac{\cfrac{\cfrac{\cfrac{\cfrac{\vdots}{\nu X(aX) \to i_a} \bullet}{a\nu X(aX) \to a i_a} h_a}{a\nu X(aX) \to a i_a + b i'_a} +\text{-}r, \text{w-}r}{a\nu X(aX) \to i'_a} \mu\text{-}r}{\nu X(aX) \to i_a} \nu\text{-}l, \nu\text{-}r \bullet$$

We have used $\bullet$ to indicate roots of identical subpreproofs. The only infinite branch along the proof, looping on $\bullet$, has a progressing RHS trace with critical formula $i_a$, according to the indicated orange trace. Note in particular that, while $i'_a$ is also infinitely often principal, it contains $i_a$ as a subformula.

Now, consider the following proof $a^\omega$ does *not* have finitely many $a$s.

---

[2] In proof systems for (linear-time) μ-calculi it makes more sense to construe the alphabet as the free Boolean algebra on finitely many propositional symbols, rather than finite sets of atomic letters, e.g. as in [28].

$$\cfrac{\cfrac{\vdots}{\cfrac{\cfrac{\overline{f_a, \nu Y(aY) \to}}{a f_a, a\nu Y(aY) \to}\, h_a \quad \cfrac{}{bf_a, a\nu Y(aY) \to}\, \text{p-}l \quad \cfrac{\cfrac{\overline{b\nu Y bY, a\nu Y(aY) \to}}{\nu Y bY, a\nu Y(aY) \to}\, \text{p-}l}{}\, \nu\text{-}l}{af_a + bf_a + \nu Y(bY), a\nu Y(aY) \to}\, \text{+-}l}{\cfrac{f_a, a\nu Y(aY) \to}{\cfrac{f_a, \nu Y(aY) \to}{f_a \cap \nu Y(aY) \to}\, \cap\text{-}l}\, \nu\text{-}l}\, \mu\text{-}l}^{\circ}$$

The only infinite branch along the right proof, looping on ∘, has a progressing LHS trace with critical formula $f_a$, according to the indicated blue path.

Our final example is a cyclic proof that any infinite word over $\{a, b\}$ has either finitely many $a$s or infinitely many $a$s.

$$\cfrac{\cfrac{\cfrac{\overline{\to f_a, i_a}}{\to f_a, i_a}\,\bullet \quad \cfrac{\cfrac{\vdots}{\to af_a, bf_a, \nu Y(bY), i'_a}^{\circ}}{\cfrac{\to f_a, \nu Y(bY), i'_a}{\to af_a, bf_a, b\nu Y(bY), ai_a, bi'_a}}\, \mu\text{-}r,+\text{-}r}{\cfrac{\to af_a, bf_a, \nu Y(bY), ai_a, bi'_a}{\to af_a, bf_a, \nu Y(bY), i'_a}^{\circ}}\, \text{+-}r}{\cfrac{\to af_a + bf_a + \nu Y(bY), i'_a}{\to f_a, i_a}\,\bullet}\, \mu\text{-}r,\nu\text{-}r}{\to f_a + i_a}\, \text{+-}r$$

Here, there are continuum many infinite branches, naturally indexed by $\{\bullet, \circ\}$. Let us again conduct a case analysis on such infinite branches:

- A branch eventually looping on ∘, has progressing RHS trace with critical formula $\nu Y(bY)$, according to the orange path (eventually).
- A branch eventually looping on •, has a progressing RHS trace with critical formula $i_a$, according to the green path (eventually).
- Otherwise, an infinite branch must repeat both • and ∘ infinitely often, in which case it has a progressing trace with critical formula $i_a$, according to the green and blue paths depending on the current loop, • or ∘ respectively. Note that this trace only 'progresses' on the • loop, along which $i_a$ is principal.

## 4 Interlude: Fischer-Ladner and Evaluation Games

As an engine for metalogical results about $\mathsf{CRLL}_\mathcal{L}$ it is useful to first develop *game-theoretic* characterisations of formula evaluation.

### 4.1 The Fischer-Ladner Closure

First let us develop some of the low-level theory of traces.

**Definition 23 (FL).** $\to_{\mathrm{FL}}$ is the smallest relation on expressions satisfying:

- $ae \to_{\mathrm{FL}} e$.
- $e_0 \star e_1 \to_{\mathrm{FL}} e_i$, for $i \in \{0,1\}$ and $\star \in \{+, \cap\}$.
- $\sigma X e(X) \to_{\mathrm{FL}} e(\sigma X e(X))$, for $\sigma \in \{\mu, \nu\}$.

Write $\to_{\mathrm{FL}}^{=}$ and $\leq_{\mathrm{FL}}$ for the reflexive and reflexive transitive closures of $\to_{\mathrm{FL}}$, respectively. We also write $e <_{\mathrm{FL}} f$ if $e \leq_{\mathrm{FL}} f \not\leq_{\mathrm{FL}} e$. The **Fischer-Ladner** (FL) **closure** of an expression $e$, written $\mathrm{FL}(e)$, is $\{f \mid f \leq_{\mathrm{FL}} e\}$. A **trace** is a sequence $e_0 \to_{\mathrm{FL}}^{=} e_1 \to_{\mathrm{FL}}^{=} e_2 \to_{\mathrm{FL}}^{=} \cdots$.

Note that any $B$-trace, as in Definition 17, is indeed a trace in the sense above.

**Fact 24 (Properties of FL, see, e.g., [27,36]).** The following hold:

1. $\mathrm{FL}(e)$ is finite, and in fact has size linear in that of $e$.
2. $\leq_{\mathrm{FL}}$ is a preorder and $<_{\mathrm{FL}}$ is well-founded.
3. Every trace has a minimum infinitely occurring element, under $\sqsubseteq$. If a trace is not eventually stable, the minimum element has form $\mu X e$ or $\nu X e$.

We call the smallest infinitely occurring element of a trace its **critical** formula. If a trace is not ultimately stable, we call it a $\mu$-**trace** or $\nu$-**trace** if its critical formula is a $\mu$-formula or a $\nu$-formula, respectively. These properties motivate the definition of 'progressing trace' in Definition 17. In particular we obtain:

**Corollary 25.** For any $\widehat{\mathsf{LRLL}}_\mathcal{C}$ preproof $P$ of a sequent of only guarded formulas:

1. $P$ has only finitely many distinct sequents.
2. Every trace of $P$ is either a $\mu$-trace or a $\nu$-trace.

*Proof.* For 1, the only formulas that may occur in a $\widehat{\mathsf{LRLL}}_\mathcal{C}$ preproof $P$ of $\Gamma \to \Delta$ belong to $\mathrm{FL}(e)$ for some $e \in \Gamma \cup \Delta$, so are finitely many, cf. Fact 24.1. As cedents are sets of formulae, there are thus only finitely many sequents occurring in $P$. 2 follows immediately from Fact 24.3 under Observation 21. □

### 4.2 The Evaluation Game

In this subsection we define games for evaluating expressions, very similar to acceptance games for APAs.

**Definition 26 (Evaluation Game).** The **Evaluation Game** is a two-player game, played by Eloise ($\exists$) and Abelard ($\forall$). Positions of the game are pairs $(w, e)$ for $w \in \mathcal{A}^\omega$ and $e$ an expression. Moves of the game are given in Fig. 2.[3]

An infinite play of the evaluation game is **won** by $\exists$ (aka **lost** by $\forall$) if the smallest expression occurring infinitely often (in the right component) is a $\nu$-formula. (Otherwise it is won by $\forall$, aka lost by $\exists$.) If a play reaches deadlock, i.e. there is no available move, the player who owns the current position loses.

| Position | Player | Available moves |
|---|---|---|
| $(aw, ae)$ | - | $(w, e)$ |
| $(aw, be)$ with $a \neq b$ | $\exists$ | |
| $(w, 0)$ | $\exists$ | |
| $(w, \top)$ | $\forall$ | |
| $(w, e + f)$ | $\exists$ | $(w, e), (w, f)$ |
| $(w, e \cap f)$ | $\forall$ | $(w, e), (w, f)$ |
| $(w, \mu X e(X))$ | - | $(w, e(\mu X e(X)))$ |
| $(w, \nu X e(X))$ | - | $(w, e(\nu X e(X)))$ |

**Fig. 2.** Rules of the evaluation game.

Note that property (3) from Proposition 24 justifies our formulation of the winning condition in the evaluation game: the right components of any infinite play always form a trace that is never stable, by inspection of the available moves. Thus it is either a $\mu$-trace or a $\nu$-trace.

Note that winning can be formulated as a parity condition, like for APAs earlier, assigning priorities consistent with formula size and with $\mu$ and $\nu$ formulas having odd and even priorities, respectively. It is well-known that parity games are positionally determined, i.e. from each position some player has a winning strategy that depends only on the current position, not the history of the play (see, e.g., [4]). Thus:

**Observation 27.** *The Evaluation Game is positionally determined.*

By a standard well-ordering argument, there is even a *universal* positional winning strategy for $\exists$, one winning from *every* winning position. Similarly for $\forall$. As suggested by its name, the Evaluation Game is adequate for $\mathcal{L}$:

**Lemma 28 (Evaluation).** $w \in \mathcal{L}(e) \iff$ *Eloise has a winning strategy from $(w, e)$. (Otherwise, by determinacy, Abelard has a winning strategy from $(w, e)$).*

The proof of this result uses relatively standard but involved techniques, exploiting the theory of approximants and signatures for fixed points, inspired by previous work on the modal $\mu$-calculus such as [30, 36]. For the $\implies$ direction, we construct a winning $\exists$-strategy by preserving language membership whenever making a choice at a +-state $(w, e + f)$. However this is not yet enough: if both $w \in \mathcal{L}(e)$ and $w \in \mathcal{L}(f)$, we must make sure to 'decrease the witness' of membership. E.g. the strategy that loops on $(w, \mu X(\top + X))$ does not win despite $w \in \mathcal{L}(\mu X(1 + X)) = \mathcal{L}(\top) = \mathcal{A}^\omega$: at some point we must choose the move $(w, \top + \mu X(\top + X)) \to (w, \top)$ to win. Formally such a 'witness' is given by an *approximant* of a fixed point. For instance if $w \in \mathcal{L}(\mu X e(X))$ then we consider the least ordinal $\alpha$ such that $w \in \mathcal{L}(e^\alpha(0))$, appropriately defined. We can give an assignment of such approximations to *every* least fixed point of an

---

[3] For positions where a player is not assigned, the choice does not matter as there is a unique available move.

expression, a concept known known as a *signatures*, which are lexicographically ordered according to a 'dependency order' induced by $\leq_{FL}$. Now an appropriate $\exists$-strategy always make choices at +-states following least signatures. The $\impliedby$ direction is entirely dual, constructing a winning $\forall$-strategy, under determinacy, by approximating greatest fixed points instead of least.

## 5 Soundness and Completeness

Both directions of Theorem 20 are ultimately established by reduction to the adequacy of evaluation games, Lemma 28, though completeness will require us to build up further game theoretic technology first. Before that, let us show the soundness argument for $\mathsf{CRLL}_\mathcal{L}$:

*Proof (of $\implies$ direction of Theorem 20, sketch).* Let $P$ be a $\widehat{\mathsf{LRLL}_\mathcal{L}}$ preproof of $\Gamma \to \Delta$ and suppose $w \in \mathcal{L}(e)$ for all $e \in \Gamma$ but $w \notin \mathcal{L}(f)$ for all $f \in \Delta$. We shall show that $P$ is not progressing.

Let $\mathfrak{e}$ be a positional $\exists$ strategy that is winning from each $(w, e)$ for $e \in \Gamma$ and $\mathfrak{a}$ a positional $\forall$ strategy winning from each $(w, f)$ for $f \in \Delta$. $\mathfrak{e}$ and $\mathfrak{a}$ induce a unique infinite branch $B_{\mathfrak{e},\mathfrak{a}}$, by always making choices in the branch construction consistent with these two strategies.

Recall from Observation 21 that, by guardedness, no trace in $P$ is ultimately stable. By inspection of the rules and definition of $B_{\mathfrak{e},\mathfrak{a}}$ we thus have:

– Every LHS trace along $B_{\mathfrak{e},\mathfrak{a}}$, restricted to principal formulas, forms the right components of a play of $\mathfrak{e}$ from $(w, e)$, for some $e \in \Gamma$.
– Every RHS trace along $B_{\mathfrak{e},\mathfrak{a}}$, restricted to principal formulas, forms the right components of a play of $\mathfrak{a}$ from $(w, f)$, for some $f \in \Delta$.

Now, $B_{\mathfrak{e},\mathfrak{a}}$ cannot have a progressing trace on the LHS as $\mathfrak{e}$ is winning for $\exists$, nor on the RHS as $\mathfrak{a}$ is winning for $\forall$. Thus $P$ is not progressing. □

*Remark 29 (Cedents as sets: the need for positionality).* Note that, in the proof above, we really must exploit positionality of $\mathfrak{e}$ and $\mathfrak{a}$ during the construction of $B_{\mathfrak{e},\mathfrak{a}}$. When cedents are sets, a formula occurrence may have multiple trace histories, as the graph of immediate ancestry is not necessarily a tree. Thus the inductive construction of $\Gamma_i \to \Delta_i$, in particular at a +-$l$ or ∩-$r$ step, is only well-defined for $\mathfrak{e}$ and $\mathfrak{a}$ positional.

### 5.1 The Proof Search Game and Determinacy

In order to prove completeness, the $\impliedby$ direction of Theorem 20, we rely on further game determinacy principles to organise bottom-up proof search appropriately.

*Remark 30 (The need for games).* We should explain why we need to rely on game determinacy to establish completeness via proof search. While usual finitary proof systems are readily shown complete by a validity preserving (bottom-up) converging proof search strategy, this is not enough for cyclic systems: we must further justify that the ultimate preproof we produce is both progressing and regular. Neither of these are local properties, and so cannot be established as an invariant of a proof search strategy. Instead determinacy of an appropriate game will guarantee progressiveness, while regularity follows by observing that winning strategies of said game need only use finite memory.

**Definition 31 (Proof search game).** *The* proof search game *(for $\widehat{\mathsf{LRLL}}_\mathcal{L}$) is a two-player game played between Prover (**P**), whose positions are inference steps of $\widehat{\mathsf{LRLL}}_\mathcal{L}$, and Denier (**D**), whose positions are sequents of $\widehat{\mathsf{LRLL}}_\mathcal{L}$. A* play *of the game starts from a particular sequent: at each turn, **P** chooses an inference step with the current sequent as conclusion, and **D** chooses a premiss of that step; the process repeats from this sequent as long as possible.*

*An infinite play of the game is* **won** *by **P** (aka* **lost** *by **D**) if the branch constructed has a progressing trace; otherwise it is won by **D** (aka lost by **P**). In the case of deadlock, the player with no valid move loses.*

Since any $\widehat{\mathsf{LRLL}}_\mathcal{L}$ preproof can have only finitely many distinct sequents, Proposition 25.1, the proof search game for $\widehat{\mathsf{LRLL}}_\mathcal{L}$ has only finitely many positions. From here it is not hard to see that the set of progressing branches forms an $\omega$-regular language over the (finite) alphabet of possible sequents. In particular we can construct a non-deterministic Büchi automaton that guesses a finite prefix and a progressing thread on the fly (along with its critical LHS-$\mu$ or RHS-$\nu$ formula), verifying that no smaller formula is unfolded after the prefix (see, e.g., [16,30], for similar developments in the setting of the modal $\mu$-calculus). Consequently, by the well-known Büchi-Landweber Theorem (see, e.g., [31, Sec. 4]):

**Proposition 32 (via Büchi-Landweber).** *The proof search game from any sequent is finite memory determined.*

Here 'finite memory', in particular, means that the strategy needs only store a bounded amount of information at any time. It is not hard to see that any finite memory **P** strategy is just a regular preproof (where the finite memory corresponds to multiple, yet finite, occurrences of the same sequent). Moreover if the strategy is winning for **P** then the corresponding preproof is progressing. Thus we have:

**Corollary 33.** *Any sequent is* $\mathsf{CRLL}_\mathcal{L}$-*provable or has a winning strategy for* **D**.

### 5.2 A Proof Search Strategy

Before giving our completeness argument, let us describe a basic validity preserving proof search algorithm, which shall serve as a 'canonical' **P** strategy in the proof search game (at least from guarded sequents).

**Definition 34 (Proof search strategy).** *The* **P** *strategy* $\mathfrak{P}$ *in the proof search game is defined as follows, bottom-up:*

- $\mathfrak{P}$ *applies left and right logical rules maximally.*
- *At a sequent* $\Gamma, ae, bf \to \Delta$ *with* $a \neq b$, $\mathfrak{P}$ *weakens* $\Gamma$ *and* $\Delta$ *then applies* p-*l to finish the proof.*
- *At a sequent* $a\Gamma \to \{b\Delta_b\}_{a \in \mathcal{A}}$, *with* $\Gamma \neq \varnothing$, $\mathfrak{P}$ *weakens all* $b\Delta_b$ *for* $b \neq a$ *and applies* $\mathsf{h}_a$ *to give the premiss* $\Gamma \to \Delta_a$.
- *At a sequent* $\to \{a\Delta_a\}_{a \in \mathcal{A}}$ $\mathfrak{P}$ *applies* p-*r*.

Note that $\mathfrak{P}$ is indeed a well defined total **P** strategy: no logical rule applies just when every formula in the sequent has form $ae$. Moreover, by invertibility of the logical rules and inspection of the other cases we have:

**Proposition 35 (Validity preservation).** $\mathfrak{P}$ *is validity-preserving. I.e. any play of* $\mathfrak{P}$ *from a* $\mathcal{L}$-*valid sequent visits only* $\mathcal{L}$-*valid sequents.*

Note also that, when playing from sequents containing only guarded formulas, no play of $\mathfrak{P}$ eventually only applies logical rules: the $\mathcal{A}$ rules must be applied infinitely often. This is critical for our upcoming countermodel construction: for unguarded sequents extra 'loop checking' required for an appropriate **P** strategy.

### 5.3 Completeness

By Corollary 33 above it suffices, for completeness, to extract a 'countermodel' from each **D** winning strategy:

**Lemma 36 (Countermodel from D winning strategy).** *If* **D** *has a winning strategy from a sequent* $\Gamma \to \Delta$, *for* $\Gamma, \Delta$ *containing only guarded expressions, there is some* $w \in \bigcap_{e \in \Gamma} \mathcal{L}(e)$ *with* $w \notin \bigcup_{f \in \Delta} \mathcal{L}(f)$.

*Proof (sketch).* Let $\mathfrak{D}$ be a winning strategy for **D** from $\Gamma \to \Delta$ and $\mathfrak{P}$ the **P** strategy from Definition 34. Play $\mathfrak{P}$ against $\mathfrak{D}$ from $\Gamma \to \Delta$ to obtain a branch $B$, which must be infinite by assumption that $\mathfrak{D}$ is winning for **D** and since $\mathfrak{P}$ is total. By guardedness, the play infinitely often applies an $\mathcal{A}$ step. For $i < \omega$ write $\mathsf{r}_i$ for the $i^{\text{th}}$ $\mathcal{A}$ step along $B$, bottom-up. We define the word $w_B := (a_i)_{i < \omega}$ by:

- if $\mathsf{r}_i$ is $\mathsf{h}_a$ then $a_i := a$;
- if $\mathsf{r}_i$ is p-*r* and $B$ follows the $a$-premiss then $a_i := a$.
- ($\mathsf{r}_i$ cannot be p-*l* as $B$ is infinite).

Now, by guardedness, $B$ has no ultimately stable traces, cf. Observation 21 so, since $\mathfrak{D}$ is **D**-winning:

1. each LHS trace along $B$ is a $\nu$-trace; and,
2. each RHS trace along $B$ is a $\mu$-trace.

Now we argue that $w_B \in \mathcal{L}(e)$ for each $e \in \Gamma$, as the LHSs of $B$ determine an $\exists$ winning strategy from $(w_B, e)$ in the Evaluation Game, under Lemma 28. Dually we can show $w_B \notin \mathcal{L}(f)$ for each $f \in \Delta$. □

We can now conclude our proof of the adequacy of $\mathsf{CRLL}_\mathcal{L}$ for $\mathcal{L}$:

*Proof (of $\impliedby$ direction of Theorem 20).* Suppose $\mathsf{CRLL}_\mathcal{L} \not\vdash \Gamma \to \Delta$, in which case there is a **D** winning strategy from $\Gamma \to \Delta$ in the proof search game, by Corollary 33. Thus by Lemma 36, we have that $\bigcap_{e \in \Gamma} \mathcal{L}(e) \not\subseteq \bigcup_{f \in \Delta} \mathcal{L}(f)$. □

## 6 Conclusions

In this work, we investigated an algebraic notation for alternating parity automata (APAs), in the form of right-linear lattice (RLL) expressions. We designed a cyclic proof system $\mathsf{CRLL}_\mathcal{L}$ manipulating RLL expressions, reasoning about inclusions between the $\omega$-languages they denote (thus also emptiness, universality, equivalence). Along the way, we developed several game-theoretic techniques, inspired by the cyclic proof theory tradition, for organising metalogical reasoning, in particular proving soundness and completeness of $\mathsf{CRLL}_\mathcal{L}$, Theorem 20.

As $\mathsf{CRLL}_\mathcal{L}$ is an analytic system,[4] it is amenable to proof search and implementation, potentially offering new algorithms for deciding APA inclusion (and emptiness, universality, equivalence). Deciding inclusion for $\omega$-regular languages is of fundamental interest in *model checking* (see, e.g., [18,19,22,37]). Typical approaches only handle Büchi automata natively, so at least one novelty offered by $\mathsf{CRLL}_\mathcal{L}$ is a new way to deal with expressions notating APAs directly, rather than their encodings by Büchi automata. A feature of proof search based algorithms in general is that they admit a notion of *certificate*: if we find a proof $P$ of $e \to f$, we can easily convince a third party ('checker') that $\mathcal{L}(e) \subseteq \mathcal{L}(f)$ by communicating $P$ as evidence, rather than requiring them to reprove it outright.

Let us point out that, while Theorem 20 indeed establishes *regular* completeness, the strategy $\mathfrak{P}$ defined in Definition 34, to facilitate countermodel extraction, does not necessarily generate regular proofs. Nonetheless, proof search in $\mathsf{CRLL}_\mathcal{L}$ is indeed effective, despite the global nature of proof checking. During proof search, we can simultaneously run a *deterministic* parity automaton recognising progressing branches to verify loop checks (a folklore fact, e.g. observed explicitly in [13]).

In parallel work [11], we proposed an axiomatisation $\mathsf{RLL}_\mathcal{L}$ for the RLL theory of $\omega$-regular languages, in particular proving its soundness and completeness with respect to $\omega$-languages, essentially by reduction to the completeness of Kaivola's axiomatisation of $\mu\mathsf{LTL}$ [23]. Naturally here the derivation of *complements* plays a crucial role in the completeness argument, allowing the simulation of Boolean reasoning.

---

[4] While $\widehat{\mathsf{LRLL}}_\mathcal{L}$ does not have the subformula property per se, any preproof of $e \to f$ has only $O(|e|, |f|)$ distinct formulas, by Fact 24.1.

# References

1. Andréka, H., Mikulás, S., Németi, I.: The equational theory of Kleene lattices. Theoret. Comput. Sci. **412**(52), 7099–7108 (2011). https://doi.org/10.1016/j.tcs.2011.09.024. https://www.sciencedirect.com/science/article/pii/S0304397511008000
2. Boffa, M.: Une remarque sur les systèmes complets d'identités rationnelles. Theor. Inform. Appl. **24**(4), 419–423 (1990)
3. Boffa, M.: Une condition impliquant toutes les identités rationnelles. Theor. Inform. Appl. **29**(6), 515–518 (1995)
4. Bojańczyk, M.: Automata, logic and games (2023), lecture course at University of Warsaw. https://www.mimuw.edu.pl/~bojan/2022-2023/automata-logic-and-games-2023
5. Bruse, F., Friedmann, O., Lange, M.: On guarded transformation in the modal $\mu$-calculus. Log. J. IGPL **23**(2), 194–216 (2015). https://doi.org/10.1093/JIGPAL/JZU030. https://doi.org/10.1093/jigpal/jzu030
6. Buchi, J.R., Landweber, L.H.: Solving sequential conditions by finite-state strategies. Trans. Am. Math. Soc. **138**, 295–311 (1969). http://www.jstor.org/stable/1994916
7. Cohen, E.: Separation and reduction. In: Backhouse, R., Oliveira, J.N. (eds.) Mathematics of Program Construction, pp. 45–59. Springer, Heidelberg (2000)
8. Cranch, J., Laurence, M.R., Struth, G.: Completeness results for omega-regular algebras. J. Log. Algebraic Methods Program. **84**(3), 402–425 (2015). https://doi.org/10.1016/J.JLAMP.2014.10.002
9. Das, A., De, A.: A proof theory of right-linear ($\omega$-)grammars via cyclic proofs. In: Sobocinski, P., Lago, U.D., Esparza, J. (eds.) Proceedings of the 39th Annual ACM/IEEE Symposium on Logic in Computer Science, LICS 2024, Tallinn, Estonia, 8–11 July 2024, pp. 30:1–30:14. ACM (2024). https://doi.org/10.1145/3661814.3662138
10. Das, A., De, A.: A proof theory of right-linear (omega-)grammars via cyclic proofs (2024). https://doi.org/10.48550/ARXIV.2401.13382
11. Das, A., De, A.: An algebraic theory of $\omega$-regular languages, via $\mu\nu$-expressions (2025). https://arxiv.org/abs/2505.10303
12. Das, A., De, A.: Cyclic system for an algebraic theory of alternating parity automata (2025). https://arxiv.org/abs/2505.09000
13. Das, A., De, A., Saurin, A.: Decision problems for linear logic with least and greatest fixed points. In: Felty, A.P. (ed.) 7th International Conference on Formal Structures for Computation and Deduction (FSCD 2022). Leibniz International Proceedings in Informatics (LIPIcs), vol. 228, pp. 20:1–20:20. Schloss Dagstuhl – Leibniz-Zentrum für Informatik, Dagstuhl, Germany (2022). https://doi.org/10.4230/LIPIcs.FSCD.2022.20. https://drops.dagstuhl.de/entities/document/10.4230/LIPIcs.FSCD.2022.20
14. Das, A., Pous, D.: A cut-free cyclic proof system for Kleene algebra. In: Schmidt, R.A., Nalon, C. (eds.) TABLEAUX 2017. LNCS (LNAI), vol. 10501, pp. 261–277. Springer, Cham (2017). https://doi.org/10.1007/978-3-319-66902-1_16
15. Dax, C., Hofmann, M., Lange, M.: A proof system for the linear time $\mu$-calculus. In: Arun-Kumar, S., Garg, N. (eds.) FSTTCS 2006. LNCS, vol. 4337, pp. 273–284. Springer, Heidelberg (2006). https://doi.org/10.1007/11944836_26
16. Dekker, M., Kloibhofer, J., Marti, J., Venema, Y.: Proof systems for the modal $\mu$-calculus obtained by determinizing automata. In: Ramanayake, R., Urban, J. (eds.) Automated Reasoning with Analytic Tableaux and Related Methods, pp. 242–259. Springer, Cham (2023)

17. Doumane, A.: Constructive completeness for the linear-time $\mu$-calculus. In: 32nd Annual ACM/IEEE Symposium on Logic in Computer Science, LICS 2017, Reykjavik, Iceland, 20–23 June 2017, pp. 1–12. IEEE Computer Society (2017). https://doi.org/10.1109/LICS.2017.8005075
18. Gastin, P., Oddoux, D.: Fast LTL to Büchi automata translation. In: Berry, G., Comon, H., Finkel, A. (eds.) Computer Aided Verification, pp. 53–65. Springer, Heidelberg (2001)
19. Gerth, R., Peled, D., Vardi, M.Y., Wolper, P.: Simple on-the-fly automatic verification of linear temporal logic. In: PSTV 1995. IAICT, pp. 3–18. Springer, Boston, MA (1996). https://doi.org/10.1007/978-0-387-34892-6_1
20. Grädel, E., Thomas, W., Wilke, T. (eds.): Automata, Logics, and Infinite Games. Lecture Notes in Computer Science, 2002 edn. Springer, New York (2003)
21. Hazard, E., Kuperberg, D.: Cyclic proofs for transfinite expressions. In: Manea, F., Simpson, A. (eds.) 30th EACSL Annual Conference on Computer Science Logic, CSL 2022, Göttingen, Germany, 14–19 February 2022 (Virtual Conference). LIPIcs, vol. 216, pp. 23:1–23:18. Schloss Dagstuhl - Leibniz-Zentrum für Informatik (2022). https://doi.org/10.4230/LIPICS.CSL.2022.23
22. Holzmann, G.: The SPIN Model Checker: Primer and Reference Manual, 1st edn. Addison-Wesley Professional (2011)
23. Kaivola, R.: Axiomatising linear time $\mu$-calculus. In: Lee, I., Smolka, S.A. (eds.) CONCUR 1995. LNCS, vol. 962, pp. 423–437. Springer, Heidelberg (1995). https://doi.org/10.1007/3-540-60218-6_32
24. Kozen, D.: A completeness theorem for Kleene algebras and the algebra of regular events. Inf. Comput. **110**(2), 366–390 (1994). https://doi.org/10.1006/inco.1994.1037. https://www.sciencedirect.com/science/article/pii/S0890540184710376
25. Kozen, D.: On Action Algebras, pp. 78–88. MIT Press, Cambridge (1994)
26. Krob, D.: Complete systems of b-rational identities. Theoret. Comput. Sci. **89**(2), 207–343 (1991). https://doi.org/10.1016/0304-3975(91)90395-I. https://www.sciencedirect.com/science/article/pii/030439759190395I
27. Kupke, C., Marti, J., Venema, Y.: Succinct graph representations of $\mu$-calculus formulas. In: Manea, F., Simpson, A. (eds.) 30th EACSL Annual Conference on Computer Science Logic (CSL 2022). Leibniz International Proceedings in Informatics (LIPIcs), vol. 216, pp. 29:1–29:18. Schloss Dagstuhl – Leibniz-Zentrum für Informatik, Dagstuhl, Germany (2022). https://doi.org/10.4230/LIPIcs.CSL.2022.29. https://drops.dagstuhl.de/entities/document/10.4230/LIPIcs.CSL.2022.29
28. Lange, M.: Weak automata for the linear time $\mu$-calculus. In: Cousot, R. (ed.) Verification, Model Checking, and Abstract Interpretation, pp. 267–281. Springer, Heidelberg (2005)
29. Laurence, M.R., Struth, G.: On completeness of omega-regular algebras. In: Kahl, W., Griffin, T.G. (eds.) RAMICS 2012. LNCS, vol. 7560, pp. 179–194. Springer, Heidelberg (2012). https://doi.org/10.1007/978-3-642-33314-9_12
30. Niwinski, D., Walukiewicz, I.: Games for the $\mu$-calculus. Theor. Comput. Sci. **163**(1&2), 99–116 (1996). https://doi.org/10.1016/0304-3975(95)00136-0
31. Perrin, D., Pin, J.: Infinite Words - Automata, Semigroups, Logic and Games, Pure and Applied Mathematics Series, vol. 141. Elsevier Morgan Kaufmann (2004)
32. Pous, D.: On the positive calculus of relations with transitive closure. In: Niedermeier, R., Vallée, B. (eds.) 35th Symposium on Theoretical Aspects of Computer Science (STACS 2018). Leibniz International Proceedings in Informatics (LIPIcs), vol. 96, pp. 3:1–3:16. Schloss Dagstuhl – Leibniz-Zentrum für Informatik, Dagstuhl, Germany (2018). https://doi.org/10.4230/LIPIcs.STACS.2018.3. https://drops.dagstuhl.de/entities/document/10.4230/LIPIcs.STACS.2018.3

33. Rabin, M.O.: Decidability of second-order theories and automata on infinite trees. Bull. Am. Math. Soc. **74**(5), 1025–1029 (1968)
34. Richard Büchi, J.: On a decision method in restricted second order arithmetic. In: Nagel, E., Suppes, P., Tarski, A. (eds.) Logic, Methodology and Philosophy of Science, Studies in Logic and the Foundations of Mathematics, vol. 44, pp. 1–11. Elsevier (1966). https://doi.org/10.1016/S0049-237X(09)70564-6. https://www.sciencedirect.com/science/article/pii/S0049237X09705646
35. Salomaa, A.: Two complete axiom systems for the algebra of regular events. J. ACM (JACM) **13**(1), 158–169 (1966)
36. Streett, R.S., Emerson, E.A.: An automata theoretic decision procedure for the propositional $\mu$-calculus. Inf. Comput. **81**(3), 249–264 (1989). https://doi.org/10.1016/0890-5401(89)90031-X
37. Vardi, M., Wolper, P.: Reasoning about infinite computations. Inf. Comput. **115**(1), 1–37 (1994). https://doi.org/10.1006/inco.1994.1092. https://www.sciencedirect.com/science/article/pii/S0890540184710923
38. Wagner, K.W.: Eine axiomatisierung der theorie der regulären folgenmengen. J. Inf. Process. Cybern. **12**, 337–354 (1976). https://api.semanticscholar.org/CorpusID:27249080

**Open Access** This chapter is licensed under the terms of the Creative Commons Attribution 4.0 International License (http://creativecommons.org/licenses/by/4.0/), which permits use, sharing, adaptation, distribution and reproduction in any medium or format, as long as you give appropriate credit to the original author(s) and the source, provide a link to the Creative Commons license and indicate if changes were made.

The images or other third party material in this chapter are included in the chapter's Creative Commons license, unless indicated otherwise in a credit line to the material. If material is not included in the chapter's Creative Commons license and your intended use is not permitted by statutory regulation or exceeds the permitted use, you will need to obtain permission directly from the copyright holder.

# A Sequent Calculus For Trace Formula Implication

Niklas Heidler[✉] and Reiner Hähnle

Technical University of Darmstadt, Darmstadt, Germany
{niklas.heidler,reiner.haehnle}@tu-darmstadt.de

**Abstract.** Specification languages are essential in deductive program verification, but they are usually based on first-order logic, hence less expressive than the programs they specify. Recently, trace specification logics with fixed points that are at least as expressive as their target programs were proposed. This makes it possible to specify not merely pre- and postconditions, but the whole trace of even recursive programs. Previous work established a sound and complete calculus to determine whether a program satisfies a given trace formula. However, the applicability of the calculus and its prospects for mechanized verification rely on the ability to prove consequence between trace formulas. We present a sound sequent calculus for proving implication (i.e. trace inclusion) between trace formulas. To handle fixed point operations with an unknown recursive bound, fixed point induction rules are used. We also employ contracts and $\mu$-formula synchronization. While this does not yet result in a complete calculus for trace formula implication, it is possible to prove many non-trivial properties.

**Keywords:** Program specification · fixed point logic · $\mu$-calculus

## 1 Introduction

There exist a variety of ways to specify and verify program properties in a mechanized fashion. In *Model Checking* [3], temporal logic, such as Linear Temporal Logic (LTL) or Computation Tree Logic (CTL) is used to specify program behaviour. During verification, a model of the given program and its temporal logic specification are finitely unwound, typically by automata constructions. *Deductive Verification* [6] uses first-order logic (FOL) to formalize procedure contracts in Hoare calculus [12] or in program logic [2] to prove that a given first-order postcondition holds in any state reachable by executing the given procedure, assuming that a precondition held in the start state.

It is interesting to note that —with few exceptions [14,18]— specification languages in deductive verification are weaker in expressiveness than the programs they are supposed to specify. Moreover, nearly all deductive verification techniques are based on reasoning about intermediate states, i.e. before and after a procedure call. In this sense, model checking is more natural, because there is a direct correspondence between the program model and its specification. However, LTL and CTL, certain extensions [1] notwithstanding, cannot express modular verification over contracts and they target *models* of programs. In consequence, an obvious question arises: Is there a logic that permits trace-based *and* contract-based specification of imperative programs with recursive procedures that has a natural correspondence between program and specification?

This was recently answered affirmatively in the form of a trace specification logic with smallest fixed points. Here, trace formulas $\Phi$ specify a (possibly infinite) set of finite computation traces generated by a program $S$ from a simple imperative language Rec with recursive procedure declarations. Judgments take the form $S:\Phi$ and mean: Any possible execution trace of $S$ is contained in the set of traces characterized by $\Phi$. Gurov & Hähnle [5] provide a sound, complete, and *compositional* proof calculus for judgments of the form $S:\Phi$, where "compositional" means that the rule premises do not introduce intermediate formulas not present in the conclusion. However *weakening* of trace formulas (i.e. prove $S:\Psi$ instead of $S:\Phi$ provided that $\Psi$ implies $\Phi$) is still necessary.

Soundness and completeness of the calculus rest on a strong correspondence between programs and trace formulas: For any Rec program $S$, there exists a *strongest trace formula* $stf(S)$ that characterizes *exactly* the traces generated by $S$.[1] Hence, $S:\Phi$ is valid iff the traces specified by $stf(S)$ are included in the traces specified by $\Phi$. This implies one can verify a judgment $S:\Phi$ by simply proving the trace formula consequence $stf(S) \models \Phi$. Alternatively, one can use the rules of the calculus to prove $S:\Phi$ directly. Thus, the correspondence between programs and trace formulas creates the opportunity to verify judgments with a program calculus *or* by trace formula consequence. It is also possible to mix both styles, of course. In either case, weakening is needed for completeness, so implication between trace formulas is a crucial ingredient. This requires a separate proof system and such a calculus was considered as future work in [5]. It is the main objective of the present paper.

The consequence relation between formulas in a fixed point logic is a difficult problem—because trace formulas are as expressive as recursive programs it is highly undecidable. Therefore, our investigation into how far one can get with such a calculus, is interesting in its own right. Existing literature has little to say about the topic. The central challenge in the design of a calculus for implication of trace formulas is the handling of fixed point formulas, i.e. formulas with a leading fixed point operator $\mu$. We propose increasingly complex strategies of how to eliminate fixed point formulas, without reaching completeness yet:

1. Straightforward *unfolding* of $\mu$-formulas is sufficient to deal with executions that have concrete bounds (Sect. 4.2).
2. Fixed point *induction* lets one prove trace inclusion of recursive executions with an unknown (or very high) bound (Sect. 4.3).

---

[1] The paper [5] even proves the reverse direction: For any trace formula $\Phi$ there is a *canonical program* $S$ having exactly the same traces as $\Phi$, establishing a Galois connection between programs and trace formulas. However, this result is not relevant for the present paper.

3. To capture the execution state *after* a fixed point formula we equip the calculus with Hoare-style state-based procedure contracts. The logic and calculus is expressive enough to prove such contracts and to propagate them inside the proofs, without the need to refer to meta theorems (Sect. 5.1).
4. When proving the consequence relation between two $\mu$-formulas, one often encounters the problem that the execution of their bodies is not *synchronized*. We equip the calculus with $\mu$-formula synchronization rules (Sect. 5.2) that are able to synchronize recursive variables inside fixed point operations in many, but not in all cases. This is one source of incompleteness.

The paper is structured as follows: In Sect. 2, we introduce Rec programs. Trace formulas are defined in Sect. 3, together with some examples of provable properties. Section 4 proposes a basic calculus for trace implication, which is the core of this paper. Section 5 extends the basic calculus with method contracts and $\mu$-formula synchronization. Section 6 refers to related work, while Sect. 7 concludes the paper and proposes future work. As noted, completeness is elusive at the moment, however, we are able to prove a range of interesting and non-trivial properties.

## 2 The Rec Language

We define a simple imperative programming language Rec [5] with (recursive) procedure calls.

**Definition 1 (Rec Program).** *A Rec Program is a pair $(S, T)$, where $S$ is a Rec Statement generated by the grammar*

$$S ::= \mathbf{skip} \mid x := a \mid S; S \mid \mathbf{if}\ b\ \mathbf{then}\ S\ \mathbf{else}\ S \mid m()$$

*and $T$ is a possibly empty sequence $M^*$ of procedure declarations, where each $M$ declares a parameter-less procedure $M \equiv m\{S\}$ consisting of procedure name $m$ and procedure body $S$. Schema variables $a$ and $b$ range over side-effect free arithmetic and boolean expressions, respectively, that are not further specified.*

The Rec language does not include syntax for **while**-loops, however, these can easily be modeled with the help of a tail-recursive procedure. There is also no parameter passing mechanism.

A program *trace* $\sigma$ is a, possibly empty, finite sequence of execution *states* $s$, partial mappings from program variables $x$ to integer values. Regarding the semantics of a program in terms of its finite $traces(S)$ of statements $S$, we refer to the standard definitions in the literature [5].

*Example 1.* The factorial Rec Program $(S_{fac}, T_{fac})$ is given by the statement $S_{fac} \equiv y := 1;\ factorial()$ and the procedure table

$$T_{fac} \equiv factorial\{\mathbf{if}\ x = 1\ \mathbf{then}\ skip\ \mathbf{else}\ y := y * x;\ x := x - 1;\ factorial()\}$$

By convention, sequential composition binds stronger that the conditional, i.e. the final three statements form the **else** block. For any start state $s = [x \mapsto i]$ with $i > 0$, the program computes the factorial of $x$ and stores the result in $y$, i.e. the program terminates in a state $s'$ where $s'(y) = x!$.

$$[\![p]\!]_\mathbb{V} = \{s \cdot \sigma \mid s \models p \land \sigma \in \mathit{State}^*\} \qquad [\![R]\!]_\mathbb{V} = \{s \cdot s' \mid R(s,s')\}$$
$$[\![\Phi_1 \land \Phi_2]\!]_\mathbb{V} = [\![\Phi_1]\!]_\mathbb{V} \cap [\![\Phi_2]\!]_\mathbb{V} \qquad [\![\Phi_1 \lor \Phi_2]\!]_\mathbb{V} = [\![\Phi_1]\!]_\mathbb{V} \cup [\![\Phi_2]\!]_\mathbb{V}$$
$$[\![\Phi_1 \frown \Phi_2]\!]_\mathbb{V} = \{\sigma \cdot s \cdot \sigma' \mid \sigma \cdot s \in [\![\Phi_1]\!]_\mathbb{V} \land s \cdot \sigma' \in [\![\Phi_2]\!]_\mathbb{V}\} \qquad [\![X]\!]_\mathbb{V} = \mathbb{V}(X)$$
$$[\![\mu X.\Phi]\!]_\mathbb{V} = \bigcap\{\gamma \subseteq \mathit{State}^+ \mid [\![\Phi]\!]_{\mathbb{V}[X \mapsto \gamma]} \subseteq \gamma\}$$

**Fig. 1.** Semantics of trace formulas

## 3 Trace Formulas

We define the *trace formula logic*. Like for Rec programs, the semantics of its formulas is given as a set of program traces.

**Definition 2 (Trace Formula Syntax).** *The grammar of trace formulas is*

$$\Phi ::= p \mid R \mid \Phi \land \Phi \mid \Phi \lor \Phi \mid \Phi \frown \Phi \mid X \mid \mu X.\Phi$$

*where $p$ ranges over first-order state predicates Pred, $R$ ranges over binary relations between states, and $X$ ranges over recursion variables RVar. The binary operator $\frown$ is called chop.*[2] *We assume $R$ contains at least the relations*

$$Id := \{(s,s) \in \mathit{State}^2\} \text{ and } Sb_x^a := \{(s,s') \in \mathit{State}^2 \mid s' = s[x \mapsto \mathbb{A}[\![a]\!](s)]\} \ .$$

Relation $Id$ models a skip and $Sb_x^a$ an assignment. $\mathbb{A}[\![a]\!](s)$ refers to the evaluation of arithmetic expression $a$ in state $s$. Observe that the logic is not closed under negation: only smallest fixed point formulas are permitted.

**Definition 3 (Trace Formula Semantics).** *Each trace formula $\Phi$ evaluates to a set of finite traces. Given a valuation function $\mathbb{V} : RVar \to P(\mathit{State}^+)$ that maps recursion variables to sets of traces, the semantics of a trace formula $\Phi$ under valuation $\mathbb{V}$, denoted $[\![\Phi]\!]_\mathbb{V}$, is defined by the equations in Fig. 1. $[\![\Phi]\!]$ abbreviates $[\![\Phi]\!]_\mathbb{V}$ when $\mathbb{V}$ does not affect the result.*

Observe that $[\![\mu X.\Phi]\!]_\mathbb{V}$ maps to the least fixed point of $\Phi$ in the powerset lattice $(P(\mathit{State}^+), \subseteq)$. This is justified by monotonicity of $\lambda \gamma.[\![\Phi]\!]_{\mathbb{V}[X \mapsto \gamma]}$ and the Knaster-Tarski theorem.

**Theorem 1 (Strongest Trace Formula [5]).** *For each Rec Program $(S, T)$ there exists a closed strongest trace formula $\Phi$ with $traces(S) = [\![\Phi]\!]$.*

The strongest trace formula can be effectively constructed from a given Rec program. The details of the construction and the proof are in [5]. The theorem implies that trace formulas are at least as expressive as the Rec language.

*Example 2.* Trace formula $\Phi_{fac}$ is the strongest trace formula for $(S_{fac}, T_{fac})$:

$$\Phi_{fac} \equiv Sb_y^1 \frown Id \frown \Phi_m, \text{ where}$$

$$\Phi_m \equiv \mu X_{fac}.((x = 1 \land Id \frown Id) \lor (x \neq 1 \land Id \frown Sb_y^{y*x} \frown Sb_x^{x-1} \frown Id \frown X_{fac}))$$

---

[2] It is inspired by Interval Temporal Logic [9] and its use in specification by [16].

**Definition 4 (Satisfiability).** *A* Rec *program $S$ satisfies a trace formula $\Phi$ (write $S:\Phi$) iff $traces(S) \subseteq [\![\Phi]\!]$.*

As noted in the introduction, a sound and complete compositional proof calculus for $S:\Phi$ is given in [5], but its applicability relies on weakening, i.e. the semantic entailment oracle $\Phi \models \Psi$, of which this paper presents the first formal investigation.

Theorem 1 implies that trace formulas can characterize the traces of a given Rec program *precisely*. But this does not mean that trace formulas are just an alternative notation for programs: Unlike programs, with the help of suitable binary predicates, formulas can conveniently abstract away from computational details.

*Example 3.* Let $S_{down}$ be a Rec program that decreases a variable $x$ by 2 until $x$ reaches the value 0. Afterwards, it further decreases variable $x$ by 1. Whether the recursion is entered depends on the initial value of $x$.

$$S_{down} \equiv down() \text{ with}$$
$$down\{\text{if } x = 0 \text{ then } x := x - 1 \text{ else } x := x - 2; down()\}$$

We illustrate how to use trace formulas as an abstract specification $S_{down}$ with two properties. None of them can be expressed with Hoare-style contracts based on pre- and postconditions.

1. For variable $x$, define the relation $R^x_{dec} := \{(s, s') \in State^2 \mid s(x) \geq s'(x)\}$ which is easy to axiomatize. The property that $x$ never increases throughout the execution of program $S_{down}$ is expressed with the fixed point formula $\mu X_{dec}.R^x_{dec} \vee R^x_{dec}\frown X_{dec}$.
2. If $x$ is *even* and *non-negative*, then $x$ will eventually reach value 0. Afterwards, $x$ will eventually reach value $-1$:

$$\overline{even(x)} \vee x < 0 \vee true \frown x = 0 \frown x = -1 \ .$$

Observe that the negated expressions $\overline{even(x)}$ and $x < 0$ serve to impose their complement as a constraint on the initial state of a trace. Trace formulas are not closed under negation, but Boolean expressions related to individual states are. Also observe that the semantics of atomic trace formulas $p$ implies that between the states with $x = 0$ and $x = -1$ an arbitrary number of intermediate states can occur.

The properties above were proven as judgments in the calculus provided in [5], while the necessary weakening steps were proven in the calculus presented in Sect. 4. The derivations can be found in [10].

## 4 A Proof Calculus for Trace Formula Consequence

### 4.1 Sequents

**Definition 5 (Sequents).** *A sequent in our calculus has the shape $\xi \diamond \Gamma \vdash \Delta$, where $\xi \subseteq RVar \times Pred \times RVar$ and $\Gamma, \Delta$ are sets of trace formulas. A triple $(X, p, X') \in \xi$ is written $(X|p, X')$ as syntactic sugar.*

$$\text{CUT} \frac{\xi \diamond \Gamma, p \vdash \Delta \quad \xi \diamond \Gamma, \overline{p} \vdash \Delta}{\xi \diamond \Gamma \vdash \Delta} \qquad \text{REL} \frac{}{\xi \diamond \Gamma, R \vdash R', \Delta} \underbrace{\{(s,s') \in R \mid s \models P_\Gamma\} \subseteq R'}_{R|_{P_\Gamma}}$$

$$\text{PRED} \frac{P_\Gamma \vdash q \quad \xi \diamond \Gamma, q \vdash \Delta}{\xi \diamond \Gamma \vdash \Delta} \qquad \text{RVAR} \frac{P_\Gamma \vdash p}{\xi, (X_1|_p, X_2) \diamond \Gamma, X_1 \vdash X_2, \Delta}$$

$$\text{CH-ID} \frac{\xi \diamond P_\Gamma, \mathit{Id} \vdash \Psi_1 \quad \cdots \quad \xi \diamond P_\Gamma, \mathit{Id} \vdash \Psi_n \quad \xi \diamond P_\Gamma, \Phi \vdash \Psi'_1, \ldots, \Psi'_n}{\xi \diamond \Gamma, \mathit{Id}^\frown \Phi \vdash \Psi_1^\frown \Psi'_1, \ldots, \Psi_n^\frown \Psi'_n, \Delta}$$

$$\text{CH-UPD} \frac{\xi \diamond P_\Gamma, Sb^a_x \vdash \Psi_1 \quad \cdots \quad \xi \diamond P_\Gamma, Sb^a_x \vdash \Psi_n \quad \xi \diamond spc_{x:=a}(P_\Gamma), \Phi \vdash \Psi'_1, \ldots, \Psi'_n}{\xi \diamond \Gamma, Sb^a_x{}^\frown \Phi \vdash \Psi_1^\frown \Psi'_1, \ldots, \Psi_n^\frown \Psi'_n, \Delta}$$

**Fig. 2.** Calculus rules for predicates and relations

The purpose of $\xi$ is to specify constraints on the recursion variables occurring in a valuation $\mathbb{V}$. We write $\Gamma \vdash \Delta$ as an abbreviation for $\emptyset \diamond \Gamma \vdash \Delta$ in case $\xi$ is empty or irrelevant. $\xi$ is always empty for a top-level sequent.

**Definition 6 (Validity of Sequents).** *A sequent $\xi \diamond \Gamma \vdash \Delta$ is valid, if for all valuations $\mathbb{V}$ with $[\![X \wedge p]\!]_\mathbb{V} \subseteq [\![X']\!]_\mathbb{V}$ for all $(X|p, X') \in \xi$, it is the case that $[\![\bigwedge \Gamma]\!]_\mathbb{V} \subseteq [\![\bigvee \Delta]\!]_\mathbb{V}$.*

*Example 4.* Let $X_1$ and $X_2$ be recursion variables. Then

$$(X_1|_{x \geq 0}, X_2) \diamond x = 0, X_1 \vdash X_2$$

is a (trivially) valid sequent, because $(X_1|_{x \geq 0}, X_2)$ already assumes trace inclusion between $X_1$ and $X_2$, whenever $x \geq 0$.

### 4.2 Base Rules

**Definition 7 (Program State).** *To extract the current state from the antecedent $\Gamma$ of a sequent, we define $P_\Gamma := \{p \in \Gamma \mid p \in Pred\}$ as the set of all first-order state predicates occurring in $\Gamma$.*

*First-order Rules.* Standard axioms such as CLOSE, TRUE and FALSE, as well as the usual rules of the first-order sequent calculus are not separately listed. They are all valid in our setting.

*Rules for Predicates and Binary Relations (Fig. 2).* The rule CUT performs a case distinction on predicate $p$. In contrast to trace formulas, first-order formulas are closed under negation. Rule PRED infers information from the program state in its first premise and adds it to the antecedent of its second premise.

Axiom REL handles trace inclusion between binary relations. Observe that the current program state $P_\Gamma$ further restricts relation $R$ in the antecedent, abbreviated as $R|_{P_\Gamma}$. Rule RVAR characterizes trace inclusion between recursion

$$\text{RVAR} \; \frac{\begin{array}{c}\vdots\\ P_\Gamma^4 \vdash \bigwedge P_\Gamma^1\end{array}}{(X_1|_{\bigwedge P_\Gamma^1}, X_2) \diamond P_\Gamma^4, X_1 \vdash X_2}$$

$$\text{REL} \; \frac{Sb_y^{y*x}|_{\mathbf{P_\Gamma^2}} \subseteq R_{inc}^y}{P_\Gamma^2, Sb_y^{y*x} \vdash R_{inc}^y} \qquad \frac{\vdots}{(X_1|_{\bigwedge P_\Gamma^1}, X_2) \diamond P_\Gamma^3, Sb_x^{x-1} \frown X_1 \vdash R_{inc}^y \frown X_2}$$

$$\text{CH-UPD} \; \frac{}{(X_1|_{\bigwedge P_\Gamma^1}, X_2) \diamond P_\Gamma^2, Sb_y^{y*x} \frown Sb_x^{x-1} \frown X_1 \vdash R_{inc}^y \frown R_{inc}^y \frown X_2}$$

**Fig. 3.** Demonstration of predicate and relation rules

variables based on $\xi$, and needs to prove the corresponding restricting predicate in its premise.

Rules CH-ID and CH-UPD handle the case where a binary relation occurs at the beginning of the current chop sequence in the antecedent. In both rules, the first $n$ premises ensure that the leading relation of the antecedent infers the leading formulas of corresponding chop operations in the succedent. The inference between the remaining trace formula composites occurs in the final premise. As the leading binary relation in the antecedent may change program variables, the program state may need to be adapted to reflect those changes. For this reason we restrict ourselves to relations $Id$ and $Sb_x^a$ in the antecedent which is sufficient to define strongest trace formulas (the rules can be easily extended to support other binary relations in the antecedent). The program state for the remaining trace is preserved when the leading relation is $Id$. In case of $Sb_x^a$, however, the program state $P_\Gamma$ needs to be updated to its strongest postcondition [4] relative to state update $x := a$, indicated by $spc_{x:=a}(P_\Gamma)$.

*Example 5.* Consider the following four state predicates $P_\Gamma^1 \equiv \{x \geq 1, y \geq 1\}$, $P_\Gamma^2 \equiv \{x > 1, y \geq 1\}$, $P_\Gamma^3 \equiv \{x > 1, y \geq x\}$ and $P_\Gamma^4 \equiv \{x \geq 1, y > x\}$, and define a new binary relation $R_{inc}^y := \{(s, s') \mid s(y) \leq s'(y)\}$, expressing that program variable $y$ does not decrease. An example derivation is in Fig. 3. It proves that for the constraints on valuations expressed in $P_\Gamma^1$, $P_\Gamma^2$, $P_\Gamma^3$, $P_\Gamma^4$, the sequence of state updates $y := y * x; x := x - 1$ can be approximated by non-decreasing predicates of program variable $y$.

*Rules for Unfolding and Lengthening (Fig. 4).* The rules UNFL and UNFR *unfold* a fixed point formula $\Phi$ in the antecedent and succedent, respectively. This is sound, because $\mu X.\Phi$ is the least fixed point, implying that an additional recursive application does not change its semantic evaluation.

Rules LENL and LENR *lengthen* fixed point formula $\Phi$ in the antecedent and succedent respectively. The repetition of fixed point formulas can be defined as

$$repeat_0(\Phi) := \Phi \text{ and } repeat_i(\Phi) := \Phi[repeat_{i-1}(\Phi)/X]) \text{ for } i \geq 1 \;.$$

The rules are sound, because for any recursive procedure $m$, procedure $m$ with $n$ recursive calls inlined has the same least fixed point as $m$ itself.

$$\text{UNFL} \frac{\xi \diamond \Gamma, \Phi[\mu X.\Phi/X] \vdash \Delta}{\xi \diamond \Gamma, \mu X.\Phi \vdash \Delta} \qquad \text{UNFR} \frac{\xi \diamond \Gamma \vdash \Psi[\mu X.\Psi/X], \Delta}{\xi \diamond \Gamma \vdash \mu X.\Psi, \Delta}$$

$$\text{LENL} \frac{\xi \diamond \Gamma, \mu X.repeat_i(\Phi) \vdash \Delta}{\xi \diamond \Gamma, \mu X.\Phi \vdash \Delta} \; i \geq 1 \qquad \text{LENR} \frac{\xi \diamond \Gamma \vdash \mu X.repeat_i(\Psi), \Delta}{\xi \diamond \Gamma \vdash \mu X.\Psi, \Delta} \; i \geq 1$$

**Fig. 4.** Calculus rules for unfoldings and lengthenings

$$\text{ARB1} \frac{\xi \diamond \Gamma \vdash \Psi, \Delta}{\xi \diamond \Gamma \vdash true\frown\Psi, \Delta} \qquad \text{ARB2} \frac{\xi \diamond \Gamma, \Phi_1\frown\Phi_2 \vdash \Phi_1\frown true\frown\Psi, \Delta}{\xi \diamond \Gamma, \Phi_1\frown\Phi_2 \vdash true\frown\Psi, \Delta}$$

**Fig. 5.** Calculus rules for arbitrary traces

*Example 6.* Let $\Phi \equiv \mu X.(R \vee R\frown X)$ be the fixed point formula modeling transitive closure of a binary relation $R$. Its unfolding is $R \vee R\frown\Phi$, while lengthening it once corresponds to $\mu X.(R \vee R\frown(R \vee R\frown X))$.

*Rules for Arbitrary Traces (Fig. 5).* According to Fig. 1, chop sequences $true\frown\Psi$ indicate an arbitrary finite trace, represented by $true$, eventually ending with a desired result $\Psi$. This closely resembles the *eventually* operator of LTL. Rule ARB1 assumes the situation that $\Psi$ already holds in the current state, while ARB2 assumes $\Psi$ does not hold yet, allowing us to skip the leading formula.

*Additional Rules.* Supplementary rules deemed not necessary to understand the central concept behind the calculus can be found in [11].

### 4.3 Fixed Point Induction

When encountering a fixed point operation $\mu X.\Phi$ in the antecedent, one possible derivation strategy is repeated usage of rule UNFL until the recursion terminates based on the current program state. However, not only does a high recursion bound blow up the proof tree size, recursion with an unknown bound may not terminate at all. This may cause the derivation strategy to be unusable, motivating an alternative approach.

*Example 7.* Trace formula $Sb_x^{10}\frown\Phi_{fac}$ can be handled by a derivation strategy with repeated unfolding. However, this does not work for just $\Phi_{fac}$, because $x$ then has an unknown value, causing the recursion to have an unknown bound.

In the remaining paper we assume a convention giving a unique name to each recursion variable.

**Theorem 2 (Fixed Point Induction).** *For recursion variables $X_1$, $X_2$, a predicate $I$, a valuation $\mathbb{V}$, and trace formulas $\mu X_1.\Phi$, $\mu X_2.\Psi$:*

*If $[\![I \wedge X_1]\!]_\mathbb{V} \subseteq [\![X_2]\!]_\mathbb{V}$ implies $[\![I \wedge \Phi]\!]_\mathbb{V} \subseteq [\![\Psi]\!]_\mathbb{V}$ then $[\![I \wedge \mu X_1.\Phi]\!]_\mathbb{V} \subseteq [\![\mu X_2.\Psi]\!]_\mathbb{V}$.*

$$\text{FPI} \quad \frac{P_\Gamma \vdash I \quad \xi, (X_1|_I, X_2) \diamond I, \Phi \vdash \Psi}{\xi \diamond \Gamma, \mu X_1.\Phi \vdash \mu X_2.\Psi, \Delta}$$

**Fig. 6.** Fixed point induction rule

*Proof.* Let recursion variables $X_1$, $X_2$, predicate $I$, valuation $\mathbb{V}$ and trace formulas $\mu X_1.\Phi$, $\mu X_2.\Psi$ be arbitrary, but fixed. Since $[\![I \wedge X_1]\!]_\mathbb{V} = [\![I]\!]_\mathbb{V} \cap \mathbb{V}(X_1)$:

$$[\![I \wedge X_1]\!]_\mathbb{V} \subseteq [\![X_2]\!]_\mathbb{V} \text{ implies } [\![I \wedge \Phi]\!]_\mathbb{V} \subseteq [\![\Psi]\!]_\mathbb{V}$$
$$\iff \forall \gamma_1, \gamma_2. \, [\![I]\!]_\mathbb{V} \cap \gamma_1 \subseteq \gamma_2 \text{ implies } [\![I]\!]_\mathbb{V} \cap [\![\Phi]\!]_{\mathbb{V}[X_1 \mapsto \gamma_1]} \subseteq [\![\Psi]\!]_{\mathbb{V}[X_2 \mapsto \gamma_2]}$$

We define the following $\gamma$-sequences:

$$(\gamma_1^i, \gamma_2^i)_{i \geq 0} \text{ with } (\gamma_1^0, \gamma_2^0) = (\varnothing, \varnothing), \, \gamma_1^{i+1} = [\![\Phi]\!]_{\mathbb{V}[X_1 \mapsto \gamma_1^i]}, \, \gamma_2^{i+1} = [\![\Psi]\!]_{\mathbb{V}[X_2 \mapsto \gamma_2^i]}$$

We prove by natural induction over $i$ that $[\![I]\!]_\mathbb{V} \cap \gamma_1^i \subseteq \gamma_2^i$ for every $i \geq 0$. In the case $i = 0$ we have $[\![I]\!]_\mathbb{V} \cap \gamma_1^0 = [\![I]\!]_\mathbb{V} \cap \varnothing = \varnothing \subseteq \gamma_2^0$.

Assume as the induction hypothesis that $[\![I]\!]_\mathbb{V} \cap \gamma_1^i \subseteq \gamma_2^i$ for a fixed $i \geq 0$. Using our premise, this implies $[\![I]\!]_\mathbb{V} \cap [\![\Phi]\!]_{\mathbb{V}[X_1 \mapsto \gamma_1^i]} \subseteq [\![\Psi]\!]_{\mathbb{V}[X_2 \mapsto \gamma_2^i]}$. Then also

$$[\![I]\!]_\mathbb{V} \cap \gamma_1^{i+1} = [\![I]\!]_\mathbb{V} \cap [\![\Phi]\!]_{\mathbb{V}[X_1 \mapsto \gamma_1^i]} \subseteq [\![\Psi]\!]_{\mathbb{V}[X_2 \mapsto \gamma_2^i]} = \gamma_2^{i+1}.$$

Both sequences must —after possibly infinitely many steps— reach their least fixed points. This means that $[\![I]\!]_\mathbb{V} \cap [\![\mu X_1.\Phi]\!]_\mathbb{V} \subseteq [\![\mu X_2.\Psi]\!]_\mathbb{V}$ must hold. This is equivalent to our proof obligation $[\![I \wedge \mu X_1.\Phi]\!]_\mathbb{V} \subseteq [\![\mu X_2.\Psi]\!]_\mathbb{V}$. □

*Fixed Point Induction Rule (Fig. 6).* Rule FPI makes use of the theorem above to infer trace inclusion between fixed point formulas. Invariant $I$ allows us to preserve program state information for the derivation of an arbitrary recursive iteration. The first premise establishes that the invariant holds initially. The second premise then takes the shape of the fixed point induction assumption as in Theorem 2, representing an arbitrary recursive iteration. Note that this premise also enforces the invariant to be preserved, as the derivation between recursion variables $X_1$, $X_2$ can only be proven if the invariant holds in the program state before $X_1$ (see rule RVAR). An alternative fixed point rule can be found in [11].[3]

*Example 8.* A derivation using rule FPI is in Fig. 7: We prove that the factorial program $S_{fac}$ never decreases variable $y$ after its initialization, or else $x$ is initialized with a negative value. For better readability, we use abbreviations

---

[3] This fixed point rule is based on an extension of the definition of triples $(X, p, X') \in \xi$ with more general triples $(X, p, \Phi) \in \xi$, where $\Phi$ matches a trace formula.

$$\text{RVAR} \; \dfrac{\vdots \\ P_\Gamma^4 \vdash \bigwedge P_\Gamma^1}{(X_{fac}|_{\bigwedge P_\Gamma^1}, X_{inc}) \diamond P_\Gamma^4, X_{fac} \vdash X_{inc}}$$

$$\text{CLOSE} \; \dfrac{}{x \geq 0, y = 1 \vdash \bigwedge P_\Gamma^1} \quad \dfrac{\vdots \\ (X_{fac}|_{\bigwedge P_\Gamma^1}, X_{inc}) \diamond P_\Gamma^1, \Phi'_{fac} \vdash repeat_3(\Phi'_{inc})}{}$$

$$\text{FPI} \; \dfrac{x \geq 0, y = 1, \mu X_{fac}.\Phi'_{fac} \vdash \mu X_{inc}.repeat_3(\Phi'_{inc})}{}$$

$$\text{LENR} \; \dfrac{}{x \geq 0, y = 1, \mu X_{fac}.\Phi'_{fac} \vdash \mu X_{inc}.\Phi'_{inc}} \; 3 \geq 1$$

$$\vdots$$

$$x \geq 0, Sb_y^1 \frown Id \frown \mu X_{fac}.\Phi'_{fac} \vdash Sb_y^1 \frown \mu X_{inc}.\Phi'_{inc}$$

$$\vdots$$

$$Sb_y^1 \frown Id \frown \mu X_{fac}.\Phi'_{fac} \vdash Sb_y^1 \frown \mu X_{inc}.\Phi'_{inc} \lor x < 0$$

**Fig. 7.** Demonstration of fixed point induction

$$\Phi'_{fac} \equiv ((x = 1 \land Id \frown Id) \lor (x \neq 1 \land Id \frown Sb_y^{y*x} \frown Sb_x^{x-1} \frown Id \frown X_{fac}))$$

$$\Phi'_{inc} \equiv R_{inc}^y \lor R_{inc}^y \frown X_{inc}$$

Before usage of FPI, trace lengthening is needed to synchronize trace lengths and positions of recursion variable occurrences. Lengthening $\Phi'_{inc}$ by a factor of three yields $R_{inc}^y \frown R_{inc}^y \frown R_{inc}^y \frown R_{inc}^y \frown X_{inc}$ as its chop sequence, which synchronizes with the right disjunct in $\Phi'_{fac}$. The left disjunct also synchronizes due to the occurrence of $R_{inc}^y \frown R_{inc}^y$.

**Theorem 3 (Soundness).** *The calculus rules presented in this section are sound, implying that only valid sequents are derivable.*

The proof of this theorem is in [11] due to its length.

## 5 Calculus Extensions

### 5.1 Contracts

The base rules of the calculus we established so far expose a major source of incompleteness: If in an antecedent the fixed point operation or the recursion variable occurs *non-tail recursively*, such as in $X \frown \Phi$ or $(\mu X.\Psi) \frown \Phi$, then there is no rule to continue a derivation. The root cause is that the effect that a fixed point or a recursion variable has on the execution state is unknown. For this reason, all the rules dealing with fixed points so far permit only a single formula in the antecedent. The standard solution in deductive verification to deal with such a situation are *contracts* [6] that summarize the execution state after a complex statement.

**Definition 8 (Procedure Contract).** *A state-based* procedure contract *for a given trace formula $\Phi$ is a pair $(pre, post)$ of precondition $pre \in Pred$ and postcondition $post \in Pred$. Postconditions may contain fresh program variables $x_{old}$ containing the value of variables $x$ in $\Phi$ in the execution state before $\Phi$ is evaluated.*

While contracts may approximate *any* kind of trace formula, we kept the attribute "procedure", because the trace formula of a contract can be thought of as the body of a procedure declaration and this is also how we use contracts. Intuitively, a procedure contract $(pre, post)$ is *valid* for a trace formula $\Phi$, if the postcondition is satisfied in the execution state after evaluation of $\Phi$, assuming the precondition is satisfied in the execution state before evaluation of $\Phi$.

*Example 9.* A valid procedure contract for trace formula $\Phi_m$ in Example 2 is

$$(x \geq 1, y = y_{old} * x_{old}! \wedge x = 1) \ .$$

We *encode* the intuitive validity of a procedure contract formally as trace inclusion.

**Definition 9 (Contract Encoding).** *Let $(v^i)_{1 \leq i \leq n}$ be all program variables occurring in $\Phi$ and $(v^i_{old})_{1 \leq i \leq n}$ fresh program variables. A procedure contract $(pre, post)$ is valid for $\Phi$ in $\mathbb{V}$ iff*

$$[\![ \underbrace{\bigwedge v^i_{old} = v^i \wedge pre \wedge \Phi\frown true}_{\langle pre(\Phi) \rangle} ]\!]_{\mathbb{V}} \subseteq [\![ \underbrace{\Phi\frown post}_{\langle post(\Phi) \rangle} ]\!]_{\mathbb{V}} \ .$$

In the following, we use abbreviations $\langle pre(\Phi) \rangle$, $\langle post(\Phi) \rangle$ for the encoding of the pre- and postcondition, respectively, as indicated above. The encoding expresses: Assuming precondition *pre* holds and the information about the execution state *before the evaluation* of $\Phi$ is memorized using fresh variables $v^i_{old}$, then after evaluating $\Phi$ we reach a state in the antecedent that implies *post* in the succedent. Observe that to model this as a trace inclusion formula, we have to copy the formula $\Phi$ into the succedent to ensure that the traces match.

**Theorem 4 (Fixed Point Induction on Contracts).** *For any recursion variable $X$, trace formula $\Phi$, valuation $\mathbb{V}$, and procedure contract $(pre, post)$, if the validity of $(pre, post)$ for $X$ in $\mathbb{V}$ implies its validity for $\Phi$ in $\mathbb{V}$, then it must also be valid for $\mu X.\Phi$ in $\mathbb{V}$.*

The proof for this theorem is in [11].

To integrate contracts into the calculus rules presented in Sect. 4, we need to remodel sequents so they include information about procedure contracts.

**Definition 10 (Sequent with Contract).** *A* procedure contract table *is a partial function $\mathbb{C} : ProcName \rightharpoonup Pred \times Pred$, assigning each procedure of a program $P$ a possible contract. $\mathbb{C}$ is called* valid in $\mathbb{V}$ *iff for all $m \in dom(\mathbb{C})$, $\mathbb{C}(m)$*

$$\text{MC} \quad \frac{v_{old}^i \in fresh(Var) \quad \mathbb{C}' = \mathbb{C}[m \mapsto (pre, post)]}{\xi \diamond \langle pre(\Phi) \rangle \vdash_{\mathbb{C}'} \langle post(\Phi) \rangle \quad \xi \diamond \Gamma, \mu X_m.\Phi \vdash_{\mathbb{C}'} \Delta}{\xi \diamond \Gamma, \mu X_m.\Phi \vdash_{\mathbb{C}} \Delta}$$

$$\text{CH-MC} \quad \frac{v_{old}^i \in fresh(Var) \quad \mathbb{C}' = \mathbb{C}[m \mapsto (pre, post)]}{\xi \diamond \langle pre(\Phi_1) \rangle \vdash_{\mathbb{C}'} \langle post(\Phi_1) \rangle \quad \xi \diamond \Gamma, (\mu X_m.\Phi_1)^\frown \Phi_2 \vdash_{\mathbb{C}'} \Delta}{\xi \diamond \Gamma, (\mu X_m.\Phi_1)^\frown \Phi_2 \vdash_{\mathbb{C}} \Delta}$$

**Fig. 8.** Calculus rules for procedure contract validity

is valid for $\mu X_m.\Phi$ in $\mathbb{V}$, where $\mu X_m.\Phi$ is the subformula of $\Gamma$ corresponding to procedure $m$. A sequent (with contract) has the form $\xi \diamond \Gamma \vdash_{\mathbb{C}} \Delta$, where a procedure contract table $\mathbb{C}$ is added as an index to $\vdash$.

Note that procedure contracts in our sequents are only available for fixed point formulas $\mu X_m.\Phi$ generated by procedures $m$ via $stf(P)$, which is sufficient for proving sequents of the form $stf(P) \vdash_{\mathbb{C}} \Psi$.

**Definition 11 (Validity of Sequent with Contract).** *A sequent $\xi \diamond \Gamma \vdash_{\mathbb{C}} \Delta$ is valid, if for all valuations $\mathbb{V}$, contract table $\mathbb{C}$ valid in $\mathbb{V}$, and $[\![X \wedge p]\!]_\mathbb{V} \subseteq [\![X']\!]_\mathbb{V}$ holding for all $(X|p, X') \in \xi$ implies $[\![\bigwedge \Gamma]\!]_\mathbb{V} \subseteq [\![\bigvee \Delta]\!]_\mathbb{V}$.*

The contract table $\mathbb{C}$ is always empty in a top-level sequent of a derivation. Procedure contracts are added to $\mathbb{C}$ on demand by the calculus rules during a derivation. The rules ensure that all added contracts are proven valid.

*Example 10.* Continuing Example 9, let $\mathbb{C}(fac) \equiv (x \geq 1, y = y_{old} * x_{old}! \wedge x = 1)$.

$$P_\Gamma^2, \Phi_m {}^\frown Sb_x^{x-1} \vdash_{\mathbb{C}} true {}^\frown x = 0$$

is a valid sequent, because the postcondition guarantees that $fac$ terminates with $x = 1$ before eventually being reduced to $x = 0$.

*Procedure Contract Validity Rules (Fig. 8).* Rules MC and CH-MC prove the validity of a procedure contract for the leading fixed point formula and add it to the procedure contract table $\mathbb{C}$, as can be seen in the right premise. The left premise assumes the procedure contract holds for the internal recursion variable $X_m$ and proves that it hence must also be valid for $\Phi$, $\Phi_1$. Theorem 4 justifies the validity of the contract for the whole fixed point formula $\mu X_m.\Phi$. The proof uses contract table $\mathbb{C}'$ that already assumes the contract for $m$, because this contract may be assumed to handle recursive calls to $m$ in $\Phi$, $\Phi_1$.

*Procedure Contract Application Rules (Fig. 9).* Rule CH-RVAR handles the occurrence of a recursion variable $X_m$ in a non-tail recursive setting. In addition to rule RVAR, it looks up the procedure contract $(pre, post)$ of $m$, as indicated by the side condition. Since the recursion variable of procedure $m$ is uniquely

$$\text{CH-RVAR} \quad \frac{\mathbb{C}(m) = (pre, post)}{\xi, (X_m|_p, X) \diamond \Gamma, X_m \frown \Phi \vdash_C X \frown \Psi, \Delta}$$

$$\text{CH-FPI} \quad \frac{\mathbb{C}(m) = (pre, post)}{\xi \diamond \Gamma, (\mu X_m.\Phi_1) \frown \Phi_2 \vdash_C (\mu X.\Psi_1) \frown \Psi_2, \Delta}$$

**Fig. 9.** Calculus rules for procedure contract application

$$\text{CLOSE} \quad \frac{}{\text{PRED} \quad \frac{y \geq 1, x = 0, y > x \vdash_C y > x}{y \geq 1, x = 0 \vdash_C y > x}}$$

$$\text{CH-MC} \quad \frac{\vdots}{\text{CH-FPI} \quad \frac{x_{old} \geq 1, y_{old} \geq 1, y = y_{old} * x_{old}! \wedge x = 1, Sb_x^{x-1} \vdash_C Sb_x^{x-1} \frown y > x}{P_\Gamma^1, \mu X_{fac}.\Phi'_{fac} \frown Sb_x^{x-1} \vdash_C \mu X_{inc}.\Phi'_{inc} \frown Sb_x^{x-1} \frown y > x}}{P_\Gamma^1, \mu X_{fac}.\Phi'_{fac} \frown Sb_x^{x-1} \vdash_\varnothing \mu X_{inc}.\Phi'_{inc} \frown Sb_x^{x-1} \frown y > x}$$

**Fig. 10.** Demonstration of calculus with procedure contracts

named as $X_m$, the correct procedure is used. The left premise additionally proves the precondition *pre*. The right premise takes the current program state, substitutes every occurrence of variable $v^i$ with variable $v_{old}^i$, as determined in the contract, and adds the postcondition *post*. This modified program state is then used to continue the derivation of the remaining trace. Rule CH-FPI behaves similarly, guaranteeing the derivation of non-tail recursive fixed point formula occurrences.

It is future work to extend the calculus to support multiple contracts for procedures by applying contracts in a hierarchical fashion. This necessitates a modification of the contract table definition and the calculus rules.

*Example 11.* The calculus with procedure contracts is illustrated by an example in Fig. 10. We use the abbreviations from Example 8, $\mathbb{C} := [fac \mapsto (pre, post)]$, $P_\Gamma^1 \equiv \{x \geq 1, y \geq 1\}$ and $(pre, post) \equiv (x \geq 1, y = y_{old} * x_{old}! \wedge x = 1)$. For readability, the derivation only follows the rightmost premises.

**Theorem 5 (Soundness of the Calculus with Procedure Contracts).**
*The calculus rules presented in this section are sound, implying that only valid sequents are derivable.*

The proof of this theorem is in [11] due to its length.

## 5.2 Synchronization

To successfully perform a fixed point induction, the trace lengths and positions of the recursion variable occurrences must align in antecedent and succedent. This is not always the case, and it motivates the following synchronization rules.

$$\text{CH-UPD} \ \dfrac{P_\Gamma^1, Sb_y^{y*x} \vdash X_{inc} \quad \begin{array}{c} \vdots \\ \text{not derivable} \\ (X_{fac}|_{\wedge P_\Gamma^1}, X_{inc}) \diamond P_\Gamma^3, Sb_x^{x-1} \frown X_{fac} \vdash R_{inc}^y \frown R_{inc}^y \end{array} \quad \begin{array}{c} \vdots \\ \text{not derivable} \\ (X_{fac}|_{\wedge P_\Gamma^1}, X_{inc}) \diamond P_\Gamma^4, X_{fac} \vdash R_{inc}^y \end{array}}{(X_{fac}|_{\wedge P_\Gamma^1}, X_{inc}) \diamond P_\Gamma^2, Sb_y^{y*x} \frown Sb_x^{x-1} \frown X_{fac} \vdash X_{inc} \frown R_{inc}^y \frown R_{inc}^y}$$

**Fig. 11.** Demonstration of recursion variable synchronization problem

*Example 12.* In fixed point formula $\Phi_{inc} := \mu X_{inc}.(R_{inc}^y \vee X_{inc} \frown R_{inc}^y)$, the recursion variable $X_{inc}$ does not occur tail recursively. So any synchronizing formula must have its recursion variable as a leading formula in its chop sequence. This issue is demonstrated in Fig. 11: The second disjunct in $\Phi_{inc}$ is expanded to $X_{inc} \frown R_{inc}^y \frown R_{inc}^y$, so that in the initial sequent of Fig. 11 the positions of recursion variables $X_{fac}, X_{inc}$ misalign.

**Definition 12 (Chop Formula).** *Let relation $R$ and recursion variable $X$ be fixed.* Primitive chop formulas *are a subclass of trace formulas consisting of chop sequences containing exclusively $R$ or $X$, specified by the grammar*

$$\Psi_{(R,X)} ::= R \mid X \mid \Psi_{(R,X)} \frown \Psi_{(R,X)} \ .$$

*The* chop formulas $CF_{(R,X)}$ *with fixed $R$ and $X$ are defined as disjunctions over primitive chop formulas, specified by the grammar*

$$\Phi_{(R,X)} ::= \Psi_{(R,X)} \mid \Psi_{(R,X)} \vee \Phi_{(R,X)} \ .$$

*All recursion variables $X$ occurring in a chop formula are* not bound.

*Example 13.* $\Phi_{sub} \equiv Id \vee Id \frown X \frown Id \frown X \vee Id \frown Id \frown Id$ is a chop formula, i.e. $\Phi_{sub} \in CF_{(Id,X)}$. The subformula $Id \frown X \frown Id \frown X$ is a primitive chop formula.

Let $\Phi \in CF_{(R,X)}$ be a chop formula. Then there exists a natural mapping $gr: CF_{(R,X)} \to G(\{X\}, \{R\}, \delta, X)$ from $\Phi = \bigvee_{1 \leq i \leq n} \varphi_i$ to a context-free grammar with *non-terminal* $X$, *terminal* $R$, *production rules* $\delta$ and *initial non-terminal* $X$, where production rules $\delta$ are defined as $X \to grammatize(\varphi_i)$ for $1 \leq i \leq n$. The function *grammatize* maps each primitive chop formula to a sequence over terminal $R$ and non-terminal $X$. It is defined by

$$grammatize(S_1 \frown S_2 \frown \ldots \frown S_n) := S_1 S_2 \cdots S_n \text{ for } S_i \in \{R, X\} \ .$$

This construction ensures that every $\Phi \in CF_{(R,X)}$ has a *unique grammar representation* $gr(\Phi)$. There is exactly one terminal symbol in $gr(\Phi)$, so we may use Parikh's theorem [17] to deduce that its specified language is regular.

**Definition 13.** *The* regular trace language *of a chop formula $\Phi$ is $L(gr(\Phi))$.*

$$\text{SYNC } \frac{\xi \diamond \Gamma \vdash \mu X.\Psi', \Delta}{\xi \diamond \Gamma \vdash \mu X.\Psi, \Delta} \ L(gr(\Psi')) \subseteq L(gr(\Psi))$$

**Fig. 12.** Calculus rule for $\mu$-formula synchronization

See Figure 3 (cf. Figure 11)
$$\vdots$$
$$(X_{fac}|_{\wedge P_\Gamma^1}, X_{inc}) \diamond P_\Gamma^2, Sb_y^{y*x} {\frown} Sb_x^{x-1} {\frown} X_{fac} \vdash R_{inc}^y {\frown} R_{inc}^y {\frown} X_{inc}$$
$$\vdots$$
$$\text{SYNC } \frac{\Phi_m \vdash \mu X_{inc}.(R_{inc}^y \vee R_{inc}^y {\frown} X_{inc})}{\Phi_m \vdash \mu X_{inc}.(R_{inc}^y \vee X_{inc} {\frown} R_{inc}^y)}$$

**Fig. 13.** Demonstration of $\mu$-formula synchronization

*Example 14.* The context-free grammar $gr(\Phi_{sub})$ of the formula from Example 13 is: $X \to Id \mid Id\ X\ Id\ X \mid Id\ Id\ Id$. Now consider the chop formula $\Phi'_{sub} \equiv Id \vee Id {\frown} Id {\frown} X {\frown} X \vee Id {\frown} Id {\frown} Id$. Its context-free grammar $gr(\Phi'_{sub})$ has the production rules: $X \to Id \mid Id\ Id\ X\ X \mid Id\ Id\ Id$. The induced regular trace languages are identical, i.e. $L(\Phi_{sub}) = L(\Phi'_{sub})$, implying that both chop formulas generate the exact same traces.

*Synchronization Rule (Fig. 12).* Rule SYNC permits to realign problematic fixed point formulas to synchronize with the antecedent. This requires the trace language of the premise to be smaller than or equal to the trace language of the conclusion. We cannot apply the synchronization rule when the fixed point formula in the premise is not a chop formula (for example, in the case of nested fixed point formulas), which is a limitation to completeness.

*Example 15.* A derivation with $\mu$-formula synchronization is in Fig. 13.

**Theorem 6 (Soundness of the Calculus with Synchronization).** *The* SYNC *rule is sound, implying that only valid sequents are derivable.*

The proof of this theorem is in [11] due to its length.

## 6 Related Work

Lange et al. [13] analyze the model checking problem over finite transition systems using a modal $\mu$-calculus logic enriched with a chop operator. They focus on providing a model checker for this extended logic and prove its soundness and completeness. The paper presents a tableau calculus that lets one verify whether a transition system $T$ satisfies a corresponding formula $\Phi$. Formula consequence is *not* addressed.

Walukiewicz [19] extends propositional modal logic with fixpoint operations, resulting in the common $\mu$-calculus. An axiomatization is provided to syntactically infer sequents $\varGamma \vdash \varDelta$ that semantically correspond to the implication between $\mu$-calculus formulas. The presented calculus is proven to be *sound* and *complete*. In contrast to the present paper, the logic syntax contains modal connectives, but neither relations nor the chop operator.

Müller-Olm [15] extends the classical modal $\mu$-calculus with chop, which is semantically interpreted using *predicate transformers*. The paper focuses on proving that any context-free process has a characteristic formula up to bisimulation or simulation. The paper further analyzes decidability and expressiveness of this logic, but reasoning about formula consequence is *not* discussed.

# 7 Conclusion

We designed a sound calculus to prove formula consequence in a trace logic with smallest fixed points, chop, and binary relations. The significance of the logic derives from the fact that it can characterize the behavior of imperative programs with recursive procedures. To prove the judgment $S : \varPhi$ that a program $S$ conforms to a trace formula specification $\varPhi$, it is necessary to infer consequence relations $\varPhi \models \varPsi$ of trace formulas [5].

As usual for a logic with smallest fixed point operator, the calculus presented here has fixed point induction as its central inference rule, but in its standard form this turns out not to be very useful. The reason is the presence of the chop operator which (i) necessitates to approximate the state *after* evaluation of the first constituent in a chop formula and (ii) may cause misalignment among the bodies of smallest fixed point formulas. We added *contracts* for fixed point formulas and grammar-based realignment, respectively, to mitigate these issues. We have not seen such mechanisms in the literature on proof systems related to $\mu$-calculus and believe these ideas constitute an interesting and viable approach to make such calculi more complete.

At the same time, both presented solutions are clearly incomplete: Regarding (i), consequence between fixed points with unbounded iterations and a formula like $true \frown \varPhi$ cannot be proven: This requires to track state changes *during* the fixed point evaluation, between iterations. Related to (ii), $\mu$-formula synchronization was defined for a specific subclass of trace formulas. Direct generalization of grammar-based alignment leads to the inclusion problem of context-free grammars which is undecidable.

In the future we want to investigate how the novel concepts —contracts and grammar-based alignment— can be generalized towards completeness and how they can be employed in automated proof search. It is also interesting to analyze the practicality of an integration of this calculus with related calculi relying on trace-based judgments [7,8].

# References

1. Alur, R., Etessami, K., Madhusudan, P.: A temporal logic of nested calls and returns. In: Jensen, K., Podelski, A. (eds.) Tools and Algorithms for the Construction and Analysis of Systems. TACAS 2004. LNCS, vol. 2988, pp. 467–481. Springer, Berlin, Heidelberg (2004). https://doi.org/10.1007/978-3-540-24730-2_35
2. Beckert, B., et al.: The Java verification tool KeY: a tutorial. In: Platzer, A., Rozier, K.Y., Pradella, M., Rossi, M. (eds.) Formal Methods. FM 2024. LNCS, vol. 14934, pp. 597–623. Springer, Cham (2024). https://doi.org/10.1007/978-3-031-71177-0_32
3. Clarke, E., Grumberg, O., Peled, D.: Model Checking. MIT Press, Cambridge (2001)
4. Dijkstra, E.W.: A Discipline of Programming. Prentice Hall Inc., Hoboken (1976)
5. Gurov, D., Hähnle, R.: An expressive trace logic for recursive programs. In: Fernandez, M. (ed.) Proceedings of the 10th International Conference on Formal Structures for Computation and Deduction, Birmingham, UK. LIPIcs, Schloss Dagstuhl - Leibniz-Zentrum fuer Informatik (2025). pre-print available at https://doi.org/10.48550/arXiv.2411.13125
6. Hähnle, R., Huisman, M.: Deductive software verification: from pen-and-paper proofs to industrial tools. In: Steffen, B., Woeginger, G. (eds.) Computing and Software Science: State of the Art and Perspectives. LNCS, vol. 10000, pp. 345–373. Springer, Cham (2019). https://doi.org/10.1007/978-3-319-91908-9_18
7. Hähnle, R., Kamburjan, E., Scaletta, M.: Context-aware trace contracts. In: De Boer, F., Damiani, F., Hähnle, R., Johnsen, E.B., Kamburjan, E. (eds.) Active Object Languages: Current Research Trends. LNCS, vol. 14360, pp. 292–325. Springer, Cham (2024). https://doi.org/10.1007/978-3-031-51060-1_11
8. Hähnle, R., Scaletta, M., Kamburjan, E.: Herding CATs. In: Ferreira, C., Willemse, T.A.C. (eds.) Software Engineering and Formal Methods. SEFM 2023. LNCS, vol. 14323, pp. 1–6. Springer, Cham (2023). https://doi.org/10.1007/978-3-031-47115-5_1
9. Halpern, J., Manna, Z., Moszkowski, B.: A hardware semantics based on temporal intervals. In: Diaz, J. (ed.) ICALP 1983. LNCS, vol. 154, pp. 278–291. Springer, Heidelberg (1983). https://doi.org/10.1007/BFb0036915
10. Heidler, N.: A Calculus for Trace Formula Implication. Master's thesis, Technical University of Darmstadt, Department of Computer Science (September 2024). https://doi.org/10.26083/tuprints-00029959
11. Heidler, N., Hähnle, R.: A Sequent Calculus for Trace Formula Implication. arXiv CoRR (May 2025). https://doi.org/10.48550/arXiv.2505.03693
12. Hoare, C.A.R.: An axiomatic basis for computer programming. Comm. ACM **12**(10), 576–580, 583 (1969)
13. Lange, M., Stirling, C.: Model checking fixed point logic with chop. In: Nielsen, M., Engberg, U. (eds.) Foundations of Software Science and Computation Structures. FoSSaCS 2002. LNCS, vol. 2303, pp. 250–263. Springer, Berlin, Heidelberg (2002). https://doi.org/10.1007/3-540-45931-6_18
14. McGuire, H., Manna, Z., Waldinger, R.J.: Annotation-based deduction in temporal logic. In: Gabbay, D.M., Ohlbach, H.J. (eds.) Temporal Logic, First International Conference, ICTL, Bonn, Germany. LNCS, vol. 827, pp. 430–444. Springer, Berlin, Heidelberg (1994). https://doi.org/10.1007/BFB0014003

15. Müller-Olm, M.: A modal fixpoint logic with chop. In: Meinel, C., Tison, S. (eds.) STACS 99. STACS 1999. LNCS, vol. 1563, pp. 510–520. Springer, Berlin, Heidelberg (1999). https://doi.org/10.1007/3-540-49116-3_48
16. Nakata, K., Uustalu, T.: Trace-based coinductive operational semantics for while. In: Berghofer, S., Nipkow, T., Urban, C., Wenzel, M. (eds.) Theorem Proving in Higher Order Logics. TPHOLs 2009. LNCS, vol. 5674, pp. 375–390. Springer, Berlin, Heidelberg (2009). https://doi.org/10.1007/978-3-642-03359-9_26
17. Parikh, R.J.: On context-free languages. J. ACM **13**(4), 570–581 (1966). https://doi.org/10.1145/321356.321364
18. Sprenger, C., Dam, M.: On global induction mechanisms in a $\mu$-calculus with explicit approximations. Theor. Inform. Appl. **37**(4), 365–391 (2003). http://www.edpsciences.org/articles/ita/pdf/2003/04/ita0317.pdf
19. Walukiewicz, I.: On completeness of the mu-calculus. In: Proceedings of the Eighth Annual Symposium on Logic in Computer Science (LICS), Montreal, Canada, pp. 136–146. IEEE Computer Society (1993). https://doi.org/10.1109/LICS.1993.287593

**Open Access** This chapter is licensed under the terms of the Creative Commons Attribution 4.0 International License (http://creativecommons.org/licenses/by/4.0/), which permits use, sharing, adaptation, distribution and reproduction in any medium or format, as long as you give appropriate credit to the original author(s) and the source, provide a link to the Creative Commons license and indicate if changes were made.

The images or other third party material in this chapter are included in the chapter's Creative Commons license, unless indicated otherwise in a credit line to the material. If material is not included in the chapter's Creative Commons license and your intended use is not permitted by statutory regulation or exceeds the permitted use, you will need to obtain permission directly from the copyright holder.

# Author Index

**A**
Acclavio, Matteo 414
Afshari, Bahareh 374

**B**
Barroso-Nascimento, Victor 3
Bjørner, Nikolaj 120
Braüner, Torben 22
Butte, Julia 278
Buzoku, Yll 318

**C**
Chaudhuri, Kaustuv 299
Ciabattoni, Agata 220
Claßen, Jens 22
Coniglio, Marcelo Esteban 181

**D**
Dalmonte, Tiziano 354
Das, Anupam 453
De, Abhishek 453

**E**
Eisenhofer, Clemens 82, 103, 120

**F**
Ferrari, Mauro 141
Fiorentini, Camillo 141

**G**
Gantait, Arunava 299
Girlando, Marianna 354
Goré, Rajeev 238
Greati, Vitor 59
Grotenhuis, Lide 374

**H**
Hähnle, Reiner 473
Heidler, Niklas 473
Horvat, Sebastijan 201

**K**
Kikkert, Cormac 238
Kloibhofer, Johannes 258
Kovács, Laura 82, 103, 120

**L**
Lang, Timo 220
Leme, Renato 181
Litak, Tadeusz 39

**M**
Marcelino, Sérgio 59
Marin, Sonia 393
Miller, Dale 299
Muñoz Pérez, Miguel 59

**N**
Nalon, Cláudia 161

**O**
Olarte, Carlos 181

**P**
Padhiar, Paaras 393
Pimentel, Elaine 3, 181
Piotrovskaya, Ekaterina 3
Platzer, André 278
Pym, David J. 318

**R**
Ramanayake, Revantha 220
Rawson, Michael 82, 103

Rivieccio, Umberto 59
Rodriguez, Ricardo Oscar 141

**S**
Samadpour Motalebi, Kiana 161
Sano, Katsuhiko 39
Schmidt, Renate A. 161
Seiser, Theodor 120
Sierra Miranda, Borja 201
Straßburger, Lutz 414
Studer, Thomas 201

**T**
Trucco Dalmas, Valentina 258

**V**
Veltri, Niccolò 433
Venema, Yde 258
Voorneveld, Niels 335

**W**
Wan, Cheng-Syuan 433

Made in the USA
Monee, IL
03 May 2026